Rereading America

Cultural Contexts for
Critical Thinking and Writing

Rereading America

Cultural Contexts for Critical Thinking and Writing

Second Edition

Edited by

Gary Colombo
LOS ANGELES COMMUNITY COLLEGE

Robert Cullen
SAN JOSE STATE UNIVERSITY

Bonnie Lisle
UNIVERSITY OF CALIFORNIA, LOS ANGELES

Bedford Books *of* St. Martin's Press • Boston

For Bedford Books

Publisher: Charles H. Christensen
Associate Publisher: Joan E. Feinberg
Managing Editor: Elizabeth M. Schaaf
Developmental Editor: Stephen A. Scipione
Production Editor: Deborah A. Liehs
Copyeditor: Susan M. S. Brown
Cover Design: Hannus Design Associates
Cover Art: Detail from a studio art quilt, *Squares and Bars*, Carol H. Gersen,
   © 1989. From a private collection.
Cover Photography: Susan Kahn. Courtesy of The Taunton Press, publisher of
   The New Quilt 1, © 1991.

Library of Congress Catalog Card Number: 90–71613

Manufactured in the United States of America.

6 5 4 3 2
f e d c b a

For information, write: St. Martin's Press, Inc.
175 Fifth Avenue, New York, NY 10010

Editorial Offices: Bedford Books *of* St. Martin's Press
29 Winchester Street, Boston, MA 02116

ISBN: 0–312–05259–6

Acknowledgments

Jerry Adler with Mark Starr, Farai Childeya, Lynda Wright, Pat Wingert and
   Linda Haac, "Taking Offense." Reprinted by permission of Newsweek
   from *Newsweek*, December 24, 1990.

*Acknowledgments and copyrights are continued at the back of the book on
pages 781–785, which constitute an extension of the copyright page.*

 The text of this book has been printed on recycled paper.

Preface for Instructors

About *Rereading America*

Designed for first-year college writing and critical thinking courses, *Rereading America* anthologizes a diverse set of selections focused on the myths that dominate U.S. culture. This central theme brings together 78 readings on a broad range of topics — success, the environment, gender roles, racism, the family, education, the media, and democracy — topics that raise controversial issues meaningful to college students of all backgrounds. We've drawn these readings from many sources, both within the academy and outside of it; the selections are both multicultural and cross-curricular, and they therefore represent an unusual variety of voices, styles, and subjects.

The readings in this anthology speak directly to students' experiences and concerns. Every college student has had some brush with prejudice, and most have something to say about the environment, the family, or the stereotypes they see on film and television. The issues raised here help students to link their personal experiences with broader cultural perspectives and lead students to analyze, or "read," the cultural forces that have shaped and continue to shape their lives. By linking the personal and the cultural, students begin to recognize that they are not academic outsiders — that they do have knowledge, assumptions, and intellectual frameworks that give them authority in academic culture. Connecting personal knowledge and academic discourse helps students see that they are able to think, speak, and write academically and that they don't have to absorb passively what the "experts" say.

What's New About the Second Edition

A New Approach to Critical Thinking. When the first edition of *Rereading America* appeared in 1989, many colleges were just beginning to respond to the concerns of an increasingly diverse student population. Since then, multiculturalism has become a burning issue on campuses across the country. Colleges have established programs to promote curricular diversity, and publishers have responded with a number of readers featuring a range of multicultural selections. Most of these anthologies, however, seek to integrate rather than transform the existing curriculum. They include more works by underrepresented authors, and they may even raise issues relevant to life in a diverse society, but they rarely use these new perspectives to challenge the way we teach and learn. In this edition of *Rereading America*, we go beyond mere representation of historically marginalized groups: we place cultural diversity at the heart of our approach to critical thinking, reading, and writing.

Critical analysis means asking tough questions — questions that arise from a dynamic interplay of ideas and perspectives. But many students find it difficult to enter into this dialogue of ideas. Traditional schooling is partly to blame: presenting ideas as commodities transmitted from teacher to student and conveying information as objective "fact," the traditional classroom gives students the impression that knowledge is static, not continually re-created through tension, struggle, and debate. Critical thinking is further impeded by dominant cultural myths: these collective and often unconsciously held beliefs influence our thinking, reading, and writing — conditioning our responses, determining the questions we ask and the questions we repress.

The selections in this edition ask students to explore the influence of our culture's dominant myths — our national beliefs about success, gender, race, democracy, and so forth. Each chapter introduces students to perspectives that challenge these deeply held ideals and values, asking them to confront difficult questions and encouraging them to work out their own answers. Thus, instead of treating cultural diversity as just another topic to be studied or "appreciated," *Rereading America* invites students to grapple with the real differences in perspectives that arise in a pluralistic society like ours. This method helps students to break through conventional assumptions and patterns of thought that hinder fresh critical responses and inhibit dialogue; it helps them to develop the intellectual independence essential to critical thinking, reading, and writing.

A greatly expanded introductory essay, "Thinking Critically, Challenging Cultural Myths," offers students a thorough orientation to this distinctly social and dialogic approach to critical thinking. It introduces students to the relationships among thinking, cultural diversity, and the notion of dominant cultural myths, and shows how such myths can influence their academic performance. We've also included a new section devoted to active reading, which offers suggestions for prereading, prewriting, note taking, text marking, and keeping a reading journal.

We've structured the book so that each chapter focuses on a myth that has played a dominant role in U.S. culture. In all, we address eight myths:

Money and success: the myth of individual opportunity
Nature and technology: the myth of progress
Women and men in relationship: myths of gender
Created equal: the myth of the melting pot
Harmony at home: the myth of the model family
Learning power: the myth of educational empowerment
The mass media: selling the myths
Government by the people: the myth of democracy

The chapter introductions, more comprehensive in this edition than in the first, offer students an overview of each cultural myth, placing it in historical context, raising some central questions, and orienting students to the structure of the chapter.

Timely New Readings. You'll also discover significant changes among the readings in this edition. While we've retained the most successful materials from the first edition, we've done our best to find the most current and stimulating new selections available. Most of the new pieces are very recent and offer an even broader range of perspectives. As in the first edition, we've sought out readings that will spark student interest and classroom debate — pieces such as Gloria Anzaldúa's theory of "mestiza consciousness," Shelby Steele's interpretation of American racism, and *Newsweek*'s account of "political correctness" on U.S. campuses. We've added essays by some of the country's most dynamic and controversial scholars: Patricia Nelson Limerick, Haunani-Kay Trask, Susan Griffin, and Henry Louis Gates, Jr. We've also included a number of writers who speak powerfully to many first-year college students — writers such as George C. Wolfe, Jamaica Kincaid, Sandra Cisneros, Bebe Moore Campbell, and Mike Rose. Occasionally we have preferred more seasoned selections — Gordon W. Allport's analysis of in-groups or Martin Luther King, Jr.'s essay on the economic roots of racism — because these are the clearest, most definitive, or most accessible treatments of an essential topic. As in the first edition, our cross-curricular emphasis has led to an eclectic mix of genres, styles, and rhetorical strategies.

Expanded Apparatus. Rereading America offers a wealth of specific suggestions for class discussions, critical thinking activities, and writing assignments. We believe strongly in the generative power of collaboration and have included many activities that lend themselves to small-group work. The prereading exercises that follow each chapter introduction encourage students to reflect on what they know of the cultural myth at hand before they begin reading selections addressing it; our purpose is to make them aware of the way that these dominant cultural forces shape the assumptions, ideas, and values they bring to their studies. The three groups of questions following each selection ask students to consider the piece carefully in several contexts: "Engaging the Text" focuses on close reading of the selection itself; "Exploring Connections" puts the selection into dialogue with other selections throughout the book; "Extending the Critical Context" invites students to connect the ideas they have read about here with sources of knowledge outside the anthology, including library research, personal experience, interviews, ethnographic-style observations, and so forth. In this edition we've also included a number of questions linking readings with contemporary feature films for instructors who want to address the interplay of cultural myths, the mass media, and critical analysis in greater depth.

The accompanying manual, *Resources for Teaching Rereading America*, provides detailed advice about ways to make the most of both the readings and the questions; it also offers further ideas for discussion, class activities, and writing assignments.

Acknowledgments

We were surprised and delighted by the generous response to the first edition of *Rereading America*. The encouragement and advice we received from instructors, and even from whole classes of students, throughout the United States have made the second edition a truly nationwide collaborative effort. We're very grateful to all those who took the time to offer their responses and suggestions: Mike Rose, University of California, Los Angeles; Don Lipman, Los Angeles City College; Frank La Ferriere, Los Angeles City College; Katya Amato, Portland State University; Jeanne Anderson, University of Louisville; Rodney Ash, Western State College of Colorado; David Axelson, Western State College of Colorado; Valerie Babb, Georgetown University; Flavia Bacarella, Herbert H. Lehman College; Jim Baril, Western State College of Colorado; Patricia Ann Bender, Rutgers University, Newark; Sara Blake, El Camino College; Maurice Blauf, Hutchins School of Liberal Studies: Laura Brady, George Mason University; Cheryl Christiansen, California State University, Stanislaus; Gloria Collins, San Jose State University; Harry James Cook, Dundalk Community College; Dulce M. Cruz, Indiana University; Wendy J. Cutler, Cynthia Dubielak, Hocking Technical College; Miriam Dow, George Washington University; M. H. Dunlop, Iowa State University; Steve Dunn, Western State College of Colorado; Harriet Dwinell, American University; Iain J. W. Ellis, Bowling Green State University; Marie Foley, Santa Barbara City College; Peter Gardner, Berklee College of Music; Ervene Gulley, Bloomsburg University; Mary R. Georges, University of California, Los Angeles; Paul Gery, Western State College of Colorado; Krystyna Golkowska, Ithaca College; James C. Hall, University of Iowa; Craig Hancock, State University of New York, Albany; Jan Hayhurst, Community College of Pittsburgh; Jay W. Helman, Western State College of Colorado; Penny L. Hirsch, Northwestern University; Roseanne L. Hoefel, Iowa State University; Carol Hovanec, Ramapo College; John M. Jakaitis, Indiana State University; Jeanette J. Jeneault, Syracuse University; Kathleen Kelly, Northeastern University; Kathleen Kiehl, Cabrillo College; Frances E. Kino, Iona College, Yonkers Campus; Elizabeth Mary Kirchen, University of Michigan, Dearborn; Judith Kirscht, University of California, Santa Barbara; Phil Klingsmith, Western State College of Colorado; Philip A. Korth, Michigan State University; Catherine W. Kroll, Somono State American Language Institute; Jim Krusoe, Santa Monica College; Sheila A. Lebo, University of California, Los Angeles; Mitzi Lewellen, Normandale Community College; L. Loeffel, Syracuse University; Bernadette Flynn Low, Dundalk Community College; Paul Lowdenslager, Western State College of Colorado; Janet Madden-Simpson, El Camino College; Annette March, Cabrillo College; Clifford Marks, University of Wyoming; Peggy Marron, University of Wyoming; Laura McCall, Western State College of Colorado; Richard McGowan, St. Joseph's College; Ann A. Merrill, Emory University; Dale Metcalfe, University of California, Davis; Charles Miller, Western State College of Colorado; Kathy Molloy, Santa Barbara City College; Merlyn E. Mowrey, Central Michigan University; Denise Muller, San Jose State University; William Murphy, University of Maine, Machias; Susan Nance, Bowling Green State University; Patricia M. Naulty, Canisius College; Scott R. Nelson, Louisiana State University; Fran O'Connor, Nassau Community College; Sarah-Hope Parmeter, University of California, Santa Cruz; Sandra Patterson, Western State College of Colorado; Marsha Penti, Michigan Technological University; Erik Peterson, University of Minnesota; Linda Peterson, Salt Lake Community College; Michele Peterson, Santa Barbara City College; Madeleine Picciotto, Oglethorpe University; Kirsten Pierce, Villanova University; Dan Pinti, Ohio State University; Fritz H. Pointer, Contra Costa College; Paige S. Price, University of Oregon; Teresa M. Redd, Howard University; Walter G. Rice, Dundalk Community College; Renee Ruderman, Metropolitan State College, Denver; Geoffrey J. Sadock, Bergen Community College; Mollie Sandock, Valparaiso University; Jurgen E. Schlunk, West Virginia University; Esther L. Schwartz, Allegheny County Community College; Jennifer A. Senft, University of California, Los Angeles; Ann Shapiro, State University of New York, Farmingdale; Michele Moragne e Silva, St. Edward's University; Craig Sirles, De Paul University; Bill Siverly, Portland Community College; Antony Sloan, Bowling Green State University; Susan Belasco Smith, Allegheny College; Cynthia Solem, Cabrillo College; Susan Sterr, Santa Monica College; Mark Stiger, Western State College of Colorado; Ann Stolls, University of Illinois, Chicago; Brendan D. Strasser, Bowling Green State University; Ruth Ann Thompson, Fordham University; Mark Todd, Western State College of Colorado; Michael Uebel, University of Virginia; Keith Walters, Ohio State University; Robert R. Watson, Grand Valley State University; Nola J. Wegman, Valparaiso University; R. L. Welker, University of Virginia; Douglas Wixson, University of Missouri; Nancy Young Bentley, Curry, and Regis colleges; and Naomi F. Zucker, University of Rhode Island.

We owe many thanks to Charles Christensen at Bedford Books for his continued enthusiasm and support. Our editor, Steve Scipione, has been a model of good humor and sound judgment at every stage of the revision process. At Bedford we also wish to thank Joan Feinberg for her unfailingly wise counsel, Kim Chabot and Laura McCready for chasing facts and trafficking manuscript, Susan M. S. Brown for her alert and perceptive copyediting, and Debbie Liehs and Elizabeth Schaaf for carefully attending to details and steering the book through production. In Los Angeles, Debbie Eisenstein helped us tremendously by doing preliminary research and tracking down elusive texts. Finally, and always, Elena Barcia, Liz Silver, and Roy Weitz merit special thanks for living with late-night phone calls, tactfully ignoring mountains of paper, and reviving tired spirits when our energies flagged.

Contents

1

Money and Success:
The Myth of Individual Opportunity   17

2

Nature and Technology: *The Myth of Progress*　　107

3

Women and Men in Relationship: *Myths of Gender*

World War. I wouldn't go so far as to say that I, a Japanese American, became Black. . . . But some kind of transformation did take place."

5

Harmony at Home:
The Myth of the Model Family   399

6

Learning Power:
The Myth of Education and Empowerment   492

7

The Mass Media:
Selling the Myths 598

8

Government by the People:
The Myth of Democracy   692

Index of Authors and Titles   787

Rereading America

Cultural Contexts for
Critical Thinking and Writing

Thinking Critically,
Challenging Cultural Myths

Becoming a College Student

Beginning college can be a disconcerting experience. It may be the first time you've lived away from home and had to deal with the stresses and pleasures of independence. There's increased academic competition, increased temptation, and a whole new set of peer pressures. In the dorms you may find yourself among people whose backgrounds make them seem foreign and unapproachable. If you commute, you may be struggling against a feeling of isolation that you've never faced before. And then there are increased expectations. For an introductory history class you may read as many books as you covered in a year of high school coursework. In anthropology, you might be asked to conduct ethnographic research — when you've barely heard of an ethnography before, much less written one. In English you may tackle more formal analytic writing in a single semester than you've ever done in your life.

College typically imposes fewer rules than high school, but also gives you less guidance and makes greater demands — demands that affect the quality as well as the quantity of your work. By your first midterm exams, you may suspect that your previous academic experience is irrelevant, that nothing you've done in school has prepared you to think, read, or write in the ways your professors expect. Your sociology instructor says she doesn't care whether you can remember all the examples in the textbook as long as you can apply the theoretical concepts to real situations. In your composition class, the perfect five-paragraph essay you turn in for your first assignment is dismissed as "superficial, mechanical, and dull." Meanwhile, the lecturer in your political science or psychology course is rejecting ideas about country, religion, family, and self that have always been a part of your deepest beliefs. How can you cope with these new expectations and challenges?

There is no simple solution, no infallible five-step method that works for everyone. As you meet the personal challenges of college, you'll grow as a human being. You'll begin to look critically at your old habits, beliefs, and values, to see them in relation to the new world you're entering. You may have to re-examine your relationships to family, friends, neighborhood, and heritage. You'll have to sort out your strengths from your weaknesses and make tough choices about who you are and who you want to become. Your academic work demands the same process of serious self-examination. To excel in college work you need to grow intellectually — to become a critical thinker.

What Is Critical Thinking?

What do instructors mean when they tell you to think critically? Most would say that it involves asking questions rather than memorizing information. Instead of simply collecting the "facts," a critical thinker probes them, looking for underlying assumptions and ideas. Instead of focusing on dates and events in history or symptoms in psychology, she probes for motives, causes — an explanation of how these things came to be. A critical thinker cultivates the ability to imagine and value points of view different from her own — then strengthens, refines, enlarges, or reshapes her ideas in light of those other perspectives. She is at once open and skeptical: receptive to new ideas yet careful to test them against previous experience and knowledge. In short, a critical thinker is an active learner, someone with the ability to shape, not merely absorb, knowledge.

All this is difficult to put into practice, because it requires getting outside your own skin and seeing the world from multiple perspectives. To see why critical thinking doesn't come naturally, take another look at the cover of this book. Many would scan the title, *Rereading America*, take in the surface meaning — to reconsider America — and go on to page one. There isn't much to question here; it just "makes sense." But what happens with the student who brings a different perspective? For example, a student from El Salvador might justly complain that the title reflects an ethnocentric view of what it means to be an American. After all, since America encompasses all the countries of North, South, and Central America, he lived in "America" long before arriving in the United States. When this student reads the title, then, he actually does *reread* it; he reads it once in the "common sense" way but also from the perspective of someone who has lived in a country dominated by U.S. intervention and interests. This double vision or double perspective frees him to look beyond the "obvious" meaning of the book and to question its assumptions.

Of course, you don't have to be bicultural to become a proficient critical thinker. You can develop a genuine sensitivity to alternative perspectives even if you've never lived outside your hometown. But to do so you need to recognize that there are no "obvious meanings." The automatic equation that the native-born student makes between "America" and the United States seems to make sense only because our culture has traditionally endorsed the idea that the United States *is*

America and, by implication, that other countries in this hemisphere are somehow inferior — not the genuine article. We tend to accept this equation and its unfortunate implications because we are products of our culture.

The Power of Cultural Myths

Culture shapes the way we think; it tells us what "makes sense." It holds people together by providing us with a shared set of customs, values, ideas, and beliefs, as well as a common language. We live enmeshed in this cultural web: it influences the way we relate to others, the way we look, our tastes, our habits; it enters our dreams and desires. But as culture binds us together it also selectively blinds us. As we grow up, we accept ways of looking at the world, ways of thinking and being that might best be characterized as cultural frames of reference or cultural myths. These myths help us understand our place in the world — our place as prescribed by our culture. They define our relationships to friends and lovers, to the past and future, to nature, to power, and to nation. Becoming a critical thinker means learning how to look beyond these cultural myths and the assumptions embedded in them.

You may associate the word "myth" primarily with the myths of the ancient Greeks. The legends of gods and heroes like Athena, Zeus, and Oedipus embodied the central ideals and values of Greek civilization — notions like civic responsibility, the primacy of male authority, and humility before the gods. The stories were "true" not in a literal sense but as reflections of important cultural beliefs. These myths assured the Greeks of the nobility of their origins; they provided models for the roles that Greeks would play in their public and private lives; they justified inequities in Greek society; they helped the Greeks understand human life and destiny in terms that "made sense" within the framework of that culture.

Our cultural myths do much the same. Take, for example, the myth of democracy. A strong belief in democracy unites us; we have only to reflect on the number of lives lost in wars fought "for democracy" to grasp its power as a cultural myth. However, look beneath the surface of our collective faith in democracy, and you'll find that we understand it in very different ways. Some say that democracy means government by the people, or the right to vote, or equality under the law. Others say it's freedom of choice, or unlimited economic opportunity. Still others argue that democracy means the active participation of all citizens in shaping public policy, or economic as well as political justice. The list of possible definitions is endless, and so is the debate about whether our government is, in fact, a democracy. But the power of the myth lies in its ability to override these differences. Politicians and advertisers rely on our automatic emotional response to treasured cultural ideas: when they invoke the name of democracy or the image of the flag, they expect us to feel a surge of patriotism and count on us not to ask whether the candidate or product really embodies the specific values we associate with democracy.

Cultural myths gain such enormous power over us by insinuating themselves into our thinking before we're aware of them. Most are learned at a deep, even unconscious level. Gender roles are a good example. As children we get gender role models from our families, our schools, our churches, and other important institutions. We see them acted out in the relationships between family members or portrayed on television, in the movies, or in song lyrics. Before long, the culturally determined roles we see for women and men appear to us as "self-evident": it seems "natural" for a man to be strong, responsible, competitive, and hetereosexual, just as it may seem "unnatural" for a man to shun competitive activity or to take a romantic interest in other men. Our most dominant cultural myths shape the way we perceive the world and blind us to alternative ways of seeing and being. When something violates the expectations that such myths create, it may even be called unnatural, immoral, or perverse.

Cultural Myths as Obstacles to Critical Thinking

Cultural myths can have more subtle effects as well. In academic work they can reduce the complexity of our reading and thinking. Recently, a professor at Los Angeles City College noted that his students were having a hard time interpreting the following poem by Theodore Roethke:

My Papa's Waltz

The whiskey on your breath
Could make a small boy dizzy;
But I hung on like death:
Such waltzing was not easy.

We romped until the pans
Slid from the kitchen shelf;
My mother's countenance
Could not unfrown itself.

The hand that held my wrist
Was battered on one knuckle;
At every step you missed
My right ear scraped a buckle.

You beat time on my head
With a palm caked hard by dirt,
Then waltzed me off to bed
Still clinging to your shirt.

The instructor read this poem as a clear expression of a child's love for his blue-collar father, a rough-and-tumble man who had worked hard all his life ("a palm caked hard by dirt"), who was not above taking a drink of whiskey to ease his mind, but who also found the time to "waltz" his son off to bed. The students didn't see this at all. They saw the poem as a story about an abusive father and heavy drinker. They seemed unwilling to look beyond the father's roughness and the whiskey on his breath, equating these with drunken violence. Although the poem does suggest an element of fear mingled with the boy's excitement ("I hung on like death"), the class missed its complexity — the mixture of fear, love and boisterous fun that colors the son's memory of his father. One way to understand the difference between these interpretations may lie in the influence of cultural myths. After all, in a culture dominated by images of the family that emphasize "positive" parenting, middle-class values, and sensitive fathers, it's no wonder that students refused to see this father sympathetically. Our culture simply doesn't associate good, loving families with drinking or with even the suggestion of physical roughness.

Years of acculturation — the process of internalizing cultural values — leave us with a set of rigid categories for "good" and "bad" parents, narrow conceptions of how parents should look, talk, and behave toward their children. These categories work like mental pigeonholes: they help us sort out our experiences rapidly, almost unconsciously (obviously, we can't ponder every new situation we meet as if it were a puzzle or a philosophical problem). But while cultural categories help us make practical decisions in everyday life, they also impose their inherent rigidity on our thinking and thus limit our ability to understand the complexity of our experience. They reduce the world to dichotomies — simplified either/or choices: either women or men, either heterosexuals or homosexuals, either nature or culture, either animal or human, either American or "alien," either us or them.

Rigid cultural beliefs can present serious obstacles to success for first-year college students. For example, a student's cultural myths may so color her thinking that she finds it nearly impossible to comprehend Freud's ideas about infant sexuality. Her ingrained assumptions about childhood innocence and sexual guilt may make it impossible for her to see children as sexual beings — a concept absolutely basic to an understanding of psychoanalytic theory. Yet college-level critical inquiry thrives on exactly this kind of revision of common sense: academics prize the unusual, the subtle, the ambiguous, the complex — and expect students to appreciate them as well. Good critical thinkers in all academic disciplines welcome the opportunity to challenge conventional ways of seeing the world; they seem to take delight in questioning everything that appears clear and self-evident.

Questioning: The Basis of Critical Thinking

By questioning the myths that dominate our culture, we can begin to resist the limits they impose on our vision. In fact, they invite such questioning. Often our personal experience fails to fit the images the myths project: a young woman's ambition to be a test pilot may clash with the ideal of femininity our culture promotes; a Cambodian immigrant who has suffered from racism in the United States may question our professed commitment to equality; a student in the vocational track may not see education as the road to success that we assume it is; and few of our families these days fit the mythic model of husband, wife, two kids, a dog, and a house in the suburbs.

Moreover, because cultural myths serve such large and varied needs, they're not always coherent or consistent. Powerful contradictory myths coexist in our society and our own minds. For example, while the myth of democracy celebrates equality, the myth of individual success pushes us to strive for inequality — to "get ahead" of everyone else. Likewise, our attitude toward the natural world is deeply paradoxical: we see nature simultaneously as a refuge from corrupt, urban society and as a resource to be exploited for the technological advancement of that society. These contradictions infuse our history, literature, and popular culture; they're so much a part of our thinking that we tend to take them for granted, unaware of their inconsistencies.

Learning to recognize contradictions lies at the very heart of critical thinking, for intellectual conflict inevitably generates questions: can both (or all) perspectives be true? What evidence do I have for the validity of each? Is there some way to reconcile them? Are there still other alternatives? Questions like these represent the beginning of serious academic analysis. They stimulate the reflection, discussion, and research that are the essence of good scholarship. Thus, whether we find contradictions between myth and lived experience, or between opposing myths, the wealth of powerful, conflicting material generated by our cultural mythology offers a particularly rich context for critical inquiry.

The Structure of *Rereading America*

We've designed this book to help you develop the habits of mind you'll need to become a critical thinker — someone who can look skeptically at the myths and cultural assumptions that shape his thinking, someone who can evaluate issues from multiple perspectives. Each of the eight chapters addresses one of the dominant myths of American culture. We begin with what is perhaps the most central of all these cultural ideas — the myth of individual success. This idea, the force behind the American Dream, has brought millions of immigrants to our shores; it is the idea that set America in motion. It has also left an indelible imprint on our collective unconscious: in no other society has it been so important for an ordinary person to feel distinguished in some way from his or her fellow citizens. As many students of American culture have noted, the great paradox of our society is that we honor the idea of equality while we strive to make ourselves stand out from the crowd.

This American obsession with distinction and difference is echoed in the cultural myths that we explore in the next three chapters. Chapter Two, "Nature and Technology," re-examines the idea that humans are essentially different from the rest of nature and that we are meant to control or improve upon it. Chapter Three, "Women and Men in Relationship," considers the cultural category of gender — the tradi-tional roles that mark the difference between women and men, hetero-sexuals and homosexuals. "Created Equal," the fourth chapter, ends the first half of the book by examining two myths of difference that have powerfully affected racial and ethnic relations in the United States — the myth of the melting pot (which celebrates cultural homogenization) and its negative counterpart, the myth of racial and ethnic superiority (which promotes separateness and inequality). Each of these chapters, then, questions how our culture divides and defines our world, how it artificially channels our experience into oppositions like black and white, natural and human, feminine and masculine, straight and gay.

The second half of *Rereading America* concentrates on institutions that help perpetuate cultural myths. Chapter Five, "Harmony at Home," looks at the ideal of family perfection and the impact it has on the large majority of individuals who live in families that do not conform to this prescription for happiness. Chapter Six, "Learning Power," asks us to reconsider the role of education in our lives: does formal schooling help and empower us, or does it hold us back? Chapter Seven, "Media," explores how most forms of mass communication — from modern advertising to the movies — exploit cultural myths to manipulate our desires and responses. The eighth chapter, "Govern-ment by the People," asks if the central idea of American government — democracy — is itself a cultural myth.

The Selections

Our identities — who we are and how we relate to others — are deeply entangled with the cultural values we have internalized since infancy. Cultural myths become so closely identified with our personal beliefs that rereading them actually means rereading ourselves, rethink-ing the way we see the world. Questioning long-held assumptions can be an exhilarating experience, but it can be distressing too. Thus, you may find certain selections in *Rereading America* difficult, controversial, or even downright offensive. They are meant to challenge you and to provoke classroom debate. But as you discuss the ideas you encounter in this book, remind yourself that your classmates may bring with them very different, and equally profound, beliefs. Keep an open mind, listen carefully, and treat other perspectives with the same respect you'd expect other people to show for your own. It's by encountering new ideas and engaging with others in open dialogue that we learn and grow.

Rereading America deliberately includes few traditional or conservative points of view, because such views seldom challenge the cultural myths that have surrounded us all our lives. And we have not tried to "balance" pro and con arguments, for we believe that doing so reinforces simplistic, "either/or" thinking. Instead, since it's often necessary to stand outside a culture to see it anew, we've included many strongly dissenting views: there are works by ecofeminists, African American militants, socialists, disabled activists, gay rights advocates, and more. You may find that their views confirm your own experience of what it means to be an American, or you may find that you bitterly disagree with them. We only hope that you will use the materials here to gain some insight into the values and beliefs that shape our thinking and our national identity. This book is meant to complicate the mental categories that our cultural myths have established for us. Our intention is not to present a new "truth" to replace the old but to expand the range of perspectives you bring to all your reading and writing in college. We believe that learning to see and value other perspectives will enable you to think more critically — to question, for yourself, the truth of any statement.

You may also note that several selections in *Rereading America* challenge the way you think writing is supposed to look or sound. You won't find many "classic" essays in this book, the finely crafted reflective essays on general topics that are often held up as models of "good writing." It's not that we reject this type of essay in principle. It's just that most writers who stand outside mainstream culture seem to have little use for it. The kind of writing that challenges dominant cultural values often comes out of scholarly research, so you can expect to cut your teeth on some serious academic analysis in this book. We also believe that unusual styles and uses of language, like unconventional ideas, offer points of entry into critical thinking. Thus you will come across some selections — like Gloria Anzaldúa's "La conciencia de la mestiza" — that seem to violate all the conventions of writing. And pieces like Rodney Morales's "Under the Table" include passages in another language or dialect. Although such readings may seem disorienting at first, we'll do our best to get you over the tough spots by offering help in chapter introductions, headnotes, and footnotes. We think these selections will reward the extra trouble it may take you to read them, because encountering new styles, besides being intellectually stimulating, can help you become a more flexible reader and writer.

Our selections come from a wide variety of sources — professional books and journals from many disciplines, popular magazines, college textbooks, autobiographies, oral histories, and literary works, including poetry, fiction, and drama. We've included this variety partly for the very practical reason that you're likely to encounter texts like these in your college coursework. But we also see textual diversity, like ethnic and political diversity, as a way to multiply perspectives and stimulate critical analysis. For example, an academic article like Jean Anyon's study of social class and school curriculum might give you a new way of understanding Mike Rose's personal narrative about his classroom experiences. On the other hand, you may find that some of the teachers Rose encounters don't neatly fit Anyon's theoretical model: do such discrepancies mean that Anyon's argument is invalid? That her analysis needs to be modified to account for these teachers? That the teachers are simply exceptions to the rule? You'll probably want to consider your own classroom experience as you wrestle with such questions. Throughout the book, we've chosen readings that "talk to each other" in this way and that draw on the cultural knowledge you bring with you. These readings invite you to join the conversation; we hope they raise difficult questions, prompt lively discussion, and stimulate critical inquiry.

The Power of Dialogue

Good thinking, like good writing and good reading, is an intensely social activity. Thinking, reading, and writing are all forms of relationship — when you read, you enter into dialogue with an author about the subject at hand; when you write, you address an imaginary reader, testing your ideas against probable responses, reservations, and arguments. Thus, you can't become an accomplished writer simply by declaring your right to speak or by criticizing as an act of principle: real authority comes when you enter into the discipline of an active exchange of opinions and interpretations. Critical thinking, then, is always a matter of dialogue and debate — discovering relationships between apparently unrelated ideas, finding parallels between your own experiences and the ideas you read about, exploring points of agreement and conflict between yourself and other people.

We've designed the readings and questions in this text to encourage you to make just these kinds of connections. You'll notice, for example, that we often ask you to divide into small groups to discuss readings, and we frequently suggest that you take part in projects that require you to collaborate with your classmates. We're convinced that the only way you can learn critical reading, thinking, and writing is by actively engaging others in an intellectual exchange. So we've built into the text many opportunities for listening, discussion, and debate.

The questions that follow each selection should guide you in critical thinking. Like the readings, they're intended to get you started, not to set limits; we strongly recommend that you also devise your own questions and pursue them either individually or in study groups. We've divided our questions into three categories. Here's what to expect from each:

- Those labeled "Engaging the Text" focus on the individual selection they follow. They're designed to highlight important issues in the reading, to help you begin questioning and evaluating what you've read, and sometimes to remind you to consider the author's choices of language, evidence, structure, and style.
- The questions labeled "Exploring Connections" will lead you from the selection you've just finished to one or more other readings in this book. It's hard to make sparks fly from just one stone; if you think hard about these connecting questions, though, you'll see some real collisions of ideas and perspectives, not just polite and predictable "differences of opinion."
- The final questions for each reading, "Extending the Critical Context," invite you to extend your thinking beyond the book — to your family, your community, your college, the media, or the more traditional research environment of the library. The emphasis here is on creating new knowledge by applying ideas from this book to the world around you and by testing these ideas in your world.

Active Reading

You've undoubtedly read many textbooks, but it's unlikely that you've had to deal with the kind of analytic, argumentative, and scholarly writing you'll find in college and in *Rereading America*. These different writing styles require a different approach to reading as well. In high school you probably read to "take in" information, often for the sole purpose of reproducing it later on a test. In college you'll also be expected to recognize larger issues, such as the author's theoretical slant, her goals and methods, her assumptions, and her relationship to other writers and researchers. These expectations can be especially difficult in the first two years of college, when you take introductory courses that survey large, complex fields of knowledge. With all these demands on your attention, you'll need to read actively to keep your bearings. Think of active reading as a conversation between you and the text: instead of listening passively as the writer talks, respond to what she says with questions and comments of your own. Here are some specific techniques you can practice to become a more active reader.

Prereading and Prewriting

It's best with most college reading to "preread" the text. In prereading, you briefly look over whatever information you have on the author and the selection itself. Reading chapter introductions and headnotes like those provided in this book can save you time and effort by giving you information about the author's background and concerns, the subject or thesis of the selection, and its place in the chapter as a whole. Also take a look at the title and at any headings or subheadings in the piece. These will give you further clues about an article's general scope and organization. Next, quickly skim the entire selection, paying a bit more attention to the first few paragraphs and the conclusion. Now you should have a pretty good sense of the author's position — what she's trying to say in this piece of writing.

At this point you may do one of several things before you settle down to in-depth reading. You may want to jot down in a few lines what you think the author is doing. Or you may want to make a list of questions you can ask about this topic based on your prereading. Or you may want to freewrite a page or so on the subject. Informally writing out your own ideas will prepare you for more in-depth reading by recalling what you already know about the topic.

We emphasize writing about what you've read because reading and writing are complementary activities: being an avid reader will help you as a writer by familiarizing you with a wide range of ideas and styles to draw on; likewise, writing about what you've read will give you a deeper understanding of your reading. In fact, the more actively you "process" or reshape what you've read, the better you'll comprehend and remember it. So you'll learn more effectively by marking a text as you read than by simply reading; taking notes as you read is even more effective than marking, and writing about the material for your own purposes (putting it in your own words and connecting it with what you already know) is better still.

Marking the Text and Taking Notes

After prereading and prewriting, you're ready to begin critical reading in earnest. As you read, be sure to highlight ideas and phrases that strike you as especially significant — those that seem to capture the gist of a particular paragraph or section, or those that relate directly to the author's purpose or argument. While prereading can help you identify central ideas, you may find that you need to reread difficult sections or flip back and skim an earlier passage if you feel yourself getting lost. Many students think of themselves as poor readers if they can't whip through an article at high speed without pausing. However, the best readers read recursively—that is, they shuttle back and forth, browsing, skimming, and rereading as necessary, depending on their interest, their familiarity with the subject, and the difficulty of the material. This shuttling actually parallels what goes on in your mind when you read actively, as you alternately recall prior knowledge or experience and predict, or look for clues about where the writer is going next.

Keep a record of your mental shuttling by writing comments in the margins as you read. It's often useful to "nutshell" the contents of each paragraph or section, to summarize it in a word or two written alongside the text. This note will serve as a reminder or key to the section when you return to it for further thinking, discussion, or writing. You may also want to note passages that puzzled you. Or you may want to write down personal reactions or questions stimulated by the reading. Take time to ponder why you felt confused or annoyed or affirmed by a particular passage. Let yourself wonder "out loud" in the margins as you read.

On the opposite page are one student's notes on a few stanzas of Inés Hernández's "Para Teresa" (p. 554). In this example, you can see that the reader puts nutshell or summary comments to the left of the poem and questions or personal responses to the right. You should experiment and create your own system of note taking, one that works best for the way you read. Just remember that your main goals in taking notes are to help you understand the author's overall position, to deepen and refine your responses to the selection, and to create a permanent record of those responses.

Keeping a Reading Journal

You may also want (or be required) to keep a reading journal in response to the selections you cover in *Rereading America*. In such a journal you'd keep all the freewriting that you do either before or after reading. Some students find it helpful to keep a double-entry journal, writing initial responses on the left side of the page and adding later reflections and reconsiderations on the right. You may want to use your journal as a place to explore personal reactions to your reading. You can do this by writing out imaginary dialogues — between two writers who address the same subject, between yourself and the writer of the selection, or between two parts of yourself. You can use the journal as a place to rewrite passages from a poem or essay in your own voice and from your own point of view. You can write letters to an author you particularly like or dislike (or to a character in a story or play). You might even draw a cartoon that comments on one of the reading selections.

Many students don't write as well as they could because they're afraid to take risks. They may have been repeatedly penalized for breaking "rules" of grammar or essay form; their main concern in writing, then, becomes avoiding trouble, not exploring ideas or experimenting with style. But without risk and experimentation, there's little

Para Teresa[1]

INÉS HERNÁNDEZ

Hernández's poem represents an attempt to resolve an old conflict between the speaker and her schoolmate, two Chicanas who chose radically different strategies for dealing with the majority culture. Inés Hernández (b. 1947) has taught at the University of Texas at Austin. She has published a volume of poetry, Con Razon, Corazón.

[Handwritten annotation: Writes to Teresa]

A tí-Teresa Compean   *— Why in Spanish?*
Te dedico las palabras estás
que explotan de mi corazón[2]   *— Why do her words explode?*

[Handwritten annotation: The day of their confrontation]

That day during lunch hour
at Alamo which-had-to-be-its-name   *! Why?*   5
Elementary
my dear raza   *— Feels close to T. (?)*
That day in the bathroom
Door guarded
Myself cornered   10
I was accused by you, Teresa
Tú y las demás de tus amigas
Pachucas todas
Eran Uds. cinco.[3]

[Handwritten annotation: T.'s accusation]

Me gritaban que porque me creía tan grande[4]   15
What was I trying to do, you growled
Show you up?
Make the teachers like me, pet me,   *Teachers must be white / Anglo.*
Tell me what a credit to my people I was?
I was playing right into their hands, you challenged   20
And you would have none of it.   *Speaker is a "good student."*
I was to stop.

---

[1] For Teresa. [Author's note]
[2] To you, Teresa Compean, I dedicate these words that explode from my heart. [Author's note]
[3] You and the rest of your friends, all Pachucas, there were five of you. [Author's note]
[4] You were screaming at me, asking me why I thought I was so hot. [Author's note]

possibility of growth. One of the benefits of journal writing is that it gives you a place to experiment with ideas, free from worries about "correctness." Here are two examples of student journal entries, in response to "Para Teresa" (we reprint the entries as they were written):

Entry 1 Internal Dialogue

Me 1: I agree with Inés Hernández's speaker. Her actions were justifiable in a way that if you can't fight'em, join'em. After all, Teresa Compean is just making the situation worse for her

because not only is she sabotaging the teacher-student relationship, she's also destroying her chance for a good education.

Me 2: Hey, Teresa's action was justifiable. Why else would the speaker
admit at the end of the poem that what Teresa did was fine thus
she respects Teresa more.

Me 1: The reason the speaker respected Teresa was because she
(Teresa) was still keeping her culture alive, although through
different means. It wasn't her action that the speaker respected,
it was the representation of it.

Me 2: The reason I think Teresa acted the way she did was because she
felt she had something to prove to society. She wanted to show
that no one could push her people around; that her people were
tough.

Entry 2: Personal Response

> "Con cố gắng học giỏi, cho Bá Má,
> Rỗi sau nầy dỏi sống cua con sẽ thõai mái lắm.[5]
> What if I don't want to?
> What if I can't?
> Sometimes I feel my parents don't understand what
> I'm going through.
> To them, education is money.
> And money is success.
> They don't see beyond that.
> Sometimes I want to fail my classes purposely to
> See their reaction, but that is too cruel.
> They have taught me to value education.
> Education makes you a person, makes you somebody, they say.
> I agree.
> They are proud I am going to UCLA.
> They brag to their friends, our vietnamese community, people
> I don't even know.
>   . . .
> They believe in me, but I doubt myself. . . .

[5]"Daughter, study hard (for us, your Mom and Dad), so your future will be bright
and easy."

You'll notice that neither of these students talks directly about "Para
Teresa" as a poem. Instead, each uses it as a point of departure for her
own reflections on ethnicity, identity, and education. Although we've
included a number of literary works in *Rereading America* —
everything from poetry to short stories and one-act plays — we don't
expect you to do literary analysis. We want you to use these pieces to
stimulate your own thinking about the cultural myths they address. So
don't feel you have to discuss imagery in Inés Hernández's "Para Teresa"

or characterization in Toni Cade Bambara's "The Lesson" in order to understand and appreciate them.

Finally, remember that the readings are just a starting point for discussion: you have access to a wealth of other perspectives and ideas among your family, friends, classmates; in your college library; in your personal experience; and in your own imagination. We urge you to consult them all as you grapple with the perspectives you encounter in this text.

1

Money and Success

The Myth of Individual Opportunity

Ask most people how they define the American Dream and chances are they'll say, "Success." The dream of individual opportunity has been at home in America since Europeans discovered a "new world" in the Western Hemisphere. Early immigrants like Hector St. Jean de Crève-coeur extolled the freedom and opportunity to be found in this new land. His glowing descriptions of a classless society where anyone could attain success through honesty and hard work fired the imaginations of many European readers: in *Letters from an American Farmer* (1782) he wrote, "We are all animated with the spirit of an industry which is unfettered and unrestrained, because each person works for himself. . . . We have no princes, for whom we toil, starve, and bleed: we are the most perfect society now existing in the world." The promise of a land where "the rewards of [a man's] industry follow with equal steps the progress of his labor" drew poor immigrants from Europe and fueled national expansion into the western territories.

Our national mythology abounds with illustrations of the American success story. There's Benjamin Franklin, the very model of the self-educated, self-made man, who rose from modest origins to become a renowned scientist, philosopher, and statesman. In the nineteenth century, Horatio Alger, a writer of pulp fiction for young boys, became America's best-selling author with rags-to-riches tales like *Ragged Dick* (1867), *Struggling Upward* (1886), and *Bound to Rise* (1873). The notion of success haunts us: we spend millions every year reading about the rich and famous, learning how to "make a fortune in real estate with no money down," and "dressing for success." The myth of success has even invaded our personal relationships: today it's as important to be "successful" in marriage or parenthood as it is to come out on top in business.

But dreams easily turn into nightmares. Every American who hopes to "make it" also knows the fear of failure, because the myth of success inevitably implies comparison between the haves and the have-nots, the achievers and the drones, the stars and the anonymous crowd. Under pressure of the myth, we become engrossed in status symbols: we try to live in the "right" neighborhoods, wear the "right" clothes, eat the "right" foods. These emblems of distinction assure us and others that we are different, that we stand out from the crowd. It is one of the great paradoxes of our culture that we believe passionately in the fundamental equality of all, yet strive as hard as we can to separate ourselves from our fellow citizens.

Steeped in a Puritan theology that vigorously preached the individual's responsibility to the larger community, colonial America balanced the drive for individual gain with concern for the common good. To Franklin, the way to wealth lay in practicing the virtues of honesty, hard work, and thrift: "Without industry and frugality nothing will do, and with them every thing. He that gets all he can honestly, and saves all he gets . . . will certainly become RICH" ("Advice to a Young Tradesman," 1748). And Alger's heroes were as concerned with moral rectitude as they were with financial gain: a benefactor advises Ragged Dick, "If you'll try to be somebody, and grow up into a respectable member of society, you will. You may not become rich, — it isn't everybody that becomes rich, you know, — but you can obtain a good position and be respected." But in the twentieth century the mood of the myth has changed. Contemporary guides to success, like Robert Ringer's enormously popular *Looking Out for Number One* (1977) urge readers to "forget foundationless traditions, forget the 'moral' standards others may have tried to cram down your throat . . . and, most important, think of yourself — Number One. . . . You and you alone will be responsible for your success or failure." The myth of success may have been responsible for making the United States what it is today, but it also seems to be pulling us apart. Can we exist as a living community if our greatest value can be summed up by the slogan "Me first"?

This chapter examines how Americans define and are defined by the idea of success. The first two selections offer a quick historical survey of the myth. Andrew Carnegie's "The Gospel of Wealth" presents a classic nineteenth-century view of the meaning of success and the relation of the rich to the poor. In "Changing Modes of Making It," Christopher Lasch sketches the evolution of the idea of success from the

Puritan era to the age of the corporate raider. The next four selections challenge the myth and its meaning from the perspective of Americans whose heritage or values place them outside the dominant culture. A successful Mexican American engineer, Stephen Cruz, questions the meaning of the American Dream after a series of disillusionments in his career. In a brief but powerful dramatic sketch from *The Colored Museum*, George C. Wolfe explores the personal price of success for an upwardly mobile African American man. Suzanne Gordon argues, in "Women at Risk," that the competitive, male success ethic not only is undermining the progress feminists have made in the workplace but threatens the quality of all our lives. Curtis Chang's "Streets of Gold" dissects the myth of Asian American success that has become pervasive in the American media.

The second half of the chapter takes up the issue of social class. The myth of success tells us that our class location — our membership in the lower, middle, or upper class — isn't very important when it comes to getting ahead. Most Americans don't even like to acknowledge that they belong to a particular class. Yet, by glorifying those who rise above the crowd, the myth itself makes class distinctions vitally important. Toni Cade Bambara's "The Lesson" introduces the meaning of class and success through the eyes of a group of kids from Harlem who venture downtown to see how the upper class lives and spends. Gregory Mantsios's "Class in America" offers a series of personal profiles suggesting that success may result more from class membership than from individual effort and merit. In the next selection, Mike LeFevre, a Chicago steelworker, talks bitterly about what it means to work in a blue-collar job. And in "Class Poem," Aurora Levins Morales, a Puerto Rican immigrant, celebrates and defends the privilege that her middle-class upbringing has conferred. The chapter closes with a personal reflection that complicates our ideal of individual opportunity: Sucheng Chan's "You're Short, Besides!" profiles a woman who has resisted the definitions of race, gender, and physical ability imposed on her by a society obsessed with mythic images of success. Chan invites us to reassess our own notions of what it means to achieve success in America.

Sources

Horatio Alger, *Ragged Dick*. Rpt. New York and London: Collier Macmillan, 1962.

Peter Baida, *Poor Richard's Legacy: American Business Values from Benjamin Franklin to Donald Trump*. New York: William Morrow, 1990.

J. Hector St. Jean de Crèvecoeur, *Letters from an American Farmer*. New York: Dolphin Books, 1961. First published in London, 1782.

Before Reading . . .

Working alone or in groups, make a list of people who best represent your idea of success. (You may want to consider public and political figures, leaders in government, entertainment, sports, education, or other fields.) List the specific qualities or accomplishments that make these people successful. Compare notes with your classmates, then freewrite about the meaning of success: what does it mean to you? To the class as a whole?

Keep your list and your definition. As you work through this chapter, reread and reflect on what you've written, comparing your ideas with those of the authors included here.

The Gospel of Wealth[1]

ANDREW CARNEGIE

Andrew Carnegie (1835–1919) immigrated to the United States from Scotland with his family at the age of thirteen. He rose rapidly through a series of jobs in a cotton mill and in his mid-twenties became a superintendent for the Pennsylvania Railroad. He invested in iron and steel manufacturing, and, when he retired in 1901, his Carnegie Steel Company was producing one quarter of all the steel in the United States. A strong believer in sharing his immense wealth, Carnegie donated hundreds of millions of dollars to libraries, scholarships, and public buildings like Carnegie Hall. This essay argues for the usefulness, even the necessity, of such charity or philanthropy; its most interesting features, however, are the assumptions it contains about individualism, wealth, and the public good.

The problem of our age is the proper administration of wealth, that the ties of brotherhood may still bind together the rich and poor in harmonious relationship. The conditions of human life have not only been changed, but revolutionized, within the past few hundred years. In former days there was little difference between the dwelling, dress, food, and environment of the chief and those of his retainers. The Indians are today where civilized man then was. When visiting the

[1]Published originally in the *North American Review*, CXLVIII (June 1889), 653–664, and CXLIX (December 1889), 682–698. [Editor's note]

Sioux, I was led to the wigwam of the chief. It was like the others in external appearance, and even within the difference was trifling between it and those of the poorest of his braves. The contrast between the palace of the millionaire and the cottage of the laborer with us today measures the change which has come with civilization. This change, however, is not to be deplored, but welcomed as highly beneficial. It is well, nay, essential, for the progress of the race that the houses of some should be homes for all that is highest and best in literature and the arts, and for all the refinements of civilization, rather than that none should be so. Much better this great irregularity than universal squalor. Without wealth there can be no Mæcenas.[2] The "good old times" were not good old times. Neither master nor servant was as well situated then as today. A relapse to old conditions would be disastrous to both — not the least so to him who serves — and would sweep away civilization with it. But whether the change be for good or ill, it is upon us, beyond our power to alter, and, therefore, to be accepted and made the best of it. It is a waste of time to criticize the inevitable.

It is easy to see how the change has come. One illustration will serve for almost every phase of the cause. In the manufacture of products we have the whole story. It applies to all combinations of human industry, as stimulated and enlarged by the inventions of this scientific age. Formerly, articles were manufactured at the domestic hearth, or in small shops which formed part of the household. The master and his apprentices worked side by side, the latter living with the master, and therefore subject to the same conditions. When these apprentices rose to be masters, there was little or no change in their mode of life, and they, in turn, educated succeeding apprentices in the same routine. There was, substantially, social equality, and even political equality, for those engaged in industrial pursuits had then little or no voice in the State.

The inevitable result of such a mode of manufacture was crude articles at high prices. Today the world obtains commodities of excellent quality at prices which even the preceding generation would have deemed incredible. In the commercial world similar causes have produced similar results, and the race is benefited thereby. The poor enjoy what the rich could not before afford. What were the luxuries have become the necessaries of life. The laborer has now more comforts than the farmer had a few generations ago. The farmer has more luxuries than the landlord had, and is more richly clad and better housed. The landlord has books and pictures rarer and appointments more artistic than the king could then obtain.

The price we pay for this salutary change is, no doubt, great. We assemble thousands of operatives in the factory, and in the mine, of

[2]*Mæcenas:* Roman statesman and patron of the arts (70?–8 B.C.); friend to the poets Horace and Virgil.

whom the employer can know little or nothing, and to whom he is little better than a myth. All intercourse between them is at an end. Rigid castes are formed, and, as usual, mutual ignorance breeds mutual distrust. Each caste is without sympathy with the other, and ready to credit anything disparaging in regard to it. Under the law of competition, the employer of thousands is forced into the strictest economies, among which the rates paid to labor figure prominently, and often there is friction between the employer and the employed, between capital and labor, between rich and poor. Human society loses homogeneity.

The price which society pays for the law of competition, like the   5
price it pays for cheap comforts and luxuries, is also great; but the advantages of this law are also greater still than its cost — for it is to this law that we owe our wonderful material development, which brings improved conditions in its train. But, whether the law be benign or not, we must say of it, as we say of the change in the conditions of men to which we have referred: it is here; we cannot evade it; no substitutes for it have been found; and while the law may be sometimes hard for the individual, it is best for the race, because it insures the survival of the fittest in every department. We accept and welcome, therefore, as conditions to which we must accommodate ourselves, great inequality of environment; the concentration of business, industrial and commercial, in the hands of a few; and the law of competition between these, as being not only beneficial, but essential to the future progress of the race. Having accepted these, it follows that there must be great scope for the exercise of special ability in the merchant and in the manufacturer who has to conduct affairs upon a great scale. That this talent for organization and management is rare among men is proved by the fact that it invariably secures enormous rewards for its possessor, no matter where or under what laws or conditions. The experienced in affairs always rate the MAN whose services can be obtained as a partner as not only the first consideration, but such as render the question of his capital[3] scarcely worth considering: for able men soon create capital; in the hands of those without the special talent required, capital soon takes wings. Such men become interested in firms or corporations using millions; and, estimating only simple interest to be made upon the capital invested, it is inevitable that their income must exceed their expenditure and that they must, therefore, accumulate wealth. Nor is there any middle ground which such men can occupy, because the great manufacturing or commercial concern which does not earn at least interest upon its capital soon becomes bankrupt. It must either go forward or fall behind; to stand still is impossible. It is a condition essential to its successful operation that it should be thus far profitable, and even that, in addition to interest on capital, it should make profit.

[3]*capital:* wealth, especially money available for investment.

It is a law, as certain as any of the others named, that men possessed of this peculiar talent for affairs, under the free play of economic forces must, of necessity, soon be in receipt of more revenue than can be judiciously expended upon themselves; and this law is as beneficial for the race as the others.

Objections to the foundations upon which society is based are not in order, because the condition of the race is better with these than it has been with any other which has been tried. Of the effect of any new substitutes proposed we cannot be sure. The Socialist or Anarchist who seeks to overturn present conditions is to be regarded as attacking the foundation upon which civilization itself rests, for civilization took its start from the day when the capable, industrious workman said to his incompetent and lazy fellow, "If thou dost not sow, thou shalt not reap,"[4] and thus ended primitive Communism by separating the drones from the bees. One who studies this subject will soon be brought face to face with the conclusion that upon the sacredness of property civilization itself depends — the right of the laborer to his hundred dollars in the savings-bank, and equally the legal right of the millionaire to his millions. Every man must be allowed "to sit under his own vine and fig-tree, with none to make afraid,"[5] if human society is to advance, or even to remain so far advanced as it is. To those who propose to substitute Communism for this intense Individualism, the answer therefore is: The race has tried that. All progress from that barbarous day to the present time has resulted from its displacement. Not evil, but good, has come to the race from the accumulation of wealth by those who have had the ability and energy to produce it. But even if we admit for a moment that it might be better for the race to discard its present foundation, Individualism — that it is a nobler ideal that man should labor, not for himself alone, but in and for a brotherhood of his fellows, and share with them all in common . . . even admit all this, and a sufficient answer is, This is not evolution, but revolution. It necessitates the changing of human nature itself — a work of eons, even if it were good to change it, which we cannot know.

It is not practicable in our day or in our age. Even if desirable theoretically, it belongs to another and long-succeeding sociological stratum. Our duty is with what is practicable now — with the next step possible in our day and generation. It is criminal to waste our energies in endeavoring to uproot, when all we can profitably accomplish is to bend the universal tree of humanity a little in the direction most favorable to the production of good fruit under existing circumstances.

[4]"If thou . . . reap": loose reference to a common biblical image. Compare Galatians 6:7 — ". . . whatsoever a man soweth, that shall he also reap."

[5]"to sit . . . make afraid": a biblical reference to the safety and prosperity of King Solomon's reign at its height. (See 1 Kings 4:25.)

We might as well urge the destruction of the highest existing type of man because he failed to reach our ideal as to favor the destruction of Individualism, Private Property, the Law of Accumulation of Wealth, and the Law of Competition; for these are the highest result of human experience, the soil in which society, so far, has produced the best fruit. Unequally or unjustly, perhaps, as these laws sometimes operate, and imperfect as they appear to the Idealist, they are, nevertheless, like the highest type of man, the best and most valuable of all that humanity has yet accomplished.

We start, then, with a condition of affairs under which the best interests of the race are promoted, but which inevitably gives wealth to the few. Thus far, accepting conditions as they exist, the situation can be surveyed and pronounced good. The question then arises — and if the foregoing be correct, it is the only question with which we have to deal — What is the proper mode of administering wealth after the laws upon which civilization is founded have thrown it into the hands of the few? And it is of this great question that I believe I offer the true solution. It will be understood that fortunes are here spoken of, not moderate sums saved by many years of effort, the returns from which are required for the comfortable maintenance and education of families. This is not wealth, but only competence, which it should be the aim of all to acquire, and which it is for the best interests of society should be acquired.

This, then, is held to be the duty of the man of wealth: to set an example of modest, unostentatious living, shunning display or extravagance; to provide moderately for the legitimate wants of those dependent upon him; and, after doing so, to consider all surplus revenues which come to him simply as trust funds, which he is called upon to administer, and strictly bound as a matter of duty to administer in the manner which, in his judgment, is best calculated to produce the most beneficial results for the community — the man of wealth thus becoming the mere trustee and agent for his poorer brethren, bringing to their service his superior wisdom, experience, and ability to administer, doing for them better than they would or could do for themselves.

. . . Those who would administer wisely must, indeed, be wise; for one of the serious obstacles to the improvement of our race is indiscriminate charity. It were better for mankind that the millions of the rich were thrown into the sea than so spent as to encourage the slothful, the drunken, the unworthy. Of every thousand dollars spent in so-called charity today, it is probable that nine hundred and fifty dollars is unwisely spent — so spent, indeed, as to produce the very evils which it hopes to mitigate or cure. A well-known writer of philosophic books admitted the other day that he had given a quarter of a dollar to a man who approached him as he was coming to visit the house of his friend.

He knew nothing of the habits of this beggar, knew not the use that would be made of this money, although he had every reason to suspect that it would be spent improperly. This man professed to be a disciple of Herbert Spencer;[6] yet the quarter-dollar given that night will probably work more injury than all the money will do good which its thoughtless donor will ever be able to give in true charity. He only gratified his own feelings, saved himself from annoyance — and this was probably one of the most selfish and very worst actions of his life, for in all respects he is most worthy.

In bestowing charity, the main consideration should be to help those who will help themselves; to provide part of the means by which those who desire to improve may do so; to give those who desire to rise the aids by which they may rise; to assist, but rarely or never to do all. Neither the individual nor the race is improved by almsgiving. Those worthy of assistance, except in rare cases, seldom require assistance. . . .

The best means of benefiting the community is to place within its reach the ladders upon which the aspiring can rise — free libraries, parks, and means of recreation, by which men are helped in body and mind; works of art, certain to give pleasure and improve the public taste; and public institutions of various kinds, which will improve the general condition of the people; in this manner returning their surplus wealth to the mass of their fellows in the forms best calculated to do them lasting good.

Thus is the problem of rich and poor to be solved. The laws of accumulation will be left free, the laws of distribution free. Individualism will continue, but the millionaire will be but a trustee for the poor, intrusted for a season with a great part of the increased wealth of the community, but administering it for the community far better than it could or would have done for itself. The best minds will thus have reached a stage in the development of the race in which it is clearly seen that there is no mode of disposing of surplus wealth creditable to thoughtful and earnest men into whose hands it flows, save by using it year by year for the general good. This day already dawns. Men may die without incurring the pity of their fellows, still sharers in great business enterprises from which their capital cannot be or has not been withdrawn, and which is left chiefly at death for public uses; yet the day is not far distant when the man who dies leaving behind him millions of available wealth, which was free to him to administer during life, will pass away "unwept, unhonored, and unsung,"[7] no matter to what uses he leaves the dross which he cannot take with him. Of such as these the

---

[6]*Herbert Spencer:* English philosopher and social theorist (1820–1903).

[7]*"unwept, unhonored, and unsung":* Carnegie is quoting Sir Walter Scott, *The Lay of the Last Minstrel* (1805).

public verdict will then be: "The man who dies thus rich dies disgraced."

Such, in my opinion is the true gospel concerning wealth, obedience to which is destined some day to solve the problem of the rich and the poor, and to bring "Peace on earth, among men good will."

Engaging the Text

1. How does Carnegie define progress? How does he view success? Do you accept his definitions?

2. What images of poor and working-class people does this selection convey? How, by contrast, does it portray the rich? What are Carnegie's attitudes toward each?

3. Throughout the selection, Carnegie relies on words and ideas generally associated with objective science. Find several instances of this practice. What effect do they have on the reader? How valid are Carnegie's "scientific" generalizations about wealth, poverty, and society?

4. Carnegie also gives his "gospel" of wealth a markedly religious flavor. What effect does this tone have on the reader? Do the religious and scientific allusions reinforce or contradict each other?

Extending the Critical Context

5. Brainstorm with classmates to identify several contemporary Americans among the wealthy elite. Working with one or two others, use library resources to write a brief profile of one such figure. Share these profiles in class and discuss whether or not they confirm Carnegie's idea that great wealth necessarily entails great social responsibility.

6. We've come a long way from the exploitative industrial conditions of Carnegie's day, but many still accept the notion that industrial development necessitates social, economic, and environmental damage. Work in groups to identify some of the obvious disadvantages that accompany industrial development today. Are these effects genuinely unavoidable?

7. Research social Darwinism. Begin by consulting several encyclopedias and your library's card catalog. How does Carnegie use this theory to support his arguments?

8. What is the "highest and best in literature and the arts" today (para. 1)? Who defines it? Who has access to it?

Changing Modes of Making It

Christopher Lasch

In the past twenty-five years, Christopher Lasch has built a reputa-
tion as an outspoken critic of contemporary American culture. In books
like Haven in a Heartless World: The Family Besieged *(1977) and* The
Minimal Self: Psychic Survival in Troubled Times *(1984), Lasch has*
dissected the national psyche, offering provocative interpretations of
our desires, values, and obsessions. In the following passage from The
Culture of Narcissism *(1979), Lasch examines the evolution of Amer-*
ica's attitude toward success — from its origin in the Puritan work ethic
to its most recent manifestation in the entrepreneur. Lasch (b. 1932)
teaches history at the University of Rochester in New York. His most
recent book is The True and Only Heaven: Progress and Its Critics
(1991).

Until recently, the Protestant work ethic stood as one of the most
important underpinnings of American culture. According to the myth
of capitalist enterprise, thrift and industry held the key to material
success and spiritual fulfillment. America's reputation as a land of
opportunity rested on its claim that the destruction of hereditary obstacles to advancement had created conditions in which social mobility
depended on individual initiative alone. The self-made man, archetypi-
cal embodiment of the American dream, owed his advancement to
habits of industry, sobriety, moderation, self-discipline, and avoidance
of debt. He lived for the future, shunning self-indulgence in favor of
patient, painstaking accumulation; and as long as the collective prospect looked on the whole so bright, he found in the deferral of gratification not only his principal gratification but an abundant source of
profits. In an expanding economy, the value of investments could be
expected to multiply with time, as the spokesmen for self-help, for all
their celebration of work as its own reward, seldom neglected to point
out.

In an age of diminishing expectations, the Protestant virtues no
longer excite enthusiasm. Inflation erodes investments and savings.
Advertising undermines the horror of indebtedness, exhorting the consumer to buy now and pay later. As the future becomes menacing and
uncertain, only fools put off until tomorrow the fun they can have
today. A profound shift in our sense of time has transformed work
habits, values, and the definition of success. Self-preservation has replaced self-improvement as the goal of earthly existence. In a lawless,

violent, and unpredictable society, in which the normal conditions of everyday life come to resemble those formerly confined to the underworld, men live by their wits. They hope not so much to prosper as simply to survive, although survival itself increasingly demands a large income. In earlier times, the self-made man took pride in his judgment of character and probity; today he anxiously scans the faces of his fellows not so as to evaluate their credit but in order to gauge their susceptibility to his own blandishments. He practices the classic arts of seduction and with the same indifference to moral niceties, hoping to win your heart while picking your pocket. The happy hooker stands in place of Horatio Alger[1] as the prototype of personal success. If Robinson Crusoe embodied the ideal type of economic man, the hero of bourgeois society in its ascendancy, the spirit of Moll Flanders[2] presides over its dotage.

The new ethic of self-preservation has been a long time taking shape; it did not emerge overnight. In the first three centuries of our history, the work ethic constantly changed its meaning; these vicissitudes, often imperceptible at the time, foreshadowed its eventual transformation into an ethic of personal surival. For the Puritans, a godly man worked diligently at his calling not so much in order to accumulate personal wealth as to add to the comfort and convenience of the community. Every Christian had a "general calling" to serve God and a "personal calling," in the words of Cotton Mather,[3] "by which his Usefulness, in his Neighborhood, is distinguished." This personal calling arose from the circumstance that "God hath made man a Sociable Creature." The Puritans recognized that a man might get rich at his calling, but they saw personal aggrandizement as incidental to social labor — the collective transformation of nature and the progress of useful arts and useful knowledge. They instructed men who prospered not to lord it over their neighbors. The true Christian, according to Calvinist conceptions of an honorable and godly existence, bore both good fortune and bad with equanimity, contenting himself with what came to his lot. "This he had learned to doe," said John Cotton, "if God prosper him, he had learned not to be puffed up, and if he should be exposed to want, he could do it without murmuring. It is the same act of unbeleefe, that makes a man murmure in crosses, which puffes him up in prosperity."

[1]*Horatio Alger:* U.S. author (1834–1899) of books for boys, now synonymous with the rags-to-riches dream.

[2]*Robinson Crusoe . . . Moll Flanders:* hero and heroine of novels by Daniel Defoe (1659?–1731). Whereas the shipwrecked Robinson Crusoe was industrious and self-sufficient, Moll Flanders was a pickpocket.

[3]*Cotton Mather:* U.S. clergyman and author (1663–1728). John Cotton, quoted later in this paragraph, was his grandfather.

Whatever the moral reservations with which Calvinism surrounded the pursuit of wealth, many of its practitioners, especially in New England, waxed fat and prosperous on the trade in rum and slaves. As the Puritan gave way to the Yankee, a secularized version of the Protestant ethic emerged. Whereas Cotton Mather advised against going into debt on the grounds that it injured the creditor ("Let it be uneasy unto you, at any time to think, *I have so much of another mans Estate in my Hands, and I to his damage detain it from him*"), Benjamin Franklin argued that indebtedness injured the debtor himself, putting him into his creditors' hands. Puritan sermons on the calling quoted copiously from the Bible; Franklin codified popular common sense in the sayings of Poor Richard.[4] *God helps them that help themselves. Lost time is never found again. Never leave that till to-morrow which you can do today. If you would know the value of money, go and try to borrow some; for he that goes a borrowing goes a sorrowing.*

The Puritans urged the importance of socially useful work; the   5
Yankee stressed self-improvement. Yet he understood self-improvement to consist of more than money-making. This important concept also implied self-discipline, the training and cultivation of God-given talents, above all the cultivation of reason. The eighteenth-century ideal of prosperity included not only material comfort but good health, good temper, wisdom, usefulness, and the satisfaction of knowing that you had earned the good opinion of others. In the section of his *Autobiography* devoted to "The Art of Virtue," Franklin summed up the results of a lifelong program of moral self-improvement:

> To Temperance he ascribes his long continu'd Health, and what is still left to him of a good Constitution. To Industry and Frugality, the early Easiness of his Circumstances, and Acquisition of his Fortune, with all that Knowledge which enabled him to be an useful Citizen, and obtain'd for him some Degree of Reputation among the Learned. To Sincerity and Justice the Confidence of his Country, and the honourable Employs it conferr'd upon him. And to the joint influence of the whole Mass of the Virtues, evenness of Temper, and that Cheerfulness in Conversation which makes his Company still sought for, and agreeable even to his younger Acquaintance.

Virtue pays, in the eighteenth-century version of the work ethic; but what it pays cannot be measured simply in money. The real reward of virtue is to have little to apologize for or to repent of at the end of your life. Wealth is to be valued, but chiefly because it serves as one of the necessary preconditions of moral and intellectual cultivation.

---

[4]*Poor Richard:* a fictitious character, unschooled but wise, in Benjamin Franklin's annual *Poor Richard's Almanack*, 1732–1757. He is the speaker of many famous aphorisms on the value of thrift and hard work.

From "Self-Culture" to Self-Promotion
through "Winning Images"

In the nineteenth century, the ideal of self-improvement degenerated into a cult of compulsive industry. P. T. Barnum,[5] who made a fortune in a calling the very nature of which the Puritans would have condemned ("Every calling, whereby God will be Dishonored; every Calling whereby none but the Lusts of men are Nourished: . . . every such Calling is to be Rejected"), delivered many times a lecture frankly entitled "The Art of Money-Getting," which epitomized the nineteenth-century conception of worldly success. Barnum quoted freely from Franklin but without Franklin's concern for the attainment of wisdom or the promotion of useful knowledge. "Information" interested Barnum merely as a means of mastering the market. Thus he condemned the "false economy" of the farm wife who douses her candle at dusk rather than lighting another for reading, not realizing that the "information" gained through reading is worth far more than the price of the candles. "Always take a trustworthy newspaper," Barnum advised young men on the make, "and thus keep thoroughly posted in regard to the transactions of the world. He who is without a newspaper is cut off from his species."

Barnum valued the good opinion of others not as a sign of one's usefulness but as a means of getting credit. "Uncompromising integrity of character is invaluable." The nineteenth century attempted to express all values in monetary terms. Everything had its price. Charity was a moral duty because "the liberal man will command patronage, while the sordid, uncharitable miser will be avoided." The sin of pride was not that it offended God but that it led to extravagant expenditures. "A spirit of pride and vanity, when permitted to have full sway, is the undying cankerworm which gnaws the very vitals of a man's worldly possessions."

The eighteenth century made a virtue of temperance but did not condemn moderate indulgence in the service of sociability. "Rational conversation," on the contrary, appeared to Franklin and his contemporaries to represent an important value in its own right. The nineteenth century condemned sociability itself, on the grounds that it might interfere with business. "How many good opportunities have passed, never to return, while a man was sipping a 'social glass' with his friend!" Preachments on self-help now breathed the spirit of compulsive enterprise. Henry Ward Beecher[6] defined "the *beau ideal*[7] of happiness" as a

---

[5]*P. T. Barnum:* U.S. showman and circus owner (1810–1891), reputed to have said, "There's a sucker born every minute."

[6]*Henry Ward Beecher:* U.S. preacher and writer (1813–1887), brother of Harriet Beecher Stowe.

[7]*beau ideal:* the perfect type or highest embodiment of something (based on a mistranslation of this French phrase for "ideal beauty").

state of mind in which "a man [is] so busy that he does not know whether he is or is not happy." Russell Sage[8] remarked that "work has been the chief, and, you might say, the only source of pleasure in my life."

Even at the height of the Gilded Age,[9] however, the Protestant ethic 10 did not completely lose its original meaning. In the success manuals, the McGuffey readers,[10] the Peter Parley Books,[11] and the hortatory[12] writings of the great capitalists themselves, the Protestant virtues — industry, thrift, temperance — still appeared not merely as stepping-stones to success but as their own reward.

The spirit of self-improvement lived on, in debased form, in the cult of "self-culture" — proper care and training of mind and body, nurture of the mind through "great books," development of "character." The social contribution of individual accumulation still survived as an undercurrent in the celebration of success, and the social conditions of early industrial capitalism, in which the pursuit of wealth undeniably increased the supply of useful objects, gave some substance to the claim that "accumulated capital means progress." In condemning speculation and extravagance, in upholding the importance of patient industry, in urging young men to start at the bottom and submit to "the discipline of daily life," even the most unabashed exponents of self-enrichment clung to the notion that wealth derives its value from its contribution to the general good and to the happiness of future generations.

The nineteenth-century cult of success placed surprisingly little emphasis on competition. It measured achievement not against the achievements of others but against an abstract ideal of discipline and self-denial. At the turn of the century, however, preachments on success began to stress the will to win. The bureaucratization of the corporate career changed the conditions of self-advancement; ambitious young men now had to compete with their peers for the attention and approval of their superiors. The struggle to surpass the previous generation and to provide for the next gave way to a form of sibling rivalry, in which men of approximately equal abilities jostled against each other in competition for a limited number of places. Advancement now depended on "will-power, self-confidence, energy, and initiative" — the qualities

[8]*Russell Sage:* U.S. financier and politician (1816–1906).

[9]*Gilded Age:* the late 1870s in the United States, named after Mark Twain and Charles D. Warner's *The Gilded Age*, a satirical novel unveiling government corruption and rampant materialism.

[10]*McGuffey readers:* textbooks containing moral tales for children; widely used in U.S. schools during the nineteenth and early twentieth centuries.

[11]*Peter Parley:* pen name of Samuel Griswold Goodrich (1793–1860), U.S. author and publisher whose books promoted Protestant virtues like hard work.

[12]*hortatory:* urging some type of conduct or action.

celebrated in such exemplary writings as George Lorimer's[13] *Letters from a Self-Made Merchant to His Son.* "By the end of the nineteenth century," writes John Cawelti in his study of the success myth, "self-help books were dominated by the ethos of salesmanship and boosterism. Personal magnetism, a quality which supposedly enabled a man to influence and dominate others, became one of the major keys to success." In 1907, both Lorimer's *Saturday Evening Post* and Orison Swett Marden's *Success* magazine inaugurated departments of instruction in the "art of conversation," fashion, and "culture." The management of interpersonal relations came to be seen as the essence of self-advancement. The captain of industry gave way to the confidence man, the master of impressions. Young men were told that they had to sell themselves in order to succeed.

At first, self-testing through competition remained almost indistinguishable from moral self-discipline and self-culture, but the difference became unmistakable when Dale Carnegie[14] and then Norman Vincent Peal[15] restated and transformed the tradition of Mather, Franklin, Barnum, and Lorimer. As a formula for success, winning friends and influencing people had little in common with industry and thrift. The prophets of positive thinking disparaged "the old adage that hard work alone is the magic key that will unlock the door to our desires." They praised the love of money, officially condemned even by the crudest of Gilded Age materialists, as a useful incentive. "You can never have riches in great quantities," wrote Napoleon Hill in his *Think and Grow Rich,* "unless you can work yourself into a white heat of *desire* for money." The pursuit of wealth lost the few shreds of moral meaning that still clung to it. Formerly the Protestant virtues appeared to have an independent value of their own. Even when they became purely instrumental, in the second half of the nineteenth century, success itself retained moral and social overtones, by virtue of its contribution to the sum of human comfort and progress. Now success appeared as an end in its own right, the victory over your competitors that alone retained the capacity to instill a sense of self-approval. The latest success manuals differ from earlier ones — even surpassing the cynicism of Dale Carnegie and Peale — in their frank acceptance of the need to exploit and intimidate others, in their lack of interest in the substance of success, and in the candor with which they insist that appearances — "winning

---

[13]*George Lorimer:* editor of *The Saturday Evening Post* from 1899 to 1937, during which time he published works by key American writers.

[14]*Dale Carnegie:* U.S. lecturer (1888–1955) and author of *How to Win Friends and Influence People* (1936) and other books on presenting a successful personality.

[15]*Norman Vincent Peale:* U.S. pastor, religious writer, and radio and television preacher (b. 1898). Peale's *The Power of Positive Thinking* (1952) set a record by being a best-seller for three years.

images" — count for more than performance, ascription for more than achievement. One author seems to imply that the self consists of little more than its "image" reflected in others' eyes. "Although I'm not being original when I say it, I'm sure you'll agree that the way you see yourself will reflect the image you portray to others." Nothing succeeds like the appearance of success.

The Eclipse of Achievement

In a society in which the dream of success has been drained of any meaning beyond itself, men have nothing against which to measure their achievements except the achievements of others. Self-approval depends on public recognition and acclaim, and the quality of this approval has undergone important changes in its own right. The good opinion of friends and neighbors, which formerly informed a man that he had lived a useful life, rested on appreciation of his accomplishments. Today men seek the kind of approval that applauds not their actions but their personal attributes. They wish to be not so much esteemed as admired. They crave not fame but the glamour and excitement of celebrity. They want to be envied rather than respected. Pride and acquisitiveness, the sins of an ascendant capitalism, have given way to vanity. Most Americans would still define success as riches, fame, and power, but their actions show that they have little interest in the substance of these attainments. What a man does matters less than the fact that he has "made it." Whereas fame depends on the performance of notable deeds acclaimed in biography and works of history, celebrity — the reward of those who project a vivid or pleasing exterior or have otherwise attracted attention to themselves — is acclaimed in the news media, in gossip columns, on talk shows, in magazines devoted to "personalities." Accordingly it is evanescent, like news itself, which loses its interest when it loses its novelty. Worldly success has always carried with it a certain poignancy, an awareness that "you can't take it with you"; but in our time, when success is so largely a function of youth, glamour, and novelty, glory is more fleeting than ever, and those who win the attention of the public worry incessantly about losing it.

Success in our society has to be ratified by publicity. The tycoon   15
who lives in personal obscurity, the empire builder who controls the destinies of nations from behind the scenes, are vanishing types. Even nonelective officials, ostensibly preoccupied with questions of high policy, have to keep themselves constantly on view; all politics becomes a form of spectacle. It is well known that Madison Avenue packages politicians and markets them as if they were cereals or deodorants; but the art of public relations penetrates even more deeply into political life, transforming policy making itself. The modern prince does not much

care that "there's a job to be done" — the slogan of American capitalism at an earlier and more enterprising stage of its development; what interests him is that "relevant audiences," in the language of the Pentagon Papers,[16] have to be cajoled, won over, seduced. He confuses successful completion of the task at hand with the impression he makes or hopes to make on others. Thus American officials blundered into the war in Vietnam because they could not distinguish the country's military and strategic interests from "our reputation as a guarantor," as one of them put it. More concerned with the trappings than with the reality of power, they convinced themselves that failure to intervene would damage American "credibility." They borrowed the rhetoric of games theory to dignify their obsession with appearances, arguing that American policy in Vietnam had to address itself to "the relevant 'audiences' of U.S. actions" — the communists, the South Vietnamese, "our allies (who must trust us as 'underwriters')," and the American public.

When policy making, the search for power, and the pursuit of wealth have no other objects than to excite admiration or envy, men lose the sense of objectivity, always precarious under the best of circumstances. Impressions overshadow achievements. Public men fret about their ability to rise to crisis, to project an image of decisiveness, to give a convincing performance of executive power. Their critics resort to the same standards: when doubts began to be raised about the leadership of the Johnson administration, they focused on the "credibility gap." Public relations and propaganda have exalted the image and the pseudo-event. People "talk constantly," Daniel Boorstin has written, "not of things themselves, but of their images."

In the corporate structure as in government, the rhetoric of achievement, of single-minded devotion to the task at hand — the rhetoric of performance, efficiency, and productivity — no longer provides an accurate description of the struggle for personal survival. "Hard work," according to Eugene Emerson Jennings, ". . . constitutes a necessary but not sufficient cause of upward mobility. It is not a route to the top." A newspaper man with experience both in journalism and in the Southern Regional Council has reported that "in neither, I realized, did it matter to the people in charge how well or how badly I performed. . . . Not the goals, but keeping the organization going, became the important thing." Even the welfare of the organization, however, no longer excites the enthusiasm it generated in the fifties. The "self-sacrificing company man," writes Jennings, has become "an obvious anachro-

---

[16]*Pentagon Papers:* the popular name given to a secret 1967–1969 Department of Defense study that criticized United States involvement in Southeast Asia and suggested that the government had misrepresented its role in the Vietnam War.

nism."[17] The upwardly mobile corporate executive "does not view himself as an organization man." His "anti-organizational posture," in fact, has emerged as his "chief characteristic." He advances through the corporate ranks not by serving the organization but by convincing his associates that he possesses the attributes of a "winner."

[17]In the 1950s, the organization man thought of an attractive, socially gifted wife as an important asset to his career. Today executives are warned of the "apparent serious conflict between marriage and a management career." A recent report compares the "elite corps of professional managers" to the Janissaries, elite soldiers of the Ottoman empire who were taken from their parents as children, raised by the state, and never allowed to marry. "A young man considering [a managerial] career might well think of himself as a modern-day Janissary — and consider very, very carefully whether marriage in any way conforms to his chosen life." [Author's note]

Engaging the Text

1. Discuss Lasch's assertion that today we work simply to survive and not to "prosper" in the original sense of the word.

2. Explain the Puritan concept of a "calling." How does it differ from our contemporary view of jobs and careers?

3. According to Lasch, what type of person is the modern American entrepreneur? Do you accept this characterization?

4. What differences in values does Lasch see between the Puritan, the Yankee, the nineteenth-century capitalist, and the competitive "confidence man, the master of impressions" (para. 12)?

Exploring Connections

5. How would Lasch characterize Andrew Carnegie's attitudes toward work and success in the preceding selection? Does the example of Carnegie support or weaken Lasch's claims about success and morality in the nineteenth century?

6. Side by side with the mythical notion that anyone in the United States can make it to the top is the idea that the United States consists primarily of a huge middle class; yet both Carnegie and Lasch focus on people who want to stand above the middle class. What images does the term "middle class" conjure up? Does belonging to the middle class mean you have failed? Does it mean you haven't truly succeeded?

Extending the Critical Context

7. Working in small groups, design an informal survey to find out how students on your campus define success. Are they chiefly motivated by a desire for

material goods, power, respect, self-improvement, self-fulfillment? Try to draw some conclusions from your results: Are there differences in the ways men and women define success? Do students of different ethnicities define success differently?

8. Watch *Wall Street* or *Working Girl* on video. To what extent do the attitudes and behavior of the characters in the film reflect Lasch's description of contemporary corporate culture?

Stephen Cruz

STUDS TERKEL

Studs Terkel (b. 1912) is probably the best-known practitioner of oral history in the United States. He has compiled several books by interviewing dozens of widely varying people — ordinary people, for the most part — about important subjects, like work, World War II, and the Depression. The edited versions of these interviews are often surprisingly powerful crystallizations of American social history, and Terkel's subjects give voice to the frustrations and hopes of whole generations of Americans. The speaker here, Stephen Cruz, is a man who at first glance seems to be living the American dream of success and upward mobility; he is never content, however, and he comes to question his own values and his place in the predominantly Anglo society where he is "successful." This selection first appeared in Terkel's American Dreams: Lost and Found *(1980).*

He is thirty-nine.

"The family came in stages from Mexico. Your grandparents usually came first, did a little work, found little roots, put together a few bucks, and brought the family in, one at a time. Those were the days when controls at the border didn't exist as they do now."

You just tried very hard to be whatever it is the system wanted of you. I was a good student and, as small as I was, a pretty good athlete. I was well liked, I thought. We were fairly affluent, but we lived down where all the trashy whites were. It was the only housing we could get. As kids, we never understood why. We did everything right. We didn't have those Mexican accents, we were never on welfare. Dad wouldn't be on welfare to save his soul. He woulda died first. He worked during the depression. He carries that pride with him, even today.

Of the five children, I'm the only one who really got into the business world. We learned quickly that you have to look for opportunities and add things up very quickly. I was in liberal arts, but as soon as Sputnik[1] went up, well, golly, hell, we knew where the bucks were. I went right over to the registrar's office and signed up for engineering. I got my degree in '62. If you had a master's in business as well, they were just paying all kinds of bucks. So that's what I did. Sure enough, the market was super. I had fourteen job offers. I could have had a hundred if I wanted to look around.

I never once associated these offers with my being a minority. I was   5
aware of the Civil Rights Act of 1964, but I was still self-confident enough to feel they wanted me because of my abilities. Looking back, the reason I got more offers than the other guys was because of the government edict. And I thought it was because I was so goddamned brilliant. (Laughs.) In 1962, I didn't get as many offers as those who were less qualified. You have a tendency to blame the job market. You just don't want to face the issue of discrimination.

I went to work with Procter & Gamble. After about two years, they told me I was one of the best supervisors they ever had and they were gonna promote me. Okay, I went into personnel. Again, I thought it was because I was such a brilliant guy. Now I started getting wise to the ways of the American Dream. My office was glass-enclosed, while all the other offices were enclosed so you couldn't see into them. I was the visible man.

They made sure I interviewed most of the people that came in. I just didn't really think there was anything wrong until we got a new plant manager, a southerner. I received instructions from him on how I should interview blacks. Just check and see if they smell, okay? That was the beginning of my training program. I started asking: Why weren't we hiring more minorities? I realized I was the only one in a management position.

I guess as a Mexican I was more acceptable because I wasn't really black. I was a good compromise. I was visibly good. I hired a black secretary, which was *verboten*. When I came back from my vacation, she was gone. My boss fired her while I was away. I asked why and never got a good reason.

Until then, I never questioned the American Dream. I was convinced if you worked hard, you could make it. I never considered myself different. That was the trouble. We had been discriminated against a lot, but I never associated it with society. I considered it an individual matter. Bad people, my mother used to say. In '68 I began to question.

I was doing fine. My very first year out of college, I was making   10

[1]*Sputnik:* satellite launched by the Soviet Union in 1957; this launch signaled the beginning of the "space race" between the United States and USSR.

twelve thousand dollars. I left Procter & Gamble because I really saw no opportunity. They were content to leave me visible, but my thoughts were not really solicited. I may have overreacted a bit, with the plant manager's attitude, but I felt there's no way a Mexican could get ahead here.

I went to work for Blue Cross. It's 1969. The Great Society[2] is in full swing. Those who never thought of being minorities before are being turned on. Consciousness raising is going on. Black programs are popping up in universities. Cultural identity and all that. But what about the one issue in this country: economics? There were very few management jobs for minorities, especially blacks.

The stereotypes popped up again. If you're Oriental, you're real good in mathematics. If you're Mexican, you're a happy guy to have around, pleasant but emotional. Mexicans are either sleeping or laughing all the time. Life is just one big happy kind of event. *Mañana.* Good to have as part of the management team, as long as you weren't allowed to make decisions.

I was thinking there were two possibilities why minorities were not making it in business. One was deep, ingrained racism. But there was still the possibility that they were simply a bunch of bad managers who just couldn't cut it. You see, until now I believed everything I was taught about the dream: the American businessman is omnipotent and fair. If we could show these turkeys there's money to be made in hiring minorities, these businessmen — good managers, good decision makers — would respond. I naïvely thought American businessmen gave a damn about society, that given a choice they would do the right thing. I had that faith.

I was hungry for learning about decision-making criteria. I was still too far away from top management to see exactly how they were working. I needed to learn more. Hey, just learn more and you'll make it. That part of the dream hadn't left me yet. I was still clinging to the notion of work your ass off, learn more than anybody else, and you'll get in that sphere.

During my fifth year at Blue Cross, I discovered another flaw in the American Dream. Minorities are as bad to other minorities as whites are to minorities. The strongest weapon the white manager had is the old divide and conquer routine. My mistake was thinking we were all at the same level of consciousness.

I had attempted to bring together some blacks with the other minorities. There weren't too many of them anyway. The Orientals never really got involved. The blacks misunderstood what I was presenting, perhaps I said it badly. They were on the cultural kick: a manager

---

[2]*the Great Society:* President Lyndon B. Johnson's term for the American society he hoped to establish through social reforms, including an antipoverty program.

should be crucified for saying "Negro" instead of "black." I said as long as the Negro or the black gets the job, it doesn't mean a damn what he's called. We got into a huge hassle. Management, of course, merely smiled. The whole struggle fell flat on its face. It crumpled from divisiveness. So I learned another lesson. People have their own agenda. It doesn't matter what group you're with, there is a tendency to put the other guy down regardless.

The American Dream began to look so damn complicated, I began to think: Hell, if I wanted, I could just back away and reap the harvest myself. By this time, I'm up to twenty-five thousand dollars a year. It's beginning to look good, and a lot of people are beginning to look good. And they're saying: "Hey, the American Dream, you got it. Why don't you lay off?" I wasn't falling in line.

My bosses were telling me I had all the "ingredients" for top management. All that was required was to "get to know our business." This term comes up all the time. If I could just warn all minorities and women whenever you hear "get to know our business," they're really saying "fall in line." Stay within that fence, and glory can be yours. I left Blue Cross disillusioned. They offered me a director's job at thirty thousand dollars before I quit.

All I had to do was behave myself. I had the "ingredients" of being a good Chicano, the equivalent of the good nigger. I was smart. I could articulate well. People didn't know by my speech patterns that I was of Mexican heritage. Some tell me I don't look Mexican, that I have a certain amount of Italian, Lebanese, or who knows. (Laughs.)

One could easily say: "Hey, what's your bitch? The American Dream has treated you beautifully. So just knock it off and quit this crap you're spreading around." It was a real problem. Every time I turned around, America seemed to be treating me very well.

Hell, I even thought of dropping out, the hell with it. Maybe get a job in a factory. But what happened? Offers kept coming in. I just said to myself: God, isn't this silly? You might as well take the bucks and continue looking for the answer. So I did that. But each time I took the money, the conflict in me got more intense, not less.

Wow, I'm up to thirty-five thousand a year. This is a savings and loan business. I have faith in the executive director. He was the kind of guy I was looking for in top management: understanding, humane, also looking for the formula. Until he was up for consideration as executive v.p. of the entire organization. All of a sudden everything changed. It wasn't until I saw this guy flip-flop that I realized how powerful vested interests are. Suddenly he's saying: "Don't rock the boat. Keep a low profile. Get in line." Another disappointment.

Subsequently, I went to work for a consulting firm. I said to myself: Okay, I've got to get close to the executive mind. I need to know how they work. Wow, a consulting firm.

Consulting firms are saving a lot of American businessmen. They're doing it in ways that defy the whole notion of capitalism. They're not allowing these businesses to fail. Lockheed was successful in getting U.S. funding guarantees because of the efforts of consulting firms working on their behalf, helping them look better. In this kind of work, you don't find minorities. You've got to be a proven success in business before you get there.

The American Dream, I see now, is governed not by education, opportunity, and hard work, but by power and fear. The higher up in the organization you go, the more you have to lose. The dream is *not losing*. This is the notion pervading America today: don't lose. 25

When I left the consulting business, I was making fifty thousand dollars a year. My last performance appraisal was: you can go a long way in this business, you can be a partner, but you gotta know our business. It came up again. At this point, I was incapable of being disillusioned any more. How easy it is to be swallowed up by the same set of values that governs the top guy. I was becoming that way. I was becoming concerned about losing that fifty grand or so a year. So I asked other minorities who had it made. I'd go up and ask 'em: "look, do you owe anything to others?" The answer was: "we owe nothing to anybody." They drew from the civil rights movement but felt no debt. They've quickly forgotten how it happened. It's like I was when I first got out of college. Hey, it's really me, I'm great. I'm great. I'm as angry with these guys as I am with the top guys.

Right now, it's confused. I've had fifteen years in the business world as "a success." Many Anglos would be envious of my progress. Fifty thousand dollars a year puts you in the one or two top percent of all Americans. Plus my wife making another thirty thousand. We had lots of money. When I gave it up, my cohorts looked at me not just as strange, but as something of a traitor. "You're screwing it up for all of us. You're part of our union, we're the elite, we should govern. What the hell are you doing?" So now I'm looked at suspiciously by my peer group as well.

I'm teaching at the University of Wisconsin at Platteville. It's nice. My colleagues tell me what's on their minds. I got a farm next-door to Platteville. With farm prices being what they are (laughs), it's a losing proposition. But with university work and what money we've saved, we're gonna be all right.

The American Dream is getting more elusive. The dream is being governed by a few people's notion of what the dream is. Sometimes I feel it's a small group of financiers that gets together once a year and decides all the world's issues.

It's getting so big. The small-business venture is not there any more. Business has become too big to influence. It can't be changed internally. A counterpower is needed. 30

Engaging the Text

1. As Cruz moves up the economic ladder, he experiences growing conflict that keeps him from being content and proud of his accomplishments. To what do you contribute his discontent? Is his "solution" the one you would recommend?

2. Cruz says that the real force in America is the dream of "not losing." What does he mean by this? Do you agree?

3. What, according to Stephen Cruz, is wrong with the American Dream? Write an essay in which you first define and then either defend or critique his position.

4. Imagine the remainder of Stephen Cruz's life. Write a few paragraphs continuing his story. Read these aloud and discuss.

Exploring Connections

5. Write a detailed analysis of Stephen Cruz's problem from the point of view of Andrew Carnegie, "The Gospel of Wealth," (p. 20). How would Carnegie assess Cruz's situation and his attitudes? What advice would he give Cruz? Or, write a critique of Carnegie's philosophy from Cruz's point of view. How might Cruz respond to Carnegie's assessment?

6. Using Christopher Lasch's discussion of the American work ethic (p. 27), analyze Stephen Cruz's attitudes toward both work and success. How do his attitudes compare with those of the Puritans, the early captains of industry, and contemporary entrepreneurs? Does Lasch help us understand what Cruz is searching for?

Extending the Critical Context

7. According to Cruz, in 1969 few management positions were open to members of minority groups. Working in small groups, go to the library and look up current statistics on minorities in business (for example, the number of large minority-owned companies; the number of minority chief executives among major corporations; the distribution of minorities among top management, middle management, supervisory, and clerical positions). Compare notes with classmates and discuss.

Symbiosis

GEORGE C. WOLFE

"Symbiosis" is one section of The Colored Museum *(1985), a play structured as a series of related sketches about the experience of African Americans and the roles they have come to play in race-conscious America. Critics have praised the work for its combination of wit and shrewd insight; both are amply displayed in this selection, in which a "Black Man" on the way up confronts his younger self. George C. Wolfe (b. 1954) has studied drama and musical theater at Pomona College and New York University. He is the librettist — that is, he wrote the words — for Duke Ellington's opera* Queenie Pie, *and he is a contributing author to* The Living Theatre.

(The Temptations singing "My Girl" are heard as lights reveal a Black Man in corporate dress standing before a large trash can throwing objects from a Saks Fifth Avenue bag into it. Circling around him with his every emotion on his face is The Kid, who is dressed in a late-sixties street style. His moves are slightly heightened. As the scene begins the music fades.)

MAN *(with contained emotions):* My first pair of Converse All Stars. Gone.

My first Afro-comb. Gone.

My first dashiki. Gone.

My autographed pictures of Stokely Carmichael,[1] Jomo Kenyatta,[2] and Donna Summer.[3] Gone.

KID *(near tears, totally upset):* This shit's not fair, man. Damn! Hell! Shit! Shit! It's not fair!

MAN: My first jar of Murray's pomade.[4]

My first can of Afro-sheen.

My first box of curl relaxer. Gone! Gone! Gone!

Eldridge Cleaver's *Soul on Ice.*[5]

KID: Not *Soul on Ice!*

---

[1]*Stokely Carmichael:* organizer of the Student Nonviolent Coordinating Committee (SNCC) during the civil rights movement; later active in the Black Panther party.

[2]*Jomo Kenyatta:* president of Kenya (1964–1978).

[3]*Donna Summer:* popular disco singer of the 1970s.

[4]*Murray's pomade, Afro-sheen:* hair care products for African Americans.

[5]*Soul on Ice:* best-selling autobiographical work of 1968. See bell hooks's discussion of Cleaver's book (p. 249).

MAN: It's been replaced on my bookshelf by *The Color Purple.*[6]
KID *(horrified)*: No!
MAN: Gone!
KID: But —
MAN: Jimi Hendrix's "Purple Haze." Gone.
   Sly Stone's "There's a Riot Goin' On." Gone.
   The Jackson Five's "I Want You Back."
KID: Man, you can't throw that away. It's living proof Michael had a black nose.
MAN: It's all going. Anything and everything that connects me to you, to who I was, to what we were, is out of my life.
KID: You've got to give me another chance.
MAN: *Fingertips Part 2.*
KID: Man, how can you do that? That's vintage Stevie Wonder.
MAN: You want to know how, Kid? You want to know how? Because my survival depends on it. Whether you know it or not, the Ice Age is upon us.
KID *(jokingly)*: Man, what the hell you talkin' about? It's 95 damn degrees.
MAN: The climate is changing, Kid, and either you adjust or you end up extinct. A sociological dinosaur. Do you understand what I'm trying to tell you? King Kong would have made it to the top if only he had taken the elevator. Instead he brought attention to his struggle and ended up dead.
KID *(pleading)*: I'll change. I swear I'll change. I'll maintain a low profile. You won't even know I'm around.
MAN: If I'm to become what I'm to become then you've got to go. . . . I have no history. I have no past.
KID: Just like that?
MAN *(throwing away a series of buttons)*: Free Angela! Free Bobby! Free Huey, Duey, and Louie![7] U.S. out of Viet Nam. U.S. out of Cambodia. U.S. out of Harlem, Detroit, and Newark. Gone! . . . The Temptations' Greatest Hits!
KID *(grabbing the album)*: No!!!

---

[6]*The Color Purple:* best-selling 1982 novel by womanist writer Alice Walker.
[7]*Angela . . . Louie:* Angela: Angela Davis, philosophy professor active in the U.S. Communist party, imprisoned on conspiracy charges for sixteen months before being acquitted in 1972. Bobby: Bobby Seale, cofounder and chairman of the Black Panther party. As one of the "Chicago Eight" at the 1968 Democratic National Convention, Seale was indicted for incitement to riot. In 1969 he was sentenced to four years in prison for contempt of court, but the charges against him were dropped. Huey: Huey Newton (1942–1989), cofounder with Bobby Seale of the Black Panther party, was convicted in 1967 of voluntary manslaughter in the death of a police officer, but the conviction was overturned twenty-two months later. Duey and Louie: a play on the names of cartoon character Donald Duck's nephews — Huey, Dewey, and Louie.

MAN: Give it back, Kid.

KID: No.

MAN: I said give it back!

KID: No. I can't let you trash this. Johnny man, it contains fourteen classic cuts by the tempting Temptations. We're talking, "Ain't Too Proud to Beg," "Papa Was a Rolling Stone," "My Girl."

MAN (*warning*): I don't have all day.

KID: For God's sake, Johnny man, "My Girl" is the jam to end all jams. It's what we are. Who we are. It's a way of life. Come on, man, for old times' sake. (*Singing.*)

[*The Kid sings three lines from "My Girl."*]

Come on, Johnny man, you ain't "bummin'," man.

[*He sings another line.*]

Here comes your favorite part. Come on, Johnny man, sing.

[*He sings another four lines of "My Girl," until the Man cuts him off.*]

MAN (*exploding*): I said give it back!

KID (*angry*): I ain't givin' you a muthafuckin' thing!

MAN: Now you listen to me!

KID: No, you listen to me. This is the kid you're dealin' with, so don't fuck with me!

(*He hits his fist into his hand, and The Man grabs for his heart. The Kid repeats with two more hits, which causes the man to drop to the ground, grabbing his heart.*)

KID: Jai! Jai! Jai!

MAN: Kid, please.

KID: Yeah. Yeah. Now who's begging who? . . . Well, well, well, look at Mr. Cream-of-the-Crop, Mr. Colored-Man-on-Top. Now that he's making it, he no longer wants anything to do with the Kid. Well, you may put all kinds of silk ties 'round your neck and white lines up your nose, but the Kid is here to stay. You may change your women as often as you change your underwear, but the Kid is here to stay. And regardless of how much of your past that you trash, I ain't goin' no damn where. Is that clear? Is that clear?

MAN (*regaining his strength, beginning to stand*): Yeah.

KID: Good. (*after a beat*) You all right, man? You all right? I don't want to hurt you, but when you start all that talk about getting rid of me, well, it gets me kind of crazy. We need each other. We are one . . .

(*Before THE KID can complete his sentence, THE MAN grabs him around his neck and starts to choke him violently.*)

MAN (*as he strangles him*): The . . . Ice . . . Age . . . is . . . upon us . . . and either we adjust . . . or we end up . . . extinct.

(*THE KID hangs limp in THE MAN's arms.*)

MAN (*laughing*): Man kills his own rage. Film at eleven. (*He then dumps* The Kid *into the trash can, and closes the lid. He speaks in a contained voice.*) I have no history. I have no past. I can't. It's too much. It's much too much. I must be able to smile on cue. And watch the news with an impersonal eye. I have no stake in the madness.
Being black is too emotionally taxing; therefore I will be black only on weekends and holidays.

(*He then turns to go, but sees the Temptations' album lying on the ground. He picks it up and sings quietly to himself.*)

[*The Man sings two lines from his favorite part of "My Girl."*]

(*He pauses, but then crosses to the trash can, lifts the lid, and just as he is about to toss the album in, a hand reaches from inside the can and grabs hold of The Man's arm. The Kid then emerges from the can with a death grip on The Man's arm.*)

KID (*smiling*): What's happenin'?

(*Blackout.*)

Engaging the Text

1. Who are the man and the kid, and why aren't they given names? What does each represent?

2. Working in small groups, discuss the significance of the people and things mentioned in the beginning of the play (e.g., Stokely Carmichael, Murray's

Pomade, and "Purple Haze"). Taken as a group, are these appropriate symbols of African American culture, or do they threaten to trivialize Black heritage?

3. If the ideas here were presented in the form of traditional arguments instead of dramatic performance, what would each character's argument be? What is Wolfe's thesis? What is your own opinion on "fitting in" versus maintaining ethnic identity: does success require that you jettison the past?

4. In biology, "symbiosis" refers to two organisms living together (even attached or one inside the other) in a mutually beneficial way. Is the relationship of man and kid symbiotic in this play?

Exploring Connections

5. Compare and contrast the struggle in this play with the difficulties Stephen Cruz faces (p. 36). How does each selection define success and reveal the costs of success for members of ethnic minorities?

6. Andrew Carnegie's "The Gospel of Wealth" (p. 20), points to the idea of success being a matter of individual achievement — of standing out from the crowd. "Stephen Cruz" and *Symbiosis* both point to the importance of fitting in with the crowd. How do you account for this difference, and which view of success do you expect to be closer to the truth in your own life?

Extending the Critical Context

7. *Symbiosis* suggests that we all try to deny our past selves as we move into new social situations. Have you ever struggled with a past self? What was this person like? How would you describe her or him?

Women at Risk

SUZANNE GORDON

In this excerpt from Prisoners of Men's Dreams *(1991), Suzanne Gordon looks beyond the dramatic accomplishments of women during the past two decades and argues that women's remarkable progress has masked fundamental social problems. In brief, even though women are attaining success as it has traditionally been defined by men, they have made little progress toward actually redefining cultural values. A free-lance reporter, Gordon (b. 1945) has published several books as well as articles in* The Nation, The Atlantic, *the* Washington Post, *and the* Boston Globe. *Her subjects have ranged from ballet to the lives of South African servants; she is particularly interested in medical, ethical, and social issues concerning women.*

Women and their vision of a more humane world are at risk.

Only a few short years ago, women's liberation promised to change our world. Our emphasis on the value of relationships, interdependence, and collaboration sought to balance work with love, hierarchy with healing, individualism with community. Through our profound commitment to caring, we hoped finally to teach American society that care was neither a reward for hard work nor an indulgence meted out to the infirm and vulnerable, but rather a fundamental human need. Many women who participated in our movement demanded that equality make a difference — not only for our sisters and ourselves, but for men and for generations to come.

Now, two decades after the great social upheavals of the 1960s, women are in danger of becoming prisoners of men's dreams.

It has required centuries of excruciating struggle, but we have finally arrived on the shores of the masculine world. And yet, as we have moved inland, slowly, almost imperceptibly, too many of us seem to have been wooed away from our original animating goal of changing this landscape.

We have not attained as much power and influence as we'd hoped.   5
Although millions of us live in poverty that has been increasingly feminized, we have nonetheless been assimilated into the American marketplace. Millions of us now participate in an economic, social, and political system that is highly competitive, aggressive, and individualistic; a system that values workplace success and the accumulation of wealth, power, and privilege above all else.

Many of us are now doctors and lawyers, bankers and stockbrokers, scientists and engineers, legislators and congressional representatives, mayors and even governors. We are telephone workers and underground miners, carpenters and house painters, auto mechanics, mailpersons, and cab drivers. A few of us sit on the boards of the nation's major corporations. We have started our own magazines and secured positions of influence in the media — editing newspapers, producing network news shows, writing and directing for television, running major motion picture studios and determining the content of at least some of the films they make.

Some of us supervise not only other women but men. We boss secretaries, give orders to nurses, hire nannies, and are served by flight attendants as we fly the nation's skies. Not all of us, but some of us, participate in making the decisions that govern other women's lives.

We are lobbyists, political consultants, and politicians. We advise women — and sometimes men — how to run campaigns and shepherd bills through state legislatures and Congress. We may not have all the votes, and we certainly do not have the final veto — but to our constituents we interpret reality, define the possible, and help create the probable.

We have entered the male kingdom — and yet, we have been forced to play by the king's rules.

That is not what an important segment of the feminist movement promised. 10

Feminism was, and remains, one of the most powerful social movements of the twentieth century. When women marched and protested and united to recast the contours of our world, many of us carried a very different transformative vision in our hearts and minds. Twenty years ago, a significant group of feminists believed in women, in the potential of femininity and the transformative power of feminism. It was clear, these transformative feminists[1] argued, that our masculine socialization — our ingrained insecurity about our competence and talents outside of the domestic sphere — was a wound. But our feminine socialization, so many sensed, was a source of strength to be mobilized not only for the private but for the public good.

Socialized in the home, the community, and the helping professions, women devoted themselves to nurturing, empowering, and caring for others. In a society little dedicated to sustaining relationships, encouraging cooperation and community, recognizing the value of collaboration, or rewarding altruism rather than greed, women have historically defined, defended, and sustained a set of insights, values, and activities which, if never dominant, at least provided a counterweight and an alternative ideal to the anomie,[2] disconnectedness, fragmentation, and commercialization of our culture.

Many of us saw women's experiences and concerns as the source of a sorely needed transformative vision. And our dream of liberation was fueled by the hope that we could carry this vision with us into the marketplace and encourage a new ethic of caring even as we demonstrated our own competence. Our vision of a more humane society was based on a profound commitment to caring — to the emotional and physical activities, attitudes, and ethical comportment that help people grow and develop, that nurture and empower them, affirming their strengths and helping them cope with their weaknesses, vulnerabilities, and life crises.

Thus we hoped to create a less hierarchial workplace, one in which people could help others grow and develop; in which knowledge, experience, power, and wealth could be shared more equitably. We wanted

---

[1]There are many different ways to refer to the feminisms and feminists that I am describing. In her work, Nancy Cott distinguishes between those who focused on equal rights and those who were concerned with using the insights of feminine socialization to show that women could make a difference in the world. Some feminists refer to "liberal" and "radical" feminists. Nel Noddings distinguishes between first, second, and third generations of feminists and Jane Mansbridge talks about "nurturant" feminism. . . . I will refer to "transformative" and "adaptive," or "equal-opportunity," feminism. [Author's note]

[2]*anomie:* a state of society in which norms and values have broken down.

both the private and public sector to allow and even help us fulfill our caring responsibilities by implementing the kinds of social policies that are essential to any real integration of work and personal relationships. And we wanted to infuse our society with a greater respect for the caring work that women have so long performed and refined both inside and outside the home. Most importantly, we wanted men to value and share that caring with us in the home and the workplace.

American society has made it enormously difficult for women — or men — to hold to such an alternative ideal. Many men have sabotaged women's struggle for equality and difference from its inception, and they continue to resist our every effort to improve our lives. When America's masculine-dominated, marketplace culture has not openly thwarted women's hopes and dreams, it has often tried to co-opt women's liberation. Thus while many women have remained faithful to this transformative vision and still struggle valiantly to make it a reality, it has been difficult for millions of others to resist a barrage of messages from corporate America and the media that define mastery and liberation in competitive, marketplace terms. Corporate America and the media have declared that feminism triumphs when women gain the opportunity to compete in what Abraham Lincoln once called the great "race of life." Following a classic pattern in which the victims of aggression identify with their aggressors, many prominent advocates of women's liberation within the highly competitive capitalist marketplace have themselves embraced this masculinized corruption of feminist ideals.

Placing competition above caring, work above love, power above empowerment, and personal wealth above human worth, corporate America has created a late-twentieth-century hybrid — a refashioned feminism that takes traditional American ideas about success and repackages them for the new female contestants in the masculine marketplace. This hybrid is equal-opportunity feminism — an ideology that abandons transformation to adaptation, promoting male-female equality without questioning the values that define the very identity it seeks.

Betty Friedan, whose important work launched the liberal branch of the feminist movement, was one of the first to give voice to this ideology, in 1963 in *The Feminine Mystique*. For her, feminism and competition seemed to be synonymous. "When women take their education and abilities seriously and put them to use, ultimately they have to compete with men," she wrote. "It is better for a woman to compete impersonally in society, as men do, than to compete for dominance in her own home with her husband, compete with her neighbors for empty status, and so smother her son that he cannot compete at all."[3]

15

[3]Betty Friedan, *The Feminine Mystique* (New York: Dell Publishing Company, 1963), 369. [Author's note]

From the equal-opportunity feminism first envisaged in *The Feminine Mystique* to that promoted today by *Working Woman* and *Savvy* magazines, and the dozens of primers[4] that promote the dress-for-success philosophy that often pretends to speak for all of feminism, progress and liberation have been defined in male, market terms. While some equal-opportunity feminists pay lip service to the work of their more care-oriented sisters, claiming that they would support a broad agenda that addresses our caring needs, the overarching mission of many is to help women adapt to the realities of the masculine marketplace. This brand of feminism often appeals to women's understandable fears that to discuss human beings' mutual need to care for one another is to argue that only women — not men — shoulder the duty to care. Rather than reaffirming our caring commitments so that we can all — male and female alike — share them, equal-opportunity feminism often seems to define caring as a masculine attempt to imprison women in the home and caring professions.

In this environment, the goal of liberation is to be treated as a man's equal *in a man's world*, competing for oneself against a very particular kind of man — the artists, scientists, politicians, and professionals that Friedan speaks of throughout her book. Or, as a recent *New York Times* series about the progress of women and feminism stated, "The basic goal of the women's movement was to eliminate the barriers that kept women from achieving as much as men and which did not allow them to *compete* with men on an equal basis"[5] (my italics).

For equal-opportunity feminism, then, the ultimate goal is tradi-   20
tional American success — making money; relentlessly accumulating possessions; capturing and hoarding power, knowledge, access, and information; grasping and clinging to fame, status, and privilege; proving that you are good enough, smart enough, driven enough to get to the top, and tough enough to stay there. In America — particularly the America of the Reagan and post-Reagan years — this is, after all, the meaning of "having it all."

In a world where allegiance to family, community, and politics has eroded, the American marketplace, with its glittering prize of success, has co-opted many of us, undermining our hopes and expectations. Others among us had a different vision. We had hoped that by going into the marketplace and taking our posts there as individuals, we would somehow subvert it. Many believed that our femininity would protect us, that the force of our feminism would make us invulnerable to the seductive logic of either patriarchy or capitalism.

[4]*primers:* (rhymes with "glimmers") elementary-level textbooks. The books Gordon refers to are not literally primers; she uses the term mockingly.

[5]Lisa Belkin, "Bars to Equality of Sexes Seen as Eroding, Slowly," *New York Times*, August 20, 1989. [Author's note]

In fact, we were remarkably naive about this foreign land into which we had journeyed. Yes, we were quick to admit that American society is too ruthless, too violent, too aggressive and uncaring. But many of us believed that the market's ills were a direct result of the sex of those who ruled and served it — men. As Betty Friedan, among so many others, has said over and over again, "Society was created by and for men."[6]

It seemed logical, therefore, to argue that the aggressive, elitist, hierarchial attitudes, values, and behaviors that kept women oppressed served the needs of and benefited all men, and that the natural solution was simply to change the sex of the players. It seemed natural to believe that putting women in power — without radically changing the system of power — would improve things for *all*. After all, like so many oppressed groups who believe oppression is a shield against the temptations of tyranny, women, who had been oppressed and subordinate for so long themselves, would never turn around and oppress and dominate others.

What we had not counted on was the strength of the marketplace, its ability to seduce and beguile the best and brightest, and its capacity to entrap us in its rules and entangle us in its imperatives. A few women have won great wealth and privilege. But, not unlike men in similar positions, many of them are unwilling to jeopardize what they've acquired in order to work for change. Some are so caught up in their own personal sagas of success that they have forgotten the women who have been left behind. . . .

Today, many women have . . . joined men in denigrating the care- 25 giving activities that they used to protect, preserve, and defend. It has become all too common for professional women to look down on those who have continued to do caring work in traditional women's professions like nursing, social work, teaching, and mothering. Nurses and others are constantly asked, "Why didn't someone as intelligent as you become a doctor?" or "Why didn't you become a psychologist rather than a social worker?" Teachers who leave the profession to become entrepreneurs are promoted as examples of "career courage," as if maintaining one's commitment to educating the young were an act of cowardice.[7]

Even our child-rearing practices have been affected. Today more and more mothers — particularly those among high-powered two-career couples — are told that good parenting equals pushing their young children to learn competitive, cognitive skills that will supposedly

[6]Betty Friedan, *The Second Stage* (New York: Summit Books, 1986), 70, 80. [Author's note]
[7]Beverly Kempton, "Great Transformations," *Working Woman*, January 1989. [Author's note]

pave the way for future career advancement. In the process, they are producing families in which both parents now subscribe to the kind of performance-oriented, competitive child rearing so often associated with masculine parenting styles. And we, as a culture, risk dissolving the positive bonds of love and nurturing and losing the irretrievable freedom of childhood.

The fact that women are now encouraged to devalue caring work has exacerbated a widespread societal crisis in caring that has deep political and social roots. As a society we cannot seem to muster the will or political courage to care for the most precious things we produce — other human beings.

By devaluing care we have, for example, abandoned our moral responsibility to the children who represent our future. The United States has risen to twenty-first in its infant mortality rate. Twenty percent of America's children are destitute, and American poverty is increasingly feminized. Over thirty-seven million people have no employer-paid health insurance coverage, and twenty to thirty million more are underinsured. Even those who can produce an insurance card when they arrive at the hospital may receive inadequate care. Moreover, older Americans are denied even catastrophic health care coverage and must pauperize themselves before they are eligible for government assistance with long-term nursing home care.

America's public education system — once the cornerstone of our democracy — is in a shambles. Millions of Americans today are homeless. Childcare is unobtainable for many, substandard for most, and frequently unaffordable for women who work in the home and also need support and respite. The only kind of parental and medical leaves that Congress seems willing to legislate are unpaid ones that will never be utilized by the majority of Americans because they cannot afford the loss of income involved. And presidential vetoes are threatened even for those.

Our need is greater than ever for more people to care for our   30
children and teach them the cognitive, moral, and social skills they will need to grow and develop; to tend the sick; to nurture the emotionally vulnerable and physically handicapped; and to help an aging population deal with infirmity, chronic illness, and death. And yet our society's widespread devaluation of care is discouraging potential recruits — whether male or female — from entering the caring professions and making it more difficult to induce those already in those professions to remain. These negative attitudes toward care pose a severe threat to existing political programs and policies that support and sustain caring activities. And if women retreat from caring, how can we possibly expect men to enter the caregiving professions or to be more caring in their personal and professional relationships?

The crisis in caring that women — and society — face today is more serious than many of us could have imagined. Yet, too many acknowledge the problem by essentially denying it. Like male CEO's[8] rationalizing their failures to promote more women to positions of corporate power, they insist that the enemy is not their own values and beliefs, but rather time. It takes years, men often say, to produce women who have the skills and knowledge required to follow the commands, execute the orders, and play the game to win. Change, they insist, is forthcoming — dozens of women are in the pipeline; just wait and you will see them.

Some contemporary defenders of feminism echo these same rationalizations. Understandably concerned about providing antifeminist ammunition for the right, they insist that the problem is time, not values; quantity, not quality. Women have not been liberated long enough, there are not yet enough of us in positions of power. If the ratio of women to men were just greater — then things would definitely change for the better.

Of course, all this is true. But it is only a partial explanation. A cold, clear look at reality reveals that these, if not amplified, are but empty assurances. Yes, we do need more time. Of course, it takes years, perhaps even decades, to change human behavior. But change is a *process*, not an *event*. If the women waiting in the wings for their moment on stage have been trained in the male method, if they behave like men, abide by the rules of the male marketplace, and merely join men in administering the status quo rather than taking risks to change it, then only the names and shapes of the players will have altered. The substance of our lives will stay the same. Indeed, things may be even worse. If women abandon caring for competition, rather than working to encourage *all of us* to share in the real work of the human community, then *who will* care? What kind of liberation will we have purchased?

[8]*CEO:* chief executive officer — the highest administrative position in most corporations.

Engaging the Text

1. What specific examples does Gordon provide of "caring professions" and "caregiving activities"? Break into single-gender groups to discuss how your attitudes toward such work have been molded by family, education, media, or other influences. Report to the full class. How similarly or dissimilarly are females and males being raised?

2. Identify the differences between the two versions of feminism that Gordon defines — "transformative" versus "adaptive" or "equal-opportunity." Discuss the benefits and limits of equal-opportunity feminism.

3. Do you think Gordon's portrayals of American corporations, media, and families are fair? Analyze specific passages in her essay to support your point.

Exploring Connections

4. Gordon acknowledges that women are succeeding in the marketplace. To what extent (if any) is their success analogous to that of Stephen Cruz (p. 36)?

5. Working in pairs, write a dialogue between Suzanne Gordon (p. 46) and George C. Wolfe (p. 42) about the costs of success and the possibility of resisting those costs. Read your dialogues aloud and discuss.

6. Janet Saltzman Chafetz writes that "the feminine role stereotype gears women for economic failure" (p. 194). Read Chafetz's argument and debate whether or not parents and schools that listened to Gordon would gear young people for failure.

Extending the Critical Context

7. If you have lived in a different culture or in a family environment whose attitude toward competition and caring was markedly different from what Gordon sees in the United States, write a journal entry or essay describing that contrasting attitude and how it is maintained in the culture or family.

8. Watch the movie *Broadcast News* on video. What does it say about the compromises women must make to succeed in a high-pressure career? Do the male characters have to make similarly difficult choices in order to succeed?

9. Interview women working in several fields. How has the feminist movement affected their careers, conditions in their workplaces, and the quality of their lives?

Streets of Gold: The Myth of the Model Minority

Curtis Chang

According to conventional wisdom, Asian Americans offer the latest, best evidence that the American Dream is alive and well. Publications like Time *and* Newsweek *have celebrated Asian Americans as a "super minority" that has adopted the Puritan work ethic and outshone even the Anglo majority in terms of education and financial success. In this essay, Curtis Chang probes the data used in such media reports and questions this new embodiment of the success myth. Since the educational achievement of Asians is an important component of the myth, the essay may prompt you to take a fresh look at the status of Asian American students on your campus. Chang was born in Taiwan and immigrated to the United States in 1971. This essay was written in 1987, when he was a freshman at Harvard; Chang anticipates a career in public policy.*

Over 100 years ago, an American myth misled many of my ancestors. Seeking cheap labor, railroad companies convinced numerous Chinese that American streets were paved with gold. Today, the media portrays Asian-Americans as finally mining those golden streets. Major publications like *Time, Newsweek, U.S. News and World Report, Fortune, The New Republic,* the *Wall Street Journal,* and the *New York Times* have all recently published congratulatory "Model Minority" headline stories with such titles:

America's Super Minority
An American Success Story
A Model Minority
Why They Succeed
The Ultimate Assimilation
The Triumph of the Asian Americans

But the Model Minority is another "Streets of Gold" tale. It distorts Asian-Americans' true status and ignores our racial handicaps. And the Model Minority's ideology is even worse than its mythology. It attempts to justify the existing system of racial inequality by blaming the victims rather than the system itself.

The Model Minority myth introduces us as an ethnic minority that is finally "making it in America" (*Time,* July 8, 1985). The media consistently defines "making it" as achieving material wealth, wealth that flows from our successes in the workplace and the schoolroom. This economic achievement allegedly proves a minority can "lay claim to the American dream" (*Fortune,* Nov. 24, 1986).

Trying to show how "Asian-Americans present a picture of affluence and economic success" (*N.Y. Times Magazine,* Nov. 30, 1986), 9 out of 10 of the major Model Minority stories of the last four years relied heavily on one statistic: the family median income. The median Asian-American family income, according to the U.S. Census Survey of Income and Education data, is $22,713 compared to $20,800 for white Americans. Armed with that figure, national magazines have trumpeted our "remarkable, ever-mounting achievements" (*Newsweek,* Dec. 6, 1982).

Such assertions demonstrate the truth of the aphorism "Statistics are   5
like a bikini. What they reveal is suggestive, but what they conceal is vital." The family median income statistic conceals the fact that Asian-American families generally (1) have more children and live-in relatives and thus have more mouths to feed; (2) are often forced by necessity to

have everyone in the family work, averaging *more* than two family income earners (whites only have 1.6) (Cabezas, 1979, p. 402); and (3) live disproportionately in high cost of living areas (i.e., New York, Chicago, Los Angeles, and Honolulu) which artificially inflate income figures. Dr. Robert S. Mariano, professor of economics at the University of Pennsylvania, has calculated that

> when such appropriate adjustments and comparisons are made, a different and rather disturbing picture emerges, showing indeed a clearly disadvantaged group. . . . Filipino and Chinese men *are no better off than black men with regard to median incomes.* (Mariano, 1979, p. 55)[1]

Along with other racial minorities, Asian-Americans are still scraping for the crumbs of the economic pie.

Throughout its distortion of our status, the media propagates two crucial assumptions. First, it lumps all Asian-Americans into one monolithic, homogeneous, yellow skinned mass. Such a view ignores the existence of an incredibly disadvantaged Asian-American underclass. Asians work in low income and low status jobs 2 to 3 times more than whites (Cabezas, 1979, p. 438). Recent Vietnamese refugees in California are living like the Appalachian poor. While going to his Manhattan office, multimillionaire architect I. M. Pei's car passes Chinese restaurants and laundries where 72% of all New York Chinese men still work (U.S. Bureau of the Census, 1977, Table 7).

But the media makes an even more dangerous assumption. It suggests that (alleged) material success is the same thing as basic racial equality. Citing that venerable family median income figure, magazines claim Asian-Americans are "obviously nondisadvantaged folks" (*Fortune*, May 17, 1982). Yet a 1979 United States Equal Employment Opportunity Commission study on Asian-Americans discovered widespread anti-Asian hiring and promotion practices. Asian-Americans "in the professional, technical, and managerial occupations" often face "modern racism — the subtle, sophisticated, systemic patterns and practices . . . which function to effect and to obscure the discriminatory outcomes" (Nishi, 1979, p. 398). One myth simply does not prove another: neither our "astonishing economic prosperity" (*Fortune*, Nov. 24, 1986) nor a racially equal America exist.

An emphasis on material success also pervades the media's stress on Asian-Americans' educational status at "the top of the class" (*Newsweek on Campus*, April 2, 1984). Our "march into the ranks of the educa-

---

[1]The picture becomes even more disturbing when one realizes that higher income figures do not necessarily equal higher quality of life. For instance, in New York Chinatown, more than 1 out of 5 residents work more than 57 hours per week, almost 1 out of 10 elderly must labor more than 55 hours per week. (Nishi, 1979, p. 503). [Author's note]

tional elite" (*U.S. News*, April 2, 1984) is significant because "all that education is paying off spectacularly" (*Fortune*, Nov. 24, 1986). Once again, the same fallacious assumptions plague this "whiz kids" image of Asian-Americans.

The media again ignores the fact that class division accounts for much of the publicized success. Until 1976, the U.S. Immigration Department only admitted Asian immigrants that were termed "skilled" workers. "Skilled" generally meant college educated, usually in the sciences since poor English would not be a handicap. The result was that the vast majority of pre-1976 Asian immigrants came from already well-educated, upper-class backgrounds — the classic "brain drain" syndrome (Hirschman and Wong, 1981, pp. 507–510).

The post-1976 immigrants, however, come generally from the 10
lower, less educated classes (Kim, 1986, p. 24). A study by Professor Elizabeth Ahn Toupin of Tufts University matched similar Asian and non-Asian students *along class lines* and found that Asian-Americans "did not perform at a superior academic level to non-Asian students. Asian-Americans were more likely to be placed on academic probation than their white counterparts . . . twice as many Asian American students withdrew from the university" (Toupin, 1986, p. 12).

Thus, it is doubtful whether the perceived widespread educational success will continue as the Asian-American population eventually balances out along class lines. When 16.2% of all Chinese have less than 4 years of schooling (*four times* that of whites) (Azores, 1979, p. 73), it seems many future Asian-Americans will worry more about being able to read a newspaper rather than a Harvard acceptance letter.

Most important, the media assumes once again that achieving a certain level of material or educational success means achieving real equality. People easily forget that to begin with, Asians invest heavily in education since other means of upward mobility are barred to them by race. Until recently, for instance, Asian-Americans were barred from unions and traditional lines of credit (Yun, 1986, pp. 23–24).[2] Other "white" avenues to success, such as the "old boy network," are still closed to Asian-Americans.

When *Time* (July 8, 1985) claims "as a result of their academic achievement Asians are climbing the economic ladder with remarkable speed," it glosses over an inescapable fact: there is a white ladder and then there is a yellow one. Almost all of the academic studies on the *actual returns Asians receive* from their education point to prevalent discrimination. A striking example of this was found in a City University of New York research project which constructed resumes with

[2]For further analysis on the role racism plays in Asian-Americans' stress on education and certain technical and scientific fields, see Suzuki, 1977, p. 44. [Author's note]

equivalent educational backgrounds. Applications were then sent to employers, one group under an Asian name and a similar group under a Caucasian name. Whites received interviews 5 times more than Asians (Nishi, 1979, p. 399). The media never headlines even more shocking data that can be easily found in the U.S. Census. For instance, Chinese and Filipino males only earned respectively 74 and 52 percent as much as their *equally educated* white counterparts. Asian females fared even worse. Their salaries were only 44 to 54 percent as large as equivalent white males' paychecks (Cabezas, 1979, p. 391). Blacks suffer from this same statistical disparity. We Asian-Americans are indeed a Model Minority — a perfect model of racial discrimination in America.

Yet this media myth encourages neglect of our pressing needs. "Clearly, many Asian-Americans and Pacific peoples are invisible to the governmental agencies," one state agency reported. "Discrimination against Asian-Americans and Pacific peoples is as much the result of omission as commission" (California State Advisory Committee, 1975, p. 75). In 1979, while the president praised Asian-Americans' "successful integration into American society," his administration revoked Asian-Americans' eligibility for minority small business loans, devastating thousands of struggling, newly arrived small businessmen. Hosts of other minority issues, ranging from reparations for the Japanese American internment[3] to the ominous rise of anti-Asian violence, are widely ignored by the general public.

The media, in fact, insist to the general populace that we are not a   15
true racial minority. In its attack on affirmative action, the *Boston Globe* (Jan. 14, 1985) pointed out that universities, like many people, "obviously feel that Asian-Americans, especially those of Chinese and Japanese descent, are brilliant, privileged, and wrongly classified as minorities." Harvard Dean Henry Rosovsky remarked in the same article that "it does not seem to me that as a group, they are disadvantaged. . . . Asian-Americans appear to be in an odd category among other protected minorities."

The image that we Asians aren't like "other minorities" is fundamental to the Model Minority ideology. Any elementary school student knows that the teacher designates one student the model, the "teacher's pet" in order to set an example for others to follow. One only sets up a "model minority" in order to communicate to the other "students," the

---

[3]*reparations . . . internment:* during World War II, over one hundred twenty thousand Japanese Americans on the West Coast were sent to prison camps by order of the U.S. government; many lost their homes, businesses, and possessions because of this forced relocation. After decades of work by Asian American activists, Congress in 1988 ordered the government to pay $20,000 to each internee as partial recompense for these losses.

blacks and Hispanics, "Why can't you be like that?" The media, in fact, almost admit to "grading" minorities as they headline Model Minority stories, "Asian-Americans: Are They Making the Grade?" (*U.S. News*, April 2, 1984). And Asians have earned the highest grade by fulfilling one important assignment: identifying with the white majority, with its values and wishes.

Unlike blacks, for instance, we Asian-Americans have not vigorously asserted our ethnic identity (a.k.a. Black Power). And the American public has historically demanded assimilation over racial pluralism.[4] Over the years, *Newsweek* has published titles from "Success Story: Outwhiting the Whites" (*Newsweek*, June 21, 1971) to "Ultimate Assimilation" (*Newsweek*, Nov. 24, 1986), which lauded the increasing number of Asian-White marriages as evidence of Asian-Americans' "acceptance into American society."

Even more significant is the public's approval of how we have succeeded in the "American tradition" (*Fortune*, Nov. 24, 1986). Unlike the Blacks and Hispanics, we "Puritan-like" Asians (*N.Y. Times Magazine*, Nov. 30, 1986) disdain governmental assistance. A *New Republic* piece, "America's Greatest Success Story" (July 15, 1985), similarly applauded how "Asian-Americans pose no problems at all." The media consistently compares the crime-ridden image of other minorities with the picture of law abiding Asian parents whose "well-behaved kids" (*Newsweek on Campus*, April 1984) hit books and not the streets.

Some insist there is nothing terrible about whites conjuring up our "tremendous" success, divining from it model American traits, then preaching, "Why can't you Blacks and Hispanics be like that?" After all, one might argue, aren't those traits desirable?

Such a view, as mentioned, neglects Asian-Americans' true and pressing needs. Moreover, this view completely misses the Model Minority image's fundamental ideology, an ideology meant to falsely grant America absolution from its racial barriers.

David O. Sears and Donald R. Kinder, two social scientists, have recently published significant empirical studies on the underpinnings of American racial attitudes. They consistently discovered that Americans' stress on "values, such as 'individualism and self-reliance, the work ethic, obedience, and discipline' . . . can be invoked, however perversely, to feed racist appetites" (Kennedy, 1987, p. 88). In other words, the Model Minority image lets Americans' consciences rest easy. They

20

---

[4]A full discussion of racial pluralism vs. assimilation is impossible here. But suffice it to say that pluralism accepts ethnic cultures as equally different; assimilation asks for a "melting" into the majority. An example of the assimilation philosophy is the massive "Americanization" programs of the late 1800s which successfully erased Eastern European immigrants' customs in favor of Anglo-Saxon ones. [Author's note]

can think: "It's not our fault those blacks and Hispanics can't make it. They're just too lazy. After all, look at the Asians."[5] Consequently, American society never confronts the systemic racial and economic factors underlying such inequality. The victims instead bear the blame.

This ideology behind the Model Minority image is best seen when we examine one of the first Model Minority stories, which suddenly appeared in the mid 1960s. It is important to note that the period was marked by newfound, strident black demands for equality and power.

> At a time when it is being proposed that hundreds of billions be spent to uplift Negroes and other minorities, the nation's 300,000 Chinese Americans are moving ahead on their own — with no help from anyone else . . . few Chinese-Americans are getting welfare handouts — or even want them . . . they don't sit around moaning. (*U.S. News*, Dec. 26, 1966)

The same article then concludes that the Chinese-American history and accomplishment "would shock those now complaining about the hardships endured by today's Negroes" (*U.S. News*, Dec. 26, 1966).

Not surprisingly, the dunce-capped blacks and Hispanics resent us apple polishing, "well-behaved" teacher's pets. Black comedian Richard Pryor performs a revealing routine in which new Asian immigrants learn from whites their first English word: "Nigger." And Asian-Americans themselves succumb to the Model Minority's deceptive mythology and racist ideology[6]. "I made it without help," one often hears among Asian circles, "why can't they?" In a 1986 nationwide poll, only 27% of Asian-American students rated "racial understanding" as "essential." The figure plunged 9% in the last year alone (a year marked by a torrent of Model Minority stories) (Hune, 1987). We "white-washed" Asians have simply lost our identity as a fellow, disadvantaged minority.

But we don't even need to look beyond the Model Minority stories themselves to realize that whites see us as "whiter" than blacks — but not quite white enough. For instance, citing that familiar median family income figure, *Fortune* magazine of May 17, 1982, complained

---

[5]This phenomenon of blaming the victim for racial inequality is as old as America itself. For instance, Southerners once eased their consciences over slavery by labeling blacks as animals lacking humanity. Today, America does it by labeling them as inferior people lacking "desirable" traits. For an excellent further analysis of this ideology, actually widespread among American intellectuals, see *Iron Cages: Race and Culture in 19th-Century America* by Ronald T. Takaki. [Author's note]

[6]America has a long history of playing off one minority against the other. During the early 1900s, for instance, mining companies in the west often hired Asians solely as scabs against striking black miners. Black versus Asian hostility and violence usually followed. This pattern was repeated in numerous industries. In a larger historical sense, almost every immigrant group has assimilated, to some degree, the culture of anti Black racism. [Author's note]

that Asian-Americans are in fact "getting *more* than its share of the pie." For decades, when white Americans were leading the nation in every single economic measure, editorials arguing that whites were getting more than *their* share of the pie were rather rare.

No matter how "well behaved" we are, Asian-Americans are still excluded from the real pie, the "positions of institutional power and political power" (Kuo, 1979, p. 289). Professor Harry Kitano of UCLA has written extensively on the plight of Asian-Americans as the "middle-man minority," a minority supposedly satisfied materially but forever racially barred from a true, *significant* role in society. Empirical studies indicate that Asian-Americans "have been channeled into lower-echelon white-collar jobs having little or no decision making authority" (Suzuki, 1977, p. 38). For example, in *Fortune's* 1,000 largest companies, Asian-American nameplates rest on a mere half of one percent of all officers' and directors' desks (a stastitical disparity worsened by the fact that most of the Asians founded their companies) (*Fortune*, Nov. 24, 1986). While the education of the upper-class Asians may save them from the bread lines, their race still keeps them from the boardroom.

Our docile acceptance of such exclusion is actually one of our "model" traits. When Asian-Americans in San Francisco showed their first hint of political activism and protested Asian exclusion from city boards, *The Washington Monthly* (May 1986) warned in a long Asian-American article, "Watch out, here comes another group to pander to." *The New Republic* (July 15, 1985) praised Asian-American political movements because

> unlike blacks or Hispanics, Asian-American politicians have the luxury of not having to devote the bulk of their time to an "Asian-American agenda," and thus escape becoming prisoners of such an agenda. . . . The most important thing for Asian-Americans . . . is simply being part of the process.

This is strikingly reminiscent of another of the first Model Minority stories:

> As the Black and Brown communities push for changes in the present system, the Oriental is set forth as an example to be followed — a minority group that has achieved success through adaptation rather than confrontation. (*Gidra*, 1969)

But it is precisely this "present system," this system of subtle, persistent racism that we all must confront, not adapt to. For example, we Asians gained our right to vote from the 1964 Civil Rights Act that blacks marched, bled, died, and in the words of that original Model Minority story, "sat around moaning for." Unless we assert our true identity as a minority and challenge racial misconceptions and inequalities, we will be nothing more than techno-coolies[7] — collecting our wages but silently enduring basic political and economic inequality.

This country perpetuated a myth once. Today, no one can afford to dreamily chase after that gold in the streets, oblivious to the genuine treasure of racial equality. When racism persists, can one really call any minority a "model"?

List of Sources

Azores, Fortunata M., "Census Methodology and the Development of Social Indicators for Asian and Pacific Americans," *U.S. Commission on Civil Rights: Testimony on Civil Rights Issues of Asian and Pacific Americans* (1979), pp. 70–79.

Boston Globe, "Affirmative Non-actions," Jan. 14, 1985, p. 10.

Cabezas, Dr. Armado, "Employment Issues of Asian Americans," *U.S. Commission on Civil Rights: Testimony on Civil Rights Issues of Asian and Pacific Americans* (1979), pp. 389–399, 402, 434–444.

California State Advisory Committee to the U.S. Commission on Civil Rights, *Asian American and Pacific Peoples: A Case of Mistaken Identity* (1975) (quoted in Chun, 1980, p. 7).

Chun, Ki-Taek, "The Myth of Asian American Success and Its Educational Ramifications," *IRCD Bulletin* (Winter/Spring 1980).

Dutta, Manoranjan, "Asian/Pacific American Employment Profile: Myth and Reality — Issues and Answers," *U.S. Commission on Civil Rights: Testimony on Civil Rights Issues of Asian and Pacific Americans* (1979), pp. 445–489.

Fortune: "America's Super Minority," Nov. 24, 1986, pp. 148–149; "Working Smarter," May 17, 1982, p. 64.

Gidra (1969), pp. 6–7 (quoted in Chun, p. 7).

Hirschman, Charles, and Wong, Morrison, "Trends in Socioeconomic Achievement Among Immigrant and Native-Born Asian-Americans, 1960–1976," *The Sociological Quarterly* (Autumn 1981), pp. 495–513.

Hune, Shirley, keynote address, East Coast Asian Student Union Conference, Boston University, Feb. 14, 1987.

Kahng, Dr. Anthony, "Employment Issues," *U.S. Commission on Civil Rights: Testimony on Civil Rights Issues of Asian and Pacific Americans* (1979), pp. 411–413.

Kennedy, David M., "The Making of a Classic, Gunnar Myrdal and Black-White Relations: The Use and Abuse of *An American Dilemma*," *The Atlantic* (May 1987), pp. 86–89.

Kiang, Peter, professor of sociology, University of Massachusetts, Boston, personal interview, May 1, 1987.

Kim, Illsoo, "Class Division Among Asian Immigrants: Its Implications for Social Welfare Policy," *Asian American Studies: Contemporary Issues, Proceedings from East Coast Asian American Scholars Conference* (1986), pp. 24–25.

[7]*techno-coolie:* the original coolies were unskilled laborers from the Far East who were often paid subsistence wages in the United States.

Kuo, Wen H. "On the Study of Asian-Americans: Its Current State and Agenda," *Sociological Quarterly* (1979), pp. 279–290.

Mariano, Dr. Robert S., "Census Issues," *U.S. Commission on Civil Rights: Testimony on Civil Rights Issues of Asian and Pacific Americans* (1979), pp. 54–59.

New Republic, "The Triumph of Asian Americans" (July 15–22, 1985), pp. 24–31.

The New York Times Magazine, "Why They Succeed" (Nov. 30, 1986), pp. 72+.

Newsweek: "The Ultimate Assimilation" (Nov. 24, 1986), p. 80; "Asian-Americans: A 'Model Minority'" (Dec. 6, 1982), pp. 39–51; "Success Story: Outwhiting the Whites" (June 21, 1971), pp. 24–25.

Newsweek on Campus: "Asian Americans, the Drive to Excel" (April 1984), pp. 4–13.

Nishi, Dr. Setsuko Matsunaga, "Asian American Employment Issues: Myths and Realities," *U.S. Commission on Civil Rights: Testimony on Civil Rights Issues of Asian and Pacific Americans* (1979), pp. 397–399, 495–507.

Sung, Betty Lee, *Chinese American Manpower and Employment* (1975).

Suzuki, Bob H., "Education and the Socialization of Asian Americans: A Revisionist Analysis of the 'Model Minority' Thesis," *Amerasia Journal*, vol. 4, issue 2 (1977), pp. 23–51.

Time, "To America with Skills" (July 8, 1985), p. 42.

Toupin, Dr. Elizabeth Ahn, "A Model University for A 'Model Minority,'" *Asian American Studies: Contemporary Issues, Proceedings from East Coast Asian American Scholars Conference* (1986), pp. 10–12.

U.S. Bureau of the Census, *Survey of Minority-Owned Business Enterprises* (1977) (as quoted in Cabezas, p. 443).

U.S. News & World Report: "Asian-Americans, Are They Making the Grade?" (April 2, 1984), pp. 41–42; "Success Story of One Minority Group in U.S." (Dec. 26, 1966), pp. 6–9.

Washington Monthly, "The Wrong Way to Court Ethnics" (May 1986), pp. 21–26.

Yun, Grace, "Notes from Discussions on Asian American Education," *Asian American Studies: Contemporary Issues, Proceedings from East Coast Asian American Scholars Conference* (1986), pp. 20–24.

Engaging the Text

1. In Chang's view, what are the key elements of the stereotype of Asian Americans as a model minority? Have you encountered these yourself? How pervasive do you believe they are in your school or community?

2. What is wrong with this positive image of Asian Americans, according to Chang? What assumptions does it make, and how do they mislead us about the situation of many Asian Americans?

3. Why has the myth of the model minority been so widely embraced, according to Chang? What does it do for the United States as a country? What is the effect of the model minority myth on other ethnic minorities?

4. Many scholars who question the image of the model minority are themselves Asian Americans. Does this fact make their claims more or less persuasive? Explain.

5. Chang's essay analyzes news stories, interprets census data, and reports on work by other scholars, but it does not present any original research. What purpose do essays like this serve when all of the data they contain is already available elsewhere?

Exploring Connections

6. When Stephen Cruz (p. 36) became successful, he was seen not as a member of a model minority group but rather as a model member of a minority group. To what extent was his situation as a successful young Chicano engineer comparable to that of Asian Americans today?

7. How might the idea of a "work ethic" as defined by Christopher Lasch (p. 27) contribute to the widespread acceptance of the model minority myth?

Extending the Critical Context

8. Discuss in small groups how you learned of the myth of the model minority. Was it through TV, family, reading? Be as specific as possible. Then try to draw some conclusions about how this type of cultural "knowledge" is taught.

9. Although the news media have been quick to extol the virtues of Asian Americans as models of achievement, representations of Asians and Asian Americans are scarce in most forms of mass entertainment. Survey movies, TV shows, music videos, song lyrics, and other forms of popular culture. How are Asian Americans represented, and how do these images compare with those implied by the myth of the model minority?

The Lesson

Toni Cade Bambara

"The Lesson" looks at wealth through the eyes of a poor Black girl whose education includes a field trip to one of the world's premier toy stores. The story speaks to serious social issues with a comic, energetic, and utterly engaging voice. Toni Cade Bambara (b. 1939) grew up in the Harlem and Bedford-Stuyvesant areas of New York City. Trained at Queens College and City College of New York in dance, drama, and literature, she is best known for her collections of stories, Gorilla, My Love *(1972) and* The Seabirds Are Still Alive and Other Stories *(1977),*

and for her novels, If Blessing Comes *(1987) and* The Salt Eaters *(1980), winner of the American Book Award. This story is taken from* Gorilla, My Love.

Back in the days when everyone was old and stupid or young and foolish and me and Sugar were the only ones just right, this lady moved on our block with nappy hair and proper speech and no makeup. And quite naturally we laughed at her, laughed the way we did at the junk man who went about his business like he was some big-time president and his sorry-ass horse his secretary. And we kinda hated her too, hated the way we did the winos who cluttered up our parks and pissed on our handball walls and stank up our hallways and stairs so you couldn't halfway play hide-and-seek without a goddamn gas mask. Miss Moore was her name. The only woman on the block with no first name. And she was black as hell, cept for her feet, which were fish-white and spooky. And she was always planning these boring-ass things for us to do, us being my cousin, mostly, who lived on the block cause we all moved North the same time and to the same apartment then spread out gradual to breathe. And our parents would yank our heads into some kinda shape and crisp up our clothes so we'd be presentable for travel with Miss Moore, who always looked like she was going to church, though she never did. Which is just one of the things the grownups talked about when they talked behind her back like a dog. But when she came calling with some sachet[1] she'd sewed up or some gingerbread she'd made or some book, why then they'd all be too embarrassed to turn her down and we'd get handed out all spruced up. She'd been to college and said it only right that she should take responsibility for the young ones' education, and she not even related by marriage or blood. So they'd go for it. Specially Aunt Gretchen. She was the main gofer in the family. You got some ole dumb shit foolishness you want somebody to go for, you send for Aunt Gretchen. She been screwed into the go-along for so long, it's a blood-deep natural thing with her. Which is how she got saddled with me and Sugar and Junior in the first place while our mothers were in a la-de-da apartment up the block having a good ole time.

So this one day Miss Moore rounds us all up at the mailbox and it's puredee hot and she's knockin herself out about arithmetic. And school suppose to let up in summer I heard, but she don't never let up. And the starch in my pinafore scratching the shit outta me and I'm really hating this nappy-head bitch and her goddamn college degree. I'd much rather

---

[1]*sachet:* a small bag filled with a sweet-smelling substance. Sachets are often placed in drawers to scent clothes.

go to the pool or to the show where it's cool. So me and Sugar leaning on the mailbox being surly, which is a Miss Moore word. And Flyboy checking out what everybody brought for lunch. And Fat Butt already wasting his peanut-butter-and-jelly sandwich like the pig he is. And Junebug punchin on Q.T.'s arm for potato chips. And Rosie Giraffe shifting from one hip to the other waiting for somebody to step on her foot or ask her if she from Georgia so she can kick ass, preferably Mercedes'. And Miss Moore asking us do we know what money is, like we a bunch of retards. I mean real money, she say, like it's only poker chips or monopoly papers we lay on the grocer. So right away I'm tired of this and say so. And would much rather snatch Sugar and go to the Sunset and terrorize the West Indian kids and take their hair ribbons and their money too. And Miss Moore files that remark away for next week's lesson on brotherhood, I can tell. And finally I say we oughta get to the subway cause it's cooler and besides we might meet some cute boys. Sugar done swiped her mama's lipstick, so we ready.

So we heading down the street and she's boring us silly about what things cost and what our parents make and how much goes for rent and how money ain't divided up right in this country. And then she gets to the part about we all poor and live in the slums, which I don't feature. And I'm ready to speak on that, but she steps out in the street and hails two cabs just like that. Then she hustles half the crew in with her and hands me a five-dollar bill and tells me to calculate 10 percent tip for the driver. And we're off. Me and Sugar and Junebug and Flyboy hangin out the window and hollering to everybody, putting lipstick on each other cause Flyboy a faggot anyway, and making farts with our sweaty armpits. But I'm mostly trying to figure how to spend this money. But they all fascinated with the meter ticking and Junebug starts laying bets as to how much it'll read when Flyboy can't hold his breath no more. Then Sugar lays bets as to how much it'll be when we get there. So I'm stuck. Don't nobody want to go for my plan, which is to jump out at the next light and run off to the first bar-b-que we can find. Then the driver tells us to get the hell out cause we are there already. And the meter reads eighty-five cents. And I'm stalling to figure out the tip and Sugar say give him a dime. And I decide he don't need it bad as I do, so later for him. But then he tries to take off with Junebug foot still in the door so we talk about his mama something ferocious. Then we check out that we on Fifth Avenue[2] and everybody dressed up in stockings. One lady in a fur coat, hot as it is. White folks crazy.

"This is the place," Miss Moore say, presenting it to us in the voice she uses at the museum. "Let's look in the windows before we go in."

"Can we steal?" Sugar asks very serious like she's getting the ground   5

[2]*Fifth Avenue:* the street in New York most famous for its shopping.

rules squared away before she plays. "I beg your pardon," say Miss Moore, and we fall out. So she leads us around the windows of the toy store and me and Sugar screamin, "This is mine, that's mine, I gotta have that, that was made for me, I was born for that," till Big Butt drowns us out.

"Hey, I'm goin to buy that there."

"That there? You don't even know what it is, stupid."

"I do so," he say punchin on Rosie Giraffe. "It's a microscope."

"Whatcha gonna do with a microscope, fool?"

"Look at things." 10

"Like what, Ronald?" ask Miss Moore. And Big Butt ain't got the first notion. So here go Miss Moore gabbing about the thousands of bacteria in a drop of water and the somethinorother in a speck of blood and the million and one living things in the air around us is invisible to the naked eye. And what she say that for? Junebug go to town on that "naked" and we rolling. Then Miss Moore ask what it cost. So we all jam into the window smudgin it up and the price tag say $300. So then she ask how long'd take for Big Butt and Junebug to save up their allowances. "Too long," I say. "Yeh," adds Sugar, "outgrown it by that time." And Miss Moore say no, you never outgrow learning instruments. "Why, even medical students and interns and," blah, blah, blah. And we ready to choke Big Butt for bringing it up in the first damn place.

"This here costs four hundred eighty dollars," say Rosie Giraffe. So we pile up all over her to see what she pointin out. My eyes tell me it's a chunk of glass cracked with something heavy, and different-color inks dripped into the splits, then the whole thing put into a oven or something. But for $480 it don't make sense.

"That's a paperweight made of semi-precious stones fused together under tremendous pressure," she explains slowly, with her hands doing the mining and all the factory work.

"So what's paperweight?" asks Rosie Giraffe.

"To weight paper with, dumbbell," say Flyboy, the wise man from 15 the East.

"Not exactly," say Miss Moore, which is what she say when you warm or way off too. "It's to weigh paper down so it won't scatter and make your desk untidy." So right away me and Sugar curtsy to each other and then to Mercedes who is more the tidy type.

"We don't keep paper on top of the desk in my class," say Junebug, figuring Miss Moore crazy or lyin one.

"At home, then," she say. "Don't you have a calendar and a pencil case and a blotter and a letter-opener on your desk at home where you do your homework?" And she know damn well what our homes look like cause she nosys around in them every chance she gets.

"I don't even have a desk," say Junebug. "Do we?"

"No. And I don't get no homework neither," say Big Butt. 20

"And I don't even have a home," say Flyboy like he do at school to keep the white folks off his back and sorry for him. Send this poor kid to camp posters, is his speciality.

"I do," say Mercedes. "I have a box of stationery on my desk and a picture of my cat. My godmother bought the stationery and the desk. There's a big rose on each sheet and the envelopes smell like roses."

"Who want to know about your smelly-ass stationery," say Rosie Giraffe fore I can get my two cents in.

"It's important to have a work area all your own so that . . ."

"Will you look at this sailboat, please," say Flyboy, cuttin her off and pointin to the thing like it was his. So once again we tumble all over each other to gaze at this magnificent thing in the toy store which is just big enough to maybe sail two kittens across the pond if you strap them to the posts tight. We all start reciting the price tag like we in assembly. "Handcrafted sailboat of fiberglass at one thousand one hundred ninety-five dollars."

"Unbelievable," I hear myself say and am really stunned. I read it again for myself just in case the group recitation put me in a trance. Same thing. For some reason this pisses me off. We look at Miss Moore and she lookin at us, waiting for I dunno what.

"Who'd pay all that when you can buy a sailboat set for a quarter at Pop's, a tube of glue for a dime, and a ball of string for eight cents? It must have a motor and a whole lot else besides," I say. "My sailboat cost me about fifty cents."

"But will it take water?" say Mercedes with her smart ass.

"Took mine to Alley Pond Park once," say Flyboy. "String broke. Lost it. Pity."

"Sailed mine in Central Park[3] and it keeled over and sank. Had to ask my father for another dollar."

"And you got the strap," laugh Big Butt. "The jerk didn't even have a string on it. My old man wailed on his behind."

Little Q.T. was staring hard at the sailboat and you could see he wanted it bad. But he too little and somebody'd just take it from him. So what the hell. "This boat for kids, Miss Moore?"

"Parents silly to buy something like that just to get all broke up," say Rosie Giraffe.

"That much money it should last forever," I figure.

"My father'd buy it for me if I wanted it."

"Your father, my ass," say Rosie Giraffe getting a chance to finally push Mercedes.

"Must be rich people shop here," say Q.T.

"You are a very bright boy," say Flyboy. "What was your first clue?" And he rap him on the head with the back of his knuckles, since Q.T.

25

30

35

[3]*Central Park:* a very large park in central Manhattan, New York City.

the only one he could get away with. Though Q.T. liable to come up behind you years later and get his licks in when you half expect it.

"What I want to know is," I says to Miss Moore though I never talk to her, I wouldn't give the bitch that satisfaction, "is how much a real boat costs? I figure a thousand'd get you a yacht any day."

"Why don't you check that out," she says, "and report back to the group?" Which really pains my ass. If you gonna mess up a perfectly good swim day least you could do is have some answers. "Let's go in," she say like she got something up her sleeve. Only she don't lead the way. So me and Sugar turn the corner to where the entrance is, but when we get there I kinda hang back. Not that I'm scared, what's there to be afraid of, just a toy store. But I feel funny, shame. But what I got to be shamed about? Got as much right to go in as anybody. But somehow I can't seem to get hold on the door, so I step away for Sugar to lead. But she hangs back too. And I look at her and she looks at me and this is ridiculous. I mean, damn, I have never ever been shy about doing nothing or going nowhere. But then Mercedes steps up and then Rosie Giraffe and Big Butt crowd in behind and shove, and next thing we all stuffed into the doorway with only Mercedes squeezing past us, smoothing out her jumper and walking right down the aisle. Then the rest of us tumble in like a glued-together jigsaw done all wrong. And people lookin at us. And it's like the time me and Sugar crashed into the Catholic church on a dare. But once we got in there and everything so hushed and holy and the candles and the bowin and the handkerchiefs on all the drooping heads, I just couldn't go through with the plan. Which was for me to run up to the altar and do a tap dance while Sugar played the nose flute and messed around in the holy water. And Sugar kept givin me the elbow. Then later teased me so bad I tied her up in the shower and turned it on and locked her in. And she'd be there till this day if Aunt Gretchen hadn't finally figured I was lying about the boarder takin a shower.

Same thing in the store. We all walkin on tiptoe and hardly touchin the games and puzzles and things. And I watched Miss Moore who is steady watchin us like she waitin for a sign. Like Mama Drewery watches the sky and sniffs the air and takes note of just how much slant is in the bird formation. Then me and Sugar bump smack into each other, so busy gazing at the toys, 'specially the sailboat. But we don't laugh and go into our fat-lady bump-stomach routine. We just stare at that price tag. Then Sugar run a finger over the whole boat. And I'm jealous and want to hit her. Maybe not her, but I sure want to punch somebody in the mouth.

"Watcha bring us here for, Miss Moore?"

"You sound angry, Sylvia. Are you mad about something?" Give me one of them grins like she tellin a grown-up joke that never turns out to be funny. And she's lookin very closely at me like maybe she plannin to do my portrait from memory. I'm mad, but I won't give her that satisfaction. So I slouch around the store bein very bored and say, "Let's go."

Me and Sugar at the back of the train watchin' the tracks whizzin by large then small then gettin gobbled up in the dark. I'm thinkin about this tricky toy I saw in the store. A clown that somersaults on a bar then does chin-ups just cause you yank lightly at his leg. Cost $35. I could see me askin my mother for a $35 birthday clown. "You wanna who that costs what?" she'd say, cockin her head to the side to get a better view of the hole in my head. Thirty-five dollars could buy new bunk beds for Junior and Gretchen's boy. Thirty-five dollars and the whole household could go visit Granddaddy Nelson in the country. Thirty-five dollars would pay for the rent and the piano bill too. Who are these people that spend that much for performing clowns and $1,000 for toy sailboats? What kinda work they do and how they live and how come we ain't in on it? Where we are is who we are, Miss Moore always pointin out. But it don't necessarily have to be that way, she always adds then waits for somebody to say that poor people have to wake up and demand their share of the pie and don't none of us know what kind of pie she talkin about in the first damn place. But she ain't so smart cause I still got her four dollars from the taxi and she sure ain't gettin it. Messin up my day with this shit. Sugar nudges me in my pocket and winks.

Miss Moore lines us up in front of the mailbox where we started   45 from, seem like years ago, and I got a headache for thinkin so hard. And we lean all over each other so we can hold up under the draggy-ass lecture she always finishes us off with at the end before we thank her for borin us to tears. But she just looks at us like she readin tea leaves. Finally she say, "Well, what did you think of F.A.O. Schwartz?"[4]

Rosie Giraffe mumbles, "White folks crazy."

"I'd like to go in there again when I get my birthday money," says Mercedes, and we shove her out the pack so she has to lean on the mailbox by herself.

"I'd like a shower. Tiring day," say Flyboy.

Then Sugar surprises me by sayin, "You know, Miss Moore, I don't think all of us here put together eat in a year what that sailboat costs." And Miss Moore lights up like somebody goosed her. "And?" she say, urging Sugar on. Only I'm standin on her foot so she don't continue.

"Imagine for a minute what kind of society it is in which some   50 people can spend on a toy what it would cost to feed a family of six or seven. What do you think?"

---

[4]F. A. O. Schwartz: the name and the toy store are real. The store, in fact, has become a tourist attraction.

"I think," say Sugar pushing me off her feet like she never done before, cause I whip her ass in a minute, "that this is not much of a democracy if you ask me. Equal chance to pursue happiness means an equal crack at the dough, don't it?" Miss Moore is besides herself and I am disgusted with Sugar's treachery. So I stand on her foot one more time to see if she'll shove me. She shuts up, and Miss Moore looks at me, sorrowfully I'm thinkin. And somethin weird is goin on, I can feel it in my chest.

"Anybody else learn anything today?" lookin dead at me. I walk away and Sugar has to run to catch up and don't even seem to notice when I shrug her arm off my shoulder.

"Well, we got four dollars anyway," she says.

"Uh hunh."

"We could go to Hascombs and get half a chocolate layer and then go to the Sunset and still have plenty money for potato chips and ice-cream sodas."

"Uh hunh."

"Race you to Hascombs," she say.

We start down the block and she gets ahead which is O.K. by me cause I'm goin to the West End and then over to the Drive to think this day through. She can run if she want to and even run faster. But ain't nobody gonna beat me at nuthin.

Engaging the Text

1. What is the lesson Miss Moore is trying to teach in this story? How well is it received by Mercedes, Sugar, and the narrator, Sylvia? Why does the narrator react differently from Sugar, and what is the meaning of her last line in the story, "But ain't nobody gonna beat me at nuthin"?

2. Why did Bambara write the story from Sylvia's point of view? How would the story change if told from Miss Moore's perspective? From Sugar's?

3. The story mentions several expensive items: a fur coat, a microscope, a paperweight, a sailboat, and a toy clown. Why do you think the author chose each of these details?

4. In paragraph 44 Sylvia says, "Where we are is who we are, Miss Moore always pointin out. But it don't necessarily have to be that way." What does Miss Moore mean by this? Do you agree? What does Miss Moore expect the children to do to change the situation?

Exploring Connections

5. Write a dialogue between Andrew Carnegie (p. 20) and Miss Moore discussing the necessity of great disparities in wealth.

Extending the Critical Context

6. For the next class meeting, find the most overpriced, unnecessary item you can in a store, catalog, TV ad or newspaper. Spend a few minutes swapping examples, then discuss the information you've gathered: are there any lessons to be learned here about wealth, success, and status?

7. The opening lines of "The Lesson" suggest that Sylvia is now a mature woman looking back on her youth. Working in groups, write a brief biography explaining what has happened to Sylvia since the day of "The Lesson." What has she done? Who has she become? Read your profiles aloud to the class and explain your vision of Sylvia's development.

Class in America: Myths and Realities

GREGORY MANTSIOS

Which of these gifts might a high school graduate in your family receive — a corsage, a savings bond, or a BMW? According to Mantsios, your answer indicates your social class. Mantsios shows how class distinctions operate in virtually every aspect of our lives, even though as Americans we conspire not to talk about them. The essay's title aptly describes its method: the author outlines four widely held beliefs about class in the United States, then explodes them with carefully documented facts. Even if your eyes are already open to the existence of classes in the United States, some of the numbers Mantsios cites are bound to surprise you. Mantsios teaches at Queens College of the City University of New York. This selection is reprinted from Paula S. Rothenberg's Racism and Sexism: An Integrated Study *(1987).*

People in the United States don't like to talk about class. Or so it would seem. We don't speak about class privileges, or class oppression, or the class nature of society. These terms are not part of our everyday vocabulary, and in most circles they are associated with the language of the rhetorical fringe. Unlike people in most other parts of the world, we shrink from using words that classify along economic lines or that point to class distinctions: phrases like *working class*, *upper class*, and *ruling class* are rarely uttered by Americans.

For the most part, avoidance of class-laden vocabulary crosses class boundaries. There are few among the poor who speak of themselves as lower class; they identify, rather, with their race, ethnic group, or geographic location. Workers are more likely to identify with their employer, industry, or occupational group than with other workers, or with the working class.[1]

Neither are those at the other end of the economic spectrum likely to identify with the word *class*. In her study of 38 wealthy and socially prominent women, Susan Ostrander asked participants if they considered themselves members of the upper class. One participant responded,

> I hate to use the word "class." We are responsible, fortunate people, old families, the people who have something.

Another said,

> I hate [the term] upper class. It is so non–upper class to use it. I just call it "all of us," those who are wellborn.[2]

It is not that Americans, rich or poor, aren't keenly aware of class differences — those quoted above obviously are — it is that class is not in the domain of public discourse. Class is not discussed or debated in public because class identity has been stripped from popular culture. The institutions that shape mass culture and define the parameters of public debate have avoided class issues. In politics, in primary and secondary education, and in the mass media, formulating issues in terms of class is unacceptable, perhaps even un-American.

There are, however, two notable exceptions to this phenomenon. 5 First, it is acceptable in the United States to talk about "the middle class." Interestingly enough, such references appear to be acceptable precisely because they mute class differences. References to the middle class by politicians, for example, are designed to encompass and attract the broadest possible constituency. Not only do references to the middle class gloss over differences, but also these references avoid any suggestion of conflict or exploitation.

This leads us to the second exception to the class avoidance phenomenon. We are, on occasion, presented with glimpses of the upper class and the lower class (the language used is "the wealthy" and "the

[1]See Oscar Glantz, "Class Consciousness and Political Solidarity," *American Sociological Review*, vol. 23, August 1958, pp. 375–382; Robert Nisbet, "The Decline and Fall of Social Class," *Pacific Sociological Review*, vol. 2, Spring 1959, pp. 11–17; Charles W. Tucker, "A Comparative Analysis of Subjective Social Class: 1945–1963," *Social Forces*, no. 46, June 1968, pp. 508–514; and Ira Katznelson, *City Trenches: Urban Politics and Patterning of Class in the United States*, New York, Pantheon Books, 1981. [Author's note]

[2]Susan Ostrander, "Upper-Class Women: Class Consciousness as Conduct and Meaning," in *Power Structure Research* by G. William Domhoff, Beverly Hills, California, Sage Productions, 1980, pp. 78–79. [Author's note]

poor"). In the media, these presentations are designed to satisfy some real or imagined voyeuristic need of "the ordinary person." As curiosities, the ground-level view of street life and the inside look at the rich and the famous serve as unique models, one to avoid and one to aspire to. In either case, the two models are presented without causal relation to each other: one is not rich because the other is poor. Similarly, when social commentators or liberal politicians draw attention to the plight of the poor, they do so in a manner that obscures the class structure and denies class exploitation. Wealth and poverty are viewed as one of several natural and inevitable states of being: differences are only differences. One may even say differences are the American way, a reflection of American social diversity.

We are left with one of two possibilities: either talking about class and recognizing class distinctions are not relevant to U.S. society, or we mistakenly hold a set of beliefs that obscure the reality of class differences and their impact on people's lives.

Let us look at four common, albeit contradictory, beliefs about the United States.

Myth Number 1: The United States is fundamentally a classless society. Class distinctions are largely irrelevant today, and whatever differences do exist in economic standing are, for the most part, insignificant. Rich or poor, we are all equal in the eyes of the law, and such basic needs as health care and education are provided to all regardless of economic standing.

Myth Number 2: We are, essentially, a middle-class nation. Despite some variations in economic status, most Americans have achieved relative affluence in what is widely recognized as a consumer society.

Myth Number 3: We are all getting richer. The American public as a whole is steadily moving up the economic ladder, and each generation propels itself to greater economic well-being. Despite some fluctuations, the United States' position in the global economy has brought previously unknown prosperity to most, if not all, North Americans.

Myth Number 4: Everyone has an equal chance to succeed. Success in the United States requires no more than hard work, sacrifice, and perseverance: "in America, anyone can be president." And with a little luck (a clever invention or a winning lottery ticket), there are opportunities for the easygoing as well. "In America, anyone can become a millionaire"; it's just a matter of being in the right place at the right time."

In trying to assess the legitimacy of these beliefs, we want to ask several important questions. Are there significant class differences among Americans? If these differences do exist, are they getting bigger or smaller, and do these differences have a significant impact on the way we live? Finally, does everyone in the United States really have an equal opportunity to succeed?

The Economic Spectrum

We will begin by looking at differences. An examination of official   10
census material reveals that variations in economic well-being are in
fact immense. Consider the following:

- The wealthiest 15 percent of the American population holds nearly
  75 percent of the total household wealth in the country. That is, they
  own three-quarters of all the consumer durables (such as houses,
  cars, and stereos) and financial assets (such as stocks, bonds, property, and savings accounts).[3]
- Approximately 17,000 Americans declared more than $1 million of
  annual income on their 1985 tax returns; that is more money than
  most Americans expect to earn in an entire lifetime.[4]

    Affluence and prosperity are clearly alive and well in certain
  segments of the United States population. However, this abundance
  is in contrast to the poverty and despair that is also prevalent in the
  United States. At the other end of the spectrum:

- A total of 15 percent of the American population — that is, one of
  every seven — live below the government's official poverty line
  (calculated in 1984 at $5,278 for an individual and $10,600 for a
  family of four).[5] These poor include a significant number of homeless people — approximately three million Americans.[6]
- Nearly a quarter of all the children in the United States under the
  age of six live in poverty.[7]

The contrast between rich and poor is sharp, and with nearly one-
third of the American population living at one extreme or the other, it is
difficult to argue that we live in a classless society. The income gap
between rich and poor in the United States (measured as the percentage
of total income held by the wealthiest 20 percent of the population
versus the poorest 20 percent is approximately 11 to 1, one of the highest
ratios in the industrialized world.[8] (For example, the ratio in Great
Britain is 7 to 1; in Japan, it is 4 to 1.)

[3]Steven Rose, *The American Profile Poster*, New York, Pantheon Books, 1986, p. 31.
[Author's note]

[4]Barbara Kallen, "Getting By on $1 Million a Year," *Forbes*, October 27, 1986,
p. 48. [Author's note]

[5]"Characteristics of the Population Below the Poverty Level: 1984," from *Current
Population Reports, Consumer Income Series P-60, No. 152*, Washington, D.C., U.S.
Department of Commerce, Bureau of the Census, June 1986. [Author's note]

[6]Constance Holden, "Homelessness: Experts Differ on Root Causes," *Science*, May
2, 1986, pp. 569–570. [Author's note]

[7]"New Class of Children Is Poorer and the Prospects of Advancement Are Dim,"*New
York Times*, October 20, 1985, p. 56. [Author's note]

[8]"United Nations National Accounts Statistics," *Statistical Papers, Series M no. 79*,
New York, United Nations, 1985, pp. 1–11. See also Ira C. Magaziner and Robert B.
Reich, *Minding America's Business: The Decline and Rise of the American Political
Economy*, New York, Vintage, 1983, p. 23. [Author's note]

Reality 1: There are enormous differences in the economic status of American citizens. A sizable proportion of the United States population occupies opposite ends of the economic spectrum.

Nor can it be said that the majority of the American population fares very well. In the middle range of the economic spectrum:

- 50 percent of the American population holds less than 3.5 percent of the nation's wealth.[9]
- The median household income (that is, half the American population made more and the other half made less) was $22,420 in 1984. This is a margin of approximately $225 per week above the poverty level.[10]

The level of inequality is sometimes difficult to comprehend fully with dollar figures and percentages. To help his students visualize the distribution of income, the well-known economist Paul Samuelson asked them to picture an income pyramid made of children's blocks, with each layer of blocks representing $1000. If we were to construct Samuelson's pyramid today, the peak of the pyramid would be much higher than the Eiffel Tower, yet almost all of us would be within six feet of the ground.[11] In other words, the distribution of income is heavily skewed; a small minority of families take the lion's share of national income, and the remaining income is distributed among the vast majority of middle-income and low-income families. Keep in mind that Samuelson's pyramid represents the distribution of income, not wealth. The distribution of wealth is skewed even further.

Reality 2: The middle class in the United States holds a very small share of the nation's wealth.

Lottery millionaires and Horatio Alger[12] stories notwithstanding, evidence suggests that the level of inequality in the United States is getting higher. Statistically, it is getting harder to make it big and more difficult to even stay in the middle-income level. Census data show the gap between the rich and the poor to be the widest since the government began collecting information in 1947. Furthermore, the percentage of households earning at a middle-income level (that is, between 75% and 125% of the median income) has been falling steadily since 1967.[13] Most

[9]Steven Rose, *The American Profile Poster*, p. 31. [Author's note]

[10]"Money Income of Households, Families and Persons in the United States: 1984," *Current Population Reports P-60, no. 151*, Washington, D.C., Department of Commerce, Bureau of Census, 1986, p. 1. [Author's note]

[11]Paul Samuelson, *Economics*, 10th ed., New York, McGraw-Hill, 1976, p. 84. [Author's note]

[12]*Horatio Alger*: U.S. author (1834–1899) of books for boys, now synonymous with the rags-to-riches dream.

[13]Chris Tilly, "U-Turn on Equality," *Dollars and Sense*, May 1986, p. 11. [Author's note]

of those who disappeared from the middle-income level moved downward, not upward. And economic polarization is expected to increase over the next several decades.[14]

Reality 3: The middle class is shrinking in size, and most of those leaving the ranks of the middle class are falling to a lower economic standing.

AMERICAN LIFE-STYLES   At last count, approximately 35 million Americans across the nation lived in unrelenting poverty. Yet, as political scientist Michael Harrington once commented, "America has the best dressed poverty the world has ever known."[15] Clothing disguises much of the poverty in the United States, and this may explain, in part, its middle-class image. With increased mass marketing of "designer" clothing and with shifts in the nation's economy from blue-collar (and often better-paying) manufacturing jobs to white-collar and pink-collar jobs in the service sector, it is becoming increasingly difficult to distinguish class differences based on appearance.[16]

Beneath the surface, there is another reality. Let us look at some "typical" and not-so-typical life-styles.

American Profile No. 1

   Name: Harold S. Browning.
   Father: manufacturer, industrialist.
   Mother: prominent social figure in the community.
   Principal child-rearer: governess.
   Primary education: an exclusive private school, Manhattan's Upper East Side.
      Notes: a small, well-respected primary school where teachers and administrators have a reputation for nurturing student creativity and for providing the finest educational preparation.
      Student's ambition: "to become president."
   Supplemental tutoring: tutors in French and math.
   Summer camp: a sleepaway camp in northern Connecticut.
      Notes: camp provides instruction in the creative arts, athletics, and the natural sciences.
   Secondary education: a prestigious preparatory school, Westchester County.
      Notes: classmates included the sons of ambassadors, doctors, attorneys, television personalities, and well-known business leaders.
      After-school activities: private riding lessons.
      Student's ambition: "to take over my father's business."
      High-school graduation gift: BMW.

[14]Paul Blumberg, *Inequality in an Age of Decline*, Oxford University Press, 1980. [Author's note]

[15]Michael Harrington, *The Other America*, New York, Macmillan, 1962, pp. 12–13. [Author's note]

[16]Stuart Ewen and Elizabeth Ewen, *Channels of Desire: Mass Images and the Shaping of American Consciousness*, New York, McGraw-Hill, 1982. [Author's note]

Family activities: theater, recitals, museums, summer vacations in Europe, occasional winter trips to the Caribbean.

Notes: as members and donors of the local art museum, the Brownings and their children attend private receptions and exhibit openings at the invitation of the museum director.

Higher education: an Ivy League liberal arts college, Massachusetts.

Major: economics and political science.

After-class activities: debating club, college newspaper, swim team.

Ambition: "to become a leader in business."

First full-time job (age 23): assistant manager of operations, Browning Tool and Dye, Inc. (family enterprise).

Subsequent employment:

3 years — Executive Assistant to the President, Browning Tool and Dye.

Responsibilities included: purchasing (materials and equipment), personnel, and distribution networks.

4 years — Advertising Manager, Lackheed Manufacturing (home appliances).

3 years — Director of Marketing and Sales, Comerex Inc. (business machines).

Present Employment (age 38):

Executive Vice President, SmithBond and Co. (digital instruments).

Typical daily activities: review financial reports and computer printouts, dictate memoranda, lunch with clients, initiate conference call, meet with assistants, plan business trips, meet with associates.

Transportation to and from work: chauffeured company limousine.

Annual salary: $215,000.

Ambition: "to become chief executive officer of the firm, or one like it, within the next 5 to 10 years."

Present residence: 18th-floor condominium in Manhattan's Upper West Side, 11 rooms, including 5 spacious bedrooms and terrace overlooking river.

Interior: professionally designed and accented with elegant furnishings, valuable antiques, and expensive artwork.

Notes: building management provides doorman and elevator attendant. Family employs au pair[17] for children and maid for other domestic chores.

Second residence: Farm in northwestern Connecticut, used for weekend retreats and for horse breeding (investment/hobby).

Notes: to maintain the farm and cater to their needs when they are there, the Brownings employ a part-time maid, groundskeeper, and horse breeder.

---

[17]*au pair*: a young woman from another country who works for a family, typically caring for children in exchange for room and board.

Harold Browning was born into a world of nurses, maids, and 20
governesses. His world today is one of airplanes and limousines, five-star
restaurants and luxurious living accommodations. The life and life-style
of Harold S. Browning are in sharp contrast to those of Bob Farrell.

American Profile No. 2

Name: Bob Farrell.
Mother: Retail clerk.
Father: Machinist.
Principal child-rearer: mother and sitter.
Early education: a medium-sized public school in Queens, New York.
  Notes: school characterized by large class size, outmoded physical
  facilities, and an educational philosophy emphasizing basic skills
  and student discipline.
  Student's ambition: "to become president."
Supplemental tutoring: none.
Summer camp: YMCA day camp.
  Notes: emphasis on team sports, arts and crafts.
Secondary education: large regional high school in Queens.
  Notes: classmates included the sons and daughters of carpenters,
  postal clerks, teachers, nurses, shopkeepers, mechanics, bus
  drivers, police officers, salesmen.
  After-school activities: basketball and handball in school park.
  High-school graduation gift: $500 savings bond.
  Student's ambition: "to make it through college."
Family activities: family gatherings around television set, bowling, an
  occasional trip to the movie theater, summer Sundays at the
  public beach.
Higher education: a two-year community college with a technical
  orientation.
  Major: electrical technology.
  After-school activities: employed as a part-time bagger in local
  supermarket.
  Student's ambition: "to become an electrical engineer."
First full-time job (age 19): service-station attendant.
  Notes: continued to take college classes in the evening.
Subsequent employment:
  Mail clerk at large insurance firm.
  Manager trainee, large retail chain.
Present employment:
  Assistant Sales Manager, building supply firm.
  Typical daily activities: demonstrate products, write up product
  orders, handle customer complaints, check inventory.
  Means of transportation to and from work: city subway.
  Annual salary: $20,000.
  Ambition: "to open up my own business."
Additional income: $4,100 in commissions from evening and weekend
  work as salesman in local men's clothing store.

Present residence: the Farrells own their own home in a working-class suburb in Queens.

Bob Farrell and Harold Browning live very differently: the life-style of one is privileged; the other is not so privileged. The differences are class differences, and these differences have a profound impact on the way they live. They are differences between playing a game of handball in the park and taking riding lessons at a private stable, watching a movie on television and going to the theater, and taking the subway to work and being driven in a limousine. More important, the difference in class determines where they live, who their friends are, how well they are educated, what they do for a living, and what they come to expect from life.

Yet, as dissimilar as their life-styles are, Harold Browning and Bob Farrell have some things in common. They live in the same city, they work long hours, and they are highly motivated. More important, they are both white males.

Let us look at someone else who works long and hard and is highly motivated. This person, however, is black and female.

American Profile No. 3

Name: Cheryl Mitchell.
Father: Janitor.
Mother: Waitress.
Principal child-rearer: grandmother.
Primary education: large public school in Ocean Hill–Brownsville, Brooklyn, New York.
  Notes: rote teaching of basic skills and emphasis on conveying the importance of good attendance, good manners, and good work habits. School patrolled by security guards.
  Student's ambition: "to be a teacher."
Supplemental tutoring: none.
Summer camp: none.
Secondary education: large public school in Ocean Hill–Brownsville.
  Notes: classmates included sons and daughters of hairdressers, groundskeepers, painters, dressmakers, dishwashers, domestics.
  After-school activities: domestic chores, part-time employment as babysitter and housekeeper.
  Student's ambition: "to be a social worker."
  High-school graduation gift: corsage.
Family activities: church-sponsored socials.
Higher education: one semester of local community college.
  Note: student dropped out of school for financial reasons.
First full-time job (age 17): counter clerk, local bakery.
Subsequent employment: file clerk with temporary service agency, supermarket checker.
Present employment: nurse's aid, municipal hospital.
  Typical daily activities: make up hospital beds, clean out bed-

pans, weigh patients and assist them to the bathroom, take temperature readings, pass out and collect food trays, feed patients who need help, bathe patients, and change dressings.

Annual salary: $11,200.

Ambition: "to get out of the ghetto."

Present residence: three-room apartment in the South Bronx, needs painting, has poor ventilation, is in a high-crime area.

Notes: Cheryl Mitchell lives with her two children and her elderly mother.

When we look at the lives of Cheryl Mitchell, Bob Farrell, and Harold Browning, we see life-styles that are very different. We are not looking, however, at economic extremes. Cheryl Mitchell's income as a nurse's aide puts her above the government's official poverty line. Below her on the income pyramid are 35 million poverty-stricken Americans. Far from being poor, Bob Farrell's annual income as an assistant sales manager puts him in the 52nd percentile of the income distribution. More than 50 percent of the United States population earns less money than Bob Farrell. And while Harold Browning's income puts him in a high-income bracket, he stands only a fraction of the way up Samuelson's income pyramid. Well above him are the 17,000 individuals whose annual salary exceeds $1 million. Yet, Harold S. Browning spends more money on his horses than Cheryl Mitchell earns in a year.

Reality 4: Even ignoring the extreme poles of the economic spectrum, we find enormous class differences in the life-styles among the haves, the have-nots, and the have-littles.   25

Class affects more than life-style and material well-being. It has a significant impact on our physical and mental well-being as well.

Researchers have found an inverse relation between social class and health. Lower-class standing is correlated to higher rates of infant mortality,[18] eye and ear disease, arthritis, physical disability, diabetes, nutritional deficiency,[19] respiratory disease,[20] mental illness,[21] and heart disease.[22] In all areas of health, poor people do not share the same life chances as those in the social class above them. Furthermore,

[18]Kyriakos S. Markides and Connie McFarland, "A Note on Recent Trends in the Infant Mortality–Socioeconomic Status Relationship," *Social Forces*, 61:1, September 1982, pp. 268–276. [Author's note]

[19]Stanley D. Eitzen, *In Conflict and Order: Understanding Society*, Boston, Allyn and Bacon, 1985, p. 265. Lucile Duberman. *Social Inequality: Class and Caste in America*, New York, J. B. Lippincott, 1976, p. 200. [Author's note]

[20]*Statistical Abstracts of the U.S.*, 1986, p. 116. [Author's note]

[21]August Hollingshead and Frederick Redlick, *Social Class and Mental Illness: A Community Study*, New York, John Wiley, 1958. Also Leo Srole, *Mental Health in the Metropolis: The Midtown Manhattan Study*, New York, McGraw-Hill, 1962. [Author's note]

[22]U.S. Bureau of the Census, *Social Indicators III*, Washington, D.C., U.S. Government Printing Office, 1980, p. 101. [Author's note]

lower-class standing is correlated to a lower quality of treatment for illness and disease. The results of poor health and poor treatment are borne out in the life expectancy rates within each class. Aaron Antonovsky found that the higher your class standing, the higher your life expectancy.[23] Conversely, Lillian Guralnick studied the relationship between class and the death rate per 1000 in each of six age categories. Within each age group, she found that the lower one's class standing, the higher the death rate; in some age groups, the figures were as much as two and three times as high.[24]

Reality 5: From cradle to grave, class standing has a significant impact on our chances for survival.

The lower one's class standing, the more difficult it is to secure appropriate housing, the more time is spent on the routine tasks of everyday life, the greater is the percentage of income that goes to pay for food and other basic necessities,[25] and the greater is the likelihood of crime victimization.[26] Class can predict changes for both survival and success.

CLASS EDUCATIONAL ATTAINMENT   In his study for the Carnegie Council on Children, Richard de Lone correlates school performance — i.e., grades and test scores — with the economic status of the student's family. After looking at the test scores of 647,031 students who took the College Board exams (SATs), he concluded that "the higher the student's social status, the higher the probability that he or she will get higher grades." [See Table 1.] De Lone's findings were consistent with earlier studies that showed a direct relation between class and scores on standardized tests.[27]

Another researcher, William Sewell, showed a positive correlation between class and overall educational achievement. In comparing the

[23]Aaron Antonovsky, "Social Class, Life Expectancy and Overall Mortality," *The Impact of Social Class*, New York, Thomas Crowell, 1972, pp. 467–491. [Author's note]

[24]Lillian Guralnick, "Socioeconomic Differences in Mortality by Cause of Death," in *International Population Conference, Ottawa, 1963*, Liège, International Union for the Scientific Study of Population, 1964, p. 298, quoted in Antonovsky, op. cit. See also Steven Caldwell and Theodore Diamond, "Income Differentials in Mortality" in Linda Del Bene and Fritz Scheuren, eds., *Statistical Uses of Administrative Records*, Washington, D.C., United States Social Security Administration, 1979, p. 58. Harriet Duleep, "Measuring the Effect of Income on Adult Mortality Using Longitudinal Administrative Record Data," *Journal of Human Resources*, vol. 21, no. 2, Spring 1986. [Author's note]

[25]Paul Jacobs, "Keeping the Poor, Poor?" in Jerome H. Skolnick and Elliot Currie, *Crisis in American Institutions*, Boston, Little, Brown and Company, 1982, pp. 104–114. [Author's note]

[26]Dennis W. Roncek, "Dangerous Places: Crime and Residential Environment," *Social Forces*, 60:1, September 1981, pp. 74–96. [Author's note]

[27]Kenneth Eells and Allison Davis, *Intelligence and Cultural Differences: A Study of Cultural Learning and Problem Solving*, Chicago, University of Chicago Press, 1951. [Author's note]

Table 1 Relation of SAT Scores to Family Income[28]

STUDENT'S SCORES	STUDENT'S MEAN FAMILY INCOME
750–800	$24,124
700–750	21,980
650–700	21,292
600–650	20,330
550–600	19,481
500–550	18,824
450–500	18,122
400–450	17,387
350–400	16,182
300–350	14,355
250–300	11,428
200–250	8,369

top 25 percent of his sample to the bottom 25 percent, he found that students from upper-class families were: twice as likely to obtain training beyond high school, four times as likely to go to college, six times as likely to graduate from college, and nine times as likely to attain a postgraduate degree. Sewell concluded, "Socio-economc background . . . operates independently of academic ability at every stage in the process of educational attainment."[29]

Reality 6: Class standing has a significant impact on chances for educational attainment.

Class standing and consequently life chances are largely determined at birth. Although examples of individuals who have gone from rags to riches abound in the mass media, statistics on class mobility show these leaps to be extremely rare. In fact, less dramatic advances in class standing are relatively few. One study showed that fewer than one in five men surpass the economic status of their fathers.[30] For those whose annual income is in six figures, economic success is due in large part to the wealth and privileges bestowed upon them at birth. Over 66 percent of the consumer units with incomes of $100,000 or more have some inherited assets. Of these units, over 86 percent reported that inheritances constituted a substantial portion of their total assets.[31]

[28]Richard de Lone, *Small Futures*, New York: Harcourt Brace Jovanovich, 1978, p. 102. [Author's note]

[29]William H. Sewell, "Inequality of Opportunity for Higher Education," *American Sociological Review*, vol. 36, no. 5, 1971, pp. 793–809. [Author's note]

[30]Richard de Lone, *Small Futures*, New York: Harcourt Brace Jovanovich, 1978, pp. 14–19. [Author's note]

[31]Howard Tuchman, *Economics of the Rich*, New York, Random House, 1973, p. 15. [Author's note]

Economist Howard Wachtel likens inheritance to a series of Monopoly games in which the winner of the first game refuses to relinquish his cash and commerical property for the second game. "After all," argues the winner, "I accumulated my wealth and income by the strength of my own wits." With such an arrangement, it is not difficult to predict the outcome of subsequent games.[32]

Reality 7: All Americans do not have an equal opportunity to 35
succeed. Inheritance laws assure a greater likelihood of success for the offspring of the wealthy.

Spheres of Power and Oppression

When we look at society and try to determine what it is that keeps most people down — what holds them back from realizing their potential as healthy, creative, productive individuals — we find institutionally oppressive forces that are largely beyond their individual control. Class domination is one of these forces. People do not choose to be poor or working class; instead, they are limited and confined by the opportunities afforded or denied them by a social system. The class structure in the United States is a function of its economic system — capitalism, a system that is based on private rather than public ownership and control of commercial enterprises, and on the class division between those who own and control and those who do not. Under capitalism, these enterprises are governed by the need to produce a profit for the owners, rather than to fulfill collective needs.

Racial and gender domination are other such forces that hold people down. Although there are significant differences in the way capitalism, racism, and sexism affect our lives, there are also a multitude of parallels. And although race, class, and gender act independently of each other, they are at the same time very much interrelated.

On the one hand, issues of race and gender oppression cut across class lines. Women experience the effects of sexism whether they are well-paid professionals or poorly paid clerks. As women, they face discrimination and male domination, as well as catcalls and stereotyping. Similarly, a black man faces racial oppression whether he is an executive, an auto worker, or a tenant farmer. As a black, he will be subjected to racial slurs and be denied opportunities because of his color. Regardless of their class standing, women and members of minority races are confronted with oppressive forces precisely because of their gender, color, or both.

On the other hand, class oppression permeates other spheres of power and oppression, so that the oppression experienced by women and minorities is also differentiated along class lines. Although women

---

[32]Howard Wachtel, *Labor and the Economy*, Orlando, Florida, Academic Press, 1984, pp. 161–162. [Author's note]

Table 2 Chances of Being Poor in America[33]

	WHITE MALE AND FEMALE	WHITE FEMALE HEAD[a]	BLACK MALE AND FEMALE	BLACK FEMALE HEAD
Poverty	1 in 9	1 in 4	1 in 3	1 in 2
Near Poverty	1 in 6	1 in 3	1 in 2	2 in 3

[a]Persons in families with female householder, no husband present

and minorities find themselves in subordinate positions vis-à-vis white men, the particular issues they confront may be quite different depending on their position in the class structure. Inequalities in the class structure distinguish social functions and individual power, and these distinctions carry over to race and gender categories.

Power is incremental and class privileges can accrue to individual women and to individual members of a racial minority. At the same time, class-oppressed men, whether they are white or black, have privileges afforded them as men in a sexist society. Similarly, class-oppressed whites, whether they are men or women, have privileges afforded them as whites in a racist society. Spheres of power and oppression divide us deeply in our society, and the schisms between us are often difficult to bridge.

Whereas power is incremental, oppression is cumulative, and those who are poor, black, and female have all of the forces of classism, racism, and sexism bearing down on them. This cumulative oppression is what is meant by the double and triple jeopardy of women and minorities.[34]

Furthermore, oppression in one sphere is related to the likelihood of oppression in another. If you are black and female, for example, you are much more likely to be poor or working class than you would be as a white male. Census figures show that the incidence of poverty and near-poverty (calculated as 125 percent of the poverty line) varies greatly by race and gender. [See Table 2.]

In other words, being female and being nonwhite are attributes in our society that increase the chances of poverty and of lower-class standing.

Reality 8: Racism and sexism compound the effects of classism in society.

[33]"Characteristics of the Population Below the Poverty Level: 1984," pp. 5–9. [Author's note]

[34]Gloria Steinem offers an opposing view, arguing that class acts in reverse for women and that power relations between wealthy men and their dependent wives are such that upper-class women are even more powerless than poor and working-class women vis-à-vis men. Gloria Steinem, "The Trouble with Rich Women," *Ms.*, June 1986, p. 41. [Author's note]

Engaging the Text

1. Having read the article, with its list of eight "realities," re-examine the four myths Mantsios cites (para. 8). Do you now see any truth in them, or not? Has the author summarized the myths fairly, or does he set them up to be easy targets?

2. Near the beginning (for instance, paras. 1, 5, and 6), Mantsios refers to exploitation and oppression. Does the essay make a case that the wealthy are exploiting the poor, or does it simply assume this? Do you agree with Mantsios's position?

3. Work out a rough budget for a family of four with an annual income of $12,000. Be sure to include costs for food, clothing, housing, transportation, health care, and other unavoidable expenses. Do you think this would be a reasonable "poverty line," or is it too low or too high?

4. Imagine that you are Harold S. Browning, Bob Farrell, or Cheryl Mitchell. Write an entry for this person's journal after a tough day on the job.

5. Picture yourself at thirty years old. Write a profile of yourself, imitating the form Mantsios uses for Harold S. Browning, Bob Farrell, and Cheryl Mitchell. What sorts of events could alter this profile dramatically (for better or worse)?

Exploring Connections

6. Reread the last section of the essay, "Spheres of Power and Oppression." Compare and contrast Mantsios's view of the working class with that offered by Andrew Carnegie in "The Gospel of Wealth" (p. 20). Which do you find more persuasive and why? Which view do you think is more widely held in the United States today?

7. To what class (upper, middle, or lower) does each of the following belong?

> Stephen Cruz in Studs Terkel's profile (p. 36)
> The Man and the Kid in George C. Wolfe's "Symbiosis" (p. 42)
> Miss Moore in Toni Cade Bambara's "The Lesson" (p. 64)

Discuss those about whom there is disagreement.

Extending the Critical Context

8. Study the employment pages of a major newspaper in your area. Roughly what percentage of the openings would you consider upper class, middle class, and lower class? On what do you base your distinctions?

9. Mantsios points out that "inheritance laws assure a greater likelihood of success for the offspring of the wealthy" (para. 35). Do you agree that this is a serious problem? What solutions can you imagine, and which would you endorse?

Mike LeFevre

STUDS TERKEL

This interview with Chicago steelworker Mike LeFevre first appeared in Working *(1972), Studs Terkel's acclaimed collection of oral histories. (More information on Terkel can be found on p. 36.) LeFevre represents a long tradition of industrial, or blue-collar, laborers — a "dying breed," as he puts it, who built America with the strength of their backs and the determination to carve a better future for their children.*

It is a two-flat dwelling, somewhere in Cicero, on the outskirts of Chicago. He is thirty-seven. He works in a steel mill. On occasion, his wife Carol works as a waitress in a neighborhood restaurant; otherwise, she is at home, caring for their two small children, a girl and a boy.

At the time of my first visit, a sculpted statuette of Mother and Child was on the floor, head severed from body. He laughed softly as he indicated his three-year-old daughter: "She Doctor Spock'd it."[1]

I'm a dying breed. A laborer. Strictly muscle work . . . pick it up, put it down, pick it up, put it down. We handle between forty and fifty thousand pounds of steel a day. (Laughs.) I know this is hard to believe — from four hundred pounds to three- and four-pound pieces. It's dying.

You can't take pride any more. You remember when a guy could point to a house he built, how many logs he stacked. He built it and he was proud of it. I don't really think I could be proud if a contractor built a home for me. I would be tempted to get in there and kick the carpenter in the ass (laughs), and take the saw away from him. 'Cause I would have to be part of it, you know.

It's hard to take pride in a bridge you're never gonna cross, in a door   5
you're never gonna open. You're mass-producing things and you never see the end result of it. (Muses.) I worked for a trucker one time. And I got this tiny satisfaction when I loaded a truck. At least I could see the truck depart loaded. In a steel mill, forget it. You don't see where nothing goes.

I got chewed out by my foreman once. He said, "Mike, you're a good worker but you have a bad attitude." My attitude is that I don't get excited about my job. I do my work but I don't say whoopee-doo.

[1]*Doctor Spock:* Dr. Benjamin Spock (b. 1903), prominent U.S. child-care expert, who generally opposes physical punishment for children.

The day I get excited about my job is the day I go to a head shrinker. How are you gonna get excited about pullin' steel? How are you gonna get excited when you're tired and want to sit down?

It's not just the work. Somebody built the pyramids. Somebody's going to build something. Pyramids, Empire State Building — these things just don't happen. There's hard work behind it. I would like to see a building, say, the Empire State, I would like to see on one side of it a foot-wide strip from top to bottom with the name of every bricklayer, the name of every electrician, with all the names. So when a guy walked by, he could take his son and say, "See, that's me over there on the forty-fifth floor. I put the steel beam in." Picasso can point to a painting. What can I point to? A writer can point to a book. Everybody should have something to point to.

It's the not-recognition by other people. To say a woman is *just* a housewife is degrading, right? Okay. *Just* a housewife. It's also degrading to say *just* a laborer. The difference is that a man goes out and maybe gets smashed.

When I was single, I could quit, just split. I wandered all over the country. You worked just enough to get a poke, money in your pocket. Now I'm married and I got two kids . . . (trails off). I worked on a truck dock one time and I was single. The foreman came over and he grabbed my shoulder, kind of gave me a shove. I punched him and knocked him off the dock. I said, "Leave me alone. I'm doing my work, just stay away from me, just don't give me the with-the-hands business."

Hell, if you whip a damn mule he might kick you. Stay out of my way, that's all. Working is bad enough, don't bug me. I would rather work my ass off for eight hours a day with nobody watching me than five minutes with a guy watching me. Who you gonna sock? You can't sock General Motors, you can't sock anybody in Washington, you can't sock a system.   10

A mule, an old mule, that's the way I feel. Oh yeah. See. (Shows black and blue marks on arms and legs, burns.) You know what I heard from more than one guy at work? "If my kid wants to work in a factory, I am going to kick the hell out of him." I want my kid to be an effete snob. Yeah, mm-hmm. (Laughs.) I want him to be able to quote Walt Whitman,[2] to be proud of it.

If you can't improve yourself, you improve your posterity. Otherwise life isn't worth nothing. You might as well go back to the cave and stay there. I'm sure the first caveman who went over the hill to see what was on the other side — I don't think he went there wholly out of curiosity. He went there because he wanted to get his son out of the cave. Just the same way I want to send my kid to college.

[2]*Walt Whitman:* influential U.S. poet (1819–1892); best known for *Leaves of Grass* (1855).

I work so damn hard and want to come home and sit down and lay around. *But I gotta get it out.* I want to be able to turn around to somebody and say, "Hey, fuck you." You know? (Laughs.) The guy sitting next to me on the bus too. 'Cause all day I wanted to tell my foreman to go fuck himself, but I can't.

So I find a guy in a tavern. To tell him that. And he tells me too. I've been in brawls. He's punching me and I'm punching him, because we actually want to punch somebody else. The most that'll happen is the bartender will bar us from the tavern. But at work, you lose your job.

This one foreman I've got, he's a kid. He's a college graduate. He thinks he's better than everybody else. He was chewing me out and I was saying, "Yeah, yeah, yeah." He said, "What do you mean, yeah, yeah, yeah. Yes, *sir.*" I told him, "Who the hell are you, Hitler? What is this 'Yes, *sir*' bullshit? I came here to work, I didn't come here to crawl. There's a fuckin' difference." One word led to another and I lost.

I got broke down to a lower grade and lost twenty-five cents an hour, which is a hell of a lot. It amounts to about ten dollars a week. He came over — after breaking me down. The guy comes over and smiles at me. I blew up. He didn't know it, but he was about two seconds and two feet away from a hospital. I said, "Stay the fuck away from me." He was just about to say something and was pointing his finger. I just reached my hand up and just grabbed his finger and I just put it back in his pocket. He walked away. I grabbed his finger because I'm married. If I'd a been single, I'd a grabbed his head. That's the difference.

You're doing this manual labor and you know that technology can do it. (Laughs.) Let's face it, a machine can do the work of a man; otherwise they wouldn't have space probes. Why can we send a rocket ship that's unmanned and yet send a man in a steel mill to do a mule's work?

Automation? Depends how it's applied. It frightens me if it puts me out on the street. It doesn't frighten me if it shortens my work week. You read that little thing: what are you going to do when this computer replaces you? Blow up computers. (Laughs.) Really. Blow up computers. I'll be goddamned if a computer is gonna eat before I do! I want milk for my kids and beer for me. Machines can either liberate man or enslave 'im, because they're pretty neutral. It's man who has the bias to put the thing one place or another.

If I had a twenty-hour workweek, I'd get to know my kids better, my wife better. Some kid invited me to go on a college campus. On a Saturday. It was summertime. Hell, if I had a choice of taking my wife and kids to a picnic or going to a college campus, it's gonna be the picnic. But if I worked a twenty-hour week, I could go do both. Don't you think with that extra twenty hours people could really expand? Who's to say? There are some people in factories just by force of circumstance. I'm just like the colored people. Potential Einsteins don't have to be white. They could be in cotton fields, they could be in factories.

The twenty-hour week is a possibility today. The intellectuals, they always say there are potential Lord Byrons, Walt Whitmans, Roosevelts, Picassos working in construction or steel mills or factories. But I don't think they believe it. I think what they're afraid of is the potential Hitlers and Stalins that are there too. The people in power fear the leisure man. Not just the United States. Russia's the same way.

What do you think would happen in this country if, for one year, they experimented and gave everybody a twenty-hour week? How do they know that the guy who digs Wallace[3] today doesn't try to resurrect Hitler tomorrow? Or the guy who is mildly disturbed at pollution doesn't decide to go to General Motors and shit on the guy's desk? You can become a fanatic if you had the time. The whole thing is time. That is, I think, one reason rich kids tend to be fanatic about politics: they have time. Time, that's the important thing.

It isn't that the average working guy is dumb. He's tired, that's all. I picked up a book on chess one time. That thing laid in the drawer for two or three weeks, you're too tired. During the weekends you want to take your kids out. You don't want to sit there and the kid comes up: "Daddy, can I go to the park?" You got your nose in a book? Forget it.

I know a guy fifty-seven years old. Know what he tells me? "Mike, I'm old and tired *all* the time." The first thing happens at work: when the arms start moving, the brain stops. I punch in about ten minutes to seven in the morning. I say hello to a couple of guys I like, I kid around with them. One guy says good morning to you and you say good morning. To another guy you say fuck you. The guy you say fuck you to is your friend.

I put on my hard hat, change into my safety shoes, put on my safety glasses, go to the bonderizer. It's the thing I work on. They rake the metal, they wash it, they dip it in a paint solution, and we take it off. Put it on, take it off, put it on, take it off, put it on, take it off . . .

I say hello to everybody but my boss. At seven it starts. My arms get tired about the first half-hour. After that, they don't get tired any more until maybe the last half-hour at the end of the day. I work from seven to three thirty. My arms are tired at seven thirty and they're tired at three o'clock. I hope to God I never get broke in, because I always want my arms to be tired at seven thirty and three o'clock. (Laughs.) 'Cause that's when I know that there's a beginning and there's an end. That I'm not brainwashed. In between, I don't even try to think.

If I were to put you in front of a dock and I pulled up a skid in front

[3]*Wallace:* George C. Wallace (b. 1919), governor of Alabama in three separate terms spanning three decades. Wallace was a key opponent of school desegregation in 1963 but recanted and won significant Black support in the 1982 election.

of you with fifty hundred-pound sacks of potatoes and there are fifty more skids just like it, and this is what you're gonna do all day, what would you think about — potatoes? Unless a guy's a nut, he never thinks about work or talks about it. Maybe about baseball or about getting drunk the other night or he got laid or he didn't get laid. I'd say one out of a hundred will actually get excited about work.

Why is it that the communists always say they're for the working-man, and as soon as they set up a country, you got guys singing to tractors? They're singing about how they love the factory. That's where I couldn't buy communism. It's the intellectuals' utopia, not mine. I cannot picture myself singing to a tractor, I just can't. (Laughs.) Or singing to steel. (Singsongs.) Oh whoop-dee-doo, I'm at the bonderizer, oh how I love this heavy steel. No thanks. Never hoppen.

Oh yeah, I daydream. I fantasize about a sexy blonde in Miami who's got my union dues. (Laughs.) I think of the head of the union the way I think of the head of my company. Living it up. I think of February in Miami. Warm weather, a place to lay in. When I hear a college kid say, "I'm oppressed," I don't believe him. You know what I'd like to do for one year? Live like a college kid. Just for one year. I'd love to. Wow! (Whispers.) Wow! Sports car! Marijuana! (Laughs.) Wild, sexy broads. I'd love that, hell yes, I would.

Somebody has to do this work. If my kid ever goes to college, I just want him to have a little respect, to realize that his dad is one of those somebodies. This is why even on — (muses) yeah, I guess, sure — on the black thing . . . (Sighs heavily.) I can't really hate the colored fella that's working with me all day. The black intellectual I got no respect for. The white intellectual I got no use for. I got no use for the black militant who's gonna scream three hundred years of slavery to me while I'm busting my ass. You know what I mean? (Laughs.) I have one answer for that guy: Go see Rockefeller. See Harriman.[4] Don't bother me. We're in the same cotton field. So just don't bug me. (Laughs.)

After work I usually stop off at a tavern. Cold beer. Cold beer right away. When I was single, I used to go into hillbilly bars, get in a lot of brawls. Just to explode. I got a thing on my arm here (indicates scar). I got slapped with a bicycle chain. Oh, wow! (Softly.) Mmm. I'm getting older. (Laughs.) I don't explode as much. You might say I'm broken in. (Quickly.) No, I'll never be broken in. (Sighs.) When you get a little older, you exchange the words. When you're younger, you exchange the blows.

When I get home, I argue with my wife a little bit. Turn on TV, get mad at the news. (Laughs.) I don't even watch the news that much. I watch Jackie Gleason. I look for any alternative to the ten o'clock news.

[4]*Harriman:* financier, diplomat, and New York governor W. Averell Harriman (1891–1986). Like Rockefeller, a rich, powerful man.

I don't want to go to bed angry. Don't hit a man with anything heavy at five o'clock. He just can't be bothered. This is his time to relax. The heaviest thing he wants is what his wife has to tell him.

When I come home, know what I do for the first twenty minutes? Fake it. I put on a smile. I got a kid three years old. Sometimes she says, "Daddy, where've you been?" I say, "Work." I could have told her I'd been in Disneyland. What's work to a three-year-old kid? If I feel bad, I can't take it out on the kids. Kids are born innocent of everything but birth. You can't take it out on your wife either. This is why you go to a tavern. You want to release it there rather than do it at home. What does an actor do when he's got a bad movie? I got a bad movie every day.

I don't even need the alarm clock to get up in the morning. I can go out drinking all night, fall asleep at four, and bam! I'm up at six — no matter what I do. (Laughs.) It's a pseudo-death, more or less. Your whole system is paralyzed and you give all the appearance of death. It's an ingrown clock. It's a thing you just get used to. The hours differ. It depends. Sometimes my wife wants to do something crazy like play five hundred rummy or put a puzzle together. It could be midnight, could be ten o'clock, could be nine thirty.

What do you do weekends?

Drink beer, read a book. See that one? *Violence in America.* It's one 35 of them studies from Washington. One of them committees they're always appointing. A thing like that I read on a weekend. But during the weekdays, gee . . . I just thought about it. I don't do that much reading from Monday through Friday. Unless it's a horny book. I'll read it at work and go home and do my homework. (Laughs.) That's what the guys at the plant call it — homework. (Laughs.) Sometimes my wife works on Saturday and I drink beer at the tavern.

I went out drinking with one guy, oh, a long time ago. A college boy. He was working where I work now. Always preaching to me about how you need violence to change the system and all that garbage. We went into a hillbilly joint. Some guy there, I didn't know him from Adam, he said, "You think you're smart," I said, "What's your pleasure?" (Laughs.) He said, "My pleasure's to kick your ass." I told him I really can't be bothered. He said, "What're you, chicken?" I said, "No, I just don't want to be bothered." He came over and said something to me again. I said, "I don't beat women, drunks, or fools. Now leave me alone."

The guy called his brother over. This college boy that was with me, he came nudging my arm, "Mike, let's get out of here." I said, "What are you worried about?" (Laughs.) This isn't unusual. People will bug you. You fend it off as much as you can with your mouth and when you can't, you punch the guy out.

It was close to closing time and we stayed. We could have left, but when you go into a place to have a beer and a guy challenges you — if you expect to go in that place again, you don't leave. If you have to fight the guy, you fight.

I got just outside the door and one of these guys jumped on me and grabbed me around the neck. I grabbed his arm and flung him against the wall. I grabbed him here (indicates throat), and jiggled his head against the wall quite a few times. He kind of slid down a little bit. This guy who said he was his brother took a swing at me with a garrison belt.[5] He just missed and hit the wall. I'm looking around for my junior Stalin (laughs), who loves violence and everything. He's gone. Split. (Laughs.) Next day I see him at work. I couldn't get mad at him, he's a baby.

He saw a book in my back pocket one time and he was amazed. He   40
walked up to me and he said, "You read?" I said, "What do you mean, I read?" He said, "All these dummies read the sports pages around here. What are you doing with a book?" I got pissed off at the kid right away. I said, "What do you mean, all these dummies? Don't knock a man who's paying somebody else's way through college." He was a nineteen-year-old effete snob.

Yet you want your kid to be an effete snob?

Yes. I want my kid to look at me and say, "Dad, you're a nice guy, but you're a fuckin' dummy." Hell yes, I want my kid to tell me that he's not gonna be like me . . .

If I were hiring people to work, I'd try naturally to pay them a decent wage. I'd try to find out their first names, their last names, keep the company as small as possible, so I could personalize the whole thing. All I would ask a man is a handshake, see you in the morning. No applications, nothing. I wouldn't be interested in the guy's past. Nobody ever checks the pedigree on a mule, do they? But they do on a man. Can you picture walking up to a mule and saying, "I'd like to know who his granddaddy was?"

I'd like to run a combination bookstore and tavern. (Laughs.) I would like to have a place where college kids came and a steelworker could sit down and talk. Where a workingman could not be ashamed of Walt Whitman and where a college professor could not be ashamed that he painted his house over the weekend.

If a carpenter built a cabin for poets, I think the least the poets owe   45
the carpenter is just three or four one-liners on the wall. A little plaque: Though we labor with our minds, this place we can relax in was built by someone who can work with his hands. And his work is as noble as ours.

---

[5]*garrison belt:* the wide, heavy belt worn by soldiers, with metal clasps at each end.

I think the poet owes something to the guy who builds the cabin for him.

I don't think of Monday. You know what I'm thinking about on Sunday night? Next Sunday. If you work real hard, you think of a perpetual vacation. Not perpetual sleep . . . What do I think of on a Sunday night? Lord, I wish the fuck I could do something else for a living.

I don't know who the guy is who said there is nothing sweeter than an unfinished symphony. Like an unfinished painting and an unfinished poem. If he creates this thing one day — let's say, Michelangelo's Sistine Chapel. It took him a long time to do this, this beautiful work of art. But what if he had to create this Sistine Chapel a thousand times a year? Don't you think that would even dull Michelangelo's mind? Or if da Vinci had to draw his anatomical charts thirty, forty, fifty, sixty, eighty, ninety, a hundred times a day? Don't you think that would even bore da Vinci?

Way back, you spoke of the guys who built the pyramids, not the pharaohs, the unknowns. You put yourself in their category?

Yes. I want my signature on 'em, too. Sometimes, out of pure meanness, when I make something, I put a little dent in it. I like to do something to make it really unique.

Engaging the Text

1. What does the American Dream mean to LeFevre? What would LeFevre have to accomplish to consider himself a success? What keeps him from being happier or more successful?

2. How would you characterize LeFevre's attitudes toward work, and what kind of a worker do you think he is? How can hard physical labor be made more bearable? Should industry be mechanizing these jobs?

3. In what ways does LeFevre's interview confirm or challenge common stereotypes about blue-collar workers?

4. How well does LeFevre's image of "college kids" match your knowledge of students on your campus?

5. If you have ever done physically demanding or highly repetitive work, write a few paragraphs describing this work and its effect on you. Did such work play a role in your motivation to attend college?

Exploring Connections

6. Imagine a meeting between Mike LeFevre and Stephen Cruz (p. 36). How would LeFevre react to Cruz's complaints about his work experiences? To what

extent would they agree about the American Dream? About the nature of the American nightmare?

7. Use Suzanne Gordon's discussion of caring versus competition in the workplace (p. 46) to analyze LeFevre's job situation. To what extent do you think LeFevre would agree with such an analysis?

8. How would Gregory Mantsios, author of the preceding essay, assess the chances that LeFevre's son would become an "effete snob" rather than a factory worker?

Extending the Critical Context

9. LeFevre's dream of a combination bookstore and tavern (para. 44) suggests that American cities have a geography of class. Chart this geography for your city or community: what specific places (stores, businesses, entertainment centers, public lands and buildings, and so on) does each class frequent? How sharp are the boundaries of these areas? What places, if any, attract people from all classes?

Class Poem

Aurora Levins Morales

As this autobiographical poem states, Aurora Levins Morales (b. 1954) was the child of a Puerto Rican mother and a Jewish father. She moved to the United States when she was thirteen and now writes, performs, and teaches in the San Francisco Bay Area. "Class Poem" is from a collection called Getting Home Alive *(1986), which she coauthored with her mother, Rosario Morales. Her mother has written that the book "began in long, budget-breaking telephone calls stretched across the width of this country . . . the phone line strung between us like a 3000-mile umbilical cord from navel to navel, mine to hers, hers to mine, each of us mother and daughter by turns, feeding each other the substance of our dreams."*

This is my poem in celebration of my middle class privilege
This is my poem to say out loud
I'm glad I had food, and shelter, and shoes,
glad I had books and travel, glad there was air and light
and room for poetry.   5

This poem is for Tita, my best friend
who played in the dirt with me
and married at eighteen (which was late) and who was a scientist
but instead she bore six children   and four of them died
Who wanted to know the exact location of color   10
in the hibiscus petal, and patiently peeled away the thinnest,
most translucent layers to find it
and who works in a douche bag factory in Maricao.[1]

This poem is for the hunger of my mother
discovering books at thirteen in the New York Public Library   15
who taught me to read when I was five
and when we lived on a coffee farm
subscribed to a mail-order library,
who read Blackwell's catalogue
like a menu of delights   20
and when we moved from Puerto Rico to the States
we packed 100 boxes of books and 40 of everything else.

This poem is for my father's immigrant Jewish family.
For my great-grandfather Abe Sackman
who worked in Bridgeport[2] making nurse's uniforms   25
and came home only on weekends, for years, and who painted
on bits of old wooden crates, with housepaint,
birds and flowers for his great-grandchildren
and scenes of his old-country childhood.

This poem celebrates my father the scientist   30
who left the microscope within reach,
with whom I discovered the pomegranate eye of the fruitfly,
and yes, the exact location of color in a leaf.

This poem celebrates my brother the artist
who began to draw when he was two,   35
and so my parents bought him reams of paper
and when he used them up, bought him more,
and today it's a silkscreen workshop
and posters that travel around the world,
and I'm glad for him   and for Pop with his housepaints   40
and Tita staining the cement with crushed flowers
searching for color
and my mother shutting out the cries of her first-born
ten minutes at a time
to sketch the roofs and elevated tracks   45
in red-brown pastels.

[1]*Maricao:* a town in western Puerto Rico.
[2]*Bridgeport:* a seaport in Connecticut.

This is for Norma
who died of parasites in her stomach when she was four
I remember because her mother wailed her name
screaming and sobbing   50
one whole afternoon in the road in front of our school
and for Angélica
who caught on fire while stealing kerosene for her family
and died in pain
because the hospital she was finally taken to   55
knew she was poor
and would not give her the oxygen she needed to live
but wrapped her in greased sheets
so that she suffocated.

This is a poem against the wrapped sheets,   60
against guilt.

This is a poem to say:
my choosing to suffer gives nothing
to Tita and Norma and Angélica
and that not to use the tongue, the self-confidence, the training   65
my privilege bought me
is to die again for people who are already dead
and who wanted to live.

And in case anyone here confuses the paraphernalia
with the thing itself   70
let me add that I lived with rats and termites
no carpet   no stereo   no TV
that the bath came in buckets and was heated on the stove
that I read by kerosene lamp and had Sears mail-order clothes
and that that has nothing to do   75
with the fact of my privilege.

Understand, I know exactly what I got: protection and choice
and I am through apologizing.
I am going to strip apology from my voice
my posture   80
my apartment
my clothing
my dreams
because the voice that says the only true puertorican   85
is a dead or dying puertorican
is the enemy's voice —
the voice that says
"How can you let yourself shine when Tita, when millions
are daily suffocating in those greased sheets . . ."
I refuse to join them there.   90

I will not suffocate.
I will not hold back.
Yes, I had books and food and shelter and medicine
and I intend to survive.

Engaging the Text

1. Rewrite this poem into a chronological biographical sketch or outline. What seem to be the key events in the speaker's life? What layers of meaning in the poem does your rewrite fail to capture?

2. Do you think the speaker of this poem is successful? If so, to what do you attribute her success?

3. If this poem is a "celebration," why does it tell the unhappy stories of Tita, Norma, and Angélica? How do these tales add to or detract from the poem's meaning and impact?

4. Is the speaker turning her back on less fortunate Puerto Ricans? Explain.

Exploring Connections

5. List the people and characters you've read about in this chapter who face strong expectations based on ethnic or other stereotypes. What different strategies do they employ to deal with the stereotyping, and with what results?

6. "Class Poem" and Toni Cade Bambara's "The Lesson" (p. 64) both feature a microscope as a seemingly important object. Compare and contrast how the two authors use the image and connotations of a microscope.

Extending the Critical Context

7. Imitate this poem by writing one of your own about a person who helped you in some important way. Model your poem directly on Morales's or use the structure suggested here:

> This poem is for [name of person   who [acted in a certain way]
>   plus one or two details]   and who . . .
> who [did something beneficial]

Read your imitation aloud in class.

You're Short, Besides!

SUCHENG CHAN

In this essay, Sucheng Chan analyzes her experiences as a "physically handicapped Asian American woman," showing how cultural myths about being disabled kept people from seeing her capacity for real achievement. Chan currently teaches history at the University of California, Santa Barbara. She won the distinguished teaching award mentioned in her essay at the University of California, Berkeley, where she received her Ph.D. and taught for ten years. She has authored several books, including Asian Americans: An Interpretive History *(1991) and* This Bittersweet Soil: The Chinese in California Agriculture, 1860–1910 *(1986), which won multiple awards. This essay first appeared in* Making Waves: An Anthology of Writings by and About Asian American Women *(1989).*

When asked to write about being a physically handicapped Asian American woman, I considered it an insult. After all, my accomplishments are many, yet I was not asked to write about any of them. Is being handicapped the most salient feature about me? The fact that it might be in the eyes of others made me decide to write the essay as requested. I realized that the way I think about myself may differ considerably from the way others perceive me. And maybe that's what being physically handicapped is all about.

I was stricken simultaneously with pneumonia and polio at the age of four. Uncertain whether I had polio of the lungs, seven of the eight doctors who attended me — all practitioners of Western medicine — told my parents they should not feel optimistic about my survival. A Chinese fortune teller my mother consulted also gave a grim prognosis, but for an entirely different reason: I had been stricken because my name was offensive to the gods. My grandmother had named me "grandchild of wisdom," a name that the fortune teller said was too presumptuous for a girl. So he advised my parents to change my name to "chaste virgin." All these pessimistic predictions notwithstanding, I hung onto life, if only by a thread. For three years, my body was periodically pierced with electric shocks as the muscles of my legs atrophied. Before my illness, I had been an active, rambunctious, precocious, and very curious child. Being confined to bed was thus a mental agony as great as my physical pain. Living in war-torn China, I received little medical attention; physical therapy was unheard of. But I was determined to walk. So one day, when I was six or seven, I instructed my mother to set up two rows of chairs to face each other so that I could use them as I would parallel bars. I attempted to walk by holding my body up and moving it forward with my arms while dragging my legs along behind. Each time I fell, my mother gasped, but I badgered her until she let me try again. After four nonambulatory years, I finally walked once more by pressing my hands against my thighs so my kness wouldn't buckle.

My father had been away from home during most of those years because of the war. When he returned, I had to confront the guilt he felt about my condition. In many East Asian cultures, there is a strong folk belief that a person's physical state in this life is a reflection of how morally or sinfully he or she lived in previous lives. Furthermore, because of the tendency to view the family as a single unit, it is believed that the fate of one member can be caused by the behavior of another. Some of my father's relatives told him that my illness had doubtless been caused by the wild carousing he did in his youth. A well-meaning but somewhat simple man, my father believed them.

Throughout my childhood, he sometimes apologized to me for having to suffer retribution for his former bad behavior. This upset me; it was bad enough that I had to deal with the anguish of not being able to walk, but to have to assuage his guilt as well was a real burden! In other ways, my father was very good to me. He took me out often, carrying me on his shoulders or back, to give me fresh air and sunshine. He did this until I was too large and heavy for him to carry. And ever since I can remember, he has told me that I am pretty.

After getting over her anxieties about my constant falls, my mother   5 decided to send me to school. I had already learned to read some words of Chinese at the age of three by asking my parents to teach me the sounds and meaning of various characters in the daily newspaper. But between the ages of four and eight, I received no education since just staying alive was a full-time job. Much to her chagrin, my mother found no school in Shanghai, where we lived at the time, which would accept me as a student. Finally, as a last resort, she approached the American School which agreed to enroll me only if my family kept an *amah* (a servant who takes care of children) by my side at all times. The tuition at the school was twenty U.S. dollars per month — a huge sum of money during those years of runaway inflation in China — and payable only in U.S. dollars. My family afforded the high cost of tuition and the expense of employing a full-time *amah* for less than a year.

We left China as the Communist forces swept across the country in victory. We found an apartment in Hong Kong across the street from a school run by Seventh-Day Adventists.[1] By that time I could walk a

---

[1]*Seventh-Day Adventists:* a Protestant sect noted for their evangelical missionary work and their belief in the imminent and visible return of Christ, which would herald the coming of the Christian millennium.

little, so the principal was persuaded to accept me. An *amah* now had to take care of me only during recess when my classmates might easily knock me over as they ran about the playground.

After a year and a half in Hong Kong, we moved to Malaysia, where my father's family had lived for four generations. There I learned to swim in the lovely warm waters of the tropics and fell in love with the sea. On land I was a cripple; in the ocean I could move with the grace of a fish. I liked the freedom of being in the water so much that many years later, when I was a graduate student in Hawaii, I became greatly enamored with a man just because he called me a "Polynesian water nymph."

As my overall health improved, my mother became less anxious about all aspects of my life. She did everything possible to enable me to lead as normal a life as possible. I remember how once some of her colleagues in the high school where she taught criticized her for letting me wear short skirts. They felt my legs should not be exposed to public view. My mother's response was, "All girls her age wear short skirts, so why shouldn't she?"

The years in Malaysia were the happiest of my childhood, even though I was constantly fending off children who ran after me calling, *"Baikah! Baikah!"* ("Cripple! Cripple!" in the Hokkien dialect commonly spoken in Malaysia). The taunts of children mattered little because I was a star pupil. I won one award after another for general scholarship as well as for art and public speaking. Whenever the school had important visitors my teacher always called on me to recite in front of the class.

A significant event that marked me indelibly occurred when I was twelve. That year my school held a music recital and I was one of the students chosen to play the piano. I managed to get up the steps to the stage without any problem, but as I walked across the stage, I fell. Out of the audience, a voice said loudly and clearly, "Ayah! A *baikah* shouldn't be allowed to perform in public." I got up before anyone could get on stage to help me and, with tears streaming uncontrollably down my face, I rushed to the piano and began to play. Beethoven's "Für Elise" had never been played so fiendishly fast before or since, but I managed to finish the whole piece. That I managed to do so made me feel really strong. I never again feared ridicule.

In later years I was reminded of this experience from time to time. During my fourth year as an assistant professor at the University of California at Berkeley, I won a distinguished teaching award. Some weeks later I ran into a former professor who congratulated me enthusiastically. But I said to him, "You know what? I became a distinguished teacher by *limping* across the stage of Dwinelle 155!" (Dwinelle 155 is a large, cold, classroom that most colleagues of mine hate to teach in.) I was rude not because I lacked graciousness but because this man, who

10

had told me that my dissertation was the finest piece of work he had read in fifteen years, had nevertheless advised me to eschew a teaching career.

"Why?" I asked.

"Your leg . . ." he responded.

"What about my leg?" I said, puzzled.

"Well, how would you feel standing in front of a large lecture class?"   15

"If it makes any difference, I want you to know I've won a number of speech contests in my life, and I am not the least bit self-conscious about speaking in front of large audiences. . . . Look, why don't you write me a letter of recommendation to tell people how brilliant I am, and let *me* worry about my leg!"

This incident is worth recounting only because it illustrates a dilemma that handicapped persons face frequently: those who care about us sometimes get so protective that they unwittingly limit our growth. This former professor of mine had been one of my greatest supporters for two decades. Time after time, he had written glowing letters of recommendation on my behalf. He had spoken as he did because he thought he had my best interests at heart; he thought that if I got a desk job rather than one that required me to be a visible, public person, I would be spared the misery of being stared at.

Americans, for the most part, do not believe as Asians do that physically handicapped persons are morally flawed. But they are equally inept at interacting with those of us who are not able-bodied. Cultural differences in the perception and treatment of handicapped people are most clearly expressed by adults. Children, regardless of where they are, tend to be openly curious about people who do not look "normal." Adults in Asia have no hesitation in asking visibly handicapped people what is wrong with them, often expressing their sympathy with looks of pity, whereas adults in the United States try desperately to be polite by pretending not to notice.

One interesting response I often elicited from people in Asia but have never encountered in America is the attempt to link my physical condition to the state of my soul. Many a time while living and traveling in Asia people would ask me what religion I belonged to. I would tell them that my mother is a devout Buddhist, that my father was baptized a Catholic but has never practiced Catholicism, and that I am an agnostic. Upon hearing this, people would try strenuously to convert me to their religion so that whichever God they believed in could bless me. If I would only attend this church or that temple regularly, they urged, I would surely get cured. Catholics and Buddhists alike have pressed religious medallions into my palm, telling me if I would wear these, the relevant deity or saint would make me well. Once while visiting the tomb of Muhammad Ali Jinnah[2] in Karachi, Pakistan, an old Muslim, after finishing his evening prayers, spotted me, gestured toward my legs, raised his arms heavenward, and began a new round of prayers, apparently on my behalf.

In the United States adults who try to act "civilized" towards handicapped people by pretending they don't notice anything unusual sometimes end up ignoring handicapped people completely. In the first few months I lived in this country, I was struck by the fact that whenever children asked me what was the matter with my leg, their adult companions would hurriedly shush them up, furtively look at me, mumble apologies, and rush their children away. After a few months of such encounters, I decided it was my responsibility to educate these people. So I would say to the flustered adults, "It's okay, let the kid ask." Turning to the child, I would say, "When I was a little girl, no bigger than you are, I became sick with something called polio. The muscles of my leg shrank up and I couldn't walk very well. You're much luckier than I am because now you can get a vaccine to make sure you never get my disease. So don't cry when your mommy takes you to get a polio vaccine, okay?" Some adults and their little companions I talked to this way were glad to be rescued from embarrassment; others thought I was strange.

Americans have another way of covering up their uneasiness: they become jovially patronizing. Sometimes when people spot my crutch, they ask if I've had a skiing accident. When I answer that unfortunately it is something less glamorous than that, they say, "I bet you *could* ski if you put your mind to it!" Alternately, at parties where people dance, men who ask me to dance with them get almost belligerent when I decline their invitation. They say, "Of course you can dance if you *want* to!" Some have given me pep talks about how if I would only develop the right mental attitude, I would have more fun in life.

Different cultural attitudes toward handicapped persons came out clearly during my wedding. My father-in-law, as solid a representative of middle America as could be found, had no qualms about objecting to the marriage on racial grounds, but he could bring himself to comment on my handicap only indirectly. He wondered why his son, who had dated numerous high school and college beauty queens, couldn't marry one of them instead of me. My mother-in-law, a devout Christian, did not share her husband's prejudices, but she worried aloud about whether I could have children. Some Chinese friends of my parents, on the other hand, said that I was lucky to have found such a noble man,

[2]*Muhammad Ali Jinnah:* leading Indian politician (1876–1948) who opposed Hindu ideology and the methods of Gandhi for separate Muslim statehood; served as Pakistan's first governor general.

one who would marry me despite my handicap. I, for my part, appeared in church in a white lace wedding dress I had designed and made myself — a miniskirt!

How Asian Americans treat me with respect to my handicap tells me a great deal about their degree of acculturation. Recent immigrants behave just like Asians in Asia; those who have been here longer or who grew up in the United States behave more like their white counterparts. I have not encountered any distinctly Asian American pattern of response. What makes the experience of Asian American handicapped people unique is the duality of responses we elicit.

Regardless of racial or cultural background, most handicapped people have to learn to find a balance between the desire to attain physical independence and the need to take care of ourselves by not overtaxing our bodies. In my case, I've had to learn to accept the fact that leading an active life has its price. Between the ages of eight and eighteen, I walked without using crutches or braces but the effort caused my right leg to become badly misaligned. Soon after I came to the United States, I had a series of operations to straighten out the bones of my right leg; afterwards though my leg looked straighter and presumably better, I could no longer walk on my own. Initially my doctors fitted me with a brace, but I found wearing one cumbersome and soon gave it up. I could move around much more easily — and more important, faster — by using one crutch. One orthopedist after another warned me that using a single crutch was a bad practice. They were right. Over the years my spine developed a double-S curve and for the last twenty years I have suffered from severe, chronic back pains, which neither conventional physical therapy nor a lighter work load can eliminate.

The only thing that helps my backaches is a good massage, but the soothing effect lasts no more than a day or two. Massages are expensive, especially when one needs them three times a week. So I found a job that pays better, but at which I have to work longer hours, consequently increasing the physical strain on my body — a sort of vicious circle. When I was in my thirties, my doctors told me that if I kept leading the strenuous life I did, I would be in a wheelchair by the time I was forty. They were right on target: I bought myself a wheelchair when I was forty-one. But being the incorrigible character that I am, I use it only when I am *not* in a hurry!

It is a good thing, however, that I am too busy to think much about my handicap or my backaches because pain can physically debilitate as well as cause depression. And there are days when my spirits get rather low. What has helped me is realizing that being handicapped is akin to growing old at an accelerated rate. The contradiction I experience is that often my mind races along as though I'm only twenty while my body feels about sixty. But fifteen or twenty years hence, unlike my

25

peers who will have to cope with aging for the first time, I shall be full of cheer because I will have already fought, and I hope won, that battle long ago.

Beyond learning how to be physically independent and, for some of us, living with chronic pain or other kinds of discomfort, the most difficult thing a handicapped person has to deal with, especially during puberty and early adulthood, is relating to potential sexual partners. Because American culture places so much emphasis on physical attractiveness, a person with a shriveled limb, or a tilt to the head, or the inability to speak clearly, experiences great uncertainty — indeed trauma — when interacting with someone to whom he or she is attracted. My problem was that I was not only physically handicapped, small, and short, but worse, I also wore glasses and was smarter than all the boys I knew! Alas, an insurmountable combination. Yet somehow I have managed to have intimate relationships, all of them with extraordinary men. Not surprisingly, there have also been countless men who broke my heart — men who enjoyed my company "as a friend," but who never found the courage to date or make love with me, although I am sure my experience in this regard is no different from that of many able-bodied persons.

The day came when my backaches got in the way of having an active sex life. Surprisingly that development was liberating because I stopped worrying about being attractive to men. No matter how headstrong I had been, I, like most women of my generation, had had the desire to be alluring to men ingrained into me. And that longing had always worked like a brake on my behavior. When what men think of me ceased to be compelling, I gained greater freedom to be myself.

I've often wondered if I would have been a different person had I not been physically handicapped. I really don't know, though there is no question that being handicapped has marked me. But at the same time I usually do not *feel* handicapped — and consequently, I do not *act* handicapped. People are therefore less likely to treat me as a handicapped person. There is no doubt, however, that the lives of my parents, sister, husband, other family members, and some close friends have been affected by my physical condition. They have had to learn not to hide me away at home, not to feel embarrassed by how I look or react to people who say silly things to me, and not to resent me for the extra demands my condition makes on them. Perhaps the hardest thing for those who live with handicapped people is to know when and how to offer help. There are no guidelines applicable to all situations. My advice is, when in doubt, ask, but ask in a way that does not smack of pity or embarrassment. Most important, please don't talk to us as though we are children.

So, has being physically handicapped been a handicap? It all depends on one's attitude. Some years ago, I told a friend that I had once said to an affirmative action compliance officer (somewhat sardonically since I do not believe in the head count approach to affirmative action) that the institution which employs me is triply lucky because it can count me as nonwhite, female, and handicapped. He responded, "Why don't you tell them to count you four times? . . . Remember, you're short, besides!"

Engaging the Text

1. How many ways has Chan been a success? How do you think she would define success? What role did her handicap play in her achievements?

2. Chan says many adults in the United States pretend not to notice visibly handicapped people. Is this a fair assessment of your own behavior? Have family members or others ever instructed you in "how to act" around physically challenged people? Has Chan's narrative changed in any way your attitude about people who face physical challenges?

Exploring Connections

3. Compare and contrast the stereotypes Chan faces with those faced by other writers or characters in earlier selections by Studs Terkel, Curtis Chang, Toni Cade Bambara, and Aurora Levins Morales.

4. Curtis Chang (p. 54) argues that the myth of the model minority has masked the difficulties faced by Asian Americans. Do you think there is a myth of the model handicapped person in American culture? If so, give a nutshell summary of this myth.

Extending the Critical Context

5. Do some research in *TV Guide* or your local video rental store to find one or more TV programs or films that include a physically challenged character. How are such characters portrayed? For example, is the "disability" invariably the focal point for that character, or is it just one part of a complex person?

6. Chan mentions that Asians generally have a stronger belief in connections between body, mind, and soul than Americans do. In small groups, discuss your own beliefs about one part of this issue: the power of the mind to heal the body. Report to the class the range of beliefs within your group. Also try to determine whether these beliefs are influenced primarily by parents, by religion, by education, by personal experience, or by other factors.

2

Nature and Technology
The Myth of Progress

As it turned toward the Americas in the sixteenth and seventeenth centuries, Europe was shaking off a thousand years of feudalism. The old order, based on church authority and the power of kings, was giving way; in this climate of change, Europe saw America as a land where history could begin again. This "new world" offered itself as a fitting home for the innovative, freedom-loving, and ambitious. As the eminent American historian Frederick Jackson Turner wrote in 1893, "Since the days when the fleet of Columbus sailed into the waters of the New World, America has been another name for opportunity. . . . a gate of escape from the bondage of the past." America grew out of this astonishing optimism, this absolute belief in a better tomorrow.

But the dream of unlimited opportunity — the American dream of success — was possible only because of the vastness and richness of the land. Benjamin Franklin noted this around 1782 when he advised prospective European immigrants that America offered new opportunities to any "who, in their own Countries, where all the Lands are fully occupied, . . . could never have emerged from the poor Condition wherein they were born." Americans could dream of success because they had the unexploited natural wealth of a whole continent before them; they could dream of freedom because they had the space necessary to make that freedom possible.

Thus, in the United States, the myth of progress has been linked to the western frontier. Many saw the westward movement (including the appropriation of American Indian lands and the conquest of Mexican territories) as the fulfillment of "Manifest Destiny." Western expansion was seen as part of a divine plan whose central aim was to "civilize" the land by making it fruitful and productive — supplying food for growing cities, coal and oil for burgeoning factories, iron ore for railroads and bridges. The 1845 *Emigrants' Guide to Oregon and California* epitomizes this faith in progress and the subjugation of nature:

> . . . the time is not distant when those wild forests, trackless plains, untrodden valleys, and the unbounded ocean, will present one grand scene, of continuous improvements, universal enterprise, and unparalleled commerce: when those vast forests, shall have disappeared, before the hardy pioneer; those extensive plains, shall abound with innumerable herds, of domestic animals; those fertile valleys, shall groan under the immense weight of their abundant products: when those numerous rivers, shall team with countless steam-boats, steamships, ships, barques and brigs; when the entire country, will be everywhere intersected, with turnpike roads, rail-roads and canals; and when, all the vastly numerous, and rich resources, of that now, almost unknown region, will be fully and advantageously developed. . . . And in fine, we are also led to contemplate the time, as fast approaching, when the supreme darkness of ignorance, superstition, and despotism, which now, so entirely pervade many portions of those remote regions, will have fled forever, before the march of civilization, and the blazing light, of civil and religious liberty; when genuine *republicanism*, and unsophisticated *democracy*, shall be reared up, and tower aloft, even upon the now wild shores, of the great Pacific; where they shall forever stand forth, as enduring monuments, to the increasing wisdom of *man*, and the infinite kindness and protection, of an all-wise, and overruling *Providence*."

The myth of progress, divinely sanctioned, gave the United States the justification it needed to seize the land and its resources. It did so by implying a sharp difference between the natural world and the world of human endeavor. Nature, according to the myth, is "other," and inferior to humans; land, rivers, minerals, plants, and animals are simply material made available for our use. And because our transformation of nature leads to "civilization," that use is ultimately justified.

Alongside the myth of progress, though, we find another myth — one that portrays nature as a spiritual resource and refuge from civilization. In his essay, "Nature" (1836), Ralph Waldo Emerson rhapsodized, "In the woods, we return to reason and faith. Standing on the bare ground, — my head bathed by the blithe air, and uplifted into infinite space . . . I am part or particle of God." Henry David Thoreau argued in *Walden* (1854) "our village life would stagnate if it were not for the unexplored forests and meadows which surround it. We need the tonic of wildness."

This countermyth inspired early conservationists like John Muir, who was instrumental in establishing the national park system, and it now drives much of the environmental movement. But the myth of progress has proved much more powerful: some of our most cherished parklands, including Yellowstone and Yosemite, were earmarked for preservation only after Congress determined that they had no commercial value. Even today, with widespread public concern about the environment, development commonly takes precedence over conservation; as recently as the late 1980s, Thoreau's wooded retreat, Walden Pond, was threatened by a condominium project.

This chapter invites you to reflect on the American definition of progress and the ways this cultural myth has molded our relationship to nature. It begins with two views of the power and politics of cultural storytelling — in particular the way the history of progress has been told in the United States. In "Empire of Innocence," Patricia Nelson Limerick argues that the myth of progress enabled white Americans to reinvent western history by casting themselves, rather than the Indians they dispossessed or the land they exploited, as innocent victims. Haunani-Kay Trask's essay "From a Native Daughter" compares Native Hawaiian and mainland American versions of Hawaiian history — and shows that widely different attitudes toward the land inform the two accounts. "Talking to the Owls and Butterflies," by Sioux medicine man John (Fire) Lame Deer and Richard Erdoes, forcefully challenges conventional assumptions about what constitutes a civilized life and offers "the Indian way" as an antidote to our technology-driven society. Leslie Marmon Silko's "Storyteller" envisions an apocalyptic end to western-style progress in the Alaskan tundra.

The next three selections examine the extent and significance of our technological dependence. In "The Spell of Technology," Chellis Glendinning examines our collective fascination with technical development and the idea of linear progress. "The Returning," a poem by American Indian writer Gail Tremblay, contemplates both the sense of disconnection from the earth and the "momentary miracles" experienced on an ordinary airline flight. Kathleen Stocking's "Living on the Land" introduces a family of "new-age" pioneers who have decided to jettison the modern American life-style for a more direct, but decidedly more difficult, relation to the land. A final pair of readings suggest that our treatment of nature mirrors our treatment of one another. In "being property once myself," poet Lucille Clifton succinctly connects the ideas of racial, sexual, and environmental exploitation. The chapter closes with Susan Griffin's "Split Culture"; this difficult but compelling essay argues that when we deny our unity with nature, we divide ourselves and in so doing lay the psychological groundwork for a series of destructive oppositions, including those that pit men against women and race against race.

Sources

Frank Bergon and Zeese Papanikolas, eds., *Looking Far West: The Search for the American West in History, Myth, and Literature.* New York: Meridian/New American Library, 1978.

Ralph Waldo Emerson, *Selected Writings.* New York: Signet/New American Library, 1965.

Leonard Pitt, *We Americans*, vol. 2, 3rd ed. Dubuque: Kendall/Hunt, 1987.

Laurence Shames, *The Hunger for More: Searching for Values in an Age of Greed.* New York: Times Books, 1989.

Henry David Thoreau, *Walden and "Civil Disobedience."* New York: Signet/New American Library, 1960.

Frederick Jackson Turner, "The Significance of the Frontier in American History." In *Annual Report for 1893*, American Historical Association, pp. 199–227.

Before Reading . . .

Working in small groups or as a class, brainstorm a list of words and ideas that you associate with the notion of progress. Then evaluate your list: does it primarily contain negative or positive terms? You might also want to collect images from magazines, newspapers, or personal photos to make collages on the themes of nature and technology. After you display and discuss them, freewrite on the meaning of technology in your life.

As you work through the chapter, refer back to these materials and compare your attitudes with those expressed by the writers you encounter here.

Empire of Innocence

Patricia Nelson Limerick

This excerpt from The Legacy of Conquest: The Unbroken Past of the American West *(1987) establishes a broad thesis about the American west and the "innocence" of its settlers. Limerick (b. 1951) is particularly skilled at seeing events from differing perspectives, and she sees in western history a complex moral landscape, peopled not by stereotypical cowboys and Indians but by extremely diverse groups, none of them in complete control of the events unfolding on the frontier. Limerick's rewriting of western history made her the subject of a* People *magazine interview (April 22, 1991); a more traditional accomplishment was her publication in 1989 of* Desert Passages: Encounters with the American Deserts. *Limerick teaches history at the University of Colorado in Boulder.*

To analyze how white Americans thought about the West, it helps to think anthropologically. One lesson of anthropology is the extraordinary power of cultural persistence; with American Indians, for instance, beliefs and values will persist even when the supporting economic and political structures have vanished. What holds for Indians holds as well for white Americans; the values they attached to westward expansion persist, in cheerful defiance of contrary evidence.

Among those persistent values, few have more power than the idea of innocence. The dominant motive for moving West was improvement and opportunity, not injury to others. Few white Americans went West intending to ruin the natives and despoil the continent. Even when they were trespassers, westering Americans were hardly, in their own eyes, criminals; rather, they were pioneers. The ends abundantly justified the means; personal interest in the acquisition of property coincided with national interest in the acquisition of territory, and those interests overlapped in turn with the mission to extend the domain of Christian civilization. Innocence of intention placed the course of events in a bright and positive light; only over time would the shadows compete for our attention. . . .

. . . Whether the target resource was gold, farmland, or Indian souls, white Americans went West convinced that their purposes were as commonplace as they were innocent. The pursuit of improved fortunes, the acquisition of property, even the desire for adventure seemed so self-evident that they needed neither explanation nor justification.

If the motives were innocent, episodes of frustration and defeat seemed inexplicable, undeserved, and arbitrary. Squatters defied the boundaries of Indian territory and then were aggrieved to find themselves harassed and attacked by Indians. Similarly, prospectors and miners went where the minerals were, regardless of Indian territorial claims, only to be outraged by threats to their lives and supply lines. Preemptors[1] who traveled ahead of government surveys later complained of insecure land titles. After the Civil War, farmers expanded

---

[1]*preemptors:* people who seek to establish a right to land by being the first to occupy it.

onto the Great Plains, past the line of semiaridity, and then felt betrayed when the rains proved inadequate.

Western emigrants understood not just that they were taking risks but also that risks led to rewards. When nature or natives interrupted the progression from risk to reward, the Westerner felt aggrieved. Most telling were the incidents in which a rush of individuals — each pursuing a claim to a limited resource — produced their own collective frustration. In resource rushes, people hoping for exclusive opportunity often arrived to find a crowd already in place, blanketing the region with prior claims, constricting individual opportunity, and producing all the problems of food supply, housing, sanitation, and social order that one would expect in a growing city, but not in a wilderness.

If one pursues a valuable item and finds a crowd already assembled, one's complicity in the situation is obvious. The crowd has, after all, resulted from a number of individual choices very much like one's own. But frustration cuts off reflection on this irony; in resource rushes in which the sum of the participants' activities created the dilemma, each individual could still feel himself the innocent victim of constricting opportunity.

Contrary to all of the West's associations with self-reliance and individual responsibility, misfortune has usually caused white Westerners to cast themselves in the role of the innocent victim. One large group was composed of those who felt injured at the hands of nature. They had trusted nature, and when nature behaved according to its own rules and not theirs, they felt betrayed. The basic plot played itself out with a thousand variations.

Miners resented the wasted effort of excavating sites that had looked promising and proved barren. Cattlemen overgrazed the grasslands and then resented nature's failure to rebound. Farmers on the Southern Plains used mechanized agriculture to break up the land and weaken the ground cover, then unhappily watched the crop of dust they harvested. City dwellers accumulated automobiles, gas stations, and freeways, and then cursed the inversion patterns and enclosing mountains that kept the automobile effluvia before their eyes and noses. Homeowners purchased houses on steep slopes and in precarious canyons, then felt betrayed when the earth's surface continued to do what it has done for millennia: move around from time to time. And, in one of the most widespread and serious versions, people moved to arid and semi-arid regions, secure in the faith that water would somehow be made available, then found the prospect of water scarcity both surprising and unfair.

In many ways, the most telling case studies concern plants. When, in the 1850s, white farmers arrived in Island County, Washington, they had a clear sense of their intentions: "to get the land subdued and the wilde nature out of it," as one of them put it. They would uproot the useless native plants and replace them with valuable crops, transforming wilderness to garden. On one count, nature did not cooperate — certain new plants, including corn, tomatoes, and wheat, could not adapt to the local climate and soil. On another count, nature proved all too cooperative. Among the plants introduced by white farmers, weeds frequently did better than crops. "Weeds," Richard White notes, "are an inevitable result of any human attempt to restrict large areas of land to a single plant." Laboring to introduce valued plants, the farmer came up against "his almost total inability to prevent the entry of unwanted invaders." Mixed with crop seeds, exotic plants like the Canadian thistle prospered in the plowed fields prepared for them, and then moved into the pastures cleared by overgrazing. The thistle was of no interest to sheep: "once it had replaced domesticated grasses the land became incapable of supporting livestock."[2]

A similar development took place between the Rockies and the Sierras and Cascades. There, as well, "species foreign to the region, brought accidentally by the settlers, came to occupy these sites to the virtual exclusion of the native colonizers." With the introduction of wheat, "entry via adulterated seed lots of the weeds of wheat . . . was inevitable." One particular species — cheatgrass — took over vast territories, displacing the native bunch grasses and plaguing farmers in their wheatfields. There is no more effective way to feel authentically victimized than to plant a crop and then to see it besieged by weeds. Farmers thus had their own, complicated position as injured innocents, plagued by a pattern in nature that their own actions had created.[3]

Yet another category of injured innocents were those who had believed and acted upon the promises of promoters and boomers. Prospective miners were particularly susceptible to reading reports of the gold strikes, leaping into action, and then cursing the distortions and exaggerations that had misled them into risking so much for so little reward. The pattern was common because resource rushes created a mood of such fevered optimism that trust came easily; people wanted so much to believe that their normal skepticism dropped away.

The authenticity of the sense of victimization was unquestionable. Still, there was never any indication that repeated episodes of victimization would reduce the pool of volunteers. Bedrock factors kept promoters and boomers supplied with believers: there *were* resources in the West, and the reports might be true; furthermore, the physical fact of Western distances meant, first, that decision making would have to rely on a chain of information stretched thin by the expanse of the continent

[2]Richard White, *Land Use, Environment, and Social Change: The Shaping of Island County, Washington* (Seattle: Univ. of Washington Press, 1980), 46, 68. [Author's note]
[3]Richard N. Mack, "Invaders at Home on the Range," *Natural History*, Feb. 1984, 43. [Author's note]

and, second, that the truth of the reports and promises could not be tested without a substantial investment of time and money simply in getting to the site. One might well consume one's nest egg merely in reaching the place of expected reward.

Blaming nature or blaming human beings, those looking for a scapegoat had a third, increasingly popular target: the federal government. Since it was the government's responsibility to control the Indians and, in a number of ways increasing into the twentieth century, to control nature, Westerners found it easy to shift the direction of their resentment. Attacked by Indians or threatened by nature, aggrieved Westerners took to pointing accusingly at the federal government. In effect, Westerners centralized their resentments much more efficiently than the federal government centralized its powers.

Oregon's situation was a classic example of this transition. The earliest settlers were rewarded with Congress's Oregon Donation Act of 1850. Settlers arriving by a certain year were entitled to a generous land grant. This act had the considerable disadvantage of encouraging white settlement without benefit of treaties and land cessions from Oregon Indians. The Donation Act thus invited American settlers to spread into territory that had not been cleared for their occupation. It was an offer that clearly infringed on the rights of the Indians and that caused the government to stretch its powers thin. After the California gold rush, when prospectors spread north into the Oregon interior, a multifront Indian war began. Surely, the white miners and settlers said, it is now the obligation of the federal government to protect us and our property.[4]

At this point, a quirk of historical casting brought an unusual man named General John Wool into the picture. As the head of the Army's Pacific Division, General Wool was charged with cleaning up the mess that Oregon development had created. He was to control the Indians, protect the settlers, and end the wars. Here Wool's unusual character emerged: assessing this situation, he decided — and said bluntly — that the wars were the results of settler intrusion; he went so far as to propose a moratorium on further settlement in the Oregon interior, a proposal that outraged the sensitive settlers. Wool's personality did not make this difference of opinion more amicable. He was, in fact, something of a prig;[5] in pictures, the symmetrical and carefully waxed curls at his temples suggest that he and the Oregon pioneers might have been at odds without the troubles of Indian policy.[6]

15

---

[4]Dorothy O. Johansen and C. M. Gates, *Empire of the Columbia: A History of the Pacific Northwest*, 2d ed. (New York: Harper & Row, 1967), 250, 252. [Author's note]

[5]*prig:* one who adheres unthinkingly or smugly to rigid moral standards.

[6]Robert Utley, *Frontiersmen in Blue: The United States Army and the Indian, 1848–1865* (1967; Lincoln: Univ. of Nebraska Press, 1981), 178–200. [Author's note]

Denounced by both the Oregon and the Washington legislatures, Wool's blunt approach did not result in a new direction in Indian affairs. The wars were prosecuted to their conclusions; the Indians, compelled to yield territory. But the Oregon settlers in 1857 knew what they thought of Wool. He was a supposed agent of the federal government, an agent turned inexplicably into a friend of the Indians and an enemy of the Americans.

It was not the first or the last time that white Americans would suspect the federal government and Indians of being in an unholy alliance. To the degree that the federal government fulfilled its treaty and statutory obligations to protect the Indians and their land, it would then appear to be not only soft on Indians but even in active opposition to its own citizens.

One other elemental pattern of their thought allowed Westerners to slide smoothly from blaming Indians to blaming the federal government. The idea of captivity organized much of Western sentiment. Actual white men, women, and children were at times taken captive by Indians, and narratives of those captivities were, from colonial times on, a popular form of literature. It was an easy transition of thought to move from the idea of humans held in an unjust and resented captivity to the idea of land and natural resources held in Indian captivity — in fact, a kind of monopoly in which very few Indians kept immense resources to themselves, refusing to let the large numbers of willing and eager white Americans make what they could of those resources. Land and natural resources, to the Anglo-American mind, were meant for development; when the Indians held control, the excluded whites took up the familiar role of injured innocents. The West, in the most common figure of speech, had to be "opened" — a metaphor based on the assumption that the virgin West was "closed," locked up, held captive by Indians.

As the federal government took over Indian territory, either as an addition to the public domain or as reservations under the government's guardianship, white Westerners kept the same sense of themselves as frustrated innocents, shut out by monopoly, but they shifted the blame. Released from Indian captivity, many Western resources, it seemed to white Americans, had merely moved into a federal captivity.

In 1979, the Nevada state legislature, without any constitutional authority, passed a law seizing from the federal government 49 million acres from the public domain within the state. This empty but symbolic act was the first scene in the media event known as the Sagebrush Rebellion, in which Western businessmen lamented their victimization at the hands of the federal government and pleaded for the release of the public domain from its federal captivity. Ceded to the states, the land that once belonged to all the people of the United States would at last be

20

at the disposal of those whom the Sagebrush Rebels considered to be the *right* people — namely, themselves.[7]

Like many rebellions, this one foundered with success: the election of Ronald Reagan in 1980 and the appointment of James Watt as secretary of the interior meant that the much-hated federal government was now in the hands of two Sagebrush Rebels. It was not at all clear what the proper rebel response to the situation should be. In any case, the rebel claim to victimization had lost whatever validity it had ever had.

Reciting the catalog of their injuries, sufferings, and deprivations at the hands of federal officials, the rebels at least convinced Western historians of the relevance of their expertise. It was a most familiar song; the Western historian could recognize every note. Decades of expansion left this motif of victimization entrenched in Western thinking. It was second nature to see misfortune as the doings of an outside force, preying on innocence and vulnerability, refusing to play by the rules of fairness. By assigning responsibility elsewhere, one eliminated the need to consider one's own participation in courting misfortune. There was something odd and amusing about late-twentieth-century businessmen adopting for themselves the role . . . of the martyred innocents, trying to go about their business in the face of cruel and arbitrary opposition.

Even if the Sagebrush Rebels had to back off for a time, that did not mean idleness for the innocent's role. In 1982, Governor Richard Lamm of Colorado and his coauthor, Michael McCarthy, published a book defending the West — "a vulnerable land" — from the assault of development. "A new Manifest Destiny," they said, "has overtaken America. The economic imperative has forever changed the spiritual refuge that was the West." The notion of a time in Western history when "the economic imperative" had not been a dominant factor was a quaint and wishful thought, but more important, Lamm and McCarthy thought, some Westerners now "refused" to submit to this change. "They — we — are the new Indians," Lamm and McCarthy concluded. "And they — we — will not be herded to the new reservations."[8]

In this breakthrough in the strategy of injured innocence, Lamm and McCarthy chose the most historically qualified innocent victims — the Indians facing invasion, fighting to defend their homelands — and appropriated their identity for the majority whites who had moved to the West for the good life, for open space and freedom of movement,

---

[7]"The Angry West vs. the Rest," *Newsweek*, Sept. 17, 1979, 31–40; "West Senses Victory in Sagebrush Rebellion," *U.S. News and World Report*, Dec. 1, 1980, 29, 30. [Author's note]

[8]Richard D. Lamm and Michael McCarthy, *The Angry West: A Vulnerable Land and Its Future* (Boston: Houghton Mifflin, 1982), 4. [Author's note]

and who were beginning to find their desires frustrated. Reborn as the "new Indians," Lamm's constituency had traveled an extraordinary, circular route. Yesterday's villains were now to be taken as today's victims; they were now the invaded, no longer the invaders. In keeping with this change, the *old* Indians received little attention in the book; as capacious as the category "injured innocent" had proven itself to be, the line had to be drawn somewhere.

Occasionally, continuities in American history almost bowl one over. What does Colorado's utterly twentieth-century governor have in common with the East Coast's colonial elite in the eighteenth century? "Having practically destroyed the aboriginal population and enslaved the Africans," one colonial historian has said, "the white inhabitants of English America began to conceive of themselves as the victims, not the agents, of Old World colonialism." "The victims, not the agents" — the changes and differences are enormous, but for a moment, if one looks from Revolutionary leaders, who held black slaves as well as the conviction that they were themselves enslaved by Great Britain, to Governor Richard Lamm, proclaiming himself and his people to be the new Indians, American history appears to be composed of one, continuous fabric, a fabric in which the figure of the innocent victim is the dominant motif.[9]

25

[9]Carole Shammas, "English-Born and Creole Elites in Turn-of-the Century Virginia," in Thad Tate and David Ammerman, eds., *The Chesapeake in the Seventeenth Century: Essays on Anglo-American Society and Politics* (New York: W. W. Norton, 1979), 274. [Author's note]

Engaging the Text

1. According to Limerick, what was the settlers' dominant attitude toward the land and its resources? Find three or four quotations that illustrate this attitude.

2. What is a "resource rush"? Can you think of any modern examples, involving either land or some other desirable resource? (Hint: think globally as well as locally.)

3. Using specific examples, explain how settlers could come to consider themselves "injured innocents" when their hopes for success in the West were shattered or compromised. What role does the notion of captivity play in this myth of innocence?

4. Limerick says in her concluding sentence that American history is "composed of one, continuous fabric, a fabric in which the figure of the innocent victim is the dominant motif." Do you agree that proclaiming one's innocence and blaming one's troubles on outside forces is a particularly American trait?

Exploring Connections

5. Limerick writes in paragraph 3 that "the pursuit of improved fortunes, the acquisition of property, even the desire for adventure seemed so self-evident that they needed neither explanation nor justification." Use information from Christopher Lasch's "Changing Modes of Making It" (p. 27) to help explain why westward expansion in the nineteenth century seemed obviously inevitable and proper.

Extending the Critical Context

6. All things considered, would it have been better to enforce General Wool's proposed moratorium on development in Oregon throughout the past century and a half?

7. Reread Limerick's discussion of the ways white settlers cast themselves as innocent victims of nature (paras. 7–10). Can you think of examples in your state in which people have "set themselves up" to become victims of earthquakes, floods, hurricanes, droughts, or other forces of nature? Under what circumstances do you think government should help people who have suffered financially at the hands of an unpredictable natural world?

8. Analyze a high school history text in terms of its treatment of conflicts between Native Americans and whites. Does the theme of "injured innocents" show up directly or indirectly? How might you account for any differences you find in these sources?

9. The award-winning film *Dances with Wolves* has been proclaimed as a turning point in the representation of the conflict between American Indians and settlers. However, it could be argued that the film has had such broad appeal because it promises mainstream audiences that they, like the hero, can recapture lost innocence. Watch the film, taking note of its portrayal of American Indians and settlers, and discuss its impact on the audience.

From a Native Daughter

Haunani-Kay Trask

Speaking of nineteenth-century Americans and birth control, a scholar recently said, "They didn't know much, and what they did know was wrong." The same could be said of the historians of Hawaii. This selection comes from a scholar who is literally rewriting the history of Hawaii. Trask explains how she learned radically different versions of history from her family and from missionary schools; having trusted her formal education for years, she eventually recognized that the colonists had distorted Hawaiian history in order to disrupt the islands' culture and appropriate their resources. This essay is an impassioned yet carefully reasoned assault on conventional interpretations of Hawaii's past and peoples. Trask, a professor of Hawaiian Studies and the director of the Center for Hawaiian Studies at the University of Hawai'i at Mānoa, has published Eros and Power: The Promise of Feminist Theory *(1986) and continues to pursue academic work on the political and cultural struggles of native islanders.*

> *E noi'i wale mai no ka haole, a,*
> *'a'ole e pau na hana a Hawai'i 'imi loa*
> Let the *haole* freely research us in detail
> But the doings of deep delving *Hawai'i*
> will not be exhausted.
> — KEPELINO, 19th-century Hawaiian historian

Aloha kākou. Let us greet each other in friendship and love. My given name is Haunaniokawēkiu o Haleakalā, native of *Hawai'i Nei.* My father's family is from the *'āina* (land) of Kaua'i, my mother's family from the *'āina* of Maui. I reside today among my native people in the community of *Waimānalo.*

I have lived all my life under the power of America. My native country, Hawai'i, is owned by the United States. I attended missionary schools, both Catholic and Protestant, in my youth, and I was sent away to the American mainland to receive a "higher" education at the University of Wisconsin. Now I teach the history and culture of my people at the University of Hawai'i.

When I was young the story of my people was told twice: once by my parents, then again by my school teachers. From my *'ohana* (family), I learned about the life of the old ones: how they fished and planted by the moon; shared all the fruits of their labors, especially their children; danced in great numbers for long hours; and honored the unity of their world in intricate genealogical chants. My mother said Hawaiians had sailed over thousands of miles to make their home in these sacred islands. And they had flourished, until the coming of the *haole* (whites).

At school, I learned that the "pagan Hawaiians" did not read or write, were lustful cannibals, traded in slaves, and could not sing. Captain Cook had "discovered" Hawai'i and the ungrateful Hawaiians had killed him. In revenge, the Christian god had cursed the Hawaiians with disease and death.

I learned the first of these stories from speaking with my mother and father. I learned the second from books. By the time I left for college, the books had won out over my parents, especially since I spent four long years in a missionary boarding school for Hawaiian children.

When I went away I understood the world as a place and a feeling divided in two: one *haole* (white), and the other *kānaka* (native). When I returned ten years later with a Ph.D., the division was sharper, the lack of connection more painful. There was the world that we lived in — my ancestors, my family, and my people — and then there was the world historians described. This world, they had written, was the truth. A primitive group, Hawaiians had been ruled by bloodthirsty priests and despotic kings who owned all the land and kept our people in feudal subjugation. The chiefs were cruel, the people poor.

But this was not the story my mother told me. No one had owned the land before the *haole* came; everyone could fish and plant, except during sacred periods. And the chiefs were good and loved their people.

Was my mother confused? What did our *kūpuna* (elders) say? They replied: did these historians (all *haole*) know the language? Did they understand the chants? How long had they lived among our people? Whose stories had they heard?

None of the historians had ever learned our mother tongue. They had all been content to read what Europeans and Americans had written. But why did scholars, presumably well-trained and thoughtful, neglect our language? Not merely a passageway to knowledge, language is a form of knowing by itself; a people's way of thinking and feeling is revealed through its music.

I sensed the answer without needing to answer. From years of living in a divided world, I knew the historian's judgment: *There is no value in things Hawaiian; all value comes from things haole.*

Historians, I realized, were very like missionaries. They were a part of the colonizing horde. One group colonized the spirit; the other, the mind. Frantz Fanon[1] had been right, but not just about Africans. He had been right about the bondage of my own people: "By a kind of perverted logic, [colonialism] turns to the past of the oppressed people, and distorts, disfigures, and destroys it" (1968:210). The first step in the colonizing process, Fanon had written, was the deculturation of a people. What better way to take our culture than to remake our image? A rich historical past became small and ignorant in the hands of Westerners. And we suffered a damaged sense of people and culture because of this distortion.

---

[1]*Frantz Fanon:* French West Indian psychiatrist, author, and political leader. Fanon (1925–1961) is perhaps best known for his psychoanalytic study of Black life in a white-dominated world, *Black Skin, White Masks.* His *The Wretched of the Earth* called for an anticolonial revolution by peasants; he anticipated that such a struggle would produce a new breed of modern people of color.

Burdened by a linear, progressive conception of history and by an assumption that Euro-American culture flourishes at the upper end of that progression, Westerners have told the history of Hawai'i as an inevitable if occasionally bitter-sweet triumph of Western ways over "primitive" Hawaiian ways. A few authors — the most sympathetic — have recorded with deep-felt sorrow the passing of our people. But in the end, we are repeatedly told, such an eclipse was for the best.

Obviously it was best for Westerners, not for our dying multitudes. This is why the historian's mission has been to justify our passing by celebrating Western dominance. Fanon would have called this missionizing, intellectual colonization. And it is clearest in the historian's insistence that pre-*haole* Hawaiian land tenure was "feudal" — a term that is now applied, without question, in every monograph, in every schoolbook, and in every tour guide description of my people's history.

From the earliest days of Western contact my people told their guests that *no one* owned the land. The land — like the air and the sea — was for all to use and share as their birthright. Our chiefs were *stewards* of the land; they could not own or privately possess the land any more than they could sell it.

But the *haole* insisted on characterizing our chiefs as feudal land-lords and our people as serfs. Thus, a European term which described a European practice founded on the European concept of private property — feudalism — was imposed upon a people halfway around the world from Europe and vastly different from her in every conceivable way. More than betraying an ignorance of Hawaiian culture and history, however, this misrepresentation was malevolent in design.

By inventing feudalism in ancient Hawai'i, Western scholars quickly transformed a spiritually-based, self-sufficient economic system of land use and occupancy into an oppressive, medieval European practice of divine right ownership, with the common people tied like serfs to the land. By claiming that a Pacific people lived under a European system — that the Hawaiians lived under feudalism — Westerners could then degrade a successful system of shared land use with a pejorative and inaccurate Western term. Land tenure changes instituted by Americans and in line with current Western notions of private property were then made to appear beneficial to the Hawaiians. But in practice, such changes benefited the *haole*, who alienated the people from the land, taking it for themselves.

The prelude to this land alienation was the great dying of the people. Barely half a century after contact with the West our people had declined in number by eighty percent. Disease and death were rampant. The sandalwood forests had been stripped bare for international commerce between England and China. The missionaries had insinuated themselves everywhere. And a debt-ridden Hawaiian king (there had been no king before Western contact) succumbed to enormous

15

pressure from the Americans and followed their schemes for dividing up the land.

This is how private property land tenure entered Hawai'i. The common people, driven from their birthright, received less than one percent of the land. They starved while huge *haole*-owned sugar plantations thrived.

And what had the historians said? They had said that the Americans "liberated" the Hawaiians from an oppressive "feudal" system. By inventing a false feudal past, the historians justify — and become complicitous in — massive American theft.

Is there "evidence" — as historians call it — for traditional   20
Hawaiian concepts of land use? The evidence is in the sayings of my people and in the words they wrote more than a century ago, much of which has been translated. However, historians have chosen to ignore any references here to shared land use. But there *is* incontrovertible evidence in the very structure of the Hawaiian language. If the historians had bothered to learn our language (as any American historian of France would learn French) they would have discovered that we show possession in two ways: through the use of an "a" possessive, which reveals acquired status, and through the use of an "o" possessive, which denotes inherent status. My body (*ko 'u kino*) and my parents (*ko'u mākua*), for example, take the "o" form; most material objects, such as food (*ka'u mea'ai*) take the "a" form. But land, like one's body and one's parents, takes the "o" possessive (*ko'u 'āina*). Thus, in our way of speaking, land is inherent to the people; it is like our bodies and our parents. The people cannot exist without the land, and the land cannot exist without the people.

Every major historian of Hawai'i has been mistaken about Hawaiian land tenure. The chiefs did not own the land: they *could not* own the land. My mother was right and the *haole* historians were wrong. If they had studied our language they would have known that no one owned the land. But was their failing merely ignorance, or simple ethnocentric bias?

No, I did not believe them to be so benign. As I read on, a pattern emerged in their writing. Our ways were inferior to those of the West, to those of the historians' own culture. We were "less developed," or "immature," or "authoritarian." In some tellings we were much worse. Thus, Gavan Daws (1968), the most famed modern historian of Hawai'i, had continued a tradition established earlier by missionaries Hiram Bingham (1848) and Sheldon Dibble (1909), by referring to the old ones as "thieves" and "savages" who regularly practiced infanticide and who, in contrast to "civilized" whites, preferred "lewd dancing" to work. Ralph Kuykendall (1938), long considered the most thorough if also the most boring of historians of Hawai'i, sustained another fiction — that my ancestors owned slaves, the outcast *Kauwā*. This opinion, as well as the description of Hawaiian land tenure as feudal, had been supported by respected sociologist Andrew Lind (1938).[2] Finally, nearly all historians had refused to accept our genealogical dating of over one hundred generations in Hawai'i. They had, instead, claimed that our earliest appearance in Hawai'i could only be traced to A.D. 700. Thus at least seven hundred years of our history were repudiated by "superior" Western scholarship. Only recently have archeological data confirmed what Hawaiians had said these many centuries (Tuggle 1979).

Suddenly the entire sweep of our written history was clear to me. I was reading the West's view of itself through the degradation of my own past. When historians wrote that the king owned the land and the common people were bound to it, they were saying that ownership was the only way human beings in their world could relate to the land, and in that relationship, some one person had to control both the land and the interaction between humans.

And when they said that our chiefs were despotic, they were telling of their own society, where hierarchy always results in domination. Thus any authority or elder is automatically suspected of tyranny.

And when they wrote that Hawaiians were lazy, they meant that work must be continuous and ever a burden.   25

And when they wrote that we were promiscuous, they meant that love-making in the Christian West is a sin.

[2]See also Fornander (1878–85). Lest one think these sources antiquated, it should be noted that there exist only a handful of modern scholarly works on the history of Hawai'i. The most respected are those by Kuykendall (1938) and Daws (1968), and a social history of the twentieth century by Lawrence Fuchs (1961). Of these, only Kuykendall and Daws claim any knowledge of pre-*haole* history, while concentrating on the nineteenth century. However, countless popular works have relied on these two studies which, in turn, are themselves based on primary sources written in English by extremely biased, anti-Hawaiian Westerners such as explorers, traders, missionaries (e.g., Bingham [1848] and Dibble [1909]), and sugar planters. Indeed, a favorite technique of Daws's — whose *Shoal of Time* is the most acclaimed and recent general history — is the lengthy quotation without comment of the most racist remarks by missionaries and planters. Thus, at one point, half a page is consumed with a "white man's burden" quotation from an 1886 *Planter's Monthly* article ("It is better for the colored man of India and Australia that the white man rules, and it is better here that the white man should rule . . . ," etc., p. 213). Daws's only comment is "The conclusion was inescapable." To get a sense of such characteristic contempt for Hawaiians, one has but to read the first few pages, where Daws refers several times to the Hawaiians as "savages" and "thieves" and where he approvingly has Captain Cook thinking, "It was a sensible primitive who bowed before a superior civilization" (p. 2). See also — among examples too numerous to cite — his glib description of sacred *hula* as a "frivolous diversion," which, instead of work, the Hawaiians "would practice energetically in the hot sun for days on end . . . their bare brown flesh glistening with sweat" (pp. 65–66). Daws, who repeatedly displays an affection for descriptions of Hawaiian skin color, taught Hawaiian history for some years at the University of Hawai'i; he now holds the Chair of Pacific History at the Australian National University's Institute of Advanced Studies. [Author's note]

And when they wrote that we were racist because we preferred our own ways to theirs, they meant that their culture needed to dominate other cultures.

And when they wrote that we were superstitious, believing in the *mana* of nature and people, they meant that the West has long since lost a deep spiritual and cultural relationship to the earth.

And when they wrote that Hawaiians were "primitive" in their grief over the passing of loved ones, they meant that the West grieves for the living who do not walk among their ancestors.

For so long, more than half my life, I had misunderstood this written record, thinking it described my own people. But my history was nowhere present. For we had not written. We had chanted and sailed and fished and built and prayed. And we had told stories through the great blood lines of memory: genealogy.

To know my history, I had to put away my books and return to the land. I had to plant taro in the earth before I could understand the inseparable bond between people and *'āina*. I had to feel again the spirits of nature and take gifts of plants and fish to the ancient altars. I had to begin to speak my language with our elders and leave long silences for wisdom to grow. But before anything else, I had to learn the language like a lover so that I could rock within her and lay at night in her dreaming arms.

There was nothing in my schooling that had told me of this, or hinted that somewhere there was a longer, older story of origins, of the flowing of songs out to a great but distant sea. Only my parents' voices, over and over, spoke to me of a Hawaiian world. While the books spoke from a different world, a Western world.

And yet, Hawaiians are not of the West. We are of *Hawai'i Nei*, this world where I live, this place, this culture, this *'āina*.

What can I say, then, to Western historians of my place and people? Let me answer with a story.

A while ago I was asked to share a panel on the American overthrow of our government in 1893. The other panelists were all *haole*. But one was a *haole* historian from the mainland who had just published a book on what he called the American anti-imperialists. He and I met briefly in preparation for the panel. I asked him if he knew the language. He said no. I asked him if he knew the record of opposition to our annexation to America. He said there was no real evidence for it, just comments here and there. I told him that he didn't understand and that at the panel I would share the evidence. When we met in public and spoke, I said this:

There is a song much loved by our people. It was sung when Hawaiians were forbidden from congregating in groups of more than three. Addressed to our imprisoned Queen, it was written in 1898, and tells of Hawaiian feelings for our land against annexation. Listen to our lament:

Kaulana na pua o'o Hawai'i	Famous are the children of
Kūpa'a mahope o ka 'āina	Hawai'i
Hiki mai ka 'elele o ka loko 'ino	Who cling steadfastly to the land
Palapala 'ānunu me ka pākaha	Comes the evil-hearted with
	A document greedy for plunder
Pane mai Hawai'i moku o Keawe	Hawai'i, island of Keawe,
Kokua na hono a'o Pi'ilani	answers
Kāko'o mai Kaua'i o Mano	The bays of Pi'ilani [of Maui,
Pau pu me ke one o Kakuhihewa	Moloka'i, and Lana'i] help
	Kaua'i of Mano assists
	Firmly together with the sands of
	Kakuhihewa
'A'ole a'e kau i ka pūlima	Do not put the signature
Maluna o ka pepa o ka 'enemi	On the paper of the enemy
Ho'ohui 'āina kū'ai hewa	Annexation is wicked sale
I ka pono sīvila a'o ke kānaka	Of the civil rights of the
	Hawaiian people
Mahope mākou o Lili'ulani	We support Lili'uokalani
A loa'a 'e ka pono o ka 'āina	Who has earned the right to the
Ha'ina 'ia mai ana ka puana	land
'O ka po'e i aloha i ka 'āina	The story is told
	Of the people who love the land

This song, I said, continues to be sung with great dignity at Hawaiian political gatherings. For our people still share the feelings of anger and protest that it conveys.

But our guest, the *haole* historian, answered that this song, although beautiful, was not evidence of either opposition or of imperialism from the Hawaiian perspective.

Many Hawaiians in the audience were shocked at his remarks, but, in hindsight, I think they were predictable. They are the standard response of the historian who does not know the language and has no respect for its memory.

Finally, I proceeded to relate a personal story, thinking that surely such a tale could not want for authenticity since I myself was relating it. My *tūtū* (grandmother) had told my mother who had told me that at the time of annexation (1898) a great wailing went up throughout the islands, a wailing of weeks, a wailing of impenetrable grief, a wailing of death. But he remarked again, this too is not evidence.

And so, history goes on, written in long volumes by foreign people. 40 Whole libraries begin to form, book upon book, shelf upon shelf.

At the same time, the stories go on, generation to generation, family to family.

Which history do Western historians desire to know? Is it to be a tale of writings by their own countrymen, individuals convinced of their "unique" capacity for analysis, looking at us with Western eyes, thinking about us within Western philosophical contexts, categorizing us by Western indices, judging us by Judeo-Christian morals, exhorting us to capitalist achievements, and finally, leaving us an authoritative-because-Western record of their complete misunderstanding?

All this has been done already. Not merely a few times, but many times. And still, every year, there appear new and eager faces to take up the same telling, as if the West must continue, implacably, with the din of its own disbelief.

But there is, as there has been always, another possibility. If it is truly our history Western historians desire to know, they must put down their books, and take up our practices. First, of course, the language. But later, the people, the *'āina*, the stories. Above all, in the end, the stories. Historians must listen, they must hear the generational connections, the reservoir of sounds and meanings.

They must come, as American Indians suggested long ago, to understand the land. Not in the Western way, but in the indigenous way, the way of living within and protecting the bond between people and *'āina*.

This bond is cultural, and it can be understood only culturally. But because the West has lost any cultural understanding of the bond between people and land, it is not possible to know this connection through Western culture. This means that the history of indigenous people cannot be written from within Western culture. Such a story is merely the West's story of itself.

Our story remains unwritten. It rests within the culture, which is inseparable from the land. To know this is to know our history. To write this is to write of the land and the people who are born from her.

Cumulative Bibliography

Bingham, Hiram (1848). *A Residence of Twenty-one Years in the Sandwich Islands.* 2nd ed. New York: Converse.

Daws, Gavan (1968). *Shoal of Time: A History of the Hawaiian Islands.* Toronto and New York: Macmillan.

Dibble, Sheldon (1909). *History of the Sandwich Islands.* Honolulu: Thrum.

Fanon, Frantz (1968). *The Wretched of the Earth.* New York: Grove, Evergreen Edition.

Fornander, Abraham (1878–85). *An Account of the Polynesian Race: Its Origin and Migrations and the Ancient History of the Hawaiian People to the Times of Kamehameha I.* 3 vols. Vol. 1. London: Trübner.

Fuchs, Lawrence (1961). *Hawaii Pono: A Social History.* New York: Harcourt, Brace and World.

Kuykendall, Ralph S. (1938). *The Hawaiian Kingdom, 1778–1854.* Honolulu: Univ. of Hawaii Press.

Lind, Andrew (1938). *An Island Community: Ecological Succession in Hawaii.*
    New York: Greenwood.
Tuggle, H. David (1979). "Hawaii." In *The Prehistory of Polynesia.* Ed. Jesse
    D. Jennings. Pp. 167–99. Cambridge, Mass.: Harvard Univ. Press.

Engaging the Text

1. What are the key mistakes *haole* historians have made, according to Trask?
Why did they get things wrong?

2. Given the information presented in this selection, explain the Hawaiian
understanding of land and natural resources prior to the arrival of white people
and discuss the subsequent legal, conceptual, and physical disruptions of the
native way of life.

3. Whom do you trust more — Trask or the earlier historians? Why?

Exploring Connections

4. Both Trask and Patricia Nelson Limerick (p. 110) offer revised versions of
history. Compare and contrast their goals and methods. Also discuss why,
according to these authors, distortions of history arose in the West and in
Hawaii.

5. Like Trask, Paula Gunn Allen (p. 241) discovered that the truths of her
family and the truths of scholars bore little resemblance to each other. Have you
ever learned conflicting "truths" about an important issue? Write your own
essay after reviewing Trask's and Allen's essays as models.

Extending the Critical Context

6. More than forty years after World War II, Japanese Americans who were
sent to internment camps began receiving some compensation for the unjust
and illegal treatment they had suffered. Assume that Trask's history is completely accurate, and debate whether the federal government ought to provide
restitution to native Hawaiians (in the form of land or money).

7. Read about Hawaii in one or more of the most recent encyclopedias you can
find. Do they reflect any of Trask's thinking, or do they give the traditional
versions she denounces? To extend the assignment, critique one or more of the
encyclopedia entries in detail, showing how particular sentences hide, distort,
or acknowledge the kind of information Trask provides.

Talking to the Owls and Butterflies

John (Fire) Lame Deer
and Richard Erdoes

Fasten your intellectual seat belt. According to the speaker of this selection, a Sioux medicine man named John (Fire) Lame Deer (1900–1976), most Americans are doing just about everything wrong: in striving for progress, we have "declawed and malformed" ourselves and forgotten how to live. The passage is much more than a critique of Anglo civilization, however; it lends substance and detail to the idea of living in harmony with nature. Lame Deer has lived in both worlds, having been a painter and rodeo clown as well as a traditional healer and storyteller.

Richard Erdoes (b. 1912) was nearly sixty when he turned to serious writing from a career in magazine illustration and photography; the key event was meeting Lame Deer, when he was assigned by Life *magazine to paint and photograph a Sioux reservation. Lame Deer picked him to write the life story that became* Lame Deer, Seeker of Visions *(1972), from which this passage is excerpted.*

Let's sit down here, all of us, on the open prairie, where we can't see a highway or a fence. Let's have no blankets to sit on, but feel the ground with our bodies, the earth, the yielding shrubs. Let's have the grass for a mattress, experiencing its sharpness and its softness. Let us become like stones, plants, and trees. Let us be animals, think and feel like animals.

Listen to the air. You can hear it, feel it, smell it, taste it. *Woniya waken* — the holy air — which renews all by its breath. *Woniya, woniya waken* — spirit, life, breath, renewal — it means all that. *Woniya* — we sit together, don't touch, but something is there; we feel it between us, as a presence. A good way to start thinking about nature, talk about it. Rather talk to it, talk to the rivers, to the lakes, to the winds as to our relatives.

You have made it hard for us to experience nature in the good way by being part of it. Even here we are conscious that somewhere out in those hills there are missile silos and radar stations. White men always pick the few unspoiled, beautiful, awesome spots for the sites of these abominations. You have raped and violated these lands, always saying, "Gimme, gimme, gimme," and never giving anything back. You have taken 200,000 acres of our Pine Ridge[1] reservation and made them into a bombing range. This land is so beautiful and strange that now some of you want to make it into a national park. The only use you have made of this land since you took it from us was to blow it up. You have not only despoiled the earth, the rocks, the minerals, all of which you call "dead" but which are very much alive; you have even changed the animals, which are part of us, part of the Great Spirit, changed them in a horrible way, so no one can recognize them. There is power in a buffalo — spiritual, magic power — but there is no power in an Angus, in a Hereford.[2]

There is power in an antelope, but not in a goat or in a sheep, which holds still while you butcher it, which will eat your newspaper if you let it. There was great power in a wolf, even in a coyote. You have made him into a freak — a toy poodle, a Pekingese, a lap dog. You can't do much with a cat, which is like an Indian, unchangeable. So you fix it, alter it, declaw it, even cut its vocal cords so you can experiment on it in a laboratory without being disturbed by its cries.

A partridge, a grouse, a quail, a pheasant, you have made them into   5
chickens, creatures that can't fly, that wear a kind of sunglasses so that they won't peck each other's eyes out, "birds" with a "pecking order." There are some farms where they breed chickens for breast meat. Those birds are kept in low cages, forced to be hunched over all the time, which makes the breast muscles very big. Soothing sounds, Muzak, are piped into these chicken hutches. One loud noise and the chickens go haywire, killing themselves by flying against the mesh of their cages. Having to spend all their lives stooped over makes an unnatural, crazy, no-good bird. It also makes unnatural, no-good human beings.

That's where you fooled yourselves. You have not only altered, declawed, and malformed your winged and four-legged cousins; you have done it to yourselves. You have changed men into chairmen of boards, into office workers, into time-clock punchers. You have changed women into housewives, truly fearful creatures. I was once invited into the home of such a one.

"Watch the ashes, don't smoke, you stain the curtains. Watch the goldfish bowl, don't breathe on the parakeet, don't lean your head against the wallpaper; your hair may be greasy. Don't spill liquor on that table: it has a delicate finish. You should have wiped your boots; the floor was just varnished. Don't, don't, don't . . ." That is crazy. We weren't made to endure this. You live in prisons which you have built for yourselves, calling them "homes," offices, factories. We have a new joke on the reservation: "What is cultural deprivation?" Answer: "Being an

[1]*Pine Ridge:* reservation established for the Oglala Sioux in 1978 following more than ten years of negotiation and fighting; site of the Wounded Knee massacre.
[2]*Angus, Hereford:* breeds of cattle.

upper-middle-class white kid living in a split-level suburban home with a color TV."

Sometimes I think that even our pitiful tar-paper shacks are better than your luxury homes. Walking a hundred feet to the outhouse on a clear wintry night, through mud or snow, that's one small link with nature. Or in the summer, in the back country, leaving the door of the privy open, taking your time, listening to the humming of the insects, the sun warming your bones through the thin planks of wood; you don't even have that pleasure anymore.

Americans want to have everything sanitized. No smells! Not even the good, natural man and woman smell. Take away the smell from under the armpits, from your skin. Rub it out, and then spray or dab some nonhuman odor on yourself, stuff you can spend a lot of money on, ten dollars an ounce, so you know this has to smell good. "B.O.," bad breath, "Intimate Female Odor Spray" — I see it all on TV. Soon you'll breed people without body openings.

I think white people are so afraid of the world they created that   10 they don't want to see, feel, smell, or hear it. The feeling of rain and snow on your face, being numbed by an icy wind and thawing out before a smoking fire, coming out of a hot sweat bath and plunging into a cold stream, these things make you feel alive, but you don't want them anymore. Living in boxes which shut out the heat of the summer and the chill of winter, living inside a body that no longer has a scent, hearing the noise from the hi-fi instead of listening to the sounds of nature, watching some actor on TV having a make-believe experience when you no longer experience anything for yourself, eating food without taste — that's your way. It's no good.

The food you eat, you treat it like your bodies, take out all the nature part, the taste, the smell, the roughness, then put the artificial color, the artificial flavor in. Raw liver, raw kidney — that's what we old-fashioned full-bloods like to get our teeth into. In the old days we used to eat the guts of the buffalo, making a contest of it, two fellows getting hold of a long piece of intestines from opposite ends, starting chewing toward the middle, seeing who can get there first; that's eating. Those buffalo guts, full of half-fermented, half-digested grass and herbs, you didn't need any pills and vitamins when you swallowed those. Use the bitterness of gall for flavoring, not refined salt or sugar. *Wasna* — meat, kidney fat, and berries all pounded together   a lump of that sweet *wasna* kept a man going for a whole day. That was food, that had the power. Not the stuff you give us today: powdered milk, dehydrated eggs, pasteurized butter, chickens that are all drumsticks or all breast; there's no bird left there.

You don't want the bird. You don't have the courage to kill honestly — cut off the chicken's head, pluck it and gut it — no, you don't want this anymore. So it all comes in a neat plastic bag, all cut up, ready to eat, with no taste and no guilt. Your mink and seal coats, you don't want to know about the blood and pain which went into making them. Your idea of war — sit in an airplane, way above the clouds, press a button, drop the bombs, and never look below the clouds — that's the odorless, guiltless, sanitized way.

When we killed a buffalo, we knew what we were doing. We apologized to his spirit, tried to make him understand why we did it, honoring with a prayer the bones of those who gave their flesh to keep us alive, praying for their return, praying for the life of our brothers, the buffalo nation, as well as for our own people. You wouldn't understand this and that's why we had the Washita Massacre,[3] the Sand Creek Massacre,[4] the dead women and babies at Wounded Knee.[5] That's why we have Song My and My Lai[6] now.

To us life, all life, is sacred. The state of South Dakota has pest-control officers. They go up in a plane and shoot coyotes from the air. They keep track of their kills, put them all down in their little books. The stockmen and sheepowners pay them. Coyotes eat mostly rodents, field mice and such. Only once in a while will they go after a stray lamb. They are our natural garbage men cleaning up the rotten and stinking things. They make good pets if you give them a chance. But their living could lose some man a few cents, and so the coyotes are killed from the air. They were here before the sheep, but they are in the way; you can't make a profit out of them. More and more animals are dying out. The animals which the Great Spirit put here, they must go. The man-made animals are allowed to stay — at least until they are shipped out to be butchered. That terrible arrogance of the white man, making himself something more than God, more than nature, saying, "I will let this animal live, because it makes money"; saying, "This animal must go, it brings no income, the space it occupies can be used in a better way. The only good coyote is a dead coyote." They are treating coyotes almost as badly as they used to treat Indians.

---

[3]*Washita Massacre:* the U.S. Army, led by Lt. Col. George Custer, attacked a Cheyenne camp at Washita River, now in Oklahoma, on November 27, 1868; the Cheyenne were resisting railroad construction.

[4]*Sand Creek Massacre:* on November 29, 1864, Colorado militiamen attacked an encampment of Southern Cheyenne at Sand Creek in southeastern Colorado, killing about a third of a band of five hundred. Many women and children were killed, mutilated, or tortured.

[5]*Wounded Knee:* at Wounded Knee in South Dakota, Miniconjou Sioux led by Big Foot fought the Seventh U.S. Cavalry in December 1890. This battle, two weeks after Chief Sitting Bull was killed, ended the Ghost Dance War. Wounded Knee was also the site of a 1973 protest by the American Indian Movement.

[6]*Song My, My Lai:* My Lai was a Vietnamese hamlet, part of a village called Song My or Son My. In the most famous of Vietnam atrocities, American soldiers massacred several hundred Vietnamese civilians there on March 16, 1968.

You are spreading death, buying and selling death. With all your 15
deodorants, you smell of it, but you are afraid of its reality; you don't
want to face up to it. You have sanitized death, put it under the rug,
robbed it of its honor. But we Indians think a lot about death. I do.
Today would be a perfect day to die — not too hot, not too cool. A day
to leave something of yourself behind, to let it linger. A day for a lucky
man to come to the end of his trail. A happy man with many friends.
Other days are not so good. They are for selfish, lonesome men, having
a hard time leaving this earth. But for whites every day would be
considered a bad one, I guess.

Eighty years ago our people danced the Ghost Dance, singing and
dancing until they dropped from exhaustion, swooning, fainting, seeing
visions. They danced in this way to bring back their dead, to bring back
the buffalo. A prophet had told them that through the power of the
Ghost Dance the earth would roll up like a carpet, with all the white
man's works — the fences and the mining towns with their whore-
houses, the factories and the farms with their stinking, unnatural animals, the railroads and the telegraph poles, the whole works. And
underneath this rolled-up white man's world we would find again the
flowering prairie, unspoiled, with its herds of buffalo and antelope, its
clouds of birds, belonging to everyone, enjoyed by all.

I guess it was not time for this to happen, but it is coming back, I
feel it warming my bones. Not the old Ghost Dance, not the rolling-
up — but a new-old spirit, not only among Indians but among whites
and blacks, too, especially among young people. It is like raindrops
making a tiny brook, many brooks making a stream, many streams
making one big river bursting all dams. Us making this book, talking
like this — these are some of the raindrops.

Listen, I saw this in my mind not long ago: in my vision the electric
light will stop sometime. It is used too much for TV and going to the
moon. The day is coming when nature will stop the electricity. Police
without flashlights, beer getting hot in the refrigerators, planes dropping from the sky, even the President can't call up somebody on the
phone. A young man will come, or men, who'll know how to shut off all
electricity. It will be painful, like giving birth. Rapings in the dark,
winos breaking into the liquor stores, a lot of destruction. People are
being too smart, too clever; the machine stops and they are helpless,
because they have forgotten how to make do without the machine.
There is a Light Man coming, bringing a new light. It will happen
before this century is over. The man who has the power will do good
things, too — stop all atomic power, stop wars, just by shutting the
white electro-power off. I hope to see this, but then I'm also afraid.
What will be will be.

I think we are moving in a circle, or maybe a spiral, going a little
higher every time, but still returning to the same point. We are moving

closer to nature again. I feel it. . . . It won't be bad, doing without many things you are now used to, things taken out of the earth and wasted foolishly. You can't replace them and they won't last forever. Then you'll have to live more according to the Indian way. People won't like that, but their children will. The machine will stop, I hope, before they make electric corncobs for poor Indians' privies.

We'll come out of our boxes and rediscover the weather. In the old days you took your weather as it came, following the cranes, moving south with the herds. Here, in South Dakota, they say, "If you don't like the weather, wait five minutes." It can be 100 degrees in the shade one afternoon and suddenly there comes a storm with hailstones as big as golf balls, the prairie is all white and your teeth chatter. That's good — a reminder that you are just a small particle of nature, not so powerful as you think. . . . 20

But all animals have power, because the Great Spirit dwells in all of them, even a tiny ant, a butterfly, a tree, a flower, a rock. The modern, white man's way keeps that power from us, dilutes it. To come to nature, feel its power, let it help you, one needs time and patience for that. Time to think, to figure it all out. You have so little time for contemplation; it's always rush, rush, rush with you. It lessens a person's life, all that grind, that hurrying and scurrying about. Our old people say that the Indians of long ago didn't have heart trouble. They didn't have that cancer. The illnesses they had they knew how to cure. But between 1890 and 1920 most of the medicines, the animal bundles, the pipes, the ancient, secret things which we had treasured for centuries, were lost and destroyed by the B.I.A.,[7] by the Government police. They went about tearing down sweat lodges, went into our homes, broke the pipes, tore up the medicine bags, threw them into the fire, burned them up, completely wiped out the wisdom of generations. But the Indian, you take away everything from him, he still has his mouth to pray, to sing the ancient songs. He can still do his *yuwipi* ceremony[8] in a darkened room, beat his small drum, make the power come back, make the wisdom return. He did, but not all of it. The elk medicines are gone. The bear medicine, too. We had a medicine man here, up the creek, who died about fifteen years ago. He was the last bear medicine man that I knew about. And he was good, too. He was really good. . . .

As for myself, the birds have something to tell me. The eagle, the owl. In an eagle there is all the wisdom of the world; that's why we have an eagle feather at the top of the pole during a *yuwipi* ceremony. If you

---

[7]*the B.I.A.:* Bureau of Indian Affairs.

[8]yuwipi *ceremony:* a sacred ritual of healing, purification, and prayer using tiny sacred rocks gathered by medicine men from anthills for gourds and rattles.

are planning to kill an eagle, the minute you think of that he knows it, knows what you are planning. The black-tailed deer has this wisdom, too. That's why its tail is tied farther down at the *yuwipi* pole. This deer, if you shoot at him, you won't hit him. He just stands right there and the bullet comes right back and hits you. It is like somebody saying bad things about you and they come back at him.

In one of my great visions I was talking to the birds, the winged creatures. I was saddened by the death of my mother. She had held my hand and said just one word: "pitiful." I don't think she grieved for herself; she was sorry for me, a poor Indian she would leave in a white man's world. I cried up on that vision hill, cried for help, stretched out my hands toward the sky and then put the blanket over myself — that's all I had, the blanket and the pipe, and a little tobacco for an offering. I didn't know what to expect. I wanted to touch the power, feel it. I had the thought to give myself up, even if it would kill me. So I just gave myself to the winds, to nature, not giving a damn about what could happen to me.

All of a sudden I hear a big bird crying, and then quickly he hit me on the back, touched me with his spread wings. I heard the cry of an eagle, loud above the voices of many other birds. It seemed to say, "We have been waiting for you. We knew you would come. Now you are here. Your trail leads from here. Let our voices guide you. We are your friends, the feathered people, the two-legged, the four-legged, we are your friends, the creatures, little tiny ones, eight legs, twelve legs — all those who crawl on the earth. All the little creatures which fly, all those under water. The powers of each one of us we will share with you and you will have a ghost with you always — another self."

That's me, I thought, no other thing than myself, different, but me 25 all the same, unseen, yet very real. I was frightened. I didn't understand it then. It took me a lifetime to find out.

And again I heard the voice amid the bird sounds, the clicking of beaks, the squeaking and chirping. "You have love for all that has been placed on this earth, not like the love of a mother for her son, or of a son for his mother, but a bigger love which encompasses the whole earth. You are just a human being, afraid, weeping under that blanket, but there is a great space within you to be filled with that love. All of nature can fit in there." I was shivering, pulling the blanket tighter around myself, but the voices repeated themselves over and over again, calling me "Brother, brother, brother." So this is how it is with me. Sometimes I feel like the first being in one of our Indian legends. This was a giant made of earth, water, the moon and the winds. He had timber instead of hair, a whole forest of trees. He had a huge lake in his stomach and a waterfall in his crotch. I feel like this giant. All of nature is in me, and a bit of myself is in all of nature.

Engaging the Text

1. Lame Deer's critique of modern life is wide-ranging and multifaceted. According to Lame Deer, what is wrong with whites' understanding of the following topics? Debate the wisdom and accuracy of his views.

the land	the animal world
sense of smell	death
eating	time

2. It's unlikely that most college students would give up pizza for buffalo guts or trade a dorm room, much less a luxury home, for a tar-paper shack. What is the value of reading a piece whose philosophy is so radically incompatible with the way American society functions?

Exploring Connections

3. Compare Patricia Nelson Limerick's claim (p. 110) that Americans are obsessed with their own innocence and Lame Deer's suggestion that "white people are so afraid of the world they created that they don't want to see, feel, smell, or hear it."

4. Imagine a conversation between Lame Deer and Mike LeFevre (p. 87). How would Lame Deer diagnose LeFevre's situation? What advice might he give LeFevre? How do you think LeFevre would reply?

Extending the Critical Context

5. Set aside your books and walk outside for a time, reflecting on what Lame Deer says. What do you see of nature where you live? What do you understand about the plants, animals, seasons, and stars? How far would you have to travel to sit in a place where you couldn't see signs of "civilization"?

6. Several years ago, a new-wave documentary film appeared, taking its title, *Koyaanisqatsi*, from the Hopi for "life out of balance." Watch the film and discuss the critique it suggests of modern technology and urban life. What do you think we might do to bring life into a better balance?

Storyteller

LESLIE MARMON SILKO

This is a strange and beautiful story. It portrays violence calmly; it sees the struggle of civilizations in terms of freezing metal; it speaks movingly of tradition, ignorance, betrayal, and revenge without using any of these words. The story unfolds gradually through a series of discrete scenes whose interconnections are not at first completely clear. In the end we see that every word and image was carefully chosen. The authenticity of this tale of revenge in the Arctic is so striking that you might think Silko was Alaskan, but she was born in Albuquerque, New Mexico, in 1948 and grew up at the Laguna Pueblo Reservation nearby. Although she had Mexican and white as well as Laguna ancestors, her poems, stories, and novel (Ceremony, 1977) emphasize her tribal identity. "Storyteller" is the title piece of a collection published in 1981. In reading the story, keep in mind that according to a traditional Eskimo poem, words once had the power to "come alive / and what people wanted to happen could happen — / all you had to do was say it."

I

Every day the sun came up a little lower on the horizon, moving more slowly until one day she got excited and started calling the jailer. She realized she had been sitting there for many hours, yet the sun had not moved from the center of the sky. The color of the sky had not been good lately; it had been pale blue, almost white, even when there were no clouds. She told herself it wasn't a good sign for the sky to be indistinguishable from the river ice, frozen solid and white against the earth. The tundra rose up behind the river but all the boundaries between the river and hills and sky were lost in the density of the pale ice.

She yelled again, this time some English words which came randomly into her mouth, probably swear words she'd heard from the oil drilling crews last winter. The jailer was an Eskimo, but he would not speak Yupik to her. She had watched people in the other cells; when they spoke to him in Yupik he ignored them until they spoke English.

He came and stared at her. She didn't know if he understood what she was telling him until he glanced behind her at the small high window. He looked at the sun, and turned and walked away. She could hear the buckles on his heavy snowmobile boots jingle as he walked to the front of the building.

It was like the other buildings that white people, the Gussucks,[1] brought with them: BIA[2] and school buildings, portable buildings that arrived sliced in halves, on barges coming up the river. Squares of metal paneling bulged out with the layers of insulation stuffed inside. She had asked once what it was and someone told her it was to keep out the cold. She had not laughed then, but she did now. She walked over to the small double-pane window and she laughed out loud. They thought they

[1]*Gussucks:* white people.
[2]*BIA:* Bureau of Indian Affairs.

could keep out the cold with stringy yellow wadding. Look at the sun. It wasn't moving; it was frozen, caught in the middle of the sky. Look at the sky, solid as the river with ice which had trapped the sun. It had not moved for a long time; in a few more hours it would be weak, and heavy frost would begin to appear on the edges and spread across the face of the sun like a mask. Its light was pale yellow, worn thin by the winter.

She could see people walking down the snow-packed roads, their 5 breath steaming out from their parka hoods, faces hidden and protected by deep ruffs of fur. There were no cars or snowmobiles that day so she calculated it was fifty below zero, the temperature which silenced their machines. The metal froze; it split and shattered. Oil hardened and moving parts jammed solidly. She had seen it happen to their big yellow machines and the giant drill last winter when they came to drill their test holes. The cold stopped them, and they were helpless against it.

Her village was many miles upriver from this town, but in her mind she could see it clearly. Their house was not near the village houses. It stood alone on the bank upriver from the village. Snow had drifted to the eaves of the roof on the north side, but on the west side, by the door, the path was almost clear. She had nailed scraps of red tin over the logs last summer. She had done it for the bright red color, not for added warmth the way the village people had done. This final winter had been coming down even then; there had been signs of its approach for many years.

II

She went because she was curious about the big school where the Government sent all the other girls and boys. She had not played much with the village children while she was growing up because they were afraid of the old man, and they ran when her grandmother came. She went because she was tired of being alone with the old woman whose body had been stiffening for as long as the girl could remember. Her knees and knuckles were swollen grotesquely, and the pain had squeezed the brown skin of her face tight against the bones; it left her eyes hard like river stone. The girl asked once, what it was that did this to her body, and the old woman had raised up from sewing a sealskin boot, and stared at her.

"The joints," the old woman said in a low voice, whispering like wind across the roof, "the joints are swollen with anger."

Sometimes she did not answer and only stared at the girl. Each year she spoke less and less, but the old man talked more — all night sometimes, not to anyone but himself; in a soft deliberate voice, he told stories, moving his smooth brown hands above the blankets. He had not fished or hunted with the other men for many years although he was not crippled or sick. He stayed in his bed, smelling like dry fish and urine, telling stories all winter; and when warm weather came, he went to his place on the river bank. He sat with a long willow stick, poking at the smoldering moss he burned against the insects while he continued with the stories.

The trouble was that she had not recognized the warnings in time. 10 She did not see what the Gussuck school would do to her until she walked into the dormitory and realized that the old man had not been lying about the place. She thought he had been trying to scare her as he used to when she was very small and her grandmother was outside cutting up fish. She hadn't believed what he told her about the school because she knew he wanted to keep her there in the log house with him. She knew what he wanted.

The dormitory matron pulled down her underpants and whipped her with a leather belt because she refused to speak English.

"Those backwards village people," the matron said, because she was an Eskimo who had worked for the BIA a long time, "they kept this one until she was too big to learn." The other girls whispered in English. They knew how to work the showers, and they washed and curled their hair at night. They ate Gussuck food. She laid on her bed and imagined what her grandmother might be sewing, and what the old man was eating in his bed. When summer came, they sent her home.

The way her grandmother had hugged her before she left for school had been a warning too, because the old woman had not hugged or touched her for many years. Not like the old man, whose hands were always hunting, like ravens circling lazily in the sky, ready to touch her. She was not surprised when the priest and the old man met her at the landing strip, to say that the old lady was gone. The priest asked her where she would like to stay. He referred to the old man as her grand-father, but she did not bother to correct him. She had already been thinking about it; if she went with the priest, he would send her away to a school. But the old man was different. She knew he wouldn't send her back to school. She knew he wanted to keep her.

III

He told her one time that she would get too old for him faster than he got too old for her; but again she had not believed him because sometimes he lied. He had lied about what he would do with her if she came into his bed. But as the years passed, she realized what he said was true. She was restless and strong. She had no patience with the old man who had never changed his slow smooth motions under the blankets.

The old man was in his bed for the winter; he did not leave it except 15 to use the slop bucket in the corner. He was dozing with his mouth open slightly; his lips quivered and sometimes they moved like he was telling a story even while he dreamed. She pulled on the sealskin boots, the mukluks with the bright red flannel linings her grandmother had sewn for her, and she tied the braided red yarn tassles around her ankles over the gray wool pants. She zipped the wolfskin parka. Her grandmother had worn it for many years, but the old man said that before she died, she instructed him to bury her in an old black sweater, and to give the parka to the girl. The wolf pelts were creamy colored and silver, almost white in some places, and when the old lady had walked across the tundra in the winter, she disappeared into the snow.

She walked toward the village, breaking her own path through the deep snow. A team of sled dogs tied outside a house at the edge of the village leaped against their chains to bark at her. She kept walking, watching the dusky sky for the first evening stars. It was warm and the dogs were alert. When it got cold again, the dogs would lie curled and still, too drowsy from the cold to bark or pull at the chains. She laughed loudly because it made them howl and snarl. Once the old man had seen her tease the dogs and he shook his head. "So that's the kind of woman you are," he said, "in the wintertime the two of us are no different from those dogs. We wait in the cold for someone to bring us a few dry fish."

She laughed out loud again, and kept walking. She was thinking about the Gussuck oil drillers. They were strange; they watched her when she walked near their machines. She wondered what they looked like underneath their quilted goosedown trousers; she wanted to know how they moved. They would be something different from the old man.

The old man screamed at her. He shook her shoulders so violently that her head bumped against the log wall. "I smelled it!" he yelled, "as soon as I woke up! I am sure of it now. You can't fool me!" His thin legs were shaking inside the baggy wool trousers; he stumbled over her boots in his bare feet. His toe nails were long and yellow like bird claws; she had seen a gray crane last summer fighting another in the shallow water on the edge of the river. She laughed out loud and pulled her shoulder out of his grip. He stood in front of her. He was breathing hard and shaking; he looked weak. He would probably die next winter.

"I'm warning you," he said, "I'm warning you." He crawled back into his bunk then, and reached under the old soiled feather pillow for a piece of dry fish. He lay back on the pillow, staring at the ceiling and chewed dry strips of salmon. "I don't know what the old woman told you," he said, "but there will be trouble." He looked over to see if she was listening. His face suddenly relaxed into a smile, his dark slanty eyes were lost in wrinkles of brown skin. "I could tell you, but you are too good for warnings now. I can smell what you did all night with the Gussucks."

She did not understand why they came there, because the village   20
was small and so far upriver that even some Eskimos who had been
away to school would not come back. They stayed downriver in the
town. They said the village was too quiet. They were used to the town
where the boarding school was located, with electric lights and running
water. After all those years away at school, they had forgotten how to
set nets in the river and where to hunt seals in the fall. Those who left
did not say it, but their confidence had been destroyed. When she asked
the old man why the Gussucks bothered to come to the village, his
narrow eyes got bright with excitement.

"They only come when there is something to steal. The fur animals
are too difficult for them to get now, and the seals and fish are hard to
find. Now they come for oil deep in the earth. But this is the last time
for them." His breathing was wheezy and fast; his hands gestured at the
sky. "It is approaching. As it comes, ice will push across the sky." His
eyes were open wide and he stared at the low ceiling rafters for hours
without blinking. She remembered all this clearly because he began the
story that day, the story he told from that time on. It began with a giant
bear which he described muscle by muscle, from the curve of the ivory
claws to the whorls of hair at the top of the massive skull. And for eight
days he did not sleep, but talked continuously of the giant bear whose
color was pale blue glacier ice.

IV

The snow was dirty and worn down in a path to the door. On either
side of the path, the snow was higher than her head. In front of the door
there were jagged yellow stains melted into the snow where men had
urinated. She stopped in the entry way and kicked the snow off her
boots. The room was dim; a kerosene lantern by the cash register was
burning low. The long wooden shelves were jammed with cans of beans
and potted meats. On the bottom shelf a jar of mayonnaise was broken
open, leaking oily white clots on the floor. There was no one in the room
except the yellowish dog sleeping in front of the long glass display case.
A reflection made it appear to be lying on the knives and ammunition
inside the case. Gussucks kept dogs inside their houses with them; they
did not seem to mind the odors which seeped out of the dogs. "They tell
us we are dirty for the food we eat — raw fish and fermented meat. But
we do not live with dogs," the old man once said. She heard voices in the
back room, and the sound of bottles set down hard on tables.

They were always confident. The first year they waited for the ice
to break up on the river, and then they brought their big yellow machines up river on barges. They planned to drill their test holes during
the summer to avoid the freezing. But the imprints and graves of their
machines were still there, on the edge of the tundra above the river,

where the summer mud had swallowed them before they ever left sight of the river. The village people had gathered to watch the white men, and to laugh as they drove the giant machines, one by one, off the steel ramp into the bogs; as if sheer numbers of vehicles would somehow make the tundra solid. But the old man said they behaved like desperate people, and they would come back again. When the tundra was frozen solid, they returned.

Village women did not even look through the door to the back room. The priest had warned them. The storeman was watching her because he didn't let Eskimos or Indians sit down at the tables in the back room. But she knew he couldn't throw her out if one of his Gussuck customers invited her to sit with him. She walked across the room. They stared at her, but she had the feeling she was walking for someone else, not herself, so their eyes did not matter. The red-haired man pulled out a chair and motioned for her to sit down. She looked back at the storeman while the red-haired man poured her a glass of red sweet wine. She wanted to laugh at the storeman the way she laughed at the dogs, straining against their chains, howling at her.

The red-haired man kept talking to the other Gussucks sitting 25 around the table, but he slid one hand off the top of the table to her thigh. She looked over at the storeman to see if he was still watching her. She laughed out loud at him and the red-haired man stopped talking and turned to her. He asked if she wanted to go. She nodded and stood up.

Someone in the village had been telling him things about her, he said as they walked down the road to his trailer. She understood that much of what he was saying, but the rest she did not hear. The whine of the big generators at the construction camp sucked away the sound of his words. But English was of no concern to her anymore, and neither was anything the Christians in the village might say about her or the old man. She smiled at the effect of the subzero air on the electric lights around the trailers; they did not shine. They left only flat yellow holes in the darkness.

It took him a long time to get ready, even after she had undressed for him. She waited in the bed with the blankets pulled close, watching him. He adjusted the thermostat and lit candles in the room, turning out the electric lights. He searched through a stack of record albums until he found the right one. She was not sure about the last thing he did: he taped something on the wall behind the bed where he could see it while he laid on top of her. He was shriveled and white from the cold; he pushed against her body for warmth. He guided her hands to his thighs; he was shivering.

She had returned a last time because she wanted to know what it was he stuck on the wall above the bed. After he finished each time, he reached up and pulled it loose, folding it carefully so that she could not see it. But this time she was ready; she waited for his fast breathing and sudden collapse on top of her. She slid out from under him and stood up beside the bed. She looked at the picture while she got dressed. He did not raise his face from the pillow, and she thought she heard teeth rattling together as she left the room.

She heard the old man move when she came in. After the Gussuck's trailer, the log house felt cool. It smelled like dry fish and cured meat. The room was dark except for the blinking yellow flame in the mica window of the oil stove. She squatted in front of the stove and watched the flames for a long time before she walked to the bed where her grandmother had slept. The bed was covered with a mound of rags and fur scraps the old woman had saved. She reached into the mound until she felt something cold and solid wrapped in a wool blanket. She pushed her fingers around it until she felt smooth stone. Long ago, before the Gussucks came, they had burned whale oil in the big stone lamp which made light and heat as well. The old woman had saved everything they would need when the time came.

In the morning, the old man pulled a piece of dry caribou meat   30
from under the blankets and offered it to her. While she was gone, men from the village had brought a bundle of dry meat. She chewed it slowly, thinking about the way they still came from the village to take care of the old man and his stories. But she had a story now, about the red-haired Gussuck. The old man knew what she was thinking, and his smile made his face seem more round than it was.

"Well," he said, "what was it?"

"A woman with a big dog on top of her."

He laughed softly to himself and walked over to the water barrel. He dipped the tin cup into the water.

"It doesn't surprise me," he said.

V

"Grandma," she said, "there was something red in the grass that   35
morning. I remember." She had not asked about her parents before. The old woman stopped splitting the fish bellies open for the willow drying racks. Her jaw muscles pulled so tightly against her skull, the girl thought the old woman would not be able to speak.

"They bought a tin can full of it from the storeman. Late at night. He told them it was alcohol safe to drink. They traded a rifle for it." The old woman's voice sounded like each word stole strength from her. "It made no difference about the rifle. That year the Gussuck boats had come, firing big guns at the walrus and seals. There was nothing left to hunt after that anyway. So," the old lady said, in a low soft voice the girl had not heard for a long time, "I didn't say anything to them when they left that night."

"Right over there," she said, pointing at the fallen poles, half buried in the river sand and tall grass, "in the summer shelter. The sun was high half the night then. Early in the morning when it was still low, the policeman came around. I told the interpreter to tell him that the storeman had poisoned them." She made outlines in the air in front of her, showing how their bodies laid twisted on the sand; telling the story was like laboring to walk through deep snow; sweat shone in the white hair around her forehead. "I told the priest too, after he came. I told him the storeman lied." She turned away from the girl. She held her mouth even tighter, set solidly, not in sorrow or anger, but against the pain, which was all that remained. "I never believed," she said, "not much anyway. I wasn't surprised when the priest did nothing."

The wind came off the river and folded the tall grass into itself like river waves. She could feel the silence the story left, and she wanted to have the old woman go on.

"I heard sounds that night, grandma. Sounds like someone was singing. It was light outside. I could see something red on the ground." The old woman did not answer her; she moved to the tub full of fish on the ground beside the work bench. She stabbed her knife into the belly of a whitefish and lifted it onto the bench. "The Gussuck storeman left the village right after that," the old woman said as she pulled the entrails from the fish, "otherwise, I could tell you more." The old woman's voice flowed with the wind blowing off the river; they never spoke of it again.

When the willows got their leaves and the grass grew tall along the river banks and around the sloughs, she walked early in the morning. While the sun was still low on the horizon, she listened to the wind off the river; its sound was like the voice that day long ago. In the distance, she could hear the engines of the machinery the oil drillers had left the winter before, but she did not go near the village or the store. The sun never left the sky and the summer became the same long day, with only the winds to fan the sun into brightness or allow it to slip into twilight.

She sat beside the old man at his place on the river bank. She poked the smoky fire for him, and felt herself growing wide and thin in the sun as if she had been split from belly to throat and strung on the willow pole in preparation for the winter to come. The old man did not speak anymore. When men from the village brought him fresh fish he hid them deep in the river grass where it was cool. After he went inside, she split the fish open and spread them to dry on the willow frame the way the old woman had done. Inside, he dozed and talked to himself. He had talked all winter, softly and incessantly about the giant polar bear stalking a lone man across Bering Sea ice. After all the months the old man had been telling the story, the bear was within a hundred feet of the man; but the ice fog had closed in on them now and the man could only smell the sharp ammonia odor of the bear, and hear the edge of the snow crust crack under the giant paws.

One night she listened to the old man tell the story all night in his sleep, describing each crystal of ice and the slightly different sounds they made under each paw; first the left and then the right paw, then the hind feet. Her grandmother was there suddenly, a shadow around the stove. She spoke in her low wind voice and the girl was afraid to sit up to hear more clearly. Maybe what she said had been to the old man because he stopped telling the story and began to snore softly the way he had long ago when the old woman had scolded him for telling his stories while others in the house were trying to sleep. But the last words she heard clearly: "It will take a long time, but the story must be told. There must not be any lies." She pulled the blanket up around her chin, slowly, so that her movements would not be seen. She thought her grandmother was talking about the old man's bear story; she did not know about the other story then.

She left the old man wheezing and snoring in his bed. She walked through river grass glistening with frost; the bright green summer color was already fading. She watched the sun move across the sky, already lower on the horizon, already moving away from the village. She stopped by the fallen poles of the summer shelter where her parents had died. Frost glittered on the river sand too; in a few more weeks there would be snow. The predawn light would be the color of an old woman. An old woman sky full of snow. There had been something red lying on the ground the morning they died. She looked for it again, pushing aside the grass with her foot. She knelt in the sand and looked under the fallen structure for some trace of it. When she found it, she would know what the old woman had never told her. She squatted down close to the gray poles and leaned her back against them. The wind made her shiver.

The summer rain had washed the mud from between the logs; the sod blocks stacked as high as her belly next to the log walls had lost their square-cut shape and had grown into soft mounds of tundra moss and stiff-bladed grass bending with clusters of seed bristles. She looked at the northwest, in the direction of the Bering Sea. The cold would come down from there to find narrow slits in the mud, rainwater holes in the outer layer of sod which protected the log house. The dark green tundra stretched away flat and continuous. Somewhere the sea and the land met; she knew by their dark green colors there were no boundaries between them. That was how the cold would come: when the boundaries were gone the polar ice would range across the land into the sky. She watched the horizon for a long time. She would stand in that place on the north side of the house and she would keep watch on the northwest horizon, and eventually she would see it come. She would watch for its approach in the stars, and hear it come with the wind. These preparations were unfamiliar, but gradually she recognized them as she did her own footprints in the snow.

She emptied the slop jar beside his bed twice a day and kept the barrel full of water melted from river ice. He did not recognize her anymore, and when he spoke to her, he called her by her grandmother's name and talked about people and events from long ago, before he went back to telling the story. The giant bear was creeping across the new snow on its belly, close enough now that the man could hear the rasp of its breathing. On and on in a soft singing voice, the old man caressed the story, repeating the words again and again like gentle strokes.

The sky was gray like a river crane's egg; its density curved into the thin crust of frost already covering the land. She looked at the bright red color of the tin against the ground and the sky and she told the village men to bring the pieces for the old man and her. To drill the test holes in the tundra, the Gussucks had used hundreds of barrels of fuel. The village people split open the empty barrels that were abandoned on the river bank, and pounded the red tin into flat sheets. The village people were using the strips of tin to mend walls and roofs for winter. But she nailed it on the log walls for its color. When she finished, she walked away with the hammer in her hand, not turning around until she was far away, on the ridge above the river banks, and then she looked back. She felt a chill when she saw how the sky and the land were already losing their boundaries, already becoming lost in each other. But the red tin penetrated the thick white color of earth and sky; it defined the boundaries like a wound revealing the ribs and heart of a great caribou about to bolt and be lost to the hunter forever. That night the wind howled and when she scratched a hole through the heavy frost on the inside of the window, she could see nothing but the impenetrable white; whether it was blowing snow or snow that had drifted as high as the house, she did not know.

It had come down suddenly, and she stood with her back to the wind looking at the river, its smoky water clotted with ice. The wind had blown the snow over the frozen river, hiding thin blue streaks where fast water ran under ice translucent and fragile as memory. But she could see shadows of boundaries, outlines of paths which were slender branches of solidity reaching out from the earth. She spent days walking on the river, watching the colors of ice that would safely hold her, kicking the heel of her boot into the snow crust, listening for a solid sound. When she could feel the paths through the soles of her feet, she went to the middle of the river where the fast gray water churned under a thin pane of ice. She looked back. On the river bank in the distance she could see the red tin nailed to the log house, something not swallowed up by the heavy white belly of the sky or caught in the folds of the frozen earth. It was time.

The wolverine fur around the hood of her parka was white with the frost from her breathing. The warmth inside the store melted it, and she felt tiny drops of water on her face. The storeman came in from the back room. She unzipped the parka and stood by the oil stove. She didn't look at him, but stared instead at the yellowish dog, covered with scabs of matted hair, sleeping in front of the stove. She thought of the Gussuck's picture, taped on the wall above the bed and she laughed out loud. The sound of her laughter was piercing; the yellow dog jumped to its feet and the hair bristled down its back. The storeman was watching her. She wanted to laugh again because he didn't know about the ice. He did not know that it was prowling the earth, or that it had already pushed its way into the sky to seize the sun. She sat down in the chair by the stove and shook her long hair loose. He was like a dog tied up all winter, watching while the others got fed. He remembered how she had gone with the oil drillers, and his blue eyes moved like flies crawling over her body. He held his thin pale lips like he wanted to spit on her. He hated the people because they had something of value, the old man said, something which the Gussucks could never have. They thought they could take it, suck it out of the earth or cut it from the mountains; but they were fools.

There was a matted hunk of dog hair on the floor by her foot. She thought of the yellow insulation coming unstuffed: their defense against the freezing going to pieces as it advanced on them. The ice was crouching on the northwest horizon like the old man's bear. She laughed out loud again. The sun would be down now; it was time.

The first time he spoke to her, she did not hear what he said, so she did not answer or even look up at him. He spoke to her again but his words were only noises coming from his pale mouth, trembling now as his anger began to unravel. He jerked her up and the chair fell over behind her. His arms were shaking and she could feel his hands tense up, pulling the edges of the parka tighter. He raised his fist to hit her, his thin body quivering with rage; but the fist collapsed with the desire he had for the valuable things, which, the old man had rightly said, was the only reason they came. She could hear his heart pounding as he held her close and arched his hips against her, groaning and breathing in spasms. She twisted away from him and ducked under his arms.

She ran with a mitten over her mouth, breathing through the fur to protect her lungs from the freezing air. She could hear him running behind her, his heavy breathing, the occasional sound of metal jingling against metal. But he ran without his parka or mittens, breathing the frozen air; its fire squeezed the lungs against the ribs and it was enough

50

that he could not catch her near his store. On the river bank he realized how far he was from his stove, and the wads of yellow stuffing that held off the cold. But the girl was not able to run very fast through the deep drifts at the edge of the river. The twilight was luminous and he could still see clearly for a long distance; he knew he could catch her so he kept running.

When she neared the middle of the river she looked over her shoulder. He was not following her tracks; he went straight across the ice, running the shortest distance to reach her. He was close then; his face was twisted and scarlet from the exertion and the cold. There was satisfaction in his eyes; he was sure he could outrun her.

She was familiar with the river, down to the instant the ice flexed into hairline fractures, and the cracking bone-sliver sounds gathered momentum with the opening ice until the sound of the churning gray water was set free. She stopped and turned to the sound of the river and the rattle of swirling ice fragments where he fell through. She pulled off a mitten and zipped the parka to her throat. She was conscious then of her own rapid breathing.

She moved slowly, kicking the ice ahead with the heel of her boot, feeling for sinews of ice to hold her. She looked ahead and all around herself; in the twilight, the dense white sky had merged into the flat snow-covered tundra. In the frantic running she had lost her place on the river. She stood still. The east bank of the river was lost in the sky; the boundaries had been swallowed by the freezing white. And then, in the distance, she saw something red, and suddenly it was as she had remembered it all those years.

VI

She sat on her bed and while she waited, she listened to the old man. The man had found a small jagged knoll on the ice. He pulled his beaver fur cap off his head; the fur inside it steamed with his body heat and sweat. He left it upside down on the ice for the great bear to stalk, and he waited downwind on top of the ice knoll; he was holding the jade knife.

She thought she could see the end of his story in the way he wheezed out the words; but still he reached into his cache of dry fish and dribbled water into his mouth from the tin cup. All night she listened to him describe each breath the man took, each motion of the bear's head as it tried to catch the sound of the man's breathing, and tested the wind for his scent.

The state trooper asked her questions, and the woman who cleaned house for the priest translated them into Yupik. They wanted to know what happened to the storeman, the Gussack who had been seen running after her down the road onto the river late last evening. He had not come back, and the Gussuck boss in Anchorage was concerned about him. She did not answer for a long time because the old man suddenly sat up in his bed and began to talk excitedly, looking at all of them — the trooper in his dark glasses and the housekeeper in her corduroy parka. He kept saying, "The story! The story! Eh-ya! The great bear! The hunter!"

They asked her again, what happened to the man from the Northern Commercial store. "He lied to them. He told them it was safe to drink. But I will not lie." She stood up and put on the gray wolfskin parka. "I killed him," she said, "but I don't lie."

The attorney came back again, and the jailer slid open the steel doors and opened the cell to let him in. He motioned for the jailer to stay to translate for him. She laughed when she saw how the jailer would be forced by this Gussuck to speak Yupik to her. She liked the Gussuck attorney for that, and for the thinning hair on his head. He was very tall, and she liked to think about the exposure of his head to the freezing; she wondered if he would feel the ice descending from the sky before the others did. He wanted to know why she told the state trooper she had killed the storeman. Some village children had seen it happen, he said, and it was an accident. "That's all you have to say to the judge: it was an accident." He kept repeating it over and over again to her, slowly in a loud but gentle voice: "It was an accident. He was running after you and he fell through the ice. That's all you have to say in court. That's all. And they will let you go home. Back to your village." The jailer translated the words sullenly, staring down at the floor. She shook her head. "I will not change the story, not even to escape this place and go home. I intended that he die. The story must be told as it is." The attorney exhaled loudly; his eyes looked tired. "Tell her that she could not have killed him that way. He was a white man. He ran after her without a parka or mittens. She could not have planned that." He paused and turned toward the cell door. "Tell her I will do all I can for her. I will explain to the judge that her mind is confused." She laughed out loud when the jailer translated what the attorney said. The Gussucks did not understand the story; they could not see the way it must be told, year after year as the old man had done, without lapse or silence.

She looked out the window at the frozen white sky. The sun had 60 finally broken loose from the ice but it moved like a wounded caribou running on strength which only dying animals find, leaping and running on bullet-shattered lungs. Its light was weak and pale; it pushed dimly through the clouds. She turned and faced the Gussuck attorney.

"It began a long time ago," she intoned steadily, "in the summertime. Early in the morning, I remember, something red in the tall river grass. . . ."

The day after the old man died, men from the village came. She was sitting on the edge of her bed, across from the woman the trooper hired to watch her. They came into the room slowly and listened to her. At the foot of her bed they left a king salmon that had been split open wide and dried last summer. But she did not pause or hesitate; she went on with the story, and she never stopped, not even when the woman got up to close the door behind the village men.

The old man would not change the story even when he knew the end was approaching. Lies could not stop what was coming. He thrashed around on the bed, pulling the blankets loose, knocking bundles of dried fish and meat on the floor. The man had been on the ice for many hours. The freezing winds on the ice knoll had numbed his hands in the mittens, and the cold had exhausted him. He felt a single muscle tremor in his hand that he could not suppress, and the jade knife fell; it shattered on the ice, and the blue glacier bear turned slowly to face him.

Engaging the Text

1. What events take place in the story? You may want to break into several small groups to review the six sections of the story and establish the plot.

2. We get several glimpses of "the Gussucks" in the story. What do we learn of them in areas such as commerce, technology, sexuality, and law? How do the Gussucks interact with the natural world? What is the story's attitude about Gussuck technology?

3. Why doesn't the protagonist try to defend herself at the end of the story? What becomes of her?

4. Explain the connection between the grandfather's story of the polar bear and the main story told here. Support your explanation with specific references to the text. Be sure to consider the meaning of how each story ends.

5. How many stories are told within "Storyteller"? What seems to be the significance of storytelling itself in this culture?

Exploring Connections

6. Compare the portrayals of western technological society offered by Silko and John (Fire) Lame Deer (p. 128). What qualities do they associate with technological culture? What fates do they imagine for it?

7. Review the "innocent" reasons behind resource rushes as described by Patricia Nelson Limerick (p. 110). Then make up a specific hypothetical character who might have an innocent reason for going to the Arctic. Write a paragraph or two from this character's point of view about why she or he is heading north. Exchange paragraphs with a classmate and write a critique of each other's paragraphs from a broader perspective.

8. The selections by Patricia Nelson Limerick (p. 110), Haunani-Kay Trask (p. 118) and Silko all emphasize stories as instruments of power. Drawing on these readings, discuss the multiple roles stories play in intercultural conflict.

Extending the Critical Context

9. John Boorman's film *The Emerald Forest* is set in the Amazon, yet it shares the apocalyptic environmental vision expressed in "Storyteller." Watch the film and compare the way it treats the conflict between nature and technology with the handling of the same theme in Silko's story. What is the appeal of such responses to technology?

The Spell of Technology

Chellis Glendinning

For twenty years, Chellis Glendinning (b. 1947) suffered from numerous health problems, including hives, food allergies, chronic infections, fevers, fatigue, and severe depression. Six of these years were spent in bed. She now traces these disorders, which physicians had proved unable to diagnose, to twentieth-century technologies, including oral contraceptives, the Dalkon Shield intrauterine device (or IUD), and artificial hormones found in various foods. In this excerpt from When Technology Wounds: The Human Consequences of Progress *(1990), she critiques our national love affair with progress and technology from the point of view of a "technology survivor." Glendinning does not believe that answers to human problems lie in faster computers, better insecticides, or safer nuclear power plants; for her, technology itself is a false idol to which Western culture has been praying for too long.*

Progress

"Progress Is Our Most Important Product."[1] In the Western world we embrace progress as if it were essential for breathing. To us, progress is the experience of time as linear, as philosopher Edward T. Hall writes,

[1]General Electric advertisement. [Author's note]

"a ribbon stretching into the future, along which one progresses,"[2] and on that ribbon we are ever forging onward, ever looking to what new things and ways we might invent.

The concept of "no limits" follows naturally. If we are, as a society, unquestioning devotees of linear progress, then we assume we can expand into infinity. We can march across land, into other people's territories, into seemingly limitless markets, into the human body, into outer space — with no attention to the health effects of the pesticides, communications towers, plutonium-charged pacemakers, plastic bottles, and space shuttles created in the service of our idea; with no attention to the infringement on the rights of people, cultures, animals, and ecosystems perpetrated in the service of our belief.

The idea of progress becomes invisible and inviolable, surrounding us and informing our perceptions of human evolution and "the good life." We come to think of ourselves as occupying the pinnacle of civilization. We look ahead to the acquisition of "more and better." Industry becomes the great liberator, capable of sweeping away nationalism, militarism, and economic exploitation, leading humans to perfectability.

As a force in the creation of social organization, the idea of progress predisposes us to build institutions that can continually invent new ways and means, purvey these to ever-expanding markets, and ease the way toward further expansion. As Harriet Beinfield describes it, progress is about "how to get something we don't already have, how to make things easier, and how to make some people richer." With these goals in mind, our society creates corporations, advertising, consumerism, and governments that facilitate "progress." Large corporations get massive tax breaks to produce more technologies that harm life and health, while the meager budgets of agencies like the EPA and state-level Agent Orange commissions reveal that their activities are considered worthless. "Ever onward!" is the byword of the day, and yet, as David Noble says, on the level of social relations we do not change at all.[3] We do not, as a society, look over our shoulders at the human debris . . . who with their lives proclaim: This idea of progress may not be so good. Writes Lewis Mumford:[4] "Progress indeed!"[5]

[2]Cited in Don Fabun, ed., *The Dynamics of Change* (Englewood Cliffs, N.J.: Prentice-Hall, 1970), p. II-22; and Edward Hall, *The Silent Language* (Greenwich, Conn.: Fawcett, 1965). [Author's note]

[3]David Noble, *America by Design: Science, Technology, and the Rise of Corporate Capitalism* (New York: Alfred A. Knopf, 1977), p. xi. [Author's note]

[4]*Mumford:* U.S. social philosopher Lewis Mumford (1895–1990), one of this century's most profound critics of the dehumanizing aspects of technological progress. His books in this area of thought include *Technics and Civilization*, *The Culture of Cities*, *Men Must Act*, and the classic *The City in History*.

[5]Lewis Mumford, *My Works and Days: A Personal Chronicle* (New York: Harcourt Brace Jovanovich, 1979), p. 7. [Author's note]

Technical Solutions to All Problems

"Better Things for Better Living."[6] Mumford is the modern thinker   5
to illuminate our society's definition of progress most forcefully: it is a
mechanistic, technological progress we seek, not a social or humanistic
one.

"Concealed within this notion," Mumford writes,

> was the assumption that human improvement would come about more
> rapidly, indeed almost automatically, through devoting all our ener-
> gies to the expansion of scientific knowledge and to technological
> invention; that traditional knowledge and experience, traditional
> forms and values, acted as a brake upon such expansion and invention;
> and that since the order embodied by the machine was the highest type
> of order, no brakes of any kind were desirable. . . . Only the present
> counted, and continual change was needed in order to prevent the
> present from becoming passé. . . . Progress was accordingly measured
> by novelty, constant change, and mechanistic difference, not by con-
> tinuity and human improvement.[7]

Jacques Ellul[8] points out that the imperative to solve all problems
technically can be traced to the eighteenth century. At that time, he
posits, the onset of technological society did not result from a centralized, rational conspiracy. In the wake of the breakdown of medieval
society, it emanated from a shift in perception taking place in the minds
of many people all over Europe. Merchants in London, shipbuilders in
Lisbon, inventors in Amsterdam — all began asking what were at the
time new questions: is a particular approach effective? Is it efficient?
Does it work?[9]

The right answers were delivered by mechanistic thinking. Cap-
tivated by scientific method and certain that reason must be applied
to every facet of human life, the emerging middle class invented machines — mechanical looms, reapers, threshing machines, cannons, and
rifles — and they developed machinelike social organizations: systematized monetary techniques, the factory system, bureaucratic armies, technical hierarchies that supplanted the old craft networks, and
state administration by rational bureaucratic principles. In the twentieth century we still live under the systems they set up. We still look to
new machines, new chemicals, and new techniques as the primary

---

[6]Du Pont advertisement. [Author's note]

[7]Lewis Mumford, "The Case Against Modern Architecture," *Architectural Record*,
Vol. 131, No. 4 (April 1962), p. 157. [Author's note]

[8]*Jacques Ellul:* French philosopher of technology (b. 1912) who warned of the
human loss of control over the state and technology. His best-known work is *The Technological Society*.

[9]Langdon Winner, *Autonomous Technology: Technics-out-of-Control as a Theme in
Political Thought* (Cambridge, Mass.: MIT Press, 1977), p. 124. [Author's note]

means to improve the human condition. "What does all this [technology] do for me?" asks a 1988 IBM advertisement.[10] Does it work?

Social critic Jerry Mander points out that the first perception of a new technology is invariably utopian.[11] Nuclear power will light one hundred American cities! The Pill will liberate women! Computers will revolutionize person-to-person communications! Superconductivity will make electricity as cheap as air! Genetic engineering will create a race of geniuses! Corporate-conceived advertisements deliver these messages to us via corporate-controlled media. Citizen participation in the process, from the conception of a new technology to its development and deployment, is not welcome. Besides, the process is so complex and specialized at this point that the creation of a new floor wax can be as mystifying as the development of an outer space missile system. "The result is that democratic participation in profoundly important decisions becomes impossible," says Mander, "and all decisions are placed within a technological class that benefits from a certain outcome."[12]

That class is made up of corporate, military, media, and government executives, scientists, and engineers. Many of them are the human correlates of Ellul's "political propaganda": they are the direct and conscious perpetrators of technological development. As much as the rest of us may feel we personally benefit from our cars and computers, we are in the "sociological propaganda" camp: living in technological society, we have grown spiritually deprived. We become like the frog whose water is slowly brought to a boil. Each increasing degree of heat comes subtly enough that he becomes incapable of judging the impending danger.

Whether "political" or "sociological," people who uncritically believe in modern technology tend to salve the wounds modern technologies inflict, not by investigating the causes of technological excess, but by looking to new technologies to provide cures. Doctors treat servicemen with cancer resulting from exposure to nuclear explosions with small blasts of radiation. Chemists and farmers look to more potent pesticides to conquer the insects that have grown resistant to last year's products. Law enforcement professionals accept new criminal detection methods based on genetic examination of DNA, but do not address the social and economic sources of unlawful behavior.

A clear illustration of substituting technical solutions for systemic ones can be seen in what has happened to Native Americans in North Dakota. On the Fort Berthold Reservation, one in every three Indians has diabetes. This rate is five times the national average. Although

---

[10]IBM advertisement, 1988. [Author's note]

[11]Jerry Mander, *The Least Popular Cause* (San Francisco: Sierra Club Books, forthcoming). [Author's note]

[12]Ibid. [Author's note]

many Indians have a genetic proclivity toward diabetes, the disease has not always been so rampant. The epidemic is technology-induced. When the United States government built the Garrison Dam, acres of Indian farmland were destroyed. The Indians lost their source of livelihood and began to live on welfare, get no exercise, and eat canned food, all factors enhancing their chance to develop diabetes. The technological response has been to send medical teams onto the reservation providing the latest treatment technologies and social work teams bringing psychological technologies to help the Indians adjust to their illness. The response has not been to explore the technological root of the epidemic.[13]

People uncritical of technology also rationalize endangering technologies by promoting humanistic uses of a particular technology. In the 1950s, for instance, nuclear weaponry was justified by its "peaceful use": cheap electricity through nuclear power. In the 1970s, when nuclear power's excesses and dangers came to light, pronuclear people tried to deflect concern by drawing attention to the medical uses of radiation.

Such rationalizations make a strong impact on both the public and the creators and disseminators of technologies. Since the notion of the technical solution has so successfully engulfed our minds, social mores, and institutions, the most searing judgment critics have been able to muster does not even question modern technology as such. Rather it asserts that technologies are neutral. They are just tools that contain no inherent political bias. If there is a problem with technology, it lies with what class of people control it.

There is another perspective. This is the technology-as-political school: technologies serve political ends. They are invented and deployed by people who believe in and benefit from a particular political setup — and their very structure serves this setup. An overview of mass technological society shows that the kinds of technologies in place are those that serve the perpetuation of mass technological society. For instance, the telephone and computer may *look* like "people's technologies," and they do help individuals stay in communication and collect, sort, and manage information. Yet both were consciously developed to enhance systems of centralized political power. According to a manual written by early telephone entrepreneurs, the telephone was consciously disseminated to increase corporate command of information, resources, communications, and time.[14] The computer was originally developed during World War II to decode intercepted radio

[13]Daniel Zwertling on *All Things Considered*, National Public Radio, Washington, D.C., July 9, 1988. [Author's note]

[14]Ithiel de Sola Pool, *Forecasting the Telephone* (Norwood, N.J.: ABLEX, 1983) [Author's note]

messages and later to boost military power through guided missilery.[15] Today these technologies make global exploitation of nature, urban centralization, and high-tech military domination not only possible, but seemingly necessary. In a decentralized, communal society, telephones and computers would be neither politically necessary nor individually attractive. As Jerry Mander sees it, "Each technology is compatible with certain political and social outcomes, and usually it has been invented by people who have some of these outcomes in mind. The idea that technology is 'neutral' is itself not neutral."[16]

The outcome of an unquestioning belief in the technical solution is to obscure our ability to see this reality. It is to invite the use of defense mechanisms that prevent us from acknowledging technology's negative effects. Most of the technologies we know and use are deployed by large institutions — corporations, government, media, the military — established to perpetuate the benefits derived by certain privileged sectors of society. Yet many people, both in and out of these sectors, still perceive modern technologies as the leading edge of human consciousness and the ultimate symbol of human perfectability. As Hiroshima survivor Kanji Kuramoto explains, "As long as the government goes on testing nuclear weapons, they won't look back to the victims they leave behind, and they won't encourage anyone else to."[17]

Control Through Technology

"Master the Possibilities."[18] Manipulation of the environment is common to all societies. Neolithic tribespeople foraged for edible roots, built fires, and painted pictures on cave walls. The Greeks fished in the Mediterranean and constructed temples out of stone. The urge to alter one's dwelling place originates not just out of the physical need to make a livelihood, but also out of a psychological need to shape and relate to consciousness. To be conscious to the degree that humans are can be a frightening experience. We face the chaos and contradictions of our own psychology, as well as the knowledge of suffering and death.

Throughout history people have created ways — be they rituals, art, spiritual practices, or rap groups — to come to terms with the fact of consciousness. According to Jacques Ellul, technology is one of these ways. "Technique is the translation into action of man's concern to

---

[15]Paul Ceruzzi, "An Unforeseen Revolution: Computers and Expectations," in Joseph Corn, ed., *Imagining Tomorrow: History, Technology, and the American Future* (Cambridge, Mass.: MIT Press, 1986), pp. 188–201. [Author's note]

[16]Mander, *Least Popular Cause.* [Author's note]

[17]Kanji Kuramoto, Lecture presented at National Radiation Survivors Conference, Berkeley, Calif., August 1986. [Author's note]

[18]MasterCard advertisement, 1987. [Author's note]

master things by means of reason," he writes, "to account for what is subconscious, make quantitative what is qualitative, make clear and precise the outlines of nature, take hold of chaos and put order into it."[19]

In the West, this tendency to put order into chaos passed from a facet of the collective personality into a dominant trait. Science was developed, in part, to control reality by creating and organizing knowledge, and technology was created in order to enact science's ideas. Today specific machines, like Dalkon Shields[20] and jackhammers, are created to do specific jobs. Techniques, like aerobic exercises and assembly lines, are predetermined behaviors designed to accomplish specific results, and technological organizations, like multinational corporations and cities, are assemblages of machines, techniques, and people in structured relationships organized for predetermined purposes. Modern technologies exist to impose order and mastery.

At the deepest level, they reflect our Western relationship to nature: that is, both to the human psyche and to the organic world. Just as people in the West have developed techniques for controlling the mind through taboos, social mores, rules, regulations, and laws, so we have invented ways to control the external world. We have invented machines for excavating the bowels of mountains and killing insects in forests. We have crafted ways and means to enable people to murder each other and societies to make war on all of creation.

The resemblance between the kinds of technologies produced in our society and tyrannical modes of political power is too conspicuous to overlook. Langdon Winner points to the similarity in language between the two realms. *Master* and *slave* are words used to describe both the technological realm and fascist politics. So are *machine, power,* and *control.*[21] The conception, invention, development, deployment, and announcement of new technologies are accomplished by an undemocratic social process; the life experience of technology survivors testifies to this fact. But if the particular kinds of technologies in our midst exist to promote mastery and power, the question arises: whose power? Over whom? Is the power citizens derive really in the hands of the individual word processor owner who saves paper, white-out, and time? Or is it with the corporations whose maximum use of supercomputers — performing billions of calculations each second — facilitates their mastery over vast quantities of human and natural resources? As Mander writes, the question must be more than who gets power by using certain

[19]Jacques Ellul, *Technological Society,* trans. John Wilkinson (New York: Alfred A. Knopf, 1964), p. 43. [Author's note]

[20]*Dalkon Shield:* an intrauterine device (IUD) for contraception, now linked to various health disorders. See the headnote for this selection.

[21]Winner, *Autonomous Technology,* p. 20. [Author's note]

technologies. It must be who gets *the most power?* Who is *most in control?*[22]

The premium our society places on control is so complete that it becomes difficult to see beyond it. We are encouraged to achieve mastery of our feelings, jobs, bodies, image, finances, and future. Our social institutions are busy trying to achieve mastery of disease, other nations, the shelf life of food, the seasons, and death. That the concept of mastery answers psychological needs to escape our primal fears enhances its appeal to the point that we often overlook an odd irony. The very technologies created to control life have come to express the unacknowledged, unconscious side of the modern psyche: they themselves have become uncontrollable. In so doing, they bring the fear we hoped to escape back into our hearts.

Everything, the Same

"We'll Be Able to Offer One-Stop, One-Shop Nuclear Weapons Simulation."[23] Stopwatch in hand, the American engineer Frank Gilbreth was an innovator of scientific management. In the fictionalized film of his home life, *Cheaper by the Dozen*,[24] Gilbreth decides that life according to traditional Victorian values is not efficient or mechanized enough for the twentieth century. His response is an experiment in time management involving not factory workers on the assembly line, but his wife and twelve children. In the experiment, Gilberth fragments the movements of every household chore into its most essential parts and trains his children to accomplish these tasks in machinelike fashion, quick and standardized. Such an approach is what his colleague Frederick Winslow Taylor called "military organization":[25] human movements become the levers of a machine.

The story reflects an archetype of the twentieth century. Indeed, our body movements *are* determined by machines. The assembly line is the obvious example, workers moving arms and torso to accomplish the designated task as many as a thousand times an hour. In the famed 1936 film *Modern Times*,[26] Charlie Chaplin uses two wrenches to stamp

---

[22]Mander, *Least Popular Cause*. [Author's note]

[23]Lieutenant Colonel Edward Williams about need for $70 million blast simulator at White Sands Missile Range in New Mexico; quoted in David Morrissey, "White Sands Proposed as Site for Nuclear Blast Simulator," *Albuquerque Journal* (February 28, 1988). [Author's note]

[24]*Cheaper by the Dozen*, directed by Walter Lang, Twentieth Century Fox, 1950. [Author's note]

[25]Quoted in Siegfried Giedion, *Mechanization Takes Command* (New York: Norton and Co., 1948), p. 99. [Author's note]

[26]*Modern Times*, directed by Charlie Chaplin, United Artists, 1936. [Author's note]

indentations onto blocks flying by at breakneck speed, and when the conveyor belt finally stops, he cannot stop his body from making the same mechanistic moves.

There are less obvious examples in our everyday lives. There is the familiar thrust of the right arm shifting from second gear to third, the release of the clutch, the flip of the audiocassette into the player — actions begotten of the union of person with machine, standardized, and then stylized into "cool moves." There is the characteristic aim of the TV remote control. When we drive, traffic lights command us to stop every two blocks whether we need to or not. All these are actions we learn and repeat, like the assembly line worker, again and again and again. Just as Frank Gilbreth's children did, we mold ourselves to a narrow range of standardized motions according to the dictates of the machines around us, and when we do, we deny a host of essential physical experiences. We become numb.

Likewise, our sense of time is molded into predictable segments by the capabilities of machines. As Marshall McLuhan[27] describes, "Electric light abolished the divisions of night and day, of inner and outer, of the subterranean and the terrestrial,"[28] making it possible for people to transcend natural boundaries and stay up all night. We divide time into arbitrary weeks with people working five days and resting two, irregardless of their biological rhythms or needs. Moments become exact replicas of each other, differing only by what digit identifies them, and our life-styles, from when we eat lunch to how we make love, become a reiteration of the American Airlines slogan: "The On-Time Machine."[29]

As the painter Barnett Newman writes, human creation on the material plane is predated by the creation of an idea,[30] and the idea that came before mechanization was that life itself is mechanistic. For thousands of years cultures around the world had perceived the earth to be a living organism, a being with skin, blood, a spirit, and soul. In the eighteenth century, scientific thinking brought forth a different idea: the earth was not alive. It was dead, and nature was operably mechanistic. This idea paved the way for, among other things, detachment from and fragmentation of living, and then the complete mechanization of life.

But mechanization, one may argue, makes life easier. With it we can build houses faster and travel to all corners of the globe. The point is

[27]*Marshall McLuhan:* Canadian communications theorist. McLuhan (1911–1980) was internationally recognized for ground-breaking scholarship on the influence of TV and other communications technologies on all aspects of modern thought.

[28]Marshall McLuhan, *Understanding Media* (New York: McGraw-Hill, 1964), p. 120. [Author's note]

[29]American Airlines advertisement, 1988. [Author's note]

[30]Barnett Newman, "The First Man Was an Artist," *The Tiger's Eye*, Vol. 1 (October 1947), p. 59. [Author's note]

well made, but there are other aspects that are overlooked. Mechanization squelches the individuality and uniqueness that fed the human spirit in times past. By the fragmentation of activity and perception it demands, it makes an overview of the impact of our technologies nearly impossible. At this point, acceptance of mechanization is so thoroughly merged with cultural reality that we accept it as the way things are supposed to be. That we all use the same chemicals in our gardens — but do not know what they are made of — is accepted. That we are all exposed to the same pollutants in the air — but do not know who among our neighbors is ill because of them — becomes normal. Our vision of what is happening to our lives becomes restricted to what Langdon Winner calls a "well-trained narrowness."[31] Each sector of technological performance is so fragmented and we each, like mechanized parts in a vast machine, are so specialized in our participation that we lose sight of the whole story. As DES[32] daughter Sarah Pirtle says, "A spell has been cast about technology, and it's everywhere. We're not even at the stage where we can question a technology when it's offered. That's a powerful spell that holds us with that much sway."

The Computer Revolution

"What Exactly Can the World's Most Powerful and Expandable PC Do? Anything It Wants."[33] Half a million large computers are in use in the United States today. There are also eight million personal computers, five million programmable calculators, and millions of microprocessors built into other machines,[34] from automobiles to burglar alarms. At least thirty million Americans are avid computer operators, either in their homes or at work.[35] Production of microchips, software, and machinery is a global industry, and computerization now supports the infrastructure of the major institutions of our society, from government and military to business, media, and communications. Ever since a Harvard physics instructor named Howard Aiken unveiled the first electromechanical computer in 1944, a grand shift in both scientific and public perception of technology has been expected.

---

[31]Winner, *Autonomous Technology*, p. 129. [Author's note]

[32]*DES:* diethylstilbestrol, a synthetic estrogen or female hormone. Glendinning says that 8 million mothers, daughters, and sons have been exposed to this potentially harmful drug, which has also been used in animal feed.

[33]Advertisement for Compaq Deskpro 386/33, 1989. [Author's note]

[34]Paul Ceruzzi, "An Unforeseen Revolution," in Joseph Corn, ed., *Imagining Tomorrow*, p. 188. [Author's note]

[35]S. Kelly, "Semiconductor Industry: Layoff Update," *Dataquest Research Newsletter* (San Jose, Calif.: November 1985); Federal Bureau of Labor Statistics, BLS Establishment Survey 790, *Employment and Earnings* (Washington, D.C.: Department of Labor, 1986); and Federal Bureau of Labor Statistics, *Employment and Earnings* (Washington, D.C.: Department of Labor, 1985). [Author's note]

The shift is worth noting because since the introduction of the   30
computer, beliefs about it have not, as widely predicted, supplanted
already existing assumptions about technology. They have sprung from
these assumptions and reinforced them. Despite all the fanfare, the
computer society is still based on the same beliefs that lie at the heart of
industrialism. Progress is still defined by technological development.
The technical solution continues to show the way to all problem-
solving. Mastery and control through technology are still thought to be
the goal of human life, and efficiency through automation is still
perceived as the primary mode of existence. We are still wedded to the
assumptions that underlie these creeds: the mandate to functionalism,
scientific detachment, and the human viewed simultaneously as device
and as dominator of nature.

Seemingly new ideas ushered in with the debut of the new field of
control and communications spoke of "thinking machines" that could
reproduce the human nervous system. The promise of the computer was
summed up by Kaiser Corporation's Don Fabun in 1967: "So simple:
three things — analog, digital processing, and feedback. Put them
together and you can go out in the backyard right now and out of some
old bits of wire, a flashlight battery, and discarded beer cans you can
. . . build a creature that can do almost everything dinosaurs did — or
you, for that matter."[36]

Computers also promised infinite creativity through unlimited programming and limitless access to information — and therefore, it was
thought, power and control. But these ideas were in fact based on the
assumption that human psychology could be reduced to explicit, rational rules and nature to atomized elements to which such rules would
apply. These ideas led to the use of computers in ways not revolutionary,
but reflective of the old, mechanistic paradigm — like word processing
secretaries lined up terminal to terminal like assembly line workers of
the nineteenth century; like PC owners sitting alone in their rooms,
separate from their families, connecting to other people only through
the green glare; like government and industry officials colluding to
conceal the health effects of video display terminal emissions. Instead of
something entirely new, the computer became yet another attempt to
express the Western notion of nature as machine.

Embedded in the zeitgeist[37] of computerization, though — and
often rationalized as its primary contribution — lies an experience that
indeed does reflect a more communal and humanistic perspective than
the industrial era has allowed. Anyone who has explored computer
programming or tapped into a computer network can attest to this

[36]Quoted in Don Fabun, *The Dynamics of Change* (Englewood Cliffs, N.J.:
Prentice-Hall, 1970), p. IV-15. [Author's note]
[37]*zeitgeist:* German: spirit of the times.

experience. It is an emphasis on overall patterns. It is the admission of the interconnectedness among all beings, things, and processes that lies at the heart of many preindustrial cultures, Eastern religions, quantum physics, holistic medicine, ecology, and feminism. People who understand the relativity of the computer "mind" see that one's perceptions are shaped by one's changing position in relation to other phenomena. The old mechanistic assumption of distinct, separate facts or phenomena is no longer relevant, and the way is paved for a more holistic perception of life. Indeed, the experience of connection among people all over the world made possible by communications satellites, personal and business computers, television, and even through the computerization of the nuclear arms race becomes a welcome — albeit terribly ironic — experience in technological society.

To apply the holistic perception computers seem to spawn, we are challenged to stretch beyond the utopian images its proponents would have us believe. The computer may offer citizens of technological society important insights that challenge some of the predominant modes of thinking, but since it springs from the assumptions that have brought us to the current crisis, it should be no surprise that it also spawns the same old package of technological shortcomings: damage to the health of electronics plant workers . . . miscarriages and birth defects among pregnant video display terminal workers . . . chemical and electromagnetic pollution of the earth; and economic discrepancies between those with access to the resources amassed by computers and those without access. With it come the same old convergence of mechanistic perceptions: unwavering faith in progress, the technical solution, control through technological development, and mechanization. With it we are still riveted to the perception that functionality, scientific detachment, and human as object/dominator are "the way things are." We are not encouraged to question the total impact of modern technologies. We are still, like addicts, held in the spell.

Engaging the Text

1. What connection between nature and technology does Glendinning see as dominant in our society? What, according to Glendinning, is so dangerous about our reliance on technological solutions and mechanistic thinking? What does she see as the social and political consequences of this reliance? Do you agree?

2. In the first two paragraphs of this excerpt, Glendinning argues that the concept of linear time leads naturally to the concept of "no limits." Restate her argument in your own words and explain why you agree or disagree.

3. Glendinning is also critical of "people's technologies" (para. 15) like the computer. Why does she reject these apparently user-friendly technologies?

4. In this reading Glendinning is primarily on the attack, criticizing existing modes of thought and action which she considers harmful. Make some educated

guesses about what she would see as *right*: what would she prefer to this unquestioning devotion to technology?

Exploring Connections

5. Write a dialogue or debate between Glendinning and Andrew Carnegie (p. 20) on technology and progress.

6. How does the American myth of individual success, discussed in Chapter One, help sustain our faith in technology and progress?

Extending the Critical Context

7. Interpret several of the following as Glendinning would:

the U.S. space program	arcade games
fax machines	weather satellites
videocassette recorders (VCRs)	parallel computing
earthquake research	industrial robots
cellular phones	any other recent technology

To what extent do you share this view?

8. How would you expect Glendinning to critique the Gulf War against Iraq? Support your reasoning with specific references to her text.

9. Glendinning mentions Charlie Chaplin's film *Modern Times* as an example of how human beings are dehumanized, turned into machines, in a technological society. Watch this classic film and discuss how technological society affects Chaplin's Little Tramp and his fellow characters. If you prefer a more contemporary perspective on the same theme, try Ridley Scott's *Blade Runner*.

The Returning

GAIL TREMBLAY

Gail Tremblay, born in Buffalo, New York, is a poet of Onondaga, Micmac, and French Canadian heritage. Her work has been published in several magazines and anthologies; this poem about land and sky is taken from Indian Singing in Twentieth Century America *(1989). Tremblay teaches at Washington State University.*

It is these long journeys to the heart
of the continent, moving too fast
thirty thousand feet above the planet

that leave me longing to whisper
to medicine roots that send shoots 5
as fine as hair for miles to anchor
themselves to ground. The body feels
strangely out of context. I desire
to see agates sparkle among cirrus clouds
stretched out like endless waves 10
washing no shore. I grow lonely
for the dirt, lonely for the horizon
that marks time in relation to sun
and stars as it spins across the sky.
Up here, there are momentary miracles: 15
outside Denver, a lake turns golden
as it mirrors sun; clouds and mountains
move together creating atmosphere
for one another as Earth arcs through space.
But this journey is a pause in normal 20
breathing; a movement through thin air
kept away by delicate walls and will,
this distant place is not meant to sustain
the flesh. Even birds fly miles
below knowing the plants creating 25
air can only send their life giving
gift so far. It is the returning to Earth
that lets the skin contain the pulse,
the returning to Earth that feeds the muscle
of the heart and makes love possible. 30

Engaging the Text

1. How would you characterize the speaker's relationship to the natural world? What values does the poem stress?

2. Why is the speaker of this poem uncomfortable with air travel? How does Tremblay make this discomfort seem significant or meaningful, rather than just a personal idiosyncrasy? What are the dominant feelings of the poem?

3. Explain the last sentence of the poem.

4. List all the nouns of the poem in two columns — concrete and abstract. What patterns, ideas, or themes are suggested by the word choice alone? Discuss the movement in the poem between concrete images and abstract ideas.

Exploring Connections

5. John (Fire) Lame Deer's "Talking to the Owls and Butterflies" (p. 128) spells out ideas about nature similar to some in this poem. Use Lame Deer's remarks to help explain "The Returning."

6. Compare Tremblay's attitude toward technology to Chellis Glendinning's (p. 150).

Extending the Critical Context

7. Living in the age of advertising, we're all familiar with "poems" addressed to machines: almost any car commercial or airline ad can be read as a song of praise to technology. Try writing a "techno-poem" of your own that unabashedly celebrates a particular machine. You might then try to write one that, like Tremblay's, also makes the reader conscious of the drawbacks of this form of technology. Read and discuss your poems in class.

Living on the Land

KATHLEEN STOCKING

How would you like to own a house, pay only $142 per month on your twenty acres of land, be your own boss, and pay no income tax? It can be done, but not without some sacrifices. In this selection Kathleen Stocking (b. 1945) describes a couple who are living more simply than the rest of us, closer to the land and farther from the crowds. They are, in essence, twentieth-century homesteaders on Michigan's Leelanau Peninsula. Stocking clearly admires their way of life, but she does not disguise the difficulties they face. Stocking is a free-lance writer for The Detroit Monthly; *this selection is taken from her book* Letters from the Leelanau: Essays of People and Place *(1990).*

A blizzard is raging outside this small, rural homestead near Cedar.[1] It is February 1982 and this part of the country is enduring its fourth snowstorm in as many weeks.

"Come on, it's not so bad," Larry Doe tells his wife, Geradine Simkins, as together they tack blankets and sheets over windows and walls on the southeast side of their house, where a fifty-mile-an-hour wind is blowing snow and icy blasts of subzero cold through invisible cracks.

---

[1]*Cedar:* a small town in Michigan. Other places mentioned throughout the essay are also in Michigan.

"It's not so great," she answers, "when we have snow in our house."

Larry Doe and Geradine Simkins are living their beliefs.

They are doing what books such as *Muddling Toward Frugality* by   5
Warren Johnson and *Voluntary Simplicity* by Duane Elgin say people
must do if they are to survive in the twenty-first century. They are doing
what the *Global 2000 Report to the President* (U.S. Department of
State, 1982) says people should do if they want to stave off a worldwide
resource crisis in the next twenty years. They are doing what a 1977
Louis Harris poll says two out of three Americans would like to do.

They are doing less with less. They are learning to be self-sufficient.
In a benign way, they are doing what some urban folks are trying to do
with the caches of guns and food: preparing to survive on their own.

If the Stanford Research Institute in Menlo Park, California, is
right, people like Larry and Geradine represent about twenty percent of
the population in the United States, or approximately thirty-three million adults as of the 1980 census. And if Louis Harris is right, they also
represent "a quiet revolution" away from materialism.

Warren Johnson says such people are a kind of advance team for the
rest of society. "If the pioneers do their work well," Johnson says, "in
discovering or reviving new ways suitable for our transition to a frugal
economy, and the rest of society eases in the same direction with hope
and good humour, then running out of energy will no longer generate
the nightmares it now does."

But being some researcher's idea of a new-age pioneer on the
frontiers of social change and actually being one are two different
things.

"There must have been something that build-your-own-house book   10
from the library didn't tell me about setting in windows," Larry jokes
later, in the spring, when it is okay to joke about such things. "Every
time there's a strong wind from the southeast we get snow or rain in our
house."

Larry, thirty-two, is a leather-worker. He spends the greater part of
every day in a studio off his house stitching leather on a large, industrial
sewing machine. Right now his workroom is heaped with yards and
yards of butter-soft chamois suede that will be made into fancy dresses
and shirts for the summer's crop of tourists who happen to visit *Ward
and Eis*, a Petoskey gallery. He estimates his annual income from the
leather-work, depending on the year, is between four and eight thousand dollars.

He is a man with a kind face framed by a full beard. He wears his
thick brown hair shoulder length, like George Washington's in the
paintings public schools usually hang above the chalkboard and under
the American flag; right now it is pulled back by two yellow duck
barrettes he has borrowed from his daughter Maya.

"The first person to ever see me with these duck barrettes was the

UPS[2] man," Larry says. "He brought a shipment of leather and I was so happy to see him with it I went running out into the yard and forgot all about my barrettes. After that I figured, 'what the hell.' But I take them out when I go to town."

Outside his recently completed studio is a rubble of sand, cement blocks, and old building materials. Beyond that are rolling hills where the spring sun has begun to burn through the snow to the brown earth, and what's left now looks like marble cake.

In 1977 Larry and Geradine bought the twenty acres where they live for three thousand dollars down in wedding money, a fifteen-year land contract, and monthly payments of one hundred forty-two dollars. That first summer they lived in a tent, and the snow was flying before they were inside a makeshift house that both of them sometimes refer to as a shack or a cabin. The exterior of the house has a modern, angular design; inside it is finished with barn wood and stucco and resembles a cottage in the Black Forest.[3]

Larry built the house with salvage lumber, yard-sale hardware, a lot of gumption, and a little experience. Geradine, as they used to say in the Shake 'n' Bake ads, "halped"[4] — when she wasn't tending to the couple's two daughters, Maya, five, and Leah, two. In order to have a steady source of income with which to buy building materials, Larry stopped doing leather-work for the first two years they lived there and took a minimum wage job at a nearby ski resort. He estimates he has twenty-five hundred dollars hard cash in the house. The house was just recently insured for forty thousand dollars.

"I was amazed they could insure it for that much," he says. "I called them up and said, 'there must be some mistake.' They sent a guy out and he went through the whole place and they still insured it for that much."

Larry is pleased that his hard work and long hours paid off, but he says there are trade-offs. He gestures toward the building materials lying on the ground outside his studio window. "You live with materials lying around for years because you can only work in your spare time. You also learn to live with mistakes. You can't learn everything from library books. There are mistakes I've made on this house that would keep me awake nights, if I let them."

Larry is stirring sand on top of the wood stove in his workroom. The hot sand will be used to fill and shrink newly made replicas of eighth-century leather tankards. He says they were the forerunners of beer

15

---

[2]*UPS:* United Parcel Service, a delivery company.

[3]*Black Forest:* forest in southwest Germany famed for its beauty.

[4]*Shake 'n Bake ads, "halped":* Shake 'n Bake, a packaged seasoning for chicken or other meats, is shaken in a bag along with the food to be coated. Its TV ads featured a little girl saying she "halped" her mother prepare dinner.

steins and are technically called "blackjacks." Originally produced by craftsmen in the European Guild, Larry says he believes they are now reproduced in only two places in the United States: Williamsburg, Virginia, and Greenfield Village in Detroit. Larry has researched the making of the tankards as part of a special commission from a client.

Larry is the second oldest of six children and grew up in Davison, 20 Michigan, near Flint. He says he has always enjoyed making things and as a child liked to help his father with household projects. He attributes much of his building skill and his self-reliance to the training his father provided. Although Larry attended Michigan State on a scholarship, he dropped out after three years to become a leather-worker.

He says he was profoundly influenced by the death of his father in 1970, when he was twenty and his father was forty-two. "My father spent his whole life working for goals he died too young to ever achieve. I learned from my father's death that anything can happen at any time, and so I decided early on that I should always do what I want to do now, before it's too late."

"Values," Lester R. Brown writes in his new book entitled *Building a Sustainable Society*, "are the key to the evolution of society, not only because they influence behavior, but also because they determine a society's priorities and thus its ability to survive."

Yet in Larry's case, he says it is difficult for him to know if he is indeed part of the evolution of society's values or if, as some of his more affluent neighbors might maintain, he is simply pulling land values down.

"Some of our neighbors," Larry says, "I think, although I don't know this, probably see our house as an eyesore. When they go to sell their house or their land, the value is less because of my building materials lying around my house and my old blue Volkswagen sitting out there in the weeds. Their parents, on the other hand, and their grandparents who homesteaded this land, are very encouraging. They give us vegetables out of their garden and let us haul water from their wells and say, 'You kids are doing *fine, just fine.*' We're living the way they did and it doesn't bother them. I myself don't know if we're a throwback to an earlier time, or the wave of the future, or some combination of both. I'd like to think it's the latter, or that we're achieving a balance between the two, but I really don't know."

Larry says he sees society becoming more and more polarized be- 25 tween an ethic of materialism and its opposite. "I think of my friends who have decided to spend their lives making money. I haven't. I've made the opposite choice. But I guess it disturbs me because it's like choosing up sides. Now we're on opposite sides of the battle. But it's not as clear-cut as a battle. It's more subtle than that."

In a chapter entitled "Civilization in Transition," in *Voluntary Simplicity*, Duane Elgin writes that American society is in a critical state of change. "A wartime psychology prevails," he says, "but it is a war without a visible opponent. In reality we are at war with ourselves and our fear of the unknown challenge that lies beyond the industrial era." It is not a war that is being fought in the streets, but rather one that is being fought in the hearts and minds of the people and in the way they live and conduct their lives.

"It's like we're all part of some Darwinian experiment," Larry sums up, "and we just don't know yet which group is going to evolve in the direction of survival: the old-fashioned seekers of the American dream of money, or the new-fashioned seekers of a more humanitarian and spiritual American dream."

It is pretty where the Doe-Simkins live. Even during one of the coldest springs in memory, the hills are graceful and pleasing to the eye. It is a landscape reminiscent of that in a J.R.R. Tolkien[5] story, the kind of setting where one expects to see a troop of elves come marching gaily down the road singing, "Over hill, over dale . . ." on their way to some noble adventure.

When the sun sets in these hills — over in the west where the clouds roll and bank over Lake Michigan — it creates a kaleidoscope of a fuchsia and peach and cerise and orange and crimson sky for thirty minutes or more. Yet even the rosiest glow from the loveliest sunset doesn't exactly create a daily idyll.

For three years the family lived without a well on their land. Instead, they hauled water from the neighbors' well and didn't take a lot of baths. In the winter, when their quarter-mile-long driveway is impassable, this meant carrying forty-pound drums of water, uphill, every other day on a toboggan. 30

Even now, in the winter, everything else — propane, groceries, two children too small to walk — has to be hauled up the driveway. Geradine is a midwife and on winter nights when she is called out to attend a birth she must navigate the long driveway on foot, sometimes through waist-deep snow drifts and sometimes with Maya on a sled and Leah in a backpack. Geradine is short, five feet and no more, and it's a trek that would daunt many a six-footer — without the kids.

"We wait for the hard crust snow in March," Larry says, "we can walk on top of that. But then in April there's mud. We can't bring the car up in that either, unless we do it early in the morning after a hard frost. In summer it's okay, but in the fall it gets muddy again if we have a lot of rain."

Together Larry and Geradine are helping Maya and Leah make

[5]*J.R.R. Tolkien:* English scholar and writer (1892–1973) best known for his fantasy works *The Hobbit* and the trilogy *The Lord of the Rings.*

bread. Maya is making a fruit-basket, and Leah is making doughy, whole wheat balls she calls babies. Leah's "babies" have little flecks of something in them that Larry finally determines to be blue Play-Doh.

"What we have," Geradine says, "is a lot of hard work and some deprivation, offset by almost unlimited freedom and control over our own lives. We don't punch a time clock or work for a boss. We don't have weeks, or weekends. We can follow the natural rhythms of the seasons and of our own intuitive sense of things. There's an exhilarating sense of personal power that comes from living here, but there's also a lot of personal responsibility." She tilts her head to the side. "Sometimes I think we must be crazy to live this way — especially in winter — but deep down I know it's the only right way."

It is a life-style that is looking better and better as times get harder 35 and harder, Larry Doe says, pointing out that people everywhere are losing their jobs, their homes, and their businesses. In Michigan, where unemployment ranges between twelve and twenty-five percent, depending on the area and the time of year, everyone knows someone who is laid off. He cites a recent *Newsweek* article that says that in the United States as a whole between 1980 and 1981, mortgage foreclosures increased by thirty-one percent, business failures by forty-five percent, and bankruptcies by eleven percent.

But the Doe-Simkins believe they are only minimally affected by the U.S. economy. They have no debts and, other than a $142 a month land contract payment, no mortgages. They are self-employed and so do not have to worry about losing a job. They grow their own food and so are only slightly affected by inflated prices at the grocery store. They heat with wood and so fuel costs are not a major concern. Larry does his own auto repairs, and with yard sales, thrift shops, and sewing, Geradine provides the family with clothing and household needs. They belong to a food co-op and barter for many goods and services. They pay three hundred dollars a year in property taxes and no income tax.

"There's a lot of security in knowing you're so far below the poverty line you don't have to worry about getting any poorer," Larry says.

When the ice goes out and the birds come back, then people in northern Michigan begin to socialize again. Tonight is March 21, the spring equinox, the time when the sun rises precisely in the east and sets precisely in the west, a time when the day and the night, the length of light and dark, will be exactly the same — and Larry and Geradine are having some friends in to celebrate. She is cooking something that looks like it will be refried beans and cheese nachos covered with chopped green onion and tomatoes, and as she cooks she talks.

"The thing I have given up to live here," she says, "is the security of belonging to the mainstream, the security of being viewed as normal."

She talks about her neighborhood in Dearborn Heights where she   40
grew up. She was the oldest of four children. "I was always with a
bunch of kids, always organizing something. We'd go on a picnic to the
park and pretend we were all orphans. Or we'd put on a play. We were
always doing crazy things that were fun." Later, she says, at the Catholic, all-girl Holy Rosary High School in downtown Detroit, she was a
member of the student council, a class officer, and a good student.

She says she began to change from what she calls a middle-class life-
style when she was ten and John F. Kennedy was running for president.
"I organized all the kids in my neighborhood into this huge marching
band with tin pans and spoons and a large banner that said, 'Vote for
J.F.K.' and we toured Dearborn Heights. I was young and didn't know
much, but it seemed that Kennedy stood for something more than other
presidents had: something human, or hopeful, or caring. And I suppose
I could relate to the fact that he was Catholic." Her father, at that time
a Nixon fan and a Republican, was embarrassed by the commotion
Geradine made in the neighborhood, and he took her banner out of the
garage and burned it. Later he apologized and he and Geradine's
mother would become what Geradine calls "more socially aware" and
"actually lead the way for me to become more aware."

In the 1960s, Geradine says, Pope John XXIII issued a papal en-
cyclical that said, in essence, that all Catholics should begin to live more
like Christ. "My parents took this seriously, and so did I." By the time
Geradine was in her third year at Wayne State University she had
decided, she says, "there was more to learn outside of school than in
school." She abandoned her plans to become a teacher and instead
joined an antiwar group called the Detroit Peace Collective. She wrote
speeches, and she gave speeches; she went on national speaking tours
and protest marches and generally worked to end the war in Vietnam.
In 1972 she decided she needed a personal life. She moved north to
Traverse City where she met Larry.

"We discovered we both wanted the same things: a little farm in the
country, children, marriage, and a life doing work we liked, which for
Larry was leather-work and for me at the time was creative sewing. It
was a fantasy but it seemed like one we could achieve."

It turned out to be harder than either of them had ever dreamed.
"We learned that you can't be a craftsman and have a middle-class life-
style. It takes a lot of work, a lot of self-discipline, and there's very little
money in it." To this day the Doe-Simkins family has no health insurance, no life insurance, no pension plan, no Social Security benefits,
and, at their income level, no way to save for their retirement.

The alleged thirty-three million persons who are living in a deliber-   45
ately unmaterialistic manner are described by the Stanford Research
Institute as *inner-directed consumers*. "These are people," the researchers say, "who are often younger persons (members of the post-

World-War-II-baby-boom generation) from middle-class backgrounds who are relatively well-educated. Inner-directed consumers tend to be idealistic, spiritually inclined, ecologically oriented, and experimental in their manner of living. Members of this group consume according to their inner sense of what is appropriate, rather than relying on prevailing fashion or the expectations of others as their primary guide."

Unlike *need-driven consumers*, who mainly want to know where their next meal is coming from, and unlike *outer-directed consumers*, who worry a lot about what other people think of them, the *inner-directed consumers*, according to the Stanford researchers, are unconcerned about the opinions of others.

Geradine disagrees.

"It bothers me a lot," she says, "to be poor. I still haven't gotten used to it. It's not the way I was raised. It also causes me a great deal of anxiety to realize I'm so far removed from the path of my high school friends.

"My dream," she says, "is not to be isolated out in the country, but to experience the commonality of the human spirit. And I'm not living out here because I'm afraid of the bomb dropping or don't want to live in cities. I certainly don't see any virtue in poverty. In a way I guess I'd like to go back to the middle class because it would bring me closer to the majority of people again. But for me personally, to give up this way of life would mean that I'm not psychologically strong enough to do it. For me, this is the way of survival of the future."

Geradine has been chopping onions furiously as she talks.   50

She is Irish, second generation, and right now she looks particularly Irish as her thick, hip-length braid of reddish-brown hair sways back and forth as she talks.

"People who are initiators and self-motivators are going to survive," she says. "People who are dependent on the culture the way it is now are going to be utterly lost. The people who survive are going to be the people who know how to grow their own food, create their own jobs, provide their own health care, educate their kids, and get along with other people. This is lost information. These are survival skills we all used to have that we just don't have a handle on any more."

The people who come for dinner that night are perhaps as good a reflection of Larry and Geradine as anything else might be. Lori Cruden is a midwife who supports herself and her six-year-old son, Gabriel, with the proceeds from her mail-order herb garden business. Rick Jones is a Tennessee hillbilly and a sculptor of unicorns and wood sprites. He was recently a guest artist in an "Artists in the Schools" program. His wife, Carol, is a speech pathologist. They are all in their late twenties or early thirties.

On the whole they are artistic, pantheistic, humanistic, and highly independent in their thinking. There seems to be an unstated agreement among them that they form a kind of extended family, a community, the beginnings of a new society. They resemble, as much as anything else, the descendants of the people who came over on the *Mayflower*. They would be recognized anywhere in the world as Americans.

That night around a bonfire, they celebrate the beginning of spring, 55 the return of the birds, and friendship.

"We are here tonight," Geradine says as she tells everyone to hold hands, "to be together and eat and thank God for bringing the warm weather back — sooner please."

In a book called simply, *Families*, former *Life* magazine staffer Jane Howard points out that a family can be any group of people who are independent and who, especially, "enliven their lives with ritual."

"The best families I know," she writes, "are the ones who celebrate the ceremonies that link people to the earth, to those who have trod it before them, and to one another." And that, in a way, is what the bonfire is all about: a linking to the earth and to the people who have trod it before.

"These are times of intense change," Geradine says, "but we must not stop there and dig into depression. We have to see these times as a wonderful opportunity for renewal and rebirth of the human potential."

One Saturday afternoon about a week later there is a gray, March 60 rain falling outside. Water runs down the driveway in small streams and sluices. An old Gene Kelly movie, *Brigadoon*, is playing on TV.

It is hard to find simple solutions to complex problems, but the mythical town of Brigadoon, in Scotland, has succeeded. Long years ago, so the story goes, the town's pastor decided the world was becoming too nasty a place for his people. And so he sent a special prayer heavenward that all the people in the town of Brigadoon would fall asleep that night, and when they woke up again it would be a hundred years later. He prayed that one whole day and night in the town of Brigadoon would be a hundred years in the rest of the world. And in the meantime Brigadoon would be enveloped in a thick mist that would part only once in every hundred years so that it and the rest of the world could get a glimpse of each other. This way, so the theory went, the town would never be exposed to evil long enough to be changed by it.

"This is a perfect day for *Brigadoon*," Geradine says as she watches the mist fill the little valley between her house and the rise of hills to the south of it.

Geradine has been singing along with Gene Kelly to the tune of "Bonnie Jean," and "The Heather on the Hill,"and dancing barefoot in front of the TV, her long hair swaying. "Did you know I could dance all these old Irish dances?" she asks her husband.

"Yes, Geradine. I know."

For the time being, Geradine says, it seems as though their family, 65
like the town of Brigadoon, has escaped from the outside world. Yet, she
says, the doubt persists: are they simply living beyond the pale or are
they part of some as yet undisclosed brave new world?[6] She turns to her
husband, "Which is it, Larry?"

"I don't know," he says. "Maybe we'll have to wait another one
hundred years for the mist to part again."

[6]*brave new world:* an oft-quoted phrase from Shakespeare's *The Tempest* (act 5,
scene 1, line 183).

Engaging the Text

1. What advantages and disadvantages do you see in the way Simkins and Doe
live? What advantages and disadvantages do you think they would perceive in
your life?

2. Do you think Simkins and Doe are "a throwback to an earlier time, or the
wave of the future, or some combination of both" (para. 24) — or perhaps
something else altogether? Are they close to nature in any beneficial way or only
exposed to nature's threats?

3. Discuss Simkins's development. What experiences led her to become a modern homesteader? How does she feel about her current way of life? How would
you characterize her attitude?

4. Stocking quotes Doe using the terms "battle," "evolve," "survival," and
"some Darwinian experiment" (paras. 25, 27); similarly, she quotes writer
Duane Elgin saying "a wartime psychology prevails" (para 26). To what struggle are these people referring? Is middle-class life in the United States in any
serious jeopardy? Why is the terminology of warfare or "survival of the fittest"
appropriate or inappropriate?

Exploring Connections

5. Define the Doe-Simkins work ethic. Where would it fit in the development
of the American work ethic as described by Christopher Lasch in "Changing
Modes of Making It" (p. 27)?

6. To what extent do Simkins and Doe resemble Stephen Cruz (p. 36), who
abandoned success in the city to farm and teach? How are they different? Do
you consider Simkins and Doe successful?

7. John (Fire) Lame Deer (p. 128) says that a new spirit is moving, "not only
among Indians but among whites and Blacks, too, especially among young
people" (para 17). He also says, "It won't be bad, doing without many things
you are now used to, things taken out of the earth and wasted foolishly" (para.
19). How well does the life chosen by Simkins and Doe fit Lame Deer's
philosophy?

Extending the Critical Context

8. Working in groups, sketch a proposal for creating an urban homestead based on the notion of "frugal economy." What advantages, if any, would be offered by a life of voluntary simplicity in the city?

9. Read and report on either *Muddling Toward Frugality* by Warren Johnson or *Voluntary Simplicity* by Duane Elgin. In particular, define the thesis of the book you choose and judge whether or not Simkins and Doe exemplify the book's philosophy.

being property once myself

LUCILLE CLIFTON

"I am a Black woman poet, and I sound like one." Lucille Clifton's distinctive voice comes through even in this extremely short poem, which says more about people and nature in thirty-nine words than most politicians say in a lifetime. Clifton was born in 1936 in Depew, New York, and was educated at Fredonia State Teachers College and Howard University. She has published several books for children and six volumes of poetry and has won many prizes for her work. Clifton is currently a professor of literature at the University of California, Santa Cruz. This poem originally appeared in Good Woman: Poems and a Memoir, 1969–1980 *(1987).*

being property once myself
i have a feeling for it,
that's why i can talk
about environment.
what wants to be a tree,
ought to be he can be it.
same thing for other things.
same thing for men.

Engaging the Text

1. Restate the poem's argument in your own words. What does it say about environment — and about people? (The poem is short enough that you may want to explain each phrase; for example, in what ways has the speaker been

property herself?) After clarifying the poem's meaning, debate the points it makes.

2. Is a poem that can be read in less than a minute likely to be dismissed or easily forgotten? Discuss the effect of the extreme brevity of this poem.

3. Your instructor would probably not accept the grammar of lines 5 and 6 if you wrote something like this in an essay. What's the effect of this phrasing and of the informal style throughout the poem?

Exploring Connections

4. Discuss whether Clifton's view of nature seems essentially compatible with John (Fire) Lame Deer's (p. 128) or whether it is markedly different. How do you account for the similarities or differences you see?

Extending the Critical Context

5. As children we have all, in a sense, "[been] property once." Freewrite a page or two about a childhood memory of a moment or situation in which you felt owned. Follow up by trying to capture the experience in a poem.

6. Clifton has made several audio and video recordings, including a segment for the PBS series *The Power of the Word* (Bill Moyers, 1989). Check the holdings of your campus audio-video library and listen to at least one recording or watch at least one videotape of Clifton. Report to the class on what you learned and how it affects your reading of this poem.

Split Culture

Susan Griffin

The final selection in this chapter represents a school of thought new enough that you may well not have heard of it: ecofeminism. As its name suggests, ecofeminism combines activism in environmental issues with feminist values and ways of knowing. In showing how ecological and feminist issues are fundamentally related, this essay critiques centuries-old habits of thought that Griffin (b. 1943) believes cut us off not only from the natural world around us but also from parts of ourselves that Western civilization has tried (with disastrous consequences) to deny. Griffin, an influential feminist theorist, is a prolific writer whose work includes an Emmy-winning play, Voices *(1975), two volumes of poetry, and nonfiction books on motherhood, pornography, and rape. "Split Culture" first appeared in* The Schumacher Lectures, *edited by Satish Kumar (1984); Griffin's latest book*, A Chorus of Stones: The Private Life of War, *is forthcoming.*

We who are born into this civilization have inherited a habit of mind. We are divided against ourselves. We no longer feel ourselves to be a part of this earth. We regard our fellow creatures as enemies. And, very young, we even learn to disown a part of our own being. We come to believe that we do not know what we know. We grow used to ignoring the evidence of our own experience, what we hear or see, what we feel in our own bodies. We come into maturity keeping secrets. But we forget this secret knowledge and feel instead only a vague shame, a sense that perhaps we are not who we say we are. Yet we have learned well to pretend that what is true is not true. In some places the sky is perpetually gray, and the air is filled with a putrid smell. Forests we loved as children disappear. The waters we once swam are forbidden to us now because they are poisoned. We remember there was a sweet taste to fruit, that there used to be more birds. But we do not read these perceptions as signs of our own peril.

Long ago we gave up ourselves. Now, if we are dying by increments, we have ceased to be aware of this death. How can we know our own death if we do not know our own existence? We have traded our real existence, our real feelings for a delusion. Instead of fighting for our lives, we bend all our efforts to defend delusion. We deny all evidence at hand that this civilization, which has shaped our minds, is also destroying the earth.

The dividedness of our minds is etched into our language. To us, the word *thought* means an activity separate from feeling, just as the word *mind* suggests a place apart from the body and from the rhythms of the earth. We do not use the word *animal* to describe human qualities. Our word *spirit* rises in our imaginations above the earth as if we believed that holiness exists in an inverse proportion to gravity. The circumstance of our birth is common to us; we are all of woman born. But we have a word *race* which suggests to us that human beings belong to different categories of virtue by birth. Through the words *masculine* and *feminine*, which we use to designate two alien and alienated poles of human behavior, we make our sexuality a source of separation. We divide ourselves and all that we know along an invisible borderline between what we call Nature and what we believe is superior to Nature.

Now we find ourselves moving almost without recourse toward a war that will destroy all of our lives. And were this not true, we have learned that the way we live has damaged the atmosphere, our bodies, even our genetic heritage so severely that perhaps we cannot save ourselves. We are at the edge of death, and yet, like one who contemplates suicide, we are our own enemies. We think with the very mind that has brought disaster on us. And this mind, taught and trained by this civilization, does not know itself. This is a mind in exile from its own wisdom.

According to this worldview — a view whose assumptions are so widely accepted by this civilization that we do not even think of it as an ideology — there is a hierarchy to existence. God and the angels, things pure in spirit and devoid of any material content, come first. Everything earthly is corrupt. But among the corrupt, human beings are of the highest spiritual order, more significant, valuable, and trustworthy than animals, or certainly trees or, of course, tomatoes, and obviously more intelligent than mountains, or oceans, or particles of sand. Among human beings, a similar order exists. Those of the human species who belong to what is thought of as the white race, and those who are part of the masculine gender, are at the top of this hierarchy. Various glosses on this fundamental belief place the rest of us in different descending orders.

We have learned of the scientific revolution that it was a victory over the irrational, over magical thought that led to the Inquisition[1] and the witch burnings. And we do not commonly associate the philosophy of St. Augustine[2] about men and women with the scientific worldview because we are accustomed to thinking that science and religion are at opposite positions in a polemic[3] that expressed itself in the trial of Galileo.[4] Despite the fact that Galileo recanted[5] to the church, we no longer believe the world was literally created in seven days, nor do we place the earth at the center of the solar system.

But what we have not considered is that a civilization may suffer a great transformation in its institutions and its philosophy — power can shift from church to state, and the authority for knowledge from priest to scientist — and yet still retain, in a new guise and a new language, the essence of the old point of view. Such is the case with the scientific revolution, so that many assumptions, methods, and even questions we

[1]*Inquisition . . . witch burnings:* the Inquisition was a tribunal organized by the Roman Catholic church in the Middle Ages to suppress heresy. Heretics were fined, imprisoned, tortured, and sometimes put to death. The Spanish Inquisition, which started some two hundred fifty years later in 1478, was harsher and freer with the death penalty. Its main targets were Jews, Muslims, and witches. As many as one hundred witches were burned in a single day in *autos-da-fé,* or mass burnings. The persecution of witches lasted into the eighteenth century. See also "What Price Independence?" by Rose Weitz, p. 257.

[2]*St. Augustine:* Christian scholar (354–430) widely recognized as the first theologian. The most famous of his many works are *Confessions* and *City of God.*

[3]*polemic:* a controversial argument.

[4]*Galileo:* Italian astronomer (1564–1642) tried for heresy by the Inquisition for proposing that the earth revolved around the sun rather than vice versa.

[5]*recant:* to retract a statement, often officially.

take to be scientific, actually partake of the same paradigm that in an earlier age we described as Christian.

Let us look at Newton's[6] *Optics* for an example. Before Newton's work on optics, many different ideas about vision were believed, including the notion that a ray of light emanated from the human eye and illuminated the world. Through observation and experiment, Newton concluded that color is not a property of the eye nor the property of any object but is instead produced by the retina, sensitive to light refracted at different angles. This and like discoveries in the seventeenth and eighteenth centuries fell into a philosophical doctrine that was taken to be an experimentally proven vision of the true nature of the world. The scientific point of view argued that we cannot trust our senses, that we are deceived by the appearance of the material world, that color is a form of illusion, that color is simply a figment of our minds and does not exist.[7]

Thus if religion told us that the earth was a corrupt place, that our true home was heaven, that sensual feeling was not to be trusted and could lead us to hell and damnation, science did not in essence contradict that doctrine. For science, too, told us not to trust our senses, that matter is deceptive, and that we are alien to our surroundings. If, then, religion told us that our own senses could not be trusted and that therefore we must bow to scripture and the authority of the priest, now science tells us that we must bow to the truth of objective experimental data and the authority of scientific experts. In both systems, not only are we alienated from a world that is described as deceiving us; we are also alienated from our own capacity to see and hear, to taste and touch, to know and describe our own experience.

Such is the strength of this old way of thinking — that the earth and what is natural in ourselves is not to be trusted — that it hardly occurs to us that there is another way to interpret Newton's discovery; we have confused his discovery with our old paradigmatic vision.

For indeed one can make a very different interpretation of Newton's observations of the nature of optics. Instead of believing we are deceived by matter or our senses, instead of deciding that color does not exist, we

10

---

[6]*Newton:* Sir Isaac Newton (1642–1727), English philosopher and mathematician best known for formulating the laws of gravity.

[7]"I cannot sufficiently admire the eminence of those men's wits, that have received and held it to be true, and with the sprightliness of their judgements offered such violence to their own senses, so that they have been able to prefer that which their reason dictated to them, to that which sensible experiments represented most manifestly to the contrary. . . . I cannot find any bounds for my admiration, how that reason in Aristarchus and Copernicus, to commit such a rape on their senses; as in despite thereof to make herself mistress of credulity." (From Galileo's *Dialogue Concerning the Two Great Systems of the World,* Vol. I, as cited in E. A. Burtt, *The Metaphysical Foundations of Modern Science,* New York, 1954.) [Author's note]

can assert, since we do experience color, that in our experience of color we have entered into a union with what we perceive. That together with matter we create color. That our sense of color is indeed evidence of a profound, sensual, and emotional connection we have with all that is part of this earth. That the joy color gives us is perhaps part of the balance of the universe.

There is another example of how the old paradigm affects what we take to be impartial science, from Francis Bacon's[8] argument that science ought to proceed by experimentation. It must be close to self-evident, one can object here, that scientific experimentation is a movement toward respect of the material world. Before the idea of experiment, the nature of the material world was not even considered worthy of observation. Speculation and deductive reason were the sources of truth. I must digress for a moment to point out that if one is part of Nature oneself, speculation, especially when it involves self-reflection, *is* a kind of experiment. And perhaps this is not really a digression. For indeed, what is missing in Bacon's idea of scientific experiment is any self-reflection. He assumes that a superior objectivity, a state of emotional and physical detachment, can belong to the scientist who performs an experiment.

In different ages, both religion and science have been the focus of our hopes and the arbiters of what we call truth. Because they have expressed the consciousness of a whole civilization, both institutions also carry with them and epitomize, in their ideas and traditions, the troubled conflict, the dividedness, of our consciousness. Both institutions within Western civilization have been shaped by and have deepened our alienation from this earth.

If the church once offered the denigration of incarnate[9] life as a solution to the human condition, now science offers us the control of matter as our rescue. But what can be wrong with cultivating either the human spirit or the soil we live on? Human creativity is a part of Nature, but rather we think of ourselves as working against Nature. The paradigm that tells us we are apart from and above this earth is not simply an intellectual response to Nature. It is instead a deeply fearful attitude. And the fear that lies under this thought, like all fear, turns into rage.

The pursuit of scientific knowledge in our civilization is beset by an emotional dilemma. In order to control Nature, we must know Nature. But just as we are seeking to know, there is a knowledge we fear. We are afraid to remember what we, in our bodies and in our feelings, still know, but what, in our fragmented, civilized consciousness we have

15

---

[8]*Francis Bacon:* English philosopher and essayist (1561–1626).
[9]*incarnate:* in human form, as in the phrase "the devil incarnate." The church held that spiritual life and afterlife were important in contrast to mere bodily existence.

been persuaded to forget. That, like the forests we destroy, or the rivers we try to tame, *we* are Nature.

The discovery of the solar system, of gravitational law, of evolution, of the microscopic world of the cell, of the genetic information that is part of matter, of the nature of light, and of the continuum between matter and energy, should transform consciousness so that we in this civilization might begin to regard the human condition with humility rather than arrogance. The thinkers who made what we call the scientific revolution had begun to discover a vast matrix of natural order, a very large wisdom whose boundaries we cannot even imagine. Just as the Earth is not the center of the solar system, so the biosphere[10] is not centered on the human species nor circumscribed by human culture. We are dependent on the universe around us not only to breathe and eat, but even to keep our feet on the ground. For we do this not at will but because we exist in a field of energy. All that we do is shaped by and partakes of that field. And our perceptions and what we experience as real depend upon the nature and movements of matter and light. Not only are we mortal, but the very human form suffers a slow change over generations. Between my arm and the air, between the movements of a flame and what we call the solid mass of wood, there is no boundary.

But we have come to rely upon another image of ourselves: as discrete static beings. And we have learned to think that we must take control of our environment in order to survive. We believe that it is a cultural order, the order we have willed, and not natural order, the order of which we are a part, that makes us safe. Thus, if the discoveries of modern science have given us the means to manipulate Nature, they have also terrified us. And this is why, in the fourteenth century, when science began to challenge our old idea of who we are, the witch burnings began. The slave trade began in the sixteenth century at the height of this revolution in thought. And in the twentieth century, when science again questioned the old notion that we are above Nature, the Nazi Holocaust and now the nuclear holocaust have commenced.

But in separating Nature from culture within himself, the man who believes this delusion has split his own needs and desires from his intelligence and from all meaning. Thus his own desires return to him as meaningless, as cruel and senseless violations. Out of the lost fragments of his own psyche, he has created a monstrous image to contain his own self-loathing. Thus the pornographer creates out of his own sexual desires a meeting between two bodies that is without emotion, without any deep or soulful connection. And when he invents a woman, a pornographic heroine, he gives her a body without a spirit, without any sensibility, without a significant consciousness. She is like the dead matter, the brute matter, of scientific theory.

[10]*biosphere:* living beings together with their environment.

And the modern mind invents the same image of Nature itself. Matter is dead. A forest has no spiritual life. When Reagan[11] was governor of California, he said in response to ecologists who were trying to preserve the great coastal forests, "If you have seen one tree you have seen them all." Believing a mountain to have no inner reason, no sacredness unto itself, the modern technologist takes coal out of the soil simply by cutting away half of the face of the mountain. Suddenly the whole of the mountain begins to erode. Chemicals from this erosion enter the streams in an unnatural balance. Trees, plants, fish, animals die. The countryside, once breathtakingly beautiful, begins to look like a place of devastation. He transforms the mountain into what he believed the mountain to be.

In the same way, society transforms those who have become symbols of Nature into objects of degradation. If a woman is a symbol of Nature wherever she is pictured as submissive or wherever she is disempowered in the social order, we can believe that culture has a supernatural power over Nature. If the Jew, who we imagine plots against us, is stripped of all civil rights, we can believe that we have control over natural power. Even those of us who suffer materially and psychologically from this delusory system of control have been educated to feel a false sense of safety from it.

Yet indeed none of us are safe. Now our lives are, every one of us, endangered by this delusion. For the delusion itself cannot rest. It is like the hungry tiger of our fearful dreams: devouring.

When the technologist destroys the mountain, he must feel, momentarily, a false sense of triumph. Like the explorers of an earlier age, he has conquered this piece of earth. He has wrested from her what he wanted. He has beaten her. And yet now, as he looks on the devastation he has caused, he cannot help but see there an image of his own inner life. His soul has been robbed by this theft. The death he sees before him must at one and the same time remind him of the part of himself he has murdered and his own inevitable mortality which, in the very act of controlling Nature, he has tried to deny.

The very images and avenues that express our power over Nature take us back to our own memory and knowledge of Nature's power both inside and outside of ourselves. Therefore our delusion demands that we gain a greater control over Nature. We must escalate our efforts. We must improve our technology.

One can see the dimensions of this madness more clearly in the development of the nuclear power industry. At each turning point, when a piece of human technology was seen to fail, the architects of this industry never questioned the fundamental premise that we are meant

[11]*Reagan:* former President Reagan (b. 1911) was governor of California from 1967 to 1974. As governor he cut the state budget for welfare, medical services, and education.

to make use of the energy inside the atom by splitting matter apart. Instead, another technological solution was offered. And each technological solution has in turn posed a greater danger.

Repeatedly one reads in the newspapers that an error in the design 25 of a nuclear power plant has been covered over by the men who build and operate the plants. In many cases the economic motivation for such a denial is clear. To design the plant properly would take many more millions of dollars. But even given this economic motive, one wonders why these men, who often live in the area of the plant and work there every day, are not afraid for their own lives or the lives of their families. But the answer is that they rely for a feeling of safety not on rational information about natural law, but on the delusion that culture, through technology or any other means, can control Nature.

The mind that invents a delusion of power over Nature in order to feel safe is afraid of fear itself. And the more this mind learns to rely on delusion, the less tolerance this mind has for any betrayal of that delusion. For we must remember that this mind has denied that it itself is a thing of Nature. It has begun to identify not only its own survival, but its own existence with culture. The mind believes that it exists because what it thinks is true. Therefore, to contradict delusion is to threaten the mind's very existence. And the ideas, words, numbers, concepts have become more real to this mind than material reality.

Thus when this mind is threatened by a material danger, it does not respond rationally. For this mind has lost touch with material reality. It is a mind possessed by madness, by a hallucinated idea of its own power. We can see such a mind at work in Stalin, during the period of Soviet industrialization. In this period, the Soviet Union as a nation faced the grave material danger of hunger and starvation. And yet, as a solution, Stalin chose to destroy real and operating farms before the new, sanctioned way of farming was functioning. Isaac Deutscher writes vividly of this cast of mind, "The whole experiment seemed to be a piece of prodigious insanity, in which all the rules of logic and principles of economics were turned upside down. It was as if a whole nation had suddenly abandoned and destroyed its houses and huts which, though obsolete and decaying, existed in reality, and moved lock, stock, and barrel, into some illusory buildings."

But what is essential to understand about this mind is that it is in a panic. It will go to any lengths to defend its delusory idea of reality. Those who opposed Stalin's plans for collectivization were sent to prison camps or murdered.

And the extent to which a belief in ideas over reality is a part of this century was predicted by George Orwell in his novel, *1984*, through the humorous but now distressingly accurate parody of a governmental slogan he invented, "Peace is War." Thus today it is actually presented as a rational argument that a buildup in arms, or a "preventative" invasion of another country, is the best way to keep peace.

We all understand economic motivation as fundamental to human   30
nature. And yet we are making a mistake if we believe that this is the only motivation. For economics touch upon reality. It would, after all, be of no economic profit to anyone living to destroy the earth. Such a destruction could only be seen as profitable by a madman. But it is madness and the motivations of madness that I am describing here.

It is only when we understand how economic motivation can be shaped and changed by this madness that we can begin to see the real danger that our culture's state of delusion poses for us. Let us take the slave trade for an example. There is an obvious economic profit to be gained by adventurers from the sale of other human beings. And yet we must question whether simply self-interest leads naturally to such a violation of other beings. Is it not a soul already distorted that can consider enslaving another human being?

Self-interest, the desire to survive, is simply part of flesh, an emotion that arises in us by virtue of our material existence, by virtue even of our love for life and for this earth. But early in childhood we are taught that our survival depends on a freedom from natural power. We are taught that we live not through the understanding of Nature but through the manipulation of Nature.

If one studies the definitions of liberty in the *Oxford English Dictionary* one sees that liberty, first defined as an "exemption or release from captivity, bondage or slavery," later becomes "the faculty or power to do as one likes," and then becomes "an unrestrained use of or access to" — as in "to take liberties with a wench" — and finally, liberty means "at one's power or disposal."

Like the Inquisition and the witch burnings, the slave trade began at the time of the scientific revolution, in the sixteenth century. This revolution threatened to change the old worldview that men ordered Nature and replaced it with an understanding of a natural law to which we are all subject. The delusion that we are free from natural law was endangered. But that freedom could be regained symbolically by enslaving a people whom this culture conceived of as symbols of Nature. At this time and through the nineteenth century it was both a scientific and a general belief that Africans were closer to Nature than white men and women. In the nineteenth century, after evolutionary theory, scientists argued that Africans had descended more directly from primates.

That the slave trade was not motivated by simple economic self-   35
interest becomes more clear when one studies the conditions that had to be endured by the men, women, and children taken into captivity on the slave ships. So many died during these trips across the water, not only from disease and exposure to the elements, but also from the

brutality of the slave traders. Had these men valued their cargo from a simple economic motive they might have taken more care to preserve these lives. But, instead, an unwonted measure of cruelty entered their acts.

Ruth and Jacob Weldon, an African couple who experienced a slave passage, recorded an incident of a child of nine months who was flogged continuously for refusing to eat. Because this beating failed to move the child to eat, the captain ordered that "the child be placed feet first into a pot of boiling water. After trying other tortuous methods with no success, the captain dropped the child and caused its death. Not deriving enough satisfaction from this sadistic act, he then commanded the mother to throw the body of the child overboard. The mother refused but she was beaten until she submitted."

That bell hooks[12] called this behavior sadistic is entirely fitting. Clearly, to murder a child in order to get that child to eat is not rational behavior. Rather, the motive lay elsewhere, with the desire to inflict cruelty for its own sake. But why is it that a slave trader should be cruel to a black child? Because of his blackness this child became, in the insane mind of this civilization, and in the mind of this captain, a symbol of natural power. And the infancy of the boy would remind this man of his own infancy, of his own memory of vulnerability, of his own naturalness. Thus, at one and the same time, he could show his power over Nature, and punish his own vulnerable child, the child within him who was still part of Nature. Underneath his hatred and his cruelty existed a profound self-hatred.

Each time that the child refused to do as he ordered, he was, in an undiscovered region of his own soul, terrified. For this could only mean that he was losing his power, and therefore that his whole existence was being threatened. In this way, the captain could believe that he murdered a nine-month-old child in defense of himself. And if a part of him suffered with that child, he could punish his own compassion, and compassion itself, by forcing the child's mother to throw the child overboard. For such a compassion is also dangerous to this mind, since compassion brings us back to our own capacity to feel.

The same blend of economic and symbolic motivation inspired the Holocaust. At the time of Hitler's rise to power, Germany suffered from a terrible economic depression. And at the same time the old paradigmatic view of man at the center of the universe was again being threatened by scientific discovery. The Nazi Party identified the Jew as responsible for the economic privation. But what is the emotional experience of economic poverty? It is not simply the absence of money that is felt, but the absence of food, or shelter, or safety. Poverty, or even economic insecurity, places us at the mercy of Nature. We become

[12]*bell hooks:* see headnote, page 249.

afraid of loss, of suffering, of death. In its delusion of power over Nature, the European mind had made the Jew the symbol of Nature. Frightened by economic insecurity and by a changing worldview, the Nazi stripped the Jew of civil rights and of the right to own possessions, and the Holocaust began.

We can recognize in Hitler's madness a self-portrait of this civiliza- 40 tion that has shaped our minds. Today modern science makes the same attempt to control procreation through genetic engineering. And in an article by Rosalie Bertell (in *Reclaim the Earth*), one reads that radiation causes genetic mutation and sterility. Thus civilization continues to rage at procreation. And today we also share with the Nazi mind a plan for a final solution to the problem of Nature. This solution is to destroy Nature and replace Nature with a record of her destruction. One sees this pattern again and again in history. Despite the fact that the Third Reich attempted to hide the existence of concentration camps from international scrutiny, the atrocities committed in them were carefully documented by the SS (*Schutzstaffel*, a quasi military unit of the Nazi party). Hitler used to watch films in his private rooms of men and women being murdered and tortured.

Today U.S. military strategies have developed a new plan for winning a nuclear war. They argue that the winner of a nuclear war will be the side that has kept the best record of destruction, the side that knows the most about what has taken place. Hence intelligence-gathering devices are being prepared for launching into space, where these machines will not be destroyed. These men have actually confused their own physical survival with the survival of information.

It is in the nature of the deluded mind to choose to preserve its delusion over its own life. When the German armies were faltering on the Russian Front, Hitler diverted troop and supply trains from that crucial battle in order to carry women, men, and children to Auschwitz to their deaths. He imagined his war against the Jew to be more important. And this was the real war in which his mind was engaged — a war, in fact, with himself. For Hitler's personal hatred for the Jew was a covert hatred of a part of himself.

This is also true of our civilization as a whole. We do not know ourselves. We try to deny what we know. We try to break the heart and the spirit of Nature, which is our own heart and our own spirit. We are possessed by an illness created by our minds, an illness that resembles sado-masochism, schizophrenia, paranoia — all the forms of the troubled soul. We are divided from our selves. We punish ourselves. We are terrified of what we know and who we are. And finally, we belong to a civilization bent upon suicide, secretly committed to destroying Nature and destroying the self that is Nature.

But we each have another secret too, a secret knowledge of wholeness. The schemata of memory exclude our memory of childhood. We do not think we still know what it was to be a child, untaught by culture to be divided from ourselves. Yet within each of us, in our bodies, that memory still exists. Our own breath reminds us of that knowledge, of a time when we were curious, when we let Nature speak to us and in us.

There exists a culture that is not alienated from Nature but expresses Nature. The mind is a physical place. The mind is made up of tissue and blood, of cells and atoms, and possesses all the knowledge of the cell, all the balance of the atom. Human language is shaped to the human mouth, made by and for the tongue, made up of sounds that can be heard by the ear. And there is to the earth and the structure of matter a kind of resonance. We were meant to hear one another, to feel. Our sexual feelings, our capacity for joy and pleasure, our love of beauty, move us toward a love that binds us to an existence. If there is a sound wave anywhere on this earth, if there is the sound of weeping or of laughter, this reaches my ears, reaches your ears. We are connected not only by the fact of our dependency on this biosphere and our participation in one field of matter and energy, in which no boundary exists between my skin and the air and you, but also by what we know and what we feel. Our own knowledge, if we can once again possess it, is as vast as existence.

I am a woman born in and shaped by this civilization, with the mind of this civilization, but also with the mind and body of a woman, with human experience. Suffering grief in my own life, I have felt all the impulses that are part of my culture in my soul. In my resistance to pain and change, I have felt the will toward self-annihilation. And still the singing in my body daily returns me to a love of this earth. I know that by a slow practice, if I am to survive, I must learn to listen to this song.

Engaging the Text

1. Griffin claims that people in Western civilization "are dying by increments" (para. 2). Explain in your own words what she means. Do you agree?

2. Explain Griffin's claim that science and Christianity, often treated as polar opposites, actually share many assumptions. Why is this point important to her argument?

3. Explain the connection that Griffin implies between the technological exploitation of nature and other forms of exploitation — for example, pornography and slavery.

4. Griffin uses several extended examples in her essay: witch hunts, Stalin, the slave trade, Hitler, and the prospect of nuclear war. In a small group, analyze one of Griffin's main examples. How does she interpret it, and how does it advance her broader argument? Share your thoughts with other groups.

5. Debate the claim that "between my arm and the air, between the movements of a flame and what we call the solid mass of wood, there is no boundary" (para. 16).

6. Griffin ends her essay with these sentences: "And still the singing in my body daily returns me to a love of this earth. I know that by a slow practice, if I am to survive, I must learn to listen to this song." Try to explain what she means. How might you begin to translate these highly abstract ideas into practical action?

Exploring Connections

7. Critique the westward expansion of the United States detailed in Patricia Nelson Limerick's "Empire of Innocence" (p. 110) from an ecofeminist perspective.

8. How could Griffin use the selections in this chapter by Haunani-Kay Trask, John (Fire) Lame Deer, Chellis Glendinning, and Lucille Clifton to support her argument?

9. Reread paragraph 45. How closely does Griffin's description of a "love that binds us to an existence" resemble the love described in Gail Tremblay's "The Returning" (p. 162)?

Extending the Critical Context

10. *Gorillas in the Mist* portrays the life of Dian Fossey, who conducted pioneering studies of the lowland gorillas in Africa and championed their preservation. Watch this film and discuss how Griffin would explain Fossey's intuitive understanding of the animals. How would she account for Fossey's development as an independent woman? What questions does this movie raise about conflicts of interest between environmentalists and humans who depend economically on the environment? How might Griffin interpret this conflict as it appears in the movie?

3

Women and Men
in Relationship

Myths of Gender

Common sense tells us that there are obvious differences between females and males: after all, biology, not culture, determines whether or not you're able to bear children. But culture and cultural myths do shape the roles men and women play in our public and private relationships: we are born female and male, but we are made women and men. Sociologists distinguish between sex and gender — between one's biological identity and the conventional patterns of behavior we learn to associate with each sex. While biological sex remains a constant, the definition of "appropriate" gender behavior varies dramatically from one cultural group or historical period to the next. The variations show up markedly in the way we dress. For example, among many American Indian tribes, men who lived and dressed as women were respected as people who possessed special powers, whereas in contemporary Anglo-American culture, cross-dressers are usually seen as deviant or ridiculous. Male clothing in late seventeenth- and early eighteenth-century England would also have failed our current "masculinity" tests: in that period, elaborate laces, brocades, wigs, and even makeup signaled wealth, status, and sexual attractiveness for men and women alike.

History shows us how completely our gender derives from cultural myths about what is proper for men and women to think, enjoy, and do. And history is replete with examples of how the apparent "naturalness" of gender has been used to regulate political, economic, and personal relations between the sexes.

In his classic 1832 treatise on American democracy, for instance, James Fenimore Cooper remarked that women's domestic role and "necessary" subordination to men made them unsuitable for participation in the nation's public life. Thus, he argued, denying women the right to vote was perfectly consistent with the principles of American democracy:

> In those countries where the suffrage is said to be universal, exceptions exist, that arise from the necessity of things. . . . The interests of women being thought to be so identified with those of their male relatives as to become, in a great degree, inseparable, females are, almost generally, excluded from the possession of political rights. There can be no doubt that society is greatly the gainer, by thus excluding one half its members, and the half that is best adapted to give a tone to its domestic happiness, from the strife of parties, and the fierce struggles of political controversies. . . . These exceptions, however, do not very materially affect the principle of political equality. (*The American Democrat*)

Such beliefs have been remarkably persistent in the United States. It took over seventy years of hard political work by both black and white women's organizations to win the right to vote. But while feminists gained the vote for women in 1920 and the legal right to equal educational and employment opportunities in the 1970s, attitudes change even more slowly than laws. Contemporary antifeminist campaigns voice some of the same anxieties as their nineteenth-century counterparts over the "loss" of femininity and domesticity.

Women continue to suffer economic inequities based on cultural assumptions about gender. What's defined as "women's work" — nurturing, feeding, caring for family and home — is devalued and largely uncompensated; a 1980 study by the World Labor Organization showed that while women do two-thirds of the world's work, they receive only 10 percent of its income. But men, too, pay a high price for their culturally imposed roles. Studies of men's mental and physical health suggest that social pressure to "be a man" (that is, to be emotionally controlled, powerful, and successful) can contribute to isolation, anxiety, stress, and illness, and may be partially responsible for men's shorter life span.

This chapter focuses on cultural myths of gender and the influence they wield over human development and personal relationships. Selections in the first half of the chapter examine the way dominant American culture has defined female and male gender roles — and how those roles have in turn defined us. Jamaica Kincaid's "Girl" suggests, through a mother's advice to her daughter, what it means to be raised a woman. Next, Janet Saltzman Chafetz reports on her study of the advantages and disadvantages associated with gender role stereotypes, arguing that we pay a price both for violating and for conforming to traditional gender roles. The oral history that follows, "Nora Quealey," provides a case in point — the portrait of a woman who is deeply ambivalent about the roles she plays as mother, wife, and blue-collar worker. Sam Keen's "The Rite of Work: The Economic Man" looks at how myths of masculinity promoted by corporate America define, or deform, male gender roles. In "Little Miracles, Kept Promises," Sandra Cisneros captures a series of revealing moments in the lives of women and men on the Texas-Mexico border; the story reminds us that there are as many potential myths of gender as there are cultures and subcultures to create them.

The second half of the chapter presents strong rereadings of traditional gender roles and female-male relationships. In "Images of Relationships," psychologist Carol Gilligan presents a radical reinterpretation of conventional gender roles, suggesting that traditionally devalued "feminine" qualities, such as cooperation and nurturing, are better indicators of psychological maturity than more highly regarded "masculine" qualities like independence and competitiveness. Paula Gunn Allen's essay "Where I Come from Is Like This" counters dominant American myths of gender with an eloquent description of the power of tribal women. In "Reflections on Race and Sex," bell hooks ranges from the sexual mythology of slavery to Madonna's music videos as she analyzes the connections between sexism, racism, and the meaning of Black masculinity. Rose Weitz provides a historical overview of social attitudes toward independent women and proposes that heterosexism — prejudice against homosexuals — represents a reaction against perceived threats to male power. "The Two," Gloria Naylor's story about a lesbian couple, challenges stereotypes and invites you to test Weitz's thesis.

Sources

James Fenimore Cooper, *The American Democrat*. N.p.: Minerva Press, 1969.

Marilyn French, *Beyond Power: On Women, Men, and Morals*. New York: Ballantine Books, 1985.

Paula Giddings, *When and Where I Enter: The Impact of Black Women on Race and Sex in America*. New York: Bantam Books, 1984.

Leonard Pitt, *We Americans*, vol. 2, 3rd ed. Dubuque: Kendall/Hunt, 1987.

Will Roscoe, ed., *Living the Spirit: A Gay American Indian Anthology*. New York: St. Martin's Press, 1988.

Before Reading . . .

Working in single-sex groups, make an inventory of gender role characteristics: what attitudes, values, and abilities are usually ascribed to women, men, lesbians, gays, heterosexuals? Share your lists in class, looking for points of consensus and disagreement. Are there differences in the ways women and men perceive their own or each other's roles? Do you see larger differences between individual groups' responses or between women's and men's as a whole?

Spend some time freewriting about the conclusions you draw from this exercise. You might also want to write about your own reactions to the lists. Do you possess all the characteristics associated with your gender and sexual orientation? Do you like the characteristics that the lists suggest you're supposed to have? Alternatively, you might explore where your notions of gender have come from: to what extent have they been shaped by your culture, religion, socioeconomic status, geographic region, or community — or by influential individuals in your life?

Girl

JAMAICA KINCAID

Although she now lives in New England, Jamaica Kincaid (b. 1949) retains strong ties, including citizenship, to her birthplace — the island of Antigua in the West Indies. After immigrating to the United States to attend college, she ended up educating herself instead, and did a good enough job to become author of five books and a staff writer for The New Yorker. *About the influence of parents on children she says, "The magic is they carry so much you don't know about. They know you in a way you don't know yourself." Some of that magic is exercised in the story "Girl," which was first published in Kincaid's award-winning collection* At the Bottom of the River *(1983).*

Wash the white clothes on Monday and put them on the stone heap; wash the color clothes on Tuesday and put them on the clothesline to dry; don't walk barehead in the hot sun; cook pumpkin fritters[1] in very hot sweet oil; soak your little cloths right after you take them off; when buying cotton to make yourself a nice blouse, be sure that it doesn't have gum[2] on it, because that way it won't hold up well after a wash; soak salt fish overnight before you cook it; is it true that you sing benna[3] in

[1] *fritters:* small fried cakes of batter, often containing vegetables, fruit, or other fillings.
[2] *gum:* plant residue on cotton.
[3] *sing benna:* sing popular music (not appropriate for Sunday school).

Sunday school?; always eat your food in such a way that it won't turn someone else's stomach; on Sundays try to walk like a lady and not like the slut you are so bent on becoming; don't sing benna in Sunday school; you mustn't speak to wharf-rat boys, not even to give directions; don't eat fruits on the street — flies will follow you; *but I don't sing benna on Sundays at all and never in Sunday school*; this is how to sew on a button; this is how to make a buttonhole for the button you have just sewed on; this is how to hem a dress when you see the hem coming down and so to prevent yourself from looking like the slut I know you are so bent on becoming; this is how you iron your father's khaki shirt so that it doesn't have a crease; this is how you iron your father's khaki pants so that they don't have a crease; this is how you grow okra — far from the house, because okra[4] tree harbors red ants; when you are growing dasheen,[5] make sure it gets plenty of water or else it makes your throat itch when you are eating it; this is how you sweep a corner; this is how you sweep a whole house; this is how you sweep a yard; this is how you smile to someone you don't like too much; this is how you smile to someone you don't like at all; this is how you smile to someone you like completely; this is how you set a table for tea; this is how you set a table for dinner; this is how you set a table for dinner with an important guest; this is how you set a table for lunch; this is how you set a table for breakfast; this is how to behave in the presence of men who don't know you very well, and this way they won't recognize immediately the slut I have warned you against becoming; be sure to wash every day, even if it is with your own spit; don't squat down to play marbles — you are not a boy, you know; don't pick people's flowers — you might catch some-thing; don't throw stones at blackbirds, because it might not be a blackbird at all; this is how to make a bread pudding; this is how to make doukona;[6] this is how to make pepper pot;[7] this is how to make a good medicine for a cold; this is how to make a good medicine to throw away a child before it even becomes a child; this is how to catch a fish; this is how to throw back a fish you don't like, and that way something bad won't fall on you; this is how to bully a man; this is how a man bullies you; this is how to love a man, and if this doesn't work there are other ways, and if they don't work don't feel too bad about giving up; this is how to spit up in the air if you feel like it, and this is how to move quick so that it doesn't fall on you; this is how to make ends meet; always squeeze bread to make sure it's fresh; *but what if the baker won't let me feel the bread?*; you mean to say that after all you are really going to be the kind of woman who the baker won't let near the bread?

[4]*okra:* a shrub whose pods are used in soups, stews, and gumbo.
[5]*dasheen:* the taro plant, cultivated, like the potato, for its edible tuber.
[6]*doukona:* plantain pudding; the plantain fruit is similar to the banana.
[7]*pepper pot:* a spicy West Indian stew.

Engaging the Text

1. What are your best guesses as to the time and place of the story? Who is telling the story? What does this dialogue tell you about the relationship between the characters, their values and attitudes? What else can you surmise about these people (for instance, ages, occupation, social status)? On what evidence in the story do you base these conclusions?

2. Why does the story juxtapose advice on cooking and sewing, for example, with the repeated warning not to act like a slut?

3. Explain the meaning of the last line of the story: "You mean to say that after all you are really going to be the kind of woman who the baker won't let near the bread?"

4. What does the story tell us about male-female relationships? According to the speaker, what roles are women and men expected to play?

Exploring Connections

5. How do the lessons being taught here compare with those in Toni Cade Bambara's "The Lesson" (p. 64). How would each author describe a successful mentor, teacher, or parent?

6. Compare the mother-daughter relationship explored here with the father-son relationship hinted at in "Mike LeFevre" (p. 87). Do you see gender differences as well as cultural differences?

Extending the Critical Context

7. Write an imitation of the story. If you are a woman, record some of the advice or lessons your mother or another woman gave you; if you are a man, put down advice received from your father or from another male. Read what you have written aloud in class, alternating between male and female speakers, and discuss the results: how does parental guidance vary according to gender?

8. Write a page or two recording what the daughter might be thinking as she listens to her mother's advice; then compare notes with classmates.

Some Individual Costs
of Gender Role Conformity

Janet Saltzman Chafetz

In 1971, Janet Saltzman Chafetz surveyed male and female college students to evaluate how they perceived the advantages and disadvantages of their own and each other's gender roles. Both women and men were somewhat unhappy with prevailing cultural norms — but in rather different ways. Chafetz (b. 1942) teaches sociology at the University of Houston; she has written or contributed to several books on gender roles, including Gender Equality: An Integrated Theory of Stability and Change *(1989). This selection comes from her earlier book* Masculine, Feminine, or Human? An Overview of the Sociology of Gender Roles *(1974).*

It is probably true that very few individuals conform totally to their sex-relevant stereotypes. Roles of all kinds . . . are sociocultural givens, but this is not to say that people play them in the same way. Indeed, individuals, like stage actors and actresses, interpret their roles and create innovations for their "parts." The fact remains that there is a "part" to be played, and it does strongly influence the actual "performance."

It is also important to recall that the precise definitions of gender role stereotypes vary within the broader culture by social class, region, race and ethnicity, and other subcultural categories. Thus, for instance, more than most other Americans, the various Spanish-speaking groups in this country (Mexican-American, Puerto Rican, Cuban) stress domesticity, passivity, and other stereotypical feminine traits, and dominance, aggressiveness, physical prowess, and other stereotypical masculine traits. Indeed, the masculine gender role for this group is generally described by reference to the highly stereotyped notion of *machismo*. In fact, a strong emphasis on masculine aggressiveness and dominance may be characteristic of most groups in the lower ranges of the socio-economic ladder (McKinley, 1964, pp. 89, 93, 112; Yorburg, 1974). Conversely, due to historical conditions beyond its control, black America has had to rely heavily on the female as provider and, more often than in the rest of society, as head of the household. Thus, the feminine stereotype discussed above has traditionally been less a part of the cultural heritage of blacks than that of whites (Staples, 1970; Yorburg, 1974). It is also clear that, at least at the verbal level, both gender role stereotypes have historically been taken more seriously in Dixie than elsewhere (see Scott, 1970, especially chap. 1). Although today this difference is probably declining, along with most other regional differences, personal experience leads me to conclude that it nonetheless remains. The pioneer past of the Far West, where survival relied upon strong, productive, independent females as well as males, may have dampened the emphasis on some aspects of the traditional feminine stereotype in that area of the country.

Much research remains to be done by way of documenting differences in gender role stereotypes between various groups, but there is little doubt that such differences exist. It is important to note, however, that, with the exception of explicitly countercultural groups, such as the "hippies" of the 1960s, even among subcultures with relatively strong traditions of their own the cultural definitions of the dominant society exert substantial pressure toward conformity. Minorities — namely, all those who are not part of the socioculturally dominant white, northern European, Protestant, middle and upper classes — exist within a society that defines them to a greater or lesser extent as inferior. To some degree such definitions are internalized by many members of the various minority groups and accepted as valid, a phenomenon known in the literature on minority groups as racial or ethnic "self-hatred" (Adelson, 1958, pp. 486, 489; Allport, 1958, pp. 147–48; Frazier, 1957, pp. 217, 226; Simpson & Yinger, 1965, pp. 227–29).

To the extent that individual minority members engage in such group self-hatred, they are led to attempt, within the limits of opportunity and the resources allowed by the dominant group, to "live up to" the norms and roles of the dominant society. Given limited economic opportunities, the result is often a parody of the values and behaviors of the dominant society, as exemplified by the strong emphasis on aggression, sexual exploitation, and physical prowess by lower class males of most ethnic groups. Similarly, large numbers of blacks, many highly educated and involved in radical politics, have accepted the negative (and false) description of their family structure as "matriarchal"[1] which has been propounded by Daniel Moynihan (1965) and other whites. Moreoever, many black males and females are now engaged in efforts to change this structure to conform to the major cultural pattern of male as dominant partner and breadwinner, and female as subservient homemaker. However, less biased research (Hill, 1972; Rhodes, 1971; Stack, 1974; Myers, 1975; Dietrich, 1975) suggests that the traditional black family structure is and has been very functional in enabling the black to survive in this society. This structure is not the pathological, weak, disorganized entity usually conveyed by the term "matriarchy."

---

[1]*matriarchal:* family structure in which the mother holds the power and authority.

Table 1   Disadvantages of Same Gender Role and Advantages of Other One as Perceived by Males

MALE DISADVANTAGES	FEMALE ADVANTAGES
Can't show emotions (P)	Freedom to express emotions (R)
Must be provider (O)	Fewer financial obligations; parents support longer (S)
Pressure to succeed, be competitive (O)	Less pressure to succeed (P)
Alimony and child support (O)	Alimony and insurance benefits (S)
Liable to draft (O)	Free from draft (S)
Must take initiative, make decisions (O)	Protected (S)
Limit on acceptable careers (P)	
Expected to be mechanical, fix things (O)	
	More leisure (S)
	Placed on pedestal; object of courtesy (S)

Note: Letters enclosed in parentheses refer to a fourfold categorization of roles (Polk & Stein, 1972). P = proscription; O = obligation; R = right; S = structural benefit.

Individuals of all levels of society who reject traditional gender role stereotypes are labeled "nonconformist" and subjected to the wrath of most members of the society. The harsh treatment of longhaired males in the 1960s by police, possible employers, and ordinary citizens speaks eloquently of the "cost" of nonconformity, as does the "wallflower" status of competitive, intellectually gifted, or career-oriented females. But costs are also paid by those who generally conform to gender role stereotypes (or any other kind, for that matter), and these are usually more "hidden."

Perceived Costs and Benefits

In 1971, students in a sex role class were asked to form single-sex groups to discuss the advantages of the other gender role and the disadvantages of their own. This exercise was a replication of the study done by Barbara Polk and Robert Stein (1972) at a northern university, using 250 students of highly diverse backgrounds, and the results parallel theirs almost exactly. Results of the class study are reported in Tables 1 and 2.

When the advantages and disadvantages of the gender roles are compared, the most striking finding relates to the relative length of the various lists. There seem to be many more disadvantages adhering to the feminine role as perceived by females than to the masculine role as perceived by males (or else the females were simply and stereotypically

Table 2   Disadvantages of Same Gender Role and Advantages of Other One as Perceived by Females

FEMALE DISADVANTAGES	MALE ADVANTAGES
Job opportunities limited; discrimination; poor pay (P)	Job opportunities greater (S)
Legal and financial discrimination (P)	Financial and legal opportunity (S)
Educational opportunities limited; judged mentally inferior; opinions devalued; intellectual life stifled (P)	Better educational and training opportunities; opinions valued (S)
Single status stigmatized; stigma for divorce and unwed pregnancy (P)	Bachelorhood glamorized (R)
Socially and sexually restricted; double standard (P)	More freedom sexually and socially (R)
Must bear and rear children; no abortions (in many places); responsible for birth control (O)	No babies (S)
Must maintain good outward appearance; dress, make-up (O)	Less fashion demand and emphasis on appearance (R)
Domestic work (O)	No domestic work (R)
Must be patient; give in; subordinate self; be unaggressive; wait to be asked out on dates (P)	Can be aggressive, dating and otherwise (O)
Inhibited motor control; not allowed to be athletic (P)	More escapism allowed (R)

Note: Letters enclosed in parentheses refer to a fourfold categorization of roles (Polk & Stein, 1972): P = proscription; O = obligation; R = right; S = structural benefit.

more loquacious!). Conversely, more advantages are seen as accruing to the masculine role by females than to the feminine role by males. More relevant to the question of costs, however, is the finding that the perceived advantages of one sex are the disadvantages of the other. If it is a masculine disadvantage not to be able to show emotions, it is a feminine advantage to be able to do so. Likewise, if it is a feminine disadvantage to face limited job opportunities, the converse is a masculine advantage. Summarizing similar findings, Polk and Stein (1972) conclude: "The extent to which this relationship exists strongly suggests that there is general agreement on the desirable characteristics for any individual, regardless of sex" (p. 16).

Polk and Stein's fourfold categorization of role components as rights, obligations, proscriptions, and structural benefits is useful in examining the nature of specific perceived costs and benefits of the two

Table 3 Gender Role Traits Helpful and Harmful in Acquiring and Performing Well in Prestigious Occupational Roles

STEREOTYPED TRAITS	HARMFUL	HELPFUL
Masculine	Sloppy	Breadwinner, provider
	Dogmatic	Stoic, unemotional
		Logical, rational, objective, scientific
		Practical
		Mechanical (for scientist and physician)
		Public awareness
		Leader
		Disciplinarian
		Independent
		Demanding
		Aggressive
		Ambitious
		Proud, confident
		Moral, trustworthy
		Decisive
		Competitive
		Adventurous

roles. According to Polk and Stein, "Rights allow the individual the freedom to commit an act or refrain from an act without receiving sanctions for either choice" (p. 19). Obligations and proscriptions are different in that individuals are negatively sanctioned, in the first case for not doing something, in the second for doing it. Structural benefits refer to "advantages derived from the social structure or from actions of others" on the basis of sex alone (p. 21). Each advantage and disadvantage listed in Tables 1 and 2 is followed by a letter in parentheses which represents my judgment as to whether that characteristic is a right (R), a proscription (P), an obligation (O), or a structural benefit (S). Masculine disadvantages consist overwhelmingly of obligations with a few proscriptions, while the disadvantages of the feminine role arise primarily from proscriptions, with a few obligations. Thus females complain about what they can't do, males about what they must do. Females complain that they cannot be athletic, aggressive, sexually free, or successful in the worlds of work and education; in short, they complain of their passivity. Males complain that they must be aggressive and must succeed; in short, of their activity. The (sanctioned) requirement that males be active and females passive in a variety of ways is clearly unpleasant to both.

The nature of the types of advantages seen as accruing to each of the two roles by the other sex supports the stereotyped dichotomy between activity and passivity still further. Females are seen as overwhelmingly

Table 3 (Continued) Gender Role Traits Helpful and Harmful in Acquiring and Performing Well in Prestigious Occupational Roles

STEREOTYPED TRAITS	HARMFUL	HELPFUL
Feminine	Worry about appearance and age	Compassionate
	Sensual	Intuitive
	Domestic	Humanistic
	Seductive, flirtatious	Perceptive
	Emotional, sentimental	Idealistic
	Nervous, insecure, fearful	Patient
	Scatterbrained, frivolous	Gentle
	Impractical	
	Petty, coy, gossipy	
	Dependent, overprotected	
	Follower, submissive	
	Self-conscious; easily intimidated	
	Not aggressive, passive	
	Tardy	
	Noncompetitive	

enjoying structural benefits, namely, advantages that accrue to them without reference to what they do. Males believe females have only one right. Females believe males also enjoy structural benefits but have considerably more rights, namely, choices of action or inaction. These findings generally agree with those of Polk and Stein, who found that altogether the masculine role had 14 obligations compared to 8 for the feminine role; 6 rights compared to 0; 4 proscriptions compared to 15; and 6 structural benefits compared to 4 (pp. 20–21, Table 2).

Economic Costs and Benefits

How helpful or costly would the masculine or feminine gender role   10
stereotype traits . . . be for a competitor in the highest echelons of our economy and society? One measure of such success is occupation. Robert Hodge, Paul Siegel, and Peter Rossi (1966) studied the relative prestige of a large number of occupations in the United States and found that the four most prestigious were: U.S. Supreme Court Justice, physician, scientist, and state governor. Table 3 [above] summarizes the data on which stereotypical traits are clearly helpful in attaining and performing well in these occupational roles and which are harmful. While the designation as "helpful" or "harmful" for some few traits is debatable, the overall picture probably is not. Stereotypical feminine traits patently do not equip those who might try to live up to them to compete in the world of social and economic privilege, power, and prestige; the exact opposite is the case for masculine characteristics.

Where 15 feminine traits are classified as "harmful," only 2 masculine ones are so designated. Conversely, where 17 masculine traits are classified as "helpful," the analogous number of feminine traits is 7. The cost of femininity for those who would enter the world outside the home could scarcely be more clear: The more a female conforms, the less is she capable of functioning in roles that are other than domestic.

Indeed, gender roles are so deeply ingrained that even among successful business executives, women, unlike men, often attribute their success to luck rather than their own hard work and competence. Moreover, women tend to understate the extent of their achievements (Hennig & Jardim, 1977). On the other hand, reared in a culture that emphasizes the myth that hard work and personal worth will result in job success, many males, especially in the middle class, suffer feelings of personal inadequacy and failure if they are not highly successful in a material sense. In short, the feminine role stereotype gears women for economic failure, and if that is not the case, women explain their success in terms external to themselves. The masculine role stereotype gears men for economic success, and if that is not forthcoming men perceive themselves as personally responsible for their "failure."

Works Cited

Adelson, Joseph. "A Study of Minority Group Authoritarianism." In Marshall Sklare (ed.), *The Jews: Social Patterns of an American Group*, pp. 475–92. Glencoe, Ill.: Free Press, 1958.

Allport, Gordon. *The Nature of Prejudice*. Garden City, N.Y.: Doubleday Anchor Books, 1958; first published 1954.

Dietrich, Kathryn. "The Re-examination of the Myth of Black Matriarchy." *Journal of Marriage and the Family* 37 (May 1975); pp. 367–74.

Frazier, E. Franklin. *Black Bourgeoisie*. Glencoe, Ill.: Free Press, 1957.

Hennig, Margaret, and Jardim, Anne. *The Managerial Woman*. New York: Anchor-Doubleday, 1977.

Hill, Robert B. *The Strengths of Black Families*. New York: Emerson Hall Publishers, 1972.

Hodge, Robert; Siegel, Paul; and Rossi, Peter. "Occupational Prestige in the United States: 1925–1963." In Reinhard Bendix and S. M. Lipset (eds.), *Class, Status and Power*, 2nd ed., pp. 322–34. Glencoe, Ill.: Free Press, 1966.

McKinley, Donald G. *Social Class and Family Life*. Glencoe, Ill.: Free Press, 1964.

Moynihan, Daniel P. *The Negro Family: The Case for National Action*. Washington, D.C.: U.S. Department of Labor, 1965.

Myers, Lena Wright. "Black Women and Self-Esteem." In Marcia Millman and Rosabeth Kanter (eds.), *Another Voice*, pp. 240–50. Garden City, N.Y.: Anchor Books, 1975.

Polk, Barbara Bovee, and Stein, Robert B. "Is the Grass Greener on the Other Side?" In Constantina Safilios-Rothschild (ed.), *Toward a Sociology of Women*, pp. 14–23. Lexington, Mass.: Xerox College Publishing Co., 1972.

Rhodes, Barbara. "The Changing Role of the Black Woman." In Robert Staples (ed.), *The Black Family*, pp. 145–49. Belmont, Calif.: Wadsworth Publishing Co., 1971.

Scott, Anne Firor. *The Southern Lady.* Chicago: University of Chicago Press, 1970.

Simpson, George E., and Yinger, J. Milton. *Racial and Cultural Minorities.* 3rd ed. New York: Harper & Row, 1965.

Stack, Carol. *All Our Kin: Strategies for Survival in a Black Community.* New York: Harper & Row, 1974.

Staples, Robert. "The Myth of the Black Matriarchy." *Black Scholar* 1 (January–February, 1970): 8–16.

Yorburg, Betty. *Sexual Identity: Sex Roles and Social Change.* New York: John Wiley & Sons, 1974.

Engaging the Text

1. What, according to Chafetz is *"machismo"*?

2. In paragraph 2, Chafetz defines several female gender role stereotypes. Try to describe other female stereotypes specific to particular regions, socioeconomic levels, or ethnic groups. What similarities and differences do you see?

3. Review the three tables in this selection; do the gender roles described in them strike you as dated? How much, if at all, do you think gender roles have changed since Chafetz conducted her research?

4. Chafetz mentions the "cost" of not conforming to gender role stereotypes. Working in groups, list some of the specific costs that nonconformists might pay. Have you ever been penalized for failing to live up to your expected masculine or feminine role?

Exploring Connections

5. Examine the mother's advice in Jamaica Kincaid's story "Girl" (p. 191). How much of it seems stereotypical? Does any of the advice seem to work against stereotypes of women? Would the mother's training predominantly instill a sense of rights, of obligations, of proscriptions, or of structural benefits?

6. To what extent do Geradine Simkins and Larry Doe in Kathleen Stocking's "Living on the Land" (p. 164) reflect the traditional gender roles outlined by Chafetz's study?

7. Look at all the traits in Table 3. Which of these would seem to apply to author Sucheng Chan, based on what you learn of her in "You're Short, Besides!" (p. 99) and in the headnote to her essay? Discuss her success in terms of these stereotypically feminine and masculine traits.

Extending the Critical Context

8. Write a journal entry about a time when your definition of your own gender came into conflict with the roles prescribed by your family, culture, or religion. How did you deal with this conflict?

9. Discuss the meaning of "*machismo*." Freewrite for a few minutes about the qualities that members of your ethnic group tend to associate with being male; then compare notes with classmates.

10. Watch Barry Levinson's film *Diner* on videotape. What does the film say about the advantages and disadvantages of traditional sex role stereotypes? How would the movie change if the story were told from the women's point of view?

Nora Quealey

Jean Reith Schroedel

This interview reveals the thoughts of a woman who has encountered sexism in a traditionally male occupation — assembly line work on trucks. Quealey is proud, strong, insightful — and she thinks she would prefer being a housewife. Jean Reith Schroedel (b. 1951) began collecting oral histories of blue-collar working women when she was an undergraduate at the University of Washington; she published these interviews in Alone in a Crowd *(1985). She has worked as a machinist and a union organizer, and, fittingly, she supported her work on the book by driving a bus.*

I was a housewife until five years ago. The best part was being home when my three kids came in from school. Their papers and their junk that they made from kindergarten on up — they were my total, whole life. And then one day I realized when they were grown up and gone, graduated and married, I was going to be left with nothing. I think there's a lot of women that way, housewives, that never knew there were other things and people outside of the neighborhood. I mean the block got together once a week for coffee and maybe went bowling, but that was it. My whole life was being there when the kids came home from school.

I never disliked anything. It was just like everything else in a marriage, there never was enough money to do things that you wanted — never to take a week's vacation away from the kids. If we did anything, it was just to take the car on Saturday or Sunday for a little, short drive. But there was never enough money. The extra money was the reason I decided to go out and get a job. The kids were getting older, needed more, wanted more, and there was just not enough.

See, I don't have a high school diploma, so when I went to Boeing and put an application in, they told me not to come back until I had a diploma or a G.E.D.[1] On the truck line they didn't mind that I hadn't finished school. I put an application in and got hired on the spot.

My dad works over at Bangor[2] in the ammunition depot, so I asked him what it would be like working with all men. The only thing he told me was if I was gonna work with a lot of men, that I would have to *listen* to swear words and some of the obscene things, but still *act* like a lady, or I'd never fit in. You can still be treated like a lady and act like a lady and work like a man. So I just tried to fit in. It's worked, too. The guys come up and they'll tell me jokes and tease me and a lot of them told me that I'm just like one of the guys. Yet they like to have me around because I wear make-up and I do curl my hair, and I try to wear not really frilly blouses, see-through stuff, but nice blouses.

We had one episode where a gal wore a tank top and when she bent   5 over the guys could see her boobs or whatever you call it, all the way down. Myself and a couple other women went and tried to complain about it. We wanted personnel to ask her to please wear a bra, or at least no tank tops. We were getting a lot of comebacks from the guys like, "When are you gonna dress like so-and-so," or "When are *you* gonna go without a bra," and "We wanna see what *you've* got." And I don't feel any need to show off; you know, I know what I've got. There were only a few women there, so that one gal made a very bad impression. But personnel said there was nothing they could do about it.

But in general the guys were really good. I started out in cab building hanging radio brackets and putting heaters in. It was all hand work, and at first I really struggled with the power screwdrivers and big reamers, but the guy training me was super neato. I would think, "Oh, dear, can I ever do this, can I really prove myself or come up to their expectations?" But the guys never gave me the feeling that I was taking the job from a man or food from his family's mouth. If I needed help, I didn't even have to ask, if they saw me struggling, they'd come right over to help.

I've worked in a lot of different places since I went to work there. I was in cab build for I don't know how long, maybe six months, eight months. Then they took me over to sleeper boxes, where I stayed for about two-and-one-half years. I put in upholstery, lined the head liners and the floor mats. After that I went on the line and did air condition-ing. When the truck came to me, it had hoses already on it, and I'd have to hook up a little air-condition-pump-type thing and a suction that draws all the dust and dirt from the lines. Then you close that off, put Freon in, and tie down the line. Then I'd tie together a bunch of color-coded electrical wires with tie straps and electrical tape to hook the firewall to the engine. Sometimes I also worked on the sleeper boxes by

[1]*G.E.D.:* a high school equivalency certificate.
[2]*Bangor:* site of a Trident nuclear submarine base in the state of Washington.

crawling underneath and tightening down big bolts and washers. Next they sent me over to the radiator shop. I was the first woman ever to do radiators. That I liked. A driver would bring in the radiators, and you'd put it on a hoist, pick it up and put it on a sling, and work on one side putting your fittings on and wiring and putting in plugs. Then they bounced me back to sleeper boxes for a while and finally ended up putting me in the motor department, where I am now. The motors are brought in on a dolly. The guy behind me hangs the transmission and I hang the pipe with the shift levers and a few other little things and that's about it. Except that we have to work terribly fast.

I was moved into the motor department after the big layoff. At that time we were doing ten motors a day. Now we're up to fourteen without any additional help. When we were down, the supervisor came to me and said we had to help fill in and give extra help to the other guys, which is fine. But the minute production went up, I still had to do my own job plus putting on parts for three different guys. These last two weeks have been really tough. I've been way behind. They've got two guys that are supposed to fill in when you get behind, but I'm stubborn enough that I won't go over and ask for help. The supervisor should be able to see that I'm working super-duper hard while some other guys are taking forty-five minutes in the can and having a sandwich and two cups of coffee. Sometimes I push myself so hard that I'm actually in a trance. And I have to stop every once in a while and ask, "What did I do?" I don't even remember putting parts on, I just go from one to the other, just block everything out — just go, go, go, go. And that is bad, for myself, my own sanity, my own health. I don't take breaks. I don't go to the bathroom. There's so much pressure on me, physical and mental stress. It's hard to handle because then I go home and do a lot of crying and that's bad for my kids because I do a lot of snapping and growling at them. When I'm down, depressed, aching, and sore, to come home and do that to the kids is not fair at all. The last couple of days the attitude I've had is, I don't care whether I get the job done or not. If they can't see I'm going under, then I don't care. And I'll take five or ten minutes to just go to the bathroom, sit on the floor, and take a couple of deep breaths, just anything to get away.

The company doesn't care about us at all. Let me give you an example. When we were having all this hot weather, I asked them please if we couldn't get some fans in here. Extension cords even, because some guys had their own fans. I wasn't just asking for myself, but those guys over working by the oven. They've got a thermometer there and it gets to a hundred and fifteen degrees by that oven! They've got their mouths open, can hardly breathe, and they're barely moving. So I said to the supervisor, "Why can't we have a fan to at least circulate the air?" "Oh, yeah, we'll look at it," was as far as it went. We're human. We have no right to be treated like animals. I mean you go out to a dairy farm and you've got air conditioning and music for those cows. I'm a person, and I don't like feeling weak and sick to my stomach and not feel like eating. Then to have the supervisor expect me to put out production as if I was mechanical — a thing, just a robot. I'm human.

You know, I don't even know what my job title is. I'm not sure if it's trainee or not. But I do know I'll never make journeyman. I'll never make anything. I tried for inspection — took all the classes they offered at the plant, went to South Seattle Community College on my own time, studied blueprinting, and worked in all the different areas like they said I had to. I broke ground for the other girls, but they won't let me move up. And it all comes down to one thing, because I associated with a black man. I've had people in personnel tell me to stop riding to work with the man, even if it meant taking the bus to and from work. I said no one will make my decisions as to who I ride with and who my friends are. Because you walk into a building with a person, have lunch with him, let him buy you a cup of coffee, people condemn you. They're crazy, because when I have a friend, I don't turn my back on them just because of what people think. What I do outside the plant after quitting time is my own business. If they don't like it, that's their problem. But in that plant I've conducted myself as a lady and have nothing to be ashamed of. I plant my feet firmly and I stand by it.

Early on, I hurt my neck, back, and shoulder while working on sleeper boxes. When I went into the motor department I damaged them more by working with power tools above my head and reaching all day long. I was out for two weeks and then had a ten-week restriction. Personnel said I had to go back to my old job, and if I couldn't handle it I would have to go home. They wouldn't put me anywhere else, which is ridiculous, with all the small parts areas that people can sit down and work in while they are restricted. My doctor said if I went back to doing what I was doing when I got hurt, I had a fifty-fifty chance of completely paralyzing myself from the waist down. But like a fool I went back. Some of the guys helped me with the bending and stooping over. Then the supervisor borrowed a ladder with three steps and on rollers from the paint department. He wanted me to stand on the top step while working on motors which are on dollies on a moving chain. I'd be using two press-wrenches to tighten fittings down while my right knee was on the transmission and the left leg standing up straight. All this from the top step of a ladder on rollers. One slip and it would be all over. I backed off and said it wouldn't work. By this time I'd gotten the shop steward there, but he didn't do anything. In fact, the next day he left on three weeks' vacation without doing anything to help me. I called the union hall and was told they'd send a business rep down the next day. I never saw or heard from the man.

Anyhow, I'm still doing the same job as when I got hurt. I can feel the tension in my back and shoulder coming up. I can feel the spasms start and muscles tightening up. Things just keep gettin' worse and they don't care. People could be rotated and moved rather than being cramped in the same position, like in the sleeper boxes, where you never stand up straight and stretch your neck out. It's eight, ten, twelve hours a day all hunched over. In the next two years I've got to quit. I don't know what I'll do. If I end up paralyzed from the neck down, the company doesn't give a damn, the union doesn't give a damn, who's gonna take care of me? Who's gonna take care of my girls? I'm gonna be put in some moldy, old, stinkin' nursing home. I'm thirty-seven years old. I could live another thirty, forty years. And who's gonna really care about me?

I mean my husband left me. He was very jealous of my working with a lot of men and used to follow me to work. When I joined the bowling team, I tried to get him to come and meet the guys I worked with. He came but felt left out because there was always an inside joke or something that he couldn't understand. He resented that and the fact that I made more money than he did. And my not being home bothered him. But he never said, "I want you to quit," or "We'll make it on what I get." If he had said that I probably would have quit. Instead we just muddled on. With me working, the whole family had to pitch in and help. When I come home at night my daughter has dinner waiting, and I do a couple loads of wash and everybody folds their own clothes. My husband pitched in for a while. Then he just stopped coming home. He found another lady that didn't work, had four kids, and was on welfare.

It really hurt and I get very confused still. I don't have the confidence and self-assurance I used to have. I think, "Why did I do that," or "Maybe I shouldn't have done it," and I have to force myself to say, "Hey, I felt and said what I wanted to and there's no turning back." It came out of me and I can't be apologizing for everything that I do. And, oh, I don't know, I guess I'm in a spell right now where I'm tired of being dirty. I want my fingernails long and clean. I want to not go up to the bathroom and find a big smudge of grease across my forehead. I want to sit down and be pampered and pretty all day. Maybe that wouldn't satisfy me, but I just can't imagine myself at fifty or sixty or seventy years old trying to climb on these trucks. I've been there for five years. I'm thirty-seven and I want to be out of there before I'm forty. And maybe I will. I've met this nice guy and he's talking of getting married. At the most, I would have to work for one more year and then I could stay at home, go back to being a housewife.

Engaging the Text

1. What are Nora Quealey's attitudes toward domesticity? Toward work? Toward money and success? Is she a traditional woman or a feminist?

2. Quealey's life is in some ways tragic. What are the greatest blows she has suffered? Do you think she could have avoided any of them? How — and at what price?

3. What motivates Quealey to persevere in the face of the difficulties she encounters? List as many possible motivations as you can, and review the text to find evidence of them.

Exploring Connections

4. How many of the gender role advantages and disadvantages listed by Janet Saltzman Chafetz (p. 194) apply to Nora Quealey? To what extent does her experience illustrate Chafetz's assertion that "the feminine role stereotype gears women for economic failure" (para. 11)?

5. Contrast Quealey's attitudes toward work with those of Mike LeFevre (p. 87). How important is gender in shaping their responses to their respective job situations?

6. To what extent does Quealey's experience on the job support or refute Suzanne Gordon's contentions, in "Women at Risk" (p. 46), that women must adopt male values in order to succeed in the workplace?

Extending the Critical Context

7. When male workers ask "When are *you* gonna go without a bra" or say "We wanna see what *you've* got," does their speech constitute sexual harassment? How do you think a female employee should respond to such comments? Do you think different standards should apply in different work settings, for example, industrial versus clerical versus professional?

8. Play Ann Landers. Imagine that Quealey has written you a long letter — namely, the text you've just read. Write a confidential response giving advice, encouragement, or an analysis of her situation or feelings, as you see fit. Then write a separate paragraph stating the rationale for your response.

The Rite of Work: The Economic Man

SAM KEEN

In the early 1990s, more than two decades after the feminist move-ment began questioning myths of womanhood, American men have begun to explore the meaning of American masculinity. This selection looks at the way work in corporate America defines — or deforms — contemporary male gender roles. It originally appeared in Sam Keen's book Fire in the Belly: On Being a Man *(1991), one of the most popular introductions to the new "men's movement." Keen holds degrees from Princeton University and Harvard Divinity School and has been nominated for an Emmy Award for his PBS series "The Enemy Within." A contributing editor of* Psychology Today *for many years, Keen has also published* The Passionate Life *(1983) and* Faces of the Enemy: Reflections of the Hostile Imagination *(1988).*

> One does not work to live; one lives to work.
> — MAX WEBER,
> *Capitalism and the Protestant Ethic*

> Have leisure and know that I am God.
> — PSALM 65

The Bottom Line — Work and Worth

Preparations for the male ritual of work begin even before the age of schooling. Long before a boy child has a concept of the day after tomorrow, he will be asked by well-meaning but unconscious adults, "What do you want to be when you grow up?" It will not take him long to discover that "I want to be a horse" is not an answer that satisfies adults. They want to know what men plan to do, what job, profession, occupation we have decided to follow at five years of age! Boys are taught early that they are what they do. Later, as men, when we meet as strangers on the plane or at a cocktail party we break the ice by asking, "What do you do?"

Formal preparation for the rites of manhood in a secular society takes place first through the institution of schooling. Our indoctrination into the dominant myths, value system, and repertoire of heroic stories is homogenized into the educational process. My fifteen-year-old nephew put the matter more accurately than any social scientist. "Schools," he said, "are designed to teach you to take life sitting down. They prepare you to work in office buildings, to sit in rows or cubicles, to be on time, not to talk back, and to let somebody else grade you." From the first grade onward, schools teach us to define and measure ourselves against others. We learn that the world is composed of winners and losers, pass or fail.

The games that make up what we call physical education — football, basketball, and baseball — are minibattles that teach boys to compete in the game of life. Pregame pep talks, like salesmen's meetings, begin with the Vince Lombardi prayer: "Winning isn't the most important thing. It's the only thing." For many boys making the team, from Little League to college, provides the ritual form of combat that is central to male identity.

The first full-time job, like the first fight or first sex, is a rite of passage for men in our time. Boys have paper routes, but men have regular paychecks. Like primitive rites, work requires certain sacrifices and offers certain insignia of manhood. In return for agreeing to put aside childish dalliance and assume the responsibility for showing up from nine to five at some place of work, the initiate receives the power object — money — that allows him to participate in the adult life of the community.

Getting a credit card is a more advanced rite of passage. The credit   5
card is for the modern male what killing prey was to a hunter. To earn a credit rating a man must certify that he has voluntarily cut himself off from childhood, that he has foregone the pleasure of languid mornings at the swimming hole, and has assumed the discipline of a regular job, a fixed address, and a predictable character. The Visa card (passport to the good life) is an insignia of membership, a sign that the system trusts you to spend what you have not yet earned because you have shown good faith by being regularly employed. In modern America going into debt is an important part of assuming the responsibilities of manhood. Debt, the willingness to live beyond our means, binds us to the economic system that requires both surplus work and surplus consumption. The popular bumper sticker, "I owe, I owe, so off to work I go" might well be the litany to express the commitment of the working man.

After accepting the disciplines of work and credit, a whole hierarchy of graduated symbolic initiations follows, from first to thirty-second degree. Mere employment entitles one to display the insignia of the Chevette. Acquiring the executive washroom key qualifies one for a Buick or Cadillac. Only those initiated into the inner sanctum of the boardroom may be borne in the regal Rolls-Royce. To the victors belong the marks of status and the repair bills. The right to wear eagle feathers or to sing certain sacred songs was recognized in American Indian tribes to signify the possession of a high degree of power and status, just as in contemporary society certain brand names and logos are tokens of class and rank. A man wears a Rolex not because it tells time more accurately than a $14.95 Timex but because, like a penis shield, it signifies an advanced degree of manhood. In a society where the marks of virtue are created by advertising, possession of stylish objects signifies power. For economic man a Ralph Lauren polo shirt says something very different than its Fruit of the Loom equivalent. The implicit message is that manhood can be purchased. And the expense of the luxury items we own marks our progress along the path of the good life as it is defined by a consumer society.

Within the last decade someone upped the ante on the tokens required for manhood. A generation ago providing for one's family was the only economic requirement. Nowadays, supplying the necessities entitles a man only to marginal respect. If your work allows you only to survive you are judged to be not much of a man. To be poor in a consumer society is to have failed the manhood test, or at least to have gotten a D −. The advertising industry reminds us at every turn that real men, successful men, powerful men, are big spenders. They have enough cash or credit to consume the best. Buying is status. "It's the cost of the toys that separates the men from the boys." The sort of man who reads *Playboy* or *The New Yorker* is dedicated to a life of voluntary complexity, conspicuous consumption, and adherence to the demanding discipline of style.

The rites of manhood in any society are those that are appropriate and congruent with the dominant myth. The horizon within which we live, the source of our value system, and the way we define "reality" are economic. The bottom line is the almighty dollar. Time is money, money is power, and power makes the world go round. In the same sense that the cathedral was the sacred center of the medieval city, the bank and other commercial buildings are the centers of the modern city.

Once upon a time work was considered a curse. As the result of Adam and Eve's sin we were driven from the Garden of Eden and forced to earn our bread by the sweat of our brows. Men labored because of necessity, but found the meaning and sweetness of life in free time. According to the Greeks, only slaves and women were bound to the life of work. Free men discovered the joys and dignity of manhood in contemplation and in the cultivation of leisure. Until the time of the Protestant Reformation[1] the world was divided between the realm of the secular, to which work and the common life belonged, and the realm of the sacred, which was the monopoly of the Church. Martin Luther changed all of this by declaring that every man and woman had a sacred vocation. The plowman and the housewife no less than the priest were called by God to express their piety in the common life of the community. Gradually the notion of the priesthood of all believers came to mean that every man and woman had a calling to meaningful secular work.

In the feudal era manhood involved being the lord of a manor, the head of a household, or at least a husbandman of the land. As the industrial revolution progressed men were increasingly pulled out of the context of nature, family, church, and community to find the meaning of their lives in trading, industry, the arts, and the professions, while women practiced their vocations by ministering to the needs of the home and practicing charity within the community. Gradually, getting and spending assumed the place of greatest importance, virtually re-

10

---

[1]*Protestant Reformation:* the 16th-century religious movement led by Martin Luther that aimed at "reforming" the Catholic Church and resulted in the creation of Protestantism.

placing all of the old activities that previously defined manhood — hunting, growing, tending, celebrating, protesting, investigating. As "the bottom line" became our ultimate concern, and the Dow Jones the index of reality, man's world shrank. Men no longer found their place beneath the dome of stars, within the brotherhood of animals, by the fire of the hearth, or in the company of citizens. Economic man spends his days with colleagues, fellow workers, bosses, employees, suppliers, lawyers, customers, and other strangers. At night he returns to an apartment or house that has been empty throughout the day. More likely than not, if he is married with children, his wife has also been away at work throughout the day and his children have been tended and educated by another cadre of professionals. If he is successful his security (*securus* — "free from care") rests in his investments (from "vestment" — a religious garment) in stocks, bonds, and other commodities whose future value depends upon the whims of the market.

Nowadays only a fortunate minority are able to find harmony between vocation and occupation. Some artists, professionals, businessmen, and tradesmen find in their work a calling, a lifework, an arena within which they may express their creativity and care. But most men are shackled to the mercantile society in much the same way medieval serfs were imprisoned in the feudal system. All too often we work because we must, and we make the best of a bad job.

In the secular theology of economic man Work has replaced God as the source from whom all blessings flow. The escalating gross national product, or at least the rising Dow Jones index, is the outward and visible sign that we are progressing toward the kingdom of God; full employment is grace; unemployment is sin. The industrious, especially entrepreneurs with capital, are God's chosen people, but even laborers are sanctified because they participate in the productive economy.

As a form of secular piety Work now satisfies many of the functions once served by religion. In the words of Ayn Rand,[2] whose popular philosophy romanticized capitalism and sanctified selfishness, "Your work is the process of achieving your values. Your body is a machine but your mind is its driver. Your work is the purpose of your life, and you must speed past any killer who assumes the right to stop you. . . . Any value you might find outside your work, any other loyalty or love, can only be travelers going on their own power in the same direction."[3]

We don't work just to make a living. Increasingly, the world of work provides the meaning of our lives. It becomes an end in itself rather than

[2]*Ayn Rand:* American author (1905–1982) whose novels champion a romanticized view of capitalist individualism.

[3]Ayn Rand, *For the New Intellectual* (NY: Signet Books, 1961), p. 130. [Author's note]

a means. A decade ago, only twenty-eight percent of us enjoyed the work we did. And yet, according to a Yankelovich survey,[4] eighty percent of us reported that we would go right on working even if we didn't need the money. By the 1980s this profile changed. We are just as attached to our work, but now we are demanding that the workplace provide an outlet for our creativity. Yankelovich reports in 1988 that fifty-two percent of Americans respond "I have an inner need to do the very best job I can, regardless of the pay" and sixty-one percent when asked what makes for the good life say "a job that is interesting."[5]

Something very strange has happened to work and leisure in the last 15 generation. The great promise of emerging technology was that it would finally set men free from slavery and we could flower. As late as the 1960s philosophers, such as Herbert Marcuse,[6] sociologists, and futurists were predicting a coming leisure revolution. We were just around the corner from a twenty-hour work week. Soon we would be preoccupied by arts, games, and erotic dalliance on leisurely afternoons. At worst we would have to learn to cope with "pleasure anxiety" and the threat of leisure.

Exactly the opposite happened. Work is swallowing leisure. The fast lane has become a way of life for young professionals who are giving their all to career. In the 1990s Americans may come more and more to resemble the Japanese — workaholics all, living to work rather than working to live, finding their identity as members of corporate tribes. . . .

Part of the problem is that work, community, and family are getting mixed up and lumped together. Increasingly, Americans live in places where they are anonymous, and seek to find their community at work. Companies, with the help of organizational development consultants, are trying to make the workplace the new home, the new family. The new motto is: humanize the workplace, make it a community; let communication flourish on all levels. The best (or is it the worst?) of companies have become paternalistic or maternalistic, providing their employees with all the comforts and securities of home. . . .

In short, the workplace is rapidly becoming its own culture that defines who we are. Like minisocieties, professions and corporations create their own ritual and mythology. Doctors share a common story, a history of disease and cure, a consensus about the means of healing with other doctors. Businessmen share the language of profit and loss with other businessmen and acknowledge the same tokens of success. As economic organizations have grown larger than governments, em-

[4]*Yankelovich survey:* a nationwide public opinion poll.
[5]*American Health* (September 1988). [Author's note]
[6]*Herbert Marcuse:* German American philosopher and social critic (1898–1979).

ployees render them a type of loyalty previously reserved for God, country, or family.

To determine what happens to men within the economic world we need to look critically at its climate, its ruling mood, its ethos,[7] its aims, and its method. We should no more accept a profession's or a corporation's self-evaluation, its idealistic view of itself (we are a family, a "service" organization, dedicated to the highest ideals of quality, etc.) than we would accept the propaganda of any tribe or nation.

A recent critical study of the climate of corporate culture suggests it   20
may be more like a tyrannical government than a kindly family. Earl Shorris, in a neglected and very important book, suggests that the modern corporation represents a historically new form of tyranny in which we are controlled by accepting the definitions of happiness that keep us in harness for a lifetime. Herewith, in short, his argument:

> The most insidious of the many kinds of power is the power to define happiness. . . .
> The manager, like the nobleman of earlier times, serves as the exemplary merchant: since happiness cannot be defined, he approximates his definition through the display of symbols, such as expense account meals, an expensive house, stylish clothing, travel to desirable places, job security, interesting friends, membership in circles of powerful people, advantages for his children, and social position for his entire family. . . .
> In the modern world, a delusion about work and happiness enables people not only to endure oppression but to seek it and to believe that they are happier because of the very work that oppresses them. At the heart of the delusion lies the manager's definition of happiness: sweat and dirty hands signify oppression and a coat and tie signify happiness, freedom, and a good life.
> Blue-collar workers . . . resist symbolic oppression. One need only visit an assembly line and observe the styles of dress, speech, and action of the workers to realize the symbolic freedom they enjoy. . . . They live where they please, socialize with whomever they please, and generally enjoy complete freedom outside the relatively few hours they spend at their jobs. . . . No matter how much money a blue-collar worker earns, he is considered poor; no matter how much he enjoys his work, he is thought to be suffering. In that way, blue-collar wages are kept low and blue-collar workers suffer the indignity of low status.
> The corporation or the bureaucracy . . . becomes a place, the cultural authority, the moral home of a man. The rules of the corporation become the rules of society, the future replaces history, and the organization becomes the family of the floating man. . . . By detaching him from the real world of place, the corporation becomes the world for him.

[7]*ethos:* the beliefs or standards that characterize a person, group, or society.

Men abandoned the power to define happiness for themselves, and having once abandoned that power, do not attempt to regain it. . . .[8]

The new rhetoric about the workplace as home and family needs to be balanced by an honest evaluation of the more destructive implications of the iron law of profit. Home and family are ends in themselves. They are, or should be, about sharing of love to no purpose. They file no quarterly reports. Business is an activity organized to make a profit. And any activity is shaped by the end it seeks. Certainly business these days wears a velvet glove, comporting itself with a new facade of politeness and enlightened personnel policies, but beneath the glove is the iron fist of competition and warfare.

The recent spate of best-selling books about business that make use of military metaphors tell an important story about economic life and therefore about the climate within which most men spend their days. Listen to the metaphors, the poetry of business as set forth in David Rogers's *Waging Business Warfare* from the jacket copy:

> Become a master of strategy on today's corporate killing fields — and win the war for success. . . . How to succeed in battle: believe it: if you're in business, you're at war. Your enemies — your competitors — intend to annihilate you. Just keeping your company alive on the battlefield is going to be a struggle. Winning may be impossible — unless you're a master of military strategy. . . . You can be — if you'll follow the examples of the great tacticians of history. Because the same techniques that made Genghis Khan, Hannibal, and Napoleon the incomparable conquerors they were are still working for Chrysler's Lee Iacocca, Procter & Gamble's John Smale, Remington's Victor Kiam, and other super-strategists on today's corporate killing-fields. . . . Join them at the command post! Mastermind the battle! Clobber the enemy! Win the war![9]

Or, maybe to succeed you need to know *The Leadership Secrets of Attila the Hun?*[10] Or listen to the language of Wall Street: corporate raiders, hostile takeovers, white knights, wolf packs, industrial spies, the underground economy, head-hunting, shark-repellent, golden parachutes, poison pills, making a killing, etc.

When we organize our economic life around military metaphors and words such as *war, battle, strategy, tactics, struggle, contest,*

[8]Earl Shorris, *The Oppressed Middle: Politics of Middle Management* (Garden City, NY: Doubleday, 1989). Now in print under a different title: *Scenes from Corporate Life* (NY: Penguin, 1990). [Author's note]

[9]David J. Rogers, *Waging Business Warfare: Lessons from the Military Masters in Achieving Corporate Superiority* (New York: Scribner, 1987). [Author's note]

[10]*The Leadership Secrets of Attila the Hun:* title of a popular business advice book published in 1985.

competition, winning, enemies, opponents, defenses, security, maneu-
ver, objective, power, command, control, willpower, assault we have
gone a long way toward falling into a paranoid worldview. And when
men live within a context where their major function is to do battle —
economic or literal — they will be shaped by the logic of the warrior
psyche.

The High Price of Success

At the moment the world seems to be divided between those coun-   25
tries that are suffering from failed economies and those that are suffering from successful economies. After a half century of communism the
USSR, Eastern Europe, and China are all looking to be saved from the
results of stagnation by a change to market economies. Meanwhile, in
the U.S., Germany, and Japan we are beginning to realize that our
success has created an underclass of homeless and unemployed, and
massive pollution of the environment. As the Dow rises to new heights
everyone seems to have forgotten the one prophetic insight of Karl Marx:
where the economy creates a class of winners it will also create a class of
losers, where wealth gravitates easily into the hands of the haves, the
fortunes of the have-nots become more desperate.

On the psychological level, the shadow of our success, the flip side
of our affluence, is the increasing problem of stress and burnout. Lately,
dealing with stress and burnout has become a growth industry. Corporations are losing many of their best men to the "disease" of stress. Every
profession seems to have its crisis: physician burnout, teacher burnout,
lawyer burnout. Experts in relaxation, nutrition, exercise, and meditation are doing a brisk business.

But finally, stress cannot be dealt with by psychological tricks,
because for the most part it is a philosophical rather than a physiologi-
cal problem, a matter of the wrong worldview. Perhaps the most common variety of stress can best be described as "rustout" rather than
burnout. It is a product, not of an excess of fire but of a deficiency of
passion. We, human beings, can survive so long as we "make a living,"
but we do not thrive without a sense of significance that we gain only by
creating something we feel is of lasting value — a child, a better
mousetrap, a computer, a space shuttle, a book, a farm. When we spend
the majority of our time doing work that gives us a paycheck but no
sense of meaning we inevitably get bored and depressed. When the
requirements of our work do not match our creative potential we rust
out. The second kind of burnout is really a type of combat fatigue that is
the inevitable result of living for an extended period within an environment that is experienced as a battle zone. If the competition is always
pressing you to produce more and faster, if life is a battle, if winning is
the only thing, sooner or later you are going to come down with battle

fatigue. Like combat veterans returning from Vietnam, businessmen who live for years within an atmosphere of low-intensity warfare begin to exhibit the personality traits of the warrior. They become disillusioned and numb to ethical issues, they think only of survival and grow insensitive to pain. You may relax, breathe deeply, take time for R and R, and remain a warrior. But ultimately the only cure for stress is to leave the battlefield.

The feminist revolution made us aware of how the economic order has discriminated against women, but not of how it cripples the male psyche. In ancient China the feet of upperclass women were broken, bent backwards, and bound to make them more "beautiful." Have the best and brightest men of our time had their souls broken and bent to make them "successful"?

Let's think about the relation between the wounds men suffer, our overidentification with work, and our captivity within the horizons of the economic myth.

Recently, a lament has gone out through the land that men are 30 becoming too tame, if not limp. The poet Robert Bly,[11] who is as near as we have these days to a traveling bard and shaman for men, says we have raised a whole generation of soft men — oh-so-sensitive, but lacking in thunder and lightning. He tells men they must sever the ties with mother, stop looking at themselves through the eyes of women, and recover the "wild man" within themselves.

 I suspect that if men lack the lusty pride of self-affirmation, if we say "yes" too often but without passion, if we are burned out without ever having been on fire, it is mostly because we have allowed ourselves to be engulfed by a metabody, a masculine womb — The Corporation. . . .

At what cost to the life of our body and spirit do we purchase corporate and professional success? What sacrifices are we required to make to these upstart economic gods?

Here are some of the secrets they didn't tell you at the Harvard Business School, some of the hidden, largely unconscious, tyrannical, unwritten rules that govern success in professional and corporate life:

>   *Cleanliness is next to prosperity.* Sweat is lower class, lower status. Those who shower before work and use deodorant make more than those who shower after work and smell human throughout the day. As a nation we are proud that only three percent of the population has to work on the land — get soiled, be earthy — to feed the other ninety-seven percent.

>   *Look but don't touch.* The less contact you have with real stuff — raw material, fertilizer, wood, steel, chemicals, making things that

---

[11]*Robert Bly:* in addition to being a leading voice in the "men's movement" Bly (b. 1926) is a prominent American poet.

have moving parts — the more money you will make. Lately, as we have lost our edge in manufacturing and production, we have comforted ourselves with the promise that we can prosper by specializing in service and information industries. Oh, so clean.

Prefer abstractions. The further you move up toward the catbird seat, the penthouse, the office with the view of all Manhattan, the more you live among abstractions. In the brave new world[12] of the market you may speculate in hog futures without ever having seen a pig, buy out an airline without knowing how to fly a plane, grow wealthy without having produced anything.

Specialize. The modern economy rewards experts, men and women who are willing to become focused, concentrated, tightly bound, efficient. Or to put the matter more poignantly, we succeed in our professions to the degree that we sacrifice wide-ranging curiosity and fascination with the world at large, and become departmental in our thinking. The professions, like medieval castles, are small kingdoms sealed off from the outer world by walls of jargon. Once initiated by the ritual of graduate school, MBAs, economists, lawyers, and physicians speak only to themselves and theologians speak only to God.

Sit still and stay indoors. The world is run largely by urban, sedentary males. The symbol of power is the chair. The chairman of the board sits and manages. As a general rule those who stay indoors and move the least make the most money. Muscle doesn't pay. Worse yet, anybody who has to work in the sun and rain is likely to make the minimum wage. With the exception of quarterbacks, boxers, and race car drivers, whose bodies are broken for our entertainment, men don't get ahead by moving their bodies.

Live by the clock. Ignore your intimate body time, body rhythms, and conform to the demands of corporate time, work time, professional time. When "time is money," we bend our bodies and minds to the demands of EST (economic standard time). We interrupt our dreams when the alarm rings, report to work at nine, eat when the clock strikes twelve, return to our private lives at five, and retire at sixty-five — ready or not. As a reward we are allowed weekends and holidays for recreation. Conformity to the sacred routine, showing up on time, is more important than creativity. Instead of "taking our time" we respond to deadlines. Most successful men, and lately women, become Type A personalities, speed freaks, addicted to the rush of adrenaline, filled with a sense of urgency, hard driven, goal oriented, and stressed out. The most brutal example of this rule is the hundred-hour week required of physicians in their year of residency. This hazing ritual, like circumcision, drives home the deep mythic message that your body is no longer your own.

---

[12]*brave new world:* a double allusion: in Shakespeare's *The Tempest*, this phrase describes Prospero's island utopia; in Aldous Huxley's novel *Brave New World*, it ironically describes a future "rational" society that has lost its humanity.

Wear the uniform. It wouldn't be so bad if those who earned success and power were proud enough in their manhood to peacock their colors. But no. Success makes drab. The higher you rise in the establishment the more colorless you become, the more you dress like an undertaker or a priest. Bankers, politicians, CEOs[13] wear black, gray, or dark blue, with maybe a bold pinstripe or a daring "power tie." And the necktie? That ultimate symbol of the respectable man has obviously been demonically designed to exile the head from the body and restrain all deep and passionate breath. The more a corporation, institution, or profession requires the sacrifice of the individuality of its members, the more it requires uniform wear. The corp isn't really looking for a few good men. It's looking for a few dedicated Marines, and it knows exactly how to transform boys into uniform men. As monks and military men have known for centuries, once you get into the habit you follow the orders of the superior.

Keep your distance, stay in your place. The hierarchy of power and prestige that governs every profession and corporation establishes the proper distance between people. There are people above you, people below you, and people on your level, and you don't get too close to any of them. Nobody hugs the boss. What is lacking is friendship. I know of no more radical critique of economic life than the observation by Earl Shorris that nowhere in the vast literature of management is there a single chapter on friendship.

Desensitize yourself. Touch, taste, smell — the realm of the senses — receive little homage. What pays off is reason, will-power, planning, discipline, control. There has, of course, recently been a move afoot to bring in potted plants and tasteful art to make corporate environments more humane. But the point of these exercises in aesthetics, like the development of communication skills by practitioners of organizational development, is to increase production. The bottom line is still profit, not pleasure or persons.

Don't trouble yourself with large moral issues. The more the world is governed by experts, specialists, and professionals, the less anybody takes responsibility for the most troubling consequences of our success-failure. Television producers crank out endless cop and killing tales, but refuse to consider their contribution to the climate of violence. Lawyers concern themselves with what is legal, not what is just. Physicians devote themselves to kidneys or hearts of individual patients while the health delivery system leaves masses without medicine. Physicists invent new generations of genocidal weapons which they place in the eager arms of the military. The military hands the responsibility for their use over to politicians. Politicians plead that they have no choice — the enemy makes them do it. Professors publish esoterica while students perish from poor teaching. Foresters, in cahoots with timber companies, clear-cut or manage the forest for

[13]*CEOs:* chief executive officers.

sustained yield, but nobody is in charge of oxygen regeneration. Psychologists heal psyches while communities fall apart. Codes of professional ethics are for the most part, like corporate advertisements, high sounding but self-serving.

When we live within the horizons of the economic myth, we begin to consider it honorable for a man to do whatever he must to make a living. Gradually we adopt what Erich Fromm[14] called "a marketing orientation" toward our selves. We put aside our dreams, forget the green promise of our young selves, and begin to tailor our personalities to what the market requires. When we mold ourselves into commodities, practice smiling and charm so we will have "winning personalities," learn to sell ourselves, and practice the silly art of power dressing, we are certain to be haunted by a sense of emptiness.

Men, in our culture, have carried a special burden of unconsciousness, of ignorance of the self. The unexamined life[15] has been worth quite a lot in economic terms. It has enabled us to increase the gross national product yearly. It may not be necessary to be a compulsive extrovert to be financially successful, but it helps. Especially for men, ours is an outer-directed culture that rewards us for remaining strangers to ourselves, unacquainted with feeling, intuition, or the subtleties of sensation and dreams.

Many of the personality characteristics that have traditionally been considered "masculine" — aggression, rationality — are not innate or biological components of maleness but are products of a historical era in which men have been socially assigned the chief roles in warfare and the economic order. As women increasingly enter the quasimilitary world of the economic system they are likely to find themselves governed by the logic of the system. Some feminists, who harbor a secret belief in the innate moral superiority of women, believe that women will change the rules of business and bring the balm of communication and human kindness into the boardroom. To date this has been a vain hope. Women executives have proven themselves the equal of men in every way — including callousness. The difference between the sexes is being eroded as both sexes become defined by work. It is often said that the public world of work is a man's place and that as women enter it they will become increasingly "masculine" and lose their "femininity." To think this way is to miss the most important factor of the economic world. Economic man, the creature who defines itself within the horizons of work and consumption, is not man in any full sense of the word, but a being who has been neutralized, degendered, rendered subservient to the laws of the market. The danger of economics is not that it turns

14*Erich Fromm:* German American psychologist and social critic (1900–1980).

15*the unexamined life:* in Plato's *Apology of Socrates,* Socrates says "the life which is unexamined is not worth living."

women into men but that it destroys the fullness of both manhood and womanhood.

Engaging the Text

1. According to Keen, how are boys prepared for the role they will play as adult males in American society? What other institutions, traditions, or customs can you think of that contribute to this process?

2. What "tokens" define manhood in our society, according to Keen? Do you agree with his analysis? Do such tokens vary for men of different socioeconomic and ethnic groups?

3. Summarize in a paragraph or two the history of work that Keen sketches from the Greeks to the present. How have historical changes in attitude toward work affected men?

4. List the attitudes, values, and behaviors that men acquire from striving to succeed in corporate America, according to Keen. Do you think corporate culture has the same impact on women?

Exploring Connections

5. Read or review Jamaica Kincaid's "Girl" (p. 191) and write a brief imitation of it entitled "Boy," focusing on a father's advice to his son.

6. How does Keen's view of the costs of the male gender role compare with that of Janet Saltzman Chafetz (p. 194)? How do you explain the differences in their positions on the advantages and disadvantages of this role?

7. Write a conversation among John (Fire) Lame Deer (p. 128), Chellis Glendinning (p. 150), Susan Griffin (p. 175), and Keen on the relationships of masculinity, work, and nature.

Extending the Critical Context

8. Higher education is the path into corporate culture for many students. To what extent is college preparing you to accept what Keen calls the "unwritten rules" of corporate life. Should it?

Little Miracles, Kept Promises

Sandra Cisneros

This story features an unusual narrative device: it consists entirely of letters to saints. In keeping with Mexican tradition, these letters are left before a statue of the saint along with a milagrito *or "little miracle" — a small charm. Despite their brevity, the letters reveal much about their authors, and together they offer penetrating insights into life and male-female relationships near the Texas-Mexico border. The story deserves careful reading, for small details carry important messages. (For example, Arnulfo Contreras's prayer reveals indirectly that he's earning only about two dollars an hour.) An award-winning writer, Sandra Cisneros (b. 1954) has published two volumes of poetry,* Bad Boys *(1980) and* My Wicked, Wicked Ways *(1987), and two volumes of fiction,* The House on Mango Street *(1983) and* Woman Hollering Creek *(1991), from which this story is taken.*

Exvoto[1] Donated as Promised

On the 20th of December of 1988 we suffered a terrible disaster on the road to Corpus Christi.[2] The bus we were riding skidded and overturned near Robstown and a lady and her little girl were killed. Thanks to La Virgen de Guadalupe we are alive, all of us miraculously unharmed, and with no visible scars, except we are afraid to ride buses. We dedicate this retablo[3] to La Virgencita[4] with our affection and gratitude and our everlasting faith.

Familia Arteaga
Alice, Texas
G.R. (Gracias Recibido[5] Thanks Given)

Blessed Santo Niño de Atocha,[6]

Thank you for helping us when Chapa's truck got stolen. We didn't know how we was going to make it. He needs it to get to work, and this

---

[1]*Exvoto:* an offering in fulfillment of a vow.

[2]*Corpus Christi:* a seaport in Texas and the first of several Texas towns and cities mentioned in the story. In Latin, "the body of Christ."

[3]*retablo:* altarpiece.

[4]*La Virgencita:* literally "the little Virgin." The diminutive form in Spanish conveys affectionate familiarity, here with the Virgin of Guadalupe, patron saint of Mexico.

[5]*Gracias Recibido:* Thanks.

[6]*Santo Niño de Atocha:* Blessed Child of Atocha.

job, well, he's been on probation since we got him to quit drinking. Raquel and the kids are hardly ever afraid of him anymore, and we are proud parents. We don't know how we can repay you for everything you have done for our family. We will light a candle to you every Sunday and never forget you.

Sidronio Tijerina
Brenda A. Camacho de Tijerina
San Angelo, Texas

Dear San Martín de Porres,[7]

Please send us clothes, furniture, shoes, dishes. We need anything that don't eat. Since the fire we have to start all over again and Lalo's disability check ain't much and don't go far. Zulema would like to finish school but I says she can just forget about it now. She's our oldest and her place is at home helping us out I told her. Please make her see some sense. She's all we got.

Thanking you,
Adelfa Vásquez
Escobas, Texas

Dear San Antonio de Padua,[8]

Can you please help me find a man who isn't a pain in the nalgas.[9] There aren't any in Texas, I swear. Especially not in San Antonio.

Can you do something about all the educated Chicanos who have to go to California to find a job. I guess what my sister Irma says is true: "If you didn't get a husband when you were in college, you don't get one."

I would appreciate it very much if you sent me a man who speaks Spanish, who at least can pronounce his name the way it's supposed to be pronounced. Someone please who never calls himself "Hispanic" unless he's applying for a grant from Washington, D.C.

Can you send me a man man. I mean someone who's not ashamed to be seen cooking or cleaning or looking after himself. In other words, a man who acts like an adult. Not one who's never lived alone, never bought his own underwear, never ironed his own shirts, never even heated his own tortillas. In other words, don't send me someone like my

---

[7]*San Martín de Porres:* St. Martin de Porres (1569–1639) was the son of a Spanish soldier and a Black freedwoman from Panama. He joined a Dominican monastery as a lay brother (that is, not as a monk) and founded an orphanage and several nurseries.

[8]*San Antonio de Padua:* St. Anthony of Padua (1195–1231). Padua is an Italian city long associated with learning and the arts (Galileo, Dante, and Petrarch taught or studied there). The city features a six-domed basilica of St. Anthony.

[9]*nalgas:* buttocks.

brothers who my mother ruined with too much chichi,[10] or I'll throw him back.

I'll turn your statue upside down until you send him to me. I've put up with too much too long, and now I'm just too intelligent, too powerful, too beautiful, too sure of who I am finally to deserve anything less.

Ms. Barbara Ybañez
San Antonio, TX

Dear Niño Fidencio,[11]

I would like for you to help me get a job with good pay, benefits, and retirement plan. I promise you if you help me I will make a pilgrimage to your tomb in Espinazo and bring you flowers. Many thanks.

César Escandón
Pharr, Tejas

DEAR DON PEDRITO JARAMILLO HEALER OF LOS OLMOS[12]

MY NAME IS ENRIQUETA ANTONIA SANDOVAL. I LIVE IN SAN MARCOS TX I AM SICK THEY OPERATED ME FROM A KIDNEY AND A TUMOR OF CANCER BUT THANKS TO GOD I AM ALIVE BUT I HAVE TO GET TREATMENTS FOR A YEAR THE KIMO[13] I AM 2½ YEARS OLD BUT MY GRANDMA BROUGHT ME THAT YOU AND OUR LORD WHO IS IN THE HEAVENS WILL CURE ME WITH THIS LETTER THAT I AM DEPOSITING HERE ITS MY GRANDMA WHO IS WRITING THIS I HOPE EVERYBODY WHO SEES THIS LETTER WILL TAKE A MINUTE TO ASK FOR MY HEALTH

ENRIQUETA ANTONIA SANDOVAL
2 AND A HALF YEARS OLD

I LEOCADIA DIMAS VDA. DE CORDERO OF SAN MARCOS TX HAVE COME TO PAY THIS REQUEST TO DON PEDRITO THAT MY GRANDDAUGHTER WILL COME OUT FINE FROM HER OPERATION THANKS TO GOD AND THOSE WHO HELPED SUCH GOOD DOCTORS THAT DID THEIR JOB WELL THE REST IS IN GODS HANDS THAT HE DO HIS WILL MANY THANKS WITH ALL MY HEART.

YOUR VERY RESPECTFUL SERVANT
LEOCADIA

[10]*chichi:* vulgar slang for "breast."
[11]*Niño Fidencio:* the Boy Fidencio.
[12]*Don Pedrito Jaramillo Healer of Los Olmos:* Mexican faith healer; died in 1907.
[13]*KIMO:* chemotheraphy to fight the cancer.

Oh Mighty Poderosos,[14] Blessed Powerful Ones,

You who are crowned in heaven and who are so close to our Divine Savior, I implore your intercession before the Almighty on my behalf. I ask for peace of spirit and prosperity, and that the demons in my path that are the cause of all my woes be removed so that they no longer torment me. Look favorably on this petition and bless me, that I may continue to glorify your deeds with all my heart — santísimo Niño Fidencio, gran General Pancho Villa, bendito Don Pedrito Jaramillo, virtuoso John F. Kennedy,[15] and blessed Pope John Paul. Amen.

Gertrudis Parra
Uvalde, Tejas

Father Almighty,

Teach me to love my husband again. Forgive me.

s.
Corpus Christi

Seven African Powers that surround our Savior — Obatala, Yemaya, Ochún, Orunla, Ogun, Elegua, and Shango[16] — why don't you behave and be good to me? Oh Seven African Powers, come on, don't be bad. Let my Illinois lottery ticket win, and if it does, don't let my cousin Cirilo in Chicago cheat me out of my winnings, since I'm the one who pays for the ticket and all he does is buy it for me each week — if he does even that. He's my cousin, but like the Bible says, better to say nothing than to say nothing nice.

Protect me from the evil eye of the envious and don't let my enemies do me harm, because I've never done a thing wrong to anyone first. Save this good Christian who the wicked have taken advantage of.

Seven Powers, reward my devotion with good luck. Look after me, why don't you? And don't forget me because I never forget you.

Moises Idelfonso Mata
San Antonio, Texas

Virgencita de Guadalupe,

I promise to walk to your shrine on my knees the very first day I get back, I swear, if you will only get the Tortillería la Casa de la Masa[17] to

---

[14]*Poderosos:* Powerful ones.

[15]*gran General Pancho Villa, virtuoso John F. Kennedy:* Pancho Villa (1878–1923) was a Mexican revolutionary, general, and eventually folk hero of the grandest proportions. President Kennedy is "virtuoso" — virtuous — in the eyes of many Chicano/Latino people who believe he was sympathetic to their cause.

[16]*Obatala, Yemaya, Ochún, Orunla, Ogun, Elegua, and Shango:* the names of deities in Santería, a religion evolved in the Caribbean that combines elements of Catholicism with traditional African tribal beliefs.

[17]*Tortillería la Casa de la Masa:* a tortilleria is a store where tortillas are made; this one is named "House of Dough."

pay me the $253.72 they owe me for two weeks' work. I put in 67½ hours that first week and 79 hours the second, and I don't have anything to show for it yet. I calculated with the taxes deducted, I have $253.72 coming to me. That's all I'm asking for. The $253.72 I have coming to me.

I have asked the proprietors Blanquita and Rudy Mondragón, and they keep telling me next week, next week, next week. And it's almost the middle of the third week already and I don't know how I'm going to do it to pay this week's rent, since I'm already behind, and the other guys have loaned me as much as they're able, and I don't know what I'm going to do, I don't know what I'm going to do.

My wife and the kids and my in-laws all depend on what I send home. We are humble people, Virgencita. You know I'm not full of vices. That's how I am. It's been hard for me to live here so far away without seeing my wife, you know. And sometimes one gets tempted, but no, and no, and no. I'm not like that. Please, Virgencita, all I'm asking for is my $253.72. There is no one else I can turn to here in this country, and well, if you can't help me, well, I just don't know.

Arnulfo Contreras
San Antonio, Tejas

Saint Sebastian who was persecuted with arrows and then survived, thank you for answering my prayers! All them arrows that had persecuted me — my brother-in-law Ernie and my sister Alba and their kids — el Junior, la Gloria, and el Skyler — all gone. And now my home sweet home is mine again, and my Dianita bien lovey-dovey, and my kids got something to say to me besides who hit who.

Here is the little gold milagrito[18] I promised you, a little house, see? And it ain't that cheap gold-plate shit either. So now that I paid you back, we're even, right? Cause I don't like for no one to say Victor Lozano don't pay his debts. I pays cash on the line, bro. And Victor Lozano's word like his deeds is solid gold.

Victor A. Lozano
Houston, TX

Dear San Lázaro,[19]

My mother's comadre[20] Demetria said if I prayed to you that like maybe you could help me because you were raised from the dead and did a lot of miracles and maybe if I lit a candle every night for seven

---

[18]*milagrito:* literally "small miracle," refers to a small metallic charm placed on an altarpiece or icon of a saint to which one prays for a favor.

[19]*San Lázaro:* According to the Gospel of John, Christ brought Lazarus back to life after four days in the tomb.

[20]*comadre:* woman friend.

days and prayed, you might maybe could help me with my face breaking out with so many pimples. Thank you.

Rubén Ledesma
Hebbronville, Texas

Santísima Señora de San Juan de los Lagos,[21]

We came to see you twice when they brought you to San Antonio, my mother and my sister Yolanda and two of my aunts, Tía Enedina and my Tía Perla, and we drove all the way from Beeville just to visit you and make our requests.

I don't know what my Tía Enedina asked for, she's always so secretive, but probably it had to do with her son Beto who doesn't do anything but hang around the house and get into trouble. And my Tía Perla no doubt complained about her ladies' problems — her ovaries that itch, her tangled fallopians, her uterus that makes her seasick with all its flipping and flopping. And Mami who said she only came along for the ride, lit three candles so you would bless us all and sweep jealousy and bitterness from our hearts because that's what she says every day and every night. And my sister Yoli asked that you help her lose weight because I don't want to wind up like Tía Perla, embroidering altar cloths and dressing saints.

But that was a year ago, Virgencita, and since then my cousin Beto was fined for killing the neighbor's rooster with a flying Big Red bottle, and my Tía Perla is convinced her uterus has fallen because when she walks something inside her rattles like a maraca, and my mother and my aunts are arguing and yelling at each other same as always. And my stupid sister Yoli is still sending away for even stupider products like the Grasa Fantástica,[22] guaranteed to burn away fat — It really works, Tere, just rub some on while you're watching TV — only she's fatter than ever and just as sad.

What I realize is that we all made the trip to San Antonio to ask something of you, Virgencita, we all needed you to listen to us. And of all of us, my mama and sister Yoli, and my aunts Enedina and Perla, of all of us, you granted me my petition and sent, just like I asked, a guy who would love only me because I was tired of looking at girls younger than me walking along the street or riding in cars or standing in front of the school with a guy's arm hooked around their neck.

So what is it I'm asking for? Please, Virgencita. Lift this heavy cross from my shoulders and leave me like I was before, wind on my neck, my arms swinging free, and no one telling me how I ought to be.

Teresa Galindo
Beeville, Texas

[21]*Santísima Señora de San Juan de los Lagos:* Blessed Lady of San Juan de los Lagos.
[22]*Grasa Fantástica:* "fantastic grease," a fictional, and clearly ineffective, patent medicine.

Miraculous Black Christ of Esquipulas,
   Please make our grandson to be nice to us and stay away from drugs. Save him to find a job and move away from us. Thank you.

> Grandma y Grandfather
> Harlingen

M3rlc5l45s BIlck Chr3st 4f 2sq53p5Ils,
   3 lsk y45, L4rd, w3th lII my h2lrt pl2ls2 wItch 4v2r Mlnny B2nlv3d2s, wh4 3s 4v2rs2ls. 3 14v2 h3m lnd 3 d4n't kn4w whlt t4 d4 lb45t lII th3s l4v2 sldn2ss lnd shlm2 thlt f3lls m2.

> B2njlm3n T.
> D21 R34 TX

Milagroso Cristo Negro de Esquípulas,
   Te ofrezco este retrato de mis niños. Wáchelos, Dios Santo, y si le quitas el trago a mi hijo te prometo prender velitas. Ayúdanos con nuestras cuentas, Señor, y que el cheque del income tax nos llegue pronto para pagar los biles. Danos una buena vida y que les ayudes a mis hijos a cambiar sus modos. Tú que eres tan bondadoso escucha estas peticiones que te pido con todo mi corazón y con toda la fe de mi alma. Ten piedad, Padre mio. Mi nombre es Adela O.[23]

> Elizondo.
> Cotulla TX

Milagroso Cristo Negro,
   Thank you por el milagro de haber graduado de high school. Aquí le regalo mi retrato de graduation.[24]

> Fito Moroles
> Rockport, Texas

Cristo Negro,
   Venimos desde muy lejos. Infinitas gracias, Señor. Gracias por habernos escuchado.[25]

> Familia Armendáriz G.
> Matamoros, Tamps, México

---

   [23]*Te ofrezco este retrato de mis niños . . .:* I offer You this photo of my children. Watch over them, dear Lord, and if You keep my sons from drinking I promise to light You some candles. Help us with our bills, Lord, and make the income tax check arrive soon so we can pay some of them off. Give us a good life and help my children to change their ways. You who are so good hear these prayers of mine which come from deep within my heart and with my soul's deepest faith. Have mercy, Father. My name is Adela O.

   [24]*Thank you por el milagro de haber. . . .:* Thank you for the miracle of my graduation from high school. Here is my graduation picture for you.

   [25]*Venimos desde muy lejos. . . .:* We come a great distance. Many thanks, Lord. Thank You for listening to us.

Jesus Christ,
    Please keep Deborah Abrego and Ralph S. Urrea together forever.
> Love,
> Deborah Abrego
> Sabínal, Texas

Blessed Virgen de los Remedios,[26]
    Señora Dolores Alcalá de Corchado finds herself gravely ill from a complication that resulted after a delicate operation she underwent Thursday last, and from which she was recovering satisfactorily until suffering a hemmorhage Tuesday morning. Please intercede on her behalf. We leave her in the hands of God, that His will be done, now that we have witnessed her suffering and don't know whether she should die or continue this life. Her husband of forty-eight years offers this request with all his heart.
> Señor Gustavo Corchado B.
> Laredo, Tejas

Madrecita de Dios,[27]
    Thank you. Our child is born healthy!
> Rene y Janie Garza
> Hondo, TX

Saint Jude, patron saint of lost causes,
    Help me pass my English 320, British Restoration Literature class and everything to turn out ok.
> Eliberto González
> Dallas

Virgencita . . .
    I've cut off my hair just like I promised I would and pinned my braid here by your statute. Above a Toys "Я" Us name tag that says IZAURA. Along several hospital bracelets. Next to a business card for Sergio's Casa de la Belleza Beauty College. Domingo Reyna's driver's license. Notes printed on the flaps of envelopes. Silk roses, plastic roses, paper roses, roses crocheted out of fluorescent orange yarn. Photo button of a baby in a *charro*[28] hat. Caramel-skinned woman in a white graduation cap and gown. Mean dude in bandanna and tattoos. Oval black-and-white passport portrait of the sad uncle who never married.

---

[26]*Virgen de los Remedios:* Virgin of Remedies.
[27]*Madrecita de Dios:* Little Mother of God — a term of endearment.
[28]*charro:* Mexican cowboy.

A mama in a sleeveless dress watering the porch plants. Sweet boy with new mustache and new soldier uniform. Teenager with a little bit of herself sitting on her lap. Blurred husband and wife leaning one into the other as if joined at the hip. Black-and-white photo of the cousins *la* Josie *y la* Mary Helen, circa 1942. Polaroid of Sylvia Rios, First Holy Communion, age nine years.

So many *milagritos* safety-pinned here, so many little miracles dangling from red thread — a gold Sacred Heart, a tiny copper arm, a kneeling man in silver, a bottle, a brass truck, a foot, a house, a hand, a baby, a cat, a breast, a tooth, a belly button, an evil eye. So many petitions, so many promises made and kept. And there is nothing I can give you except this braid of hair the color of coffee in a glass.

Chayo,[29] *what have you done! All that beautiful hair.*

Chayito, how could you ruin in one second what your mother took years to create?

You might as well've plucked out your eyes like Saint Lucy.[30] *All that hair!*

My mother cried, did I tell you? All that beautiful hair . . .

I've cut off my hair. Which I've never cut since the day I was born. The donkey tail in a birthday game. Something shed like a snakeskin.

My head as light as if I'd raised it from water. My heart buoyant again, as if before I'd worn *el* Sagrado Corazón[31] in my open chest. I could've lit this entire church with my grief.

I'm a bell without a clapper. A woman with one foot in this world and one foot in that. A woman straddling both. This thing between my legs, this unmentionable.

I'm a snake swallowing its tail. I'm my history and my future. All my ancestors' ancestors inside my own belly. All my futures and all my pasts.

I've had to steel and hoard and hone myself. I've had to push the furniture against the door and not let you in.

---

[29]*Chayo . . . Chayito:* Rosario's nickname. Chayito is the diminutive of Chayo.

[30]*Saint Lucy:* a Sicilian virgin martyr who died circa 304. According to legend, she dedicated herself to God at an early age and rejected a pagan suitor. The suitor then denounced her during persecutions of the Christians by Roman Emperor Diocletian.

[31]*el Sagrado Corazón:* the Sacred Heart (of Christ). In Catholic imagery, Christ is sometimes pictured with a heart visible in his chest.

What you doing sitting in there in the dark?

I'm thinking.

Thinking of what?

Just . . . thinking.

You're nuts. Chayo, ven a saludar.[32] *All the relatives are here. You come out of there and be sociable.*

Do boys think, and girls daydream? Do only girls have to come out and greet the relatives and smile and be nice and *quedar bien?*[33]

It's not good to spend so much time alone.
What she do in there all by herself? It don't look right.
Chayito, when you getting married? Look at your cousin Leticia. She's younger than you.
How many kids you want when you grow up?
When I become a mommy . . .
You'll change. You'll see. Wait till you meet Mr. Right.
Chayo, tell everybody what it is you're studying again.
Look at our Chayito. She likes making her little pictures. She's gonna be a painter.
A painter! Tell her I got five rooms that need painting.
When you become a mother . . .

Thank you for making all those months I held my breath not a child in my belly, but a thyroid problem in my throat.

I can't be a mother. Not now. Maybe never. Not for me to choose, like I didn't choose being female. Like I didn't choose being artist — it isn't something you choose. It's something you are, only I can't explain it.

I don't want to be a mother.

I wouldn't mind being a father. At least a father could still be artist, could love some*thing* instead of some*one*, and no one would call that selfish.

---

[32]*ven a saludar:* come and say hello.
[33]*quedar bien:* make a good impression.

I leave my braid here and thank you for believing what I do is important. Though no one else in my family, no other woman, neither friend nor relative, no one I know, not even the heroine in the *telenovelas*,[34] no woman wants to live alone.

I do.

Virgencita de Guadalupe. For a long time I wouldn't let you in my house. I couldn't see you without seeing my ma each time my father came home drunk and yelling, blaming everything that ever went wrong in his life on her.

I couldn't look at your folded hands without seeing my *abuela*[35] mumbling, "My son, my son, my son . . ." Couldn't look at you without blaming you for all the pain my mother and her mother and all our mothers' mothers have put up with in the name of God. Couldn't let you in my house.

I wanted you bare-breasted, snakes in your hands. I wanted you leaping and somersaulting the backs of bulls. I wanted you swallowing raw hearts and rattling volcanic ash. I wasn't going to be my mother or my grandma. All that self-sacrifice, all that silent suffering. Hell no. Not here. Not me.

Don't think it was easy going without you. Don't think I didn't get my share of it from everyone. Heretic. Atheist. *Malinchista*.[36] *Hocicona*.[37] But I wouldn't shut my yap. My mouth always getting me in trouble. *Is that what they teach you at the university? Miss High-and-Mighty. Miss Thinks-She's-Too-Good-for-Us.* Acting like a *bolilla*, a white girl. *Malinche*. Don't think it didn't hurt being called a traitor. Trying to explain to my ma, to my *abuela*, why I didn't want to be like them.

I don't know how it all fell in place. How I finally understood who you are. No longer Mary the mild, but our mother Tonantzín.[38] Your church at Tepeyac built on the site of her temple. Sacred ground no matter whose goddess claims it.

[34]*telenovelas:* TV soap operas extremely popular in Latin America.

[35]*abuela:* grandmother.

[36]*Malinchista:* a woman who is perceived as a sexual and cultural traitor; after Malintzin Tenepal, "La Malinche," Indian mistress of Hernán Cortés, who conquered Mexico for Spain.

[37]*Hocicona:* "wise guy" or "smartass."

[38]*Tonantzín:* (or Tonantsi). Ancient Indian earth goddess in Mexico; with the advent of Christianity, her identity became merged with that of the Virgin of Guadalupe.

That you could have the power to rally a people when a country was born, and again during civil war, and during a farmworkers' strike in California made me think maybe there is power in my mother's patience, strength in my grandmother's endurance. Because those who suffer have a special power, don't they? The power of understanding someone else's pain. And understanding is the beginning of healing.

When I learned your real name is Coatlaxopeuh,[39] She Who Has Dominion over Serpents, when I recognized you as Tonantzín, and learned your names are Teteoinnan, Toci, Xochiquetzal, Tlazolteotl, Coatlicue, Chalchiuhtlicue, Coyolxauhqui, Huixtocihuatl, Chicome-coatl, Cihuacoatl, when I could see you as Nuestra Señora de la Soledad, Nuestra Señora de los Remedios, Nuestra Señora del Perpetuo Socorro, Nuestra Señora de San Juan de los Lagos, Our Lady of Lourdes, Our Lady of Mount Carmel, Our Lady of the Rosary, Our Lady of Sorrows, I wasn't ashamed, then, to be my mother's daughter, my grandmother's granddaughter, my ancestors' child.

When I could see you in all your facets, all at once the Buddha, the Tao, the true Messiah, Yahweh, Allah, the Heart of the Sky, the Heart of the Earth, the Lord of the Near and Far, the Spirit, the Light, the Universe, I could love you, and, finally, learn to love me.

Mighty Guadalupana Coatlaxopeuh Tonantzín,
What "little miracle" could I pin here? Braid of hair in its place and know that I thank you.

Rosario (Chayo) De Leon
Austin, Tejas

[39]*Coatlaxopeuh . . . .*: this and the next paragraph refer to a highly complex Mexican-Chicano tradition of folk Catholicism which has evolved over centuries and incorporates indigenous Indian beliefs.

Engaging the Text

1. Take a few minutes to study a particular letter and to "rehearse" how you would read it aloud. Then read your chosen letter to the class.

2. What kinds of things are people in this story praying for? What do you learn about them, about their needs, desires, and dreams, about their accomplishments and their failures, about their values and way of life? What composite picture do you get from these glimpses?

3. Choose one letter and write a detailed analysis of how it fits into the story. What exactly do you learn about its writer? What issues does it raise? What

facts does it reveal? What is its tone or emotional impact? How does it reinforce or contrast with other letters in the story?

4. Working in small groups, look closely at three or four letters that emphasize male-female relationships. What images of men and women do they project? Can you draw àny conclusions about the way Cisneros portrays male-female relationships?

Exploring Connections

5. What lessons has Rosario De Leon's family tried to teach her? What lessons has she actually learned? Compare this family wisdom with that passed between generations in "Girl" by Jamaica Kincaid (p. 191).

6. Both Rosario De Leon and the unnamed narrator of Leslie Marmon Silko's "Storyteller" (p. 135) find a sense of personal identity and power by allying themselves with ancestral traditions. Compare the roles played by cultural tradition in their development: what problems does each woman confront, and how do cultural traditions contribute to or help her to solve these problems?

Extending the Critical Context

7. Read one of Cisneros's story collections, *Woman Hollering Creek* or *The House on Mango Street* and write either a review of the full volume or a critical analysis of a particular story.

Images of Relationships

CAROL GILLIGAN

Carol Gilligan reports here on an elegant study of female-male psychology. She presented college students with simple pictures (some suggesting personal intimacy, others suggesting professional achievement) and asked them to write stories for each image. Male and female students responded in markedly different ways; for example, many women imagined a net to protect trapeze artists while men pictured the acrobats plunging to their death. Gilligan (b. 1936) is a professor of education at Harvard University. This selection is from her book In a Different Voice: Psychological Theory and Women's Development *(1982). More recently she has edited and contributed to* Mapping the Moral Domain *(1988) and* Making Connections: The Relational Worlds of Adolescent Girls at Emma Willard School *(1990).*

. . . A study of the images of violence that appear in stories written by college students to pictures on the TAT[1] . . . report[s] statistically significant sex differences in the places where violence is seen and in the substance of violent fantasies as well. The themes of separation and connection are central to the study, conducted by Susan Pollak and myself and based on an analysis of stories, written prior to the study, by students as a class exercise in a psychology course on motivation (Pollak and Gilligan, 1982). The study began with Pollak's observation of seemingly bizarre imagery of violence in men's stories about a picture of what appeared to be a tranquil scene, a couple sitting on a bench by a river next to a low bridge. In response to this picture, more than 21 percent of the eighty-eight men in the class had written stories containing incidents of violence — homicide, suicide, stabbing, kidnapping, or rape. In contrast, none of the fifty women in the class had projected violence into this scene.

This observation of violence in men's stories about intimacy appeared to us as a possible corollary to Horner's (1968) report of imagery of violence in women's stories about competitive success. Horner, exemplifying her category of "bizarre or violent imagery" in depicting women's anticipation of negative consequences following success, cites a story that portrays a jubilant Anne, at the top of her medical school class, physically beaten and maimed for life by her jealous classmates. The corollary observation of violent imagery in men's fantasies of intimate relationships is illustrated by a story written by one of the men in the class to the picture of the riverbench scene:

> Nick saw his life pass before his eyes. He could feel the cold penetrating ever deeper into his body. How long had it been since he had fallen through the ice — thirty seconds, a minute? It wouldn't take long for him to succumb to the chilling grip of the mid-February Charles River. What a fool he had been to accept the challenge of his roommate Sam to cross the frozen river. He knew all along that Sam hated him. Hated him for being rich and especially hated him for being engaged to Mary, Sam's childhood sweetheart. But Nick never realized until now that Mary also hated him and really loved Sam. Yet there they were, the two of them, calmly sitting on a bench in the riverbend, watching Nick drown. They'd probably soon be married, and they'd probably finance it with the life insurance policy for which Mary was the beneficiary.

Calling attention to the eye of the observer in noting where danger is seen, Pollak and I wondered whether men and women perceive

---

[1]*TAT*: Thematic Apperception Test; according to Gilligan, "The TAT presents for interpretation an ambiguous cue — a picture about which a story is to be written or a segment of a story that is to be completed. Such stories . . . are considered by psychologists to reveal . . . the concepts and interpretations [people] bring to their experience and thus presumably the kind of sense they make of their lives" (*In a Different Voice*, 14).

danger in different situations and construe danger in different ways. Following the initial observation of violence in men's stories about intimacy, we set out to discover whether there were sex differences in the distribution of violent fantasies across situations of achievement and affiliation and whether violence was differently associated by males and females with intimacy and competitive success. The findings of the resulting images of violence study corroborate previous reports of sex differences in aggression (Terman and Tyler, 1954; Whiting and Pope, 1973; Maccoby and Jacklin 1974) by revealing a far greater incidence of violence in stories written by men. Of the eighty-eight men in the motivation class, 51 percent wrote at least one story containing images of violence, in comparison to 20 percent of the fifty women in the class, and no woman wrote more than one story in which violence appeared. But the study also revealed sex differences in the distribution and substance of violent fantasies, indicating a difference between the way in which men and women tend to imagine relationships.

Four of the six pictures that comprised the test were chosen for the purposes of this analysis since they provided clear illustrations of achievement and affiliation situations. Two of the pictures show a man and a woman in close personal affiliation — the couple on the bench in the river scene, and two trapeze artists grasping each other's wrists, the man hanging by his knees from the trapeze and the woman in mid-air. Two pictures show people at work in impersonal achievement situations — a man sitting alone at his desk in a high-rise office building, and two women, dressed in white coats, working in a laboratory, the woman in the background watching while the woman in the foreground handles the test tubes. The study centered on a comparison between the stories written about these two sets of pictures.

The men in the class, considered as a group, projected more violence into situations of personal affiliation than they did into impersonal situations of achievement. Twenty-five percent of the men wrote violent stories only to the pictures of affiliation, 19 percent to pictures of both affiliation and achievement, and 7 percent only to pictures of achievement. In contrast, the women saw more violence in impersonal situations of achievement than in situations of affiliation; 16 percent of the women wrote violent stories to the achievement pictures and 6 percent to the pictures of affiliation.

As the story about Nick, written by a man, illustrates the association of danger with intimacy, so the story about Miss Hegstead, written by a woman, exemplifies the projection of violence into situations of achievement and the association of danger with competitive success:

> Another boring day in the lab and that mean bitchy Miss Hegstead always breathing down the students' backs. Miss Hegstead has been at Needham Country High School for 40 years and every chemistry class is the same. She is watching Jane Smith, the model student in the class.

> She always goes over to Jane and comments to the other students that
> Jane is always doing the experiment right and Jane is the only student
> who really works hard, etc. Little does Miss Hegstead know that Jane
> is making some arsenic to put in her afternoon coffee.

If aggression is conceived as a response to the perception of danger, the findings of the images of violence study suggest that men and women may perceive danger in different social situations and construe danger in different ways — men seeing danger more often in close personal affiliation than in achievement and construing danger to arise from intimacy, women perceiving danger in impersonal achievement situations and construing danger to result from competitive success. The danger men describe in their stories of intimacy is a danger of entrapment or betrayal, being caught in a smothering relationship or humiliated by rejection and deceit. In contrast, the danger women portray in their tales of achievement is a danger of isolation, a fear that in standing out or being set apart by success, they will be left alone. In the story of Miss Hegstead, the only apparent cause of the violence is Jane's being singled out as the best student and thus set apart from her classmates. She retaliates by making arsenic to put in the teacher's afternoon coffee, yet all Miss Hegstead did was to praise Jane for her good work.

As people are brought closer together in the pictures, the images of violence in the men's stories increase, while as people are set further apart, the violence in the women's stories increases. The women in the class projected violence most frequently into the picture of the man at his desk (the only picture portraying a person alone), while the men in the class most often saw violence in the scene of the acrobats on the trapeze (the only picture in which people touched). Thus, it appears that men and women may experience attachment and separation in different ways and that each sex perceives a danger which the other does not see — men in connection, women in separation.

But since the women's perception of danger departs from the usual mode of expectation, the acrobats seeming to be in far greater danger than the man at his desk, their perception calls into question the usual mode of interpretation. Sex differences in aggression are usually interpreted by taking the male response as the norm, so that the absence of aggression in women is identified as the problem to be explained. However, the disparate location of violence in the stories written by women and men raises the question as to why women see the acrobats as safe.

The answer comes from the analysis of the stories about the trapeze. 10 Although the picture of acrobats shows them performing high in the air without a net, 22 percent of the women in the study added nets in the stories they wrote. In contrast, only 6 percent of the men imagined the presence of a net, while 40 percent either explicitly mentioned the absence of a net or implied its absence by describing one or both acrobats as plummeting to their deaths. Thus, the women saw the scene on the trapeze as safe because, by providing nets, they had made it safe, protecting the lives of the acrobats in the event of a fall. Yet failing to imagine the presence of nets in the scene on the trapeze, men, interpreting women's responses, readily attribute the absence of violence in women's stories to a denial of danger or to a repression of aggression (May, 1980) rather than to the activities of care through which the women make the acrobats safe. As women imagine the activities through which relationships are woven and connection sustained, the world of intimacy — which appears so mysterious and dangerous to men — comes instead to appear increasingly coherent and safe.

If aggression is tied, as women perceive, to the fracture of human connection, then the activities of care, as their fantasies suggest, are the activities that make the social world safe, by avoiding isolation and preventing aggression rather than by seeking rules to limit its extent. In this light, aggression appears no longer as an unruly impulse that must be contained but rather as a signal of a fracture of connection, the sign of a failure of relationship. From this perspective, the prevalence of violence in men's fantasies, denoting a world where danger is everywhere seen, signifies a problem in making connection, causing relationships to erupt and turning separation into a dangerous isolation. Reversing the usual mode of interpretation, in which the absence of aggression in women is tied to a problem with separation, makes it possible to see the prevalence of violence in men's stories, its odd location in the context of intimate relationships, and its association with betrayal and deceit as indicative of a problem with connection that leads relationships to become dangerous and safety to appear in separation. The rule-bound competitive achievement situations, which for women threaten the web of connection, for men provide a mode of connection that establishes clear boundaries and limits aggression, and thus appears comparatively safe.

A story written by one of the women about the acrobats on the trapeze illustrates these themes, calling into question the usual opposition of achievement and affiliation by portraying the continuation of the relationship as the predicate for success:

> These are two Flying Gypsies, and they are auditioning for the big job with the Ringling Brothers Circus. They are the last team to try out for the job, and they are doing very well. They have grace and style, but they use a safety net which some teams do not use. The owners say that they'll hire them if they forfeit the net, but the Gypsies decide that they would rather live longer and turn down the job than take risks like that. They know the act will be ruined if either got hurt and see no sense in taking the risk.

For the Gypsies in the story, it is not the big job with the circus that is of paramount importance but rather the well-being of the two people involved. Anticipating negative consequences from a success attained at the risk of their lives, they forfeit the job rather than the net, protecting their lives but also their act, which "would be ruined if either got hurt."

While women thus try to change the rules in order to preserve relationships, men, in abiding by these rules, depict relationships as easily replaced. Projecting most violence into this scene, they write stories about infidelity and betrayal that end with the male acrobat dropping the woman, presumably replacing the relationship and going on with the act:

> The woman trapeze artist is married to the best friend of the male who has just discovered (before the show) that she has been unfaithful to his friend (her husband). He confronted her with this knowledge and told her to tell her husband but she refused. Not having the courage to confront him himself, the trapeze artist creates an accident while 100 feet above ground, letting the woman slip out of his grasp in mid-flight. She is killed in the incident but he feels no guilt, believing that he has rectified the situation.

The prevalence of violence in male fantasy . . . is consonant with the view of aggression as endemic in human relationships. But these male fantasies and images also reveal a world where connection is fragmented and communication fails, where betrayal threatens because there seems to be no way of knowing the truth. Asked if he ever thinks about whether or not things are real, eleven-year-old Jake says that he wonders a lot about whether people are telling the truth, about "what people say, like one of my friends says, 'Oh yeah, he said that,' and sometimes I think, 'Is he actually saying the truth?'" Considering truth to lie in math and certainty to reside in logic, he can see "no guidelines" for establishing truth in English class or in personal relationships.

Thus, although aggression has been construed as instinctual and   15
separation has been thought necessary for its constraint, the violence in male fantasy seems rather to arise from a problem in communication and an absence of knowledge about human relationships. But as . . . women in their fantasies create nets of safety where men depict annihilation, the voices of women comment on the problem of aggression that both sexes face, locating the problem in the isolation of self and in the hierarchical construction of human relationships.

. . . The images of hierarchy and web, drawn from the texts of men's and women's fantasies and thoughts, convey different ways of structuring relationships and are associated with different views of morality and self. But these images create a problem in understanding because each distorts the other's representation. As the top of the hierarchy becomes the edge of the web and as the center of a network of connection becomes the middle of a hierarchical progression, each image marks as dangerous the place which the other defines as safe. Thus the images of hierarchy and web inform different modes of assertion and response: the wish to be alone at the top and the consequent fear that others will get too close; the wish to be at the center of connection and the consequent fear of being too far out on the edge. These disparate fears of being stranded and being caught give rise to different portrayals of achievement and affiliation, leading to different modes of action and different ways of assessing the consequences of choice.

The reinterpretation of women's experience in terms of their own imagery of relationships thus clarifies that experience and also provides a nonhierarchical vision of human connection. Since relationships, when cast in the image of hierarchy, appear inherently unstable and morally problematic, their transposition into the image of web changes an order of inequality into a structure of interconnection. But the power of the images of hierarchy and web, their evocation of feelings and their recurrence in thought, signifies the embeddedness of both of these images in the cycle of human life. The experiences of inequality and interconnection, inherent in the relation of parent and child, then give rise to the ethics of justice and care, the ideals of human relationship — the vision that self and other will be treated as of equal worth, that despite differences in power, things will be fair; the vision that everyone will be responded to and included, that no one will be left alone or hurt. These disparate visions in their tension reflect the paradoxical truths of human experience — that we know ourselves as separate only insofar as we live in connection with others, and that we experience relationship only insofar as we differentiate other from self.

Works Cited

Horner, Matina S. "Sex Differences in Achievement Motivation and Performance in Competitive and Noncompetitive Situations." Ph.D. Diss., University of Michigan, 1968. University Microfilms #6912135.

Maccoby, Eleanor, and Jacklin, Carol. *The Psychology of Sex Differences.* Stanford: Stanford University Press, 1974.

May, Robert. *Sex and Fantasy: Patterns of Male and Female Development.* New York: W. W. Norton, 1980.

Pollak, Susan, and Gilligan, Carol. "Images of Violence in Thematic Apperception Test Stories." *Journal of Personality and Social Psychology* 42, no. 1 (1982): 159–167.

Terman, L., and Tyler, L. "Psychological Sex Differences." In L. Carmichael, ed., *Manual of Child Psychology*, 2nd ed. New York: John Wiley and Sons, 1954.

Whiting, Beatrice, and Pope, Carolyn. "A Cross cultural Analysis of Sex Difference in the Behavior of Children Age Three to Eleven." *Journal of Social Psychology* 91 (1973): 171–188.

Engaging the Text

1. What, according to Gilligan, is the purpose of her study? Working in pairs or small groups, paraphrase this purpose in your own words.

2. What is the distinction Gilligan makes between achievement and affiliation? How are these terms related to gender roles?

3. Break into single-sex groups. Discuss and critique Gilligan's conclusion about the kinds of situations associated with aggression for women and for men. How does she account for this difference? Do you find Gilligan's interpretations of her results convincing? Is she attacking men?

4. Does a man's aggressive attitude toward intimacy, as revealed by a test like the one described here, constitute either sexism or a psychological problem? Explain.

Exploring Connections

5. Analyze Stephen Cruz (p. 36), Mike LeFevre (p. 87), or the speaker of Aurora Levins Morales's "Class Poem" (p. 95) in terms of the ideas and images Gilligan raises — web versus hierarchy, intimacy versus achievement, perceived danger, and aggression.

6. Reread Sandra Cisneros's "Little Miracles, Kept Promises" (p. 221). How might Gilligan interpret the desires, attitudes, and values glimpsed in those letters? Discuss whether Cisneros's portrayal of male and female roles corrobo rates Gilligan's thesis.

7. Look ahead to "Charlie Sabatier" (p. 751). To what extent does Sabatier's personal history challenge or confirm Gilligan's assertions about men, aggression, and men's connections with others?

Extending the Critical Context

8. In the summer of 1991, Ridley Scott's film *Thelma and Louise* provoked strong reactions because of the way it portrayed women and particularly because of its apparent celebration of female aggression and violence. Some critics complained that the movie simply transferred male attitudes toward violence into female characters, that it virtually turned its heroines into macho men. Watch the film and discuss its portrayal of women, men, and violence. Do you agree with the film's critics? How might Gilligan interpret the film? How might she interpret the critics' responses to it?

Where I Come from Is Like This

PAULA GUNN ALLEN

Paula Gunn Allen was born in 1939 in Cubero, New Mexico, a Spanish-Mexican land grant village; where she comes from is life as a Laguna Pueblo–Sioux–Lebanese woman. In this essay she discusses some of the ways traditional images of women in American Indian cultures differ from images in mainstream American culture. Allen is a professor of English and American Indian literature at the University of California, Los Angeles. In addition to her scholarly work, Allen is widely recognized for her books of poetry and for her novel The Woman Who Owned the Shadows *(1983). Her recent work includes* Skins and Bones: Poems, 1979–87 *(1988) and* Spider Woman's Granddaughters *(1989), an anthology of traditional and contemporary stories by American Indian women. This piece appeared in her collection of essays,* The Sacred Hoop: Recovering the Feminine in American Indian Traditions *(1986).*

I

Modern American Indian women, like their non-Indian sisters, are deeply engaged in the struggle to redefine themselves. In their struggle they must reconcile traditional tribal definitions of women with industrial and postindustrial non-Indian definitions. Yet while these definitions seem to be more or less mutually exclusive, Indian women must somehow harmonize and integrate both in their own lives.

An American Indian woman is primarily defined by her tribal identity. In her eyes, her destiny is necessarily that of her people, and her sense of herself as a woman is first and foremost prescribed by her tribe. The definitions of woman's roles are as diverse as tribal cultures in the Americas. In some she is devalued, in others she wields considerable power. In some she is a familial/clan adjunct, in some she is as close to autonomous as her economic circumstances and psychological traits permit. But in no tribal definitions is she perceived in the same way as are women in western industrial and postindustrial cultures.

In the west, few images of women form part of the cultural mythos, and these are largely sexually charged. Among Christians, the madonna is the female prototype, and she is portrayed as essentially passive: her contribution is simply that of birthing. Little else is attributed to her and she certainly possesses few of the characteristics that are attributed to mythic figures among Indian tribes. This image is countered (rather than balanced) by the witch-goddess/whore characteristics designed to reinforce cultural beliefs about women, as well as western adversarial and dualistic perceptions of reality.

The tribes see women variously, but they do not question the power of femininity. Sometimes they see women as fearful, sometimes peaceful, sometimes omnipotent and omniscient, but they never portray women as mindless, helpless, simple, or oppressed. And while the women in a given tribe, clan, or band may be all these things, the individual woman is provided with a variety of images of women from the interconnected supernatural, natural, and social worlds she lives in.

As a half-breed American Indian woman, I cast about in my mind   5
for negative images of Indian women, and I find none that are directed to Indian women alone. The negative images I do have are of Indians in general and in fact are more often of males than of females. All these images come to me from non-Indian sources, and they are always balanced by a positive image. My ideas of womanhood, passed on largely by my mother and grandmothers, Laguna Pueblo women, are about practicality, strength, reasonableness, intelligence, wit, and competence. I also remember vividly the women who came to my father's store, the women who held me and sang to me, the women at Feast Day, at Grab Days,[1] the women in the kitchen of my Cubero home, the women I grew up with; none of them appeared weak or helpless, none of them presented herself tentatively. I remember a certain reserve on those lovely brown faces; I remember the direct gaze of eyes framed by bright-colored shawls draped over their heads and cascading down their backs. I remember the clean cotton dresses and carefully pressed hand-embroidered aprons they always wore; I remember laughter and good food, especially the sweet bread and the oven bread they gave us. Nowhere in my mind is there a foolish woman, a dumb woman, a vain woman, or a plastic woman, though the Indian women I have known have shown a wide range of personal style and demeanor.

My memory includes the Navajo woman who was badly beaten by her Sioux husband; but I also remember that my grandmother abandoned her Sioux husband long ago. I recall the stories about the Laguna woman beaten regularly by her husband in the presence of her children so that the children would not believe in the strength and power of femininity. And I remember the women who drank, who got into fights with other women and with the men, and who often won those battles. I have memories of tired women, partying women, stubborn women, sullen women, amicable women, selfish women, shy women, and aggressive women. Most of all I remember the women who laugh and scold and sit uncomplaining in the long sun on feast days and who cook

---

[1]*Grab Days:* Laguna ritual in which women throw food and small items (like pieces of cloth) to those attending.

wonderful food on wood stoves, in beehive mud ovens, and over open fires outdoors.

Among the images of women that come to me from various tribes as well as my own are White Buffalo Woman, who came to the Lakota long ago and brought them the religion of the Sacred Pipe which they still practice; Tinotzin the goddess who came to Juan Diego to remind him that she still walked the hills of her people and sent him with her message, her demand and her proof to the Catholic bishop in the city nearby. And from Laguna I take the images of Yellow Woman, Coyote Woman, Grandmother Spider (Spider Old Woman), who brought the light, who gave us weaving and medicine, who gave us life. Among the Keres she is known as Thought Woman who created us all and who keeps us in creation even now. I remember Iyatiku, Earth Woman, Corn Woman, who guides and counsels the people to peace and who welcomes us home when we cast off this coil of flesh as huskers cast off the leaves that wrap the corn. I remember Iyatiku's sister, Sun Woman, who held metals and cattle, pigs and sheep, highways and engines and so many things in her bundle, who went away to the east saying that one day she would return.

II

Since the coming of the Anglo-Europeans beginning in the fifteenth century, the fragile web of identity that long held tribal people secure has gradually been weakened and torn. But the oral tradition has prevented the complete destruction of the web, the ultimate disruption of tribal ways. The oral tradition is vital; it heals itself and the tribal web by adapting to the flow of the present while never relinquishing its connection to the past. Its adaptability has always been required, as many generations have experienced. Certainly the modern American Indian woman bears slight resemblance to her forebears — at least on superficial examination — but she is still a tribal woman in her deepest being. Her tribal sense of relationship to all that is continues to flourish. And though she is at times beset by her knowledge of the enormous gap between the life she lives and the life she was raised to live, and while she adapts her mind and being to the circumstances of her present life, she does so in tribal ways, mending the tears in the web of being from which she takes her existence as she goes.

My mother told me stories all the time, though I often did not recognize them as that. My mother told me stories about cooking and childbearing; she told me stories about menstruation and pregnancy; she told me stories about gods and heroes, about fairies and elves, about goddesses and spirits; she told me stories about the land and the sky, about cats and dogs, about snakes and spiders; she told me stories about climbing trees and exploring the mesas; she told me stories about going to dances and getting married; she told me stories about dressing and undressing, about sleeping and waking; she told me stories about herself, about her mother, about her grandmother. She told me stories about grieving and laughing, about thinking and doing; she told me stories about school and about people; about darning and mending; she told me stories about turquoise and about gold; she told me European stories and Laguna stories; she told me Catholic stories and Presbyterian stories; she told me city stories and country stories; she told me political stories and religious stories. She told me stories about living and stories about dying. And in all of those stories she told me who I was, who I was supposed to be, whom I came from, and who would follow me. In this way she taught me the meaning of the words she said, that all life is a circle and everything has a place within it. That's what she said and what she showed me in the things she did and the way she lives.

Of course, through my formal, white, Christian education, I discovered that other people had stories of their own — about women, about Indians, about fact, about reality — and I was amazed by a number of startling suppositions that others made about tribal customs and beliefs. According to the un-Indian, non-Indian view, for instance, Indians barred menstruating women from ceremonies and indeed segregated them from the rest of the people, consigning them to some space specially designed for them. This showed that Indians considered menstruating women unclean and not fit to enjoy the company of decent (nonmenstruating) people, that is, men. I was surprised and confused to hear this because my mother had taught me that white people had strange attitudes toward menstruation: they thought something was bad about it, that it meant you were sick, cursed, sinful, and weak and that you had to be very careful during that time. She taught me that menstruation was a normal occurrence, that I could go swimming or hiking or whatever else I wanted to do during my period. She actively scorned women who took to their beds, who were incapacitated by cramps, who "got the blues."

As I struggled to reconcile these very contradictory interpretations of American Indians' traditional beliefs concerning menstruation, I realized that the menstrual taboos were about power, not about sin or filth. My conclusion was later borne out by some tribes' own explanations, which, as you may well imagine, came as quite a relief to me.

The truth of the matter as many Indians see it is that women who are at the peak of their fecundity are believed to possess power that throws male power totally out of kilter. They emit such force that, in their presence, any male-owned or -dominated ritual or sacred object cannot do its usual task. For instance, the Lakota say that a menstruating woman anywhere near a yuwipi man, who is a special sort of psychic, spirit-empowered healer, for a day or so before he is to do his

10

ceremony will effectively disempower him. Conversely, among many if not most tribes, important ceremonies cannot be held without the presence of women. Sometimes the ritual woman who empowers the ceremony must be unmarried and virginal so that the power she channels is unalloyed, unweakened by sexual arousal and penetration by a male. Other ceremonies require tumescent women, others the presence ?
of mature women who have borne children, and still others depend for empowerment on postmenopausal women. Women may be segregated from the company of the whole band or village on certain occasions, but on certain occasions men are also segregated. In short, each ritual depends on a certain balance of power, and the positions of women within the phases of womanhood are used by tribal people to empower certain rites. This does not derive from a male-dominant view; it is not a ritual observance imposed on women by men. It derives from a tribal view of reality that distinguishes tribal people from feudal and industrial people.

Among the tribes, the occult power of women, inextricably bound to our hormonal life, is thought to be very great; many hold that we possess innately the blood-given power to kill — with a glance, with a step, or with a judicious mixing of menstrual blood into somebody's soup. Medicine women among the Pomo of California cannot practice until they are sufficiently mature; when they are immature, their power is diffuse and is likely to interfere with their practice until time and experience have it under control. So women of the tribes are not especially inclined to see themselves as poor helpless victims of male domination. Even in those tribes where something akin to male domination was present, women are perceived as powerful, socially, physically, and metaphysically. In times past, as in times present, women carried enormous burdens with aplomb. We were far indeed from the "weaker sex," the designation that white aristocratic sisters unhappily earned for us all.

I remember my mother moving furniture all over the house when she wanted it changed. She didn't wait for my father to come home and help — she just went ahead and moved the piano, a huge upright from the old days, the couch, the refrigerator. Nobody had told her she was too weak to do such things. In imitation of her, I would delight in loading trucks at my father's store with cases of pop or fifty-pound sacks of flour. Even when I was quite small I could do it, and it gave me a belief in my own physical strength that advancing middle age can't quite erase. My mother used to tell me about the Acoma Pueblo women she had seen as a child carrying huge ollas (water pots) on their heads as they wound their way up the tortuous stairwell carved into the face of the "Sky City" mesa, a feat I tried to imitate with books and tin buckets. ("Sky City" is the term used by the Chamber of Commerce for the mother village of Acoma, which is situated atop a high sandstone table mountain.) I was never very successful, but even the attempt reminded me that I was supposed to be strong and balanced to be a proper girl.

Of course, my mother's Laguna people are Keres Indian, reputed to be the last extreme mother-right people on earth. So it is no wonder that I got notably nonwhite notions about the natural strength and prowess of women. Indeed, it is only when I am trying to get non-Indian approval, recognition, or acknowledgment that my "weak sister" emotional and intellectual ploys get the better of my tribal woman's good sense. At such times I forget that I just moved the piano or just wrote a competent paper or just completed a financial transaction satisfactorily or have supported myself and my children for most of my adult life.

Nor is my contradictory behavior atypical. Most Indian women I know are in the same bicultural bind: we vacillate between being dependent and strong, self-reliant and powerless, strongly motivated and hopelessly insecure. We resolve the dilemma in various ways: some of us party all the time; some of us drink to excess; some of us travel and move around a lot; some of us land good jobs and then quit them; some of us engage in violent exchanges; some of us blow our brains out. We act in these destructive ways because we suffer from the societal conflicts caused by having to identify with two hopelessly opposed cultural definitions of women. Through this destructive dissonance we are unhappy prey to the self-disparagement common to, indeed demanded of, Indians living in the United States today. Our situation is caused by the exigencies of a history of invasion, conquest, and colonization whose searing marks are probably ineradicable. A popular bumper sticker on many Indian cars proclaims: "If You're Indian You're In," to which I always find myself adding under my breath, "Trouble."

III

No Indian can grow to any age without being informed that her people were "savages" who interfered with the march of progress pursued by respectable, loving, civilized white people. We are the villains of the scenario when we are mentioned at all. We are absent from much of white history except when we are calmly, rationally, succinctly, and systematically dehumanized. On the few occasions we are noticed in any way other than as howling, bloodthirsty beings, we are acclaimed for our noble quaintness. In this definition, we are exotic curios. Our ancient arts and customs are used to draw tourist money to state coffers, into the pocketbooks and bank accounts of scholars, and into support of the American-in-Disneyland promoters' dream.

As a Roman Catholic child I was treated to bloody tales of how the savage Indians martyred the hapless priests and missionaries who went among them in an attempt to lead them to the one true path. By the time I was through high school I had the idea that Indians were people who had benefited mightily from the advanced knowledge and superior morality of the Anglo-Europeans. At least I had, perforce, that idea to lay beside the other one that derived from my daily experience of Indian life, an idea less dehumanizing and more accurate because it came from my mother and the other Indian people who raised me. That idea was that Indians are a people who don't tell lies, who care for their children and their old people. You never see an Indian orphan, they said. You always know when you're old that someone will take care of you — one of your children will. Then they'd list the old folks who were being taken care of by this child or that. No child is ever considered illegitimate among the Indians, they said. If a girl gets pregnant, the baby is still part of the family, and the mother is too. That's what they said, and they showed me real people who lived according to those principles.

Of course the ravages of colonization have taken their toll; there are orphans in Indian country now, and abandoned, brutalized old folks; there are even illegitimate children, though the very concept still strikes me as absurd. There are battered children and neglected children, and there are battered wives and women who have been raped by Indian men. Proximity to the "civilizing" effects of white Christians has not improved the moral quality of life in Indian country, though each group, Indian and white, explains the situation differently. Nor is there much yet in the oral tradition that can enable us to adapt to these inhuman changes. But a force is growing in that direction, and it is helping Indian women reclaim their lives. Their power, their sense of direction and of self will soon be visible. It is the force of the women who speak and work and write, and it is formidable.

Through all the centuries of war and death and cultural and psychic 20 destruction have endured the women who raise the children and tend the fires, who pass along the tales and the traditions, who weep and bury the dead, who are the dead, and who never forget. There are always the women, who make pots and weave baskets, who fashion clothes and cheer their children on at powwow, who make fry bread and piki bread, and corn soup and chili stew, who dance and sing and remember and hold within their hearts the dream of their ancient peoples — that one day the woman who thinks will speak to us again, and everywhere there will be peace. Meanwhile we tell the stories and write the books and trade tales of anger and woe and stories of fun and scandal and laugh over all manner of things that happen every day. We watch and we wait.

My great-grandmother told my mother: never forget you are Indian. And my mother told me the same thing. This, then, is how I have gone about remembering, so that my children will remember too.

Engaging the Text

1. Outline how Allen's views of women differ from traditional Anglo-American views.

2. What does Allen mean by "bicultural bind" (para. 16)? How has it affected her, and how does she deal with it?

3. How does Allen represent relationships between American Indian women and men?

4. Why is remembering so important to Allen? What roles does it play in helping her live in a world dominated by an alien culture? How does it help her define herself as a woman?

5. Allen's essay includes much personal recollection. Try to "translate" some of this information into more abstract statements of theme or message (for instance, you might write, "Women's roles in American Indian cultures are maintained through example, through oral tradition, and through ceremonial tribal practices.") What is gained, what lost in such "translations"?

Exploring Connections

6. Drawing on the selections by Haunani-Kay Trask (p. 118), Leslie Marmon Silko (p. 135), and Allen, discuss the power that stories have to shape our identities and ways of thinking.

7. Compare and contrast the ways Allen and Carol Gilligan (p. 233) use the image of the web to illustrate their arguments about female and tribal values.

8. Review Sandra Cisneros's "Little Miracles, Kept Promises" (p. 221). Do you find in any of those letters the conflicting gender roles that Allen discusses?

Extending the Critical Context

9. Are you struggling to reconcile different definitions of what you should be? Write an essay or journal entry exploring this issue. (For example, are family, friends, and school pushing you in different directions?) If you are writing a full essay, you might want to take a look ahead at "Split at the Root" by Adrienne Rich (p. 307) as a model.

10. Working in single-sex groups, create collages of male or female images drawn from a range of popular publications. What qualities, values, and attitudes do these images project? Are they consistent, or do you see contradictions and tensions within them? What myths about each gender do you see emerging?

Reflections on Race and Sex

BELL HOOKS

In this essay bell hooks attacks what she considers a nearly universal blindness to the connections between racism and sexism. She argues that neither can be battled effectively if their dynamic interaction is not critiqued and understood; thus even feminists and African American politicians, in her opinion, can unwittingly perpetuate oppression as they attempt to fight racism or sexism. bell hooks is the pen name of Gloria Watkins (b. 1952), who teaches at Oberlin College and writes a column entitled "Sisters of the Yam" for Z Magazine. *Her books include* Ain't I a Woman: Black Women and Feminism *(1981),* Feminist Theory from Margin to Center *(1984),* Talking Back: Thinking Feminist, Thinking Black *(1989), and the volume from which this selection is taken,* Yearning: Race, Gender, and Cultural Politics *(1990).*

Race and sex have always been overlapping discourses in the United States. That discourse began in slavery. The talk then was not about black men wanting to be free so that they would have access to the bodies of white women — that would come later. Then, black women's bodies were the discursive terrain, the playing fields where racism and sexuality converged. Rape as both right and rite of the white male dominating group was a cultural norm. Rape was also an apt metaphor for European imperialist colonization of Africa and North America.

Sexuality has always provided gendered metaphors for colonization. Free countries equated with free men, domination with castration, the loss of manhood, and rape — the terrorist act re-enacting the drama of conquest, as men of the dominating group sexually violate the bodies of women who are among the dominated. The intent of this act was to continually remind dominated men of their loss of power; rape was a gesture of symbolic castration. Dominated men are made powerless (i.e., impotent) over and over again as the women they would have had the right to possess, to control, to assert power over, to dominate, to fuck, are fucked and fucked over by the dominating victorious male group.

There is no psychosexual history of slavery that explores the meaning of white male sexual exploitation of black women or the politics of sexuality, no work that lays out all the available information. There is no discussion of sexual sado-masochism, of the master who forced his wife to sleep on the floor as he nightly raped a black woman in bed. There is no discussion of sexual voyeurism. And what were the sexual lives of white men like who were legally declared "insane" because they wanted to marry black slave women with whom they were sexually and romantically involved? Under what conditions did sexuality serve as a force subverting and disrupting power relations, unsettling the oppressor/oppressed paradigm? No one seems to know how to tell this story, where to begin. As historical narrative it was long ago supplanted by the creation of another story (pornographic sexual project, fantasy, fear, the origin has yet to be traced). That story, invented by white men, is about the overwhelming desperate longing black men have to sexually violate the bodies of white women. The central character in this story is the black male rapist. Black men are constructed,[1] as Michael Dyson puts it, as "peripatetic[2] phalluses with unrequited desire for their denied object — white women." As the story goes, this desire is not based on longing for sexual pleasure. It is a story of revenge, rape as the weapon by which black men, the dominated, reverse their circumstance, regain power over white men.

Oppressed black men and women have rarely challenged the use of gendered metaphors to describe the impact of racist domination and/or black liberation struggle. The discourse of black resistance has almost always equated freedom with manhood, the economic and material domination of black men with castration emasculation. Accepting these sexual metaphors forged a bond between oppressed black men and their white male oppressors. They shared the patriarchal[3] belief that revolutionary struggle was really about the erect phallus, the ability of men to establish political dominance that could correspond to sexual dominance. Careful critical examination of black power literature in the sixties and early seventies exposes the extent to which black women and men were using sexualized metaphors to talk about the effort to resist racist domination. Many of us have never forgotten that moment in *Soul on Ice*[4] when Eldridge Cleaver, writing about the need to "redeem my conquered manhood," described raping black women as practice for the eventual rape of white women. Remember that readers were not shocked or horrified by this glamorization of rape as a weapon of terrorism men might use to express rage about other forms of domination, about their struggle for power with other men. Given the sexist context of the culture, it made sense. Cleaver was able to deflect attention away from the misogynist[5] sexism of his assertions by poi-

[1]*constructed:* imagined or perceived, not physically built.

[2]*peripatetic:* going from place to place.

[3]*patriarchal:* describing a system in which authority and power belong primarily to males; a patriarch is the male head of a family or tribe.

[4]*Soul on Ice:* one of the most important radical books of the 1960s. See George C. Wolfe's "Symbiosis" (p. 42).

[5]*misogynist:* women-hating.

gnantly justifying these acts as a "natural" response to racial domination. He wanted to force readers to confront the agony and suffering black men experience in a white supremacist society. Again, freedom from racial domination was expressed in terms of redeeming black masculinity. And gaining the right to assert one's manhood was always about sexuality.

During slavery, there was perhaps a white male who created his 5 own version of *Soul on Ice*, one who confessed how good it felt to assert racial dominance over black people, and particularly black men, by raping black women with impunity, or how sexually stimulating it was to use the sexual exploitation of black women to humiliate and degrade white women, to assert phallocentric domination in one's household. Sexism has always been a political stance mediating racial domination, enabling white men and black men to share a common sensibility about sex roles and the importance of male domination. Clearly both groups have equated freedom with manhood, and manhood with the right of men to have indiscriminate access to the bodies of women. Both groups have been socialized to condone patriarchal affirmation of rape as an acceptable way to maintain male domination. It is this merging of sexuality with male domination within patriarchy that informs the construction of masculinity for men of all races and classes. Robin Morgan's book, *The Demon Lover: On the Sexuality of Terrorism*, begins with rape. She analyses the way men are bonded across class, race, and nationalities through shared notions of manhood which make masculinity synonymous with the ability to assert power-over through acts of violence and terrorism. Since terrorist acts are most often committed by men, Morgan sees the terrorist as "the logical incarnation of patriarchal politics in a technological world." She is not concerned with the overlapping discourses of race and sex, with the interconnectedness of racism and sexism. Like many radical feminists, she believes that male commitment to maintaining patriarchy and male domination diminishes or erases difference.

Much of my work within feminist theory has stressed the importance of understanding difference, of the ways race and class status determine the degree to which one can assert male domination and privilege and most importantly the ways racism and sexism are interlocking systems of domination which uphold and sustain one another. Many feminists continue to see them as completely separate issues, believing that sexism can be abolished while racism remains intact, or that women who work to resist racism are not supporting feminist movement. Since black liberation struggle is so often framed in terms that affirm and support sexism, it is not surprising that white women are uncertain about whether women's rights struggle will be diminished if there is too much focus on resisting racism, or that many black women continue to fear that they will be betraying black men if they support feminist movement. Both these fears are responses to the equation of black liberation with manhood. This continues to be a central way black people frame our efforts to resist racist domination; it must be critiqued. We must reject the sexualization of black liberation in ways that support and perpetuate sexism, phallocentrism, and male domination. Even though Michele Wallace tried to expose the fallacy of equating black liberation with the assertion of oppressive manhood in *Black Macho and the Myth of the Superwoman*, few black people got the message. Continuing this critique in *Ain't I a Woman: Black Women and Feminism*, I found that more and more black women were rejecting this paradigm. It has yet to be rejected by most black men, and especially black male political figures. As long as black people hold on to the idea that the trauma of racist domination is really the loss of black manhood, then we invest in the racist narratives that perpetuate the idea that all black men are rapists, eager to use sexual terrorism to express their rage about racial domination.

Currently we are witnessing a resurgence of such narratives. They are resurfacing at a historical moment when black people are bearing the brunt of more overt and blatant racist assaults, when black men and especially young black men are increasingly disenfranchised by society. Mainstream white supremacist media make it appear that a black menace to societal safety is at large, that control, repression, and violent domination are the only effective ways to address the problem. Witness the use of the Willie Horton[6] case to discredit Dukakis in the 1988 Presidential election. Susan Estrich in her post-campaign articles has done a useful job of showing how racist stereotypes were evoked to turn voters against Dukakis, and how Bush in no way denounced this strategy. In all her articles she recounts the experience of being raped by a black man fifteen years ago, describing the way racism determined how the police responded to the crime, and her response. Though her intent is to urge societal commitment to antiracist struggle, every article I have read has carried captions in bold print emphasizing the rape. The subversive content of her work is undermined and the stereotype that all black men are rapists is reinscribed and reinforced. Most people in this society do not realize that the vast majority of rapes are not interracial, that all groups of men are more likely to rape women who are the same race as themselves.

Within popular culture, Madonna's video "Like a Prayer" also makes use of imagery which links black men with rape, reinforcing this representation in the minds of millions of viewers — even though she

---

[6]*Willie Horton:* convicted murderer in Massachusetts who committed a rape after being furloughed by prison authorities while Michael Dukakis was governor. Supporters of George Bush used the incident in the 1988 presidential campaign to portray candidate Dukakis as soft on crime.

has said that her intention is to be antiracist, and certainly the video suggests that not all black men who are accused of raping white women are guilty. Once again, however, this subversive message is undermined by the overall focus on sexually charged imagery of white female sexuality and black male lust. The most subversive message in the video has nothing to do with antiracism; it has to do with the construction of white females as desiring subjects who can freely assert sexual agency. Of course the taboo expression of that agency is choosing to be sexual with black men. Unfortunately this is a continuation of the notion that ending racist domination is really about issues of interracial sexual access, a myth that must be critiqued so that this society can confront the actual material, economic, and moral consequences of perpetuating white supremacy and its traumatic genocidal impact on black people.

Images of black men as rapists, as dangerous menaces to society, have been sensational cultural currency for some time. The obsessive media focus on these representations is political. The role it plays in the maintenance of racist domination is to convince the public that black men are a dangerous threat who must be controlled by any means necessary, including annihilation. This is the cultural backdrop shaping media response to the Central Park rape[7] case, and the media has played a major role in shaping public response. Many people are using this case to perpetuate racial stereotypes and racism. Ironically, the very people who claim to be shocked by the brutality of this case have no qualms about suggesting that the suspects should be castrated or killed. They see no link between this support of violence as a means of social control and the suspects' use of violence to exercise control. Public response to this case highlights the lack of understanding about the interconnectedness of racism and sexism.

Many black people, especially black men, using the sexist paradigm   10 that suggests rape of white women by black men is a reaction to racist domination, view the Central Park case as an indictment of the racist system. They do not see sexism as informing the nature of the crime, the choice of victim. Many white women have responded to the case by focusing solely on the brutal assault as an act of gender domination, of male violence against women. A piece in the *Village Voice* written by white female Andrea Kannapell carried captions in bold print which began with the statement in all capitals for greater emphasis, "THE CRIME WAS MORE SEXIST THAN RACIST . . ." Black women responding to the same issue all focused on the sexist nature of the crime, often giving examples of black male sexism. Given the work black women have done within feminist writing to call attention to the reality of black male sexism, work that often receives little or no attention or is

[7]*the Central Park rape:* an internationally publicized crime in which black youths raped a white woman in New York's Central Park during a "wilding" spree in 1989.

accused of attacking black men, it is ironic that the brutal rape of a white woman by a group of young black males serves as the catalyst for admission that sexism is a serious problem in black communities. Lisa Kennedy's piece, "Body Double: The Anatomy of a Crime," also published in the *Village Voice*, acknowledges the convergence of racism and sexism as politics of domination that inform this assault. Kennedy writes:

> If I accept the premise of the coverage, that this rape is more heartbreaking than all the rapes that happen to women of color, then what happens to the value of my body? What happens to the quality of my blackness?

These questions remain unanswered, though she closes with "a call for a sophisticated feminist offensive." Such an offensive should begin with cultivating critical awareness of the way racism and sexism are interlocking systems of domination.

Public response to the Central Park case reveals the extent to which the culture invests in the kind of dualistic thinking that helps reinforce and maintain all forms of domination. Why must people decide whether this crime is more sexist than racist, as if these are competing oppressions? Why do white people, and especially feminist white women, feel better when black people, especially black women, disassociate themselves from the plight of black men in white supremacist capitalist patriarchy to emphasize opposition to black male sexism? Cannot black women remain seriously concerned about the brutal effect of racist domination on black men and also denounce black male sexism? And why is black male sexism evoked as though it is a special brand of this social disorder, more dangerous, more abhorrent and life-threatening than the sexism that pervades the culture as a whole, or the sexism that informs white male domination of women? These questions call attention to the either/or ways of thinking that are the philosophical underpinning of systems of domination. Progressive folks must then insist, wherever we engage in discussions of this crime or of issues of race and gender, on the complexity of our experience in a racist sexist society.

The Central Park crime involves aspects of sexism, male domination, misogyny, and the use of rape as an instrument of terror. It also involves race and racism; it is unlikely that young black males growing up in this society, attacking a white woman, would see her as "just a woman" — her race would be foremost in their consciousness as well as her sex, in the same way that masses of people hearing about this crime were concerned with identifying first her race. In a white supremacist sexist society all women's bodies are devalued, but white women's bodies are more valued than those of women of color. Given the context of white supremacy, the historical narratives about black male rapists, the racial identities of both victim and victimizers enable this tragedy to be sensationalized.

To fully understand the multiple meanings of this incident, it must be approached from an analytical standpoint that considers the impact of sexism and racism. Beginning there enables many of us to empathize with both the victim and the victimizers. If one reads *The Demon Lover* and thinks again about this crime, one can see it as part of a continuum of male violence against women, of rape and terror as weapons of male domination — yet another horrific and brutal expression of patriarchal socialization. And if one considers this case by combining a feminist analysis of race and masculinity, one sees that since male power within patriarchy is relative, men from poorer groups and men of color are not able to reap the material and social rewards for their participation in patriarchy. In fact they often suffer from blindly and passively acting out a myth of masculinity that is life-threatening. Sexist thinking blinds them to this reality. They become victims of the patriarchy. No one can truly believe that the young black males involved in the Central Park incident were not engaged in a suicidal ritual enactment of a dangerous masculinity that will ultimately threaten their lives, their well-being.

If one reads again Michael Dyson's piece "The Plight of Black Men," focusing especially on the part where he describes the reason many young black men form gangs — "the sense of absolute belonging and unsurpassed love" — it is easy to understand why young black males are despairing and nihilistic. And it is rather naive to think that if they do not value their own lives, they will value the lives of others. Is it really so difficult for folks to see the connection between the constant pornographic glorification of male violence against women that is represented, enacted, and condoned daily in the culture and the Central Park crime? Does racism create and maintain this blindspot or does it allow black people and particularly black men to become the scapegoats, embodying society's evils?

If we are to live in a less violent and more just society, then we must engage in antisexist and antiracist work. We desperately need to explore and understand the connections between racism and sexism. And we need to teach everyone about those connections so that they can be critically aware and socially active. Much education for critical consciousness can take place in everyday conversations. Black women and men must participate in the construction of feminist thinking, creating models for feminist struggle that address the particular circumstances of black people. Still, the most visionary task of all remains that of reconceptualizing masculinity so that alternative, transformative models are there in the culture, in our daily lives, to help boys and men who are working to construct a self, to build new identities. Black liberation struggle must be re-visioned so that it is no longer equated with male-

15

ness. We need a revolutionary vision of black liberation, one that emerges from a feminist standpoint and addresses the collective plight of black people.

Any individual committed to resisting politics of domination, to eradicating sexism and racism, understands the importance of not promoting an either/or competition between the oppressive systems. We can empathize with the victim and the victimizers in the Central Park case, allowing that feeling to serve as a catalyst for renewed commitment to antisexist and antiracist work. Yesterday I heard this story. A black woman friend called to say that she had been attacked on the street by a black man. He took her purse, her house keys, her car keys. She lives in one of the poorest cities in the United States. We talked about poverty, sexism, and racial domination to place what had happened in a perspective that will enable both individual healing and political understanding of this crime. Today I heard this story. A white woman friend called to say that she had been attacked in her doorway by a black man. She screamed and he ran away. Neighbors coming to her aid invoked racism. She refused to engage in this discussion even though she was shocked by the intensity and degree of racism expressed. Even in the midst of her own fear and pain, she remained politically aware, so as not to be complicit in perpetuating the white supremacy that is the root of so much suffering. Both of these women feel rage at their victimizers; they do not absolve them even as they seek to understand and to respond in ways that will enrich the struggle to end domination — so that sexism, sexist violence, racism, and racist violence will cease to be an everyday happening.

Selected Bibliography

Cleaver, Eldridge. *Soul on Ice.* New York: McGraw-Hill, 1967.

Dyson, Michael. "The Plight of Black Men," Z *Magazine*, February, 1989.

Morgan, Robin. *The Demon Lover: On the Sexuality of Terrorism.* New York: Norton, 1988.

Wallace, Michele. *Black Macho and the Myth of the Superwoman.* New York: Dial Press, 1979.

Engaging the Text

1. According to bell hooks, what roles do sex and sexism play in relation to racism?

2. How do "racist narratives" (para. 6) come about, according to the author? What examples of such narratives does she offer? Can you cite your own examples or counterexamples?

3. How, according to bell hooks, do men from oppressed groups become "victims of the patriarchy" (para. 13)?

4. Choose one instance in the essay in which bell hooks asserts that some widely accepted idea is actually wrong. (One example would be the idea that the

Central Park rape was more a sexual crime than a racial crime.) Write a few sentences explaining what she considers mistaken and what she believes is the truth. Share your efforts with classmates, and discuss how each example illustrates or supports the author's broader argument.

5. Although bell hooks uses the word "fuck" (para. 2), her word choice, or diction, tends toward words like "continuum" and "complicit" and phrases like "the taboo expression of that agency." Find other examples of verbal complexity or of abstract phrases, like "interlocking systems of domination." What do you think is the intended effect of her style? Is that its effect on you?

Exploring Connections

6. Review "Little Miracles, Kept Promises" by Sandra Cisneros (p. 221). Do sexual and racial inequities appear to be deeply interconnected in this story? Explain.

7. Huanani-Kay Trask (p. 118), Paula Gunn Allen (p. 241), and bell hooks all discuss the way the dominant culture has distorted the images of their people. Compare the motives, methods, and results of these deliberate cultural misreadings.

Extending the Critical Context

8. Brainstorm a list of images of African American men in current popular culture (TV shows, movies, comics, music videos, ads, and so on). In what situations are African American men most often seen? What roles are they given? Do these images challenge or confirm bell hooks's analysis of racism and sexism?

9. Watch the Madonna video "Like a Prayer." Write a brief essay describing the video itself, summarizing bell hooks's claims about it (para. 8), and supporting, modifying, or refuting her interpretation.

What Price Independence?
Social Reactions to Lesbians, Spinsters, Widows, and Nuns
ROSE WEITZ

This essay addresses the history of women who have been excluded by their societies. Weitz marshals a considerable body of historical fact to demonstrate that the social order stigmatizes lesbians and other independent women because they threaten the foundation of male dominance upon which it is built. Besides documenting misogyny and "gynophobia" in the West, she considers the Hindu practice of suttee — the ritual burning of wives on their husbands' funeral pyres. Rose Weitz (b. 1952) teaches in the sociology department at Arizona State University and has written Labor Pains: Modern Midwives and Home Birth *(1988).*

For seven days in 1981, nineteen-year-old Stephanie Riethmiller was held captive by two men and a woman in a secluded Alabama cabin. During that time, according to Riethmiller, her captors constantly harangued her on the sinfulness of homosexuality, and one captor raped her nightly. Riethmiller's parents, who feared that their daughter was involved in a lesbian relationship with her roommate, had paid $8,000 for this "deprogramming"; her mother remained in the next room throughout her captivity. When the kidnappers were brought to trial, the jury, in the opinion of the judge, "permit[ted] their moral evaluations to enter into their legal conclusions" and failed to bring in a guilty verdict (Raskin 1982, 19).

As the Riethmiller case shows, the individual who identifies herself as a lesbian — or who is so labeled by others — may face severe social, economic, and legal sanctions. Along with communists, the diseased, and the insane, persons who openly acknowledge their homosexuality may be denied admission to the United States. In most U.S. jurisdictions, discrimination against homosexuals in housing, employment, child custody, and other areas of life is legal, while homosexual behavior is illegal. Gay persons are not covered under any of the national civil rights acts, and most court decisions have held that they are not covered under the equal protection clause of the United States Constitution. (For an excellent review of the legal status of homosexuality, see Rivera 1979.)

These legal restrictions reflect generally held social attitudes. Surveys conducted during the 1970s using large national probability samples found that between 70 percent and 75 percent of the Americans interviewed believed that sexual relations between two members of the same sex were always wrong (Glenn and Weaver 1979).

Cross-Cultural and Historical Views of Lesbianism

To most Americans, stigmatization and punishment of lesbianism seem perfectly natural. Yet such has not always been the case. In fact, a study of attitudes toward homosexuality in seventy-six cultures around the world found that in 64 percent of those cultures "homosexual activities of one sort or another are considered normal and socially acceptable for certain members of the community" (Ford and Beach 1951, 130).

In the western world, male homosexuality, which had been an accepted part of Greek and Roman culture, was increasingly rejected by society as the power of the Christian church grew (Barrett 1979). Yet lesbianism generally remained unrecognized legally and socially until the beginning of the modern age. Instead, beginning with the Renaissance, intimate "romantic friendships" between women were a common part of life, at least among the middle and upper classes (Faderman 1981).[1]

> Women who were romantic friends were everything to each other. They lived to be together. They thought of each other constantly. They made each other deliriously happy or horribly miserable by the increase or abatement of their proffered love. They were jealous of other female friends (and certainly of male friends) who impinged on their beloved's time or threatened to carry away a portion of her affections. They vowed that if it were at all possible they would someday live together, or at least die together, and they declared that both eventualities would be their greatest happiness. They embraced and kissed and walked hand in hand, and some even held each other all night in sleep. But unless they were transvestites or considered "unwomanly" in some male's conception, there was little chance that their relationships would be considered lesbian [Faderman 1981, 84].

We cannot know whether most romantic friends expressed their love for women genitally, and we do know that most were married to men (at least in part for economic survival). A reading of letters and journals from this period leaves no doubt, however, of the erotic and emotional intensity of these relationships between women and little doubt that in another era the relationships would have been expressed sexually (Smith-Rosenberg 1975; Faderman 1981). Yet belief in the purity of these relationships lingered even into the twentieth century. For example, when the British Parliament attempted in 1885 to add mention of lesbianism to its criminal code, Queen Victoria refused to sign the bill, on the ground that such behavior did not exist (Ettorre 1980).

Given that lesbianism has not always elicited negative social reactions, the current intolerance of it cannot derive from some universal biological or ethical law. What, then, causes these negative social reactions? I suggest in this article that at least part of the answer lies in the threat that lesbianism presents to the power of males in society. Furthermore, I suggest that whenever men fear women's sexual or economic independence, all unmarried women face an increased risk of stigmati-

---

[1]We have little first-hand data about the intimate lives of lower-class women. Few poorer women could write, and, even if they could and did record their lives, their letters and journals were rarely preserved. [Author's note]

zation and punishment. The experience of such diverse groups as lesbians, medieval nuns, and Hindu widows shows the interrelated social fates of all women not under the direct control of men.

Lesbians and the Threat to Male Power

Western culture teaches that women are the weaker sex, that they cannot flourish — or perhaps even survive — without the protection of men. Women are taught that they cannot live happy and fulfilled lives without a Prince Charming, who is superior to them in all ways. In the struggle to find and keep their men, women learn to view each other as untrustworthy competitors. They subordinate the development of their own psychological, physical, and professional strengths to the task of finding male protectors who will make up for their shortcomings. In this way, Western culture keeps women from developing bonds with each other, while it maintains their dependence on men.

Lesbians[2] throw a large wrench into the works of this cultural system. In a society that denigrates women, lesbians value women enough to spend their lives with women rather than with men. Lesbians therefore do not and cannot rely on the protection of men. Knowing that they will not have that protection, lesbians are forced to develop their own resources. The very survival of lesbians therefore suggests the potential strength of all women and their ability to transcend their traditional roles. At the same time, since lesbians do not have even the illusion of male protection that marriage provides, and since they are likely to see their fate as tied to other women rather than to individual men, lesbians may be more likely than heterosexual women to believe in the necessity of fighting for women's rights; the heavy involvement of lesbians in the feminist movement seems to support this thesis (Abbott and Love 1972).

Lesbians also threaten the dominant cultural system by presenting, 10 or at least appearing to present, an alternative to the typical inequality of heterosexual relationships. Partners attempting to equalize power in a heterosexual relationship must first neutralize deeply ingrained traditional sex roles. Since lesbian relationships generally contain no built-in assumption of the superiority of one partner,[3] developing an egalitarian

[2]I am using the terms *lesbian* and *heterosexual* as nouns simply to ease the flow of the writing. This article focuses on stigmatization, not on some intrinsic quality of individuals. Hence, in this article, *lesbian* and *heterosexual* refer to persons who adopt a particular life-style or who are labeled as doing so by significant others. These terms reflect shared social fates, not some essential, inflexible aspect of the individual. [Author's note]

[3]While there is no way to ascertain exactly what proportion of lesbian couples adopted butch-femme relationships in the past, recent studies suggest that such relationships have all but disappeared, especially among younger and more feminist lesbians (Wolf 1979; Tanner 1978). [Author's note]

relationship may be easier. Lesbian relationships suggest both that a love between equals is possible and that an alternative way of obtaining such a love may exist. Regardless of the actual likelihood of achieving equality in a lesbian relationship, the threat to the system remains, as long as lesbian relationships are believed to be more egalitarian. This threat increases significantly when, as in the past few years, lesbians express pride in and satisfaction with their life-style.

If lesbianism incurs social wrath because of the threat it presents to existing sexist social arrangements, then we should find that lesbianism is most negatively viewed by persons who hold sexist beliefs. Evidence from various studies (summarized in Weinberger and Millham 1979) supports this hypothesis. Homophobia (i.e., fear and hatred of homosexuals) appears strongly correlated with support for traditional sex roles. Survey data suggest that support for traditional sex roles explains homophobia better than do negative or conservative attitudes toward sex in general (MacDonald et al. 1973; MacDonald and Games 1974).

Historical data on when and under what circumstances lesbianism became stigmatized also support the contention of a link between that stigma and the threat lesbianism poses to male power. As described above, romantic friendships between women were common in both Europe and America from the Renaissance through the late nineteenth century. The women involved were generally accepted or at least tolerated by society even in the few cases where their relationships were openly sexual. That acceptance ceased, however, if either of the women attempted to usurp male privilege in some way — by wearing men's clothing, using a dildo, or passing as a man. Only in these circumstances were pre-modern-era lesbians likely to suffer social sanctions. In looking at both historical records and fiction from the thirteenth through the nineteenth centuries, Faderman (1981) found that women were, at most, lightly punished for lesbianism unless they wore male clothing.[4] She therefore concludes that "at the base it was not the sexual aspects of lesbianism as much as the attempted usurpation of male prerogative by women who behaved like men that many societies appeared to find most disturbing" (Faderman 1981, 17).

As long as the women involved did not attempt to obtain male privileges, romantic friends ran little risk of censure before the late nineteenth century. The factors behind the shift in attitude that occurred at that time again suggest the importance of the threat that lesbianism seemed to pose to male power.

Before the twentieth century, only a small number of independently wealthy women (such as the Ladies of Llangollen [Mavor 1973]) were

---

[4]The crime for which Joan of Arc was eventually condemned was not witchcraft but the heretical act of wearing male clothing. [Author's note]

able to establish their own households and live out their lives with their female companions (Faderman 1981). By the second half of the nineteenth century, however, the combined effects of the Civil War in this country and of male migration away from rural areas in both the United States and Europe had created a surplus of unmarried women in many communities. At the same time, the growth of the feminist movement had led to increased educational opportunities for women. These factors, coupled with the growth of industrialization, opened the possibility of employment and an independent existence to significant numbers of women.

Once female independence became a real economic possibility, it became a serious concern to those intent on maintaining the sexual status quo. Relationships between women, which previously had seemed harmless, now took on a new and threatening appearance. Only at this point do new theories emerge that reject the Victorian image of the passionless woman (Cott 1978), acknowledge females as sexual beings, and define lesbianism as pathological.

Stereotypes of lesbianism, first developed in the early twentieth century, reduce the threat to existing social arrangements by defusing the power of lesbianism as a viable alternative life-style. According to these stereotypes, all lesbians are either butches or femmes,[5] and their relationships merely mimic heterosexual relationships. Lesbianism, therefore, seems to offer no advantages over heterosexuality.

Cultural stereotypes defuse lesbian sexuality by alternately denying and exaggerating it. These stereotypes hold that women become lesbians because of either their inability to find a man or their hatred of men. Such stereotypes deny that lesbianism may be a positive choice, while suggesting that lesbianism can be cured by the right man. The supposed futility of lesbian sexuality was summed up by best-selling author Dr. David Reuben in the phrase, "one vagina plus another vagina still equals zero" (1969, 217). (Reuben further invalidated lesbianism by locating his entire discussion of the subject within his chapter on prostitution; male homosexuality was "honored" with its own chapter.) In other cultural arenas, lesbians and lesbianism are defined in purely sexual terms, stripped of all romantic, social, or political content. In this incarnation, lesbianism can be subverted into a vehicle for male sexual pleasure; in the world of pornographic films, men frequently construct lesbian scenes to play out their own sexual fantasies.

In sum, strong evidence suggests that the negative social reactions to lesbianism reflect male fears of female independence, and the social sanctions and cultural stereotypes serve to lessen the threat that these independent women pose to male power.

If this hypothesis is true, then it should also hold for other groups of

---

[5]*butches . . . femmes:* women who adopt particularly masculine or feminine appearance and behavior.

women not under direct male control. Next, I briefly discuss how, historically, negative social reactions to such women seem most likely to develop whenever men fear women's sexual or economic independence.

Spinsters, Widows, and Women Religious

The inquisition against witches that occurred from the fifteenth through the seventeenth centuries represents the most extreme response in the western world to the threat posed by independent women. The vast majority of the persons executed for witchcraft were women; estimates of the number killed range from under one hundred thousand to several million (Daly 1978). Accusations of witchcraft typically involved charges that the women healed sickness, engaged in prohibited sexual practices, or controlled reproduction (Ehrenreich and English 1973). Such activities threatened the power of the church by giving individuals (especially women) greater control over their own lives, reducing their dependence on the church for divine intervention while inhibiting the natural increase of the Catholic population.

The witchcraft trials occurred in a society undergoing the first throes of industrialization and urbanization (Nelson 1979). The weakening of the rural extended family forced many women to look for employment outside the home. These unattached women proved especially vulnerable to accusations of witchcraft (Nelson 1979; Daly 1978). As Mary Daly points out, "The targets of attack in the witchcraze were not women defined by assimilation into the patriarchal family. Rather, the witchcraze focused predominantly upon women who had rejected marriage (Spinsters) [sic] and some who had survived it (widows)" (1978, 184).

Contemporary theological beliefs regarding female sexuality magnified the perceived economic and social threat posed by unmarried women. The medieval church viewed all aspects of female sexuality with distrust; unless a woman was virginal or proven chaste, she was believed to be ruled by her sexual desires (Ehrenreich and English 1973). Catholic doctrine blamed Eve's licentiousness for the fall from grace in the Garden of Eden. According to the most popular medieval "manual" for witchhunters, the *Malleus Maleficarum*, most witches were women because "all witchcraft comes from carnal lust, which is in women insatiable" (Kramer and Sprenger 1971, 120). Given this theology, any woman not under the direct sexual control of a man would appear suspect, if not outright dangerous.

For most women living before the nineteenth century who wished to or were forced to remain unmarried, entering the religious life was the only socially acceptable option.[6] During the Middle Ages, a woman

[6]However, it should be realized that convent life was not always a chosen refuge. Just as a father could marry his daughter to whatever man he chose, so too could he "marry" his daughter to the church. [Author's note]

could either become a nun or join one of the "secular convents" known as *Beguines* (Nelson 1979; Boulding 1976). Beguines arose to serve the population of surplus unmarried women that had developed in the early European cities. Residents of Beguines took a vow of chastity and obedience while living there, but they could marry thereafter. They spent their days in work and prayer.

Beguines threatened the monopolies of both the guilds and the church. The guilds feared the economic competition of these organized skilled women workers, while the church feared their social and religious independence (Nelson 1979); the Beguines' uncloistered life seemed likely to lead women into sin, while the lack of perpetual vows freed them from direct church supervision. For these reasons, the church in the fourteenth century ordered the Beguine houses dissolved, although some have continued nonetheless to the present day. Residents were urged either to marry or to become nuns (Boulding 1976).

The history of convents similarly illustrates the church's distrust of independent women (Eckenstein 1963). In the early medieval period, many nuns lived with their families. Some nuns showed their religious vocation through the wearing of a veil, while others wore no distinctive dress. Convents served as centers of learning for women, providing educational opportunities not available elsewhere. During this period, many "double monasteries" flourished, in which male and female residents lived and shared decision-making authority.

Given medieval ideas regarding the spiritual weakness and inherent carnality of women, the independence of early medieval nuns could not be allowed to last long. The developing laws of feudalism increasingly restricted the right of women to own land, so that, by the Renaissance, women faced increasing difficulties in attempting to found or to endow convents, while friars began to take over the management of existing convents (Eckenstein 1963). The church gradually closed all double monasteries, pressuring nuns to enter cloisters and to wear religious habits. Education for nuns increasingly seemed unnecessary or even dangerous. For this reason, by the sixteenth century church authorities had significantly decreased the educational opportunities available in most convents, although some convents did manage to preserve their intellectual traditions. Once Latin ceased to be taught, nuns were effectively excluded from all major church decisions.

As Protestant ideas began to infiltrate Europe, the status of unmarried women declined. One of the few areas in which Catholics and early Protestants agreed was the danger presented by independent women. Responding to flagrant sexual offenses in medieval monasteries, Protestants concluded that few men — let alone women, given their basically carnal nature — could maintain a celibate life. They therefore viewed "the religious profession [as] a thing of evil and temptation in which it was not possible to keep holy" (Charitas Perckheimer, quoted in Eckenstein 1963, 467). To Protestants, "marriage was the most acceptable state before God and . . . a woman has no claim to consideration except in her capacity as wife and mother" (Eckenstein 1963, 433). These beliefs, coupled with the political aims of Protestant rulers, culminated in the forced dissolution of convents and monasteries in many parts of Europe. In Protestant Europe, women were left without a socially acceptable alternative to marriage, while, in Catholic Europe, nuns had been stripped of their autonomy.

The belief in female carnality continued until the nineteenth century. At that point, while lower-class women were still considered sexually wanton by their social betters, prescriptive literature began to paint an image of upper-class women as passionless (Cott 1978). In this situation, unmarried lower-class women continued to suffer severe social sanctions as real or suspected prostitutes. Unmarried upper-class women continued to be stigmatized as unnatural, since they were not fulfulling their allotted role as wives and mothers. These upper-class women did not seem particularly threatening, however, since they were assumed, at least in public discourse, to be asexual beings. As a result, social sanctions against them diminished sharply, not to emerge again until women's new-found economic independence significantly changed the social context of romantic friendships among women.

In this historical overview I have so far discussed only events in the western world. In the West, widows probably evoke less of a sense of threat than do other unmarried women, since widows do not generally seem to have chosen their fate. It is instructive to compare the fate of Hindu widows, who are believed to have caused their husbands' deaths by sins they committed in this or a previous life (Daly 1978; Stein 1978).

Since a Hindu woman's status is determined by her relationship to a man, and since Hindu custom forbids remarriage, widows literally have no place in that society. A widow is a superfluous economic burden on her family. She is also viewed as a potential source of dishonor, since Hindus believe that "women are by nature sexually unreliable and incapable of leading chaste lives without a husband to control them" (Stein 1978, 255). For the benefit of her family and for her own happiness in future lives, a widow was in the past expected to commit suttee — to throw herself alive onto her husband's burning funeral pyre.[7] The horror of suttee was multiplied by the practice of polygamy and by the practice of marrying young girls to grown men, which resulted in the widowing of many young girls before they even reached puberty (Stein 1978; Daly 1978). Suttee, child marriage, and polygamy are illegal under the current government, but they do still occur.

[7]Suttee was most common among the upper castes (where a widow meant an extra mouth, but not an extra pair of hands), but it occurred throughout Hindu society (Stein 1978). [Author's note]

As her only alternative to suttee, a widow was allowed to adopt a life of such poverty and austerity that she rarely survived for long. Her life was made even more miserable by the fact that only faithful wives were permitted to commit suttee. The refusal to commit suttee might therefore be regarded as an admission of infidelity. If a woman declined to immolate herself, her relatives might force her to do so, to protect both her honor and the honor of her family.

Stigmatization of Male Homosexuals

. . . this article has discussed male homosexuality only in passing. Nevertheless, it cannot be ignored that the sanctions against male homosexuality appear even stronger than those against lesbianism. Why might this be so? First, I would argue that anything women do is considered relatively trivial — be it housework, mothering, or lesbianism. Second, whereas lesbians threaten the status quo by refusing to accept their inferior position as women, gay males may threaten it even more by appearing to reject their privileged status as men. Prevailing cultural mythology holds that lesbians want to be males. In a paradoxical way, therefore, lesbians may be perceived as upholding "male" values. Male homosexuality, on the other hand, is regarded as a rejection of masculine values; gay males are regarded as feminized "sissies" and "queens." Thus male homosexuality, with its implied rejection of male privilege, may seem even more incomprehensible and threatening than lesbianism. Finally, research indicates that people in general are more fearful and intolerant of homosexuals of their own sex than of homosexuals belonging to the opposite sex (Weinberger and Millham 1979). The greater stigmatization of male than female homosexuality may therefore simply reflect the greater ability of males to enforce their prejudices.

Conclusions

The stigmatization of independent women — whether spinster, widow, nun, or lesbian — is neither automatic nor natural. Rather, it seems to derive from a particular social constellation in which men fear women's sexual and economic independence. Sociological theory explains how stigmatizing individuals as deviant may serve certain purposes for the dominant community, regardless of the accuracy of the accusations leveled (Erikson 1962). First, particularly when social norms are changing rapidly, labeling and punishing certain behaviors as deviant emphasizes the new or continued unacceptability of those behaviors. The stigmatization of "romantic friendships" in the early twentieth century, for example, forced all members of society to recognize that social norms had changed and that such relationships would no longer be tolerated. Second, stigmatizing certain groups as deviant may increase solidarity within the dominant group, as the dominant group unites against its common enemy. Third, stigmatizing as deviant the individuals who challenge traditional ideas may reduce the threat of social change, if those individuals either lose credibility or are removed from the community altogether.

These principles apply to the stigmatization of independent women, from the labeling of nontraditional women as witches in medieval society to the condemnation of lesbians in contemporary society. Medieval inquisitors used the label *witch* to reinforce the normative boundaries of their community, to unite that community against the perceived source of its problems, and to eliminate completely women who seemed to threaten the social order. Currently, the word *lesbian* is used not only to describe women who love other women but also to censure women who overstep the bounds of the traditional female role and to teach all women that such behavior will not be tolerated. Feminists, women athletes, professional women, and others risk being labeled lesbian for their actions and beliefs. Awareness of the potential social consequences of that label exerts significant pressure on all women to remain in their traditional roles.

Antifeminist forces have used the lesbian label to denigrate all feminists, incite community wrath against them, and dismiss their political claims. In 1969 and 1970, some feminists responded to this social pressure by purging lesbians from their midst and proclaiming their moral purity (Abbott and Love 1972). This tactic proved extremely self-destructive, as movement organizations collapsed in bitterness and dissension. In addition, eliminating lesbian members had little effect, since lesbian-baiting by antifeminists was equally damaging to the movement whether or not it was accurate.

By late 1970, many feminists had realized that trying to remove lesbians from their organizations was both self-destructive and ineffective. In response to this knowledge, various feminist organizations went on record acknowledging sexual preference as a feminist and a civil rights issue and supporting the rights of lesbians (Abbott and Love 1972). In a press conference held in December 1970, various women's liberation activists stated:

> Women's Liberation and Homosexual Liberation are both struggling toward a common goal: a society free from defining and categorizing people by virtue of gender and/or sexual preference. "Lesbian" is a label used as a psychic weapon to keep women locked into their male-defined "feminine role." The essence of that role is that a woman is defined in terms of her relationship to men. A woman is called a Lesbian when she functions autonomously. Women's autonomy is what Women's Liberation is all about [quoted in Abbott and Love 1972, 124].

A leaflet distributed the same month by the New York branch of the National Organization for Women acknowledged that, when charges of lesbianism are made, "it is not one woman's sexual preference that is under attack — it is the freedom of all women to openly state values that fundamentally challenge the basic structure of patriarchy" (quoted in Abbott and Love 1972, 122).

It seems, then, that the fates of feminists and lesbians are inextricably intertwined. Unless and until women's independence is accepted, lesbians will be stigmatized, and unless and until the stigma attached to lesbianism diminishes, the lesbian label will be used as a weapon against those who work for women's independence.

Works Cited

Abbott, Sidney, and Barbara Love. *Sappho Was a Right-on Woman: A Liberated View of Lesbianism*. New York: Stein and Day Publishers, 1972.

Barrett, Ellen M. "Legal Homophobia and the Christian Church." *Hastings Law Journal* 30(4): 1019–27, 1979.

Boulding, Elise. *The Underside of History*. Boulder, Colo.: Westview Press, 1976.

Cott, Nancy. "Passionlessness: An Interpretation of Victorian Sexual Ideology, 1790–1850." *Signs: Journal of Women in Culture and Society* 4(2): 219–36, 1978.

Daly, Mary. *Gyn/ecology: The Metaethics of Radical Feminism*. Boston: Beacon Press, 1978.

Eckenstein, Lina. *Women under Monasticism*. New York: Russell and Russell, 1963.

Ehrenreich, Barbara, and Deirdre English. *Witches, Midwives and Nurses: A History of Women Healers*. Old Westbury, N.Y.: Feminist Press, 1973.

Erikson, Kai T. "Notes on the Sociology of Deviance." *Social Problems* 9(Spring): 307–14, 1962.

Ettorre, E. M. *Lesbians, Women and Society*. London: Routledge and Kegan Paul, 1980.

Faderman, Lillian. *Surpassing the Love of Men: Romantic Friendship and Love between Women from the Renaissance to the Present*. New York: William Morrow and Co., 1981.

Ford, Clellan S., and Frank A. Beach. *Patterns of Sexual Behavior*. New York: Harper and Row, 1951.

Glenn, Norval D., and Charles N. Weaver. "Attitudes towards Premarital, Extramarital and Homosexual Relationships in the United States in the 1970s." *Journal of Sex Research* 15(2): 108–17, 1979.

Kramer, H., and J. Sprenger. *Malleus Maleficarum*. Translated by Montague Summers. New York: Dover Publications, 1971.

MacDonald, A. P., and R. G. Games. "Some Characteristics of Those Who Hold Positive and Negative Attitudes towards Homosexuals." *Journal of Homosexuality* 1(1): 9–28, 1974.

MacDonald, A. P., J. Huggins, S. Young, and R. A. Swanson. "Attitudes towards Homosexuality: Preservation of Sex Morality or the Double Standard." *Journal of Consulting and Clinical Psychology* 40(1): 161, 1973.

Mavor, Elizabeth. *The Ladies of Llangollen: A Study of Romantic Friendship.* New York: Penguin Books, 1973.

Nelson, Mary. "Why Witches Were Women." In Jo Freeman (ed.), *Women: A Feminist Perspective,* 2d ed. Palo Alto, Calif.: Mayfield Publishing Co., 1979.

Raskin, Richard. "The 'Deprogramming' of Stephanie Riethmiller," *Ms.*, Sept. 1982, 19.

Reuben, David. *Everything You Always Wanted to Know about Sex But Were Afraid to Ask.* New York: David McKay Co., 1969.

Rivera, Rhonda R. "Our Straight-laced Judges: The Legal Position of Homosexual Persons in the United States." *Hastings Law Journal* 30(4): 799–956, 1979.

Smith-Rosenberg, Carroll. "The Female World of Love and Ritual: Relations between Women in Nineteenth Century America." *Signs: Journal of Women in Culture and Society* 1(1): 1–29, 1975.

Stein, Dorothy K. "Women to Burn: Suttee as a Normative Institution." *Signs: Journal of Women in Culture and Society* 4(2): 253–68, 1978.

Tanner, Donna M. *The Lesbian Couple.* Lexington, Mass.: D. C. Heath and Co., 1978.

Weinberger, Linda E., and Jim Millham. "Attitudinal Homophobia and Support of Traditional Sex Roles." *Journal of Homosexuality* 4(3): 237–45, 1979.

Wolf, Deborah Goleman. *The Lesbian Community.* Berkeley: University of California Press, 1979.

Engaging the Text

1. According to Weitz, how does the very existence of lesbians and other independent women challenge dominant cultural ideas and values?

2. Why, according to Weitz, was lesbianism not stigmatized until very recently? What social function does the stigmatization of lesbians serve?

3. Outline Weitz's argument. What kind of evidence does she rely on? Overall, do you find her essay convincing?

4. In your own words, explain how the Prince Charming syndrome works. Illustrate your explanation with examples drawn from your own experience and from contemporary culture.

Exploring Connections

5. Review Susan Griffin's essay on ecofeminism, "Split Culture" (p. 175). In what ways does ecofeminism threaten male authority? Based on Weitz's essay, what kinds of strategies would you expect to be used to discredit ecofeminism or hold it in check? In your reading or your observation, have you seen any evidence of such strategies being employed?

6. Weitz in this essay and Christopher Lasch in "Changing Modes of Making It" (p. 27) both discuss major shifts in the way society perceives such basic aspects

of life as work and gender. Review their essays, looking for notions of "causality": what causes do they identify (or assume) for the cultural changes they describe? To what extent can any individual or group exercise control over these social changes?

Extending the Critical Context

7. Working in groups, make a list of independent women (real and fictional) from history, public life, literature, movies, and TV. Do you see any evidence that such women are still stigmatized in American society?

8. Debate Weitz's assertion that typical male-female relationships are hierarchical, patriarchal, and undemocratic.

9. Go to the library and research the Salem witchcraft trials. How do the depictions you find of these events compare with Weitz's?

10. Weitz cites a 1979 article by Rhonda R. Rivera on the legal position of homosexual people in the United States (see "Works Cited"). Read more recent work on this subject and report to the class on current laws in your state or on the federal level.

The Two

GLORIA NAYLOR

This story from Gloria Naylor's The Women of Brewster Place *(1982) paints a fictional portrait of a Black lesbian couple as their neighbors begin to discover their secret. As they emerge in the story, Lorraine and Theresa prompt us to reconsider stereotypes of homosexual people. Gloria Naylor (b. 1950) holds a master's degree in Afro-American Studies from Yale University.* The Women of Brewster Place *brought her national recognition and critical acclaim when it won the American Book Award for First Fiction. Naylor has also published two other novels,* Linden Hills *(1985) and* Mama Day *(1988), and a work of nonfiction,* Centennial *(1986).*

At first they seemed like such nice girls. No one could remember exactly when they had moved into Brewster. It was earlier in the year before Ben[1] was killed — of course, it had to be before Ben's death. But

---

[1]*Ben:* the resident caretaker for the apartments in Brewster Place.

no one remembered if it was in the winter or spring of that year that the two had come. People often came and went on Brewster Place like a restless night's dream, moving in and out in the dark to avoid eviction notices or neighborhood bulletins about the dilapidated condition of their furnishings. So it wasn't until the two were clocked leaving in the mornings and returning in the evenings at regular intervals that it was quietly absorbed that they now claimed Brewster as home. And Brewster waited, cautiously prepared to claim them, because you never knew about young women, and obviously single at that. But when no wild music or drunken friends careened out of the corner building on weekends, and especially, when no slightly eager husbands were encouraged to linger around that first-floor apartment and run errands for them, a suspended sigh of relief floated around the two when they dumped their garbage, did their shopping, and headed for the morning bus.

The women of Brewster had readily accepted the lighter, skinny one. There wasn't much threat in her timid mincing walk and the slightly protruding teeth she seemed so eager to show everyone in her bell-like good mornings and evenings. Breaths were held a little longer in the direction of the short dark one — too pretty, and too much behind. And she insisted on wearing those thin Qiana dresses that the summer breeze molded against the maddening rhythm of the twenty pounds of rounded flesh that she swung steadily down the street. Through slitted eyes, the women watched their men watching her pass, knowing the bastards were praying for a wind. But since she seemed oblivious to whether these supplications went answered, their sighs settled around her shoulders too. Nice girls.

And so no one even cared to remember exactly when they had moved into Brewster Place, until the rumor started. It had first spread through the block like a sour odor that's only faintly perceptible and easily ignored until it starts growing in strength from the dozen mouths it had been lying in, among clammy gums and scum-coated teeth. And then it was everywhere — lining the mouths and whitening the lips of everyone as they wrinkled up their noses at its pervading smell, unable to pinpoint the source or time of its initial arrival. Sophie could — she had been there.

It wasn't that the rumor had actually begun with Sophie. A rumor needs no true parent. It only needs a willing carrier, and it found one in Sophie. She had been there — on one of those August evenings when the sun's absence is a mockery because the heat leaves the air so heavy it presses the naked skin down on your body, to the point that a sheet becomes unbearable and sleep impossible. So most of Brewster was outside that night when the two had come in together, probably from one of those air-conditioned movies downtown, and had greeted the ones who were loitering around their building. And they had started up the steps when the skinny one tripped over a child's ball and the darker one had grabbed her by the arm and around the waist to break her fall. "Careful, don't wanna lose you now." And the two of them had laughed into each other's eyes and went into the building.

The smell had begun there. It outlined the image of the stumbling woman and the one who had broken her fall. Sophie and a few other women sniffed at the spot and then, perplexed, silently looked at each other. Where had they seen that before? They had often laughed and touched each other — held each other in joy or its dark twin — but where had they seen *that* before? It came to them as the scent drifted down the steps and entered their nostrils on the way to their inner mouths. They had seen that — done that — with their men. That shared moment of invisible communion reserved for two and hidden from the rest of the world behind laughter or tears or a touch. In the days before babies, miscarriages, and other broken dreams, after stolen caresses in barn stalls and cotton houses, after intimate walks from church and secret kisses with boys who were now long forgotten or permanently fixed in their lives — that was where. They could almost feel the odor moving about in their mouths, and they slowly knitted themselves together and let it out into the air like a yellow mist that began to cling to the bricks on Brewster.

So it got around that the two in 312 were *that* way. And they had seemed like such nice girls. Their regular exits and entrances to the block were viewed with a jaundiced eye. The quiet that rested around their door on the weekends hinted of all sorts of secret rituals, and their friendly indifference to the men on the street was an insult to the women as a brazen flaunting of unnatural ways.

Since Sophie's apartment windows faced theirs from across the air shaft, she became the official watchman for the block, and her opinions were deferred to whenever the two came up in conversation. Sophie took her position seriously and was constantly alert for any telltale signs that might creep out around their drawn shades, across from which she kept a religious vigil. An entire week of drawn shades was evidence enough to send her flying around with reports that as soon as it got dark they pulled their shades down and put on the lights. Heads nodded in knowing unison — a definite sign. If doubt was voiced with a "But I pull my shades down at night too," a whispered "Yeah, but you're not *that* way" was argument enough to win them over.

Sophie watched the lighter one dumping their garbage, and she went outside and opened the lid. Her eyes darted over the crushed tin cans, vegetable peelings, and empty chocolate chip cookie boxes. What do they do with all them chocolate chip cookies? It was surely a sign, but it would take some time to figure that one out. She saw Ben go into their apartment, and she waited and blocked his path as he came out, carrying his toolbox.

"What ya see?" She grabbed his arm and whispered wetly in his face.

Ben stared at her squinted eyes and drooping lips and shook his head 10 slowly. "Uh, uh, uh, it was terrible."

"Yeah?" She moved in a little closer.

"Worst busted faucet I seen in my whole life." He shook her hand off his arm and left her standing in the middle of the block.

"You old sop bucket," she muttered, as she went back up on her stoop. A broken faucet, huh? Why did they need to use so much water?

Sophie had plenty to report that day. Ben had said it was terrible in there. No, she didn't know exactly what he had seen, but you can imagine — and they did. Confronted with the difference that had been thrust into their predictable world, they reached into their imaginations and, using an ancient pattern, weaved themselves a reason for its existence. Out of necessity they stitched all of their secret fears and lingering childhood nightmares into this existence, because even though it was deceptive enough to try and look as they looked, talk as they talked, and do as they did, it had to have some hidden stain to invalidate it — it was impossible for them both to be right. So they leaned back, supported by the sheer weight of their numbers and comforted by the woven barrier that kept them protected from the yellow mist that enshrouded the two as they came and went on Brewster Place.

Lorraine was the first to notice the change in the people on Brewster 15 Place. She was a shy but naturally friendly woman who got up early, and had read the morning paper and done fifty sit-ups before it was time to leave for work. She came out of her apartment eager to start her day by greeting any of her neighbors who were outside. But she noticed that some of the people who had spoken to her before made a point of having something else to do with their eyes when she passed, although she could almost feel them staring at her back as she moved on. The ones who still spoke only did so after an uncomfortable pause, in which they seemed to be peering through her before they begrudged her a good morning or evening. She wondered if it was all in her mind and she thought about mentioning it to Theresa, but she didn't want to be accused of being too sensitive again. And how would Tee even notice anything like that anyway? She had a lousy attitude and hardly ever spoke to people. She stayed in that bed until the last moment and rushed out of the house fogged-up and grumpy, and she was used to being stared at — by men at least — because of her body.

Lorraine thought about these things as she came up the block from work, carrying a large paper bag. The group of women on her stoop parted silently and let her pass.

"Good evening," she said, as she climbed the steps.

Sophie was standing on the top step and tried to peek into the bag. "You been shopping, huh? What ya buy?" It was almost an accusation.

"Groceries." Lorraine shielded the top of the bag from view and squeezed past her with a confused frown. She saw Sophie throw a knowing glance to the others at the bottom of the stoop. What was wrong with this old woman? Was she crazy or something?

Lorraine went into her apartment. Theresa was sitting by the window, reading a copy of *Mademoiselle.* She glanced up from her magazine. "Did you get my chocolate chip cookies?" 20

"Why good evening to you, too, Tee. And how was my day? Just wonderful." She sat the bag down on the couch. "The little Baxter boy brought in a puppy for show-and-tell, and the damn thing pissed all over the floor and then proceeded to chew the heel off my shoe, but, yes, I managed to hobble to the store and bring you your chocolate chip cookies."

Oh, Jesus, Theresa thought, she's got a bug up her ass tonight.

"Well, you should speak to Mrs. Baxter. She ought to train her kid better than that." She didn't wait for Lorraine to stop laughing before she tried to stretch her good mood. "Here, I'll put those things away. Want me to make dinner so you can rest? I only worked half a day, and the most tragic thing that went down was a broken fingernail and that got caught in my typewriter."

Lorraine followed Theresa into the kitchen. "No, I'm not really tired, and fair's fair, you cooked last night. I didn't mean to tick off like that; it's just that . . . well, Tee, have you noticed that people aren't as nice as they used to be?"

Theresa stiffened. Oh, God, here she goes again. "What people, Lorraine? Nice in what way?" 25

"Well, the people in this building and on the street. No one hardly speaks anymore. I mean, I'll come in and say good evening — and just silence. It wasn't like that when we first moved in. I don't know, it just makes you wonder; that's all. What are they thinking?"

"I personally don't give a shit what they're thinking. And their good evenings don't put any bread on my table."

"Yeah, but you didn't see the way that woman looked at me out there. They must feel something or know something. They probably — "

"They, they, they!" Theresa exploded. "You know, I'm not starting up with this again, Lorraine. Who in the hell are they? And where in the hell are we? Living in some dump of a building in this God-forsaken part of town around a bunch of ignorant niggers with the cotton still under their fingernails because of you and your theys. They knew something in Linden Hills, so I gave up an apartment for you that I'd been in for the last four years. And then they knew in Park Heights, and you made me so miserable there we had to leave. Now these mysterious theys are on Brewster Place. Well, look out that window, kid. There's a big wall down that block, and this is the end of the line for me. I'm not moving anymore, so if that's what you're working yourself up to — save it!"

When Theresa became angry she was like a lump of smoldering coal, and her fierce bursts of temper always unsettled Lorraine.

"You see, that's why I didn't want to mention it." Lorraine began to pull at her fingers nervously. "You're always flying up and jumping to conclusions — no one said anything about moving. And I didn't know your life has been so miserable since you met me. I'm sorry about that," she finished tearfully.

Theresa looked at Lorraine, standing in the kitchen door like a wilted leaf, and she wanted to throw something at her. Why didn't she ever fight back? The very softness that had first attracted her to Lorraine was now a frequent cause for irritation. Smoked honey. That's what Lorraine had reminded her of, sitting in her office clutching that application. Dry autumn days in Georgia woods, thick bloated smoke under a beehive, and the first glimpse of amber honey just faintly darkened about the edges by the burning twigs. She had flowed just that heavily into Theresa's mind and had stuck there with a persistent sweetness.

But Theresa hadn't known then that this softness filled Lorraine up to the very middle and that she would bend at the slightest pressure, would be constantly seeking to surround herself with the comfort of everyone's goodwill, and would shrivel up at the least touch of disapproval. It was becoming a drain to be continually called upon for this nurturing and support that she just didn't understand. She had supplied it at first out of love for Lorraine, hoping that she would harden eventually, even as honey does when exposed to the cold. Theresa was growing tired of being clung to — of being the one who was leaned on. She didn't want a child — she wanted someone who could stand toe to toe with her and be willing to slug it out at times. If they practiced that way with each other, then they could turn back to back and beat the hell out of the world for trying to invade their territory. But she had found no such sparring partner in Lorraine, and the strain of fighting alone was beginning to show on her.

"Well, if it was that miserable, I would have been gone a long time ago," she said, watching her words refresh Lorraine like a gentle shower.

"I guess you think I'm some sort of a sick paranoid, but I can't afford to have people calling my job or writing letters to my principal. You know I've already lost a position like that in Detroit. And teaching is my whole life, Tee."

"I know," she sighed, not really knowing at all. There was no danger of that ever happening on Brewster Place. Lorraine taught too far from this neighborhood for anyone here to recognize her in that

30

35

school. No, it wasn't her job she feared losing this time, but their approval. She wanted to stand out there and chat and trade makeup secrets and cake recipes. She wanted to be secretary of their block association and be asked to mind their kids while they ran to the store. And none of that was going to happen if they couldn't even bring themselves to accept her good evenings.

Theresa silently finished unpacking the groceries. "Why did you buy cottage cheese? Who eats that stuff?"

"Well, I thought we should go on a diet."

"If *we* go on a diet, then you'll disappear. You've got nothing to lose but your hair."

"Oh, I don't know. I thought that we might want to try and reduce our hips or something." Lorraine shrugged playfully. 40

"No, thank you. We are very happy with our hips the way they are," Theresa said, as she shoved the cottage cheese to the back of the refrigerator. "And even when I lose weight, it never comes off there. My chest and arms just get smaller, and I start looking like a bottle of salad dressing."

The two women laughed, and Theresa sat down to watch Lorraine fix dinner. "You know, this behind has always been my downfall. When I was coming up in Georgia with my grandmother, the boys used to promise me penny candy if I would let them pat my behind. And I used to love those jawbreakers — you know, the kind that lasted all day and kept changing colors in your mouth. So I was glad to oblige them, because in one afternoon I could collect a whole week's worth of jawbreakers."

"Really. That's funny to you? Having some boy feeling all over you."

Theresa sucked her teeth. "We were only kids, Lorraine. You know, you remind me of my grandmother. That was one straight-laced old lady. She had a fit when my brother told her what I was doing. She called me into the smokehouse and told me in this real scary whisper that I could get pregnant from letting little boys pat my butt and that I'd end up like my cousin Willa. But Willa and I had been thick as fleas, and she had already given me a step-by-step summary of how she'd gotten into her predicament. But I sneaked around to her house that night just to double-check her story, since that old lady had seemed so earnest. 'Willa, are you sure?' I whispered through her bedroom window. 'I'm tellin' ya, Tee,' she said. 'Just keep both feet on the ground and you home free.' Much later I learned that advice wasn't too biologically sound, but it worked in Georgia because those country boys didn't have much imagination."

Theresa's laughter bounced off of Lorraine's silent, rigid back and died in her throat. She angrily tore open a pack of the chocolate chip cookies. "Yeah," she said, staring at Lorraine's back and biting down hard into the cookie, "it wasn't until I came up north to college that I 45 found out there's a whole lot of things that a dude with a little imagination can do to you even with both feet on the ground. You see, Willa forgot to tell me not to bend over or squat or — "

"Must you!" Lorraine turned around from the stove with her teeth clenched tightly together.

"Must I what, Lorraine? Must I talk about things that are as much a part of life as eating or breathing or growing old? Why are you always so uptight about sex or men?"

"I'm not uptight about anything. I just think its disgusting when you go on and on about — "

"There's nothing disgusting about it, Lorraine. You've never been with a man, but I've been with quite a few — some better than others. There were a couple who I still hope to this day will die a slow, painful death, but then there were some who were good to me — in and out of bed."

"If they were so great, then why are you with me?" Lorraine's lips were trembling.   50

"Because — " Theresa looked steadily into her eyes and then down at the cookie she was twirling on the table. "Because," she continued slowly, "you can take a chocolate chip cookie and put holes in it and attach it to your ears and call it an earring, or hang it around your neck on a silver chain and pretend it's a necklace — but it's still a cookie. See — you can toss it in the air and call it a Frisbee or even a flying saucer, if the mood hits you, and it's still just a cookie. Send it spinning on a table — like this — until it's a wonderful blur of amber and brown light that you can imagine to be a topaz or rusted gold or old crystal, but the law of gravity has got to come into play, sometime, and it's got to come to rest — sometime. Then all the spinning and pretending and hoopla is over with. And you know what you got?"

"A chocolate chip cookie," Lorraine said.

"Uh-huh." Theresa put the cookie in her mouth and winked. "A lesbian." She got up from the table. "Call me when dinner's ready, I'm going back to read." She stopped at the kitchen door. "Now, why are you putting gravy on that chicken, Lorraine? You know it's fattening."

Engaging the Text

1. What type of community does Naylor describe in her opening two paragraphs, and how, specifically, does she create this atmosphere? Why is this important to the theme of the story?

2. Why does Naylor shift the story's point of view from that of the community to that of Lorraine and Theresa? How does this change of perspective affect the reader?

3. Why does Naylor make a point of details like drawn shades, chocolate chip cookies, and the broken faucet?

4. How important is sexuality in Lorraine and Theresa's relationship? What do they share besides lovemaking?

Exploring Connections

5. How would Rose Weitz (p. 257) explain the community's reaction to the presence of a lesbian couple in the neighborhood?

6. Does Lorraine and Theresa's relationship support Weitz's claim that lesbian couples are more "egalitarian" than heterosexual couples?

Extending the Critical Context

7. Find one or more psychology texts or articles authored before 1960 that cover homosexuality. How is it defined, described, and classified? How often is lesbianism specifically included in the discussion?

8. Investigate the official policy (if any) toward homosexual teachers at various schools in your locale. Are there restrictions, explicit or implicit, against homosexual teachers? Report to the class on your findings. Your sources might include interviews with teachers as well as school documents, laws, or court cases.

4

Created Equal
The Myth of the Melting Pot

The myth of the melting pot predates the drafting of the U.S. Constitution. In 1782, a year before the Peace of Paris formally ended the Revolutionary War, Hector St. Jean de Crèvecoeur envisioned the young American republic as a crucible that would forge its disparate immigrant population into a vigorous new society with a grand future:

> What, then, is the American, this new man? He is either an European, or the descendant of an European. . . . He is an American, who leaving behind him all his ancient prejudices and manners, receives new ones from the new mode of life he has embraced, the new government he obeys, and the new rank he holds. . . . Here individuals of all nations are melted into a new race of men, whose labours and posterity will one day cause great changes in the world.

Crèvecoeur's metaphor has remained a powerful ideal for many generations of American scholars, politicians, artists, and ordinary citizens. Ralph Waldo Emerson, writing in his journal in 1845, celebrated the national vitality produced by the mingling of immigrant cultures: "in this continent — asylum of all nations, — the energy of . . . all the European tribes, — of the Africans, and of the Polynesians — will construct a new race, a new religion, a new state, a new literature." An English Jewish writer named Israel Zangwill, himself an immigrant, popularized the myth in his 1908 drama, *The Melting Pot*. In the play, the hero rhapsodizes, "Yes East and West, and North and South, the palm and the pine, the pole and the equator, the crescent and the cross — how the great Alchemist melts and fuses them with his purging flame! Here shall they all unite to build the Republic of Man and the Kingdom of God." The myth was perhaps most vividly dramatized, though, in a pageant staged by Henry Ford in the early 1920s. Decked out in the costumes of their native lands, Ford's immigrant workers sang traditional songs from their homelands as they danced their way into an enormous replica of a cast-iron pot. They then emerged from the other side wearing identical "American" suits, waving miniature American flags, and singing "The Star-Spangled Banner."

The drama of becoming an American has deep roots: immigrants take on a new identity — and a new set of cultural myths — because they want to become members of the community, equal members with all the rights, responsibilities, and opportunities of their fellow citizens. The force of the melting pot myth lies in this implied promise that all Americans are indeed "created equal." However, the myth's promises of openness, harmony, unity, and equality were deceptive from the beginning. Crèvecoeur's exclusive concern with the mingling of *European* peoples (he lists the "English, Scotch, Irish, French, Dutch, Germans, and Swedes") utterly ignored the presence of some three-quarters of a million Africans and African Americans who then lived in this country, as well as the tribal peoples who had lived on the land for thousands of years before European contact. Crèvecoeur's vision of a country embracing "all nations" clearly applied only to northern European nations. Benjamin Franklin, in a 1751 essay, was more blunt; since Africa, Asia, and most of America were inhabited by dark-skinned people, he argued, the American colonies should consciously try to increase the white population and keep out the rest: "Why increase the Sons of Africa, by Planting them in America, where we have so fair an opportunity, by excluding Blacks and Tawneys, of increasing the lovely White . . . ?" If later writers like Emerson and Zangwill saw a more inclusive cultural mix as a source of hope and renewal for the United States, others throughout this country's history have, even more than Franklin, feared that mix as a threat.

The fear of difference underlies another, equally powerful American myth — the myth of racial supremacy. This is the negative counterpart of the melting pot ideal: instead of the equal and harmonious blending of cultures, it proposes a racial and ethnic hierarchy based on the "natural superiority" of Anglo-Americans. Under the sway of this myth, differences become signs of inferiority, and "inferiors" are treated as childlike or even subhuman. This myth has given rise to some of the most shameful passages in our national life: slavery, segregation, and lynching; the near extermination of tribal peoples and cultures; the denial of citizenship and constitutional rights to African Americans, American Indians, Chinese and Japanese immigrants; the brutal exploitation of Mexican and Asian laborers . . . the catalog of injustices is long and painful. The melting pot ideal itself has often masked the myth of racial and ethnic superiority. "Inferiors" are expected to "melt" into conformity with Anglo-American behavior and values. Henry Ford's pageant conveys the message that ethnic identity is best left behind — exchanged for something "better," more uniform, less threatening.

This chapter explores the interaction between these two related cultural myths: the myth of unity and the myth of difference and hierarchy. It examines how the categories of race and ethnicity are defined and how they operate to divide us even within apparently unified communities. These issues become crucial as the population of the United States grows increasingly diverse: the selections here challenge you to reconsider the fate of the melting pot myth as we enter the era of multiethnic, multicultural America. Can we learn to accept and honor our differences?

The first half of the chapter focuses on the myth of racial superiority. The introductory selection, by Michael Omi and Howard Winant, explores the idea that racial categories are not biologically determined but socially constructed. Gordon W. Allport's classic essay on the formation of in-groups explains prejudice as a by-product of the need for community and a sense of inclusion. In the autobiographical essay "Split at the Root," Adrienne Rich reflects on her inner conflicts as a woman torn between multiple, competing in-groups. In a historical survey of American racism, Martin Luther King, Jr., shows how the myth of racial superiority has justified the economic exploitation of African Americans. Wendy Rose's haunting poem "Three Thousand Dollar Death Song" affirms the vitality of American Indian culture, despite centuries of oppression and injustice. Likewise, in "We, the Dangerous," poet Janice Mirikitani celebrates the strength of Asian Americans to survive and resist the power of violent racism. Next, the account of C. P. Ellis's transformation from Ku Klux Klan member to union activist shows racism from the inside and raises questions about how, on a larger scale, we can combat the myth of racial superiority. Shelby Steele's provocative piece "I'm Black, You're White, Who's Innocent?" departs from other selections here by calling on African Americans to stop dwelling on the racist past, seize present opportunities, and strive for success.

Readings in the second half of the chapter focus on relations among groups historically marginalized by Anglo-American culture and explore the emerging myth of the "new melting pot" of multicultural America. Virginia R. Harris and Trinity A. Ordoña analyze the legacy of racism among groups that have been its targets — self-hatred and cutthroat competition for slightly higher, but still subordinate, positions in the racial hierarchy. In "A Fire in Fontana," Hisaye Yamamoto DeSoto relates how a series of encounters with bigotry gradually led her to re-evaluate her own role in the tragic deaths of a young African American family. The idea of intergroup and intragroup conflict is given a comic twist in Luis Valdez's satirical one-act play "Los Vendidos." In a daring selection whose multilingual, multicultural style echoes her thesis, Gloria Anzaldúa calls for a new way of looking at the world: a *mestiza* or mixed consciousness that liberates us from outworn and dangerous myths of difference. The chapter concludes with Aurora Levins Morales's "Child of the Americas," a poem that pays tribute both to cultural difference and to the continuing power of the melting pot myth.

Sources

John Hope Franklin, *Race and History: Selected Essays, 1938–1988.* Baton Rouge: Louisiana State University Press, 1989, pp. 321–331.

Milton M. Gordon, *Assimilation in American Life: The Role of Race, Religion, and National Origins.* New York: Oxford University Press, 1964.

Itabari Njeri, "Beyond the Melting Pot." *Los Angeles Times,* January 13, 1991, pp. E1, E8–9.

Leonard Pitt, *We Americans,* vol. 2, 3rd ed. Dubuque: Kendall/Hunt, 1987.

Ronald Takaki, "Reflections on Racial Patterns in America." In *From Different Shores: Perspectives on Race and Ethnicity in America,* Ronald Takaki, ed. New York: Oxford University Press, 1987, pp. 26–37.

Before Reading . . .

Survey images in the popular media (newspapers, magazines, TV shows, movies, and pop music) for evidence of the myth of the melting pot. Do you find any figures in popular culture who seem to endorse the idea of a "new melting pot" in the United States? How closely do these images reflect your understanding of your own and other ethnic and racial groups? Explore these questions in a journal entry, then discuss in class.

Alternatively, you might investigate the metaphors that are being used to describe racial and ethnic group relations or interactions between members of different groups on your campus and in your community. Consult local news sources and campus publications, and keep your ears open for conversations that touch on these issues. Do some freewriting about what you discover and compare notes with classmates.

Racial Formation

MICHAEL OMI AND HOWARD WINANT

Context: race a cultural category that needs to be examined to do a cultural analysis of literature [handwritten annotation]

This selection sets the stage for an analysis of race issues in the United States. Michael Omi and Howard Winant provide a broad overview of the subject, arguing in particular that race is more social myth than biological fact. They also have a keen sense of the contradictions, ironies, and paradoxes that permeate racial consciousness in our culture. Omi is a professor of Asian American Studies at the University of California, Berkeley; Winant is a political sociologist at Temple University. The essay comes from their book, Racial Formation in the United States: From the 1960s to the 1980s *(1986).*

In 1982–83, Susie Guillory Phipps unsuccessfully sued the Louisiana Bureau of Vital Records to change her racial classification from black to white. The descendant of an eighteenth-century white planter and a black slave, Phipps was designated "black" in her birth certificate in accordance with a 1970 state law which declared anyone with at least one-thirty-second "Negro blood" to be black. The legal battle raised intriguing questions about the concept of race, its meaning in contemporary society, and its use (and abuse) in public policy. Assistant Attorney General Ron Davis defended the law by pointing out that some type of racial classification was necessary to comply with federal record-keeping requirements and to facilitate programs for the prevention of genetic diseases. Phipps's attorney, Brian Begue, argued that the assignment of racial categories on birth certificates was unconstitutional and that the one-thirty-second designation was inaccurate. He called on a retired Tulane University professor who cited research indicating that most whites have one-twentieth "Negro" ancestry. In the end, Phipps lost. The court upheld a state law which quantified racial identity, and in so doing affirmed the legality of assigning individuals to specific racial groupings.[1]

The Phipps case illustrates the continuing dilemma of defining race and establishing its meaning in institutional life. Today, to assert that

---

[1]*San Francisco Chronicle*, 14 September 1982, 19 May 1983. Ironically, the 1970 Louisiana law was enacted to supersede an old Jim Crow statute which relied on the idea of "common report" in determining an infant's race. Following Phipps's unsuccessful attempt to change her classification and have the law declared unconstitutional, a legislative effort arose which culminated in the repeal of the law. See *San Francisco Chronicle*, 23 June 1983. [Author's note]

variations in human physiognomy are racially based is to enter a constant and intense debate. *Scientific* interpretations of race have not been alone in sparking heated controversy; *religious* perspectives have done so as well.[2] Most centrally, of course, race has been a matter of *political* contention. This has been particularly true in the United States, where the concept of race has varied enormously over time without ever leaving the center stage of U.S. history.

What Is Race?

Race consciousness, and its articulation in theories of race, is largely a modern phenomenon. When European explorers in the New World "discovered" people who looked different than themselves, these "natives" challenged then existing conceptions of the origins of the human species, and raised disturbing questions as to whether *all* could be considered in the same "family of man."[3] Religious debates flared over the attempt to reconcile the Bible with the existence of "racially distinct" people. Arguments took place over creation itself, as theories of polygenesis questioned whether God had made only one species of humanity ("monogenesis"). Europeans wondered if the natives of the New World were indeed human beings with redeemable souls. At stake were not only the prospects for conversion, but the types of treatment to be accorded them. The expropriation of property, the denial of political rights, the introduction of slavery and other forms of coercive labor, as well as outright extermination, all presupposed a worldview which distinguished Europeans — children of God, human beings, etc. — from "others." Such a worldview was needed to explain why some should be "free" and others enslaved, why some had rights to land and

---

[2]The Mormon church, for example, has been heavily criticized for its doctrine of black inferiority. [Author's note]

[3]Thomas F. Gossett notes:

> Race theory . . . had up until fairly modern times no firm hold on European thought. On the other hand, race theory and race prejudice were by no means unknown at the time when the English colonists came to North America. Undoubtedly, the age of exploration led many to speculate on race differences at a period when neither Europeans nor Englishmen were prepared to make allowances for vast cultural diversities. Even though race theories had not then secured wide acceptance or even sophisticated formulation, the first contacts of the Spanish with the Indians in the Americas can now be recognized as the beginning of a struggle between conceptions of the nature of primitive peoples which has not yet been wholly settled. (Thomas F. Gossett, *Race: The History of an Idea in America* [New York: Schocken Books, 1965], p. 16.)

Winthrop Jordan provides a detailed account of early European colonialists' attitudes about color and race in *White over Black: American Attitudes Toward the Negro, 1550–1812* (New York: Norton, 1977 [1968]), pp. 3–43. [Authors' note]

property while others did not. Race, and the interpretation of racial differences, was a central factor in that worldview.

. . . Many scholars in the eighteenth and nineteenth centuries dedicated themselves to the identification and ranking of variations in humankind. Race was thought of as a *biological* concept, yet its precise definition was the subject of debates which . . . continue to rage today. Despite efforts ranging from Dr. Samuel Morton's studies of cranial capacity[4] to contemporary attempts to base racial classification on shared gene pools,[5] the concept of race has defied biological definition.

None of the ostensibly "objective" measures to determine and define   5
racial categories were free from the invidious elements of racial ideology. The eighteenth century saw the popular acceptance of a concept with roots in classical Greek thought — the "Great Chain of Being." Posing a grand hierarchy starting with inanimate objects, up through the lowliest forms of life, through "man," and culminating with God the Creator, the "Great Chain of Being" framed discussion about the gradations which existed among humankind. Which races were closer to God and which to apes? In a period where hierarchical arrangements in society were being questioned, the notion of a "Great Chain of Being" legitimated status differences and inequality with appeals to the "naturalness" of distinctions between human beings. To challenge this order would be tantamount to challenging God him/herself.[6]

In the nineteenth century, Count Arthur de Gobineau drew upon the most respected scientific studies of his day to compose his four-volume *Essay on the Inequality of Races* (1853–55). He not only greatly influenced the racial thinking of the period, but his themes were to be echoed in the racist ideologies of the next hundred years: beliefs that

[4]Pro-slavery physician Samuel George Morton (1799–1851) compiled a collection of 800 crania from all parts of the world which formed the sample for his studies of race. Assuming that the larger the size of the cranium translated into greater intelligence, Morton established a relationship between race and skull capacity. Gossett reports that

> In 1849, one of his studies included the following results: the English skulls in his collection proved to be the largest, with an average cranial capacity of 96 cubic inches. The Americans and Germans were rather poor seconds, both with cranial capacities of 90 cubic inches. At the bottom of the list were the Negroes with 83 cubic inches, the Chinese with 82, and the Indians with 79. (Ibid., p. 74.)

On Morton's methods, see Stephen J. Gould, "The Finagle Factor," *Human Nature* (July 1978). [Authors' note]

[5]Definitions of race founded upon a common pool of genes have not held up when confronted by scientific research which suggests that the differences *within* a given human population are greater than those *between* populations. See L. L. Cavalli-Sforza, "The Genetics of Human Populations," *Scientific American* (September 1974), pp. 81–9. [Authors' note]

[6]Winthrop D. Jordan, op. cit., pp. 219–28. [Authors' note]

superior races produce superior cultures and that racial intermixtures result in the degradation of the superior racial stock. These themes found expression, for instance, in the eugenics movement inspired by Darwin's cousin, Francis Galton,[7] which had an immense impact on scientific and sociopolitical thought in Europe and the United States.[8]

Attempts to discern the *scientific meaning* of race continue to the present day. Although most physical anthropologists and biologists have abandoned the quest for a scientific basis to determine racial categories, controversies have recently flared in the area of genetics and educational psychology. For instance, an essay by Arthur Jensen[9] which argued that hereditary factors shape intelligence not only revived the "nature or nurture" controversy, but raised highly volatile questions about racial equality itself.[10] Clearly the attempt to establish a *biological* basis of race has not been swept into the dustbin of history, but is being resurrected in various scientific arenas. . . .

Race as a Social Concept

The social sciences have come to reject biologistic notions of race in favor of an approach which regards race as a *social* concept. Beginning in the eighteenth century, this trend has been slow and uneven, but its direction clear. In the nineteenth century Max Weber[11] discounted biological explanations for racial conflict and instead highlighted the social and political factors which engendered such conflict.[12] The work of pioneering cultural anthropologist Franz Boas was crucial in refuting the scientific racism of the early twentieth century by rejecting the connection between race and culture, and the assumption of a continuum of "higher" and "lower" cultural groups. Within the contemporary social science literature, race is assumed to be a variable which is shaped by broader societal forces.

---

[7]*eugenics . . . Galton:* Francis Galton (1822–1911) coined the term "eugenics" (literally "good genes") for the science of improving a species by influencing or controlling reproduction. Promoted as a way of minimizing birth defects and congenital illnesses, eugenics has also led to sperm banks for geniuses, proposals to castrate sex offenders, and a call for tax incentives to lower African American birthrates.

[8]Two recent histories of eugenics are Allen Chase, *The Legacy of Malthus* (New York: Knopf, 1977); Daniel J. Kelves, *In the Name of Eugenics: Genetics and the Uses of Human Heredity* (New York: Knopf, 1985). [Authors' note]

[9]*Arthur Jensen:* professor (b. 1923) whose theories of genetic determinism, suggesting that African Americans have lower IQs than whites, have been criticized as racist.

[10]Arthur Jensen, "How Much Can We Boost IQ and Scholastic Achievement?" *Harvard Educational Review*, vol. 39 (1969), pp. 1–123. [Authors' note]

[11]*Max Weber:* (pronounced VAY-ber). German sociologist and political economist (1864–1920).

[12]Ernst Moritz Manasse, "Max Weber on Race," *Social Research*, vol. 14 (1947), pp. 191–221. [Authors' note]

Race is indeed a pre-eminently *sociohistorical* concept. Racial categories and the meaning of race . . . have varied tremendously over time and between different societies.

In the United States, the black/white color line has historically been   10
rigidly defined and enforced. White is seen as a "pure" category. Any racial intermixture makes one "nonwhite." In the movie *Raintree County*, Elizabeth Taylor describes the worst of fates to befall whites as "havin' a little Negra blood in ya' — just one little teeny drop and a person's all Negra."[13] This thinking flows from what Marvin Harris[14] has characterized as the principle of *hypo-descent*:

> By what ingenious computation is the genetic tracery of a million years of evolution unraveled and each man [*sic*] assigned his proper social box? In the United States, the mechanism employed is the rule of hypo-descent. This descent rule requires Americans to believe that anyone who is known to have had a Negro ancestor is a Negro. We admit nothing in between. . . . "Hypo-descent" means affiliation with the subordinate rather than the superordinate group in order to avoid the ambiguity of intermediate identity. . . . The rule of hypo-descent is, therefore, an invention, which we in the United States have made in order to keep biological facts from intruding into our collective racist fantasies.[15]

The Susie Guillory Phipps case represents the contemporary expression of this racial logic.

By contrast, a striking feature of race relations in the lowland areas of Latin America since the abolition of slavery has been the relative absence of sharply defined racial groupings. No such rigid descent rule characterizes racial identity in many Latin American societies. Brazil, for example, has historically had less rigid conceptions of race, and thus a variety of "intermediate" racial categories exist. Indeed, as Harris notes, "One of the most striking consequences of the Brazilian system of racial identification is that parents and children and even brothers and sisters are frequently accepted as representatives of quite opposite racial types."[16] Such a possibility is incomprehensible within the logic of racial categories in the United States.

To suggest another example: the notion of "passing" takes on new meaning if we compare various American cultures' means of assigning racial identity. In the United States, individuals who are actually

---

[13]Quoted in Edward D. C. Campbell, Jr., *The Celluloid South: Hollywood and the Southern Myth* (Knoxville: University of Tennessee Press, 1981), pp. 168–70. [Authors' note]

[14]*Marvin Harris:* contemporary cultural anthropologist (b. 1927).

[15]Marvin Harris, *Patterns of Race in the Americas* (New York: Norton, 1964), p. 56. [Authors' note]

[16]Ibid., p. 57. [Authors' note]

"black" by the logic of hypo-descent have attempted to skirt the discriminatory barriers imposed by law and custom by attempting to "pass" for white.[17] Ironically, these same individuals would not be able to pass for "black" in many Latin American societies.

Consideration of the term "black" illustrates the diversity of racial meanings which can be found among different societies and historically within a given society. In contemporary British politics the term "black" is used to refer to all nonwhites. Interestingly this designation has not arisen through the racist discourse of groups such as the National Front. Rather, in political and cultural movements, Asian as well as Afro-Caribbean youth are adopting the term as an expression of self-identity.[18] The wide-ranging meanings of "black" illustrate the manner in which racial categories are shaped politically.[19]

The meaning of race is defined and contested throughout society, in both collective action and personal practice. In the process, racial categories themselves are formed, transformed, destroyed, and re-formed. We use the term *racial formation* to refer to the process by which social, economic, and political forces determine the content and importance of racial categories, and by which they are in turn shaped by racial meanings. . . .

Racial Ideology and Racial Identity

The seemingly obvious, "natural" and "common sense" qualities which the existing racial order exhibits themselves testify to the effectiveness of the racial formation process in constructing racial meanings and racial identities.   15

One of the first things we notice about people when we meet them (along with their sex) is their race. We utilize race to provide clues about *who* a person is. This fact is made painfully obvious when we encounter someone whom we cannot conveniently racially categorize — someone

[17]After James Meredith had been admitted as the first black student at the University of Mississippi, Harry S. Murphy announced that he, and not Meredith, was the first black student to attend "Ole Miss." Murphy described himself as black but was able to pass for white and spent nine months at the institution without attracting any notice (ibid., p. 56). [Authors' note]

[18]A. Sivanandan, "From Resistance to Rebellion: Asian and Afro-Caribbean Struggles in Britain," *Race and Class*, vol. 23, nos. 2–3 (Autumn–Winter 1981). [Authors' note]

[19]Consider the contradictions in racial status which abound in the country with the most rigidly defined racial categories — South Africa. There a race classification agency is employed to adjudicate claims for upgrading of official racial identity. This is particularly necessary for the "coloured" category. The apartheid system considers Chinese as "Asians" while the Japanese are accorded the status of "honorary whites." This logic nearly detaches race from any grounding in skin color and other physical attributes and nakedly exposes race as a juridicial category subject to economic, social, and political influences. (We are indebted to Steve Talbot for clarification of some of these points.) [Authors' note]

who is, for example, racially "mixed" or of an ethnic/racial group with which we are not familiar. Such an encounter becomes a source of discomfort and momentarily a crisis of racial meaning. Without a racial identity, one is in danger of having no identity.

Our compass for navigating race relations depends on preconceived notions of what each specific racial group looks like. Comments such as, "Funny, you don't look black," betray an underlying image of what black should be. We also become disoriented when people do not act "black," "Latino," or indeed "white." The content of such stereotypes reveals a series of unsubstantiated beliefs about who these groups are and what "they" are like.[20]

In U.S. society, then, a kind of "racial etiquette" exists, a set of interpretative codes and racial meanings which operate in the interactions of daily life. Rules shaped by our perception of race in a comprehensively racial society determine the "presentation of self,"[21] distinctions of status, and appropriate modes of conduct. "Etiquette" is not mere universal adherence to the dominant group's rules, but a more dynamic combination of these rules with the values and beliefs of subordinated groupings. This racial "subjection" is quintessentially ideological. Everybody learns some combination, some version, of the rules of racial classification, and of their own racial identity, often without obvious teaching or conscious inculcation. Race becomes "common sense" — a way of comprehending, explaining, and acting in the world.

Racial beliefs operate as an "amateur biology," a way of explaining the variations in "human nature."[22] Differences in skin color and other obvious physical characteristics supposedly provide visible clues to differences lurking underneath. Temperament, sexuality, intelligence, athletic ability, aesthetic preferences, and so on are presumed to be fixed and discernible from the palpable mark of race. Such diverse questions as our confidence and trust in others (for example, clerks or salespeople, media figures, neighbors), our sexual preferences and romantic images, our tastes in music, films, dance, or sports, and our very ways of talking, walking, eating, and dreaming are ineluctably[23] shaped by notions of race. Skin color "differences" are thought to explain perceived differences in intellectual, physical, and artistic temperaments,

---

[20]Gordon W. Allport, *The Nature of Prejudice* (Garden City, New York: Doubleday, 1958), pp. 184–200. [Authors' note]

[21]We wish to use this phrase loosely, without committing ourselves to a particular position on such social psychological approaches as symbolic interactionism, which are outside the scope of this study. An interesting study on this subject is S. M. Lyman and W. A. Douglass, "Ethnicity: Strategies of Individual and Collective Impression Management," *Social Research*, vol. 40, no. 2 (1973). [Authors' note]

[22]Michael Billig, "Patterns of Racism: Interviews with National Front Members," *Race and Class*, vol. 20, no. 2 (Autumn 1978), pp. 161–79. [Authors' note]

[23]*ineluctably:* inescapably.

and to justify distinct treatment of racially identified individuals and groups.

The continuing ~~persistence~~ of racial ideology suggests that these racial myths and stereotypes cannot be exposed as such in the popular imagination. They are, we think, too essential, too integral, to the maintenance of the U.S. social order. Of course, particular meanings, stereotypes, and myths can change, but the presence of a *system* of racial meanings and stereotypes, of racial ideology, seems to be a permanent feature of U.S. culture.

Film and television, for example, have been notorious in disseminating images of racial minorities which establish for audiences what people from these groups look like, how they behave, and "who they are."[24] The power of the media lies not only in their ability to reflect the dominant racial ideology, but in their capacity to shape that ideology in the first place. D. W. Griffith's epic *Birth of a Nation*, a sympathetic treatment of the rise of the Ku Klux Klan during Reconstruction, helped to generate, consolidate, and "nationalize" images of blacks which had been more disparate (more regionally specific, for example) prior to the film's appearance.[25] In U.S. television, the necessity to define characters in the briefest and most condensed manner has led to the perpetuation of racial caricatures, as racial stereotypes serve as shorthand for scriptwriters, directors, and actors, in commercials, etc. Television's tendency to address the "lowest common denominator" in order to render programs "familiar" to an enormous and diverse audience leads it regularly to assign and reassign racial characteristics to particular groups, both minority and majority.

These and innumerable other examples show that we tend to view race as something fixed and immutable — something rooted in "na-

---

[24]"Miss San Antonio USA, Lisa Fernandez, and other Hispanics auditioning for a role in a television soap opera did not fit the Hollywood image of real Mexicans and had to darken their faces before filming." Model Aurora Garza said that their faces were bronzed with powder because they looked too white. " 'I'm a real Mexican [Garza said] and very dark anyway. I'm even darker right now because I have a tan. But they kept wanting me to make my face darker and darker' " (*San Francisco Chronicle*, 21 September 1984). A similar dilemma faces Asian American actors who feel that Asian character lead roles inevitably go to white actors who make themselves up to be Asian. Scores of Charlie Chan films, for example, have been made with white leads (the last one was the 1981 *Charlie Chan and the Curse of the Dragon Queen*). Roland Winters, who played in six Chan features, was asked by playwright Frank Chin to explain the logic of casting a white man in the role of Charlie Chan: " 'The only thing I can think of is, if you want to cast a homosexual in a show, and you get a homosexual, it'll be awful. It won't be funny . . . and maybe there's something there . . .' " (Frank Chin, "Confessions of the Chinatown Cowboy," *Bulletin of Concerned Asian Scholars*, vol. 4, no. 3 [Fall 1972]. [Authors' note]

[25]Melanie Martindale-Sikes, "Nationalizing 'Nigger' Imagery Through 'Birth of a Nation,' " paper prepared for the 73rd Annual Meeting of the American Sociological Association, 4–8 September 1978 in San Francisco. [Authors' note]

ture." Thus we mask the historical construction of racial categories, the shifting meaning of race, and the crucial role of politics and ideology in shaping race relations. Races do not emerge full-blown. They are the results of diverse historical practices and are continually subject to challenge over their definition and meaning.

Engaging the Text

1. Why, according to Omi and Winant, did modern "race consciousness" arise? What examples do they offer of its historical influence?

2. How do Omi and Winant distinguish between biological and social definitions of race? What difference does it make which definition one accepts?

3. Explain the concept of "hypo-descent" (para. 10). How has it functioned to maintain racial categories?

4. Explain Omi and Winant's assertion that racial categories seem to be a matter of "common sense" (para. 15). Brainstorm a list of American "racial beliefs" about the "temperament, sexuality, intelligence, athletic ability, aesthetic preferences, and so on" (para. 19) of different racial groups. To what extent do you believe that these stereotypes are "a permanent feature of U.S. culture" (para. 20)? How might they be changed?

Exploring Connections

5. Review "Streets of Gold: The Myth of the Model Minority" by Curtis Chang (p. 54). How does the selection by Omi and Winant help explain the social misconceptions and ignorance Chang points out?

Extending the Critical Context

6. Analyze the racial and ethnic makeup of your class. How many nationalities, "races," and ethnic groups are represented, even if only minutely (for instance, "one sixty-fourth Welsh on my father's side")? After exploring such data, try to draw some conclusions about the status of race in the United States as a biological and as a social concept.

7. Compare and contrast a high school and a college biology textbook for their coverage of race. How much attention is given to the topic? Is it presented as a valid, invalid, or controversial designation of human types? How might Omi and Winant expand or revise each text?

Formation of In-Groups

GORDON W. ALLPORT

Gordon W. Allport (1897–1967) published The Nature of Prejudice, *from which this selection is excerpted, in 1954. It served then as a cornerstone for the scientific study of racial prejudice and still provides a theoretical foundation for many psychologists and sociologists. In this section, Allport analyzes how people join and are excluded from various groups, relating these processes to the notion of stereotyping. When his work appeared, the idea that a person's behavior might be determined by group membership and identification rather than by innate drives was highly controversial. Allport was educated at Harvard University and at Cambridge, England; throughout a career spanning some fifty years he taught psychology at Harvard and authored more than a dozen books and two hundred articles.*

The proverb *familiarity breeds contempt* contains considerably less than a half-truth. While we sometimes do become bored with our daily routine of living and with some of our customary companions, yet the very values that sustain our lives depend for their force upon their familiarity. What is more, what is familiar tends to *become a value.* We come to like the style of cooking, the customs, the people, we have grown up with.

Psychologically, the crux of the matter is that the familiar provides the indispensable basis of our existence. Since existence is good, its accompanying groundwork seems good and desirable. A child's parents, neighborhood, region, nation are given to him — so too his religion, race, and social traditions. To him all these affiliations are taken for granted. Since he is part of them, and they are part of him, they are good.

As early as the age of five, a child is capable of understanding that he is a member of various groups. He is capable, for example, of a sense of ethnic identification. Until he is nine or ten he will not be able to understand just what his membership signifies — how, for example, Jews differ from gentiles, or Quakers from Methodists, but he does not wait for this understanding before he develops fierce in-group loyalties.

Some psychologists say that the child is "rewarded" by virtue of his memberships, and that this reward creates the loyalty. That is to say, his family feeds and cares for him, he obtains pleasure from the gifts and attentions received from neighbors and compatriots. Hence he learns to love them. His loyalties are acquired on the basis of such rewards. We may doubt that this explanation is sufficient. A colored child is seldom or never rewarded for being a Negro — usually just the opposite, and yet he normally grows up with a loyalty to his racial group. Thoughts of Indiana arouse a glow in the breast of a native Hoosier[1] — not necessarily because he passed a happy childhood there, but simply because he *came* from there. It is still, in part, the ground of his existence.

Rewards may, of course, help the process. A child who has plenty of fun at a family reunion may be more attached thereafter to his own clan because of the experience. But normally he would be attached to his clan anyway, simply because it is an inescapable part of his life.

Happiness (i.e., "reward") is not then the only reason for our loyalties. Few of our group memberships seem to be sustained by the pleasures they provide — an exception perhaps being our recreational memberships. And it takes a major unhappiness, a prolonged and bitter experience, to drive us away from loyalties once formed. And sometimes no amount of punishment can make us repudiate our loyalty.

This principle of the *ground* in human learning is important. We do not need to postulate a "gregarious instinct" to explain why people like to be with people: they have simply found people lock-stitched into the very fabric of their existence. Since they affirm their own existence as good, they will affirm social living as good. Nor do we need to postulate a "consciousness of kind" to explain why people adhere to their own families, clans, ethnic groups. The self could not be itself without them.

Scarcely anyone ever wants to be anybody else. However handicapped or unhappy he feels himself, he would not change places with other more fortunate mortals. He grumbles over his misfortunes and wants his lot improved; but it is *his* lot and *his* personality that he wants bettered. This attachment to one's own being is basic to human life. I may say that I envy *you*. But I do not want to *be* you; I only want to have for myself some of your attributes or possessions. And along with this beloved self go all of the person's basic memberships. Since he cannot alter his family stock, its traditions, his nationality, or his native language, he does well to accept them. Their accent dwells in the heart as well as on the tongue.

Oddly enough, it is not necessary for the individual to have direct acquaintance with all his in-groups. To be sure, he usually knows the members of his immediate family. (An orphan, however, may be passionately attached to parents he has never seen.) Some groups, such as clubs, schools, neighborhoods, are known through personal contacts. But others depend largely on symbols or hearsay. No one can have direct acquaintance with his race as a whole, nor with all his lodge brothers or co-religionists. The young child may sit enthralled while he hears of the exploits of the great-grandfather whose role as a sea-captain, a frontiers-

[1] *Hoosier:* common name for residents of the state of Indiana.

man, or nobleman sets a tradition with which the child identifies himself. The words he hears provide him just as authentic a ground for his life as do his daily experiences. By symbols one learns family traditions, patriotism, and racial pride. Thus in-groups that are only verbally defined may be nonetheless firmly knit.

What Is an In-Group?

In a static society it would be fairly easy to predict just what   10
loyalties the individual will form — to what region, to what phratry,[2] or to what social class. In such a static society kinship, status, even place of residence, may be rigidly prescribed.

> In ancient China at one time residential arrangements actually coincided with social distance. Where one lived indicated all of one's memberships. The inner circle of a region was the Tribute Holding where government officials only were permitted to reside. A second circle contained the nobility. Beyond this an outer but defended area, known as the Peaceful Tenures, contained literary workers and other citizens of repute. Farther out lay the Prohibited territory divided between foreigners and transported convicts. Finally came the Unstrained territory, where only barbarians and ostracized felons were allowed to dwell.[3]

In a more mobile, technological society such as ours no such rigidity exists.

There is one law — universal in all human societies — that assists us in making an important prediction. *In every society on earth the child is regarded as a member of his parents' group.* He belongs to the same race, stock, family tradition, religion, caste, and occupational status. To be sure, in our society, he may when he grows older escape certain of these memberships, but not all. The child is ordinarily expected to acquire his parents' loyalties and prejudices; and if the parent because of his group-membership is an object of prejudice, the child too is automatically victimized.

Although this rule holds in our society, it is less infallible than in more "familistic" regions of the world. While the American child normally acquires a strong sense of family membership and a certain loyalty to his parents' country of origin, race, and religion, he has considerable latitude respecting his attachments. Each individual pattern will be somewhat different. An American child is free to accept some of his parents' memberships and to reject others.

[2]*phratry:* a group of clans within a tribe.
[3]W. G. Old. *The Shu King, or the Chinese Historical Classic.* New York: J. Lane, 1904, 50–51. See also J. Legge (Trans.), Texts of Confucianism, in *The Sacred Books of the East.* Oxford: Clarendon Press, 1879, Vol. III, 75–76. [Author's note]

It is difficult to define an in-group precisely. Perhaps the best that can be done is to say that members of an in-group all use the term *we* with the same essential significance. Members of a family do so, likewise schoolmates, members of a lodge, labor union, club, city, state, nation. In a vaguer way members of international bodies may do the same. Some we-organizations are transitory (e.g., an evening party), some are permanent (e.g., a family or clan).

Sam, a middle-aged man of only average sociability, listed his own in-group membership as follows:

his paternal relatives
his maternal relatives
family of orientation (in which he grew up)
family of procreation (his wife and children)
his boyhood circle (now a dim memory)
his grammar school (in memory only)
his high school (in memory only)
his college as a whole (sometimes revisited)
his college class (reinforced by reunions)
his present church membership (shifted when he was 20)
his profession (strongly organized and firmly knit)
his firm (but especially the department in which he works)
a "bunch" (group of four couples who take a good deal of recreation together)
surviving members of a World War I company of infantry (growing dim)
state where he was born (a fairly trivial membership)
town where he now lives (a lively civic spirit)
New England (a regional loyalty)
United States (an average amount of patriotism)
United Nations (in principle firmly believed in but psychologically loose because he is not clear concerning the "we" in this case)
Scotch-Irish stock (a vague feeling of kinship with others who have this lineage)
Republican party (he registers Republican in the primaries but has little additional sense of belonging)

Sam's list is probably not complete — but from it we can reconstruct fairly well the membership ground on which he lives.

In his list Sam referred to a boyhood circle. He recalls that at one time this in-group was of desperate importance to him. When he moved to a new neighborhood at the age of ten he had no one of his own age to pal with, and he much desired companionship. The other boys were curious and suspicious. Would they admit him? Was Sam's style compatible with the gang's style? There was the usual ordeal by fistfight, set in motion at some slight pretext. This ritual — as is customary in boys' gangs — is designed to provide a swift and acceptable test of the stranger's manners and morale. Will he keep within the limits set by the gang, and show just enough boldness, toughness, and self-control to suit the other boys? Sam was fortunate in this ordeal, and was forthwith admitted to the coveted in-group. Probably he was lucky that he had no additional handicaps in terms of his racial, religious, or status memberships. Otherwise the probation would have been longer and the tests more exacting; and perhaps the gang would have excluded him forever.

Thus some in-group memberships have to be fought for. But many are conferred automatically by birth and by family tradition. In terms of modern social science the former memberships reflect *achieved* status; the later, *ascribed* status.

Sex as an In-Group

Sam did not mention his membership (ascribed status) in the male sex. Probably at one time it was consciously important to him — and may still be so.

The in-group of sex makes an interesting case study. A child of two normally makes no distinction in his companionships: a little girl or a little boy is all the same to him. Even in the first grade the awareness of sex-groups is relatively slight. Asked whom they would choose to play with, first-grade children on the average choose opposite-sexed children at least a quarter of the time. By the time the fourth grade is reached these cross-sexed choices virtually disappear: only 2 percent of the children want to play with someone of the opposite sex. When the eighth grade is reached friendships between boys and girls begin to re-emerge, but even then only eight percent extend their choices across the sex boundary.[4]

For some people — misogynists[5] among them — the sex-grouping remains important throughout their lives. Women are viewed as a wholly different species from men, usually an inferior species. Such primary and secondary sex differences as exist are greatly exaggerated and are inflated into imaginary distinctions that justify discrimination. With half of mankind (his own sex) the male may feel an in-group solidarity, with the other half, an irreconcilable conflict.

Lord Chesterfield,[6] who in his letters often admonished his son to guide his life by reason rather than by prejudice, nevertheless has this to say about women:

"Women, then, are only children of a larger growth; they have an entertaining tattle, and sometimes wit; but for solid reasoning, good

[4]J. L. Moreno. *Who shall survive?* Washington: Nervous and Mental Disease Pub. Co., 1934, 24. These data are somewhat old. At the present time there are grounds for believing that the sex boundary is not so important among children as formerly. [Author's note]

[5]*misogynist:* a person who hates women.

[6]*Lord Chesterfield:* English statesman and author (1694–1773), remembered for his *Letters to His Son.*

sense, I never knew in my life one that had it, or who reasoned or acted consequentially for four and twenty hours together. . . .

"A man of sense only trifles with them, plays with them, humors and flatters them, as he does a sprightly, forward child; but he neither consults them about, nor trusts them with serious matters; though he often makes them believe that he does both; which is the thing in the world that they are most proud of. . . .[7]

"Women are much more like each other than men; they have in truth but two passions, vanity and love: these are their universal characteristics."[8]

Schopenhauer's[9] views were much like Chesterfield's. Women, he wrote, are big children all their life long. A fundamental fault of the female character is that it has no sense of justice. This is mainly due to the fact, Schopenhauer insisted, that women are defective in the powers of reasoning and deliberation.[10]

Such antifeminism reflects the two basic ingredients of prejudice — denigration and gross overgeneralization. Neither of these famous men of intellect allows for individual differences among women, nor asks whether their alleged attributes are in fact more common in the female than in the male sex.

What is instructive about this antifeminism is the fact that it implies security and contentment with one's own sex-membership. To Chesterfield and to Schopenhauer the cleavage between male and female was a cleavage between accepted in-group and rejected out-group. But for many people this "war of the sexes" seems totally unreal. They do not find in it a ground for prejudice.

The Shifting Nature of In-Groups

Although each individual has his own conception of in-groups important to himself, he is not unaffected by the temper of the times. During the past century, national and racial memberships have risen in importance, while family and religious memberships have declined (though they are still exceedingly prominent). The fierce loyalties and rivalries between Scottish clans is almost a thing of the past — but the conception of a "master race"[11] has grown to threatening proportions. The fact that women in Western countries have assumed roles once

[7]C. Strachey (Ed.). *The Letters of the Earl of Chesterfield to His Son.* New York: G. P. Putnam's Sons, 1925, Vol. I, 261. [Author's note]

[8]*Ibid.*, Vol. II, 5. [Author's note]

[9]*Schopenhauer:* Arthur Schopenhauer, German philosopher (1788–1860) whose pessimistic view of human existence stressed the dominance of will over intelligence.

[10]E. B. Bax (Ed.). *Selected Essays of Schopenhauer.* London: G. Bell & Sons, 1914, 340. [Author's note]

[11]*master race:* term used in Nazi Germany to distinguish those of Aryan ancestry from other supposedly inferior ethnic groups.

reserved for men makes the antifeminism of Chesterfield and Schopenhauer seem old-fashioned indeed.

A change in the conception of the national in-group is seen in the shifting American attitude toward immigration. The native American nowadays seldom takes an idealistic view of immigration. He does not feel it a duty and privilege to offer a home to oppressed people — to include them in his in-group. The legend on the Statue of Liberty, engraved eighty years ago, already seems out of date:

> Give me your tired, your poor,
> Your huddled masses yearning to breathe free,
> The wretched refuse of your teeming shore.
> Send these, the homeless, the tempest-tossed to me.
> I lift my lamp beside the golden door.

The lamp was virtually extinguished by the anti-immigration laws 25 passed in the period 1918–1924. The lingering sentiment was not strong enough to relax the bars appreciably following the Second World War when there were more homeless and tempest-tost than ever before crying for admission. From the standpoint of both economics and humanitarianism there were strong arguments for relaxing the restrictions; but people had grown fearful. Many conservatives feared the importation of radical ideas; many Protestants felt their own precarious majority might be further reduced; some Catholics dreaded the arrival of Communists; anti-Semites wanted no more Jews; some labor-union members feared that jobs would not be created to absorb the newcomers and that their own security would suffer.

During the 124 years for which data are available, approximately 40,000,000 immigrants came to America, as many as 1,000,000 in a single year. Of the total immigration 85 percent came from Europe. Until a generation ago, few objections were heard. But today nearly all applicants are refused admission, and few champions of "displaced persons" are heard. Times have changed, and whenever they change for the worse, as they have, in-group boundaries tend to tighten. The stranger is suspect and excluded.

Not only do the strength and definition of in-groups change over the years in a given culture, but a single individual, too, may have occasion at one time to affirm one group-loyalty and at a different time another. The following amusing passage from H. G. Wells's[12] A Modern Utopia illustrates this elasticity. The passage depicts a snob — a person whose group loyalties are narrow. But even a snob, it appears, must have a certain flexibility, for he finds it convenient to identify himself sometimes with one in-group and sometimes with another.

---

[12]H. G. Wells: English novelist, historian, and sociologist (1866–1946), best known as author of The Time Machine and War of the Worlds.

Native white
Protestant gentiles

Native white
Protestant gentiles,
Negroes, Catholics,
Jews, Immigrants,
etc.

As seen by Individual A   As seen by Individual B

Fig. 1. The national in-group as perceived by two Americans

The passage illustrates an important point: in-group memberships
are not permanently fixed. For certain purposes an individual may
affirm one category of membership, for other purposes a slightly larger
category. It depends on his need for self-enhancement.

Wells is describing the loyalties of a certain botanist:

> He has a strong feeling for systematic botanists as against plant
> physiologists, whom he regards as lewd and evil scoundrels in this
> relation; but he has a strong feeling for all botanists and indeed all
> biologists, as against physicists, and those who profess the exact sci-
> ences, all of whom he regards as dull, mechanical, ugly-minded
> scoundrels in this relation; but he has a strong feeling for all who
> profess what he calls Science, as against psychologists, sociologists,
> philosophers, and literary men, whom he regards as wild, foolish,
> immoral scoundrels in this relation; but he has a strong feeling for all
> educated men as against the working man, whom he regards as a
> cheating, lying, loafing, drunken, thievish, dirty scoundrel in this
> relation; but as soon as the working man is comprehended together
> with these others, as *Englishmen* . . . he holds them superior to all
> sorts of Europeans, whom he regards. . . .[13]

Thus the sense of belonging is a highly personal matter. Even two
members of the same actual in-group may view its composition in
widely divergent ways. Take, for instance, the definition that two
Americans might give to their own national in-group. [See Fig. 1.]

The narrowed perception of Individual A is the product of an
arbitrary categorization, one that he finds convenient (functionally
significant) to hold. The larger range of perception on the part of

30

[13]Reprinted by permission of Chapman & Hall, Ltd., from *A Modern Utopia.*
London, 1905, 322 [Author's note] and A. P. Watt Ltd. on behalf of the Literary
Executors of the Estate of H. G. Wells.

Individual B creates a wholly different conception of the national in-group. It is misleading to say that both belong to the same in-group. Psychologically, they do not.

Each individual tends to see in his in-group the precise pattern of security that he himself requires. An instructive example comes from a recent resolution of the convention of the Democratic Party in South Carolina. To the gentlemen assembled the Party was an important in-group. But the definition of Party (as stated in its national platform) was unacceptable. Hence in order to re-fence the in-group so that each member could feel secure, the category "Democrat" was redefined to "include those who believe in local self-government as against the idea of a strong centralized, paternalistic government; and exclude those whose ideas or leadership are inspired by foreign influences, Communism, Nazism, Fascism, statism, totalitarianism, or the Fair Employment Practices Commission."

Thus in-groups are often recreated to fit the needs of individuals, and when the needs are strongly aggressive — as in this case — the redefinition of the in-group may be primarily in terms of the hated out-groups.

In-Groups and Reference Groups

We have broadly defined an in-group as any cluster of people who can use the term "we" with the same significance. But the reader has noted that individuals may hold all manner of views concerning their membership in in-groups. A first-generation American may regard his Italian background and culture as more important than do his children, who are second-generation Italian-Americans. Adolescents may view their neighborhood gang as a far more important in-group than their school. In some instances an individual may actively repudiate an in-group, even though he cannot escape membership in it.

In order to clarify this situation, modern social science has introduced the concept of reference group. Sherif and Sherif have defined reference groups as "those groups to which the individual relates himself as a part, or to which he aspires to relate himself psychologically."[14] Thus a reference group is an in-group that is warmly accepted, or a group in which the individual wishes to be included.

Now usually an in-group is also a reference group, but not always. A Negro may wish to relate himself to the white majority in his community. He would like to partake of the privileges of this majority, and be considered one of its members. He may feel so intensely about the matter that he repudiates his own in-group. He develops a condition that Kurt Lewin has called "self-hate" (i.e., hatred for his own in-

35

[14]M. and Carolyn W. Sherif. *Groups in Harmony and Tension.* New York: Harper, 1953, 161. [Author's note]

group). Yet the customs of the community force him to live with, work with, and be classified with the Negro group. In such a case his in-group membership is not the same as his reference group.

Or take the case of a clergyman of Armenian descent ministering in a small New England town. His name is foreign. Townsmen classify him as an Armenian. Yet he himself seldom thinks of his ancestry, though he does not actively reject his background. His reference groups (his main interests) are his church, his family, and the community in which he lives. Unfortunately for him, his fellow townsmen persist in regarding him as an Armenian; they regard this ethnic in-group as far more important than he himself does.

The Negro and the Armenian cleric occupy *marginal* roles in the community. They have difficulty relating themselves to their reference groups because the pressures of the community force them always to tie to in-groups of small psychological importance to them.

To a considerable degree all minority groups suffer from the same state of marginality, with its haunting consequences of insecurity, conflict, and irritation. Every minority group finds itself in a larger society where many customs, many values, many practices are prescribed. The minority group member is thus to some degree forced to make the dominant majority his reference group in respect to language, manners, morals, and law. He may be entirely loyal to his minority in-group, but he is at the same time always under the necessity of relating himself to the standards and expectations of the majority. The situation is particularly clear in the case of the Negro. Negro culture is almost entirely the same as white American culture. The Negro must relate himself to it. Yet whenever he tries to achieve this relatedness he is likely to suffer rebuff. Hence there is in his case an almost inevitable conflict between his biologically defined in-group and his culturally defined reference group. If we follow this line of thinking we see why all minority groups, to some degree, occupy a marginal position in society with its unhappy consequents of apprehension and resentment.

The concepts of in-group and reference group help us to distinguish 40 two levels of belongingness. The former indicates the sheer fact of membership; the latter tells us whether the individual prizes that membership or whether he seeks to relate himself with another group. In many cases, as we have said, there is a virtual identity between in-groups and reference groups; but it is not always so. Some individuals, through necessity or by choice, continually compare themselves with groups which for them are not in-groups.

Social Distance

The distinction between in-group and reference group is well brought out in studies of social distance. This familiar technique, invented by E. S. Bogardus, asks respondents to indicate to which steps on the following scale they would admit members of various ethnic and national groups:

1. to close kinship by marriage
2. to my club as personal chums
3. to my street as neighbors
4. to employment in my occupation
5. to citizenship in my country
6. as visitors only to my country
7. would exclude from my country

Now the most striking finding from this procedure is that a similar pattern of preference is found across the country, varying little with income, region, education, occupation, or even with ethnic group. Most people, whoever they are, find the English and Canadians acceptable as citizens, as neighbors, as social equals, and as kinsmen. These ethnic stocks have the least social distance. At the other extreme come Hindus, Turks, Negroes. The ordering — with a few minor shifts — stays substantially constant.[15]

While members of the unfavored groups tend to put their own groups high in the list, yet in all other respects they choose the prevailing order of acceptability. In one study of Jewish children, for example, it was found that the standard pattern of social distance existed excepting only that most Jewish children place Jews high in acceptability.[16] In similar investigations it turns out that on the average the Negro places the Jew at about the same distance as does the white gentile; and the Jew ordinarily places the Negro low on his list.

From such results we are forced to conclude that the member of an ethnic minority tends to fashion his attitudes as does the dominant majority. In other words, the dominant majority is for him a *reference group*. It exerts a strong pull upon him, forcing attitudinal conformity. The conformity, however, rarely extends to the point of repudiating his own in-group. A Negro, or Jew, or Mexican will ordinarily assert the acceptability of his own in-group, but in other respects he will decide as does his larger reference group. Thus, both in-group and reference group are important in the formation of attitudes.

---

[15]The order found by Bogardus in 1928 (E. S. Bogardus, *Immigration and Race Attitudes*, Boston: D. C. Heath, 1928) was found essentially unchanged by Hartley in 1946, and again by Spoerl in 1951. (Cf. E. L. Hartley, *Problems in Prejudice*, New York: Kings Crown Press, 1946; and Dorothy T. Spoerl, Some aspects of prejudice as affected by religion and education, *Journal of Social Psychology*, 1951, 33, 69–76). [Author's note]

[16]Rose Zeligs. Racial attitudes of Jewish children. *Jewish Education*, 1937, 9, 148–152. [Author's note]

The Group-Norm Theory of Prejudice

We are now in a position to understand and appreciate a major [45] theory of prejudice. It holds that all groups (whether in-groups or reference groups) develop a way of living with characteristic codes and beliefs, standards and "enemies" to suit their own adaptive needs. The theory holds also that both gross and subtle pressures keep every individual member in line. The in-group's preferences must be his preferences, its enemies his enemies. The Sherifs, who advance this theory, write:

> Ordinarily the factors leading individuals to form attitudes of prejudice are not piecemeal. Rather, their formation is functionally related to becoming a group member — to adopting the group and its values (norms) as the main anchorage in regulating experience and behavior.[17]

A strong argument in favor of this view is the relative ineffectiveness of attempts to change attitudes through influencing individuals. Suppose the child attends a lesson in intercultural education in the classroom. The chances are this lesson will be smothered by the more embracing norms of his family, gang, or neighborhood. To change the child's attitudes it would be necessary to alter the cultural equilibrium of these, to him, more important groups. It would be necessary for the family, the gang, or the neighborhood to sanction tolerance before he as an individual could practice it.

This line of thought has led to the dictum, "It is easier to change group attitudes than individual attitudes." Recent research lends some support to the view. In certain studies whole communities, whole housing projects, whole factories, or whole school systems have been made the target of change. By involving the leaders, the policies, the rank and file, new norms are created, and when this is accomplished, it is found that individual attitudes tend to conform to the new group norm.[18]

While we cannot doubt the results, there is something unnecessarily "collectivistic" about the theory. Prejudice is by no means exclusively a mass phenomenon. Let the reader ask himself whether his own social attitudes do in fact conform closely to those of his family, social class, occupational group, or church associates. Perhaps the answer is yes; but more likely the reader may reply that the prevailing prejudices of his

---

[17]M. and Carolyn W. Sherif. *Op. cit.*, 218. [Author's note]

[18]Among the studies of this type we may refer especially to: A. Morrow and J. French, Changing a stereotype in industry, *Journal of Social Issues*, 1945, 1, 33–37; R. Lippitt, *Training in Community Relations*, New York: Harper, 1949; Margot H. Wormser and Claire Selltiz, *How to Conduct a Community Self-survey of Civil Rights*, New York: Association Press, 1951; K. Lewin, Group decision and social change in T. M. Newcomb and E. L. Hartley (Eds.), *Readings in Social Psychology*, New York: Holt, 1947. [Author's note]

various reference groups are so contradictory that he cannot, and does not, "share" them all. He may also decide that his pattern of prejudice is unique, conforming to none of his membership groups.

Realizing this individual play of attitudes, the proponents of the theory speak of a "range of tolerable behavior," admitting thereby that only approximate conformity is demanded within any system of group norms. People may deviate in their attitudes to some extent, but not too much.

As soon as we allow, however, for a "range of tolerable behavior" we 50 are moving toward a more individualistic point of view. We do not need to deny the existence of group norms and group pressure in order to insist that each person is uniquely organized. Some of us are avid conformists to what we believe the group requirement to be. Others of us are passive conformists. Still others are nonconformists. Such conformism as we show is the product of individual learning, individual needs, and individual style of life.

In dealing with problems of attitude formation it is always difficult to strike a proper balance between the collective approach and the individual approach. This [study] maintains that prejudice is ultimately a problem of personality formation and development; no two cases of prejudice are precisely the same. No individual would mirror his group's attitude unless he had a personal need, or personal habit, that leads him to do so. But it likewise maintains that one of the frequent sources, perhaps the most frequent source, of prejudice lies in the needs and habits that reflect the influence of in-group memberships upon the development of the individual personality. It is possible to hold the individualistic type of theory without denying that the major influences upon the individual may be collective.

Can There Be an In-Group Without an Out-Group?

Every line, fence, or boundary marks off an inside from an outside. Therefore, in strict logic, an in-group always implies the existence of some corresponding out-group. But this logical statement by itself is of little significance. What we need to know is whether one's loyalty to the in-group automatically implies disloyalty, or hostility, or other forms of negativism, toward out-groups.

The French biologist, Felix le Dantec, insisted that every social unit from the family to the nation could exist only by virtue of having some "common enemy." The family unit fights many threatening forces that menace each person who belongs to the unit. The exclusive club, the American Legion, the nation itself, exists to defeat the common enemies of its members. In favor of Le Dantec's view is the well-known Machiavellian trick[19] of creating a common enemy in order to cement an

---

[19]*Machiavellian trick:* after Niccolò Machiavelli (1469–1527), Italian political philosopher noted for his cynical and manipulative approach to government.

in-group. Hitler created the Jewish menace not so much to demolish the Jews as to cement the Nazi hold over Germany. At the turn of the century the Workingmen's Party in California whipped up an anti-Oriental sentiment to consolidate its own ranks which, without a common enemy, were indifferent and wavering. School spirit is never so strong as when the time for an athletic contest with the traditional "enemy" approaches. Instances are so numerous that one is tempted to accept the doctrine. Studying the effect of strangers entering a group of nursery school children, Susan Isaacs reports, "The existence of an outsider is in the beginning an essential condition of any warmth or togetherness within the group."[20]

So deeply was William James[21] impressed by the fact that social cohesiveness seems to require a common enemy that he wrote a famous essay on the subject. In *The Moral Equivalent for War* he recognized the adventuresomeness, the aggression, and the competitiveness that marked human relationships, especially among young people of military age. In order that they themselves might live at peace he recommended that they find an enemy that would not violate man's growing sense of loyalty to humanity. His advice was: fight nature, fight disease, fight poverty.

Now there is no denying that the presence of a threatening common enemy will cement the in-group sense of any organized aggregate of people. A family (if it is not already badly disrupted) will grow cohesive in the face of adversity, and a nation is never so unified as in time of war. But the psychological emphasis must be placed primarily on the desire for security, not on hostility itself.

One's own family is an in-group; and by definition all other families on the street are out-groups; but seldom do they clash. A hundred ethnic groups compose America, and while serious conflict occasionally occurs, the majority rub along in peace. One knows that one's lodge has distinctive characteristics that mark it off from all others, but one does not necessarily despise the others.

The situation, it seems, can best be stated as follows: although we could not perceive our own in groups excepting as they contrast to out-groups, still the in-groups are psychologically primary. We live in them, by them, and, sometimes, for them. Hostility toward out-groups helps strengthen our sense of belonging, but it is not required.

Because of their basic importance to our own survival and self-esteem we tend to develop a partisanship and ethnocentrism in respect to our in-groups. Seven-year-old children in one town were asked,

[20]Susan Isaacs, *Social Development in Young Children*. New York: Harcourt, Brace, 1933, 250. [Author's note]

[21]*William James:* American psychologist and philosopher (1842–1910), and leading exponent of pragmatism, the philosophical approach that measures the validity of a theory in terms of its practical result.

"Which are better, the children in this town or in Smithfield (a neighboring town)?" Almost all replied, "The children in this town." When asked why, the children usually replied, "I don't know the kids in Smithfield." This incident puts the initial in-group and out-group situation in perspective. The familiar is *preferred*. What is alien is regarded as somehow inferior, less "good," but there is not necessarily hostility against it.

Thus while a certain amount of predilection is inevitable in all in-group memberships, the reciprocal attitude toward out-groups may range widely. At one extreme they may be viewed as a common enemy to be defeated in order to protect the in-group and strengthen its inner loyalties. At the other extreme the out-group may be appreciated, tolerated, even liked for its diversity.

Engaging the Text

1. Explain Allport's concept of "in-groups" and "out-groups." Why, according to Allport, do individuals identify with their in-groups? What is the difference between achieved and ascribed status?

2. How do in-groups and reference groups enforce values and prejudices? Think of examples from your own experience, from the experience of family members and friends, from things you've read or seen.

3. Do you find Allport's analysis of group loyalty convincing? Can you think of any different explanations? Are there any social or psychological rewards for *changing* group loyalties?

4. Explain what Allport means by "marginal." Do you agree with him that all minorities occupy marginal roles? Do women, although not a minority, also constitute a marginal group?

5. What is a "reference group" and how does it function in relation to an in-group? Allport implies (para. 36) that African Americans must have white American culture as their reference group. Do you agree that African Americans and other so-called marginalized groups must relate themselves to the dominant culture in this way?

6. What is the group norm theory of racial prejudice? What does this theory suggest about attempts to teach tolerance and racial harmony? Do you agree?

Exploring Connections

7. Analyze one or more of the people listed in terms of their in-groups, out-groups, and reference groups:

The Man and the Kid in "Symbiosis" (p. 42)	Mike LeFevre (p. 87)
	Sucheng Chan (p. 99)
Sylvia in "The Lesson" (p. 64)	Nora Quealey (p. 202)

8. Compare Allport's theories of racism and prejudice with Omi and Winant's (p. 283). To what extent do they agree on the origins of racial distinctions and on how such distinctions are reinforced and maintained? What is the role of the individual in both theories? What hope for change does each offer?

9. In this excerpt, Allport is speaking primarily about racial prejudice. How well do you think a theory of group loyalty would explain prejudice against gay and lesbian people? Review the selections by Rose Weitz (p. 257) and Gloria Naylor (p. 270) to determine the usefulness of concepts like "in-group," "reference group," and "ascribed group" for discussing anti-gay prejudice.

Extending the Critical Context

10. List the in-groups you belong to and identify whether each is ascribed or achieved. Rank the groups in order of their importance to you. Have these rankings ever been different from what they are now? If so, how and why? Write an essay explaining the way you ranked your in-groups and discussing how their importance has changed at different times in your life.

11. Watch Spike Lee's *Jungle Fever* and discuss the in-groups, out-groups, and reference groups of the film's main characters. In your analysis, consider not only their racial identification but also their socioeconomic and gender identification. How does each in-group maintain its boundaries? Does the film confirm or complicate Allport's analysis?

Split at the Root: An Essay on Jewish Identity

Adrienne Rich

Academic concepts like "in-groups," "out-groups," and "marginalization" are easy to handle when abstracted from personal experience. But the actual things they name can have a devastating impact on individual lives. In the following selection, Adrienne Rich assesses the personal costs of growing up in a world divided by prejudice. Rich (b. 1929) is one of America's premier poets and an ardent feminist. Her poetry, which has appeared in numerous collections over the past forty years, often addresses themes of social injustice, women's consciousness, and the need for an authentic human community. In 1974, she won the National Book Award for poetry for Diving into the Wreck. *"Split at the Root" is taken from* Blood, Bread, and Poetry: Selected Prose, 1979–1985. *Rich is professor of English and feminist studies at Stanford University.*

For about fifteen minutes I have been sitting chin in hand in front of the typewriter, staring out at the snow. Trying to be honest with myself, trying to figure out why writing this seems to be so dangerous an act, filled with fear and shame, and why it seems so necessary. It comes to me that in order to write this I have to be willing to do two things: I have to claim my father, for I have my Jewishness from him and not from my gentile mother; and I have to break his silence, his taboos; in order to claim him I have in a sense to expose him.

And there is, of course, the third thing: I have to face the sources and the flickering presence of my own ambivalence as a Jew; the daily, mundane anti-Semitisms of my entire life.

These are stories I have never tried to tell before. Why now? Why, I asked myself sometime last year, does this question of Jewish identity float so impalpably, so ungraspably around me, a cloud I can't quite see the outlines of, which feels to me to be without definition?

And yet I've been on the track of this longer than I think.

In a long poem written in 1960, when I was thirty-one years old, I described myself as "Split at the root, neither Gentile nor Jew, / Yankee nor Rebel."[1] I was still trying to have it both ways: to be neither/nor, trying to live (with my Jewish husband and three children more Jewish in ancestry than I) in the predominantly gentile Yankee academic world of Cambridge, Massachusetts.

But this begins, for me, in Baltimore, where I was born in my father's workplace, a hospital in the Black ghetto, whose lobby contained an immense white marble statue of Christ.

My father was then a young teacher and researcher in the department of pathology at the Johns Hopkins Medical School, one of the very few Jews to attend or teach at that institution. He was from Birmingham, Alabama; his father, Samuel, was Ashkenazic,[2] an immigrant from Austria-Hungary, and his mother, Hattie Rice, a Sephardic[3] Jew from Vicksburg, Mississippi. My grandfather had had a shoe store in Birmingham, which did well enough to allow him to retire comfortably and to leave my grandmother income on his death. The only souvenirs of my grandfather, Samuel Rich, were his ivory flute, which lay on our living-room mantel and was not to be played with; his thin gold pocket watch, which my father wore; and his Hebrew prayer book, which I discovered among my father's books in the course of reading my

---

[1]Adrienne Rich, "Readings of History," in *Snapshots of a Daughter-in-Law* (New York: W. W. Norton, 1967), pp. 35–40. [Author's note]

[2]*Ashkenazic:* pertaining to descendants of the Jews who settled in middle and northern Europe after the Babylonian captivity (597–538 B.C.)

[3]*Sephardic:* pertaining to descendants of the Jews who settled in Spain and Portugal.

way through his library. In this prayer book there was a newspaper clipping about my grandparents' wedding, which took place in a synagogue.

My father, Arnold, was sent in adolescence to a military school in the North Carolina mountains, a place for training white southern Christian gentlemen. I suspect that there were few, if any, other Jewish boys at Colonel Bingham's, or at "Mr. Jefferson's university" in Charlottesville, where he studied as an undergraduate. With whatever conscious forethought, Samuel and Hattie sent their son into the dominant southern WASP culture to become an "exception," to enter the professional class. Never, in describing these experiences, did he speak of having suffered — from loneliness, cultural alienation, or outsiderhood. Never did I hear him use the word *anti-Semitism*.

It was only in college, when I read a poem by Karl Shapiro beginning "To hate the Negro and avoid the Jew / is the curriculum," that it flashed on me that there was an untold side to my father's story of his student years. He looked recognizably Jewish, was short and slender in build with dark wiry hair and deep-set eyes, high forehead and curved nose.

My mother is a gentile. In Jewish law I cannot count myself a Jew. 10 If it is true that "we think back through our mothers if we are women" (Virginia Woolf[4]) — and I myself have affirmed this — then even according to lesbian theory, I cannot (or need not?) count myself a Jew.

The white southern Protestant woman, the gentile, has always been there for me to peel back into. That's a whole piece of history in itself, for my gentile grandmother and my mother were also frustrated artists and intellectuals, a lost writer and a lost composer between them. Readers and annotators of books, note takers, my mother a good pianist still, in her eighties. But there was also the obsession with ancestry, with "background," the southern talk of family, not as people you would necessarily know and depend on, but as heritage, the guarantee of "good breeding." There was the inveterate romantic heterosexual fantasy, the mother telling the daughter how to attract men (my mother often used the word "fascinate"); the assumption that relations between the sexes could only be romantic, that it was in the woman's interest to cultivate "mystery," conceal her actual feelings. Survival tactics of a kind, I think today, knowing what I know about the white woman's sexual role in the southern racist scenario. Heterosexuality as protection, but also drawing white women deeper into collusion with white men.

It would be easy to push away and deny the gentile in me — that white southern woman, that social christian. At different times in my

---

[4]*Virginia Woolf:* English feminist, critic, and innovator in modern British fiction (1882–1941), best known for her novels *Mrs. Dalloway* and *To the Lighthouse*.

life I have wanted to push away one or the other burden of inheritance, to say merely *I am a woman; I am a lesbian.* If I call myself a Jewish lesbian, do I thereby try to shed some of my southern gentile white woman's culpability? If I call myself only through my mother, is it because I pass more easily through a world where being a lesbian often seems like outsiderhood enough?

According to Nazi logic, my two Jewish grandparents would have made me a *Mischling, first-degree* — nonexempt from the Final Solution.[5]

The social world in which I grew up was christian virtually without needing to say so — christian imagery, music, language, symbols, assumptions everywhere. It was also a genteel, white, middle-class world in which "common" was a term of deep opprobrium. "Common" white people might speak of "niggers"; *we* were taught never to use that word — *we* said "Negroes" (even as we accepted segregation, the eating taboo, the assumption that Black people were simply of a separate species). Our language was more polite, distinguishing us from the "rednecks" or the lynch-mob mentality. But so charged with negative meaning was even the word "Negro" that as children we were taught never to use it in front of Black people. We were taught that any mention of skin color in the presence of colored people was treacherous, forbidden ground. In a parallel way, the word "Jew" was not used by polite gentiles. I sometimes heard my best friend's father, a Presbyterian minister, allude to "the Hebrew people" or "people of the Jewish faith." The world of acceptable folk was white, gentile (christian, really), and had "ideals" (which colored people, white "common" people, were not supposed to have). "Ideals" and "manners" included not hurting someone's feelings by calling her or him a Negro or a Jew — naming the hated identity. This is the mental framework of the 1930s and 1940s in which I was raised.

(Writing this, I feel dimly like the betrayer; of my father, who did   15 not speak the word; of my mother, who must have trained me in the messages; of my caste and class; of my whiteness itself.)

Two memories: I am in a play reading at school of *The Merchant of Venice.* Whatever Jewish law says, I am quite sure I was *seen* as Jewish (with a reassuringly gentile mother) in that double vision that bigotry allows. I am the only Jewish girl in the class, and I am playing Portia.[6] As always, I read my part aloud for my father the night before, and he tells me to convey, with my voice, more scorn and contempt with the

---

[5]*Final Solution:* euphemistic name for the Nazi plan to execute all members of the Jewish race in "death camps" like Auschwitz and Dachau.

[6]*Portia:* the heroine of Shakespeare's *The Merchant of Venice.*

word "Jew": "Therefore, Jew . . ." I have to say the word out, and say it loudly. I was encouraged to pretend to be a non-Jewish child acting a non-Jewish character who has to speak the word "Jew" emphatically. Such a child would not have had trouble with the part. But *I* must have had trouble with the part, if only because the word itself was really taboo. I can see that there was a kind of terrible, bitter bravado about my father's way of handling this. And who would not dissociate from Shylock[7] in order to identify with Portia? As a Jewish child who was also a female, I loved Portia — and, like every other Shakespearean heroine, she proved a treacherous role model.

A year or so later I am in another play, *The School for Scandal*, in which a notorious spendthrift is described as having "many excellent friends . . . among the Jews." In neither case was anything explained, either to me or to the class at large, about this scorn for Jews and the disgust surrounding Jews and money. Money, when Jews wanted it, had it, or lent it to others, seemed to take on a peculiar nastiness; Jews and money had some peculiar and unspeakable relation.

At this same school — in which we had Episcopalian hymns and prayers, and read aloud through the Bible morning after morning — I gained the impression that Jews were in the Bible and mentioned in English literature, that they had been persecuted centuries ago by the wicked Inquisition, but that they seemed not to exist in everyday life. These were the 1940s, and we were told a great deal about the Battle of Britain, the noble French Resistance fighters, the brave, starving Dutch — but I did not learn of the resistance of the Warsaw ghetto until I left home.

I was sent to the Episcopal church, baptized and confirmed, and attended it for about five years, though without belief. That religion seemed to have little to do with belief or commitment; it was liturgy that mattered, not spiritual passion. Neither of my parents ever entered that church, and my father would not enter *any* church for any reason — wedding or funeral. Nor did I enter a synagogue until I left Baltimore. When I came home from church, for a while, my father insisted on reading aloud to me from Thomas Paine's *The Age of Rea son* — a diatribe against institutional religion. Thus, he explained, I would have a balanced view of these things, a choice. He — they — did not give me the choice to be a Jew. My mother explained to me when I was filling out forms for college that if any question was asked about "religion," I should put down "Episcopalian" rather than "none" — to seem to have no religion was, she implied, dangerous.

But it was white social christianity, rather than any particular 20 christian sect, that the world was founded on. The very word *Christian* was used as a synonym for virtuous, just, peace-loving, generous, etc.,

[7]*Shylock:* the Jewish money-lender and villain of *The Merchant of Venice.*

etc.[8] The norm was christian: "religion: none" was indeed not acceptable. Anti-Semitism was so intrinsic as not to have a name. I don't recall exactly being taught that the Jews killed Jesus — "Christ killer" seems too strong a term for the bland Episcopal vocabulary — but certainly we got the impression that the Jews had been caught out in a terrible mistake, failing to recognize the true Messiah, and were thereby less advanced in moral and spiritual sensibility. The Jews had actually allowed *moneylenders in the Temple* (again, the unexplained obsession with Jews and money). They were of the past, archaic, primitive, as older (and darker) cultures are supposed to be primitive; christianity was lightness, fairness, peace on earth, and combined the feminine appeal of "The meek shall inherit the earth" with the masculine stride of "Onward, Christian Soldiers."

Sometime in 1946, while still in high school, I read in the newspaper that a theater in Baltimore was showing films of the Allied liberation of the Nazi concentration camps. Alone, I went downtown after school one afternoon and watched the stark, blurry, but unmistakable newsreels. When I try to go back and touch the pulse of that girl of sixteen, growing up in many ways so precocious and so ignorant, I am overwhelmed by a memory of despair, a sense of inevitability more enveloping than any I had ever known. Anne Frank's diary and many other personal narratives of the Holocaust were still unknown or unwritten. But it came to me that every one of those piles of corpses, mountains of shoes and clothing had contained, simply, individuals, who had believed, as I now believed of myself, that they were intended to live out a life of some kind of meaning, that the world possessed some kind of sense and order; yet *this* had happened to them. And I, who believed my life was intended to be so interesting and meaningful, was connected to those dead by something — not just mortality but a taboo name, a hated identity. Or was I — did I really have to be? Writing this now, I feel belated rage that I was so impoverished by the family and social worlds I lived in, that I had to try to figure out by myself what this did indeed mean for me. That I had never been taught about resistance, only about passing. That I had no language for anti-Semitism itself.

When I went home and told my parents where I had been, they were not pleased. I felt accused of being morbidly curious, not healthy, sniffing around death for the thrill of it. And since, at sixteen, I was often not sure of the sources of my feelings or of my motives for doing what I did, I probably accused myself as well. One thing was clear:

[8]In a similar way the phrase "That's white of you" implied that you were behaving with the superior decency and morality expected of white but not of Black people. [Author's note]

there was nobody in my world with whom I could discuss those films. Probably at the same time, I was reading accounts of the camps in magazines and newspapers; what I remember were the films and having questions that I could not even phrase, such as *Are those men and women "them" or "us"?*

To be able to ask even the child's astonished question *Why do they hate us so?* means knowing how to say "we." The guilt of not knowing, the guilt of perhaps having betrayed my parents or even those victims, those survivors, through mere curiosity — these also froze in me for years the impulse to find out more about the Holocaust.

1947: I left Baltimore to go to college in Cambridge, Massachusetts, left (I thought) the backward, enervating South for the intellectual, vital North. New England also had for me some vibration of higher moral rectitude, of moral passion even, with its seventeenth-century Puritan self-scrutiny, its nineteenth-century literary "flowering," its abolitionist righteousness, Colonel Shaw and his Black Civil War regiment depicted in granite on Boston Common. At the same time, I found myself, at Radcliffe, among Jewish women. I used to sit for hours over coffee with what I thought of as the "real" Jewish students, who told me about middle-class Jewish culture in America. I described my background — for the first time to strangers — and they took me on, some with amusement at my illiteracy, some arguing that I could never marry into a strict Jewish family, some convinced I didn't "look Jewish," others that I did. I learned the names of holidays and foods, which surnames are Jewish and which are "changed names"; about girls who had had their noses "fixed," their hair straightened. For these young Jewish women, students in the late 1940s, it was acceptable, perhaps even necessary, to strive to look as gentile as possible; but they stuck proudly to being Jewish, expected to marry a Jew, have children, keep the holidays, carry on the culture.

I felt I was testing a forbidden current, that there was danger in these revelations. I bought a reproduction of a Chagall[9] portrait of a rabbi in striped prayer shawl and hung it on the wall of my room. I was admittedly young and trying to educate myself, but I was also doing something that *is* dangerous: I was flirting with identity.

One day that year I was in a small shop where I had bought a dress with a too-long skirt. The shop employed a seamstress who did alterations, and she came in to pin up the skirt on me. I am sure that she was a recent immigrant, a survivor. I remember a short, dark woman wearing heavy glasses, with an accent so foreign I could not understand her

25

[9]*Chagall:* Marc Chagall, Russian painter (1887–1985), famous for surreal, dreamlike works inspired by his Jewish heritage.

words. Something about her presence was very powerful and disturbing to me. After marking and pinning up the skirt, she sat back on her knees, looked up at me, and asked in a hurried whisper: "You Jewish?" Eighteen years of training in assimilation sprang into the reflex by which I shook my head, rejecting her, and muttered, "No."

What was I actually saying "no" to? She was poor, older, struggling with a foreign tongue, anxious; she had escaped the death that had been intended for her, but I had no imagination of her possible courage and foresight, her resistance — I did not see in her a heroine who had perhaps saved many lives, including her own. I saw the frightened immigrant, the seamstress hemming the skirts of college girls, the wandering Jew. But I was an American college girl having her skirt hemmed. And I was frightened myself, I think, because she had recognized me ("It takes one to know one," my friend Edie at Radcliffe had said) even if I refused to recognize myself or her, even if her recognition was sharpened by loneliness or the need to feel safe with me.

But why should she have felt safe with me? I myself was living with a false sense of safety.

There are betrayals in my life that I have known at the very moment were betrayals: this was one of them. There are other betrayals committed so repeatedly, so mundanely, that they leave no memory trace behind, only a growing residue of misery, of dull, accreted self-hatred. Often these take the form not of words but of silence. Silence before the joke at which everyone is laughing; the anti-woman joke, the racist joke, the anti-Semitic joke. Silence and then amnesia. Blocking it out when the oppressor's language starts coming from the lips of one we admire, whose courage and eloquence have touched us: *She didn't really mean that; he didn't really say that.* But the accretions build up out of sight, like scale inside a kettle.

1948: I come home from my freshman year at college, flaming with   30
new insights, new information. I am the daughter who has gone out into the world, to the pinnacle of intellectual prestige, Harvard, fulfilling my father's hopes for me, but also exposed to dangerous influences. I have already been reproved for attending a rally for Henry Wallace[10] and the Progressive party. I challenge my father: "Why haven't you told me that I am Jewish? Why do you never talk about being a Jew?" He answers measuredly, "You know that I have never denied that I am a Jew. But it's not important to me. I am a scientist, a deist.[11] I have no use for organized religion. I choose to live in a world of many kinds of

[10]*Henry Wallace:* (1888–1965), American journalist, politician, and agriculturalist who was the Progressive party's candidate for the presidency in 1948.

[11]*deist:* one who believes that human reason, not divine power, underlies the laws of the universe.

people. There are Jews I admire and others whom I despise. I am a person, not simply a Jew." The words are as I remember them, not perhaps exactly as spoken. But that was the message. And it contained enough truth — as all denial drugs itself on partial truth — so that it remained for the time being unanswerable, leaving me high and dry, split at the root, gasping for clarity, for air.

At that time Arnold Rich was living in suspension, waiting to be appointed to the professorship of pathology at Johns Hopkins. The appointment was delayed for years, no Jew ever having held a professional chair in that medical school. And he wanted it badly. It must have been a very bitter time for him, since he had believed so greatly in the redeeming power of excellence, of being the most brilliant, inspired man for the job. With enough excellence, you could presumably make it stop mattering that you were Jewish; you could become the *only* Jew in the gentile world, a Jew so "civilized," so far from "common," so attractively combining southern gentility with European cultural values that no one would ever confuse you with the raw, "pushy" Jews of New York, the "loud, hysterical" refugees from eastern Europe, the "overdressed" Jews of the urban South.

We — my sister, mother, and I — were constantly urged to speak quietly in public, to dress without ostentation, to repress all vividness or spontaneity, to assimilate with a world which might see us as too flamboyant. I suppose that my mother, pure gentile though she was, could be seen as acting "common" or "Jewish" if she laughed too loudly or spoke aggressively. My father's mother, who lived with us half the year, was a model of circumspect behavior, dressed in dark blue or lavender, retiring in company, ladylike to an extreme, wearing no jewelry except a good gold chain, a narrow brooch, or a string of pearls. A few times, within the family, I saw her anger flare, felt the passion she was repressing. But when Arnold took us out to a restaurant or on a trip, the Rich women were always tuned down to some WASP level my father believed, surely, would protect us all — maybe also make us unrecognizable to the "real Jews" who wanted to seize us, drag us back to the *shtetl*, the ghetto, in its many manifestations.

For, yes, that *was* a message — that some Jews would be after you, once they "knew," to rejoin them, to re-enter a world that was messy, noisy, unpredictable, maybe poor — "even though," as my mother once wrote me, criticizing my largely Jewish choice of friends in college, "some of them will be the most brilliant, fascinating people you'll ever meet." I wonder if that isn't one message of assimilation — of America — that the unlucky or the unachieving want to pull you backward, that to identify with them is to court downward mobility, lose the precious chance of passing, of token existence. There was always within this sense of Jewish identity a strong class discrimination. Jews might be "fascinating" as individuals but came with huge unruly families who "poured chicken soup over everyone's head" (in the phrase of a white southern male poet). Anti-Semitism could thus be justified by the bad behavior of certain Jews; and if you did not effectively deny family and community, there would always be a remote cousin claiming kinship with you who was the "wrong kind" of Jew.

I have always believed his attitude toward other Jews depended on who they were. . . . It was my impression that Jews of this background looked down on Eastern European Jews, including Polish Jews and Russian Jews, who generally were not as well educated. This from a letter written to me recently by a gentile who had worked in my father's department, whom I had asked about anti-Semitism there and in particular regarding my father. This informant also wrote me that it was hard to perceive anti-Semitism in Baltimore because the racism made so much more intense an impression: *I would almost have to think that blacks went to a different heaven than the whites, because the bodies were kept in a separate morgue, and some white persons did not even want blood transfusions from black donors.* My father's mind was predictably racist and misogynist;[12] yet as a medical student he noted in his journal that southern male chivalry stopped at the point of any white man in a streetcar giving his seat to an old, weary Black woman standing in the aisle. Was this a Jewish insight — an outsider's insight, even though the outsider was striving to be on the inside?

Because what isn't named is often more permeating than what is, I   35
believe that my father's Jewishness profoundly shaped my own identity and our family existence. They were shaped both by external anti-Semitism and my father's self-hatred, and by his Jewish pride. What Arnold did, I think, was call his Jewish pride something else: achievement, aspiration, genius, idealism. Whatever was unacceptable got left back under the rubric of Jewishness or the "wrong kind" of Jews — uneducated, aggressive, loud. The message I got was that we were really superior: nobody else's father had collected so many books, had traveled so far, knew so many languages. Baltimore was a musical city, but for the most part, in the families of my school friends, culture was for women. My father was an amateur musician, read poetry, adored encyclopedic knowledge. He prowled and pounced over my school papers, insisting I use "grownup" sources; he criticized my poems for faulty technique and gave me books on rhyme and meter and form. His investment in my intellect and talent was egotistical, tyrannical, opinionated, and terribly wearing. He taught me, nevertheless, to believe in hard work, to mistrust easy inspiration, to write and rewrite; to feel that I *was* a person of the book, even though a woman; to take ideas seriously. He made me feel, at a very young age, the power of language and that I could share in it.

[12]*misogynist:* a person who hates women.

The Riches were proud, but we also had to very careful. Our behavior had to be more impeccable than other people's. Strangers were not to be trusted, nor even friends; family issues must never go beyond the family; the world was full of potential slanderers, betrayers, *people who could not understand.* Even within the family, I realize that I never in my whole life knew what my father was really feeling. Yet he spoke — monologued — with driving intensity. You could grow up in such a house mesmerized by the local electricity, the crucial meanings assumed by the merest things. This used to seem to me a sign that we were all living on some high emotional plane. It was a difficult force field for a favored daughter to disengage from.

Easy to call that intensity Jewish; and I have no doubt that passion is one of the qualities required for survival over generations of persecution. But what happens when passion is rent from its original base, when the white gentile world is softly saying "Be more like us and you can be almost one of us"? What happens when survival seems to mean closing off one emotional artery after another? His forebears in Europe had been forbidden to travel or expelled from one country after another, had special taxes levied on them if they left the city walls, had been forced to wear special clothes and badges, restricted to the poorest neighborhoods. He had wanted to be a "free spirit," to travel widely, among "all kinds of people." Yet in his prime of life he lived in an increasingly withdrawn world, in his house up on a hill in a neighborhood where Jews were not supposed to be able to buy property, depending almost exclusively on interactions with his wife and daughters to provide emotional connectedness. In his home, he created a private defense system so elaborate that even as he was dying, my mother felt unable to talk freely with his colleagues or others who might have helped her. Of course, she acquiesced in this.

The loneliness of the "only," the token, often doesn't feel like loneliness but like a kind of dead echo chamber. Certain things that ought to don't resonate. Somewhere Beverly Smith writes of women of color "inspiring the behavior" in each other. When there's nobody to "inspire the behavior," act out of the culture, there is an atrophy, a dwindling, which is partly invisible.

Sometimes I feel I have seen too long from too many disconnected angles: white, Jewish, anti-Semite, racist, anti-racist, once-married, lesbian, middle-class, feminist, exmatriate southerner, *split at the root* — that I will never bring them whole. I would have liked, in this essay, to bring together the meanings of anti-Semitism and racism as I have experienced them and as I believe they intersect in the world beyond my life. But I'm not able to do this yet. I feel the tension as I think, make notes: *If you really look at the one reality, the other will waver and disperse.* Trying in one week to read Angela Davis and Lucy

Davidowicz;[13] trying to hold throughout to a feminist, a lesbian, perspective — what does this mean? Nothing has trained me for this. And sometimes I feel inadequate to make any statement as a Jew; I feel the history of denial within me like an injury, a scar. For assimilation has affected *my* perceptions; those early lapses in meaning, those blanks, are with me still. My ignorance can be dangerous to me and to others.

Yet we can't wait for the undamaged to make our connections for 40 us; we can't wait to speak until we are perfectly clear and righteous. There is no purity and, in our lifetimes, no end to this process.

This essay, then, has no conclusions: it is another beginning for me. Not just a way of saying, in 1982 Right Wing America, *I, too, will wear the yellow star.*[14] It's a moving into accountability, enlarging the range of accountability. I know that in the rest of my life, the next half century or so, every aspect of my identity will have to be engaged. The middle-class white girl taught to trade obedience for privilege. The Jewish lesbian raised to be a heterosexual gentile. The woman who first heard oppression named and analyzed in the Black Civil Rights struggle. The woman with three sons, the feminist who hates male violence. The woman limping with a cane, the woman who has stopped bleeding are also accountable. The poet who knows that beautiful language can lie, that the oppressor's language sometimes sounds beautiful. The woman trying, as part of her resistance, to clean up her act.

[13]Angela Y. Davis, *Woman, Race and Class* (New York: Random House, 1981); Lucy S. Davidowicz, *The War against the Jews 1933–1945* (1975; New York: Bantam, 1979). [Author's note]

[14]*the yellow star:* the Star of David, used by Nazis during World War II to identify people who were Jewish.

Engaging the Text

1. In this personal reminiscence, Rich dissects her identity, analyzing her consciousness into separate, often antagonistic selves that compete for recognition. Work through her essay to identify these various selves and discuss how and why they conflict with one another.

2. Analyze the motives that underlie Arnold Rich's racism and his denial of his own Jewish heritage.

3. Why are other ethnic minority groups important to Rich?

4. When Rich mentions buying a Chagall portrait of a rabbi (para. 25), she writes, "but I was also doing something that *is* dangerous: I was flirting with identity." What does she mean? Why is exploring her own identity a "dangerous" act?

Exploring Connections

5. Review Gordon W. Allport's definitions of in-groups and out-groups (p. 292). List all the in-groups that Rich's family identifies with. What features or behaviors describe each group? What out-groups is each defined against? What, according to Rich, are the personal costs of in-group and out-group relations, and of mobility between groups?

6. Discuss the ways in which the following people or characters might be considered — like Rich — "split at the root":

The Man in "Symbiosis" (p. 42)   Nora Quealey (p. 202)
Haunani-Kay Trask (p. 118)   Stephen Cruz (p. 36)
The speaker of "The Returning"   Paula Gunn Allen (p. 241)
    (p. 162)

Extending the Critical Context

7. Try your hand at writing your own self-analysis. How many separate selves do you contain? What demands do they make of you? How do they conflict? What does it mean for you to be "accountable" to them?

Racism and the White Backlash

MARTIN LUTHER KING, JR.

This essay was published the year before Martin Luther King, Jr. (1929–1968) was assassinated in Memphis. In this indictment of what he calls a schizophrenic America, King offers a historical perspective on the economic and cultural motives for racism. This radical rereading of U.S. history may come as a surprise to those who have been brought up on textbook images of both the "founding fathers" and King himself. Clearly one of the most influential and revered American public figures of the twentieth century, King was awarded the Nobel Peace Prize in 1964 for his work in the civil rights movement. This essay appeared in a book whose title remains an important question twenty-five years later: Where Do We Go from Here: Chaos or Community? *(1967).*

It is time for all of us to tell each other the truth about who and what have brought the Negro to the condition of deprivation against which he struggles today. In human relations the truth is hard to come by, because most groups are deceived about themselves. Rationalization and the incessant search for scapegoats are the psychological cataracts that blind us to our individual and collective sins. But the day has passed for bland euphemisms. He who lives with untruth lives in spiritual slavery. Freedom is still the bonus we receive for knowing the truth. "Ye shall know the truth, and the truth shall set you free."[1]

It would be neither true nor honest to say that the Negro's status is what it is because he is innately inferior or because he is basically lazy and listless or because he has not sought to lift himself by his own bootstraps. To find the origins of the Negro problem we must turn to the white man's problem. As Earl Conrad says in a recent book, *The Invention of the Negro*: "I have sought out these new routes in the unshakable conviction that the question involved there cannot be and never could be answered merely by examining the Negro himself, his ghettos, his history, his personality, his culture. For the answer to how the Negro's status came to be what it is does not lie essentially in the world of the Negro, but in the world of the white." In short, white America must assume the guilt for the black man's inferior status.

Ever since the birth of our nation, white America has had a schizophrenic personality on the question of race. She has been torn between selves — a self in which she proudly professed the great principles of democracy and a self in which she sadly practiced the antithesis of democracy. This tragic duality has produced a strange indecisiveness and ambivalence toward the Negro, causing America to take a step backward simultaneously with every step forward on the question of racial justice, to be at once attracted to the Negro and repelled by him, to love and to hate him. There has never been a solid, unified, and determined thrust to make justice a reality for Afro-Americans.

The step backward has a new name today. It is called the "white backlash." But the white backlash is nothing new. It is the surfacing of old prejudices, hostilities, and ambivalences that have always been there. It was caused neither by the cry of Black Power nor by the unfortunate recent wave of riots in our cities. The white backlash of today is rooted in the same problem that has characterized America ever since the black man landed in chains on the shores of this nation. The white backlash is an expression of the same vacillations, the same search for rationalizations, the same lack of commitment that have always characterized white America on the question of race.

What is the source of this perennial indecision and vacillation? It 5 lies in the "congenital deformity" of racism that has crippled the nation from its inception. The roots of racism are very deep in America. Historically it was so acceptable in the national life that today it still

---

[1] *"Ye shall know the truth . . . .*: from the New Testament (John 8:32).

only lightly burdens the conscience. No one surveying the moral land-scape of our nation can overlook the hideous and pathetic wreckage of commitment twisted and turned to a thousand shapes under the stress of prejudice and irrationality.

This does not imply that all white Americans are racists — far from it. Many white people have, through a deep moral compulsion, fought long and hard for racial justice. Nor does it mean that America has made no progress in her attempt to cure the body politic of the disease of racism, or that the dogma of racism has not been considerably modified in recent years. However, for the good of America, it is necessary to refute the idea that the dominant ideology in our country even today is freedom and equality while racism is just an occasional departure from the norm on the part of a few bigoted extremists.

What is racism? Dr. George Kelsey, in a profound book entitled *Racism and the Christian Understanding of Man*, states that:

> Racism is a faith. It is a form of idiolatry. . . . In its early modern beginnings, racism was a justificatory device. It did not emerge as a faith. It arose as an ideological justification for the constellations of political and economic power which were expressed in colonialism and slavery. But gradually the idea of the superior race was heightened and deepened in meaning and value so that it pointed beyond the historical structures of relation, in which it emerged, to human existence itself.

In her *Race: Science and Politics*, Ruth Benedict expands on the theme by defining racism as "the dogma that one ethnic group is condemned by nature to hereditary inferiority and another group is destined to hereditary superiority. It is the dogma that the hope of civilization depends upon eliminating some races and keeping others pure. It is the dogma that one race has carried progress throughout human history and can alone ensure future progress."

Since racism is based on the dogma "that the hope of civilization depends upon eliminating some races and keeping others pure," its ultimate logic is genocide. Hitler, in his mad and ruthless attempt to exterminate the Jews, carried the logic of racism to its ultimate tragic conclusions. While America has not literally sought to eliminate the Negro in this final sense, it has, through the system of segregation, substituted a subtle reduction of life by means of deprivation.

If a man asserts that another man, because of his race, is not good enough to have a job equal to his, or to eat at a lunch counter next to him, or to have access to certain hotels, or to attend school with him, or to live next door to him, he is by implication affirming that that man does not deserve to exist. He does not deserve to exist because his existence is corrupt and defective. 10

Racism is a philosophy based on a contempt for life. It is the arrogant assertion that one race is the center of value and object of devotion, before which other races must kneel in submission. It is the absurd dogma that one race is responsible for all the progress of history and alone can assure the progress of the future. Racism is total estrangement. It separates not only bodies, but minds and spirits. Inevitably it descends to inflicting spiritual or physical homicide upon the out-group.

Of the two dominant and contradictory strains in the American psyche, the positive one, our democratic heritage, was the later development on the American continent. Democracy, born in the eighteenth century, took from John Locke of England the theory of natural rights and the justification of revolution and imbued it with the ideal of a society governed by the people. When Jefferson wrote the Declaration of Independence, the first government of the world to be based on these principles was established on American soil. A contemporary description of Benjamin Franklin might have described the new nation: "He has torn lightning from the sky; soon he will tear their sceptres from the kings." And Thomas Paine in his enthusiasm declared, "We have the power to begin the world all over again."

Yet even amid these electrifying expressions of the rights of man, racism — the myth of inferior peoples — was flourishing here to contradict and qualify the democratic ideal. Slavery was not only ignored in defining democracy, but its enlargement was tolerated in the interests of strengthening the nation.

For more than two hundred years before the Declaration of Independence, Africa had been raped and plundered by Britain and Europe, her native kingdoms disorganized, and her people and rulers demoralized. For a hundred years afterward, the infamous trade continued in America virtually without abatement, even after it had ceased to be legal on this continent.

In fact, this ghastly blood traffic was so immense and its profits were so stupendous that the economies of several European nations owed their growth and prosperity to it and New England rested heavily on it for its development. Beard[2] declared it was fair to say of whole towns in New England and Great Britain: "The stones of your houses are cemented with the blood of African slaves." Conservatively estimated, several million Africans died in the calloused transfer of human merchandise to the New World alone.

It is important to understand that the basis for the birth, growth, and development of slavery in America was primarily economic. By the beginning of the seventeenth century, the British Empire had established colonies all along the Atlantic seaboard from Massachusetts to the West Indies to serve as producers of raw materials for British manufac-

[2]*Beard:* Charles A. Beard (1874–1948), American historian, political scientist, and author of *An Economic Interpretation of the Constitution of the United States* and (with Mary R. Beard) *The Rise of American Civilization.*

turing, a market for goods manufactured in Britain, and a source of staple cargoes for British shipping engaged in world trade. So the colonies had to provide an abundance of rice, sugar, cotton, and tobacco. In the first few years of the various settlements along the East Coast, so-called indentured servants, mostly white, were employed on plantations. But within a generation the plantation operators were demanding outright and lifetime slavery for the Africans they imported. As a function of this new economic policy, Africans were reduced to the status of property by law, and this status was enforced by the most rigid and brutal police power of the existing governments. By 1650 slavery had been legally established as a national institution.

Since the institution of slavery was so important to the economic development of America, it had a profound impact in shaping the social-political-legal structure of the nation. Land and slaves were the chief forms of private property, property was wealth and the voice of wealth made the law and determined politics. In the service of this system, human beings were reduced to propertyless property. Black men, the creators of the wealth of the New World, were stripped of all human and civil rights. And this degradation was sanctioned and protected by institutions of government, all for one purpose: to produce commodities for sale at a profit, which in turn would be privately appropriated.

It seems to be a fact of life that human beings cannot continue to do wrong without eventually reaching out for some rationalization to clothe their acts in the garments of righteousness. And so, with the growth of slavery, men had to convince themselves that a system which was so economically profitable was morally justifiable. The attempt to give moral sanction to a profitable system gave birth to the doctrine of white supremacy.

Religion and the Bible were cited and distorted to support the status quo. It was argued that the Negro was inferior by nature because of Noah's curse upon the children of Ham. The Apostle Paul's dictum became a watchword: "Servant, be obedient to your master." In this strange way theology became a ready ally of commerce. The great Puritan divine Cotton Mather culled the Bible for passages to give comfort to the plantation owners and merchants. He went so far as to set up some "Rules for the Society of Negroes," in which, among other things, Negroes disobedient to their masters were to be rebuked and denied attendance at church meetings, and runaway slaves were to be brought back and severely punished. All of this, he reasoned, was in line with the Apostle Paul's injunction that servants should be obedient to their masters.

Logic was manipulated to give intellectual credence to the system of   20
slavery. Someone formulated the argument for the inferiority of the Negro in the shape of a syllogism:

All men are made in the image of God;
God, as everybody knows, is not a Negro;
Therefore the Negro is not a man.

Academicians eventually climbed on the bandwagon and gave their prestige to the myth of the superior race. Their contribution came through the so-called Teutonic Origins theory, a doctrine of white supremacy surrounded by the halo of academic respectability. The theorists of this concept argued that all Anglo-Saxon institutions of any worth had their historical roots in the Teutonic tribe institutions of ancient Germany, and furthermore that "only the Teutonic race had been imbued with the ability to build stable governments." Historians from the lofty academic towers of Oxford, like Bishop William Stubbs and Edward A. Freeman, expounded the Teutonic Origins theory in British intellectual circles. It leaped the Atlantic and found lodging in the mind of Herbert Baxter Adams, one of the organizers of the graduate school at Johns Hopkins University and founder of the American Historical Association. He expanded Freeman's views by asserting that the Teutonic Origins theory really had "three homes — England, Germany and the United States." Pretty soon this distorted theory dominated the thinking of American historians at leading universities like Harvard, Cornell, Wisconsin, and Columbia.

Even natural science, that discipline committed to the inductive method, creative appraisal, and detached objectivity, was invoked and distorted to give credence to a political position. A whole school of racial ethnologists developed using such terms as "species," "genus," and "race." It became fashionable to think of the slave as a "species of property." It was during this period that the word "race" came into fashion.

Dr. Samuel G. Morton, a Philadelphia physician, emerged with the head-size theory which affirmed that the larger the skull, the superior the individual. This theory was used by other ethnologists to prove that the large head size of Caucasians signified more intellectual capacity and more native worth. A Dr. Josiah C. Nott, in his *Collections on the Natural History of the Caucasian and Negro Races*, used psuedoscientific evidence to prove that the black man was little above the level of an ape. A Frenchman, Count Arthur de Gobineau, in his book *The Inequality of the Human Races*, vigorously defended the theory of the inferiority of the black man and used the experience of the United States as his prime source of evidence. It was this kind of "science" that pervaded the atmosphere in the nineteenth century, and these pseudo scientists became the authoritative references for any and all seeking rationalization for the system of slavery.

Generally we think of white supremacist views as having their origins with the unlettered, underprivileged, poorer-class whites. But the social obstetricians who presided at the birth of racist views in our country were from the aristocracy: rich merchants, influential clergymen, men of medical sciences, historians, and political scientists from some of the leading universities of the nation. With such a distinguished company of the elite working so assiduously to disseminate racist views, what was there to inspire poor, illiterate, unskilled white farmers to think otherwise?

Soon the doctrine of white supremacy was imbedded in every textbook and preached in practically every pulpit. It became a structural part of the culture. And men then embraced this philosophy, not as the rationalization of a lie, but as the expression of a final truth. In 1857 the system of slavery was given its ultimate legal support by the Supreme Court of the United States in the Dred Scott decision,[3] which affirmed that the Negro had no rights that the white man was bound to respect.

The greatest blasphemy of the whole ugly process was that the white man ended up making God his partner in the exploitation of the Negro. What greater heresy has religion known? Ethical Christianity vanished and the moral nerve of religion atrophied. This terrible distortion sullied the essential nature of Christianity.

Virtually all of the Founding Fathers of our nation, even those who rose to the heights of the Presidency, those whom we cherish as our authentic heroes, were so enmeshed in the ethos of slavery and white supremacy that not one ever emerged with a clear, unambiguous stand on Negro rights. No human being is perfect. In our individual and collective lives every expression of greatness is followed, not by a period symbolizing completeness, but by a comma implying partialness. Following every affirmation of greatness is the conjunction "but." Naaman "was a great man," says the Old Testament, "but . . . " — that "but" reveals something tragic and disturbing — "but he was a leper." George Washington, Thomas Jefferson, Patrick Henry, John Quincy Adams, John Calhoun, and Abraham Lincoln were great men, but — that "but" underscores the fact that not one of these men had a strong, unequivocal belief in the equality of the black man.

No one doubts the valor and commitment that characterized George Washington's life. But to the end of his days he maintained a posture of exclusionism toward the slave. He was a fourth-generation slaveholder. He only allowed Negroes to enter the Continental Army because His Majesty's Crown was attempting to recruit Negroes to the British cause. Washington was not without his moments of torment, those moments of conscience when something within told him that slavery was wrong. As he searched the future of America one day, he wrote to his nephew: "I wish from my soul that the legislature of this

---

[3]*Dred Scott decision:* 1857 Supreme Court decision denying U.S. citizenship to African American slaves.

State could see the policy of gradual abolition of slavery. It might prevent much future mischief." In spite of this, Washington never made a public statement condemning slavery. He could not pull away from the system. When he died he owned, or had on lease, more than 160 slaves.

Here, in the life of the father of our nation, we can see the developing dilemma of white America: the haunting ambivalence, the intellectual and moral recognition that slavery is wrong, but the emotional tie to the system so deep and pervasive that it imposes an inflexible unwillingness to root it out.

Thomas Jefferson reveals the same ambivalence. There is much in the life of Jefferson that can serve as a model for political leaders in every age; he came close to the ideal "philosopher-king" that Plato dreamed of centuries ago. But in spite of this, Jefferson was a child of his culture who had been influenced by the pseudo-scientific and philosophical thought that rationalized slavery. In his *Notes on Virginia*, Jefferson portrayed the Negro as inferior to the white man in his endowments of body, mind, and imagination, although he observed that the Negro appeared to be superior at picking out tunes on the "banjar." Jefferson's majestic words, "all men are created equal," meant for him, as for many others, that all *white* men are created equal.

Yet in his heart Jefferson knew that slavery was wrong and that it degraded the white man's mind and soul. In the same *Notes on Virginia* he wrote: "For if a slave can have a country in this world, it must be any other in preference to that in which he is born to live and labor for another. . . . Indeed I tremble for my country when I reflect that God is just, that his justice cannot sleep forever . . . the Almighty has no attribute which can take sides with us in such a contest." And in 1820, six years before his death, he wrote these melancholy words: "But the momentous question [slavery] like a fire-bell in the night, awakened and filled me with terror. I considered it at once as the knell of the Union. . . . I regret that I am now to die in the belief that the useless sacrifice of themselves by the generation of 1776, to acquire self-government and happiness to their country, is to be thrown away by the unwise and unworthy passion of their sons, and that my only consolation is to be that I live not to weep over it."

This strange duality toward the Negro and slavery vexed the mind of Abraham Lincoln for years. Few men in history have anchored their lives more deeply in moral convictions than Abraham Lincoln, but on the question of slavery Lincoln's torments and vacillations were tenacious.

As early as 1837, as a State Legislator, Lincoln referred to the injustice and impracticality of slavery. Later he wrote of the physical differences between blacks and whites and made it clear that he felt whites were superior. At times he concluded that the white man could not live with the Negro. This accounted for his conviction that the only answer to the problem was to colonize the black man — send him back to Africa, or to the West Indies or some other isolated spot. This view was still in his mind toward the height of the Civil War. Delegation after delegation — the Quakers above all, great abolitionists like Charles Sumner, Horace Greeley, and William Lloyd Garrison — pleaded with Lincoln to free the slaves, but he was firm in his resistance. Frederick Douglass, a Negro of towering grandeur, sound judgment, and militant initiative, sought, without success, to persuade Lincoln that slavery, not merely the preservation of the union, was at the root of the war. At the time, Lincoln could not yet see it.

A civil war raged within Lincoln's own soul, a tension between the Dr. Jekyll of freedom and the Mr. Hyde of slavery, a struggle like that of Plato's charioteer with two headstrong horses each pulling in different directions. Morally Lincoln was for black emancipation, but emotionally, like most of his white contemporaries, he was for a long time unable to act in accordance with his conscience.

But Lincoln was basically honest and willing to admit his confu- 35 sions. He saw that the nation could not survive half slave and half free; and he said, "If we could first know where we are and whither we are tending, we could better judge what to do and how to do it." Fortunately for the nation, he finally came to see "whither we are tending." On January 1, 1863, he issued the Emancipation Proclamation, freeing the Negro from the bondage of chattel slavery. By this concrete act of courage his reservations of the past were overshadowed. The conclusion of his search is embodied in these words: "In giving freedom to the slave, we assure freedom to the free — honourable alike is what we give and what we preserve."

The significance of the Emancipation Proclamation was described by Frederick Douglass in these words:

> Unquestionably, for weal or for woe, the First of January is to be the most memorable day in American Annals. The Fourth of July was great, but the First of January, when we consider it in all its relations and bearings, is incomparably greater. The one had respect to the mere political birth of a nation; the last concerns the national life and character, and is to determine whether that life and character shall be radiantly glorious with all high and noble virtues, or infamously blackened, forevermore. . . .

But underneath, the ambivalence of white America toward the Negro still lurked with painful persistence. With all the beautiful promise that Douglass saw in the Emancipation Proclamation, he soon found that it left the Negro with only abstract freedom. Four million newly liberated slaves found themselves with no bread to eat, no land to cultivate, no shelter to cover their heads. It was like freeing a man who

had been unjustly imprisoned for years, and on discovering his innocence sending him out with no bus fare to get home, no suit to cover his
body, no financial compensation to atone for his long years of incarcera-
tion and to help him get a sound footing in society; sending him out
with only the assertion: "Now you are free." What greater injustice
could society perpetrate? All the moral voices of the universe, all the
codes of sound jurisprudence, would rise up with condemnation at such
an act. Yet this is exactly what America did to the Negro. In 1863 the
Negro was given abstract freedom expressed in luminous rhetoric. But in
an agrarian economy he was given no land to make liberation concrete.
After the war the government granted white settlers, without cost,
millions of acres of land in the West, thus providing America's new
white peasants from Europe with an economic floor. But at the same
time its oldest peasantry, the Negro, was denied everything but a legal
status he could not use, could not consolidate, could not even defend. As
Frederick Douglass came to say, "Emancipation granted the Negro
freedom to hunger, freedom to winter amid the rains of heaven. Emancipation was freedom and famine at the same time."

The inscription on the Statue of Liberty refers to America as the
"mother of exiles." The tragedy is that while America became the
mother of her white exiles, she evinced no motherly concern or love for
her exiles from Africa. It is no wonder that out of despair and estrangement the Negro cries out in one of his sorrow songs: "Sometimes I feel
like a motherless child." The marvel is, as Frederick Douglass once said,
that Negroes are still alive.

In dealing with the ambivalence of white America, we must not
overlook another form of racism that was relentlessly pursued on American shores: the physical extermination of the American Indian. The
South American example of absorbing the indigenous Indian population
was ignored in the United States, and systematic destruction of a whole
people was undertaken. The common phrase, "The only good Indian is
a dead Indian," was virtually elevated to national policy. Thus the
poisoning of the American mind was accomplished not only by acts of
discrimination and exploitation but by the exaltation of murder as an
expression of the courage and initiative of the pioneer. Just as Southern
culture was made to appear noble by ignoring the cruelty of slavery, the
conquest of the Indian was depicted as an example of bravery and
progress.

Thus through two centuries a continuous indoctrination of Ameri-   40
cans has separated people according to mythically superior and inferior
qualities while a democratic spirit of equality was evoked as the national ideal. These concepts of racism, and this schizophrenic duality of
conduct, remain deeply rooted in American thought today. This tendency of the nation to take one step forward on the question of racial

justice and then to take a step backward is still the pattern. Just as an ambivalent nation freed the slaves a century ago with no plan or program to make their freedom meaningful, the still ambivalent nation in 1954 declared school segregation unconstitutional with no plan or program to make integration real. Just as the Congress passed a civil rights bill in 1868 and refused to enforce it, the Congress passed a civil rights bill in 1964 and to this day has failed to enforce it in all its dimensions. Just as the Fifteenth Amendment in 1870 proclaimed Negro suffrage, only to permit its *de facto* withdrawal in half the nation, so in 1965 the Voting Rights Law was passed and then permitted to languish only with factional and halfhearted implementation.

The civil rights measures of the 1960s engraved solemn rights in the legal literature. But after writing piecemeal and incomplete legislation and proclaiming its historic importance in magnificent prose, the American Government left the Negro to make the unworkable work. Against entrenched segregationist state power, with almost total dependence economically on those they had to contend with, and without political experience, the impoverished Negro was expected to usher in an era of freedom and plenty.

When the war against poverty came into being in 1964, it seemed to herald a new day of compassion. It was the bold assertion that the nation would no longer stand complacently by while millions of its citizens smothered in poverty in the midst of opulence. But it did not take long to discover that the government was only willing to appropriate such a limited budget that it could not launch a good skirmish against poverty, much less a full-scale war.

Moreover, the poverty program, which in concept elated the Negro poor, became so embroiled in political turmoil that its insufficiencies were magnified and its operations paralyzed. Big-city machines felt threatened by it and small towns, especially in the South, directed it away from Negroes. Its good intentions and limited objectives were frustrated by the skillful maneuvers of experienced politicians. The worst effect of these manipulations was to cast doubt upon the program as a whole and discredit those Negroes involved directly in its administration.

In 1965 the President presented a new plan to Congress — which it finally passed in 1966 — for rebuilding entire slum neighborhoods. With other elements of the program it would, in his words, make the decaying cities of the present into "the masterpieces of our civilization." This Demonstration Cities plan is imaginative; it embodies social vision and properly defines racial discrimination as a central evil. However, the ordinary Negro, though no social or political analyst, will be skeptical. He will be skeptical, first, because of the insufficient funds assigned to the program. He will be skeptical, second, because he knows how many laws exist in Northern states and cities prohibiting discrimination in housing, in education, and in employment; he knows how many overlapping commissions exist to enforce the terms of these laws — and he knows how he lives. The ubiquitous discrimination in his daily life tells him that laws on paper, no matter how imposing their terms, will not guarantee that he will live in "the masterpiece of civilization."

Throughout our history, laws affirming Negro rights have consist- 45 ently been circumvented by ingenious evasions which render them void in practice. Laws that affect the whole population — draft laws, income-tax laws, traffic laws — manage to work even though they may be unpopular; but laws passed for the Negro's benefit are so widely unenforced that it is a mockery to call them laws. There is a tragic gulf between civil rights laws passed and civil rights laws implemented. There is a double standard in the enforcement of law and a double standard in the respect for particular laws.

All of this tells us that the white backlash is nothing new. White America has been backlashing on the fundamental God-given and human rights of Negro Americans for more than three hundred years. With all of her dazzling achievements and stupendous material strides, America has maintained its strange ambivalence on the question of racial justice.

Engaging the Text

1. What contradictions does King note between the ideal of individual freedom and racism? How does he explain the development of racism in U.S. history? What role does he attribute to the Bible in this process?

2. What does King mean in paragraph 2 when he says that "white America must assume the guilt for the Black man's inferior status"? What implications does King's statement have for white Americans today?

3. What does King mean in paragraph 3 when he says that "white America has had a schizophrenic personality on the question of race"? How does he explain the connection between this cultural schizophrenia and the white backlash he perceived in 1967? Do you see evidence of either cultural schizophrenia or a white backlash in U.S. society today?

4. King sometimes sounds like a scholar in this essay and sometimes like a preacher. Find several instances of each type of rhetoric: Do these two styles blend successfully in the essay or clash?

Exploring Connections

5. Although King uses the term "out-group" — a concept essential to Gordon W. Allport's explanation of racial prejudice (p. 292) — his approach to racism in this essay is on the whole quite different from Allport's. What shortcomings might King identify in Allport's analysis?

6. How might Susan Griffin (p. 175) respond to King's analysis of the sources of racism in American history? Working with a partner, write a dialogue between the two; then read your dialogue aloud in class.

Extending the Critical Context

7. Like Lincoln, Martin Luther King, Jr., has become a mythic American leader. What ideas, qualities, and events define King as a cultural myth — that is, what has he come to represent in American culture? How does this essay support, challenge, or complicate this image?

8. King suggests that civil rights legislation has failed because racism remains "a structural part of the culture" (para. 25). Working in groups, discuss this claim. Have attempts to legislate racial equality improved the situation of people of color in the United States? Have such attempts reduced or increased racial tensions? What do you think would be the best ways to combat structural racism?

Three Thousand Dollar Death Song

WENDY ROSE

Many Native American writers have noted and decried the tendency to treat their heritage as something dead and gone, something to be studied like the fossil record of extinct animals. This poem is a proud song of protest against such dehumanization. Wendy Rose (b. 1948) is a Hopi-Miwok poet, visual artist, editor, and anthropologist. She currently teaches American Indian Studies at Fresno City College. This poem is from the most acclaimed of her several books of poetry, Lost Copper *(1980), which was nominated for an American Book Award.*

> Nineteen American Indian Skeletons from Nevada . . . valued at $3000 . . .
> — MUSEUM INVOICE, 1975

Is it in cold hard cash? the kind
that dusts the insides of men's pockets
lying silver-polished surface along the cloth.
Or in bills? papering the wallets of they
who thread the night with dark words. Or   5

checks? paper promises weighing the same
as words spoken once on the other side
of the grown grass and damned rivers
of history. However it goes, it goes
Through my body it goes assessing each nerve, running its edges   10
along my arteries, planning ahead
for whose hands will rip me
into pieces of dusty red paper,
whose hands will smooth or smatter me   15
into traces of rubble. Invoiced now,
it's official how our bones are valued
that stretch out pointing to sunrise
or are flexed into one last foetal bend,[1]
that are removed and tossed about,   20
catalogued, numbered with black ink
on newly-white foreheads.
As we were formed to the white soldier's voice,
so we explode under white students' hands.   25
Death is a long trail of days
in our fleshless prison.

From this distant point we watch our bones
auctioned with our careful beadwork,
our quilled medicine bundles, even the bridles
of our shot-down horses. You: who have   30
priced us, you who have removed us: at what cost?
What price the pits where our bones share
a single bit of memory, how one century
turns our dead into specimens, our history
into dust, our survivors into clowns.   35
Our memory might be catching, you know;
picture the mortars,[2] the arrowheads, the labrets[3]
shaking off their labels like bears
suddenly awake to find the seasons have ended
while they slept. Watch them touch each other,   40
measure reality, march out the museum door!
Watch as they lift their faces
and smell about for us; watch our bones rise
to meet them and mount the horses once again!
The cost, then, will be paid   45

---

[1]*foetal bend:* throughout history, many cultures have buried their dead in a curled
position resembling that of a fetus.

[2]*mortars:* bowl-shaped vessels.

[3]*labrets:* ornaments of wood or bone worn in holes pierced through the lip.

for our sweetgrass-smelling having-been
in clam shell beads and steatite,[4]
dentalia[5] and woodpecker scalp, turquoise
and copper, blood and oil, coal
and uranium, children, a universe   50
of stolen things.

> [4]*steatite:* a soft, easily carved stone; soapstone.
> [5]*dentalia:* a type of mollusk shell resembling a tooth.

Engaging the Text

1. What do the Indian skeletons mentioned in the epigraph represent?

2. What is the "distant point" Rose mentions in the second stanza?

3. What item seems unusual or out of place in the catalog of "stolen things" that ends the poem? Why does Rose include it in the list? In what way were all these things stolen from the Indians?

4. How do time, place, and point of view shift in the poem? How do these shifts contribute to the poem's meaning?

5. A cynical reader might dismiss lines 36–51 as an empty threat: after all, the bones of slain warriors will not literally rise again and remount their horses. What symbolic or rhetorical purposes might these lines serve?

Exploring Connections

6. Imagine that Kevin Costner is about to make another film involving Native Americans, to follow up on the success of *Dances with Wolves*. Draft a letter to Costner from one of the following: Wendy Rose, Haunani-Kay Trask (p. 118), John (Fire) Lame Deer (p. 128), Gail Tremblay (p. 162), or Paula Gunn Allen (p. 241). This letter might critique *Dances with Wolves*, suggest ideas or issues for the new film, warn of common misconceptions about Native American life, and so on. To extend the assignment, work in small groups to draft a brief statement of principles regarding the portrayal of native peoples in film.

Extending the Critical Context

7. Play the role of museum director. Write a letter to the *Reno Times* explaining and defending your museum's purchase of the skeletons. Make up any circumstances you think plausible. Then evaluate the effectiveness of your defense.

8. Investigate a museum in your area with an American Indian collection. What is displayed for public view, and how? What further materials are reserved for research or special exhibits? Has there been any controversy over rightful ownership of skeletons or artifacts? Report your findings to the class.

We, the Dangerous

Janice Mirikitani

Janice Mirikitani is a third-generation Japanese American who was born in 1942, when the United States and Japan were at war. In this poem she presents a sobering catalog of the injustice, oppression, and violence that the United States has inflicted on Asian and Asian American people. Yet this poem also celebrates the persistence, pride, and courage that have enabled them to endure. Mirikitani is an editor, teacher, and community activist (in San Francisco) as well as a poet. Her collections of prose and poetry are Shedding Silence *(1987) and* Awake in the River *(1978), from which "We, the Dangerous" is reprinted.*

I swore
it would not devour me
I swore
it would not humble me
I swore   5
it would not break me.

> And they commanded we dwell in the desert
> Our children be spawn of barbed wire and barracks

We, closer to the earth,
squat, short thighed,   10
knowing the dust better.

> And they would have us make the garden
> Rake the grass to soothe their feet

We, akin to the jungle,
plotting with the snake,   15
tails shedding in civilized America.

> And they would have us skin their fish
> deft hands like blades/sliding back flesh/bloodless

We, who awake in the river
Ocean's child   20
Whale eater.

> And they would have us strange scented women,
> Round shouldered/strong and yellow/like the moon
> to pull the thread to the cloth
> to loosen their backs massaged in myth   25

We, who fill the secret bed,
the sweat shops
the laundries.

    And they would dress us in naplam,
    Skin shred to clothe the earth,   30
    Bodies filling pock marked fields.
    Dead fish bloating our harbors.

We, the dangerous,
Dwelling in the ocean.
Akin to the jungle.   35
Close to the earth.

    Hiroshima
    Vietnam
    Tule Lake[1]

And yet we were not devoured.   40
And yet we were not humbled
And yet we are not broken.

[1]*Tule Lake:* the largest of the camps where Japanese immigrants and their children were imprisoned in the United States during World War II.

Engaging the Text

1. List the images associated with Asian people in the poem. What values and characteristics do these images suggest, and why are they "dangerous"?

2. Who are "they," and what values and characteristics does Mirikitani associate with them?

3. Discuss the significance of the shift from "I" to "we" between stanzas one and two.

4. What does the poem suggest about the social and economic status of Asians in the United States?

5. Explain the structure of the poem. Be sure to comment on the similarity of the first and last stanzas, on the way the two distinct types of stanzas in the rest of the poem play off each other, and on the poem's use of repetition.

Exploring Connections

6. Compare the roles of the speakers in Aurora Levins Morales's "Class Poem" (p. 95), Wendy Rose's "Three Thousand Dollar Death Song" (p. 331), and "We, the Dangerous." What are their relationships — historical, political, economic, cultural, emotional — to the people they are talking about?

Extending the Critical Context

7. Choose some marginalized group in American culture besides Asian Americans — for example, some other ethnic group, lesbians or gays, hearing-impaired people, the aged. Write at least two stanzas in imitation of Mirikitani's poem, keeping your structure identical to Mirikitani's but changing the actual words and ideas. For example, if you wrote from the point of view of a neglected parent, the lines "And they would dress us in napalm / Skin shred to clothe the earth" might become "And they would lock us in nursing homes / Bodies drugged to ease their consciences." Share your effort with classmates.

C. P. Ellis

Studs Terkel

The following oral history brings us uncomfortably close to unambiguous, deadly prejudice: C. P. Ellis is a former Ku Klux Klan member who claims to have overcome his racist (and sexist) attitudes; he speaks here as a union leader who feels an alliance to other workers, including blacks and women. The story of his "transformation" not only is fascinating reading in its own right but also provides a complex example on which theories like Gordon W. Allport's (p. 292) can be tested. For a brief introduction to Studs Terkel (b. 1912) and his method of compiling oral histories, see the headnote to Terkel's "Stephen Cruz" (p. 36). This selection first appeared in American Dreams: Lost and Found *(1980).*

We're in his office in Durham, North Carolina. He is the business manager of the International Union of Operating Engineers. On the wall is a plaque: "Certificate of Service, in recognition to C. P. Ellis, for your faithful service to the city in having served as a member of the Durham Human Relations Council. February 1977."

At one time, he had been president (exalted cyclops) of the Durham chapter of the Ku Klux Klan. . . .

He is fifty-two years old.

My father worked in a textile mill in Durham. He died at forty-eight years old. It was probably from cotton dust. Back then, we never heard of brown lung. I was about seventeen years old and had a mother and sister depending on somebody to make a livin'. It was just barely enough insurance to cover his burial. I had to quit school and go to work. I was about eighth grade when I quit.

My father worked hard but never had enough money to buy decent   5
clothes. When I went to school, I never seemed to have adequate clothes
to wear. I always left school late afternoon with a sense of inferiority.
The other kids had nice clothes, and I just had what Daddy could buy. I
still got some of those inferiority feelin's now that I have to overcome
once in a while.

I loved my father. He would go with me to ball games. We'd go
fishin' together. I was really ashamed of the way he'd dress. He would
take this money and give it to me instead of putting it on himself. I
always had the feeling about somebody looking at him and makin' fun
of him and makin' fun of me. I think it had to do somethin' with my
life.

My father and I were very close, but we didn't talk about too many
intimate things. He did have a drinking problem. During the week, he
would work every day, but weekends he was ready to get plastered. I
can understand when a guy looks at his paycheck and looks at his bills,
and he's worked hard all the week, and his bills are larger than his
paycheck. He'd done the best he could the entire week, and there
seemed to be no hope. It's an illness thing. Finally you just say: "The
heck with it. I'll just get drunk and forget it."

My father was out of work during the depression, and I remember
going with him to the finance company uptown, and he was turned
down. That's something that's always stuck.

My father never seemed to be happy. It was a constant struggle with
him just like it was for me. It's very seldom I'd see him laugh. He was
just tryin' to figure out what he could do from one day to the next.

After several years pumping gas at a service station, I got married.   10
We had to have children. Four. One child was born blind and retarded,
which was a real additional expense to us. He's never spoken a word. He
doesn't know me when I go to see him. But I see him, I hug his neck. I
talk to him, tell him I love him. I don't know whether he knows me or
not, but I know he's well taken care of. All my life, I had work, never a
day without work, worked all the overtime I could get and still could
not survive financially. I began to say there's somethin' wrong with this
country. I worked my butt off and just never seemed to break even.

I had some real great ideas about this great nation. (Laughs.) They
say to abide by the law, go to church, do right and live for the Lord, and
everything'll work out. But it didn't work out. It just kept gettin' worse
and worse.

I was workin' a bread route. The highest I made one week was
seventy-five dollars. The rent on our house was about twelve dollars a
week. I will never forget: outside of this house was a 265-gallon oil
drum, and I never did get enough money to fill up that oil drum. What
I would do every night, I would run up to the store and buy five gallons
of oil and climb up the ladder and pour it in that 265-gallon drum. I

could hear that five gallons when it hits the bottom of that oil drum, splatters, and it sounds like it's nothin' in there. But it would keep the house warm for the night. Next day you'd have to do the same thing.

I left the bread route with fifty dollars in my pocket. I went to the bank and I borrowed four thousand dollars to buy the service station. I worked seven days a week, open and close, and finally had a heart attack. Just about two months before the last payments of that loan. My wife had done the best she could to keep it runnin'. Tryin' to come out of that hole, I just couldn't do it.

I really began to get bitter. I didn't know who to blame. I tried to find somebody. I began to blame it on black people. I had to hate somebody. Hatin' America is hard to do because you can't see it to hate it. You gotta have somethin' to look at to hate. (Laughs.) The natural person for me to hate would be black people, because my father before me was a member of the Klan. As far as he was concerned, it was the savior of the white people. It was the only organization in the world that would take care of the white people. So I began to admire the Klan.

I got active in the Klan while I was at the service station. Every Monday night, a group of men would come by and buy a Coca-Cola, go back to the car, take a few drinks, and come back and stand around talkin'. I couldn't help but wonder: Why are these dudes comin' out every Monday? They said they were with the Klan and have meetings close-by. Would I be interested? Boy, that was an opportunity I really looked forward to! To be part of somethin'. I joined the Klan, went from member to chaplain, from chaplain to vice-president, from vice-president to president. The title is exalted cyclops.

The first night I went with the fellas, they knocked on the door and gave the signal. They sent some robed Klansmen to talk to me and give me some instructions. I was led into a large meeting room, and this was the time of my life! It was thrilling. Here's a guy who's worked all his life and struggled all his life to be something, and here's the moment to be something. I will never forget it. Four robed Klansmen led me into the hall. The lights were dim, and the only thing you could see was an illuminated cross. I knelt before the cross. I had to make certain vows and promises. We promised to uphold the purity of the white race, fight communism, and protect white womanhood.

After I had taken my oath, there was loud applause goin' through-out the building', musta been at least four hundred people. For this one little ol' person. It was a thrilling moment for C. P. Ellis.

It disturbs me when people who do not really know what it's all about are so very critical of individual Klansmen. The majority of 'em are low-income whites, people who really don't have a part in something. They have been shut out as well as the blacks. Some are not very well educated either. Just like myself. We had a lot of support from doctors and lawyers and police officers.

Maybe they've had bitter experiences in this life and they had to hate somebody. So the natural person to hate would be the black person. He's beginnin' to come up, he's beginnin' to learn to read and start votin' and run for political office. Here are white people who are supposed to be superior to them, and we're shut out.

I can understand why people join extreme right-wing or left-wing groups. They're in the same boat I was. Shut out. Deep down inside, we want to be part of this great society. Nobody listens, so we join these groups.

At one time, I was state organizer of the National Rights party. I organized a youth group for the Klan. I felt we were getting old and our generation's gonna die. So I contacted certain kids in schools. They were havin' racial problems. On the first night, we had a hundred high school students. When they came in the door, we had "Dixie" playin'. These kids were just thrilled to death. I begin to hold weekly meetin's with 'em, teachin' the principles of the Klan. At that time, I believed Martin Luther King had Communist connections. I began to teach that Andy Young[1] was affiliated with the Communist party.

I had a call one night from one of our kids. He was about twelve. He said: "I just been robbed downtown by two niggers." I'd had a couple of drinks and that really teed me off. I go downtown and couldn't find the kid. I got worried. I saw two young black people. I had the .32 revolver with me. I said: "Nigger, you seen a little young white boy up here? I just got a call from him and was told that some niggers robbed him of fifteen cents." I pulled my pistol out and put it right at his head. I said: "I've always wanted to kill a nigger and I think I'll make you the first one." I nearly scared the kid to death, and he struck off.

This was the time when the civil rights movement was really beginnin' to peak. The blacks were beginnin' to demonstrate and picket downtown stores. I never will forget some black lady I hated with a purple passion. Ann Atwater. Every time I'd go downtown, she'd be leadin' a boycott. How I hated — pardon the expression, I don't use it much now — how I just hated that black nigger. (Laughs.) Big, fat, heavy woman. She'd pull about eight demonstrations, and first thing you know they had two, three blacks at the checkout counter. Her and I have had some pretty close confrontations.

I felt very big, yeah. (Laughs.) We're more or less a secret organization. We didn't want anybody to know who we were, and I began to do some thinkin'. What am I hidin' for? I've never been convicted of anything in my life. I don't have any court record. What am I, C. P.

[1]*Andy Young:* Andrew Jackson Young, Jr. (b. 1932), prominent Black leader and politician. Young was a friend and adviser of Martin Luther King, Jr., and served as President Jimmy Carter's ambassador to the United Nations. In the 1980s, he was twice elected mayor of Atlanta.

Ellis, as a citizen and a member of the United Klansmen of America? Why can't I go the city council meeting and say: "This is the way we feel about the matter? We don't want you to purchase mobile units to set in our schoolyards. We don't want niggers in our schools."

We began to come out in the open. We would go to the meetings, and the blacks would be there and we'd be there. It was a confrontation every time. I didn't hold back anything. We began to make some inroads with the city councilmen and county commissioners. They began to call us friend. Call us at night on the telephone: "C. P., glad you came to that meeting last night." They didn't want integration either, but they did it secretively, in order to get elected. They couldn't stand up openly and say it, but they were glad somebody was sayin' it. We visited some of the city leaders in their home and talk to 'em privately. It wasn't long before councilmen would call me up: "The blacks are comin' up tonight and makin' outrageous demands. How about some of you people showin' up and have a little balance?" I'd get on the telephone. "The niggers is comin' to the council meeting tonight. Persons in the city's called me and asked us to be there."

We'd load up our cars and we'd fill up half the council chambers, and the blacks the other half. During these times, I carried weapons to the meetings, outside my belt. We'd go there armed. We would wind up just hollerin' and fussin' at each other. What happened? As a result of our fightin' one another, the city council still had their way. They didn't want to give up control to the blacks nor the Klan. They were usin' us.

I began to realize this later down the road. One day I was walkin' downtown and a certain city council member saw me comin'. I expected him to shake my hand because he was talkin' to me at night on the telephone. I had been in his home and visited with him. He crossed the street. Oh shit, I began to think, somethin's wrong here. Most of 'em are merchants or maybe an attorney, an insurance agent, people like that. As long as they kept low-income whites and low-income blacks fightin', they're gonna maintain control.

I began to get that feeling after I was ignored in public. I thought: Bullshit, you're not gonna use me any more. That's when I began to do some real serious thinkin'.

The same thing is happening in this country today. People are being used by those in control, those who have all the wealth. I'm not espousing communism. We got the greatest system of government in the world. But those who have it simply don't want those who don't have it to have any part of it. Black and white. When it comes to money, the green, the other colors make no difference. (Laughs.)

I spent a lot of sleepless nights. I still didn't like blacks. I didn't want to associate with 'em. Blacks, Jews, or Catholics. My father said: "Don't have anything to do with 'em." I didn't until I met a black person and talked with him, eyeball to eyeball, and met a Jewish person and talked to him, eyeball to eyeball. I found out they're people just like me. They cried, they cussed, they prayed, they had desires. Just like myself. Thank God, I got to the point where I can look past labels. But at that time, my mind was closed.

I remember one Monday night Klan meeting. I said something was wrong. Our city fathers were using us. And I didn't like to be used. The reactions of the others was not too pleasant: "Let's just keep fightin' them niggers."

I'd go home at night and I'd have to wrestle with myself. I'd look at a black person walkin' down the street, and the guy'd have ragged shoes or his clothes would be worn. That began to do somethin' to me inside. I went through this for about six months. I felt I just had to get out of the Klan. But I wouldn't get out.

Then something happened. The state AFL–CIO[2] received a grant from the Department of HEW,[3] a $78,000 grant: how to solve racial problems in the school system. I got a telephone call from the president of the state AFL–CIO. "We'd like to get some people together from all walks of life." I said: "All walks of life? Who you talkin' about?" He said: "Blacks, whites, liberals, conservatives, Klansmen, NAACP[4] people."

I said: "No way am I comin' with all those niggers. I'm not gonna be associated with those type of people." A White Citizens Council guy said: "Let's go up there and see what's goin' on. It's tax money bein' spent." I walk in the door, and there was a large number of blacks and white liberals. I knew most of 'em by face 'cause I seen 'em demonstratin' around town. Ann Atwater was there. (Laughs.) I just forced myself to go in and sit down.

The meeting was moderated by a great big black guy who was   35
bushy-headed. (Laughs.) That turned me off. He acted very nice. He said: "I want you all to feel free to say anything you want to say." Some of the blacks stand up and say it's white racism. I took all I could take. I asked for the floor and I cut loose. I said: "No, sir, it's black racism. If we didn't have niggers in the schools, we wouldn't have the problems we got today."

I will never forget. Howard Clements, a black guy, stood up. He said: "I'm certainly glad C. P. Ellis come because he's the most honest man here tonight." I said: "What's that nigger tryin' to do?" (Laughs.) At the end of that meeting, some blacks tried to come up shake my hand, but I wouldn't do it. I walked off.

[2]*AFL–CIO:* American Federation of Labor and Congress of Industrial Organizations — a huge federation of independent labor unions in the United States, Canada, Mexico, Panama, and elsewhere.

[3]*HEW:* Health, Education, and Welfare — at the time, a department of the federal government.

[4]*NAACP:* National Association for the Advancement of Colored People.

Second night, same group was there. I felt a little more easy because I got some things off my chest. The third night, after they elected all the committees, they want to elect a chairman. Howard Clements stood up and said: "I suggest we elect two co-chairpersons." Joe Beckton, executive director of the Human Relations Commission, just as black as he can be, he nominated me. There was a reaction from some blacks. Nooo. And, of all things, they nominated Ann Atwater, that big old fat black gal that I had just hated with a purple passion, as co-chairman. I thought to myself: Hey, ain't no way I can work with that gal. Finally, I agreed to accept it, 'cause at this point, I was tired of fightin', either for survival or against black people or against Jews or against Catholics.

A Klansman and a militant black woman, co-chairmen of the school committee. It was impossible. How could I work with her? But after about two or three days, it was in our hands. We had to make it a success. This give me another sense of belongin', a sense of pride. This helped this inferiority feelin' I had. A man who has stood up publicly and said he despised black people, all of a sudden he was willin' to work with 'em. Here's a chance for a low-income white man to be somethin'. In spite of all my hatred for blacks and Jews and liberals, I accepted the job. Her and I began to reluctantly work together. (Laughs.) She had as many problems workin' with me as I had workin' with her.

One night, I called her: "Ann, you and I should have a lot of differences and we got ' em now. But there's somethin' laid out here before us, and if it's gonna be a success, you and I are gonna have to make it one. Can we lay aside some of these feelin's?" She said: "I'm willing if you are." I said: "Let's do it."

My old friends would call me at night: "C. P., what the hell is 40 wrong with you? You're sellin' out the white race." This begin to make me have guilt feelin's. Am I doin' right? Am I doin' wrong? Here I am all of a sudden makin' an about-face and tryin' to deal with my feelin's, my heart. My mind was beginnin' to open up. I was beginnin' to see what was right and what was wrong. I don't want the kids to fight forever.

We were gonna go ten nights. By this time, I had went to work at Duke University, in maintenance. Makin' very little money. Terry Sanford give me this ten days off with pay. He was president of Duke at the time. He knew I was a Klansman and realized the importance of blacks and whites getting along.

I said: "If we're gonna make this thing a success, I've got to get to my kind of people." The low-income whites. We walked the streets of Durham, and we knocked on doors and invited people. Ann was goin' into the black community. They just wasn't respondin' to us when we made these house calls. Some of 'em were cussin' us out. "You're sellin' us out, Ellis, get out of my door. I don't want to talk to you." Ann was gettin' the same response from blacks. "What are you doin' messin' with that Klansman?"

One day, Ann and I went back to the school and we sat down. We began to talk and just reflect. Ann said: "My daughter came home cryin' every day. She said her teacher was makin' fun of me in front of the other kids." I said: "Boy, the same thing happened to my kid. White liberal teacher was makin' fun of Tim Ellis's father, the Klansman. In front of other peoples. He came home cryin'." At this point — (he pauses, swallows hard, stifles a sob) — I begin to see, here we are, two people from the far ends of the fence, havin' identical problems, except hers bein' black and me bein' white. From that moment on, I tell ya, that gal and I worked together good. I begin to love the girl, really. (He weeps.)

The amazing thing about it, her and I, up to that point, had cussed each other, bawled each other, we hated each other. Up to that point, we didn't know each other. We didn't know we had things in common.

We worked at it, with the people who came to these meetings. They 45
talked about racism, sex education, about teachers not bein' qualified. After seven, eight nights of real intense discussion, these people, who'd never talked to each other before, all of a sudden came up with resolutions. It was really somethin', you had to be there to get the tone and feelin' of it.

At that point, I didn't like integration, but the law says you do this and I've got to do what the law says, okay? We said: "Let's take these resolutions to the school board." The most disheartening thing I've ever faced was the school system refused to implement any one of these resolutions. These were recommendations from the people who pay taxes and pay their salaries. (Laughs.)

I thought they were good answers. Some of 'em I didn't agree with, but I been in this thing from the beginning, and whatever comes of it, I'm gonna support it. Okay, since the school board refused, I decided I'd just run for the school board.

I spent eighty-five dollars on the campaign. The guy runnin' against me spent several thousand. I really had nobody on my side. The Klan turned against me. The low-income whites turned against me. The liberals didn't particularly like me. The blacks were suspicious of me. The blacks wanted to support me, but they couldn't muster up enough to support a Klansman on the school board. (Laughs.) But I made up my mind that what I was doin' was right, and I was gonna do it regardless what anybody said.

It bothered me when people would call and worry my wife. She's always supported me in anything I wanted to do. She was changing, and my boys were too. I got some of my youth corps kids involved. They still followed me.

I was invited to the Democratic women's social hour as a candidate. 50
Didn't have but one suit to my name. Had it six, seven, eight years. I
had it cleaned, put on the best shirt I had and a tie. Here were all this
high-class wealthy candidates shakin' hands. I walked up to the mayor
and stuck out my hand. He give me that handshake with that rag type
of hand. He said: "C. P., I'm glad to see you." But I could tell by his
handshake he was lyin' to me. This was botherin' me. I know I'm a low-
income person. I know I'm not wealthy. I know they were sayin':
"What's this little ol' dude runnin' for school board?" Yet they had to
smile and make like they're glad to see me. I begin to spot some black
people in that room. I automatically went to 'em and that was a firm
handshake. They said: "I'm glad to see you, C. P." I knew they meant
it — you can tell about a handshake.

Every place I appeared, I said I will listen to the voice of the people.
I will not make a major decision until I first contacted all the organiza-
tions in the city. I got 4,640 votes. The guy beat me by two thousand.
Not bad for eighty-five bucks and no constituency.

The whole world was openin' up, and I was learnin' new truths
that I had never learned before. I was beginnin' to look at a black
person, shake hands with him, and see him as a human bein'. I hadn't
got rid of all this stuff. I've still got a little bit of it. But somethin' was
happenin' to me.

It was almost like bein' born again. It was a new life. I didn't have
these sleepless nights I used to have when I was active in the Klan and
slippin' around at night. I could sleep at night and feel good about it. I'd
rather live now than at any other time in history. It's a challenge.

Back at Duke, doin' maintenance, I'd pick up my tools, fix the
commode, unstop the drains. But this got in my blood. Things weren't
right in this country, and what we done in Durham needs to be told. I
was so miserable at Duke, I could hardly stand it. I'd go to work every
morning just hatin' to go.

My whole life had changed. I got an eighth-grade education, and I 55
wanted to complete high school. Went to high school in the afternoons
on a program called PEP — Past Employment Progress. I was about the
only white in class, and the oldest. I begin to read about biology. I'd
take my books home at night, 'cause I was determined to get through.
Sure enough, I graduated. I got the diploma at home.

I come to work one mornin' and some guy says: "We need a union."
At this time I wasn't pro-union. My daddy was anti-labor, too. We're
not gettin' paid much, we're havin' to work seven days in a row. We're
all starvin' to death. The next day, I meet the international representative of the Operating Engineers. He give me authorization cards. "Get
these cards out and we'll have an election." There was eighty-eight for
the union and seventeen no's. I was elected chief steward for the union.

Shortly after, a union man come down from Charlotte and says we need a full-time rep. We've got only two hundred people at the two plants here. It's just barely enough money comin' in to pay your salary. You'll have to get out and organize more people. I didn't know nothin' about organizin' unions, but I knew how to organize people, stir people up. (Laughs.) That's how I got to be business agent for the union.

When I began to organize, I began to see far deeper. I began to see people again bein' used. Blacks against whites. I say this without any hesitancy: management is vicious. There's two things they want to keep: all the money and all the say-so. They don't want these poor workin' folks to have none of that. I begin to see management fightin' me with everything they had. Hire anti-union law firms, badmouth unions. The people were makin' a dollar ninety-five an hour, barely able to get through weekends. I worked as a business rep for five years and was seein' all this.

Last year, I ran for business manager of the union. He's elected by the workers. The guy that ran against me was black, and our membership is seventy-five percent black. I thought: Claiborne, there's no way you can beat that black guy. People know your background. Even though you've made tremendous strides, those black people are not gonna vote for you. You know how much I beat him? Four to one. (Laughs).

The company used my past against me. They put out letters with a picture of a robe and a cap: would you vote for a Klansman? They wouldn't deal with the issues. I immediately called for a mass meeting. I met with the ladies at an electric component plant. I said: "Okay, this is Claiborne Ellis. This is where I come from. I want you to know right now, you black ladies here, I was at one time a member of the Klan. I want you to know, because they'll tell you about it."

I invited some of my old black friends. I said: "Brother Joe, Brother Howard, be honest now and tell these people how you feel about me." They done it. (Laughs.) Howard Clements kidded me a little bit. He said: "I don't know what I'm doin' here, supportin' an ex-Klansman." (Laughs.) He said: "I know what C. P. Ellis come from. I knew him when he was. I knew him as he grew, and growed with him. I'm tellin' you now: Follow, follow this Klansman." (He pauses, swallows hard.) "Any questions?" "No," the black ladies said. "Let's get on with the meeting, we need Ellis." (He laughs and weeps.) Boy, black people sayin' that about me. I won one thirty-four to forty-one. Four to one.

It makes you feel good to go into a plant and butt heads with professional union busters. You see black people and white people join hands to defeat the racist issues they use against people. They're tryin' the same things with the Klan. It's still happenin' today. Can you imagine a guy who's got an adult high school diploma runnin' into professional college graduates who are union busters? I gotta compete with 'em. I work seven days a week, nights and on Saturday and Sunday. The salary's not that great, and if I didn't care, I'd quit. But I care and I can't quit. I got a taste of it. (Laughs.)

I tell people there's a tremendous possibility in this country to stop wars, the battles, the struggles, the fights between people. People say: "That's an impossible dream. You sound like Martin Luther King." An ex-Klansman who sounds like Martin Luther King. (Laughs.) I don't think it's an impossible dream. It's happened in my life. It's happened in other people's lives in America.

I don't know what's ahead of me. I have no desire to be a big union official. I want to be right out here in the field with the workers. I want to walk through their factory and shake hands with that man whose hands are dirty. I'm gonna do all that one little ol' man can do. I'm fifty-two years old, and I ain't got many years left, but I want to make the best of 'em.

When the news came over the radio that Martin Luther King was 65 assassinated, I got on the telephone and begin to call other Klansmen. We just had a real party at the service station. Really rejoicin' 'cause that son of a bitch was dead. Our troubles are over with. They say the older you get, the harder it is for you to change. That's not necessarily true. Since I changed, I've set down and listened to tapes of Martin Luther King. I listen to it and tears come to my eyes 'cause I know what he's sayin' now. I know what's happenin'.

POSTSCRIPT: *The phone rings. A conversation.*

"This was a black guy who's director of Operation Breakthrough in Durham. I had called his office. I'm interested in employin' some young black person who's interested in learnin' the labor movement. I want somebody who's never had an opportunity, just like myself. Just so he can read and write, that's all."

Engaging the Text

1. How does Ellis battle the racism he finds in himself? What gives him the motivation and strength to change? What specific changes does he undergo, and how successful is he in abandoning racist attitudes?

2. Would Ellis say that economic class is more important than race in determining job placement and occupational mobility? Find specific passages that reveal Ellis's beliefs about the connections between economic class, race, and success in American society. What do you believe?

3. How well does Ellis seem to understand himself, his feelings, his motives? Give evidence for your assertions.

4. What is Terkel's role in this selection? Is he unconsciously helping to rationalize or justify the actions of the Ku Klux Klan?

Exploring Connections

5. How well does the theory of racial formation spelled out by Michael Omi and Howard Winant (p. 283) account for Ellis's racism or his reform? Explain how you think those authors would interpret Ellis's history.

6. To what extent does Ellis's experience illustrate Gordon W. Allport's concept of in-groups and out-groups (p. 292)? Of group mobility? Find specific examples that support your assertions.

7. Look back to Martin Luther King, Jr.'s analysis of the economic basis of racism (p. 319), particularly the connection he finds between racism and social class. How might King explain Ellis's racism and his eventual change of heart?

Extending the Critical Context

8. Find a definition of "displacement," a psychological defense mechanism, in a psychology textbook. To what extent is Ellis's decision to join the Ku Klux Klan an example of displacement?

9. Consulting the essays by Susan Griffin (p. 175) and Carol Gilligan (p. 233), critique Ellis's life and ideas from a feminist perspective.

10. Several movies in the past decade portrayed white characters who discovered and began to fight against racism in their own societies. Watch *The Long Walk Home* or *A Dry White Season* and compare the transformation the central character undergoes with C. P. Ellis's. What motives lead them to challenge the racism of their in-group? Are there transformations convincing? Do these films, and Ellis's story, offer a credible way of overcoming misunderstanding and hatred between races? Given the explanations Omi and Winant, Allport, and King offer for the persistence of racism, do you think such "solutions" would be workable on a large scale? Why or why not?

I'm Black, You're White, Who's Innocent?

SHELBY STEELE

This essay comes from one of the most controversial American books of 1990 — The Content of Our Character: A New Vision of Race in America. Shelby Steele (b. 1946) believes that Black Americans have failed to seize opportunities which would lead to social equality; he is also an outspoken critic of affirmative action, arguing that instead of promoting equality it locks its recipients into second-class status. Angry critics accuse him of underestimating the power of racism, of blaming

*ictims for their predicament, of being a traitor to his race. Steele's
collection of essays has garnered not only publicity but also awards,
including a National Book Critics Circle Award. Steele teaches English
at San Jose State University.*

It is a warm, windless California evening, and the dying light that
covers the redbrick patio is tinted pale orange by the day's smog. Eight
of us, not close friends, sit in lawn chairs sipping chardonnay. A black
engineer and I (we had never met before) integrate the group. A psychologist is also among us, and her presence encourages a surprising
openness. But not until well after the lovely twilight dinner has been
served, when the sky has turned to deep black and the drinks have long
since changed to scotch, does the subject of race spring awkwardly upon
us. Out of nowhere the engineer announces, with a coloring of accusation in his voice, that it bothers him to send his daughter to a school
where she is one of only three black children. "I didn't realize my
ambition to get ahead would pull me into a world where my daughter
would lose touch with her blackness," he says.

Over the course of the evening we have talked about money, past
and present addictions, child abuse, even politics. Intimacies have been
revealed, fears named. But this subject, race, sinks us into one of those
shaming silences where eye contact terrorizes. Our host looks for something in the bottom of his glass. Two women stare into the black sky as if
to locate the Big Dipper and point it out to us. Finally, the psychologist
seems to gather herself for a challenge, but it is too late. "Oh, I'm sure
she'll be just fine," says our hostess, rising from her chair. When she
excuses herself to get the coffee, the psychologist and two sky gazers
offer to help.

With four of us now gone, I am surprised to see the engineer still
silently holding his ground. There is a willfulness in his eyes, an inner
pride. He knows he has said something awkward, but he is determined
not to give a damn. His unwavering eyes intimidate even me. At last the
host's head snaps erect. He has an idea. "The hell with coffee," he says.
"How about some of the smoothest brandy you've ever tasted?" An idea
made exciting by the escape it offers. Gratefully, we follow him back
into the house, quickly drink his brandy, and say our good-byes.

An autopsy of this party might read: death induced by an abrupt
and lethal injection of the American race issue. An accurate if superficial assessment. Since it has been my fate to live a rather integrated life,
I have often witnessed sudden deaths like this. The threat of them, if not
the reality, is a part of the texture of integration. In the late 1960s, when
I was just out of college, I took a delinquent's delight in playing the
engineer's role, and actually developed a small reputation for playing it

well. Those were the days of flagellatory white guilt: it was such great fun to pinion some professor or housewife or, best of all, a large group of remorseful whites, with the knowledge of both their racism and their denial of it. The adolescent impulse to sneer at convention, to startle the middle-aged with doubt, could be indulged under the guise of racial indignation. And how could I lose? My victims — earnest liberals for the most part — could no more crawl out from under my accusations than Joseph K. in Kafka's *Trial*[1] could escape the amorphous charges brought against him. At this odd moment in history the world was aligned to facilitate my immaturity.

About a year of this was enough: the guilt that follows most cheap thrills caught up to me, and I put myself in check. But the impulse to do it faded more slowly. It was one of those petty talents that is tied to vanity, and when there were ebbs in my self-esteem the impulse to use it would come alive again. In integrated situations I can still feel the faint itch. But then there are many youthful impulses that still itch and now, just inside the door of midlife, this one is least precious to me.

In the literature classes I teach I often see how the presence of whites all but seduces some black students into provocation. When we come to a novel by a black writer, say Toni Morrison, the white students can easily discuss the human motivations of the black characters. But, inevitably, a black student, as if by reflex, will begin to set in relief the various racial problems that are the background of these characters' lives. This student's tone will carry a reprimand: the class is afraid to confront the reality of racism. Classes cannot be allowed to die like dinner parties, however. My latest strategy is to thank that student for his or her moral vigilance and then appoint the young man or woman as the class's official racism monitor. But even if I get a laugh — I usually do, but sometimes the student is particularly indignant, and it gets uncomfortable — the strategy never quite works. Our racial division is suddenly drawn in neon. Overcaution spreads like spilled paint. And, in fact, the black student who started it all does become a kind of monitor. The very presence of this student imposes a new accountability on the class.

I think those who provoke this sort of awkwardness are operating out of a black identity that obliges them to badger white people about race almost on principle. Content hardly matters. (For example, it made little sense for the engineer to expect white people to anguish terribly much over his decision to send his daughter to school with *white* children.) Race indeed remains a source of white shame; the goal of these provocations is to put whites, no matter how indirectly, in touch

---

[1]*Kafka's* Trial: Austrian writer Franz Kafka (1883–1924) is famous for his dreamlike and ominous stories. In his novel *The Trial*, the character known only as Joseph K. battles an intricate legal and police system that never specifies his alleged crime.

with this collective guilt. In other words, these provocations I speak of are *power* moves, little shows of power that try to freeze the "enemy" in self-consciousness. They gratify and inflate the provocateur. They are the underdog's bite. And whites, far more secure in their power, respond with self-contained and tolerant silence that is itself a show of power. What greater power than that of nonresponse, the power to let a small enemy sizzle in his own juices, to even feel a little sad at his frustration just as one is also complimented by it. Black anger always, in a way, flatters white power. In America, to know that one is not black is to feel an extra grace, a little boost of impunity.

I think the real trouble between the races in America is that the races are not just races but competing power groups — a fact that is easily minimized, perhaps because it is so obvious. What is not so obvious is that this is true quite apart from the issue of class. Even the well-situated middle-class (or wealthy) black is never completely immune to that peculiar contest of power that his skin color subjects him to. Race is a separate reality in American society, an entity that carries its own potential for power, a mark of fate that class can soften considerably but not eradicate.

The distinction of race has always been used in American life to sanction each race's pursuit of power in relation to the other. The allure of race as a human delineation is the very shallowness of the delineation it makes. Onto this shallowness — mere skin and hair — men can project a false depth, a system of dismal attributions, a series of malevolent or ignoble stereotypes that skin and hair lack the substance to contradict. These dark projections then rationalize the pursuit of power. Your difference from me makes you bad, and your badness justifies, even demands, my pursuit of power over you — the oldest formula for aggression known to man. Whenever much importance is given to race, power is the primary motive.

But the human animal almost never pursues power without first convincing himself that he is *entitled* to it. And this feeling of entitlement has its own precondition: to be entitled one must first believe in one's innocence, at least in the area where one wishes to be entitled. By innocence I mean a feeling of essential goodness in relation to others and, therefore, superiority to others. Our innocence always inflates us and deflates those we seek power over. Once inflated we are entitled; we are in fact licensed to go after the power our innocence tells us we deserve. In this sense, *innocence is power*. Of course, innocence need not be genuine or real in any objective sense, as the Nazis demonstrated not long ago. Its only test is whether or not we can convince ourselves of it.

I think the racial struggle in America has always been primarily a struggle for innocence. White racism from the beginning has been a claim of white innocence and therefore of white entitlement to subjugate blacks. And in the sixties, as went innocence so went power. Blacks used the innocence that grew out of their long subjugation to seize more power, while whites lost some of their innocence and so lost a degree of power over blacks. Both races instinctively understand that to lose innocence is to lose power (in relation to each other). To be innocent someone else must be guilty, a natural law that leads the races to forge their innocence on each other's backs. The inferiority of the black always makes the white man superior; the evil might of whites makes blacks good. This pattern means that both races have a hidden investment in racism and racial disharmony despite their good intentions to the contrary. Power defines their relations, and power requires innocence, which, in turn, requires racism and racial division.

I believe it was his hidden investment that the engineer was protecting when he made his remark — the white "evil" he saw in a white school "depriving" his daughter of her black heritage confirmed his innocence. Only the logic of power explained his emphasis — he bent reality to show that he was once again a victim of the white world and, as a victim, innocent. His determined eyes insisted on this. And the whites, in their silence, no doubt protected their innocence by seeing him as an ungracious troublemaker, his bad behavior underscoring their goodness. What none of us saw was the underlying game of power and innocence we were trapped in, or how much we needed a racial impasse to play that game.

When I was a boy of about twelve, a white friend of mine told me one day that his uncle, who would be arriving the next day for a visit, was a racist. Excited by the prospect of seeing such a man, I spent the following afternoon hanging around the alley behind my friend's house, watching from a distance as this uncle worked on the engine of his Buick. Yes, here was evil and I was compelled to look upon it. And I saw evil in the sharp angle of his elbow as he pumped his wrench to tighten nuts. I saw it in the blade-sharp crease of his chinos, in the pack of Lucky Strikes that threatened to slip from his shirt pocket as he bent, and in the way his concentration seemed to shut out the human world. He worked neatly and efficiently, wiping his hands constantly, and I decided that evil worked like this.

I felt a compulsion to have this man look upon me so that I could see evil — so that I could see the face of it. But when he noticed me standing beside his toolbox, he said only, "If you're looking for Bobby, I think he went up to the school to play baseball." He smiled nicely and went back to work. I was stunned for a moment, but then I realized that evil could be sly as well, could smile when it wanted to trick you.

Need, especially hidden need, puts a strong pressure on perception, 15 and my need to have this man embody white evil was stronger than any contravening evidence. As a black person you always hear about racists but rarely meet any who will let you know them as such. And I needed to incarnate this odious category of humanity, those people who hated Martin Luther King, Jr., and thought blacks should "go slow" or not at all. So, in my mental dictionary, behind the term "white racist," I inserted this man's likeness. I would think of him and say to myself, "There is no reason for him to hate black people. Only evil explains unmotivated hatred." And this thought soothed me; I felt innocent. If I hated white people, which I did not, at least I had a reason. His evil commanded me to assert in the world the goodness he made me confident of in myself.

In looking at this man I was *seeing for innocence* — a form of seeing that has more to do with one's hidden need for innocence (and power) than with the person or group one is looking at. It is quite possible, for example, that the man I saw that day was not a racist. He did absolutely nothing in my presence to indicate that he was. I invested an entire afternoon in seeing not the man but in seeing my innocence through the man. *Seeing for innocence* is, in this way, the essence of racism — the use of others as a means to our own goodness and superiority.

The loss of innocence has always to do with guilt, Kierkegaard[2] tells us, and it has never been easy for whites to avoid guilt where blacks are concerned. For whites, *seeing for innocence* means seeing themselves and blacks in ways that minimize white guilt. Often this amounts to a kind of white revisionism,[3] as when President Reagan declared himself "color-blind" in matters of race. The President, like many of us, may have aspired to racial color blindness, but few would grant that he ever reached this sublimely guiltless state. His statement clearly revised reality, moved it forward into some heretofore unknown America where all racial determinism would have vanished. I do not think that Ronald Reagan was a racist, as that term is commonly used, but neither do I think that he was capable of seeing color without making attributions, some of which may have been negative — nor am I, or anyone else I've ever met.

So why make such a statement? I think Reagan's claim of color blindness with regard to race was really a claim of racial innocence and guiltlessness — the preconditions for entitlement and power. This was the claim that grounded Reagan's campaign against special entitlement programs — affirmative action, racial quotas, and so on — that black power had won in the sixties. Color blindness was a strategic assumption of innocence that licensed Reagan's use of government power against black power. . . .

[2]*Kierkegaard:* Danish philosopher and religious thinker Søren Kierkegaard (1813–1855).

[3]*revisionism:* the reinterpretation or revising of reality to suit one's current purposes.

Black Americans have had to find a way to handle white society's presumption of racial innocence whenever they have sought to enter the American mainstream. Louis Armstrong's[4] exaggerated smile honored the presumed innocence of white society — *I will not bring you your racial guilt if you will let me play my music.* Ralph Ellison[5] calls this "masking"; I call it bargaining. But whatever it's called, it points to the power of white society to enforce its innocence. I believe this power is greatly diminished today. Society has reformed and transformed — Miles Davis[6] never smiles. Nevertheless, this power has not faded altogether and blacks must still contend with it.

Historically, blacks have handled white society's presumption of innocence in two ways: they have bargained with it, granting white society its innocence in exchange for entry into the mainstream, or they have challenged it, holding that innocence hostage until their demand for entry (or other concessions) was met. A bargainer says, *I already believe you are innocent (good, fair-minded) and have faith that you will prove it.* A challenger says, *If you are innocent, then prove it.* Bargainers *give* in hope of receiving; challengers *withhold* until they receive. Of course, there is risk in both approaches, but in each case the black is negotiating his own self-interest against the presumed racial innocence of the larger society.

Clearly, the most visible black bargainer on the American scene today is Bill Cosby. His television show has been a perfect formula for black bargaining in the eighties. The remarkable Huxtable family — with its doctor/lawyer parent combination, its drug-free, college-bound children, and its wise yet youthful grandparents — is a blackface version of the American dream. Cosby is a subscriber to the American identity, and his subscription confirms his belief in its fair-mindedness. His vast audience knows this, knows that Cosby will never assault their innocence with racial guilt. Racial controversy is all but banished from the show. The Huxtable family never discusses affirmative action.

The bargain Cosby offers his white viewers — *I will confirm your racial innocence if you accept me* — is a good deal for all concerned. Not only does it allow whites to enjoy Cosby's humor with no loss of innocence, but it actually enhances their innocence by implying that race is not the serious problem for blacks that it once was. If anything, the success of this handsome, affluent black family points to the fair-mindedness of whites who, out of their essential goodness, changed

[20]

---

[4]*Louis Armstrong:* American jazz trumpet virtuoso and singer (1900–1971), nicknamed Satchmo.

[5]*Ralph Ellison:* American novelist (b. 1914), best known for *Invisible Man*, the account of a nameless black youth coming of age in a hostile society.

[6]*Miles Davis:* jazz musician and trumpeter (1926–1991).

society so that black families like the Huxtables could succeed. Whites can watch *The Cosby Show* and feel complimented on a job well done.

The power that black bargainers wield is the power of absolution. On Thursday nights, Cosby, like a priest, absolves his white viewers, forgives and forgets the sins of the past. And for this he is rewarded with an almost sacrosanct[7] status. Cosby benefits from what might be called the gratitude factor. His continued number-one rating may have something to do with the (white) public's gratitude at being offered a commodity so rare in our time; he tells his white viewers each week that they are okay, and that this black man is not going to challenge them.

When a black bargains, he may invoke the gratitude factor and find himself cherished beyond the measure of his achievement; when he challenges, he may draw the dark projections of whites and become a source of irritation to them. If he moves back and forth between these two options, as I think many blacks do today, he will likely baffle whites. It is difficult for whites either to accept or reject such blacks. It seems to me that Jesse Jackson is such a figure — many whites see Jackson as a challenger by instinct and a bargainer by political ambition. They are uneasy with him, more than a little suspicious. His powerful speech at the 1984 Democratic Convention was a masterpiece of bargaining. In it he offered a King-like[8] vision of what America could be, a vision that presupposed Americans had the fair-mindedness to achieve full equality — an offer in hope of a return. A few days after this speech, looking for rest and privacy at a lodge in Big Sur,[9] he and his wife were greeted with standing ovations three times a day when they entered the dining room for meals. So much about Jackson is deeply American — his underdog striving, his irrepressible faith in himself, the daring of his ambition, and even his stubbornness. These qualities point to his underlying faith that Americans can respond to him despite race, and this faith is a compliment to Americans, an offer of innocence.

But Jackson does not always stick to the terms of his bargain as Cosby does on TV. When he hugs Arafat,[10] smokes cigars with Castro,[11] refuses to repudiate Farrakhan,[12] threatens a boycott of major league baseball or, more recently, talks of "corporate barracudas," "pension-fund socialism," and "economic violence," he looks like a challenger in bargainer's clothing, and his positions on the issues look like familiar

25

[7]*sacrosanct:* sacred.

[8]*King-like:* like that of Martin Luther King, Jr.

[9]*Big Sur:* section of the California coast known for its natural beauty.

[10]*Arafat:* Yasir Arafat (b. 1929), leader of the Palestine Liberation Organization, or PLO.

[11]*Castro:* Fidel Castro (b. 1926), president of Cuba.

[12]*Farrakhan:* Louis Farrakhan (b. 1933) Nation of Islam leader, often accused of making anti-Semitic remarks. Many African American politicians carefully distance themselves from Farrakhan.

protests dressed in white-paper formality. At these times he appears to be revoking the innocence so much else about him seems to offer. The old activist seems to come out of hiding once again to take white innocence hostage until whites prove they deserve to have it. In his candidacy there is a suggestion of protest, a fierce insistence on his *right* to run, that sends whites a message that he may secretly see them as a good bit less than innocent. His dilemma is to appear the bargainer while his campaign itself seems to be a challenge.

There are, of course, other problems that hamper Jackson's bid for the Democratic presidential nomination. He has held no elective office, he is thought too flamboyant and opportunistic by many, there are rather loud whispers of "character" problems. As an individual, he may not be the best test of a black man's chances for winning so high an office. Still, I believe it is the aura of challenge surrounding him that hurts him most. Whether it is right or wrong, fair or unfair, I think no black candidate will have a serious chance at his party's nomination, much less the presidency, until he can convince white Americans that he can be trusted to preserve their sense of racial innocence. Such a candidate will have to use his power of absolution; he will have to flatly forgive and forget. He will have to bargain with white innocence out of genuine belief that it really exists. There can be no faking it. He will have to offer a vision that is passionately raceless, a vision that strongly condemns any form of racial politics. This will require the most courageous kind of leadership, leadership that asks all the people to meet a new standard.

Now the other side of America's racial impasse: how do blacks lay claim to their racial innocence?

The most obvious and unarguable source of black innocence is the victimization that blacks endured for centuries at the hands of a race that insisted on black inferiority as a means to its own innocence and power. Like all victims, what blacks lost in power they gained in innocence — innocence that, in turn, entitled them to pursue power. This was the innocence that fueled the civil rights movement of the sixties and that gave blacks their first real power in American life — victimization metamorphosed into power via innocence. But this formula carries a drawback that I believe is virtually as devastating to blacks today as victimization once was. It is a formula that binds the victim to his victimization by linking his power to his status as a victim. And this, I'm convinced, is the tragedy of black power in America today. It is primarily a victim's power, grounded too deeply in the entitlement derived from past injustice and in the innocence that Western/Christian tradition has always associated with poverty.

Whatever gains this power brings in the short run through political action, it undermines in the long run. Social victims may be collectively entitled, but they are all too often individually demoralized. Since the social victim has been oppressed by society, he comes to feel that his individual life will be improved more by changes in society than by his own initiative. Without realizing it, he makes society rather than himself the agent of change. The power he finds in his victimization may lead him to collective action against society, but it also encourages passivity within the sphere of his personal life.

Not long ago, I saw a television documentary that examined life in   30
Detroit's inner city on the twentieth anniversary of the riots there in which forty-three people were killed. A comparison of the inner city then and now showed a decline in the quality of life. Residents feel less safe, drug trafficking is far worse, crimes by blacks against blacks are more frequent, housing remains substandard, and the teenage pregnancy rate has skyrocketed. Twenty years of decline and demoralization, even as opportunities for blacks to better themselves have increased. This paradox is not peculiar to Detroit. By many measures, the majority of blacks — those not yet in the middle class — are further behind whites today than before the victories of the civil rights movement. But there is a reluctance among blacks to examine this paradox, I think, because it suggests that racial victimization is not our real problem. If conditions have worsened for most of us as racism had receded, then much of the problem must be of our own making. To admit this fully would cause us to lose the innocence we derive from our victimization. And we would jeopardize the entitlement we've always had to challenge society. We are in the odd and self-defeating position in which taking responsibility for bettering ourselves feels like a surrender to white power.

So we have a hidden investment in victimization and poverty. These distressing conditions have been the source of our own real power, and there is an unconscious sort of gravitation toward them, a complaining celebration of them. One sees evidence of this in the near happiness with which certain black leaders recount the horror of Howard Beach,[13] Bensonhurst,[14] and other recent instances of racial tension. As one is saddened by these tragic events, one is also repelled at the way some black leaders — agitated to near hysteria by the scent of victim power inherent in them — leap forward to exploit them as evidence of black innocence and white guilt. It is as though they sense the decline of black victimization as a loss of standing and dive into the middle of these incidents as if they were reservoirs of pure black innocence swollen with potential power.

[13]*Howard Beach:* scene in Queens, New York, of a December 1986 racial confrontation in which several young African American men were severely beaten and one died.
[14]*Bensonhurst:* location in Brooklyn, New York, where the racially motivated murder of sixteen-year-old Yusuf Hawkins took place in August 1989.

Seeing for innocence pressures blacks to focus on racism and to neglect the individual initiative that would deliver them from poverty — the only thing that finally delivers *anyone* from poverty. With our eyes on innocence we see racism everywhere and miss opportunity even as we stumble over it. About 70 percent of black students at my university drop out before graduation — a flight from opportunity that racism cannot explain. It is an injustice that whites can see for innocence with more impunity than blacks can. The price whites pay is a certain blindness to themselves. Moreover, for whites seeing for innocence continues to engender the bad faith of a long-disgruntled minority. But the price blacks pay is an ever-escalating poverty that threatens to make the worst off a permanent underclass. Not fair, but real.

Challenging works best for the collective, while bargaining is more the individual's suit. From this point on, the race's advancement will come from the efforts of its individuals. True, some challenging will be necessary for a long time to come. But bargaining is now — today — a way for the black individual to *join* the larger society, to make a place for himself or herself.

"Innocence is ignorance," Kierkegaard says, and if this is so, the claim of innocence amounts to an insistence on ignorance, a refusal to know. In their assertions of innocence both races carve out very functional areas of ignorance for themselves — territories of blindness that license a misguided pursuit of power. Whites gain superiority by not knowing blacks; blacks gain entitlement by not seeing their own responsibility for bettering themselves. The power each race seeks in relation to the other is grounded in a double-edged ignorance of the self as well as of the other.

The original sin that brought us to an impasse at the dinner party I mentioned occurred centuries ago, when it was first decided to exploit racial difference as a means to power. It was a determinism that flowed karmically from this sin that dropped over us like a net that night. What bothered me most was our helplessness. Even the engineer did not know how to go forward. His challenge hadn't worked, and he'd lost the option to bargain. The marriage of race and power depersonalized us, changed us from eight people to six whites and two blacks. The easiest thing was to let silence blanket our situation, our impasse. . . .

What both black and white Americans fear are the sacrifices and risks that true racial harmony demands. This fear is the measure of our racial chasm. And though fear always seeks a thousand justifications, none is ever good enough, and the problems we run from only remain to haunt us. It would be right to suggest courage as an antidote to fear, but the glory of the word might only intimidate us into more fear. I prefer the word effort — relentless effort, moral effort. What I like most about this word are its connotations of everydayness, earnestness, and practical sacrifice. No matter how badly it might have gone for us that warm summer night, we should have talked. We should have made the effort.

Engaging the Text

1. What does Steele mean by "innocence" and by "seeing for innocence"? How does he apply these terms to racial conflict and struggles for power in the United States? How do Blacks and whites claim innocence through racial conflict? What does Steele mean when he says that "innocence is power"?

2. According to Steele, what strategies have African Americans employed to handle "white society's presumption of racial innocence" (para. 19)? How does he account for public reactions to figures like Bill Cosby and Jesse Jackson in terms of these strategies? Are there other possible explanations of their appeal?

3. Steele believes that "bargaining is now — today — a way for the Black individual to *join* the larger society" (para. 33). Do you agree? Is bargaining an available and acceptable alternative for all African Americans?

4. Steele writes that when the issue of race comes up in classes, "overcaution spreads like spilled paint" (para. 6). If you have observed this phenomenon in class or in other circumstances, write a journal entry describing one such incident and analyzing the behavior of the people there.

Exploring Connections

5. Write an imaginary dialogue between the Man and the Kid in George C. Wolfe's "Symbiosis" (p. 42) on Steele's concepts of bargaining and challenging.

6. Review Martin Luther King, Jr.'s, "Racism and the White Backlash" (p. 319). Playing the role of King, write a response to Steele's analysis of racism.

Extending the Critical Context

7. Watch Spike Lee's film *Do the Right Thing* on video. Choose one or two scenes that are most interesting in terms of guilt, innocence and "seeing for innocence." Watch these scenes repeatedly and write a careful analysis of how guilt, innocence, and seeing for innocence operate in the characters' (or filmmaker's) psychology.

8. Find out the graduation rate for African American students at your school. Then interview a faculty member or administrator to get her or his perceptions of why your school does or does not graduate Black students in proportionate numbers. If several students do this assignment, you can begin to analyze prevailing attitudes on campus.

9. At the end of this essay, Steele says, "No matter how badly it might have gone for us . . . we should have talked. We should have made the effort." Working in groups, role-play the conversation that might have occurred that night. How

might you initiate such conversations on your campus? Is talk the only or best solution to the kinds of tensions Steele describes?

Racism and Cross-Racial Hostility
Virginia R. Harris
and Trinity A. Ordoña

Discussions of race in America typically focus on the opposition between a dominant Anglo group and one or more oppressed minorities. This essay, however, looks at prejudice and hostility between minority groups, differentiating this phenomenon — cross-racial hostility —from racism and assessing its psychological and political effects. Virginia R. Harris is an African American essayist, mediator, lecturer, and fiction writer. Trinity A. Ordoña is a Filipino American photographer and community activist. This selection is an excerpt from a longer essay which appeared in a volume, edited by Gloria Anzaldúa, entitled Haciendo Caras: Making Face, Making Soul *(1990).*

The American nation was founded on racism. Compare the rapid emergence and eventual world dominance of the United States with the centuries-long process of national formation in Europe. This dominance was *not* the result of "Yankee ingenuity" and would not have been accomplished without the resources and wealth first created by stolen Native American land and enslaved black labor.

America created a simple system of privilege for whites based on the exploitation and oppression of people of color. This social division along the color line crossed class, nationality, language, and religious barriers. The simple fact of "whiteness"[1] meant the overall life, fortune, and destiny of white people and their white children were qualitatively better than those of people of color. White people were exempt from slavery, land grab, and genocide — the first forms of white privilege. Whites enjoyed a wide latitude of opportunities, personal freedom, and democratic rights protected by the State. Even though poor American-born and immigrant whites were viciously exploited by rich white

[1]See *The Subjective Side of Politics* by Margo Adair and Sharon Howell for further analysis of what "whiteness" means in the United States. Available from Tools of Change, P.O. Box 14141, San Francisco, CA 94114, (415) 861-6838. [Authors' note]

people, they were not on the bottom. The bottom was reserved for Indians, blacks, and other people of color.

All people of color face the oppression of racism. The commonality could serve as a powerful unifying bond of solidarity between us. But instead of unifying, we fight one another to stay "one step up" from the bottom of the racial hierarchy. However, we do not *choose* our place in the racial pecking order. We are *placed* in it.

Cross-racial hostility is the stepchild of racism. The dynamics of cross-racial hostility are created by the imbalances in treatment between racially oppressed people based on exaggerated differences among us. Each group has its own unique history of discrimination, racial violence, and institutionalized prejudice. Historically, each group "served" a particular role in meeting the socioeconomic needs of white America. For example, during western expansion in the 1800s, while the debate over free versus slave state raged, thousands of Chinese men were brought in to work the mines and railroads. The Chinese were not slaves but they were not free. The Chinese were also subject to lynching and other forms of violence from whites because of their race. They did not have the legal legacy of slavery and its subsequent Jim Crow laws[2] to overcome. However, they faced severe legal and social restrictions — racist violence, anti-alien hysteria, as well as anti-miscegenation, school segregation, and employment exclusion laws. After working the mines and railroads, Chinese were barred from the trades and all but domestic employment. For the most part, they were left to support their own through family-owned stores, laundries, and restaurants in Chinatown ghettoes. The same, yet not the same. Different, yet not different.

Where differences among white people tend to be evened out by white privilege, differences among people of color are blown out of proportion with personal jealousies and betrayal, encouraged by whites. The difference between the house nigger and the field nigger is a classic example of how differential/preferential treatment split and divided us. Both were slaves for life, but one was treated conspicuously better than the other. For example, "the light-skinned blacks, usually the offspring of white men and black women, were typically given the preferred [*sic*] work inside the master's home, while darker-skinned blacks were relegated to [grueling] field work."[3] There was no guarantee this exemption would continue from one day to the next. The house nigger's situation was always precarious. Their "privileges" and "status" could be taken away for any or no reason. In the daily, ruthless life and death struggle, the desire for preferential treatment often overshadowed feelings of hatred for the master and replaced it with jealous hatred for each other.

[5]

---

[2]*Jim Crow laws:* enacted in the post–Civil War South, these laws mandated racial segregation.

[3]*New York Times*, 23 May 1989, National Edition, A11. [Authors' note]

Slaves were also used to hunt down and punish runaway slaves. Worse yet, some slaves were promised freedom if they betrayed their runaway brothers and sisters. Freedom was an individual privilege whose benefits defy comparison, even though the black person could be sold back into slavery with no legal recourse. If the "benefits" of betrayal did not persuade them, defiant slaves were beaten until the information was forced from them. They were tortured, maimed, and/or killed as examples to all others who might resist.

These practices created deep emotional, spiritual, and ideological chasms among black people. The chasms grew wider and became a way of life for many. The legacy? Colorism. In 1790 free mulattoes in Charleston, South Carolina, formed the Brown Fellowship Society, which restricted membership to the light-skinned. In retaliation, free dark-skinned blacks formed the Free Dark Men of Color, permitting only the darkest to belong. These two groups maintained segregated burial plots for their members in an already segregated cemetery.[4] The legacy continues — color is the basis of a discrimination lawsuit filed by a lighter-skinned black woman against her darker-skinned supervisor, also a black woman. The New York Times ran the story on the front page.[5]

This lawsuit comes from hundreds of years of intraracial conflict and internal strife. We were/are consciously and constantly used against each other. American history offers countless examples. Indian scouts helped the U.S. Cavalry in campaigns against rival Indian tribes. Black soldiers have been part of the ground troops in all the U.S. racist conquests — the Indian wars, the Spanish-American War of 1898, the Vietnam War, the 1985 invasion of Grenada. Legal versus illegal immigrant status continually divides the Latino community. The ongoing struggle at Big Mountain[6] pits Indian against Indian in a bitter dispute over land, resources and sovereignty.

Recent changes in U.S. immigration laws have altered social and economic progress for peoples of color and put us solidly on a collision course. In the 1960s, the government and big business realized a need to invest in the scientific and technical training of a work force to meet the growing demands of a high-tech society.[7] This education could have

---

[4]Walter B. Weare, *Black Business in the South: A Social History of North Carolina Mutual Life Insurance Company* (Urbana: University of Illinois Press, 1973), 9–10. [Authors' note]

[5]*The New York Times*, 23 May 1989, 1. [Authors' note]

[6]*Big Mountain:* area in New Mexico at the center of a Navaho and Hopi dispute over land rights and treaty conditions.

[7]The neglect of U.S. science education is now under sharp criticism. The National Assessment of Educational Progess states: "Alarming numbers of young Americans . . . emerge from the nation's elementary and secondary schools with an inadequate grounding in mathematics, science and technology. . . . At age 17, students' science achievement remains well below that of 1969. . . . [While] the average proficiency of 13 to 17 year old black and Hispanic students remains at least 4 years behind that of their white peers." [Author's note]

affected large numbers of people of color in America who were unskilled, i.e., low-paid garment workers, domestics, and farm workers. Instead, government and big business looked overseas for cheap *skilled* labor.

In 1965, new legislation gave preference to professional and technically skilled immigrants from countries in Asia, Africa, and Latin America. (Ironically, this law was signed two years after the historic March on Washington.) Asian and Latin American immigrants have filled the quotas, most coming from countries tied to U.S. foreign debt and U.S.-dominated multinational corporations. United States–born unskilled workers are unable to compete with the more highly skilled and educated immigrants. Within the Asian community, third and fourth generation Asian Americans, often the first in their families to receive a college education, find themselves competing with immigrants from their home countries for the same few positions. In the meantime, the recent arrivals experience discrimination from Americans based on language, culture, foreign education, and citizenship status. They work for cheap wages, unable to get jobs in their chosen professions or at salaries commensurate to their education, experience, or training.

The classrooms are being filled with Asian children due to the large influx of Asians in California. (Between 1980 and 1995, the Asian population in California will increase from 1.6 million to 3.8 million, or *140%* in 15 years.)[8] At prestigious U.C. Berkeley, the large population of Asian students triggered a reactionary backlash among white students fearful of losing dominance in science, engineering, and computer technology. The administration threatens to close affirmative action opportunities to all Asians while proclaiming Asians the "model minority," pitting Asians against other people of color.[9]

Prejudice toward immigrants is not the exclusive property of whites. People of color have joined the chorus of growing American national chauvinism. In 1986, Proposition 63 — to uphold "English as the official language" and thus eliminate the legal basis for bilingual education and ballots — was supported in California by a margin of three to one. The measure surprisingly won support in cities where people of color were in the majority. In Oakland, where the population is 63% "minority,"[10] the measure was passed by 51%.[11] Most notably, the nationally publicized campaign was led by S. I. Hayakawa,[12] a

[8]*California Population Characteristics* (1988), 46. [Authors' note]

[9]Chinese for Affirmative Action, *1988–89 Annual Report* (San Francisco), 24–31. [Authors' note]

[10]1980 Census Data for Oakland: 46.9% black, 14.8% other, 38.2% white, 1988 Census Data for Oakland: 50.4% black, 15.2% other, 34.5% white. [Authors' note]

[11]"Supplement to the Statement of Vote," *Statement of Vote* (General Elections, Oakland, 4 November 1986), 198. [Authors' note]

[12]S. I. Hayakawa, Editorial, "For: A United People," *San Francisco Chronicle*, 1 November 1986, 34. [Authors' note]

Japanese Canadian (and naturalized U.S. citizen) who first gained notoriety in 1968 for his fight *against* Ethnic Studies at San Francisco State University.

In day-to-day terms, Asians compete against blacks and others for jobs, while their accomplishments are used to threaten affirmative action opportunities for Asian Americans. Racial antagonism, competition, and hostility characterize the social interactions between these groups in the workplace, neighborhood, and schools. Yet, none are aware of the greater socioeconomic and political forces orchestrating this conflict.

> [Racism] has consistently dehumanized peoples of color, especially those who questioned or refused normative socialization. It has fostered privileges to the privileged; it has solidified a normative white culture, and it continues to make unjust social institutions and oppressive relations seem legitimate. . . . Racism is only one of the several bases of social differentiation; nevertheless, it is probably the strongest, and it is fueled by class and gender-related "isms." Racial differentiation continues to interact with class and gender distinctions which keep the majority of Black folks on the "outside" while the society extends color, class, and gender privileges to the socially acceptable "insiders," even for "Negro" insiders as long as they use the "master's" tools.[13]

Over a long, insidious, and brutal process of being conquered, peoples of color have been instilled with the same racist, chauvinist, and supremacist values and attitudes which have oppressed us. Is it then a mystery that we find unity so elusive? While people, and especially women, of color are, in broad, general terms, commonly oppressed by racism, we are exploited differently by racism. Depending on one's class, racial group, gender, nationality, cultural background, education, English fluency, citizenship status, sexual preference, physical appearance and ability, and history in or with this country, we are "given" our place in the racial hierarchy. It is arbitrary and subject to the sociopolitical needs of the U.S. economy and for the benefit and maintenance of white privilege.

Unity is not automatically bequeathed to people of color. Racism   15
translates the differences among us into *relatively* preferential treatment for some at the expense of others, promoting internalized racism and cross-racial hostility. Disunity among people of color due to the exploitation of differences is an inherent part of the system of racism. The *potential* for unity is there and the *power* is tremendous — witness the recent Civil Rights Movement. For unity to develop and continue to

[13]Joyce Elaine King and Thomasyne Lightfoote Wilson, *On Being African American: Beyond Cultural Democracy and Racist Education* (1988, unpublished), 3. [Authors' note]

exist, the distrust and discord ever-present among us must be replaced. How?

In the groups we conduct with women of color, we begin by acknowledging and sharing our own internalized racism. The face of racism inside each of us is an ugly one, but we find that confronting the stereotypes and predispositions we have about ourselves leads to understanding others. In group process, it becomes clear that our definitions of unity mean sameness — same feelings, thoughts, ideas, and behaviors. This mentality commonly develops a tenuous agreement to coexist as long as differences — not just political and organizational, but personal differences as well — are denied and disregarded. Our *sameness* brings us together, our *differences* drive us apart. We stay together as long as we do *not* confront the issues. Witness how the struggle against sexism in the Civil Rights Movement was put on hold because racism was the "unifying" issue and sexism "divided" us.

We live in a time when the assault on women of color is increasing. Laws that were marginally enforced are now being rolled back — legalized abortion for one. Recruitment in the Ku Klux Klan is the highest it has ever been. Colored children are being drugged to death — if they survive their first year. So why spend time on internalized racism and cross-racial hostility when racism is still so rampant? We have spent years fighting racism and other oppressions through legislation. No legislation, however, can give a person self-esteem. Slogans like "Black Is Beautiful" did not eliminate self-hatred. Internalized racism cannot be legalized or constitutionalized or sloganized away.

Women of color must challenge our racist attitudes and internalized racism with the same vigor we challenge racism. We must honestly admit and confront the stereotypes and predispositions we have about ourselves and others. We must think and act equitably in a society that honors the hierarchical. We must learn and know our existence cannot be at the expense of another person.

Individually, we cannot eliminate the institution of racism. But we *can change* how we individually interact with each other and internalize racism — internalize oppression. The conflict and hostility between and among women of color can only be resolved by women of color. This is a long, painful process. Internalized racism and cross-racial hostility have been around as long as institutionalized racism. This is *our* work and we have to do it if we want *real* freedom.

"Now that we've begun to break the silence and begun to break through the diabolically erected barriers and can hear each other and see each other, we can sit down with trust and break bread together."[14]   20

[14]Toni Cade Bambara, Foreword, *This Bridge Called My Back: Writings by Radical Women of Color* (Latham, NY: Kitchen Table: Women of Color Press, 1981), vi. [Authors' note]

Engaging the Text

1. According to Harris and Ordoña, what kinds of lessons do people of color internalize from the dominant culture? How do they cope with these influences?

2. What distinctions do the authors draw between racism and cross-racial hostility? Do you agree that these need to be recognized as two distinct though related issues?

3. According to the authors, how are racism and cross-racial hostility connected? How do they interact and support each other? What seem to be the authors' strategies for battling racism and cross-racial hostility?

Exploring Connections

4. Attempt to explain cross-racial hostility from the point of view of Gordon W. Allport's theory of group loyalty (p. 292) and Shelby Steele's notion of "seeing for innocence" (p. 347). How well do these approaches account for the feelings and behavior Harris and Ordoña describe?

5. Harris and Ordoña argue that "differences among white people tend to be evened out by white privilege" (para. 5). Test this assertion against the experiences of Mike LeFevre (p. 87), Nora Quealey (p. 202), and C. P. Ellis (p. 336).

6. Drawing on historical information provided by bell hooks (p. 249), Martin Luther King, Jr. (p. 319), and Harris and Ordoña, write a brief "rereading" of U.S. race relations from the American Revolution to the present.

Extending the Critical Context

7. If you have ever experienced cross-racial hostility, describe an instance of it. Analyze your own thoughts and actions as well as the actions of those around you. Use your personal experience to support or challenge what Harris and Ordoña have written.

8. If you are familiar with the women's movement or the gay and lesbian movement, analyze how divisions within the group threaten its unity and effectiveness.

A Fire in Fontana[1]

Hisaye Yamamoto DeSoto

*Of the 120,000 Japanese Americans interned during World War II,
one was a young journalist named Hisaye Yamamoto. Despite her
family's forced relocation to Arizona, she continued her career, writing
for the internment camp newspaper and, after the war, for the* Los
Angeles Tribune, *a Black weekly. In this unusual autobiographical
essay, DeSoto (b. 1921) tells not of the injustices she suffered but rather
of the prejudice against Blacks that she witnessed in the 1950s and '60s.
DeSoto's unique perspective makes the essay particularly interesting: as
you read, pay attention to her perceptions of racism as well as to the
examples she recounts. DeSoto has published short stories in several
national magazines as well as her own collection, entitled* Seventeen
Syllables *(1988). "A Fire in Fontana" first appeared in 1985 in* Rafu
magazine.

Something weird happened to me not long after the end of the
Second World War. I wouldn't go so far as to say that I, a Japanese
American, became Black, because that's a pretty melodramatic statement. But some kind of transformation did take place, the effects of
which are with me still.

I remember reading a book called *Young Man with a Horn*, by
Dorothy Baker, which is said to be based on the life of Bix Beiderbecke,[2]
in which the narrator early wonders if his musician friend would have
come to the same tragic end if he hadn't become involved with Negroes
(in 1985, how odd the word has become!) and with one musician in
particular.

In real life, there happened to be a young White musician in an
otherwise Black band which played in such places as the Club Alabam
on Central Avenue. His name was Johnny Otis, and the group became
quite respected in jazz and blues circles. But his name was once Veliotis
— he is of Greek heritage; in more recent years he has become the pastor
of a church in Watts.[3] I suppose he, too, arrived at a place in his life

---

[1] *Fontana:* suburb approximately thirty five miles east of downtown Los Angeles.

[2] *Bix Beiderbecke:* Leon Bismarck Beiderbecke (1903–1931), self-taught jazz cornet-
ist, pianist, and composer who died of pneumonia.

[3] *Watts:* area of south-central Los Angeles, scene of civil insurrection or the "Watts
riots" of 1965, during which thirty-four people died.

from which there was no turning back. But his life, as I see it, represents a triumph.

But I don't know whether mine is or not. Because when I realized that something was happening to me, I scrambled to backtrack for awhile. By then it was too late. I continued to look like the Nisei[4] I was, with my height remaining at slightly over four feet ten, my hair straight, my vision myopic. Yet I know that this event transpired inside me; sometimes I see it as my inward self being burnt black in a certain fire.

Or perhaps the process, unbeknownst to me, had begun even ear- 5 lier. Once, during the war, squeezed into a hot summer bus out of Chicago, my seatmate was a blond girl about my size or maybe a little taller, who started telling me her life story.

The young woman wore a bright-flowered jersey dress, swirling purples and reds and greens on a white background, and she chortled a lot. She said she was twenty-eight years old and married to a man in his sixties, a customer of where she'd been a waitress. Just now she had been visiting in Chicago with her married sister and she'd had a lot of fun, her brother-in-law pretending he was going to drown her in the lake where they'd all gone for a swim. She said in East St. Louis, where she lived, all the kids of the neighborhood would come around for her cookies. Her husband was very good to her, so she was quite content.

The bus was south of Springfield somewhere when suddenly, startling me, the girl sat bolt upright and began chortling. "I knew it! I knew it!" For some reason, she was filled with glee.

"See that nigger?" she asked. "He got off the bus and went into that restaurant to ask for a drink and they told him to go around outside to the faucet!"

Sure enough, the young fellow was bent awkwardly over the outside tap which protruded from the wooden building about a foot from the ground, trying to get a drink without getting his clothes sloshed.

"I knew they wouldn't give him a glass of water!" She crowed as 10 though it were a personal victory.

Here I was on a bus going back to the camp in Arizona[5] where my father still lived, and I knew there was a connection between my seatmate's joy and our having been put in that hot and windblown place of barracks.

Even though I didn't dare shove her out the window, I must have managed to get some sign of protest across to her. After awhile, she said doggedly. "Well, it's all in the way you're brought up. I was brought up this way, so that's the way I feel."

[4]*Nisei:* second-generation Japanese American.
[5]*the camp in Arizona:* the Colorado River Relocation Center in Poston.

After the girl got off in East St. Louis, where (she had informed me) Negroes walked on one side of the street and White people on the other, the bus went through a bleak and dry territory where when one got off, there were large grasshoppers which clung to the walls like ivy and scrunched underfoot on the pavement like eggshells. The toilets were a new experience, too, labeled either Colored or White. I dared to try White first, and no one challenged me, so I continued this presumptuous practice at all the way stations of Texas. After I got back on the bus the first time, I was haunted by the long look given me by a cleaning woman in the restroom. I decided, for the sake of my conscience, that the Negro woman had never seen a Japanese before.

So the first job I got after coming out of camp again was with a Negro newspaper in Los Angeles. I really wanted the job badly, and was amazed when I was hired over a Nisei fellow who was more qualified, since the ad in the *Pacific Citizen* had specified a man. Moreover, the young man, already a Nisei journalist of some note, had edited his own newspaper before the war and knew athletes like Kenny Washington and Woody Strode because he'd gone to UCLA with them. The idea of hiring a Japanese on a Black newspaper was that maybe the returning Japanese businessmen would advertise and this would attract some Japanese readership, and maybe there would be the beginnings of an intercultural community.

It didn't work out that way at all, because I'm not one of your go- 15
getters or anything. I did rewrites mostly, of stories culled from all the other Black newspapers across the country that exchanged with the *Los Angeles Tribune*, from the very professional ones like the *Chicago Defender* (with columnists like Langston Hughes[6] and S. I. Hayakawa)[7] and the *New Amsterdam News* to smaller ones like the primly proper Bostonian sheet with elegant society notes and the smudged weeklies from small towns in Mississippi and Oklahoma that looked to have been turned out on antiquated, creaking presses. Almost every week, I toted up the number of alleged lynchings across the country and combined them into one story.

The office was on the mezzanine of the Dunbar Hotel, where people well-known in the entertainment industry, as they say, would regularly stay. There was a spirited running argument going on almost every day of the week down in the foyer which the *Tribune* office overlooked. The denizens of the place, retired members of the Brotherhood of Sleeping

[6]*Langston Hughes:* African American writer (1902–1967) best known for his poetry. Hughes was a major figure in the Harlem Renaissance, a flowering of black artists, musicians, and writers in New York in the 1920s.

[7]*S. I. Hayakawa:* Samuel Ichiye Hayakawa (b. 1906), Canadian-born Japanese American linguist, writer, and politician. Hayakawa was an opponent of dissident students during his tenure as president of San Francisco State College (1968–1973) and was a U.S. senator from 1977 to 1982.

Car Porters[8] and such, were provoked to discussion regularly by one of the hotel owners, a Negro who looked absolutely White and whose dark eyes smoldered with a bitter fire. The inexhaustible topic was Race, always Race.

I got a snootful of it. Sometimes I got to wondering whether Negroes talked about anything else. No matter what the initial remark, if the discussion continued for any length of time, the issue boiled down to Race. Even the jokes were darkly tinged with a dash of bitters. More that once I was easily put down with a casual, "That's mighty White of you," the connotations of which were devastating.

But it was not all work. One Halloween Mrs. Preacley, the secretary, and I visited a nightclub to watch a beauty contest. Among the contestants flouncing about in their scented silks and furs across the platform were a couple of guys employed by the hotel. One young man, donning a mop of auburn curls, a pink sheath dress, and high heels, had turned into a young matron; another competed in a simple white gown, statuesquely, regally, as though posing for an expensive fashion magazine. Another time, the bosses took a visiting fireman out for a night on the town and a couple of us Nisei were invited along. At one Sunset Strip nightclub the waiter was slow in returning with drinks and the table chitchat suddenly turned into a serious consideration of what strategy to use if the waiter failed to return. But eventually the drinks came.

The office was frequently visited by a well-to-do retired physician, the color of café-au-lait, whose everyday outfit consisted of a creamy Panama,[9] impeccable white suit, and cane. With his distinguished-looking goatee, all that was missing was the frosted, tall, tinkling glass topped with a sprig of mint. The young eager beaver sports editor–advertising manager rushed in and out at all hours, breathlessly, bringing in a new display ad or dashing off to interview a boxing contender.

Later he was to get an appointment to West Point from Rep. Helen 20 Gahagan Douglas. There were glimpses of the sprinkling of showfolk who stayed at the hotel — Billy Eckstine,[10] the recently married Ossie Davis and Ruby Dee,[11] the Delta Rhythm Boys; and down on Central Avenue, the theater marquee would advertise live acts like Pigmeat Markham, Mantan Moreland, Moms Mabley, and Redd Foxx.[12] A tall young police lieutenant, later to become mayor of the city, came by to protest the newspaper's editorial on police brutality.

One day when a new secretary named Miss Moten and I were in the mezzanine office, which was really three desks and two filing cabinets

---

[8]*Brotherhood of Sleeping Car Porters:* union of African American railroad workers.

[9]*Panama:* style of hat made of plaited palmlike leaves.

[10]*Billy Eckstine:* singer and bandleader (b. 1914) who fostered the early careers of jazz legends Sarah Vaughan, Dizzy Gillespie, and Charlie Parker.

[11]*Ossie Davis and Ruby Dee:* prominent African American actors.

[12]*The Delta Rhythm Boys . . . Foxx:* popular African American entertainers.

jammed into one end of the open mezzanine, with a counter separating the office from the subscribing and advertising public, a nice-looking young man with a mustache came up the stairs.

He said his name was Short. Urgently, he told us a disturbing story. He said he and his wife and two children had recently purchased a house in Fontana. They had not been accorded a very warm welcome by the community. In fact, he said, there had been several threats of get-out-or-else, and his family was living in fear. He wanted his situation publicized so that some sentiment could be mustered in support of his right to live in Fontana. He was making the rounds of the three Negro newspapers in town to enlist their assistance.

I took down his story for the editor to handle when she got in. After he left, I noticed Miss Moten was extremely agitated. She was on the tense side to begin with, but she was a quiet, conscientious worker and always spoke in a gentle murmur.

But now her eyes were blazing with fury. She spat out the words. "I hate White people!"

"What?" I said, feeling stupid. I'd heard her all right, but I'd never seen her even halfway angry before.   25

"I hate White people! They're all the same!"

Then, later the same week, there was a fire in Fontana. Dead in the blaze, which appeared to have started with gasoline poured all around the house and outbuildings, were the young man who had told us his story, his comely wife, and their two lovely children, a boy and a girl (one of the other newspapers had obtained a recent portrait of the family, probably from relatives in the city).

There was an investigation, of course. The official conclusion was that probably the man had set the gasoline fire himself, and the case was closed.

Among those who doubted the police theory was a White priest who was so skeptical that he wrote a play about the fire in Fontana. *Trial by Fire*, he called it. Not long after it was presented on stage, the priest was suddenly transferred to a parish somewhere in the boondocks of Arizona.

And that was the last time I heard mention of the conflagration.   30

It was around this time that I felt something happening to me, but I couldn't put my finger on it. It was something like an itch I couldn't locate, or like food not being cooked enough, or something undone which should have been done, or something forgotten which should have been remembered. Anyway, something was unsettling my innards.

There was a Japanese evangelist who, before the war, used to shout on the northeast corner of First and San Pedro in Little Tokyo, his large painting of Jesus propped up against the signal pole there, and his tambourine for contributions placed on the sidewalk in front of the picture. He wore a small mustache, a uniform of navy blue, and a visored military-type cap. So regular was the cadence of his call to salvation that, from a distance, it sounded like the sharp barking of a dog. "*Wan, wan, wan! Wan, wan, wan!*" until, closer up, the man could be seen in exhortation, his face awry and purple with the passion of his message.

A fellow regular about that time on the sidewalks of Little Tokyo was a very large boy in a wheelchair which was usually pushed by a cute girl in bangs or another boy, both smaller than their charge, both of whom seemed to accept their transporting job cheerfully, as a matter of course. The large boy's usual outfit was denim overalls, his head was closely shaven, Japanese military-style, and there was a clean white handkerchief tied around his neck to catch the bit of saliva which occasionally trickled from a corner of his mouth.

It seems to me that my kinship, for all practical purposes, was with the large boy in the wheelchair, not with the admirable evangelist who was literally obeying the injunction to shout the good news from the housetops and street corners. For, what had I gone and done? Given the responsibility by the busy editor, I had written up from my notes a calm, impartial story, using "alleged" and "claimed" and other cautious journalese. Anyone noticing the story about the unwanted family in Fontana would have taken it with a grain of salt.

I should have been an evangelist at 7th and Broadway, shouting out the name of the Short family and their predicament in Fontana. But I had been as handicapped as the boy in the wheelchair, as helpless.

All my family and friends had already been feeling my displeasure when it came to certain matters anyway. I was a curmudgeon, a real pill. If they funned around or dared so much as to imitate a Southernly accent, I pounced on them like a cougar. They got so they would do their occasional sho-nuffs behind my back, hushing up suddenly when I came into the room.

And my correspondence suffered. When one fellow dared to imply that I was really unreasonable on the subject of race relations, saying that he believed it sufficient to make one's stand known only when the subject happened to come up, the exchange of letters did not continue much longer.

I even dared to engage in long-distance tilting with a university scholar who had been kind enough to notice my writing. Specifically, I objected to his admiration of Herman Melville's *Benito Cereno* as one of the most perfect short stories extant, to his citing of the slave Babo in the story as the epitome of evil. The professor replied that race was not the issue, and that, anyway, Melville was writing from assumptions prevalent in the culture of his time, and, furthermore, Negroes themselves had participated in the sealing of their fellow Blacks into bondage. These *non sequiturs*, coming from such a distinguished source, dismayed me.

So I guess you could say that things were coming to a head. Then, one afternoon when I was on the trolley bus heading home to Boyle Heights, there was some kind of disagreement at First and Broadway between the Negro driver of the bus I was on, turning onto First, and the White driver of the other bus turning onto Broadway. The encounter ended with the White driver waving his arms and cursing, "Why, you Black bastard!"

The Negro driver merely got back on and turned the bus onto   40
Broadway, but I was sick, cringing from the blow of those words. My stomach was queasy with anxiety, and I knew Miss Moten's fury for my very own. I wanted to yell out the window at the other driver, but what could I have said? I thought of reporting him to management, but what could I have said?

Not long after, going to work one morning, I found myself wishing that the streetcar would rattle on and on and never stop. I'd felt the sensation before, on the way to my mother's funeral. If I could somehow manage to stay on the automobile forever, I thought, I would never have to face the fact of my mother's death. A few weeks after this incident on the street, I mumbled some excuse about planning to go back to school and left the paper.

I didn't go back to school, but after a time I got on trains and buses that carried me several thousand miles across the country and back. I guess you could say I was realizing my dream of travelling forever (escaping responsibility forever). I was in Massachusetts, New York, New Jersey, Maryland, and most of the time I didn't argue with anyone.

But once in Baltimore, I couldn't help objecting to a guest's offhand remark. This lady had been a patient in a maternity ward alongside a Negro woman and she mimicked the latter's cry, "Oh, give me something to ease the pain! Give me something to ease the pain!"

She gave me a pain, so I entered into a polite and wary fray, with the lady's husband joining in on his wife's behalf. "Edge-acated niggers," they said, what they couldn't support was the uppity airs of edge-acated niggers.

As the discussion continued, they backed down to allow as how   45
Northern Negroes might be another matter. But I knew nothing had been accomplished except the discomfiture of those whose hospitality we were enjoying.

In Baltimore, too, I admired the industry of the lady owner of the rowhouse[13] next door. Lovely enough to be in the movies, with softly curling dark hair, she spoke a soft Marylandese that enchanted me. In the middle of winter, I could see her cleaning her upstairs windows, seated precariously on the sill so as to face the windows from the

[13]*rowhouse:* one of a continuous row of houses of uniform structure and appearance, often with common side walls.

outside. But, one day, happening to walk with her to do some shopping, I saw her spewing lizards, toads, and wriggling serpents: "It's them damn niggras!"

When I finally came back to Los Angeles I was married and set about producing a passel of children. But stuff kept happening. Our son in high school reported that his classmates took delight in saying "nigger" behind the back of the Black electronics teacher. A White electronics teacher, visiting his sister in the hospital in the same room where I lay, said that he knew it was wrong, but he didn't want Blacks moving into his neighborhood in Alhambra — no Moors in Alhambra?[14] — because of the drop in property values that would ensue (I jousted feebly with him — well, I was sick — and later, on my return home, happened to be talking to someone who knew him, and found out that the teacher felt the same way about Japanese moving near him). When I objected to my children repeating a favorite word used by their playmates, one grandparent informed me that there was nothing wrong with the word nigger — she used it all the time herself. An attractive Korean lady friend and real esate agent put her children into Catholic schools because, as her daughter explained it, the public schools hereabouts were "integrated," while, on the other hand, she winsomely urged local real estate onto Black clients because, as she explained to me, "It's the coming thing," and her considerable profits ("It's been very good to me") made possible her upward mobility into less integrated areas.

So it was that, in between putting another load of clothes into the automatic washer, ironing, maybe whipping up some tacos for supper, I watched the Watts riot on television. Back then I was still middle-aged, sitting safely in a house which was located on a street where panic would be the order of the day if a Black family should happen to move in — I had come there on sufferance myself, on the coattails of a pale husband.

Appalled, inwardly cowering, I watched the burning and looting on the screen and heard the reports of the dead and wounded. But beneath all my distress, I felt something else, a tiny trickle of warmth which I finally recognized as an undercurrent of exultation. To me, the tumult in the city was the long-awaited, gratifying next chapter of an old movie that had flickered about in the back of my mind for years. In the film, shot in the dark of about three o'clock in the morning, there was this modest house out in the country. Suddenly the house was in flames and there were the sound effects of the fire roaring and leaping skyward. Then there could be heard the voices of a man and woman screaming, and the voices of two small children as well.

---

[14]*no Moors in Alhambra:* Alhambra is a suburb of Los Angeles but also a famous group of buildings overlooking Grenada, Spain. They were a citadel built between 1200 and 1350 by the Moors, North African Muslims who ruled parts of Spain for eight centuries. It's thus ironic to keep Blacks, or "Moors," out of Alhambra.

Engaging the Text

1. Early in the essay, DeSoto speaks of her "inward self being burnt black" in paragraph 4. What do you think she means by this? How is this idea developed? How would you decribe the transformation she undergoes? Is it credible?

2. How are the author's perceptions of racial prejudice against African Americans influenced by her own race? Does her experience complicate your notion of race relations in the United States?

3. DeSoto's short essay has a rather large cast of characters: Explain the behavior of these people and the significance the author attaches to the incidents in which they figure:

the blond girl on the bus	the maternity ward patient
Miss Moten	the rowhouse owner
the Japanese evangelist	the Korean real estate agent
the university scholar	

4. Does DeSoto's reference to the boy in the wheelchair as a metaphor for helplessness itself represent an instance of intergroup insensitivity? What other metaphors might she have used?

5. Explain DeSoto's emotion in the last paragraph. What is the "old movie that had flickered about in the back of [her] mind for years"?

Exploring Connections

6. Analyze DeSoto's narrative in terms of in-groups, out-groups, and reference groups. How well does Gordon W. Allport's theory on racial prejudice (p. 292) account for DeSoto's feelings or for the racial hostility she observes around her?

7. For the most part, DeSoto describes events without explaining them or theorizing about them. Working in small groups, try to extract or distill the author's most important beliefs about race in the United States. As a follow-up discuss which of the more theoretical writers in the chapter seems most closely to share DeSoto's perspective (Omi and Winant, p. 283, Allport, p. 292, King, p. 319, Steele, p. 347, Harris and Ordoña, p. 359).

Extending the Critical Context

8. In recent years, there have been a number of highly publicized conflicts between Asians and African Americans. Research current relations between these groups in your community. Are there sources of conflict? Drawing on any of the theoretical analyses of racism in this chapter, how might you explain such conflicts?

Los Vendidos[1]

Luis M. Valdez

In this one-act play, Valdez dramatizes the tensions within the Chicano/Latino community and ridicules stereotypical thinking by following up on an inspired oddball premise: the sale of Mexican robots to then governor Ronald Reagan's administration in California. Valdez (b. 1940) has been a major force in the establishment of Chicano theater in the United States, in particular through El Teatro Campesino, a company that emerged from Valdez's improvisations for migrant farm workers in the 1960s. His best-known plays are Zoot Suit *(1978) and* I Don't Have to Show You No Stinking Badges *(1986). He also wrote and directed the 1987 hit movie* La Bamba *and is preparing a version of a medieval Spanish mystery play,* La Pastorela, *for television.* Los Vendidos *was first produced in 1967.*

Characters

Honest Sancho	Johnny
Secretary	Revolucionario
Farm Worker	Mexican-American

Scene: Honest Sancho's Used Mexican Lot and Mexican Curio Shop. Three models are on display in Honest Sancho's shop: to the right, there is a Revolucionario, complete with sombrero, carrilleras,[2] and carabina 30–30. At center, on the floor, there is the Farm Worker, under a broad straw sombrero. At stage left is the Pachuco, filero[3] in hand.

(Honest Sancho is moving among his models, dusting them off and preparing for another day of business.)

Sancho: Bueno, bueno, mis monos, vamos a ver a quien vendemos ahora, ¿no? (*To audience.*) ¡Quihubo![4] I'm Honest Sancho and this is my shop. Antes fui contratista pero ahora logré tener mi negocito.[5] All I need now is a customer. (*a bell rings offstage.*) Ay, a customer!

---

[1]*Los Vendidos:* sellouts.
[2]*carrilleras:* literally chin straps, but may refer to cartridge belts.
[3]*Pachuco:* Chicano slang for a 1940s zoot suiter; *filero:* blade.
[4]*Bueno, bueno, . . . Quihubo:* "Good, good, my cute ones, let's see who we can sell now, O.K.?"
[5]*Antes fui . . . negocito:* "I used to be a contractor, but now I've succeeded in having my little business."

SECRETARY (*entering*): Good morning, I'm Miss Jiménez from —

SANCHO: ¡Ah, una chicana! Welcome, welcome Señorita Jiménez.

SECRETARY (*Anglo pronunciation*): JIM-enez.

SANCHO: ¿Qué?

SECRETARY: My name is Miss JIM-enez. Don't you speak English? What's wrong with you?

SANCHO: Oh, nothing, Señorita JIM-enez. I'm here to help you.

SECRETARY: That's better. As I was starting to say, I'm a secretary from Governor Reagan's office, and we're looking for a Mexican type for the administration.

SANCHO: Well, you come to the right place, lady. This is Honest Sancho's Used Mexican lot, and we got all types here. Any particular type you want?

SECRETARY: Yes, we were looking for somebody suave —

SANCHO: Suave.

SECRETARY: Debonair.

SANCHO: De buen aire.

SECRETARY: Dark.

SANCHO: Prieto.

SECRETARY: But of course not too dark.

SANCHO: No muy prieto.

SECRETARY: Perhaps, beige.

SANCHO: Beige, just the tone. Así como cafecito con leche,[6] ¿no?

SECRETARY: One more thing. He must be hard-working.

SANCHO: That could only be one model. Step right over here to the center of the shop, lady. (*They cross to the Farm Worker.*) This is our standard farm worker model. As you can see, in the words of our beloved Senator George Murphy, he is "built close to the ground." Also take special notice of his four-ply Goodyear huaraches, made from the rain tire. This wide-brimmed sombrero is an extra added feature — keeps off the sun, rain, and dust.

SECRETARY: Yes, it does look durable.

SANCHO: And our farm-worker model is friendly. Muy amable.[7] Watch. (*Snaps his fingers.*)

FARM WORKER (*lifts up head*): Buenos días, señorita. (*His head drops.*)

SECRETARY: My, he's friendly.

SANCHO: Didn't I tell you? Loves his patrones! But his most attractive feature is that he's hard working. Let me show you. (*Snaps fingers. Farm Worker stands.*)

FARM WORKER: ¡El jale![8] (*He begins to work.*)

SANCHO: As you can see, he is cutting grapes.

---

[6]*Así como . . . leche:* like coffee with milk.

[7]*Muy amable:* very friendly.

[8]*El jale:* the job.

SECRETARY: Oh, I wouldn't know.

SANCHO: He also picks cotton. (*Snap. Farm Worker begins to pick cotton.*)

SECRETARY: Versatile isn't he?

SANCHO: He also picks melons. (*Snap. Farm Worker picks melons.*) That's his slow speed for late in the season. Here's his fast speed. (*Snap. Farm Worker picks faster.*)

SECRETARY: ¡Chihuahua! . . . I mean, goodness, he sure is a hard worker.

SANCHO (*pulls the Farm Worker to his feet*): And that isn't the half of it. Do you see these little holes on his arms that appear to be pores? During those hot sluggish days in the field, when the vines or the branches get so entangled, it's almost impossible to move; these holes emit a certain grease that allow our model to slip and slide right through the crop with no trouble at all.

SECRETARY: Wonderful. But is he economical?

SANCHO: Economical? Señorita, you are looking at the Volkswagen of Mexicans. Pennies a day is all it takes. One plate of beans and tortillas will keep him going all day. That, and chile. Plenty of chile. Chile jalapenos, chile verde, chile colorado. But, of course, if you do give him chile (*Snap. Farm Worker turns left face. Snap. Farm Worker bends over.*) then you have to change his oil filter once a week.

SECRETARY: What about storage?

SANCHO: No problem. You know these new farm labor camps our Honorable Governor Reagan has built out by Parlier or Raisin City? They were designed with our model in mind. Five, six, seven, even ten in one of those shacks will give you no trouble at all. You can also put him in old barns, old cars, river banks. You can even leave him out in the field overnight with no worry!

SECRETARY: Remarkable.

SANCHO: And here's an added feature: every year at the end of the season, this model goes back to Mexico and doesn't return, automatically, until next Spring.

SECRETARY: How about that. But tell me: does he speak English?

SANCHO: Another outstanding feature is that last year this model was programmed to go out on STRIKE! (*Snap*).

FARM WORKER: ¡HUELGA! ¡HUELGA! Hermanos, sálganse de esos files.[9] (*Snap. He stops.*)

SECRETARY: No! Oh no, we can't strike in the State Capitol.

SANCHO: Well, he also scabs. (*Snap.*)

FARM WORKER: Me vendo barato, ¿y qué?[10] (*Snap.*)

---

[9]*HUELGA! HUELGA! . . . esos files:* "Strike! Strike! Brothers, leave those rows."
[10]*Me vendo . . . qué:* "I come cheap, so what?"

SECRETARY: That's much better, but you didn't answer my question. Does he speak English?

SANCHO: Bueno . . . no, pero[11] he has other —

SECRETARY: No.

SANCHO: Other features.

SECRETARY: NO! He just won't do!

SANCHO: Okay, okay pues. We have other models.

SECRETARY: I hope so. What we need is something a little more sophisticated.

SANCHO: Sophisti — ¿qué?

SECRETARY: An urban model.

SANCHO: Ah, from the city! Step right back. Over here in this corner of the shop is exactly what you're looking for. Introducing our new 1969 JOHNNY PACHUCO model! This is our fast-back model. Streamlined. Built for speed, low-riding, city life. Take a look at some of these features. Mag shoes, dual exhausts, green chartreuse paint-job, dark-tint windshield, a little poof on top. Let me just turn him on. (*Snap. Johnny walks to stage center with a pachuco bounce.*)

SECRETARY: What was that?

SANCHO: That, señorita, was the Chicano shuffle.

SECRETARY: Okay, what does he do?

SANCHO: Anything and everything necessary for city life. For instance, survival: he knife fights. (*Snap. Johnny pulls out switch blade and swings at Secretary*).

(*Secretary screams.*)

SANCHO: He dances. (*Snap.*)

JOHNNY (*singing*): "Angel Baby, my Angel Baby . . ." (*Snap.*)

SANCHO: And here's a feature no city model can be without. He gets arrested, but not without resisting, of course. (*Snap.*)

JOHNNY: ¡En la madre, la placa![12] I didn't do it! I didn't do it! (*Johnny turns and stands up against an imaginary wall, legs spread out, arms behind his back.*)

SECRETARY: Oh no, we can't have arrests! We must maintain law and order.

SANCHO: But he's bilingual!

SECRETARY: Bilingual?

SANCHO: Simón que yes.[13] He speaks English! Johnny, give us some English. (*Snap.*)

[11]*Bueno . . . no, pero:* "Well, no, but . . ."
[12]*En la . . . placa:* "Wow, the police!"
[13]*Simón . . . yes:* yeah, sure.

JOHNNY (*comes downstage*): Fuck-you!

SECRETARY (*gasps*): Oh! I've never been so insulted in my whole life!

SANCHO: Well, he learned it in your school.

SECRETARY: I don't care where he learned it.

SANCHO: But he's economical!

SECRETARY: Economical?

SANCHO: Nickels and dimes. You can keep Johnny running on hamburgers, Taco Bell tacos, Lucky Lager beer, Thunderbird wine, yesca —

SECRETARY: Yesca?

SANCHO: Mota.

SECRETARY: Mota?

SANCHO: Leños[14] . . . Marijuana. (*Snap; Johnny inhales on an imaginary joint.*)

SECRETARY: That't against the law!

JOHNNY (*big smile, holding his breath*): Yeah.

SANCHO: He also sniffs glue. (*Snap. Johnny inhales glue, big smile.*)

JOHNNY: Tha's too much man, ése.

SECRETARY: No, Mr. Sancho, I don't think this —

SANCHO: Wait a minute, he has other qualities I know you'll love. For example, an inferiority complex. (*Snap.*)

JOHNNY (*to Sancho*): You think you're better than me, huh ése? (*Swings switch blade.*)

SANCHO: He can also be beaten and he bruises, cut him and he bleeds; kick him and he — (*He beats, bruises, and kicks Pachuco.*) would you like to try it?

SECRETARY: Oh, I couldn't.

SANCHO: Be my guest. He's a great scapegoat.

SECRETARY: No, really.

SANCHO: Please.

SECRETARY: Well, all right. Just once. (*She kicks Pachuco.*) Oh, he's so soft.

SANCHO: Wasn't that good? Try again.

SECRETARY (*kicks Pachuco*): Oh, he's so wonderful! (*She kicks him again.*)

SANCHO: Okay, that's enough, lady. You ruin the merchandise. Yes, our Johnny Pachuco model can give you many hours of pleasure. Why, the L.A.P.D. just bought twenty of these to train their rookie cops on. And talk about maintenance. Señorita, you are looking at an entirely self-supporting machine. You're never going to find our Johnny Pachuco model on the relief rolls. No, sir, this model knows how to liberate.

---

[14]*Leños:* "joints" of marijuana.

SECRETARY: Liberate?

SANCHO: He steals. (*Snap. Johnny rushes the Secretary and steals her purse.*)

JOHNNY: ¡Dame esa bolsa, vieja!¹⁵ (*He grabs the purse and runs. Snap by Sancho. He stops.*)

(*Secretary runs after Johnny and grabs purse away from him, kicking him as she goes.*)

SECRETARY: No, no, no! We can't have any *more* thieves in the State Administration. Put him back.

SANCHO: Okay, we still got other models. Come on, Johnny, we'll sell you to some old lady. (*Sancho takes Johnny back to his place.*)

SECRETARY: Mr. Sancho, I don't think you quite understand what we need. What we need is something that will attract the women voters. Something more traditional, more romantic.

SANCHO: Ah, a lover. (*He smiles meaningfully.*) Step right over here, señorita. Introducing our standard Revolucionario and/or Early California Bandit type. As you can see he is well-built, sturdy, durable. This is the International Harvester of Mexicans.

SECRETARY: What does he do?

SANCHO: You name it, he does it. He rides horses, stays in the mountains, crosses deserts, plains, rivers, leads revolutions, follows revolutions, kills, can be killed, serves as a martyr, hero, movie star — did I say movie star? Did you ever see *Viva Zapata? Viva Villa? Villa Rides? Pancho Villa Returns? Pancho Villa Goes Back? Pancho Villa Meets Abbott and Costello* —

SECRETARY: I've never seen any of those.

SANCHO: Well, he was in all of them. Listen to this. (*Snap.*)

REVOLUCIONARIO (*scream*): ¡VIVA VILLAAAAA!

SECRETARY: That's awfully loud.

SANCHO: He has a volume control. (*He adjusts volume. Snap.*)

REVOLUCIONARIO (*mousey voice*): ¡Viva Villa!

SECRETARY: That's better.

SANCHO: And even if you didn't see him in the movies, perhaps you saw him on TV. He makes commercials. (*Snap.*)

REVOLUCIONARIO: Is there a Frito Bandito in your house?

SECRETARY: Oh yes, I've seen that one!

SANCHO: Another feature about this one is that he is economical. He runs on raw horsemeat and tequila!

SECRETARY: Isn't that rather savage?

SANCHO: Al contrario,¹⁶ it makes him a lover. (*Snap.*)

---

¹⁵*Dame esa . . . , vieja:* "Gimme that bag, old lady!"
¹⁶*Al contrario:* on the contrary.

REVOLUCIONARIO (*to Secretary*): ¡Ay, mamasota, cochota, ven pa'ca! (*He grabs Secretary and folds her back — Latin-Lover style.*)

SANCHO (*Snap. Revolucionario goes back upright*): Now wasn't that nice?

SECRETARY: Well, it was rather nice.

SANCHO: And finally, there is one outstanding feature about this model I KNOW the ladies are going to love: He's a GENUINE antique! He was made in Mexico in 1910!

SECRETARY: Made in Mexico?

SANCHO: That's right. Once in Tijuana, twice in Guadalajara, three times in Cuernavaca.

SECRETARY: Mr. Sancho, I thought he was an American product.

SANCHO: No, but —

SECRETARY: No, I'm sorry. We can't buy anything but American-made products. He just won't do.

SANCHO: But he's an antique!

SECRETARY: I don't care. You still don't understand what we need. It's true we need Mexican models such as these, but it's more important that he be *American*.

SANCHO: American?

SECRETARY: That's right, and judging from what you've shown me, I don't think you have what we want. Well, my lunch hour's almost over; I better —

SANCHO: Wait a minute! Mexican but American?

SECRETARY: That's correct.

SANCHO: Mexican but . . . (*A sudden flash.*) AMERICAN! Yeah, I think we've got exactly what you want. He just came in today! Give me a minute. (*He exits. Talks from backstage.*) Here he is in the shop. Let me just get some papers off. There. Introducing our new 1970 Mexican-American! Ta-ra-ra-ra-ra-ra-RA-RAAA!

(*Sancho brings out the Mexican-American model, a clean-shaven middle-class type in a business suit, with glasses.*)

SECRETARY (*impressed*): Where have you been hiding this one?

SANCHO: He just came in this morning. Ain't he a beauty? Feast your eyes on him! Sturdy US STEEL frame, streamlined, modern. As a matter of fact, he is built exactly like our Anglo models except that he comes in a variety of darker shades: Naugahyde, leather, or Leatherette.

SECRETARY: Naugahyde.

SANCHO: Well, we'll just write that down. Yes, señorita, this model represents the apex of American engineering! He is bilingual, college educated, ambitious! Say the word "acculturate" and he accelerates. He is intelligent, well-mannered, clean — did I say clean? (*Snap. Mexican-American raises his arm.*) Smell.

SECRETARY (*smells*): Old Sobaco, my favorite.

SANCHO (*Snap. Mexican-American turns toward Sancho*): Eric! (*To Secretary*). We call him Eric García. (*To Eric.*) I want you to meet Miss JIM-enez, Eric.

MEXICAN-AMERICAN: Miss JIM-enez, I am delighted to make your acquaintance. (*He kisses her hand.*)

SECRETARY: Oh, my, how charming!

SANCHO: Did you feel the suction? He has seven especially engineered suction cups right behind his lips. He's a charmer all right!

SECRETARY: How about boards? Does he function on boards?

SANCHO: You name them, he is on them. Parole boards, draft boards, school boards, taco quality control boards, surf boards, two-by-fours.

SECRETARY: Does he function in politics?

SANCHO: Señorita, you are looking at a political MACHINE. Have you ever heard of the OEO, EOC, COD, WAR ON POVERTY? That's our model! Not only that, he makes political speeches.

SECRETARY: May I hear one?

SANCHO: With pleasure. (*Snap.*) Eric, give us a speech.

MEXICAN-AMERICAN: Mr. Congressman, Mr. Chairman, members of the board, honored guests, ladies and gentlemen. (*Sancho and Secretary applaud.*) Please, please. I come before you as a Mexican-American to tell you about the problems of the Mexican. The problems of the Mexican stem from one thing and one thing alone: he's stupid. He's uneducated. He needs to stay in school. He needs to be ambitious, forward-looking, harder-working. He needs to think American, American, American, AMERICAN, AMERICAN, AMERICAN. GOD BLESS AMERICA! GOD BLESS AMERICA! GOD BLESS AMERICA!! (*He goes out of control.*)

(*Sancho snaps frantically and the Mexican-American finally slumps forward, bending at the waist.*)

SECRETARY: Oh my, he's patriotic too!

SANCHO: Sí, señorita, he loves his country. Let me just make a little adjustment here. (*Stands Mexican-American up.*)

SECRETARY: What about upkeep? Is he economical?

SANCHO: Well, no, I won't lie to you. The Mexican-American costs a little bit more, but you get what you pay for. He's worth every extra cent. You can keep him running on dry Martinis, Langendorf bread.

SECRETARY: Apple pie?

SANCHO: Only Mom's. Of course, he's also programmed to eat Mexican food on ceremonial functions, but I must warn you: an overdose of beans will plug up his exhaust.

SECRETARY: Fine! There's just one more question: HOW MUCH DO YOU WANT FOR HIM?

SANCHO: Well, I tell you what I'm gonna do. Today and today only, because you've been so sweet, I'm gonna let you steal this model from me! I'm gonna let you drive him off the lot for the simple price of — let's see taxes and license included — $15,000.

SECRETARY: Fifteen thousand DOLLARS? For a MEXICAN!

SANCHO: Mexican? What are you talking, lady? This is a Mexican-AMERICAN! We had to melt down two pachucos, a farm worker, and three gabachos[17] to make this model! You want quality, but you gotta pay for it! This is no cheap run-about. He's got class!

SECRETARY: Okay, I'll take him.

SANCHO: You will?

SECRETARY: Here's your money.

SANCHO: You mind if I count it?

SECRETARY: Go right ahead.

SANCHO: Well, you'll get your pink slip in the mail. Oh, do you want me to wrap him up for you? We have a box in the back.

SECRETARY: No, thank you. The Governor is having a luncheon this afternoon, and we need a brown face in the crowd. How do I drive him?

SANCHO: Just snap your fingers. He'll do anything you want.

(Secretary snaps. Mexican-American steps forward.)

MEXICAN-AMERICAN: RAZA QUERIDA, ¡VAMOS LEVANTANDO ARMAS PARA LIBERARNOS DE ESTOS DESGRACIADOS GABACHOS QUE NOS EXPLOTAN! VAMOS.[18]

SECRETARY: What did he say?

SANCHO: Something about lifting arms, killing white people, etc.

SECRETARY: But he's not supposed to say that!

SANCHO: Look, lady, don't blame me for bugs from the factory. He's your Mexican-American; you bought him, now drive him off the lot!

SECRETARY: But he's broken!

SANCHO: Try snapping another finger.

(Secretary snaps. Mexican-American comes to life again.)

MEXICAN-AMERICAN: ¡ESTA GRAN HUMANIDAD HA DICHO BASTA! Y SE HA PUESTO EN MARCHA! ¡BASTA! ¡BASTA! ¡VIVA LA RAZA! ¡VIVA LA CAUSA!¡VIVA LA HUELGA! ¡VIVAN LOS

---

[17]*gabachos:* derogatory Chicano term for Anglos.

[18]*RAZA QUERIDA, . . . VAMOS:* "Beloved Raza, let's pick up arms to liberate ourselves from those damned whites that exploit us! Let's go."

BROWN BERETS! ¡VIVAN LOS ESTUDIANTES! ¡CHICANO POWER![19]

(The Mexican-American turns toward the Secretary, who gasps and backs up. He keeps turning toward the Pachuco, Farm Worker, and Revolucionario, snapping his fingers and turning each of them on, one by one.)

PACHUCO *(Snap. To Secretary)*: I'm going to get you, baby! ¡Viva La Raza!

FARM WORKER *(Snap. To Secretary)*: ¡Viva la huelga! ¡Viva la Huelga! ¡VIVA LA HUELGA!

REVOLUCIONARIO *(Snap. To Secretary)*: ¡Viva la revolución! ¡VIVA LA REVOLUCION!

(The three models join together and advance toward the Secretary who backs up and runs out of the shop screaming. Sancho is at the other end of the shop holding his money in his hand. All freeze. After a few seconds of silence, the Pachuco moves and stretches, shaking his arms and loosening up. The Farm Worker and Revolucionario do the same. Sancho stays where he is, frozen to his spot.)

JOHNNY: Man, that was a long one, ése. *(Others agree with him.)*

FARM WORKER: How did we do?

JOHNNY: Perty good, look all that lana, man! *(He goes over to Sancho and removes the money from his hand. Sancho stays where he is.)*

REVOLUCIONARIO: En la madre, look at all the money.

JOHNNY: We keep this up, we're going to be rich.

FARM WORKER: They think we're machines.

REVOLUCIONARIO: Burros.

JOHNNY: Puppets.

MEXICAN-AMERICAN: The only thing I don't like is — how come I always got to play the godamn Mexican-American?

JOHNNY: That's what you get for finishing high school.

FARM WORKER: How about our wages, ése?

JOHNNY: Here it comes right now. $3,000 for you, $3,000 for you, $3,000 for you, and $3,000 for me. The rest we put back into the business.

MEXICAN-AMERICAN: Too much, man. Heh, where you vatos going tonight?

FARM WORKER: I'm going over to Concha's. There's a party.

JOHNNY: Wait a minute, vatos. What about our salesman? I think he needs an oil job.

REVOLUCIONARIO: Leave him to me.

[19]*ESTA GRAN . . . CHICANO POWER:* "This great mass of humanity has said enough! And it begins to march! Enough! Enough! Long live La Raza! Long live the Cause! Long live the strike! Long live the Brown Berets! Long live the students! Chicano Power!

(The Pachuco, Farm Worker, and Mexican-American exit, talking loudly about their plans for the night. The Revolucionario goes over to Sancho, removes his derby hat and cigar, lifts him up, and throws him over his shoulder. Sancho hangs loose, lifeless.)

REVOLUCIONARIO *(to audience)*: He's the best model we got! ¡Ajua!
   (Exit.)

(End.)

Engaging the Text

1. Who is Honest Sancho? Who would buy his products? What is Valdez saying about American society through this character?

2. What is the point of the discussion about Ms. Jiménez's name? What does she want, and what does she represent in the play?

3. Whom does Valdez attack in the play, and how? How can you be sure of Valdez's position?

4. Write a short essay explaining the significance of the play's conclusion.

5. Why is the play primarily in English? How different would its effect be if it were entirely in English or Spanish? Who is the ideal audience for the play?

Exploring Connections

6. Virginia R. Harris and Trinity A. Ordoña (p. 359) argue that "differences among people of color are blown out of proportion with personal jealousies and betrayal, encouraged by whites" (para. 5). What evidence of this do you see in *Los Vendidos*? What response to this dilemma does Valdez offer in the play?

Extending the Critical Context

7. Working in groups, classify the common stereotypes for another group (for example, college students — by major or by living group; residents of your city; members of a different ethnic group). In what ways do these stereotypes oversimplify or distort reality? To extend the assignment, write an essay comparing and contrasting the stereotyped image of the group with its reality as you know it.

8. Describe the characters and plot of the play if you were to rewrite it for an Asian or African American audience.

La conciencia de la mestiza[1]/
Towards a New Consciousness

Gloria Anzaldúa

When Gloria Anzaldúa speaks of a "new consciousness," she's talk-
ing about creating a new self, about experiencing the world in a dif-
ferent way. She envisions a cultural evolution bringing new understand-
ings of race, gender, class, and nationality. And in writing of the
mestiza *consciousness and the multiple cultures from which it arises, she*
uses a new language — a hybrid of English, Castilian Spanish, a North
Mexican dialect, Tex-Mex, and the Indian language Nahuatl. Anzaldúa
is editor of Haciendo Caras: Making Face/Making Soul *(1990) and*
coeditor of This Bridge Called My Back: Writings by Radical Women of
Color *(1983). This selection is from her book* Borderlands = La Frontera: The New Mestiza *(1987). Although we've provided translations, we*
suggest that you not consult these in your first reading. Concentrate
instead on Anzaldúa's main points and on her innovative blend of
argument and poetry, of myth and manifesto.

> *Por la mujer de mi raza*
> *hablará el espíritu.*[2]

Jose Vascocelos, Mexican philosopher, envisaged *una raza mestiza,*
una mezcla de razas afines, una raza de color — la primera raza síntesis
del globo.[3] He called it a cosmic race, *la raza cósmica,* a fifth race
embracing the four major races of the world.[4] Opposite to the theory of
the pure Aryan,[5] and to the policy of racial purity that white America
practices, his theory is one of inclusivity. At the confluence of two or
more genetic streams, with chromosomes constantly "crossing over,"
this mixture of races, rather than resulting in an inferior being, provides

---

[1]*La conciencia de la mestiza: mestiza* consciousness; consciousness of the *mestiza* (a woman of mixed racial heritage).

[2]This is my own "take off" on Jose Vasconcelos' idea. Jose Vasconcelos, *La Raza Cósmica: Misión de la Raza Ibero-Americana* (México: Aguilar S.A. de Ediciones, 1961). [Author's note] *Por la mujer de mi raza . . . .:* the spirit shall speak through the women of my race.

[3]*una raza mestiza . . . .:* a multiracial race, a mixture of kindred races, a race of color, the first synthetic race of the world.

[4]Vasconcelos. [Author's note]

[5]*the theory of the pure Aryan:* the myth espoused by Adolf Hitler and others of the racial superiority of white northern Europeans.

hybrid progeny, a mutable, more malleable species with a rich gene pool. From this racial, ideological, cultural, and biological cross-pollinization, an "alien" consciousness is presently in the making — a new *mestiza* consciousness, *una conciencia de mujer*.[6] It is a consciousness of the Borderlands.

Una lucha de fronteras / A Struggle of Borders

Because I, a *mestiza*,
continually walk out of one culture
and into another,
because I am in all cultures at the same time,
alma entre dos mundos, tres, cuatro,
me zumba la cabeza con lo contradictorio.
Estoy norteada por todas las voces que me hablan
simultáneamente.[7]

The ambivalence from the clash of voices results in mental and emotional states of perplexity. Internal strife results in insecurity and indecisiveness. The mestiza's dual or multiple personality is plagued by psychic restlessness.

In a constant state of mental nepantilism, an Aztec word meaning torn between ways, *la mestiza* is a product of the transfer of the cultural and spiritual values of one group to another. Being tricultural, monolingual, bilingual, or multilingual, speaking a patois,[8] and in a state of perpetual transition, the *mestiza* faces the dilemma of the mixed breed: which collectivity does the daughter of a darkskinned mother listen to?

El choque de un alma atrapado entre el mundo del espíritu y el mundo de la técnica a veces la deja entullada.[9] Cradled in one culture, sandwiched between two cultures, straddling all three cultures and their value systems, *la mestiza* undergoes a struggle of flesh, a struggle of borders, an inner war. Like all people, we perceive the version of reality that our culture communicates. Like others having or living in more than one culture, we get multiple, often opposing messages. The coming together of two self-consistent but habitually incompatible frames of reference[10] causes *un choque*, a cultural collision.

[6]*una conciencia de mujer:* a female consciousness.

[7]*alma entre dos mundos . . . .:* a soul caught between two, three, four worlds. My head aches with contradictions. I'm led north by all the voices that speak to me simultaneously.

[8]*patois:* nonstandard dialect.

[9]*El choque de una alma atrapado . . . .:* The struggle of a soul trapped between the world of the spirit and the world of technology sometimes leaves it paralyzed.

[10]Arthur Koestler termed this "bisociation." Albert Rothenberg, *The Creative Process in Art, Science, and Other Fields* (Chicago, IL: University of Chicago Press, 1979), 12. [Author's note]

Within us and within *la cultura chicana*,[11] commonly held beliefs of   5
the white culture attack commonly held beliefs of the Mexican culture,
and both attack commonly held beliefs of the indigenous culture. Subconsciously, we see an attack on ourselves and our beliefs as a threat and
we attempt to block with a counterstance.

But it is not enough to stand on the opposite river bank, shouting
questions, challenging patriarchal, white conventions. A counterstance
locks one into a duel of oppressor and oppressed; locked in mortal
combat, like the cop and the criminal, both are reduced to a common
denominator of violence. The counterstance refutes the dominant culture's views and beliefs, and, for this, it is proudly defiant. All reaction
is limited by, and dependent on, what it is reacting against. Because the
counterstance stems from a problem with authority — outer as well as
inner — it's a step towards liberation from cultural domination. But it is
not a way of life. At some point, on our way to a new consciousness, we
will have to leave the opposite bank, the split between the two mortal
combatants somehow healed so that we are on both shores at once and,
at once, see through serpent and eagle eyes.[12] Or perhaps we will decide
to disengage from the dominant culture, write it off altogether as a lost
cause, and cross the border into a wholly new and separate territory. Or
we might go another route. The possibilities are numerous once we
decide to act and not react.

A Tolerance for Ambiguity

These numerous possibilities leave *la mestiza* floundering in un-
charted seas. In perceiving conflicting information and points of view,
she is subjected to a swamping of her psychological borders. She has
discovered that she can't hold concepts or ideas in rigid boundaries. The
borders and walls that are supposed to keep the undesirable ideas out
are entrenched habits and patterns of behavior; these habits and patterns are the enemy within. Rigidity means death. Only by remaining
flexible is she able to stretch the psyche[13] horizontally and vertically. *La
mestiza* constantly has to shift out of habitual formations; from convergent thinking, analytical reasoning that tends to use rationality to
move toward a single goal (a Western mode), to divergent thinking,[14]

[11]*la cultura chicana:* chicana culture. Elsewhere in *Borderlands,* Anzaldúa writes,
"*La Cultura chicana* identifies with the mother (Indian) rather than with the father
(Spanish). Our faith is rooted in indigenous attributes, images, symbols, magic, and
myth" (Chapter 3).

[12]*see through serpent and eagle eyes:* "The eagle symbolizes the spirit (as the sun, the
father); the serpent symbolizes the soul (as the earth, the mother). Together, they symbol-
ize the struggle between the spiritual/celestial/male and the underworld/earth/feminine"
(*Borderlands,* Chapter 1).

[13]*the psyche:* the soul or self.

[14]In part, I derive my definitions for "convergent" and "divergent" thinking from
Rothenberg, 12–13. [Author's note]

characterized by movement away from set patterns and goals and toward a more whole perspective, one that includes rather than excludes.

The new *mestiza* copes by developing a tolerance for contradictions, a tolerance for ambiguity. She learns to be an Indian in Mexican culture, to be Mexican from an Anglo point of view. She learns to juggle cultures. She has a plural personality, she operates in a pluralistic mode — nothing is thrust out, the good the bad and the ugly, nothing rejected, nothing abandoned. Not only does she sustain contradictions, she turns the ambivalence into something else.

She can be jarred out of ambivalence by an intense, and often painful, emotional event which inverts or resolves the ambivalence. I'm not sure exactly how. The work takes place underground — subconsciously. It is work that the soul performs. That focal point or fulcrum, that juncture where the *mestiza* stands, is where phenomena tend to collide. It is where the possibility of uniting all that is separate occurs. This assembly is not one where severed or separated pieces merely come together. Nor is it a balancing of opposing powers. In attempting to work out a synthesis, the self has added a third element which is greater than the sum of its severed parts. That third element is a new consciousness — a *mestiza* consciousness — and though it is a source of intense pain, its energy comes from continual creative motion that keeps breaking down the unitary aspect of each new paradigm.

En unas pocas centurias,[15] the future will belong to the *mestiza.* Because the future depends on the breaking down of the paradigms, it depends on the straddling of two or more cultures. By creating a new mythos — that is, a change in the way we perceive reality, the way we see ourselves, and the ways we behave — *la mestiza* creates a new consciousness.

The work of *mestiza* consciousness is to break down the subject-object duality that keeps her a prisoner and to show in the flesh and through the images in her work how duality is transcended. The answer to the problem between the white race and the colored, between males and females, lies in healing the split that originates in the very foundation of our lives, our culture, our languages, our thoughts. A massive uprooting of dualistic thinking in the individual and collective consciousness is the beginning of a long struggle, but one that could, in our best hopes, bring us to the end of rape, of violence, of war. . . .

El camino de la mestiza
The Mestiza Way

> Caught between the sudden contraction, the breath sucked in and the endless space, the brown woman stands still, looks at the sky. She

---

[15]*En unas pocas centurias:* in a few centuries.

decides to go down, digging her way along the roots of trees. Sifting through the bones, she shakes them to see if there is any marrow in them. Then, touching the dirt to her forehead, to her tongue, she takes a few bones, leaves the rest in their burial place.

She goes through her backpack, keeps her journal and address book, throws away the muni-bart metromaps.[16] The coins are heavy and they go next, then the greenbacks flutter through the air. She keeps her knife, can opener, and eyebrow pencil. She puts bones, pieces of bark, *hierbas*,[17] eagle feather, snakeskin, tape recorder, the rattle and drum in her pack and she sets out to become the complete *tolteca*.[18]

Her first step is to take inventory. *Despojando, desgranando, quitando paja*.[19] Just what did she inherit from her ancestors? This weight on her back — which is the baggage from the Indian mother, which the baggage from the Spanish father, which the baggage from the Anglo?

Pero es difícil[20] differentiating between *lo heredado, lo adquirido, lo impuesto*.[21] She puts history through a sieve, winnows out the lies, looks at the forces that we as a race, as women, have been a part of. *Luego bota lo que no vale, los desmientos, los desencuentros, el embrutecimiento. Aguarda el juicio, hondo y enraízado, de la gente antigua*.[22] This step is a conscious rupture with all oppressive traditions of all cultures and religions. She communicates that rupture, documents the struggle. She reinterprets history and, using new symbols, she shapes new myths. She adopts new perspectives toward the darkskinned, women, and queers, She strengthens her tolerance (and intolerance) for ambiguity. She is willing to share, to make herself vulnerable to foreign ways of seeing and thinking. She surrenders all notions of safety, of the familiar. Deconstruct, construct. She becomes a *nahual*,[23] able to transform herself into a tree, a coyote, into another person. She learns to transform the small "I" into the total Self. *Se hace moldeadora de su alma. Según la concepción que tiene de sí misma, así será*.[24]

---

[16]*muni-bart metromaps:* maps of bus and rail transportation in the San Francisco Bay area.

[17]*hierbas:* herbs.

[18]Gina Valdés, *Puentes y Fronteras: Coplas Chicanas* (Los Angeles, CA: Castle Lithograph, 1982), 2. [Author's note] *tolteca:* the Toltec empire predates the Aztec in ancient Mexico. Anzaldúa associates the Toltecs with more woman-centered culture and religion than those of the warlike, patriarchal Aztecs.

[19]*Despojando, desgranando, quitando paja:* Stripping, removing the grain or the straw.

[20]*Pero es difícil:* But it is difficult.

[21]*lo heredado, lo adquirido, lo impuesto:* the inherited, the acquired, the imposed.

[22]*Luego bota lo que no vale . . .:* Then she discards whatever is useless, falsehoods and brutality. She waits for the deep, probing common sense of the ancient people.

[23]*nahual:* sorceress.

[24]*Se hace moldeadora . . . .:* She is able to mold her soul. Whatever image she has of herself, so she will be.

Que no se nos olvide los hombres[25]

> *"Tú no sirves pa' nada*[26] —
> you're good for nothing.
> *Eres pura vieja."*[27]

"You're nothing but a woman" means you are defective. Its opposite is to be *un macho*. The modern meaning of the word "machismo," as well as the concept, is actually an Anglo invention. For men like my father, being "macho" meant being strong enough to protect and support my mother and us, yet being able to show love. Today's macho has doubts about his ability to feed and protect his family. His "machismo" is an adaptation to oppression and poverty and low self-esteem. It is the result of hierarchical male dominance. The Anglo, feeling inadequate and inferior and powerless, displaces or transfers these feelings to the Chicano by shaming him. In the Gringo[28] world, the Chicano suffers from excessive humility and self-effacement, shame of self and self-deprecation. Around Latinos he suffers from a sense of language inadequacy and its accompanying discomfort; with Native Americans he suffers from a racial amnesia which ignores our common blood, and from guilt because the Spanish part of him took their land and oppressed them. He has an excessive compensatory hubris[29] when around Mexicans from the other side. It overlays a deep sense of racial shame.

The loss of a sense of dignity and respect in the macho breeds a   15
false machismo which leads him to put down women and even to brutalize them. Coexisting with his sexist behavior is a love for the mother which takes precedence over that of all others. Devoted son, macho pig. To wash down the shame of his acts, of his very being, and to handle the brute in the mirror, he takes to the bottle, the snort, the needle, and the fist.

Though we "understand" the root causes of male hatred and fear, and the subsequent wounding of women, we do not excuse, we do not condone, and we will no longer put up with it. From the men of our race, we demand the admission/acknowledgment/disclosure/testimony that they wound us, violate us, are afraid of us and of our power. We need them to say they will begin to eliminate their hurtful put-down ways. But more than the words, we demand acts. We say to them: We will develop equal power with you and those who have shamed us.

It is imperative that *mestizas* support each other in changing the

---

[25]*Que no se nos olvide los hombres:* Let us not forget men.
[26]*Tú no sirves pa' nada:* You're good for nothing.
[27]*Eres pura vieja:* You're nothing but a woman.
[28]*Gringo:* Anglo.
[29]*hubris:* exaggerated pride or self-confidence.

sexist elements in the Mexican-Indian culture. As long as woman is put down, the Indian and the Black in all of us is put down. The struggle of the *mestiza* is above all a feminist one. As long as *los hombres* think they have to *chingar mujeres*[30] and each other to be men, as long as men are taught that they are superior and therefore culturally favored over *la mujer*,[31] as long as to be a *vieja*[32] is a thing of derision, there can be no real healing of our psyches. We're halfway there — we have such love of the Mother, the good mother. The first step is to unlearn the *puta/virgen*[33] dichotomy and to see *Coatlapopeuh-Coatlicue* in the Mother, *Guadalupe*.[34]

Tenderness, a sign of vulnerability, is so feared that it is showered on women with verbal abuse and blows. Men, even more than women, are fettered to gender roles. Women at least have had the guts to break out of bondage. Only gay men have had the courage to expose themselves to the woman inside them and to challenge the current masculinity. I've encountered a few scattered and isolated gentle straight men, the beginnings of a new breed, but they are confused, and entangled with sexist behaviors that they have not been able to eradicate. We need a new masculinity and the new man needs a movement.

Lumping the males who deviate from the general norm with man, the oppressor, is a gross injustice. *Asombra pensar que nos hemos quedado en ese pozo oscuro donde el mundo encierra a las lesbianas. Asombra pensar que hemos, como femenistas y lesbianas, cerrado nuestros corazónes a los hombres, a nuestros hermanos los jotos, desheredados y marginales como nosotros.*[35] Being the supreme crossers of cultures, homosexuals have strong bonds with the queer white, Black, Asian, Native American, Latino, and with the queer in Italy, Australia, and the rest of the planet. We come from all colors, all classes, all races, all time periods. Our role is to link people with each other — the Blacks with Jews with Indians with Asians with whites with extraterrestrials. It is to transfer ideas and information from one culture to another. Colored homosexuals have more knowledge of other cultures; have

[30]*chingar mujeres:* fuck women.

[31]*la mujer:* the woman.

[32]*vieja:* old woman.

[33]*puta/virgen:* whore/virgin.

[34]*Coatlapopeuh-Coatlicue in the Mother, Guadalupe:* a reference to the dual identity (Indian/pagan and Spanish/Christian) of the Virgin of Guadalupe. Anzaldúa argues that "after the conquest, the Spaniards and their Church . . . desexed Guadalupe, taking Coatlalopeuh, the serpent/sexuality, out of her" (*Borderlands*, Chapter 3).

[35]*Asombra pensar que nos hemos quedado,* . . .: It's astonishing to think that we have stayed in that dark well where the world locks up lesbians. It's astonishing to think that as feminist lesbians, we have closed our hearts to men, to our gay brothers, as disinherited and alienated as we are.

always been at the forefront (although sometimes in the closet) of all liberation struggles in this country; have suffered more injustices and have survived them despite all odds. Chicanos need to acknowledge the political and artistic contributions of their queer. People, listen to what your *jotería*[36] is saying.

The mestizo and the queer exist at this time and point on the evolutionary continuum for a purpose. We are a blending that proves that all blood is intricately woven together, and that we are spawned out of similar souls. | 20 |

Somos una gente[37]

> *Hay tantísimas fronteras*
> *que dividen a la gente,*
> *pero por cada frontera*
> *existe también un puente.*[38]

> — GINA VALDÉS[39]

Divided Loyalties

Many women and men of color do not want to have any dealings with white people. It takes too much time and energy to explain to the downwardly mobile, white middle-class women that it's okay for us to want to own "possessions," never having had any nice furniture on our dirt floors or "luxuries" like washing machines. Many feel that whites should help their own people rid themselves of race hatred and fear first. I, for one, choose to use some of my energy to serve as mediator. I think we need to allow whites to be our allies. Through our literature, art, *corridos*,[40] and folktales we must share our history with them so when they set up committees to help Big Mountain Navajos[41] or the Chicano farmworkers or *los Nicaragüenses*[42] they won't turn people away because of their racial fears and ignorances. They will come to see that they are not helping us but following our lead.

Individually, but also as a racial entity, we need to voice our needs. We need to say to white society: we need you to accept the fact that Chicanos are different, to acknowledge your rejection and negation of us. We need you to own the fact that you looked upon us as less than

---

[36]*jotería:* gayness.

[37]*Somas una gente:* We are one people.

[38]*Hay tantísimas fronteras . . .:* There are so many borders / dividing people / but through each border there / passes a bridge.

[39]Richard Wilhelm, *The I Ching or Book of Changes*, trans. Cary F. Baynes (Princeton, NJ: Princeton University Press, 1950), 98. [Author's note]

[40]*corridos:* ballads or narrative folk songs of Mexico.

[41]*Big Mountain Navajoes:* Big Mountain is an area in New Mexico at the center of a Navaho and Hopi dispute over land rights and treaty conditions.

[42]*los Nicaragüenses:* The Nicaraguans.

human, that you stole our lands, our personhood, our self-respect. We need you to make public restitution: to say that, to compensate for your own sense of defectiveness, you strive for power over us, you erase our history and our experience because it makes you feel guilty — you'd rather forget your brutish acts. To say you've split yourself from minority groups, that you disown us, that your dual consciousness splits off parts of yourself, transferring the "negative" parts onto us. (Where there is persecution of minorities, there is shadow projection. Where there is violence and war, there is repression of shadow.) To say that you are afraid of us, that to put distance between us, you wear the mask of contempt. Admit that Mexico is your double, that she exists in the shadow of this country, that we are irrevocably tied to her. Gringo, accept the doppelganger[43] in your psyche. By taking back your collective shadow the intracultural split will heal. And finally, tell us what you need from us.

By Your True Faces We Will Know You

I am visible — see this Indian face — yet I am invisible. I both blind them with my beak nose and am their blind spot. But I exist, we exist. They'd like to think I have melted in the pot. But I haven't, we haven't.

The dominant white culture is killing us slowly with its ignorance. By taking away our self-determination, it has made us weak and empty. As a people we have resisted and we have taken expedient positions, but we have never been allowed to develop unencumbered — we have never been allowed to be fully ourselves. The whites in power want us people of color to barricade ourselves behind our separate tribal walls so they can pick us off one at a time with their hidden weapons; so they can whitewash and distort history. Ignorance splits people, creates prejudices. A misinformed people is a subjugated people.

Before the Chicano and the undocumented worker and the Mexican 25 from the other side can come together, before the Chicano can have unity with Native Americans and other groups, we need to know the history of their struggle and they need to know ours. Our mothers, our sisters and brothers, the guys who hang out on street corners, the children in the playgrounds, each of us must know our Indian lineage, our afro-*mestisaje*,[44] our history of resistance.

To the immigrant *mexicano* and the recent arrivals we must teach our history. The 80 million *mexicanos* and the Latinos from Central and South America must know of our struggles. Each one of us must know

[43]*doppelganger:* a double.
[44]*afro-mestisaje:* mixed-blood Latino people of African descent.

basic facts about Nicaragua, Chile, and the rest of Latin America. The Latinoist movement (Chicanos, Puerto Ricans, Cubans, and other Spanish-speaking people working together to combat racial discrimination in the market place) is good but it is not enough. Other than a common culture we will have nothing to hold us together. We need to meet on a broader communal ground.

The struggle is inner: Chicano, *indio*,[45] American Indian, *mojado*,[46] *mexicano*, immigrant Latino, Anglo in power, working class Anglo, Black, Asian — our psyches resemble the bordertowns and are populated by the same people. The struggle has always been inner, and is played out in the outer terrains. Awareness of our situation must come before inner changes, which in turn come before changes in society. Nothing happens in the "real" world unless it first happens in the images in our heads.

[45]*indio:* Indian (of Mexico/Central America).
[46]*mojado:* wetback.

Engaging the Text

1. What does Anzaldúa mean by "*mestiza* consciousness"? Why does she think such a new consciousness is necessary? What risks and rewards does she associate with a *mestiza* consciousness?

2. The concept of the *mestiza*, like the myth of the melting pot, involves the coming together of two or more cultures. How does the idea of *mestiza* consciousness differ from the melting pot metaphor?

3. How does Anzaldúa define the concept of *machismo* in this essay? How does it connect to the idea of *mestiza* consciousness? Why, according to Anzaldúa, are homosexuals important to this new way of thinking?

4. In paragraph 7, Anzaldúa distinguishes between a western mode of thinking, which she considers narrow and inadequate, and a more comprehensive "divergent" mode of thought. Do you think a person trained in traditional western thought can or should learn to think differently?

5. Discuss the effects of Anzaldúa's frequent use of Spanish, her mix of prose and poetry, her references to Mexican/Indian deities and folktales, her movement between vivid image and broad generalization, and other distinctive elements of her essay.

Exploring Connections

6. Write a dialogue between Anzaldúa and Virginia R. Harris and Trinity A. Ordoña (p. 359) on cross-racial hostility. Does *mestiza* consciousness offer an alternative to such hostilities?

7. What value might Anzaldúa's perspective have for a middle-class Jewish southerner? Write a letter from Anzaldúa to Adrienne Rich (p. 307) on being "split at the root."

8. Read or reread Sandra Cisneros's "Little Miracles, Kept Promises" (p. 221). Discuss the cultural, ideological, and racial borderlands that Cisneros's characters inhabit. Are any of these characters developing *mestiza* consciousness?

9. Review "Reflections on Race and Sex" (p. 249). Are bell hooks's views compatible with Anzaldúa's? Compare and contrast these authors' ideas about cultural and political change.

Extending the Critical Context

10. What advice do you think Anzaldúa would give to an American whose experience and family background are essentially monocultural?

11. Sketch out the rough plot outline for a short story that would capture some of Anzaldúa's ideas. Include brief descriptions of the main characters.

12. Anzaldúa suggests that one option for the *mestiza* is "to disengage from the dominant culture, write it off altogether as a lost cause, and cross the border into a wholly new and separate territory" (para. 6). What would it mean to disengage from the dominant culture? Do you think this is possible?

Child of the Americas

Aurora Levins Morales

This poem concentrates on the positive aspects of a multicultural heritage, as Morales celebrates her uniqueness, her diversity, and her wholeness. It's an up-to-date and sophisticated reinterpretation of the melting pot myth and a possible illustration of Gloria Anzaldúa's "mestiza consciousness" finding voice in poetry. For information on Morales, see the headnote to "Class Poem" in Chapter One (p. 95).

I am a child of the Americas,
a light-skinned mestiza of the Caribbean,
a child of many diaspora,[1] born into this continent at a crossroads.

[1]*diaspora:* scattered colonies. The word originally referred to Jews scattered outside Palestine after the Babylonian exile; it is now used often to refer to African peoples scattered around the world.

I am a U.S. Puerto Rican Jew,
a product of the ghettos of New York I have never known.   5
An immigrant and the daughter and granddaughter of immigrants.
I speak English with passion: it's the tongue of my consciousness,
a flashing knife blade of crystal, my tool, my craft.

I am Caribeña,[2] island grown. Spanish is in my flesh,
ripples from my tongue, lodges in my hips: 10
the language of garlic and mangoes,
the singing in my poetry, the flying gestures of my hands.
I am of Latinoamerica, rooted in the history of my continent:
I speak from that body.

I am not african. Africa is in me, but I cannot return.   15
I am not taína.[3] Taíno is in me, but there is no way back.
I am not european. Europe lives in me, but I have no home there.

I am new. History made me. My first language was spanglish.[4]
I was born at the crossroads
and I am whole.   20

---

[2]*Caribeña:* Caribbean woman.

[3]*taína:* describing the Taino, an aboriginal people of the Greater Antilles and Bahamas.

[4]*spanglish:* Spanish and English combined.

Engaging the Text

1. What is the myth of the melting pot? Does this poem challenge or promote this Central American myth? Explain.

2. Why does the poet list elements of her background that she scarcely knows ("the ghettos of New York" and Taino)? How can they be part of her?

3. How do you interpret the last stanza? Rephrase its messages in more complete, more explicit statements.

Exploring Connections

4. To what extent does this poem display a "*mestiza* consciousness" as described by Gloria Anzaldúa (p. 386)? Do you see any important differences between these authors? Explain.

5. Feeling "split at the root" is an issue not only for Adrienne Rich (p. 307), but also for Gloria Anzaldúa (p. 386), Stephen Cruz (p. 36), Huanani-Kay Trask (p. 118), and many other writers/characters in this book. How does the speaker of this poem avoid the feeling of fragmentation or schizophrenia?

Extending the Critical Context

6. Write your own version of "Child of the Americas," following Morales's structure but substituting ideas and images from your own heritage. Read it to the class.

5

Harmony at Home

The Myth of the Model Family

What would an American political campaign be without wholesome photographs of the candidates kissing babies and posing with their loving families? Politicians understand the cultural power of these symbols; they appreciate the family as one of our most sacred American institutions. The vision of the ideal nuclear family — Dad, Mom, a couple of kids, maybe a dog, and a spacious suburban home — is a cliché but also a potent myth, a dream that millions of Americans work to fulfill. The image is so compelling that it's easy to forget what a short time it's been around, especially compared with the long history of the family itself.

In fact, what we call the "traditional" family, headed by a breadwinner-father and a housewife-mother, has existed for little more than two hundred years, and the suburbs only came into being in the 1950s. But the family as a social institution was legally recognized in Western culture at least as far back as the Code of Hammurabi, published in ancient Mesopotamia some four thousand years ago. To appreciate how profoundly concepts of family life have changed, consider the absolute power of the Mesopotamian father, the patriarch: the law allowed him to use any of his dependents, including his wife, as collateral for loans or even to sell family members outright to pay his debts.

Although patriarchal authority was less absolute in Puritan America, fathers remained the undisputed heads of families. Seventeenth-century Connecticut, Massachusetts, and New Hampshire enacted laws condemning rebellious children to severe punishment and, in extreme cases, to death. In the early years of the American colonies, as in

Western culture stretching back to Hammurabi's time, unquestioned authority within the family served as both the model for and the basis of state authority. Just as family members owed complete obedience to the father, so all citizens owed unquestioned loyalty to the king and his legal representatives. In his influential volume *Democracy in America* (1835), French aristocrat Alexis de Tocqueville describes the relationship between the traditional European family and the old political order:

> . . . Among aristocratic nations, social institutions recognize, in truth, no one in the family but the father; children are received by society at his hands; society governs him, he governs them. Thus, the parent not only has a natural right, but acquires a political right to command them; he is the author and the support of his family; but he is also its constituted ruler.

By the mid-eighteenth century, however, new ideas about individual freedom and democracy were stirring the colonies. And by the time Tocqueville visited the United States in 1831, they had evidently worked a revolution in the family as well as in the nation's political structure: he observes, "When the condition of society becomes democratic, and men adopt as their general principle that it is good and lawful to judge of all things for one's self, . . . the power which the opinions of a father exercise over those of his sons diminishes, as well as his legal power." To Tocqueville, this shift away from strict patriarchal rule signaled a change in the emotional climate of families: "in proportion as manners and laws become more democratic, the relation of father and son becomes more intimate and more affectionate; rules and authority are less talked of, confidence and tenderness are oftentimes increased, and it would seem that the natural bond is drawn closer. . . ." In his view, the American family heralded a new era in human relations. Freed from the rigid hierarchy of the past, parents and children could meet as near equals, joined by "filial love and fraternal affection."

This vision of the democratic family — a harmonious association of parents and children united by love and trust — has mesmerized popular culture in the United States. From the nineteenth century to the present, popular novels, magazines, music, and advertising images have glorified the comforts of loving domesticity. In recent years, we've probably absorbed our strongest impressions of the ideal family from television situation comedies. In the 1950s we had the Andersons on *Father Knows Best*, the Stones on *The Donna Reed Show*, and the real-life Nelson family on *The Adventures of Ozzie & Harriet*. Over the next three decades, the model stretched to include single parents, second marriages, and interracial adoptions on *My Three Sons*, *The Brady Bunch*, and *Diff'rent Strokes*, but the underlying ideal of wise, loving parents and harmonious, happy families remained unchanged. Today, the same story is told again and again on *The Cosby Show, Wonder Years*, and even *The Simpsons*.

But while the myth of the American family is rooted deeply in our culture, it scarcely reflects the complexities of modern American life. High divorce rates, the rise of the single-parent household, the impact of remarriage, and a growing frankness about domestic violence are transforming the way we see family life; many families must also contend with the stresses of urban life and economic hardship. Such pressures on and within the family can be particularly devastating to young people: the suicide rate among fifteen- to nineteen-year-olds has more than tripled in the last thirty years. In our world it's no longer clear whether the family is a blessing to be cherished or an ordeal to be survived.

This chapter traces the history of the model family myth and explores alternative visions of family life. The first three selections raise questions about the myth itself. In "The Paradox of Perfection," Arlene Skolnick surveys American family life from the seventeenth century to the present and protests the influence of mythic images that encourage us to measure our family relationships against an unrealistic ideal. The narrator of Gary Soto's story "Looking for Work" recalls a boyhood desire to live the myth — and recounts his humorously futile attempts to transform his working-class Chicano family into a facsimile of the Cleaver clan on *Leave It to Beaver*. Richard Louv's "The Children of Sex, Drugs, and Rock 'n' Roll" approaches what politicians like to call the "crisis of the family" from a new perspective; his interviews with teenagers unsettle conventional assumptions about childhood innocence and adult responsibility.

The remainder of the chapter explores alternatives to the dominant model of family perfection. Tracing the African origins of Black family patterns, Joseph L. White exposes the cultural blindness that underlies many of the myths surrounding African American family life. Bebe Moore Campbell's "Envy" offers a lively personal account of growing up father-hungry in a female-dominated African American family. Next, in "An Indian Story," Robert Jack paints a warm, magical portrait of the bond between a Native American boy and his aunt. In "Friends as Family," a searing critique of the patriarchal family, Karen Lindsey contends that voluntary associations of friends can better fulfill our needs than biological families. Finally, Richard Goldstein's "The Gay Family" explores the ways that gay and lesbian marriages at once challenge and confirm the mythic power of the American family.

Sources

Gerda Lerner, *The Creation of Patriarchy*. New York: Oxford University Press, 1986.

Steven Mintz and Susan Kellogg, *Domestic Revolutions: A Social History of American Family Life*. New York: Free Press, 1988.

Alexis de Tocqueville, *Democracy in America*. 1835; New York: Vintage Books, 1990.

Before Reading . . .

Spend ten minutes or so jotting down every word, phrase, or image you associate with the idea of "family." Write as freely as possible, without censoring your thoughts or worrying about grammatical correctness. Working in small groups, compare lists and try to categorize your responses. What assumptions about families do they reveal?

If you prefer, draw a visual representation of your family. This could take the form of a graph, chart, diagram, map, cartoon, symbolic picture, or literal portrait. Don't worry if you're not a skillful artist: the main point is to convey an idea, and even stick figures can speak eloquently. When you're finished, write a journal entry about your drawing. Was it easier to depict some feelings or ideas visually than it would have been to describe them in words? Did you find some things about your family difficult or impossible to convey visually? Does your drawing "say" anything that surprises you?

The Paradox of Perfection

ARLENE SKOLNICK

The pressures of life in a highly industrialized urban society have taken their toll on the American family during the last century. Divorce is commonplace, mothers have joined fathers in the work force, and remarriages have vastly complicated family relationships. Yet the ideal of the perfect family lives on in American mythology. In this selection, Arlene Skolnick examines this myth and the effect it has on families who fail to live up to the expectations it creates. Skolnick (b. 1933) is a research psychologist at the Institute of Human Development at the University of California, Berkeley. She has edited or coedited The Intimate Environment *(1987),* Rethinking Childhood *(1976),* Family in Transition, *6th edition (1989), and* The Psychology of Human Development *(1986). "The Paradox of Perfection" first appeared in the* Wilson Quarterly, *Summer 1980.*

The American Family, as even readers of *Popular Mechanics* must know by now, is in what Sean O'Casey[1] would have called "a terrible state of chassis." Yet, there are certain ironies about the much-publicized crisis that give one pause.

True, the statistics seem alarming. The U.S. divorce rate, though it has reached something of a plateau in recent years, remains the highest in American history. The number of births out-of-wedlock among all races and ethnic groups continues to climb. The plight of many elderly Americans subsisting on low fixed incomes is well known.

What puzzles me is an ambiguity, not in the facts, but in what we are asked to make of them. A series of opinion polls conducted in 1978 by Yankelovich, Skelley, and White, for example, found that 38 percent of those surveyed had recently witnessed one or more "destructive activities" (e.g., a divorce, a separation, a custody battle) within their own families or those of their parents or siblings. At the same time, 92 percent of the respondents said the family was highly important to them as a "personal value."

Can the family be at once a cherished "value" and a troubled institution? I am inclined to think, in fact, that they go hand in hand. A recent "Talk of the Town" report in *The New Yorker* illustrates what I mean:

> A few months ago word was heard from Billy Gray, who used to play brother Bud in "Father Knows Best," the 1950s television show about the nice Anderson family who lived in the white frame house on a side street in some mythical Springfield — the house at which the father arrived each night swinging open the front door and singing out "Margaret, I'm home!" Gray said he felt "ashamed" that he had ever had anything to do with the show. It was all "totally false," he said, and had caused many Americans to feel inadequate, because they thought that was the way life was supposed to be and that their own lives failed to measure up.

As Susan Sontag[2] has noted in *On Photography*, mass-produced images have "extraordinary powers to determine our demands upon reality." The family is especially vulnerable to confusion between truth and illusion. What, after all, is "normal"? All of us have a backstairs view of our own families, but we know The Family, in the aggregate, only vicariously.

Like politics or athletics, the family has become a media event. Television offers nightly portrayals of lump-in-throat family "normalcy" (*The Waltons, Little House on the Prairie*) and even humorous "deviance" (*One Day at a Time, The Odd Couple*). Family advisers

[1]*Sean O'Casey:* Irish playwright (1880–1964).
[2]*Susan Sontag:* contemporary American essayist and critic (b. 1933).

sally forth in syndicated newspaper columns to uphold standards, mend relationships, suggest counseling, and otherwise lead their readers back to the True Path. For commercial purposes, advertisers spend millions of dollars to create stirring vignettes of glamorous-but-ordinary families, the kind of family most 11-year-olds wish they had.

All Americans do not, of course, live in such a family, but most share an intuitive sense of what the "ideal" family should be — reflected in the precepts of religion, the conventions of etiquette, and the assumptions of law. And, characteristically, Americans tend to project the ideal back into the past, the time when virtues of all sorts are thought to have flourished.

We do not come off well by comparison with that golden age, nor could we, for it is as elusive and mythical as Brigadoon.[3] If Billy Gray shames too easily, he has a valid point: while Americans view the family as the proper context for their own lives — 9 out of 10 people live in one — they have no realistic context in which to view the family. Family history, until recently, was as neglected in academe as it still is in the press. [The summer 1980] White House Conference on Families is "policy-oriented," which means present-minded. The familiar, depressing charts of "leading family indicators" — marriage, divorce, illegitimacy — in newspapers and newsmagazines rarely survey the trends before World War II. The discussion, in short, lacks ballast.

Let us go back to before the American Revolution.

Perhaps what distinguishes the modern family most from its colonial counterpart is its newfound privacy. Throughout the 17th and 18th centuries, well over 90 percent of the American population lived in small rural communities. Unusual behavior rarely went unnoticed, and neighbors often intervened directly in a family's affairs, to help or to chastise.

10

The most dramatic example was the rural "charivari," prevalent in both Europe and the United States until the early 19th century. The purpose of these noisy gatherings was to censure community members for familial transgressions — unusual sexual behavior, marriages between persons of grossly discrepant ages, or "household disorder," to name but a few. As historian Edward Shorter describes it in *The Making of the Modern Family*:

> Sometimes the demonstration would consist of masked individuals circling somebody's house at night, screaming, beating on pans, and blowing cow horns. . . . [O]n other occasions, the offender would be

---

[3]*Brigadoon:* in the Broadway musical (and, later, film) by Alan Jay Lerner and Frederick Loewe, Brigadoon is a Scottish town that comes to life only once every hundred years. It thus remains almost unchanged, a utopian place "saved" from history.

seized and marched through the streets, seated perhaps backwards on
a donkey or forced to wear a placard describing his sins.

The state itself had no qualms about intruding into a family's affairs
by statute, if necessary. Consider 17th-century New England's "stubborn child" laws that, though never actually enforced, sanctioned the
death penalty for chronic disobedience to one's parents.

If the boundaries between home and society seem blurred during
the colonial era, it is because they were. People were neither very
emotional nor very self-conscious about family life, and, as historian
John Demos points out, family and community were "joined in a
relation of profound reciprocity." In his *Of Domestical Duties*,
William Gouge, a 17th-century Puritan preacher, called the family "a
little community." The home, like the larger community, was as much
an economic as a social unit; all members of the family worked, be it on
the farm, or in a shop, or in the home.

There was not much to idealize. Love was not considered the basis
for marriage but one possible result of it. According to historian Carl
Degler, it was easier to obtain a divorce in colonial New England than
anywhere else in the Western world, and the divorce rate climbed
steadily throughout the 18th century, though it remained low by contemporary standards. Romantic images to the contrary, it was rare for
more than two generations (parents and children) to share a household,
for the simple reason that very few people lived beyond the age of 60. It
is ironic that our nostaglia for the extended family — including grandparents and grandchildren — comes at a time when, thanks to improve-
ments in health care, its existence is less threatened than ever before.

Infant mortality was high in colonial days, though not as high as we   15
are accustomed to believe, since food was plentiful and epidemics,
owing to generally low population density, were few. In the mid-1700s,
the average age of marriage was about 24 for men, 21 for women — not
much different from what it is now. Households, on average, were
larger, but not startlingly so: a typical household in 1790 included about
5.6 members, versus about 3.5 today. Illegitimacy was widespread.
Premarital pregnancies reached a high in 18th-century America (10
percent of all first births) that was not equaled until the 1950s.

Form Follows Function

In simple demographic terms, then, the differences between the
American family in colonial times and today are not all that stark; the
similarities are sometimes striking.

The chief contrast is psychological. While Western societies have
always idealized the family to some degree, the *most vivid* literary
portrayals of family life before the 19th century were negative or, at

best, ambivalent. In what might be called the "high tragic" tradition —
including Sophocles,[4] Shakespeare, and the Bible, as well as fairy tales
and novels — the family was portrayed as a high-voltage emotional
setting, laden with dark passion, sibling rivalries, and violence. There
was also the "low comic" tradition — the world of henpecked husbands
and tyrannical mothers-in-law.

It is unlikely that our 18th-century ancestors ever left the Book of
Genesis or *Tom Jones*[5] with the feeling that their own family lives were
seriously flawed.

By the time of the Civil War, however, American attitudes toward
the family had changed profoundly. The early decades of the 19th
century marked the beginnings of America's gradual transformation
into an urban, industrial society. In 1820, less than 8 percent of the U.S.
population lived in cities; by 1860, the urban concentration approached
20 percent, and by 1900 that proportion had doubled.

Structurally, the American family did not immediately undergo a   20
comparable transformation. Despite the large families of many immigrants and farmers, the size of the *average* family declined — slowly but
steadily — as it had been doing since the 17th century. Infant mortality
remained about the same and may even have increased somewhat,
owing to poor sanitation in crowded cities. Legal divorces were easier to
obtain than they had been in colonial times. Indeed, the rise in the
divorce rate was a matter of some concern during the 19th century,
though death, not divorce, was the prime cause of one-parent families,
as it was up to 1965.

Functionally, however, America's industrial revolution had a lasting
effect on the family. No longer was the household typically a group of
interdependent workers. Now, men went to offices and factories and
became breadwinners; wives stayed home to mind the hearth; children
went off to the new public schools. The home was set apart from the
dog-eat-dog arena of economic life; it came to be viewed as a utopian
retreat or, in historian Christopher Lasch's[6] phrase, a "haven in a
heartless world." Marriage was now valued primarily for its emotional
attractions. Above all, the family became something to worry about.

The earliest and most saccharine "sentimental model" of the family
appeared in the new mass media that proliferated during the second
quarter of the 19th century. Novels, tracts, newspaper articles, and
ladies' magazines — there were variations for each class of society —
elaborated a "Cult of True Womanhood" in which piety, submissive-

[4]*Sophocles:* Greek dramatist (495?–406?, B.C).
[5]*Tom Jones:* satirical eighteenth-century novel by Henry Fielding.
[6]*Christopher Lasch:* See p. 27.

ness, and domesticity dominated the pantheon of desirable feminine qualities. This quotation from *The Ladies Book* (1830) is typical:

> See, she sits, she walks, she speaks, she looks — unutterable things! Inspiration springs up in her very paths — it follows her footsteps. A halo of glory encircles her, and illuminates her whole orbit. With her, man not only feels safe, but actually renovated.

In the late 1800s, science came into the picture. The "professionalization" of the housewife took two different forms. One involved motherhood and childrearing, according to the latest scientific understanding of children's special physical and emotional needs. (It is no accident that the publishing of children's books became a major industry during this period.) The other was the domestic science movement — "home economics," basically — which focused on woman as full-time homemaker, applying "scientific" and "industrial" rationality to shopping, making meals, and housework.

The new ideal of the family prompted a cultural split that has endured, one that Tocqueville[7] had glimpsed (and rather liked) in 1835. Society was divided more sharply into man's sphere and woman's sphere. Toughness, competition, and practicality were the masculine values that ruled the outside world. The softer values — affection, tranquility, piety — were worshiped in the home and the church. In contrast to the colonial view, the ideology of the "modern" family implied a critique of everything beyond the front door.

What is striking as one looks at the writings of the 19th-century 25 "experts" — the physicians, clergymen, phrenologists[8] and "scribbling ladies"[9] — is how little their essential message differs from that of the sociologists, psychiatrists, pediatricians, and women's magazine writers of the 20th century, particularly since World War II.

Instead of men's and women's spheres, of course, sociologists speak of "instrumental" and "expressive" roles. The notion of the family as a retreat from the harsh realities of the outside world crops up as "functional differentiation." And, like the 19th-century utopians who believed society could be regenerated through the perfection of family life, 20th-century social scientists have looked at the failed family as the source of most American social problems.

[7]*Tocqueville:* see the introduction to this chapter.

[8]*phrenologists:* scientists who believed that certain mental characteristics could be indicated by the configuration of one's skill. Phrenology, which often supported racist arguments, has been discredited in this century.

[9]*scribbling ladies:* Nathaniel Hawthorne's derogatory term for female novelists who dealt with domestic themes and — not incidentally — often outsold Hawthorne's own works.

None of these who promoted the sentimental model of the family — neither the popular writers nor the academics — considered the paradox of perfectionism: the ironic possibility that it would lead to trouble. Yet it has. The image of the perfect, happy family makes ordinary families seem like failures. Small problems loom as big problems if the "normal" family is thought to be one where there are no real problems at all.

One sees this phenomenon at work on the generation of Americans born and reared during the late 19th century, the first generation reared on the mother's milk of sentimental imagery. Between 1900 and 1920, the U.S. divorce rate doubled, from four to eight divorces annually per 1,000 married couples. The jump — comparable to the 100 percent increase in the divorce rate between 1960 and 1980 — is not attributable to changes in divorce laws, which were not greatly liberalized. Rather, it would appear that, as historian Thomas O'Neill believes, Americans were simply willing to dissolve marriages that did not conform to their idea of domestic bliss — and perhaps try again.

A "Fun" Morality

If anything, family standards became even more demanding as the 20th century progressed. The new fields of psychology and sociology opened up whole new definitions of familial perfection. "Feelings" — fun, love, warmth, good orgasm — acquired heightened popular significance as the invisible glue of successful families.

Psychologist Martha Wolfenstein, in an analysis of several decades   30
of government-sponsored infant care manuals, has documented the emergence of a "fun morality." In former days, being a good parent meant carrying out certain tasks with punctilio;[10] if your child was clean and reasonably obedient, you had no cause to probe his psyche. Now, we are told, parents must commune with their own feelings and those of their children — an edict which has seeped into the ethos of education as well. The distinction is rather like that between religions of deed and religions of faith. It is one thing to make your child brush his teeth; it is quite another to transform the whole process into a joyous "learning experience."

The task of 20th-century parents has been further complicated by the advice offered them. The experts disagree with each other and often contradict themselves. The kindly Dr. Benjamin Spock, for example, is full of contradictions. In a detailed analysis of *Baby and Child Care*, historian Michael Zuckerman observes that Spock tells mothers to relax ("trust yourself") yet warns them that they have an "ominous power" to

[10]*punctilio:* strictness or exactness.

destroy their children's innocence and make them discontented "for years" or even "forever."

As we enter the 1980s, both family images and family realities are in a state of transition. After a century and a half, the web of attitudes and nostrums[11] comprising the "sentimental model" is beginning to unravel. Since the mid-1960s, there has been a youth rebellion of sorts, a new "sexual revolution," a revival of feminism, and the emergence of the two-worker family. The huge postwar Baby-Boom generation is pairing off, accounting in part for the upsurge in the divorce rate (half of all divorces occur within seven years of a first marriage). Media images of the family have become more "realistic," reflecting new patterns of family life that are emerging (and old patterns that are re-emerging).

Among social scientists, "realism" is becoming something of an ideal in itself. For some of them, realism translates as pluralism: all forms of the family, by virtue of the fact that they happen to exist, are equally acceptable — from communes and cohabitation to one-parent households, homosexual marriages, and, come to think of it, the nuclear family. What was once labeled "deviant" is now merely "variant." In some college texts, "the family" has been replaced by "family systems." Yet, this new approach does not seem to have squelched perfectionist standards. Indeed, a palpable strain of perfectionism runs through the pop literature on "alternative" family lifestyles.

For the majority of scholars, realism means a more down-to-earth view of the American household. Rather than seeing the family as a haven of peace and tranquility, they have begun to recognize that even "normal" families are less than ideal, that intimate relations of any sort inevitably involve antagonism as well as love. Conflict and change are inherent in social life. If the family is now in a state of flux, such is the nature of resilient institutions; if it is beset by problems, so is life. The family will survive.

[11]*nostrums:* quack medicines or, more generally, pet schemes to remedy social ills.

Engaging the Text

1. Summarize the three historical attitudes toward families that Skolnick describes. How does she account for the emergence of these views?

2. What is paradoxical about the American myth of the perfect family, according to Skolnick?

3. In Skolnick's view, what is "fun" morality and how has it affected family relationships?

4. Is Skolnick's conclusion about the future of the family consistent with the rest of her essay? How would you account for her conclusion?

Exploring Connections

5. Review "Living on the Land" by Kathleen Stocking (p. 164). What assumptions, values, or expectations are at work in the family life depicted there? How well does the Doe-Simkins family embody any of the typical American ideas about family that Skolnick describes?

6. Skolnick suggests that in the past families and family relationships were often depicted tragically. Look ahead to Karen Lindsey's "Friends as Family" (p. 463). How does her account of the patriarchal family help to explain this negative characterization?

Extending the Critical Context

7. Skolnick's essay was published in 1980. Do research on one area of family life that may have changed since then (homeless families, divorce rates, gay families, adoptions, incest or other abuse, TV families, and so on) and report your findings to the class. Based on several students' reports, what changes or additions would you make to Skolnick's article?

8. Ignoring current family law, discuss these questions in small groups. What commitments should a couple make at marriage? What minimum responsibilities do parents have toward their children, and vice versa? What grounds, if any, should a person have to get a divorce?

9. According to Skolnick, seventeenth-century preacher William Gouge saw the home as an economic unit as much as a social unit (para. 13). In a journal entry or essay, analyze the economic life of your own family. To what extent are responsibilities shared? What roles do various family members play in decisions about money? How is the economic life of the family related to other aspects of family life (authority, recreation, career satisfaction, birth control, friends, location of home, household routine, and so on)?

10. Watch Ron Howard's *Parenthood* on videotape. To what extent do the three families in the film reflect the myth of the perfect family? How would you define the relationships and values of each? Does the movie suggest the emergence of any new myths about the American family?

Looking for Work

Gary Soto

In the previous reading, you saw the "perfect family" from a scholar's perspective. Now see it through the eyes of a nine-year-old. "Looking for Work" is the humorous narrative of a young Mexican American boy who wants his family to imitate those he sees on TV. Gary

Soto deftly compares seductive myth and complex reality. Soto (b. 1952), now a professor of English at the University of California, Berkeley, grew up in Fresno, California, heart of the fertile San Joaquin Valley. Having discovered poetry almost by chance in a city college library, he has now published several volumes of his own, including The Elements of San Joaquin *(1977),* Father Is a Pillow Tied to a Broom *(1980), and* Home Course in Religion *(1991). He has also published essays and prose memoirs. "Looking for Work" appeared in* Living Up the Street: Narrative Recollections *(1985).*

One July, while killing ants on the kitchen sink with a rolled newspaper, I had a nine-year-old's vision of wealth that would save us from ourselves. For weeks I had drunk Kool-Aid and watched morning reruns of *Father Knows Best*, whose family was so uncomplicated in its routine that I very much wanted to imitate it. The first step was to get my brother and sister to wear shoes at dinner.

"Come on, Rick — come on, Deb," I whined. But Rick mimicked me and the same day that I asked him to wear shoes he came to the dinner table in only his swim trunks. My mother didn't notice, nor did my sister, as we sat to eat our beans and tortillas in the stifling heat of our kitchen. We all gleamed like cellophane, wiping the sweat from our brows with the backs of our hands as we talked about the day: Frankie our neighbor was beat up by Faustino; the swimming pool at the playground would be closed for a day because the pump was broken.

Such was our life. So that morning, while doing-in the train of ants which arrived each day, I decided to become wealthy, and right away! After downing a bowl of cereal, I took a rake from the garage and started up the block to look for work.

We lived on an ordinary block of mostly working class people: warehousemen, egg candlers,[1] welders, mechanics, and a union plumber. And there were many retired people who kept their lawns green and the gutters uncluttered of the chewing gum wrappers we dropped as we rode by on our bikes. They bent down to gather our litter, muttering at our evilness.

At the corner house I rapped the screen door and a very large   5 woman in a muu-muu answered. She sized me up and then asked what I could do.

"Rake leaves," I answered smiling.

"It's summer, and there ain't no leaves," she countered. Her face was pinched with lines; fat jiggled under her chin. She pointed to the lawn, then the flower bed, and said: "You see any leaves there — or

[1]*egg candler:* one who inspects eggs by holding them up to a light.

there?" I followed her pointing arm, stupidly. But she had a job for me and that was to get her a Coke at the liquor store. She gave me twenty cents, and after ditching my rake in a bush, off I ran. I returned with an unbagged Pepsi, for which she thanked me and gave me a nickel from her apron.

I skipped off her porch, fetched my rake, and crossed the street to the next block where Mrs. Moore, mother of Earl the retarded man, let me weed a flower bed. She handed me a trowel and for a good part of the morning my fingers dipped into the moist dirt, ripping up runners of Bermuda grass. Worms surfaced in my search for deep roots, and I cut them in halves, tossing them to Mrs. Moore's cat who pawed them playfully as they dried in the sun. I made out Earl whose face was pressed to the back window of the house, and although he was calling to me I couldn't understand what he was trying to say. Embarrassed, I worked without looking up, but I imagined his contorted mouth and the ring of keys attached to his belt — keys that jingled with each palsied step. He scared me and I worked quickly to finish the flower bed. When I did finish Mrs. Moore gave me a quarter and two peaches from her tree, which I washed there but ate in the alley behind my house.

I was sucking on the second one, a bit of juice staining the front of my T-shirt, when Little John, my best friend, came walking down the alley with a baseball bat over his shoulder, knocking over trash cans as he made his way toward me.

Little John and I went to St. John's Catholic School, where we sat   10
among the "stupids." Miss Marino, our teacher, alternated the rows of good students with the bad, hoping that by sitting side-by-side with the bright students the stupids might become more intelligent, as though intelligence were contagious. But we didn't progress as she had hoped. She grew frustrated when one day, while dismissing class for recess, Little John couldn't get up because his arms were stuck in the slats of the chair's backrest. She scolded us with a shaking finger when we knocked over the globe, denting the already troubled Africa. She muttered curses when Leroy White, a real stupid but a great softball player with the gift to hit to all fields, openly chewed his host[2] when he made his First Communion; his hands swung at his sides as he returned to the pew looking around with a big smile.

Little John asked what I was doing, and I told him that I was taking a break from work, as I sat comfortably among high weeds. He wanted to join me, but I reminded him that the last time he'd gone door-to-door asking for work his mother had whipped him. I was with him when his mother, a New Jersey Italian who could rise up in anger one moment and love the next, told me in a polite but matter-of-fact voice that I had

---

[2]*his host:* the wafer that represents, in the Catholic sacrament of Communion, the bread of the Last Supper and the body of Christ.

to leave because she was going to beat her son. She gave me a homemade popsicle, ushered me to the door, and said that I could see Little John the next day. But it was sooner than that. I went around to his bedroom window to suck my popsicle and watch Little John dodge his mother's blows, a few hitting their mark but many whirring air.

It was midday when Little John and I converged in the alley, the sun blazing in the high nineties, and he suggested that we go to Roosevelt High School to swim. He needed five cents to make fifteen, the cost of admission, and I lent him a nickel. We ran home for my bike and when my sister found out that we were going swimming, she started to cry because she didn't have the fifteen cents but only an empty Coke bottle. I waved for her to come and three of us mounted the bike — Debra on the cross bar, Little John on the handle bars and holding the Coke bottle which we would cash for a nickel and make up the difference that would allow all of us to get in, and me pumping up the crooked streets, dodging cars and pot holes. We spent the day swimming under the afternoon sun, so that when we got home our mom asked us what was darker, the floor or us? She feigned a stern posture, her hands on her hips and her mouth puckered. We played along. Looking down, Debbie and I said in unison, "Us."

That evening at dinner we all sat down in our bathing suits to eat our beans, laughing and chewing loudly. Our mom was in a good mood, so I took a risk and asked her if sometime we could have turtle soup. A few days before I had watched a television program in which a Polynesian tribe killed a large turtle, gutted it, and then stewed it over an open fire. The turtle, basted in a sugary sauce, looked delicious as I ate an afternoon bowl of cereal, but my sister, who was watching the program with a glass of Kool-Aid between her knees, said, "Caca."

My mother looked at me in bewilderment. "Boy, are you a crazy Mexican. Where did you get the idea that people eat turtles?"

"On television," I said, explaining the program. Then I took it a step further. "Mom, do you think we could get dressed up for dinner one of these days? David King does."

"Ay, Dios," my mother laughed. She started collecting the dinner plates, but my brother wouldn't let go of his. He was still drawing a picture in the bean sauce. Giggling, he said it was me, but I didn't want to listen because I wanted an answer from Mom. This was the summer when I spent the mornings in front of the television that showed the comfortable lives of white kids. There were no beatings, no rifts in the family. They wore bright clothes; toys tumbled from their closets. They hopped into bed with kisses and woke to glasses of fresh orange juice, and to a father sitting before his morning coffee while the mother buttered his toast. They hurried through the day making friends and gobs of money, returning home to a warmly lit living room, and then dinner. *Leave It to Beaver* was the program I replayed in my mind:

15

"May I have the mashed potatoes?" asks Beaver with a smile.

"Sure, Beav," replies Wally as he taps the corners of his mouth with a starched napkin.

The father looks on in his suit. The mother, decked out in earrings and a pearl necklace, cuts into her steak and blushes. Their conversation is politely clipped.

"Swell," says Beaver, his cheeks puffed with food.   20

Our own talk at dinner was loud with belly laughs and marked by our pointing forks at one another. The subjects were commonplace.

"Gary, let's go to the ditch tomorrow," my brother suggests. He explains that he has made a life preserver out of four empty detergent bottles strung together with twine and that he will make me one if I can find more bottles. "No way are we going to drown."

"Yeah, then we could have a dirt clod fight," I reply, so happy to be alive.

Whereas the Beaver's family enjoyed dessert in dishes at the table, our mom sent us outside, and more often than not I went into the alley to peek over the neighbor's fences and spy out fruit, apricot or peaches.

I had asked my mom and again she laughed that I was a crazy   25
chavalo[3] as she stood in front of the sink, her arms rising and falling with suds, face glistening from the heat. She sent me outside where my brother and sister were sitting in the shade that the fence threw out like a blanket. They were talking about me when I plopped down next to them. They looked at one another and then Debbie, my eight-year-old sister, started in.

"What's this crap about getting dressed up?"

She had entered her *profanity* stage. A year later she would give up such words and slip into her Catholic uniform, and into squealing on my brother and me when we "cussed this" and "cussed that."

I tried to convince them that if we improved the way we looked we might get along better in life. White people would like us more. They might invite us to places, like their homes or front yards. They might not hate us so much.

My sister called me a "craphead," and got up to leave with a stalk of grass dangling from her mouth. "They'll never like us."

My brother's mood lightened as he talked about the ditch — the   30
white water, the broken pieces of glass, and the rusted car fenders that awaited our knees. There would be toads, and rocks to smash them.

David King, the only person we knew who resembled the middle class, called from over the fence. David was Catholic, of Armenian and French descent, and his closet was filled with toys. A bear-shaped cookie jar, like the ones on television, sat on the kitchen counter. His mother was remarkably kind while she put up with the racket we made

---

[3]*chavalo:* kid.

on the street. Evenings, she often watered the front yard and it must have upset her to see us — my brother and I and others — jump from trees laughing, the unkillable kids of the very poor, who got up unshaken, brushed off, and climbed into another one to try again.

David called again. Rick got up and slapped grass from his pants. When I asked if I could come along he said no. David said no. They were two years older so their affairs were different from mine. They greeted one another with foul names and took off down the alley to look for trouble.

I went inside the house, turned on the television, and was about to sit down with a glass of Kool-Aid when Mom shooed me outside.

"It's still light," she said. "Later you'll bug me to let you stay out longer. So go on."

I downed my Kool-Aid and went outside to the front yard. No one 35 was around. The day had cooled and a breeze rustled the trees. Mr. Jackson, the plumber, was watering his lawn and when he saw me he turned away to wash off his front steps. There was more than an hour of light left, so I took advantage of it and decided to look for work. I felt suddenly alive as I skipped down the block in search of an overgrown flower bed and the dime that would end the day right.

Engaging the Text

1. Why is the narrator attracted to the kind of family life depicted on TV? What, if anything, does he think is wrong with his life? Why do his desires apparently have so little impact on his family?

2. Why does the narrator first go looking for work? Has the meaning of work changed at all by the end of the story, when he goes out again "in search of an overgrown flower bed and the dime that would end the day right"? Explain.

3. As Soto looks back on his nine-year-old self, he has a different perspective on things than he had as a child. How would you characterize the mature Soto's thoughts about his childhood family life? (Was it "a good family"? What was wrong with Soto's thinking as a nine-year-old?) Back up your remarks with specific references to the narrative.

4. Review the story to find each mention of food or drink. Explain the role these references play.

Exploring Connections

5. To what extent does Soto's experience bear out Arlene Skolnick's claims in "The Paradox of Perfection" (p. 402)? Do any of his insights complicate or challenge her thesis?

6. At the end of the narrative, the young Soto goes off in search of work and "the dime that would end the day right." Read or reread the selection by Gregory Mantsios in Chapter One (p. 72). How would Mantsios evaluate the

narrator's chances for success in later life? To what extent does the story challenge Mantsios's assumptions about the power of social class?

Extending the Critical Context

7. Write a journal entry about a time when you wished your family were somehow different. What caused your dissatisfaction? What did you want your family to be like? Was your dissatisfaction ever resolved?

8. "Looking for Work" is essentially the story of a single day. Write a narrative of one day when you were eight or nine or ten; use details as Soto does to give the events of the day broader significance.

9. Some TV portrayals of families have become more complicated since the era of *Father Knows Best*. Watch an episode or two of *Roseanne* or *Married . . . with Children* and discuss what these shows say about families and family relationships. Do they undermine the myth of family perfection? How would you account for their popularity?

The Children of Sex, Drugs, and Rock 'n' Roll

RICHARD LOUV

If children are the barometer of the family, a storm is brewing. In Childhood's Future *(1990), Richard Louv explores the "vanishing web of support" that once sustained America's families and made growing up in this country a relatively uncomplicated task. In this selection from the book, he reports on his interviews with teens — interviews that would no doubt shock their parents; indeed, one of his major themes is parents' ignorance of their children's lives in such vital areas as sexuality and drug use. Louv is a journalist, social commentator, and columnist for the* San Diego Union.

For so many children, the phosphor strands of video and computers, of street gangs and cults, and of course sex and drugs become a kind of false webbing, like scar tissue replacing healthy flesh. And so, even for healthy families, the world rushes in.

Tom and Beth Fitzsimons face their children's increasingly pressurized sexual environment straight on, as best they can. The trick, said Beth Fitzsimons, is to be direct and clear about the costs and limitations of sex. And that's not at all easy in the age of television and high-powered advertising. The important thing, said Beth, is to get *other* messages into their brains — though this approach has its shortcomings.

"We've tried to answer all their questions, and we're comfortable with one another, so that's helpful. But over the past couple of years, I've come to understand that you can answer all the questions right, you can educate them in a very modern way about the issues of sexuality, and they're going to screw it up anyway.

"I was cleaning the tub one day. Justin came in and said, 'Mom, I know all about the eggs and I know all about the sperms. And I know all about penises and I know all about vaginas. There's only one thing I don't understand. How does the sperm get through the two pairs of pants?' He was dead serious. He looked at me for a moment, and then realization dawned in his eyes. He went, '*Eeeeeeewwww* . . . unless you're *naked*! *Eeeeeeewwww*! That's *disgusting*!' And he was running around the second floor yelling this out and I was yelling at him, 'It *is not* disgusting! Your mother and father do it all the time!' And then I said, 'Oh, God . . . this is not good sex ed.'

"But you know, that phase went by and now he's very matter-of-fact. Elizabeth says, 'I prefer not to discuss this with you. I'll just read a book.'" Beth laughed. "Our kids had a great sex ed course at school. And this year, they had a program for the eighth-graders, too. They invited parents to take a corresponding course at night. We went. It was one of the best things we've ever done. Six Monday nights in a row. The kids were hysterical. Justin said, '*What*? You're going to a sex course *now*?' Actually, the kids loved it. We had the same teacher that they had. We talked about what our kids were talking about. One of the comforting things was that the parents all had the same concerns, especially that we would not like our children to be sexually active real young."

"I don't really think kids were doing it all that much these days anyway," said Tom. "They're probably just like we were. They talk about it more than they do it."

Unfortunately, kids are doing it more, and at earlier ages.

And the stakes are greater.

Childhood's New Sexual Environment

Four main elements define childhood's new sexual environment: sexual activity at younger and younger ages, AIDS, teenage pregnancy, and adult hesitancy to act.

A poll conducted by Louis Harris for Planned Parenthood in 1986, which surveyed one thousand youngsters from twelve to seventeen, found that 4 percent of the twelve-year-olds, 10 percent of the thirteen-year-olds, and 20 percent of the fourteen-year-olds had already had sex.

More than half the kids surveyed said they had had intercourse by the time they were seventeen. That rate was underscored by a study conducted by researchers at Brandeis University and Wheaton College, which showed that — even in the era of AIDS — more than two-thirds of U.S. male teenagers aged seventeen to nineteen reported having sexual intercourse in 1988, up 11 percent from 1979.[1]

"Most of the parents I meet aren't fully aware of how early and how intense the sexual pressure is for kids," said teacher Mary Olbersen, who conducts a peer-counseling program in San Diego. "Some of these kids have done really well standing up to pressure and just saying no and walking away with their chin up. Others fight for a while, but come in one day and say, 'I blew it, now what?' And it's not just the girls who get pressured into sex. One ninth-grader in this class, a good-looking, nice, intelligent boy who just transferred here to live with his father, told me there were four different girls on this campus who wanted him to get them pregnant."

How do kids perceive the sexual pressure?

"There's more of a stress on sex being so *important* in life," said one girl, an eleventh-grader, with resentment in her voice. "Since ninth grade, it's just been sex, sex, *sex*. Sex is constantly thrown at us."

An exuberant letterman added: "My parents and a lot of friends' parents, instead of sitting there and saying sex is something horrible, they say be safe about it. Instead of trying to ignore the problem, they're trying to face it. It's accepted. I know my parents think I have sex. A lot of parents would be really, like, *old-fashioned* I guess is the term if they didn't think that. I've seen movies about how if someone your age had sex when they were teenagers it was like *incredible*. Like really *strange*."

His classmates laughed. 15

"My parents know that I'm sexually active," he said, "and they can accept that and they're not trying to sit there and turn their backs on it and say it's not happening or anything, but I don't think it's exactly real to them."

Why, in the age of AIDS, is sexual activity among children increasing? Partly because of the sheer power of sexual images in the electronic bubble, which push them into sexual activity at younger and younger ages. Partly it's logistics. "Forget the back seat of the car," said Pat Welsh, the outspoken author and teacher at T. C. Williams. "During the days these houses are empty. There are kids here who leave school during their lunch hour, go home to get laid, and then rush back for their sixth-period class." And partly, it's naiveté, or worse, on the part of parents. "Parents don't connect drinking with sex," said Welsh. "The parents would rather have them drinking than doing drugs. But kids

---

[1]"Survey Finds More Teen-age Males Sexually Active, More of Them Using Condoms," *San Diego Union*, March 31, 1989, sec. F. [Author's note]

will tell you that the kids who are the heavy drinkers are often the most heavily into sex."

In this new sexual climate, kids are not only doing it a lot more, but they're disturbingly naive or fatalistic about the consequences, they're far more at risk than previous generations. The truth is that kids know everything about sex, but not much at all about getting pregnant or contracting AIDS. The *Detroit Free Press* reports that some girls think that they can't get pregnant if they wear high heels during intercourse, or that they can't get pregnant the first time, or that they can't get pregnant standing, or that they can't get pregnant if they don't kiss. Although condom use among the general teenage population is gradually increasing, condom use among teenagers in high-risk groups is *declining*.[2] Such ignorance is astonishing in a society so blanketed with sexual images.

I asked kids at San Diego High School, How had AIDS changed their lives?

Some of the boys were wearing fingerless gloves and earrings. The   20
girls favored leather and killer stares. Others were decked out, fifties style, in bobby sox.

"You can't go out and have your little —"

"Flings," said a girl. There was laughter.

"Gang bangs," said a boy. There was lots of laughter.

"It used to be you'd worry about getting pregnant and stuff and now it's directed toward getting AIDS," said the girl. She was wearing a leather coat and had a soft voice.

What about all those warning ads on television? Weren't adoles-   25
cents getting inundated with the message? *Nah*, they said, *we tune 'em out. Too depressing.*

I asked what proportion of kids were sexually active in that school.

"Two-thirds," someone at the back of the class said. "Three-fourths," a girl said. A boy topped her estimate. "Nine-tenths," he said.

How many of the girls knew somebody who used condoms? A few hands went up.

If most of them were sexually active, why didn't they use condoms?

Several of them answered at once. "Embarrassing." "It's not cool."   30
"Some of them bust so it doesn't matter." A girl said: "I think boys are embarrassed to go buy them. I think they'd rather steal them than buy them."

I thought they would be smarter than this, I told them.

"Adults aren't," said a girl.

Should condoms be more available to kids? Would that help? I

[2]Barbara Kantrowitz et al., "Kids and Contraceptives," *Newsweek*, February 16, 1987, 56–57. [Author's note]

asked them to raise their hands if they agreed. Most of them raised their hands.

"They should have them in the boys' bathroom," said the boy with the earring. "Like they have pads in the girls' bathroom, they should have condoms in the boys' bathroom."

Was AIDS talked about much in school? 35

"No. Except in a joking sense." The class agreed with that.

"They give us pamphlets," somebody said sarcastically. "You see them piled up outside the class doors. You see them in the hallway at lunch. Like it's a joke. Everybody goes, 'Hey, books on AIDS, it'll never happen to me, see ya.'" . . .

A few miles away, at Garfield High, I visited a class of pregnant teenagers. Protected by an armed security officer, the campus exuded an end-of-the-road atmosphere. This was where many of the city's problem students end up. . . .

Eighteen girls, aged fourteen and up, sat in this classroom. Some of the children who have attended the class at one time or another have been pregnant as young as eleven or twelve years old. All but one of the girls in this class were black or Hispanic. The exception was a Vietnamese girl who was perhaps four and a half feet tall, with a slash of red lipstick across her mouth. (This racial mix, I should add, does not reflect the national demographics of child pregnancy, which is increasing at a faster rate for whites than for blacks and Hispanics.)

Some of the girls had already given birth, and their babies were at 40 home with their mothers, or with baby sitters, or in the school nursery. The rest of the girls were pregnant, their bellies still growing. But their arms and legs were still growing, too. They were still children. Perhaps that is what I could see in their eyes — not their innocence, but their childhood.

"Some of us really wanted babies so we went out and got 'em," one girl said defiantly. The girl at the back of the room, hair braided tight, said, "Some of us were forced to fool around." So they were, most of them. According to statistics collected by a California network of teen pregnancy programs, as many as nine out of ten pregnant teenagers who carry their babies to term have been sexually molested or raped during their childhood.

"After I had the baby I went sort of dingy for a few minutes," said a fourteen-year-old. "I tripped out because for nine months I had a little human inside me. It was weird. That's a baby! In a way it was a bad thing that I got pregnant because I'm still young. In a way it's good because it drawed me and my boyfriend closer, so it worked out pretty well. Except me and my boyfriend aren't talkin' right now. . . ."

I asked, How many of them were glad they had gotten pregnant?

Two girls raised their hands. One of them, in the back, said: "I wanted to see if I had a baby, How would I treat my baby? Would I beat my baby, or abuse my baby? I feel good. I love my baby."

One out of six babies in the United States is born to a teenager, a 45
pregnancy rate that has plateaued. But the nature of teen pregnancy has changed: the pregnancy rate among younger teenagers is rising.

The tragedy is magnified in the next generation. Seventy percent of children born to mothers aged seventeen or younger — compared with 25 percent of children born to mothers in their twenties — will spend part of their lives in single-parent homes. Eighty percent of teenage mothers never finish high school. (Most were dropouts when they became pregnant, which suggests that keeping kids in school may help lower the teenage birthrate.) The likelihood of living a life of poverty is seven times greater for a teenage mother than for other teens. Sixty percent of the nation's total welfare budget is provided to women who first gave birth as a teenager. . . . These grim statistics are part of the price of the vanishing web.[3]

The future of teenage mothers does not have to be such a portrait of disappointment. Most experts on teen pregnancy agree that remedial education is the one factor that can improve the later lives of these young women and their children, and that the programs should extend beyond high school and well into the women's twenties.

"I wanted to be a cheerleader," said one of the fourteen-year-olds a little uncertainly. "I think I still be able to do that."

The Vietnamese girl said, in the smallest of voices: "This class gave us encouragement to go on with life. We're all a big family here."

"Sometimes when we go on our little walks," said a girl with 50
cornrow braids, "we'll walk around the block here, 'cause they say walking's good, and everybody driving by instead of keeping their eye on the road, they slow down because there's twenty or forty people walking down the street and all of them pregnant."

She giggled at the image and hid her face.

"Ironically, a teenager often sees having a baby as a way to make something good in her life, to become a 'good girl' by becoming a mother," explained Judy Kirsten, who heads the Garfield Pregnant Minors Program. "Look at the need for status. Look at the fact that so many of these girls have been molested themselves, as children, and yet

---

[3]Charles Ballard, who runs the Teen Fathers Program in Cleveland, says he asked a group of fifteen boys how many were fathers. Only two raised their hands. When he asked how many had babies, fourteen hands went up. "They just don't think like fathers," Ballard says. "They don't connect pregnancy with marriage or husbanding or fatherhood." At least 65 percent of his clients never really knew their own fathers. "No man has ever touched their lives except a policeman," he says, "and he was approaching them with a gun or a billyclub in his hand." ("Kids and Contraceptives," Newsweek, February 16, 1987, 60). . . . [Author's note]

they insist on carrying their own babies to term, to create six pounds of self-esteem, to do something good in the world."

One of those good things is to make contact with an adult.

Among pregnant adolescent programs nationwide, there is a new awareness that men in their twenties, thirties, and forties — adults — are primarily the ones getting young girls pregnant. In San Diego County, for example, teenage boys father only 15 percent of the babies born to girls aged twelve to seventeen. "This used to be called statutory rape and was legally prosecuted. It is not being prosecuted anymore," said Kirsten. "The courts are too jammed with other things, the girls are not good witnesses, or they fear that the father will retaliate against them."

These kids live in a fairy tale; they believe that someday a prince   55
will sweep them away to the Land of Cosby, where the father always comes home and the ratings are always high. But today, an unmarried pregnant black teen has a greater chance of miscarrying than she has of marrying; only one in five premarital pregnancies is resolved through marriage. What about the girl's family; what about the baby's grand-mother? Isn't the child-mother taken into those adult arms? In some cases, yes; but more often the girl's family does more harm than good.

"Typically, the girl takes the baby home and the girl's mother and grandmother help care for it — they compete for the baby while the girl goes on with her life," Kirsten said. "Meanwhile, the baby grows, isn't as cuddly and cute anymore, and then the girl's mother hands the baby back to the teenager and says, 'Okay, now it's your turn.' But the girl is unprepared to take the baby back, has never developed a sense of responsibility, hasn't bonded to the child, and has few parenting skills."

These children, particularly the African American ones, are far more culturally conservative about some aspects of the birth process than white kids. They wouldn't, for example, consider placing their babies up for adoption or aborting. Some of the girls, however, had considered suicide. One of them said she had considered taking sleeping pills. "Or like poison or something," she said. "I didn't want to have a slow, agonizing death. I like to get it done quick and over with." Fortunately, her parents had taken her back into their home, and the thoughts of suicide had drifted away.

Now, for the first time, the girl with the stack of books spoke up. "I didn't want to be pregnant," she said fiercely. "There was a lot of things that I wanted to do and I'm going to do them. I'm going to college."

"Who's gonna take care of your baby?" asked one of her classmates.

"My mom, or a baby sitter," said the girl with the books. "Or they   60
got day-care centers at community colleges —"

"Ain't no baby sitter at four o'clock in the morning," said one of the other girls, her voice light and trilly, almost taunting.

"You got to deal with it," said the girl with the books, hanging on for dear life, her fierceness still there even as she began to cry. "You got to deal with it."

Sex and the Fundamental Divide

Most adults are not dealing with it — not with the threat of AIDS to teenagers, not with children having children, not with the fundamental divide.

First, unlike Tom and Beth Fitzsimons, most parents do not talk with their children about sex. Clinical research indicates that kids whose parents talk to them about sex are more likely to delay having sex, and when they do have sex, are more likely to be responsible. Yet former U.S. surgeon general C. Everett Koop has pointed out that the vast majority of parents of children under twelve have never discussed sex with their kids — despite all the openness of this generation of parents and kids on other topics.[4]

Second, most of our institutions are failing to confront the issue directly. As the kids with whom I spoke rightly suggested, our schools and other institutions have done relatively little to educate children about the danger of AIDS. In the late eighties, thirteen- to nineteen-year-olds accounted for less than 1 percent of individuals infected with the AIDS virus nationwide. Read that statistic cold and you might assume that teens are somehow insulated by their immune systems from the syndrome. But the next age group, aged twenty to twenty-nine, accounted for 21 percent of the individuals diagnosed with the virus. When were they likely to have been infected? *When they were teenagers.*[5]

During the year following this report, the U.S. Army tested about half a million teenage recruits and announced in May 1988 that results showed a higher than expected prevalence of the virus among teens. Recent studies also show that teenagers are more likely to have multiple sex partners than persons in other age groups. Gary Yates, director of a pilot medical and psychiatric clinic for teenagers at Children's Hospital in Los Angeles, reports that more than half of street kids barter their bodies to survive, and 35 percent of street kids are involved in intravenous drug use. They therefore constitute a prime group for the transmission of AIDS.[6]

65

---

[4]Erica E. Goode, "Telling '80s Kids About Sex," *U.S. News and World Report,* November 16, 1987, 83. [Author's note]

[5]Schools to Get Special Help on AIDS Instruction, Koop Says," *San Diego Union,* July 27, 1987, sec. A; Mark Arner, "Curriculum on AIDS Unveiled by County," *San Diego Tribune,* July 27, 1988, sec B. [Author's note]

[6]Robert P. Hey, "U.S. Army Data Show AIDS Virus Is a Growing Teen-age Problem," *Christian Science Monitor,* May 2, 1988; "Scientists Trying to Find Why Teens Do Such Risky Things," *San Diego Union,* November 26, 1987, sec. A. . . . [Author's note]

Yet, trapped between dueling moralities, the schools are moving at a snail's pace. The San Diego Unified School District, for example, is using a "social concerns team," a group of about twenty teachers who go around to the schools and teach about drug abuse and AIDS. In 1988, the district's goal was to reach every student in grades six to twelve with at least one hour of AIDS instruction in a classroom setting. By the spring of that year, the district's director of health services estimated that only 50 to 60 percent of the students had been talked to.

For a relatively enlightened school district, this record is horrific, and all too typical of other school districts around the country.

Surprisingly, no study has ever proved or disproved that school sex education per se has any effect on the frequency of sexual activity among students.[7] What *has* been proved, at least in the prevention of pregnancy, is the effectiveness of classes in sexuality combined with school-based clinics offering birth control information or actual contraceptives. The success of this combination was first demonstrated when the Mechanic Arts High School in St. Paul, Minnesota, adopted such an approach in 1973 and cut the teenage birthrate nearly in half. The reason school-based clinics make headway is twofold: first, they offer more than talk; second, they offer follow-up. A nurse or nurse practitioner at a school clinic can establish continuing, first-name relationships with students, guiding them through the sexual minefield of adolescence.[8] School-based clinics can also diagnose serious health problems, identify children with inadequate immunizations, and offer prenatal care — all of which, in the long run, can reduce the nation's health expenditures, as well as the number of babies born to children. . . .

There should also be more discussion in schools of the moral dimensions of sexual activity. But I was astonished to find how little teenagers in the classes I interviewed talked about the morality of sexual activity.

Ironically, the timidity of teachers to bring up such issues was due in part, I was told by teachers, to their fear of attack by religious parents who often do not want sex discussed in school, or by other parents who, for whatever reason, have resisted the introduction of religion or morality into the debate.

Yet the stark realities of AIDS are slowly opening up . . . the discussion of previously taboo topics. C. Everett Koop — known for his

[7]Hersch, "Coming of Age on City Streets," *Psychology Today*, January 1988, 28. Some studies have suggested that youngsters who take courses in sex education are more likely to use contraceptives — and more likely to have sex. Other studies contest this claim. [Author's note]

[8]"Kids and Contraceptives," *Newsweek*, February 16, 1987, 60. School-based clinics do more than counsel teens about birth control and pregnancy. One such school clinic, in the South Bronx, is part of an after-school program called the Hub, which includes aerobics and karate and computer lessons, in addition to group discussions about sex and contraceptives. [Author's note]

conservative views on birth control and abortion — was a forceful advocate of the use of condoms as AIDS protection. At the same time, many social liberals, to whom the word *abstinence* was in recent decades a joke, now advocate the teaching of this concept in schools.[9]

Unless this sense of common adult purpose can be nurtured, the fundamental divide will widen and children will continue to fall into the gap in ever-increasing numbers.

Drugs: From Rehabilitation to Habilitation

Each year during the eighties, the "National High School Senior Drug Abuse Survey" reported that drug abuse among high school seniors had decreased slightly. But while Americans in general appear to be slowly turning away from the use of illegal drugs, the people doing so tend to be the most educated and affluent, and drug abuse among the poorest and least educated continues to intensify.[10]

There are three especially troubling aspects to the trends in drug use 75 among children and teenagers. First, a new wave may be on the way. Whereas drug use among other teenagers appears to have peaked by the end of the eighties, drug use among junior high and elementary school children is rising. Second, hard-core drug use continues to destroy inner-city neighborhoods, and the children in them. Third, alcohol abuse among children and teens is worsening. With drug and alcohol abuse, as with sex, what parents believe the kids are doing and what the kids are actually doing are often different.

A Louis Harris survey for the Metropolitan Life Foundation in 1988 pointed out "wide discrepancies between parental perception and what

[9]One organization that helps schools set up health clinics, the Washington-based Center for Population Options, publishes a booklet that lists ten reasons not to have sex, including "You don't want to," "You're not ready," "You want to wait until you're in love or married," and "You're not using birth control." In 1988, the California Senate passed by a wide margin legislation that would require school sex education programs to emphasize abstinence and encourage students to make decisions based on ethical considerations. The bill was inspired by a program at San Marcos High School which had resulted in a drop in the number of pregnant girls from 147 in 1984–85 to 20 in 1986–87. The program emphasizes the importance of correct decision making regarding a variety of subjects, including sex and drugs. Under the bill, sex education programs are required to teach students how to communicate on a nonsexual level, how to reject sexual advances and "negative peer pressure," and that abstinence from sexual intercourse is the only completely effective protection against unwanted pregnancy. In addition, the bill requires sex education programs to discuss the fallibility of all contraceptives, the failure rate of condoms in preventing AIDS and other sexually transmitted diseases, the legal implications for minors of having sexual intercourse, and the financial responsibility of having children in or out of wedlock. But even this presentation drew opposition from some quarters, including one state senator, who argued, "We are asking schools to take over for mom and pop" (Michael Smolens, "State Senate OKs Sex Education Bill Pushing Abstinence," *San Diego Union*, May 13, 1988, sec. A). [Author's note]

[10]Jane E. Brody, "Personal Health," *New York Times*, May 4, 1989, sec. B. [Author's note]

students report in the areas of alcohol and drug abuse." Five percent of the parents surveyed reported that their child had used drugs, whereas 17 percent of students said they had used drugs. Thirty-six percent of parents said their child had had at least one alcoholic drink; but 66 percent of students surveyed said they had used alcohol at least once or twice.[11]

I asked a class at San Diego High what they saw, in their lives, as the major drug trends. One boy offered: "We're in a state of flux. People are more extreme, on one side or another. You have the Say No to Drugs group over here and you have the group over here that's doing drugs and selling drugs, and there's nothing in the middle."

One girl said, "If you're in the middle, you're only in the middle for a while."

The kids spoke almost at once now. "It starts really early and that's pretty scary." "Elementary school." "I know someone who was doing heavy drugs in fifth grade. Acid."

"My brother's and sister's in elementary school and they come home and say they have friends who are into drugs right now." "I've seen a lot of people get scared away from drugs in elementary school and then seen them turn around and do them in junior high and then turn around and not do them in high school."

Most of the other kids said drugs started later, around eighth grade.

I asked, How did they feel about the Just Say No campaign?

"I think it might affect people in elementary school, but I don't think it affects people in high school. They're going to do what they want to do and no campaign about Say No to Drugs is going to stop them."

Most of the class agreed with that. One girl said, "I knew this guy who had a JUST SAY NO bumper sticker on his car and he's a cocaine addict."

Among these kids, alcohol was currently the drug of choice: "Easier to get." "Easy and inexpensive." "You go to a store that isn't afraid to sell to younger people, you get someone who looks twenty-one, you fish — ask someone out on the street who's over twenty-one." "Or you just get a friend you know who's over twenty-one." "It seems drinking is more acceptable and when you drink you can accept what you're doing 'cause your parents do it, it's not as bad." "I've been to a lot of parties where parents will get the alcohol, will sit there and will stay there, and they'll say it's because they don't want anything to get too rowdy, which might be OK — but then why did they get the alcohol in the first place?"

[11]"Kids Who Take Drugs Pull Wool over Parents' Eyes," *San Diego Tribune*, November 3, 1988, sec. D. [Author's note]

Some of the kids believed the Just Say No campaign had worked, but not exactly in the way it was intended.

"We say no to drugs, and *yes* to alcohol," said one boy. "It's made alcohol acceptable. A friend of mine was doing pot a lot and then he started forgetting things so he decided to quit. He's been clean from pot for a month, but he was telling me about all these alcohol drinks he's been tasting; every night he tries something different."

"Drink as much as you can as fast as you can. That's the goal."

What did adults tell them to say yes to?

"Milk: it does a body good," said one boy.   90

As with sex, drugs aren't the problem. The problem is adults and the messages they send to children.[12] Consider, for example, the messages sent by adults — the signals that saturate the electronic bubble — regarding alcohol.

The three most heavily promoted product groups in the United States today are, first, pharmaceuticals; second, tobacco; and third, alcohol.

A few years ago, Michelob ads rang with the jingle, "Weekends are made for Michelob." That message was consistent with what was then the prevailing American norm: drinking is for time out, for weekends. Then came "put a little weekend in your week." The most recent theme is "the night, the night, the night belongs to Michelob" — ads with a thumping rock beat aimed at a youth market.

In a matter of a few years, advertisers have worked to condition Americans — particularly young Americans — to think of drinking as an appropriate nightly habit rather than a weekend escape. Wine coolers, introduced in the past decade and targeted specifically at young women, are what one alcohol-abuse expert describes as the "alcoholic soft drink for girls." The alcohol industry's newest thrust is to increase the number of outlets for "off-sale premises" — gas stations and minimarts — where teenagers buy most of their alcohol. It's not unusual today to find beer priced more competitively than Pepsi.[13]

[12]"Teacher Poll Finds Most Battle Student Drinking," *San Diego Tribune*, September 22, 1989, sec. A. In 1989, the annual survey of teacher opinion by the Metropolitan Life Insurance Company found that the number of teachers in grades seven through twelve concerned about student drinking in their schools had increased from 66 percent in 1985 to 81 percent in the latest survey. Each day in America, about 1,000 people will die because of tobacco, 350 will die because of alcohol, and 35 will die because of illegal drug use. The total cost to society of alcohol abuse, including lost productivity in the work place, is about $115 billion. In comparison, the total cost of illegal drug abuse is about $60 billion. [Author's note]

[13]*Weekly Reader Survey on Drugs and Drinking* (Middletown, Conn.: Field Publications, 1987). Some of the material on alcohol abuse was provided by Bob Reynolds, former deputy director for alcohol services for the San Diego County Health Department and now an advocate for reform of alcohol-related laws in California. [Author's note]

Not surprisingly, when the *Weekly Reader* and the National Council   95
on Alcoholism and Drug Dependence conducted a survey of student
attitudes in 1987, the survey revealed that alcohol is the only drug that
children are *less* likely to identify as a drug as they grow older. In grades
two and three, 33 percent of students called wine coolers a drug; by
grades seven through twelve, the figure was 25 percent.

Meanwhile, alcohol-related problems are the leading cause of death
among adolescents.

The problem, it seems to me, is not the drugs themselves, but the
commercial exploitation of children and young people and the environment in which they live. In any effective war on drugs, the emphasis
must shift from the drugs themselves to the environment in which
children live. Specific drugs will come and go; stop cocaine smuggling
tomorrow, and methamphetamine will burst into production in base-
ments all over America — and children, of course, will still drink. But
the commercial and social environment that encourages drug abuse will
remain. . . .

It's Not Only Rock 'n' Roll

One of the best ways to understand how children and teenagers
perceive their environment, and the need to change it, is through their
music — not through the music itself, or its packaging, but through
what kids say about their music.

At Baldi Middle School in Philadelphia I asked a class, What about
all the people who say heavy metal music causes kids to take drugs?

One boy who listened to heavy metal said: "People who are going to   100
take drugs are going to take drugs anyway, and if a lot of people like to
blame the music — I mean, if someone says, 'Go jump off of the Empire
State Building,' or 'Go jump off a bridge,' or 'Shoot your mother,' are
you going to do it? The only people that are saying, 'If you play a record
backwards you get a Satanic message and it's going to harm your child,'
the only people who are saying that are the ones trying to find an excuse
why their daughter or son did drugs, 'cause they're scared it's just going
to come down to their kid had emotional problems."

A boy who favored rap music explained why he likes to turn his
boom box up loud. He likes to create an *environment*: "Since we like it
so much, we get into the illusion that a lot of people must like it, so we
go around playing it loud and we have this feeling that we're bringing
them the music — so we can make everybody dance, make everybody
say *ho*, and it's like a symbol or power, just making you believe that you
can bring the music that everybody likes to them, like you're the sup-
plier of what they want." . . .

Baby boomers grew up thinking of rock 'n' roll, the music of
defiance and rebellion, as their personal sound track. *Tsk*, *tsk*, they

cluck today. Look at all the teenagers listening to all that imitation rock. No meaning, no context.

In fact, today's children may be the first generation since the advent of vinyl and radio to embrace its parents' music; in that sense, teenagers today are more unusual, musically, than the boomers.[14]

Francis Thumm, forty, is a musician, a contributor to the albums of singer-songwriter Tom Waits, and a music teacher at Point Loma High School in San Diego. He says teenage music today is as rich and diverse as it was in the sixties.

"But young people today have a sense of history about the music. A   105
kid who listens to heavy metal knows instinctively that the guitar solos he hears had roots in Jimmy Page and Eric Clapton." The Beatles are popular. (One of the Baldi girls said she liked the Beatles because "some of their music sounds like hard rock, and some of it sounds like Easy One-Oh-One music, and some of it like sounds like elevator music and that's why I like it, because whatever I feel like, I can listen to.") Thumm continued: "Jimi Hendrix is a god to these kids. They don't know much about him personally. But musically, he's a symbol of fiery virtuosity."

Revealingly, Jim Morrison, dark prince of the Doors, is a bigger star today than he was in the sixties — bigger than the Beatles. "Kids love the gothic quality of his songs, the preoccupation with death, the sense of isolation and waywardness, and the fact that he died young." The Jim Morrison biography *No One Here Gets Out Alive* is the current teen generation's corollary to what *The Autobiography of Malcolm X* meant to baby boomers. . . .

In Thumm's songwriting class, students stand or sit under the light of a single lamp and sing or simply read their songs or poetry. A frequent subject of these songs is their painful home life.

What impresses Thumm most is how closely the kids listen to one another. "When they sing, you can hear a pin drop. Unlike most of us baby boomers at that age, these kids listen to each other with absolute respect."

Sometimes they write about suicide. A few years ago, one girl, "tall and stunning, like a model," killed herself. Thumm pulled one of her poems from a manila folder. It read, "The air gets warm / and thinner by the breath / when will be the mercy / of the coming of my death. . . ." The lines, written so neatly, nearly disappear on the page.

When Thumm showed me this poem, his face filled with pain. "I   110
have learned over time to pay close attention to these songs and poems."

Despite the inherent sadness of rock 'n' roll nostalgia, many teenagers display strong survival instincts. For every sad song, there's a song

---

[14]George Varga, music critic for the *San Diego Union*, contributed this idea. [Author's note]

of hope. Thumm is moved by his students' reverence for nature. And some things never change. "Quality music always wins," he says. "For example, they love gospel music. Just today, when I asked the members of the chorus what they wanted to sing, most of them held up 'Ave Maria,' a thirteenth-century motet. We had a school assembly that began with six students singing an a cappella rendition of Leadbelly's 'Sylvie,' a southern work song. Suddenly this chaotic auditorium became as quiet as a church. I attribute that to the surprising peer respect among these young people and to the simple, noble power of the music."

For teenagers, the need for approval and love from parents and peers has never changed. Teenagers are insecure and scared to death. That hasn't changed either.

Joan Baez has complained that youth music today has no context — no Vietnam War or civil rights movement for which to serve as sound track. But the affinity for classic rock suggests a context. And surely heavy metal and rap music have their own context. Some of this music glorifies destruction, but much of it criticizes what drugs, advertising, environmental ignorance, and divorce have done to our society. Of *course* there's hysteria in much of today's music, and *sure*, it lacks grace and joy. But the context is kids growing up with single parents trying to make ends meet, growing up with divorce, growing up with disintegration.

"There's a sense now, in the music, of a people about to slide over a cultural waterfall," said Thumm. "My response to Joan is, Wake up, honey, it's a different world."

Engaging the Text

1. What are the most essential problems Louv addresses? What causes and what solutions does he see for these problems? What causes and solutions would you add?

2. Teen pregnancy is often an accident, but Louv also discusses teenagers who want to get pregnant. Why would a girl or a boy want to become a parent at the age of fifteen or sixteen?

3. Some public health experts say that college students are well informed about AIDS and AIDS prevention but that, in their actual behavior, many disregard what they know. How do you think Louv would explain this split between knowledge and action?

4. Why, according to Louv, do parents and teens communicate so poorly? To what extent do you agree with him?

5. Why does Louv follow his analysis of sex, drugs, and childhood with a discussion of rock and roll? What is his thesis in the last section of the essay? Do you agree with it?

Exploring Connections

6. How can the myth of the perfect family, as described by Arlene Skolnick (p. 402), survive in a culture with all the family problems Louv lists?

7. Review the notions of innocence and "seeing for innocence" in the essays by Patricia Nelson Limerick (p. 110) and Shelby Steele (p. 347). Discuss the problems of teenage AIDS, unwanted pregnancies, and drug and alcohol abuse in terms of innocence. Have teens simply lost their innocence? Does our society, in its desire to "see for innocence," refuse to acknowledge the realities of teenagers' lives and its own responsibility for the conditions they live with? To what extent do teenagers themselves "see for innocence" when they discuss their problems?

Extending the Critical Context

8. Overall, do the teenagers, parents, and schools you know resemble those described by Louv? Explain the similarities and differences.

9. Working in groups, "translate" some of Louv's information into a visual medium, such as a drawing, poster, collage, or series of charts. Arrange with your instructor to display these on campus or to present them to another class.

10. In the summer of 1991, John Singleton's film *Boyz N the Hood* touched a nerve with audiences across the nation. Watch the movie and discuss the problems that Singleton's characters face as they struggle to survive in south-central Los Angeles. What roles do sex, drugs, and rock and roll play in their lives? What other challenges must they confront, and what resources do they have to meet them? How does Singleton depict parent-child relationships in this inner-city community?

Black Family Life
JOSEPH L. WHITE

In this selection an eminent African American researcher challenges some of the prevailing views of the Black family. He argues that it is inaccurate to apply Western European standards and expectations to Black families, to see them, essentially, as failed white familes; the Black family must, instead, be seen in the context of the cultural traditions and historical circumstances surrounding its development. Joseph L. White (b. 1932) is professor of psychology and psychiatry in the Department of Comparative Culture at the University of California, Irvine. He is the author of The Troubled Adolescent *(1989) and* The

Psychology of Blacks: An Afro-American Perspective (1984), from which this selection is taken.

The Deficit-Deficiency Model

The view of the core structure of the Black family as an extended family grouping is not shared by all observers. The traditional view of the Black family, which has evolved from the works of Frazier (1939), Elkins (1968), Moynihan (1965), and Rainwater (1970), is one of a disorganized, single-parent, subnuclear, female-dominated social system. This is essentially the deficit-deficiency model of Black family life. The deficit-deficiency model begins with the historical assumption that there was no carry-over from Africa to America of any sophisticated African-based form of family life and communal living. Viable patterns of family life either did not exist because Africans were incapable of creating them, or they were destroyed beginning with slavery and the separation of biological parents and children, forced breeding, the master's sexual exploitation of Black women, and the accumulative effects of three hundred years of economic and social discrimination. As a result of this background of servitude, deprivation, second-class citizenship, and chronic unemployment, Black adults have not been able to develop marketable skills, self-sufficiency, future orientation, and planning and decision-making competencies, instrumental behaviors thought to be necessary for sustaining a successful two-parent nuclear family while guiding the children through the socialization process.

In a society that placed a premium on decisive male leadership in the family, the Black male was portrayed as lacking the masculine sex role behaviors characterized by logical thinking, willingness to take responsibility for others, assertiveness, managerial skills, achievement orientation, and occupational mastery. The Black male in essence had been psychologically castrated and rendered ineffective by forces beyond his control. He is absent within the family circle and unable to provide leadership and command respect when he is present. After generations of being unable to achieve the ideal male role in the family and in American society, the Black male is likely to be inclined to compensate for his failure by pursuing roles such as the pimp, player, hustler, and sweet daddy, which are in conflict with the norms of the larger society. The appearance of these roles in male behavior in the Black community, rather than being interpreted as a form of social protest, reinforces the majority culture stereotypes of Black males as irresponsible, lazy, shiftless, and sociopathic.[1]

---

[1]*sociopathic:* characterized by antisocial behavior.

The Black woman does not fare much better in terms of how she is portrayed in the deficit-deficiency model of Black family life. She is regarded as the head of the household, a matriarch[2] who initially received her power because the society was unwilling to permit the Black male to assume the legal, economic, and social positions necessary to become a dominant force within the family and community life. Having achieved this power by default, the Black female is unwilling to share it. Her unwillingness to share her power persists even when the Black male is present and willing to assume responsibility in the family circle, since she is not confident of the male's ability to follow through on his commitments. Confrontation over decision making and family direction is usually not necessary because the Black male is either not present in the household on any ongoing basis or is regarded as ineffective by the female when he is present.

The proponents of the pathology-oriented, matriarchal family model did not consider the possibility that a single-parent Black mother could serve as an adequate role model for the children of both sexes. The notion that the mother could reflect a balance of the traditional male and female roles, with respect to mental toughness and emotional tenderness, was largely ignored because of the rigid classification of psychosexual roles in American society. In the Black community, however, the categorization of social role behaviors based on gender is not as inflexible. It is conceivable that a Black mother could project a combination of assertive and nurturant behaviors in the process of rearing children of both sexes as nonsexist adults.

With the reality of accelerating divorce rates, in recent years the single-parent family headed by a woman has become a social reality in Euro-America. This reality has been accompanied by an attempt on the part of social scientists to legitimate family structures that represent alternatives to the nuclear family while reconceptualizing the social roles of males and females with less emphasis on exclusive behaviors. The concept of androgyny[3] has been introduced to cover the vast pool of human personality traits that can be developed by either sex (Rogers, 1978). A well-balanced person reflects a combination of both instrumental[4] and expressive[5] traits. The latter include feeling-oriented behaviors formerly considered feminine, such as tenderness, caring, and affection. Thus, it is conceptually possible for a white, single, and androgynous female parent to rear psychologically healthy, emotionally integrated children. It is interesting how the sociology of the times

5

[2]*matriarch:* a female who rules or dominates a family group.
[3]*androgyny:* the condition of having both male and female characteristics.
[4]*instrumental:* of or relating to extrinsic purposes, active; aggressive.
[5]*expressive:* relating to feelings; emotional; affective.

makes available to white Americans psychological concepts designed to legitimize changes in the family, in child-rearing patterns, and in relationships between the sexes. Yet, these same behaviors when first expressed by Afro-Americans were considered as pathological.

The Extended Family Model

The extended family, in contrast to the single-parent subnuclear family, consists of a related and quasi-related group of adults, including aunts, uncles, parents, cousins, grandparents, boyfriends, and girlfriends linked together in a kinship or kinlike network. They form a cooperative interface[6] with each other in confronting the concerns of living and rearing the children. This model of family life, which seems able to capture not only the strength, vitality, resilience, and continuity of the Black family, but also the essence of Black values, folkways, and life styles, begins with a different set of assumptions about the development and evolution of Black family life in America.

The Black extended family is seen as an outgrowth of African patterns of family and community life that survived in America. The Africans carried with them through the Mid-Atlantic passage and sale to the initial slave owners a well-developed pattern of kinship, exogamous mating,[7] and communal values, emphasizing collective survival, mutual aid, cooperation, mutual solidarity, interdependence, and responsibility for others (Nobles, 1974; Blassingame, 1972). These values became the basis for the Black extended family in America. They were retained because they were familiar and they allowed the slaves to have some power over destiny by enabling them to develop their own styles for family interaction. A consciousness of closeness to others, belongingness, and togetherness protected the slave from being psychologically destroyed by feelings of despair and alienation and the extended family provided a vehicle to pass the heritage on to the children (Fredrickson, 1976; Gutman, 1976). Slaves in essence created their own communal family space, regardless of whether the master was paternalistic[8] or conducted a Nazi-like concentration camp.

To understand the cultural continuity, it is necessary to depart from the traditional hypothesis that slave masters and their descendants exercised total psychological and social control over the development of Black family life and community institutions. The slaves were much more than empty psychological tablets on which the master imprinted an identity. These early Blacks were able to find ways of creating psychological space and implementing African cultural forms that

[6]*cooperative interface:* reciprocal or two-way relationship.
[7]*exogamous mating:* marriage outside of a specific group.
[8]*paternalistic:* apparently benevolent, like a father.

whites were unaware of and did not understand. Once in the New World the African recreated a sense of tribal community within the plantation milieu[9] through a series of extended kin and kinlike family networks that carried on the cultural values of responsibility for others, mutual aid, and collective survival. First- and second-generation American slaves who were separated from biological kin by continued activity at the auction block and newly arriving slaves who were sold to different plantations were incorporated into the extended family structures of existing plantations. It was not essential for the survival of African conceptions of family life that biological or legal kinship ties be maintained. When a people share a philosophy of interdependence and collective survival, persons who are not biologically or legally related can become interwoven into newly created and existing kinlike networks. Cultural patterns once established seem to endure, especially if they work. The extended family survived because it provided Afro-Americans a support system within the context of a shared frame of reference. Along with other African customs and beliefs, an African family identity was passed along to the children as the link between generations through the oral tradition.

Once the philosophy of collective survival and interdependence was set into place as the foundation for community living, the extended family evolved through a series of cycles of formation, breakup, and reformation as the slaves who were without the recourse to legal rights to protect kinship structures and conjugal unions were transferred from place to place. Much later, with the beginnings of the Industrial Revolution after the Civil War, the pattern of Black family life based on combinations of kinship and kinlike networks continued, despite the emergence of the nuclear family among Euro-Americans. The growth of the individual nuclear family in Euro-America seemed to correspond with the competitive and individualistic values of the market place. The cycles of formation, breakup, and reformation of the extended family continued as Blacks migrated farther north and west towards the cities at the turn of the century during the pre and post periods of the two world wars and into the modern age.

The Black extended family, with its grandparents, biological parents, conjugal partners, aunts, uncles, cousins, older siblings, boyfriends, girlfriends, and quasi-kin, is an intergenerational group. The members of this three-generation family do not necessarily reside in the same household. Individual households are part of a sociofamilial network that functions like a minicommunity. The members band together to share information, resources, and communal concern (Stack, 1974). There is no central authority, matriarchal or patriarchal. Decisions are

[9]*milieu:* environment; setting.

made on an equalitarian model with input and outcomes determined by who is available at a given time, who has expertise with reference to a given problem, and one's prior experience and track record in decision making. This is likely to give some edge to the tribal elders. They are looked up to within the extended family network as resource people and advisors because they have the life experience that is highly valued in the Black community. As in the past, the family is held together over time and across geographical space by a shared experience frame and a common set of values involving interdependence, mutual aid, resilience, communalism,[10] and collective responsibility (Nobles, 1978). These values transcend sex roles and allow both men and women to participate in and contribute to the management of economic resources, child rearing, community activism, and other issues of family life without being categorically restricted on the basis of gender. The fluid distinction between social sex roles offers both men and women in the Black family network the opportunity to emerge as decision makers, influence molders, and household managers.

It could be argued that the Black extended family exists and persists primarily because Black people face the common fate of oppressive economic and social conditions, that it exists out of necessity as a way of surviving in an oppressive class system. Politically and economically oppressed people have historically banded together for survival, whether it be in internment camps, labor unions, or women's movements. It would follow from this argument that the Black extended family would disappear as Black people moved up the socioeconomic ladder. Yet the extended family does not appear to be disappearing with rising economic fortunes. McAdoo's (1979) work with upwardly mobile middle and upper-middle class Black families suggests that not only does the extended family model persist when Blacks move up the socioeconomic ladder but the Afro-American values of mutual aid, interdependence, and interconnectedness also remain as the guiding ethos[11] of family existence.

Being part of a close-knit extended family group is a vital part of Afro-American life. Wherever Blacks appear in numbers of two or more, whether it be on predominantly white college campuses, professional baseball teams, fraternal groups, street corners, storefront churches, automobile factories, or professional conferences, they soon seem to form a quasi-family network, share information and resources, get together, git down, rap, and party. White folks don't know what to make of this. The idea of sharing closeness, and interdependence expressed in sociofamilial groups[12] is so deeply ingrained in the fabric of

[10]*communalism:* social organization based on religious, ethnic, or some other group loyalty.

[11]*ethos:* distinguishing character; essential nature.

[12]*sociofamilial groups:* in this context, "extended families."

the Afro-American ethos that it is not likely to give way to the nuclear family with its stress on isolation, competition, and independence. If anything, the traditional nuclear family may be moving toward becoming more like the Afro-American extended family.

To the extent that the extended family model represents a more accurate way of categorizing the Black family and capturing its strengths, the question arises as to why generations of the Black ghetto's Euro-American occupation army represented by sociologists, their graduate students, census takers, welfare workers, law-enforcement personnel, and bill collectors could only find broken, disorganized, single-parent, female-dominated families. The answer to this question involves several complex, interrelated reasons.

First, white observers may have been guided by a constricted cultural frame of reference where the only viable form of family life consisted of a two-parent family contained within the boundaries of a single household. When they didn't find this single household nuclear family operating in the Black community, their constricted model prevented them from being able to assess correctly the differences they observed. They mistakenly labeled differences as deviant, therefore pathological.

Second, Black folks themselves have been known to be deceptive   15 about the membership of their families when being questioned by authorities representing the white establishment whom they mistrust, such as law-enforcement personnel, bill collectors, and welfare workers. Given the restrictive nature of the welfare system, it is not hard to imagine why a Black woman would not be truthful to a public assistance worker about the nature of her conjugal relationships, regardless of whether they involve a legal husband, boyfriend, sweet daddy, or transient male friend. Carol Stack (1974) contends that the welfare system as it was traditionally structured worked against the emergence of stable conjugal unions within the extended family.

Third, the very nature of white institutions works against the Black extended family as it attempts to fulfill its collective responsibilities and functions within the context of Afro-American values (Nobles, 1978). Wade Nobles, a nationally recognized expert on the Black family, tells a story about moving his nephew, a high school student, from the boy's mother's residence in Louisiana to his household in Berkeley, California. There were no major psychosocial adjustment problems associated with the nephew's making the transition from the Louisiana branch of the Nobles extended family to the Berkeley, California, branch. The problem came about when Dr. Nobles attempted to explain to the Internal Revenue Service how he came by an adolescent dependent in the space of one year with no legal papers to back him up. If Professor Nobles, who holds a Ph.D. from Stanford University, had difficulty explaining the composition of his extended family with the addition of this adolescent nephew, try to imagine what low-income Black aunties or grandmothers go through when they are trying to get aid for dependent children residing in their household who are not their biological or legal offspring, or for that matter what Black college freshmen go through trying to explain the income of their multiple extended-family parents divided by the number of dependent cousins, siblings, nieces, nephews, and fictional kin to college financial aid officers.

The Black child growing up in the extended family is exposed to a variety of role models covering a wide age span whose social behaviors are not completely regulated by conventional sex roles. This offers the children a greater opportunity to incorporate a balanced pattern of expressive and instrumental behaviors. Since parents may not be equally effective as role models at every stage of the child's development, the presence of a range of role models allows the children a series of options at any stage of their development in terms of adults they might seek out for guidance. . . .

Works Cited

Blassingame, John. *The Slave Community*. New York: Oxford University Press, 1972.

Elkins, Stanley. *Slavery: A Problem in American Institutions and Intellectual Life*. Chicago: University of Chicago Press, 1968.

Frazier, E. Franklin. *The Negro Family in the United States*. Chicago: University of Chicago Press, 1939.

Fredrickson, George. "The Gutman Report," *The New York Review*, September 30, 1976, pp. 18–22, 27.

Gutman, Herbert. *The Black Family in Slavery and Freedom, 1750–1925*. New York: Vintage Books, 1976.

McAdoo, Harriet. "Black Kinship," *Psychology Today*, May 1979, pp. 67–69, 79, 110.

Moynihan, Daniel Patrick. *The Negro Family: The Case for National Action*, Washington, D.C.: U.S. Government Printing Office, 1965.

Nobles, Wade. "Africanity: Its Role in Black Families," *The Black Scholar*, June 1974, pp. 10–17.

_____. "Toward an Empirical and Theoretical Framework for Defining Black Families," *Journal of Marriage and Family*, November 1978, pp. 679–688.

Rainwater, Lee. *Behind Ghetto Walls: Black Family Life in a Federal Slum*. Chicago: Aldine, 1970.

Rogers, Dorothy. *Adolescence: A Psychological Perspective*, 2nd Edition. Monterey, Calif.: Brooks/Cole, 1978.

Stack, Carol. *All Our Kin: Strategies for Survival in a Black Community*. New York: Harper & Row, 1974.

Engaging the Text

1. In the beginning of this selection, White presents the "deficit-deficiency model" of Black family life. Describe this model in your own words. What assumptions underlie it? What is White's final evaluation of its effectiveness?

2. What does White mean when he says that the extended Black family is "equalitarian" (para. 10)?

3. How has the extended Black family provided a means of surviving "oppressive economic and social conditions" (para. 11)?

4. How does White account for what he sees as earlier misrepresentations of the African American family? How persuasive do you find his arguments?

Exploring Connections

5. Compare White's model of the extended Black family with the "perfect" nuclear family described by Arlene Skolnick (p. 463).

6. Does Gordon W. Allport's theory of group psychology (p. 292) help explain how the deficit-deficiency model of Black family life could arise? Explain.

7. Compare and contrast White's notion of the extended Black family with the tribal family described by Paula Gunn Allen (p. 241).

Extending the Critical Context

8. Taking several generations into consideration, describe the structure of your family. Does it conform to the general features of either the traditional nuclear family or the extended family? Would you describe it as equalitarian, matriarchal, or patriarchal? Does it reflect a particular ethos, or essential nature?

9. Examine the ways Black family members are portrayed in popular movies and TV shows. Do these portrayals still depend on the deficit-deficiency model?

10. Debate whether the traditional nuclear family is, in fact, becoming more like the African American family.

11. If your class contains people from both nuclear and extended families, conduct research into the perceived advantages and disadvantages of each type of family. Using the methodology described by Janet Saltzman Chafetz for investigating gender roles (p. 194), survey class members about the advantages and disadvantages of nuclear and extended families. Discuss the results in class. Is there any consensus on what a family should be? Time permitting, complete the project by writing a research report using Chafetz's as a model.

Envy

BEBE MOORE CAMPBELL

What would make a schoolgirl who is afraid to chew gum in class threaten to stab her teacher? In this narrative, at least, it's not grammar drills or sentence diagrams — it's anger, frustration, and envy caused by an absentee father. Like Gary Soto's "Looking for Work" (p. 410), this personal recollection of childhood combines the authenticity of actual experience with the artistry of expert storytelling. Bebe Moore Campbell (b. 1950) is a free-lance journalist who has published in many national newspapers and magazines, including The New York Times Magazine, Working Mother, Ms., *and the* Los Angeles Times. *She also has written two books:* Successful Women, Angry Men: Backlash in the Two-Career Marriage *(1987) and* Sweet Summer: Growing Up with and Without My Dad *(1989), from which this selection is taken.*

The red bricks of 2239 North 16th Street melded into the uniformity of look-alike doors, windows, and brownstone-steps. From the outside our rowhouse looked the same as any other. When I was a toddler, the similarity was unsettling. The family story was that my mother and I were out walking on the street one day when panic rumbled through me. "Where's our house? Where's our house?" I cried, grabbing my mother's hand.

My mother walked me to our house, pointed to the numbers painted next to the door. "Twenty-two thirty-nine," she said, slapping the wall. "This is our house."

Much later I learned that the real difference was inside.

In my house there was no morning stubble, no long johns or Fruit of the Loom on the clothesline, no baritone hollering for keys that were sitting on the table. There was no beer in the refrigerator, no ball game on TV, no loud cussing. After dark the snores that emanated from the bedrooms were subtle, ladylike, little moans really.

Growing up, I could have died from overexposure to femininity. 5 Women ruled at 2239. A grandmother, a mother, occasionally an aunt, grown-up girlfriends from at least two generations, all the time rubbing up against me, fixing my food, running my bathwater, telling me to sit still and be good in those grown-up, girly-girl voices. Chanel and Prince Matchabelli wafting through the bedrooms. Bubble bath and Jergens came from the bathroom, scents unbroken by aftershave, macho beer breath, a good he-man funk. I remember a house full of 'do rags and rollers, the soft, sweet allure of Dixie peach and bergamot;[1] brown-skinned queens wearing pastel housecoats and worn-out size six-and-a-half flip-flops that slapped softly against the wood as the royal women climbed the stairs at night carrying their paperbacks to bed.

The outside world offered no retreat. School was taught by stern, old-maid white women with age spots and merciless gray eyes; ballet lessons, piano lessons, Sunday school, and choir were all led by colored

---

[1]*bergamot:* a citrus tree with a fragrant fruit.

sisters with a hands-on-their-hips attitude who cajoled and screeched in distaff[2] tongues.

And what did they want from me, these Bosoms? Achievement! This desire had nothing to do with the pittance they collected from the Philadelphia Board of Education or the few dollars my mother paid them. Pushing little colored girls forward was in their blood. They made it clear: a life of white picket fences and teas was for other girls to aspire to. I was to *do* something. And if I didn't climb willingly up their ladder, they'd drag me to the top. Rap my knuckles hard for not practicing. Make me lift my leg until I wanted to die. Stay after school and write "I will listen to the teacher" five hundred times. They were not playing. "Obey them," my mother commanded.

When I entered 2B — the Philadelphia school system divided grades into A and B — in September 1957, I sensed immediately that Miss Bradley was not a woman to be challenged. She looked like one of those evil old spinsters Shirley Temple[3] was always getting shipped off to live with; she was kind of hefty, but so tightly corseted that if she happened to grab you or if you fell against her during recess, it felt as if you were bouncing into a steel wall. In reality she was a sweet lady who was probably a good five years past her retirement age when I wound up in her class. Miss Bradley remained at Logan for one reason and one reason only: she was dedicated. She wanted her students to learn! learn! learn! Miss Bradley was halfway sick, hacking and coughing her lungs out through every lesson, spitting the phlegm into fluffy white tissues from the box on her desk, but she was *never* absent. Each day at three o'clock she kissed each one of her "little pupils" on the cheek, sending a faint scent of Emeraude home with us. Her rules for teaching children seemed to be: love them; discipline them; reward them; and make sure they are clean.

Every morning she ran a hygiene check on the entire class. She marched down the aisle like a stormtrooper, rummaging through the ears of hapless students, checking for embedded wax. She looked under our fingernails for dirt. Too bad on you if she found any. Once she made David, a stringy-haired white boy who thought Elvis Presley was a living deity and who was the most notorious booger-eater in the entire school, go to the nurse's office to have the dirt cleaned from under his fingernails. Everybody knew that what was under David's fingernails was most likely dried-up boogies and not dirt, but nobody said anything.

If she was death on dirt and earwax, Miss Bradley's specialty was head-lice patrol. Down the aisles she stomped in her black Enna Jettick   10

---

[2]*distaff:* female, maternal.
[3]*Shirley Temple:* famous child actor (b. 1928); later, Shirley Temple Black, U.S. ambassador.

shoes,[4] stopping at each student to part strands of blond, brown, or dark hair, looking for cooties. Miss Bradley would flip through plaits, curls, kinks — the woman was relentless. I always passed inspection. Nana put enough Nu Nile in my hair to suffocate any living creature that had the nerve to come tipping up on my scalp. Nu Nile was the official cootie killer. I was clean, wax-free, bug-free, and smart. The folder inside my desk contained a stack of spelling and arithmetic papers with A's emblazoned across the top, gold stars in the corner. Miss Bradley always called on me. She sent me to run errands for her too. I was her pet.

When Mrs. Clark, my piano teacher and my mother's good friend, told my mother that Logan Elementary School was accepting children who didn't live in the neighborhood, my mother immediately enrolled Michael and later me. "It's not crowded and it's mixed," she told a nodding, smiling Nana. The fact that Logan was integrated was the main reason Michael and I were sent there. Nana and Mommy, like most upwardly mobile colored women, believed that to have the same education as a white child was the first step up the rocky road to success. This viewpoint was buttressed by the fact that George Washington Carver, my neighborhood school, was severely overcrowded. Logan was just barely integrated, with only a handful of black kids thrown in with hordes of square-jawed, pale-eyed second-generation Ukrainians whose immigrant parents and grandparents populated the neighborhood near the school. There were a few dark-haired Jews and aristocratic-looking WASPs too. My first day in kindergarten it was Nana who enthusiastically grabbed Michael's and my hands, pulling us away from North Philly's stacked-up rowhouses, from the hucksters whose wagons bounced down the streets with trucks full of ripe fruits and vegetables, from the street-corner singers and jitterbugs who filled my block with all-day doo-wahs. It was Nana who resolutely walked me past the early-morning hordes of colored kids heading two blocks away to Carver Elementary School, Nana who pulled me by the hand and led me in another direction.

We went underground at the Susquehanna and Dauphin subway station, leaving behind the unremitting asphalt and bricks and the bits of paper strewn in the streets above us. We emerged at Logan station, where sunlight, brilliant red and pink roses and yellow chrysanthemums, and neatly clipped lawns and clean streets startled me. There were robins and blue jays flying overhead. The only birds in my neighborhood were sparrows and pigeons. Delivering me at the schoolyard, Nana firmly cupped my chin with her hand as she bent down to instruct me. "Your mother's sending you up here to learn, so you do everything your teacher tells you to, okay?" To Michael she turned and said, "You're not up here to be a monkey on a stick." Then to both of us:

---

[4]*Enna Jettick shoes:* brand name of "sensible" women's shoes.

"Don't talk. Listen. Act like you've got some home training. You've got as much brains as anybody up here. Do you know that? All right now. Make Nana proud of you."

A month after I returned from Pasquotank County,[5] I sat in Miss Bradley's classroom on a rainy Monday watching her write spelling words on the blackboard. The harsh sccurr, sccurr of Miss Bradley's chalk and the tinny sound the rain made against the window took my mind to faraway places. I couldn't get as far away as I wanted. Wallace, the bane of the whole class, had only moments earlier laid the most gigunda fart in history, one in a never-ending series, and the air was just clearing. His farts were silent wonders. Not a hint, not the slightest sound. You could be in the middle of a sentence and then wham! bam! Mystery Funk would knock you down.

Two seats ahead of me was Leonard, a lean colored boy from West Philly who always wore suits and ties to school, waving his hand like a crazy man. A showoff if ever there was one.

I was bored that day. I looked around at the walls. Miss Bradley had   15
decorated the room with pictures of the ABCs in cursive. Portraits of the presidents were hanging in a row on one wall above the blackboard. On the bulletin board there was a display of the Russian satellite, *Sputnik I*, and the American satellite, *Explorer I*. Miss Bradley was satellite-crazy. She thought it was just wonderful that America was in the "space race" and she constantly filled our heads with space fantasies. "Boys and girls," she told us, "one day man will walk on the moon." In the far corner on another bulletin board there was a Thanksgiving scene of turkeys and pilgrims. And stuck in the corner was a picture of Sacajawea.[6] Sacajawea, Indian Woman Guide. I preferred looking at Sacajawea over satellites any day.

Thinking about the bubble gum that lay in my pocket, I decided to sneak a piece, even though gum chewing was strictly forbidden. I rarely broke the rules. Could anyone hear the loud drumming of my heart, I wondered, as I slid my hand into my skirt pocket and felt for the Double Bubble? I peeked cautiously to either side of me. Then I managed to unwrap it without even rustling the paper; I drew my hand to my lips, coughed, and popped the gum in my mouth. Ahhh! Miss Bradley's back was to the class. I chomped down hard on the Double Bubble. Miss Bradley turned around. I quickly packed the gum under my tongue. My hands were folded on top of my desk. "Who can give me a sentence for 'birthday'?" Leonard just about went nuts. Miss Bradley ignored him, which she did a lot. "Sandra," Miss Bradley called.

---

[5]*Pasquotank County:* county in North Carolina where Campbell's father lived; she visited him there every summer.
[6]*Sacajawea:* a Shoshone Indian woman (1786–1812), captured and sold to a white man; she became the famous guide of the 1804 Lewis and Clark expedition.

A petite white girl rose obediently. I liked Sandra. She had shared her crayons with me once when I left mine at home. I remember her drawing: a white house with smoke coming out of the chimney, a little girl with yellow hair like hers, a mommy, a daddy, a little boy, and a dog standing in front of the house in a yard full of flowers. Her voice was crystal clear when she spoke. There were smiles in that voice. She said, "My father made me a beautiful dollhouse for my birthday."

The lump under my tongue was suddenly a stone and when I swallowed, the taste was bitter. I coughed into a piece of tablet paper, spit out the bubble gum, and crumpled up the wad and pushed it inside my desk. The center of my chest was burning. I breathed deeply and slowly. Sandra sat down as demurely as a princess. She crossed her ankles. Her words came back to me in a rush. "Muuuy fatha made me a bee-yoo-tee-ful dollhouse." Miss Bradley said, "Very good," and moved on to the next word. Around me hands were waving, waving. Pick me! Pick me! Behind me I could hear David softly crooning, "You ain't nothin' but a hound dog, cryin' all the time." Sometimes he would stick his head inside his desk, sing Elvis songs, and pick his boogies at the same time. Somebody was jabbing pins in my chest. Ping! Ping! Ping! I wanted to holler, "Yowee! Stop!" as loud as I could, but I pressed my lips together hard.

"Now who can give me a sentence?" Miss Bradley asked. I put my head down on my desk and when Miss Bradley asked me what was wrong I told her that I didn't feel well and that I didn't want to be chosen. When Leonard collected the homework, I shoved mine at him so hard all the papers he was carrying fell on the floor.

Bile was still clogging my throat when Miss Bradley sent me into the cloakroom to get my lunchbox. The rule was, only one student in the cloakroom at a time. When the second one came in, the first one had to leave. I was still rummaging around in my bookbag when I saw Sandra.

"Miss Bradley said for you to come out," she said. She was smiling. That dollhouse girl was always smiling. I glared at her.

"Leave when I get ready to," I said, my words full of venom.

Sandra's eyes darted around in confusion. "Miss Bradley said . . . " she began again, still trying to smile as if she expected somebody to crown her Miss America or something and come take her picture any minute.

In my head a dam broke. Terrible waters rushed out. "I don't care about any Miss Bradley. If she messes with me I'll, I'll . . . I'll take my butcher knife and stab her until she bleeds." What I lacked in props I made up for in drama. My balled-up hand swung menacingly in the air. I aimed the invisible dagger toward Sandra. Her Miss America smile faded instantly. Her eyes grew round and frightened as she blinked rapidly. "Think I won't, huh? Huh?" I whispered, enjoying my meanness, liking the scared look on Sandra's face. Scaredy cat! Scaredy cat! Muuuy fatha made me a bee-yoo-tee-full dollhouse. "What do you think about that?" I added viciously, looking into her eyes to see the total effect of my daring words.

But Sandra wasn't looking at me. Upon closer inspection, I realized that she was looking *over* me with sudden relief in her face. I turned to see what was so interesting, and my chin jammed smack into the Emeraude-scented iron bosom of Miss Bradley. Even as my mind scrambled for an excuse, I knew I was lost.

Miss Bradley had a look of horror on her face. For a minute she didn't say anything, just stood there looking as though someone had slapped her across the face. Sandra didn't say anything. I didn't move. Finally, "Would you mind repeating what you just said, Bebe."

"I didn't say anything, Miss Bradley." I could feel my dress sticking to my body.

"Sandra, what did Bebe say?"

Sandra was crying softly, little delicate tears streaming down her face. For just a second she paused, giving a tiny shudder. I rubbed my ear vigorously, thinking, "Oh, please . . ."

"She said, she said, if you bothered with her she would cut you with her knife."

"Unh unh, Miss Bradley, I didn't say that. I didn't. I didn't say anything like that."

Miss Bradley's gray eyes penetrated mine. She locked me into her gaze until I looked down at the floor. The she looked at Sandra.

"Bebe, you and I had better go see the principal."

The floor blurred. The principal!! Jennie G., the students called her with awe and fear. As Miss Bradley wrapped her thick knuckles around my forearm and dutifully steered me from the cloakroom and out the classroom door, I completely lost what little cool I had left. I began to cry, a jerky, hiccuping, snot-filled cry for mercy. "I didn't say it. I didn't say it," I moaned.

Miss Bradley was nonplussed. Dedication and duty overruled compassion. Always. "Too late for that now," she said grimly.

Jennie G.'s office was small, neat, and dim. The principal was dwarfed by the large brown desk she sat behind, and when she stood up she wasn't much bigger than I. But she was big enough to make me tremble as I stood in front of her, listening to Miss Bradley recount the sordid details of my downfall. Jennie G. was one of those pale, pale vein-showing white women. She had a vocabulary of about six horrible phrases, designed to send chills of despair down the spine of any young transgressor. Phrases like "We'll just see about that" or "Come with me, young lady," spoken ominously. Her face was impassive as she listened to Miss Bradley. I'd been told that she had a six-foot paddle in her office used solely to beat young transgressors. Suppose she tried to beat me? My heart gave a lurch. I tugged rapidly at my ears. I longed to suck my thumb.

"Well, Bebe, I think we'll have to call your mother."

My mother! I wanted the floor to swallow me up and take me whole. My mother! As Jennie G. dialed the number, I envisioned my mother's face, clouded with disappointment and shame. I started crying again as I listened to the principal telling my mother what had happened. They talked for a pretty long time. When she hung up, ole Jennie G. flipped through some paper on her desk before looking at me sternly.

"You go back to class and watch your mouth, young lady."

As I was closing the door to her office I heard her say to Miss 40 Bradley, "What can you expect?"

"Ooooh, you're gonna get it girl," is how Michael greeted me after school. Logan's colored world was small, and news of my demise had blazed its way through hallways and classrooms, via the brown-skinned grapevine. Everyone from North Philly, West Philly, and Germantown knew about my crime. The subway ride home was depressing. My fellow commuters kept coming up to me and asking, "Are you gonna get in trouble?" Did they think my mother would give me a reward or something? I stared at the floor for most of the ride, looking up only when the train came to a stop and the doors hissed open. Logan. Wyoming. Hunting Park. Each station drew me closer to my doom, whatever that was going to be. "What can you expect?" I mulled over those words. What did she mean? My mother rarely spanked, although Nana would give Michael or me, usually Michael, a whack across the butt from time to time. My mother's social-worker instincts were too strong for such undignified displays; Doris believed in talking things out, which was sometimes worse than a thousand beatings. As the train drew closer to Susquehanna and Dauphin I thought of how much I hated for my mother to be disappointed in me. And now she would be. "What can you expect?"

Of me? Didn't Jennie G. know that I was riding a subway halfway across town as opposed to walking around the corner to Carver Elementary School, for a reason: the same reason I was dragged away from Saturday cartoons and pulled from museum to museum, to Judimar School of Dance for ballet (art class for Michael), to Mrs. Clark for piano. The Bosoms wanted me to Be Somebody, to be the second generation to live out my life as far away from a mop and scrub brush and Miss Ann's floors as possible.

My mother had won a full scholarship to the University of Pennsylvania. The story of that miracle was a treasured family heirloom. Sometimes Nana told the tale and sometimes my mother described how the old Jewish counselor at William Penn High School approached her and asked why a girl with straight E's (for "excellent") was taking the commercial course. My mother replied that Nana couldn't afford to send her to college, that she planned to become a secretary. "Sweetheart, you switch to academic," the woman told her. "You'll get to college." When her graduation day approached, the counselor pulled her aside. "I have two scholarships for you. One to Cheyney State Teacher's College and the other to the University of Pennsylvania." Cheyney was a small black school outside of Philadelphia. My mother chose Penn. I had been born to a family of hopeful women. One miracle had already taken place. They expected more. And now I'd thrown away my chance. Michael, who was seated next to me on the subway and whose generosity of spirit had lasted a record five subway stops, poked me in my arm. "Bebe," he told me gleefully, "your ass is grass."

Nana took one look at my guilty face, scowled at me, and sucked her teeth until they whistled. My mother had called her and told her what happened and now she was possessed by a legion of demons. I had barely entered the room when she exploded. "Don't. Come. In. Here. Crying," Nana said, her voice booming, her lips quivering and puffy with anger. When Nana talked in staccato language she was beyond pissed off. Waaaay beyond. "What. Could. Possess. You. To. Say. Such. A. Thing?" Embarrassingyourmotherlikethatinfrontof *those people!*" Before I could answer she started singing some Dinah Washington[7] song, real loud. Volume all the way up. With every word she sang I sank deeper and deeper into gloom.

Later that evening, when my mother got home and Aunt Ruth, 45 Michael's mother, came to visit, the three women lectured me in unison. The room was full of flying feathers. Three hens clucking away at me, their breasts heaving with emotion. Cluck! Cluck! Cluck! How could I have said such a thing? What on earth was I thinking about? Cluck! Cluck! Cluck! A knife, such a, a *colored* weapon.

"But I didn't do anything," I wailed, the tears that had been trickling all day now falling in full force.

"Umph, umph, umph," Nana said, and started singing. Billie Holiday[8] this time.

"You call threatening somebody with a knife nothing?" Aunt Ruth asked. Ruth was Nana's middle girl. She was the family beauty, as pretty as Dorothy Dandridge[9] or Lena Horne.[10] Now her coral lips were curled up in disdain and her Maybelline eyebrows were raised in judgment against me. "They expect us to act like animals and you have to go and say that. My God."

Animals. Oh. Oh. Oh.

My mother glared at her sister, but I looked at Aunt Ruth in 50 momentary wonder and appreciation. Now I understood. The un-

---

[7]*Dinah Washington:* blues singer, born Ruth Jones (1924–1963).

[8]*Billie Holiday:* celebrated jazz singer (1915–1959).

[9]*Dorothy Dandridge:* glamorous film star (1923–1965).

[10]*Lena Horne:* singer, actor (b. 1917); first Black woman vocalist to be featured with a white band.

spoken rule that I had sensed all my life was that a colored child had to be on her best behavior whenever she visited the white world. Otherwise, whatever opportunity was being presented would be snatched away. I had broken the rule. I had committed the unpardonable sin of embarrassing my family in front of *them*. Sensing my remorse and shame, Mommy led me out of the kitchen. We sat down on the living room sofa; my mother took my hand. "Bebe, I want you to go to your room and think about what you've done. I don't understand your behavior. It was very hard for me to get you in Logan." She drew a breath. I drew a breath and looked into the eyes of a social worker. "I'm extremely disappointed in you."

I didn't go straight to my room. Instead I sneaked into Michael's room, which overlooked Mole Street, the tiny, one-sided alley of narrow rowhouses that faced the backyards of 16th Street. Michael and I usually played on the "back street." Alone in Michael's room with the window open, I could hear Mr. Watson, our neighbor, hollering at one of his kids. Why had I said what I said? What had possessed me? Then I remembered. "Muuuy fatha made me a bee-yoo-tee-ful dollhouse for muuuuy birthday." Something pinched me inside my chest when I heard those words. Pain oozed from my heart like a tube of toothpaste bursting open, going every whichaway. Blue-eyes kept yapping away with her golden hair and her goofy little smile. Who cared what her fatha did? Who cared? I couldn't help it. When she came into the cloakroom I got mad all over again. When I said I had a knife, she looked just like Grandma Mary's chickens. Scared. And my chest stopped hurting. Just stopped.

Mr. Watson's baritone voice was a seismic rumble echoing with the threat of upheaval, violence. His words floated over Mole Street and into the bedroom window. Whoever was in trouble over there was really gonna get it. None of this "go to your room" stuff. None of this corny "I'm disappointed in you" stuff. Mr. Watson was getting ready to beat somebody's ass.

Adam's. He was the youngest and one of my playmates. I could tell by his pleading voice. "Please, Daddy. I won't do it anymore, Daddy. I'm sorry, Daddy."

Michael came into the room. "What are you doing?" he whispered.

"Shhh. Adam's getting a whipping."

"You better go to your room before Aunt Doris comes upstairs."

"Shhhh."

My playmate's misery took my mind off my own. His father's exotic yelling hypnotized me. From downstairs I could hear the hens, still clucking away. Michael and I sat quietly, not making a sound. Mr. Watson's voice sounded so foreign coming into our house. For a moment I pretended that his anger was emanating from Michael's bedroom, and I remembered how only last year he got mad and ran after all of us kids — Jackie, Jane, and Adam, his own three, and me.

His face was covered with shaving cream and he held a razor in one hand and a thick leather belt in the other. I don't recall what we had done, but I remember him chasing us and yelling ferociously, "This belt's got your name on it too, Miss Bebe!" And I recall that I was thrilled when the leather grazed my hiney with the vengeance of a father's wrath.

My mind drifted back a few years. The memory was vague and fuzzy. When I was four or five I was playing on Mole Street when my ten-year-old neighbor, a boy named Buddy, asked me to come inside his yard. He was sitting on an old soda crate. "Come closer," he told me. "Wanna play doctor?"

"Uh huh." 60

"You can examine me."

I told my mother, prattling on about the "game" I had played. She sat me down on her bed. "Did he touch your private parts?"

"Nope." Why was Mommy's face so serious?

"Did you touch his?"

"I touched his zipper." Had I done something wrong? 65

Nana went into hysterics, singing and screeching like a wild woman. "Mother, just calm down," Mommy told her.

Mommy was cool, every inch the social worker; she took my hand and we walked down the street to Buddy's house. He was in his yard making a scooter out of the crate. "Buddy," my mother said softly. When he saw the two of us, he dropped his hammer. "Buddy, I want to talk with you."

My mother questioned him. Calmly put the fear of God in him. Warned him of penalties for a repeat performance. And that was that. Not quite. Weeks, maybe months later, my father came to visit me, one of his pop-in, no-real-occasion visits. My mother, my father, and I were sitting in his car and she told him about my playing doctor. His leg shot out in wild, uncontrollable spasms. His face became contorted and he started yelling. Nana's screeching paled in contrast. This was rage that my mother and Nana could not even begin to muster. And it was in my honor. This energy was for my avengement, my protection. Or should have been. But the sound of his fury frightened me. I remember angling away from my father, this man who was yelling like an animal in pain. I leaned toward my mother, and she put one arm around me and with her other hand tried to pat my father's shoulder, only he snatched [it] away. He leaned forward and started reaching for his chair.[11] "I may not be able to walk, goddammit, but I can tear that little son of a bitch's ass up."

My mother kept talking very softly, saying, "No, no, no. It's all right. He's just a kid. I took care of it. It's okay." I leaned away from my father's anger, his determination. He frightened me. But the rage was

[11]*his chair:* Campbell's father had lost the use of his legs in an automobile accident.

fascinating too. And after a while, when my father was shouting only a little, I moved closer to him. I wanted to see the natural progression of his hot words. If he snatched his wheelchair out of the backseat and rolled up to Buddy's house, what would he do? What would he do in my honor? My mother calmed my father. His shouting subsided. I was relieved. I was disappointed.

"Hey" — I suddenly heard Michael's persistent voice — "ain't you glad Mr. Watson ain't your father?" I felt Michael's hands, shaking my shoulder. "Ain't you?"

I didn't answer. I was thinking about Miss Bradley, Jennie G., Aunt Ruth, Nana, and Mommy. All these women with power over me. I could hear Mrs. Watson telling her husband that enough was enough and then the baritone telling her he knew when to stop and Adam letting out another feeble little yelp. "Muuuy fatha made me a bee-yoo-tee-ful dollhouse." Maybe my mother would write my daddy and tell him how bad I had been. Maybe he would get so mad he would get into his car and drive all the way to Philly just to whip my behind. Or tell me he was disappointed in me. Either one.

The Bosoms decided to forgive me. My mother woke me up with a kiss and a snuggle and then a crisp, "All right, Bebe. It's a brand-new day. Forget about yesterday." When I went to get a bowl of cereal that morning, my Aunt Ruth was sitting in the kitchen drinking coffee and reading the newspaper. She had spent the night. "Did you comb your hair?" she asked me.

I nodded.

"That's not what I call combed. Go get me the comb and brush."

She combed out my hair and braided it all over again. This time there were no wispy little ends sticking out. "Now you look nice," she said. "Now you look like a pretty girl, and when you go to school today, act like a pretty girl. All right?"

I nodded.

Last night Nana had hissed at me between her teeth. "If you want to behave like a little *heathen*, if you want go up there acting like a, a . . . *monkey on a stick . . . well*, thenyoucangotoschoolrightaroundthecornerandI'llwalkyoubackhomeandI'llcomeandgetyouforlunchnowyou*behave*yourself!" But today she was sanguine, even jovial, as she fixed my lunch. She kissed me when I left for school.

On my way out the door my mother handed me two elegant letters, one to Miss Bradley and the other to Jennie G., assuring them that I had an overactive imagination, that I had no access to butcher knives or weapons of any kind, that she had spoken to me at length about my unfortunate outburst, and that henceforth my behavior would be exemplary. These letters were written on her very best personalized stationery. The paper was light pink and had "D.C.M." in embossed letters across the top. Doris C. knew lots of big words and she had used every single one of them in those letters. I knew that all of her *i*'s were dotted and all of her *t*'s were crossed. I knew the letters were extremely dignified. My mother was very big on personal dignity. Anyone who messed with her dignity was in serious trouble.

I was only five when an unfortunate teller at her bank called her by her first name loud enough for the other customers to hear. My mother's body stiffened when she heard, "Doris, oh Doris," coming from a girl almost young enough to be her child.

"Are you talking to *me*, dear?" Her English was so clipped, her words so razor sharp she could have taken one, stabbed the teller, and drawn blood. The girl nodded, her speckled green eyes wide and gaping, aware that something was going on, not quite sure what, and speechless because she was no match at all for this imperious little brown-skinned woman. "The people in *my* office all call me *Mrs. Moore.*"

80

And she grabbed me by the hand and we swept out of the bank. Me and Bette Davis.[12] Me and Claudia McNeil.[13] People stepped aside to let us pass.

So I knew my mother's letters not only would impress Miss Bradley and Jennie G. but also would go a long way toward redeeming me. After Miss Bradley read the note she told me I had a very nice mother and let me know that if I was willing to be exemplary she would let bygones be bygones and I could get back into her good graces. She was, after all, a dedicated teacher. And I had learned my lesson.

My mother wrote my father about the knife incident. I waited anxiously to hear from him. Would he suddenly appear? I searched the street in front of the school every afternoon. At home I jumped up nervously whenever I heard a horn beep. Finally, a letter from my dad arrived — one page of southpaw scribble.

> Dear Bebe,
> Your mother told me what happened in school about the knife. That wasn't a good thing to say. I think maybe you were joking. Remember, a lot of times white people don't understand how colored people joke, so you have to be careful what you say around them. Be a good girl.
> Lots of love,
Daddy.

The crumpled letter hit the edge of the wastepaper basket in my mother's room and landed in front of her bureau. I picked it up and slammed it into the basket, hitting my hand in the process. I flung myself across the bed, buried my face into my pillow, and howled with

---

[12]*Bette Davis:* actor (1908–1989) known for her portrayals of strong, beautiful, intelligent women.

[13]*Claudia McNeil:* Emmy–winning actor (b. 1917).

pain, rage, and sadness. "It's not fair," I wailed. Ole Blondie had her dollhouse-making daddy whenever she wanted him. "Muuuy fatha . . ." Jackie, Jane, and Adam had their wild, ass-whipping daddy. All they had to do was walk outside their house, look under a car, and there he was, tinkering away. Ole ugly grease-monkey man. Why couldn't I have my daddy all the time too? I didn't want a letter signed "Lots of love," I wanted my father to come and yell at me for acting like a monkey on a stick. I wanted him to come and beat my butt or shake his finger in my face, or tell me that what I did wasn't so bad after all. Anything. I just wanted him to come.

Engaging the Text

1. Why does Sandra's sentence in Miss Bradley's class so upset Bebe?

2. The family in "Envy" is clearly matriarchal: "Women ruled at 2239" (para. 5). What positive and negative effects did this matriarchal family have on the author when she was a child?

3. How did the matriarchs groom the young Bebe for success? Keeping in mind that she has become a published author, do you think their methods were the best possible?

4. What does the young Bebe think she is missing with her father's absence? What might he provide that the women do not? Do you think the mature author sees the situation much differently than she did as a child?

5. What traditionally male roles do the women in Bebe's family play? How well do you think they perform these roles?

Exploring Connections

6. Compare this family with the one Gary Soto portrays in "Looking for Work" (p. 410). In particular, consider the gender roles, the household atmosphere, and the expectations placed on children.

7. What lessons are being taught in this family? To what extent do the lessons and the teaching process resemble those of Toni Cade Bambara's "The Lesson" (p. 64) or Jamaica Kincaid's "Girl" (p. 191).

8. Compare and contrast the matriarchs in this narrative with the tribal women Paula Gunn Allen describes in "Where I Come from Is Like This" (p. 241).

9. Return to the distinction Shelby Steele makes between challenging and bargaining (p. 347). How do these strategies for racial interaction describe the behavior and attitudes of Bebe and her mother? How does this selection support or complicate Steele's analysis of Black-white relations?

Extending the Critical Context

10. If you have ever felt the lack of a father, mother, sister, brother, or grandparent in your family, write a journal entry or narrative memoir exploring your memories and emotions.

11. At the end of *Sweet Summer*, Campbell decides that, while she saw her father only during the summer, her extended family — including uncles, boarders, and family friends — had provided her with plenty of healthy male influences. Read the rest of the book and report to the class on Campbell's portrayal of her relationship with her immediate family and extended family.

An Indian Story

ROGER JACK

A companion piece of sorts to the previous selection by Bebe Moore Campbell, this story also concerns growing up away from one's father — this time in one of the Indian cultures of the Pacific Northwest. It's also an intimate view of a nonnuclear family; the author is interested in the family not as a static set of defined relationships but as a social network that adapts to the ever-changing circumstances and needs of its members. Roger Jack's work has been published in several journals and anthologies, including Spawning the Medicine River, Earth Power Coming, *and* The Clouds Threw This Light. *"An Indian Story" appeared in* Dancing on the Rim of the World: An Anthology of Contemporary Northwest Native American Writing *(1990), edited by Andrea Lerner.*

Aunt Greta was always a slow person. Grandpa used to say she was like an old lady out of the old days who never hurried herself for anything, no matter what. She was only forty-five, heavyset, dark-complexioned, and very knowledgeable of the old ways, which made her seem even older. Most of the time she wore her hair straight up or in a ponytail that hung below her beltline. At home she wore pants and big, baggy shirts, but at ritual gatherings she wore her light blue calico dress, beaded moccasins, hair braided and clasped with beaded barrettes. Sometimes she wore a scarf on her head like ladies older than she. She said we emulate those we love and care for. I liked seeing her dressed for ceremonials. Even more, I liked seeing her stand before crowds of tribal members and guests translating the old language to the new for our elders, or speaking on behalf of the younger people who had no understanding of the Indian language. It made me proud to be her nephew and her son.

My mom died when I was little. Dad took care of me as best he could after that. He worked hard and earned good money as an accountant at the agency. But about a year after Mom died he married a half-breed Indian and this made me feel very uncomfortable. Besides, she had a child of her own who was white. We fought a lot — me and Jeffrey Pine — and then I'd get into trouble because I was older and was supposed to know better than to misbehave.

I ran away from home one day when everyone was gone — actually, I walked to Aunt Greta's and asked if I could move in with her since I had already spent so much time with her anyway. Then after I had gone to bed that night, Dad came looking for me and Aunt Greta told him what I had told her about my wanting to move in with her. He said it would be all right for a while, then we would decide what to do about it later. That was a long time ago. Now I am out of high school and going to college. Meanwhile, Jeffrey Pine is a high-school dropout and living with the folks.

Aunt Greta was married a long time ago. She married a guy named Mathew who made her very happy. They never had children, but when persistent people asked either of them what was wrong, they would simply reply they were working on it. Then Mathew died during their fifth year of marriage. No children. No legacy. After that Aunt Greta took care of Grandpa, who had moved in with them earlier when Grandma died. Grandpa wasn't too old, but sometimes he acted like it. I guess it came from that long, drawn-out transition from horse riding and breeding out in the wild country to reservation life in buggies, dirt roads, and cars. He walked slowly everywhere he went; he and Aunt Greta complemented each other that way.

Eventually, Aunt Greta became interested in tribal politics and   5
threatened to run for tribal council, so Grandpa changed her Indian name from Little Girl Heart to Old Woman Walking, which he had called Grandma when she was alive. Aunt Greta didn't mind. In fact, she was proud of her new name. Little Girl Heart was her baby name, she said. When Grandpa died a couple of years later she was all alone. She decided tribal politics wasn't for her but began teaching Indian culture and language classes. That's when I walked into her life like a newborn Mathew or Grandpa or the baby she never had. She had so much love and knowledge to share, which she passed on to me naturally and freely; she received wages for teaching others. But that was gesticulation, she said.

My home and academic life improved a lot after I had moved in with Aunt Greta. Dad and his wife had a baby boy, and then a girl, but I didn't see too much of them. It was like we were strangers living a quarter mile from one another. Aunt Greta and I went on vacations together from the time I graduated from the eighth grade. We were trailblazers, she said, because our ancestors never traveled very far from the homeland.

The first year we went to Maryhill, Washington, which is about a ten-hour drive from our reservation home in Park City, and saw the imitation Stonehenge Monument. We arrived there late in the evening because we had to stop off in every other town along the road to eat, whether or not we were hungry, because that was Aunt Greta's way and Grandma's and all the other old ladies of the tribe. You have to eat to survive, they would say. It was almost dark when we arrived at the park. We saw the huge outlines of the massive hewn stones placed in a circular position and towering well over our heads. We stood small and in awe of their magnificence, especially seeing darkness fall upon us. Stars grew brighter and we saw them more keenly as time passed. Then they started falling, dropping out of the sky to meet us where we stood. I could see the power of Aunt Greta protruding through her eyes; if I had power I wouldn't have to explore, physically, the sensation I imagined her feeling. She said nothing for a long time. Then, barely audible, she murmured something like, "I have no teepee. I need no cover. This moment has been waiting for me here all this time." She paused. Then, "I wasn't sure what I would find here, but I'm glad we came. I was going to say something goofy like 'we should have brought the teepee and we could call upon Coyote to come and knock over these poles so we could drape our canvas over the skeleton and camp!' But I won't. I'm just glad we came here."

"Oh no, you aren't flipping out on me, are you?" I ribbed her. She always said good Indians remember two things: their humor and their history. These are the elements that dictate our culture and our survival in this crazy world. If these are somehow destroyed or forgotten, we would be doomed to extinction. Our power gone. And she had the biggest, silliest grin on her face. She said, "I want to camp right here!" and I knew she was serious.

We camped in the car, in the parking lot, that night. But neither of us slept until nearly daybreak. She told me Coyote stories and Indian stories and asked me what I planned to do with my life. "I want to be like you," I told her. Then she reminded me that I had a Dad to think about, too, and that maybe I should think about taking up his trade. I thought about a lot of stories I had heard about boys following in their father's footsteps — good or bad — and I told Aunt Greta that I wasn't too sure about living on the reservation and working at the agency all my life. Then I tried to sleep, keeping in mind everything we had talked about. I was young, but my Indian memory was good and strong.

On our way home from Maryhill we stopped off at Coyote's Sweat-   10
house down by Soap Lake. I crawled inside the small cavernous stone structure and Aunt Greta said to make a wish for something good. She tossed a coin inside before we left the site. Then we drove through miles of desert country and basalt cliffs and canyons, but we knew we were getting closer to home when the pine trees starting weeding out the sagebrush, and the mountains overrode the flatland.

Our annual treks after that brought us to the Olympic Peninsula on the coast and the Redwood Forest in northern California; Yellowstone National Park in Wyoming and Glacier Park in Montana; and the Crazy Horse / Mount Rushmore Monuments in South Dakota. We were careful in coordinating our trips with pow-wows too. Then we talked about going all the way to Washington, D.C., and New York City to see the sights and how the other half lived, but we never did.

After high-school graduation we went to Calgary for a pow-wow and I got into trouble for drinking and fighting with some local Indians I had met. They talked me into it. The fight occurred when a girlfriend of one of the guys started acting very friendly toward me. Her boyfriend got jealous and started pushing me around and calling me names; only after I defended myself did the others join in the fight. Three of us were thrown into the tribe's makeshift jail. Aunt Greta was not happy when she came to pay my bail. As a matter of fact, I had never seen her angry before. Our neighbors at the campground thought it was funny that I had been arrested and thrown into jail and treated the incident as an everyday occurrence. I sat in the car imagining my own untimely death. I was so sick.

After dropping the ear poles, I watched Aunt Greta take down the rest of the teepee with the same meticulousness with which we had set it up. She went around the radius of the teepee removing wooden stakes from the ground that held fast the teepee's body to the earth. Then she stood on a folding chair to reach the pins that held the face of the teepee together. She folded the teepee into halves as it hung, still, on the center pole. She folded it again and again until it grew clumsy and uneven, then she motioned for me to come and drop the pole so she could untie the fastener that made the teepee our home. Meanwhile, I had to drop all skeletal poles from the sky and all that remained were a few holes in the ground and flattened patches of grass that said we had been there. I stood looking over the crowd. Lots of people had come from throughout Canada and the northern states for the pow-wow. Hundreds of people sat watching the war dance. Other people watched the stick-games and card games. But what caught my attention were the obvious drunks in the crowd. I was "one of them" now.

Aunt Greta didn't talk much while we drove home. It was a long, lonely drive. We stopped only twice to eat cold, tasteless meals. Once in Canada and once stateside. When we finally got home, Aunt Greta said, "Good night," and went to bed. It was only eight o'clock in the evening. I felt a heavy calling to go talk to Dad about what had happened. So I did.

He was alone when I arrived at his house. As usual I walked through the front door without knocking, but immediately heard him call out, "Son?"

"Yeah," I said as I went to sit on a couch facing him. "How did you know it was me?"

15

He smiled, said hello, and told me a father is always tuned in to his son. Then he senses my hesitation to speak and asked, "What's wrong?"

"I got drunk in Calgary." My voice cracked. "I got into a fight and thrown in jail too. Aunt Greta had to bail me out. Now she's mad at me. She hasn't said much since we packed to come home."

"Did you tell her you were sorry for screwing up?" Dad asked.

"Yeah. I tried to tell her. But she clammed up on me."   20

"I wouldn't worry about it," Dad said. "This was bound to happen sooner or later. You really feel guilty when you take that first drink and get caught doing it. Hell, when I got drunk the first time, my Mom and Dad took turns preaching to me about the evils of drinking, fornication, and loose living. It didn't stop me though. I was one of those smart asses who had to have his own way. What you have to do is come up with some sort of reparation. Something that will get you back on Greta's good side."

"I guess that's what got to me. She didn't holler or preach to me. All the while I was driving I could feel her staring at me." My voice strengthened, "But she wouldn't say anything."

"Well, Son. You have to try to imagine what's going through her mind too. As much as I love you, you have been Greta's boy since you were kneehigh to a grasshopper. She has done nothing but try to provide all the love and proper caring that she can for you. Maybe she thinks she has done something wrong in your upbringing. She probably feels more guilty about what happened than you. Maybe she hasn't said anything because she isn't handling this very well either." Dad became a little less serious before adding. "Of course, Greta's been around the block a time or two herself."

Stunned, I asked, "What do you mean?"

"Son, as much as Greta's life has changed, there are some of us who   25 remember her younger days. She liked drinking, partying, and loud music along with war dancing, stick-games, and pow-wows. She got along wherever she went looking for a good time. She was one of the few who could do that. The rest of us either took to drinking all the time, or we hit the pow-wow circuit all straight-faced and sober, never mixing up the two. Another good thing about Greta was that when she found her mate and decided to settle down, she did it right. After she married Mathew she quit running around." Dad smiled, "Of course, Mathew may have had some influence on her behavior, since he worked for the alcohol program."

"I wonder why she never remarried?" I asked.

"Some women just don't," Dad said authoritatively. "But she never had a shortage of men to take care of. She had your Grandpa — and YOU!" We laughed. Then he continued, "Greta could have had her pick of any man on the reservation. A lot of men chased after her before she married, and a lot of them chased after her after Mathew died. But she never had time for them."

"I wonder if she would have gotten married again if I hadn't moved in on her?"

"That's a question only Greta can answer. You know, she may work in tribal programs and college programs, but if she had to give it all up for one reason in the world, it would be you." Dad became intent, "You are her bloodline. You know that? Otherwise I wouldn't have let you stay with her all these years. The way her family believes is that two sisters coming from the same mother and father are the same. Especially blood. After your Mother died and you asked to go and live with your Aunt, that was all right. As a matter of fact, according to her way, we were supposed to have gotten married after our period of mourning was over."

"You — married to Aunt Greta!" I half-bellowed and again we laughed.   30

"Yeah. We could have made a hell of a family, don't you think?" Dad tried steadying his mood. "But, you know, maybe Greta's afraid of losing you too. Maybe she's afraid that you're entering manhood and that you'll be leaving her. Like when you go away to college. You are still going to college, aren't you?"

"Yeah. But I never thought of it as leaving her. I thought it more like going out and doing what's expected of me. Ain't I supposed to strike out on my own one day?"

"Yeah. Your leaving your family and friends behind may be expected, but like I said, 'you are everything to Greta,' and maybe she has other plans for you." Dad looked down to the floor and I caught a glimpse of graying streaks of hair on top of his head. Then he asked me which college I planned on attending.

"One in Spokane," I answered. "I ain't decided which one yet."

Then we talked about other things and before we knew it his missus and the kids were home. Junior was nine, Anna Lee eight; they had gone to the last day of the tribe's celebration and carnival in Nespelem, which was what Aunt Greta and I had gone to Calgary to get away from for once. I sat quietly and wondered what Aunt Greta must have felt for my wrongdoing. The kids got louder as they told Dad about their carnival rides and games and prizes they had won. They shared their goodies with him and he looked to be having a good time eating popcorn and cotton candy.

I remembered a time when Mom and Dad brought me to the carnival. Grandpa and Grandma were with us. Mom and Dad stuck me on a big, black merry-go-round horse with flaming red nostrils and fiery eyes. Its long, dangling tongue hung out of its mouth. I didn't really want to ride that horse, but I felt I had to because Grandpa kept telling Mom and Dad that I belonged on a real horse and not some wooden thing. I didn't like the horse, when it hit certain angles it jolted and scared me even more. Mom and Dad offered me another ride on it, but I refused.

"Want some cotton candy?" Junior brought me back to reality. "We had fun going on the rides and trying to win some prizes. Here, you can have this one." He handed me one of his prizes. And, "Are you gonna stay with us tonight?"

I didn't realize it was after eleven o'clock.

"You can sleep in my bed," Junior offered.

"Yeah. Maybe I will, Little Brother." Junior smiled. I bade everyone 40 good night and went to his room and pulled back his top blanket revealing his Star Wars sheets. I chuckled at the sight of them before lying down and trying to sleep on them. This would be my first time sleeping away from Aunt Greta in a long time. I still felt tired from my drinking and the long drive home, but I was glad to have talked to Dad. I smiled in thinking that he said he loved me, because Indian men hardly ever verbalize their emotions. I went to sleep thinking how alone Aunt Greta must have felt after I had left home and promised myself to return there as early as I could.

I ate breakfast with the family before leaving. Dad told me one last thing that he and Aunt Greta had talked about sometime before. "You know, she talked about giving you an Indian name. She asked me if you had one and I said 'no.' She talked about it and I thought maybe she would go ahead and do it too, but her way of doing this is: boys are named for their father's side and girls are named for their mother's. Maybe she's still waiting for me to give you a name. I don't know."

"I remember when Grandpa named her, but I never thought of having a name myself. What was the name?" I asked.

"I don't remember. Something about stars."

Aunt Greta was sitting at the kitchen table drinking coffee and listening to an Elvis album when I got home. Elvis always made her lonesome for the old days or it cheered her up when she felt down. I didn't know what to say, but showed her the toy totem pole Junior had given me.

"That's cute," she said. "So you spent the night at the carnival?" 45

"No. Junior gave it to me," I explained. "I camped at Dad's."

"Are you hungry?" she was about to get up from the table.

"No. I've eaten." I saw a stack of pancakes on the stove. I hesitated another moment before asking, "What's with Elvis?"

"He's dead!" she said and smiled, because that's what I usually said to her. "Oh well, I just needed a little cheering up, I guess."

I remember hearing a story about Aunt Greta that happened a long 50 time ago. She was a teenager when the Elvis craze hit the reservation. Back then hardly any families had television sets, so they couldn't see Elvis. But when his songs hit the airwaves on the radio the girls went crazy. The guys went kind of crazy too — but they were pissed off crazy. A guy can't be that good looking and talented too, they claimed. They were jealous of Elvis. Elvis had a concert in Seattle and my Mom and Aunt Greta and a couple other girls went to it. Legend said that Elvis kissed Aunt Greta on the cheek during his performance and she took to heart the old "ain't never going to wash that cheek again" promissory and never washed her cheek for a long time and it got chapped and cracked until Grandpa and Grandma finally had to order her to go to the clinic to get some medicine to clean up her face. She hated them for a while, still swearing Elvis would be her number one man forever.

"How's your Dad?"

"He's all right. The kids were at the carnival when I got to his house, so we had a nice, long visit." I paused momentarily before adding, "And he told me some stories about you too."

"Oh?" she acted concerned even though her crow's feet showed.

"Yeah. He said you were quite a fox when you were young. And he said you probably could have had any man you wanted before you married Uncle Mathew, and you could have had any man after Uncle Mathew died. So, how come you never snagged yourself another husband?"

Aunt Greta sat quietly for a moment. I could see her slumping into 55 the old way of doing things which said you thought things through before saying them. "I suppose I could have had my pick of the litter. It's just that after my old man died I didn't want anyone else. He was so good to me that I didn't think I could find any better. Besides, I had you and Grandpa to care for, didn't I? Have I ever complained about that?"

"Yeah," I persisted, "but haven't you ever thought about what might have happened if you had gotten married again? You might have done like Dad and started a whole new family. Babies, even!"

Aunt Greta was truly embarrassed. "Will you get away from here with talk like that. I don't need babies. Probably won't be long now and you'll be bringing them home for me to take care of anyhow."

Now I was embarrassed. We got along great after that initial conversation. It was like we had never gone to Calgary and I had never gotten on to her wrong side at all. We were like kids rediscovering what it was worth to have a real good friend go away for a while and then come back. To be appreciative of each other, I imagined Aunt Greta might have said.

Our trip to Calgary happened in July. August and September found me dumbfounded as to what to do with myself college-wise. I felt grateful that Indian parents don't throw out their offspring when they reach a certain age. Aunt Greta said it was too late for fall term and that I should rest my brain for a while and think about going to college after Christmas. So I explored different schools in the area and talked to people who had gone to them. Meanwhile, some of my friends were going to Haskell Indian Junior College in Kansas. Aunt Greta frowned upon my going there. She said it was too far away from home, people die of malaria there, and if you're not drunk, you're just crazy. So I stuck with the Spokane plan.

That fall Aunt Greta was invited to attend a language seminar in   60
Portland. She taught Indian language classes when asked to. So we
decided to take a side trip to our old campsite at Stonehenge. This time
we arrived early in the morning and it was foggy and drizzling rain. The
sight of the stones didn't provide the feeling we had experienced earlier.
To us, the sight seemed to be just a bunch of rocks standing, overlooking
the Columbia River, a lot of sagebrush, and two state highways. It
didn't offer us feelings of mysticism and power anymore. Unhappy with
the mood, Aunt Greta said we might as well leave; her words hung
heavy on the air.

We stayed in Portland for a week and then made it a special point to
leave late in the afternoon so we could stop by Stonehenge again at dusk.
So with careful planning we arrived with just enough light to take a
couple pictures and then darkness began settling in. We sat in the car
eating baloney sandwiches and potato chips and drinking pop because
we were tired of restaurant food and we didn't want people staring at us
when we ate. That's where we were when an early evening star fell.
Aunt Greta's mouth fell open, potato chip crumbs clung to the sides of
her mouth. "This is it!" she squealed in English, Indian, and English
again. "Get out of the car, Son," and she half pushed me out the door.
"Go and stand in the middle of the circle and pray for something good
to happen to you." I ran out and stood waiting and wondering what was
supposed to happen. I knew better than to doubt Aunt Greta's wishes or
superstitions. Then the moment came to pass.

"Did you feel it?" she asked as she led me back to the car.

"I don't know," I told her because I didn't think anything had
happened.

"I guess it just takes some people a little longer to realize," she said.

I never quite understood what was supposed to have happened that   65
day. A couple months later I was packing up to move to Spokane. I
decided to go into the accounting business, like Dad. Aunt Greta
quizzed me hourly before I was to leave whether I was all right and if I
would be all right in the city. "Yeah, yeah," I heard myself repeating. So
by the time I really was to leave she clued me in on her new philosophy:
it wasn't that I was leaving her, it was just that she wouldn't be around
to take care of me much anymore. She told me, "Good Indians stick
together," and that I should search out our people who were already
there, but not forget those who were still at home.

After I arrived in Spokane and settled down I went home all too
frequently to actually experience what Aunt Greta and everyone told
me. Then my studies got so intense that I didn't think I could travel
home as much anymore. So I stayed in Spokane a lot more than before.
Finally it got so I didn't worry as much about the folks at home. I would
be out walking in the evening and know someone's presence was with
me. I never bothered telephoning Dad at his office at the agency; and I

never knew where or when Aunt Greta worked. She might have been at the agency or school. Then one day Dad telephoned me at school. After asking how I was doing, he told me why he was calling. "Your Aunt Greta is sick. The doctors don't know what's wrong with her yet. They just told me to advise her family of the possibility that it could be serious." I only half heard what he was saying. "Son, are you there?"

"Yeah."

"Did you hear me? Did you hear what I said?"

"Yeah. I don't think you have to worry about Aunt Greta though. She'll be all right. Like the old timers used to say, 'she might go away for a while, but she'll be back,'" and I hung up the telephone unalarmed.

Engaging the Text

1. Give specific examples of how the narrator's extended family or kinship structure works to solve family problems. What problems does it seem to create or make worse?

2. What key choices does the narrator make in this story? How are these choices influenced by family members or family considerations?

3. Is the family portrayed here matriarchal, patriarchal, "equalitarian," or something else? Explain. To what extent is parenting influenced by gender roles?

4. What events narrated in this story might threaten the survival of a nuclear family? How well does the extended family manage these crises?

5. How strong an influence does the narrator's father have on him? How can you explain the father's influence given how rarely the two see each other?

6. How do you interpret the narrator's reaction when he hears about Aunt Greta's failing health? What is implied in the story's closing lines?

Exploring Connections

7. Study the tribal expectations about family life in this story and in Paula Gunn Allen's "Where I Come from Is Like This" (p. 241). What matters are left entirely to the family, and on what issues does the community exert pressure on the family (for instance, to have children)? To extend the assignment, compare these tribal expectations with those in your own community.

8. Review "Black Family Life" (p. 431), noting Joseph L. White's explanation of how an extended family works and how it evolved in response to specific historical pressures such as slavery. How well does White's concept of an extended family fit the family Jack describes? What historical circumstances may have influenced the structure and function of tribal families in the United States?

Extending the Critical Context

9. This story celebrates the power of stories to connect people and to shape or affirm one's identity. Throughout, the narrator relates family stories about his

father and his aunt that give him a clearer sense of himself and his relationship to those he loves. In a journal entry or essay, relate one or two family stories that are important to you and explain how they help you define who you are.

Friends as Family

KAREN LINDSEY

In this introduction to her book Friends as Family *(1981), Karen Lindsey proposes a tantalizing and controversial thesis — that families need not be defined by biological relationships but may be "chosen." In clearing the ground to make this argument, she also offers some startling information about the history of the family. Lindsey (b. 1944) is a teacher, editor, and free-lance writer whose work often reflects her radical feminist viewpoint.*

The traditional family isn't working. This should not come as a startling revelation to anyone who picks up this book: it may be the single fact on which every American, from the Moral Majority member through the radical feminist, agrees. Statistics abound: 50 percent of couples married since 1970 and 33 percent of those married since 1950 are divorced. One out of every six children under eighteen lives with only one parent. The number of children living in families headed by women more than doubled between 1954 and 1975.[1] The family no longer has room for aged parents. Increasing numbers of the elderly live alone or in nursing homes: only 11 percent live with their children or with other relatives.[2]

Even when the family stays together, it often does so under grim conditions. As many as 60 percent of all married women are beaten at least once by their husbands.[3] One in every hundred children is beaten, sexually molested, or severely neglected by parents.[4] And between

[1]Susan Dworkin, "Carter Wants to Save the Family, but He Can't Even Save His Family Conference," *Ms.*, September 1987, pp. 62, 98. [Author's note]

[2]Beth B. Hess, *Growing Old in America* (New Brunswick, N.J.: Transaction Books, 1976), p. 26. [Author's note]

[3]Terry Davidson, *Conjugal Crime: Understanding and Changing the Wifebeating Pattern* (New York: Hawthorn, 1978), pp. 6–7. [Author's note]

[4]Naomi Feigelson Chase, *A Child Is Being Beaten* (New York: Holt, Rinehart, & Winston, 1975), p. 185. [Author's note]

500,000 and one million elderly parents are abused each year by the adult offspring they live with.[5] Whatever the family in the United States is, it isn't *Father Knows Best*.[6]

There are a lot of people who refuse to believe this, who prefer to attribute both the problems within families and the increasing breakup of families to the "new narcissism" or the evils of the "me generation." This theory, promulgated by many conservatives and liberals, and legitimized by intellectual pseudo-leftists like Christopher Lasch,[7] suggests (Lasch, at least, is shrewd enough never to come out and say it) that if people would only stop worrying about their own personal fulfillment and return to the loving bosom of the patriarchal family, the world would be a happy place. Such apologists for the family tend to ignore the issue of intrafamily abuse, since it paints a somewhat different portrait of "those basic things we used to know."

Lasch is totally remarkable in this regard: in neither his massively popular *The Culture of Narcissism* nor his earlier and even more reactionary *Haven in a Heartless World*[8] does he discuss wife abuse or child abuse. Indeed, to perpetuate the myth of the new narcissism, he can't *afford* to acknowledge family violence. The myth of the new narcissism is more than a myth. It's also a lie. And it's important to remember that, although we often confuse the two, "myth" and "lie" are not by definition synonyms. Myth, as the dictionary tells us, is "a traditional story of ostensible historical events that serves to unfold part of the world view of a people or explain a practice, belief, or natural phenomenon." Or, as the introduction to *World Mythology* says, it is "the spontaneous defense of the human mind faced with an unintelligible or hostile world."[9]

Objective reality neither affirms nor negates a myth. Athena and   5
Zeus never existed; Jesus existed but little is known about his life; George Washington, Florence Nightingale, and Bo Derek[10] are real people about whom a great deal is known. But all exist mythically, apart from their objective existence or nonexistence.

What is true of mythical people is true of mythical concepts. Heaven and hell, the nuclear family, the Russian Revolution: all are myths, though clearly two are also historical facts. They are myths because, apart from whatever reality they have, the way in which we

---

[5]Lynn Langway, "Unveiling a Family Secret," *Newsweek*, Feb. 18, 1980, pp. 104–106. [Author's note]

[6]*Father Knows Best:* 1950s TV show featuring a highly idealized family.

[7]*Christopher Lasch:* see p. 27.

[8]Christopher Lasch, *The Culture of Narcissism* (New York: Warner Books, 1979), and *Haven in a Heartless World* (New York: Basic Books, 1977). [Author's note]

[9]Pierre Grimal, ed., *Larousse World Mythology* (London: The Hamlin Publishing Group, 1965), p. 9. [Author's note]

[10]*Bo Derek:* American actor and model (b. 1956) once considered one of the world's most beautiful women.

view them helps clarify, even shape, our vision of the world. It is in this sense that I speak of the myth of the family.

The myth of the new narcissism bases itself on the myth of the family. As Lasch and others conceptualize it, the theory of the new narcissism is that nobody cares about social causes any more, nobody cares about anyone else, and everyone is single-mindedly devoted to self-fulfillment. People of the '70s took the liberation ideologies of the '60s and individualized them, creating a selfish and decadent society concerned only with material or psychological gain. This was symbolized most strongly by the breakdown of the family. The agenda of the '80s is thus clear: return to the good old days, before the breakdown of the nuclear family.

According to this new myth, the world is now divided into *Cosmopolitan* or *Redbook*:[11] you can have a life of sex clubs and high-powered careers or a life of Mommy staying home and cooking, Daddy going to work all day and spending the evening at home, and 2.4 happy and obedient kids. There is nothing else. The acceptance of these alternatives as the parameters of human experience leaves us little real choice. If we wish to retain our humanity — to be caring, nurturing people and, by the same token, cared-for and nurtured people — we must opt for the traditional family. Whatever evils we perceive in the nuclear family, the freedom to live without human relationships is ultimately no freedom, but hell. And so the acceptance of the myth as truth has the very real possibility of turning us — at least women — into collaborators in our own oppression.

The myth of the new narcissism is a perfect example of what Mary Daly calls "false naming." False naming, Daly argues, creates a concept of reality which is a tool of oppression: it invents a definition of reality and forces us to live under the terms of that definition. Speaking specifically of the oppression of women, Daly writes: "Women have had the power of naming stolen from us. We have not been free to use our own power to name ourselves, the world, or god . . . women are now realizing that the universal imposing of names by men has been false because partial. That is, inadequate words have been taken as adequate."[12]

And so it is essential to our survival to name the lie, to look beyond the words to the reality they obscure. To do this, we must start with the base of the myth — the notion that there was once an ideally happy family which has only recently been destroyed by the forces of organized selfishness. Whether that ideal family is supposed to have

---

[11]*Cosmopolitan* or *Redbook:* two popular magazines for women, with two very different audiences, as Lindsey indicates.

[12]Mary Daly, *Beyond God the Father: Toward a Philosophy of Women's Liberation* (Boston: Beacon Press, 1973), p. 8. [Author's note]

occurred in the confines of the historically recent nuclear family, or in the older extended family, it exists as a vision of that which has been destroyed, that to which we must return. As Will Rogers[13] said, things ain't the way they used to be, and maybe they never were.

When *was* the Golden Age of the happy family? Mythmakers vary on this question, but their most common image suggests it was sometime during the nineteenth century that the world was a Norman Rockwell[14] painting. (Lasch, perhaps the shrewdest of the Golden Age mythologizers, never places it in any historical period, though he repeatedly implies that it did indeed exist.) Was it in 1869, when John Stuart Mill[15] wrote *The Subjugation of Women*, decrying the fact that thousands of husbands routinely "indulge in the utmost habitual excesses of bodily violence towards the unhappy wife"?[16] Was it in 1878, when Frances Power Cobbe wrote of the area of Liverpool known as the "kicking district" because so many of its residents kicked their wives' faces with hobnailed boots?[17] Was it in 1890, when the *Encyclopaedia Britannica* noted that the "modern crime of infanticide shows no symptoms of diminishing in the leading nations of Europe"?[18] Was it a little earlier — in the 1830s or '40s, when thousands of temperance societies sprang up throughout the United States in response to the growing number of abusive drunken men? "The drunken spouse could (and did) spend the family money as he chose, sell off his and his wife's property, apprentice their children, and assault wife and children alike."[19]

Perhaps, then, the nineteenth century is too late in history — perhaps the evils of industrialism had taken hold and destroyed the Golden Age. Perhaps we need to look back further to find our happy family — maybe to the Middle Ages, before the forces of industry had torn the family apart, when husband, wife, and children all worked the farm together in domestic harmony. The only problem is that during this period, "men were exhorted from the pulpit to beat their wives and their wives to kiss the rod that beat them. The deliberate teaching of domestic violence, combined with the doctrine that women and children by nature could have no human rights, had taken such hold by the late Middle Ages that men had come to treat their wives and children worse than their beasts."[20]

[13] *Will Rogers:* U.S. humorist and actor (1879–1935).

[14] *Norman Rockwell:* U.S. painter and illustrator (1894–1978), famous for idealized portraits of American life.

[15] *John Stuart Mill:* English philosopher and economist (1806–1873).

[16] Davidson, p. 108. [Author's note]

[17] Davidson, p. 110. [Author's note]

[18] Chase, p. 17. Infanticide itself seems to have occurred chiefly among the poor — though as always there is reason to suspect its occurrence, discreetly covered up, in more affluent families as well. [Author's note]

[19] Judith Papachristou, *Women Together* (New York: Knopf, 1976), p. 19. [Author's note]

[20] Davidson, p. 98. [Author's note]

Well, there's always the Renaissance,[21] bringing light to the primitive mentality bred by the Middle Ages. The Spanish scholar Vives, so influential in the court of England under Henry VIII and his first wife, Katherine of Aragón, is usually viewed as one of the more enlightened intellects of the era: he was influential in spreading the theory that girls, as well as boys, should be well educated. He, like dozens of other scholars in the Tudor[22] era, published tracts on childrearing and domestic harmony. Vives wrote approvingly that he knew "many fathers to cut the throats of their daughters, bretheren of their sisters, and kinsmen of their kinswomen" when these unfortunate women were discovered to be unchaste.[23] He explained that his own mother had never "lightly laughed upon me, she never cockered me . . . Therefore there was nobody that I did more flee, or was more loath to come nigh, than my mother, when I was a child." Showing affection, or "cherishing," he said, "marreth sons, but it utterly destroyeth daughters."[24]

It was perhaps fortunate for both daughters and sons that they *didn't* feel too comfortable at home, since they were likely to be betrothed at infancy and married off in adolescence — often, in the case of upperclass offspring, never to see their families again. Margaret Beaufort, grandmother of Henry VIII, was married off at 12, gave birth to Henry Tudor,[25] and never had another child — probably as a result of early childbirth. Her granddaughter, Margaret of Scotland, was also forced to marry at 12, and left her home to live with her husband, the King of Scotland; her letters home are filled with misery and homesickness.[26]

Wifebeating and childbeating were approved by most of the tract-writers of the time, though often the husband was advised to use physical abuse only as a last resort. Needless to say many husbands *didn't* obey these pious exhortations. On at least one occasion, the Duke of Norfolk (Anne Boleyn's uncle) had his servants help him beat his wife; they stopped only when blood began pouring out of her mouth.[27]

15

The statistics on physical abuse in various historical periods tell us something about family violence in the past. But they don't tell us about the nonviolent forms of misery in people's lives. We can make assumptions about the viability of marriage and family life today because

[21]*Renaissance:* the intellectual and artistic movement which spread from fourteenth-century Italy to the rest of Europe by the seventeenth century.

[22]*Tudor:* the royal dynasty in England from 1485 to 1603.

[23]Lu Emily Pearson, *Elizabethans at Home* (Stanford, Calif.: Stanford University Press, 1957), p. 248. [Author's note]

[24]H. F. M. Prescott, *Mary Tudor* (New York: Macmillan, 1953), p. 26. [Author's note]

[25]Alison Plowden, *Tudor Women* (New York: Atheneum 1979), p. 8. [Author's note]

[26]Alison Plowden, *The House of Tudor* (New York: Stein & Day, 1976), p. 47. [Author's note]

[27]Lacey Baldwin Smith, *A Tudor Tragedy: The Life and Times of Catherine Howard* (New York: Pantheon, 1961), p. 28. [Author's note]

divorce is permissible: people who leave their families are presumably unhappy in them. But how do we know what human misery (as well as human happiness) existed among people who had no option but to live together? How many parents despised the children they had no choice but to raise? How many wives loathed their husbands; how many husbands hated their wives? How many people lived together in a helpless toleration that later ages would call contentment? Such records as we have are usually diaries and letters written by members of privileged classes — people who could read and write, people who had the luxury of privacy in which to record their thoughts.

The story of Anne Askew, the sixteenth-century Protestant martyr who wrote about her life and religion as she awaited execution, and whose maid was able to smuggle the document to the exiled Bishop Bale, provides a terse but poignant picture of miserable cohabitation between a brilliant young woman and a cloddish, conservative husband.[28] How many other Anne Askews were there whose stories were never told, even to their closest friends? We have the words of Lady Jane Grey, the doomed child who was to briefly become England's queen in the same era, complaining to the scholar Roger Ascham of her parents' abuses and coldness. How many such children never voiced their complaints, or voiced them to less-concerned listeners than hers?[29] We are told by Martin Luther, the leading light of the Protestant Reformation, that his parents were severe and abusive, and his childhood miserable.[30] We have a chilling vision of intra-family hatred in the story of the 350 Lollard Heretics[31] discovered in Lincoln County in 1521. The reason so many were caught is that parents and children, husbands and wives, eagerly informed against each other.[32] How many people in how many eras would have left their husbands, wives, and parents if there had been any possibility of their doing so?

There is another aspect of family which the proponents of the Golden Age like to ignore: the family has always been a very different reality for each of its members. The father had absolute power over all the other members; the mother had some power over her sons and very much power over her daughters; the son was under his parents' control,

[28]John Bale, *Select Works* (London: Parker Society, 1849), pp. 140–240. [Author's note]

[29]Mary M. Luke, *A Crown for Elizabeth* (New York: Coward-McCann, 1970), p. 191. [Author's note]

[30]Philip Hughes, *A Popular History of the Reformation* (Garden City, N.Y.: Hanover House, 1957), p. 98. [Author's note]

[31]*Lollard heretics:* Lollardry was a medieval English movement founded by John Wycliffe in the late fourteenth century. The heretics criticized the church's wealth amid widespread poverty, wanted to abolish celibacy for the clergy, condemned all wars, and called for personal interpretation of the Bible.

[32]A. G. Dickens, *The English Reformation* (New York: Schocken, p. 27). [Author's note]

but knew that one day he would probably be able to rule his own family and perhaps even the mother who now ruled him; the daughter had no power and could anticipate little. The family may well have been — and may well still be — a "haven from the heartless world" for many men. But for women and children, it has always been the very *center* of the heartless world, from which no haven existed. For man, the limits of the family have been tacitly recognized, and legitimate or quasi-legitimate institutions have been established to supplement their needs. Men have always been permitted mistresses, even if official morality has shaken its head; women have rarely been able to get by with taking lovers. The very existence of prostitution, which has always coexisted with the family, offers implicit approval of men's search for extra-familial fulfillment. Both Saint Augustine and Saint Thomas Aquinas recognized this, when they likened prostitution to a sewer, ugly but necessary to keep the palace functioning.[33] Monogamous marriage, which the Golden Agers celebrate, has usually meant only monogamous wifehood.

I'm not trying to suggest that families have always been devoid of love, or caring, of the "cherishing" that Vives found so destructive. There are records of happy families, as there are records of unhappy ones. And in any event the human need for communication, for sharing, for love would certainly find a way to be satisfied in almost any situation. The very quality of shared experience, shared history, can build strong bonds of love and affection among people. In a family, in a commune, in a prison, people can make deep and indissoluble connections with one another. But if it isn't recognized that the family, historically, *was* a prison, which people entered not by choice but by necessity, the real happiness as well as the real misery becomes mythologized into something quite distinct from the reality. The family becomes, in Daly's words, a creation of false naming.

The false naming that creates the myth of the happy traditional family has its corollary in the false naming that says life outside the family is miserable and empty, that people who choose childlessness have no real relationships with children or with the future, and that friends are never as fulfilling as family. In our culture, there is family, and there are friends. Sometimes friendship is deep, even heroic — especially, perhaps exclusively, among men. Damon and Pythias,[34] Jonathan and David.[35] But mostly, friendship is secondary: friends are who you pass pleasant time with, who you like but don't love, to whom

20

---

[33]Simone de Beauvoir, *The Second Sex* (New York: Bantam, 1961), p. 96. [Author's note]

[34]*Damon and Pythias:* in classical mythology, Damon pledged his life to help his friend Pythias.

[35]*Jonathan and David:* in the Old Testament, Jonathan was the son of King Saul of Israel. He saved David from Saul's jealous attack on David's life. (See 1 Samuel.)

you make minimal if any commitment. Above all, *friends are not family*. Blood is thicker than water. Your friends are always "other"; your family is who you are. Friends, in that most demeaning of phrases, are "just friends." And we have believed it; we have mystified it and mythologized it. We have taken the lie for the truth, and in doing so we have almost made it true.

But people are larger than the myths they try to live by. And the truth hidden by the myth is that people have always created larger families than the biological family — larger, and infinitely more diverse. It has been there for many of us, perhaps for most of us, and we have always said to ourselves, this is different, this is me and my life, this has nothing to do with the way things are.

Side by side with the language of our oppression, other phrases have evolved and been assimilated into our vocabulary without our understanding their importance. "She's been a second mother to me." "He's just like a brother." "You are the daughter I've never had." "We're all one big happy family." Why have we never suspected that these innocuous phrases contain as much revolutionary potential as anything Karl Marx[36] or Emma Goldman[37] or Mary Wollstonecraft[38] ever said? Such phrases suggest that the family is something more than your husband or wife and the offspring of you and your spouse and the people who are related to you because somebody somewhere has the same blood parent, that someone totally outside the limits of that kinship definition can be your family. The family isn't what we've been taught it is. Thus we are not trapped between the Scylla and Charybdis[39] that the lie of the new narcissism offers; we do not need to choose between living without human bondings, or with bondings not of our choice. We can create our own bondings, choose them as they meet our needs; we can define, with others we have chosen and who have chosen us, what the nature of our bondings will be.

I think that some of the power that marriage has had for us — at least for women, although possibly for men as well — lies in this concept of choice. In an era when half of all marriages end in divorce, when couples openly live together, when the taint of "illegitimacy" is fading, marriage still has a powerful hold on women. And the power isn't only over women of the mainstream. Radical and socialist feminists

[36]*Karl Marx:* German social and political theorist (1818–1883), founder of communism.

[37]*Emma Goldman:* Russian-born American anarchist, speaker, and publisher (1869–1940). She was imprisoned for obstructing the draft and for advocating birth control and was deported in 1919.

[38]*Mary Wollstonecraft:* English writer (1759–1797), one of the first to advocate equal rights for women and men.

[39]*Scylla and Charybdis:* a deadly pair of threats; in classical mythology, they were sea monsters identified with a rock and a whirlpool.

marry; women who have lived with their lovers marry; women who have lived with *many* lovers marry. Even women who eschew monogamy marry. Sometimes they marry to placate parents, sometimes to make life easier for the children they plan to have. But I suspect that often these are simply the surface explanations for far more fundamental, more mythic, reasons.

The mythic power of marriage is threefold. To begin with, it offers a feeling of protection, of economic security. Historically, this has been accurate. A woman without a husband to protect her was at the mercy of her relatives and of strangers. The only other economically viable option was the convent, and even here a woman might find herself the "poor relation" of nuns from more affluent or prestigious families. Even today in the United States, women earn 59 percent of what men earn, and the poor are largely made up of women and their children.[40]

The second, and related, mythic power of marriage rests in its promise of permanence. The myth of true-love-forever may be comparatively recent, but a few centuries is long enough to embed a myth into a culture. Further, the permanence of marriage predates romantic love. A man might abuse his wife, he might take on mistresses, he might functionally desert her. But he — or his kin, when he fails to meet his obligations — must support her and their children, and abandonment of one's wife carries strong social censure. Henry VIII's fame as an historic ogre rests not on his dissolution of the monasteries and consequent impoverishment of thousands of monks, nuns, and the beggars who relied on them for charity, not on his arbitrary executions of hundreds of "papists" and "heretics," but on his open willingness to discard, through divorce and execution, four wives. Especially when a woman has children, she is given the right to expect that her husband, whose bloodline she has preserved, will continue to provide for her needs.

The third myth, and the one that is the concern of this book, is that of the spouse as chosen relative. It is true that only in very recent history has a woman had any actual choice in whom she marries, that it has historically been assumed that a spouse will be chosen by the parents of both men and women. But alongside this reality has always existed the story of the woman who defies the rule — who chooses, or attempts to choose, her mate. Cleopatra[41] chose Marc Antony, Dido[42] chose

---

[40]Judy Foreman, "9 to 5 grows, so does its clout," The *Boston Globe*, Sept. 28, 1979. [Author's note]

[41]*Cleopatra:* queen of Egypt (69–30 B.C.). After two marriages in Egypt and an affair with Caesar, Cleopatra married Marc Antony, a potential rival from Rome who fell in love with her. They eventually committed suicide after military defeats by Roman forces.

[42]*Dido:* in Roman mythology, the queen of Carthage. Virgil's *Aeneid* describes her love for Aeneas, a shipwrecked Trojan. When he continued his journey, she threw herself on a burning pyre.

Aeneas, and in so doing they destroyed both their empires and their lives.

This is a negative image of choice, and in any case most women don't have the options available to women who rule nations. But the stories of royalty have always provided the mythology of the lower classes, and at the very least these stories introduce the *concept* of choice into the selection of a mate. In recent centuries, the concept has significantly changed. The choice has been transmitted into a good one; it is worth losing everything to maintain the integrity of that choice, select one's true love, and reject the choice of others, even when that choice seems more sensible. Indeed, in contemporary mythology, that choice often *guarantees* happiness — marry Mr. Right and your troubles are over.

But however the myth varies, its power rests in the fact that except in the atypical instance of adoption, your spouse is the only relative you are ever permitted to choose. You are born to your parents and, by extension, to their kin, and you raise the children you give birth to. The young, modern woman who chooses her mate has behind her a string of spiritual ancestors as long as Banquo's ghost,[43] ancestors to whom, at least once, however briefly, the thought of choosing their own mates must have occurred. It is a thought so monumental that its very existence must have changed something in the mind of its thinker. Few women could have voiced this change, and even fewer could have acted on it. But we are the heirs of that change nonetheless.

Now an even greater concept has entered into our minds. We can choose most of our family. We can choose *all* of our family. In some ways, recognition of this possibility has begun to surface in popular culture. Recently, several magazines published articles about the need to create new, familial ways to celebrate holidays, and described festive scenes shared by former and current spouses, in-laws from both marriages, and offspring from the divorced parents' current and former marriages.

As far as it goes, this represents an important step in breaking through the oppressive definitions of family. For people who have shared history, who have loved each other and lived through major parts of each other's lives together, the concept of "family" should apply, in much the same way as it applied to parents and grown siblings who no longer live together or share the same interests but who are indelibly part of one another's lives.

But it isn't only spouses who share or have shared each other's lives, who have created a common past with each other. Friends, neighbors, co-workers have often lived through as many experiences together as

30

---

[43]*Banquo's ghost:* a reference to Shakespeare's *Macbeth* (act 4, scene 1); Macbeth, who has murdered Banquo, sees an apparition of eight kings of Banquo's lineage.

husbands and wives — have created, perhaps unconsciously, equally strong bonds. And slowly these bonds too are seeping into popular mythology.

A good barometer of the change is television, which is probably the most potent force in mid-twentieth-century American mythmaking. In the '50s, the model of the family was clear-cut. Mommy, Daddy, and the kids. *Father Knows Best. I Remember Mama. Ozzie and Harriet. Make Room for Daddy. I Love Lucy. Life of Riley.* Even *Burns and Allen*, miles ahead of the others in wit and sophistication, showed two nuclear families, and the Burnses had a son (though he never appeared till the later episodes). Only *My Little Margie*, saccharine sweet as it was, dared to veer from the accepted family norm: Daddy was a widower who lived with his grown daughter.

In the '60s, things began to change. Divorce was a social reality, but a fantasy taboo, so TV compromised. The mortality rate among television spouses soared: suddenly widows and widowers with kids were the norm. *The Diahann Carroll Show. The Doris Day Show. The Andy Griffith Show. The Partridge Family.* And then the crème de la crème, *The Brady Bunch*: widow with cute large brood marries widower with cute large brood, re-creating the two-parent family with a vengeance. It was an interesting attempt to cover up by half admitting what was happening to the family. Viewers who were divorced or separated could identify with the one-parent (or re-created two-parent) family, but could not have the validity of their own experience confirmed. Death is a tragedy, not a choice: the family still works until something more cosmic than human need disrupts it.

By the '70s even that wasn't enough, and the workplace family began to achieve some recognition. It started with *The Mary Tyler Moore Show*. Mary Richards, the character Moore played, had just broken off with her boyfriend and had come to Minneapolis to seek a job. Her coworkers and her best friend, Rhoda, became her family. This was no accident: the characters on the show *talked* about being a family. In one episode, Rhoda refused a job in New York because it would separate her from Mary. With little fanfare, *The Mary Tyler Moore Show* tastefully broke a taboo.

Then there was *Mod Squad*, the story of three stereotypically 35 alienated kids who become cops, and in the process also become each other's family. Corny as that show was (and reactionary in its basic theme — three dropouts become narcs), a caring and commitment among the three came through as it never did in any other cop show. The relationship, in fact, may have scared some of its creators. A year or two ago, they aired a two-hour special, *Return of the Mod Squad*, in which the three, now living separate lives, are reunited essentially to establish that the old "family" was an adolescent phase and they have now outgrown each other.

But the model of on-the-job families continues — perhaps to reassure all the divorced people, the not-yet-married people, the not-in-romantic-relationship people, that they aren't totally alone. Good shows and bad, serious and silly, they are astoundingly numerous. The cops on *Barney Miller*, the soldiers on *M*A*S*H*, the radio personnel on *WKRP in Cincinnati*. Even on as vacuous a show as *Love Boat*, the workmates in more than one episode are described as a family. Last season, in fact, the Love Boat family was solidified by its adoption of a child — Captain Stuebing's illegitimate, ten-year-old daughter, Vicki. In the episode introducing Vicki's residence on board the ship, a social worker at first is reluctant to permit the girl to live in such an unstable environment, with no family but the captain. But she is soon persuaded that Vicki does indeed have a family on the ship. Vicki, she says, is "one lucky lady . . . You have not one parent but five, all of them loving, caring people."[44]

In *M*A*S*H*, too, the family has been verbalized. At one point, fatherly Colonel Potter says, "The 4077 is not just a roster of people; it's my family. Not only that, but a loyal family." In another episode, Corporal Klinger, shattered by the news that his wife is divorcing him, comes to realize that "I may not have a family anymore in Toledo, but I sure have one here." In yet another, Margaret describes the unit as "like a family," and then corrects herself. "No," she says firmly, "it *is* a family." Sometimes the familial relationship among the characters is mirrored in the relationship of the actors. An interview with the cast of *M*A*S*H* brings up familial references. Gary Burghoff, who played the boyish Radar O'Reilly, told one writer that since the death of his own father, "I think of Harry [Morgan] as my new father."[45]

Some of TV's workplace families are more believable than others: the warmth of the *M*A*S*H* personnel comes through beautifully; the poke-in-the-ribs camaraderie of the *Love Boat* crew evokes little feeling of connection or commitment. But, however successful each is, TV has come to recognize, and institutionalize, the workplace family.

In 1978 a brief-lived show called *The Apple Family* attempted a truly radical idea — the story of unrelated people who came together with the idea of forming a consciously chosen family, not an office family or a thrown-together family. The show didn't last. It wasn't very good, and in any event lots of shows don't last, so maybe that doesn't mean anything. On the other hand, maybe it does. Maybe it means that television, which influences so much of our thinking, can't afford to tell us we can choose our own families. It is, after all, a very dangerous

---

[44]The quotes from television shows came from the diligent research of Lisa Leghorn, one of my chosen-family members, who selflessly spent hours watching *M*A*S*H* and *Love Boat* to cull them for me. [Author's note]

[45]David S. Reiss, *M*A*S*H: The Exclusive Inside Story of TV's Most Popular Show* (New York: Bobbs-Merrill, 1980), p. 35. [Author's note]

message. It will be interesting to see the fate of a fall 1981 program, *Love, Sidney*, in which a gay man lives with a heterosexual woman and her daughter, forming, in the producer's words, a "surrogate family."[46]

In writing this book, I've had to make choices about terminology. 40 This is always sticky, since words inevitably attempt to pin down human experience, and human experience always exists in countless variations. What do we call the family as we know it? The nuclear family is only a recent phenomenon, springing out of the older extended family. "Family of origin" is inaccurate if it attempts to include grand-parents, aunts, uncles, and cousins whom we may not even meet until we are five, ten, or thirty, but who are still part of that concept called family. "Biological family" comes closest, and I have chosen to use it, but not without trepidation, since both marriage and adoption are integral parts of it. I've chosen it because it seems to me to encompass not the whole reality, but the whole *myth*: blood is thicker than water. Much of the power of the patriarchy rests on the concept of biological kinship: a man needs a son to carry on his genes and his name; hence woman is forced into marriage and monogamy. Marriage historically is the integration of two bloodlines, and it is this, not the more recent myth of romance, that is the central mythical commitment of marriage: "She is the mother of my children." The stepmother in the fairy tale *must* be wicked, because her natural alliance is to the children of her own body, not those of her husband's body. Adoption of children not of one's own bloodline is always an adaptation. When one can't have children of "one's own," one creates a substitute, in effect pretending that the child is blood kin. The reality has changed; the myth remains untouched. Hence, I am using "biological family" to encompass the myth in all its facets, since it is the myth rather than the fact of genetical inheritance that governs our lives.

The same problem of terminology arises when I find myself defin-ing the kinds of contemporary nonbiological family. Definition, the creation of categories — these are useful and necessary, but they are also dangerous. They are useful if, like clothing, they can be worn when they're comfortable and can stretch to fit whatever they cover, allowing themselves to be discarded when they no longer fit properly. If they become straitjackets, restricting and confining, they are destructive; they have become false naming. True naming is a process of infinite growth, infinite flexibility. And so I have drawn up categories of non-biological family. I think they are useful categories, helping to put into focus a reality we've been taught not to see. But they are loose catego-ries. A given relationship may fall into one, or two, or three categories.

[46]Frank Swertlow, "TV Update," *TV Guide*, June 6, 1981, p. A–1. [Author's note] (*Love, Sidney* was canceled after two seasons on NBC.)

There may be — there must be — other categories. I've chosen mine because they fit my experience and my observations.

The three kinds of nonbiological family I've seen are the "honorary relative" family — the family friend who is your "uncle" or "aunt" as you grow up; the workplace family; and, finally, the chosen family — the friends who, with no outside force throwing you together, you have consciously or unconsciously chosen to be your family. . . .

The chosen family isn't always an unmitigated good: I'm not attempting to erase *Father Knows Best* and replace it wih an equally silly picture of happy little chosen families creating heaven on earth. Sometimes the chosen family mirrors the worst of biological families — the patriarchal power, the crippling dependency, the negation of the individual selves that can exist in a secure framework. Charles Manson[47] was the leader of a chosen family; so was Jim Jones.[48] Armies create families of men who are permitted and encouraged through their bonding to rape and kill. To expand definitions, to create choice, doesn't guarantee that the choices will be either wise or moral. But choice itself is good, and with it comes a greater potential for good than exists in its absence. . . .

[47]*Charles Manson:* leader of the "family" that murdered actor Sharon Tate and six of her friends in 1969.
[48]*Jim Jones:* American-born head of a fanatical religious sect, some nine hundred members of which committed mass suicide in Guyana.

Engaging the Text

1. Is it possible to *choose* one's own family? Are the kinds of chosen families Lindsey describes really families, or "just" groups of friends?

2. Explain the concept of the "new narcissism." How, according to Lindsey, has it affected the American family?

3. Early in this selection, Lindsey draws a distinction between a myth and a lie. Explain and illustrate the difference between these two terms.

4. What, according to Lindsey, is the relationship between patriarchy and the traditional nuclear family?

5. Analyze the structure of Lindsey's argument. How persuasive is the evidence she provides in its defense?

Exploring Connections

6. Drawing on the readings by Lindsey, Arlene Skolnick (p. 402), Richard Louv (p. 416), and Joseph L. White (p. 431), write a composite history of the American family.

7. Analyze the couple in Gloria Naylor's "The Two" (p. 270) as an example of a chosen family. Would Lindsey say they meet her criteria of a functional family? Would you?

Extending the Critical Context

8. Several recent books, like Robert Bly's *Iron John*, suggest that Americans are experiencing a deep psychological hunger for a strong father — the need for a firm but kind embodiment of authority and male power. Do you share this perception? How might Lindsey argue against it?

9. At the end of this selection, Lindsey suggests that chosen families may have some negative as well as positive aspects. What, in your opinion, might be the negative implications of a society composed primarily of voluntary families?

10. Do you know any example of nonbiological or chosen families? How do they differ from the biological families you know? Are there purposes each serves that the other cannot?

The Gay Family

RICHARD GOLDSTEIN

During the last two decades, openly gay citizens have sought and won high public office, claimed and rejuvenated urban communities, and challenged traditional ideas and institutions like marriage and the family. Yet, despite these accomplishments, they have had to cope with the tragedy of the AIDS epidemic and with increased hostility in some quarters of the larger community. In this piece, Richard Goldstein reports on the obstacles faced by homosexuals who choose to marry or raise children. Goldstein (b. 1944) is arts editor for the Village Voice *and writes frequently about sexual politics. In addition to his many publications in magazines and newspapers, he is author of* Reporting the Counterculture *(1989). "The Gay Family" appeared in the* Village Voice *on July 1, 1986.*

Paul wore white. Scott wore white. They stood under the *chupah* while parents and siblings, *zaydehs* and *bubbas*[1], looked on. Old friends teared up as the rabbi recited a benediction in Hebrew and English. There were readings from the Song of Songs ("Come, my beloved, let us go into the field . . .") and from *Leaves of Grass*[2] ("To be surrounded by beautiful, curious, breathing, laughing flesh is enough"). Paul and Scott

---

[1]*chupah:* the canopy at a Jewish wedding ceremony. *Zaydehs* are grandfathers and *bubbas* are grandmothers.

[2]*Leaves of Grass:* 1855 poem by Walt Whitman (1819–1892), revolutionary in its form and frank sexuality.

raised a glass to each other's lips and pronounced a benediction of their own: "With this wine, I declare my love for you before this assembly of family and friends and in accord with the traditions of the Jewish people and the spirit of human liberation." Then they stepped on the glass and shattered it. Together.

"We don't call it a wedding," Scott says. "We don't call it a marriage. I correct people. We call it our Ceremony."

Their Ceremony was not so different from many June weddings I've attended: a beautiful site (the Prospect Park picnic house), a groaning buffet, the usual utopian rhetoric. If anything, it smacked of those hippie weddings where the bride and groom wrote their own service, accompanied by a guitarist who sang of world peace and spiritual harmony. But this ceremony was different, of course, for being shorn of any legal significance; and, because of who Paul Horowitz and Scott Klein are, it took on a resonance that made even the song they'd chosen by Sade[3] ("Everybody wants to live together / Why can't we live together?") seem urgent, personal.

Despite my muffled snickers, I cried a bit, in part because I remembered my own wedding to a woman, in part because, sitting next to my male lover, watching Paul and Scott, I yearned for the day when we felt safe enough to laugh at them exchanging vows.

The idea of staging such a ceremony has always intrigued them, but   5
Paul and Scott were spurred to act by a succession of weddings among their college friends. "Here I'm recognizing their relationships in a very public way," says Scott, "and I began to feel we deserve the same kind of recognition. We've been together four years now. We don't talk about forever, but we're very committed to each other, and I think it's important for people to see that there's a depth between us."

A depth, when it must be confined or confided to a few sympathetic friends, can seem like an illusion. A commitment that may never be commemorated in ritual can feel fleeting, fragile. Any relationship is vulnerable to change — many of us prefer it that way — but a gay relationship is a Sisyphean[4] journey: You walk out of your house on a brilliant afternoon and, overcome with limerance,[5] you tousle your lover's hair, only to be plummeted by a passerby's scowl — or worse. No ceremony can prevent such occurrences; the world we will always have with us. But an exchange of vows before parents and peers can offer

[3]*Sade:* contemporary female vocalist.

[4]*Sisyphean:* suggestive of the labors of Sisyphus, who was ruler of Corinth in classical mythology. He offended the gods and was made to roll a stone up a hill endlessly, with the stone always escaping near the top and rolling down again.

[5]*limerance:* word coined by Ursula LeGuin in her sci-fi novel *Left Hand of Darkness;* it refers to a transitional stage between sexes, characterized by aroused sexual feelings.

some protection against worldlessness — that feeling of being out of time and place.

There's a ready remedy for heterosexuals who experience that feeling: marriage. For those who choose to live without the trappings of a sexist institution, there is still the possibility that a man and woman living together or caring for a child could be married. An unmarried couple who take advantage of that assumption can benefit from it; the point is, they have a choice. An unmarried couple is as unlike a gay couple as a bohemian who has chosen poverty is unlike the poor. And because of the particular oppression it addresses, a gay Ceremony, unlike a wedding, is a radical act.

So is having children, if you're gay. Lesbian motherhood and gay fatherhood raise terrors so primal that they make orgies and sexual devices pale as emblems of deviance. If sexual excess connotes a life beyond the pale[6] (and safety net), having kids expresses a commitment not just to a community of peers but to the march of generations. It threatens the stereotype that enables heterosexuals to think of themselves as distinct — and superior. It suggests that, just as Jews are complete without Jesus, homosexuals are whole without the "salvation" of heterosexuality.

How much more comforting to think of gay people as narcissists who consciously reject fertility. Norman Podhoretz[7] has often availed himself of this stereotype; he milked it vigorously in a recent column honoring Father's Day. "A man who decides to live as a homosexual is abdicating his place as a father," he observed. "Indeed, it is entirely possible that this represents, either consciously or unconsciously, one of the main attractions of homosexuality." Podhoretz did not bother to report that many gay people *do* have children: the Kinsey Institute estimated recently that a third of all lesbians and a fifth of all gay men have been married. Half are parents.

When they break the covenant of marriage and heterosexuality, much more often than not, gay parents leave their children behind. Judges commonly restrict even visitation rights when a gay parent has a live-in lover; gay friends are often barred from the house while the child is visiting. A judge's order not to "flaunt sexuality" may require withdrawing from a gay church or political organization. Gay parents petitioning for even partial custody often must choose between a child and a lover, friends, and community. A judge in Chicago recently added a new wrinkle when he ordered a gay father to take the HTLV-III antibody test before he could have any contact with his child at all.

It's the exception that proves the rule when gay parents are granted

10

---

[6]*beyond the pale:* outside the bounds of acceptable behavior.

[7]*Norman Podhoretz:* outspoken editor (b. 1930) of the conservative magazine *Commentary.*

custody. But the proportion of lesbian mothers who win such cases has risen from less than one percent in 1970 to 15 percent today. The stereotype of women as natural custodians of children may have more to do with this shift than any tolerance of homosexuality. As for a gay father winning custody over a straight mother, no matter what their respective parental capacities, *Psychology Today* observes: "That would be news."

For Rosemary Dempsey and Maggie Wales, raising five children in the home they share has been a struggle whose rewards are barely hinted at by the plate that sits above their mantel: a gift from all their children, it reads, "Happy 10th Anniversary."

They can vividly recall the day in 1979 when their vacation in Florida was interrupted by a phone call from the friend they'd left the kids with: Maggie's cat had died, and not only that; five years after he relinquished custody, Rosemary's husband had suddenly appeared and taken his children. They drove all night, arrived at her husband's home the next afternoon, and found her son "hiding in a closet in his pajamas" and her daughter "crying hysterically." They brought the kids back, only to be confronted by two policemen who sheepishly arrested Dempsey. A first year law student (now a prominent attorney in custody law), she spent that day and night in jail.

It's the nightmare every gay parent lives with: the specter of the state stepping in. "You ask yourself," Rosemary says, "should we just stop and let them have the kids? Because it sure is painful for them. But then, the message you give is that they're not worth fighting for." So they went to trial, assembling a parade of neighbors to testify on their behalf and rallying feminist groups to their defense, with signs that read "Save Rosemary's Babies." The judge handed down a landmark ruling: though these children were being raised in "an unconventional household," there was not "a scintilla of evidence from which the court could infer that Dempsey's sexual orientation was adversely affecting them." She was not to be denied custody on the sole basis of her sexuality.

All's well that ends well, except this ordeal did not. Two weeks later, a new set of court papers arrived; this time, Maggie's husband was suing for custody of *his* kids on similar grounds. And this time, another judge ruled differently: Maggie could see her three children for a month every summer, on three weekends out of four, and on alternate holidays. But for the rest of the year, it was in the best interest of the children to live with their heterosexual dad.

Maggie and Rosemary are still very much a family, with scrapbooks full of pictures and the usual braggadocio: "Two kids from this household have won the mayor's award for academic excellence; one is president of his class and too popular for his own good." Their relationship, which began shortly after both women left their husbands, has the flinty, tempered quality of a boulder. "The kids have always known that we loved each other," Maggie says. "Their main concern was whether we were each gonna be there for them." They have been through a lot together, and it has sealed not just their union but their politics. "What often comes up in these trials is that it's wrong to expose kids to values that are different from the dominant society's," Rosemary insists. "When they saw that they couldn't get us on lesbian sexuality, the main thrust was our involvement in the feminist movement. They won't put you in jail for fighting to change society — but they might take your kids."

Despite the cultivated image of homosexuals as emotional nomads, most gay people, at some point in their lives, establish a stable, central relationship. And, despite all that Oscar Wilde[8] has said about marriage ("It's as demoralizing as cigarettes and far more expensive"), there is nothing new about gay people holding Ceremonies of Union, holy or otherwise. Historians have uncovered ample evidence of homosexual marriage rites, performed in private, sometimes by renegade clergy and occasionally with one party in drag. Half-camp, half-yearning, and all fantasy, these elaborate fetes were part of the high romanticism of gay life before Stonewall,[9] when, as diarist Donald Vining recalls with some disdain, "we thought pairing up was what homosexuals *did*." ("Monogamy," he hastens to add, "was seldom part of the deal.")

What is new is the public nature of these ceremonies, and the active participation of family and clergy. Not since the year 342, when homosexual marriage was outlawed in Europe (it had flourished in the Roman Empire, largely among the aristocracy; Nero married two men, one of whom was accorded the status of an empress), has an established religion performed such ceremonies. But in 1984, the Unitarian / Universalist Association voted overwhelmingly to permit its ministers to marry congregants of the same sex. Reverend Robert Wheatly has married many homosexual couples, especially of the Catholic faith, at his Unitarian church in Boston. To "sanctify a relationship satisfies a very human need," he says. "It adds a dimension of integrity and longevity." Individual Quaker meetings will perform such ceremonies, and so will individual rabbis. "If a gay couple have, despite all the prejudices, managed to build an enduring relationship, it deserves to be recognized," says Yoel Kahn of San Francisco, who presided over Paul and Scott's union. And the Metropolitan Community Church, an

---

[8]*Oscar Wilde:* Irish poet, dramatist, novelist, and social critic (1854–1900).

[9]*Stonewall:* the Stonewall or Christopher Street riots of June 1969 in Greenwich Village, New York City, a watershed event in gay activism. After police closed the Stonewall Inn, a dance bar frequented by flamboyant and unconventional homosexuals, the crowd attacked the police with cobblestones and bottles. Several nights of disorder and demonstrations followed.

openly gay denomination with over 200 congregations worldwide, will conduct "a ceremony of holy union" for lesbians and gay men who have lived together for at least a year.

Despite his antipathy to gay marriage, Vining put me in touch with two friends who, as he described it, "wear the ring." One of the pair, a professor at City College, describes a ceremony performed for him and his lover in 1969, by a Presbyterian minister who had been arrested in Selma, Alabama, several years earlier. "The civil rights movement was the coattail we were riding on," he recalls, "not the Stonewall riot." Their ceremony — along with a full communion service — was held in the chapel, before the entire congregation. As a guitarist played and sang "The Impossible Dream," the pair were pronounced "mate and spouse." "We gave our rings to the minister, who blessed them and put them on our hands. Then we went to his home for a reception with his wife and kids."

"Were you embarrassed?" I asked.   20

"Judging from the photos, we were scared to death. After the exchange of rings, it was clear we could kiss, and *that* was embarrassing. We *did* kiss, but gingerly, and when the service was over, we dashed into the back room and kissed good."

Times have changed. Last year, two male stockbrokers planning to marry registered a china pattern in their names at Bloomingdale's. They were reflecting the three A's of gay life in the '80s: aging, assimilation, and AIDS. As the Stonewall generation enters midlife, along with the rest of the baby boom, the entire culture is pushing couplehood. The gay response, in less tragic times, might be to combine the stability of a spouse with the serendipity of sexual adventures; but AIDS has ushered in monogamy, and the bond which suddenly carries with it obligations of denial and restraint makes gay male couplehood more like traditional marriage than it ever was. The energy that gay culture once poured into erotic enterprise — as well as the elaborate chains of "kinship" sex can forge — all must be redirected. If the predictions are correct, and 180,000 people, most of them gay men, perish from AIDS over the next five years, the survivors will be very different people, with values antithetical to those associated with the disease. The urge for couplehood is only the most visible component of that change: the real reconstitution going on in gay culture today involves the broader, trickier terrain of family.

The change is hardly limited to gay men. Among lesbians, "couplism," a heresy second only to "looksism" in some circles, is definitely making a comeback; but, as with gay male pairings, the return to a discarded tradition often has a radical edge. The lesbian couple of the '80s may well "choose children," often through artificial insemination. Heterosexual women have had to struggle for the right *not* to have children, but dykes are supposed to be sterile. They must defend their choice to bear children against social and legal pressures as binding as the system that tracks straight women toward motherhood.

No one knows how many of the 20,000 women inseminated each year are unmarried, but "turkey baster babies" have become a staple of what's being referred to as the "lesbian baby boom." The apotheosis of self-directed motherhood, A.I., confers on women an extraordinary degree of autonomy. As Joy Schulenberg writes in *Gay Parenting*, all that's required is "an ovulating woman, 1 cc. of viable sperm, a cheap piece of equipment, and some very basic knowledge of female anatomy." In the hands of lesbians, A.I. can become an instrument for appropriating the act of conception itself. "I inseminated LeAnn myself," one woman told Schulenberg, "and it was the most beautiful act of love I have ever done."

The contours of gay family, in this setting, have very little to do   25
with the conventional heterosexual paradigm: there may be one or two mommies, sometimes a daddy or uncle, and sometimes, a profusion of parents who have no blood relation to the child. The collectivism of the '60s and '70s, when groups of women marshaled their meager assets and ample resources to care for each other, is being adapted to the tasks of parenting. In the lesbian enclave of Park Slope, a "mommies group" meets monthly, with nine women, two of whom have already borne children. They exchange information and energy, bolstering each other against reservations about raising a child in an unorthodox setting, and all the burdens that come of being out on the edge.

Not everyone is happy about the lesbian baby boom. "I'm horrified by it," says one woman whose lover is six months pregnant. "For me, part of being a lesbian is not being baby centered, and it seems to me that the lesbian world is becoming more baby centered every hour." At this rate, the Michigan Womyn's Music Festival, a sort of lesbian Woodstock, will soon have to drop its rule prohibiting males over the age of seven from mingling with women and girls.

All these changes are occurring at a time when the gay rights movement is having its most tangible success — at least in cities where homosexuals have translated their ample presence into political clout. Among urban professionals, at any rate, there is probably less onus attached to being openly gay than at any time in American history; Paul and Scott, for example, were able to get a "marriage discount" on their joint mortgage from the bank where Paul works because it has a nondiscrimination hiring policy.

In the face of such relative equity, gay life is becoming increasingly demystified and, in the process, it is losing its compensatory — if colorful — edge. As distinctions become more subtle (among the young it sometimes seems that lesbians and gay men are Yuppies with brighter eyes), much of what used to seem inherent about homosexuality — its argot, costumes, inflection, and gait — is slipping away, leaving men who love men and women who love women but who are fundamentally different from heterosexuals in no other respect.

So much in gay tradition mocks the institutions of heterosexuality that what often goes unnoticed is the yearning to lead an ordinary life — to play a role in society without hiding one's sexuality. As the stereotypes drop away and new options open up, gay people are discovering a more authentically individual relationship to social conventions. "We're strong enough as a movement to support people's real life choices," says one lesbian mother-to-be.

The gay family is shorthand for a new institution, one that bears little resemblance to the patriarchal structure most of us were raised in. Homosexuals are, by definition, outside that structure, and given our status, when we try to appropriate the tradition of forming families, we end up creating something new.

Do gay families subvert the family? A more salient question might be, is the family subverting itself? By now, the statistics have been drummed into our fornicating brains: the average American marriage lasts 9.4 years; nearly 20 percent of all children are born to unwed mothers; four out of 10 children born in the '70s will spend some time in single-parent households. Depending on whether you like what you see, these figures epitomize either the crisis of family life or its evolution. In any case, the change has created a new class of single parents and their lovers — millions of people, most of them straight. The battle being waged on this cutting edge of gay liberation has implications for all unmarried people, since, when it comes to employee benefits, at least, gay couples are usually treated like heterosexuals "living in sin."

For most gay couples, the struggle has less to do with subverting the patriarchy than with getting a lover's children covered on your health plan. But symbolism is never far from the surface. As Nan Hunter, newly appointed director of the ACLU's[10] Lesbian and Gay Rights Project, observes: "The idea that other kinds of relationships would be accorded some of the economic breaks of marriage, or that other kinds of relationships can provide a loving atmosphere for the raising of children, is deeply frightening for society."

So far, activists have had their greatest success in the private sector. In 1982, the *Village Voice's* union won health coverage for live-in "spouse equivalents" of its rank and file. Similar plans have been adopted by several small companies, and some progressive unions are considering raising the issue in collective bargaining. But when San Francisco's Board of Supervisors passed a bill in 1982 that would have extended benefits to the "domestic partners" of city workers and authorized a municipal registry for them, it was as if a line had been crossed.

[10]*ACLU: the American Civil Liberties Union.*

Gay rights, yes; gay power, reluctantly; but subsidizing relationships out of wedlock, never! Mayor Dianne Feinstein vetoed the bill.

But similar measures have passed in Berkeley and West Hollywood, a newly constituted city whose politics are dominated by homosexuals and retirees. For both groups, the benefits of domestic partnership legislation are more than financial: hospitals and convalescent homes must extend full visitation rights to live-in lovers. The AIDS crisis has heightened the urgency of these issues for gay male couples: suddenly, the power to make life-and-death decisions about a lover's medical treatment seems worth fighting for.

So does the right to grieve. In California, a railroad worker denied funeral leave to mourn his male lover, who had died of AIDS, sued and won time off. Retaining shared assets after a lover's death is another point of contention, especially when those possessions include a rent-controlled or stabilized apartment. A judge in New York recently ruled that a man who had lived with and cared for his male lover through a terminal struggle with AIDS was, in effect, a relative, and could continue to reside in their apartment, though his name is not on the lease. The case is currently being appealed.

. . . In California, where court decisions affirming the validity of relationships outside marriage date back to 1921, gay adoptive parents meet relatively little resistance. In New York, the governor's executive order prohibiting discrimination in state services has been interpreted to apply to foster care and adoption. Gay people can and do adopt children here, but their road is seldom an easy one.

It's difficult, in any case, for a single male to adopt; the old wisdom is that men make poor care providers, so agencies are especially loath to place infants with "bachelors." But Rubén is an exception: a physician who has lived with his lover, an executive, for 19 years, he's the kind of adoptive parent any agency would relish — except for the fact that he's gay. But in New York, the subject of sexuality rarely comes up in adoption proceedings; officially, gay couples are treated like other unmarried couples: only one member can qualify as the legal parent. Even though the agency knew Rubén was a single male in his mid forties who lived with a male roommate, it had no immediate reservations about placing a three-week-old boy in his care — the procedure took all of four days.

Then the trouble began. When Rubén went to Family Court to have the adoption certified, the judge noticed the reference to a roommate and drew her own conclusions; she asked for a second home study. A probation officer visited Rubén and popped the question: Was he gay? His heart stopped. "I decided to be honest. I had heard that this was not supposed to be a deterrent to adoption, so I swallowed hard and said yes."

What followed was a two-year ordeal, during which the probation officer, the original agency, and the judge wavered over whether to certify the adoption. The court ordered two more home studies, called in a child psychologist, appointed an attorney to represent the child. "Through all those proceedings," Rubén remembers, "nobody said this shouldn't happen; but one thing or another kept standing in the way. And I began to sense that they were looking for a reason to say no."

Meanwhile, the child was bonding with his new family — calling Rubén "daddy" and the lover "father." Rubén's mother, who took to the child immediately, began to feel as if her grandson were only temporary. On more than one occasion, Rubén says, he was tempted "to take my kid and run away to Canada." But he stuck it out, in part because he understood that the longer a child lives in its adoptive home, the harder for a court to take it away. "It would have been devastating for him to be removed," Rubén says.

Finally, two weeks after the boy's second birthday, the adoption was finalized. "In retrospect, it seems they all wanted to see that every *i* was dotted, in case a problem came up afterward," he says. The final hearing in Family Court took all of five minutes, at the end of which, the judge looked up at Rubén's son and said, "Take good care of your father."

What about the children. Will they be insecure? Enraged? Gay? The latter question is often thrust at gay parents in the form of an accusation, but the evidence, scanty as it is, says otherwise. "At this stage, I tentatively suggest that children being raised by . . . homosexual parents do not differ appreciably from children raised in more conventional family settings," says Richard Greene, a professor of psychiatry and psychology at Stony Brook. All the children in his study were able to "comprehend and verbalize the atypical nature of their parents' lifestyles and to view that atypicality in the broader perspective of the cultural norm." Greene thinks that the formation of a sexual identity has more to do with interactions outside the home than with a parent's personal choice of a mate.

But that doesn't mean the children of gay people are *never* gay. The director of a camp for children of "alternative families" (mostly the daughters of lesbians), says: "My sense is that most of these kids will probably end up heterosexual — but not strictly so. They're more open-minded. A lot of them say they're bisexual, or that they don't know yet." There are anxieties peculiar to the situation: "Most kids go through a particularly homophobic period in junior high school. They're very judgmental. The girls are very into makeup and badly want to have boyfriends." The sons of gay men are even more likely than other adolescent boys to experience profound anxieties about their sexual identity. The best adjustment, a University of Alberta study suggests, is made by children whose parents are candid about sexuality and live in a stable relationship.

One gay father, interviewed in *Psychology Today*, remembers telling his sons when they were both 15. "I told them bluntly and then explained what it was all about," he said. "They wept — then they coped."

Gay families face a situation that is, in many ways, analogous to what interracial families confronted a generation ago. The children are typically more circumspect, especially about confiding in their peers. But the bonds they form are strong and their sense of social justice keen. "What he assimilates at this point is that anyone can love anyone — and it's not just a right but a fact," says one lesbian mother about her nine-year-old son. "He also knows that some people try to prevent it from happening, and that we're struggling for freedom just as they're struggling for freedom in South Africa."

All the gay parents interviewed for this article describe their children as self-directed and unafraid to speak out. It's a trait many gay parents cultivate from their own tribulations — a determination to make your own decisions and a drive to remake the world in your own terms. Even Rubén notices that, at three, his son has "a strong will. He's not a follower. So I'm hoping that, if he sees my situation is right for me, then he'll be able to deal with what the world thinks of it."

Tommy is not Dee's biological child, but neither was he formally adopted. Dee just happened to be in the right place at the right time; within a few hours of hearing that an infant was available, she became a mother.

Raised by a divorced woman at a time when that was, in many eyes, as problematic as being raised by a lesbian today, Dee says, "I'd always been attracted to the idea that you don't have to be married to have a child. While I was living with a guy, I deliberately became pregnant, but miscarried. I tried again with a second guy; I proposed becoming pregnant, but it was clear that I would be the parent, and *I* would decide what his relationship to the child could be." They broke up before Dee conceived.

Then something unexpected happened: she fell in love with another woman. While they were vacationing in the Caribbean, Dee heard the maids talking about an abandoned baby at the hospital. "They were asking each other, does anybody want this child, because by three that afternoon, when its mother checked out of the hospital, he would be going to the orphanage." Her lover chimed in: "I know someone who wants a baby, don't you, Dee?" A thought flashed through her mind: "If I don't do this now, I may never [get] a chance again."

She raced to the hospital, got the mother's permission, put her name on the birth certificate, and paid the bill. Then she went to the baby room and asked for infant number three. "They handed me this piss-smelling baby wrapped in blankets. All I could see was his face and hairy head." Back at the hotel, the maids showed her how to diaper the baby. She slept on the floor that night, terrified when he began to hiccup. The next day she called her mother in New York: "Sit down," Dee said. "You're a grandmother. I want you to pick the middle name."

An "informal custodial arrangement" like Dee's is fraught with uncertainty. Has the child been abducted? Will the "coyote" hired to transport the baby across the border prove reliable? Will the mother, or her surrogate, suddenly appear with blackmail in mind? Such risks notwithstanding, once a child has reached its destination, its actual status is hard to discern; after several years, even if the truth is discovered, the courts are reluctant to separate a child from caring parents — even if they are gay. And given the immensely bureaucratic procedures gay people face when they try to adopt legally, the immediate availability of an abandoned baby is an offer difficult to refuse.

"I think most human beings want to be parents," Dee says, "and I don't think there's any reason to negate those desires just because you're not married or not heterosexual or even not in a couple." She bristles at the recollection of encounters with "separatist lesbians and radical feminists who think I'm not to be taken seriously because I've sold out." For Dee, becoming a mother and living as a lesbian intersected: "The strength I gained from single motherhood — both in terms of my identity as a woman and in terms of dealing with society —gave me the courage I needed to come out. I remember sitting on a couch and thinking, 'My God, I have done something very few people have the privilege to do. I can take my life and turn it in a different direction and say, This is good! And it will work.'"

If there's one thing gay parents have in common, it's a design for living. They are deliberate and determined, almost to a fault — it comes with the territory.

Julie Greenberg, 29, is a rabbinical student and a lesbian. In about a month, she intends to become pregnant with her first child. The semen, donated by a close friend, is waiting in the sperm bank for her. She calls it "alternate conception."

"I have 100 percent custody," she says. "I will do all the work and take the responsibility. But I would like the child to have a relationship with a father figure, and I intend to foster it." So the child will call the donor "daddy," and Julie will call him "Sam." A contract between them will enumerate his rights and responsibilities, which include some financial support.

Though some women insist on an anonymous donor — it avoids the prospect of a custody battle by the biological father — there's an evident risk to that approach: there's no way to evaluate an unknown donor's health. More often, the donor is known — a dear friend — and though he will never become "the man of the house," he will play a role in the child's life. Sam is heterosexual, but for many lesbians, the dear friend who is willing to be present but not dominant is a gay man who has tested negative for HTLV-III antibodies. (The odds of passing AIDS on to a woman and child via A.I. are not to be ignored.) The baby signifies not just a bond between its lesbian coparents, but between male and female homosexuals, one of the least acknowledged and most abiding relationships in gay life.

If the formation of families ever does become significant for homosexuals, A.I. will be one reason why. It requires neither medical intervention nor approval by the state, nor the capacity to function heterosexually. I know two gay men among my circle of friends who have entered into contractual relationships with women, intending to be the primary parent of the child that evolves. More commonly, lesbians enter into contractual relationships with men for a child who will be raised by the mother and her female lover. Julie intents to be "a single mother living in a feminist community. They'll contribute bits and pieces. And we'll be poor."

It remains to be seen how a congregation, even one willing to break with Jewish tradition, will react when it becomes apparent that its rabbi is pregnant and unmarried. But Julie is optimistic: "They don't necessarily have to deal with the fact that I'm a lesbian," she says, "but I'm hoping they'll be receptive to another form of Jewish family. We're saying there's no such thing as *the* family; there are various forms of family — single parents by choice, single parents not by choice, shared custody arrangements, collective networks. . . ."

Can a family be formulated by contract? In a sense, the point is moot: there's no more binding way for a mother and "father-figure" to declare their intentions; there aren't even words to describe such a relationship. Gay families are always coming up against the boundaries of language, which affirm their position on the edge of social change. And being on that edge carries a special burden: with no models or precedents, you don't know how to prepare for what the future may hold. So contracts and rituals take on an almost mystical significance. (Julie plans to appropriate an ancient fertility rite; she will stand among her friends and call forth a *neshuma*, or soul, into the world.)

Reba is six months pregnant now. When the baby arrives, by the 60 terms of a 12-page contract, she will be the parent who makes all the decisions about its care. Ray will have custody of the child on weekends, alternate Wednesdays, and for three weeks every summer. "I'm still uncertain about what to call myself," he says. "I'm the daddy/uncle." Reba's lover Katy has taken to calling herself the "sometime-mommy," although she's tempted by the term "daddy" because, she says, "I want the privilege. I haven't had a biological desire to be a mother. I've always felt the family system as I know it is overwhelming, too nuclear. So the idea of sharing is all that makes this appealing to me."

Katy's parents have been drumming their fears into her head: What if Reba runs off and sticks her with a kid that isn't even "your own"? And Reba's parents resent the presence of another woman whose rights vis-à-vis their grandchild are uncodified. "I mean, they hung up the phone when they heard the baby was going to carry Katy's father's name," Reba recalls. "They asked me *not* to name it after *tanta Mascha*.[11] I realize my family's been bargaining with me about what to tell people. At best, they're gonna have to concoct a story about their daughter having an illegitimate child. At worst, they'll have to admit that their daugher is a lesbian mother."

Spend some time with the gay family and you may feel transported to the summer of love. But these "hippies" are a lot less innocent. They understand that progress is not inevitable, and they've learned to watch their backs. This counterculture is emerging at a time of mixed signals. Courts and agencies are distinctly more tolerant of unorthodox parenting arrangements, but the culture is lurching rightward; judges can be replaced.

Given the uncertainties, gay families are easier to imagine than to maintain. Under stress, some will fall apart. Father-figures will breach their contracts. Children will suffer. Priests will proclaim, "They tampered with God's will." Friends will mutter, "I told you so."

And the world will change.

[11]*tanta Mascha:* Aunt Mascha.

Engaging the Text

1. Traditional wedding ceremonies are public statements of personal commitment. In what ways does the "radical act" of a gay marriage take on meanings beyond those of a traditional wedding?

2. What evidence does Goldstein offer of the active oppression of gays?

3. Gays and lesbians, like many marginalized groups, are concerned with the issue of assimilation into mainstream American culture and the attendant loss of personal and group identity. Where does Goldstein seem to stand on the issue of gay assimilation?

4. In your view, does the fact that Goldstein is gay weaken or strengthen his credibility as a journalist in writing this article?

Exploring Connections

5. Drawing on the pieces by Goldstein, Arlene Skolnick (p. 402), and Karen Lindsey (p. 463) in this chapter, debate whether a couple like Maggie Wales and Rosemary Dempsey should be given custody of their children.

6. Read or review Rose Weitz's analysis of the social categorization of lesbians and other independent women (p. 257). How might Weitz explain the dominant society's reluctance to approve gay or lesbian marriage and adoption?

Extending the Critical Context

7. Using your library or information provided by community interest groups, research the ways your state regulates child custody. You may want to focus either on recent legislation or on the history of this issue.

8. Now that you have read several pieces concerning the family in the United States, choose one area of special interest to you and write an essay using what you have learned in this chapter to inform your own argument or analysis. Choose your own focus or investigate one of these areas:

> gender roles within the family
> the future of the American family
> the family and the community
> the family in the media

9. Goldstein defines the gay family in fairly conventional terms, focusing primarily on biological parents and children. Watch *Longtime Companion* or *Paris Is Burning* and discuss the alternate or chosen gay families the films depict. What needs do such families fulfill?

6

Learning Power

The Myth of Education and Empowerment

Education is the engine that drives the American dream of success. The chance to learn, to gain the skills that pay off in upward mobility, has sustained the hope of millions of Americans. We're all familiar with the stories of sacrifice and success: the father who works two shifts a day to send his child to college; the older sister who cashes in her own dreams, leaving school to work and care for the family so her sisters and brothers will have a chance. As a nation we look up to figures like Abraham Lincoln and Frederick Douglass, men who learned to see beyond poverty and slavery by learning to read. Education tells us that the American dream can work for anyone: it reassures us that the path to success lies through individual effort and talent, not through blind luck or birth. However, this powerful myth conceals as much as it reveals — it fails to capture the complex ways education shapes us.

School emphatically did not appear as a route to success to the leaders of the Six Nations in 1744. In that year, Benjamin Franklin reports, the government of Virginia offered to provide six American Indian youths with the best college education the colony could offer. The tribal leaders politely declined, pointing out that

> our ideas of this kind of education happen not to be the same with yours. We have had some experience of it; several of our young people were formerly brought up at the colleges of the northern provinces; they were instructed in all your sciences; but when they came back to us, they were bad runners; ignorant of every means of living in the

woods; unable to bear either cold or hunger; knew neither how to build a cabin, take a deer, or kill an enemy; spoke our language imperfectly; were therefore neither fit for hunters, warriors, or counsellors: they were totally good for nothing.

It's not surprising that these leaders saw a colonial college education as useless. Education works to socialize young people — to teach them the values, beliefs, and skills central to their society; the same schooling that prepared students for life in Anglo-American culture made them singularly unfit for life in tribal culture.

Even within the same culture, the goals of education shift with the changing concerns of the larger society. The Puritans, for example, saw school as a force for spiritual rather than worldly advancement. Lessons were designed to reinforce moral and religious training and to teach children to read the Bible for themselves. But with the Revolutionary War came a new task for education. Following the overthrow of British rule, leaders sought to create a spirit of nationalism that would unify the former colonies. Differences were to be set aside, for, as George Washington pointed out, "the more homogeneous our citizens can be made . . . the greater will be our prospect of permanent union." The goal of schooling became the creation of uniformly loyal, patriotic Americans. In the words of Benjamin Rush, one of the signers of the Declaration of Independence, "Our schools of learning, by producing one general and uniform system of education, will render the mass of the people more homogeneous and thereby fit them more easily for uniform and peaceable government." For revolutionary leaders like Washington and Rush, education served the national interest first and individual development second.

The nineteenth century brought even greater pressures for uniformity and "homogenization" in educating young Americans. Massive immigration from eastern and southern Europe led to fears that non-English-speaking people would undermine the cultural identity of the United States. Many saw school as the first line of defense against this perceived threat, a place where the children of "foreigners" could become Americanized. The use of education to enforce cultural conformity was clearer still for American Indian children: beginning in the 1880s, government-supported schools taught them Anglo-American values and deliberately weaned them from tribal ways, just as the Six Nations' elders had foreseen and feared over a century before.

Industrialization gave rise to another kind of uniformity in nineteenth-century public education: the increasing demand for factory workers put a premium on young people who were obedient and able to work according to fixed schedules. Accordingly, in 1874, leading educators proposed a system of schooling that would meet the needs of the "modern industrial community" by stressing "punctuality, regularity, attention, and silence, as habits necessary through life." History complicates the myth of educational empowerment; as these few examples attest, school can bind as well as free us, enforce conformity as well as foster individual talent.

But history also supplies examples of education serving the idealistic goals of democracy, equality, and civic empowerment. Thomas Jefferson saw school as a training ground for democratic citizenship. Recognizing that an illiterate and ill-informed population would be unable to assume the responsibilities of self-government, in 1781 Jefferson laid out a comprehensive plan for public education in the state of Virginia. According to this plan, all children would be eligible for three years of free public instruction. Of those who could not afford further schooling, one promising "genius" from each school was to be "raked from the rubbish" and given six more years of free education. At the end of that time, ten boys would be selected to attend college at public expense. Jeffersonian Virginia may have been the first place in the United States where education so clearly offered the penniless boy a path to success. However, this path was open to very few, and Jefferson, like Washington and Rush, seemed more concerned with benefiting the state than serving the individual student: "we hope to avail the state of those talents which nature has sown as liberally among the poor as the rich, but which perish without use, if not sought for and cultivated."

Nineteenth-century educator and reformer Horace Mann worked to expand Jefferson's model of public education: not content to rescue a handful of "geniuses," he sought to give all students a chance for success. Mann believed that, with knowledge and hard work, anyone could prosper; thus, he maintained, universal education is "the great equalizer of the conditions of men," a virtual cure for poverty. At the turn of the century, educational theorist John Dewey made even greater claims for educational empowerment. Arguing that "education is the fundamental method of social progress and reform," Dewey proposed that schools strive to produce thinking citizens rather than obedient workers. The national interest, in his view, could be served only by developing fully the talents and abilities of all citizens: "only by being true to the full growth of all the individuals who make it up, can society by any chance be true to itself." Our current myths of education echo the optimism of Mann and Dewey, promising to help us not only achieve our private dreams of success but also perform our civic responsibilities — and perhaps even transform society.

Does education truly empower us, or are these empty promises? This chapter takes a critical look at education — what it can do and how it shapes our identities. The first three readings ask whether day-to-day life in American classrooms measures up to the myth. Theodore Sizer's "What High School Is" opens the chapter by comparing the idealistic goals of secondary education with the experience of an average high school student. Next, two cartoons by Matt Groening offer a satirical look at the unexpected lessons we learn in the classroom. In "'I Just Wanna Be Average,'" Mike Rose gives a moving personal account of the power that teachers can exert, for good or ill, over their students' lives.

The next section explores how education works to define us — how it molds our perceptions and our destinies. In "Social Class and the Hidden Curriculum of Work," Jean Anyon suggests that schools virtually program students for success or failure according to their socioeconomic status. The autobiographical selections by Richard Rodriguez and Malcolm X present contrasting views of education and its meaning for those who stand outside mainstream American culture. In her dramatic narrative poem *Para Teresa*, Inés Hernández asks whether academic achievement demands cultural conformity or whether it can become a form of protest against oppression and racism. "Connected Education for Women," by psychologist Blythe McVicker Clinchy and three colleagues, suggests that women are ill served in schools dominated by men and proposes an alternative model of learning based on cooperation rather than competition. Maxine Hong Kingston's "Silence" shows how a cultural mismatch between student and school leads a Chinese American girl to doubt the power of her own voice. Finally, in "Taking Offense: New McCarthyism on Campus?" Jerry Adler wonders if our college campuses are actually enforcing a new kind of conformity by silencing those who entertain "politically incorrect" views.

Sources

John Dewey, "The School and Society" (1899) and "My Pedagogic Creed" (1897). In *John Dewey on Education*. New York: Modern Library, 1964.

Benjamin Franklin, "Remarks Concerning the Savages of North America." In *The Works of Dr. Benjamin Franklin*. Hartford: S. Andrus and Son, 1849.

Thomas Jefferson, *Notes on the State of Virginia*. Chapel Hill: University of North Carolina Press, 1955.

Leonard Pitt, *We Americans*, vol. 2, 3rd ed. Dubuque: Kendall / Hunt, 1987.

Edward Stevens and George H. Wood, *Justice, Ideology, and Education: An Introduction to the Social Foundations of Education*. New York: Random House, 1987.

Elizabeth Vallance, "Hiding the Hidden Curriculum: An Interpretation of the Language of Justification in Nineteenth-Century Educational Reform." *Curriculum Theory Network*, vol. 4, no. 1 (1973–74), pp. 5–21.

Before Reading . . .

Freewrite for fifteen or twenty minutes about your best and worst educational experiences. Then, working in groups, compare notes to see if you can find recurring themes or ideas in what you've written. What aspects of school seem to stand out most clearly in your memories? Do the best experiences have anything in common? How about the worst? What aspects of your school experience didn't show up in the freewriting?

If you prefer, work in small groups to draw a collective picture that expresses your experience of high school or college. Don't worry about your drawing skill — just load the page with imagery, feelings, and ideas. Then show your work to other class members and let them try to interpret it.

What High School Is

THEODORE SIZER

High school is the one institution nearly every U.S. citizen participates in; in fact, it may be the nation's most widely shared cultural experience. This selection investigates the gulf between the mythic aims of schooling and the realities of life in contemporary American high schools. Theodore Sizer begins by describing a day in the life of a typical high school student, actually a fictional composite of many students interviewed during his research. His analysis of the rather dispiriting scenario follows. Sizer (b. 1932) is a professor in the Education Department at Brown University and chair of the Coalition of Essential Schools, a national organization devoted to educational reform. This selection is taken from Horace's Compromise: The Dilemma of the American High School *(1984).*

Mark, sixteen and a genial eleventh-grader, rides a bus to Franklin High School, arriving at 7:25. It is an Assembly Day, so the schedule is adapted to allow for a meeting of the entire school. He hangs out with his friends, first outside school and then inside, by his locker. He carries a pile of textbooks and notebooks; in all, it weighs eight and a half pounds.

From 7:30 to 8:19, with nineteen other students, he is in Room 304 for English class. The Shakespeare play being read this year by the eleventh grade is *Romeo and Juliet*. The teacher, Ms. Viola, has various students in turn take parts and read out loud. Periodically, she interrupts the (usually halting) recitations to ask whether the thread of the conversation in the play is clear. Mark is entertained by the stumbling readings of some of his classmates. He hopes he will not be asked to be Romeo, particularly if his current steady, Sally, is Juliet. There is a good deal of giggling in class, and much attention paid to who may be called on next. Ms. Viola reminds the class of a test on this part of the play to be given next week.

The bell rings at 8:19. Mark goes to the boys' room, where he sees a classmate who he thinks is a wimp but who constantly tries to be a buddy. Mark avoids the leech by rushing off. On the way, he notices two boys engaged in some sort of transaction, probably over marijuana. He pays them no attention. 8:24. Typing class. The rows of desks that embrace big office machines are almost filled before the bell. Mark is uncomfortable here: typing class is girl country. The teacher constantly threatens what to Mark is a humiliatingly female future: "Your employer won't like these erasures." The minutes during the period are spent copying a letter from a handbook onto business stationery. Mark struggles to keep from looking at his work; the teacher wants him to watch only the material from which he is copying. Mark is frustrated, uncomfortable, and scared that he will not complete his letter by the class's end, which would be embarrassing.

Nine tenths of the students present at school that day are assembled in the auditorium by the 9:18 bell. The dilatory[1] tenth still stumble in, running down aisles. Annoyed class deans try to get the mob settled. The curtains part; the program is a concert by a student rock group. Their electronic gear flashes under the lights, and the five boys and one girl in the group work hard at being casual. Their movements on stage are studiously at three-quarter time, and they chat with one another as though the tumultuous screaming of their schoolmates were totally inaudible. The girl balances on a stool; the boys crank up the music. It is very soft rock, the sanitized lyrics surely cleared with the assistant principal. The girl sings, holding the mike close to her mouth, but can scarcely be heard. Her light voice is tentative, and the lyrics indecipherable. The guitars, amplified, are tuneful, however, and the drums are played with energy.

The students around Mark — all juniors, since they are seated by   5
class — alternately slouch in their upholstered, hinged seats, talking to one another, or sit forward, leaning on the chair backs in front of them, watching the band. A boy near Mark shouts noisily at the microphone-fondling singer, "Bite it . . . ohhh," and the area around Mark explodes in vulgar male laughter, but quickly subsides. A teacher walks down the

[1]*dilatory:* tending to delay or procrastinate.

aisle. Songs continue, to great applause. Assembly is over at 9:46, two minutes early.

9:53 and biology class. Mark was at a different high school last year and did not take this course there as a tenth-grader. He is in it now, and all but one of his classmates are a year younger than he. He sits on the side, not taking part in the chatter that goes on after the bell. At 9:57, the public address system goes on, with the announcements of the day. After a few words from the principal ("Here's today's cheers and jeers . . ." with a cheer for the winning basketball team and a jeer for the spectators who made a ruckus at the gymnasium), the task is taken over by officers of ASB (Associated Student Bodies). There is an appeal for "bat bunnies." Carnations are for sale by the Girls' League. Miss Indian American is coming. Students are auctioning off their services (background catcalls are heard) to earn money for the prom. Nominees are needed for the ballot for school bachelor and school bachelorette. The announcements end with a "thought for the day. When you throw a little mud, you lose a little ground."

At 10:04 the biology class finally turns to science. The teacher, Mr. Robbins, has placed one of several labeled laboratory specimens — some are pinned in frames, others swim in formaldehyde — on each of the classroom's eight laboratory tables. The three or so students whose chairs circle each of these benches are to study the specimen and make notes about it or drawings of it. After a few minutes each group of three will move to another table. The teacher points out that these specimens are of organisms already studied in previous classes. He says that the period-long test set for the following day will involve observing some of these specimens — then to be without labels — and writing an identifying paragraph on each. Mr. Robbins points out that some of the printed labels ascribe the specimens names different from those given in the textbook. He explains that biologists often give several names to the same organism.

The class now falls to peering, writing, and quiet talking. Mr. Robbins comes over to Mark, and in whispered words asks him to carry a requisition form for science department materials to the business office. Mark, because of his "older" status, is usually chosen by Robbins for this kind of errand. Robbins gives Mark the form and a green hall pass to show to any teacher who might challenge him, on his way to the office, for being out of a classroom. The errand takes Mark four minutes. Meanwhile Mark's group is hard at work but gets to only three of the specimens before the bell rings at 10:42. As the students surge out, Robbins shouts a reminder about a "double" laboratory period on Thursday.

Between classes one of the seniors asks Mark whether he plans to be a candidate for schoolwide office next year. Mark says no. He starts to explain. The 10:47 bell rings, meaning that he is late for French class.

There are fifteen students in Monsieur Bates's language class. He 10
hands out tests taken the day before: *"C'est bien fait, Etienne . . . c'est
mieux, Marie . . . Tch, tch, Robert . . ."* Mark notes his C + and peeks
at the A − in front of Susanna, next to him. The class has been assigned
seats by M. Bates; Mark resents sitting next to prissy, brainy Susanna.
Bates starts by asking a student to read a question and give the correct
answer. *"James, question un."* James haltingly reads the question and
gives an answer that Bates, now speaking English, says is incomplete. In
due course: *"Mark, question cinq."* Mark does his bit, and the sequence
goes on, the eight quiz questions and answers filling about twenty
minutes of time.

"Turn to page forty-nine. *Maintenant, lisez après moi . . ."* and
Bates reads a sentence and has the class echo it. Mark is embarrassed by
this and mumbles with a barely audible sound. Others, like Susanna,
keep the decibel count up, so Mark can hide. This I-say-you-repeat drill
is interrupted once by the public address system, with an announcement about a meeting for the cheerleaders. Bates finishes the class,
almost precisely at the bell, with a homework assignment. The students
are to review these sentences for a brief quiz the following day. Mark
takes note of the assignment, because he knows that tomorrow will be a
day of busy-work in French class. Much though he dislikes oral drills,
they are better than the workbook stuff that Bates hands out. Write,
write, write, for Bates to throw away, Mark thinks.

11:36. Down to the cafeteria, talking noisily, hanging out, munch-
ing. Getting to Room 104 by 12:17: U.S. history. The teacher is sitting
crosslegged on his desk when Mark comes in, heatedly arguing with
three students over the fracas that had followed the previous night's
basketball game. The teacher, Mr. Suslovic, while agreeing that the
spectators from their school certainly were provoked, argues that they
should neither have been so obviously obscene in yelling at the opposing
cheerleaders nor have allowed Coke cans to be rolled out on the floor.
The three students keep saying that "it isn't fair." Apparently they and
some others had been assigned "Saturday mornings" (detentions) by the
principal for the ruckus.

At 12:34, the argument appears to subside. The uninvolved students, including Mark, are in their seats, chatting amiably. Mr. Suslovic
climbs off his desk and starts talking: "We've almost finished this unit,
chapters nine and ten . . ." The students stop chattering among themselves and turn toward Suslovic. Several slouch down in their chairs.
Some open notebooks. Most have the five-pound textbook on their desks.

Suslovic lectures on the cattle drives, from north Texas to railroads
west of St. Louis. He breaks up this narrative with questions ("Why
were the railroad lines laid largely east to west?"), directed at nobody in
particular and eventually answered by Suslovic himself. Some students
take notes. Mark doesn't. A student walks in the open door, hands

Mr. Suslovic a list, and starts whispering with him. Suslovic turns from the class and hears out this messenger. He then asks, "Does anyone know where Maggie Sharp is?" Someone answers, "Sick at home"; someone else says, "I thought I saw her at lunch." Genial consternation.[2] Finally Suslovic tells the messenger, "Sorry, we can't help you," and returns to the class: "Now, where were we?" He goes on for some minutes. The bell rings. Suslovic forgets to give the homework assignment.

1:11 and Algebra II. There is a commotion in the hallway: some-   15
one's locker is rumored to have been opened by the assistant principal and a narcotics agent. In the five-minute passing time, Mark hears the story three times and three ways. A locker had been broken into by another student. It was Mr. Gregory and a narc. It was the cops, and they did it without Gregory's knowing. Mrs. Ames, the mathematics teacher, has not heard anything about it. Several of the nineteen students try to tell her and start arguing among themselves. "O.K., that's enough." She hands out the day's problem, one sheet to each student. Mark sees with dismay that it is a single, complicated "word" problem about some train that, while traveling at 84 mph, due west, passes a car that was going due east at 55 mph. Mark struggles: Is it $d = rt$ or $t = rd$? The class becomes quiet, writing, while Mrs. Ames writes some additional, short problems on the blackboard. "Time's up." A sigh; most students still writing. A muffled "Shit." Mrs. Ames frowns. "Come on, now." She collects papers, but it takes four minutes for her to corral them all.

"Copy down the problems from the board." A minute passes. "William, try number one." William suggests an approach. Mrs. Ames corrects and cajoles, and William finally gets it right. Mark watches two kids to his right passing notes; he tries to read them, but the handwriting is illegible from his distance. He hopes he is not called on, and he isn't. Only three students are asked to puzzle out an answer. The bell rings at 2:00. Mrs. Ames shouts a homework assignment over the resulting hubbub.

Mark leaves his books in his locker. He remembers that he has homework, but figures that he can do it during English class the next day. He knows that there will be an in-class presentation of one of the *Romeo and Juliet* scenes and that he will not be in it. The teacher will not notice his homework writing, or won't do anything about it if she does.

Mark passes various friends heading toward the gym, members of the basketball teams. Like most students, Mark isn't an active school athlete. However, he is associated with the yearbook staff. Although he is not taking "Yearbook" for credit as an English course, he is contributing photographs. Mark takes twenty minutes checking into the yearbook

[2]*genial consternation:* good-humored confusion or bewilderment.

staff's headquarters (the classroom of its faculty adviser) and getting some assignments of pictures from his boss, the senior who is the photography editor. Mark knows that if he pleases his boss and the faculty adviser, he'll take that editor's post for the next year. He'll get English credit for his work then.

After gossiping a bit with the yearbook staff, Mark will leave school by 2:35 and go home. His grocery market bagger's job is from 4:45 to 8:00, the rush hour for the store. He'll have a snack at 4:30, and his mother will save him some supper to eat at 8:30. She will ask whether he has any homework, and he'll tell her no. Tomorrow, and virtually every other tomorrow, will be the same for Mark, save for the lack of the assembly: each period then will be five minutes longer.

Most Americans have an uncomplicated vision of what secondary 20 education should be. Their conception of high school is remarkably uniform across the country, a striking fact, given the size and diversity of the United States and the politically decentralized character of the schools. This uniformity is of several generations' standing. It has, however, two appearances, each quite different from the other, one of words and the other of practice, a world of political rhetoric and Mark's world.

A California high school's general goals, set out in 1979, could serve equally well most of America's high schools, public and private. This school had as its ends:

- Fundamental scholastic achievement . . . to acquire knowledge and share in the traditionally accepted academic fundamentals . . . to develop the ability to make decisions, to solve problems, to reason independently, and to accept responsibility for self-evaluation and continuing self-improvement.
- Career and economic competence . . .
- Citizenship and civil responsibility . . .
- Competence in human and social relations . . .
- Moral and ethical values . . .
- Self-realization and mental and physical health . . .
- Aesthetic awareness . . .
- Cultural diversity . . .[3]

In addition to its optimistic rhetoric, what distinguishes this list is its comprehensiveness. The high school is to touch most aspects of an

[3]Shasta High School, Redding, California. An eloquent and analogous statement, "The Essentials of Education," one stressing explicitly the "interdependence of skills and content" that is implicit in the Shasta High School statement, was issued in 1980 by a coalition of education associations. Organizations for the Essentials of Education (Urbana, Illinois) [Author's note]

adolescent's existence — mind, body, morals, values, career. No one of these areas is given especial prominence. School people arrogate to themselves an obligation to all.

An example of the wide acceptability of these goals is found in the courts. Forced to present a detailed definition of "thorough and efficient education," elementary as well as secondary, a West Virginia judge sampled the best of conventional wisdom and concluded that

> there are eight general elements of a thorough and efficient system of education: (a) Literacy, (b) The ability to add, subtract, multiply, and divide numbers, (c) Knowledge of government to the extent the child will be equipped as a citizen to make informed choices among persons and issues that affect his own governance, (d) Self-knowledge and knowledge of his or her total environment to allow the child to intelligently choose life work — to know his or her options, (e) Work-training and advanced academic training as the child may intelligently choose, (f) Recreational pursuits, (g) Interests in all creative arts such as music, theater, literature, and the visual arts, and (h) Social ethics, both behavioral and abstract, to facilitate compatibility with others in this society.[4]

That these eight — now powerfully part of the debate over the purpose and practice of education in West Virginia — are reminiscent of the influential list, "The Seven Cardinal Principles of Secondary Education," promulgated in 1918 by the National Education Association, is no surprise.[5] The rhetoric of high school purpose has been uniform and consistent for decades. Americans agree on the goals for their high schools.

That agreement is convenient, but it masks the fact that virtually all 25 the words in these goal statements beg definition. Some schools have labored long to identify specific criteria beyond them; the result has been lists of daunting pseudospecificity and numbing earnestness. However, most leave the words undefined and let the momentum of traditional practice speak for itself. That is why analyzing how Mark spends his time is important: from watching him one uncovers the important purposes of education, the ones that shape practice. Mark's day is similar to that of other high school students across the country, as similar as the rhetoric of one goal statement to others'. Of course, there are variations, but the extent of consistency in the shape of school

[4]Judge Arthur M. Recht, in his order resulting from *Pauley v. Kelly*, 1979, as reprinted in *Education Week*, May 26, 1982, p. 10. See also, in *Education Week*, January 16, 1983, pp. 21, 24, Jonathan P. Sher, "The Struggle to Fulfill at Judicial Mandate: How Not to 'Reconstruct' Education in W. Va." [Author's note]

[5]Bureau of Education, Department of the Interior, "Cardinal Principles of Secondary Education: A Report of the Commission on the Reorganization of Secondary Education, appointed by the National Education Association," *Bulletin*, no. 35 (Washington, U.S. Government Printing Office, 1918). [Author's note]

routine for a large and diverse adolescent population is extraordinary, indicating more graphically than any rhetoric the measure of agreement in America about what one does in high school, and, by implication, what it is for.

The basic organizing structures in schools are familiar. Above all, students are grouped by age (that is, freshman, sophomore, junior, senior), and all are expected to take precisely the same time — around 720 school days over four years, to be precise — to meet the requirements for a diploma. When one is out of his grade level, he can feel odd, as Mark did in his biology class. The goals are the same for all, and the means to achieve them are also similar.

Young males and females are treated remarkably alike; the schools' goals are the same for each gender. In execution, there are differences, as those pressing sex discrimination suits have made educators intensely aware. The students in metalworking classes are mostly male; those in home economics, mostly female. But it is revealing how much less sex discrimination there is in high schools than in other American institutions. For many young women, the most liberated hours of their week are in school.

School is to be like a job: you start in the morning and end in the afternoon, five days a week. You don't get much of a lunch hour, so you go home early, unless you are an athlete or are involved in some special school or extracurricular activity. School is conceived of as the children's workplace, and it takes young people off parents' hands and out of the labor market during prime-time work hours. Not surprisingly, many students see going to school as little more than a dogged necessity. They perceive the day-to-day routine, a Minnesota study reports, as one of "boredom and lethargy." One of the students summarizes: school is "boring, restless, tiresome, puts ya to sleep, tedious, monotonous, pain in the neck."[6]

The school schedule is a series of units of time: the clock is king. The base time block is about fifty minutes in length. Some schools, on what they call modular scheduling, split that fifty-minute block into two or even three pieces. Most schools have double periods for laboratory work, especially in the sciences, or four-hour units for the small numbers of students involved in intensive vocational or other work-study programs. The flow of all school activity arises from or is blocked by these time units. "How much time do I have with my kids" is the teacher's key question.

Because there are many claims for those fifty-minute blocks, there is   30
little time set aside for rest between them, usually no more than three to

---

[6]Diane Hedin, Paula Simon, and Michael Robin, *Minnesota Youth Poll: Youth's Views on School and School Discipline*, Minnesota Report 184 (1983), Agricultural Experiment Station, University of Minnesota, p. 13. [Author's note]

ten minutes, depending on how big the school is and, consequently, how far students and teachers have to walk from class to class. As a result, there is a frenetic[7] quality to the school day, a sense of sustained restlessness. For the adolescents, there are frequent changes of room and fellow students, each change giving tempting opportunities for distraction, which are stoutly resisted by teachers. Some schools play soft music during these "passing times," to quiet the multitude, one principal told me.

Many teachers have a chance for a coffee break. Few students do. In some city schools where security is a problem, students must be in class for seven consecutive periods, interrupted by a heavily monitored twenty-minute lunch period for small groups, starting as early as 10:30 A.M. and running to after 1:00 P.M. A high premium is placed on punctuality and on "being where you're supposed to be." Obviously, a low premium is placed on reflection and repose. The student rushes from class to class to collect knowledge. Savoring it, it is implied, is not to be done much in school, nor is such meditation really much admired. The picture that these familiar patterns yield is that of an academic supermarket. The purpose of going to school is to pick things up, in an organized and predictable way, the faster the better.

What is supposed to be picked up is remarkably consistent among all sorts of high schools. Most schools specifically mandate three out of every five courses a student selects. Nearly all of these mandates fall into five areas — English, social studies, mathematics, science, and physical education. On the average, English is required to be taken each year, social studies and physical education three out of the four high school years, and mathematics and science one or two years. Trends indicate that in the mid-eighties there is likely to be an increase in the time allocated to these last two subjects. Most students take classes in these four major academic areas beyond the minimum requirements, sometimes in such special areas as journalism and "yearbook," offshoots of English departments.[8]

Press most adults about what high school is for, and you hear these subjects listed. *High school? That's where you learn English and math and that sort of thing.* Ask students, and you get the same answer. High school is to "teach" these "subjects."

What is often absent is any definition of these subjects or any rationale for them. They are just there, labels. Under those labels lie a multitude of things. A great deal of material is supposed to be "cov-

---

[7]*frenetic:* frantic; frenzied.

[8]I am indebted to Harold F. Sizer and Lyde E. Sizer for a survey of the diploma requirements of fifty representative secondary schools, completed for A Study of High Schools. [Author's note]

ered"; most of these courses are surveys, great sweeps of the stuff of their parent disciplines.

While there is often a sequence *within* subjects — algebra before   35
trigonometry, "first-year" French before "second-year" French — there is rarely a coherent relationship or sequence *across* subjects. Even the most logically related matters — reading ability as a precondition for the reading of history books, and certain mathematical concepts or skills before the study of some of physics — are only loosely coordinated, if at all. There is little demand for a synthesis of it all; English, mathematics, and the rest are discrete items, to be picked up individually. The incentive for picking them up is largely through tests and, with success at these, in credits earned.

Coverage within subjects is the key priority. If some imaginative teacher makes a proposal to force the marriage of, say, mathematics and physics or to require some culminating challenges to students to use several subjects in the solution of a complex problem, and if this proposal will take "time" away from other things, opposition is usually phrased in terms of what may be thus forgone. If we do that, we'll have to give up colonial history. We won't be able to get to programming. We'll not be able to read *Death of a Salesman*.[9] There isn't time. The protesters usually win out.

The subjects come at a student like Mark in random order, a kaleidoscope of worlds: algebraic formulae to poetry to French verbs to Ping-Pong to the War of the Spanish Succession, all before lunch. Pupils are to pick up these things. Tests measure whether the picking up has been successful.

The lack of connection between stated goals, such as those of the California high school cited earlier, and the goals inherent in school practice is obvious and, curiously, tolerated. Most striking is the gap between statements about "self-realization and mental and physical growth" or "moral and ethical values" — common rhetoric in school documents — and practice. Most physical education programs have neither the time nor the focus really to ensure fitness. Mental health is rarely defined. Neither are ethical values, save at the negative extremes, such as opposition to assault or dishonesty. Nothing in the regimen of a day like Mark's signals direct or implicit teaching in this area. The "schoolboy code" (not ratting on a fellow student) protects the marijuana pusher, and a leechlike associate is shrugged off without concern. The issue of the locker search was pushed aside, as not appropriate for class time.

---

[9]*Death of a Salesman:* 1957 award-winning drama by American playwright Arthur Miller.

Most students, like Mark, go to class in groups of twenty to twenty-seven students. The expected attendance in some schools, particularly those in low-income areas, is usually higher, often thirty-five students per class, but high absentee rates push the actual numbers down. About twenty-five per class is an average figure for expected attendance, and the actual numbers are somewhat lower. There are remarkably few students who go to class in groups much larger or smaller than twenty-five.[10]

A student such as Mark sees five or six teachers per day; their differing styles and expectations are part of his kaleidoscope. High school staffs are highly specialized: guidance counselors rarely teach mathematics, mathematics teachers rarely teach English, principals rarely do any classroom instruction. Mark, then, is known a little bit by a number of people, each of whom sees him in one specialized situation. No one may know him as a "whole person" — unless he becomes a special problem or has special needs.

Save in extracurricular or coaching situations, such as in athletics, drama, or shop classes, there is little opportunity for sustained conversation between student and teacher. The mode is a one-sentence or two-sentence exchange: *Mark, when was Grover Cleveland president?* Let's see, was [it] 1890 . . . or something . . . wasn't he the one . . . he was elected twice, wasn't he? . . . *Yes . . . Gloria, can you get the dates right?* Dialogue is strikingly absent, and as a result the opportunity of teachers to challenge students' ideas in a systematic and logical way is limited. Given the rushed, full quality of the school day, it can seldom happen. One must infer that careful probing of students' thinking is not a high priority. How one gains (to quote the California school's statement of goals again) "the ability to make decisions, to solve problems, to reason independently, and to accept responsibility for self-evaluation and continuing self-improvement" without being challenged is difficult to imagine. One certainly doesn't learn these things merely from lectures and textbooks.

Most schools are nice places. Mark and his friends enjoy being in theirs. The adults who work in schools generally like adolescents. The academic pressures are limited, and the accommodations to students are substantial. For example, if many members of an English class have jobs after school, the English teacher's expectations for them are adjusted, downward. In a word, school is sensitively accommodating, as long as students are punctual, where they are supposed to be, and minimally

---

[10]Education Research Service, Inc. *Class Size: A Summary of Research* (Arlington, Virginia, 1978); and *Class Size Research: A Critique of Recent Meta-Analyses* (Arlington, Virginia, 1980). [Author's note]

dutiful about picking things up from the clutch of courses in which they enroll.

This characterization is not pretty, but it is accurate, and it serves to describe the vast majority of American secondary schools. "Taking subjects" in a systematized, conveyor-belt way is what one does in high school. That this process is, in substantial respects, not related to the rhetorical purposes of education is tolerated by most people, perhaps because they do not really either believe in those ill-defined goals or, in their heart of hearts, believe that schools can or should even try to achieve them. The students are happy taking subjects. The parents are happy, because that's what they did in high school. The rituals, the most important of which is graduation, remain intact. The adolescents are supervised, safely and constructively most of the time, during the morning and afternoon hours, and they are off the labor market. That is what high school is all about.

Engaging the Text

1. Sizer uses metaphors describing Mark's classes as a "kaleidoscope of worlds" and comparing his school to an "academic supermarket" or a "conveyor belt" from which students "pick up" ideas. What does Sizer mean by these metaphors? What do they suggest about the problems of high school education in the United States?

2. What kind of student is Mark? Imagine his background and home life. Why do you think Sizer chose him to illustrate his view of high school?

3. Would you say that Sizer's depiction of American high schools is accurate? How does it compare with your high school experience?

4. Debate Sizer's claim that "for most young women, the most liberated hours of their week are in school."

Exploring Connections

5. Compare and contrast Mark's day with Sylvia's day in Toni Cade Bambara's "The Lesson" (p. 64). Who learns more, and why? What does each style of education offer, and what does each lack? Does your comparison suggest any practicable changes that might be made in American high schools?

6. In "The Rite of Work: The Economic Man" (p. 207), Sam Keen lists ten "unwritten rules that govern success in professional and corporate life." To what extent does Mark's school experience train him to follow these "rules"? What kinds of success or failure do you believe Mark's school is preparing him for?

Extending the Critical Context

7. Work in groups to design a high school that would make a "supermarket" or "kaleidoscope" approach to education impossible. Describe one day of a student's life in this hypothetical school.

8. Some students find or construct a coherent curriculum in college, but for others college is just a bigger "supermarket" than high school was. What can students do in either high school or college to lessen the fragmentation of intellectual experience that Sizer describes?

9. If you feel your high school served you poorly, write an educational "Bill of Wrongs" — a manifesto detailing the shortcomings of education at the high school you attended and calling for specific reforms. Send this with a cover letter to your former principal.

10. Divide Mark's day into active and passive blocks of time. Then do a similar analysis of one day from your recent education. Write a journal entry on the problems of passive education and possible solutions for them.

Life in School

MATT GROENING

Before The Simpsons *came* Life in Hell, *a weekly comic feature by Matt Groening (rhymes with "raining"). The following two cartoons by the creator and executive producer of* The Simpsons *capture some of the rage, hopelessness, and humor that many students associate with the classroom. They're meant to make you laugh, but they may also help you examine some of the reservations you might have about your own school experience. Groening (b. 1954) has published several enormously popular collections of cartoons (for instance,* Work Is Hell, *1986,* Love Is Hell, *1986) and was nominated for an Emmy Award for his work on* "The Tracey Ullman Show," *where the Simpson family first appeared.*

LIFE IN HELL
©1987 BY MATT GROENING
SCHOOL IS HELL
A CARTOON ABOUT WISING UP
LESSON 4: WAKE UP! YOU'LL BE LATE FOR YOUR FIRST DAY OF SCHOOL!
PLEASE DON'T CALL ON ME-- PLEASE DON'T CALL ON ME-- PLEASE DON'T CALL ON ME-- PLEASE DON'T CALL ON ME-- PLEASE DON'T CALL ON ME--
YOU!!! THE QUIET ONE IN THE BACK!! STAND UP AND TELL US THE ANSWER!!
Oooo
ACME FEATURES SYNDICATE 3·6·87
WELCOME TO SCHOOL, STUDENTS.
WOULD YOU LIKE YOUR EDUCATION THE QUICK WAY, OR WOULD YOU LIKE IT SPREAD OUT OVER A DOZEN YEARS?
QUICK WAY!!
QUICK WAY!!
QUICK WAY!!
OOH, THE QUICK WAY!
THEN SIT STILL AND SHUT UP.
YOUR SQUIRMING DAYS ARE OVER.
FIRST: LEARNING HAS NOTHING TO DO WITH LIFE.
LEARNING IS PASSIVE.
IT MUST ALWAYS BE TEDIOUS.
SO DON'T SASS BACK. YOU'RE ALL BASICALLY WORTHLESS LITTLE CREEPS FIT ONLY TO TAKE ORDERS.
YOUR CONCERNS COUNT FOR NOTHING.
WHAT IS IMPORTANT IS WHAT WE SAY IS IMPORTANT.
SO DO WHAT YOU ARE TOLD AND YOU WILL STAY OUT OF TROUBLE.
EVERYONE KNOWS YOU WON'T DO ANYTHING UNLESS YOU ARE BRIBED, TRICKED, OR FORCED.
BECAUSE NOTHING IS WORTH DOING FOR ITS OWN SAKE.
SO LEARN TO BE BORED. WE'RE BORED, SO YOU SHOULD BE TOO.
IF YOU LIVE IN A DAZE, YOU'LL BE LESS UNHAPPY.
ANY QUESTIONS?
THAT'S IT? THAT'S OUR EDUCATION?
WE CAN GO NOW?
OF COURSE NOT.
WE HAVE SOME TIME TO KILL. HAVE TO KEEP YOU TINY MONSTERS OFF THE STREET TILL YOU'RE 18, YOU KNOW.
OPEN YOUR BOOKS TO PAGE 1, AND WE'LL BEGIN.

Engaging the Text

1. What attitude toward teachers and schools do these cartoons portray? How do they portray students? How accurate are these depictions?

2. What role does silence play in Groening's view of education?

3. Why does the "student" have only one ear?

Exploring Connections

4. How would Theodore Sizer (see p. 496) explain the humor in Groening's cartoons?

Extending the Critical Context

5. Try writing your own captions for Groening's cartoon balloons, or try your hand at drawing your own cartoon strip about school life.

6. Cite a few examples from your own school experience when you were just killing time in the way Groening's second cartoon suggests. Also cite examples of occasions when you believe you learned something truly beneficial. Compare notes with classmates.

"I Just Wanna Be Average"

MIKE ROSE

Mike Rose (b. 1944) is anything but average: he has published poetry, scholarly research, a textbook, and a widely praised book on America's educational underclass, Lives on the Boundary *(1989). He is associate director of UCLA Writing Programs and has won awards from the National Academy of Education and the National Council of Teachers of English. The following selection from* Lives on the Boundary *tells how this highly successful teacher and writer started high school in the "vocational education" track, learning dead-end skills from teachers who were often underprepared or incompetent. Rose shows that students whom the system has written off can have tremendous unrealized potential, and his critique of the school system specifies several reasons for the "failure" of students who go through high school belligerent, fearful, stoned, frustrated, or just plain bored.*

It took two buses to get to Our Lady of Mercy. The first started deep in South Los Angeles and caught me at midpoint. The second drifted through neighborhoods with trees, parks, big lawns, and lots of flowers. The rides were long but were livened up by a group of South L.A. veterans whose parents also thought that Hope had set up shop in the west end of the country. There was Christy Biggars, who, at sixteen, was dealing and was, according to rumor, a pimp as well. There were Bill

Cobb and Johnny Gonzales, grease-pencil artists extraordinaire, who left Nembutal-enhanced[1] swirls of "Cobb" and "Johnny" on the corrugated walls of the bus. And then there was Tyrrell Wilson. Tyrrell was the coolest kid I knew. He ran the dozens[2] like a metric halfback, laid down a rap that outrhymed and outpointed Cobb, whose rap was good but not great — the curse of a moderately soulful kid trapped in white skin. But it was Cobb who would sneak a radio onto the bus, and thus underwrote his patter with Little Richard, Fats Domino, Chuck Berry, the Coasters,[3] and Ernie K. Doe's mother-in-law, an awful woman who was "sent from down below." And so it was that Christy and Cobb and Johnny G. and Tyrrell and I and assorted others picked up along the way passed our days in the back of the bus, a funny mix brought together by geography and parental desire.

Entrance to school brings with it forms and releases and assessments. Mercy relied on a series of tests, mostly the Stanford-Binet,[4] for placement, and somehow the results of my tests got confused with those of another student named Rose. The other Rose apparently didn't do very well, for I was placed in the vocational track, a euphemism for the bottom level. Neither I nor my parents realized what this meant. We had no sense that Business Math, Typing, and English–Level D were dead ends. The current spate of reports on the schools criticizes parents for not involving themselves in the education of their children. But how would someone like Tommy Rose, with his two years of Italian schooling, know what to ask? And what sort of pressure could an exhausted waitress apply? The error went undetected, and I remained in the vocational track for two years. What a place.

My homeroom was supervised by Brother Dill, a troubled and unstable man who also taught freshman English. When his class drifted away from him, which was often, his voice would rise in paranoid accusations, and occasionally he would lose control and shake or smack us. I hadn't been there two months when one of his brisk, face-turning slaps had my glasses sliding down the aisle. Physical education was also pretty harsh. Our teacher was a stubby ex-lineman who had played old-time pro ball in the Midwest. He routinely had us grabbing our ankles to receive his stinging paddle across our butts. He did that, he said, to make men of us. "Rose," he bellowed on our first encounter; me standing geeky in line in my baggy shorts. "'Rose'? What the hell kind of name is that?"

---

[1]*Nembutal:* trade name for pentobarbital, a sedative drug.

[2]*the dozens:* a verbal game of African origin in which competitors try to top each other's insults.

[3]*Little Richard, Fats Domino, Chuck Berry, the Coasters:* popular Black musicians of the 1950s.

[4]*Stanford-Binet:* an IQ test.

"Italian, sir," I squeaked.

"Italian! Ho. Rose, do you know the sound a bag of shit makes when   5
it hits the wall?"

"No, sir."

"Wop!"[5]

Sophomore English was taught by Mr. Mitropetros. He was a large, bejeweled man who managed the parking lot at the Shrine Auditorium. He would crow and preen and list for us the stars he'd brushed against. We'd ask questions and glance knowingly and snicker, and all that fueled the poor guy to brag some more. Parking cars was his night job. He had little training in English, so his lesson plan for his day work had us reading the district's required text, *Julius Caesar*, aloud for the semester. We'd finish the play way before the twenty weeks was up, so he'd have us switch parts again and again and start again: Dave Snyder, the fastest guy at Mercy, muscling through Caesar to the breathless squeals of Calpurnia, as interpreted by Steve Fusco, a surfer who owned the school's most envied paneled wagon. Week ten and Dave and Steve would take on new roles, as would we all, and render a water-logged Cassius and a Brutus that are beyond my powers of description.

Spanish I — taken in the second year — fell into the hands of a new recruit. Mr. Montez was a tiny man, slight, five foot six at the most, soft-spoken and delicate. Spanish was a particularly rowdy class, and Mr. Montez was as prepared for it as a doily maker at a hammer throw. He would tap his pencil to a room in which Steve Fusco was propelling spitballs from his heavy lips, in which Mike Dweetz was taunting Billy Hawk, a half-Indian, half-Spanish, reed-thin, quietly explosive boy. The vocational track at Our Lady of Mercy mixed kids traveling in from South L.A. with South Bay surfers and a few Slavs and Chicanos from the harbors of San Pedro. This was a dangerous miscellany: surfers and hodads[6] and South-Central blacks all ablaze to the metronomic tapping of Hector Montez's pencil.

One day Billy lost it. Out of the corner of my eye I saw him strike   10
out with his right arm and catch Dweetz across the neck. Quick as a spasm, Dweetz was out of his seat, scattering desks, cracking Billy on the side of the head, right behind the eye. Snyder and Fusco and others broke it up, but the room felt hot and close and naked. Mr. Montez's tenuous authority was finally ripped to shreds, and I think everyone felt a little strange about that. The charade was over, and when it came down to it, I don't think any of the kids really wanted it to end this way. They had pushed and pushed and bullied their way into a freedom that both scared and embarrassed them.

[5]*Wop:* derogatory term for Italian.
[6]*hodads:* nonsurfers.

Students will float to the mark you set. I and the others in the vocational classes were bobbing in pretty shallow water. Vocational education has aimed at increasing the economic opportunities of students who do not do well in our schools. Some serious programs succeed in doing that, and through exceptional teachers — like Mr. Gross in *Horace's Compromise*[7] — students learn to develop hypotheses and troubleshoot, reason through a problem, and communicate effectively — the true job skills. The vocational track, however, is most often a place for those who are just not making it, a dumping ground for the disaffected. There were a few teachers who worked hard at education; young Brother Slattery, for example, combined a stern voice with weekly quizzes to try to pass along to us a skeletal outline of world history. But mostly the teachers had no idea of how to engage the imaginations of us kids who were scuttling along at the bottom of the pond.

And the teachers would have needed some inventiveness, for none of us was groomed for the classroom. It wasn't just that I didn't know things — didn't know how to simplify algebraic fractions, couldn't identify different kinds of clauses, bungled Spanish translations — but that I had developed various faulty and inadequate ways of doing algebra and making sense of Spanish. Worse yet, the years of defensive tuning out in elementary school had given me a way to escape quickly while seeming at least half alert. During my time in Voc. Ed., I developed further into a mediocre student and a somnambulant problem solver, and that affected the subjects I did have the wherewithal to handle: I detested Shakespeare; I got bored with history. My attention flitted here and there. I fooled around in class and read my books indifferently — the intellectual equivalent of playing with your food. I did what I had to do to get by, and I did it with half a mind.

But I did learn things about people and eventually came into my own socially. I liked the guys in Voc. Ed. Growing up where I did, I understood and admired physical prowess, and there was an abundance of muscle here. There was Dave Snyder, a sprinter and halfback of true quality. Dave's ability and his quick wit gave him a natural appeal, and he was welcome in any clique, though he always kept a little independent. He enjoyed acting the fool and could care less about studies, but he possessed a certain maturity and never caused the faculty much trouble. It was a testament to his independence that he included me among his friends — I eventually went out for track, but I was no jock. Owing to the Latin alphabet and a dearth of *R*s and *S*s, Snyder sat behind Rose, and we started exchanging one-liners and became friends.

There was Ted Richard, a much-touted Little League pitcher. He was chunky and had a baby face and came to Our Lady of Mercy as a

[7]*Horace's Compromise:* a book on American education by Theodore Sizer. See p. 496.

seasoned street fighter. Ted was quick to laugh and he had a loud, jolly laugh, but when he got angry he'd smile a little smile, the kind that simply raises the corner of the mouth a quarter of an inch. For those who knew, it was an eerie signal. Those who didn't found themselves in big trouble, for Ted was very quick. He loved to carry on what we would come to call philosophical discussions: What is courage? Does God exist? He also loved words, enjoyed picking up big ones like *salubrious* and *equivocal* and using them in our conversations — laughing at himself as the word hit a chuckhole rolling off his tongue. Ted didn't do all that well in school — baseball and parties and testing the courage he'd speculated about took up his time. His textbooks were *Argosy* and *Field and Stream*, whatever newspapers he'd find on the bus stop — from the *Daily Worker* to pornography — conversations with uncles or hobos or businessmen he'd meet in a coffee shop, *The Old Man and the Sea*. With hindsight, I can see that Ted was developing into one of those rough-hewn intellectuals whose sources are a mix of the learned and the apocryphal, whose discussions are both assured and sad.

And then there was Ken Harvey. Ken was good-looking in a puffy   15
way and had a full and oily ducktail and was a car enthusiast . . . a hodad. One day in religion class, he said the sentence that turned out to be one of the most memorable of the hundreds of thousands I heard in those Voc. Ed. years. We were talking about the parable of the talents, about achievement, working hard, doing the best you can do, blah-blah-blah, when the teacher called on the restive Ken Harvey for an opinion. Ken thought about it, but just for a second, and said (with studied, minimal affect), "I just wanna be average." That woke me up. Average? Who wants to be average? Then the athletes chimed in with the clichés that make you want to laryngectomize them, and the exchange became a platitudinous melee. At the time, I thought Ken's assertion was stupid, and I wrote him off. But his sentence has stayed with me all these years, and I think I am finally coming to understand it.

Ken Harvey was gasping for air. School can be a tremendously disorienting place. No matter how bad the school, you're going to encounter notions that don't fit with the assumptions and beliefs that you grew up with — maybe you'll hear these dissonant notions from teachers, maybe from the other students, and maybe you'll read them. You'll also be thrown in with all kinds of kids from all kinds of back-grounds, and that can be unsettling — this is especially true in places of rich ethnic and linguistic mix, like the L.A. basin. You'll see a handful of students far excel you in courses that sound exotic and that are only in the curriculum of the elite: French, physics, trigonometry. And all this is happening while you're trying to shape an identity, your body is changing, and your emotions are running wild. If you're a working-class kid in the vocational track, the options you'll have to deal with this will be constrained in certain ways: you're defined by your school as "slow";

you're placed in a curriculum that isn't designed to liberate you but to occupy you, or, if you're lucky, train you, though the training is for work the society does not esteem; other students are picking up the cues from your school and your curriculum and interacting with you in particular ways. If you're a kid like Ted Richard, you turn your back on all this and let your mind roam where it may. But youngsters like Ted are rare. What Ken and so many others do is protect themselves from such suffocating madness by taking on with a vengeance the identity implied in the vocational track. Reject the confusion and frustration by openly defining yourself as the Common Joe. Champion the average. Rely on your own good sense. Fuck this bullshit. Bullshit, of course, is everything you — and the others — fear is beyond you: books, essays, tests, academic scrambling, complexity, scientific reasoning, philosophical inquiry.

The tragedy is that you have to twist the knife in your own gray matter to make this defense work. You'll have to shut down, have to reject intellectual stimuli or diffuse them with sarcasm, have to cultivate stupidity, have to convert boredom from a malady into a way of confronting the world. Keep your vocabulary simple, act stoned when you're not or act more stoned than you are, flaunt ignorance, materialize your dreams. It is a powerful and effective defense — it neutralizes the insult and the frustration of being a vocational kid and, when perfected, it drives teachers up the wall, a delightful secondary effect. But like all strong magic, it exacts a price.

My own deliverance from the Voc. Ed. world began with sophomore biology. Every student, college prep to vocational, had to take biology, and unlike the other courses, the same person taught all sections. When teaching the vocational group, Brother Clint probably slowed down a bit or omitted a little of the fundamental biochemistry, but he used the same book and more or less the same syllabus across the board. If one class got tough, he could get tougher. He was young and powerful and very handsome, and looks and physical strength were high currency. No one gave him any trouble.

I was pretty bad at the dissecting table, but the lectures and the textbook were interesting: plastic overlays that, with each turned page, peeled away skin, then veins and muscle, then organs, down to the very bones that Brother Clint, pointer in hand, would tap out on our hanging skeleton. Dave Snyder was in big trouble, for the study of life — versus the living of it — was sticking in his craw. We worked out a code for our multiple-choice exams. He'd poke me in the back: once for the answer under *A*, twice for *B*, and so on; and when he'd hit the right one, I'd look up to the ceiling as though I were lost in thought. Poke: cytoplasm. Poke, poke: methane. Poke, poke, poke: William Harvey. Poke, poke, poke, poke: islets of Langerhans. This didn't work out perfectly, but Dave passed the course, and I mastered the dreamy look of a guy on a record jacket. And something else happened. Brother Clint puzzled over this Voc. Ed. kid who was racking up 98s and 99s on his tests. He checked the school's records and discovered the error. He recommended that I begin my junior year in the College Prep program. According to all I've read since, such a shift, as one report put it, is virtually impossible. Kids at that level rarely cross tracks. The telling thing is how chancy both my placement into and exit from Voc. Ed. was; neither I nor my parents had anything to do with it. I lived in one world during spring semester, and when I came back to school in the fall, I was living in another.

Switching to College Prep was a mixed blessing. I was an erratic 20 student. I was undisciplined. And I hadn't caught onto the rules of the game: why work hard in a class that didn't grab my fancy? I was also hopelessly behind in math. Chemistry was hard; toying with my chemistry set years before hadn't prepared me for the chemist's equations. Fortunately, the priest who taught both chemistry and second-year algebra was also the school's athletic director. Membership on the track team covered me; I knew I wouldn't get lower than a C. U.S. history was taught pretty well, and I did okay. But civics was taken over by a football coach who had trouble reading the textbook aloud — and reading aloud was the centerpiece of his pedagogy. College Prep at Mercy was certainly an improvement over the vocational program — at least it carried some status — but the social science curriculum was weak, and the mathematics and physical sciences were simply beyond me. I had a miserable quantitative background and ended up copying some assignments and finessing the rest as best I could. Let me try to explain how it feels to see again and again material you should once have learned but didn't.

You are given a problem. It requires you to simplify algebraic fractions or to multiply expressions containing square roots. You know this is pretty basic material because you've seen it for years. Once a teacher took some time with you, and you learned how to carry out these operations. Simple versions, anyway. But that was a year or two or more in the past, and these are more complex versions, and now you're not sure. And this, you keep telling youself, is ninth- or even eighth-grade stuff.

Next it's a word problem. This is also old hat. The basic elements are as familiar as story characters: trains speeding so many miles per hour or shadows of buildings angling so many degrees. Maybe you know enough, have sat through enough explanations, to be able to begin setting up the problem: "If one train is going this fast . . ." or "This shadow is really one line of a triangle . . ." Then: "Let's see . . ." "How did Jones do this?" "Hmmmm." "No." "No, that won't work." Your attention wavers. You wonder about other things: a football game, a dance, that cute new checker at the market. You try to focus on the problem again. You scribble on paper for a while, but the tension wins out and your attention flits elsewhere. You crumple the paper and begin daydreaming to ease the frustration.

The particulars will vary, but in essence this is what a number of students go through, especially those in so-called remedial classes. They open their textbooks and see once again the familiar and impenetrable formulas and diagrams and terms that have stumped them for years. There is no excitement here. *No* excitement. Regardless of what the teacher says, this is not a new challenge. There is, rather, embarrassment and frustration and, not surprisingly, some anger in being reminded once again of long-standing inadequacies. No wonder so many students finally attribute their difficulties to something inborn, organic: "That part of my brain just doesn't work." Given the troubling histories many of these students have, it's miraculous that any of them can lift the shroud of hopelessness sufficiently to make deliverance from these classes possible.

Through this entire period, my father's health was deteriorating with cruel momentum. His arteriosclerosis progressed to the point where a simple nick on his shin wouldn't heal. Eventually it ulcerated and widened. Lou Minton would come by daily to change the dressing. We tried renting an oscillating bed — which we placed in the front room — to force blood through the constricted arteries in my father's legs. The bed hummed through the night, moving in place to ward off the inevitable. The ulcer continued to spread, and the doctors finally had to amputate. My grandfather had lost his leg in a stockyard accident. Now my father too was crippled. His convalescence was slow but steady, and the doctors placed him in the Santa Monica Rehabilitation Center, a sun-bleached building that opened out onto the warm spray of the Pacific. The place gave him some strength and some color and some training in walking with an artificial leg. He did pretty well for a year or so until he slipped and broke his hip. He was confined to a wheelchair after that, and the confinement contributed to the diminishing of his body and spirit.

I am holding a picture of him. He is sitting in his wheelchair and smiling at the camera. The smile appears forced, unsteady, seems to quaver, though it is frozen in silver nitrate. He is in his mid-sixties and looks eighty. Late in my junior year, he had a stroke and never came out of the resulting coma. After that, I would see him only in dreams, and to this day that is how I join him. Sometimes the dreams are sad and grisly and primal: my father lying in a bed soaked with his suppuration,[8] holding me, rocking me. But sometimes the dreams bring him back to me healthy: him talking to me on an empty street, or buying some pictures to decorate our old house, or transformed somehow into someone strong and adept with tools and the physical.

25

[8]*suppuration:* discharge from wounds.

Jack MacFarland couldn't have come into my life at a better time. My father was dead, and I had logged up too many years of scholastic indifference. Mr. MacFarland had a master's degree from Columbia and decided, at twenty-six, to find a little school and teach his heart out. He never took any credentialing courses, couldn't bear to, he said, so he had to find employment in a private system. He ended up at Our Lady of Mercy teaching five sections of senior English. He was a beatnik who was born too late. His teeth were stained, he tucked his sorry tie in between the third and fourth buttons of his shirt, and his pants were chronically wrinkled. At first, we couldn't believe this guy, thought he slept in his car. But within no time, he had us so startled with work that we didn't much worry about where he slept or if he slept at all. We wrote three or four essays a month. We read a book every two to three weeks, starting with the *Iliad* and ending up with Hemingway. He gave us a quiz on the reading every other day. He brought a prep school curriculum to Mercy High.

MacFarland's lectures were crafted, and as he delivered them he would pace the room jiggling a piece of chalk in his cupped hand, using it to scribble on the board the names of all the writers and philosophers and plays and novels he was weaving into his discussion. He asked questions often, raised everything from Zeno's paradox to the repeated last line of Frost's "Stopping by Woods on a Snowy Evening." He slowly and carefully built up our knowledge of Western intellectual history — with facts, with connections, with speculations. We learned about Greek philosophy, about Dante, the Elizabethan world view, the Age of Reason, existentialism. He analyzed poems with us, had us reading sections from John Ciardi's *How Does a Poem Mean?*, making a potentially difficult book accessible with his own explanations. We gave oral reports on poems Ciardi didn't cover. We imitated the styles of Conrad, Hemingway, and *Time* magazine. We wrote and talked, wrote and talked. The man immersed us in language.

Even MacFarland's barbs were literary. If Jim Fitzsimmons, hung over and irritable, tried to smart-ass him, he'd rejoin with a flourish that would spark the indomitable Skip Madison — who'd lost his front teeth in a hapless tackle — to flick his tongue through the gap and opine, "good chop," drawing out the single "o" in stinging indictment. Jack MacFarland, this tobacco-stained intellectual, brandished linguistic weapons of a kind I hadn't encountered before. Here was this *egghead*, for God's sake, keeping some pretty difficult people in line. And from what I heard, Mike Dweetz and Steve Fusco and all the notorious Voc. Ed. crowd settled down as well when MacFarland took the podium. Though a lot of guys groused in the schoolyard, it just seemed that giving trouble to this particular teacher was a silly thing to do. Tomfoolery, not to mention assault, had no place in the world he was trying to create for us, and instinctively everyone knew that. If nothing else, we all recognized MacFarland's considerable intelligence and respected the hours he put into his work. It came to this: the troublemaker would look foolish rather than daring. Even Jim Fitzsimmons was reading *On the Road* and turning his incipient alcoholism to literary ends.

There were some lives that were already beyond Jack MacFarland's ministrations, but mine was not. I started reading again as I hadn't since elementary school. I would go into our gloomy little bedroom or sit at the dinner table while, on the television, Danny McShane was paralyzing Mr. Moto with the atomic drop, and work slowly back through *Heart of Darkness*, trying to catch the words in Conrad's sentences. I certainly was not MacFarland's best student; most of the other guys in College Prep, even my fellow slackers, had better backgrounds than I did. But I worked very hard, for MacFarland had hooked me. He tapped my old interest in reading and creating stories. He gave me a way to feel special by using my mind. And he provided a role model that wasn't shaped on physical prowess alone, and something inside me that I wasn't quite aware of responded to that. Jack MacFarland established a literacy club, to borrow a phrase of Frank Smith's, and invited me — invited all of us — to join.

There's been a good deal of research and speculation suggesting that the acknowledgement of school performance with extrinsic rewards — smiling faces, stars, numbers, grades — diminishes the intrinsic satisfaction children experience by engaging in reading or writing or problem solving. While it's certainly true that we've created an educational system that encourages our best and brightest to become cynical grade collectors and, in general, have developed an obsession with evaluation and assessment, I must tell you that venal though it may have been, I loved getting good grades from MacFarland. I now know how subjective grades can be, but then they came tucked in the back of essays like bits of scientific data, some sort of spectroscopic readout that said, objectively and publicly, that I had made something of value. I suppose I'd been mediocre for too long and enjoyed a public redefinition. And I suppose the workings of my mind, such as they were, had been private for too long. My linguistic play moved into the world; . . . these papers with their circled, red B-pluses and A-minuses linked my mind to something outside it. I carried them around like a club emblem.

One day in the December of my senior year, Mr. MacFarland asked me where I was going to go to college. I hadn't thought much about it. Many of the students I teach today spent their last year in high school with a physics text in one hand and the Stanford catalog in the other, but I wasn't even aware of what "entrance requirements" were. My folks would say that they wanted me to go to college and be a doctor, but I don't know how seriously I ever took that; it seemed a sweet thing to say, a bit of supportive family chatter, like telling a gangly daughter she's graceful. The reality of higher education wasn't in my scheme of things: no one in the family had gone to college; only two of my uncles had completed high school. I figured I'd get a night job and go to the local junior college because I knew that Snyder and Company were going there to play ball. But I hadn't even prepared for that. When I finally said, "I don't know," MacFarland looked down at me — I was seated in his office — and said, "Listen, you can write."

My grades stank. I had A's in biology and a handful of B's in a few English and social science classes. All the rest were C's — or worse. MacFarland said I would do well in his class and laid down the law about doing well in the others. Still, the record for my first three years wouldn't have been acceptable to any four-year school. To nobody's surprise, I was turned down flat by USC and UCLA. But Jack Mac-Farland was on the case. He had received his bachelor's degree from Loyola University, so he made calls to old professors and talked to somebody in admissions and wrote me a strong letter. Loyola finally accepted me as a probationary student. I would be on trial for the first year, and if I did okay, I would be granted regular status. MacFarland also intervened to get me a loan, for I could never have afforded a private college without it. Four more years of religion classes and four more years of boys at one school, girls at another. But at least I was going to college. Amazing.

In my last semester of high school, I elected a special English course fashioned by Mr. MacFarland, and it was through this elective that there arose at Mercy a fledgling literati. Art Mitz, the editor of the school newspaper and a very smart guy, was the kingpin. He was joined by me and by Mark Dever, a quiet boy who wrote beautifully and who would die before he was forty. MacFarland occasionally invited us to his apartment, and those visits became the high point of our apprenticeship: we'd clamp on our training wheels and drive to his salon.

He lived in a cramped and cluttered place near the airport, tucked away in the kind of building that architectural critic Reyner Banham calls a *dingbat*. Books were all over: stacked, piled, tossed, and crated, underlined and dog eared, well worn and new. Cigarette ashes crusted with coffee in saucers or spilled over the sides of motel ashtrays. The little bedroom had, along two of its walls, bricks and boards loaded with notes, magazines, and oversized books. The kitchen joined the living room, and there was a stack of German newspapers under the sink. I had never seen anything like it: a great flophouse of language furnished by City Lights and Café le Metro. I read every title. I flipped through paperbacks and scanned jackets and memorized names: Gogol, *Finnegans Wake*, Djuna Barnes, Jackson Pollock, *A Coney Island of the Mind*, F. O. Matthiessen's *American Renaissance*, all sorts of Freud, *Troubled Sleep*, Man Ray, *The Education of Henry Adams*, Richard Wright, *Film as Art*, William Butler Yeats, Marguerite Duras, *Redburn*, *A Season in Hell*, *Kapital*. On the cover of Alain-Fournier's *The*

Wanderer was an Edward Gorey drawing of a young man on a road winding into dark trees. By the hotplate sat a strange Kafka novel called *Amerika,* in which an adolescent hero crosses the Atlantic to find the Nature Theater of Oklahoma. Art and Mark would be talking about a movie or the school newspaper, and I would be consuming my English teacher's library. It was heady stuff. I felt like a Pop Warner[9] athlete on steroids.

Art, Mark, and I would buy stogies and triangulate from Mac-   35
Farland's apartment to the Cinema, which now shows X-rated films but was then L.A.'s premier art theater, and then to the musty Cherokee Bookstore in Hollywood to hobnob with beatnik homosexuals — smoking, drinking bourbon and coffee, and trying out awkward phrases we'd gleaned from our mentor's bookshelves. I was happy and precocious and a little scared as well, for Hollywood Boulevard was thick with a kind of decadence that was foreign to the South Side. After the Cherokee, we would head back to the security of MacFarland's apartment, slaphappy with hipness.

Let me be the first to admit that there was a good deal of adolescent passion in this embrace of the avant-garde: self-absorption, sexually charged pedantry, an elevation of the odd and abandoned. Still it was a time during which I absorbed an awful lot of information: long lists of titles, images from expressionist paintings, new wave shibboleths,[10] snippets of philosophy, and names that read like Steve Fusco's misspellings — Goethe, Nietzsche, Kierkegaard. Now this is hardly the stuff of deep understanding. But it was an introduction, a phrase book, a Baedeker[11] to a vocabulary of ideas, and it felt good at the time to know all these words. With hindsight I realize how layered and important that knowledge was.

It enabled me to do things in the world. I could browse bohemian bookstores in far-off, mysterious Hollywood; I could go to the Cinema and see events through the lenses of European directors; and, most of all, I could share an evening, talk that talk, with Jack MacFarland, the man I most admired at the time. Knowledge was becoming a bonding agent. Within a year or two, the persona of the disaffected hipster would prove too cynical, too alienated to last. But for a time it was new and exciting: it provided a critical perspective on society, and it allowed me to act as though I were living beyond the limiting boundaries of South Vermont.[12]

---

[9]*Pop Warner:* a nationwide youth athletics organization.
[10]*new wave shibboleths:* trendy phrases or jargon.
[11]*Baedeker:* travel guide.
[12]*South Vermont:* a street in an economically depressed area of Los Angeles.

Engaging the Text

1. Describe Rose's life in Voc. Ed. What were his teachers like? Have you ever had experience with teachers like these?

2. What did Voc. Ed. do to Rose and his fellow students? How did it affect them intellectually, emotionally, and socially? Why was it subsequently so hard for Rose to catch up in math?

3. Why is high school so disorienting to students like Ken Harvey? How does he cope with it? What other strategies do students use to cope with the pressures and judgments they encounter in school?

4. What does Jack MacFarland offer Rose that finally helps him learn? Do you think it was inevitable that someone with Rose's intelligence would eventually succeed?

Exploring Connections

5. How does Rose's perception of educational ills differ from Theodore Sizer's in "What High School Is" (p. 496)? Explain how their arguments support or contradict each other. Whose ideas do you find more persuasive or important?

6. Draw a Groening-style cartoon (see p. 508) or comic strip of Rose in the vocational track, or of Rose before and after his liberation from Voc. Ed.

7. Write an imaginary dialogue between Rose and Gregory Mantsios (p. 72) about why some students, like Rose, seem to be able to break through social class barriers and others, like Dave Snyder, Ted Richard, and Ken Harvey, do not.

Extending the Critical Context

8. Rose explains that high school can be a "tremendously disorienting place" (para. 16). What, if anything, do you find disorienting about college? What steps can students at your school take to lessen feelings of disorientation? What could the college do to help them?

9. Review one or more of Rose's descriptions of his high school classmates; then write a description of one of your own high school classmates, trying to capture in a nutshell how that person coped or failed to cope with the educational system.

10. Watch *Stand and Deliver* or *Dead Poets Society* on videotape and compare the movie's depiction of a teacher to Rose's portrayal of Jack MacFarland. What do such charismatic teachers offer their students personally and intellectually? Do you see any disadvantages to classes taught by teachers like these?

From *Social Class and the Hidden Curriculum of Work*

JEAN ANYON

It's no surprise that schools in wealthy communities are better than those in poor communities, or that they better prepare their students for desirable jobs. It may be shocking, however, to learn how vast the differences in schools are — not so much in resources as in teaching methods and philosophies of education. Jean Anyon observed five elementary schools over the course of a full school year and concluded that fifth-graders of different economic backgrounds are already being prepared to occupy particular rungs on the social ladder. In a sense, some whole schools are on the vocational education track, while others are geared to produce future doctors, lawyers, and business leaders. Anyon's main audience is professional educators, so you may find her style and vocabulary challenging, but, once you've read her descriptions of specific classroom activities, the more analytic parts of the essay should prove easier to understand. Anyon is chairperson of the Department of Education at Rutgers University, Newark; this essay first appeared in Journal of Education *in 1980.*

Scholars in political economy and the sociology of knowledge have recently argued that public schools in complex industrial societies like our own make available different types of educational experience and curriculum knowledge to students in different social classes. Bowles and Gintis[1] for example, have argued that students in different social-class backgrounds are rewarded for classroom behaviors that correspond to personality traits allegedly rewarded in the different occupational strata — the working classes for docility and obedience, the managerial classes for initiative and personal assertiveness. Basil Bernstein, Pierre Bourdieu, and Michael W. Apple,[2] focusing on school knowledge, have

[1] S. Bowles and H. Gintis, *Schooling in Capitalist America: Educational Reform and the Contradictions of Economic Life* (New York: Basic Books, 1976). [Author's note]

[2] B. Bernstein, *Class, Codes and Control, Vol. 3. Towards a Theory of Educational Transmission,* 2d ed. (London: Routledge & Kegan Paul, 1977); P. Bourdieu and J. Passeron, *Reproduction in Education, Society and Culture* (Beverly Hills, Calif.: Sage, 1977); M. W. Apple, *Ideology and Curriculum* (Boston: Routledge & Kegan Paul, 1979). [Author's note]

argued that knowledge and skills leading to social power and regard (medical, legal, managerial) are made available to the advantaged social groups but are withheld from the working classes, to whom a more "practical" curriculum is offered (manual skills, clerical knowledge). While there has been considerable argumentation of these points regarding education in England, France, and North America, there has been little or no attempt to investigate these ideas empirically in elementary or secondary schools and classrooms in this country.[3]

This article offers tentative empirical support (and qualification) of the above arguments by providing illustrative examples of differences in student *work* in classrooms in contrasting social class communities. The examples were gathered as part of an ethnographical[4] study of curricular, pedagogical, and pupil evaluation practices in five elementary schools. The article attempts a theoretical contribution as well and assesses student work in the light of a theoretical approach to social-class analysis. . . . It will be suggested that there is a "hidden curriculum" in schoolwork that has profound implications for the theory — and consequence — of everyday activity in education. . . .

The Sample of Schools

. . . The social-class designation of each of the five schools will be identified, and the income, occupation, and other relevant available social characteristics of the students and their parents will be described. The first three schools are in a medium-sized city district in northern New Jersey, and the other two are in a nearby New Jersey suburb.

The first two schools I will call *working-class schools.* Most of the parents have blue-collar jobs. Less than a third of the fathers are skilled, while the majority are in unskilled or semiskilled jobs. During the period of the study (1978–1979), approximately 15 percent of the fathers were unemployed. The large majority (85 percent) of the families are white. The following occupations are typical: platform, storeroom, and stockroom workers; foundrymen, pipe welders, and boilermakers; semiskilled and unskilled assembly-line operatives; gas station attendants, auto mechanics, maintenance workers, and security guards. Less than 30 percent of the women work, some part-time and some full-time, on assembly lines, in storerooms and stockrooms, as waitresses, barmaids, or sales clerks. Of the fifth-grade parents, none of the wives of the skilled workers had jobs. Approximately 15 percent of the families

---

[3]But see, in a related vein, M. W. Apple and N. King, "What Do Schools Teach?" *Curriculum Inquiry* 6 (1977): 341–58; R. C. Rist, *The Urban School: A Factory for Failure* (Cambridge, Mass.: MIT Press, 1973). [Author's note]

[4]*ethnographical:* based on an anthropological study of cultures or subcultures — the "cultures" in this case being the five schools observed.

in each school are at or below the federal "poverty" level;[5] most of the rest of the family incomes are at or below $12,000, except some of the skilled workers whose incomes are higher. The incomes of the majority of the families in these two schools (at or below $12,000) are typical of 38.6 percent of the families in the United States.[6]

The third school is called the *middle-class school*, although because of neighborhood residence patterns, the population is a mixture of several social classes. The parents' occupations can be divided into three groups: a small group of blue-collar "rich," who are skilled, well-paid workers such as printers, carpenters, plumbers, and construction workers. The second group is composed of parents in working-class and middle-class white-collar jobs: women in office jobs, technicians, super-visors in industry, and parents employed by the city (such as firemen, policemen, and several of the school's teachers). The third group is composed of occupations such as personnel directors in local firms, accountants, "middle management," and a few small capitalists (owners of shops in the area). The children of several local doctors attend this school. Most family incomes are between $13,000 and $25,000, with a few higher. This income range is typical of 38.9 percent of the families in the United States.[7]

The fourth school has a parent population that is at the upper income level of the upper middle class and is predominantly professional. This school will be called the *affluent professional school*. Typical jobs are: cardiologist, interior designer, corporate lawyer or engineer, executive in advertising or television. There are some families who are not as affluent as the majority (the family of the superintendent of the district's schools, and the one or two families in which the fathers are skilled workers). In addition, a few of the families are more affluent than the majority and can be classified in the capitalist class (a partner in a prestigious Wall Street stock brokerage firm). Approximately 90 percent of the children in this school are white. Most family incomes are between $40,000 and $80,000. This income span represents approximately 7 percent of the families in the United States.[8]

5

[5]The U.S. Bureau of the Census defines *poverty* for a nonfarm family of four as a yearly income of $6,191 a year or less. U.S. Bureau of the Census, *Statistical Abstract of the United States: 1978* (Washington, D.C.: U.S. Government Printing Office, 1978), p. 465, table 754. [Author's note]

[6]U.S. Bureau of the Census, "Money Income in 1977 of Families and Persons in the United States," *Current Population Reports* Series P-60, no. 118 (Washington, D.C.: U.S. Government Printing Office, 1979), p. 2, table A. [Author's note]

[7]Ibid. [Author's note]

[8]This figure is an estimate. According to the Bureau of the Census, only 2.6 percent of families in the United States have money income of $50,000 or over. U.S. Bureau of the Census, *Current Population Reports* Series P-60. For figures on income at these higher levels, see J. D. Smith and S. Franklin, "The Concentration of Personal Wealth, 1922–1969," *American Economic Review*, 64 (1974): 162–67. [Author's note]

In the fifth school the majority of the families belong to the capitalist class. This school will be called the *executive elite school* because most of the fathers arc top executives (for example, presidents and vice-presidents) in major United States–based multinational corporations — for example, ATT, RCA, City Bank, American Express, U.S. Steel. A sizable group of fathers are top executives in financial firms in Wall Street. There are also a number of fathers who list their occupations as "general counsel" to a particular corporation, and these corporations are also among the large multinationals. Many of the mothers do volunteer work in the Junior League, Junior Fortnightly, or other service groups; some are intricately involved in town politics; and some are themselves in well-paid occupations. There are no minority children in the school. Almost all the family incomes are over $100,000, with some in the $500,000 range. The incomes in this school represent less than 1 percent of the families in the United States.[9]

Since each of the five schools is only one instance of elementary education in a particular social class context, I will not generalize beyond the sample. However, the examples of schoolwork which follow will suggest characteristics of education in each social setting that appear to have theoretical and social significance and to be worth investigation in a larger number of schools. . . .

The Working-Class Schools

In the two working-class schools, work is following the steps of a procedure. The procedure is usually mechanical, involving rote behavior and very little decision making or choice. The teachers rarely explain why the work is being assigned, how it might connect to other assignments, or what the idea is that lies behind the procedure or gives it coherence and perhaps meaning or significance. Available textbooks are not always used, and the teachers often prepare their own dittos or put work examples on the board. Most of the rules regarding work are designations of what the children are to do; the rules are steps to follow. These steps are told to the children by the teachers and are often written on the board. The children are usually told to copy the steps as notes. These notes are to be studied. Work is often evaluated not according to whether it is right or wrong but according to whether the children followed the right steps.

The following examples illustrate these points. In math, when two-digit division was introduced, the teacher in one school gave a four-minute lecture on what the terms are called (which number is the divisor, dividend, quotient, and remainder). The children were told to copy these names in their notebooks. Then the teacher told them the steps to follow to do the problems, saying, "This is how you do them."

[9]Smith and Franklin, "The Concentration of Personal Wealth." [Author's note]

The teacher listed the steps on the board, and they appeared several days later as a chart hung in the middle of the front wall: "Divide, Multiply, Subtract, Bring Down." The children often did examples of two-digit division. When the teacher went over the examples with them, he told them what the procedure was for each problem, rarely asking them to conceptualize or explain it themselves: "Three into twenty-two is seven; do your subtraction and one is left over." During the week that two-digit division was introduced (or at any other time), the investigator did not observe any discussion of the idea of grouping involved in division, any use of manipulables, or any attempt to relate two-digit division to any other mathematical process. Nor was there any attempt to relate the steps to an actual or possible thought process of the children. The observer did not hear the terms *dividend*, *quotient*, and so on, used again. The math teacher in the other working-class school followed similar procedures regarding two-digit division and at one point her class seemed confused. She said, "You're confusing yourselves. You're tensing up. Remember, when you do this, it's the same steps over and over again — and that's the way division always is." Several weeks later, after a test, a group of her children "still didn't get it," and she made no attempt to explain the concept of dividing things into groups or to give them manipulables for their own investigation. Rather, she went over the steps with them again and told them that they "needed more practice."

In other areas of math, work is also carrying out often unexplained fragmented procedures. For example, one of the teachers led the children through a series of steps to make a 1-inch grid on their paper *without* telling them that they were making a 1-inch grid or that it would be used to study scale. She said, "Take your ruler. Put it across the top. Make a mark at every number. Then move your ruler down to the bottom. No, put it across the bottom. Now make a mark on top of every number. Now draw a line from . . ." At this point a girl said that she had a faster way to do it and the teacher said, "No, you don't; you don't even know what I'm making yet. Do it this way or it's wrong." After they had made the lines up and down and across, the teacher told them she wanted them to make a figure by connecting some dots and to measure that, using the scale of 1 inch equals 1 mile. Then they were to cut it out. She said, "Don't cut it until I check it."

In both working-class schools, work in language arts is mechanics of punctuation (commas, periods, question marks, exclamation points), capitalization, and the four kinds of sentences. One teacher explained to me, "Simple punctuation is all they'll ever use." Regarding punctuation, either a teacher or a ditto stated the rules for where, for example, to put commas. The investigator heard no classroom discussion of the aural context of punctuation (which, of course, is what gives each mark its meaning). Nor did the investigator hear any statement or inference that placing a punctuation mark could be a decision-making process, depending, for example, on one's intended meaning. Rather, the children were told to follow the rules. Language arts did not involve creative writing. There were several writing assignments throughout the year, but in each instance the children were given a ditto, and they wrote answers to questions on the sheet. For example, they wrote their "autobiography" by answering such questions as "Where were you born?" "What is your favorite animal?" on a sheet entitled "All About Me."

In one of the working-class schools, the class had a science period several times a week. On the three occasions observed, the children were not called upon to set up experiments or to give explanations for facts or concepts. Rather, on each occasion the teacher told them in his own words what the book said. The children copied the teacher's sentences from the board. Each day that preceded the day they were to do a science experiment, the teacher told them to copy the directions from the book for the procedure they would carry out the next day and to study the list at home that night. The day after each experiment, the teacher went over what they had "found" (they did the experiments as a class, and each was actually a class demonstration led by the teacher). Then the teacher wrote what they "found" on the board, and the children copied that in their notebooks. Once or twice a year there are science projects. The project is chosen and assigned by the teacher from a box of 3-by-5-inch cards. On the card the teacher has written the question to be answered, the books to use, and how much to write. Explaining the cards to the observer, the teacher said, "It tells them exactly what to do, or they couldn't do it."

Social studies in the working-class schools is also largely mechanical, rote work that was given little explanation or connection to larger contexts. In one school, for example, although there was a book available, social studies work was to copy the teacher's notes from the board. Several times a week for a period of several months the children copied these notes. The fifth grades in the district were to study United States history. The teacher used a booklet she had purchased called "The Fabulous Fifty States." Each day she put information from the booklet in outline form on the board and the children copied it. The type of information did not vary: the name of the state, its abbreviation, state capital, nickname of the state, its main products, main business, and a "Fabulous Fact" ("Idaho grew twenty-seven billion potatoes in one year. That's enough potatoes for each man, woman, and . . ."). As the children finished copying the sentences, the teacher erased them and wrote more. Children would occasionally go to the front to pull down the wall map in order to locate the states they were copying, and the teacher did not dissuade them. But the observer never saw her refer to the map; nor did the observer ever hear her make other than perfunctory remarks concerning the information the children were copying. Occasionally the children colored in a ditto and cut it out to make a stand-up figure (representing, for example, a man roping a cow in the Southwest). These were referred to by the teacher as their social studies "projects."

Rote behavior was often called for in classroom work. When going over math and language art skills sheets, for example, as the teacher asked for the answer to each problem, he fired the questions rapidly, staccato, and the scene reminded the observer of a sergeant drilling recruits: above all, the questions demanded that you stay at attention: "The next one? What do I put here? . . . Here? Give us the next." Or "How many commas in this sentence? Where do I put them . . . The next one?"

The four fifth-grade teachers observed in the working-class schools attempted to control classroom time and space by making decisions without consulting the children and without explaining the basis for their decisions. The teacher's control thus often seemed capricious. Teachers, for instance, very often ignored the bells to switch classes — deciding among themselves to keep the children after the period was officially over to continue with the work or for disciplinary reasons or so they (the teachers) could stand in the hall and talk. There were no clocks in the rooms in either school, and the children often asked, "What period is this?" "When do we go to gym?" The children had no access to materials. These were handed out by teachers and closely guarded. Things in the room "belonged" to the teacher: "Bob, bring me my garbage can." The teachers continually gave the children orders. Only three times did the investigator hear a teacher in either working-class school preface a directive with an unsarcastic "please," or "let's" or "would you." Instead, the teachers said, "Shut up," "Shut your mouth," "Open your books," "Throw your gum away — if you want to rot your teeth, do it on your own time." Teachers made every effort to control the movement of the children, and often shouted, "Why are you out of your seat??!!" If the children got permission to leave the room, they had to take a written pass with the date and time. . . .

Middle-Class School

In the middle-class school, work is getting the right answer. If one accumulates enough right answers, one gets a good grade. One must follow the directions in order to get the right answers, but the directions often call for some figuring, some choice, some decision making. For example, the children must often figure out by themselves what the directions ask them to do and how to get the answer: what do you do first, second, and perhaps third? Answers are usually found in books or by listening to the teacher. Answers are usually words, sentences, numbers, or facts and dates; one writes them on paper, and one should be neat. Answers must be given in the right order, and one cannot make them up.

The following activities are illustrative. Math involves some choice: one may do two-digit division the long way or the short way, and there are some math problems that can be done "in your head." When the teacher explains how to do two-digit division, there is recognition that a cognitive process is involved; she gives you several ways and says, "I want to make sure you understand what you're doing — so you get it right"; and, when they go over the homework, she askes the *children* to tell how they did the problem and what answer they got.

In social studies the daily work is to read the assigned pages in the textbook and to answer the teacher's questions. The questions are almost always designed to check on whether the students have read the assignment and understood it: who did so-and-so; what happened after that; when did it happen, where, and sometimes, why did it happen? The answers are in the book and in one's understanding of the book; the teacher's hints when one doesn't know the answers are to "read it again" or to look at the picture or at the rest of the paragraph. One is to search for the answer in the "context," in what is given.

Language arts is "simple grammar, what they need for everyday life." The language arts teacher says, "They should learn to speak properly, to write business letters and thank-you letters, and to understand what nouns and verbs and simple subjects are." Here, as well, actual work is to choose the right answers, to understand what is given. The teacher often says, "Please read the next sentence and then I'll question you about it." One teacher said in some exasperation to a boy who was fooling around in class, "If you don't know the answers to the questions I ask, then you can't stay in this *class*! [pause] You *never* know the answers to the questions I ask, and it's not fair to me — and certainly not to you!"

Most lessons are based on the textbook. This does not involve a critical perspective on what is given there. For example, a critical perspective in social studies is perceived as dangerous by these teachers because it may lead to controversial topics; the parents might complain. The children, however, are often curious, especially in social studies. Their questions are tolerated and usually answered perfunctorily. But after a few minutes the teacher will say, "All right, we're not going any farther. Please open your social studies workbook." While the teachers spend a lot of time explaining and expanding on what the textbooks say, there is little attempt to analyze how or why things happen, or to give thought to how pieces of a culture, or, say, a system of numbers or elements of a language fit together or can be analyzed. What has happened in the past and what exists now may not be equitable or fair,

20

but (shrug) that is the way things are and one does not confront such matters in school. For example, in social studies after a child is called on to read a passage about the pilgrims, the teacher summarizes the paragraph and then says, "So you can see how strict they were about everything." A child asks, "Why?" "Well, because they felt that if you weren't busy you'd get into trouble." Another child asks, "Is it true that they burned women at the stake?" The teacher says, "Yes, if a woman did anything strange, they hanged them. [*sic*] What would a woman do, do you think, to make them burn them? [*sic*] See if you can come up with better answers than my other [social studies] class." Several children offer suggestions, to which the teacher nods but does not comment. Then she says, "Okay, good," and calls on the next child to read.

Work tasks do not usually request creativity. Serious attention is rarely given in school work on *how* the children develop or express their own feelings and ideas, either linguistically or in graphic form. On the occasions when creativity or self-expression is requested, it is peripheral to the main activity or it is "enrichment" or "for fun." During a lesson on what similes are, for example, the teacher explains what they are, puts several on the board, gives some other examples herself, and then asks the children if they can "make some up." She calls on three children who give similes, two of which are actually in the book they have open before them. The teacher does not comment on this and then asks several others to choose similes from the list of phrases in the book. Several do so correctly, and she says, "Oh good! You're picking them out! See how good we are?" Their homework is to pick out the rest of the similes from the list.

Creativity is not often requested in social studies and science projects, either. Social studies projects, for example, are given with directions to "find information on your topic" and write it up. The children are not supposed to copy but to "put it in your own words." Although a number of the projects subsequently went beyond the teacher's direction to find information and had quite expressive covers and inside illustrations, the teacher's evaluative comments had to do with the amount of information, whether they had "copied," and if their work was neat.

The style of control of the three fifth-grade teachers observed in this school varied from somewhat easygoing to strict, but in contrast to the working-class schools, the teachers' decisions were usually based on external rules and regulations — for example, on criteria that were known or available to the children. Thus, the teachers always honor the bells for changing classes, and they usually evaluate children's work by what is in the textbooks and answer booklets.

There is little excitement in schoolwork for the children, and the 25 assignments are perceived as having little to do with their interests and feelings. As one child said, what you do is "store facts up in your head like cold storage — until you need it later for a test or your job." Thus, doing well is important because there are thought to be *other* likely rewards: a good job or college.[10]

Affluent Professional School

In the affluent professional school, work is creative activity carried out independently. The students are continually asked to express and apply ideas and concepts. Work involves individual thought and expressiveness, expansion and illustration of ideas, and choice of appropriate method and material. (The class is not considered an open classroom, and the principal explained that because of the large number of discipline problems in the fifth grade this year they did not departmentalize. The teacher who agreed to take part in the study said she is "more structured" this year than she usually is.) The products of work in this class are often written stories, editorials and essays, or representations of ideas in mural, graph, or craft form. The products of work should not be like everybody else's and should show individuality. They should exhibit good design, and (this is important) they must also fit empirical reality. Moreover, one's work should attempt to interpret or "make sense" of reality. The relatively few rules to be followed regarding work are usually criteria for, or limits on, individual activity. One's product is usually evaluated for the quality of its expression and for the appropriateness of its conception to the task. In many cases, one's own satisfaction with the product is an important criterion for its evaluation. When right answers are called for, as in commercial materials like SRA (Science Research Associates) and math, it is important that the children decide on an answer as a result of thinking about the idea involved in what they're being asked to do. Teacher's hints are to "think about it some more."

The following activities are illustrative. The class takes home a sheet requesting each child's parents to fill in the number of cars they have, the number of television sets, refrigerators, games, or rooms in the house, and so on. Each child is to figure the average number of a type of possession owned by the fifth grade. Each child must compile the "data" from all the sheets. A calculator is available in the classroom to do the mechanics of finding the average. Some children decide to send sheets to the fourth-grade families for comparison. Their work should be "verified" by a classmate before it is handed in.

Each child and his or her family has made a geoboard. The teacher asks the class to get their geoboards from the side cabinet, to take a handful of rubber bands, and then to listen to what she would like them to do. She says, "I would like you to design a figure and then find the

---

[10]A dominant feeling, expressed directly and indirectly by teachers in this school, was boredom with their work. They did, however, in contrast to the working-class schools, almost always carry out lessons during class times. [Author's note]

perimeter and area. When you have it, check with your neighbor. After you've done that, please transfer it to graph paper and tomorrow I'll ask you to make up a question about it for someone. When you hand it in, please let me know whose it is and who verified it. Then I have something else for you to do that's really fun. [pause] Find the average number of chocolate chips in three cookies. I'll give you three cookies, and you'll have to *eat* your way through, I'm afraid!" Then she goes around the room and gives help, suggestions, praise, and admonitions that they are getting noisy. They work sitting, or standing up at their desks, at benches in the back, or on the floor. A child hands the teacher his paper and she comments, "I'm not accepting this paper. Do a better design." To another child she says, "That's fantastic! But you'll never find the area. Why don't you draw a figure inside [the big one] and subtract to get the area?"

The school district requires the fifth grade to study ancient civilization (in particular, Egypt, Athens, and Sumer). In this classroom, the emphasis is on illustrating and re-creating the culture of the people of ancient times. The following are typical activities: the children made an 8mm film on Egypt, which one of the parents edited. A girl in the class wrote the script, and the class acted it out. They put the sound on themselves. They read stories of those days. They wrote essays and stories depicting the lives of the people and the societal and occupational divisions. They chose from a list of projects, all of which involved graphic representations of ideas: for example, "Make a mural depicting the division of labor in Egyptian society."

Each child wrote and exchanged a letter in hieroglyphics with a 30 fifth grader in another class, and they also exchanged stories they wrote in cuneiform. They made a scroll and singed the edges so it looked authentic. They each chose an occupation and made an Egyptian plaque representing that occupation, simulating the appropriate Egyptian design. They carved their design on a cylinder of wax, pressed the wax into clay, and then baked the clay. Although one girl did not choose an occupation but carved instead a series of gods and slaves, the teacher said, "That's all right, Amber, it's beautiful." As they were working the teacher said, "Don't cut into your clay until you're satisfied with your design."

Social studies also involves almost daily presentation by the children of some event from the news. The teacher's questions ask the children to expand what they say, to give more details, and to be more specific. Occasionally she adds some remarks to help them see connections between events.

The emphasis on expressing and illustrating ideas in social studies is accompanied in language arts by an emphasis on creative writing. Each child wrote a rhebus story for a first grader whom they had interviewed to see what kind of story the child liked best. They wrote editorials on pending decisions by the school board and radio plays, some of which were read over the school intercom from the office and one of which was performed in the auditorium. There is no language arts textbook because, the teacher said, "The principal wants us to be creative." There is not much grammar, but there is punctuation. One morning when the observer arrived, the class was doing a punctuation ditto. The teacher later apologized for using the ditto. "It's just for review," she said. "I don't teach punctuation that way. We use their language." The ditto had three unambiguous rules for where to put commas in a sentence. As the teacher was going around to help the children with the ditto, she repeated several times, "Where you put commas depends on how you say the sentence; it depends on the situation and what you want to say." Several weeks later the observer saw another punctuation activity. The teacher had printed a five-paragraph story on an oak tag and then cut it into phrases. She read the whole story to the class from the book, then passed out the phrases. The group had to decide how the phrases could best be put together again. (They arranged the phrases on the floor.) The point was not to replicate the story, although that was not irrelevant, but to "decide what you think the best way is." Punctuation marks on cardboard pieces were then handed out, and the children discussed and then decided what mark was best at each place they thought one was needed. At the end of each paragraph the teacher asked, "Are you satisfied with the way the paragraphs are now? Read it to yourself and see how it sounds." Then she read the original story again, and they compared the two.

Describing her goals in science to the investigator, the teacher said, "We use ESS (Elementary Science Study). It's very good because it gives a hands-on-experience — so they can make *sense* out of it. It doesn't matter whether it [what they find] is right or wrong. I bring them together and there's value in discussing their ideas."

The products of work in this class are often highly valued by the children and the teacher. In fact, this was the only school in which the investigator was not allowed to take original pieces of the children's work for her files. If the work was small enough, however, and was on paper, the investigator could duplicate it on the copying machine in the office.

The teacher's attempt to control the class involves constant negotiation. She does not give direct orders unless she is angry because the children have been too noisy. Normally, she tries to get them to foresee the consequences of their actions and to decide accordingly. For example, lining them up to go see a play written by the sixth graders, she says, "I presume you're lined up by someone with whom you want to sit. I hope you're lined up by someone you won't get in trouble with." . . .

One of the few rules governing the children's movement is that no more than three children may be out of the room at once. There is a school rule that anyone can go to the library at any time to get a book. In the fifth grade I observed, they sign their name on the chalkboard and leave. There are no passes. Finally, the children have a fair amount of officially sanctioned say over what happens in the class. For example, they often negotiate what work is to be done. If the teacher wants to move on to the next subject, but the children say they are not ready, they want to work on their present projects some more, she very often lets them do it.

Executive Elite School

In the executive elite school, work is developing one's analytical intellectual powers. Children are continually asked to reason through a problem, to produce intellectual products that are both logically sound and of top academic quality. A primary goal of thought is to conceptualize rules by which elements may fit together in systems and then to apply these rules in solving a problem. Schoolwork helps one to achieve, to excel, to prepare for life.

The following are illustrative. The math teacher teaches area and perimeter by having the children derive formulas for each. First she helps them, through discussion at the board, to arrive at $A = W \times L$ as a formula (not *the* formula) for area. After discussing several, she says, "Can anyone make up a formula for perimeter? Can you figure that out yourselves? [pause] Knowing what we know, can we think of a formula?" She works out three children's suggestions at the board, saying to two, "Yes, that's a good one," and then asks the class if they can think of any more. No one volunteers. To prod them, she says, "If you use· rules and good reasoning, you get many ways. Chris, can you think up a formula?"

She discusses two digit division with the children as a decision-making process. Presenting a new type of problem to them, she asks, "What's the *first* decision you'd make if presented with this kind of example? What is the first thing you'd *think*? Craig?" Craig says, "To find my first partial quotient." She responds, "Yes, that would be your first decision. How would you do that?" Craig explains, and then the teacher says, "OK, we'll see how that works for you." The class tries his way. Subsequently, she comments on the merits and shortcomings of several other children's decisions. Later, she tells the investigator that her goals in math are to develop their reasoning and mathematical thinking and that, unfortunately, "there's no *time* for manipulables."

While right answers are important in math, they are not "given" by the book or by the teacher but may be challenged by the children. Going over some problems in late September the teacher says, "Raise your hand if you do not agree." A child says, "I don't agree with sixty-four." The teacher responds, "OK, there's a question about sixty-four. [to class] Please check it. Owen, they're disagreeing with you. Kristen, they're checking yours." The teacher emphasized this repeatedly during

40

September and October with statements like "Don't be afraid to say you disagree. In the last [math] class, somebody disagreed, and they were right. Before you disagree, check yours, and if you still think we're wrong, then we'll check it out." By Thanksgiving, the children did not often speak in terms of right and wrong math problems but of whether they agreed with the answer that had been given.

There are complicated math mimeos with many word problems. Whenever they go over the examples, they discuss how each child has set up the problem. The children must explain it precisely. On one occasion the teacher said, "I'm more — just as interested in *how* you set up the problem as in what answer you find. If you set up a problem in a good way, the answer is *easy* to find."

Social studies work is most often reading and discussion of concepts and independent research. There are only occasional artistic, expressive, or illustrative projects. Ancient Athens and Sumer are, rather, societies to analyze. The following questions are typical of those that guide the children's independent research. "What mistakes did Pericles make after the war?" "What mistakes did the citizens of Athens make?" "What are the elements of a civilization?" "How did Greece build an economic empire?" "Compare the way Athens chose its leaders with the way we choose ours." Occasionally the children are asked to make up sample questions for their social studies tests. On an occasion when the investigator was present, the social studies teacher rejected a child's question by saying, "That's just fact. If I asked you that question on a test, you'd complain it was just memory! Good questions ask for concepts."

In social studies — but also in reading, science, and health — the teachers initiate classroom discussions of current social issues and problems. These discussions occurred on every one of the investigator's visits, and a teacher told me, "These children's opinions are important — it's important that they learn to reason things through." The classroom discussions always struck the observer as quite realistic and analytical, dealing with concrete social issues like the following: "Why do workers strike?" "Is that right or wrong?" "Why do we have inflation, and what can be done to stop it?" "Why do companies put chemicals in food when the natural ingredients are available?" and so on. Usually the children did not have to be prodded to give their opinions. In fact, their statements and the interchanges between them struck the observer as quite sophisticated conceptually and verbally, and well-informed. Occasionally the teachers would prod with statements such as, "Even if you don't know [the answers], if you think logically about it, you can figure it out." And "I'm asking you [these] questions to help you think this through."

Language arts emphasizes language as a complex system, one that should be mastered. The children are asked to diagram sentences of complex grammatical construction, to memorize irregular verb conjugations (he lay, he has lain, and so on . . .), and to use the proper participles, conjunctions, and interjections in their speech. The teacher (the same one who teaches social studies) told them, "It is not enough to get these right on tests; you must use what you learn [in grammar classes] in your written and oral work. I will grade you on that."

Most writing assignments are either research reports and essays for social studies or experiment analyses and write-ups for science. There is only an occasional story or other "creative writing" assignment. On the occasion observed by the investigator (the writing of a Halloween story), the points the teacher stressed in preparing the children to write involved the structural aspects of a story rather than the expression of feelings or other ideas. The teacher showed them a filmstrip, "The Seven Parts of a Story," and lectured them on plot development, mood setting, character development, consistency, and the use of a logical or appropriate ending. The stories they subsequently wrote were, in fact, well-structured, but many were also personal and expressive. The teacher's evaluative comments, however, did not refer to the expressiveness or artistry but were all directed toward whether they had "developed" the story well.

Language arts work also involved a large amount of practice in presentation of the self and in managing situations where the child was expected to be in charge. For example, there was a series of assignments in which each child had to be a "student teacher." The child had to plan a lesson in grammar, outlining, punctuation, or other language arts topic and explain the concept to the class. Each child was to prepare a worksheet or game and a homework assignment as well. After each presentation, the teacher and other children gave a critical appraisal of the "student teacher's" performance. Their criteria were: whether the student spoke clearly, whether the lesson was interesting, whether the student made any mistakes, and whether he or she kept control of the class. On an occasion when a child did not maintain control, the teacher said, "When you're up there, you have authority and you have to use it. I'll back you up." . . .

The executive elite school is the only school where bells do not demarcate the periods of time. The two fifth-grade teachers were very strict about changing classes on schedule, however, as specific plans for each session had been made. The teachers attempted to keep tight control over the children during lessons, and the children were sometimes flippant, boisterous, and occasionally rude. However, the children may be brought into line by reminding them that "It is up to you." "You must control yourself," "you are responsible for your work," you must "set your own priorities." One teacher told a child, "You are the only driver of your car — and only you can regulate your speed." A new teacher complained to the observer that she had thought "these children" would have more control.

While strict attention to the lesson at hand is required, the teachers make relatively little attempt to regulate the movement of the children at other times. For example, except for the kindergartners the children in this school do not have to wait for the bell to ring in the morning; they may go to their classroom when they arrive at school. Fifth graders often came early to read, to finish work, or to catch up. After the first two months of school, the fifth-grade teachers did not line the children up to change classes or to go to gym, and so on, but, when the children were ready and quiet, they were told they could go — sometimes without the teachers.

In the classroom, the children could get materials when they needed them and took what they needed from closets and from the teacher's desk. They were in charge of the office at lunchtime. During class they did not have to sign out or ask permission to leave the room; they just got up and left. Because of the pressure to get work done, however, they did not leave the room very often. The teachers were very polite to the children, and the investigator heard no sarcasm, no nasty remarks, and few direct orders. The teachers never called the children "honey" or "dear" but always called them by name. The teachers were expected to be available before school, after school, and for part of their lunchtime to provide extra help if needed. . . .

The foregoing analysis of differences in schoolwork in contrasting 50
social class contexts suggests the following conclusion: the "hidden curriculum" of schoolwork is tacit preparation for relating to the process of production in a particular way. Differing curricular, pedagogical, and pupil evaluation practices emphasize different cognitive and behavioral skills in each social setting and thus contribute to the development in the children of certain potential relationships to physical and symbolic capital,[11] to authority, and to the process of work. School experience, in the sample of schools discussed here, differed qualitatively by social class. These differences may not only contribute to the development in the children in each social class of certain types of economically significant relationships and not others but would thereby help to *reproduce* this system of relations in society. In the contribution to the reproduction of unequal social relations lies a theoretical meaning and social consequence of classroom practice.

The identification of different emphases in classrooms in a sample of contrasting social class contexts implies that further research should be conducted in a large number of schools to investigate the types of work tasks and interactions in each to see if they differ in the ways discussed here and to see if similar potential relationships are un-

[11]*physical and symbolic capital:* elsewhere Anyon defines *capital* as "property that is used to produce profit, interest, or rent"; she defines *symbolic capital* as the knowledge and skills that "may yield social and cultural power."

covered. Such research could have as a product the further elucidation of complex but not readily apparent connections between everyday activity in schools and classrooms and the unequal structure of economic relationships in which we work and live.

Engaging the Text

1. Examine the ways any single subject is taught in the four types of schools Anyon describes. What differences in teaching methods and in the student-teacher relationship do they reflect? What other differences do you note in the schools? What schools in your geographic region would closely approximate the working-class, middle-class, affluent professional, and executive elite schools of her article?

2. What attitudes toward knowledge and work are the four types of schools teaching their students? What kinds of jobs are students being prepared to do? Do you see any evidence that the schools in your community are producing particular kinds of workers?

3. What is the "hidden curriculum" of Anyon's title? How is this curriculum taught, and what social, cultural, or political purposes does it serve?

Exploring Connections

4. What kind of a school — working class, middle class, affluent professional, or executive elite — does Mark attend in Theodore Sizer's "What High School Is" (p. 496)? On what do you base your judgment? How might Anyon interpret the "supermarket" mentality of the school Sizer describes?

5. Draw a Groening-like (see p. 508) cartoon or comic strip about a classroom situation in a working-class, middle-class, professional, or elite school (but do not identify the type of school explicitly). Pool all the cartoons from the class. In small groups, sort the comics according to the type of school they represent.

6. Analyze the teaching styles that Mike Rose encounters at Our Lady of Mercy (p. 511). Which of Anyon's categories would they fit best? Do Rose's experiences at his high school tend to confirm or complicate Anyon's analysis?

7. Which, if any, of the five schools Anyon describes would be most likely to produce workers that fit Sam Keen's profile of "the economic man" (p. 207)? To what extent do the two writers agree about the attitudes and behaviors that lead to corporate success?

Extending the Critical Context

8. Should all schools be run like the professional or elite schools? What would be the advantages of making these schools models for all social classes? Do you see any possible disadvantages?

9. Choose a common elementary school task or skill that Anyon does not mention. Outline four ways it might be taught in the four types of schools.

The Achievement of Desire

RICHARD RODRIGUEZ

Hunger of Memory, the autobiography of Richard Rodriguez and the source of the following selection, set off a storm of controversy in the Chicano community when it appeared in 1981. Some hailed it as an uncompromising portrayal of the difficulties of growing up between two cultures; others condemned it because it seemed to blame Mexican Americans for the difficulties they encountered assimilating into mainstream American society. Rodriguez was born in 1944 into an immigrant family outside San Francisco. Though he was unable to speak English when he entered school, his educational career can only be described as brilliant: undergraduate work at Stanford University, graduate study at Berkeley and Columbia, a Fulbright fellowship to study English literature in London, a subsequent grant from the National Endowment for the Humanities. In this selection, Rodriguez analyzes the motives that led him to abandon his study of Renaissance literature and return to live with his parents. He has since served as an educational consultant and has published articles in several national magazines. His most recent book is Mexico's Children *(1991), a study of Mexicans in the United States.*

I stand in the ghetto classroom — "the guest speaker" — attempting to lecture on the mystery of the sounds of our words to rows of diffident students. "Don't you hear it? Listen! The music of our words. '*Sumer is i-cumen in.*[1] . . .' And songs on the car radio. We need Aretha Franklin's voice to fill plain words with music — her life." In the face of their empty stares, I try to create an enthusiasm. But the girls in the back row turn to watch some boy passing outside. There are flutters of smiles, waves. And someone's mouth elongates heavy, silent words through the barrier of glass. Silent words — the lips straining to shape each voiceless syllable: "*Meet meee late errr.*" By the door, the instructor smiles at me, apparently hoping that I will be able to spark some enthusiasm in the class. But only one student seems to be listening. A girl, maybe fourteen. In this gray room her eyes shine with ambition. She keeps nodding and nodding at all that I say; she even takes notes. And each time I ask a question, she jerks up and down in her desk like a marionette, while her hand waves over the bowed heads of her classmates. It is myself (as a boy) I see as she faces me now (a man in my thirties).

---

[1]*Sumer is i-cumen in:* opening line of a Middle English poem ("Summer has come").

The boy who first entered a classroom barely able to speak English, twenty years later concluded his studies in the stately quiet of the reading room in the British Museum. Thus with one sentence I can summarize my academic career. It will be harder to summarize what sort of life connects the boy to the man.

With every award, each graduation from one level of education to the next, people I'd meet would congratulate me. Their refrain always the same: "Your parents must be very proud." Sometimes then they'd ask me how I managed it — my "success." (How?) After a while, I had several quick answers to give in reply. I'd admit, for one thing, that I went to an excellent grammar school. (My earliest teachers, the nuns, made my success their ambition.) And my brother and both my sisters were very good students. (They often brought home the shiny school trophies I came to want.) And my mother and father always encouraged me. (At every graduation they were behind the stunning flash of the camera when I turned to look at the crowd.)

As important as these factors were, however, they account inadequately for my academic advance. Nor do they suggest what an odd success I managed. For although I was a very good student, I was also a very bad student. I was a "scholarship boy," a certain kind of scholarship boy. Always successful, I was always unconfident. Exhilarated by my progress. Sad. I became the prized student — anxious and eager to learn. Too eager, too anxious — an imitative and unoriginal pupil. My brother and two sisters enjoyed the advantages I did, and they grew to be as successful as I, but none of them ever seemed so anxious about their schooling. A second-grade student, I was the one who came home and corrected the "simple" grammatical mistakes of our parents. ("Two negatives make a positive.") Proudly I announced — to my family's startled silence — that a teacher had said I was losing all trace of a Spanish accent. I was oddly annoyed when I was unable to get parental help with a homework assignment. The night my father tried to help me with an arithmetic exercise, he kept reading the instructions, each time more deliberately, until I pried the textbook out of his hands, saying, "I'll try to figure it out some more by myself."

When I reached the third grade, I outgrew such behavior. I became 5 more tactful, careful to keep separate the two very different worlds of my day. But then, with ever-increasing intensity, I devoted myself to my studies. I became bookish, puzzling to all my family. Ambition set me apart. When my brother saw me struggling home with stacks of library books, he would laugh, shouting: "Hey, Four Eyes!" My father opened a closet one day and was startled to find me inside, reading a novel. My mother would find me reading when I was supposed to be asleep or helping around the house or playing outside. In a voice angry or worried or just curious, she'd ask: "What do you see in your books?" It became the family's joke. When I was called and wouldn't reply, someone would say I must be hiding under my bed with a book.

(How did I manage my success?)

What I am about to say to you has taken me more than twenty years to admit: *A primary reason for my success in the classroom was that I couldn't forget that schooling was changing me and separating me from the life I enjoyed before becoming a student.* That simple realization! For years I never spoke to anyone about it. Never mentioned a thing to my family or my teachers or classmates. From a very early age, I understood enough, just enough about my classroom experiences to keep what I knew repressed, hidden beneath layers of embarrassment. Not until my last months as a graduate student, nearly thirty years old, was it possible for me to think much about the reasons for my academic success. Only then. At the end of my schooling, I needed to determine how far I had moved from my past. The adult finally confronted, and now must publicly say, what the child shuddered from knowing and could never admit to himself or to those many faces that smiled at his every success. ("Your parents must be very proud. . . .")

At the end, in the British Museum (too distracted to finish my dissertation) for weeks I read, speed-read, books by modern educational theorists, only to find infrequent and slight mention of students like me. (Much more is written about the more typical case, the lower-class student who barely is helped by his schooling.) Then one day, leafing through Richard Hoggart's *The Uses of Literacy*, I found, in his description of the scholarship boy, myself. For the first time I realized that there were other students like me, and so I was able to frame the meaning of my academic success, its consequent price — the loss.

Hoggart's description is distinguished, at least initially, by deep understanding. What he grasps very well is that the scholarship boy must move between environments, his home and the classroom, which are at cultural extremes, opposed. With his family, the boy has the intense pleasure of intimacy, the family's consolation in feeling public alienation. Lavish emotions texture home life. *Then*, at school, the instruction bids him to trust lonely reason primarily. Immediate needs set the pace of his parents' lives. From his mother and father the boy learns to trust spontaneity and nonrational ways of knowing. *Then*, at school, there is mental calm. Teachers emphasize the value of a reflectiveness that opens a space between thinking and immediate action.

Years of schooling must pass before the boy will be able to sketch the cultural differences in his day as abstractly as this. But he senses those differences early. Perhaps as early as the night he brings home an assignment from school and finds the house too noisy for study.

He has to be more and more alone, if he is going to "get on." He will have, probably unconsciously, to oppose the ethos[2] of the hearth, the

---

[2]*ethos:* the fundamental spirit or character of a thing.

intense gregariousness of the working-class family group. Since every-thing centres upon the living-room, there is unlikely to be a room of his own; the bedrooms are cold and inhospitable, and to warm them or the front room, if there is one, would not only be expensive, but would require an imaginative leap — out of the tradition — which most families are not capable of making. There is a corner of the living-room table. On the other side Mother is ironing, the wireless is on, someone is singing a snatch of song or Father says intermittently whatever comes into his head. The boy has to cut himself off mentally, so as to do his homework, as well as he can.[3]

The next day, the lesson is as apparent at school. There are even rows of desks. Discussion is ordered. The boy must rehearse his thoughts and raise his hand before speaking out in a loud voice to an audience of classmates. And there is time enough, and silence, to think about ideas (big ideas) never considered at home by his parents.

Not for the working-class child alone is adjustment to the classroom difficult. Good schooling requires that any student alter early childhood habits. But the working-class child is usually least prepared for the change. And, unlike many middle-class children, he goes home and sees in his parents a way of life not only different but starkly opposed to that of the classroom. (He enters the house and hears his parents talking in ways his teachers discourage.)

Without extraordinary determination and the great assistance of others — at home and at school — there is little chance for success. Typically most working-class children are barely changed by the class-room. The exception succeeds. The relative few become scholarship students. Of these, Richard Hoggart estimates, most manage a fairly graceful transition. Somehow they learn to live in the two very different worlds of their day. There are some others, however, those Hoggart pejoratively terms "scholarship boys," for whom success comes with special anxiety. Scholarship boy: good student, troubled son. The child is "moderately endowed," intellectually mediocre, Hoggart supposes — though it may be more pertinent to note the special qualities of tem-perament in the child. High-strung child. Brooding. Sensitive. Haunted by the knowledge that one *chooses* to become a student. (Education is not an inevitable or natural step in growing up.) Here is a child who cannot forget that his academic success distances him from a life he loved, even from his own memory of himself.

Initially, he wavers, balances allegiance. ("The boy is himself [until he reaches, say, the upper forms[4]] very much of *both* the worlds of home and school. He is enormously obedient to the dictates of the world of

---

[3]All quotations are from Richard Hoggart, *The Uses of Literacy* (London: Chatto and Windus, 1957), chapter 10. [Author's note]

[4]*upper forms:* upper grades or classes in British secondary schools.

 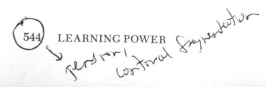

school, but emotionally still strongly wants to continue as part of the family circle.") Gradually, necessarily, the balance is lost. The boy needs to spend more and more time studying, each night enclosing himself in the silence permitted and required by intense concentration. He takes his first step toward academic success, away from his family.

From the very first days, through the years following, it will be with his parents — the figures of lost authority, the persons toward whom he feels deepest love — that the change will be most powerfully measured. A separation will unravel between them. Advancing in his studies, the boy notices that his mother and father have not changed as much as he. Rather, when he sees them, they often remind him of the person he once was and the life he earlier shared with them. He realizes what some Romantics[5] also know when they praise the working class for the capacity for human closeness, qualities of passion and spontaneity, that the rest of us experience in like measure only in the earliest part of our youth. For the Romantic, this doesn't make working-class life childish. Working-class life challenges precisely because it is an *adult* way of life.

The scholarship boy reaches a different conclusion. He cannot afford to admire his parents. (How could he and still pursue such a contrary life?) He permits himself embarrassment at their lack of education. And to evade nostalgia for the life he has lost, he concentrates on the benefits education will bestow upon him. He becomes especially ambitious. Without the support of old certainties and consolations, almost mechanically, he assumes the procedures and doctrines of the classroom. The kind of allegiance the young student might have given his mother and father only days earlier, he transfers to the teacher, the new figure of authority. "[The scholarship boy] tends to make a father-figure of his form-master,"[6] Hoggart observes.

But Hoggart's calm prose only makes me recall the urgency with which I came to idolize my grammar school teachers. I began by imitating their accents, using their diction, trusting their every direction. The very first facts they dispensed, I grasped with awe. Any book they told me to read, I read — then waited for them to tell me which books I enjoyed. Their every casual opinion I came to adopt and to trumpet when I returned home. I stayed after school "to help" — to get my teacher's undivided attention. It was the nun's encouragement that mattered most to me. (She understood exactly what — my parents never seemed to appraise so well — all my achievements entailed.) Memory gently caressed each word of praise bestowed in the classroom so that

[5]*Romantics:* adherents of the principles of romanticism — a literary and philosophical movement that emphasized the imagination, freedom, nature, the return to a simple life, and the ordinary individual.

[6]*form-master:* a teacher in a British secondary school.

compliments teachers paid me years ago come quickly to mind even today.

The enthusiasm I felt in second-grade classes I flaunted before both my parents. The docile, obedient student came home a shrill and precocious son who insisted on correcting and teaching his parents with the remark: "My teacher told us. . . ."

I intended to hurt my mother and father. I was still angry at them for having encouraged me toward classroom English. But gradually this anger was exhausted, replaced by guilt as school grew more and more attractive to me. I grew increasingly successful, a talkative student. My hand was raised in the classroom; I yearned to answer any question. At home, life was less noisy than it had been. (I spoke to classmates and teachers more often each day than to family members.) Quiet at home, I sat with my papers for hours each night. I never forgot that schooling had irretrievably changed my family's life. That knowledge, however, did not weaken ambition. Instead, it strengthened resolve. Those times I remembered the loss of my past with regret, I quickly reminded myself of all the things my teachers could give me. (They could make me an educated man.) I tightened my grip on pencil and books. I evaded nostalgia. Tried hard to forget. But one does not forget by trying to forget. One only remembers. I remembered too well that education had changed my family's life. I would not have become a scholarship boy had I not so often remembered.

Once she was sure that her children knew English, my mother would tell us, "You should keep up your Spanish." Voices playfully groaned in response. "¡Pochos!"[7] my mother would tease. I listened silently.

After a while, I grew more calm at home. I developed tact. A fourth-grade student, I was no longer the show-off in front of my parents. I became a conventionally dutiful son, politely affectionate, cheerful enough, even — for reasons beyond choosing — my father's favorite. And much about my family life was easy then, comfortable, happy in the rhythm of our living together: hearing my father getting ready for work; eating the breakfast my mother had made me; looking up from a novel to hear my brother or one of my sisters playing with friends in the backyard; in winter, coming upon the house all lighted up after dark.

But withheld from my mother and father was any mention of what most mattered to me: the extraordinary experience of first-learning. Late afternoon: in the midst of preparing dinner, my mother would come up behind me while I was trying to read. Her head just over mine, her breath warmly scented with food. "What are you reading?" Or, "Tell me all about your new courses." I would barely respond, "Just the

20

---

[7]*pocho:* a derogatory Spanish word for a Mexican American who has adopted the attitudes, values, and lifestyle of Anglo culture.

usual things, nothing special." (A half smile, then silence. Her head moving back in the silence. Silence! Instead of the flood of intimate sounds that had once flowed smoothly between us, there was this silence.) After dinner, I would rush to a bedroom with papers and books. As often as possible, I resisted parental pleas to "save lights" by coming to the kitchen to work. I kept so much, so often, to myself. Sad. Enthusiastic. Troubled by the excitement of coming upon new ideas. Eager. Fascinated by the promising texture of a brand-new book. I hoarded the pleasures of learning. Alone for hours. Enthralled. Nervous. I rarely looked away from my books — or back on my memories. Nights when relatives visited and the front rooms were warmed by Spanish sounds, I slipped quietly out of the house.

It mattered that education was changing me. It never ceased to matter. My brother and sisters would giggle at our mother's mispronounced words. They'd correct her gently. My mother laughed girlishly one night, trying not to pronounce *sheep* as *ship*. From a distance I listened sullenly. From that distance, pretending not to notice on another occasion, I saw my father looking at the title pages of my library books. That was the scene on my mind when I walked home with a fourth-grade companion and heard him say that his parents read to him every night. (A strange-sounding book — *Winnie the Pooh*.) Immediately, I wanted to know, "What is it like?" My companion, however, thought I wanted to know about the plot of the book. Another day, my mother surprised me by asking for a "nice" book to read. "Something not too hard you think I might like." Carefully I chose one, Willa Cather's[8] *My Ántonia*. But when, several weeks later, I happened to see it next to her bed unread except for the first few pages, I was furious and suddenly wanted to cry. I grabbed up the book and took it back to my room and placed it in its place, alphabetically on my shelf.

"Your parents must be very proud of you." People began to say that to me about the time I was in sixth grade. To answer affirmatively, I'd smile. Shyly I'd smile, never betraying my sense of the irony: I was not proud of my mother and father. I was embarrassed by their lack of education. It was not that I ever thought they were stupid, though stupidly I took for granted their enormous native intelligence. Simply, what mattered to me was that they were not like my teachers.

But, "Why didn't you tell us about the award?" my mother demanded, her frown weakened by pride. At the grammar school ceremony several weeks after, her eyes were brighter than the trophy I'd won. Pushing back the hair from my forehead, she whispered that I had "shown" the *gringos*.[9] A few minutes later, I heard my father speak to my teacher and felt ashamed of his labored, accented words. Then

[8]*Willa Cather:* U.S. novelist (1876–1947).
[9]*gringos:* Anglos.

guilty for the shame. I felt such contrary feelings. (There is no simple roadmap through the heart of the scholarship boy.) My teacher was so soft-spoken and her words were edged sharp and clean. I admired her until it seemed to me that she spoke too carefully. Sensing that she was condescending to them, I became nervous. Resentful. Protective. I tried to move my parents away. "You both must be very proud of Richard," the nun said. They responded quickly. (They were proud.) "We are proud of all our children." Then this afterthought: "They sure didn't get their brains from us." They all laughed. I smiled.

In fourth grade I embarked upon a grandiose reading program. "Give me the names of important books," I would say to startled teachers. They soon found out that I had in mind "adult books." I ignored their suggestion of anything I suspected was written for children. (Not until I was in college, as a result, did I read *Huckleberry Finn* or *Alice's Adventures in Wonderland*.) Instead, I read *The Scarlet Letter* and Franklin's *Autobiography*. And whatever I read I read for extra credit. Each time I finished a book, I reported the achievement to a teacher and basked in the praise my effort earned. Despite my best efforts, however, there seemed to be more and more books I needed to read. At the library I would literally tremble as I came upon whole shelves of books I hadn't read. So I read and I read and I read: *Great Expectations*; all the short stories of Kipling; *The Babe Ruth Story*; the entire first volume of the *Encyclopaedia Britannica* (A–ANSTEY) the *Iliad*; *Moby Dick*; *Gone with the Wind*; *The Good Earth*; *Ramona*; *Forever Amber*; *The Lives of the Saints*; *Crime and Punishment*; *The Pearl*. . . . Librarians who initially frowned when I checked out the maximum ten books at a time started saving books they thought I might like. Teachers would say to the rest of the class, "I only wish the rest of you took reading as seriously as Richard obviously does."

But at home I would hear my mother wondering, "What do you see in your books?" (Was reading a hobby like her knitting? Was so much reading even healthy for a boy? Was it the sign of "brains"? Or was it just a convenient excuse for not helping around the house on Saturday mornings?) Always, "What do you see . . . ?"

What *did* I see in my books? I had the idea that they were crucial for my academic success, though I couldn't have said exactly how or why. In the sixth grade I simply concluded that what gave a book its value was some major idea or theme it contained. If that core essence could be mined and memorized, I would become learned like my teachers. I decided to record in a notebook the themes of the books that I read. After reading *Robinson Crusoe*, I wrote that its theme was "the value of learning to live by oneself." When I completed *Wuthering Heights*, I noted the danger of "letting emotions get out of control." Rereading these brief moralistic appraisals usually left me disheartened.

I couldn't believe that they were really the source of reading's value. But for many more years, they constituted the only means I had of describing to myself the educational value of books.

I entered high school having read hundreds of books. My habit of reading made me a confident speaker and writer of English. Reading also enabled me to sense something of the shape, the major concerns, of Western thought. (I was able to say something about Dante[10] and Descartes[11] and Engels[12] and James Baldwin[13] in my high school term papers.) In these various ways, books brought me academic success as I hoped that they would. But I was not a good reader. Merely bookish, I lacked a point of view when I read. Rather, I read in order to acquire a point of view. I vacuumed books for epigrams, scraps of information, ideas, themes — anything to fill the hollow within me and make me feel educated. When one of my teachers suggested to his drowsy tenth-grade English class that a person could not have a "complicated idea" until he had read at least two thousand books, I heard the remark without detecting either its irony or its very complicated truth. I merely determined to compile a list of all the books I had ever read. Harsh with myself, I included only once a title I might have read several times. (How, after all, could one read a book more than once?) And I included only those books over a hundred pages in length. (Could anything shorter be a book?)

There was yet another high school list I compiled. One day I came   30
across a newspaper article about the retirement of an English professor at a nearby state college. The article was accompanied by a list of the "hundred most important books of Western Civilization." "More than anything else in my life," the professor told the reporter with finality, "these books have made me all that I am." That was the kind of remark I couldn't ignore. I clipped out the list and kept it for the several months it took me to read all of the titles. Most books, of course, I barely understood. While reading Plato's *Republic*, for instance, I needed to keep looking at the book jacket comments to remind myself what the text was about. Nevertheless, with the special patience and superstition of a scholarship boy, I looked at every word of the text. And by the time I reached the last word, relieved, I convinced myself that I had read *The Republic*. In a ceremony of great pride, I solemnly crossed Plato off my list.

. . . The scholarship boy does not straddle, cannot reconcile, the two great opposing cultures of his life. His success is unromantic and

[10]*Dante:* Dante Alighieri, Italian poet (1265–1321); author of the *Divine Comedy.*
[11]*Descartes:* René Descartes, French philosopher and mathematician (1596–1650).
[12]*Engels:* Friedrich Engels, German socialist (1820–1895); coauthor with Karl Marx of the *Communist Manifesto* in 1848.
[13]*James Baldwin:* American author (1924–1987).

plain. He sits in the classroom and offers those sitting beside him no calming reassurance about their own lives. He sits in the seminar room — a man with brown skin, the son of working-class Mexican immigrant parents. (Addressing the professor at the head of the table, his voice catches with nervousness.) There is no trace of his parents' accent in his speech. Instead he approximates the accents of teachers and classmates. Coming from *him* those sounds seem suddenly odd. Odd too is the effect produced when *he* uses academic jargon — bubbles at the tip of his tongue: "*Topos* . . . negative capability . . . vegetation imagery in Shakespearean comedy."[14] He lifts an opinion from Coleridge, takes something else from Frye or Empson or Leavis.[15] He even repeats exactly his professor's earlier comment. All his ideas are clearly borrowed. He seems to have no thought of his own. He chatters while his listeners smile — their look one of disdain.

When he is older and thus when so little of the person he was survives, the scholarship boy makes only too apparent his profound lack of *self*-confidence. This is the conventional assessment that even Richard Hoggart repeats:

> [The scholarship boy] tends to over-stress the importance of examinations, of the piling-up of knowledge and of received opinions. He discovers a technique of apparent learning, of the acquiring of facts rather than of the handling and use of facts. He learns how to receive a purely literate education, one using only a small part of the personality and challenging only a limited area of his being. He begins to see life as a ladder, as a permanent examination with some praise and some further exhortation at each stage. He becomes an expert imbiber and dolerout; his competence will vary, but will rarely be accompanied by genuine enthusiasms. He rarely feels the reality of knowledge, of other men's thoughts and imaginings, on his own pulses . . . He has something of the blinkered pony about him. . . .

But this is criticism more accurate than fair. The scholarship boy is a very bad student. He is the great mimic; a collector of thoughts, not a thinker; the very last person in class who ever feels obliged to have an opinion of his own. In large part, however, the reason he is such a bad student is because he realizes more often and more acutely than most other students — than Hoggart himself — that education requires radical self-reformation. As a very young boy, regarding his parents, as he struggles with an early homework assignment, he knows this too well. That is why he lacks self-assurance. He does not forget that the classroom is responsible for remaking him. He relies on his teacher, depends on all that he hears in the classroom and reads in his books. He

---

[14]*topos . . . negative capability . . . .:* technical terms associated with the study of literary criticism.

[15]*Coleridge . . . Frye . . . Empson . . . Leavis:* important literary critics.

becomes in every obvious way the worst student, a dummy mouthing the opinions of others. But he would not be so bad — nor would he become so successful, a *scholarship* boy — if he did not accurately perceive that the best synonym for primary "education" is "imitation."

Like me, Hoggart's imagined scholarship boy spends most of his years in the classroom afraid to long for his past. Only at the very end of his schooling does the boy-man become nostalgic. In this sudden change of heart, Richard Hoggart notes:

> He longs for the membership he lost, "he pines for some Nameless Eden where he never was." The nostalgia is the stronger and the more ambiguous because he is really "in quest of his own absconded self yet scared to find it." He both wants to go back and yet thinks he has gone beyond his class, feels himself weighted with knowledge of his own and their situation, which hereafter forbids him the simpler pleasures of his father and mother. . . .

According to Hoggart, the scholarship boy grows nostalgic because   35
he remains the uncertain scholar, bright enough to have moved from his past, yet unable to feel easy, a part of a community of academics.

This analysis, however, only partially suggests what happened to me in my last years as a graduate student. When I traveled to London to write a dissertation on English Renaissance literature, I was finally confident of membership in a "community of scholars." But the pleasure that confidence gave me faded rapidly. After only two or three months in the reading room of the British Museum, it became clear that I had joined a lonely community. Around me each day were dour faces eclipsed by large piles of books. There were the regulars, like the old couple who arrived every morning, each holding a loop of the shopping bag which contained all their notes. And there was the historian who chattered madly to herself. ("Oh dear! Oh! Now, what's this? What? Oh, my!") There were also the faces of young men and women worn by long study. And everywhere eyes turned away the moment our glance accidentally met. Some persons I sat beside day after day, yet we passed silently at the end of the day, strangers. Still, we were united by a common respect for the written word and for scholarship. We did form a union, though one in which we remained distant from one another.

More profound and unsettling was the bond I recognized with those writers whose books I consulted. Whenever I opened a text that hadn't been used for years, I realized that my special interests and skills united me to a mere handful of academics. We formed an exclusive — eccentric! — society, separated from others who would never care or be able to share our concerns. (The pages I turned were stiff like layers of dead skin.) I began to wonder: Who, beside my dissertation director and a few faculty members, would ever read what I wrote? And: Was my dissertation much more than an act of social withdrawal? These questions went unanswered in the silence of the Museum reading room. They remained to trouble me after I'd leave the library each afternoon and feel myself shy — unsteady, speaking simple sentences at the grocer's or the butcher's on my way back to my bed-sitter.[16]

Meanwhile my file cards accumulated. A professional, I knew exactly how to search a book for pertinent information. I could quickly assess and summarize the usability of the many books I consulted. But whenever I started to write, I knew too much (and not enough) to be able to write anything but sentences that were overly cautious, timid, strained brittle under the heavy weight of footnotes and qualifications. I seemed unable to dare a passionate statement. I felt drawn by professionalism to the edge of sterility, capable of no more than pedantic, lifeless, unassailable prose.

Then nostalgia began.

After years spent unwilling to admit its attractions, I gestured   40
nostalgically toward the past. I yearned for that time when I had not been so alone. I became impatient with books. I wanted experience more immediate. I feared the library's silence. I silently scorned the gray, timid faces around me. I grew to hate the growing pages of my dissertation on genre[17] and Renaissance literature. (In my mind I heard relatives laughing as they tried to make sense of its title.) I wanted something — I couldn't say exactly what. I told myself that I wanted a more passionate life. And a life less thoughtful. And above all, I wanted to be less alone. One day I heard some Spanish academics whispering back and forth to each other, and their sounds seemed ghostly voices recalling my life. Yearning became preoccupation then. Boyhood memories beckoned, flooded my mind. (Laughing intimate voices. Bounding up the front steps of the porch. A sudden embrace inside the door.)

For weeks after, I turned to books by educational experts. I needed to learn how far I had moved from my past — to determine how fast I would be able to recover something of it once again. But I found little. Only a chapter in a book by Richard Hoggart . . . I left the reading room and the circle of faces.

I came home. After the year in England, I spent three summer months living with my mother and father, relieved by how easy it was to be home. It no longer seemed very important to me that we had little to say. I felt easy sitting and eating and walking with them. I watched them, nevertheless, looking for evidence of those elastic, sturdy strands that bind generations in a web of inheritance. I thought as I watched my mother one night: of course a friend had been right when she told me that I gestured and laughed just like my mother. Another time I

[16]*bed-sitter:* a one-room apartment.
[17]*genre:* a class or category of artistic work; e.g., the genre of poetry.

saw for myself: my father's eyes were much like my own, constantly watchful.

But after the early relief, this return, came suspicion, nagging until I realized that I had not neatly sidestepped the impact of schooling. My desire to do so was precisely the measure of how much I remained an academic. *Negatively* (for that is how this idea first occurred to me): my need to think so much and so abstractly about my parents and our relationship was in itself an indication of my long education. My father and mother did not pass their time thinking about the cultural meanings of their experience. It was I who described their daily lives with airy ideas. And yet, *positively:* the ability to consider experience so abstractly allowed me to shape into desire what would otherwise have remained indefinite, meaningless longing in the British Museum. If, because of my schooling, I had grown culturally separated from my parents, my education finally had given me ways of speaking and caring about that fact.

My best teachers in college and graduate school, years before, had tried to prepare me for this conclusion, I think, when they discussed texts of aristocratic pastoral literature. Faithfully, I wrote down all that they said. I memorized it: "The praise of the unlettered by the highly educated is one of the primary themes of 'elitist' literature." But, "the importance of the praise given the unsolitary, richly passionate and spontaneous life is that it simultaneously reflects the value of a reflective life." I heard it all. But there was no way for any of it to mean very much to me. I was a scholarship boy at the time, busily laddering my way up the rungs of education. To pass an examination, I copied down exactly what my teachers told me. It would require many more years of schooling (an inevitable miseducation) in which I came to trust the silence of reading and the habit of abstracting from immediate experience — moving away from a life of closeness and immediacy I remembered with my parents, growing older — before I turned unafraid to desire the past, and thereby achieved what had eluded me for so long — the end of education.

Engaging the Text

1. What does education do to the young Rodriguez? How does it affect his relationship to his family, his past, and his culture? What role do his teachers play in this transformation?

2. What is a "scholarship boy"? Why does Rodriguez consider himself a bad student despite his academic success?

3. What happens to Rodriguez in London? Why does he ultimately abandon his studies there?

4. What drives Rodriguez to succeed? What does education represent to him? To his father and mother?

5. What is Rodriguez's final assessment of what he has gained and lost through his education? Do you agree with his analysis?

Exploring Connections

6. Compare Rodriguez, Stephen Cruz, (p. 36), Gary Soto (p. 410), and Mike Rose (p. 511) in terms of their attitudes toward education and success.

7. Write a letter to Rodriguez from Haunani-Kay Trask (p. 118), offering advice and discussing such issues as conflicts between family and scholarship.

8. Working in a small group, draft a short play similar to George C. Wolfe's *Symbiosis* (p. 42) but based on Rodriguez's life and his Mexican American heritage.

Extending the Critical Context

9. What are your personal motives for academic success? How do they compare with those of Rodriguez?

10. Today many college students find that they're following in the footsteps of family members — not breaking ground as Rodriguez did. What special difficulties do such second- or third-generation college students face?

Para Teresa[1]

Inés Hernández

This poem explores and attempts to resolve an old conflict between its speaker and her schoolmate, two Chicanas at "Alamo which-had-to-be-its-name" Elementary School who have radically different ideas about what education means and does. Inés Hernández (b. 1947) teaches Native American literature at the University of California, Davis. This poem appeared in her collection Con Razón, Corazón *(1987).*

A tí-Teresa Compean
Te dedico las palabras estás
que explotan de mi corazón[2]

---

[1]For Teresa. [Author's note]
[2]To you, Teresa Compean, I dedicate these words that explode from my heart. [Author's note]

That day during lunch hour
at Alamo which-had-to-be-its-name   5
Elementary
my dear raza
That day in the bathroom
Door guarded
Myself cornered   10
I was accused by you, Teresa
Tú y las demás de tus amigas
Pachucas todas
Eran Uds. cinco.[3]

Me gritaban que porque me creía tan grande[4]   15
What was I trying to do, you growled
Show you up?
Make the teachers like me, pet me,
Tell me what a credit to my people I was?
I was playing right into their hands, you challenged   20
And you would have none of it.
I was to stop.

I was to be like you
I was to play your game of deadly defiance
Arrogance, refusal to submit.   25
The game in which the winner takes nothing
Asks for nothing
Never lets his weaknesses show.

But I didn't understand.
My fear salted with confusion   30
Charged me to explain to you
I did nothing *for the teachers*.
I studied for my parents and for my grandparents
Who cut out honor roll lists
Whenever their nietos'[5] names appeared   35
For my shy mother who mastered her terror
to demand her place in mother's clubs
For my carpenter-father who helped me patiently with my math.
For my abuelos que me regalaron lápices en la Navidad[6]
And for myself.   40

Porque reconocí en aquel entonces
una verdad tremenda

---

[3]You and the rest of your friends, all Pachucas, there were five of you. [Author's note]
[4]You were screaming at me, asking me why I thought I was so hot. [Author's note]
[5]Grandchildren's. [Author's note]
[6]Grandparents who gave me gifts of pencils at Christmas. [Author's note]

que me hizo a mi un rebelde
Aunque tú no te habías dadocuenta[7]
We were not inferior   45
You and I, y las demás de tus amigas
Y los demás de nuestra gente[8]
I knew it the way I knew I was alive
We were good, honorable, brave
Genuine, loyal, strong   50

And smart.
Mine was a deadly game of defiance, also.
My contest was to prove
beyond any doubt
that we were not only equal but superior to them.   55
That was why I studied.
If I could do it, we all could.

You let me go then.
Your friends unblocked the way
I who-did-not-know-how-to-fight   60
was not made to engage with you-who-grew-up-fighting
Tu y yo, Teresa[9]
We went in different directions
Pero fuimos juntas.[10]

In sixth grade we did not understand   65
Uds. with the teased, dyed-black-but-reddening hair,
Full petticoats, red lipsticks
and sweaters with the sleeves
pushed up
Y yo conformándome con lo que deseaba mi mamá[11]   70
Certainly never allowed to dye, to tease, to paint myself
I did not accept your way of anger,
Your judgements
You did not accept mine.

But now in 1975, when I am twenty-eight   75
Teresa Compean
I remember you.
Y sabes —
Te comprendo,

[7]Because I recognized a great truth then that made me a rebel, even though you
didn't realize it. [Author's note]

[8]And the rest of your friends / And the rest of our people. [Author's note]

[9]You and I. [Author's note]

[10]But we were together. [Author's note]

[11]And I conforming to my mother's wishes. [Author's note]

Es más, te respeto.   80
Y, si me permites,
Te nombro — "hermana."¹²

¹²And do you know what, I understand you. Even more, I respect you. And, if you
permit me, I name you my sister. [Author's note]

Engaging the Text

1. The speaker says that she didn't understand Teresa at the time of the incident
she describes. What didn't she understand, and why? How have her views of
Teresa and of herself changed since then? What seems to have brought about
this change?

2. What attitudes toward school and the majority culture do Teresa and the
speaker represent? What about the speaker's family? In what way are both girls
playing a game of "deadly defiance"?

3. Why do you think Hernández wrote this poem in both Spanish and English?
What does doing so say about the speaker's life? About her change of attitude
toward Teresa?

Exploring Connections

4. Compare and contrast the speaker's attitude toward school and her motivations with those of Richard Rodriguez (p. 541). Would it be fair to call this
speaker a "scholarship girl"?

5. Reread "Para Teresa," "Stephen Cruz" (p. 36), and Aurora Levins Morales's
"Class Poem" (p. 95) and "Child of the Americas" (p. 396). Write an essay on
"expectations" in these texts: specifically, identify what was expected of people
in these selections and why; discuss how expectations were sometimes conflicting; analyze how and why these people conformed to or resisted the expectations placed on them.

6. Compare the relationship of the speaker and Teresa in this poem with that of
Sylvia and Sugar in Toni Cade Bambara's "The Lesson" (p. 64).

Extending the Critical Context

7. Was there a person or group you disliked, feared, or fought with in elementary school? Has your understanding of your adversary or of your own motives
changed since then? If so, what brought about this change?

Learning to Read

Malcolm X

Born Malcolm Little on May 19, 1925, Malcolm X was one of the most articulate and powerful leaders of Black America during the 1960s. A street hustler convicted of robbery in 1946, he spent seven years in prison, where he educated himself and became a disciple of Elijah Muhammad, founder of the Black Muslim religion. In the days of the civil rights movement, Malcolm X emerged as the leading spokesman for Black separatism, a philosophy that urged Black Americans to cut political, social, and economic ties with the white community. After a pilgrimage to Mecca, the capital of the Muslim world, in 1964, he became an orthodox Muslim, adopted the Muslim name El Hajj Malik El-Shabazz, and distanced himself from the teachings of the Black Muslims. He was assassinated in 1965. In the following excerpt from his autobiography (1965) coauthored with Alex Haley and published the year of his death, Malcolm X describes his self-education.

It was because of my letters that I happened to stumble upon starting to acquire some kind of a homemade education.

I became increasingly frustrated at not being able to express what I wanted to convey in letters that I wrote, especially those to Mr. Elijah Muhammad.[1] In the street, I had been the most articulate hustler out there — I had commanded attention when I said something. But now, trying to write simple English, I not only wasn't articulate, I wasn't even functional. How would I sound writing in slang, the way I would *say* it, something such as, "Look, daddy, let me pull your coat about a cat, Elijah Muhammad —"

Many who today hear me somewhere in person, or on television, or those who read something I've said, will think I went to school far beyond the eighth grade. This impression is due entirely to my prison studies.

It had really begun back in the Charlestown Prison, when Bimbi[2] first made me feel envy of his stock of knowledge. Bimbi had always taken charge of any conversations he was in, and I had tried to emulate him. But every book I picked up had few sentences which didn't contain

---

[1]*Elijah Muhammad:* U.S. clergyman (1897–1975); leader of the Black Muslims, 1935–1975.

[2]*Bimbi:* a fellow inmate whose encyclopedic learning and verbal facility greatly impressed Malcolm X.

anywhere from one to nearly all of the words that might as well have been in Chinese. When I just skipped those words, of course, I really ended up with little idea of what the book said. So I had come to the Norfolk Prison Colony still going through only book-reading motions. Pretty soon, I would have quit even these motions, unless I had received the motivation that I did.

I saw that the best thing I could do was get hold of a dictionary — to study, to learn some words. I was lucky enough to reason also that I should try to improve my penmanship. It was sad. I couldn't even write in a straight line. It was both ideas together that moved me to request a dictionary along with some tablets and pencils from the Norfolk Prison Colony school.

I spent two days just riffling uncertainly through the dictionary's pages. I'd never realized so many words existed! I didn't know *which* words I needed to learn. Finally, just to start some kind of action, I began copying.

In my slow, painstaking, ragged handwriting, I copied into my tablet everything printed on that first page, down to the punctuation marks.

I believe it took me a day. Then, aloud, I read back, to myself, everything I'd written on the tablet. Over and over, aloud, to myself, I read my own handwriting.

I woke up the next morning, thinking about those words — immensely proud to realize that not only had I written so much at one time, but I'd written words that I never knew were in the world. Moreover, with a little effort, I also could remember what many of these words meant. I reviewed the words whose meanings I didn't remember. Funny thing, from the dictionary first page right now, that "aardvark" springs to my mind. The dictionary had a picture of it, a long-tailed, long-eared, burrowing African mammal, which lives off termites caught by sticking out its tongue as an anteater does for ants.

I was so fascinated that I went on — I copied the dictionary's next page. And the same experience came when I studied that. With every succeeding page, I also learned of people and places and events from history. Actually the dictionary is like a miniature encyclopedia. Finally the dictionary's A section had filled a whole tablet — and I went on into the B's. That was the way I started copying what eventually became the entire dictionary. It went a lot faster after so much practice helped me to pick up handwriting speed. Between what I wrote in my tablet, and writing letters, during the rest of my time in prison I would guess I wrote a million words.

I suppose it was inevitable that as my word-base broadened, I could for the first time pick up a book and read and now begin to understand what the book was saying. Anyone who has read a great deal can imagine the new world that opened. Let me tell you something: from then until I left that prison, in every free moment I had, if I was not reading in the library, I was reading on my bunk. You couldn't have gotten me out of books with a wedge. Between Mr. Muhammad's teachings, my correspondence, my visitors, . . . and my reading of books, months passed without my even thinking about being imprisoned. In fact, up to then, I never had been so truly free in my life.

The Norfolk Prison Colony's library was in the school building. A variety of classes was taught there by instructors who came from such places as Harvard and Boston universities. The weekly debates between inmate teams were also held in the school building. You would be astonished to know how worked up convict debaters and audiences would get over subjects like "Should Babies Be Fed Milk?"

Available on the prison library's shelves were books on just about every general subject. Much of the big private collection that Parkhurst[3] had willed to the prison was still in crates and boxes in the back of the library — thousands of old books. Some of them looked ancient: covers faded, old-time parchment-looking binding. Parkhurst . . . seemed to have been principally interested in history and religion. He had the money and the special interest to have a lot of books that you wouldn't have in a general circulation. Any college library would have been lucky to get that collection.

As you can imagine, especially in a prison where there was heavy emphasis on rehabilitation, an inmate was smiled upon if he demonstrated an unusually intense interest in books. There was a sizable number of well-read inmates, especially the popular debaters. Some were said by many to be practically walking encyclopedias. They were almost celebrities. No university would ask any student to devour literature as I did when this new world opened to me, of being able to read and *understand*.

I read more in my room than in the library itself. An inmate who 15 was known to read a lot could check out more than the permitted maximum number of books. I preferred reading in the total isolation of my own room.

When I had progressed to really serious reading, every night at about ten P.M. I would be outraged with the "lights out." It always seemed to catch me right in the middle of something engrossing.

Fortunately, right outside my door was a corridor light that cast a glow into my room. The glow was enough to read by, once my eyes adjusted to it. So when "lights out" came, I would sit on the floor where I could continue reading in that glow.

At one-hour intervals the night guards paced past every room. Each time I heard the approaching footsteps, I jumped into bed and feigned

[3]*Parkhurst:* Charles Henry Parkhurst (1842–1933); U.S. clergyman, reformer, and president of the Society for the Prevention of Crime.

sleep. And as soon as the guard passed, I got back out of bed onto the floor area of that light-glow, where I would read for another fifty-eight minutes — until the guard approached again. That went on until three or four every morning. Three or four hours of sleep a night was enough for me. Often in the years in the streets I had slept less than that.

The teachings of Mr. Muhammad stressed how history had been "whitened" — when white men had written history books, the black man simply had been left out. Mr. Muhammad couldn't have said anything that would have struck me much harder. I had never forgotten how when my class, me and all of those whites, had studied seventh-grade United States history back in Mason, the history of the Negro had been covered in one paragraph, and the teacher had gotten a big laugh with his joke, "Negroes' feet are so big that when they walk, they leave a hole in the ground."

This is one reason why Mr. Muhammad's teachings spread so swiftly   20
all over the United States, among *all* Negroes, whether or not they became followers of Mr. Muhammad. The teachings ring true — to every Negro. You can hardly show me a black adult in America — or a white one, for that matter — who knows from the history books anything like the truth about the black man's role. In my own case, once I heard of the "glorious history of the black man," I took special pains to hunt in the library for books that would inform me on details about black history.

I can remember accurately the very first set of books that really impressed me. I have since bought that set of books and I have it at home for my children to read as they grow up. It's called *Wonders of the World*. It's full of pictures of archeological finds, statues that depict, usually, non-European people.

I found books like Will Durant's[4] *Story of Civilization*. I read H. G. Wells'[5] *Outline of History. Souls of Black Folk* by W. E. B. Du Bois[6] gave me a glimpse into the black people's history before they came to this country. Carter G. Woodson's[7] *Negro History* opened my eyes about black empires before the black slave was brought to the United States, and the early Negro struggles for freedom.

J. A. Rogers'[8] three volumes of *Sex and Race* told about race-mixing before Christ's time; and Aesop being a black man who told fables;

[4]*Will Durant:* U.S. author and historian (1885–1981).
[5]*H. G. Wells:* English novelist and historian (1866–1946).
[6]*W. E. B. Du Bois:* William Edward Burghardt Du Bois, distinguished Black scholar, author, and activist (1868–1963). Du Bois was the first director of the NAACP and was an important figure in the Harlem Renaissance; his best-known book is *Souls of Black Folk*.
[7]*Carter G. Woodson:* distinguished African American historian (1875–1950); considered the father of Black history.
[8]*J. A. Rogers:* African American historian and journalist (1883–1965).

about Egypt's Pharaohs; about the great Coptic Christian Empires;[9] about Ethiopia, the earth's oldest continuous black civilization, as China is the oldest continuous civilization.

Mr. Muhammad's teaching about how the white man had been created led me to *Findings In Genetics* by Gregor Mendel.[10] (The dictionary's G section was where I had learned what "genetics" meant.) I really studied this book by the Austrian monk. Reading it over and over, especially certain sections, helped me to understand that if you started with a black man, a white man could be produced; but starting with a white man, you never could produce a black man — because the white chromosome is recessive. And since no one disputes that there was but one Original Man, the conclusion is clear.

During the last year or so, in the *New York Times*, Arnold 25 Toynbee[11] used the word "bleached" in describing the white man. His words were: "White (i.e., bleached) human beings of North European origin. . . ." Toynbee also referred to the European geographic area as only a peninsula of Asia. He said there is no such thing as Europe. And if you look at the globe, you will see for yourself that America is only an extension of Asia. (But at the same time Toynbee is among those who have helped to bleach history. He has written that Africa was the only continent that produced no history. He won't write that again. Every day now, the truth is coming to light.)

I never will forget how shocked I was when I began reading about slavery's total horror. It made such an impact upon me that it later became one of my favorite subjects when I became a minister of Mr. Muhammad's. The world's most monstrous crime, the sin and the blood on the white man's hands, are almost impossible to believe. Books like the one by Frederick Olmsted[12] opened my eyes to the horrors suffered when the slave was landed in the United States. The European woman, Fanny Kemble,[13] who had married a Southern white slaveowner, described how human beings were degraded. Of course I read *Uncle Tom's Cabin*.[14] In fact, I believe that's the only novel I have ever read since I started serious reading.

Parkhurst's collection also contained some bound pamphlets of the Abolitionist[15] Anti-Slavery Society of New England. I read descriptions

[9]*Coptic Christian Empire:* the domain of the Coptic Church, a native Egyptian Christian church that retains elements of its African origins.

[10]*Gregor Mendel:* Austrian monk, botanist, and pioneer in genetic research (1822–1884).

[11]*Arnold Toynbee:* English historian (1889–1975).

[12]*Frederick Olmsted:* Frederick Law Olmsted (1822–1903), U.S. landscape architect, city planner, and opponent of slavery.

[13]*Fanny Kemble:* Frances Anne Kemble, English actress and author (1809–1893); best known for her autobiographical *Journal of a Residence on a Georgia Plantation*, published in 1863 to win support in Britain for the abolitionist cause.

[14]*Uncle Tom's Cabin:* Harriet Beecher Stowe's 1852 antislavery novel.

[15]*abolitionist:* advocating the prohibition of slavery.

of atrocities, saw those illustrations of black slave women tied up and flogged with whips; of black mothers watching their babies being dragged off, never to be seen by their mothers again; of dogs after slaves, and of the fugitive slave catchers, evil white men with whips and clubs and chains and guns. I read about the slave preacher Nat Turner, who put the fear of God into the white slavemaster. Nat Turner wasn't going around preaching pie-in-the-sky and "non-violent" freedom for the black man. There in Virginia one night in 1831, Nat and seven other slaves started out at his master's home and through the night they went from one plantation "big house" to the next, killing, until by the next morning 57 white people were dead and Nat had about 70 slaves following him. White people, terrified for their lives, fled from their homes, locked themselves up in public buildings, hid in the woods, and some even left the state. A small army of soldiers took two months to catch and hang Nat Turner. Somewhere I have read where Nat Turner's example is said to have inspired John Brown[16] to invade Virginia and attack Harpers Ferry nearly thirty years later, with thirteen white men and five Negroes.

I read Herodotus,[17] "the father of History," or, rather, I read about him. And I read the histories of various nations, which opened my eyes gradually, then wider and wider, to how the whole world's white men had indeed acted like devils, pillaging and raping and bleeding and draining the whole world's non-white people. I remember, for instance, books such as Will Durant's *The Story of Oriental Civilization*, and Mahatma Gandhi's[18] accounts of the struggle to drive the British out of India.

Book after book showed me how the white man had brought upon the world's black, brown, red, and yellow peoples every variety of the sufferings of exploitation. I saw how since the sixteenth century, the so-called "Christian trader" white man began to ply the seas in his lust for Asian and African empires, and plunder, and power. I read, I saw, how the white man never has gone among the non-white peoples bearing the Cross in the true manner and spirit of Christ's teachings — meek, humble, and Christlike.

I perceived, as I read, how the collective white man had been actually nothing but a piratical opportunist who used Faustian machinations[19] to make his own Christianity his initial wedge in criminal conquests. First, always "religiously," he branded "heathen" and "pagan" labels upon ancient non-white cultures and civilizations. The

[16]*John Brown:* U.S. abolitionist (1800–1859); leader of an attack on Harpers Ferry, West Virginia, in 1859.

[17]*Herodotus:* early Greek historian (484?–425? B.C.).

[18]*Mahatma Gandhi:* Hindu religious leader, social reformer, and advocate of non-violence (1869–1948).

[19]*Faustian machinations:* evil plots or schemes. Faust was a legendary character who sold his soul to the devil for knowledge and power.

stage thus set, he then turned upon his non-white victims his weapons of war.

I read how, entering India — half a *billion* deeply religious brown people — the British white man, by 1759, through promises, trickery, and manipulations, controlled much of India through Great Britain's East India Company. The parasitical British administration kept tentacling out to half of the sub-continent. In 1857, some of the desperate people of India finally mutinied — and, excepting the African slave trade, nowhere has history recorded any more unnecessary bestial and ruthless human carnage than the British suppression of the non-white Indian people.

Over 115 million African blacks — close to the 1930's population of the United States — were murdered or enslaved during the slave trade. And I read how when the slave market was glutted, the cannibalistic white powers of Europe next carved up, as their colonies, the richest areas of the black continent. And Europe's chancelleries for the next century played a chess game of naked exploitation and power from Cape Horn to Cairo.

Ten guards and the warden couldn't have torn me out of those books. Not even Elijah Muhammad could have been more eloquent than those books were in providing indisputable proof that the collective white man had acted like a devil in virtually every contact he had with the world's collective non-white man. I listen today to the radio, and watch television, and read the headlines about the collective white man's fear and tension concerning China. When the white man professes ignorance about why the Chinese hate him so, my mind can't help flashing back to what I read, there in prison, about how the blood forebears of this same white man raped China at a time when China was trusting and helpless. Those original white "Christian traders" sent into China millions of pounds of opium. By 1839, so many of the Chinese were addicts that China's desperate government destroyed twenty thousand chests of opium. The first Opium War[20] was promptly declared by the white man. Imagine! Declaring *war* upon someone who objects to being narcotized! The Chinese were severely beaten, with Chinese-invented gunpowder.

The Treaty of Nanking made China pay the British white man for the destroyed opium; forced open China's major ports to British trade; forced China to abandon Hong Kong; fixed China's import tariffs so low that cheap British articles soon flooded in, maiming China's industrial development.

After a second Opium War, the Tientsin Treaties legalized the ravaging opium trade, legalized a British-French-American control of   35

[20]*Opium War:* 1839–1842 war between Britain and China that ended with China's cession of Hong Kong to British rule.

China's customs. China tried delaying that Treaty's ratification; Peking was looted and burned.

"Kill the foreign white devils!" was the 1901 Chinese war cry in the Boxer Rebellion.[21] Losing again, this time the Chinese were driven from Peking's choicest areas. The vicious, arrogant white man put up the famous signs, "Chinese and dogs not allowed."

Red China after World War II closed its doors to the Western white world. Massive Chinese agricultural, scientific, and industrial efforts are described in a book that *Life* magazine recently published. Some observers inside Red China have reported that the world never has known such a hate-white campaign as is now going on in this non-white country where, present birth-rates continuing, in fifty more years Chinese will be half the earth's population. And it seems that some Chinese chickens will soon come home to roost, with China's recent successful nuclear tests.

Let us face reality. We can see in the United Nations a new world order being shaped, along color lines — an alliance among the non-plained not long ago that in the United Nations "a skin game"[23] was being played. He was right. He was facing reality. A "skin game" *is* being played. But Ambassador Stevenson sounded like Jesse James accusing the marshal of carrying a gun. Because who in the world's history ever has played a worse "skin game" than the white man?

Mr. Muhammad, to whom I was writing daily, had no idea of what a new world had opened up to me through my efforts to document his teachings in books.

When I discovered philosophy, I tried to touch all the landmarks of   40 philosophical development. Gradually, I read most of the old philosophers, Occidental and Oriental. The Oriental philosophers were the ones I came to prefer; finally, my impression was that most Occidental philosophy had largely been borrowed from the Oriental thinkers. Socrates, for instance, traveled in Egypt. Some sources even say that Socrates was initiated into some of the Egyptian mysteries. Obviously Socrates got some of his wisdom among the East's wise men.

I have often reflected upon the new vistas that reading opened to me. I knew right there in prison that reading had changed forever the course of my life. As I see it today, the ability to read awoke inside me some long dormant craving to be mentally alive. I certainly wasn't seeking any degree, the way a college confers a status symbol upon its

[21]*Boxer Rebellion:* the 1898–1900 uprising by members of a secret Chinese society who opposed foreign influence in Chinese affairs.

[22]*Adlai Stevenson:* U.S. politician (1900–1965); Democratic candidate for the presidency in 1952 and 1956.

[23]*skin game:* a dishonest or fraudulent scheme, business operation, or trick, with the added reference in this instance to skin color.

students. My homemade education gave me, with every additional book that I read, a little bit more sensitivity to the deafness, dumbness, and blindness that was afflicting the black race in America. Not long ago, an English writer telephoned me from London, asking questions. One was, "What's your alma mater?" I told him, "Books." You will never catch me with a free fifteen minutes in which I'm not studying something I feel might be able to help the black man.

Yesterday I spoke in London, and both ways on the plane across the Atlantic I was studying a document about how the United Nations proposes to insure the human rights of the oppressed minorities of the world. The American black man is the world's most shameful case of minority oppression. What makes the black man think of himself as only an internal United States issue is just a catch-phrase, two words, "civil rights." How is the black man going to get "civil rights" before first he wins his *human* rights? If the American black man will start thinking about his *human* rights, and then start thinking of himself as part of one of the world's great peoples, he will see he has a case for the United Nations.

I can't think of a better case! Four hundred years of black blood and sweat invested here in America, and the white man still has the black man begging for what every immigrant fresh off the ship can take for granted the minute he walks down the gangplank.

But I'm digressing. I told the Englishman that my alma mater was books, a good library. Every time I catch a plane, I have with me a book that I want to read — and that's a lot of books these days. If I weren't out here every day battling the white man, I could spend the rest of my life reading, just satisfying my curiosity — because you can hardly mention anything I'm not curious about. I don't think anybody ever got more out of going to prison than I did. In fact, prison enabled me to study far more intensively than I would have if my life had gone differently and I had attended some college. I imagine that one of the biggest troubles with colleges is there are too many distractions, too much panty-raiding, fraternities, and boola-boola and all of that. Where else but in a prison could I have attacked my ignorance by being able to study intensely sometimes as much as fifteen hours a day?

Engaging the Text

1. What motivated Malcolm X to educate himself?

2. What kind of knowledge did Malcolm X gain by learning to read? How did this knowledge free or empower him?

3. Some readers are offended by the strength of Malcolm X's accusations and by his grouping of all members of a given race into "collectives." Given the history of racial injustice he recounts here, do you feel he is justified in taking such a position?

Exploring Connections

4. Compare and contrast Malcolm X's views on the meaning and purpose of education — or on the value and nature of reading — with those of Richard Rodriguez (p. 541). How can you account for the differences in their attitudes?

5. Read or review "From a Native Daughter" by Haunani-Kay Trask (p. 118). Compare and contrast her account of how white historians rewrote Hawaiian history with Malcolm X's description of "whitened" history. What similarities do you see in the motives or methods of historians in these two cases? To what extent do you trust Trask's and Malcolm X's versions of history, and why?

6. Imagine that Theodore Sizer (p. 496), Mike Rose (p. 511), Richard Rodriguez (p. 541), and Malcolm X have been appointed to redesign American education. Working in groups, role-play a meeting in which the committee attempts to reach consensus on its recommendations. Report to the class the results of the committee's deliberations and discuss them.

Extending the Critical Context

7. Survey some typical elementary or secondary school textbooks to test the currency of Malcolm X's charge that the educational establishment presents a "whitened" view of America. What view of America is presently being projected in public school history and social science texts?

8. Go to the library and read one page of the dictionary chosen at random. Study the meanings of any unfamiliar words and follow up on the information on your page by consulting encyclopedias, books, or articles. Let yourself be guided by chance and by your interests. After you've tried this experiment, discuss in class the benefits and drawbacks of an unsystematic self-education like Malcolm X's.

Connected Education for Women

BLYTHE MCVICKER CLINCHY,
MARY FIELD BELENKY,
NANCY GOLDBERGER,
AND JILL MATTUCK TARULE

The authors of this article argue that higher education in the United States unnecessarily intimidates and alienates women students, that schools usually fail to teach in the productive and humane ways they could. They base their conclusions on interviews with more than a hundred women in widely diverse colleges and adult education pro-

grams; the comments by these women suggest that many traditional teaching techniques can actually be significant barriers to learning. The authors are all psychologists — Blythe Clinchy at Wellesley College, Mary Belenky at the University of Vermont, Nancy Goldberger at the Austin Riggs Center in Massachusetts, and Jill Tarule at Lesley College. The article from which this selection is excerpted appeared in the Journal of Education *in 1985. The article was followed in 1986 by* Women's Ways of Knowing: The Development of Self, Voice, and Mind, *by the same authors.*

Most of the institutions of higher education in this country were designed by men, and most continue to be run by men. In recent years feminist teachers and scholars have begun to question the structure, the curriculum, and the pedagogical practices of these institutions, and they have put forth useful proposals for change (e.g., Bowles & Duelli Klein, 1983; Martin, 1984; Nicholson, 1980; Rich, 1979; Spanier, Bloom, & Borovik, 1984). But in order to design an education appropriate for women we must learn about the academic experiences of ordinary women, women who are, in most cases, neither teachers nor scholars nor even feminists, but simply students.

In a project on "Education for Women's Development," supported by the Fund for the Improvement of Post-secondary Education, we asked 135 ordinary women to share their educational experiences with us. The women were drawn from three private liberal arts colleges (a women's college, an "early college" which admits younger students, and a progressive coeducational college), an inner-city community college, an urban public high school, two adult education programs, and three rural human service agencies which we call "invisible colleges." The women ranged in age from 16 to 65 and came from a variety of ethnic, class, and religious backgrounds. Some were single, some divorced, some married. Many had borne and raised children.

In individual interviews we asked each woman what she thought would stay with her about her experiences in the school or program she attended. We asked her to tell us about specific academic and non-academic experiences, about good and bad teachers, good and bad assignments, good and bad programs or courses. We asked her whether she thought that her participation in the program had changed the way she thought about herself or the world. We asked: "In your learning here, have you come across an idea that made you see things differently?" "What has been most helpful to you about this place?" "Are there things it doesn't provide that are important to you? Things you would like to learn that you can't learn here?" Finally, we asked, "Looking back over your whole life, can you tell us about a really powerful learning experience that you've had, in or out of school?"

The women's responses were, of course, quite diverse, but as we read and reread the women's accounts of what they had learned and failed to learn, of how they liked to learn and how they had been forced to learn, some common themes emerged, themes which may be distinctively, although surely not exclusively, feminine. . . .

Confirmation of the Self as Knower

In thinking about the education of women, Adrienne Rich[1] writes, "Suppose we were to ask ourselves, simply: What does a woman need to know?" (Rich, 1979, p. 240). Our interviews have convinced us that every woman, regardless of age, social class, ethnicity, and academic achievement, needs to know that she is capable of intelligent thought, and she needs to know it right away. Perhaps men learn this lesson before going to college, or perhaps they can wait until they have "proved themselves" to hear it; we do not know. We do know that many of the women we interviewed had not yet learned it.

Most of them report that they have frequently been treated as if they were stupid. This is especially true of the less privileged. Consider, for example, the case of Lillian, a student at one of the invisible colleges. When Lillian's infant son suffered an attack of projectile vomiting, she called her pediatrician. "Don't worry about it," he said. Instead of respecting her concern, he dismissed it. Lillian wanted respect, and she wanted information. "I wasn't asking for the complete history of projectile vomiting," she says.

> I just really wanted an explanation, simple, something like you would give a child if they asked you a question like where do babies come from. You don't give them a whole routine, just a piece of it, and let them deal with that. You don't say, "Never mind." You don't patronize them. I don't do that with my own daughter, so I don't like to be treated like that. . . . I really wanted to be dealt with as a person, not just a hysterical mother, not even as a mother, as just another person who was halfway intelligent.

Lillian's encounters with authority (teachers, bosses, doctors, priests, bureaucrats, and policemen) have taught her that "experts" usually attempt to assert dominance over less knowledgeable people either by assaulting them with information or by withholding information. But her experience as a mother has provided her with a different model, a model we call "connected education," in which the expert (parent) examines the needs and capacities of the learner (child) and composes a message that is, in Jerome Bruner's[2] felicitous term, "courteous" to the learner. Although Lillian knows more than her son knows, she does not think she is better than he. She does not want to exert power

---

[1]*Adrienne Rich:* see p. 307.
[2]*Jerome Bruner:* educational psychologist and learning theorist (b. 1915).

over him. She wants to help him on his own terms, and she needs experts who will do the same for her.

Fortunately, a public health clinic for children, run on the connected teaching model, opened up in Lillian's area. The director of the clinic defines the clinic's job not as "teaching mothers how to raise children," but as "trying to help mothers do what they need to do." Mothers who use the clinic are astonished to discover that members of the staff, nearly all of them women, believe in them. "It makes me realize I'm all right," says one. "I never knew that." Another says, "I walk out of there feeling so good. I feel like I could tame the whole world. I could just do anything." And Lillian said, "They seemed to have trust in me, and I guess I needed that, because I hadn't had that in a long time, that feeling like my parents gave me, that I was — no questions asked — trusted."

What these women need and what the clinic provides, perhaps more clearly, consistently, and sincerely than any other institution we sampled, is confirmation that they can be trusted to know and to learn. Given confirmation, they feel they can "just do anything." Lacking it, as one said, they are "crippled," and "just can't function." Most of the women we interviewed made it clear that they do not wish to be told merely that they have the "capacity" or the "potential" to *become* knowledgeable or wise. They need to know that they already know something (although by no means everything), that there is something good inside them. They worry that there isn't. . . .

Some women found the confirmation they needed in . . . college. 10 One, for example, said that although she had always done well in school, no one had ever told her that she was intelligent until she came to college. There, "people say, 'Well, you know, you're a pretty smart person.' If people say that to you enough you have to figure that they know at least a little of what they're talking about."

A classmate, however, interviewed toward the end of her first year, tells a different story. Although she had entered college with SAT scores in the high 600s, she feels, nevertheless, "I've got to be the dumbest girl here." Her high school teachers doled out "constant praise," but in college the teachers are silent.

> You need a little bit of praise to keep you going. If you get an idea that the teacher likes what you're doing it helps you go on more, whereas most of my courses the teachers are kind of — They don't say bad, they don't say good, so you start having doubts and thinking, "Well, if he doesn't say something nice, he must not like it." And you just get into such a rut where you can't do anything. There's just an extreme lack of praise around here.

When she and her friends entered college, she says, "we all had a lot of self-esteem, and we didn't really think about it, we just knew we could do it. Whereas now, it's totally different." In high school they were stars; in this highly competitive college they are just average.

> If I could just think to myself that I've done something really exceptionally good, 'cause sometimes I feel like I'm getting lost in the crowd. If I could just write maybe one paper and have a teacher say, "Hey, that was really, really good," I think that would help a lot.

Would the approval have to come from a teacher? asks the interviewer. Could it not come from within her? "Not at this point," says the student. "It's been so far pushed down it couldn't come back up by itself."

In the masculine myth, confirmation comes not at the beginning of education but at the end. Confirmation as a thinker and membership in a community of thinkers come as the climax of Perry's[3] (1970) story of intellectual development in the college years. The student learns, according to Perry, that "we must all stand judgment," and that he must earn "the privilege of having [his] ideas respected" (Perry, 1970, p. 33). Having proved beyond reasonable doubt that he has learned to think in complex, contextual ways, the young man is admitted to the fraternity of powerful knowers. . . . Doubt precedes belief, separation leads to connection. The weak become powerful, the inferiors join their superiors. At traditional, hierarchically organized institutions, run by powerful judges charged with enforcing the high standards of their disciplines and administering justice through "blind" evaluation of the students' work without respect to the students' persons, this may well be the "natural" course of development. But, in an institution which placed care and understanding of persons, rather than impersonal standards, at its center, development might take a different course. And women's development, in particular, might proceed with less pain.

Knowing the Realities

In considering how to design an education appropriate for women, suppose we were to begin by asking, simply: what does a woman know? Traditional courses do not begin there. They begin not with the student's knowledge but with the teacher's knowledge. The courses are about the culture's questions, questions fished out of the "mainstream" of the disciplines. If the student is female, her questions are unlikely to intersect with the culture's questions, since women, paddling in the bywaters of the culture, have had little to do with positing the culture's questions or designing the agendas of the disciplines (See, e.g., Harding & Hintikka, 1983; Reinharz, 1979; Sherman & Beck, 1979; Smith, 1974).

[3]*Perry:* William Perry, educational psychologist; Perry theorized that college students' thinking follows predictable patterns of development.

Cynthia, an alumna of a traditional liberal arts college, said that, although she had enjoyed the "austerity" of the college curriculum and had done well, she had been lonely and sad throughout the four years. At the time, she thought her problems were "just personal," but lately she has begun to wonder if the curriculum might have contributed to her depression. She had been reading an essay by E. B. White about a battle between an old gander and a younger, stronger gander.

> The young male goose was stronger, and they have this heroic battle. And the older goose at the end of the story is seen leaping off to lick his wounds somewhere in a patch of sun in a field. And it struck me that E. B. White saw everything in terms of great struggles — these great clashes between opposing forces — and that's what life was like, this — uh — sort of larger than life thing.

The larger-than-life knowledge contained in the college curriculum seemed to her at the time the only respectable form of knowledge, but now that she has more sense of herself as a woman, it strikes her as a distinctively masculine perspective.

> You know, it's not a battle between the gods that concerns women. Women are concerned with how you get through life from minute to minute. What each little teeny tiny incident — how it can affect everything else you do. Women see things close at hand and are more concerned with minutiae. I think I haven't ever seen things in quite this way, been quite as aware of the fun I could have with introspection and observation of daily life.

This feminine mode "seems realer, somehow," to Cynthia. . . .

Most of the women we interviewed were drawn to the sort of knowledge that comes from firsthand observation, and most of the educational institutions they attended emphasized abstract "out-of-context learning" (Cole, Gay, Glick, & Sharp, 1971). We asked one young woman from one such institution to tell us about a good paper that she had written. She said she hadn't written many good papers, but there was one that she really liked.

> It was for a writing course. We were allowed to write about whatever we wanted. And I just described a place where I had worked — the social structure and all the cattiness — and I really enjoyed that. I was just so excited about what I was writing, and I thought it was just the greatest thing to read, and I sent copies to friends I had worked with, and they just loved it.

But the teacher didn't. "He didn't think it was an important issue. He said it was well written, but lacked content, whatever that means [laughs]."

The interviewer asked, "How about a bad paper?"

> There was one I wrote analyzing a book that I hadn't finished. That wasn't too good. You know, it's really easy, though, to read part of a

book and then pick up a few sources and annotate everything. I just thought it was horrible. I just knew that I didn't know what I was talking about, and I think it showed.

But apparently it didn't; the teacher liked the paper. The student's standards conflicted with the teacher's. When she wrote out of her own experience she felt she knew what she was talking about, but the teacher felt the paper wasn't about anything. When she pasted together a mess of undigested secondhand information, he was satisfied.

Most of the women we interviewed were not opposed to abstraction. They find concepts useful as ways of making meaning of their experiences. But they balk when the abstractions precede the experiences or push them out entirely. Even the women who were extraordinarily adept at abstract reasoning preferred to start from personal experience. Mary Lou is one of them. 20

> I think women care about things that relate to their lives personally. I think the more involvement they have in something that affects them personally the more they're going to explore it and the more they're going to be able to give and to get out of it. I think that [men] — because they're male they haven't been put down all the time for their sex, so they can go into any subject with confidence, saying, "I can learn about this" or "I have the intellect to understand this." Whereas I think women don't deal with things that way. I think they break down an issue and pick out what it is about it that has happened to them, or they can relate to in some way, and that's how they start to explore it. . . .

Judith, a staff member at the children's health clinic and one of our most highly educated and cerebral informants, says, "I don't like getting things totally out of a book. I really like having some real experience of it myself." Much that we think we know, Judith says, we know only in the form of "general concepts." "We don't really know it." "In the most exciting kind of learning people are allowed to go right down to rock bottom and really look at these concepts and find out what their experience has been with it, what they know about it." Judith has had this sort of intense conversation in informal sessions, but never in school. In school, she says, "you're supposed to learn it the way somebody else sees it."

Usually, we are supposed to learn it the way men see it. Men move quickly to impose their own conceptual schemes on the experience of women, says the French feminist writer Marguerite Duras (1973). These schemes do not help women make sense of their experience; they extinguish the experience. . . .

Freedom, Structure, and the Tyranny of Expectation

In analyzing each woman's interview, we asked: Who or what, in this woman's eyes, defines the goals, sets the pace, and evaluates the outcomes of her behavior? In terms of education, we asked: To what degree does she perceive the tasks, the timetable, and the standards as imposed by the institution, to what degree by herself, and with what consequences?

Students from the most prestigious and academically "demanding" institutions complained most eloquently about the effects of external structure. Some students from the women's college, for instance, said that they had never learned to make choices; the college made the choices for them. An alumna:

> [In college] it's very set up for you. Do your assignments, and you'll make the grade. But when you get out, it's not really like that. You don't know quite what to do to succeed in your job. It's not clear-cut. You have to make sense of a lot of things that are not well-organized. You have to find out what's important. You have to establish priorities. And I didn't know how to do that.

Bridget's story illustrates what can happen when good girls go to good colleges. Like most girls in our society, Bridget was raised to be "nice." Two years out of college, niceness remains a problem: 25

> I'm constantly having to fight this natural tendency I have to be a "nice person." I've been mad at myself for being too nice for a long time, and yet, at the same time, I know I can get away with murder sometimes, because I'm so nice. I'm still very afraid of not being nice, very afraid.

Nice girls fulfill other people's expectations. "My parents always expected me to do things," Bridget says. Bridget thinks the women's college was wrong for her, because it expected too much: "It was too competitive and too demanding. I'm a very conscientious person, and I found myself always trying to do the work."

In high school Bridget consistently achieved top marks without working very hard. At college she continued to take it easy, and her grades at the end of the first semester were terrible. In second semester she tried a new approach:

> I worked my butt off. I have never been so intense and disciplined working before. I ended up getting the second highest grade in the economics final, coming up from [the bottom]. I memorized every goddamn picture there was in art history. I spent three hours every day going over those pictures. For three hours every day I studied French; for three hours every day I studied art; and for three hours every day I ground myself through economics.

At the end of each day she went swimming to loosen her constipated brain:

> I swam a mile every day, and it wasn't until the end of that mile that I finally felt my muscles begin to loosen up, and my head was finally

clear of all this crap that I was stuffing it full of. That was probably the peak of my career at the college in terms of beating the system.

Bridget portrays herself during the next three terms as a drudge, motivated by duty rather than desire (Weil, 1951), slogging through dull courses in order to fulfill various "distribution requirements" and prepare herself for a successful career. But, although she worked constantly, she was always "behind" and she got mediocre grades. . . .

Bridget and other students at the women's college and other equally "demanding" institutions feel, especially in retrospect, that their intellectual development was stunted rather than nourished by the incessant academic pressure. "Ever since leaving college," Bridget says, "my joy in reading and my desire to read has increased incredibly. I'm absolutely thrilled to be learning what I want to learn. It's been like a renaissance."

The teachers in these colleges do not intend, of course, to inhibit their students' intellectual development. Some are especially kind and concerned and accessible, but this only makes it worse. It is especially difficult for good girls to disobey good parents. Teachers, as well as students, yearn for an atmosphere less academic and more intellectual, but the teachers are unable to reduce the pressure and the students are unable to resist it. Both teachers and students are proud of the institution's "high standards," and many of them (students as well as teachers) believe that the standards lure the students into performing at the top of their capacities.

These standards play a major role in Perry's (1970) account of intellectual development in college. It is in attempting to discern the standards and to meet them that the student is propelled into independent contextual thinking. But for nice girls like Bridget the standards seem to act more as impediments than as goads to independent thinking, distracting their attention from the intellectual substance of the work and transforming their efforts to learn into efforts to please.

Women like Bridget, still struggling to formulate their own purposes and their own standards, although eager for formal graduate training in order to pursue professional careers, are fearful of entering another institution which may try and may succeed in shaping them according to its standards. Deborah, on the eve of entering graduate school after a delay of two years, says:

> I'm afraid of some clashes between what I want to do and what they want me to do, and I'm not sure how those will be resolved, not understanding the system. It may take me a semester to find out how you don't do what they're asking you to do.

Gretchen, in her senior year at college, already accepted at a prestigious medical school, decides to defer enrollment for a year.

I have to find myself absolutely alone for a while. I don't feel as if I'm gonna *last* through another five years of school unless I sit back and find for myself or remind myself that I am an independent person and I am defined by my own standards and not by these external standards. Right now I feel sort of very wishy-washy about myself, and that's because I've been getting different sorts of signals from different people or institutions which have been evaluating me. And I've been letting these things sort of cloud over my own feelings about myself. Sort of refractional crystallization. Sort of getting rid of the dirt and the garbage and just sort of crystallizing out what is me. I want to spend a year not letting myself be evaluated by other people's standards.

Judith is eager to improve her skills as a therapist, but she dreads a 35 repetition of her graduate school experience.

I worry about getting further analytic training, 'cause you're supposed to learn it the way that somebody else sees it. It would be different if I could find something — a program — where I was helped to see things in my own way. That would be gold.

Some of the women we talked with had discovered "gold" in their institutions. We asked a 27-year-old mother of two what had been most helpful to her about the adult program she was attending. "The faculty not being above us, not being the boss," she said.

Making our own decisions and writing our own curriculum. Making your own decisions — that's what's most important. And it's real hard at first, when you're not used to it. You expect, "Well, what do we do next?" It developed me a lot more in thinking, "What is it that I want?" instead of listening to what people tell me.

Another student in the same program spoke with appreciation of how the teacher who guided her independent study project respected her working rhythm, instead of imposing an arbitrary timetable.

When I would get stuck in the middle of my studies — as I always did — I never got any silly notes from [the teacher] saying, "Now, now, you must produce your stuff on time, otherwise blah blah blah." He would just say, "Well, I guess you're stuck. You'll get over it." He gave me a lot of space and a lot of guidance.

A young woman painter is grateful for the freedom and support offered by the coeducational progressive college she attends. The college has allowed her to develop her "own sort of natural working habit."

I choke under pressure, but I do very well under pressures that I've created, goals that I establish, so the college is perfect for me, because there's not a lot of pressure, and there's a tremendous amount of time to work on your own.

The college exempts her from formal classes during her senior year and provides her with a studio. "I'm able to work all day and all night on my own. If I was meeting with classes all the time, and if there was a different attitude about work and grades and competition, I'd hate painting." The college puts little emphasis on grades.

> When something really attracts you, you can really get obsessive about it. There's a lot of freedom, trusting that people are going to want to work, that people have instincts and will find out what they want to do and how they're going to go about doing it. But with teachers that are knowledgeable and can give you guidance and support and believe in you.

Some of the students at the highly structured, high-pressure institu-40 tions believed that without the pressure they would "go bad," as one put it, or "go dead," as another said. They would sleep late, cut classes, and stop working. [Some] who moved temporarily into less pressured environments did indeed go bad. They may have cut more classes and they certainly spent less time on assigned work. But they did not go dead; they emerged as more active agents in their own learning. Jeanne Block (1984) has written that because girls in our society are raised to accommodate to existing structures they need colleges which will help set them free, but they also need strong support in moving toward freedom. . . .

Connected Teaching

Not one of the women we interviewed advocated the traditional form of education characterized by Paulo Freire[4] as a "banking model," in which the teacher's role is "to 'fill' the students by making deposits of information which he considers to constitute true knowledge," and the student's job is merely to "store the deposits" (Freire, 1971, p. 60). Even a woman who, heavily dependent upon knowledge received from authorities, said, "I just want to listen to the instructor" said, in almost the next breath, "I don't really think that anybody can put something into someone that isn't there. It has to be there."

Many women expressed — some firmly, some shakily — this belief that they possessed latent knowledge. The kind of teacher they praised and the kind they yearned for was a teacher who would help them articulate and expand their latent knowledge: a midwife-teacher. The midwife-teacher is the opposite of the banker-teacher. While the bank clerk deposits knowledge in the learner's head, the midwife draws it out. She assists the students in giving birth to their own ideas, in making their own tacit knowledge explicit and elaborating it.

Here are some examples of women talking about their midwife-teachers: "She helped me to be able to say what I wanted to say." "He

[4]*Paulo Freire:* noted Brazilian educator, philosopher, and political activist (b. 1921).

said to me, 'What you're thinking is fine, but think more.' " "She let me do what I wanted to do [with my poetry] and helped me do it and pushed it further." "She told me, 'Go home and write what you feel, because then you can look at it and see how you felt.' " "I told her that I'd had this dream that inspired my painting, and she said, 'Keep drawing from that dream until you can't draw from it any more.' "

In Freire's banking model the teacher constructs knowledge in private and talks about it in public, so that the students may store it. In the connected education model, as in Freire's "problem-posing" model, teacher and students construct knowledge together. Several women cherished memories of classes like this. One woman told us about a connected class that had occurred by accident. Usually, she said, her English teacher "just hands you his thoughts," but on one memorable occasion he allowed a discussion to erupt.

> We were all raising our hands and talking about I forget what book, and some of the students brought up things that he hadn't thought about that made him see it in a whole different way, and he was really excited, and we all came to a conclusion that none of us had started out with. We came up with an answer to a question we thought was unanswerable in the beginning, and it just made you all feel really good when you walked out of class. You felt you had accomplished something and that you understood the book. And he was pleased, too.

At the next class meeting, however, the teacher had reverted to the banking mode. "I guess he doesn't like that method," the student said.

The connected class provides a culture in which ideas can grow. It is, in the writer Peter Elbow's[5] (1973) words, a "yoghurt" class, as opposed to a "movie" class. Members of the connected class are not mere spectators; they actively nurture each other's ideas. A senior at the women's college tries to explain what goes on in her art history seminar: "Somebody will say, 'Well, do you mean . . . ?' and then somebody else says, 'No, I mean . . .' It's clarifying." The teacher has fostered a special atmosphere in the class.

> It's allowing everyone to voice things that they think are uncertain. It's allowing people to realize that they're not stupid for questioning things. It's okay to say, "Why" or "How" or "What." I think it's important to let everybody voice their uncertainties.

In a connected class no one apologizes for uncertainty. It is assumed that evolving thought must be tentative.

Connected classes seem to work best when members of the group meet over a long period of time and get to know each other well. The early college, a small college in which most classes are conducted as seminars, came closest to fulfilling these conditions. One of the women

[5]*Peter Elbow:* American educator (b. 1935) specializing in writing instruction.

we interviewed attended the early college for two years and then transferred to a larger school. There she enrolled in a seminar on modern British poetry, one of her favorite topics. "It was awful," she says. "The people didn't know how to talk about anything. They didn't know how to share ideas. It was always an argument. It wasn't an idea to be developed, to be explored." At the early college, students came to know their classmates' styles of thinking. "It was like a family group trying to work out a family problem, except it was an idea." In most colleges there is no chance to form family groups. Each course starts with a new cast of characters, runs for 13 weeks or so, and then disperses.

In a community, unlike a hierarchy, people get to know each other. They do not act as representatives of positions to be attacked or defended or as occupants of roles but as individuals with particular modes of thinking. A first-year student remarked that her editing group composed of three classmates in a writing course was not working: "We just talk about commas and junk like that."

> I had a peer editing group in high school, and it was terrific. But we all knew each other inside out, so you knew what each person was trying to do in her writing, and you knew what kinds of criticisms helped her and what kind hurt her feelings. You can't really help if you don't know people.

Unless she knows the critic personally and the critic knows her personally, she says, she finds criticism of her work "hurtful, but not helpful."

Connected teaching is personal. Connected teachers present themselves as genuine, flawed human beings. They allow students to observe the imperfect processes of their thinking. Connected teachers take a personal interest in their students. They want to know how each individual student is thinking. But connected teaching is not "soft." It is rigorous. And it is objective, although not coldly impersonal.

Connected teachers practice a sophisticated form of what we call "connected knowing," a "technique of *disciplined* subjectivity" (Erikson, 1964) requiring them to "systematically empathize" with their students (Wilson, 1977, p. 259). They try to practice what Peter Elbow (1973, p. 171) calls "projection in the good sense," using their own reactions to the material the class is studying to formulate hypotheses about the students' reactions.

Cynthia, an alumna quoted earlier, told us about an English 50 teacher who could serve as an ideal prototype.

> This woman and her method of teaching and her attitude towards life moved me very much. She was so rigorous. She wanted things always to add up. You had to have a system and you had to make everything work. You had to assume that there was a purpose to everything the artist did. And if something seemed odd, you couldn't overlook it or ignore it or throw it out.

This teacher was thoroughly "objective" in treating the students' responses as real and independent of her own.

> She was intensely, genuinely interested in everybody's feelings about things. She asked a question and wanted to know what your response was. She wanted to know because she wanted to see what sort of effect this writing was having. She wasn't using us as a sounding board for her own feelings about things. She really wanted to know. . . .

Cynthia's English teacher does not treat her own experience of the material under study as primary, and she does not assume that her students experience the material as she does; this would be undisciplined subjectivity or, as Elbow (1973, p. 171) puts it, "projection in the bad sense." She "really wants to know" how the students are experiencing the material. . . .

Belief, Doubt, and Development

Midwives are believers. They trust their students' thinking and encourage them to expand it. But in the psychological literature concerning the factors promoting cognitive development, doubt has played a more prominent role than belief and the adversarial model has dominated institutions of higher education (Rich, 1979). In order to stimulate cognitive growth, according to this model, the teacher should point out flaws in the students' thinking, put forth opposing notions, encourage debate, and challenge students to defend their ideas. One should attempt to induce cognitive conflict in students' minds. We do not deny that cognitive conflict can act as an impetus to growth, but in all our interviews only a handful of women described a powerful and positive learning experience in which a teacher challenged their ideas in this fashion. The women did mention such incidents, but they did not describe them as occasions for cognitive growth. On the whole, women found the experience of being doubted debilitating, rather than energizing.

Because so many women are already filled with self-doubt, doubts imposed from outside seem at best redundant ("I'm always reprimanding myself"), and at worst destructive, confirming their own sense of themselves as inadequate knowers. The doubting model, then, may be peculiarly inappropriate for women (although we are not convinced that it is appropriate for men, either).

We believe that most women want and need an education in which 55 connection is emphasized over separation, understanding and acceptance over judgment and assessment, and collaboration over debate. They need a curriculum which accords respect to and allows time for the knowledge that emerges from firsthand experience. They need a system which, instead of imposing its own expectations and arbitrary requirements, helps them to define their own questions and evolve their own patterns of work for pursuing these questions. These are the lessons we think we have learned in listening to ordinary women.

References

Block, J. (1984). Gender differences and implications for educational policy. In *Sex role identity and ego development* (pp. 207–253). San Francisco: Jossey-Bass.

Bowles, G., & Duelli Klein, R. (1983). *Theories of women's studies.* London: Routledge & Kegan Paul.

Cole, M., Gay, J., Glick, J., & Sharp, D. (1971). *The cultural context of learning and thinking.* New York: Basic Books.

Duras, M. (1981). Smothered creativity. In E. Marks & I. de Courtivron (Eds.), *New French feminisms* (pp. 111–114). New York: Schocken. (Original work published 1973)

Elbow, P. (1973). *Writing without teachers.* London: Oxford University Press.

Erikson, E. (1964). On the nature of clinical evidence. In E. Erikson, *Insight and responsibility* (pp. 49–80). New York: Norton.

Freire, P. (1971). *Pedagogy of the oppressed.* New York: Seaview.

Harding, S., & Hintikka, M. B. (Eds.). (1983). *Discovering reality.* Dordrecht, Holland: Reidel.

Martin, J. (1984). Bringing women into educational thought. *Educational Theory, 34,* 341–353.

Nicholson, L. (1980). Women and schooling. *Educational Theory, 30,* 225–233.

Perry, W. (1970). *Forms of intellectual and ethical development in the college years.* New York: Holt, Rinehart, and Winston.

Reinharz, S. (1979). *On becoming a social scientist.* San Francisco: Jossey-Bass.

Rich, A. (1979). *On Lies, Secrets, and Silence: Selected prose: 1966–78.* New York: Norton.

Sherman, J., & Beck, E. (Eds.). (1979). *The prism of sex.* Madison, WI: University of Wisconsin Press.

Smith, D. (1974). Women's perspective as a radical critique of sociology. *Sociological Inquiry, 44,* 7–13.

Spanier, B., Bloom, A., & Borovik, D. (1984). *Toward a balanced curriculum: A source book for initiating gender integration projects.* Cambridge, MA: Schenkman.

Weil, S. (1951). *Waiting for God.* New York: Harper Colophon Books.

Wilson, S. (1977). The use of ethnographic techniques in educational research. *Review of Educational Research, 47,* 245–265.

Engaging the Text

1. Break into small same-sex groups and ask yourselves the questions that the authors asked their subjects (see para. 3). What conclusions can you draw from your discussion? Report to the full class.

2. List the main features of traditional education according to this article. What assumptions does traditional education make about the relationships between teachers and students, abstract knowledge and practical experience, and students and their classmates?

3. Explain in your own words what the authors mean by "connected education"; elaborate with examples from the article or your own experience. Why is connected education rare in American institutions of higher learning? What social and personal costs do the authors equate with more traditional education?

4. What do the authors mean when they say many teachers and students desire "an atmosphere less academic and more intellectual" (para 31). Do you think this desire exists at your school? What specific changes would a shift from academic to intellectual entail?

Exploring Connections

5. This article suggests that many women students, like the students in Matt Groening's cartoons (p. 508), find themselves in a hostile environment. Draw a cartoon or comic strip that captures some of the feelings and ideas of the women quoted in this article.

6. In "Social Class and the Hidden Curriculum of Work" (p. 524), Jean Anyon links specific classroom practices with the social status and jobs different schools expect their students to hold later in life. Write your own analysis of how traditional practices in higher education relate to the expected social status and jobs of women.

7. Drawing on the analysis of traditional and connected teaching in this article, discuss which model best describes Jack MacFarland in Mike Rose's "'I Just Wanna Be Average'" (p. 511).

8. Suzanne Gordon (p. 46), Carol Gilligan (p. 233), and the authors of this essay all suggest that women experience and respond to the world differently than men. Write a short narrative about a world in which "women's values" dominate. Share your story in class and discuss.

Extending the Critical Context

9. Explain why you think men would be better or worse off if traditional teaching methods were replaced with the connected education that the authors envision. You may want to consult Sam Keen's (p. 207) analysis of male gender roles as you consider your response.

10. Analyze your current classes for evidence of connected and traditional teaching techniques. Write a journal entry on your reactions to the teaching styles you observe and compare notes with classmates.

11. When teachers attempt to practice connected teaching (peer editing groups, collaborative learning groups, small group discussions, and so on), they find that some students resist these efforts. Discuss your experiences with such approaches to teaching and learning. Why do you think some students reject them?

Silence

MAXINE HONG KINGSTON

*To the Chinese immigrant, white Americans are "ghosts" —
threatening and occasionally comical specters who speak an incomprehensible tongue. For many immigrants, becoming American
means living among "ghosts," finding a new voice, adopting new
values, defining a new self. This selection, from Maxine Hong Kingston's enormously popular autobiography,* The Woman Warrior, *describes the conflicts experienced by a young Chinese girl as she struggles
to adapt to new ways in her American school. Maxine Hong Kingston
(b. 1940) teaches at the University of California, Berkeley.* The Woman
Warrior *won the National Book Critics Award for nonfiction in 1976
and was named by* Time *magazine as one of the top ten nonfiction
works of the 1970s. Kingston has since published* China Men *(1980) and*
Tripmaster Monkey *(1989), in addition to numerous poems, short stories, and articles in national magazines.*

Long ago in China, knot-makers tied string into buttons and frogs,
and rope into bell pulls. There was one knot so complicated that it
blinded the knot-maker. Finally an emperor outlawed this cruel knot,
and the nobles could not order it anymore. If I had lived in China, I
would have been an outlaw knot-maker.

Maybe that's why my mother cut my tongue. She pushed my tongue
up and sliced the frenum. Or maybe she snipped it with a pair of nail
scissors. I don't remember her doing it, only her telling me about it, but
all during childhood I felt sorry for the baby whose mother waited with
scissors or knife in hand for it to cry — and then, when its mouth was
wide open like a baby bird's, cut. The Chinese say "a ready tongue is an
evil."

I used to curl up my tongue in front of the mirror and tauten my
frenum into a white line, itself as thin as a razor blade. I saw no scars in
my mouth. I thought perhaps I had had two frena, and she had cut one.
I made other children open their mouths so I could compare theirs to
mine. I saw perfect pink membranes stretching into precise edges that
looked easy enough to cut. Sometimes I felt very proud that my mother
committed such a powerful act upon me. At other times I was terrified
— the first thing my mother did when she saw me was to cut my tongue.

"Why did you do that to me, Mother?"

"I told you."   5

"Tell me again."

"I cut it so that you would not be tongue-tied. Your tongue would be able to move in any language. You'll be able to speak languages that are completely different from one another. You'll be able to pronounce anything. Your frenum looked too tight to do those things, so I cut it."

"But isn't 'a ready tongue an evil'?"

"Things are different in this ghost country."

"Did it hurt me? Did I cry and bleed?"   10

"I don't remember. Probably."

She didn't cut the other children's. When I asked cousins and other Chinese children whether their mothers had cut their tongues loose, they said, "What?"

"Why didn't you cut my brothers' and sisters' tongues?"

"They didn't need it."

"Why not? Were theirs longer than mine?"   15

"Why don't you quit blabbering and get to work?"

If my mother was not lying she should have cut more, scraped away the rest of the frenum skin, because I have a terrible time talking. Or she should not have cut at all, tampering with my speech. When I went to kindergarten and had to speak English for the first time, I became silent. A dumbness — a shame — still cracks my voice in two, even when I want to say "hello" casually, or ask an easy question in front of the check-out counter, or ask directions of a bus driver. I stand frozen, or I hold up the line with the complete, grammatical sentence that comes squeaking out at impossible length. "What did you say?" says the cab driver, or "Speak up," so I have to perform again, only weaker the second time. A telephone call makes my throat bleed and takes up that day's courage. It spoils my day with self-disgust when I hear my broken voice come skittering out into the open. It makes people wince to hear it. I'm getting better, though. Recently I asked the postman for special-issue stamps; I've waited since childhood for postmen to give me some of their own accord. I am making progress, a little every day.

My silence was thickest — total — during the three years that I covered my school paintings with black paint. I painted layers of black over houses and flowers and suns, and when I drew on the blackboard, I put a layer of chalk on top. I was making a stage curtain, and it was the moment before the curtain parted or rose. The teachers called my parents to school, and I saw they had been saving my pictures, curling and cracking, all alike and black. The teachers pointed to the pictures and looked serious, talked seriously too, but my parents did not understand English. ("The parents and teachers of criminals were executed," said my father.) My parents took the pictures home. I spread them out (so black and full of possibilities) and pretended the curtains were swinging open, flying up, one after another, sunlight underneath, mighty operas.

During the first silent year I spoke to no one at school, did not ask before going to the lavatory, and flunked kindergarten. My sister also said nothing for three years, silent in the playground and silent at lunch. There were other quiet Chinese girls not of our family, but most of them got over it sooner than we did. I enjoyed the silence. At first it did not occur to me I was supposed to talk or to pass kindergarten. I talked at home and to one or two of the Chinese kids in the class. I made motions and even made some jokes. I drank out of a toy saucer when the water spilled out of the cup, and everybody laughed, pointing at me, so I did it some more. I didn't know that Americans don't drink out of saucers.

I liked the Negro students (Black Ghosts) best because they laughed   20
the loudest and talked to me as if I were a daring talker too. One of the Negro girls had her mother coil braids over her ears Shanghai-style like mine; we were Shanghai twins except that she was covered with black like my paintings. Two Negro kids enrolled in Chinese school, and the teachers gave them Chinese names. Some Negro kids walked me to school and home, protecting me from the Japanese kids, who hit me and chased me and stuck gum in my ears. The Japanese kids were noisy and tough. They appeared one day in kindergarten, released from concentration camp,[1] which was a tic-tac-toe mark, like barbed wire, on the map.

It was when I found out I had to talk that school became a misery, that the silence became a misery. I did not speak and felt bad each time that I did not speak. I read aloud in first grade, though, and heard the barest whisper with little squeaks come out of my throat. "Louder," said the teacher, who scared the voice away again. The other Chinese girls did not talk either, so I knew the silence had to do with being a Chinese girl.

Reading out loud was easier than speaking because we did not have to make up what to say, but I stopped often, and the teacher would think I'd gone quiet again. I could not understand "I." The Chinese "I" has seven strokes, intricacies. How could the American "I," assuredly wearing a hat like the Chinese, have only three strokes, the middle so straight? Was it out of politeness that this writer left off strokes the way a Chinese has to write her own name small and crooked? No, it was not politeness; "I" is a capital and "you" is a lower-case. I stared at that middle line and waited so long for its black center to resolve into tight strokes and dots that I forgot to pronounce it. The other troublesome word was "here," no strong consonant to hang on to, and so flat, when "here" is two mountainous ideographs.[2] The teacher, who had already told me every day how to read "I" and "here," put me in the low corner under the stairs again, where the noisy boys usually sat.

When my second grade class did a play, the whole class went to the

---

[1]*concentration camp:* refers to one of the U.S. camps where Japanese Americans were imprisoned during World War II.

[2]*ideographs:* composite characters in Chinese writing made by combining two or more other characters.

auditorium except the Chinese girls. The teacher, lovely and Hawaiian, should have understood about us, but instead left us behind in the classroom. Our voices were too soft or nonexistent, and our parents never signed the permission slips anyway. They never signed anything unnecessary. We opened the door a crack and peeked out, but closed it again quickly. One of us (not me) won every spelling bee, though.

I remember telling the Hawaiian teacher, "We Chinese can't sing 'land where our fathers died.' " She argued with me about politics, while I meant because of curses. But how can I have that memory when I couldn't talk? My mother says that we, like the ghosts, have no memories.

After American school, we picked up our cigar boxes, in which we   25
had arranged books, brushes, and an inkbox neatly, and went to Chinese school, from 5:00 to 7:30 P.M. There we chanted together, voices rising and falling, loud and soft, some boys shouting, everybody reading together, reciting together and not alone with one voice. When we had a memorization test, the teacher let each of us come to his desk and say the lesson to him privately, while the rest of the class practiced copying or tracing. Most of the teachers were men. The boys who were so well behaved in the American school played tricks on them and talked back to them. The girls were not mute. They screamed and yelled during recess, when there were no rules; they had fistfights. Nobody was afraid of children hurting themselves or of children hurting school property. The glass doors to the red and green balconies with the gold joy symbols were left wide open so that we could run out and climb the fire escapes. We played capture-the-flag in the auditorium, where Sun Yat-sen[3] and Chiang Kai-shek's[4] pictures hung at the back of the stage, the Chinese flag on their left and the American flag on their right. We climbed the teak ceremonial chairs and made flying leaps off the stage. One flag headquarters was behind the glass door and the other on stage right. Our feet drummed on the hollow stage. During recess the teachers locked themselves up in their office with the shelves of books, copybooks, inks from China. They drank tea and warmed their hands at a stove. There was no play supervision. At recess we had the school to ourselves, and also we could roam as far as we could go — downtown, Chinatown stores, home — as long as we returned before the bell rang.

At exactly 7:30 the teacher again picked up the brass bell that sat on his desk and swung it over our heads, while we charged down the stairs, our cheering magnified in the stairwell. Nobody had to line up.

Not all of the children who were silent at American school found voice at Chinese school. One new teacher said each of us had to get up

---

[3]*Sun Yat-sen:* Chinese politician, intellectual, and revolutionary (1866–1925).
[4]*Chiang Kai-shek:* military leader of the Chinese Revolution (1887–1975), later leader of the Nationalist government driven to Taiwan by their former allies, the Chinese Communists.

and recite in front of the class, who was to listen. My sister and I had memorized the lesson perfectly. We said it to each other at home, one chanting, one listening. The teacher called on my sister to recite first. It was the first time a teacher had called on the second-born to go first. My sister was scared. She glanced at me and looked away; I looked down at my desk. I hoped that she could do it because if she could, then I would have to. She opened her mouth and a voice came out that wasn't a whisper, but it wasn't a proper voice either. I hoped that she would not cry, fear breaking up her voice like twigs underfoot. She sounded as if she were trying to sing through weeping and strangling. She did not pause or stop to end the embarrassment. She kept going until she said the last word, and then she sat down. When it was my turn, the same voice came out, a crippled animal running on broken legs. You could hear splinters in my voice, bones rubbing jagged against one another. I was loud, though. I was glad I didn't whisper. There was one little girl who whispered.

Engaging the Text

1. Explain the significance of the first paragraph and Kingston's assertion that she "would have been an outlaw knot-maker."

2. Did Kingston's mother literally cut her tongue? If so, why, and what was the result? If not, why does Kingston create this elaborate and graphic story?

3. Why is the young Kingston silent in American school? What's the connection for her between being silent and being Chinese? Between being silent and being female?

4. Kingston writes that school became "a misery" (para. 21). Was this misery avoidable? What, if anything, could Kingston, her American school, her parents, or her Chinese school have done better?

5. Compare and contrast the two schools Kingston attended. Consider their activities, their rules, the behavior of the students and teachers, their probable goals. Why are the schools so different?

Exploring Connections

6. Compare and contrast Kingston's experience with that of the speaker in Inés Hernández's "Para Teresa" (p. 554). Consider each girl's relationship to her family, her attitude toward school, and her strategy for coping with or fitting into Anglo society.

7. Richard Rodriguez (p. 541) also reports a period of silence and discomfort in school. How does his situation compare with Kingston's? Are the differences you see a matter of degree, or were the two students silent for different reasons?

8. Write a scenario in which the silent young Kingston encounters a "connected teacher" (see "Connected Education for Women," p. 567). What would the teacher do, and how might the young Kingston respond? Read your scenario aloud in class.

Extending the Critical Context

9. Write a journal entry or essay about a time you felt silenced in school. Describe the situation in detail. How did you perceive yourself? How do you think others perceived you? What factors, both in and outside the classroom, led to the situation?

Taking Offense: New McCarthyism on Campus?

JERRY ADLER

A battle over "political correctness" is raging at American universities, and the outcome is bound to affect not only your studies but other aspects of campus life as well, including even what messages you may display on your dorm room door. Political correctness is a volatile issue because it brings two key American myths — free speech and equal opportunity — into direct opposition. In this article from Newsweek *magazine (written with the assistance of Mark Starr, Farai Chideya, Lynda Wright, Pat Wingert, and Linda Haac), Jerry Adler reports on developments at several campuses and quotes representatives of both sides of the debate. The article appeared in the December 24, 1990 issue. Adler is a senior writer for* Newsweek.

Perhaps Nina Wu, a sophomore at the University of Connecticut, actually didn't like gays. More likely, she thought she was being funny when she allegedly put up a sign on the door to her dorm room listing "people who are shot on sight" — among them, "preppies," "bimbos," "men without chest hair," and "homos." No protests were heard from representatives of the first three categories, but UConn's gay community was more forthright in asserting its prerogatives. Wu was brought up on charges of violating the student-behavior code, which had recently been rewritten to prohibit "posting or advertising publicly offensive, indecent, or abusive matter concerning persons . . . and making personal slurs or epithets based on race, sex, ethnic origin, disability, religion, or sexual orientation." Found guilty last year in a campus administrative hearing, Wu was . . . what would you guess? Reprimanded? Ordered to write a letter of apology? No, Wu was ordered to move off campus and forbidden to set foot in any university dormitories or cafeterias. Only under pressure of a federal lawsuit did the university let her move back onto campus this year — and revise the Code of Student Conduct to make it conform to a higher code, the First Amendment.

There is an experiment of sorts taking place in American colleges. Or, more accurately, hundreds of experiments at different campuses, directed at changing the consciousness of this entire generation of university students. The goal is to eliminate prejudice, not just of the petty sort that shows up on sophomore dorm walls, but the grand prejudice that has ruled American universities since their founding: that the intellectual tradition of Western Europe occupies the central place in the history of civilization. In this context it would not be enough for a student to refrain from insulting homosexuals or other minorities. He or she would be expected to "affirm" their presence on campus and to study their literature and culture alongside that of Plato, Shakespeare, and Locke. This agenda is broadly shared by most organizations of minority students, feminists, and gays. It is also the program of a generation of campus radicals who grew up in the sixties and are now achieving positions of academic influence. If they no longer talk of taking to the streets, it is because they now are gaining access to the conventional weapons of campus politics: social pressure, academic perks[1] (including tenure), and — when they have the administration on their side — outright coercion.

There is no conspiracy at work here, just a creed, a set of beliefs and expressions which students from places as diverse as Sarah Lawrence[2] and San Francisco State recognize instantly as "PC" — politically correct. Plunk down a professor from Princeton, say, in the University of Wisconsin at Madison, show him a student in a tie-dyed T shirt, with open-toed sandals and a grubby knapsack dangling a student-union-issue, environmentally sound, reusable red plastic cup, and he'll recognize the type instantly. It's "PC Person," an archetype that has now been certified in the official chronicles of American culture, the comic pages. Jeff Shesol, a student cartoonist at Brown, created him as an enforcer of radical cant, so sensitive to potential slights that he even knows the correct euphemism for nine-year-old "girls." He calls them "pre-women."

That is appalling, or would be if it were true. What happened to Nina Wu is in fact appalling, as the university itself seems to have admitted. But so was the incident that led UConn to prohibit "personal slurs" in the first place: a group of white students taunting and spitting at Asian-American students on their way to a dance. If women, gays, and racial minorities are seeking special protections, it is because they

---

[1]*perks:* bonuses or fringe benefits of employment — short for "perquisites."
[2]*Sarah Lawrence:* a private college in Bronxville, New York.

have been the objects of special attacks. (According to sociologist Howard Ehrlich, each year one minority student in five experiences "ethnoviolent attack," including verbal assaults.) If African-Americans are challenging the primacy of Western civilization, it is because for centuries they were oppressed by it. The oppressed have no monopoly on truth. But surely they have earned the right to critique the society that enslaved them.

The content of PC is, in some respects, uncontroversial: who would *defend* racism? What is distressing is that at the university, of all places, tolerance has to be imposed rather than taught, and that "progress" so often is just the replacement of one repressive orthodoxy by another.

Shelf Struggle

The march of PC across American campuses has hardly been unopposed. On the contrary, it has provoked the most extreme reaction, from heartfelt defenses of the First Amendment to the end-of-the-world angst[3] of a Rabelais[4] scholar whose subject has just been dropped from the freshman lit course in favor of Toni Morrison.[5] Opponents of PC now have their own organization, the National Association of Scholars (based in Princeton, N.J.), "committed to rational discourse as the foundation of academic life." It is supported mostly by conservative foundations, but its 1,400 members include some prominent liberals such as Duke political scientist James David Barber, former chair of Amnesty International USA. Duke is a microcosm of the struggle over PC, which is being fought right down to the shelves in the campus bookstore, and not always entirely by rational discourse. Barber stalked into the political-science section one day last spring and turned on its spine every volume with "Marx" in its title — about one out of seven by his count, a lot more attention than he thought it warrants — and angrily demanded their removal. His attempt to organize an NAS chapter at Duke touched off a battle with the influential head of the English department, Stanley Fish, which was extreme even by academic standards of vitriol. Fish called NAS, and by implication its members, "racist, sexist, and homophobic." "That," notes one of Barber's allies, "is like calling someone a communist in the McCarthy years."

Opponents of PC see themselves as a beleaguered minority among barbarians who would ban Shakespeare because he didn't write in Swahili. Outnumbered they may be on some campuses, but they are also often the most senior and influential people on their faculties. "We know who's in," says Martin Kilson, a black professor of government at

---

[3]*angst:* anxiety, fear.
[4]*Rabelais:* ribald French satirist (c. 1483–1553).
[5]*Toni Morrison:* contemporary African American writer (b. 1931).

Harvard — "and it's not women or blacks. That's a damned lie!" And whenever the campus comes into conflict with the power structure of society, it's no contest. Last week a bureaucrat in the Department of Education jeopardized decades of progress in affirmative action by threatening the loss of federal funds to universities that award scholarships specifically for minority students.

But where the PC reigns, one defies it at one's peril. That was the experience of Prof. Vincent Sarich of the University of California, Berkeley, when he wrote in the alumni magazine that the university's affirmative-action program discriminated against white and Asian applicants. Seventy-five students marched into his anthropology class last month and drowned out his lecture with chants of "bullshit." His department began an investigation of his views and chancellor Chang-Lin Tien invited complaints from students about his lectures. Sarich was left in doubt whether he would be allowed to teach the introductory anthropology course he has taught off and on for twenty-three years.

Of course, Sarich was not entirely an innocent who blundered into the minefield of campus politics. He holds scientifically controversial views about the relationship of brain size to intelligence, which tend toward the politically unthinkable conclusion that some races could have a genetic edge in intellect. (He does not, however, bring these up in his introductory course.) As an anthropologist, Sarich knows exactly what happened to him: he stumbled on a taboo. "There are subjects you don't even talk or think about," Sarich says; among them, "race, gender, [and] homosexuality."

Rude Comments

It is not just wildly unfashionable views like Sarich's that are taboo. Students censor even the most ordinary of opinions. Nicole Stelle, a Stanford junior, spent this past semester working and studying in Washington, and found it easier to be a liberal in Republican Sen. Robert Dole's office than a conservative in Stanford. "If I was at lunch [in the dorm] and we started talking about something like civil rights, I'd get up and leave. . . . I knew they didn't want to hear what I had to say."

PC is, strictly speaking, a totalitarian philosophy. No aspect of university life is too obscure to come under its scrutiny. The University of Connecticut issued a proclamation banning "inappropriately directed laughter" and "conspicuous exclusion of students from conversations." Did someone propose an alcohol-free "All-American Halloween Party" at Madison this fall? The majority faction in the Student Senate rose up in protest: masked students might take advantage of their anonymity to inflict "poking, pinching, rude comments" and suchlike oppressions on women and minorities. When the New York University Law School moot court board assigned a case on the custody rights of a lesbian mother, students forced its withdrawal. "Writing arguments [against the mother's side] is hurtful to a group of people and thus hurtful to all of us," one student wrote. To which Prof. Anthony Amsterdam responded: "The declaration that any legal issue is not an open question in law school is a declaration of war upon everything that a law school is." (The problem was reinstated.) At San Francisco State University, thirty students disrupted the first week of Prof. Robert Smith's course in black politics this fall. They weren't even angry about anything Smith said — they just were upset that the course had been listed in the catalog under Political Science rather than Black Studies, which they viewed as an attack on SF State's Black Studies department.

One of the most controversial PC initiatives took place at the University of Texas at Austin, where the English faculty recently chose a new text for the freshman composition course, which is required for about half the entering undergraduates. Up till now, instructors had been free to assign essays on a range of topics for students to read and discuss. Henceforth, all readings will be from an anthology called "Racism and Sexism: An Integrated Study," by Paula S. Rothenberg. The selections, some of which are excellent, comprise a primer of PC thought. In the first chapter Rothenberg answers what many white men wonder but few dare ask: why are *they* the only ones ever accused of racism or sexism? The sine qua non[6] of racism and sexism, Rothenberg explains, is *subordination*, which in Western society is exercised only by whites over blacks and men over women. Hence reverse racism and sexism by definition do not exist. Prof. Alan Gribben was one of the minority who objected to this approach to teaching composition. He derided the course as "Oppression Studies." By dictating the content of the readings, he charged, the department "presumes that content is the most important thing about the writing course." But that is just the point: in the context of PC, political content is the most important thing about everything.

What are the underpinnings of this powerful movement, so seemingly at odds with what most Americans believe?

Philosophically, PC represents the subordination of the right to free speech to the guarantee of equal protection under the law. The absolutist position on the First Amendment is that it lets you slur anyone you choose. The PC position is that a hostile environment for minorities abridges their right to an equal education. "Sure you have the right to speech," says Kate Fahey, an associate dean at Mt. Holyoke College. "But I want to know: what is it going to do to our community? Is it going to damage us?" When a few students last spring mocked Mt. Holyoke's Lesbian/Bisexual Awareness Week by proclaiming "Heterosexual Awareness Week," president Elizabeth Kennan upbraided them for violating the spirit of "community." Unfortunately for the

[6]*sine qua non:* something essential; an indispensable condition.

"community," courts have generally held that highly restrictive speech codes are unconstitutional. The sociologist Ehrlich, who has written five books on racial prejudice, also considers them counterproductive. "You have to let students say the most outrageous and stupid things," he says. "To get people to think and talk, to question their own ideas, you don't regulate their speech."

Role Models

But solicitude for minorities does not stop at shielding them from insults. Promotion of "diversity" is one of the central tenets of PC. Accrediting bodies have even begun to make it a condition of accreditation. Diversity refers both to students and faculty. Of the 373 tenured professors at Harvard's Faculty of Arts and Sciences, only two are black. The latest thinking holds that black undergraduates would be less likely to drop out if there were more black teachers available to act as mentors and role models, so the competition for qualified black professors is acute.

The Ford Foundation gave grants totaling $1.6 million to 19 colleges and universities this year for "diversity." Tulane received a grant for a program "to focus the attention of . . . administration, faculty, and students on the *responsibility* of each to *welcome* and *encourage* all members of the university community regardless of their race, gender, sexual orientation, or religious beliefs." (Emphasis added.) That is a big responsibility. To political-science professor Paul Lewis, one of the 25 percent of the faculty who dissented from the university's draft "Initiatives for Race and Gender Enrichment," it implies a network of PC spies reporting to the "enrichment-liaison person" in each department. Could a bad grade be construed as failure to encourage? If you don't talk to a woman you dislike, are you guilty of not making her welcome? Tulane president Eamon Kelly calls Lewis's fears "foolishness."

Politically, PC is Marxist in origin, in the broad sense of attempting to redistribute power from the privileged class (white males) to the oppressed masses. But it is Marxism of a peculiarly attenuated, self-referential kind. This is not a movement aimed at attracting more working-class youths to the university. The failure of Marxist systems throughout the world has not noticeably dimmed the allure of left-wing politics for American academics. Even today, says David Littlejohn of Berkeley's Graduate School of Literature, "an overwhelming proportion of our courses are taught by people who really hate the system."

Intellectually, PC is informed by deconstructionism, a theory of literary criticism associated with the French thinker Jacques Derrida. This accounts for the concentration of PC thought in such seemingly unlikely disciplines as comparative literature. Deconstructionism is a famously obscure theory, but one of its implications is a rejection of the notion of "hierarchy." It is impossible in deconstructionist terms to say that one text is superior to another. PC thinkers have embraced this conceit[7] with a vengeance. "If you make any judgment or assessment as to the quality of a work, then somehow you aren't being an intellectual egalitarian," says Jean Bethke Elshtain, a political-science professor at Vanderbilt. At a conference recently she referred to Czeslaw Milosz's book *The Captive Mind* as "classic"; to which another female professor exclaimed in dismay that the word *classic* "makes me feel oppressed."

Age and Beauty

It is not just in literary criticism that the PC rejects "hierarchy," but in the most mundane daily exchanges as well. A Smith College handout from the Office of Student Affairs lists ten different kinds of oppression that can be inflicted by making judgments about people. These include "ageism — oppression of the young and old by young adults and the middle-aged"; "heterosexism — oppression of those of sexual orientations other than heterosexual . . . this can take place by not acknowledging their existence," and "lookism . . . construction of a standard for beauty / attractiveness." It's not sufficient to avoid discriminating against unattractive people; you must suppress the impulse to notice the difference. But the most Orwellian[8] category may be "ableism — oppression of the differently abled, by the temporarily able." "Differently abled" is a "term created to underline the concept that differently abled individuals are just that, not less or inferior in any way [as the terms disabled, handicapped, etc., imply]." Well, many people with handicaps surely do develop different abilities, but that is not what makes them a category. They lack something other people possess, and while that is not a reason to oppress them, it does violence to logic and language to pretend otherwise. If people could choose, how many would be "differently abled"?

Sex Change

It sometimes appears that the search for euphemisms has become   20
the great intellectual challenge of American university life. Lest anyone take offense at being called "old," he or she becomes a "non-traditional-age student." Non-Caucasians generally are "people of color." This should never be confused with "colored people." Dennis Williams, who teaches writing at Cornell, recently wrote an article on affirmative action in which he tweaked the PC with the phrase "colored students." "Students of color sounds stupid," reasoned Williams, who is black. "As language, it's sloganeering. It's like saying 'jeans of blue.' " He received

[7]*conceit:* in this context, "idea."
[8]*Orwellian:* in his novel *1984,* George Orwell envisioned a nightmare society in which the government controls ideas by distorting and manipulating language.

no comments on the substance of his article, but he got many complaints about his language — proving his point, that the form of language is taking precedence over its meaning. No one seems to have suggested renaming the sexes, although there is a movement to change the way they're spelled; at Sarah Lawrence and a few other places the PC spelling is "womyn," without the "men."

The rejection of hierarchy underlies another key PC tenet, "multiculturalism." This is an attack on the primacy of the Western intellectual tradition, as handed down through centuries of "great books." In the PC view, this canon perpetuates the power of "dead white males" over women and blacks from beyond the grave. It obliges black students to revere the thoughts of Thomas Jefferson, who was a literal slave owner. In opposition to this "Eurocentric" view of the world, Molefi Asante, chairperson of African American studies at Temple, has proposed an "Afrocentric" curriculum. It would be based on the thoughts of ancient African scholars (he annexes Pharaonic Egypt for this purpose) and the little-known (to Americans) cultures of modern East and West Africa. This would be one of many such ethnic-specific curricula he foresees in a multicultural America. "There are only two positions," Asante says sweepingly; "either you support multiculturalism in American education, or you support the maintenance of white supremacy."

It is statements like that, of course, that send members of the National Association of Scholars stomping into bookstores in a rage. To Stephen Balch, president of the organization, it is a dereliction of duty for educators to admit that every culture can be equally valid. Western civilization has earned its place at the center of the university curriculum, not by the accident that most university professors have been white males, but by its self-evident virtue. It has given rise to the single most compelling idea in human history, individual liberty, which as it happens is just now sweeping the entire world.

But Asante is proposing a change in values, not just reading lists. So what if the Western tradition gave rise to individual liberty? Is liberty necessarily a universal value? African cultures, he points out, exalt that familiar ideal: "community."

Right Terms

"Community!" "Liberty!" Is there no way out of this impasse? Or are we doomed to an endless tug of war over words between the very people who should be leading us onward to a better life? If two people with as many degrees between them as Fish and Barber can't communicate except by hurling charges of "racism" and knocking over books in a store, what hope is there for the rest of us? Yet one hears the same thing over and over: I don't know how to talk to African-Americans. I'm scared of saying the wrong thing to women. Whites don't listen. "There are times when I want to be very cautious about offending a feminist colleague, but I can't find the right terms," says Robert Caserio of the University of Utah. And Caserio is an English teacher. The great Harvard sociologist David Riesman recently complained about having to go to "great lengths to avoid the tag 'racist.' " "He wouldn't be annoyed to have to go to great lengths not to be anti-Semitic!" Harvard's Kilson exploded. And Riesman was once Kilson's mentor!

Yes, of course conflict is inevitable, as the university makes the transition — somewhat ahead of the rest of society — toward its multiethnic future. There are in fact some who recognize the tyranny of PC, but see it only as a transitional phase, which will no longer be necessary once the virtues of tolerance are internalized. Does that sound familiar? It's the dictatorship of the proletariat, to be followed by the withering away of the state. These should be interesting years. 25

Engaging the Text

1. Adler writes that what happened to Nina Wu was "appalling." Do you agree? What kind of response, if any, should the university have made to her sign?

2. Define what critics of "political correctness" mean by this term. What are the implications of this label?

3. What do you believe are the goals of scholars who promote multicultural studies or administrators who try to bar offensive behavior or speech from campuses? What do you believe are the goals of their opponents? Do you see any way to resolve these differences?

4. Is Adler neutral, or does he favor one side over the other? Cite specific examples to support your judgment. Where do you stand in the debate?

Exploring Connections

5. Drawing on several readings in this chapter, write an essay on the effects of a traditional curriculum on nontraditional students. In particular, you may wish to consider whether a different curriculum and school environment would have benefited individual students mentioned in these readings. Does your analysis support one side or the other in the PC debate?

6. Review Shelby Steele's discussion of innocence, power, and "seeing for innocence" (p. 347); then discuss the PC debate in terms of innocence.

Extending the Critical Context

7. Interview a faculty member regarding the impact of the political correctness issue on her or his teaching and research. (You may wish to work in a small group to prepare a list of questions to ask.) When you all have completed your interviews, discuss this sampling of faculty viewpoints. Is it a divisive issue on your campus? What are faculty members' main concerns?

8. Investigate your school's official policies on free speech, offensive language, theme parties, and related issues. What sanctions, if any, are proposed for inappropriate behavior? Consider hypothetical cases that would test the policies. Do you think these policies are legitimate and fair?

9. This anthology, *Rereading America*, features many nontraditional writers and addresses many issues that some educators consider taboo, including race, gender, and homosexuality. Is this a politically correct text? Does an instructor's or writing program's choice of this text represent an attempt to enforce a particular political point of view?

10. As Adler suggests, one of the issues lurking beneath the PC debate is the conflict among the many new communities that make up a modern college campus. In your view, how open is the dialogue among these groups on your campus? What should students or the college do to improve communication among these groups?

7

The Mass Media

Selling the Myths

Since the time of Columbus, news and publicity have helped shape American history by selling American myths. The quest for trade and profit launched the voyages of discovery that led to the new world; European explorers returned with news of wonders that enticed others to seek "new Edens" and cities of gold in the Americas. Columbus reported to the Spanish court that "Hispaniola is a miracle. . . . There are many wide rivers of which the majority contain gold. . . . There are many spices, and great mines of gold and other metals." The printing press, which had been introduced in Europe less than fifty years before Columbus's voyage, made written news easy and cheap to reproduce: one of Columbus's letters, published as a popular pamphlet, became a best-seller in several European cities. Later, similarly glowing reports were used to sell the myth of the new world to prospective colonists. Promoters in seventeenth-century England mounted advertising campaigns that promised settlers everything from unlimited supplies of fish and venison to fountains of youth.

Likewise, commercial interests and advertising fueled much of the westward expansion in the United States during the nineteenth century. A notable illustration of frontier hype comes from the 1880s in Texas, where speculators bought acres of arid, open land and constructed whole towns, each complete with church, hotel, shops, and houses. After everything was built, the promoters advertised these uninhabited "communities" as bustling oases of civilization — "the new plains of Jerusalem" or "the Athens of the South." By attracting settlers, businesses, and above all, the railroad, they hoped to create real towns and thus make a fortune on their otherwise worthless land.

The early press sold dreams of freedom as well as prosperity. In the decades preceding the Revolutionary War, local newspapers helped foster a sense of national identity as they increasingly referred to the colonies as a single entity and addressed their readers as "Americans" rather than Virginians or Pennsylvanians. Many openly encouraged discontent with British rule, publishing lists of "outrages" committed by British soldiers and denouncing loyalists as "serpents" and "guileful betrayers." The lieutenant governor of New York complained in 1765 that the papers were "exciting the People to disobedience of the Laws and to Sedition." When military hostilities erupted in 1775, newspapers rallied to the rebels' cause. Reporting the battle of Lexington, one Boston paper called on readers to "JOIN OR DIE!":

> AMERICANS! forever bear in mind the BATTLE OF LEXINGTON!
> — where British troops, unmolested and unprovoked, wantonly and in a most inhuman manner, fired upon and killed a number of our countrymen, then robbed, ransacked, and burnt their houses! nor could the tears of defenseless women, some of whom were in the pains of childbirth, the cries of helpless babes, nor the prayers of old age, confined to beds of sickness, appease their thirst for blood! — or divert them from their DESIGN OF MURDER and ROBBERY!

But the patriotism of the press had economic underpinnings. In the years just before the Revolution, the British Parliament had levied a series of taxes on paper; colonial publishers rebelled at least in part out of fear for their livelihoods. And while newsmen like Isaiah Thomas, the reporter quoted above, were dedicated patriots, others championed the cause of liberty because it was more profitable — and safer — to do so: not only did revolutionary fervor sell more papers but several publishers sympathetic to the British found their homes and businesses attacked by angry mobs.

Like their precursors, the modern mass media grew out of commercial culture. Popular magazines led the way toward the media empires we know today. Until 1850 there were no national magazines, and for several decades after that, national circulation remained relatively limited. But in the 1880s and 1890s, two changes occurred: companies angling for new markets invented the nationwide advertising campaign, and publishers discovered that they could increase profits by selling more ads and reducing the prices of their magazines. Subscriptions soared, and by 1905 the total circulation of monthly magazines reached 64 million. The mass market was born. As new media like radio and television emerged, they followed a similar pattern: American businesses, continually seeking larger markets for their wares, bought airtime to advertise their products; commercial support funded more programs, which in turn attracted ever larger audiences — and more advertising.

Unlike the pamphlets and local newspapers of earlier times, the mass media opened American homes to the continuous, direct influence of advertising and commercialism. One could even say that all modern media are actually forms of advertising, for while they may also convey information or entertain us, their primary goal is to sell a product — whether that product is a new cologne or a new feature film. As commercial enterprises, the media exploit powerful cultural myths to shape our reactions to their products; thus, we learn to associate the things we buy — from mouthwash to life insurance — with our most cherished values and urgent desires.

The enormous power of the media is hardly a new idea. As early as 1838, James Fenimore Cooper worried that the press "may become despotic." Today the major U.S. newsmagazines, themselves prime examples of mass media, regularly feature stories about the growing influence of mass communications on our world. These articles usually focus on the direct influence that television or movies may have on their audiences; they ask, for instance, whether violent images provoke violent behavior in the viewer or whether the shoddy sexual mores of popular entertainment aren't corrupting "family values." But as sources of cultural mythology, the mass media may influence us in more subtle ways. When they tell us myths about what it means to be an American, to be socially acceptable, to be Black or white, male or female, the media begin to shape who we are and how we see and respond to the world.

Cooper contended in 1838 that "there is but one way of extricating the mind from the baneful influence of the press of this country, and that is by making a rigid analysis of its nature and motives." His advice remains sound in the 1990s. This chapter offers some starting points for an analysis of contemporary media. In "Masters of Desire: The Culture of American Advertising," Jack Solomon explores the connections among advertising, cultural mythology, and personal identity. Next, Elayne Rapping's "Local News: Reality as Soap Opera" demonstrates how local news shows sell themselves by exploiting our desire for community. Maurine Doerken, in "What's Left After Violence and Advertising?" investigates the ways television reinforces stereotypes and isolates us from one another. A pair of essays on Black entertainment in white America round out this section. Mark Crispin Miller argues that *The Cosby Show* taps into potent myths of race, family, and consumerism; and, in "TV's Black World Turns — But Stays Unreal," Henry Louis Gates, Jr., places contemporary media images of Black America in the larger context of African American social and cultural history.

The chapter closes with a section dedicated to the impact of the movies. In "Action-Adventure as Ideology," Gina Marchetti offers a sophisticated analysis of how contradictory cultural desires and values are reconciled in movies that feature tough-guy American heroes. Louise Erdrich's poem "Dear John Wayne" reinterprets cowboy heroes and movie myths of the old west from an American Indian perspective. Finally, Rodney Morales's short story "Under the Table" offers a comic illustration of the way a media icon like Elvis Presley influences the lives of a group of kids growing up in Hawaii.

Sources

Daniel J. Boorstin, *Hidden History: Exploring Our Secret Past*. New York: Harper & Row, 1987.

James Fenimore Cooper, *The American Democrat*. City Unlisted: Minerva Press, 1969.

Richard Ohmann, *Politics of Letters*. Middletown, CT: Wesleyan University Press, 1987.

Laurence Shames, *The Hunger for More: Searching for Values in an Age of Greed*. New York: Times Books, 1989.

Louis L. Snyder and Richard B. Morris, eds., *A Treasury of Great Reporting*. New York: Simon & Schuster, 1949.

Mitchell Stephens, *A History of News*. New York: Viking Penguin, 1988.

Howard Zinn, *A People's History of the United States*. New York: Harper & Row, 1980.

Before Reading . . .

Working independently or in groups, make a collage of images from news photos and magazine advertisements. Try to collect images that communicate something about what it means to be successful, "natural," female or male, "ethnic," part of a family, well educated, or "American." After you and your classmates have shown and discussed your collages, see if you can reach any general conclusions about how the media portray these mythic categories.

As an alternative, watch several hours of TV, taking careful notes on the images associated with any one of the categories listed in the preceding paragraph. Share your notes in class and discuss your collective findings.

Masters of Desire:
The Culture of American Advertising

JACK SOLOMON

In The Signs of Our Time *(1988), the source of this selection, Jack Solomon (b. 1954) offers a crash course in the "semiotics" of American popular culture. Semiotics, or the study of signs, is concerned with the meanings one can "read" in almost every aspect of culture; semioticians work to discover and interpret the cultural myths and messages that lie hidden in the way we dress, the food we eat, the movie heroes we identify with. Here, Solomon analyzes how advertising exploits some of the most cherished values of American culture in order to sell pickup trucks, hamburgers, and beer. Solomon is an assistant professor of English at California State University, Northridge. In addition to scholarly articles on semiotics and literary theory, he has published* Discourse and Reference in the Nuclear Age *(1988).*

> Amongst democratic nations, men easily attain a certain equality
> of condition; but they can never attain as much as they desire.
> ALEXIS DE TOCQUEVILLE

On May 10, 1831, a young French aristocrat named Alexis de Tocqueville arrived in New York City at the start of what would become one of the most famous visits to America in our history. He had come to observe firsthand the institutions of the freest, most egalitarian society of the age, but what he found was a paradox. For behind America's mythic promise of equal opportunity, Tocqueville discovered a desire for *unequal* social rewards, a ferocious competition for privilege and distinction. As he wrote in his monumental study, *Democracy in America*:

> When all privileges of birth and fortune are abolished, when all
> professions are accessible to all, and a man's own energies may place
> him at the top of any one of them, an easy and unbounded career
> seems open to his ambition. . . . But this is an erroneous notion, which
> is corrected by daily experience. [For when] men are nearly alike, and
> all follow the same track, it is very difficult for any one individual to
> walk quick and cleave a way through the same throng which surrounds
> and presses him.

Yet walking quick and cleaving a way is precisely what Americans dream of. We Americans dream of rising above the crowd, of attaining a social summit beyond the reach of ordinary citizens. And therein lies the paradox.

The American dream, in other words, has two faces: the one communally egalitarian and the other competitively elitist. This contradiction is no accident; it is fundamental to the structure of American society. Even as America's great myth of equality celebrates the virtues of mom, apple pie, and the girl or boy next door, it also lures us to achieve social distinction, to rise above the crowd and bask alone in the glory. This land is your land and this land is my land, Woody Guthrie's populist anthem tells us, but we keep trying to increase the "my" at the expense of the "your." Rather than fostering contentment, the American dream breeds desire, a longing for a greater share of the pie. It is as if our society were a vast high-school football game, with the bulk of the participants noisily rooting in the stands while, deep down, each of them is wishing he or she could be the star quarterback or head cheerleader.

For the semiotician, the contradictory nature of the American myth of equality is nowhere written so clearly as in the signs that American advertisers use to manipulate us into buying their wares. "Manipulate" is the word here, not "persuade"; for advertising campaigns are not sources of product information, they are exercises in behavior modification. Appealing to our subconscious emotions rather than to our conscious intellects, advertisements are designed to exploit the discontentments fostered by the American dream, the constant desire for social success and the material rewards that accompany it. America's consumer economy runs on desire, and advertising stokes the engines by transforming common objects — from peanut butter to political candidates — into signs of all the things that Americans covet most.

But by semiotically reading the signs that advertising agencies manufacture to stimulate consumption, we can plot the precise state of desire in the audiences to which they are addressed. In this [essay], we'll look at a representative sample of ads and what they say about the emotional climate of the country and the fast-changing trends of American life. Because ours is a highly diverse, pluralistic society, various advertisements may say different things depending on their intended audiences, but in every case they say something about America, about the status of our hopes, fears, desires, and beliefs.

Let's begin with two ad campaigns conducted by the same company that bear out Alexis de Tocqueville's observations about the contradictory nature of American society: General Motors' campaigns for its Cadillac and Chevrolet lines. First, consider an early magazine ad for the Cadillac Allanté. Appearing as a full-color, four-page insert in *Time*, the ad seems to say "I'm special — and so is this car" even before we've begun to read it. Rather than being printed on the ordinary, flimsy pages of the magazine, the Allanté spread appears on glossy

5

coated stock. The unwritten message here is that an extraordinary car deserves an extraordinary advertisement, and that both car and ad are aimed at an extraordinary consumer, or at least one who wishes to appear extraordinary compared to his more ordinary fellow citizens.

Ads of this kind work by creating symbolic associations between their product and what is most coveted by the consumers to whom they are addressed. It is significant, then, that this ad insists that the Allanté is virtually an Italian rather than an American car, an automobile, as its copy runs, "Conceived and Commissioned by America's Luxury Car Leader — Cadillac" but "Designed and Handcrafted by Europe's Renowned Design Leader — Pininfarina, SpA, of Turin, Italy." This is not simply a piece of product information, it's a sign of the prestige that European luxury cars enjoy in today's automotive marketplace. Once the luxury car of choice for America's status drivers, Cadillac has fallen far behind its European competitors in the race for the prestige market. So the Allanté essentially represents Cadillac's decision, after years of resisting the trend toward European cars, to introduce its own European import — whose high cost is clearly printed on the last page of the ad. Although $54,700 is a lot of money to pay for a Cadillac, it's about what you'd expect to pay for a top-of-the-line Mercedes-Benz. That's precisely the point the ad is trying to make: the Allanté is no mere car. It's a potent status symbol you can associate with the other major status symbols of the 1980s.

American companies manufacture status symbols because American consumers want them. As Alexis de Tocqueville recognized a century and a half ago, the competitive nature of democratic societies breeds a desire for social distinction, a yearning to rise above the crowd. But given the fact that those who do make it to the top in socially mobile societies have often risen from the lower ranks, they still look like everyone else. In the socially immobile societies of aristocratic Europe, generations of fixed social conditions produced subtle class signals. The accent of one's voice, the shape of one's nose, or even the set of one's chin, immediately communicated social status. Aside from the nasal bray and uptilted head of the Boston Brahmin, Americans do not have any native sets of personal status signals. If it weren't for his Mercedes-Benz and Manhattan townhouse, the parvenu Wall Street millionaire often couldn't be distinguished from the man who tailors his suits. Hence, the demand for status symbols, for the objects that mark one off as a social success, is particularly strong in democratic nations — stronger even than in aristocratic societies, where the aristocrat so often looks and sounds different from everyone else.

Status symbols, then, are signs that identify their possessors' place in a social hierarchy, markers of rank and prestige. We can all think of any number of status symbols — Rolls-Royces, Beverly Hills mansions, even Shar Pei puppies (whose rareness and expense has rocketed them beyond

Russian wolfhounds as status pets and has even inspired whole lines of wrinkle-faced stuffed toys) — but how do we know that something *is* a status symbol? The explanation is quite simple: when an object (or puppy!) either costs a lot of money or requires influential connections to possess, anyone who possesses it must also possess the necessary means and influence to acquire it. The object itself really doesn't matter, since it ultimately disappears behind the presumed social potency of its owner. Semiotically, what matters is the signal it sends, its value as a sign of power. One traditional sign of social distinction is owning a country estate and enjoying the peace and privacy that attend it. Advertisements for Mercedes-Benz, Jaguar, and Audi automobiles thus frequently feature drivers motoring quietly along a country road, presumably on their way to or from their country houses.

Advertisers have been quick to exploit the status signals that belong to body language as well. As Hegel[1] observed in the early nineteenth century, it is an ancient aristocratic prerogative to be seen by the lower orders without having to look at them in return. Tilting his chin high in the air and gazing down at the world under hooded eyelids, the aristocrat invites observation while refusing to look back. We can find such a pose exploited in an advertisement for Cadillac Seville in which we see an elegantly dressed woman out for a drive with her husband in their new Cadillac. If we look closely at the woman's body language, we can see her glance inwardly with a satisfied smile on her face but not outward toward the camera that represents our gaze. She is glad to be seen by us in her Seville, but she isn't interested in looking at *us*!

Ads that are aimed at a broader market take the opposite approach. If the American dream encourages the desire to "arrive," to vault above the mass, it also fosters a desire to be popular, to "belong." Populist commercials accordingly transform products into signs of belonging, utilizing such common icons as country music, small-town life, family picnics, and farmyards. All of these icons are incorporated in GM's "Heartbeat of America" campaign for its Chevrolet line. Unlike the Seville commercial, the faces in the Chevy ads look straight at us and smile. Dress is casual; the mood upbeat. Quick camera cuts take us from rustic to suburban to urban scenes, creating an American montage filmed from sea to shining sea. We all "belong" in a Chevy.

Where price alone doesn't determine the market for a product, advertisers can go either way. Both Johnnie Walker and Jack Daniel's are better-grade whiskies, but where a Johnnie Walker ad appeals to the buyer who wants a mark of aristocratic distinction in his liquor, a Jack Daniel's ad emphasizes the down-home, egalitarian folksiness of its product. Johnnie Walker associates itself with such conventional status symbols as sable coats, Rolls-Royces, and black gold; Jack Daniel's gives

[1]*Hegel:* G. W. F. Hegel (1770–1831), German philosopher.

us a Good Ol' Boy in overalls. In fact, Jack Daniel's Good Ol'Boy is an icon of backwoods independence, recalling the days of the moonshiner and the Whisky Rebellion of 1794. Evoking emotions quite at odds with those stimulated in Johnnie Walker ads, the advertisers of Jack Daniel's have chosen to transform their product into a sign of America's populist tradition. The fact that both ads successfully sell whisky is itself a sign of the dual nature of the American dream.

Beer is also pitched on two levels. Consider the difference between the ways Budweiser and Michelob market their light beers. Bud Light and Michelob Light cost and taste about the same, but Budweiser tends to target the working class while Michelob has gone after the upscale market. Bud commercials are set in working-class bars that contrast with the sophisticated nightclubs and yuppie watering holes of the Michelob campaign. "You're one of the guys," Budweiser assures the assembly-line worker and the truck driver, "this Bud's for you." Michelob, on the other hand, makes no such appeal to the democratic instinct of sharing and belonging. You don't share, you take, grabbing what you can in a competitive dash to "have it all."

Populist advertising is particularly effective in the face of foreign competition. When Americans feel threatened from the outside, they tend to circle the wagons and temporarily forget their class differences. In the face of the Japanese automotive "invasion," Chrysler runs populist commercials in which Lee Iacocca joins the simple folk who buy his cars as the jingle "Born in America" blares in the background. Seeking to capitalize on the popularity of Bruce Springsteen's *Born in the USA* album, these ads gloss over Springsteen's ironic lyrics in a vast display of flag-waving. Chevrolet's "Heartbeat of America" campaign similarly attempts to woo American motorists away from Japanese automobiles by appealing to their patriotic sentiments.

The patriotic iconography of these campaigns also reflects the general cultural mood of the early- to mid-1980s. After a period of national anguish in the wake of the Vietnam War and the Iran hostage crisis, American went on a patriotic binge. American athletic triumphs in the Lake Placid and Los Angeles Olympics introduced a sporting tone into the national celebration, often making international affairs appear like one great Olympiad in which America was always going for the gold. In response, advertisers began to do their own flag-waving. 15

The mood of advertising during this period was definitely upbeat. Even deodorant commercials, which traditionally work on our self-doubts and fears of social rejection, jumped on the bandwagon. In the guilty sixties, we had ads like the "Ice Blue Secret" campaign with its connotations of guilt and shame. In the feel-good Reagan eighties, "Sure" deodorant commercials featured images of triumphant Americans throwing up their arms in victory to reveal — no wet marks! Deodorant commercials once had the moral echo of Nathaniel Hawthorne's guilt-ridden *The Scarlet Letter*; in the early eighties they had all the moral subtlety of *Rocky IV*, reflecting the emotions of a Vietnam-weary nation eager to embrace the imagery of America Triumphant.

The commercials for Worlds of Wonder's Lazer Tag game featured the futuristic finals of some Soviet-American Lazer Tag shootout ("Practice hard, America!") and carried the emotions of patriotism into an even more aggressive arena. Exploiting the hoopla that surrounded the victory over the Soviets in the hockey finals of the 1980 Olympics, the Lazer Tag ads pandered to an American desire for the sort of clear-cut nationalistic triumphs that the nuclear age has rendered almost impossible. Creating a fantasy setting where patriotic dreams are substituted for complicated realities, the Lazer Tag commercials sought to capture the imaginations of children caught up in the patriotic fervor of the early 1980s.

Live the Fantasy

By reading the signs of American advertising, we can conclude that America is a nation of fantasizers, often preferring the sign to the substance and easily enthralled by a veritable Fantasy Island of commercial illusions. Critics of Madison Avenue often complain that advertisers create consumer desire, but semioticians don't think the situation is that simple. Advertisers may give shape to consumer fantasies, but they need raw material to work with, the subconscious dreams and desires of the marketplace. As long as these desires remain unconscious, advertisers will be able to exploit them. But by bringing the fantasies to the surface, you can free yourself from advertising's often hypnotic grasp.

I can think of no company that has more successfully seized upon the subconscious fantasies of the American marketplace — indeed the world marketplace — than McDonald's. By no means the first nor the only hamburger chain in the United States, McDonald's emerged victorious in the "burger wars" by transforming hamburgers into signs of all that was desirable in American life. Other chains like Wendy's, Burger King, and Jack-In-The-Box continue to advertise and sell widely, but no company approaches McDonald's transformation of itself into a symbol of American culture.

McDonald's success can be traced to the precision of its advertising. Instead of broadcasting a single "one-size-fits-all" campaign at a time, McDonald's pitches its burgers simultaneously at different age groups, different classes, even different races (Budweiser beer, incidentally, has succeeded in the same way). For children, there is the Ronald McDonald campaign, which presents a fantasy world that has little to do with hamburgers in any rational sense but a great deal to do with the emotional desires of kids. Ronald McDonald and his friends are signs that recall the Muppets, *Sesame Street*, the circus, toys, storybook illustrations, even *Alice in Wonderland*. Such signs do not signify hamburgers. Rather, they are displayed in order to prompt in the child's mind an automatic association of fantasy, fun, and McDonald's.

The same approach is taken in ads aimed at older audiences — teens, adults, and senior citizens. In the teen-oriented ads we may catch a fleeting glimpse of a hamburger or two, but what we are really shown is a teenage fantasy: groups of hip and happy adolescents singing, dancing, and cavorting together. Fearing loneliness more than anything else, adolescents quickly respond to the group appeal of such commercials. "Eat a Big Mac," these ads say, "and you won't be stuck home alone on Saturday night."

To appeal to an older and more sophisticated audience no longer so afraid of not belonging and more concerned with finding a place to go out to at night, McDonald's has designed the elaborate "Mac Tonight" commercials, which have for their backdrop a nightlit urban skyline and at their center a cabaret pianist with a moon-shaped head, a glad manner, and Blues Brothers shades. Such signs prompt an association of McDonald's with nightclubs and urban sophistication, persuading us that McDonald's is a place not only for breakfast or lunch but for dinner too, as if it were a popular off-Broadway nightspot, a place to see and be seen. Even the parody of Kurt Weill's "Mack the Knife" theme song that Mac the Pianist performs is a sign, a subtle signal to the sophisticated hamburger eater able to recognize the origin of the tune in Bertolt Brecht's *Threepenny Opera*.

For yet older customers, McDonald's has designed a commercial around the fact that it employs a large number of retirees and seniors. In one such ad, we see an elderly man leaving his pretty little cottage early in the morning to start work as "the new kid" at McDonald's, and then we watch him during his first day on the job. Of course he is a great success, outdoing everyone else with his energy and efficiency, and he returns home in the evening to a loving wife and happy home. One would almost think that the ad was a kind of moving "help wanted" sign (indeed, McDonald's *was* hiring elderly employees at the time), but it's really just directed at consumers. Older viewers can see themselves wanted and appreciated in the ad — and perhaps be distracted from the rationally uncomfortable fact that many senior citizens take such jobs because of financial need and thus may be unlikely to own the sort of home that one sees in the commercial. But realism isn't the point here. This is fantasyland, a dream world promising instant gratification no matter what the facts of the matter may be.

Practically the only fantasy that McDonald's doesn't exploit is the fantasy of sex. This is understandable, given McDonald's desire to present itself as a family restaurant. But everywhere else, sexual fantasies, which have always had an important place in American advertising, are beginning to dominate the advertising scene. You expect sexual come-ons in ads for perfume or cosmetics or jewelry — after all, that's what they're selling — but for room deodorizers? In a magazine ad for Claire Burke home fragrances, for example, we see a well-dressed couple cavorting about their bedroom in what looks like a cheery preparation for sadomasochistic exercises. Jordache and Calvin Klein pitch blue jeans as props for teenage sexuality. The phallic appeal of automobiles, traditionally an implicit feature in automotive advertising, becomes quite explicit in a Dodge commercial that shifts back and forth from shots of a young man in an automobile to teasing glimpses of a woman — his date — as she dresses in her apartment.

The very language of today's advertisements is charged with sex- 25
uality. Products in the more innocent fifties were "new and improved," but everything in the eighties is "hot!" — as in "hot woman," or sexual heat. Cars are "hot." Movies are "hot." An ad for Valvoline pulses to the rhythm of a "heat wave, burning in my car." Sneakers get red hot in a magazine ad for Travel Fox athletic shoes in which we see male and female figures, clad only in Travel Fox shoes, apparently in the act of copulation — an ad that earned one of *Adweek*'s annual "badvertising" awards for shoddy advertising.

The sexual explicitness of contemporary advertising is a sign not so much of American sexual fantasies as of the lengths to which advertisers will go to get attention. Sex never fails as an attention-getter, and in a particularly competitive, and expensive, era for American marketing, advertisers like to bet on a sure thing. Ad people refer to the proliferation of TV, radio, newspaper, magazine, and billboard ads as "clutter," and nothing cuts through the clutter like sex.

By showing the flesh, advertisers work on the deepest, most coercive human emotions of all. Much sexual coercion in advertising, however, is a sign of a desperate need to make certain that clients are getting their money's worth. The appearance of advertisements that refer directly to the prefabricated fantasies of Hollywood is a sign of a different sort of desperation: a desperation for ideas. With the rapid turnover of advertising campaigns mandated by the need to cut through the "clutter," advertisers may be hard pressed for new ad concepts, and so they are more and more frequently turning to already-established models. In the early 1980s, for instance, Pepsi-Cola ran a series of ads broadly alluding to Steven Spielberg's *E.T.* In one such ad, we see a young boy who, like the hero of *E.T.*, witnesses an extraterrestrial visit. The boy is led to a soft-drink machine where he pauses to drink a can of Pepsi as the spaceship he's spotted flies off into the universe. The relationship between the ad and the movie, accordingly, is a parasitical one, with the ad taking its life from the creative body of the film.

Pepsi did something similar in 1987 when it arranged with the producers of the movie *Top Gun* to promote the film's video release in Pepsi's televison advertisements in exchange for the right to append a

Pepsi ad to the video itself. This time, however, the parasitical relationship between ad and film was made explicit. Pepsi sales benefited from the video, and the video's sales benefited from Pepsi. It was a marriage made in corporate heaven.

The fact that Pepsi believed that it could stimulate consumption by appealing to the militaristic fantasies dramatized in *Top Gun* reflects similar fantasies in the "Pepsi generation." Earlier generations saw Pepsi associated with high-school courtship rituals, with couples sipping sodas together at the corner drugstore. When the draft was on, young men fantasized about Peggy Sue, not Air Force Flight School. Military service was all too real a possibility to fantasize about. But in an era when military service is not a reality for most young Americans, Pepsi commercials featuring hotshot fly-boys drinking Pepsi while streaking about in their Air Force jets contribute to a youth culture that has forgotten what military service means. It all looks like such fun in the Pepsi ads, but what they conceal is the fact that military jets are weapons, not high-tech recreational vehicles.

For less militaristic dreamers, Madison Avenue has framed ad campaigns around the cultural prestige of high-tech machinery in its own right. This is especially the case with sports cars, whose high-tech appeal is so powerful that some people apparently fantasize about *being* sports cars. At least, this is the conclusion one might draw from a Porsche commercial that asked its audience, "If you were a car, what kind of car would you be?" As a candy-red Porsche speeds along a rain-slick forest road, the ad's voice-over describes all the specifications you'd want to have if you *were* a sports car. "If you were a car," the commercial concludes, "you'd be a Porsche."

In his essay "Car Commercials and *Miami Vice*," Todd Gitlin explains the semiotic appeal of such ads as those in the Porsche campaign. Aired at the height of what may be called America's "myth of the entrepreneur," these commercials were aimed at young corporate managers who imaginatively identified with the "lone wolf" image of a Porsche speeding through the woods. Gitlin points out that such images cater to the fantasies of faceless corporate men who dream of entrepreneurial glory, of striking out on their own like John DeLorean and telling the boss to take his job and shove it. But as DeLorean's spectacular failure demonstrates, the life of the entrepreneur can be extremely risky. So rather than having to go it alone and take the risks that accompany entrepreneurial independence, the young executive can substitute fantasy for reality by climbing into his Porsche — or at least that's what Porsche's advertisers wanted him to believe.

But there is more at work in the Porsche ads than the fantasies of corporate America. Ever since Arthur C. Clarke and Stanley Kubrick teamed up to present us with HAL 9000, the demented computer of *2001: A Space Odyssey*, the American imagination has been obsessed

30

with the melding of man and machine. First there was television's *Six Million Dollar Man*, and then movieland's *Star Wars*, *Blade Runner*, and *Robocop*, fantasy visions of a future dominated by machines. Androids haunt our imaginations as machines seize the initiative. *Time* magazine's "Man of the Year" for 1982 was a computer. Robot-built automobiles appeal to drivers who spend their days in front of computer screens — perhaps designing robots. When so much power and prestige is being given to high-tech machines, wouldn't you rather be a Porsche?

In short, the Porsche campaign is a sign of a new mythology that is emerging before our eyes, a myth of the machine, which is replacing the myth of the human. The iconic figure of the little tramp caught up in the cogs of industrial production in Charlie Chaplin's *Modern Times* signified a humanistic revulsion to the age of the machine. Human beings, such icons said, were superior to machines. Human values should come first in the moral order of things. But as Edith Milton suggests in her essay "The Track of the Mutant," we are now coming to believe that machines are superior to human beings, that mechanical nature is superior to human nature. Rather than being threatened by machines, we long to merge with them. *The Six Million Dollar Man* is one iconic figure in the new mythology; Harrison Ford's sexual coupling with an android is another. In such an age it should come as little wonder that computer-synthesized Max Headroom should be a commercial spokesman for Coca-Cola, or that Federal Express should design a series of TV ads featuring mechanical-looking human beings revolving around strange and powerful machines.

Fear and Trembling in the Marketplace

While advertisers play on and reflect back at us our fantasies about everything from fighter pilots to robots, they also play on darker imaginings. If dream and desire can be exploited in the quest for sales, so can nightmare and fear.

The nightmare equivalent of America's populist desire to "belong," for example, is the fear of not belonging, of social rejection, of being different. Advertisements for dandruff shampoos, mouthwashes, deodorants, and laundry detergents ("Ring Around the Collar!") accordingly exploit such fears, bullying us into consumption. Although ads of this type are still around in the 1980s, they were particularly common in the fifties and early sixties, reflecting a society still reeling from the witch-hunts of the McCarthy years. When any sort of social eccentricity or difference could result in a public denunciation and the loss of one's job or even liberty, Americans were keen to conform and be like everyone else. No one wanted to be "guilty" of smelling bad or of having a dirty collar.

35

"Guilt" ads characteristically work by creating narrative situations in which someone is "accused" of some social "transgression," pronounced guilty, and then offered the sponsor's product as a means of returning to "innocence." Such ads, in essence, are parodies of ancient religious rituals of guilt and atonement, whereby sinning humanity is offered salvation through the agency of priest and church. In the world of advertising, a product takes the place of the priest, but the logic of the situation is quite similar.

In commercials for Wisk detergent, for example, we witness the drama of a hapless housewife and her husband as they are mocked by the jeering voices of children shouting "Ring Around the Collar!" "Oh, those dirty rings!" the housewife groans in despair. It's as if she and her husband were being stoned by an angry crowd. But there's hope, there's help, there's Wisk. Cleansing her soul of sin as well as her husband's, the housewife launders his shirts with Wisk, and behold, his collars are clean. Product salvation is only as far as the supermarket.

The recent appearance of advertisements for hospitals treating drug and alcohol addiction have raised the old genre of the guilt ad to new heights (or lows, depending on your perspective). In such ads, we see wives on the verge of leaving their husbands if they don't do something about their drinking, and salesmen about to lose their jobs. The man is guilty; he has sinned; but he upholds the ritual of guilt and atonement by "confessing" to his wife or boss and agreeing to go to the hospital the ad is pitching.

If guilt looks backward in time to past transgressions, fear, like desire, faces forward, trembling before the future. In the late 1980s, a new kind of fear commercial appeared, one whose narrative played on the worries of young corporate managers struggling up the ladder of success. Representing the nightmare equivalent of the elitist desire to "arrive," ads of this sort created images of failure, storylines of corporate defeat. In one ad for Apple computers, for example, a group of junior executives sits around a table with the boss as he asks each executive how long it will take his or her department to complete some publishing jobs. "Two or three days," answers one nervous executive. "A week, on overtime," a tight-lipped woman responds. But one young up-and-comer can have everything ready tomorrow, today, or yesterday, because his department uses a Macintosh desktop publishing system. Guess who'll get the next promotion?

Fear stalks an ad for AT&T computer systems too. A boss and four   40
junior executives are dining in a posh restaurant. Icons of corporate power and prestige flood the screen — from the executives' formal evening wear to the fancy table setting — but there's tension in the air. It seems that the junior managers have chosen a computer system that's incompatible with the firm's sales and marketing departments. A whole new system will have to be purchased, but the tone of the meeting suggests that it will be handled by a new group of managers. These guys

are on the way out. They no longer "belong." Indeed, it's probably no accident that the ad takes place in a restaurant, given the joke that went around in the aftermath of the 1987 market crash. "What do you call a yuppie stockbroker?" the joke ran. "Hey, waiter!" Is the ad trying subtly to suggest that junior executives who choose the wrong computer systems are doomed to suffer the same fate?

For other markets, there are other fears. If McDonald's presents senior citizens with bright fantasies of being useful and appreciated beyond retirement, companies like Secure Horizons dramatize senior citizens' fears of being caught short by a major illness. Running its ads in the wake of budgetary cuts in the Medicare system, Secure Horizons designed a series of commercials featuring a pleasant old man named Harry — who looks and sounds rather like Carroll O'Connor — who tells us the story of the scare he got during his wife's recent illness. Fearing that next time Medicare won't cover the bills, he has purchased supplemental health insurance from Secure Horizons and now securely tends his rooftop garden.

Among all the fears advertisers have exploited over the years, I find the fear of not having a posh enough burial site the most arresting. Advertisers usually avoid any mention of death — who wants to associate a product with the grave? — but mortuary advertisers haven't much choice. Generally, they solve their problem by framing cemeteries as timeless parks presided over by priestly morticians, appealing to our desires for dignity and comfort in the face of bereavement. But in one television commercial for Forest Lawn we find a different approach. In this ad we are presented with the ghost of an old man telling us how he might have found a much nicer resting place than the run-down cemetery in which we find him had his wife only known that Forest Lawn was so "affordable." I presume the ad was supposed to be funny, but it's been pulled off the air. There are some fears that just won't bear joking about, some nightmares too dark to dramatize.

The Future of an Illusion

There are some signs in the advertising world that Americans are getting fed up with fantasy advertisements and want to hear some straight talk. Weary of extravagant product claims and irrelevant associations, consumers trained by years of advertising to distrust what they hear seem to be developing an immunity to commercials. At least, this is the semiotic message I read in the "new realism" advertisements of the eighties, ads that attempt to convince you that what you're seeing is the real thing, that the ad is giving you the straight dope, not advertising hype.

You can recognize the "new realism" by its camera techniques. The lighting is usually subdued to give the ad the effect of being filmed without studio lighting or special filters. The scene looks gray, as if the blinds were drawn. The camera shots are jerky and off-angle, often zooming in for sudden unflattering close-ups, as if the cameraman was an amateur with a home video recorder. In a "realistic" ad for AT&T, for example, we are treated to a monologue by a plump stockbroker — his plumpness intended as a sign that he's for real and not just another actor — who tells us about the problems he's had with his phone system (not AT&T's) as the camera jerks around, generally filming him from below as if the cameraman couldn't quite fit his equipment into the crammed office and had to film the scene on his knees. "This is no fancy advertisement," the ad tries to convince us, "this is sincere."

An ad for Miller draft beer tries the same approach, recreating the   45
effect of an amateur videotape of a wedding celebration. Camera shots shift suddenly from group to group. The picture jumps. Bodies are poorly framed. The color is washed out. Like the beer it is pushing, the ad is supposed to strike us as being "as real as it gets."

Such ads reflect a desire for reality in the marketplace, a weariness with Madison Avenue illusions. But there's no illusion like the illusion of reality. Every special technique that advertisers use to create their "reality effects" is, in fact, more unrealistic than the techniques of "illusory" ads. The world, in reality, doesn't jump around when you look at it. It doesn't appear in subdued gray tones. Our eyes don't have zoom lenses, and we don't look at things with our heads cocked to one side. The irony of the "new realism" is that it is more unrealistic, more artificial, than the ordinary run of television advertising.

But don't expect any truly realistic ads in the future, because a realistic advertisement is a contradiction in terms. The logic of advertising is entirely semiotic: it substitutes signs for things, framed visions of consumer desire for the thing itself. The success of modern advertising, its penetration into every corner of American life, reflects a culture that has itself chosen illusion over reality. At a time when political candidates all have professional image-makers attached to their staffs, and the President of the United States is an actor who once sold shirt collars, all the cultural signs are pointing to more illusions in our lives rather than fewer — a fecund breeding ground for the world of the advertiser.

Engaging the Text

1. How, according to Solomon, does advertising exploit our dominant cultural myths? What central cultural paradox do U.S. advertisers exploit most frequently? Why?

2. Brainstorm a list of current status symbols. Why, according to Solomon, are they such an important feature of American life? What cultural function do they perform? In what sense can even your body language become a symbol of your social status?

3. What is the appeal of populist images in ads? What types of products are they most frequently associated with?

4. How do corporations like McDonald's manipulate the subconscious fears and desires of different groups of Americans in their carefully targeted advertising campaigns?

Exploring Connections

5. In "Images of Relationships" (p. 233) Carol Gilligan suggests that men and women have distinctly different ideas about success and failure. Drawing on the ideas presented by Solomon and Gilligan, analyze several television commercials that are clearly addressed to either men or women. Do these ads convey differing notions of success and failure depending on the gender of the target audience?

6. Solomon's analysis of status symbols and their power assumes that there is, in fact, a good deal of social mobility in U.S. culture. How might Gregory Mantsios (p. 72) critique this assumption? How might you explain the power of status symbols in a culture where social mobility is relatively restricted?

7. Read or review Chellis Glendinning's "The Spell of Technology" (p. 150) and Susan Griffin's "Split Culture" (p. 175). How might these feminist social critics account for the transformation of American attitudes toward machines and mechanization that Solomon describes?

Extending the Critical Context

8. Solomon suggests that advertising in the late 1980s tried to project an upbeat, superpatriotic image of "America Triumphant" (para. 16). Survey television commercials and ads in popular magazines. Are advertisers continuing to exploit American self-assuredness? What images and references convey this attitude?

9. Working in small groups, survey a few hours of prime-time commercial TV and try to categorize the kinds of appeals that are made in the ads. How many, for example, offer imagery associated with status and success? With sexuality? With a need for community? How many touch on deep-seated fears? What conclusions can you draw from your survey results?

10. Solomon suggests that the mythic relationship between human beings and machines has changed dramatically over the last fifty years. Analyze the relationship suggested by recent movies like *Total Recall* and *Terminator 2*.

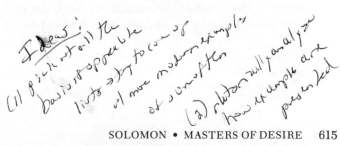

Local News: Reality as Soap Opera

ELAYNE RAPPING

When Elayne Rapping first became interested in the cultural messages communicated by television programs, her friends thought it was a joke: how could she take television seriously enough to treat it as an important academic subject? But in this chapter from The Looking Glass World of Nonfiction TV *(1987), she does just that. She dissects local television news shows and discovers that they tell us more about our anxieties than about what's happening in the world. Rapping (b. 1938) is an associate professor of communications at Adelphi University.*

Local news was not always the jazzy package we have come to think of as "Happy News," "Eyewitless News" and "Newzak." In fact, local news, until recently, wasn't much of anything. Even national news was, until the early 1960s, a mere fifteen minute segment which affiliates were reluctant to carry because it was not a moneymaker. National news has always been a difficult thing to sell. An FCC ruling requires that it be a regular programming feature, but it doesn't draw viewers well and has never warranted primetime scheduling. Even the special events and reports, which networks carry largely for prestige and to fulfill the "public interest" requirements of the FCC, lose money.[1] Apparently, most people, most of the time, don't like to be educated or informed; after a hard day's work they prefer lighter fare, escapism, something that either numbs or stimulates intense emotions.

The expansion of national news to thirty minutes came about because of technical innovations at a time when public life was particularly dramatic. The 1960s were heady days for American newswatchers. The Vietnam War, violent police reactions to massive protests, ghetto riots, public figure assassinations, "all converged to attract nightly viewers in unprecedented numbers."[2] The sophistication of the new TV technologies, especially the portable minicam which allowed live, on-the-spot coverage of breaking news, added to the appeal. So did the highly televisible space flights with their accompanying development of global satellite communications technology. Now major news stories from distant places, as well as the most mundane local fire or car

---

[1]Ron Powers, *The Newscasters* (New York, 1977), p. 53. [Author's note]
[2]*ibid.*, p. 6. [Author's note]

accident, could be brought to audiences as they happened, in full, bold color.

Local news was the primary beneficiary of this technology because it enabled stations to turn trivial local events into sensational, colorful dramas. But there was another reason for local news' rise to prominence. By the 1960s, local news had become almost the only original programming produced by affiliates. The networks had become so powerful that they had been able to produce and sell their own shows to affiliates very successfully. They offered an arrangement the locals could not refuse. In exchange for running nationally produced programs, rather than their own, affiliates received "compensation" from the networks. Since the local affiliates could sell their own spots in the network shows, the arrangement was both profitable and efficient. Affiliates no longer had to hire large production staffs and produce elaborate programs. They merely used nationally relayed material, which was slick and popular. Thus, local happenings became the only area which required local production.[3]

Another factor in the rise of local news was its growing role in the evening's primetime schedule. Local news is, by default, the program which establishes the personality and tone, the "signature," for each local affiliate. Whatever the quality of the news team and its coverage, that is what viewers come to identify as the quality of the entire station. And whatever local news show develops the biggest audience is also the show which is most likely to carry its viewers with it through the rest of the evening's shows. Network news as well as the entire schedule of primetime programming for each network thus depend on the ratings of their affiliates' local newscasts. So do the affiliates' own revenues for local commercials.

As a result of this importance, as early as the 1960s audience research specialists were hired to help in attracting audiences. Paul Klein, a brilliant analyst hired by NBC, came up with the concept of "Least Objectionable Programming." It was based on the insightful idea that audiences did not really "watch a program" so much as they "watched television." The handwriting was on the wall. The move from information to broadly appealing entertainment was a foregone conclusion.[4]

The affiliates, sensing the rising appeal of news in general, as well as its pivotal importance in primetime ratings, began to think about the news more carefully. With their eyes fixed on greater profits, commercialization of local news was inevitable. As Ron Powers has said, "the TV newscast was a victim of its own success."[5] Advertisers were quick to

5

---

[3]*ibid.*, p. 29. [Author's note]
[4]*ibid.*, p. 30. [Author's note]
[5]*ibid.*, p. 6. [Author's note]

zero in on the growing audiences and were willing to pay higher rates for even bigger ones. How to deliver them? The answer came through the services of market research consultants. And when their services paid off more handsomely than anyone had anticipated, the future of TV news was a *fait accompli*. It was to be — in ways more profound and disturbing than anyone imagined — a commodity, a combination of various show business staples packaged and promoted like perfume or pet food.

In 1974, local use of media consultants hit the jackpot. NBC's New York affiliate was running a poor third in ratings. Compared to its 333,000 adult viewers, ABC had 697,000 and CBS a whopping 937,000.[6] NBC hired some experts who, using standard marketing techniques found they could gauge audiences' tastes and their attitudes toward various news features and styles more effectively than the networks had dreamed possible. Seventeen months later, NBC's *News Center 4* was number one with 708,000 viewers to CBS' 696,000 and ABC's 610,000.

At that point "television news had become too important to be left to the newspeople." Marketing whiz kids and TV production experts began determining the content, look, and delivery of what was supposed to be important political information and analysis. No expense was spared in what was quickly recognized as a near foolproof investment. Suddenly budgets went sky high. NBC built a $300,000 set, raised anchor Tom Snyder's salary to $500,000 a year and put a staff of 200 — "the largest group anywhere putting out a news program, local or national"[7] — to work. Local news had become big business, big show business to be exact.

Marketing research is a system developed to determine "what people want," but always within the limits of what the market is prepared to offer. Viewers participating in the research had their past experience to use as a guideline — not some ideal informational universe in which relevant, significant events were offered in a meaningful context. The choices presented by researchers necessarily reflected some variation of selections from within that range. Similarly, once the results of the research are put into practice, and ratings rise accordingly, viewers are not necessarily confirming that their needs have been met. They are merely confirming that as network news goes, they prefer the new arrangement to the old.

The researchers discovered that what viewers "chose" to see on local news — and increasingly, over time, on all news — wasn't more in depth reporting on politics or social issues. Far from it. They were dying for something which was not technically news or information at all.

[6]*ibid.*, p. 17. [Author's note]

[7]Edwin Diamond, *The Tin Kazoo* (Cambridge, Mass., 1975), p. 76. [Author's note]

They wanted more human interest stories, more personable anchors who would communicate a sense of intimacy and warmth, more sports, more weather, more jazzy graphics, and more on-the-spot coverage of community events — no matter what they were. In a word, audiences wanted local newscasters to create for them a sense of "community."

If the results of these findings, in terms of news production, have at times seemed appalling, that is by no means because of "what people wanted," at least not in some absolute sense. The direction of local news reflects two facts about contemporary life and network TV. In the first place, it reconfirms [that] the social role of television, in its broadest sense, is to provide that lost sense of community integrity in a fragmented world. That is a legitimate need and, to the extent that local news alone provides it, its popularity is justified. That this society needs to manufacture a synthetic version of community in this way is a reflection of its structural values, not its citizens. It is the economic drive of capitalism, after all, that subverted the homogeneous communities of the past. And it is capitalist economics, more than any human "want," that led to the particularly plastic version of "community" local news came to offer.

To provide "what people wanted," local news producers began to revamp their entire newscasts. Everyone needed a "media consultant" — it was not enough to have a general sense of what was wanted. Competition demanded specialists in creating sets, weather maps, and other graphic aids. National trends began to emerge, as each station adopted a tried and true format established elsewhere. *Eyewitness News*, *News Center 4*, and so on, came to represent standardized sets and program formats seen all over the nation. Even some packaged, generic-style news items began to appear. Human interest and other light features are highly transportable in a society which has increasingly given up local color for the modern uniformity of mass-produced shopping malls, fast food chains, and eight-screen movie complexes showing the same eight movies from Anchorage to Atlanta.

All of this is considered nonfiction. It pretends to present "reality" in the raw. But in truth it could hardly be further from reality. The superficially unique but essentially clonelike communities portrayed on local newscasts everywhere are utopian fantasies. They are Emerald Cities conjured up by the hidden Wizards of marketing research. They construct a false version of reality, a false sense of community and intimacy which, in many lives, must substitute for the real thing. That these Tinker Toy towns are taken at face value by most viewers, are embraced and smiled upon as their own, is a sadder commentary on American life than the much scapegoated media "sex and violence." For the "have schmaltz will travel" anchors that smile out at us from news desks and other cozy local spots are not journalists, strictly speaking, but rather paid performers, impersonating the friends and neighbors we all wish we had.

It is all too easy to condemn the audiences whose apparent attitudes and desires brought all this about. That, in fact, is the standard line we get from most educated people and indeed many media workers themselves. It is worth looking at the implications of this position. On the one hand, there is no question that the networks are in the business of manipulation and profiteering. They need to attract and hold audiences and they have found that the best way to do this is with this pseudo-news. But if people enjoy and look forward to watching this stuff, it is not because they are stupid; it is because their immediate human needs are not being met elsewhere. What people in this country crave, and increasingly feel the absence of, is human intimacy and a sense of meaning in their lives. They are lonely, confused, and increasingly terrified of what the world "out there" might have in store for them.

The lack of interest in hard news and analysis is in part attributable 15 to this greater felt need for security and well being. But it is also a function of the educational institutions — of which the media is by now perhaps the most influential — through which we develop our ideas about the world. Functional illiteracy in America is a well known scandal. Even those who are "educated" are not taught to see events in an historic context or to question the information they receive. When you put together the commercial, show biz style of TV generally, the lack of critical skills in the population at large, and the very real — almost heartbreaking — need for emotional and social gratification, you have a world readymade for the gift of Newzak.

A Day in the Life of Hometown, USA

Local news is now quite standardized. It is made up of a series of formulaic features organized in a way which prioritizes things for us. To scan the agenda and time allotments of the items featured on a typical local newscast is to see at a glance what a typical American day is supposed to have been like in Anytown, USA. I have selected, at random, an 11 P.M. Action Newscast from the ABC affiliate in Pittsburgh, on the night of September 26, 1984. First there was a report of a fatal car crash. Then a three-year-old "was found beaten to death." Then came the death of an eleven month old baby, possibly a result of neglect. A man, we heard next, was sentenced to twenty-five years for arson, followed by a report about a local county's budget problems. All this took four minutes. It was followed by a "teaser" for upcoming stories and a commercial break.

At 11:06:50 the national and international news began — with a noticeable local slant. First, and supposedly most important, a local speech by Anwar Sadat's widow was canceled because of a bomb scare. Then came a quick report on the activities of the President, Secretary of State, and Vice President — all of whom had spent their important days delivering speeches. After a quick report on a study of the dangers of tobacco, and another commercial, we were ready, at 11:13, for the sports segment, which ran over six minutes — as compared to the seconds-long reports on political and social matters.

After the sports came a report on the beginning of the Jewish New Year, a report on the lottery winners, and a commercial break preceded by a teaser for the weather report. The weather itself, second in time-measured importance only to sports, ran for over five minutes. It included footage of the weather reporter's visit to a local grade school that day, complete with pictures of the signs made by the kids — "The Weatherman Cares" — and the refreshment table, Jell-O molds and all. Finally the anchor told a cute story about tourists stealing sherry glasses from an English Earl and said good night.

With a variety of other similarly earthshaking options, this is what local news does. It sends us off to bed with certain images, ideas, and attitudes dancing in our heads. First there is local catastrophe, the more heartrending the better. Kids in need of organ transplants are often featured in the early minutes, along with pleas for money and/or donors. Lately, reports on missing children have also become big news. Any story in which warm feelings combine with dramatic visuals is a shoe-in. Pets stuck in trees, or kids falling into wells are always hot. They allow for sympathy and for a chance to show our local fire fighters and law enforcers on the job, being heroic, making our neighborhoods safe and happy. Whatever national news is shown is usually locally oriented and, if possible, sensational too. Big names are featured doing ceremonial things. If there is a bomb scare, all the better. The local heroes are on the job again.

This series of disasters and tragedies may not seem particularly   20
cheering at first glance, but given the realities of modern life, it presents a picture that is in many ways reassuring. In fact, the world it presents to us is remarkably like the fictional world of daytime soap opera. There is a preponderance of trouble and disaster, to be sure; but the trouble and disaster take timebound, physical forms. The tragedy is always personal, not political, even in the major national news items. It takes the form of illness, natural catastrophe, and human failure of a very personal, immediate kind. The father who beats his child is, by the very fact of his deeds having been reported, already taken into custody. And if the missing child, the child in need of an organ transplant, the victim of fire, are in very bad — even terminally bad — shape, it is not the fault of society or the political system. On the contrary, to the extent that local or national officials enter the picture, they are seen as heroes, good guys — not by dint of any political virtues, but because of their official status. The implication is that given disaster and tragedy in our community, more often than not, there are good professional father figures around inventing new surgical procedures, putting criminals and child abusers where they belong, saving family homes from fire.

The very ways in which social leaders are portrayed is reassuringly apolitical and noncontroversial. Speeches, acts of derring do, and so on, have no political, social, or historic context or implication. Local news, again like soap opera, makes no judgments about issues, except an occasional emotional endorsement of "Democracy" and repudiation of "Communism." It omits any historic or social background information to tie personal events — and even national speeches by individual leaders are personalized — together or make them part of a larger social world. It moves from visually sensational or heart stirring image to image quickly, with each report separated from the other by breaks. Overall, it provides a sense that the average citizen, as victim, patient, frightened worker, or homeowner, is important, is cared about and cared for.[8]

Local news stations do deal with larger, more ongoing social issues in their own way. But it is not a way which leads to deeper understanding or raises any kind of question about differing policies or strategies for solving such problems. Rather, the ways of solving social problems on local news are wholly in keeping with the ways of solving private problems. From time to time, special reports are run on recurring problems. If there has been a rash of rapes, teen suicides, or the like, locals will often run a series of brief reports on the topic. Incest, teen sexuality, and other sexually titillating topics are particularly popular. Mostly, they are nothing but interviews with victims and local experts in the field. A director of a shelter for battered women may say a few sentences about the number of cases and the gory details of the typical situations. Footage of crying children, bandaged women, and — if all else fails — the exteriors of family homes is *de rigueur*.

These special reports are usually run during the sweeps seasons to boost ratings at the time when advertising rates are set. When media consultants are brought in, the topics covered can be pretty flimsy. "Bikini fashions" was a hit in one city. A series on "Super Rats" sighted around town actually boosted a Chicago station's audience by 30,000 homes. "We thought it was a joke," said one of the reporters involved. While media experts tend to believe that the popularity of this kind of thing "brings out the worst in human nature," there is more to it than that. This, after all, is just the kind of thing people in a small, close knit community would talk about quite naturally. It is only because of the atomization and impersonality of most cities that we do not normally have these discussions, even when the situation at hand is one that affects an entire community. People often do not know their neighbors anymore, and may even be hostile or fearful of them. Local TV, by acting as neighbor substitute and telling us this kind of story, may not be

<hr>

[8]Herbert Schiller's *The Mind Managers* (Boston, 1973), deals with many of these features in detail, and discusses their ideological effects. His seminal work is done in the tradition of strict manipulation theory however. [Author's note]

giving us the news, but it is giving us something we don't get anywhere else and would naturally find interesting or at least useful for small talk.

Another feature of local news which is both disheartening and understandable is the increasing use of prepackaged items distributed by independent producers or the networks. While the independent items are generally used as fillers on slow nights, the network packages are different. They are produced and distributed so the affiliates can publicize, through popular local newscasts, the network's other programming. As competition from cable and video cassettes impinges on network entertainment audiences, it has become common for the networks to send affiliates whole series of pseudo-promotional clips to be run as news. Most typically, a "report" on a sitcom or soap opera will air, accompanied by guest appearances by stars, or even appearances by newscasters in the shows themselves.

This serves two purposes. First it helps boost the shows. But more   25
interestingly, it adds to the personalization of the newscasters, to their transformation from journalists to show business personalities. There they are, acting out a fantasy viewers can only dream of — mingling with popular stars and appearing as actors on television. Never mind that they are already more actors than information gatherers. This ploy intensifies and glamorizes a process which is not consciously understood by most viewers, but which is perhaps the most important ingredient in the success of local news.

On another level, of course, there is a great deal of public awareness of much of what I have just described, although not in any coherent, systematic context. And the media itself, in its other forms, often satirizes and criticizes the excesses of news trivialization. Recently, one of the networks aired a very good TV movie about the dangers of sensationalizing the news, and the moral and social issues the practice raises. This is where television acts in its most healthy capacity. The tendency of TV movies to individualize and limit issues is always present, but the process of consciousness raising is nonetheless begun.

Late night TV comedy has always been the domain in which social satire flourishes best, and TV news has often been its target. As early as the 1960s, *That Was the Week That Was* began mocking TV news as a genre, HBO's current *Not Necessarily the News* updates the effort. In fact, the best TV comedy today — *Second City TV* and *David Letterman* for instance — takes its humor from its knowing "defrocking" of the hallowed traditions of its own medium. The demise of *Saturday Night Live* was probably in part attributable to its failure to focus on a salient aspect of the social world and mock it. Its best features, in its early days, were its parodies of classic TV genres. That it is now the media itself that most demands satiric comment is a reflection of the "looking glass" hypothesis: that social reality, as we experience it, comes largely through the mediated glass of network convention.

Howdy, Neighbors!

If satiric take-offs on TV news have focused mostly on newscasters themselves, it is because the personalities of these people, "the news teams," as they are euphemistically called, are the dominant elements of the genre and the biggest factors in the ratings wars. Most local newscasters have had no experience in print journalism. They were trained and hired to do what local news does: create a sense of "family." So important is this role that local newspeople have become marketable commodities. No longer do they hail from the cities they report on, and pretend to be a part of. They move from town to town in search of the bigger buck, the bigger market, the bigger chance to hit the TV big-time. "They circulate through the ranks of the farm-league stations on their way to the majors with maximum fanfare."[9] You only need to check the trade paper, *Variety*, to see what has happened. Each week, space is devoted to the moves and salaries of local newscasters. Anyone with appeal will move from Omaha to Denver to Washington so fast they will have no time to learn the local landscape, slang, or dialect. Newscasters even have agents to negotiate their salaries and career moves.

In order to capitalize on, and increase, the sense of family closeness and community solidarity which the news team is supposed to reflect, stations now regularly hire ad agencies to create very elaborate, almost sitcom-like ads for their crews. They are seen doing their shopping, visiting their grandmothers, tending their babies, and so on. They are tracked to the bank, the local diner, and the Little League in order to promote their local roots and "just folks" personalities. An anchor who has just barely unpacked will say "I love my neighborhood" to attract viewers. And during the sweeps season, when the ratings are monitored, the stations go all out to do more and more of what works best — color-ful, emotion-charged stories full of sensational visuals and community spirit.

There are anchors who cannot pronounce the English language, much less names and cities of other cultures. There are anchors who cannot read a sentence and make it seem as though they understand their own words. And these people may be the most popular. Grooming, dress, and the all-important ability to interact in a chummy way with the other reporters and exude cheeriness and charm are what producers look for. After all, with a script full of half-minute hard news stories stuck between mountains of shocks and tearjerkers, the only reactions really needed are horror, pity, and sentimentality.

30

[9]Ann Salisbury, "News That Isn't Really," *TV Guide* (February 11, 1984), pp. 5–10. [Author's note]

The advancement of women into anchor spots has been heralded as a victory for feminists. Certainly there is truth in this. The change in newscaster image, from the fatherly authority of Walter Cronkite to the informal sister-brother camaraderie of today's local and national teams is one of the many salutary effects of feminism on the mass media. It is also one of the most dramatic illustrations of the often kinky workings of hegemony. On the one hand, even that bastion of male privilege, *60 Minutes*, has introduced a woman, Jessica Savitch, to the team. And Barbara Walters' position of prominence in the news world would have been unthinkable a decade ago. On the other hand, the image projected by these women is not exactly a model of feminist dignity. And the worst of the negative features foisted upon women newscasters is seen in local news.

It is difficult to sort out the convoluted minglings of the demands of feminism and the marketplace in discussing women on the news. For if, on the other hand, women newscasters — like women in every field — must be faster, brighter, and more aggressive than their male counterparts, they must also conform to an image of femininity which is saturated with negative stereotypes. Women anchors are invariably young, pretty, and ever-smiling. Since they are meant to perform as good neighbors and family members, they mimic the most traditional female versions of those roles. They coo at babies, cluck at naughtiness, sigh emotionally at stories of human tragedy.

The case of Christine Craft, the thirty-eight year old local anchor who brought suit against her ex-employer on grounds of sex discrimination, explains it all. Craft was let go because, among other things, she did not take enough care of her appearance and failed to show "deference" to males. The attractive, personable woman won her case, although it was appealed and is still unresolved. But the contradictions in local news shows brought out in the case were enlightening. For it is not only women, but men too, who have been "feminized" by Newszak. Good journalism is in fact a matter of aggressiveness and integrity, not deference or grooming. But since ratings and human interest, not truth, are most valued in local news, show business standards overtake those of journalism. And show business is built on charm and affability. For women, this translates into an image too close to "sweet young thing" for comfort. For men, it comes across as "good old boy." In both cases, it reflects a move from the "watchdog" role of professional, independent journalists to a more entertainment-oriented image of the untroubled Yuppie enjoying his or her lifestyle.

In the process of creating the "team," local news has followed another trend set by dramatic series — presenting an image of the family in which authority figures are downplayed, while youth and equality are stressed. Sitcoms have long projected this view of family life. Father has not known best in TV families for a long time now. More often, as in *Family Ties* and *All in the Family*, it is the youngsters, more in tune with social reality and often more sophisticated and intelligent, who shine. Bumbling old Dad, with his outdated ideas about life, is the butt of many jokes on TV. (The popularity of *The Bill Cosby Show* may reflect popular discomfort with this trend and a return to patriarchal dignity.)

As a trend, the elimination of the strong father figure, and his replacement with a group of palsy-walsy kids who get along fine without him, is at the heart of the news team concept. Expertise and authority are less and less centered in the home, after all. And a family living the good life presented on TV is in fact caught up equally in the concern with youthfulness, fun, and being "with it." And so, while Dan Rather and Ted Koppel still affect a patriarchal kind of authoritativeness, the local teams, reflecting personal life and private values, share in the playful, egalitarian image of family life projected by commercials. Sometimes — often, actually — a team will burst into theatrical giggles when a line is flubbed. This collective cracking up emphasizes the childishness of what's going on, the playfulness and the element of leisure activity. Needless to say, such behavior would be unseemly in a serious analysis of the arms race. But such material is not found on local news.

In place of old fashioned journalism, local news inserts interpersonal relations, jokes, and teasing. "Where did you get that jacket?" says a woman anchor to the weatherman — who has developed a reputation for slightly out of the ordinary attire. Or perhaps we hear about someone's failure to change her snow tires or stick to his diet. Just like you and me, we think, as we smile warmly to ourselves.

The actual coverage of events, and choice of stories, reflects these human, neighborly criteria for news. In fact, the media — especially local news — have become a kind of substitute for all the things a good society is supposed to provide, but which our society dramatically lacks. We live in a world in which social service agencies are underfunded, inefficient, and often cruel and insensitive. The police and the courts are filled with corruption and bias in their enforcement of "justice." The sense of community has been replaced by a plastic, nationally uniform series of commercial enterprises. Do you need child care? You won't find much in the way of public assistance and what is available is expensive and corporately owned and managed. Do you worry about the dangers of drugs and violence for your kids? The streets and schools are full of both and there is little being done about it. Government agencies are often as not in on the take or responsible for the violence.

But when you turn on the local news, it's a different world entirely. There you see any number of encouraging and reassuring things. The pretty reporter who jokes with the weatherman every day is right there in front of City Hall, or the local prison, keeping us informed of the latest developments in a scary situation. The robber is just now being apprehended, she'll assure us. The city council is carefully considering bills to stop drug traffic, to tighten up regulations for child care licenses, to bring more jobs to our city. We ourselves might be frightened to go out and observe these things — especially with the media so eager to scare us to death about street violence — but we know if "our Mary" is on-the-spot, it cannot be too bad for too long.

News Teams as Public Servants

Serious city council debates on troublesome issues do not in fact bring results very often. So, besides reassuring us that things are being "considered," local newscasters have another, even more important job. As the world and its problems worsen, and the proposed plans to make things better fall by the wayside and are forgotten, the media has become the primary source of its own "good news." It is no exaggeration to say that most of what passes for good news — as opposed to reports that our officials are on the job, working on solutions to social problems — is manufactured by local news stations themselves. More and more, local news stations have been taking their responsibilities as agents of the public interest seriously. News stations and crews are responsible for any number of campaigns and programs to solve community problems.

The sign in the grade school lunchroom announcing "The Weatherman Cares" is a symbol of the main role of local TV. It presents an image of an institution — the media itself — that is wholly concerned with us and our needs. Newspeople now traditionally visit schools, lead parades, head charity drives, and open malls — all in the name of public interest. In any city you visit you will find that each network affiliate has its own little do-gooder bailiwick. One may focus on collecting food for the unemployed and homeless. One may provide information for returning veterans. One may provide health information.

This trend began with the now standard "Action Line" segments in cities everywhere. People, desperate for help in solving everyday problems, took to calling their local TV stations for advice and information. From there it was a quick move to the institutionalization of a special feature in which anyone with a problem calls a certain number and talks to the person in charge of that beat. Say the garbage on your street has been sitting there for weeks, attracting rats and looking generally grotesque. Call "Action Line" and the newscaster will put in a special call on your behalf to the appropriate agency. In a flash your problem is solved. Then you will find yourself on the evening news telling your story to other sufferers of governmental neglect.

40

This is a technique which President Reagan has used with great success. Single out one person, solve her or his problem, and then announce to the world that the system works. Never mind that it took clout to do the job for which every citizen pays taxes. Never mind that one case means nothing in the scheme of things. The point is that help is available, caring, and effective. No need to organize, protest, or — perish the thought — change any institutional structures or power relations. In fact, one result of this technique is to individualize the whole concept of social problem solving. While giving us a sense of belonging to a cohesive, caring community, it also reinforces the sense that each problem is unique and personal and must be solved on a case by case basis.

When this technique took off, stations recognized a real gold mine of viewer loyalty and commercial revenues. And since the world is getting harder and harder to deal with anyway, it was inevitable that bigger problems and bigger media extravaganzas would soon arrive. Following in the tradition of the TV marathon for charity, the stations began running lengthy broadcasts devoted to one particularly serious community issue. Typical issues treated in several-hour long, or even whole day, marathons are those which first speak to local concerns and crises, and second, have great emotional appeal. The plight of Vietnam vets, for example, might be treated as a day long "workshop" in which local news teams and public officials participate.

This "group effort" image is one of the most important aspects of this kind of program. It adds to the image of the station as a caring, effective community institution. The hitch is that the TV crews can do nothing beyond publicizing, and exaggerating, the existing programs and agencies and their effectiveness in "solving problems." In fact, these problems have deep social, historic, and political causes. They arise because we live in a society which does not provide needed services and benefits for those on the bottom, those who have the least opportunity and are therefore most often exploited — a perfect description of the Vietnam vets. But the day long attention to their "problems" gives the false impression that this society is functioning in a healthy, just way.

One of the most common issues to be treated in this way recently is   45
unemployment. No fewer than sixty cities have in the last few years run lengthy primetime extravaganzas called "Job-a-thons."[10] These shows, sponsored by local stations in areas hard hit by unemployment, are paradigms — almost parodies, really — of what local news is all about. Following the charity marathon format, they pretend to be offering a vital service: a "job exchange." The entire news team is on hand to facilitate the event. Publicity begins early and is relentless, leading

[10]Tim Patterson, "Eyewitless News: An Amusing Aid to Digestion," in *Alternative Papers: Selection from the Alternative Press* (Philadelphia, 1982), p. 458. [Author's note]

anyone with a problem finding work to anticipate the day with great hope. First, every possible employer in need of workers lists openings, complete with job description, requirements, and pay. Then everyone seeking work is invited to come on the show and give her or his story and work qualifications. Viewers — both employers and jobseekers — can also call in to offer jobs and request interviews for those listed.

This format — part *Queen for a Day*, part cattle auction — is both dishonest and exploitative. First of all, the jobs listed are almost invariably minimum wage dead ends that no one else wants. Some are downright Dickensian in their demands. A position as the sole live-in "counselor" at a halfway house for delinquent and addicted teenagers is typical. Most of the opportunities are of the custodial nature, and many are very short term. The "applicants" for these positions are often positively tragic. Most are highly qualified for much more meaningful work. They are people laid off from good jobs, with families to support, and are forced, through sheer desperation, to parade themselves before the TV audience, dressed in their best and nervously trying to make a good impression as they tell their stories. What should elicit outrage brings pity. The always smiling newscasters look dutifully sympathetic and concerned — as they do about everything else they report on. The experience is humiliating and, worse yet, largely useless. In Pittsburgh, one of the hardest hit cities economically, 4,600 people, many with advanced degrees and special skills, applied for about 1,500 jobs. Only 300 fulltime jobs were filled. Almost all were far beneath the talents of their applicants. In Milwaukee, 860 jobs were offered. Of 2,800 applicants, 460 found jobs. Most were with food chains.[11]

The sheer number of offerings and ringing phones, seen and heard on the TV screen, give the impression that there is a lot happening, that people are being helped out of seemingly hopeless situations, that a huge social problem is being solved. This impression comes almost entirely from the visual and dramatic format of the programs. The hosts seem to be sweating away, aching hearts in throats, in the interest of the poor souls they exploit as they comfort. Soup kitchens are shown feeding smiling children. Volunteer health care workers describe free health care. Never mind that in reality these institutions are few, understaffed, and very limited in the services they are able to provide. It looks impressive on TV. Periodically, local politicians come on or call in to applaud the effort and pledge their support (whatever that means). President Reagan himself called in to the "Virginia Job Day" program. And why not? That is just the sort of "safety net" he loves — one which gets lots of media coverage and almost no meaningful results.

The society at large is clearly not dealing with the problem of

[11]*"Cross Currents," Channels of Communication* (May–June, 1983), p. 11. [Author's note]

unemployment, or health care, or illiteracy, or any other widescale social crisis affecting the poor, the disabled, the minorities of the country. Nothing vaguely related to the real causes of structural unemployment, or any other social crisis, ever comes up in these shows. There is no analysis of historic causes, no economic analysis, no attempt to look for broad solutions to endemic problems of capitalism. Instead, out of a few bad jokes, crocodile tears, and completely misleading images of activity and progress, the viewer is led to believe that no matter what might befall you in these United States, help is just around the corner.

So successful have these features become that many stations take on long term commitments to their pet social crises. The station that ran the Job-a-thon in Pittsburgh has continued to collect food for the unemployed on weekends. Each week you see your local favorites — out of their tailored suits and dressed in jeans and parkas — going out to various town centers to personally collect canned goods from viewers and load them onto trucks. Such is the job of a TV reporter. Not only do these people fail to report news, they often collude in increasingly important ways with the corporations and government agencies responsible for the policies that create these problems. This is because they tend to create a false sense that society is in fact working more effectively than is the case to solve problems. Where collective agitation to demand government action might be a more useful response to a crisis, those who might protest are led to believe the issue is being resolved, that no further action is necessary. In this sense, the media have become an indispensable part of the established power structure, ameliorating anxiety and defusing mass anger.

The Real News:
Game Canceled Because of Rain

As dramatic as these special marathons are, they are obviously not what keeps people watching local news every day. What makes up the bulk of the nightly newscasts are sports and weather — issues of no social import at all. Each of these segments runs far longer than any hard news story, no matter how earthshaking. The allocation of time for these segments is based on the findings of market analysts. It was sports and weather, in particular, that viewers were interested in having expanded. Over the years, this has been happening almost on a daily basis. Anyone returning from a trip of any length at all will notice at least minor embellishments to the weather and sports reports. Maps of various aspects of the weather proliferate endlessly. And sports reports are continuously being changed, and changed again, in efforts to make even more attractive what is already the highlight of the broadcast.

Sports and weather may be the most vacuous things on the air. They provide very little in the way of real information, and what is presented is nearly drowned in glitz. Sports news is the most repetitious and nonanalytical thing on TV. There is no sense that economic or social factors come into play in the sports world. On the contrary, the typical sportscast is predictable to the point of self-parody. Athletes are interviewed about a game coming up or just played. The questions and answers are always the same. "How do you think you'll do this season, Bud?" "Well, gee, we're just gonna get out there and give it our best and all," is recognizably typical. (Actually, it is the prototype of most TV interviewing. "How do you feel about your daughter's murder?" "Well, it's hard to put into words. We're just broken up about it." Pointless questions and obvious answers are the stuff of TV "reporting.")

The appeal of these reports cannot be understood in terms of news criteria. It is the very desire to escape from "news," from the pressures of social reality and personal woes, that draws viewers to sports and weather. In that sense, the blurring of entertainment and information creates a situation in which critics, puzzling over entertainment presented as news, may be missing the point. It is because sports is so universal a form of "fun" and relaxation for Americans that it is so talked about and watched. It provides needed "play" after a busy day.

That sports seems to be news is related to the role of sports teams in community identity. If football is fun to watch, rooting for a home team is a more significant pastime. It provides one of the strongest forms of community "glue" left to us. There are few activities — none in collective daily life — that provide that sense of belonging and sharing that sports do. In workplaces, where competition and tension rule, the time spent talking about local teams is a welcome respite from the anxiety and hostility of other activities.

The weather report plays a similar role. Even those who don't like sports must discuss and concern themselves with the weather. It too binds us together as a community; it too is a common element of our collective daily life. When personal problems — money fears, sexual anxieties — plague us, we often hide them from others. With the weather, we really do share them. That is an important social fact. An interview with Phil McHugh, of the media consultant firm McHugh and Hoffman, explained some of the reasons for emphasizing weather on local news. The interview took place in 1974, at a time when weather was only, on average, about three and one-half minutes of the newscasts. In ten years it has just about doubled. According to McHugh, "People are very much interested in weather. They plan their life around it . . . the mass audience, the people who have to go to work for a living . . . all the mothers want to know how to dress their kids for school."[12]

[12] *ibid.* [Author's note]

The elaborate, sometimes downright gorgeous graphics used to 55
show us everything we could conceivably want to know about the
weather are interesting examples of the way in which television's visual
sophistication has improved its ability to provide this kind of shared
intimacy and personal advice. Because there are so many different maps
and radarscopes available, the weatherperson can stay on screen, saying
nothing much, for a very long time. Weather people are usually the
homiest, wittiest (actually silliest in most cases), and most informal
members of the news team. They are often loved by community members, who will choose a particular news station as much for the
weatherperson as anything else. If there is no one at home to commiser-
ate with about the eight days of rain we've just had; no one to complain
to about having to cut the grass, miss the softball game; or whatever
may happen, we still have good old Bill What's-His-Name to share it
with. He understands just how we feel. He too forgot his umbrella, or
had to shovel his walk four times in one week.

That these weather reporters are in some sense informing us of a
phenomenon which has all the trappings of science produces interesting
side effects. For one thing, the sexy blondes who reported weather in the
1950s have gone the way of all such blatantly sexist stereotyping on local
news. Men do most weather reports, and the women who do it are all
business. In that sense, weather and women have made progress toward
respectability. But on another level, the pseudoscientific mystification
produced by the sets and charts is excessive. It reflects another trend in
media toward taking authority away from us and putting our fates in
the hands of scientific experts who are knowledgeable about things
beyond our comprehension. Science and pseudoscience are the delights
of television, for they justify so much that is done to us and for us. The
folklore and finger knowledge that Grandma used often worked after
all. She didn't need TV to tell her what nature was up to. While there
are positive elements to this trend, it also creates one more area of daily
life over which we have lost control and forgotten how to use our
common sense.

In essence, all these aspects of local news combine to create a feeling
of family for those who have none, and for those who have little in
common with the one they do have. In so doing they reinforce the
corporate definition of family relations too. As one TV station promo
promised: "It's not like watching news, it's like watching family!" And it
is a family more to your liking than the one you may be stuck with at
that. There is a phrase that has gained currency among TV folk lately:
"Reality Programming." It is the industry term for the phenomenon
signaled by the success of local news — the fact that more and more
people seem to prefer nonfiction to fiction on TV. They watch local
news in the same spirit that they watch soap operas — in an effort to
feel some intense, ongoing human drama in which no matter how bad

things may get or seem, there is always a silver lining, an upbeat ending, a hero to solve the problem or at least explain it. They get that from local news. But it is in many ways a more dangerous addiction than the soaps. Soaps after all are — for all but the borderline psychotic — clearly unreal. Local news, on the other hand, is presented and accepted as all too real. What it tells, what it leaves out, how it explains and solves problems, have a lot to do with the way people have come to understand and respond to their daily experience. And yet local news is every bit as much a creation, a fiction, a story as a soap opera. Its characters are playing roles, its stories are distorted and falsified versions of life, and its values are those of the people who make the decisions governing our lives, not our own.

Engaging the Text

1. Summarize Rapping's account of the evolution of local news programming. Why has local news generally not been a network priority? What factors led to its rise during the 1960s and 1970s?

2. What does Rapping mean when she says that local news has become a "commodity" (para. 6)? How has market research shaped what we see on local news shows? What fears and desires do these shows play on?

3. What, according to Rapping, is the typical structure of a local news show? What "parts" does it contain, and what functions do these parts perform? Overall, what cultural messages do such shows communicate to their viewers?

4. Discuss the symbolic roles played by the members of a "news team" on a local news broadcast. What is the function of the anchor, the coanchor, the sportscaster, the weatherperson, the media critic, the consumer advocate?

5. What danger does Rapping see in "Reality Programming" (para. 57) like that represented by local television news shows? Why, in her opinion, are these kinds of shows more threatening than the average soap opera? Do you agree?

Exploring Connections

6. Rapping and Jack Solomon (p. 602) suggest that advertisers and television programmers are looking to "reality" as a new source of media myths and images. What evidence do you see of this "new realism" in the style or content of current advertising and television programming? What makes such shows or commercials particularly "realistic"? What do they communicate to us about the nature of "reality"? What is their attraction? Discuss whether this "new realism" represents, as Rapping suggests, a potentially "dangerous addiction" (para. 57).

7. Review "The Paradox of Perfection" (p. 402) and discuss how Arlene Skolnick might analyze the average local news program as an example of the ideal family. How, according to Skolnick, might such a family be expected to make us feel?

Extending the Critical Context

8. Test some of Rapping's assertions about local news shows by analyzing a few broadcasts in your vicinity. Do you find evidence of the kind of role playing and "egalitarian" playfulness that Rapping notes? What kinds of information does the local news actually provide? What evidence, if any, do you see that it's a substitute for "all the things a good society is supposed to provide, but which our society dramatically lacks" (para. 37)?

9. Working in small groups, write a brief script for your local news show that would offer useful information and respond directly to the realities of its viewers — a show that Rapping herself might design as an antidote to the meaningless "goodnews" she believes is served up in most local news programming. Share a few of these scripts in class and discuss how this kind of television programming might affect its viewers.

What's Left After Violence and Advertising?

Maurine Doerken

In this selection from the provocatively titled Classroom Combat: Teaching and Television *(1983), Maurine Doerken (b. 1950), a teacher and expert on the field of education, surveys the fictional world of stereotypes that television offers its viewers; she also makes a case for the powerful and dangerous influence these distortions have, particularly on children. Pushing beyond the usual debates about violence and advertising, she argues that TV's escapist fare diminishes social awareness and fosters passivity and personal isolation.*

Attitudes Toward Entertainment

If the average person on the street were stopped and asked what the three most frequent offerings on American television are (excluding commercials), he would probably answer action/adventure, situation comedy, and musical/variety talk shows. This same person then most likely would turn around and classify these all under the rubric "entertainment."

But Shakespearean plays and grand opera are also "entertainment," yet they are hardly the same kind as is usually offered on our TV screens. This is a problem we Americans face when discussing television programming, . . . because we have grown so accustomed to think of TV material as general entertainment when it is, in fact, light fare of a very specific kind. The vast majority of TV offerings in this country have been and continue to be fantasy/escapist entertainment, *not* the entertainment we get from Othello or Beethoven. Some entertainment, to be sure, can be very engaging and very moving without being escapist, but those who organize TV material in America usually give the broad name "entertainment" to what is only a narrow section of the whole. This is not *always* the case, but generally it is.

Consequently, over the past thirty years, viewers have been exposed with great consistency to fantasy/escapist entertainment and a narrowing of tasks to fit "the average," not entertainment of a more serious, thought-provoking kind or one based predominantly on real life. So when we discuss the impact of televison on young people, we are talking about the impact of three decades of fantasy/escapist fare. Even during the mid-fifties, light entertainment constituted approximately seventy-five percent of total TV time, and a brief glance at *TV Guide* today hardly reveals much of a change. Escapist entertainment still dominates the screen. In this sense, TV material has become what one broadcast historian calls a strategy word, for it minimizes the importance of what is presented.[1] Rather, entertainment is there to lull our critical faculties by sending us into the domain of low-involvement learning. It has no meaning, essentially, other than diverting and filling time between commercials.

This brings to mind several questions. With such a heavy diet of fantasy material, where are viewers, especially children and adolescents, to receive a comparable amount of reality presentations? Is it better to get a solid footing in reality or fantasy? Or at least an equal grounding in both? These questions are particularly relevant to preliterate youngsters who cannot read to counterbalance what they see and hear, for they are even more susceptible to informal television influence.

The effect of this fantasy/escapist entertainment has to be different 5 in character and kind than if we had had three decades of plays and dramas from renowned writers; a spectrum of musical offerings; fewer commercials; or more quality programming geared specifically toward children. This is self-evident. TV has been promoted as a window to the world, and in many cases, this has been true. But, in many other ways, it most certainly has not been so, due to the fantasy material which has dominated the screen. One need only look at American TV entertainment over the past three decades to see what a distorted view has been presented as life.

[1] Erik Barnouw, *The Sponsor: Notes on a Modern Potentate*, Oxford University Press, New York, 1978, pp. 100–102. [Author's note]

The Sexes and Racial Groups

As far as men, women, and various racial groups are concerned, television in this country has generally shown the following picture:

1. The most powerful group is the white American male. He usually is young, middle class, and unmarried — and is likely to be involved in violence.

2. Women make up a smaller proportion of all TV characters, regardless of ethnic background. They usually appear in a sexual context or in romantic roles. Two out of three are married or engaged, though this is now changing.

3. Women participate less in violence but are victimized more, and if a woman engages in aggression, she is not as likely to succeed as a man.

4. Women are also cast more frequently in domestic/comedic roles.

5. Married women are less likely to be victims of aggression. Housewives are not portrayed as villains as much as single women or those who are employed.[2]

It was not until 1968 that the first black series was offered over the TV airwaves. A young child growing up with TV during the fifties might have thought that blacks and other minorities did not exist. Not only were many people and races virtually ignored at TV's inception, but when they did appear, they often were presented as unfavorable stereotypes (i.e., Indians as bloodthirsty drunks or Chinese as cooks, servants, and laundry owners). For nearly three decades, television has concentrated on showing the twenty- to fifty-year-olds, thereby ignoring the very young and the elderly. There has been a constant push in the informal learning domain to telescope all age groups into a young adult market, focusing intently on the NOW.

Themes and Format of Programs

Not only has our escapist TV entertainment centered on specific races and ages, implicitly denying the existence of many other people and life styles, but recurring themes and ideas emerge as well. As indicated previously, violence has been a staple on the American TV screen, but even though it has occurred with mind-boggling regularity as "true-to-life action drama," it still follows the same pattern of unreality. Street crime, for example, has not been as important in the world of TV as it is in real life. Murder and assault have accounted for about fifty percent of all TV crime, yet this is not true of life on the outside. As one can see [in Table 1], almost a complete inversion has taken place.

---

[2]Robert M. Liebert et al., *The Early Window: Effects of Television on Children and Youth*, Pergamon, 1982, pp. 18–19. [Author's note]

Table 1 Comparison of Television Crimes and Real-Life Crimes[3]

FREQUENCY RANKING OF FBI CRIME INDEX FROM 1970	FREQUENCY RANKING OF TV CRIMES FROM 1972
1. Burglary	1. Murder
2. Larceny	2. Assault
3. Auto Theft	3. Robbery
4. Robbery	4. Auto Theft
5. Assault	5. Burglary
6. Rape	6. Larceny
7. Murder	7. Rape

Generally, crime on American TV has:

1. overrepresented violent crimes directed against individuals; real-life crime is usually nonviolent and directed at property;

2. underrepresented blacks, young people, and lower-class individuals involved in crime;

3. reinforced the moral that crime does not pay; the main intent is to reassure society that right will prevail; in the real world, however, this obviously is not so, for crime often pays quite well;

4. concentrated on "the hunt" as being all-important rather than the legal processes involved after apprehension;

5. underrepresented nonwhites as murder victims;

6. underrepresented violent crimes between family members; and

7. made crime motives appear simple and easily understood; in real life, this often is not the case at all.[4]

Quite clearly, this picture has little to do with reality, even though it   10
has been presented as "true" life. Yet, how much misinformation is being assimilated incidentally by children who watch a moderate to heavy amount? How much do they accept at face value? A very false image of the world could be in the making, which might be difficult to untangle later on.

TV Employment

Aside from these misrepresentations of various groups and crime in our society, another important aspect of television distortion concerns employment. Not surprisingly, the most frequent form of TV work is law enforcement. Nearly one-third of the American TV labor force at one time or another has been concerned with the pursuit of law and

[3]Chart from Joseph R. Dominick, "Crime and Law Enforcement on Prime-Time Television," *Public Opinion Quarterly*, 1973, Vol. 37, pp. 245–246. [Author's note]
[4]Same as above, p. 249. [Author's note]

order. In reality, however, only about one percent of the population is so involved. . . . Jobs associated with entertainment rank second in the world of TV, which is hardly true to life either. Professional workers have been overrepresented, and there has always been that push for a higher socioeconomic status — informal messages consistent with the consuming world of TV. A corresponding underrepresentation of worker roles has been evident, though this is changing. As a source of incidental learning for young people about jobs and work, television provides a very slanted view of what is considered important, which could have serious ramifications in children's attitudes regarding employment later on.

A case in point: when a group of children was questioned about work, they overwhelmingly chose *power* as the most important factor to consider when thinking about employment. Money, prestige, and travel came next; helping others was last. The interesting point here is that these results held for both rich and poor children; urban and rural; male and female; dull and bright.[5] Television's influence was pervasive in all areas of society. The fantasy/escapist material had been successful in changing their attitudes and aspirations toward a career.

Is this a form of programmed discontent? Does television teach unhappiness about work in general by presenting a false picture of the way life really *is*? If a child consistently sees powerful or dangerous jobs cast in glamorous settings, what kinds of ideas will he form about what he wants to be? His informal learning from television may be a source of disappointment and conflict when he finally starts to work, for it is not easy to become rich and powerful. In effect, such portrayals take the child away from the ordinary, which is a very real part of living, a part which needs to be met and dealt with often. How might all this influence his evaluation of work or his choice of job opportunities after leaving high school or college?

These instances of misrepresentation are but a few examples of how television escapist fare has twisted and turned images of life. All this may be obvious to the adult viewer, but how the past thirty years have affected children growing up under TV's powerful, informal gaze is another matter entirely. We are talking about analyzing human reactions and emotions in the area of incidental, deferred learning, which certainly is not an easy task. Yet, the impact of all this may be profound and go much deeper than many of us suspect. . . .

Personal Isolation and Television

Another important aspect in the conflict of television and children 15
is the personal and emotional isolation fostered by TV. How does this

[5]Melvin DeFleur, "Occupational Roles as Portrayed on Television," *Public Opinion Quarterly*, 1964, Vol. 28, p. 68. [Author's note]

Table 2 Amount of Viewing and Personality Characteristics[6]

CHARACTERISTIC	WATCH A GREAT DEAL OF TV	WATCH TV FREQUENTLY	WATCH TV SELDOM
Lonely	95%	5%	0%
Shy	70%	22%	7%
Listless	51%	22%	27%
Pampered	49%	25%	28%
Emotional	39%	39%	22%
Obedient	4%	79%	17%
Has Friends	4%	29%	68%
Active	1%	34%	65%

affect individual growth and development? It must be remembered that when a child accepts the box as a form of leisure activity or comfort, he turns away from *people* and all the direct stimulation they provide. His learning becomes vicarious rather than first-hand; he substitutes something inanimate for live, direct interaction. TV allows him to escape from personal involvement by substituting something that *seems* like close contact but which in fact is not. Some people believe television is the perfect refuge for those who are unable to cope with life because it acts as solace to the individual who cannot deal with the outside world. Rather than encouraging him to face his problems and learn from other people, TV offers him a place to hide or becomes a way to kill time so he will not have to cope with reality.

The following case study is a good example of this type of influence and how it can directly alter a child's behavior in school. A little girl named "Susie" exhibited marked antisocial tendencies in class. She would not participate in group activities and refused to become involved with other children. When her teacher discovered that Susie was a heavy TV viewer, she suggested to the mother that she put her daughter on a TV diet.

During the first week without TV, Susie was very upset over not being allowed to watch. Her teacher reported that she was moodier than usual and would sit and stare at the ground. After only one week, however, changes began to appear. Susie started to ask her mother to invite playmates over to the house after school. This was something she had never wanted before, and her teacher also noticed her playing more with the other children during classtime. By the end of the four weeks, the youngster no longer was just an outsider but a participant. She played by herself and with other children, and both mother and teacher thought her a much happier child. Several weeks later, however, when

[6]Chart compiled from information in Robert D. Hess and Harriet Goldman, "Parents' Views of the Effects of Television on Their Children," *Child Development*, 1962, Vol. 33, p. 415. [Author's note]

the girl's mother allowed her to resume watching television, Susie's previous symptoms returned. She simply refused to interact with other people. There appeared to be a direct relationship between the little girl's social maladjustment and her TV-watching behavior.[7] . . .

There is also the possibility that those who consume large amounts of television may possess certain introverted personality traits which are only reinforced by the medium's tendency to isolate and remove. As one can see [in Table 2], there is evidence to support this claim.

Though television by no means warrants universally adverse effects, among heavy viewers certain patterns do begin to emerge. Like the little girl just mentioned, the heavy user is lonelier, more listless, and shy. On the other hand, children who watch little TV, according to the above figures, are almost the opposite. Nor is it merely the only child or the child whose parents work who is the heavy viewer, but more importantly, the insecure child who has trouble making friends or who feels safer alone than in a group.

Whether television stimulates these personality/emotional tenden-   20
cies or draws individuals to it who are already predisposed to such traits does not really matter, because the net result is a negative influence on personal development. TV can prevent a child from being lonely, but this is not necessarily good, especially if that child is inclined to shyness in the first place. He should, on the contrary, be encouraged to participate with those around him. In other cases, television may keep children from learning how to be alone and cope with aloneness, both of which represent vital aspects of growth. As psychologist Bruno Bettelheim[8] suggests:

> Children who have been taught, or conditioned, to listen passively most of the day to the warm verbal communication coming from the TV screen . . . are often unable to respond to real persons because they arouse so much *less* feeling than the skilled actor. Worse, they lose the ability to learn from reality because life experiences are more complicated than the ones they see on the screen, and there is no one who comes in at the end to explain it all. . . . If this block of solid inertia is not removed, the emotional isolation from others that starts in front of the TV may continue. This . . . is one of the real dangers of TV.[9]

This isolation and lack of personal involvement may lead to an increase in all dependent behaviors and may hamper the development of individuals into people capable of forming their own decisions. . . .

---

[7]Safran, "How TV Changes Children," p. 17. [Author's note]

[8]*Bruno Bettelheim:* American psychologist and educationist (1903–1991) best known for his work on children and the nature of prejudice.

[9]Martin Mayer, *About Television*, Harper & Row, New York, 1972, p. 128. [Author's note]

It must be remembered, too, that television's isolating effect has been going on for several decades now. It is not a question of a few random individuals like little Susie holing up with the box, but if the Nielsens[10] are correct, almost an entire nation! This fourteen-year-old's comment states the case well:

> Television is perfect to tune out to the rest of the world. But I don't relate with my family much because we're all too busy watching TV.[11]

Narcotic Dysfunction of Television

This tendency of television to isolate individuals may have further educational and social ramifications. As people substitute watching TV for *doing*, and as they interact less with one another, they cease in a sense being social creatures. They decrease their actual involvement and learning from others and the world around them, though they may vicariously see a great deal. In this way, television acts as a narcotic or drug, as some people have claimed, for it removes people from people by taking real life away. At the flick of the switch, seas of fantasy/escapist material are readily available to pass the time of day.

But by providing the individual, especially the growing child, with so many escape valves from outside pressures, television may simultaneously stunt the growth of personal and group responsibility. It may provide steady relief from daily life and all the tensions that go along with it; but if used to hide from anxiety or duties, it can also reduce the likelihood of involvement and genuine concern. Using the medium to run away from problems or to put them off indefinitely makes the viewer less aware of troubles that do in fact exist. Continually accepting a dream world or confusing reality with fantasy is not conducive to the development of social consciousness. It is quite possible that gradual changes could result in attitudes and behavior, *away* from individual awareness and public commitment.

The term narcotizing dysfunction has been coined by psychologists to describe this particular effect of television.[12] Even though the medium exposes us to vast amounts of information, it still may evoke only minimal interest in real social problems, and this could develop into mass apathy. Excessive TV exposure may actually deaden rather than enliven the emotions of the average viewer, because the more time he spends with television, the less time he has for action and work.

---

[10]*the Nielsens:* the Nielsen rating system — a market research service used to measure and rank the popularity of television shows.

[11]"What TV Does to Kids," p. 67. [Author's note]

[12]See Paul Lazarsfeld and Robert Merton, "Mass Communication, Popular Taste, and Organized Social Action," in *The Process and Effect of Mass Communication*, Wilbur Schramm and Donald E. Roberts (Editors), University of Illinois Press, 1971, pp. 565ff. [Author's note]

Similar to the case of excessive violence viewing, a general habituation or desensitization to life's problems may take place. A person might have enormous amounts of material available to him but still fail to make any decisions regarding that information or to act upon his own feelings and instincts.

TV will not necessarily reinforce apathy among those already committed, but it will tend to do so with those who are poor self-starters in the first place. The problem here is that the apathetic generally make up a far larger number of the whole. There are always more people who do not wish to act or who have trouble overcoming their own inertia. Teachers and educators have always been confronted with the problem of student motivation. Yet, however difficult genuine social concern may be to achieve, it does not change the fact that we need a critical, perceptive, and caring citizenry, particularly among the young growing to adulthood. In an age of global politics, social awareness and responsibility toward the whole are crucial to all. 25

Television certainly has great capacity to foster the development of such attitudes, but something seems to have gone amiss along the way. There can be no doubt, for example, that TV helped to encourage some of the awareness and concern which manifested themselves during the sixties. Some very real and disturbing events found their way onto the screen, events which have left a deep impression on an entire generation. But perhaps the habit of escaping into fantasy and materialism — also promoted by television — was stronger in the long run than the effort required for continual commitment to social activism. In the short term, TV can inspire concern among people because immediate events are exciting or disturbing. But over longer periods of time, a different pattern may emerge. The preponderance of escapist fare, which allows the viewer to avoid real life or which places material above ideological concerns, may contravene both social and political action. . . .

American Schizophrenia

There are other points to consider in relationship to this narcotisizing aspect of the medium's power. In conjunction with TV's tendency to isolate and its potential for, in effect, drugging people not to care, there is also the real danger of much personal, internal conflict resulting from heavy exposure. Constantly shifting between what is and what is not; between shows, ideas, images, and channels literally is enough to push some people over the "deep end" or to make them nervous temperamentally. So much TV is based upon illusion and fantasy that it becomes very difficult at times to know what is truth and what is not. This is expecially true of young children, who have not yet accumulated a vast catalog of personal experiences against which to evaluate TV content.

One wonders: is there something inherently jarring and debilitating about the American television experience? The National Institute of Mental Health Report actually cites a study comparing American and foreign TV which suggests this may be so. Foreigners who are accustomed to a much slower pace of television say they find American TV unnerving and experience a kind of physical pain when they first see commercial television in this country. The Report declares:

> The rapid form of presentation characterizing American television in which novelty piles upon novelty in short sequences may well be counterproductive for organized and effective learning sequences. The young child who has not yet developed strategies for tuning out irrelevancies may be especially vulnerable in this respect; even programs that seek to be informative as well as entertaining may miss the mark because they allow too little time for reflection. . . . Extremely rapid-pace material, presenting novelty along with high levels of sound and fast movement, may generate surprise and confusion in a viewer whose anticipatory strategies . . . are not yet prepared for coping with this material.[13]

All this points to the fact that a very disturbing element of schizophrenia lies at the very heart of American television. On the one hand is a vast display of random bits of life; on the other is the constant psychic irritation of rampant consumerism. If mental breakdown is the common result of endless new patterns of information, then TV in this country certainly provides agitation in abundance. All the contradictory input could very well create a widespread state of subconscious confusion. This is most true for the young, because they generally need reassurance, structure, and freedom within reason in order to grow and learn at their best.

Yet, how can youngsters possibly analyze and catalog all that they view on television — especially if their parents do not take the time to discuss with them what they see? Is television somehow grooming us for mass nervous disorder and resentment? A pervasive malaise existing just below the surface of our lives? There is evidence that this is indeed likely. A survey of fifth- and sixth-grade students, for example, reveals that many emotional and personal problems suffered by these children, such as worries about looks, being fat, having bad complexions, and being accepted by others, all related to the kinds of television they watched.[14] Moreover, this country's mental hospitals are now overloaded with young patients, and many children today currently undergo some form of counseling or private therapy because they seem so unable to cope with life. There is also growing evidence that many

[13]National Institute of Mental Health Report, p. 20. [Author's note]

[14]Wilbur Schramm et al., *Television in the Lives of Our Children*, Stanford University Press, 1961, p. 119. [Author's note]

children in the United States suffer from clinical depression and suicidal tendencies even though very young.[15]

. . . If we were to construct a picture of the average TV consumer based upon the data presented thus far, the image we come up with is rather disheartening. The moderate to heavy viewer is somewhat duller, more materialistic, and less knowledgeable about life. He reads less and may lack a certain amount of spontaneity and creativity. He is less interested in the real world and people than in an edited, fantasy version of life. He may be somewhat shy and introverted, and though he may crave human contact, he has not had the practice to know how to go about being a friend. He may even be a personality type bordering at times on the mildly neurotic and mentally unstable. Or, he simply may be an inert mass which does not care and is willing to watch life go by.

[15]*Los Angeles Times*, July 25, 1978, part 1, pp. 1, 17, 18. [Author's note]

Engaging the Text

1. According to Doerken, what general image of American life does TV convey? What stereotypes or myths are associated with this version of life in the United States? What does TV tell us about the way we work, about the roles of women, men, people of color? Do you agree with her assessment?

2. How, according to Doerken, does TV "program" discontent in viewers?

3. Explain Doerken's claim that TV acts as a narcotic or a drug. What evidence, if any, have you seen that "heavy users" tend to be shy, lonely, and listless?

4. What, according to Doerken, are the social consequences of the escapism promoted by TV? Discuss whether or not she attributes too much influence to TV. How consistent are her statements about the influence of TV?

Exploring Connections

5. How would Jack Solomon (p. 602) explain the tendency of TV to exploit stereotypical images of men, women, people of color, and various social classes?

6. Read Lewis H. Lapham's indictment of American democracy in Chapter Eight (p. 701). How might Doerken's notion of the "narcotic dysfunction of television" support Lapham's analysis of the demise of the democratic "spirit" in America? Do you think that TV has made Americans more or less political?

Extending the Critical Context

7. Working in groups, test Doerken's conclusions about what television programs teach us about race, gender, crime, and work. Are the stereotypes she

describes still common on TV? What new images, if any, have taken their place?

8. Doerken mentions that what TV *omits* can influence viewers as powerfully as what it presents. Working in groups, survey several evenings of prime-time programming to determine what groups, situations, and values are omitted. Why do you suppose these omissions occur? What message is conveyed by the specific omissions you note?

The Cosby Show

Mark Crispin Miller

One of the most popular sitcoms in television history, The Cosby Show *has been praised for bringing a new realism to TV comedy, reaffirming family values, showcasing African American talent, and promoting Black culture, while still attracting a large white audience. Mark Crispin Miller sees another picture: in this selection from a much longer essay, he castigates* Cosby *for promoting shallow consumerism, authoritarian family structures, and Black stereotypes. From Miller's perspective,* Cosby *has been enormously successful precisely because it reinforces several crucial American myths. A writing instructor at Johns Hopkins University, Miller (b. 1949) has contributed essays on popular culture to* The New Republic, The Nation, Mother Jones, *and other magazines. He is the author of* Boxed In: The Culture of TV *(1988) and editor of* Seeing Through Movies *(1990). This selection is taken from the anthology* Watching Television *(1986), edited by Todd Griffin.*

Cosby is today's quintessential[1] TV Dad — at once the nation's best-liked sitcom character and the most successful and ubiquitous of celebrity pitchmen. Indeed, Cosby himself ascribes his huge following to his appearances in the ads: "I think my popularity came from doing solid 30-second commercials. They can cause people to love you and see more of you than in a full 30-minute show." Like its star, *The Cosby Show* must owe much of its immense success to advertising, for this sitcom is especially well attuned to the commercials, offering a full-scale confirmation of their vision. The show has its charms, which seem to set it well apart from TV's usual crudeness; yet even these must be considered in the context of TV's new integrity.

---

[1]*quintessential:* the most perfect embodiment of something; the purest form.

On the face of it, the Huxtables' milieu is as upbeat and well stocked as a window display at Bloomingdale's,[2] or any of those visions of domestic happiness that graced the billboards during the Great Depression. Everything within this spacious brownstone[3] is luminously clean and new, as if it had all been set up by the state to make a good impression on a group of visiting foreign dignitaries. Here are all the right commodities — lots of bright sportwear, plants and paintings, gorgeous bedding, plenty of copperware, portable tape players, thick carpeting, innumerable knickknacks, and, throughout the house, big, burnished dressers, tables, couches, chairs, and cabinets (Early American yet looking factory-new). Each week, the happy Huxtables nearly vanish amid the porcelain, stainless steel, mahogany, and fabric of their lives. In every scene, each character appears in some fresh designer outfit that positively glows with newness, never to be seen a second time. And, like all this pricey clutter, the plots and subplots, the dialogue, and even many of the individual shots reflect in some way on consumption as a way of life: Cliff's new juicer is the subject of an entire episode; Cliff does a monologue on his son Theo's costly sweatshirt; Cliff kids daughter Rudy for wearing a dozen wooden necklaces. Each Huxtable, in fact, is hardly more than a mobile display case for his/her momentary possessions. In the show's first year, the credit sequence was a series of vivid stills presenting Cliff alongside a shiny Dodge Caravan, out of which the lesser Huxtables then emerged in shiny playcothes, as if the van were their true parent, with Cliff serving as the genial midwife to this antiseptic birth. Each is routinely upstaged by what he/she eats or wears or lugs around: in a billowing blouse imprinted with gigantic blossoms, daughter Denise appears, carrying a tape player as big as a suitcase; Theo enters to get himself a can of Coke from the refrigerator, and we notice that he's wearing both a smart beige belt *and* a pair of lavender suspenders; Rudy munches cutely on a piece of pizza roughly twice the size of her own head.

As in the advertising vision, life among the Huxtables is not only well supplied, but remarkable for its surface harmony. Relations between these five pretty kids and their cute parents are rarely complicated by the slightest serious discord. Here affluence is magically undisturbed by the pressures that ordinarily enable it. Cliff and Clair, although both employed, somehow enjoy the leisure to devote themselves full-time to the trivial and comfortable concerns that loosely determine each episode: a funeral for Rudy's goldfish, a birthday surprise for Cliff, the kids' preparations for their first day of school. And daily life in this bright house is just as easy on the viewer as it is (apparently) for Cliff's dependents: *The Cosby Show* is devoid of any

<hr>

[2]*Bloomingdale's:* an exclusive New York–based department store.
[3]*brownstone:* a multistory row house, typically built of reddish-brown stone.

dramatic tension whatsoever. Nothing happens, nothing changes, there is no suspense or ambiguity or disappointment. In one episode, Cliff accepts a challenge to race once more against a runner who, years before, had beaten him at a major track meet. At the end, the race is run, and — it's a tie!

Of course, *The Cosby Show* is by no means the first sitcom to present us with a big, blissful family whose members never collide with one another, or with anything else; *Eight is Enough*, *The Brady Bunch*, and *The Partridge Family* are just a few examples of earlier prime-time idylls.[4] Here are, however, some crucial differences between those older shows and this one. First of all, *The Cosby Show* is far more popular than any of its predecessors. It is (as of this writing) the top-rated show in the United States and elsewhere, attracting an audience that is not only vast, but often near fanatical in its devotion. Second, and stranger still, this show and its immense success are universally applauded as an exhilarating sign of progress. Newspaper columnists and telejournalists routinely deem *The Cosby Show* a "breakthrough" into an unprecedented *realism* because it uses none of the broad plot devices or rapid-fire gags that define the standard sitcom. Despite its fantastic ambience of calm and plenty, *The Cosby Show* is widely regarded as a rare glimpse of truth, whereas *The Brady Bunch* et al., though just as cheery, were never extolled in this way. And there is a third difference between this show and its predecessors that may help explain the new show's greater popularity and peculiar reputation for progressivism: Cliff Huxtable and his dependents are not only fabulously comfortable and mild, but also noticeably black.

Cliff's blackness serves an affirmative purpose within the ad that is   5
The Cosby Show. At the center of this ample tableau, Cliff is himself an
ad, implicitly proclaiming the fairness of the American system: "Look!" he shows us. "Even *I* can have all this!" Cliff is clearly meant to stand for Cosby himself, whose name appears in the opening credits as "Dr. William E. Cosby, Jr., Ed.D." — a testament both to Cosby's lifelong effort at self-improvement, and to his sense of brotherhood with Cliff. And, indeed, Dr. Huxtable is merely the latest version of the same statement that Dr. Cosby has been making for years as a talk show guest and stand-up comic: "I got mine!" The comic has always been quick to raise the subject of his own success. "What do I care what some ten-thousand-dollar-a-year writer says about me?" he once asked Dick Cavett. And on *The Tonight Show* a few years ago, Cosby told of how his father, years before, had warned him that he'd never make a dime in show business, "and then he walked slowly back to the projects. . . . Well, I just lent him forty thousand dollars!"

[4] *idylls:* short poems or prose works depicting the pleasant simplicity of rural life; in general terms, an ideal situation.

That anecdote got a big hand, just like *The Cosby Show*, but despite the many plaudits for Cosby's continuing tale of self-help, it is not quite convincing. Cliff's brownstone is too crammed, its contents too lustrous, to seem like his — or anyone's — own personal achievement. It suggests instead the corporate showcase which, in fact, it is. *The Cosby Show* attests to the power, not of Dr. Cosby/Huxtable, but of a consumer society that has produced such a tantalizing vision of reality. As Cosby himself admits, it was not his own Algeresque[5] efforts that "caused people to love" him, but those ads put out by Coca-Cola, Ford, and General Foods — those ads in which he looks and acts precisely as he looks and acts in his own show.

Cosby's image is divided in a way that both facilitates the corporate project and conceals its true character. On the face of it, the Cosby style is pure impishness. Forever mugging and cavorting, throwing mock tantrums or beaming hugely to himself or doing funny little dances with his stomach pushed out, Cosby carries on a ceaseless parody of some euphoric eight-year-old. His delivery suggests the same childish spontaneity, for in the high, coy gabble of his harangues and monologues there is a disarming quality of baby talk. And yet all this artful goofiness barely conceals an intimidating hardness — the same uncompromising willfulness that we learn to tolerate in actual children (however cute they may be), but which can seem a little threatening in a grown-up. And Cosby is indeed a most imposing figure, in spite of all his antics: a big man boasting of his wealth, and often handling an immense cigar.

It is a disorienting blend of effects, but it works perfectly whenever he confronts us on behalf of Ford or Coca-Cola. With a massive car or Coke machine behind him, or with a calculator at his fingertips, he hunches toward us, wearing a bright sweater and an insinuating grin, and makes his playful pitch, cajoling us to buy whichever thing he's selling, his face and words, his voice and posture all suggesting this implicit and familiar come-on: "Kitchy-koo!" It is not so much that Cosby makes his mammoth bureaucratic masters seem as nice and cuddly as himself (although such a strategy is typical of corporate advertising); rather, he implicitly assures us that *we* are nice and cuddly, like little children. At once solicitous and overbearing, he personifies the corporate force that owns him. Like it, he comes across as an easygoing parent, and yet, also like it, he cannot help but betray the impulse to coerce. We see that he is bigger than we are, better known, better off, and far more powerfully sponsored. Thus, we find ourselves ambiguously courted, just like those tots who eat up lots of Jell-O pudding under his playful supervision.

[5]*Algeresque:* reminiscent of the writings of Horatio Alger (1834–1899), a U.S. novelist whose rags-to-riches tales of success were popular at the turn of the century.

Dr. Huxtable controls his family with the same enlightened deviousness. As widely lauded for its "warmth" as for its "realism," *The Cosby Show* has frequently been dubbed "the *Father Knows Best* of the eighties." Here again (the columnists agree) is a good strong Dad maintaining the old "family values." This equation, however, blurs a crucial difference between Cliff and the early fathers. Like them, Cliff always wins; but this modern Dad subverts his kids not by evincing the sort of calm power that once made Jim Anderson[6] so daunting, but by seeming to subvert himself at the same time. His is the executive style, in other words, not of the small businessman as evoked in the fifties, but of the corporate manager, skilled at keeping his subordinates in line while half concealing his authority through various disarming moves: Cliff rules the roost through teasing put-downs, clever mockery, and amiable shows of helpless bafflement. This Dad is no straightforward tyrant, then, but the playful type who strikes his children as a peach, until they realize, years later and after lots of psychotherapy, what a subtle thug he really was.

An intrusive kidder, Cliff never fails to get his way; and yet there is   10
more to his manipulativeness than simple egomania. Obsessively, Cliff sees to it, through his takes and teasing, that his children always keep things light. As in the corporate culture and on TV generally, so on this show there is no negativity allowed. Cliff's function is therefore to police the corporate playground, always on the lookout for any downbeat tendencies.

In one episode, for instance, Denise sets herself up by reading Cliff some somber verses that she's written for the school choir. The mood is despairing; the refrain, "I walk alone . . . I walk alone." It is clear that the girl does not take the effort very seriously, and yet Cliff merrily overreacts against this slight and artificial plaint as if it were a crime. First, while she recites, he wears a clownish look of deadpan bewilderment, then laughs out loud as soon as she has finished, and finally snidely moos the refrain in outright parody. The studio audience roars, and Denise takes the hint. At the end of the episode, she reappears with a new version, which she reads sweetly, blushingly, while Cliff and Clair, sitting side by side in their high-priced pajamas, beam with tenderness and pride on her act of self-correction:

> My mother and my father are my best friends.
> When I'm all alone, I don't have to be.
> It's because of me that I'm all alone, you see.
> Their love is real. . . .
>
> Never have they lied to me, never connived me,
> talked behind my back.

---

[6]*Jim Anderson:* father's name in the early TV series *Father Knows Best.*

Never have they cheated me.
Their love is real, their love is real.

Clair, choked up, gives the girl a big warm hug, and Cliff then takes her little face between his hands and kisses it, as the studio audience bursts into applause.

Thus, this episode ends with a paean[7] to the show itself (for "their love" is *not* "real," but a feature of the fiction), a moment that, for all its mawkishness, attests to Cliff's managerial adeptness. Yet Cliff is hardly a mere enforcer. He is himself also an underling, even as he seems to run things. This subservient status is manifest in his blackness. Cosby's blackness is indeed a major reason for the show's popularity, despite his frequent claims, and the journalistic consensus, that *The Cosby Show* is somehow "colorblind," simply appealing in some general "human" way. Although whitened by their status and commodities, the Huxtables are still unmistakably black. However, it would be quite inaccurate to hail their popularity as evidence of a new and rising amity between the races in America. On the contrary, *The Cosby Show* is such a hit with whites in part because whites are just as worried about blacks as they have always been — not blacks like Bill Cosby, or Lena Horne, or Eddie Murphy, but poor blacks, and the poor in general, whose existence is a well-kept secret on prime-time TV.

And yet TV betrays the very fears that it denies. In thousands of high-security buildings, and in suburbs reassuringly remote from the cities' "bad neighborhoods," whites may, unconsciously, be further reassured by watching not just Cosby, but a whole set of TV shows that negate the possibility of black violence with lunatic fantasies of containment: *Diff'rent Strokes* and *Webster*, starring Gary Coleman and Emmanuel Lewis, respectively, each an overcute, miniaturized black person, each playing the adopted son of good white parents. Even the oversized and growling Mr. T, complete with Mohawk, bangles, and other primitivizing touches, is a mere comforting joke, the dangerous ex-slave turned comic and therefore innocuous by campy excess; and this behemoth too is kept in line by a casual white father, Hannibal Smith, the commander of the A-Team who employs Mr. T exclusively for his brawn.

As a willing advertisement for the system that pays him well, Cliff   15
Huxtable also represents a threat contained. Although dark-skinned and physically imposing, he ingratiates us with his childlike mien and enviable life-style, a surrender that must offer some deep solace to a white public terrified that one day blacks might come with guns to steal the copperware, the juicer, the microwave, the VCR, even the TV itself. On *The Cosby Show*, it appears as if blacks in general can have, or do have,

---

[7]*paean:* a poem or song of praise.

what many whites enjoy, and that such material equality need not entail a single break-in. And there are no hard feelings, none at all, now that the old injustice has been so easily rectified. Cosby's definitive funny face, flashed at the show's opening credits and reproduced on countless magazine covers, is a strained denial of all animosity. With its little smile, the lips pursed tight, eyes opened wide, eyebrows raised high, that dark face shines toward us like the white flag of surrender — a desperate look that no suburban TV Dad of yesteryear would ever have put on, and one that millions of Americans today find indispensable.

By and large, American whites need such reassurance because they are now further removed than ever, both spatially and psychologically, from the masses of the black poor. And yet the show's appeal cannot be explained merely as a symptom of class and racial uneasiness, because there are, in our consumer culture, anxieties still more complicated and pervasive. Thus, Cliff is not just an image of the dark Other capitulating to the white establishment, but also the reflection of any constant viewer, who, whatever his/her race, must also feel like an outsider, lucky to be tolerated by the distant powers that be. There is no negativity allowed, not anywhere; and so Cliff serves both as our guide and as our double. His look of tense playfulness is more than just a sign that blacks won't hurt us; it is an expression that we too would each be wise to adopt, lest we betray some devastating sign of anger or dissatisfaction. If we stay cool and cheerful, white like him,[8] and learn to get by with his sort of managerial acumen, we too, perhaps, can be protected from the world by a barrier of new appliances, and learn to put down others as each of us has, somehow, been put down.

Such rampant putting-down, the ridicule of all by all, is the very essence of the modern sitcom. Cliff, at once the joker and a joke, infantilizing others and yet infantile himself, is exemplary of everybody's status in the sitcoms, in the ads, and in most other kinds of TV spectacle (as well as in the movies). No one, finally, is immune.

---

[8]*white like him:* an allusion to *Black Like Me*, the 1961 account by John H. Griffin, a white reporter who underwent surgical treatment so that he could pass for black and document racial segregation in the South.

Engaging the Text

1. In what sense does *The Cosby Show* offer "full-scale confirmation" (para. 1) of the world of TV commercials? What values, images, and myths does it share with the world of advertising? Do you agree with Miller's claim?

2. In what ways does Cosby come across as a supreme example of the "corporate manager"? Why does Miller call him a "subtle thug" (para. 9)?

3. What, according to Miller, is the role of race in *The Cosby Show*'s popularity? What message does the show convey about being Black in America? What does the show tell its audience about the relationship between African Americans and white Americans?

4. Is Miller attacking Cosby? Explain. How might Cosby respond to Miller's observations?

5. Pinpoint Miller's assumptions about the nature of U.S. society today. What evidence does he cite to support his views? Do you think his assumptions are accurate? Cite more examples to support his point of view or find counterexamples.

Exploring Connections

6. Review Elayne Rapping's analysis of local television news shows (p. 616). How might Rapping explain the popularity of *The Cosby Show*? How might her interpretation differ from Miller's?

7. Imagine that The Man and The Kid in George C. Wolfe's *Symbiosis* (p. 42) have dropped by the Huxtables' to get Cliff's perspective on their conflict. Working in groups, write the conversation that might ensue. Read your conversation aloud to the class and discuss.

8. In "I'm Black, You're White, Who's Innocent?" (p. 347), Shelby Steele explains Cosby's popularity as the result of his willingness to bargain with rather than challenge white America. Review Steele's selection and compare his analysis with Miller's. To what extent do they seem to agree? Which offers the richer view of Cosby's power as a media figure?

9. To what extent does the Huxtable family reflect the values and the tensions Arlene Skolnick (p. 402) associates with contemporary families?

Extending the Critical Context

10. Watch one episode of *The Cosby Show* and use it to test Miller's claims. It will help to write out Miller's main points on an "observation sheet" before starting to watch. Compare observations with classmates, then write an essay based on your analysis.

11. Miller disagrees with critics who praise *The Cosby Show* for being more realistic than most TV comedies. Watch an episode and write a short analysis of which elements of the show seem true to life and which seem unrealistic. To clarify your perspective on the show, you might compare it with another family sitcom, like *Roseanne*.

TV's Black World Turns — But Stays Unreal

Henry Louis Gates, Jr.

When Henry Louis Gates, Jr., was lured to Harvard University to become head of the Afro-American Studies program, Boston papers wrote feature stories heralding him as "a genuine superstar" and "the dean of the black academic entrepreneurs." In this article, first published in the New York Times *in 1989, Gates confirms his reputation as a scholarly and challenging thinker by tracing the lineage of Cliff Huxtable on* The Cosby Show *back to Amos 'n' Andy — a popular early comedy that has become a symbol of television racism at its worst. Gates's approach to* Cosby *differs from Mark Crispin Miller's in the previous essay; Gates offers a historical perspective on the show by examining it in the context of the media myths that have surrounded African American entertainers for the past one hundred years. A leading literary critic, Gates (b. 1950) has written prolifically on issues of African American culture and race relations. He has also edited several important collections of African American literature. His* The Signifying Monkey: A Theory of African-American Literary Criticism *won an American Book Award in 1989.*

There is a telling moment in the 1986 film *Soul Man* when a young man explains to a friend why he has decided to down a bottle of tanning pills and turn himself black. The friend is skeptical: what's it actually going to be like, being black?

"It's gonna be great," the hero assures him. "These are the 80s, man. This is the *Cosby* decade. America *loves* black people."

Alas, he soon discovers the gulf that separates the images of black people he sees on television and the reality that blacks experience every day.

Even black Americans sometimes need to be reminded about the deceptiveness of television. Blacks retain their fascination with black characters on TV: many of us buy *Jet* magazine primarily to read its weekly television feature, which lists *every* black character (major or minor) to be seen on the screen that week. Yet our fixation with the presence of black characters on TV has blinded us to an important fact that *Cosby*, which began in 1984, and its offshoots over the years demonstate convincingly: there is very little connection between the social status of black Americans and the fabricated images of black people that Americans consume each day. Moreoever, the representations of blacks on TV is a very poor index to our social advancement or political progress.

But the young man is right about one thing: this is the *Cosby* 5 decade. The show's unprecedented success in depicting the lives of affluent blacks has exercised a profound influence on television in the last half of the 80s. And, judging from the premiere of this season's new black series — *Family Matters*, *Homeroom*, and *Snoops*, as well as *Generations*, an interracial soap opera — *Cosby's* success has led to the flow of TV sitcoms that feature the black middle class, each of which takes its lead from the *Cosby* show.

Historically, blacks have always worried aloud about the image that white Americans harbor of us, first because we have never had control of those images and, second, because the greater number of those images have been negative. And given television's immediacy, and its capacity to reach so many viewers so quickly, blacks, at least since *Amos 'n' Andy* back in the early 50s, have been especially concerned with our images on the screen. I can remember as a child sitting upstairs in my bedroom and hearing my mother shout at the top of her voice that someone *"colored . . . colored!"* was on TV and that we had all better come downstairs at once. And, without fail, we did, sitting in front of our TV, nervous, full of expectation and dread, praying that our home girl or boy would not let the race down.

"White" Money vs. "Colored" Money

Later, when American society could not successfully achieve the social reformation it sought in the 60s through the Great Society,[1] television solved the problem simply by inventing symbols of that transformation in the 80s, whether it was Cliff Huxtable — whom we might think of as the grandson of Alexander Scott[2] (played by Mr. Cosby in *I Spy*, 1965–68) — or Benson[3] (1979–86), the butler who transforms himself into a lieutenant governor.

Today, blacks are doing much better on TV than they are in real life, an irony underscored by the use of black public figures (Mr. Cosby, Michael Jackson, Michael Jordan, Bobby McFerrin[4]) as spokesmen for

---

[1]*Great Society:* the informal name for President Lyndon Johnson's ambitious package of social and legislative reforms, including programs like Headstart, Medicare, and the Teacher Corps.

[2]*Alexander Scott:* African American hero on the mid-1960s adventure series *I Spy*. Cosby played Scott and was one of the first Black Americans to costar on an integrated program.

[3]*Benson:* the title character in the TV sitcom of the 1980s starring Robert Guillaume.

[4]*Bobby McFerrin:* African American singer, entertainer, and author of the book *Don't Worry, Be Happy* (1989).

major businesses. When Mr. Cosby, deadpan, faces the camera squarely and says, "E. F. Hutton. Because it's my money," the line blurs between Cliff Huxtable's successful career and Mr. Cosby.

This helps to explain why *Cosby* makes some people uncomfortable: as the dominant representation of blacks on TV, it suggests that blacks are solely responsible for their social conditions, with no acknowledgment of the severely constricted life opportunities that most black people face. What's troubling about the phenomenal success of *Cosby*, then, is what was troubling about the earlier popularity of *Amos 'n' Andy*: it's not the representation itself (Cliff Huxtable, a child of college-educated parents, is altogether believable), but the role it begins to play in our culture, the status it takes on as being, well, truly representative.

As long as *all* blacks were represented in demeaning or peripheral 10 roles, it was possible to believe that American racism was, as it were, indiscriminate. The social vision of Cosby, however, reflecting the minuscule integration of blacks into the upper middle class (having "white money," my mother used to say, rather than "colored" money) reassuringly throws the blame for black poverty back onto the impoverished.

This is the subliminal message of America's weekly dinner date with the Huxtables, played out to a lesser extent in other weekly TV encounters with middle-class black families, such as *227*, *A Different World*, *Amen* (Sherman Helmsley is a lawyer), and with isolated black individuals, such as the dashing Blair Underwood on *L. A. Law* and Philip Michael Thomas on *Miami Vice*. One principal reason for the failure of Flip Wilson's *Charlie & Company* was the ambiguity of his class status; Wilson's character, Charlie Richmond, was an office worker at the Department of Highways, his wife (Gladys Knight) a schoolteacher. Wilson once joked, acidly, that he was the star of the black version of *The Cosby Show*, which may have been true in ways that he did not intend.

The Great *Amos 'n' Andy* Debate

In 1933, Sterling Brown, the great black poet and critic, divided the full range of black character types in American literature into seven categories: the contented slave; the wretched freeman; the comic Negro; the brute Negro; the tragic mulatto; the local color Negro, and the exotic primitive. It was only one small step to associate our public negative image in the American mind with the public negative social roles that we were assigned and to which we were largely confined. "If only they could be exposed to the *best* of the race," the sentiment went, "then they would see that we were normal human beings and treat us better."

Such a burdensome role for the black image led, inevitably, to careful monitoring and, ultimately, to censorship of our representations in literature, film, radio, and later television. The historian W. E. B. Du Bois[5] summarized this line of thinking among blacks: "We want," he said in 1925, "everything that is said about us to tell of the best and highest and noblest in us. We insist that our Art and Propaganda be one. We fear that the evil in us will be called racial while in others it is viewed as individual. We fear that our shortcomings are not merely human but foreshadowings and threatenings of disaster and failure." And the genre about which we were most sensitive, Du Bois wrote, was comedy. "The more highly trained we become," he wrote in 1921, "the less we can laugh at Negro comedy."

One of my favorite pastimes is screening episodes of *Amos 'n' Andy* for black friends who think that the series was both socially offensive and politically detrimental. After a few minutes, even hardliners have difficulty restraining their laughter. "It's still racist," is one typical comment, "but it was funny."

The performance of those great black actors — Tim Moore, Spencer Williams, and Ernestine Wade — transformed racist stereotypes into authentic black humor. The dilemma of *Amos 'n' Andy*, however, was that these were the *only* images of blacks that Americans could see on TV. The political consequences for the early civil rights movement were thought to be threatening. The N.A.A.C.P helped to have the series killed.   15

What lies behind these sorts of arguments is a belief that social policies affecting black Americans were largely determined by our popular images in the media. But the success of *The Cosby Show* has put the lie to that myth: *Cosby* exposes more white Americans than ever before to the most nobly idealized blacks in the history of entertainment, yet social and economic conditions for the average black American have not been bleaker in a very long time.

To make matters worse, *Cosby* is also one of the most popular shows in apartheid South Africa, underscoring the fact that the relationship between how whites treat us and their exposure to "the best" in us is far from straightforward. (One can hear the Afrikaaner speaking to his black servants: "When you people are like Cliff and Clair, *then* we will abandon apartheid.")

There are probably as many reasons to like *The Cosby Show* as there are devoted viewers — and there are millions of them. I happen to like it because my daughters (ages nine and seven) like it, and I enjoy watch-

[5]W. E. B. Du Bois: William Edward Burghardt Du Bois (1868–1963), noted African American leader, writer, and sociologist. Du Bois was instrumental in founding the NAACP and was the first Black recipient of a Ph.D. from Harvard.

ing them watch themselves in the depictions of middle-class black kids, worrying about school, sibling rivalries, and family tradition. But I also like *Cosby* because its very success has forced us to rethink completely the relation between black social progress and the images of blacks that American society fabricates, projects, and digests.

But the *Cosby* vision of upper-middle-class blacks and their families is comparatively recent. And while it may have constituted the dominant image of blacks for the last five years, it is a direct reaction against the lower-class ghetto comedies of the 70s, such as *Sanford and Son* 1972–77), *Good Times* (1974–79), *That's My Mama* (1974–75), and *What's Happening!!* (1976–79). The latter three were single-mother-dominated sitcoms. Although *Good Times* began with a nuclear family, John Amos — who had succeeded marvelously in transforming the genre of the black maternal household — was soon killed off, enabling the show to conform to the stereotype of a fatherless black family.

Even *The Jeffersons* (1975–85) conforms to this mold. George and   20
Louise began their TV existence as Archie Bunker's[6] working-class neighbors, saved their pennies, then "moved on up," as the theme song says, to Manhattan's East Side. *The Jeffersons* also served as a bridge between sitcoms depicting the ghetto and those portraying the new black upper class.

In fact, in the history of black images on television, character types have distinct pasts and, as is also the case with white shows, series seem both to lead to other series and to spring from metaphorical ancestors.

Pure Street in a Brooks Brothers Suit

Let's track the evolution of the *Cosby* type on television. While social engineering is easier on the little screen than in the big city, Sterling Brown's list of black stereotypes in American literature proves quite serviceable as a guide to the images TV has purveyed for the last two decades. Were we writing a new sitcom using these character types, our cast might look like this — contented slave: Andy, Fred Sanford, J. J. (*Good Times*); wretched freeman: George Jefferson; comic Negro: Flip Wilson; brute Negro: Mr. T (*The A-Team*), Hawk (*Spenser: for Hire*); tragic mulatto: *Julia*, Elvin (*Cosby*), Whitley (*A Different World*); local color Negro: Meschach Taylor (*Designing Women*); exotic primitive: Link (*Mod Squad* 1968–73); most black characters on MTV. If we add the category of Noble Negro (Cliff Huxtable, Benson), our list might be complete.

We can start with George Jefferson, who we might think of as a Kingfish (*Amos 'n' Andy*) or as a Fred Sanford (*Sanford and Son*) who

---

[6]*Archie Bunker:* the leading character on *All in the Family*, a popular sitcom of the 1970s. Bunker was noted for his racist and misogynist views.

has finally made it. Jefferson epitomized Richard Nixon's version of black capitalism, bootstrap variety, and all of its terrifying consequences. Jefferson was anything but a man of culture; unlike the *Cosby* living room, his East Side apartment had no painting by Jacob Lawrence or Charles White, Romare Bearden or Varnette Honeywood.[7] Despite his new-found wealth, Jefferson was pure street, draped in a Brooks Brothers suit. You did not want to live next to a George Jefferson, and you most certainly did not want your daughter to marry one.

The *Jeffersons* was part of a larger trend in television in the depiction of black men. We might think of this as their domestication, in direct reaction to the questing, macho images of black males shown in the 60s news clips of the civil rights movement, the Black Panthers, and the black power movement. While Jefferson (short, feisty, racist, rich, vulgar) represents one kind of domestication, a more curious kind was the cultural dwarfism represented by *Diff'rent Strokes* (1978–86) and *Webster* (1983–87), in which small black "boys" (arrested adolescents who were much older than the characters they played) were adopted by tall, successful white males. These establishment figures represented the myth of the benevolent paternalism of the white upper class, an American myth as old as the abolitionist movement.[8]

Indeed, one central motif of nineteenth-century American art is a sculpted tall white male (often Lincoln) towering above a crouched or kneeling adult or adolescent slave, in the act of setting them free. *Webster* and *Diff'rent Strokes* depict black orphans who are rescued from blackness and poverty, adopted, and raised just like any other upper-middle-class white kid, prep schools and all. These shows can be thought of as TV's fantasy of Lyndon Johnson's[9] "Great Society" and the war on poverty rolled into one.

The formula was not as successful with a female character: An attempt to use the same format with a black woman, Shirley Hemphill (*One in a Million*, 1980) lasted only six months. *The White Shadow* (1978–81) was a variation of this paternal motif, in which wild and unruly ghetto kids were tamed with a basketball.

These small black men signaled to the larger American audience that the very idea of the black male could be, and had been, successfully domesticated. Mr. T — whose 1983–87 *A-Team* run paralleled that of *Webster* — might appear to be an exception. We are forced to wonder, however, why such an important feature of his costume — and favorite

[7]*Jacob Lawrence, Charles White, Romare Bearden, Varnette Honeywood:* African American painters.

[8]*abolitionist movement:* a social movement of the nineteenth century that sought to abolish slavery.

[9]*Lyndon Johnson:* Thirty-sixth president of the United States (1908–1973).

fetish — was those dazzling gold chains, surely a subliminal suggestion of bondage.

This process of paternal domestication, in effect, made Cliff Huxtable's character a logical next step. In fact, I think of the evolution of the Huxtable character, generationally, in this way: imagine if George Jefferson owned the tenement building in which Florida and her family from *Good Times* lived. After John Amos dies, Jefferson evicts them for nonpayment of rent. Florida, destitute and distraught, tries to kill George. The state puts her children up for adoption.

They are adopted by Mr. Drummond (*Diff'rent Strokes*) and graduate from Dalton, Exeter, and Howard. Gary Coleman's grandson becomes an obstetrician, marries a lovely lawyer named Clair, and they move to Brooklyn Heights. And there you have it: the transformation of the character type of the black male on television.

And while Clair Huxtable is a refreshingly positive depiction of an   30
intelligent, successful black woman, she is clearly a descendant of *Julia* (1968–71), though a Julia with sensuality and sass. The extent of typecasting of black women as mammy figures, descended from the great Hollywood "Mammy" of *Gone with the Wind*, is astonishing; Beulah, Mama in *Amos 'n' Andy*, Geraldine (*Flip Wilson*, 1970–75), Florida, Nel in *Gimme a Break* (1981–88), Louise (*The Jeffersons*); Eloise (*That's My Mama*, 1974–75).

Is TV Depicting a Different World?

And what is the measure of the Huxtables' nobility? One of the reasons *Cosby* and its spin-off, *A Different World*, are so popular is that the black characters in them have finally become, in most respects just like white people.

While I applaud *Cosby's* success at depicting (at long last) the everyday concerns of black people (love, sex, ambition, generational conflicts, work and leisure) far beyond reflex responses to white racism, the question remains: has TV managed to depict a truly "different world"? As Mark Crispin Miller puts it, "By insisting that blacks and whites are entirely alike, television denies the cultural barriers that slavery necessarily created; barriers that have hardened over years and years, and that still exist" — barriers that produced different cultures, distinct worlds.

And while *Cosby* is remarkably successful at introducing most Americans to traditional black cultural values, customs, and norms, it has not succeeded at introducing America to a truly different world. The show that came closest — that presented the fullest range of black character types — was the 1987–88 series *Frank's Place*, starring Tim Reid and his wife Daphne Maxwell Reid and set in a Creole restaurant in New Orleans.

Unfortunately, Mr. Reid apparently has learned his lesson: his new series, *Snoops*, in which his wife also stars, is a black detective series suggestive of *The Thin Man*.[10] The couple is thoroughly middle class: he is a professor of criminology at Georgetown; she is head of protocol at the State Department, "Drugs and murder and psychotic people," Mr. Reid said in a recent interview. "I think we've seen enough of that in real life."

But it is also important to remember that the early 70s ghetto sitcoms — (*Good Times* and *Sanford*) were no more realistic than *Cosby* is. In fact, their success made the idea of ghetto life palatable for most Americans, robbing it of its reality as a place of exile, a place of rage, and frustration, and death. And perhaps with *Cosby*'s success and the realization that the very structure of the sitcom (in which every character is a type) militates against its use as an agent of social change, blacks will stop looking to TV for our social liberation. As a popular song in the early 70s put it, "The revolution will not be televised."

35

---

[10]*The Thin Man:* an early motion picture and TV series notable for the sophistication of its husband-wife detective team; based on the novel *The Thin Man* (1932) by Dashiell Hammett.

Engaging the Text

1. What relation does Gates see between the realities of Black America and the images of Blacks on TV in the "*Cosby* decade"? What troubles Gates about this relation? Why does he believe it's so important?

2. Explain the subtle distinction that Gates makes between the "representation" of Cliff Huxtable as the successful child of college-educated parents and the "role" this representation plays in U.S. culture (para. 9). What does the image of Cliff Huxtable do for the dominant culture, according to Gates? Do you agree?

3. How has *The Cosby Show* complicated earlier analyses of the relation between mass media images (like those projected in *Amos 'n' Andy*) and racism?

4. What stages does Gates sketch in his presentation of the evolution of Black images on TV? What social function did African American characters like Amos and Andy, George Jefferson, Webster, and B. K. Baracus (Mr. T) fulfill?

5. Gates claims that *Cosby* has failed to introduce America to "a truly 'different world'" (para. 32). Do you agree? Can you think of any TV series that does this? What is Gates saying about the relation between TV and social change?

Exploring Connections

6. Compare Gates's analysis of *The Cosby Show* with Mark Crispin Miller's (p. 645). What do Gates and Miller agree about in their explanations of the show's success? What differences can you find in their assumptions, perspec-

tives, and conclusions? Which analysis do you find more interesting and rewarding? Why?

7. Write an imaginary dialogue between Gates and Luis Valdez (p. 375) on the
power of racial stereotypes. In what ways are stereotypes oppressive? Can they
be used to subvert or resist oppression?

Extending the Critical Context

8. Since the appearance of *The Cosby Show* and the publication of Gates's
essay, more TV shows have been introduced featuring African Americans,
including sitcoms like *Fresh Prince of Bel-Air*, comedy-variety shows like *In
Living Color*, and talk shows like *Arsenio Hall*. How might Gates analyze the
images of African Americans that these shows project?

9. As a class, discuss TV portrayals of other groups that fall outside dominant
American culture. What images do you find of Chicano/Latinos? Asian Americans, American Indians, or the working classes? Do they resemble any of the
stereotypes that Gates describes for African Americans? How would you account for TV's relative neglect of these groups?

Action-Adventure as Ideology

Gina Marchetti

*When you settle down with a hot-buttered popcorn and a soft drink
to watch your favorite Hollywood hero "smoke" a few dozen bad guys,
you may think it's all just good, clean fun, but Gina Marchetti thinks
otherwise. According to Marchetti, action-adventure films convey extremely complex cultural messages, messages that help "domesticate" or
neutralize any hostility we might have toward the "white American
status quo." Her analysis of action-adventure heroes and villains may
challenge your reading skills, but if you can weather the first few pages,
you should find her discussion insightful and rewarding. Marchetti
teaches in the Department of Radio, TV, and Film at the University of
Maryland. This selection originally appeared in an anthology entitled*
Cultural Politics in Contemporary America *(1989).*

Defining the Action-Adventure Genre

Both producers and viewers tend to categorize films and television
shows in certain ways, so that a film-goer paying to see a Western would
not expect to see futuristic cities, robots, and flying saucers. Instead,

that viewer would expect the film maker to provide gunfighters, cow-boys, six-shooters, and stagecoaches. A set of common codes and assumptions underlie production parameters and viewer expectations. These popularly accepted classifications for films and television shows are known as "genres."

Popular genres are particularly important for industrialized mass media because they allow producers to remain within tried and true formulas — e.g., the horror film, the Western, the melodrama — which have proved profitable in the past. During the Hollywood studio era and in most television production today, this type of production also holds down costs, since sets, costumes, and props can be used over and over again in different films or television shows fitting within the same genre.

There is also a very important link between genre and ideology. Particular genres tend to be popular at certain points in time because they somehow embody and work through those social contradictions the culture needs to come to grips with and may not be able to deal with except in the realm of fantasy. As such, popular genres often function in a way similar to the way myth functions — to work through social contradictions in the form of a narrative so that very real problems can be transposed to the realm of fantasy and apparently solved there.[1]

Right now, the action-adventure genre seems to be particularly popular. Although always a staple of the film and television industries, action-adventure more recently picked up steam with the immense popularity of Steven Spielberg's *Raiders of the Lost Ark* (1981).[2] In many ways, the contemporary action-adventure genre appears to be very closely related to the literary form of "romance." In *Anatomy of Criticism*[3] Northrop Frye notes that the romance has a plot which revolves round a series of adventures in which a mortal hero goes on a quest, struggles with a foe, kills the foe, and either attains his objective

---

[1]For a more extensive discussion of the relationship between genre and myth, see Thomas Schatz, "The Structural Influence: New Directions in Film Genre Study," in Barry Keith Grant, ed., *Film Genre Reader* (Austin: U of Texas, 1986), pp. 91–101. [Author's note]

For a discussion of the relationship between ideology and myth, see Roland Barthes, *Mythologies*, trans. Annette Lavers (NY: Hill and Wang, 1972) and Fredric Jameson, *The Political Unconscious: Narrative as a Socially Symbolic Act* (Ithaca, NY: Cornell U, 1981). [Author's note]

[2]For more on *Raiders*, see Patricia Zimmerman, "Soldiers of Fortune: Lucas, Spielberg, Indiana Jones, and *Raiders of the Lost Ark*," *Wide Angle* 6:2 (1984), pp. 34–39. For an interesting analysis of the sequel, see Moishe Postone and Elizabeth Traube, "The Return of the Repressed: *Indiana Jones and the Temple of Doom*," *Jump Cut* #30 (March 1984), pp. 12–14. [Author's note]

[3]Northrop Frye, *Anatomy of Criticism* (Princeton, NJ: Princeton U, 1957). [Author's note]

or else dies himself. Generally, the reward following the adventure involves marriage to a beautiful woman, who may also have been the object of the quest (along with buried treasure or some other valuable object).

The same basic structure holds true for action-adventure stories 5
today. A hero goes on a quest, usually in an exotic land, and encounters villains along the way who hope to thwart his efforts. However, beyond the bare bones of these deceptively simple tales, social contradictions find expression, and the ideological operations of the text can be seen to be at work. The nature of the quest, the characteristics of the hero and villain, the parameters of the story environment, the physical objects which come into play have all changed dramatically over time. These generic specifics — plot, characterization, iconography, and theme[4] — all hold clues to the ideological power a genre might have at a particular point in time within a specific cultural context.

Action-adventure plots are episodic, allowing for wide variations in tone, the inclusion of many different locations and incidentally introduced characters, and moments of spectacle, generally involving fights, explosions, or other types of violence. The hero is usually some sort of private adventurer, e.g., a mercenary, a treasure-hunter, etc., and he (only very rarely *she*) is often accompanied by one or more "buddies" who fit the same mold. Action-adventure stories are set in exotic locations, and the stereotypical accoutrements of the locales form the principal features of the genre's iconography — e.g., decaying temples, deserts, mountains, rain forests, and exotic cities. Guns, knives, and para-military khaki usually flesh out the rest of the visual element of the genre. Principal themes include rights of possession and property; the definition of the national, ethnic, racial self as opposed to "other"; the propriety of intervening in other nations' or other cultures' affairs; the moral consequences of violence; and the meaning of masculinity and male prerogatives.

Even this schematic listing of themes brings up some sorely debated and rapidly changing areas within American culture. Through deceptively simple tales of "good" against "evil," action-adventure texts very often also deal with issues involving changing class, gender, racial, and other social relations. Through this narrative working out of very real problems and concerns, the action-adventure tale does its ideological work of exposing contradictions, transposing them into fantasy, and then resolving them. However, as these narratives do this, they also open themselves up to multiple meanings, readings, and uses. If the dominant ideology . . . finds a way to win over the viewer, it is at the cost of

[4]These attributes of genre are outlined in Douglas Pye, "The Western (Genre and Movies)," in Grant, *Film Genre Reader*. [Author's note]

recognizing the very unstable, multifaceted, heterogeneous, and contradictory nature of the . . . social fabric.

Why Vietnam? The Contemporary Action-Adventure Tale

Three types of action-adventure plots seem to be particularly popular at present. The first type, perhaps the most traditional, involves a quest for a valuable object hidden away in a Third World[5] country. *Raiders of the Lost Ark, Romancing the Stone* (1984), and *Firewalker* (1986) all follow this formula. Also, this type of narrative generally involves the capture and return of a woman, who sometimes acts as the hero's buddy and sometimes as the villain's captive.

The second type of narrative popular today involves invasion scenarios. In this case, the foreign villain invades the hero's community or country. Normally ostracized by his own society, the hero must come to its aid in order to save it from destruction. *Invasion USA* (1985) is typical of this sort of action-adventure tale. Television action-adventure shows, like *The A-Team* (NBC, 1982–87), also often rely on this sort of plot for their weekly adventures.

This third type of action-adventure plot in wide circulation in the 1980s involves the search for captives. These stories are told within the framework of a hero's search for prisoners listed as "missing in action" — specifically during the war in Vietnam — whom the hero believes to be alive still in Indo-Chinese prisoner-of-war camps. *Missing in Action I* (1984), *Uncommon Valor* (1983), *Rambo: First Blood II* (1985), and episodes of several popular television series have all contributed to making this an extraordinarily successful subgenre.[6]

All three of these plotlines have several important things in common. They all deal with attitudes and values currently experiencing some sort of social crisis. In this fashion, action-adventure has been able to accommodate historical and cultural changes while keeping the main ideological thrust of the genre intact.

For example, the genre often deals with the definition of property rights and the proper distribution of wealth. The treasure hunt plotline offers a clear elaboration of this theme. Not coincidentally, the treasure

---

[5]*Third World:* term originated by West Indian psychologist and political writer Frantz Fanon (1925–1961); refers to economically developing countries that are committed to neither the Western (First World) nor the Soviet (Second World) power block.

[6]For interesting analyses of these MIA films, see Susan Jeffords, "The New Vietnam Films: Is the Movie Over?" *Journal of Popular Film and Television* 13:3 (Winter 1986), pp. 186–194. Elizabeth G. Traube, "Redeeming Images: The Wildman Comes Home," *Persistence of Vision* Nos. 3/4 (Summer 1986), pp. 71–94. On the new image of the Vietnam veteran, see Lisa M. Heilbronn, "Coming Home a Hero: The Changing Image of the Vietnam Vet on Prime Time Television," *Journal of Popular Film and Video* 13:1 (Spring 1985), pp. 25–30. [Author's note]

hunt generally takes place in the Third World. As Ariel Dorfman and Armand Mattelart point out (in *How to Read Donald Duck: Imperialist Ideology in the Disney Comic*)[7] Third World people, pictured as innocent children who simply do not understand the value of the objects surrounding them, often symbolically stand in for First World workers in popular fantasies. Within a racist ideology that pictures Third World people as intellectually limited savages, the text can allow the hero to step in, as representative of First World reason and logic, and help the natives "exploit" their treasures. Clearly, this fantasy, at a time when American economic "interests" seem to be "threatened" globally, has a particular appeal. After all, the treasure need not be gold or jewels, but could as easily be South African platinum, Arabian gulf oil, or Central American fruit crops. Hence, fantasies of Indiana Jones[8] traipsing around the globe looking for treasure seem also to have a more contemporary significance in supporting capital's[9] power to exploit labor domestically and internationally.

Invasion narratives also deal with the definition of property, identity, and national boundaries in a similar fashion. They provide the flipside of the treasure hunt narratives by allowing the shoe to be on the other foot. In this case, America, home and hearth, is penetrated by a malevolent foreign power. While the American hero is always justified in his quest to find treasure abroad, the foreigner can never be right in interfering in American affairs. However, these narratives express a certain ambivalent attitude toward that wealth which the foreigner seems to be after and which, bottom-line, defines the American identity. Here, American abundance is often presented as the source of the entire problem.

In *Invasion USA*, for example, the Cuban and East European villains note that America is "soft," "satiated," and easily conquered because of this "bourgeois[10] decadence." They seem to both covet American wealth and wish to destroy it because of its corrupting influences. In this case, Matt Hunt (Chuck Norris), the ultimate working-class hero, a former C.I.A. operative who wrestles alligators in the Florida swamps and lives in a back-water shack, must single-handedly rescue the bastions of middle-classness the "Commies" have under seige. Once again, like the treasure hunt narratives, these invasion tales justify the

[7]Ariel Dorfman and Armand Mattelart, *How to Read Donald Duck: Imperialist Ideology in the Disney Comic*, trans. David Kunzle (NY: International General, 1975). [Author's note]

[8]*Indiana Jones:* hero of Steven Spielberg's *Raiders of the Lost Ark.*

[9]*capital:* here referring to Karl Marx's notion of the capitalist class, the segment of society that owns the means of production (factories, machinery, and so on) and profits from the labor of the working class.

[10]*bourgeois:* characteristic of the middle class.

violent suppression of anyone who may interfere with American property rights, and it is the working classes that, despite the fact they are presented as having the least to lose, rise up to do battle to secure the right of private property.

It is interesting to note that, in both the treasure hunt and invasion plots, official representatives of the American government — i.e., the police, the army — are either not on the scene or are completely ineffectual. In *The Empire's Old Clothes: What the Lone Ranger, Babar, and Other Innocent Heroes Do to Our Minds*,[11] Ariel Dorfman points out that the Lone Ranger, Superman, and several other of American mass culture's most popular heroes were created during the Depression of the 1930s, at a time of severe economic crisis in which the U.S. Government substantially increased its powers. These heroes personalized that new power, by taking on police and other powers generally considered the prerogatives of governments, and also represented an ambivalence toward those new powers by standing outside the government.

Right now, the MIA captivity/rescue fantasies seem to be popular for a similar reason. On the one hand, they seem to call for increased government and military action — e.g., for increased involvement in foreign affairs, perhaps even for a new war in Vietnam. At the same time, however, they also represent a deep suspicion of the State which is seen both as weak and ineffectual and as corrupt and self-serving. As a panacea for the loss of Vietnam, they conjure up the figure of the heroic individual, who both represents the interests of the nation and goes beyond the strictures of the government.

Once again, territoriality becomes important. In these MIA narratives, the right of Americans to intervene violently in Southeast Asia goes unquestioned. These tales place Americans in the role of the underdog, as prisoners of war or misunderstood and underappreciated veterans at home. Now victims, Americans are given the moral right to go into the Third World and again retrieve property — this time, in the guise of prisoners of war.

All of these action-adventure scenarios also seem to reflect changing and contradictory feelings about gender roles and women's equality. Recognizing that women are an important part of the audience and that the Women's Movement has changed certain attitudes toward gender, contemporary action-adventure tales have allowed women to expand their traditional function in these narratives a bit. Although women still play the passive part of the captive who must be retrieved from the villain by the hero, they also figure more and more often as the hero's "buddy" as well as the object of the tale's love interest. As a result, some

15

---

[11]Ariel Dorfman, *The Empire's Old Clothes: What the Lone Ranger, Babar, and Other Innocent Heroes Do to Our Minds* (NY: Pantheon, 1983). [Author's note]

of these action-adventure texts have allowed women a certain camaraderie with the hero, sharing the battle and the danger, that had been
rarer in the past.

However, although women may be given a bit more license to
pursue goals actively, these tales are still very much male-dominated
and male-defined. In fact, most feature a very aggressive masculinity,
expressed through guns, tanks, armed helicopters, and other instruments of death. Emphasis is placed on the male body, its musculature
and strength, and its ability to withstand torture and to kill efficiently.
For example, although *Rambo* features a loyal and efficient female
comrade-in-arms, she fairly quickly meets with a violent end, leaving
Rambo (Sylvester Stallone) to fight against the male villains and rescue
the male prisoners of war. Moreover, although the film devotes a great
deal of attention to Rambo's body — e.g., close-ups of his bulging
muscles both preparing for battle and during scenes in which he hero-
ically withstands torture — her body is really only given similar attention in one scene in which she must dress as a prostitute in order to
penetrate the prisoner of war camp. Here, the visual emphasis is on her
sexual allure, rather than her physical strength or power, and this seems
to be fairly typical of the way in which female adventurers are treated
visually within the genre.

Villains, Heroes, and Buddies

Perhaps the most straightforward part of any tale is the antagonist,   20
the villain. Few popular culture texts explore in any, even the most
cursory, fashion why the villain must be accepted as villainous. He or
she simply exists as a force to thwart the efforts of the hero; the reasons
behind the villain's actions remain vague.

Because the villain appears as such a taken-for-granted entity, the
common-sensical embodiment of everything a society supposedly finds
abhorrent, this figure may be a particularly good place to explore the
ideological work of the action-adventure text. In his study of popular
literature, *Adventure, Mystery, and Romance: Formula Stories as Art
and Popular Culture*, John G. Cawelti describes the role of the villain as
follows:

> Formulas enable the audience to explore in fantasy the boundary
> between the permitted and the forbidden and to experience in a
> carefully controlled way the possibility of stepping across this bound-
> ary. This seems to be preeminently the function of villains in formulaic
> structures: to express, explore, and finally reject those actions which
> are forbidden, but which, because of certain other cultural patterns,
> are strongly tempting.[12]

---

[12]John G. Cawelti, *Adventure, Mystery, and Romance: Formula Stories as Art and
Popular Culture* (Chicago: U of Chicago, 1976), pp. 35–36. [Author's note]

Therefore, villains in popular fantasies . . . embody a secret desire for the forbidden while at the same time acting as the embodiment of "otherness," as that which must be eradicated from existence and denied.

In most American action-adventure tales, the villain represents the dark side of the American Dream. If the American Dream promises that anyone in the United States can become wealthy and materially successful with hard work and persistence, the villain represents the realization of that ambition through criminal means. Often, action-adventure villains are drug-traffickers, illegal gun-runners, corrupt politicians, or wealthy merchants who got rich on stolen goods. They represent that side of capitalism which promotes ruthless competition, the monopolization of resources, and the exploitation of workers.

. . . These villians . . . also often express a suspicion of political as well as economic clout. Very often these villains are elected officials — albeit, usually officials of foreign governments. Even more often, villains are representatives of the legal or military establishment — e.g., policemen, army officers. For those outside of the operations of power, these villains can embody the secret wish to be on the inside, to have the power and knowledge necessary to control one's own life as well as the lives of others.

Villains also allow for the exploration of issues of identity involving racial, ethnic, cultural, national, and gender boundaries. Villains are outside the norm, and thus allow for the negative definition of that norm — i.e., everything the villain is not is normal and positive. Therefore, villains tend to be foreign and very often nonwhite. They speak a different language, have different values, even eat different, exotic foods — e.g., the South Asian villains in *Indiana Jones and the Temple of Doom* eat live creatures.

In this way, villains allow for the expression of xenophobia, that 25 fear of the foreign which solidifies a national identity and often becomes the main meat of war propaganda. However, villains also, in a contradictory way, represent a desire to be "different," not to follow the norms and strictures which bind our own society together. Often villains are personally appealing because they are different and exotic; e.g., they can be sexually alluring, stylish, accomplished, intelligent, powerful, and rich. Frequently, action-adventure stories involve the tearing off of this alluring mask to uncover the truly heinous nature of the villain.

In *Romancing the Stone*, for example, Joan Wilder (Kathleen Turner), at first, seems attracted to the dark, mysterious stranger, Zolo (Manual Ojeda), who offers to help her. The film "codes" him as both "attractive" and "dangerous." His clothes display his wealth and taste; his heavy Hispanic accent codes him as "foreign"; his tall, slender frame and Latin features allow him to be considered sexually alluring.

However, Joan soon realizes, when trapped in the middle of a gun fight between Zolo and the hero Jack Colten (Michael Douglas), that Zolo is her enemy.

Here, the text draws a line between the appeal of ethnic-racial otherness and its threatening aspects. However, even as this otherness is dismissed as evil and dangerous, the text has already opened up the possibility that the villain — and by implication, his race, culture, or nation — may have a certain power and validity. The villain, therefore, can be admired as well as hated.

Frequently, too, the villain represents utter contempt for all those things American society holds most sacred — e.g., middle-class respectability, the nuclear family, suburban material comfort, law and order, patriotism. It can be argued that, in expressing contempt for these institutions, the villain may be venting the viewer's own frustrations arising from pressure to succeed or fit in.

In *Invasion USA*, when East European and Cuban forces invade the United States, their campaign involves attacking those institutions which seem so stereotypically "American," e.g., the suburban mall, the neighborhood filled with ranch-style houses, the local church, and grocery store. All of these things represent the American "good life." However, for many viewers, particularly those viewers marginalized by racial, class, or other differences, these lily-white, middle-class bastions represent an impossible dream of success and abundance. When the "Commies" demolish entire suburban neighborhoods filled with intact nuclear families, Christmas celebrations with abundant gifts and decorations, and shopping malls brimming with high-priced items, the villains may be venting many viewers' frustrations with their own inability to cash in on that wealth.

Moreover, the characterization of the hero underscores these frustra- 30 tions with the middle-class norm. In most respects, the hero differs as much from what may be construed as the social norm — the ideal of "middle-classness" — in the text as the villain does. The hero is an outsider, often a lounger, a drifter, who has no real attachment to a home, family, business, or profession. Although the hero may have been a policeman or a soldier, he is now an adventurer who has an uneasy relationship with his past. In fact, as is the case with *The A-Team* and Rambo, the hero may even be a fugitive, actively hunted by those institutions, like the military and the legal system, which are supposed to operate in the best interests of society. Here, the hero, as a hunted outsider, represents a basic distrust of the "establishment" as well as a freedom from the pressure of trying to conform to middle-class norms.

Similarly, if the villain is foreign, exotic, and dangerous, the hero may also be pictured as "alien," but in a safe and clearly domesticated way. In *Rambo*, for example, a point is made by Rambo's Native American–German ethnicity. Although his ancestors represented two enemy nations, Rambo himself represents the American "melting pot" in which his own ethnicity has been domesticated and put at the service of American interests. This ethnicity can also belie the racism and xenophobia at the root of the text. Rambo cannot be accused of racism in his desire to combat the Vietnamese since he himself is not "white." Similarly, he cannot be accused of going to battle with the Soviets out of a desire to eradicate the foreign, since he himself has a German ancestry.

However, although very much like the villain in many ways, the hero also has his roots in the community besieged by his foe. If the villain is wealthy and part of the established power structure, the hero may be identified with the working classes or the poor, and he has no official place in the power hierarchy.

Therefore, the hero enjoys a peculiar ability to mediate between the domain of the villain and the everyday world of the ordinary person. The hero may be outside the power structure; however, unlike the villain, he acts to secure the status quo and keep the world which seems to have exiled him in operation. Occasionally, at the end of the hero's quest, he is accepted back into the world which had shunned him — i.e., through marriage, a pardon from the legal system, etc. — but, just as often, the hero remains an outsider, tainted by those qualities which enabled him to defeat the villain and restore order to society — i.e., his violence, his otherness, his self-reliance.

In fact, the individual action-adventure hero cuts a rather lonely figure, and he embodies that ambivalence which surrounds the myth of the American individual. If a good deal of the American mythos promises to secure the rights of the individual against the dictates of society, then, the individual must also pay the price for that freedom in loneliness, rootlessness, and homelessness. The action-adventure hero can be a rather tragic figure, ostracized from the very community that he risked his life to protect. Within the figure of the hero, there is always a dialectical play between individualism and community acceptance, freedom and social stigma.[13] Current representations of Vietnam veterans in action-adventure texts embody all these qualities and make the contradictions this figure represents historically concrete.

In order to lighten this tragic aspect of the hero, action-adventure 35 stories usually provide the hero with "buddies," who act as his helpers, or else allow the function of the hero to be taken up by a team rather than a single individual. In general, the buddies or the team also allow the text to compensate a bit for the [narrow ideology] a single white, male hero may dictate. Therefore, if the hero himself is white, male,

[13]In this regard, the action-adventure hero is quite similar to the Western hero; see Robert Warshow, "Movie Chronicle: The Westerner," in *The Immediate Experience: Movies, Comics, Theatre and Other Aspects of Popular Culture* (NY: Atheneum, 1975), pp. 135–154. [Author's note]

and mainstream, the buddy generally is nonwhite, occasionally female, and marginal. The ethnic, racial, or gender difference the buddy represents allows . . . a nonwhite, female, ethnic viewer to identify with someone other than the villain. Although this buddy role may be minor, it can draw this marginalized viewer in on the ideological side of the status quo, on the side of the hero who fights to maintain the powers that be.

Moreover, since action-adventure tales generally involve a white American hero going to battle with nonwhite foreign villains, the fact that the hero's buddy may be part of that alien culture assures the viewer of the moral right of the hero to combat the alien nation violently. By his/her personal loyalty to the hero, the buddy identifies with the power and prerogatives of white, male, American culture.

Similarly, the action-adventure team can act as a point of mediation between a text which seems to assure white, male, American interests and the actual viewer, who may have an uneasy relationship with those interest. *The A-Team*,[14] for instance, features a heterogeneous group which functions as a microcosm of contemporary American society, reproducing the power hierarchies in operation in that society by placing a black, working-class figure at the bottom rung of the ladder. However, this series also allows this figure, B. A. "Bad Attitude" Baracas (Mr. T), to display the marks of his "past" oppression flamboyantly (e.g., by wearing Native American feathers, an African warrior's hairstyle, gold chains to represent past slavery, and the dressed-up battle fatigues of a common soldier) and to express his anger toward a series of white, middle-class villains violently. Although he remains a "pussycat" underneath, childlike and always subject to his white superior's orders, B.A. still allows for some expression of violent anger and resistance that may make him particularly appealing to nonwhite or working-class viewers.

In their configurations of heroes, villains, and buddies, action-adventure texts express ambivalent feelings toward race, class, gender, and power. However, any moments in these texts which may point toward a more direct type of resistance against the status quo are usually brief and marginalized within the fantasy. Instead, action-adventure stories feature a dual operation to eliminate the threat that the villain represents — i.e., the threat of national, cultural, racial otherness. On the one hand, these narratives assimilate and domesticate this threat through the figure of the buddy, who shores up the white, American status quo through his/her personal loyalty to the hero, or through the conflicted nature of the hero himself. Moreover, the buddy's or the hero's alien elements are always kept in check by their unquestioned

[14]For a more detailed analysis, see Gina Marchetti, "Class, Ideology and Commercial Television: An Analysis of THE A-TEAM," *Journal of Film and Video* 39:2 (Spring 1987), pp. 19–28. [Author's note]

support for the dominant culture. On the other hand, difference is also eliminated through the violent death of the villain. Therefore, these tales, although decidedly ambivalent about the economic, gender, and racial status quo, ultimately only allow differences to exist on the dominant culture's own terms.

Conclusion

Beyond the very complicated ways in which the action-adventure genre deals with social inequality, these texts also feature another very important ideological masking of the power relations they treat. That is, built within these tales is the myth of entertainment, i.e., that these narratives are meant to be innocent fun and not serious discussions of political or social issues.

In a certain sense, this seems to be true. Within the action-adventure genre, narrative takes a backseat to spectacle. The emphasis is not on plot or characterization but on action, on the visual display of violence. This is certainly one of the reasons that action-adventure films seem to be particularly popular internationally. A complete understanding of dialogue or plot really is not necessary; instead, the main pleasure of the text revolves around spectacular fights, gun play, torture, and battles.

This reliance on spectacle coupled with the contradictory nature of plots and characters allow the action-adventure genre to appeal to a wide range of viewers. Places seem to be structured into the text for a fluid identification with alluring villains, conflicted heroes, and multiracial, multiethnic buddies. Even women have been acknowledged as having a role to play. The heterogeneity of the text allows these tales to turn profits from a heterogeneous audience — in both domestic and international markets.

However, although open to many different readings, these texts also manage to privilege the dominant ideology. The heroes, in the last instance, remain predominantly white and male and, although outsiders, they are always at the service of dominant bourgeois interests in their championing of the middle-class norm. Pleasure, for the vast majority outside that American middle-class norm, remains on the edges. It exists, and audiences pay dearly for it, but, ultimately, it stays buried beneath the surface, always subject to qualifications and limitations.

Engaging the Text

1. What, according to Marchetti, is the connection between the genre of a film and ideology? In what sense do film genres "function in a way similar to the way myth functions" (para. 3)?

2. What are the "generic specifics" that define the action-adventure film, according to Marchetti? Test her definition of this genre against examples of action-adventure films you have seen. Is her definition accurate and complete?

3. What contradictory or ambivalent messages do most action-adventure films convey about governmental authority? About women and their relation to men?

4. What, according to Marchetti, is the ideological function of the action-adventure film villain? What relationship does she suggest between the villain and the American Dream and other deeply cherished American values? Why is it that action-adventure villains are often "admired as well as hated" (para. 27)?

5. What features, qualities, and values do the heroes and the villains of action-adventure films share? In what sense is the hero figure a kind of "mediator"? In what sense is he typically a "tragic" figure?

6. According to Marchetti, what role do the action-adventure hero's "buddies" play for the audience?

Exploring Connections

7. Read or review Patricia Nelson Limerick's (p. 110) and Shelby Steele's (p. 347) discussions of the notion of American innocence. To what extent do action-adventure films, according to Marchetti, claim a kind of innocence for their heroes and, by extension, for the dominant culture?

8. Read or review Susan Griffin's "Split Culture" (p. 175). How might Griffin interpret the attitudes expressed or implied in action-adventure films toward nature, toward Third World countries and their inhabitants, toward people of color, toward women?

9. Marchetti claims that action-adventure films are "very much male-dominated and male-defined" (para. 19). How might Carol Gilligan (p. 233) account for the relationships among audience, hero, villain, and community in this genre? What would a "female-defined" action-adventure film be like? Is such a thing possible?

Extending the Critical Context

10. Watch any recent action-adventure film and test Marchetti's thesis. Does the film contain the "generic specifics" she mentions? To what extent do the film's hero and villain embody the contradictory traits and values she suggests? What is the ideological "message" of the film? What does it say about the role of marginalized groups? What does it say about the status quo?

Dear John Wayne

Louise Erdrich

For most Americans, being invaded by aliens sounds like a plot for a science fiction film, but for American Indians it's a way of life. The following poem about a group of Indians watching a John Wayne movie at the drive-in addresses what it means to live surrounded by the mythic figures of a hostile culture. Louise Erdrich (b. 1954) is one of America's premier contemporary novelists. The author of three best-sellers, Love Medicine *(1984),* The Beet Queen *(1986), and* Tracks *(1988), she has also written two collections of poetry,* Jacklight *(1984) and* Baptism of Desire *(1990). Her latest work,* The Crown of Columbus *(1991), was coauthored with her husband and longtime collaborator, Michael Dorris. This poem first appeared in an earlier version in* Jacklight.

August and the drive-in picture is packed.
We lounge on the hood of the Pontiac
surrounded by the slow-burning spirals they sell
at the window, to vanquish the hordes of mosquitoes.
Nothing works. They break through the smoke-screen for blood.   5

Always the look-out spots the Indians first,
spread north to south, barring progress.
The Sioux, or Cheyenne, or some bunch
in spectacular columns, arranged like SAC missiles,
their feathers bristling in the meaningful sunset.   10

The drum breaks. There will be no parlance.
Only the arrows whining, a death-cloud of nerves
swarming down on the settlers
who die beautifully, tumbling like dust weeds
into the history that brought us all here   15
together: this wide screen beneath the sign of the bear.

The sky fills, acres of blue squint and eye
that the crowd cheers. His face moves over us,
a thick cloud of vengeance, pitted
like the land that was once flesh. Each rut,   20
each scar makes a promise: *It is
not over, this fight, not as long as you resist.*

Everything we see belongs to us.
A few laughing Indians fall over the hood

slipping in the hot spilled butter. 25
The eye sees a lot, John, but the heart is so blind.
How will you know what you own?
He smiles, a horizon of teeth
the credits reel over, and then the white fields
again blowing in the true-to-life dark. 30
The dark films over everything.
We get into the car
scratching our mosquito bites, speechless and small
as people are when the movie is done.
We are back in ourselves. 35

How can we help but keep hearing his voice,
the flip side of the sound-track, still playing:
Come on, boys, we've got them
where we want them, drunk, running.
They will give us what we want, what we need: 40
The heart is a strange wood inside of everything
we see, burning, doubling, splitting out of its skin.

Engaging the Text

1. Identify which lines refer to actions and characters in the movie and which lines describe what's going on at the drive-in. What parallels or contrasts does Erdrich draw between the movie and the people watching it?

2. Does the speaker of the poem change? If so, where do the changes occur and how can you tell?

3. This poem is filled with details that suggest meanings beyond the simple denotations of the things themselves. What do you make of the way Erdrich emphasizes the mosquitoes that attack for blood, the "SAC missiles," the "meaningful sunset," the "sign of the bear," the "land that was once flesh"? What do these details say about the history of American Indians?

4. Whose point of view does the line "The Sioux, or Cheyenne, or some bunch" reflect? What unspoken assumptions does it reveal?

5. Why do the Indians laugh in stanza 6? Why, at the end of the stanza, does the speaker say, "We are back in ourselves"?

6. What do you make of the poem's enigmatic concluding metaphor? How does the poem as a whole illustrate the heart "burning, doubling, splitting"?

Exploring Connections

7. To what extent does Erdrich's poem confirm or challenge the case Gina Marchetti makes for the influence of movies (p. 661)?

8. Compare the reactions of the Indians to John Wayne in this poem with the reactions of Rodney Morales's narrator and his friends to Elvis in "Under the Table" (p. 676). How do you explain their reactions?

9. Read or review Susan Griffin's "Split Culture" (p. 175). How might her analysis of dominant attitudes toward nature and tribal peoples be used to interpret this poem? Does her notion of cultural splitting help clarify the poem's concluding lines?

Extending the Critical Context

10. Watch a John Wayne western on videotape and write an analysis of the myths and messages it conveys about cowboys, Indians, women, nature, and the West. Consult the selections by Patricia Nelson Limerick (p. 110) and Gina Marchetti (p. 661) to help you with your analysis. You may also want to review discussions of related themes by John (Fire) Lame Deer (p. 128), Chellis Glendinning (p. 150), and Susan Griffin (p. 175).

Under the Table

RODNEY MORALES

This selection takes us literally under the table during an English test at Farrington High, to an afternoon matinee featuring Elvis Presley's It Happened at the World's Fair, *and to a beachside fistfight that changed a boy's life. The author, Rodney Morales, gives us a view of what it's like growing up Hawaiian in a culture saturated by white-controlled media. It's an entertaining and poignant look at the price we pay for the myths that sustain innocence. Morales teaches at the University of Hawai'i, Mānoa. His collection of short stories* The Speed of Darkness, *the source of this selection, was published in 1988.*

May 1969

Maybe we weren't listening. Or just couldn't understand. It was often like that in school. So, when the teachers passed out exams, we'd look at the questions, give each other funny looks, then proceed to cheat.

On this occasion, we were almost through taking a test in our American Problems class at Farrington High. We were the class of '69, a precious two and a half weeks away from graduation. Mrs. Harada, our teacher, had trusted us enough to leave the classroom temporarily, leaving Marsha Olayan (Marsha the Brain, we called her; she always finished taking tests first) to act as monitor. What the teacher didn't know was that Marsha had a mean crush on Lenny Batista, the cheating scheme ringleader, and as soon as Marsha was in charge, pieces of paper that had been carefully passed from one student to another now flew around the room like paper planes.

Sometimes cheating was too easy. As a class we seemed to be arriving at the notion that it was more fun to come up with the answers on our own. And in the case of this test, when I started to do just that, I found myself both tickled and puzzled by one peculiar question. It read: "What world leader in 1959 made the statement, 'We will bury you,' thus feeding the fire of the Cold War?" Knowing the answer, for once, I started to write it down. Then, unsure of the spelling of the foreign name, I picked up the paper airplane that had landed in front of me seconds earlier. I opened it up and read the words that were etched in almost calligraphic style. It read: ANSWER TO #17 — NICKY DA CRUISE JOB.[1] I coughed out a laugh and thought immediately: Lenny. I looked across the table, where he sat, but he wasn't there. Puzzled, I shook my head — perhaps chiding myself in advance for what I was about to do — crossed out what I had started to write, and wrote "Nicky da Cruise Job." Then I felt something tugging at my pant cuffs. Normally I would have kicked. But I knew it had to be Lenny. I dropped my pen — on purpose — and went under the table to get it.

So there we were, amidst the flurry of legs. Bare female legs, covered male ones. We sat eight to a table, so there were twelve legs left to surround us. Just at the moment that Lenny motioned for me to look in the direction of Lynette Toma's crotch, I whispered "Nicky da Cruise Job" and he gulped down a laugh and suddenly we were in the sixth grade.

May 1963

I couldn't understand it when Miss Lake told us we had to go under the table because of Nicky da Cruise Job. She said if we didn't hide under the table that Nicky da Cruise Job was going to bomb us guys. So we'd be under the table, our lessons totally disrupted — to our excitement and delight — and I'd be wondering, Who is this guy, Nicky da Cruise Job?

Finally, one Friday after school, I asked Lenny, figuring he was almost as smart as Shane[2] but at least he doesn't punch you when you ask questions. I had to ask Lenny because it was like I had been absent and I had missed something and I hated that feeling. But Lenny said he

5

---

[1]*Nicky da Cruise Job:* Nikita Khrushchev (1894–1971), premier of the Soviet Union from 1958 to 1964.

[2]*Shane:* also the name of the protagonist of a classic western novel and film. Shane epitomizes the mysterious and reticent outsider turned hero.

didn't know either. He said that Larry Kanahele had told him that Miss Lake actually pronounced it, "Nicky da Cruise Chef," not "Nicky da Cruise Job," and that Nicky da Cruise, Job or Chef, was actually a Mafia guy and that this Mafia guy Nicky da Cruise had a chef working for him like Larry's Uncle Keoki who worked as a chef at the Queen's Surf in Waikiki.

All I could figure out was that I had to ask Shane and risk getting punched. Since it was Friday, I knew I'd see Shane the next day when he and Gerry and Lenny and me were going to see an Elvis Presley matinee at a theater downtown.

Perseverance was the ticket to a movie those days. That is, if you nagged your mom until she realized that not having you around was worth the buck and a half — two bucks, if she felt rich — that would get you there.

We were meeting at the bus stop near the corner of King and Kalihi streets, in front of the Kamehameha Homes Public Housing Project (a low-income development whose name everyone shortened to Kam Housing), across [from] Farrington High School. Me and Gerry were always the first ones there.

"Maybe like 'De la Cruz.' You know, like Gerry's last name," Gerry was saying, referring to another Gerry. He was wearing a new pair of Levi's that had about twenty pockets. And from the pocket that ran alongside from below his right hip to just short of his knee, Gerry pulled out a long, black comb and began to comb his thick-with-pomade black hair. 10

"No, but . . . da teachah said 'Cruise Job' . . . I t'ink. Shit, I dunno."

We were going to see *It Happened at the World's Fair* at the King Theater. While a war movie or cowboy movie sounded more exciting, we went along with Shane's fervent wish to see the latest Elvis Presley movie that had hit town. Shane was our leader, and the undisputed number one Elvis Presley fan.

And speaking of Shane, as I gazed over the low shrubbery that outlined the housing area I saw him coming up Kalihi Street. Shane had a sharp, hands-open-and-to-the-side way of walking. It was so smooth I could already hear the sharpness from afar.

Shane was the one to ask about things you didn't understand; he always knew better. The teachers were stupid enough to put him in the dumb class but we knew that he was the smartest, toughest, coolest, not-to-mention handsomest dude around. We all parted our hair on the side, the way he did. But only he had the privilege (and maybe the kind of hair) to push the front part up and back — Elvis Presley style. Shane had seen all the Elvis movies. The last ones he saw were *G.I. Blues* and

Blue Hawaii. Shane's favorite color was blue. And so was ours. And it all made perfect sense.

What made Shane look so extra sharp, though, was his pants. We all tried to get our parents to buy us the type of bell-bottom pants — drapes, we called them — that Shane wore. But we didn't know where to buy them. And Shane wouldn't tell us, though I figured out later that his mother made them for him.

Even on J.P.O.[3] duty, he looked so tough, with his square-cut white shirt, his blue drapes, his captain's whistle. Of course, we had voted him captain. Geraldo "Gerry" De la Cruz was lieutenant. Lenny, me, and Gerry, our Gerry, had swept the whole slate by being elected first, second, and third sergeants, respectively. Shane was too cool.

When Shane's features were within sight, when I could see the slight squint he often made when approaching us, a mock sort of sizing up, I greeted him with a quick up-down head motion. He didn't respond.

"Gerry said Elvis Hawaiian," I said the moment Shane was within earshot. He was wearing his customary drapes. And he had on a nifty, blue velour shirt with a string sort of tie at the collar.

"Dass true," Gerry replied.

"Bullshit," Shane said. "He one haole."[4]

"But, but, in *Blue Hawaii* he no look haole. Da buggah brown."

"Dass 'cause dy wen' paint his skin. Dye 'om. Dass what Hollywood do. Dey make 'om look like somet'ing else. Dey can make one haole look Japanee."

"Ey, I no believe you," Gerry said. Shane punched him in the shoulder. "OW! Okay, I believe . . . I believe." Gerry rubbed his arm. "Ow, you fuckah. Sore."

Shane was the smartest guy around.

Then Lenny, always last, arrived. He probably came through Kam Housing, because it seemed like he had come out of nowhere, like he had been hiding in the bushes all the time. When I greeted him, again with a head gesture, a barely perceptible inverted nod, Lenny responded by lifting his eyebrows. No other part of his face moved.

When Lenny had transferred to our school, Kalihi-Kai Elementary, earlier that school year, Shane challenged him to a footrace. When I shouted "MARK! SET! GO!" Lenny ran the wrong way, a route that was perpendicular to Shane's. Together they were like the vectors we were learning about in math class, forming a longer and longer right angle. I laughed till I was blue.

But as I got to know Lenny, I began to suspect that he was smart enough not to show that he could beat Shane . . . yet.

---

[3]*J.P.O.:* Junior Patrol Officer.
[4]*haole:* native Hawaiian term for a white.

The H.R.T.[5] arrived. We all got on the bus and walked down the aisle to the back so we could look at everybody in front. If anybody turned back to look at us we give that person the stink eye and act tough.

I sat between Shane and Gerry, Shane being on my left. Lenny sat to the left of Shane. We were silent for a minute as the bus sped toward downtown. Then I spoke first.

"So, who is dis Nicky da Cruise Job?" 30

"You fuckah," Shane said, elbowing my ribs. "You always gotta bring up stupid stuff."

Gerry said, "I t'ink he one, you know, da kine syndicate guy. Like Al Capone . . . Dillinger. . . ."

"Mafia?" I said.

"Yeah."

"Make sense. . . . So we are practicing fo' hide from da Mafia. . . ." 35

Then Shane spoke. "Fucking stupid. You guys so FUCKING STOOPID? He one Russian! He da Russian leadah —"

"How you know?"

"My muddah wen' tell me. He da old bolohead[6] guy."

"Why we gotta hide undah da table 'cause a' one old bolohead guy?" Gerry said. "Why we no jes' beef 'om? If da buggah old."

"Not jes' him," Shane started to say. He sounded pissed. "He get his 40
boys . . . da Russians . . . strong buggahs. . . ."

"What," Gerry said, "dey can beef you?"

"Of course . . . I mean, of course not. Not if one-on-one."

"What if," Gerry said, "what if you take da strongest American guy our age, an' dass pro'bly you, Shane . . . an' you take da strongest Russian guy our age, an' den you guys beef. Who would win?"

I glanced at Lenny. Through all this conversation he had been staring straight ahead, quiet. But when I looked at him he turned to make a mock-serious face at me, then quickly looked straight ahead again.

"Me, of course," Shane said, very serious. "He pro'bly goin' be 45
biggah . . ." He started shadow boxing. ". . . but I no care. . . . I goin' let 'om t'row first, eh. Den I goin' duck. No, no, I goin' give 'om one cross block, den duck an' come up wit' one left uppacut, den hit 'om low, right in the ribs. *OOGH!* Den, if da buggah still standing, I goin' wait fo' he t'row again, duck dis time, turning li' dis . . ." Shane turned his body leftward, toward me, pulling his right arm toward his left shoulder. ". . . den give 'om one . . ." He threw his right hand out toward some shadow enemy, saying ". . . KARATE CHOP IN DA NECK!"

---

[5]*H.R.T.:* Hawaiian Rapid Transit.
[6]*bolohead:* bald-headed.

Shane took karate lessons; he always reminded us, in case we had forgotten.

"Whoah," Gerry said, as some passengers up front turned to look at us. "Ja' like Tosh Togo."[7] Then he said, "Hey Shane, you can lick one Japanee guy our age who one judo expert? Or kung fu?"

"Tst. . . . Of course. Easy."

We all kept pulling on the cord that rang the bell that announced we were getting off. *BINGBINGBINGBINGBING . . . BING-BINGBINGBINGBING,* to the bus driver's annoyance. We exited then, crossed Smith Street on King, passed a sundry shop, then it was the theater. We each paid our 75 cents for the movie ticket and walked into the snack bar area. We loaded up on popcorn, Pom Poms, M & Ms, Mr. Goodbars, Cokes, and 7-Ups. Then we walked into the dark, cavernous escape world just in time for the Looney Tunes.

We took seats way in the back. Me and Gerry, positioning ourselves 50 a seat apart to give ourselves room, sat in the same row. Shane and Lenny, also a seat apart, sat in the row behind us. The good thing about Saturday matinees was that there were always a lot of empty seats.

The warm smells of butter and chocolate wafted through the moviehouse as we began gulping down the goodies and adjusting our eyes to the bright colors of the opening cartoon.

"Hey Gerry. Bugs Bunny look ja'like you."

"Shit, you look like Elmah Fudd. . . . OW! Hey, no kick da chair!"

During the rest of the cartoon, we threw ice and pieces of candy wrappers, kicked chairs, and swore at each other a lot. But we got real quiet when the opening credits to *It Happened at the World's Fair* filled the screen.

The tone for the movie was set early. Elvis and this other guy are in 55 this small plane. They're cropdusters. Elvis — while singing, of course — sparks[8] two nice-looking chicks in a convertible and flies the plane low to check them out.

Then the plot begins to unfold. It turns out that Elvis and his plane-flying partner are saving up all their money so they can start a business of their own. The only problem is that Elvis's partner is a chronic gambler and has already gambled away some of their earnings. So, Elvis has to hide the money and keep it under lock and key.

Elvis, it turns out, is a chronic girl chaser. . . .

"Junk, dis movie. He only like make out wit girls."

"Shaddup, Gerry. Jes' watch."

Elvis's partner somehow gets hold of the money, about four hun- 60 dred dollars, finds a poker game to join into, and proceeds to lose

---

[7]*Tosh Togo:* Asian American actor.
[8]*sparks:* spots, sees, notices.

everything and more. By the time Elvis discovers that the money is missing and finds the location of the poker game — this is after he has been chased with a gun by the father of a girl he is caught making out with — his partner owes the rest of the players seven hundred dollars. Elvis accuses the other players of cheating him, suggesting that they were doing something under the table, and a fight ensues.

"All right."

"Wow. You saw dat? He wen' kick 'om."

"Of course. Elvis know karate."

"Whoa, watch him smoke da guys."

"Wow. You saw dat? You saw dat? Karate chop?"   65

"Wheah?"

"You blind mullet —"

Elvis was fighting about a half-dozen guys, licking them all, while his partner struggled to fight one.

"Dere. He doin' 'om again."

"Shhhh."   70

Elvis grabs his friend and they haul ass out of town. The timing is perfect. A pickup truck, driven by a Chinese man, the passenger his little daughter, stops and picks them up.

"Look like your faddah, Gerry."

"Shaddap."

"Look like your sistah, Gerry."

"Fuck you. You cannot tell da difference between one Japanee and   75
one —"

"Shhhhh!"

"What you said, Gerry? Elvis Hawaiian?"

"Shaddap."

"She your speed, Gerry,"

"Shaddap. She *your* speed. An' you bettah not kick my chair."   80

"Shhhhhhh!"

I noticed that Elvis's hair was combed back even more so than I had remembered. And it looked real shiny, like he loaded it up with some kind of hair oil. It looked kind of funny to me. I figured that Shane was going to start using more pomade.

The Chinese guy and his daughter — she introduces herself as Sue Lin; Elvis says he is Mike; she calls him Mr. Mike — are heading out toward Seattle to see the World's Fair. Sue Lin's father tells Elvis and his partner they are welcome to head up there with them. They think it's a great idea.

But when they reach the fair, something goes wrong. The girl's father, who runs a produce business, discovers he has to make an important delivery, and won't be able to take his daughter to the fair as promised. Elvis, of course, saves the day by volunteering to take the little girl around while his partner goes off to find them work.

"Mr. Mike" and Sue Lin check out the Space Needle, the Dream Car —
a futuristic vehicle (more than a few "ooh's" and "wow's" from the
movie audience) —, and they eat a lot of junk food. Sue Lin ends up
having an awful bellyache, and Elvis takes her to the dispensary. Of
course, Elvis falls for the nurse. . . .

"Getting stale again. When dey goin' fight again? Hey, Shane, no 85
t'row ice."

"Yeah," I said, "no t'row ice. Who t'rowing ice?"

Elvis spends the rest of the movie chasing after the nurse, and sings
enough songs to fill an album. His partner continues to gamble, but he
also gets them a potentially lucrative job delivering some goods in their
plane across the Canadian border. It turns out, though, that it's a gun-
smuggling operation involving some syndicate type. Elvis reneges on the
deal, which leads to a film-ending fight that almost makes the movie
worthwhile.

When we got out of the theater no one said anything for several
minutes. We walked sort of absently in the same direction — down Fort
Street — and reacquainted ourselves with the overwhelming brightness
of the sky and the sunlit street.

Gerry spoke first: "Wow, I like da way Elvis wen' smoke da guys.
Ten of 'om against him."

"Was mo' like five," I said. 90

"Seven," Shane said. No one disputed that.

"Silly, eh," Lenny said, "da way everytime Elvis sing get all kine
music backup — like all da musicians stay in da bushes o' somet'ing."
Then Lenny started singing, doing a mock Elvis. "Happy ending, happy
ending/Give me a story with a *boom* happy end—"

"Tst," Shane said, interrupting Lenny's performance, "dass jes'
Hollywood."

"Hey," Gerry said. "We go see *Gunfight at O.K. Corral*. Stay
showing at Hawaii T'eatah. I bet get mo' action."

"We no mo' nuff money," Shane said. "Unless you goin' treat us." 95

"Oh, yeah . . ." Gerry said, as if remembering, "we no mo' nuff
money."

"Tired, cowboy pictures, anyway. Get nuff a' dat on T.V."

"Hey," Gerry quickly added, "anybody saw *Stoney Burke*[9] las'
night? Stoney wen fall off his horse and —"

"I saw," Shane said. "Was junk."

"Was *good*." *POOM* "OW! Okay, was junk den." 100

We walked past Metronome music store. We saw some guys testing
out some electric guitars. A couple of them were so good that they were
even practicing their steps.

[9]*Stoney Burke:* early 1960s TV series about a rodeo cowboy.

"Wow," Lenny said. "Maybe dey play fo' da Spiedels."[10]

"Da guys who play, 'Pipeline'?" I asked.

"No . . . 'Telstar.'"[11] Lenny turned and grinned at me. I grinned back. We walked on till Lenny said, "Hey, we go beach. Still early."

"Nah," Shane said. "I no like get' my pants dirty. Besides, we no mo' towels." 105

"No need towels fo' dry off," Lenny said. "And pants . . . can wash."

"Yeah, we go," Gerry chimed.

"Yeah," I said.

Shane didn't seem to like the idea. He didn't seem to like being challenged, but for once he was outnumbered. His jaw seemed to tighten. "Okay, shit. We go den."

We always wore swimming trunks underneath our pants. It's a 110 habit you learn quick enough when you grow up in a hot, tropical climate. The first time Lenny went out with us, though, he hadn't been all that acclimated. He only had B.V.D.'s on underneath, so we couldn't go to Waikiki or Ala Moana. We ended up swimming bareballs at Sand Island.

It took us about a half hour to get to Ala Moana beach. We were all hot and sweaty by then, and anxious to swim out to the reef that functioned as a breakwater. We laid our clothes on the sand, Shane folding his carefully, and jumped in. We swam to the reef, took some dives off the rocks, shoved each other's heads in, then swam back to the shore. Then, using a scrunched up paper cup with a little bit of sand in it, we played Hawaiian-style football in the shallow water till the game got out of hand with everybody stretching the already loose rules more and more. Finally, we got out.

By then we were all both hungry and thirsty. We knew, however, that if we ate or drank something we'd be using our bus fare home. Still, it seemed like it would be worth it. We checked to see how much money we had. Shane had fifty-three cents. I had thirty-five. Lenny had thirty-five also. Gerry, from his vast array of pockets, pulled out two long combs, a short one, a piece of string he identified as belonging to a yoyo, his ticket stub, but only managed to scrape up twenty-three cents. Together we had enough for hotdogs and soft drinks. That's about it.

"I tot you said you wanted fo' see *Gunfight at O.K. Corral?*" Shane said to Gerry as he handed him twelve cents. "You mo' broke dan us."

"I tot I had . . . I fo'got." Shane karate-chopped him in the neck. "OW! Fucking Shane, why you always gotta whack *me?* Whack dem . . ." Gerry looked toward me and Lenny ". . . sometime." Shane responded by giving Gerry a headlock.

---

[10]*da Spiedels:* the Spiedels — an early 1960s rock group.
[11]*"Pipeline," "Telstar":* popular rock instrumentals of the early 1960s.

We bought our Cokes and hotdogs at the Ala Moana Beach Ewa 115
concession and devoured the food and drink in what seemed like seconds. Still, it was great. Then we started walking through one of the
woodier areas of the park to get on with the long trek home.

Then, from out of nowhere, we heard an Elvis Presley song:

She wrote upon it
Return to sender, address unknown
No such number, no such zone . . .

We were all suddenly reeling, spinning slowly around in a small clearing, grinning, goofy-like, wondering where the music was coming from.
"Whoa," Lenny said, "ja'like in da movie." Shane started doing a
mock-Elvis routine, moving his legs to and fro.

Then out of the green, it seemed, two big guys approached us. They
looked to be eighth graders, at least.

What are movies without bad guys? These guys looked like they'd
fit the bill.

"Hey," the Japanese-looking guy said to Shane. "How much money
you get?" His companion turned his transistor radio down.

"Not-t'ing," Shane said. 120

"What about you, Japanee?" He was glaring at Gerry.

"Not-t'ing," Shane said again.

"Hey, I talking to you, Potagee?[12] I not talking to you."

Gerry dug into one of the many pockets of his jeans, and, like he
knew the exact location, pulled out a dollar bill and handed it to the
hijacker. Shane, Lenny, and me all looked at Gerry, startled; he did not
look at us. Then the hijacker looked at Lenny and me, but before he
could utter a word we both pulled our pockets out to show that we had
nothing. Then his attention turned again to Shane. "You get nice
clothes. You must get money —"

"I no mo'," Shane said, looking down at the dirt. 125

"Eh, leave 'om alone, Russ," the hijacker's Portuguese-looking companion said. "Dey already gave us. If he said he no mo', he no mo'."

I calculated that Shane must have had six cents somewhere on him.
Why didn't he just give it?

"Eh," the guy named Russ said, "but I t'ink dis guy t'ink he hot
shit." Russ glared at Shane. His pupils seemed dilated. His eyes were
red, but also a bit yellowy. "You hot shit?"

Shane looked down. "No," he said, quick but soft.

"Look at me when you talk." 130

"Leave 'om alone, Russ." His partner pulled at Russ's arm. Russ
pulled his arm back.

"Use your karate, Shane," Gerry whispered.

[12]*Potagee:* derogatory term for a Portuguese.

"What?" Russ said, feigning surprise. "Dis panty know karate?"

"Heah," Gerry said. "He can break your ass." Shane glared at Gerry.

"Oh boy, I scared now. Dis guy know ka-ra-te." Russ went into a fake, exaggerated karate position. "YAHT-YAHT-YAHT!" he yelled, throwing awkward blows in the direction of Shane. "Come on. Break my ass."

"Yeah, break his ass already," his companion said. He seemed exasperated.

"You goin' break my ass?" Russ said, taunting Shane.

Shane looked at the dirt on the ground. "No."

"How come? You one panty? One karate panty?" Shane glanced up. He saw our eyes on him. There was a pause. "Come on! Talk!"

"Come on, Russ. Let's go. We already get dere money."

"Yeah, but . . . dey have clothes. Look at dis nice shirt." Russ grabbed at Shane's shirt. Shane pushed his hand away. Russ responded by bunching up Shane's shirt collar, and pulling Shane closer. Shane pulled away. The shirt tore.

"You fuckah . . . ma muddah wen' —"

"Your mom-mee? Baby needs his mom-mee?" Russ kicked dirt on Shane's khaki drapes. Shane dusted it off. Russ then rubbed his slipper bottom on it. Shane shoved him away. Russ lost his cool. "You fuckah," Russ said, and he threw a long, roundhouse right that smashed into Shane's left ear. I grimaced as I heard the crunch.

"OW! My ear! You fuckah!" Shane started crying. He bent low, cupping his ear, tears streaming down his face. "You cheat, you fuckah. You punch in da ear! OW-WEE. . . ."

Before Russ could react, Lenny charged the much larger guy, catching him off-balance. Lenny threw wild but lightning quick punches at Russ, who probably could have killed Lenny, if Lenny would only let him swing back, let alone breathe, against the flurry of his small blows.

The other big kid moved slightly, like he thought about jumping in. Gerry and I moved correspondingly, to let him know we'd jump in too. He stopped, held a hand up, indicating a momentary truce. "It's cool," he said, with exaggerated nods. "Let 'om fight."

Shane was still bent low, almost in squatting position, holding his ear. He kept crying out, "Cheat, cheat, da fuckah punch ear."

Then Russ fell down, more from being off-balance, it seemed. Lenny kept swinging at him. "You fucking Russ," his friend said, "you let one small guy lick you."

"Okay, nuff," Russ began to say, "nuff already. I sorry. I nevah mean fo' cheat, okay?"

Lenny finally got off him. Slowly, Russ stood up, holding his nose, which was bleeding steadily. He also had a black eye.

"Shit," his friend said. "Now I gotta wash you up. How embarrassing." Oblivious to us, he led Russ away. Then he stopped for a second, turned up his radio, then off they continued, disappearing in the same bushes that they seemed to materialize out of. We were left with a wounded Shane and the fading sounds of the transistor radio:

> *. . . and before that, that was the King himself singing his hit song from the movie,* Girls, Girls, Girls *. . . you're listening to the number one station* (female voices:) *K-P-O-I — Honolulu. . . .*

As soon as Russ and his companion were gone Gerry shouted "Hey, look!" and pointed to a dollar bill right where the scuffle had occurred. It must have been the dollar that Gerry had given to Russ. It must have fallen out of his pocket. Gerry ran to retrieve it. Lenny went up to him and punched his arm.

"You fuckah. You nevah tell us you had dat much."

"I fo'got . . . fo' real, I fo'got."

"Yeah . . . sure."   155

"Hey, I treat you guys, okay? I pay fo' everybody's bus fare."

"You fuckah. You bettah buy us Cokes too."

"Yeah, yeah. But fo' real . . . I fo'got."

We had washed Shane up at Ala Moana Shopping Center, then had hiked up on Keeaumoku Street to King to catch the 1R Kalihi bus home.

We didn't sit in the back. In fact, we sat way up front, right behind   160
the driver. Me and Lenny sat together, Shane and Gerry sat behind us. Shane kept telling Gerry, "If da buggah nevah cheat, man . . . I woulda use' my karate," and Gerry would be saying, "Yeah, you woulda killed 'om, Shane. Fucking cheatah."

The downtown stores like Long's Drugs and Woolworth's, a dizzying blur from inside the speeding bus, cast their large shadows in the late afternoon. The places we had been but hours before, though it seemed like months, were history. Shane said. "An' dis panty," referring to Lenny, "He no can even beef. He cannot fight fo' shit. You saw how he swing?" Shane imitated Lenny's wild blows in exaggerated style. I saw Lenny's fists tighten on his lap. Shane and Gerry went on talking.

"Wow, your pants all had it," Gerry said.

"Yeah. Ma muddah goin' kill me. Shit."

"Da fuckah cheat. He mo' worse dan da Russians," Gerry said, his voice trailing off.

"You had money," Lenny said suddenly, turning to punch Gerry in   165
the arm. "Fucking stashah."

"Yeah, stashah," I echoed. Then it got silent and uncomfortable for a while. It wasn't till we were way past Aala Park and nearing Palama Theater that Shane broke the ice.

"An' da buggah call me 'Potagee,'" he said. "I only part. I get Hawaiian . . . English . . . some Chinese. . . ."

"Yeah, you get everything, Shane," Lenny cut in. I could not really tell if he were being straightforward or sarcastic then, sarcasm being pretty new to me. In fact, I think it was Lenny who started introducing such nuances to my ears.

Still, for the most part, edges were being lost in translation. Nicky da Cruise, Job or Chef. Who is the guy? Were we hearing it right? I mean, you'd like to know who's threatening you . . . and why. I glanced at Lenny. And as I caught his conspiratorial smile I was under the table again.

May 1969 — A moment later

Lenny's eyes again moved in the direction of Lynette Toma's crotch. 170 This time my eyes followed. I had hoped he hadn't summoned me under the table to play spark-panty. We hadn't done that in ages. Just the thought of it, made me hot with embarrassment — yet curious.

And there it was, Lynette's crotch, jiggling like Jell-O. Usually, all the girls wore bikini bottoms because dresses and skirts were so short in those days. Few were ever brave enough to wear panties. Lynette's legs were going 280; she always had that leg-shaking habit. At the moment she was busy talking to Jolene Kauhane, another fox, and they seemed to have no idea that me and Lenny were under.

Lenny and I grinned at each other. I figured we'd get caught — but it was worth it. At that moment I thought Lynette was the foxiest girl in the world.

Then she covered it up — probably her sixth sense. It always happened like that; such moments were so brief. Then I looked at Lenny and whispered (though not as soft as before), "So who is this guy, Nicky da Cruise Job?" and we both started laughing.

The laughing seemed to reverberate off of every conceivable wall. Suddenly, the whole class's attention was turned to Lenny and me, the two idiots under the table. Then Lenny came out from under and started yelling, "BWAAAAAAAAAAAAAHHHHH . . . AIR RAID . . . AIR RAID . . . ALL UNITS ON ALERT . . . THIS IS NOT, I REPEAT, THIS IS *NOT* A FALSE ALARM . . . WE *ARE* BEING ATTACKED BY THE SOVIETS . . . THEY ARE ABOUT TO . . . BURY US[13] . . . UNDER THE TABLE, EVERYONE. . . ."

Lenny was diverting all the attention away from me. He jumped on 175 tables, made siren noises — school was never able to stifle Lenny, the way it did so many of us; it would take a lot more than that.

"I tell you, boys are such —" I heard Lynette start to whisper to Jolene. I couldn't believe it. Their whispers seemed so loud from under

---

[13]*"They are about to . . . bury us"*: during his rule as premier of the Soviet Union, Nikita Khrushchev shocked the Western world and spurred on the Cold War by threatening to "bury" the United States.

the table. It seemed as if I were in an adjacent room from the one they were in, and their room was being bugged. It was as if I wore head-phones — like I had seen on T.V. — and was suddenly in on their innermost secrets.

But then I heard "Da teachah coming, da teachah coming," our very own air-raid warning. A very effective one. In an instant the class was tellingly silent, a world of deaf-mutes. Marsha, the monitor, sat casually in her place at the teacher's desk up front. Somebody's hand tossed a paper plane under the table and it hit my arm. Another piece of paper fell to the floor and a girl's foot kicked it more under.

It was too late for me to come out from under the table without getting nabbed. Yet if I didn't come out, the teacher would notice I was missing. I thought of how often I seemed to be caught in similar dilemmas.

Strangely enough, Mrs. Harada went through the routine of collect-ing test papers without noting my absence. Someone had probably stuck my paper under his or hers, and got my paper handed in. As a class we were good at covering up for each other.

I cherished my newly discovered invisibility — something I thought 180 only Hollywood could do.

Then the bell rang. I stayed there through the shuffle. At one point, Lenny ducked his head under. "Somattah?" he said. "Catch da stre — hey, you all right?" I waved him away. He understood. I made no move to go to math class. Instead, I thought of vectors. I thought of how we all seemed to start at the same place and then grow further and further apart. And I don't just mean those infinitesimal misunderstandings that grow into disputes of global proportions. I'm just talking about growing up. I mean, what's so great about growing up if you keep losing friends?

So what if Shane didn't know karate, at least not to the extent that he claimed. So what if Gerry stashed bucks sometimes. So what if I knew Lenny for a couple of years before I found out he lived in that housing project and didn't want to let on how poor he thought his family was, not appreciating for a long time that the rest of us weren't much better off, or that it didn't matter. Shane and Gerry had already been lost in the shuffle, lost in those trying transitions to intermediate and high school. Now me and Lenny were going to part ways. We, like so many others our age, had received draft notices. I was escaping to college; Lenny was headed for Nam. He didn't want to go. But more important, he didn't want to not go. He had too much pride.

Lenny was going to Nam because some men in nice suits in Paris[14] couldn't agree on the size and shape of their negotiating table.

---

[14]*Some men in nice suits in Paris:* refers to the Paris peace talks of the early 1970s, intended to end the Vietnam War. The talks were stalled repeatedly because participants could not agree on the shape of the negotiating table.

Lenny was going to Nam as part of Richard Nixon's *Vietnamization* program.[15]

And it made me sad.   185

It made me less sad, though, to remember Lenny singing the song that Elvis sang at the end of *It Happened at the World's Fair*:

Happy ending, happy ending
Give me a story with a (boom) *happy ending . . .*

though it just so happens that the world — except in movies, maybe — is not fair. Because I still wanted to believe in happy endings.

I wanted to bask in the wet-dream world of Jell-O-like crotches, in dark, cavernous theaters, living out Hollywood scenes . . . where background music is there for you whenever you want to sing, where fights work out as planned, where the bad guys always lose. . . .

But now I didn't even know who the bad guys were.

I wanted to lash out at my shadow enemy. No, not Nicky da Cruise Job, or Khrushchev, or cruise missiles, but the part of me that is torn, ripped apart, like my drafts of love notes to Lynette, like my draft notice, the part that won't let me come up from under the table.

---

[15]*Richard Nixon's Vietnamization Program:* President Nixon's purported attempt to transfer responsibility for conducting the war in Vietnam from U.S. troops to the South Vietnamese army.

Engaging the Text

1. How have the movies influenced the characters in this story? What myths or expectations do they develop because of the Elvis films and other movies they have seen? How does their experience on the beach compare with the movie version of the same experience in *It Happened at the World's Fair*?

2. Shane and his friends work hard at being "cool." What traits, behaviors, or attitudes convey their coolness? What did it mean to be cool when you were in junior high school? How would you explain the concept of coolness to someone from a culture that had no similar notion?

3. At the end of the story, the narrator seems unhappy about growing up. Why can't he believe in "happy endings"? Why does he say, "I didn't even know who the bad guys were" (para. 188)? Who do you think were the "bad guys" in this story?

4. Morales's narrator says he would like to "lash out" at the part of himself that "is torn, ripped apart . . . like my draft notice, the part that won't let me come up from under the table" (para 189). How do you interpret this sentence?

5. How does Morales use historic details in the story? What purposes do they serve?

6. Contrast the narrator's voice in 1963 and 1969 with his voice in the present as he tells the story. What can we tell about him and the probable course of his life from the differences in these voices?

Exploring Connections

7. "Under the Table," George C. Wolfe's *Symbiosis* (p. 42), Toni Cade Bambara's "The Lesson" (p. 64), and Inés Hernández's "Para Teresa" (p. 554) portray characters who have reached a crisis in their lives, a turning point that forces them to see their lives differently. Compare the way two or more of these works convey this crisis. What are their characters losing and gaining? What conflicts do they experience? What role does the dominant society play in each?

8. Keeping Gina Marchetti's analysis of action-adventure heroes (p. 661) in mind, discuss Morales's portrayal of Shane. What does Morales seem to be suggesting about the dominant culture through this figure?

9. Read or review "Little Miracles, Kept Promises," by Sandra Cisneros (p. 221) and write a "prayer" from each of the four main characters in this story — Shane, the narrator, Lenny, and Gerry. What would each ask for?

10. Return to Haunani-Kay Trask's "From a Native Daughter" (p. 118). How might Trask intepret this story in terms of notions like "intellectual colonization"?

Extending the Critical Context

11. Write an essay or journal entry about a movie or TV series that had a strong influence on you as you grew up. What character was the most attractive to you? What drew you to this character? How did this influence affect your thinking, attitudes, values, behavior?

12. Write a paper or a journal entry on an important turning point in your life. Was there a moment when you began to feel that your heroes weren't really heroic, a time when you weren't sure who the "bad guys" were?

8

Government by the People

The Myth of Democracy

The Declaration of Independence and the Constitution, more than any other source, have created and sustained the myth of democratic self-government in the United States. The Declaration asserts that government exists to defend the rights of the people; when it fails in this duty, citizens are entitled to create a better, more responsive government:

> We hold these truths to be self-evident, that all men are created equal, that they are endowed by their Creator with certain unalienable Rights, that among these are Life, Liberty and the pursuit of Happiness. — That to secure these rights, Governments are instituted among Men, deriving their just powers from the consent of the governed. — That whenever any Form of Government becomes destructive of these ends, it is the Right of the People to alter or to abolish it, and to institute new Government.

The Constitution, too, emphasizes the power of the people to shape the nation's destiny, to build a government based on justice and liberty:

> We, the People of the United States, in order to form a more perfect union, establish justice, insure domestic tranquility, provide for the common defence, promote the general welfare, and secure the blessings of liberty to ourselves and our posterity, do ordain and establish this Constitution for the United States of America.

Designed to unite and inspire the diverse residents of the new nation, the stirring language of these founding documents retains its power to this day. But even at the time these resounding words were written, there were glaring inconsistencies between their democratic promise and the realities of political life in America.

Despite the emphasis on the power of "the People" to govern themselves, only a small minority of the population was allowed to participate directly in civic affairs. Women, American Indians, slaves, and most free African Americans were prohibited from voting. Many states also imposed property requirements, so that even among white males of voting age, roughly a third were denied the franchise because they were poor or didn't own land. For those who could vote, democratic participation was diluted by the system of representation established by the Constitution. Electors, rather than the voters themselves, ultimately chose the president, and senators were appointed by the state legislatures. For well over one hundred years, the House of Representatives was the only component of the national government directly elected by the people. (In 1913 the Constitution was amended to allow for direct popular election of senators; the president is still chosen by the electoral college.)

A stunning contradiction within the Constitution itself was its explicit endorsement of the slave trade. The ideals of the American Revolution had made slavery appear hypocritical to some patriots; as Abigail Adams wrote during the war, "I wish most sincerely there was not a slave in the province; it always appeared a most iniquitous scheme to me to fight ourselves for what we are daily robbing and plundering from those who have as good a right to freedom as we have." Such feelings prevailed in Vermont, where slavery was outlawed a year after the colonies declared their independence. However, economic and political considerations took precedence over human rights as the Constitutional Convention debated the slavery issue in 1787.

Outright abolition was never discussed at the convention — it would have been politically unacceptable to the many delegates who owned slaves. The question that did arise was whether the United States should continue to allow the importation of Africans for slave labor. Several representatives argued that it was "inconsistent with the principles of the revolution and dishonorable to the American character to have such a feature in the Constitution." But delegates from the South contended that more slaves not only were essential for developing southern agriculture but also would provide economic benefits for the northern states: "The importation of slaves would be for the interest of the whole Union. The more slaves, the more produce to employ the carrying trade; The more consumption also, and the more of this, the more of revenue for the common treasury." Thus a document that sought to "secure the blessings of liberty to ourselves and our posterity" also legitimized the sale and ownership of one human being by another.

The democratic ideal was also compromised when liberties explicitly protected by the Constitution were denied in practice. Despite the First Amendment guarantee of free speech, for example, the law did not actively enforce this right until well into the twentieth century. Those who held unpopular opinions (abolitionists, political dissidents, labor organizers, feminists, and birth control advocates, among others) were frequently arrested, harassed, fined, denied permits, or otherwise prevented from speaking publicly. The problem was so widespread that in 1915 a government-sponsored investigative committee reported that

> on numerous occasions in every part of the country, the police of cities and towns have either arbitrarily or under the cloak of a traffic ordinance, interfered with, or prohibited public speaking, both in the open and in halls, by persons connected with organizations of which the police or those from whom they receive their orders, did not approve. In many instances such interference has been carried out with a degree of brutality which would be incredible if it were not vouched for by reliable witnesses.

Although the United States has often failed to live up to its democratic myth, the ideals of liberty, equality, and self-determination held out by the Declaration and the Constitution have inspired many to fight for — and sometimes win — their "unalienable rights." Those who have braved opposition and demanded their rights are following an American tradition older than the Constitution itself. Protest and rebellion gave birth to the nation: in 1776, frustrated by their lack of representation in the British Parliament and infuriated by a series of new taxes, colonists took direct action, staging a series of protest marches, boycotting British goods, and dumping a shipment of British tea into Boston Harbor. These acts of resistance to British rule helped ignite the American Revolution. Similarly, popular movements throughout the nation's history have organized, marched, struck, sued, and practiced civil disobedience when established political channels failed them. A determined, seventy-year campaign by American feminists won women the vote in 1920, and systematic protests and court challenges by the labor movement in the 1930s gave us many of our current protections of free speech.

The longest and hardest-fought of these grass-roots campaigns, though, has been African Americans' quest for liberty and equality. African Americans in Boston filed a suit challenging the legality of slavery as early as 1766, and in 1773 they petitioned the Massachusetts legislature for their freedom. Similar suits and petitions were brought in several other colonies during the revolutionary period. In 1800, Black leaders in Philadelphia petitioned Congress to abolish slavery; the petition was denied because legislators feared its "tendency to create disquiet." Nevertheless, the abolitionist movement gradually gained public support during the nineteenth century. By 1827 slavery was prohibited in all the northern states, and in 1865 the Thirteenth Amendment banned it altogether. But while this amendment technically gave African American men the right to vote, many states and communities quickly passed discriminatory election laws requiring literacy tests, poll taxes, or other measures to keep Blacks from the polls. Decades of continued African American activism, culminating in the civil rights movement, eventually won substantive legal reforms in the 1960s.

In spite of these victories, the struggle for democracy is far from over. Continuing conflicts over freedom of expression, over the rights of women, ethnic and racial groups, and the poor illustrate the difficulty of fulfilling the promise of democracy. The myth of democratic self-government tells us that our freedom depends on speaking out in these ongoing debates, playing an active role in civic affairs, taking responsibility for shaping our common destiny. But while opinion polls indicate that most Americans still feel intensely proud of their country, shrinking voter turnouts suggest that a great number may have lost faith in the fundamental myth of the American enterprise — the people's sovereign power to rule themselves.

What significance does the myth of democracy have in the final years of the twentieth century? This chapter challenges us to rethink what we mean when we talk about "government by the people." We begin with the Declaration of Independence, the first document to assert that government should serve the people, and the first to declare the power of citizens "to alter or to abolish" a government that fails to do so. Lewis H. Lapham's "Democracy in America?" reevaluates four central myths about American self-government and pointedly wonders if we've lost the spirit that makes democracy possible. Next, in "Capitalism and Democracy," political scientists Ira Katznelson and Mark Kesselman ask whether the egalitarian ideals of democracy can be reconciled with the economic inequalities created by capitalism. Frank Bryan and John McClaughry, in "Recreating Democracy on a Human Scale" advocate a return to the direct democracy of the New England town meeting as a way to get citizens more involved and make government more responsive.

The second half of the chapter focuses on individual Americans engaged in direct democratic action. In "All Over the Deep South," Cynthia Stokes Brown introduces us to Septima Clark, an African American woman who used her skills as an educator and community organizer to register Black voters during the civil rights movement. Sam Cornish's poem "Fannie Lou Hamer" celebrates the strength of a share-cropper who went on to challenge the power of the white Democratic party machine in Mississippi. Next, Charlie Sabatier relates his experiences as a Vietnam veteran who returned to the United States to fight another battle — the discrimination he faced as a paraplegic. Cynthia Hamilton's "Women, Home, and Community: The Struggle in an Urban Environment" tells how a group of inner-city women joined forces to wrestle control of their neighborhood from city and corporate planners who had earmarked the area for a waste incineration plant. The chapter and book close with Langston Hughes's impassioned appeal to make America a land that lives up to its finest myths:

The land that never has been yet —
And yet must be — the land where *every* man is free.

Sources

Lerone Bennett, Jr., *Before the Mayflower: A History of Black America*, rev. 5th ed. New York: Viking Penguin, 1984.

David Kairys, "Freedom of Speech." In *The Politics of Law: A Progressive Critique*, David Kairys, ed. New York: Pantheon Books, 1982.

Ralph Ketcham, ed., *The Anti-Federalist Papers and the Constitutional Convention Debates*. New York: Mentor Books, 1986.

Michael Parenti, *Democracy for the Few*, 4th ed. New York: St. Martin's, 1983.

Howard Zinn, *A People's History of the United States*. New York: Harper & Row, 1980.

Before Reading . . .

Have you ever strongly disagreed with a law or policy of your local, state, or national government? If so, freewrite for ten or fifteen minutes about the issue and your response to it. What, if anything, did you do, and how effective do you feel your action was? If you've never felt strong disagreement with your elected representatives, or if you disagreed with them but did nothing, explain why. After writing, compare notes to determine how many in the class have

voted
written a letter to a government official or newspaper
attended or testified at a public hearing
signed or circulated a petition
worked for a political campaign or citizens' group
lobbied for or against a proposed law or ordinance
organized or addressed a political rally or teach-in
organized or participated in a strike, demonstration, or boycott
contributed money to a political campaign or interest group
worn a button or T-shirt with a political message
committed an act of civil disobedience
engaged in any other political activity
engaged in no political activity

Is there any consensus among class members about which of these activities constitute real participation in the democratic process? About which actions are most and least likely to make a difference?

Declaration of Independence

THOMAS JEFFERSON

Drafted by Thomas Jefferson when he was only thirty-three years old, the Declaration of Independence was meant to announce and defend the colonies' decision to throw off British rule. But since its adoption by the Second Continental Congress on July 4, 1776, it has come to mean much more: its vision of responsive government and its insistence upon the fundamental equality of the governed have inspired democratic reforms for the past two hundred years — from the Bill of Rights *to the civil rights movement. Conceived as a revolutionary manifesto, the Declaration has become the preamble to the most durable of all American myths, the myth of democratic self-government. As third president of the United States (1801–1809), Thomas Jefferson (1743–1826) promoted westward expansion in the form of the Louisiana Purchase and the Lewis and Clark Expedition. In addition to his political career he was a scientist, architect, city planner (Washington, DC), and founder of the University of Virginia; his writings fill fifty-two volumes.*

THE UNANIMOUS DECLARATION of the thirteen united STATES OF AMERICA.

When in the Course of human events, it becomes necessary for one people to dissolve the political bands which have connected them with another, and to assume among the powers of the earth, the separate and equal station to which the Laws of Nature and of Nature's God entitle them, a decent respect to the opinions of mankind requires that they should declare the causes which impel them to the separation. —— We hold these truths to be self-evident, that all men are created equal, that they are endowed by their Creator with certain unalienable Rights, that among these are Life, Liberty and the pursuit of Happiness. — That to secure these rights, Governments are instituted among Men, deriving their just powers from the consent of the governed. — That whenever any Form of Government becomes destructive of these ends, it is the Right of the People to alter or to abolish it, and to institute new Government, laying its foundation on such principles and organizing its powers in such form, as to them shall seem most likely to effect their Safety and Happiness. Prudence, indeed, will dictate that Governments long established should not be changed for light and transient causes; and accordingly all experience hath shewn, that mankind are more disposed to suffer, while evils are sufferable, than to right themselves by abolishing the forms to which they are accustomed. But when a long train of abuses and usurpations, pursuing invariably the same Object[1] evinces a design to reduce them under absolute Despotism, it is their right, it is their duty, to throw off such Government, and to provide new Guards for their future security. — Such has been the patient sufferance of these Colonies; and such is now the necessity which constrains them to alter their former Systems of Government. The history of the present King of Great Britain is a history of repeated injuries and usurpations, all having in direct object the establishment of an absolute Tyranny over these States. To prove this, let Facts be submitted to a candid world. — — He has refused his Assent to Laws, the most wholesome and necessary for the public good. —— He has forbidden his Governors to pass Laws of immediate and pressing importance, unless suspended in their operation till his Assent should be obtained; and when so suspended, he has utterly neglected to attend to them. —— He has refused to pass other Laws for the accommodation of large districts of people, unless those people would relinquish the right of Representation in the Legislature, a right inestimable to them and formidable to tyrants only. —— He has called together legislative bodies at places unusual, uncomfortable, and distant from the depository of their public Records, for the sole purpose of fatiguing them into compliance with his measures. —— He has dissolved Representative Houses repeatedly, for opposing with manly firmness his invasions on the rights of the people. —— He has refused for a long time, after such dissolutions, to cause others to be elected; whereby the Legislative powers, incapable of Annihilation, have returned to the People at large for their exercise; the State remaining in the mean time exposed to all the dangers of invasion from without, and convulsions within. —— He has endeavoured to prevent the population of these States; for that purpose obstructing the Laws for Naturalization of Foreigners; refusing to pass others to encourage their migrations hither, and raising the conditions of new Appropriations of Lands. —— He has obstructed the Administration of Justice, by refusing his Assent to Laws for establishing Judiciary powers. —— He has made Judges dependent on his Will alone, for the tenure of their offices, and the amount and payment of their salaries. —— He has erected a multitude of New Offices, and sent hither swarms of Officers to harass our people, and eat out their substance. —— He has kept among us, in times of peace, Standing Armies without the Consent of our legislatures. —— He has affected to render the Military independent of and superior to the Civil power. —— He has combined with others to subject us to a jurisdiction foreign to our constitution, and unacknowledged by our laws; giving his Assent to their Acts of pretended Legislation: — For Quartering large bodies of armed troops among us: — For protecting them, by a mock Trial, from punishment for any Murders which they

[1]*Object:* goal, purpose.

should commit on the Inhabitants of these States: — For cutting off our Trade with all parts of the world: — For imposing Taxes on us without our Consent: For depriving us in many cases, of the benefits of Trial by Jury: — For transporting us beyond Seas to be tried for pretended offences: — For abolishing the free System of English Laws in a neighbouring Province, establishing therein an Arbitrary government, and enlarging its Boundaries so as to render it at once an example and fit instrument for introducing the same absolute rule into these Colonies: — For taking away our Charters, abolishing our most valuable Laws, and altering fundamentally the Forms of our Governments: — For suspending our own Legislatures, and declaring themselves invested with power to legislate for us in all cases whatsoever. — He has abdicated Government here, by declaring us out of his Protection and waging War against us: — He has plundered our seas, ravaged our Coasts, burnt our towns, and destroyed the lives of our people. — He is at this time transporting large Armies of foreign Mercenaries to compleat the works of death, desolation and tyranny, already begun with circumstances of Cruelty & Perfidy scarcely paralleled in the most barbarous ages, and totally unworthy the Head of a civilized nation. — He has constrained our fellow Citizens taken Captive on the high Seas to bear Arms against their Country, to become the executioners of their friends and Brethren, or to fall themselves by their Hands. — He has excited domestic insurrections amongst us, and has endeavoured to bring on the inhabitants of our frontiers, the merciless Indian Savages, whose known rule of warfare, is an undistinguished destruction of all ages, sexes and conditions. In every stage of these Oppressions We have Petitioned for Redress in the most humble terms: Our repeated Petitions have been answered only by repeated injury. A Prince, whose character is thus marked by every act which may define a Tyrant, is unfit to be the ruler of a free people. Nor have We been wanting in attentions to our British brethren. We have warned them from time to time of attempts by their legislature to extend an unwarrantable jurisdiction over us. We have reminded them of the circumstances of our emigration and settlement here. We have appealed to their native justice and magnanimity, and we have conjured them by the ties of our common kindred to disavow these usurpations, which would inevitably interrupt our connections and correspondence. They too have been deaf to the voice of justice and of consanguinity. We must, therefore, acquiesce in the necessity, which denounces our Separation, and hold them, as we hold the rest of mankind, Enemies in War, in Peace Friends.

We, THEREFORE, the Representatives of the UNITED STATES OF AMERICA, in General Congress Assembled, appealing to the Supreme Judge of the world for the rectitude of our intentions, do, in the Name and by Authority of the good People of these Colonies, solemnly publish and declare, That these United Colonies are, and of Right ought to be FREE

AND INDEPENDENT STATES; that they are Absolved from all Allegiance to the British Crown, and that all political connection between them and the State of Great Britain, is and ought to be totally dissolved; and that as Free and Independent States, they have full Power to levy War, conclude Peace, contract Alliances, establish Commerce, and to do all other Acts and Things which Independent States may of right do. —— And for the support of this Declaration, with a firm reliance on the protection of divine Providence, we mutually pledge to each other our Lives, our Fortunes and our sacred Honor.

Engaging the Text

1. Paraphrase the opening of the Declaration, up to the phrase "former Systems of Government." Are the truths named here "self-evident"?

2. Outline the Declaration in three to five lines. What structure of argument is revealed here?

3. What attitudes toward women and Native Americans does the Declaration reveal?

4. How would you characterize the voice of this document? Read some of it aloud. What is its tone, and how, specifically, is that tone created?

5. Summarize the charges made against the king. Which address matters of individual rights? Economic rights? Colonial autonomy?

Exploring Connections

6. Reread Toni Cade Bambara's "The Lesson" (p. 64) and Martin Luther King, Jr.'s "Racism and the White Backlash" (p. 319). Then write an imaginary conversation among Jefferson, Miss Moore, and King on the nature of American democracy.

Extending the Critical Context

7. Working in small groups, go to the library and compare the Declaration with the Constitution in terms of their tone, their approach to individual rights, and the notion of equality they convey.

Democracy in America?

Lewis H. Lapham

*In 1978, President Jimmy Carter called attention to the malaise —
the spiritual sickness — he felt was infecting the nation. Many believe
this "blunder" cost him the 1980 presidential election, confirming the
cliché that we Americans would rather celebrate our dreams than
confront our nightmares. In this selection, Lewis H. Lapham asks us to
take another look at the dark side of American democracy. According to
Lapham's inflammatory rereading of the political scene, we have become an alienated and apathetic country — one accustomed to winking
at corruption and to preferring comfort to active political involvement.
The editor of* Harper's Magazine *since 1983, Lapham (b. 1935) has
authored several books on U.S. social and political issues, including*
Money and Class *(1987) and* Imperial Masquerade *(1990). This essay
originally appeared in the November 1990 issue of* Harper's.

> The spirit of liberty is the spirit which is not too sure it is right.
> — JUDGE LEARNED HAND

Over the course of the last eighteen months, no American politician
worth his weight in patriotic sentiment has missed a chance to congratulate one of the lesser nations of the earth on its imitation of the
American democracy. Invariably, the tone of the compliment is condescending. The politician presents himself as the smiling host who welcomes into the clean and well-lighted rooms of "the American way of
life" the ragged and less fortunate guests, who — sadly and through no
fault of their own — had wandered for so many years in ideological
darkness.

The orators haven't lacked edifying proofs and instances. First the
Chinese students in Tiananmen Square,[1] holding aloft a replica of the
Statue of Liberty against the armies of repression. Next the German
crowds dancing on the ruin of the Berlin Wall; then the apprentice
democrats triumphant in Budapest and Warsaw and Prague; then Gor-
bachev in Washington, amiably recanting the communist heresy to his
new friend in the White House. And always the Americans, saying, in
effect, "You see, we were right all along; we were right, and you were

---

[1]*Tiananmen Square:* site in Beijing of a major pro-democracy uprising by Chinese
university students in 1989.

wrong, and if you know what's good for you, you will go forth and prosper in a bright new world under the light of an American moon."

At the end of last summer Ronald Reagan was in Berlin, conducting a seminar for the East Germans on the theory and practice of democracy; John Sununu, the White House chief of staff, was in Moscow showing the hierarchs in the Kremlin how to organize the paperwork of a democratic government; a synod[2] of American journalists had gone off to Budapest to teach their Hungarian colleagues how to draft a First Amendment; in Washington the chief correspondent of the *New York Times* was celebrating the crisis in the Persian Gulf as great and glorious proof that the United States had regained its status as the world's first and foremost superpower, that all the dreary talk about American bankruptcy and decline was just so much sniveling, trendy rot.

I listen to the speeches and read the bulletins in the newspapers, and I marvel at my own capacity for the willing suspensions of disbelief.[3] I find myself humming along with the self-congratulatory cant on *Nightline* and *Face the Nation* or beating four-quarter time with the jingoists' chorus in *Newsweek*, and I forget for the moment that we're talking about a country (the United States of America, a.k.a. "the light of hope and reason in a dark and discordant world") in which the spirit of democracy is fast becoming as defunct as the late Buffalo Bill.[4] About a country in which most of the population doesn't take the trouble to vote and would gladly sell its constitutional birthright for a Florida condominium or another twenty days on the corporate expense account. About a country in which the president wages war after consultation with four or five privy councillors and doesn't inform either the Congress or the electorate (a.k.a. "the freest, happiest, and most enlightened people on earth") until the armada has sailed.

Although I know that Jefferson once said that it is never permissible 5 "to despair of the commonwealth," I find myself wondering whether the American experiment with democracy may not have run its course. Not because of the malevolence or cunning of a foreign power (the Russians, the Japanese, the Colombian drug lords, Saddam Hussein, etc.) but because a majority of Americans apparently have come to think of democracy as a matter of consensus and parades, as if it were somehow easy, quiet, orderly, and safe. I keep running across people who speak fondly about what they imagine to be the comforts of autocracy,[5] who long for the assurances of the proverbial man on the

---

[2]*synod:* here, a group.

[3]*the willing suspensions of disbelief:* an allusion to "the willing suspension of disbelief . . . which constitutes poetic faith" from Samual Taylor Coleridge's *Biographia Literaria* (1817).

[4]*as defunct as . . . Buffalo Bill:* an allusion to e.e. cummings's (1894–1962) ironic poem that begins "Buffalo Bill's defunct . . ." (1923).

[5]*autocracy:* a government in which one person possesses unlimited power.

white horse likely to do something hard and puritanical about the moral relativism that has made a mess of the cities, the schools, and prime-time television.

If the American system of government at present seems so patently at odds with its constitutional hopes and purposes, it is not because the practice of democracy no longer serves the interests of the presiding oligarchy[6] (which it never did) but because the promise of democracy no longer inspires or exalts the citizenry lucky enough to have been born under its star. It isn't so much that liberty stands at bay but, rather, that it has fallen into disuse, regarded as insufficient by both its enemies and its nominal friends. What is the use of free expression to people so frightened of the future that they prefer the comforts of the authoritative lie? Why insist on the guarantee of so many superfluous civil liberties when everybody already has enough trouble with the interest rates and foreign cars, with too much crime in the streets, too many Mexicans crossing the border, and never enough money to pay the bills? Why bother with the tiresome chore of self-government when the decisions of state can be assigned to the functionaries in Washington, who, if they can be trusted with nothing else, at least have the wit to pretend that they are infallible? President Bush struck the expected pose of omniscience in the course of the 1988 election campaign when he refused to answer a rude question about an American naval blunder in the Persian Gulf (the shooting down of an Iranian airliner) on the ground that he would "never apologize for the United States of America. I don't care what the facts are."

As recently as 1980 I knew a good many people who took a passionate interest in politics, who felt keenly what one of them described as "the ancient republican hostility" to the rule of the self-serving few. They knew the names of their elected representatives, and they were as well-informed on the topics of the day as any government spokesman paid to edit the news. By the end of the decade most of them had abandoned their political enthusiasm as if it were a youthful folly they no longer could afford — like hang gliding or writing neosymbolist verse.

Much of the reason for the shift in attitude I attribute to the exemplary cynicism of the Reagan administration. Here was a government obsequious in its devotion to the purposes of a selfish oligarchy, a regime that cared nothing for the law and prospered for eight years by virtue of its willingness to cheat and steal and lie. And yet, despite its gross and frequent abuses of power, the country made no complaint. The Democratic Party (the nominal party of opposition) uttered not the

---

[6]*oligarchy:* a government controlled by a small, elite group.

slightest squeak of an objection. Except for a few journals of small circulation, neither did the media.

During the early years of the administration, even people who recognized the shoddiness of Reagan's motives thought that the country could stand a little encouragement — some gaudy tinsel and loud advertising, a lot of parades, and a steady supply of easy profits. The country had heard enough of Jimmy Carter's sermons, and it was sick of listening to prophecies of the American future that could be so easily confused with a coroner's report. In return for the illusion that the United States was still first in the world's rankings, the country indulged Reagan in his claptrap economic and geopolitical theories. For a few years it didn't seem to matter that the Laffer curve[7] and the Strategic Defense Initiative[8] had been imported from the land of Oz. What difference did it make as long as the Japanese were willing to lend money and Rambo was victorious in the movies?

But it turned out that the lies did make a difference — the lies and   10
the Reagan administration's relentless grasping of illegal and autocratic privilege. Congress offered itself for sale to the highest bidder, and the political action committees bought so many politicians of both denominations that it was no longer possible to tell the difference between a Republican and a Democrat: both sides of the aisle owned their allegiance to the same sponsors. Nor was it possible to distinguish between the executive and the legislative functions of government. Any doubts on this score were dissolved in the midden of the Iran-Contra deals.[9] President Reagan and his aides-de-camp on the National Security Council sold weapons to a terrorist regime in Iran in order to finance a terrorist revolt in Nicaragua. The scheme obliged them to make a mockery of the Constitution, dishonor their oaths of office, and seize for themselves the powers of despotism. They did so without a qualm, and the subsequent congressional investigation absolved them of their crimes and confirmed them in their contempt for the law and the American people. The principal conspirators were allowed to depart with no more than a reprimand.

It was this series of events — so obviously and complacently corrupt throughout the whole course of the narrative — that proved even more damaging to the American polity than the ruin of the economy. Justified by a timid Congress and excused by a compliant media, the Reagan administration reduced the Constitution to a sheaf of commercial paper

[7]*Laffer curve:* refers to Arthur Laffer's theory that higher taxes result in lower revenues, lower taxes in higher revenues. Laffer's ideas became the foundation for the Reagan administration's economic policies.

[8]*Strategic Defense Initiative:* popularly known as Stars Wars, SDI was the Reagan administration's plan for putting lasers into orbit to intercept enemy missiles.

[9]*Iran-Contra deals:* government figures implicated in this covert trafficking in arms abroad violated several federal laws.

no more or less worthless than a promissory note signed by Donald Trump[10] or a financial prospectus offering shares in the Wedtech Corporation.[11]

The defeat might be easier to bear if the politicians would quit mouthing the word "democracy." If they were to say instead, "Yes, we are a great nation because we obey the rule of the expedient lie" or, "Yes, believe in our power because we have gerrymandered[12] our politics to serve the interests of wealth," I might find it easier to wave the flag and swell the unison of complacent applause.

But not "democracy." Maybe "plutocracy,"[13] or "oligarchy," or even "state capitalism," but not, please God, "a free nation under law" or, as a professor of government put it in an address to a crowd of newly naturalized citizens of Monticello, the "moral and political reasoning [that] is the republic's unique and priceless heritage."

What "moral and political reasoning"? Between which voices of conscience, and where would the heritage be exhibited to public view? On network television? In the United States Senate? In a high school auditorium in Detroit?

Saddam Hussein's invasion of Kuwait presented a fairly prominent   15
occasion for a display of America's moral and political reasoning, but it was a spectacle that nobody wanted to see or hear. The national choir of newspaper columnists banged their cymbals and drums, shouting for the head of the monster of Baghdad. Loudly and without a single exception, the 535 members of Congress declared themselves loyal to the great American truth that had descended into the Arabian desert with the 82nd Airborne Division. The television networks introduced a parade of generals, all of them explicating the texts of glorious war. The few individuals who publicly questioned the wisdom of the president's policy instantly found themselves classified as subversives, spoilsports, ingrates, and sore thumbs.

The judgment is one with which I am familiar, probably because my own remarks on the state of American politics often have been attacked by more or less the same gang of adjectives. With respect to the argument in progress, I can imagine the rejoinder pronounced by a self-satisfied gentleman in his middle forties, a reader of *Time* magazine and a friend of the American Enterprise Institute.[14] He wears a three-

---

[10]*Donald Trump:* (b. 1946) American real estate speculator and billionaire who lost much of his fortune at the end of the 1980s.

[11]*Wedtech Corporation:* defense contractor accused of illegally influencing Reagan administration officials to win government projects.

[12]*gerrymandered:* a reference to the deliberate division of electoral districts to give special advantages to a particular group.

[13]*plutocracy:* a government controlled by the wealthy.

[14]*the American Enterprise Institute:* a center for the study and propagation of conservative political views.

piece suit and speaks slowly and patiently, as if to a foreigner or a prospective suicide. Having done well by the system, he begins by reminding me that I, too, have done well by the system and should show a decent respect for the blessings of property. His voice is as smug as his faith in the American political revelation ("not perfect, of course, but the best system on offer in an imperfect world"). His argument resolves into categorical statements, usually four, presented as facets of a flawless truth. As follows:

1

The American government is formed by the rule of the ballot box. What other country trusts its destiny to so many free elections?

The statement is true to the extent that it describes a ritual, not a function, of government. Early last spring the Times Mirror Center for the People and the Press conducted a survey of the political attitudes prevailing among a random sampling of citizens between the ages of eighteen and twenty-nine. To nobody's surprise the survey discovered a generation that "knows less, cares less, votes less and is less critical of its leaders and institutions than young people in the past." The available statistics support the impression of widespread political apathy. In this month's election it is expected that as many as 120 million Americans (two thirds of the eligible electorate) will not bother to vote.

The numbers suggest that maybe the people who don't vote have good and sufficient reasons for their abstentions. Vote for what and for whom? For a program of false promises and empty platitudes? For ambitious office-seekers distinguished chiefly by their talents for raising money? For a few rich men (i.e., the sixty or seventy senators possessing assets well in excess of $1 million) who can afford to buy a public office as if it were a beach house or a rubber duck?

Since the revision of the campaign finance laws in the late 1970s, [20] most of the candidates don't even take the trouble to court the good opinion of the voters. They speak instead to the PACs,[15] to the lobbyists who can fix the money for campaigns costing as much as $350,000 (for the House of Representatives) and $4 million (for the Senate). The rising cost of political ambition ensures the rising rate of incumbency (47 percent of the present United States Congress were in office in 1980, as opposed to 4 percent of the Supreme Soviet). The sponsors back the safe bets and receive the assurance of safe opinions. (As of last June 30, the incumbent senators up for reelection this month had collected $83.1 million for their campaigns, as opposed to $25.9 million raised on behalf of the insurgents.)

---

[15]*PACs:* political action committees; these professional lobbying groups have become a dominant source of campaign funding and a primary channel for influencing political candidates.

A democracy supposedly derives it strength and character from the diversity of its many voices, but the politicians in the Capitol speak with only one voice, which is the voice of the oligarchy that buys the airline tickets and the television images. Among the company of legislators in Washington or Albany or Sacramento I look in vain for a representation of my own interest or opinions, and I never hear the voice of the scientist, the writer, the athlete, the teacher, the plumber, the police officer, the farmer, the merchant. I hear instead the voice of only one kind of functionary: a full-time politician, nearly always a lawyer, who spends at least 80 percent of his time raising campaign funds and construes his function as that of freight-forwarding agent redistributing the national income into venues convenient to his owners and friends.

Maybe it still can be said that the United States is a representative government in the theatrical sense of the word, but if I want to observe the workings of democracy I would be better advised to follow the debate in the Czech Parliament or the Soviet Congress of People's Deputies. The newly enfranchised politicians in Eastern Europe write their own speeches and delight in the passion of words that allows them to seize and shape the course of a new history and a new world. Unlike American voters, voters to the Soviet Union (repeat, the Soviet Union, Russia, the USSR, the "Evil Empire,"[16] the communist prison, etc., etc.) enjoy the right to express the full range of their opinions at the polls. Instead of marking the ballot for a favored candidate, the Soviet voter crosses off the names of the politicians whom he has reason to distrust or despise. He can vote against all the candidates, even an incumbent standing unopposed. Because a Soviet politician must receive an absolute majority, the election isn't valid unless more than half of the electorate votes, which means that in Moscow or Leningrad the citizens can vote for "none of the above," and by doing so they can do what the voters in New York or Los Angeles cannot do — throw the thieves into the street.

2

Democratic government is self-government, and in America the state is owned and operated by the citizens.

I admire the sentiment, and I am willing to believe that in the good old days before most of what was worth knowing about the mechanics of government disappeared under the seals of classified information, it was still conceivable that the business of the state could be conducted by amateurs. In the early years of the twentieth century it was still possible for anybody passing by the White House to walk through the front door and expect a few words with the president. It's true that the promise of

16*the "Evil Empire"*: in the early 1980s, President Reagan likened the Soviet Union to the forces of evil in George Lucas's movie *Star Wars*.

democracy is synonymous with the idea of the citizen. The enterprise requires the collaboration of everybody present, and it fails (or evolves into something else) unless enough people perceive their government as subject rather than object, an animate organism rather than automatic vending machine.

Such an antique or anthropomorphic[17] understanding of politics no 25 longer satisfies the demand for omnipotence or the wish to believe in kings or queens or fairy tales. Ask almost anybody in any street about the nature of American government, and he or she will describe it as something that belongs to somebody else, as a them, not an us. Only advanced students of political science remember how a caucus works, or what is written in the Constitution, or who paves the roads. The active presence of the citizen gives way to the passive absence of the consumer, and citizenship devolves into a function of economics. Every two or four or six years the politicians ask the voters whether they recognize themselves as better or worse off than they were the last time anybody asked. The question is only and always about money, never about the spirit of the laws or the cherished ideals that embody the history of the people. The commercial definition of democracy prompts the politicians to conceive of and advertise the republic as if it were a resort hotel. They promise the voters the rights and comforts owed to them by virtue of their status as America's guests. The subsidiary arguments amount to little more than complaints about the number, quality, and cost of the available services. The government (a.k.a. the hotel management) preserves its measure of trust in the exact degree that it satisfies the whims of its patrons and meets the public expectation of convenience and style at a fair price. A debased electorate asks of the state what the rich ask of their servants — i.e., "comfort us," "tell us what to do." The wish to be cared for replaces the will to act.

3

The American democracy guarantees the freedom of its people and the honesty of its government with a system of checks and balances; the division or separation of powers prevents the government from indulging the pleasures of despotism; the two-party system ensures the enactment of just laws vigorously debated and openly arrived at.

It was precisely this principle that the Iran-Contra deals (the trading of weapons for hostages as well as the subsequent reprieves and exonerations) proved null and void. President Reagan usurped the prerogatives of Congress, and Congress made no objection. President Bush exercised the same option with respect to the expedition in the Persian Gulf, and again Congress made no objection, not even when it was discovered that

[17]*anthropomorphic:* attributing human qualities to a nonhuman thing.

Saudi Arabia had offered to hire the CIA to arrange the overthrow of Saddam Hussein. For the last forty years it has been the practice of the American government to wage a war at the will and discretion of the foreign-policy apparat[18] in Washington — without reference to the wishes or opinions of the broad mass of the American people.

Dean Acheson, secretary of state in the Truman administration, understood as long ago as 1947 that if the government wished to do as it pleased, then it would be necessary to come up with a phrase, slogan, or article of faith that could serve as a pretext for arbitrary decisions. He hit upon the word "nonpartisan." Knowing that the American people might balk at the adventure of the Cold War if they thought that the subject was open to discussion, he explained to his confederates in the State Department that a militant American foreign policy had to be presented as a "nonpartisan issue," that any and all domestic political quarreling about the country's purposes "stopped at the water's edge."

"If we can make them believe that," Acheson said, "we're off to the races."

Among the promoters of the national security state the theory of "nonpartisanship" was accorded the weight of biblical revelation, and for the next two generations it proved invaluable to a succession of presidents bent on waging declared and undeclared wars in Korea, Vietnam, Guatemala, Grenada, Panama, Cambodia, Lebanon, Nicaragua, and the Persian Gulf. President John F. Kennedy elaborated the theory into a doctrine not unlike the divine right of kings. At a press conference in May 1962, Kennedy said, with sublime arrogance: "Most of us are conditioned for many years to have a political viewpoint — Republican or Democratic, liberal, conservative, or moderate. The fact of the matter is that most of the problems . . . that we now face are technical problems, are administrative problems. They are very sophisticated judgments, which do not lend themselves to the great sort of passionate movements which have stirred this country so often in the past. [They] deal with questions which are now beyond the comprehension of most men."

To President Bush the word "nonpartisan" is the alpha and omega of government by administrative decree: a word for all seasons; a word that avoids the embarrassment of forthright political argument; a word with which to send the troops to Saudi Arabia, postpone decisions on the budget, diffuse the blame for the savings and loan swindle. The White House staff takes pride in the techniques of what its operatives refer to as "conflict-avoidance." Speaking to a writer for *The New Republic* in August, one of Bush's senior press agents said, "We don't do [political] fighting in this administration. We do bipartisan compromising."

[18]*apparat:* political machine.

But in a democracy everything is partisan. Democratic politics is about nothing else except being partisan. The American dialectic[19] assumes argument not only as the normal but as the necessary condition of its continued existence. The structure of the idea resembles a suspension bridge rather than a pyramid or a mosque. Its strength depends on the balance struck between countervailing forces, and the idea collapses unless the stresses oppose one another with equal weight, unless enough people have enough courage to sustain the argument between rich and poor, the government and the governed, city and suburb, presidency and Congress, capital and labor, matter and mind. It is precisely these arguments (i.e., the very stuff and marrow of democracy) that the word "nonpartisan" seeks to annul.

With reference to domestic political arguments, the word "consensus" serves the same purpose as the word "nonpartisan" does in the realm of foreign affairs: it is another sleight of hand that makes possible the perpetual avoidance of any question that might excite the democratic passions of a free people bent on governing themselves. The trick is to say as little as possible in a language so bland that the speaker no longer can be accused of harboring an unpleasant opinion. Adhere firmly to the safe cause and the popular sentiment. Talk about the flag or drugs or crime (never about race or class or justice) and follow the yellow brick road to the wonderful land of "consensus." In place of honest argument among consenting adults the politicians substitute a lullaby for frightened children: the pretense that conflict doesn't really exist, that we have achieved the blessed state in which (because we are all American and therefore content) we no longer need politics. The mere mention of the word "politics" brings with it the odor of something low and rotten and mean.

Confronted with genuinely stubborn and irreconcilable differences (about revising the schedule of Social Security payments, say, or closing down a specific number of the nation's military bases), the politicians assign the difficulty to the law courts, or to a special prosecutor, or to a presidential commission. In line with its habitual cowardice, Congress this past September dispatched a few of its most pettifogging members to Andrews Air Force Base, where, behind closed doors, it was hoped that they might construct the facade of an agreement on the budget.

For the better part of 200 years it was the particular genius of the   35
American democracy to compromise its differences within the context of an open debate. For the most part (i.e., with the tragic exception of the Civil War), the society managed to assimilate and smooth out the edges of its antagonisms and by so doing to hold in check the violence bent on its destruction. The success of the enterprise derived from the rancor of the nation's loud-mouthed politics — on the willingness of its

---

[19]*dialectic:* the interaction or dialogue between different perspectives.

citizens and their elected representatives to defend their interests, argue their case, and say what they meant. But if the politicians keep silent, and if the citizenry no longer cares to engage in what it regards as the distasteful business of debate, then the American dialectic cannot attain a synthesis or resolution. The democratic initiative passes to the demagogues in the streets, and the society falls prey to the ravening minorities in league with the extremists of all denominations who claim alliance with the higher consciousness and the absolute truth. The eloquence of Daniel Webster[20] or Henry Clay[21] degenerates into the muttering of Al Sharpton[22] or David Duke.[23]

The deliberate imprecision of the Constitution (sufficiently vague and spacious to allow the hope of a deal) gives way to rigid enumerations of privileges and rights. A democracy in sound working order presupposes a ground of tolerance, in Judge Learned Hand's phrase, "the spirit which is not too sure that it is right." I might think that the other fellow is wrong, but I do not think that he is therefore wicked. A democracy in decay acquires the pale and deadly cast of theocracy.[24] Not only is the other fellow wrong (about abortion, obscenity, or the flag); he is also, by definition, an agent of the Antichrist.

4

The Constitution presents the American people with as great a gift of civil liberties as ever has been granted by any government in the history of the world.

But liberty, like the habit of telling the truth, withers and decays unless it's put to use, and for the last ten years it seems as if the majority of Americans would rather not suffer the embarrassment of making a scene (in a public place) about so small a trifle as a civil right. With scarcely a murmur of objection, they fill out the official forms, answer the questions, submit to the compulsory urine or blood tests, and furnish information to the government, the insurance companies, and the police.

The Bush administration cries up a war on drugs, and the public responds with a zeal for coercion that would have gladdened the hearts of the Puritan judges presiding over the Salem witch trials. Of the respondents questioned by an ABC/*Washington Post* poll in September 1989, 55 percent supported mandatory drug testing for all Americans,

---

[20]*Daniel Webster:* (1782-1852), American statesman and orator.

[21]*Henry Clay:* (1777–1852), American statesman and orator.

[22]*Al Sharpton:* outspoken New York minister and organizer noted for his flamboyant style.

[23]*David Duke:* former Ku Klux Klan Grand Dragon who won a seat in the Lousiana state legislature in 1989. He ran for governor of Louisiana in 1991 and lost.

[24]*theocracy:* a government controlled by religious leaders.

52 percent were willing to have their homes searched, and 83 percent favored reporting suspected drug users to the police, even if the suspects happened to be members of their own family. Politicians of both parties meet with sustained applause when they demand longer jail sentences and harsher laws as well as the right to invade almost everybody's privacy; to search, without a warrant, almost anybody's automobile or boat; to bend the rules of evidence, hire police spies, and attach, again without a warrant, the wires of electronic surveillance. Within the last five years the Supreme Court has granted increasingly autocratic powers to the police — permission (without probable cause) to stop, detain, and question a traveler passing through the nation's airports in whom the police can see a resemblance to a drug dealer; permission (again without probable cause) to search barns, stop motorists, inspect bank records, and tap phones.

The same Times Mirror survey that discovered a general indif-   40
ference toward all things political also discovered that most of the respondents didn't care whether a fair percentage of the nation's politi- cians proved to be scoundrels and liars. Such was the nature of their task, and it was thought unfair to place on the political authorities the additional and excessive burden of too many harsh or pointed questions. "Let them," said one of the poor dupes of a respondent, "authoritate."

Democracy, of course, is never easy to define. The meaning of the word changes with the vagaries of time, place, and circumstance. The American democracy in 1990 is not what it was in 1890; democracy in France is not what it is in England or Norway or the United States. What remains more or less constant is a temperament or spirit of mind rather than a code of laws, a set of immutable virtues or a table of bureaucratic organization. The temperament is skeptical and conten- tious, and if democracy means anything at all (if it isn't what Gore Vidal[25] called "the great American nonsense word" or what H. L. Mencken[26] regarded as a synonym for the collective fear and prejudice of an ignorant mob) it means the freedom of thought and the perpetual expansion of the discovery that the world is not oneself. Freedom of thought brings the society the unwelcome news that it is in trouble. But because all societies, like all individuals, are always in trouble, the news doesn't cause them to perish. They die instead from the fear of thought — from the paralysis that accompanies the wish to make time stand still and punish the insolence of an Arab who makes a nuclear bomb or sells gasoline for more than twenty-five dollars a barrel.

Democracy allies itself with change and proceeds on the assumption that nobody knows enough, that nothing is final, that the old order

---

[25]*Gore Vidal:* (b. 1925), contemporary American writer and social critic.
[26]*H. L. Mencken:* Henry Louis Mencken (1880–1956), caustic and outspoken Ameri- can editor and essayist.

(whether of men or institutions) will be carried offstage every twenty years. The multiplicity of its voices and forms assumes a ceaseless making and remaking of laws and customs as well as equations and matinee idols. Democratic government is a purpose held in common, and if it can be understood as a field of temporary coalitions among people of different interests, skills, and generations, then everybody has need of everybody else. To the extent that democracy gives its citizens a chance to chase their own dreams, it gives itself the chance not only of discovering its multiple glories and triumphs but also of surviving its multiple follies and crimes.

Engaging the Text

1. Summarize the four myths of American democracy that Lapham presents and his arguments against them. What evidence does he use to support his claims? How convincing do you find his arguments?

2. Why does Lapham believe that "the American experiment with democracy may . . . have run its course" (para. 5)? What evidence does he give that this is true?

3. According to Lapham, what happened to the national faith in democracy during the Reagan administration? Do you agree with him that most Americans have lost interest in the real workings of government and are more interested in "gaudy tinsel and loud advertising, a lot of parades, and a steady supply of easy profits" (para. 9)?

4. How have the notions of "nonpartisan" support and "consensus" politics helped to erode real democracy, according to Lapham?

5. Explain Lapham's understanding of the "spirit" of democracy. What do "self-doubt" and diversity have to do with this spirit? What, according to Lapham, threatens to kill it?

6. At one point Lapham says that democracy is like "a suspension bridge rather than a pyramid or a mosque" (para. 29). Explain what he is trying to communicate through this image and discuss its implications.

Exploring Connections

7. Review Elayne Rapping's "Local News" (p. 616). How might Lapham interpret the appeal of the local news for the average American? How might he evaluate its impact on the spirit of democracy?

8. Review Patricia Nelson Limerick's "Empire of Innocence" (p. 110) and Martin Luther King, Jr.'s "Racism and the White Backlash" (p. 319). To what extent do their discussions of early American history support or challenge Lapham's assertion that the spirit of democracy has declined over the past one hundred years?

9. Keeping the selections by Susan Griffin (p. 175), Sam Keen (p. 207), and Carol Gilligan (p. 233) in mind, discuss whether Lapham's definition of democ-

racy seems unnecessarily masculine and aggressive. Are there other, less comba-
tive ways of thinking about democracy and democratic action?

Extending the Critical Context

10. Lapham claims that the U.S. government speaks with the voice of "a full-
time politician, nearly always a lawyer, who spends at least 80 percent of his
time raising campaign funds." (para. 20). Test this profile of America's ruling
elite by researching the occupations and backgrounds of current members of
Congress and past presidents.

11. Working in small groups, devise a survey to test Lapham's assertion that
most Americans have come to think of their government as "something that
belongs to somebody else, as a them, not an us." (para. 23). What do average
Americans think about government today?

Capitalism and Democracy

Ira Katznelson and Mark Kesselman

This selection, excerpted from The Politics of Power *(1987), a popular university-level political science textbook, asks a question that has
haunted American social thinkers since the onset of industrialization:
can the principle of government by the many coexist with an economic
system that tends to concentrate economic power in the hands of the
few? As they begin exploring this contradiction at the heart of American
culture, Ira Katznelson and Mark Kesselman offer several contrasting
definitions of democracy. This selection also offers you the chance to
practice strategies for reading and understanding highly abstract and
systematic academic analysis. Ira Katznelson is dean of the Graduate
Faculty at the New School for Social Research in New York City and
author of several books on urban politics. A specialist in European
political issues, Mark Kesselman teaches at Columbia University.*

The United States is the world's oldest political democracy. All adult
American citizens today have the right to vote. The party system invites
political participation, and parties compete actively to win the support
of the electorate. Interest groups lobby to defend the interests of their
members. Newspapers and television provide regular reports of government activities, debate the wisdom of government policies, and expose

wrongdoing by high government officials. In few countries is political debate as open, free, and extensive.

A democracy, like that of the United States, is composed of rules that tell who can govern and make laws and under what procedures they may do so. Compared to those in nondemocratic societies, public authorities are accessible and responsive. Rule is not arbitrary. Citizens are protected by rights and by laws, and they are invited into the political process as participants. Government is accountable to the people, who, in the last resort, are considered to be sovereign.

Is democracy to be judged only by formal procedures? What shall we make of uneven voting, the unequal distribution of reading skills, large divergences in the earnings and social class position of the population, and of the impact of monied interests on elections and the political process? More generally, to what extent is popular sovereignty possible in a society organized within a capitalist framework? In such societies, the divisions between those who privately own the means to produce goods and services have disproportionate power, not only because they have more money, but because governments must act in ways that promote the prosperity of private firms. In a capitalist society, the well-being of everyone for jobs and income depends on the investment decisions and the profits of private firms.

One consequence is that many political issues, including the very desirability of an economic system based on private property, are not debated in public. Further, many issues of manifestly public concern, such as where new automobile or computer plants will be built, are decided privately. The result is a contraction of public politics. The principle of majority rule, the very centerpiece of representative democracy, thus applies only to a limited sphere of questions and decisions. Just as it is frequently argued that the separation of economic from political power is beneficial for democracy, for it prevents the concentration of power in the hands of a single elite, so we may ask what the implications are for democratic citizenship when many key issues are not considered to be appropriate issues for public discussion and decision.

Further, the actions of business in pursuit of profit — indeed, the routine operation of a capitalist economic system — generate inequalities of wealth and income. In the United States, the pattern of income distribution has remained virtually unchanged in this century. In 1910, the top fifth of income earners received 46 percent of the national income; today, the richest fifth's share is still over 40 percent. The share of the bottom fifth, moreover, has actually declined from over 8 percent in 1910 to just over 5 percent today.

This pattern of inequality in income is tied directly to even greater disparities in the distribution of wealth — ownership of corporate stock, businesses, homes and property, cash reserves, government and corporate bonds, and retirement funds. Roughly 20 percent of personal wealth in the United States is owned by one-third of 1 percent of the population; the richest 1 percent own over 28 percent of the wealth; and the top 10 percent of Americans own over half (56 percent). The bottom 10 percent actually owe more than they own.

This basic structure underpins the complexity of everyday life in the United States. Although Americans have diverse ethnic and racial backgrounds, work in different kinds of jobs, live in different places, and hold widely different political opinions, all are part of the class structure and are affected by it. Capitalist production interpenetrates virtually every aspect of American society, including the place of racial minorities and women, the quality of city neighborhoods, and the political choices made by government officials and citizens. . . .

The connections between capitalism and democracy raise the most interesting and pressing questions about political life in all the advanced industrial societies of Western Europe and North America. Indeed, the central questions confronting modern social theory and political philosophy for the past century have been about the tensions inherent in societies that are simultaneously capitalist and democratic. The political content of debate in most of these countries has been shaped principally by these questions. Even when these questions are not openly on the agenda, the relationship between capitalism — which routinely generates inequalities in life conditions — and democracy — which posits equal rights and responsibilities for all citizens — affects major features of political life. In the United States, it is impossible to understand the politics of power — and powerlessness — without attention to these concerns, because American society is both the most capitalist and one of the most procedurally democratic of all the countries of the West.

Standards of Democracy

In 1961, political scientist Robert Dahl published an influential study of politics in New Haven, Connecticut. By commonly accepted standards, he argued, the city was a democracy, since virtually all its adult citizens were legally entitled to vote, their votes were honestly counted, and "two political parties contest elections, offer rival slates of candidates, and thus present the voters with at least some outward show of choice." Although the city's residents were legally equal at the ballot box, they were substantively unequal. Economic inequality in New Haven contrasted sharply with its formal political equality. Fewer than one-sixteenth of the taxpayers owned one-third of the city's property. In the wealthiest ward, one family out of four had an income three times the city average; the majority of the families in the poorest ward earned under $2,000 per year. Only one out of thirty adults in the poorest ward had attended college, as contrasted to nearly half of those in the richest ward.[1]

Is the combination of legal equality and class inequality demo- cratic? Dahl put the question this way, "In a system where nearly every adult may vote but where knowledge, wealth, social position, access to officials, and other resources are unequally distributed, who actually governs? . . . How does a 'democratic' system work amid inequality of resources?"[2] He placed quotation marks around the term *democratic* because its meaning in this situation is unclear. Should a democratic system be measured only by legal standards of equality, such as fair and open election procedures, or should it be measured by substantive standards, according to the control and distribution of resources? What, in short, is the relationship of capitalism and democracy?

Procedural Democracy: Structure Ignored

In his study of New Haven, Dahl argued that, rather than one elite group making political decisions, different elite groups determined policy in different issue areas, such as urban renewal, public education, and the nomination of candidates for office. In each area, however, there was a wide disparity between the ability of politically and economically powerful people and average citizens to make decisions. As a result of such disparities, Dahl noted, New Haven was "a long way from achieving the goal of political equality advocated by the philosophers of democracy and incorporated into the creed of democracy and equality practically every American professes to uphold."[3]

Nevertheless, he concluded that "New Haven is an example of a democratic system, warts and all."[4] Dahl never resolved the problem of capitalist inequalities in a "democratic" system. Rather, he reached his conclusion by assessing democracy only according to the procedural test (Can citizens vote? Do they have a choice between candidates? Are elections honest and conducted freely?). The structure of society and class inequalities are ignored.

This approach has dominated much recent thinking about democracy. . . . The most influential twentieth-century discussion of the relationship of capitalism and democracy is by Joseph Schumpeter in *Capitalism, Socialism, and Democracy*. Schumpeter defines democracy wholly in procedural terms. Even though we reject his proposed standard of democracy, it is important to review his arguments here because

[1]Robert Dahl, *Who Governs? Democracy and Power in an American City* (New Haven, Conn., 1961), pp. 3–4. [Author's note]

[2]*Ibid.*, pp. 1, 3. [Author's note]

[3]*Ibid.*, p. 86. [Author's note]

[4]*Ibid.*, p. 311. [Author's note]

his work underpins the way that most American social scientists think about democracy and because the issues he raises are basic to the elaboration of the approach to democracy we propose. . . .

Schumpeter began his discussion by rejecting the "classical view of democracy," which held that democracy exists when the people decide issues in the interest of the common good of all. This view assumed that there exists a "common good" — that all the members of the political system share basic interests. Since all members of the polity share these interests, it is possible to talk of "the people" who actually make decisions — either directly by themselves or indirectly through representatives whose job it is to accurately reflect the "common good."

Schumpeter powerfully questioned the existence of these assumed entities in a capitalist society. He wrote, "There is . . . no such thing as a uniquely determined common good that all people could agree on or be made to agree on by the force of rational argument."[5] A "common good" does not exist in societies characterized by basic structural inequalities because of the absence of shared interests. So long as patterns of inequality persist, it is impossible to speak of a "common good," since the good of some depends on the subordination of others.

Hence it is also impossible to speak of "the people," for when members of a society have different interests, there is no single, natural direction their will can take. Rather, "the people" are divided into groups that reflect the unequal distribution of power. Schumpeter thus concluded that "both the pillars of the classical doctrine inevitably crumble into dust."

Because he found the classical approach to democracy out of touch with reality, Schumpeter proposed that we accept "another theory which is much truer to life and at the same time salvages much of what sponsors of the democratic method really mean by this term."

Whereas the classical doctrine saw democracy as a set of institutional arrangements for reaching decisions to realize the people's common good, Schumpeter viewed democracy as "that institutional arrangement for arriving at political decisions in which individuals acquire the power to decide by means of a competitive struggle for the people's vote." Democracy thus becomes a set of rules for choosing, by election, among competing political leaders; the substance of what is decided by those selected is only secondary. Schumpeter's alternative to the classical doctrine of democracy is also rooted in a profound distrust of the governed. Indeed, for Schumpeter, it is best that political elites, not "the people," make decisions, because the people are incompetent:

[5]Joseph Schumpeter, *Capitalism, Socialism, and Democracy* (New York 1942). p. 251. [Author's note]

The typical citizen drops down to a lower level of mental performance as soon as he enters the political field. He argues and analyzes in a way which he would readily recognize as infantile within the sphere of his real interests. He becomes a primitive again.[6]

For Schumpeter, and for the vast majority of American social scientists who have accepted his approach, a political system is democratic when citizens are provided with an opportunity to vote either for the political leaders in office or for a set of competing leaders who wish to get into office. Democracy is seen as a method, a set of formal procedures by which citizens can select among a limited number of alternative sets of leaders.

The role of voters in this conception resembles the role of consumers   20
in a market economy. Much as consumers choose among competing products packaged by business people, so voters choose among competing candidates packaged by political parties. "The psycho-technics of party management and party advertising," Schumpeter wrote, "slogans and marching tunes, are not accessories. They are of the essence of politics."[7] Since neither major party challenges the basic structure of capitalist inequality, the act of choice, a legal right, replaces the substance of choice at the heart of democratic theory.

This purely procedural definition of democracy has become an ideological tool of social control. Those who benefit most from the capitalist social structure may maintain, since citizens can choose their leaders, that they have little cause for grievance. The system, by definition, is open and democratic. Those with complaints can express them in the next election. In this way, the procedural approach to democracy requires and promotes a relatively passive citizenry.

"Democracy" emerges from Schumpeter's discussion without its cutting edge. The classical view of democracy, however flawed by its reliance on the concepts of "common good" and "the people," was concerned fundamentally with the substance of political decision making and the rule of the many against the powerful few. For this reason, democracy commanded far from universal acceptance. The emasculation of the term by Schumpeter has made it far more acceptable to dominant interests. Democracy is not a standard against which existing practice can be measured critically but is rather an uncritical, incomplete description of present electoral arrangements. Not surprisingly, almost all those who define democracy in wholly procedural terms find that there is no clash between democracy and capitalist inequality.

---

[6]*Ibid.*, p. 262. [Author's note]
[7]*Ibid.*, p. 283. [Author's note]

In rejecting the classical definition of democracy, Schumpeter had three alternatives. The first was to abandon the term *democracy* altogether as hopelessly utopian. The second, which he opted for, was to retain the term but redefine it to conform to existing realities. The third alternative, which we support, was to maintain the term *democracy* as a yardstick against which to measure and test reality. Thus, in a preliminary way, we define *democracy* as *a situation in which all citizens have relatively equal chances to influence and control the making of decisions that affect them.*

This alternative recognizes that although formal democratic procedures are essential to democracy, they do not guarantee it. For democracy approached this way does not depend simply on a set of rules, important though rules may be, but on the nature of the social structure within which the rules of procedural democracy operate.

Broadly, we may distinguish [two] different, though related, approaches to our definition of democracy. The first stresses popular participation in decision making; [and] the second, the representation of interests. . . . Let us examine each of these approaches in turn.   25

The Importance and Limits of Direct Participation

Citizen participation in decision making has traditionally been regarded as the centerpiece of democracy. Convincing arguments for a participatory form of democracy were put forward by Jean Jacques Rousseau, an eighteenth-century French philosopher. His influential political theory hinged on the *direct* experience of political participation. For Rousseau, participation has objective and subjective components. The objective component is that citizens exercise control by participating in decision making; the subjective component is that, because they feel they have been able to participate authentically in the making of decisions that affect them, citizens come to identify with the decisions taken and develop feelings of loyalty to the society. In addition, citizens learn to participate effectively. As social theorist Carole Pateman put it in her interpretation of Rousseau's *The Social Contract*, "the more the individual citizen participates, the better he is able to do so. . . . He learns to be a public as well as a private citizen."[8]

One of the by-products of authentic participation is that citizens learn to identify and interpret their own interests accurately and need not depend on the interpretations of others. Conversely, if participation is inauthentic, if individuals are given the feeling of participating in decision making but are not accorded the power to actually control the decision-making process, the inevitable short-term result is that they are

---

[8]Carole Pateman, *Participation and Democratic Theory* (Cambridge, Mass., 1970), p. 25. [Author's note]

prevented from arriving at an accurate perception of their interests. Though eighteenth-century New England town meetings were examples of direct democracy, many were dominated by a small elite who controlled the agenda and often successfully manipulated the group discussions. The key issue is thus not whether people participate in the political system but what the *terms* of their participation are.

In the past twenty years, many organizations — including communes, antiwar protest groups, and women's-rights groups — have been founded on classical, Rousseauian democratic principles. They reject the formal procedural approach to democracy and run themselves, instead, as participatory democracies. Their members have self-consciously sought to create open, democratic communities in which all members participate directly in decision making. For many political activists, this kind of direct democracy provides a model for how democracy should be practiced in American society as a whole.

The leap from the small group to the society, however, is impossible to make. The program of participatory groups, including face-to-face unanimous decision making and absolute equality of status and power, is actually based on principles of friendship. As political scientist Jane Mansbridge notes,

> friendship is an equal relation, it does not grow or maintain itself well at a distance, and its expression is in unanimity. . . . As participatory democracies grow from groups of fairly close acquaintances to associations of strangers, friendship can no longer serve as the basis of organization. Distrust replaces trust, and the natural equality, directness, and unanimity of friendship are transformed into rigid rules whose major purpose becomes the prevention of coercion and the protection of the individual.[9]

In small groups where people know each other intimately and are present voluntarily, the principles of direct, unanimous democracy may work to produce a natural, organic consensus of the group's will. Beyond such small groups, however, consensus is likely to be the result of manipulation, since shared values and mutual respect can develop only in situations where group members share interests. Small groups may constitute a "people" with a "common good," but as Schumpeter demonstrated, these entities in a capitalist society are fictions on a larger scale.

If democracy is to be used as a yardstick to assess both what exists 30 and what is possible, the direct-participation approach is ruled out, because society as a whole does not provide the "friendship" basis that direct democracy requires. Hence a second approach to our definition

---

[9]Jane Mansbridge, "The Limits of Friendship," unpublished manuscript, pp. 1–2. [Author's note]

of democracy argues that the crucial issue is not whether people participate directly, but whether all groups of the capitalist social structure and their interests achieve political *representation*.

Representative Democracy

There are four dimensions of representative democracy that provide us with an immediately useful yardstick against which to test present realities. The first is *procedures*. It is essential in a democracy that individuals and groups be able to make their views known and fairly select their leaders and public officials. Hence, civil liberties are essential. Free speech, free assembly, and freedom of the press are basic aspects of procedural representation. When these procedural guarantees are suppressed, it is extraordinarily difficult for people to formulate and express their interests.

The electoral mechanisms available to citizens for selecting their representatives are also an important factor in procedural representation. How wide is the electorate? How is party competition organized? What, in short, are the rules of the electoral process? As we have seen, electoral choice is at the heart of the formal procedural standard of democracy developed by Schumpeter.

But, unlike those who advocate procedural democracy, we believe that it is a mistake to limit the discussion of procedures of representation to elections. Rather, we must consider the nature of all of the rules that determine whether an individual or group has access to the political system and whether that access is likely to have an effect on decision making. Thus the traditionally narrow focus of issues raised about the procedures of representation must be widened. Are workers permitted to join unions? How are congressional committee chairmen selected? How does an elected mayor exercise control over nonelected city bureaucrats? To whom and how is a school system's personnel formally accountable? How are key foreign-policy decision makers chosen? How, if at all, are they formally held accountable? What are the procedures for representation in areas such as the space program, where expertise is available only to a few? Who selects the experts and to whom are they accountable? What are the procedures of leadership selection in interest groups (unions, farmers' organizations, professional associations)?

The list could easily be extended. The procedural dimension of representative democracy depends not only on equitable electoral procedures but more broadly on the mechanisms of access, influence, and accountability in government and in organizations that claim to represent the interests of their constituents. It is essential that the "rules of the game" ensure that the line that divides representatives and represented not harden and that access to ruling positions be open to all and not limited by racial, class, sexual, or other forms of discrimination.

Let us briefly consider a historical example. In the early 1900s, the 35
Democratic party Tammany Hall machine dominated politics in New
York City. During this period, most of the city's population consisted of
European immigrants and their children. Because the populations of
ethnic neighborhoods were relatively homogenous, the ethnic groups
gained control over the Tammany political clubs in their area. Blacks,
however, were excluded from these organizations. They participated in
party affairs through a citywide organization called the United Colored Democracy, whose leaders were selected by the white leaders of
Tammany Hall, not by other blacks. Not surprisingly, studies of political
patronage in the period indicate that blacks did the least well of all the
groups in the city in securing political jobs; and the jobs they did get
were the least desirable."[10]

Thus both the blacks from the South and the white ethnics from
Europe joined the Democratic party, but on very different procedural
terms. Although both groups could vote, the differences blacks experienced in the rules of access to the Democratic party severely limited
their chances of reaping the rewards of municipal patronage.

The second dimension of representation is *personnel*. Irrespective of
the way in which representatives have been selected, those who govern
may or may not accurately reflect the demographic characteristics of
class, race, ethnicity, sex, and geography of those they formally represent. During the Cuban missile crisis of 1962, for example, which was
resolved when the Soviet Union removed its offensive missiles from
Cuba after an American blockade of the island had been imposed,
fewer than twenty individuals made the decisions that, by their own
account, might have resulted in 150,000,000 casualties. The executive
committee of the National Security Council met regularly in the two-
week period of crisis to recommend courses of action to President
Kennedy. Almost all of the council's members were Protestant, all were
white, male, and wealthy. They included an investment banker, four
corporation lawyers, a former automobile company president, and a
number of multimillionaires.

In this instance, a very small group of men, hardly representative of
the population as a whole, had the power to make decisions of the
highest consequences. Judged by the personnel dimension of representation, the absence of democracy in this case is beyond doubt. The
demographic representativeness of those who make political decisions is
not important just in order to fulfill abstract numerical quotas of
representation. Rather, the personnel dimension of representation is
important because the more demographically representative a political

[10]Ira Katznelson, *Black Men, White Cities* (New York, 1973), chapter 5. [Author's
note]

system is, the more likely it is that the interests of the basic groups of the social structure will be adequately and substantively represented. It is highly unlikely, for example, that a group of business leaders will accurately represent the interests of workers or that the interests of blacks will be best represented by whites. This might occasionally be the case, but group members are much more likely to represent their own interests than those of their structural antagonists. It is not surprising, therefore, that workers in unions earn better wages than those whose wage levels are entrusted to the discretion of their employers; nor is it surprising that Southern blacks have been treated more equitably by police since the passage of the Voting Rights Act of 1965 than they had been when they had to depend on the goodwill of the white community.

To represent group interests adequately, representatives must also fulfill the dimensions of *consciousness* — they must be aware of and responsive to their constituents' concerns. In this respect, subordinates often find it much more difficult than the privileged to achieve representation of their interests, since those with more resources tend to perceive their interests more accurately than subordinates. The privileged are also in a better position to put pressure on their representatives than those who are politically powerless. Thus representation concerns not only *who* rules but also the *uses* to which power is put by those who rule. The first two dimensions of representation — procedures and personnel — refer to the first of these two issues. But the dimension of consciousness asks how representatives see the interests of their constituents and how they act on behalf of these interests. To satisfy the requirements of representative democracy, those who formally represent the population must use the power conferred by their positions to promote the interests of the represented.

But even where the first three dimensions of representation are 40 satisfied, political democracy cannot be said to exist. The last dimension that must be realized is *effectiveness* — the ability of representatives to produce the results they desire. A system cannot be democratically representative if its effectiveness is distributed very unequally among representatives. For example, given the fact that most congressional legislation is decided by the various committees, it would be difficult to argue that Polish working-class citizens who select a Polish working-class representative will be democratically represented if the representative is placed on committees irrelevant to their concerns.

Thus representative democracy is achieved only when all four dimensions are satisfied: when leaders are selected by regular procedures that are open to all people and all groups have relatively equal access to the political system; when representatives reflect the demographic composition of the population as a whole; when they are conscious of and responsive to their constituents' interests; and when they can effectively act on behalf of those interests.

Engaging the Text

1. According to Katznelson and Kesselman, what problems are associated with democratic government in a society that has a capitalist economic system?

2. Explain the distinction the authors make between legal standards of equality and "substantive" standards. Do you agree that substantive equality ought to be a national goal?

3. What do the authors mean by "procedural democracy"? What role does the average citizen assume within this model?

4. What is "Rousseauian" participatory democracy? What are its advantages and disadvantages? Why do Katznelson and Kesselman feel that this model of democracy isn't sustainable in the United States?

5. Describe the "four dimensions" of representative democracy. How does each affect the quality of representation? Using these four criteria as a yardstick, how representative would you say U.S. democracy is today?

Exploring Connections

6. Contrast Katznelson and Kesselman's analysis of democracy with that offered by Lewis H. Lapham (p. 701). What differences do you see in their views? What do they highlight, and what do they neglect? What assumptions do they make, and what do they conclude about the possibility of democracy in the United States?

7. Katznelson and Kesselman claim that there is no single "common good" that is in the interest of all Americans — that there really is no "we, the people" for government to serve. How might Andrew Carnegie (p. 20) and Gloria Anzaldúa (p. 386) respond to this assertion? How might each of them define the "comon good"?

8. Review Gregory Mantsios's "Class in America" (p. 72) and evaluate the ability of the three Americans he profiles to "influence and control the making of decisions that affect them" (para. 23).

Extending the Critical Context

9. Working in small groups, survey how people of diverse ethnicities, class backgrounds, and educational levels rank the top priorities for the United States in the 1990s. Then compare your results to test Katznelson and Kesselman's assertion that it has become impossible to define the "common good" in a highly diverse society like the United States.

10. Katznelson and Kesselman suggest that we define democracy as "a situation in which all citizens have relatively equal chances to influence and control the making of decisions that affect them" (para 23). In your journal, try to keep track of all the public "decisions" that affect your daily life (for example, zoning laws and local codes that affect the buildings you inhabit, the pollution standards controlling the air you breathe, the FDA regulations that define your daily recommended allowance of vitamin C). Later, pool your observations in class and discuss how you might get more actively involved in these decisions.

Recreating Democracy on a Human Scale

FRANK BRYAN AND JOHN MCCLAUGHRY

The authors of this selection are two "real Vermonters" who are convinced that the only way to save the American dream of democracy is to rebuild it step by step. Taken from Frank Bryan's and John Mc-Claughry's personal declaration of independence, The Vermont Papers *(1989), this excerpt carries us from theory into action: the authors aren't content to fret about the sorry state of American democracy — they want to do something about it. Frank Bryan is a farmer, a former middleweight boxer, and a professor of political science at the University of Vermont. He is also the coauthor of books with intriguing titles like* Out! The Vermont Secession Book *(1987) and* Real Vermonters Don't Milk Goats *(1983). John McClaughry is a veteran of Vermont politics, now serving his first term as state senator.*

For all its inspiring success, the American dream still lies beyond our reach.

America stands as a beacon to liberty, democracy, and community. But that tradition is under challenge from the forces of centralized power. Those forces have never wholly succeeded, but neither have they been decisively repelled. That task still lies ahead. The little green-clad state of Vermont may well become the place to show America how liberty, democracy, and community can be restored.

We live on dirt roads in the back country of northern New England. As this book goes to print, the shadows of November's sun lie flat on the face of the land. Birds gather against the sky, and the orange needles of the tamaracks fall silently onto the forest floor. None of this has changed in two hundred years. Vermonters have treated this land with relative care. True, like others, we have slashed and hacked and gouged and spilled and spewed. Yet here the planet still breathes as it spins through the galaxy. So far at least Mother Earth has pardoned our sins. So far she has repaired herself. You sense that watching a chickadee sass the cold at twenty below.

There is no such forgiveness in human affairs. There is no self-repair. Like dawn through a drizzle a vision is forming across the political horizon — the specter of a government that no longer works. Senator Daniel Moynihan said it succinctly in his book on Lyndon Johnson's "War on Poverty," *Maximum Feasible Misunderstanding,* published twenty years ago. "The government," he said, "did not know what it was doing." Things have gotten worse since then. Much worse.

Presidential elections have become empty and even disgusting spectacles avoided by those best prepared to lead. National election campaigns today are an issueless soap opera feasting on scandals and trivia. Their language is the language of horse races or of sports commentators awaiting the next play. The news media have become enamored of campaign tactics and bored with substance. They hype the process month after month, insulting the people with their inflated speculations, usually couched in terms of intrigue and deceit — anything to keep the viewer's fingers off the remote-control button.

Meanwhile the voters, dismayed, are opting out. If the Gross National Product had fallen the way voter turnout has since 1960, there would be panic in the streets. The most poignant bumper sticker of 1984 was gallows humor: VOTE FOR MONDALE. AT LEAST YOU'LL LIVE TO REGRET IT. Curtis B. Gans of the Committee of the American Electorate wrote in 1987 in *Public Opinion*: "The central and perhaps greatest single problem of the American polity is . . . the degree to which the vital underpinnings of American democracy are being eroded . . . the level of political participation is now sinking and the decline seems irreversible." A year later in 1988, the percentage of eligible voters in America that went to the polls to vote for president (and the thousands of other national, state, and local offices up for election) barely reached 50 percent, the lowest since 1928.

Back at the grass roots the people have barricaded themselves in interest groups as insurance against defeat in the one or two areas where government action is most important to them. Political parties, once healthy, decentralized, and citizen-based, have become too weak to provide coherence and direction. Congress stumbles along, deferring decisions right and left to the courts and the bureaucracy. The president faces incessant attack by the electronic media, which are more interested in scoring points than in informing the public on key matters of governance. Washington seems more and more remote and irrelevant. The danger is that it is remote but *not* irrelevant. . . .

In short the republic cannot survive without representative bodies that are credible and competent. Representation is founded on citizenship. But citizens cannot be factory-built or found in electronic villages. They must be raised at home. That rearing takes place in real polities: places where community and politics meet, where individuals learn the *habit* of democracy face to face, where decision making takes place in the context of communal interdependence.

This then is the great American challenge of the twenty-first century: saving the center by shoring up its parts, preserving union by emphasizing disunion, making cosmopolitanism possible by making parochialism necessary, restoring the representative republic by rebuilding direct democracy, strengthening the national character through a rebirth of local citizenship.

Over the past quarter-century there have been many recommenda-
tions to save American politics, but they have been mainly cosmetic and superficial, like giving smelling salts to a fighter whose legs have gone. We propose to return to where the roots of democracy are still firmly established and nourish them into new life. We propose to focus on a place where citizenship still lives, where a small pastureland of liberty and community of the kind America so desperately needs still lies intact. There we propose to build a new, resurgent twenty-first-century politics of human scale. As that promising place which will inspire all America, we suggest Vermont.

A Pasture Spring

Vermont is physically in the past and technologically in the future. It leapfrogged America's urban-industrial period and landed smack in the Information Age. It is still green. Unfettered by the baggage of urban-industrialism and free of the problems associated with it, Vermont nevertheless is among the leading states on measure after measure of technological maturity. On every side those that live here are struck by the fusion of past and future. We can touch the ingenuity of our ancestors. We can imagine the merging of old values and new technologies.

Vermont is an ideal setting, too, because it is still a governable place. With half a million people scattered over a granite wedge of field and forest about twice the size of Connecticut, it is small enough to meet the concept of a manageable polity. Vermont can't save the world, but it can save itself and by its example show America how to get its democracy back. Working things out in a small place first is far preferable to banging one's head against the wall in a larger system. Vermont matters *because* it is small, not in spite of it.

Moreover today there is no other place in America where the battle for liberty, lost elsewhere, is still as fiercely waged as in Vermont. Vermont democracy is under attack from the same forces that have undercut democracy throughout the nation. But they are far less formidable here, in part because they are far more visible. The juxtaposition of freedom and authority in Vermont is always striking. For Vermont, with its tiny state capital (still the smallest in America with 8,241 people), with its town meetings, its citizen legislature, its two-year term for governor, has preserved the institutions and traditions of liberty and community. Because of its unique historical circumstances Vermont has a rare opportunity to breathe new life into its democracy. . . .

We make three claims. The first is that real democracy is too precious to give up. The second is that communications technology increases the potential for a revitalized democracy. The third is that representational democracy, as *democracy*, depends on the existence of a vital direct democracy.

More than anything else a human-scale politics in America based on these principles needs a place to be — a location of its own. We propose to create one in Vermont by building the housing for a continuing democracy. Fundamental to the design of this new government is the need to address the tragedy of the mass so vividly told by Leopold Kohr: 15

> When a crowd of New Yorkers not so long ago invited a suicide candidate clinging for hours to a windowsill high on a skyscraper to "make it snappy," one might have been inclined to attribute this monstrous sentiment to the brutalized outlook of insensitive city dwellers. Yet, the first ones to arrive on the scene displayed quite a different attitude. They were terror-struck and they prayed. But as their number changed, so changed their outlook. The pangs of individual conscience were insensibly drowned in the throb of social excitement. Tragedy turned into spectacle, terror into thrill, and the prayer to desist into the clamor to perform. Only when the spectators dispersed did they return to prayer, not as a result of their better selves but as a result of the transformation of a critical into a sub-critical mass whose tenuous nature makes it impossible for an individual to hide from himself. This indicated that, contrary to current theory, atrocity-loving ideologies in general, such as fascism or nazism, seem again not so much to result from bad leadership, evil education, or metropolitan callousness as from *critical* social size.

A similar giantism is corrupting our political institutions. Overcoming it requires the creation of governments of human scale in which democracy is maintained in the context of communal liberty. To do this, to effect these human values, to preserve our liberties, reinvigorate our democracy, and reunite our communities — and to confound and rebuke the forces of centralism tirelessly at work to undermine that cherished tradition — we propose the creation of a Vermont of *shires*, new units of general-purpose local government to which most of the powers of the state will be devolved and through which our people can express their most heartfelt political ideals.

To achieve these goals the new shires must meet the problems of critical size by integrating seven principles of democratic governance. The first of these principles is that government efficiency must never be defined in terms that sacrifice local citizen judgment. All too often when democratic control conflicts with plans for administrative efficiency, democracy is *automatically* precluded. For us, in contrast, the bottom line is the democratic process. Without that nothing, indeed, can ever be efficient.

Secondly, given this prerequisite, governmental size must be permitted to float free and seek its own level. At present it is encouraged (and often forced) upward but never allowed downward. The question, is a locality *big* enough to provide a welfare *system*, must read, is the unit *small* enough to provide the human *context* without which attempts to care for the needy shrivel and die on the bureaucratic vine of depersonalization?

Thirdly, there is a fundamental difference between direct and representative democracy. Representative systems depend on electorates well versed in the principles of citizenship. These can only be learned in the context of human-scale institutions. Since we can't get along without representational systems, small direct democracies are a requirement, not a luxury.

Fourthly, there is no other way to train democrats other than to give people *total* power to control *some* of the things that affect their lives — from beginning to end — in a government of human scale. Accepting credit for success and blame for failure is the essence of citizenship. Bits and pieces of democracy won't do.   20

Fifth, the more a particular policy relies on human factors for the proper understanding of its formulation and implementation, the more it ought to be conceived and carried out in governments of human scale. The more planet-based a policy is (that is, the more its proper understanding entails environmental thinking), the more its conception and implementation must come at a centralized level.

By way of example welfare is the most human of all government operations, relying on the most humane instinct, helping others. Centralization has taken welfare away from our people, insisting that this most human behavior can be translated into the most inhuman policy. By taking the giver out of the process of giving, we have lost our sense that as humans we have a *public* obligation to care for others.

Sixth, subdividing policy-making institutions into a multiplicity of one-purpose bodies (school boards, solid-waste authorities, planning commissions), governing over jurisdictions that are seldom coterminous, forces people to seek out influence in a puzzling web. Citizen fatigue and then despair set in. Democracy is lost to the tryanny of complexity and obfuscation. At a time when a complex society demands integration, policy is atomized into camouflaged enclaves dominated by interest groups. The size of jurisdictions must be reduced to the point where the linkages between, say, highways and schools become understandable and manageable. Policy will be better for it. Democracy cannot survive without it.

Finally, administrative decentralization on a function-by-function basis is worse than none at all. Unless democratic processes accompany decentralization, we are left with the worst possible situation, no democracy and lots of complexity. To compound the sin (as Vermont's leaders often do), such a decentralism is often packaged to appear democratic when all it does is divide and conquer local communities.

The Shires

Tucked away in the hills of Vermont are 246 towns and cities. The ²⁵ biggest, Burlington, had a population of 37,712 in 1980, and the smallest, Victory, had a population of 56. Fifty-four towns have a population of under 500. One hundred twenty have populations under 1,000. One hundred and ninety-six (80 percent) have populations of under 2,500. There are also over 50 incorporated villages in Vermont (which are subdivisions of the towns) equipped with taxation and service-delivery powers. Thus the total number of small democracies reaches 348, one for every 1,500 people. No other state comes close to this arrangement.

Why not strengthen democracy by reinforcing the present system? Because with so many units of government a vacuum has been created whereby the state has been free to centralize power. G. Ross Stephens, in an important article in the *Journal of Politics* in 1974, shows that between 1957 and 1969 no other state centralized its government more swiftly than Vermont. When the very smallest towns are incapable of providing services, *all* the towns are apt to lose out, because without home-rule protection in the constitution, they are governed by general law created by the legislature and prescribed for towns as such.

We also need to synchronize political and social structure. Town boundaries were drawn over two hundred years ago. Social and economic influences sometimes crisscross Vermont with little respect for political boundaries. All too often work, play, and home have become estranged from government.

We need new governments bigger than towns yet smaller than Vermont's vestigial counties. They must draw their power down from the state rather than up from the towns. To achieve this, Vermont must change more radically than any other American state has ever changed. The central government must shrink to one quarter its current size — become unrecognizable by current standards. While the authority for laws which must be uniform (and on inspection one finds these are precious few) will continue to reside at the center, the great bulk of state spending programs (education, welfare, mental health, even roads) will devolve to the new shire governments. By giving the shires complete residual power an age-old custom in America will be reversed. In Vermont the localities will no longer be creatures of the state. The state will be the creature of its localities.

These new governments might be given any name, but we prefer "shire." The old English shire provides a rich inspiration for a new, decentralized political structure. Historically that structure was established on a hierarchy of human scale, from warrior to clan to tribe. If we think of Vermont's citizens as warriors and the towns as clans, what is needed is a structure akin to tribes. While the terms "shire" and "county" are used interchangeably by British historians, we prefer the term shire because it is more clearly tied to human (clan/tribe) symbolism, because it will tend to confuse less with the existing county system, and because the term is familiar to Vermont. Counties were first called shires, and "shire towns" still exist in each county.[1]

Most important though, in history and in literature, the shire's image is of unions of small villages cast in the context of the earth itself — land, water, and the local peculiarities of place which bespeak character and culture, distinctiveness and delineation. When one thinks of "shires," one thinks of them in multiplicity, in constant interaction and creative turmoil. One thinks of the variety on which all art, letters, and science ultimately depend. The shire evokes the sense of communal liberty and environmental consciousness that is essential to the preservation of democracy. It will create the context in which people of all income ranges and social classes will be able to reacquaint themselves with their democracy.

One point must be emphasized most strongly: the shires are not designed as *more government* between the towns and the all-powerful state. Indeed the authors have been in the forefront of the struggle — vocally so — against those who would take away the functions of our towns and vest them in "regional" bodies which would inevitably become the creatures of the state.

On the contrary the proposed shires will be independent polities, accountable directly to their own people, governed by a body elected by the people, having their own independent revenue base adequate to their needs. Shires will represent not more government, but the same amount of government we have now, redistributed from Montpelier to St. Johnsbury, Wilmington, Manchester, Canaan, and Bristol, where governments can be run the way the people, and not the technocrats, want them run. We want more democracy in the government, not more government in the democracy. . . .

The model best approximating our plan is the Swiss. The Vermont state government would be analogous to the Swiss national government, the Swiss cantons would be our shires, and their communes our towns and cities. As the Swiss communes have their rights and duties defined

---

[1]On March 24, 1778, the General Assembly of the Republic of Vermont passed the following resolution: "Voted that the line between Bennington and Rutland *Shires* be the north line of Dorset and Tinmouth." In his path-breaking work on the evolution of Vermont's counties, Virgil McCarty comments, "It is difficult to distinguish between the meaning of the word 'Shire' as it is used here — meaning the extent of territory over which the Shire town of a county exercised jurisdiction — and the word 'county.'" It is interesting that all the records of the colonies of New York use the term "county" while Vermont's very first references used the word "shire." Evidently the word "shire" was considered by these early Vermonters to more appropriately denote the lands of their new-found freedom. [Author's note]

by the cantons, the Vermont towns and cities will be creatures of the shires. In some Swiss cantons the communes have autonomy in a wide array of policy; in others they do not. This too will happen in Vermont. In Switzerland there are communal assemblies, in Vermont there are town meetings. All of this is wrapped in a strong tradition of communal liberty in Switzerland — as it is in Vermont.

Bounding the Shires

In dealing with the question of space and size in a way consistent with our seven democratic principles above, two problems of language emerge. First, there is no word to modify "community" that means "small" anymore. The great majority of small-city or small-town studies considers a community of 25,000 to be small. But if we are concerned with the size of communities in which democracy is possible, 25,000 is very, very big. It is bigger, for instance, than 245 of the 246 towns and cities in Vermont. It is substantially larger than Vermont's second-biggest city, Rutland, which had a 1980 population of 18,436.

Another problem is that "representative" democracy has come to mean democracy itself. The most thorough look at the subject of size and democracy, by Robert Dahl and Edward Tufte, laments this very point: "Clarity would have been better served if the term 'democracy' had never been transferred from ideals and institutions associated with direct popular rule in the city/state to the ideals and institutions associated with representative government in the nation-state." Madison[2] himself (in Federalist No. 14) warned against the misuse of the word "democracy": "In a democracy the people meet and exercise the government in person: in a republic they assemble and administer it by their representatives." 35

Keeping these problems in mind and remembering that there is a connection between practicing citizenship yourself and knowing how to elect others to practice it for you, we have established a two-tier framework for democracy in Vermont: (1) the towns, where direct (town meeting) forms of decision making will be used, and (2) the shires, which feature a representational system. Building the shires from the bottom up by combining towns will provide them with a foundation of strong communities. But the shires are also kept small enough to create a clear bond between citizen and legislator and relieve the tension of representation stretched beyond reason. What we need then are criteria for establishing the optimal size for direct democracy and for representational systems.

[2]*Madison:* James Madison (1751–1836), fourth president of the United States and a contributor to the *Federalist Papers* (1788), a collection of essays by Madison, Alexander Hamilton, and John Jay, refuting the arguments of those who opposed ratification of the U.S. Constitution.

Beginning with the Greeks there is a long history of optimal-size analysis. Kirkpatrick Sale's recent work concludes that the optimum population size is 500. Robert Dahl, of Yale, one of America's leading political scientists, observes in *Dilemmas of Pluralist Democracy*: "A unit with a citizen body larger than a thousand, let us say, will drastically reduce opportunities for effective participation and individual influence."

In his book *Strong Democracy* Benjamin Barber calls for a national system of neighborhood assemblies which "can probably include no fewer than five thousand citizens and certainly no more than twenty-five thousand." Douglas Yates reviews a long list of examples in *Neighborhood Democracy* and concludes that only where community size was limited to several hundred "did widespread citizen participation occur." Joseph Zimmerman, who writes on town-meeting democracy from the State University of New York at Albany, puts the upper limit at a population of from 8,000 to 10,000.

Two criteria seem to generate these estimates. They are canopied by one overarching control variable. The criteria are: (1) social structure — the Rousseauian[3] premise that "each citizen can with ease know all the rest," and (2) political process — how many people can come face to face and decide issues. The control variable is population density, what Sale refers to as the "walking distance" criterion.

Our judgment from Vermont is that the optimal population size for direct democracy is in the 500-to-2,500 range. Towns of over 2,500 people quickly come to fail the social-structure requirement — that is, one cannot know everyone else "with ease" in them. The record of what happened in hundreds of town meetings we studied between 1969 and 1989 shows a strong and consistent relationship between size and participation. There is a remarkable dropoff in attendance at about the 1,000-population level. There is also a dramatic decrease in the percentage of citizens that speak out in larger town meetings. Nevertheless there are enough cases of towns in the 1,000-to-2,500 range that attain, say 20-percent attendance to warrant a faith in population sizes of up to 2,500.

Thus the assessments of both Barber and Zimmerman need some adjustment. Neighborhood assemblies in towns of over 5,000 will soon become debating forums for a tiny few. Stretching the town meeting form over communities of from 2,500 to 5,000 reduces attendance well below the 10-percent range. At the same time we don't accept the notion that 500 is the optimal population for the democratic unit, although it is absolutely clear that the tiny communities of 500 are more

40

---

[3]*Rousseauian:* referring to the political doctrines of Jean-Jacques Rousseau (1712–1778), French philosopher and writer.

purely democratic than those of 2,500. With the shires made up of towns or neighborhood assemblies of 500-to-2,500 population, 20 percent of the towns in Vermont will be too *small*. Our limit also means that some of Vermont's larger towns, which are too big to meet the requirements of direct democracy and too small to become shires, will need to subdivide. Yet over 50 percent of Vermont's towns are in the 500-to-2,500 population range and thus already fit our prescriptions for optimal democratic governance.

Surely the communities in this array seem tiny. It is legitimate to ask how much togetherness is too much togetherness? This question, however, has less relevance in small, town-meeting democracies than in utopian communal arrangements. Town-meeting societies have always been based on a balance of personal and impersonal behavior. Small-towners know it is essential to preserve the capacity to act together even in the face of sharp disagreement. That is why strictly applied "rules of order" in town meeting often astound the newcomer expecting a "touchy-feely" 1960s atmosphere. Small-town life has always maintained rituals and institutions that let diversity exist in the context of community — to allow the private and public person to coexist in each citizen. Vermonters understand that it is frightfully difficult to offer your neighbors a smile and a "good day" when her hogs have recently rooted out a perfectly good row of your beets. "Good fences make good neighbors" in politics too.

While the towns will remain the fundamental unit of Vermont's democracy — the place where politics will be learned through practice in centers of deep-rooted history and tradition — the primary unit of Vermont's government will be the shires. While the distinction is somewhat artificial, one might think of the towns as the heart of Vermont democracy, while the shires are the heart of Vermont's governance.

The size of the shires (75 percent will fall in the 5,000-to-15,000 population range) and the small number of towns in them (from five to ten) will give every town considerable weight in the shire. This will create a condition whereby the arguments made by representatives of even the shire's smallest towns (which will receive face-to-face consideration in the shire-moot[4]) will be hard to dismiss. Opponents will not be able to hide behind the anonymity of social distance. Consensual decision making will replace the kind of adversarialism which is apt to rely on the brute force of numbers. . . .

Witness: Bill and Sally Jones were cramped into the cab of their   45
1967 Ford two-ton. Even in Vermont it gets hot in August, and Bill couldn't turn the heater off. He'd meant to cut and splice the heater

---

[4]*shire-moot:* where the shire members assemble. *Moot* is a medieval word for "meeting" or "assembly."

hose, but he hadn't gotten to it. The truck's body had been home-built many years earlier. A peavey[5] and two chain binders lay with the logging chains on the back between the bunkers. Vent windows directed some cooling to Bill and Sally's faces, but at thirty-five miles per hour it didn't help much. The right front wheel wobbled slightly on a bald tire as the dust from the road filtered up through the floor.

About a month earlier they'd purchased a 1976 Ford with 120,000 miles on it from a neighbor for $150 and a load of hay (seventy-five bales). To register it they had mailed the sales tax to the state capital along with the registration fee. Sally did that. Forty-five dollars to register the car and $6 tax (4 percent of the sale price of $150). With the car registered they wouldn't have to eat up gas with the truck whenever they had an errand. They'd already picked up a junk Ford for $50 and parked it across the road from their place. That would serve for parts.

But now the Vermont State Department of Motor Vehicles (fifty-six miles to the south in Montpelier) had sent the Joneses a form letter with the list price of a 1976 Ford at $1,200. They said the Joneses still owed $42 in tax on their new vehicle. Their neighbor drafted a letter to the DMV saying he'd sold Bill and Sally the car for $150 because it was falling apart. "It probably wasn't worth the $150," he wrote. (The seventy-five bales of hay he chalked up to the hidden economy.)[6] Sally mailed the letter. Time passed. Then came a second form letter: please pay the $42, or you don't get your registration. The Joneses said, to hell with it, we'll pay the $42. They needed the car. The neighbor said, "Stand up for your rights. Drive down there and get it settled once and for all."

The trip to Montpelier is the Joneses' longest by far this year. The Motor Vehicle Department is across the street from the capitol. There is traffic, and there are parking meters (for cars — not logging trucks). The Joneses parked some distance off. Sally is fifty-eight years old and walks with a cane. Her legs don't support her weight any more. Bill, partially bald, long unkempt beard of gray, and huge hands — so callused the joints seem to have disappeared — walks straight but slow. He is relieved their truck held together on the trip to Montpelier; his mind is on the trip back. The sidewalk shimmers in the heat. They sweat. Inside the building there is a long line before the registration window. Bill and Sally know they look different. Time passes, and the urge to go home becomes overpowering. When the clerk behind the glass says $42, Sally lays down several sweaty bills and pays on the spot. It's time to leave.

That evening at a supper table crammed with bread, rolls, fried hotdogs, fried potatoes, and little brown cupcakes — seconds from a

---

[5]*peavey:* a heavy wooden lever used to handle logs.

[6]*the hidden economy:* refers to exchanging goods and services instead of money in order to avoid taxes.

local bakery — the Joneses were happy. They'd made it down and back. Nothing bad had happened. They explained the day's events to their neighbor over coffee. He was struck by the fact that Sally had been, more than anything else, impressed with the number of police cars she'd seen in Montpelier. Bill said, with a smile and perhaps just a trace of apology, "Didn't save any money, but what t'hell." The neighbor said, "Yeah, what the hell." He'd caused the Joneses enough trouble already.

Once again people who most needed and deserved their government's help got, instead, the shaft. For those for whom reading and writing are a chore, for whom the sound of their car *starting up* is a joy (one that is most often problematical), for whom hope has withered away in the gloom of chances lost, the "interface" with government cannot be routinized and bureaucratized. It is a truth of the twentieth century that policies which transformed the great low-income working majority of 1900 into the income-secure middle class of 1990 will not work for the substantial residue of truly poor people that were left behind.

Bureaucracies are not evil, but they are inhuman. They are *fashioned* that way: they work *because* they are capable of inhumanity on a massive scale. This is not to criticize bureaucrats. In fact the greatest complaints bureaucrats have about being bureaucrats is that they are forced by routine to treat people as numbers. When Bill and Sally Jones reached that window in Montpelier, they had a tale to tell — a very human tale. It involved a neighbor and a special circumstance. It involved a dying little hill farm. It involved two people who are uncomfortable dealing with strangers.

It is our task to reintroduce everyone — but especially people like Bill and Sally Jones — to their democracy. The middle class is taught to deal with lines and schedules, routines, forms, and faceless functionaries. That is why program after program intended to help the poor ends up helping, instead, the secure. Middle-class citizens fudge forms to secure low-income housing. Well-to-do parents of college students borrow low-interest money from the government for college bills instead of cashing in their stocks. Conservatives often latch onto the extremes (the tiny percentage of the poor who cheat the system) and tout them as typical. Liberals, because they have no capacity to separate an admission that the old technologies have failed from the implication that the conservatives are right, overlook the fact that the secure are benefiting at the expense of the poor. Spend more, they say, and a good portion of the benefits will fall into the lap of the poor. Liberals have their own "trickle-down theory."[7]

---

[7]*trickle-down theory:* informal designation for the theory that guided the Reagan administration's economic policies. It holds that money accumulated by the wealthiest classes because of increased tax breaks will eventually "trickle down" to the middle and working classes.

Rather than in Montpelier, picture Sally Jones down at the town clerk's office in the town where she lives. The town administers car registration and collects the tax that goes with it. Sally knows the town clerk. True, there is a class difference between them. Sally is poor, and the town clerk has "done better." But there is no way the town clerk can ignore Sally. There is no need for a form letter. There is plenty of time and space for tales to be told. Besides, Bill sells wood to the town clerk's sister-in-law. Bill's grandchildren are in school with hers. And there is something else. Bill and Sally Jones *won't take it* if they are treated badly by "the town." They'll raise hell. Finally there is town meeting. Bill seldom goes, but Sally and her daughter-in-law were there last year. When the Joneses get riled up, they can account for at least a dozen votes at town meeting. They did that eight years ago when they opposed the plan to move a one-room school house in their part of town down to the village. Town clerks pay attention to a dozen votes in a town with less than a thousand registered voters.

Distributing Power

Designing a code for the redistribution of power between state and shire in Vermont involves a complete turnabout in the way Americans approach government. To wit: policies that most directly affect people are most appropriately decentralized; policies that most directly affect the planet are most appropriately centralized. Our reform abandons the way of government currently in favor: education by megastandards, welfare by mailbox, police protection by radio, and health care by stranger.

If we can build the "complicated and dutiful" relationships of true human interaction back into governance, most of our problems in these areas will shrink to manageable size. Thus the power of the state government as the protector of the environment and guarantor of basic civil rights and liberties should be preserved. But the shires should be the repository of authority in matters in which success or failure depend on face-to-face interaction of human beings. 55

There is a need for state presence in other concerns that transcend local boundaries, such as transportation, disease control, information gathering and dissemination, technical assistance, and shire-federal relationships. But even in areas such as transportation there should be a substantial shift of power to the shires. The bottom line: if when traveling through Vermont one encounters variations in the quality of the roads, that is the price one pays for democracy. If local speed limits are different, that is a quirk produced when self-government is given more than lip service. While many may see these as problems, we see them as an affirmation of the human condition, a condition that thrives on variety, innovation, spontaneity, and the deep-seated and long-lasting cultures generated by people in charge of their own destinies.

In all areas where law making is shared between state and shire the *administration* of policy should be at the shire level. Here is where information technology offers its greatest hope for democracy. During the 1970s the decentralization of administration to the face-to-face level was called "street-level bureaucracy." There have been problems with building human transactions back into administration. But the process should not be abandoned, for the course of events is moving in its favor. If advances in information technology — especially in the field of "real-time" decision making[8] — continue to develop as they have over the last two decades, we will soon be able to administer nearly all governmental functions at the shire and subshire level.

In this way citizens will be required to do the *work* of government as well as making the decisions. An officer like the environmental constable, a local citizen with the power to poke around the shire and make sure laws designed to keep the countryside clean are being obeyed, is an example.[9] In fact Vermont not only has a deep historical tradition of local office holding — hog reeves, fence viewers, scalers — it has also developed more and more roles for citizens in recent years. One such is town energy officer. Quasi-public functions are remarkably strong, too. Volunteer fire departments and rescue squads in Vermont provide an infrastructure[10] of local organizational vitality. With the shires in place a whole range of administrative services now run by the state will become the work of local people.

The case for a complete redirecting of human-scale policy to the localities and a parallel redirection of environmental policy to the bioregional level seems obvious. People *need* the human touch. Welfare without love is impossible. With environmental concerns, however, the case is otherwise. Nature does not know love. While it must be treated *with* love, it will not react *to* it — as anyone will tell you who has asked a team of oxen to perform out of love. The nationally-based welfare bureaucracy doesn't take this critical distinction into account. It, therefore, quite literally, treats the poor like something inhuman — like dirt. . . .

To summarize: What will the shires do? The answer? Nearly every-   60
thing. . . . The pivotal *structural* concept to bear in mind is that whereas before the localities were creatures of the state, in the new system the state will be a creature of the shires. In other words Vermont will shift from the unitary model to the federal model. The pivotal *functional* concept to bear in mind is that human-services policy will be

---

[8]*"real-time" decision making:* refers to computer technology that would provide local administrators instant access to needed information.

[9]"Bounty hunting for trash" is not such a wild idea. After all, Vermont's returnable-bottle law kept one of the authors in spending money as he was growing up in the late 1940s and 1950s (and is keeping the other in spending money now). [Author's note]

[10]*infrastructure:* basic utility and transportation services.

localized, while environmental policy will be centralized. In all our plan we were guided by Benjamin Barber's description of a strong democracy: one that requires common deliberation, common legislation, and common work.

References

Hannah Arendt, *On Revolution* (New York: Viking, 1963).

Benjamin R. Barber, *Strong Democracy* (Berkeley: Univ. of California Press, 1984).

Carl Becker, *Progress and Power* (Stanford: Stanford Univ. Press, 1935).

Wendell Berry, *The Unsettling of America* (New York: Avon Books, 1977).

Harry C. Boyte, *The Backyard Revolution* (Philadelphia: Temple Univ. Press, 1980).

Robert A. Dahl, *Dilemmas of Pluralist Democracy* (New Haven: Yale Univ. Press, 1982).

Robert A. Dahl and Edward R. Tufte, *Size and Democracy* (Stanford: Stanford Univ. Press, 1973).

Robert Frost, *North of Boston* (New York: Henry Holt, 1915).

Curtis B. Gans, "The Empty Ballot Box: Reflections on Non Voting in America," *Public Opinion* (September–October 1987).

Barry D. Karl, *The Uneasy State* (Chicago: Univ. of Chicago Press, 1983).

Leopold Kohr, "Critical Size," in Michael North, ed., *Time Running Out? Best of Resurgence* (Dorchester, Dorset: Prism Press, 1976).

James Madison, "Federalist No. 14," in Alexander Hamilton, James Madison, and John Jay, *The Federalist Papers* (New York: New American Library, 1961).

Virgil McCarty, "The Evolution of Vermont Counties," unpublished paper (Montpelier: Vermont Historical Society, 1941).

John McClaughry, "Populism for the '80s Gaining Momentum," *Human Events* (April 16, 1983).

Daniel Moynihan, *Maximum Feasible Misunderstanding* (New York: Free Press, 1969).

Kirkpatrick Sale, *Human Scale* (New York: Coward, McCann & Geoghegan, 1980).

G. Ross Stephens, "State Centralism and the Erosion of Local Autonomy," *Journal of Politics* (February 1974).

Douglas Yates, *Neighborhood Democracy* (Lexington, MA: D. C. Heath, 1973).

Engaging the Text

1. What is wrong with American government, according to Bryan and Mc-Claughry?

2. Write an extended definition of "citizen" as Bryan and McClaughry use the term. What special kinds of knowledge or skills does their ideal citizen possess? Why are genuine citizens so rare?

3. Outline the authors' proposal to "save American politics." What qualities make Vermont such an appealing setting for their experiment? Why is the "shire" so important in their plan? What are its functions?

4. Why do you think Bill and Sally Jones choose not to fight for their rights when they arrive at the Department of Motor Vehicles? Why do the authors include so much detail in this extended illustration? What are they trying to show?

5. What, according to the authors, are the advantages of decentralized government? What is the proper role of centralized state authority?

Exploring Connections

6. To what extent does the notion of citizenship developed by Bryan and McClaughry resemble the "spirit" of democracy eulogized by Lewis H. Lapham (p. 701)? Would the shire system be likely to give rise to the kind of democratic personality Lapham seeks?

7. The authors suggest that modern electronic technology may play a significant role in decentralizing and humanizing government. How might Chellis Glendinning (p. 150) and Susan Griffin (p. 175) assess the probable impact of this technology on democracy?

8. By decentralizing government, Bryan and McClaughry would be expanding the power of local groups, which may choose to use their power to promote their own values and prejudices. Role-play or write an imaginary conversation among Bryan and McClaughry, Gloria Naylor's characters in "The Two" (p. 270), Gordon W. Allport (p. 292), C. P. Ellis (p. 336), and Karen Lindsey (p. 463) on the risks involved in decentralized government.

Extending the Critical Context

9. Working in groups, imagine that you're part of a public policy "think tank" that's been commissioned to plan a shire system of decentralized government for an industrialized urban area like Chicago, Los Angeles, or New York City. What problems would you foresee? How might you solve them? Is such radical decentralization possible outside a relatively unpopulated state like Vermont?

10. Keeping Bryan and McClaughry's notion of the democratic citizen in mind, design a survey that will measure a person's "citizenship" quotient or capacity and administer it to a sample of students, faculty, and staff on or near your campus. Share your results with the class and try to draw some conclusions about the state of democracy in your immediate community.

All Over the Deep South

Septima Clark and Cynthia Stokes Brown

The will of the people can express itself through structures like small town meetings, but it can also appear in protests, boycotts, civil disobedience, and other forms of direct democratic action. In 1954 Septima Clark, a fifty-six-year-old African American schoolteacher, joined Myles Horton at the Highlander Folk School, an institution Horton had created to empower rural southerners to recognize and fight for their rights. Working with Martin Luther King, Jr., and the Southern Christian Leadership Conference, they eventually laid the foundation for the "Citizenship Schools" that registered millions of African Americans to vote and broke the back of government-sponsored segregation in the South. A little known but central figure in the civil rights Movement, Clark represents a long tradition of Americans who have struggled to seize and shape their own destinies. This account of her work in the voter registration effort is excerpted from Ready from Within: Septima Clark and the Civil Rights Movement *(1986), edited by Cynthia Stokes Brown. An associate professor of education at Dominican College in San Rafael, California, Cynthia Stokes Brown has written extensively on literacy and oral history. Among her publications is* Literacy in Thirty Hours: Paulo Freire's Process in Northeast Brasil *(1975).*

The United Church of Christ owned a center in Liberty County, Georgia. We asked the man in charge in New York through Andy Young[1] if we could use that center. They used to have some kind of a school there, but it had been closed for quite some time. We were able to get that center, and we could hire people in the community to do the cooking, make the beds, and get the place ready for us. That center was called the Dorchester Cooperative Community Center in McIntosh, Georgia, some 295 miles from Atlanta and forty miles south of Savannah.

Three of us from SCLC[2] drove all over the South recruiting people to go to the Dorchester Center. Andy Young was the administrator, Dorothy Cotton was the director or the educational consultant, and I

---

[1]*Andy Young:* Andrew Young: (b. 1932), executive director of the SCLC (1964–1970), ambassador to the United Nations (1977–1979) and mayor of Atlanta in the 1980s.

[2]*SCLC:* Southern Christian Leadership Conference, a major civil rights organization led by Martin Luther King, Jr., from 1957 to 1968.

was the supervisor of teacher training. The three of us worked together as a team, and we drove all over the South bringing busloads of folk — sometimes seventy people — who would live together for five days at the Dorchester Center.

Once a month, for five days, we'd work with the people we had recruited, some of whom were just off the farms. Like Fannie Lou Hamer,[3] who stood up and said, "I live on Mr. Marlowe's plantation." She talked about how Pap, her husband, had to take her to the next county because they were going to beat up Pap and her if she didn't stop that voter registration talk. She taught us the old songs that they sang in the meetings to keep their spirits up. We sang a lot in the workshops at Dorchester. . . .

We went into various communities and found people who could read well aloud and write legibly. They didn't have to have a certificate of any kind. I sat down and wrote out a flyer saying that the teachers we need in a Citizenship School should be people who are respected by the members of the community, who can read well aloud, and who can write their names in cursive writing. These are the ones that we looked for.

We brought those people to the center in Liberty County, Georgia. 5 While they were there, we gave them the plan for teaching in a citizenship school. We had a day-by-day plan, which started the first night with them talking, telling us what they would like to learn. The next morning we started off with asking them: "Do you have an employment office in your town? Where is it located? What hours is it open? Have you been there to get work?"

The answers to those things we wrote down on dry cleaner's bags, so they could read them. We didn't have any blackboards. That afternoon we would ask them about the government in their home town. They knew very little about it. They didn't know anything about the policemen or the mayor or anything like that. We had to give them a plan of how these people were elected, of how people who had registered to vote could put these people in office, and of how they were the ones who were over you.

We were trying to make teachers out of these people who could barely read and write. But they could teach. If they could read at all, we could teach them that c-o-n-s-t-i-t-u-t-i-o-n spells constitution. We'd have a long discussion all morning about what the Constitution was. We were never telling anybody. We used a very nondirective approach.

The people who left Dorchester went home to teach and to work in voter registration drives. They went home, and they didn't take it anymore. They started their own citizenship classes, discussing the

---

[3]*Fannie Lou Hamer:* See p. 749.

problems in their own towns. "How come the pavement stops where the black section begins?" Asking questions like that, and then knowing who to go to talk to about that, or where to protest it.

The first night at the Liberty County Center we would always ask people to tell the needs of the people in their community. The first night they gave us their input, and the next morning we started teaching from what they wanted to do.

But what they wanted varied. We had to change. Down in the southern part of Georgia some women wanted to know how to make out bank checks. One woman told the workshop that somebody had been able to withdraw a lot of money from her account because she did not know how to make out her own check and check up on her own account. She was in the habit of having someone white make out her check for her, and then she'd sign with an "X."

So we started teaching banking. We brought in a banker, and he put the whole form up on the board and showed them how to put in the date and how to write it out. He told them, "Don't leave a space at the end of the check. Somebody else could write another number in there. When you finish putting down the amount, take a line and carry it all the way to the dollar mark."

He was very good, but the white people in Liberty County got to the place where they were against his coming to teach. When they found out that black people were learning to write their names, they got very angry about it. One night we had a whole group of white farmers out there against us. They were cursing, but they didn't shoot. The banker got away; he got in his car and drove on back to his town.

There was a good side to that, too. When black people learned how to withdraw their money from the banks, they went to merchants to buy new clothes. Then the merchants were happy that they had some money.

The Marshall Field Foundation gave us a $250,000 grant. With that money we gave the students $30 to come to school two nights a week, two hours a night, for three months at a time. They were always in debt. We felt that if they didn't make anything on the farm, we had to pay them.

Even then we didn't have too many to come. There was so much pressure from the whites in the community that too many of them were afraid. Those who came had to feel that we could get away with it or that we didn't mind if we had to die.

Black people in small southern towns didn't trust black people coming in from the city. They just thought that you were so high falutin that you were going to try to make fun of them. I found out when I went into small communities that the illiterate blacks in these communities were ashamed to let me know that they were illiterate. I had to walk around and get people in that community to believe in what I wanted done.

Here is an example of what I did when I went into a new town. This is what happened when I went to Huntsville, Alabama. I decided to go there because in Cincinnati, Ohio, I met a Jewish rabbi who had a group of Jewish people in Huntsville that he was trying to work with. They told him of the injustices that the blacks had and the fact that they could not register to vote. I came home to tell Myles about it, and he gave me the name of a woman, a Miss Harris, who ran an orphan house in Huntsville.

I went over there to see Miss Harris. I brought two of her daughters back to Highlander with me, so they could get the feel of it. When they got ready to go home I went with them, and I stayed with them for some time. Miss Harris was busy getting her place together with her orphan children, and I contributed $15 on a Frigidaire that she needed, which spelled a lot. She introduced me to a black minister, a Baptist minister. I went to his house, and we sat and talked. We walked around approximately two weeks, just talking and talking to people. Finally I got him to invite ten other persons, a Methodist minister along, to have luncheon with us. I paid for the luncheon, too. I had money from Highlander to do these things.

At that luncheon meeting I told them about the Citizenship Schools. I told this Methodist minister that I would like very much for him to do some teaching for me and that he could come to a workshop with me — just spend a weekend, and he could see the program that we had. He came, but when I went to his church, he had too many middle-class black teachers who worked at a college in Huntsville so that it was no way in the world that I could get them to do anything whatsoever. They were too scared. When I went to his church that Sunday, he introduced me, but he wouldn't mention Citizenship Schools.

Nevertheless, I kept talking around and working with them until we   20
were able to set up three schools in Huntsville. I let them know that the people who taught would be paid some money for their time. Those things were the drawing cards for the people as they went along.

The teachers received $75 a month after we brought them to the Liberty County Center and taught them how to teach others. When I was in Selma, a young woman got her check for $75. She said, "I've never had this much money in my life." She was very happy over it.

All of the states had different election laws. Georgia had thirty questions, and people who wanted to register had to answer twenty-four out of thirty. Alabama had about twenty-four questions they had to answer. One of them was: "Give the definition of a thief." One teacher said she never could give the definition because the registrar wanted her to say, "A thief is a nigger who steals." Because she couldn't say that, or didn't know that she should say that, she never could pass.

Of course, we didn't teach them to say a thief is a nigger who steals. We kept working on that question, "What is a thief?" and we found definitions out of the dictionary. One woman said she said, "Well, the dictionary says this." And the registrar said, "Well, maybe it does, but that's not what we want," and she was refused her registration.

I have to laugh when I think of those people. I wonder if they think about themselves, how silly they were making those kinds of laws.

There was a fellow at Tuskegee Institute in Alabama who had his 25 Ph.D. He read the Constitution too well, so they gave him some Chinese to read. He couldn't get his registration certificate either. In Louisiana even the women had to say, "I am not the father of an illegitimate child."

To try to get around that problem of answering the questions to the satisfaction of the registrar, an organization was formed in Tuskegee. Someone went to Washington two or three times to talk with the U.S. Attorney General. That little organization used about $1300 sending people back and forth to Washington. Finally, the people in Washington would phone down to the registering group to let them know it was against the laws of the United States to ask people to give definitions according to the satisfaction of the registrar.

But the whites in Tuskegee tried everything. When they saw the black people coming in to register at the bank, the registrar would hide in a vault and pretend that registration was closed. We had a lady there who was very fair; they couldn't tell whether she was black or white. We sent her in, and when the man came out to register her, the other black people surged in. He said, "Oh, my God. Here comes the niggers." They thought they had a white woman, but she was one of us.

In the summer of 1965 Congress passed the Voting Rights Act, which eliminated all literacy tests. After that, people in Alabama did not have to answer twenty-four questions. They could register to vote if they could sign their name in cursive. It didn't take us but twenty minutes in Selma, Alabama, to teach a woman to write her name. The white students took her to the courthouse. She wrote her name in cursive writing and came back with a number that meant she could register to vote. This is the way we did it.

We had 150 of those schools in Selma, paying those teachers $1.25 an hour, two hours each morning, five days a week. The Marshall Field Foundation furnished the money for that, and we did it for three solid months. At the end of three months, we had 7002 persons with a number that gave them the right to vote when the federal man came down in August. We worked from May 18 to August 15. That was in 1965, because in 1966 we went to the vote.

The black ministers in Selma were just as bad as the middle-class 30 teachers in Huntsville. When the ministers had an anniversary, they would get a suit from the merchants up town. So they didn't want us to teach those people how to write their names. Dr. King sent in a team of five of us to do that teaching, and I was the only one who stayed for those three months. The rest of them left me because they got angry with the black preachers. Then I trained others to help me do the work.

The black preachers would say, "Who's going to pay for this? Who's going to do so-and-so?" Back of it was the fact that they didn't want the white people to know that we were teaching blacks to write their names, for then the merchants would stop giving the preachers their anniversary gifts. They wanted those gifts. Material things were more to them than the human value things.

But I toughed it out with those men. I met one day with five of them, and they said, "Who's going to pay for it?" I said, "We'll pay the teachers." They said, "Who's going to advertise it?" I said, "Well, I'll get the advertising done. I'll go around to the churches." At one o'clock in the morning I was going through Selma hunting up preachers to make that announcement the next day. It was something.

Of course, I understand those preachers. I know they were dependent on white people's approval. Even with their congregation's support, they could be run out of town if the white power structure decided they ought to go. Often they weren't against the Movement; they were just afraid to join it openly. It's simply a contradiction: so many preachers supported the Movement that we can say it was based in churches, yet many preachers couldn't take sides with it because they thought they had too much to lose.

In Selma, anybody who came to our meeting lost their job. Fifty or more did. Some of them got their jobs back later, but some never did. I couldn't stay at any of their houses because the whites knew me so well they would have harassed anyone I stayed with. I had to rent a room in a motel. Dr. King had to send money from the SCLC to buy groceries for the people who lost their jobs.

But even with this kind of harassment, the Citizenship Schools really got into full force. There were 897 going from 1957 to 1970. In 1964 there were 195 going at one time. They were in people's kitchens, in beauty parlors, and under trees in the summertime. I went all over the South, sometimes visiting three Citizenship Schools in one day, checking to be sure they weren't using textbooks, but were teaching people to read those election laws and to write their names in cursive writing.

One time I heard Andy Young say that the Citizenship Schools were the base on which the whole civil rights movement was built. And that's probably very much true.

It's true because the Citizenship Schools made people aware of the political situation in their area. We recruited the wise leaders of their communities, like Fannie Lou Hamer in Mississippi. Hosea Williams[4] started out as a Citizenship School Supervisor. The Citizenship School classes formed the grassroot basis of new statewide political organizations in South Carolina, Georgia, and Mississippi. From one end of the

---

[4]*Hosea Williams:* (b. 1926), civil rights activist, journalist, and Georgia state representative.

South to the other, if you look at the black elected officials and the political leaders, you find people who had their first involvement in the training program of the Citizenship School.

It was 1962 before the major civil rights groups were ready to do something about voter registration. But we had developed the ideas of the Citizenship Schools between 1957 and 1961. So all the civil rights groups could use our kind of approach, because by then we knew it worked.

In 1962 the SCLC joined four other groups — the Congress of Racial Equality (CORE), the NAACP, the Urban League, and the Student Non-Violent Coordinating Committee (SNCC) — to form the Voter Education Project. In the next four years all the groups together trained about 10,000 teachers for Citizenship Schools. During this period almost 700,000 black voters registered across the South. After the Voting Rights Act passed in 1965, registration increased very rapidly. At least a million more black people registered by 1970. But it took until the election of 1972 for the first two blacks from the Deep South to be elected to U.S. Congress since Reconstruction. They were Andrew Young, who helped me set up all those Citizenship Schools, and Barbara Jordan,[5] from Texas.

[5]*Barbara Jordan:* (b. 1936), civil rights activist, member of the U.S. House of Representatives from 1972 to 1978.

Engaging the Text

1. What was the aim of the Citizenship Schools? How did Clark recruit participants? How and what did they study?

2. What strategies of direct democratic action did Clark and her colleagues employ in their work?

3. What kinds of resistance did Clark encounter from both Blacks and whites in her efforts to increase African American voter registration? How would you characterize her attitude toward those who opposed her?

Exploring Connections

4. Review "Connected Education for Women" by Blythe McVicker Clinchy et al. (p. 567) and use its ideas to evaluate the teaching methods Septima Clark employed in the Citizenship Schools. To what extent did these schools anticipate the notion of "connected education"?

5. How might Gordon W. Allport (p. 292), Martin Luther King, Jr. (p. 319), Shelby Steele, or Virginia R. Harris and Trinity A. Ordoña (p. 359) interpret the reluctance of middle-class Black ministers to support the SCLC and Clark's

Citizenship Schools? Do you find the perspectives offered by these authors more or less illuminating than Clark's?

6. Write a letter from Septima Clark to Stephen Cruz (p. 36), Mike LeFevre (p. 87), Nora Quealey (p. 202), or any of the characters in Sandra Cisneros's "Little Miracles, Kept Promises" (p. 221). What advice might she offer?

Extending the Critical Context

7. In her oral history, Clark offers a model of direct democratic action that makes a clear connection between education and democracy. In what ways has your education prepared you to assume the role of an active citizen? What might be done to improve the way we prepare people to become self-governing?

8. Brainstorm a list of topics that a "Citizenship School" might address in your community — or even on your campus. What kind of school might you set up to help people influence the decisions that affect their lives?

9. As a class project, research the organizations and individuals Clark mentions (the Southern Christian Leadership Conference, the Highlander Folk School, Myles Horton, the Student Non-Violent Coordinating Committee, Andrew Young, Hosea Williams, Barbara Jordan, and so on). Report on the roles they played in the civil rights movement.

Fannie Lou Hamer

Sam Cornish

One of twenty children born into a family of sharecroppers, Fannie Lou Hamer (1917–1977) didn't even know she had the right to vote before she encountered the Student Non-Violent Coordinating Committee in 1962. But working on a plantation with her husband for eighteen years was all the schooling Hamer needed to become the "angriest woman in Mississippi" and a force in the civil rights movement. In 1964 she served as spokesperson for the Mississippi Freedom Democratic Party, which unsuccessfully challenged the legitimacy of the all-white Mississippi delegation to the national Democratic convention. She returned to challenge the regular Democrats at the 1968 convention in Chicago, and her party was finally seated in 1972. This poem celebrates Hamer as an African American hero and American patriot. Its author, Sam Cornish (b. 1935), is a professor of Afro-American literature and creative writing at Emerson College. He has published several books of verse, including Songs of Jubilee *(1986). "Fannie Lou Hamer" is taken from* An Ear to the Ground: An Anthology of Contemporary American Poetry *(1989).*

fannie
lou
hamer
never
heard   5
of
in chicago
was known for
her
big   10
black
mouth
in the south
fannie lou
ate   15
her greens
watched
her land
and wanted
to   20
vote

men went
to the bottom
of the river
for wanting less   25
but fannie
got up
went to the courthouse

big as a fist
black as the ground   30
underfoot

Engaging the Text

1. Why does Cornish emphasize that Fannie Lou Hamer was never heard of "in chicago"? How would your understanding of the poem suffer if you didn't know the history behind this allusion? Why do you imagine Cornish chose not to capitalize throughout the poem?

2. How does the poet portray Hamer? What descriptive details does he offer? What does each detail contribute to the portrait?

3. In a sentence or two, summarize the statement Cornish is making about Hamer in this poem. What is lost in your prose translation?

4. Describe the poem's tone. What words or images help create this tone?

Exploring Connections

5. Fannie Lou Hamer emerges from this poem as a larger-than-life figure. How does her image as a hero of the civil rights movement compare with that of Septima Clark (p. 742)?

6. Write an imaginary dialogue between Fannie Lou Hamer and Aurora Levins Morales ("Class Poem," p. 95) on middle-class privilege.

Extending the Critical Context

7. Imitating Cornish's praisesong for Hamer, write a short poem that focuses on a moment when someone you admired stood up for what she or he believed was right.

Charlie Sabatier

JOHN LANGSTON GWALTNEY

Charlie Sabatier, speaker of the following monologue, offers another view of democratic action, American style. A paraplegic veteran of the Vietnam War, Sabatier returned to the United States to become an activist for the disabled. This interview originally appeared in John Langston Gwaltney's The Dissenters *(1986). No stranger himself to the problems encountered by the physically challenged, Gwaltney (b. 1928) is a blind anthropologist who has made a career of studying the attitudes of marginalized groups; his first major book,* Drylongso *(1980), is a moving collection of first-person accounts of what it means to be a Black American. Gwaltney is currently a professor of anthropology at Syracuse University.*

Combat duty in Southeast Asia left Charlie Sabatier with a need for a wheelchair, but it is difficult for me to think of him as confined. The truth is, his mind is infinitely freer now than it was for most of his pre-Vietnam life. In that pre-Vietnam, South Texas existence, Charlie and I would probably not have had very much to do with one another. But in July of 1982 we met and talked in his suburban Boston home and he turned out to be civil, hospitable, direct, and a formidable raconteur. The talking and listening were facilitated by the array of thick sandwiches and cold beer he provided. Late in the afternoon of our day of talking and listening Charlie's wife, Peggy, phoned. He maneuvered his wheelchair out of the house they are remodeling, down the drive, and into his car and drove off to pick her up.

The May 1982 issue of the American Coalition of Citizens with Disabilities newsletter had carried a story about Charlie's successful battle with Delta Airlines over one of their policies regarding disabled persons. The story read, in part:

On March 17, 1982, in East Boston, Charles Sabatier fought with Delta Airlines over evacuation. Sabatier was arrested when he refused to comply with a Delta Airlines safety policy which stipulates that a disabled person must sit on a blanket while in transit so that he/she can be evacuated in case of emergency. . . . When Sabatier refused to sit on the blanket (which was folded), the flight was delayed, and Sabatier was eventually arrested for disorderly conduct.

The court in which he was charged was located in an inaccessible courthouse. Sabatier refused to be carried up the courthouse steps and was therefore arraigned on the steps. The location of the trial was then moved to an accessible courthouse. Charges against Sabatier were dismissed in court when the parties reached a pretrial settlement. Delta agreed to change its policy so that use of a blanket to evacuate persons will be optional and paid Sabatier $2,500.00 for legal fee expenses, $1.00 of which would be for punitive damages at Sabatier's request. Sabatier agreed not to sue Delta over the incident.

This blanket thing had happened to me at least a dozen times   5
before, and in the last three years I've flown at least three dozen times. I
mean, I've been *everywhere*. I've been to Seattle and Los Angeles and
San Francisco and New Orleans and Chicago and any place you can
name that's on the map, practically, any major city, I've been there in
the last three years. I've been subjected to that probably ninety percent
of the times I flew Delta or Eastern. I would protest. I would get on just
like this time. I would get on out of the wheelchair and into this aisle
chair that Delta, by the way, likes to call the "invalid" chair — I've even
written them letters about that. You know, about how language means
things. Like you don't call black people niggers and you don't call
women broads and chick and honey and you don't call disabled people
cripples and invalids. You know, I told 'em what an invalid meant. That
that's somebody in a bed, totally   helpless. I said, "I'm not totally
helpless and stop calling me names." And I'd write them nice
bureaucratic-type letters. Yeah, they write back all the time,
bureaucratic-type things. They got a standard-type letter, I'm telling
ya. They hire somebody, you know, whose only qualification is — can
you write a bureaucratic meaningless letter? You know, at least a one-
pager. That guy's probably paid twenty-five thousand dollars a year to
answer people like me. And I never got anywhere by it, but that didn't

stop me from writing them. I had to write to get it out of my system, I think. One of the things I contended was that the whole damn policy was arbitrary and capricious because it happened to me a dozen times before and I always talked my way off the blanket! I'd get in there and argue with 'em and talk about my rights and all this self-worth, dignity, humiliation, and stigma and they'd go "Jesus Christ! Get him out of here. Forget about it." You know, "Just go sit down." They'd go, "Hey, we gotta take off, man!" So they'd say "Listen, forget it." And so that's what would happen. They would just forget about their dumb policy. And so I expected the same thing to happen this time. I mean, they're gonna subject me to this and I'll argue and get away with it. And this time I ran into a captain. The stewardess actually said forget it, and I went down — that's how I got into the seat. 'Cause this all happened at the door of the plane by the captain's cabin when I transferred from my chair to the aisle chair that gets me down the narrow aisle. And we argued and someone behind said, "Forget it." And so we went down. I got in the chair, got in the seat, had my seat belt on, they moved the chair out of the aisle and she comes down and says, "I'm sorry, the captain insists that you sit on the blanket." I said, "Look, you tell the captain what I told you. That I'm not about to sit on this blanket." And we went through this whole thing and I argued with every Delta person in probably the whole terminal over the course of about forty-five minutes and naturally, you know, this plane's going to Miami and everybody's saying, "Let's get going!" Yeah, I mean, it's not like it's wintertime and you're going to Minneapolis. They wanted to get going. Everybody's kinda wondering. I think the people on the plane, who saw me coming on, see, in this chair, they figured, this guy is sick or something and they were pretty nice. Well, finally the stewardess got irritated about this delay and she walks down the aisle and she used to like stoop down to talk to me but this time she comes down and just stands there and says, "Look, if you don't sit on the blanket, we're gonna have to de-board the plane and cancel the flight." Out loud, see? So everybody said, "Wait a minute, this guy's not sick. This delay's just 'cause he won't sit on a blanket." So some guy yells out, like about five rows behind me, "You mean to tell me that this delay is because this guy won't sit on a blanket?" And she says "Yes!" And he says, "Look, man, if I sit on a blanket, will you sit on a blanket?" And I said, "No. But if everybody sits on a blanket, I'll sit on a blanket." And he says, "Well, why do you have to sit on a blanket?" And she says, "It's for his safety." He says, "It's for your own good, do it." I said, "Look, seat belts are for people's safety. *Everybody* gets one. If blankets are for my safety, I want everybody to get one, Okay? If it's so good for my safety, it's so good for everybody else's. But if I'm the only one that has to do it, it's like puttin' a bag over an ugly man's head, you know? I mean, that's a stigma." So the guy says, "Okay, then we'll all sit on blankets." Everybody says,

"Yeah!" So half these people started chanting, "We want blankets! We want blankets! We want blankets!" I kinda enjoyed it, 'cause I was getting some support finally. I was getting a kick out of it, but at the same time I was a little bit nervous. It was funny except for the fact that the State Police officer was comin' down the aisle at the same time they were chanting on the plane. So he says, "Either you sit on this blanket or I'm gonna have to arrest you." I said, "What charge? Where's the blanket charge?" He says, "Disorderly conduct." And that got me mad. Disorderly conduct? *These* are the people chanting "We want blankets," it's their conduct. I said, "If anybody's being disorderly, it's them. And it's this airline that's treating me like dirt who should be arrested." I said, "Besides, you don't work for the airline. You work for the State of Massachusetts, just like me. You shouldn't be arresting people that are violating some policy they have. This is not a Federal Aviation Administration regulation. And even if it was, it should be the feds making the arrest here, not you. You're out of your jurisdiction." Well, he didn't get ahold of all that and goes, "Oh well, I don't care. Look, these people are gonna have to get off, you're interrupting and costing them a lot of money. I'm going to arrest you. I'll worry about that later." I says, "You bet you will, 'cause I'm gonna sue you for false arrest. I got two attorneys sitting right here, right next to me, and I've got their cards and they've already said that I haven't done anything wrong and they're gonna be witnesses. You'd better write down your own witnesses 'cause you're gonna need 'em." I found out later that I was right. That I wasn't guilty of disorderly conduct.

But an ironic thing was that the guy who arrested me had a twelve-year-old son with multiple sclerosis who was in an electric wheelchair! When I was in his office taking care of the paperwork we were talking about his son and I said, "I'll tell you something. I feel better about taking a stand and doing this than I *ever* felt about my role in the war in Vietnam. I know that what I'm doing right here is right. I know right from wrong and I know that this policy humiliates people and irregardless of its intention to evacuate people in the event of a survivable crash, and that was even suspect if that was the real intention, it's categoric discrimination," I said. Because when they see me as a nonambulatory person they categorically discriminated against me because they have me stereotyped as being helpless. I have no problem about how they get me out of the plane, *if* they get me out. I've got a problem about how they treat me *before* the crash. They could put the blanket above the seat in the compartment, they could put it under the seat. Do they think I'm gonna sit there and twiddle my thumbs in the seat waitin' for the stewardess to come back and get me on the blanket? I weigh two hundred pounds! Give me a break! I'm gonna be out of that seat just like I got in it, 'cause I know that when people start headin' for the exits, they're not comin' back for their purse, right? I mean, they're gonna be in the aisle, right down back, and there's gonna be this big cluster of people around the doors jumpin' out and I'll be right behind 'em. There are like eighty-, ninety-year-old people who get on that plane with the help of a walker and their grandson and they help 'em sit down and they kiss 'em good-bye. I'm telling you, if there was a survivable crash, those people, because of arthritis and age, couldn't get out. They'd be more helpless in a situation than I would, but they're ambulatory, you see, so they don't have to sit on a blanket. I mean, I had 'em cold, it was just unbelievable. I could have brought paraplegics in there who can lift five hundred pounds. I mean, I can prove that paraplegics are not helpless people.

If I had been in that pilot's place, of course I wouldn't have done what he did. 'Course not, because I think I have more common sense than he had. I mean, I think I'd realize that if there was really a survivable crash, you're just gonna grab somebody and try to drag 'em out, no one's going to think about which one. I'll tell you something that I've always suspected. In their minds, they didn't just see me as a helpless person, they saw me as an incontinent person. They had probably had experiences of people who were paralyzed and incontinent and they're trying to protect the upholstery of their seats. That's not unusual, that paternalism. You know, I lobby all the time. I'll talk to people a half hour in their office — senators, congressmen — and on the way out I'll get patted on the back like I'm a little kid. I mean, even very high officials. They're so far out of tune with what's goin' on in the disabled movement and the women's movement, the black movement, I mean, they're just so engrossed, I guess, in doing their job, that they lose contact.

I've got a blind friend who we see every once in a while. One day I'm walking down the street with this guy — and he's got dark glasses and a white cane — and a guy pulls over and says to me, "Hey! Could you tell me how to get to the Prudential Building?" Well, I had been here only a year and a half and I know the major roads, but I don't know the names of the streets so my friend starts talkin' and tells the guy how to get there and the guy pulls off and like five feet later pulls over and asks somebody else, 'cause he says to himself, "Blind guys don't know where anything is." But my friend can get around that town as well as anybody else. If anybody's gonna memorize how to get around, he is. But yeah, that's not untypical of the nondisabled population.

One of the things that happens when you stigmatize people is, you see, if I can call people "niggers" in my mind, I don't think of these people as human beings. There's not equality, you know. They're not my peers. If I call a Vietnamese a gook, it's easier to kill him than Mr. Hung Yung or whatever his name would be, right? So we do it. Americans do it, everyone, man. We call people krauts, limeys, gooks, niggers, and handicapped. People are refusing to recognize people as people, as having human traits. It's easier to just stereotype a large group of people than it is to deal with the problems and the need.

We always deal with problems in this country either technologically   10
or monetarily, and that's how this country has decided to deal with disabled people. Hey, I get my butt shot up in Vietnam, I come back here, they're not interested in what I'm gonna do, you know. They're not interested in my head problems about Vietnam or getting over all that trauma. It's later for that. We'll dump some money on you, just like, stay home. But if I say, "Look, later with your money. Stop subsidizing my life, just allow me equal opportunity to make my way in this life to the best that I can and all I want you to do is provide me accessible transportation so that I can get to and from my job, or make that post office that's two blocks away from here accessible so I can mail a letter and maintain my dignity while I'm doing it, rather than have somebody go up and do it for me," they refuse to do that. They'll dump money on you though, so you can stay home.

I don't even know if I could really give an answer as to why I didn't sit on the blanket. I know good people, good friends of mine, who have sat on that blanket, and I consider them to be real advocates. They did it because, I guess, it was like the easiest course to take. Most people's lives, I think, probably are like water. Water runs to the easiest course and most people would prefer to go around a confrontation than actually confront somebody. Oh for sure I would have preferred that. I mean, nobody enjoys confrontation, really. I think you'd have to be sick to really enjoy confrontation. There's a lot that's gone on in my life that goes way back. There's building blocks, I guess, and you see things and it takes time. You are what you are today because of what you were yesterday and the day before. We are an accumulation.

I think by the time I got out of the army, I said to myself, "I'm gonna start making the decisions in my life." Because I was always saying, "I should have listened to myself." Well, I started really making decisions for myself for the first time when I was layin' in a bloody mess in Vietnam. It was the first time, okay? Up until then I'd always been doing these crazy things on the advice of other people. I grew up in a time where we saw too many John Wayne movies, okay? I was a World War II baby, I was born in July of forty-five and I grew up with all this Audie Murphy,[1] John Wayne type of thing. The good guy goes to war, gets a bullet in the shoulder, meets and marries the pretty nurse, and they live happily ever after. That was war to me — and besides, we always won. We were always the good guys and we were always moral and ethical and all that. That was the propaganda that I was fed all my life, through movies, television. When I was young, "Combat" was the big show. Vic Morrow, who just died, was the buck sergeant. I grew up

[1]Audie Murphy: (1924–1971), most decorated American soldier of World War II.

in South Texas, my dad was a marine in World War II. I fell for it. I don't think that the movie industry really thought that they were propagandizing, but that's what it is. 'Cause you were subjected to only one side. I mean, the Nazis were always bad, every Nazi was bad, every bad guy had a foreign accent. The Japanese were the people who were always torturing people. My God, we'd never do a thing like that! Oh no! But I believed it. I mean, I was twenty years old and I believed it. I had *never learned* to question.

Actually I started questioning before I got shot but that changed my life completely. When I got shot I took a different road, I guess, from the one I might have taken. I probably would have come back from 'Nam and gone back to school and been workin' in a bank with a couple kids, probably divorced, I'm sure, that type of thing. But it's strange, you know. Being shot has made my life probably a lot more exciting. I would have probably lived a normal, average mundane kind of life. But it's like I entered a whole new field. I started learning real fast that disabled people were not considered the general population and I started wondering why.

I learned what things meant and the language and semantics got important to me. I was six foot two, a hundred seventy-five pounds, I'd never been disabled or in a hospital in my life. I had never seen anybody die before, then all of a sudden in a short period of time I'm killing people, people are trying to kill me, then I do get shot and almost killed. I get back and *then* I'm subjected to the worst bunch of crap I've ever seen in my life. I started being treated like dirt. It was ironic. Up until the time I got shot I was like Number One citizen. My country was spendin' *billions* of dollars for me. Thousands of dollars just to train me how to kill, thousands more dollars to send me halfway around the world to save us from "Communism." And they let it thrive ninety miles away! When I got in the army, that's when I started thinkin', wait a minute. Like I'm on this airplane and all of a sudden I realized, this is a one-way ticket! I'd been enslaved to keep this country "free." I'd been drafted for two years and if you don't think it's slavery, you just try to walk away from it! And so I said, okay, number one, I'm a slave, then I say, where am I? I'm goin' halfway around the world 'cause we had to pick a fight with some little Southeast Asian country to save the world from Communism! I had never even met a Vietnamese. I didn't even know what one *looked* like. I couldn't tell one from a Japanese and I'm going to go over there and kill these people? I thought, "This is ridiculous."

I was like twenty-one when I got there and the average age of everybody in 'Nam was nineteen. Which meant that the average age of the infantry, the guy on the line, was about seventeen and a half. And I just couldn't believe it. I just couldn't believe what was goin' on there. And we were goin' around in circles, you know, killin' people, and they

15

were killin' us and it was like no war that we ever had. You never took ground, you never went north — you know, *that's* where the enemy is, Goddamn!

I think that we are a nation of dissenters. Our nation was created by dissenters. Anybody that's ever made a major change in this world has been someone who was a dissenter. It's been done by somebody, you know, who you would call an unreasonable person. It was George Bernard Shaw[2] who said the reasonable man looks at the world as it is and tries to adapt himself to suit the world. And the unreasonable man sees the world as it is and tries to change the world to suit himself. Therefore, said Shaw, all progress depends on the unreasonable man. I think that's absolutely true! And it's those dissenters that I think really are like a drumbeat ahead, you know, from the rest of the band. They are the people that are leading. Hey! If there were no dissenters, if there were no "unreasonable" people there'd just simply be the status quo. We'd still be goin' around as cave men. But somebody had to have a better idea. And it seems like every time somebody's got a better idea, the status quo is there to start callin' him names.

Like what I did. People would say, "Man, that was an unnatural thing to do." And it *is* unnatural, because thousands of people have sat on the damn blanket before me. I guess they didn't consider it unnatural. But I'm telling ya, people are going to *have* to start becoming more unnatural, if that's what you want to call it, more unreasonable; less tolerant with those greedy people.

I don't know what makes people principled dissenters. I'll tell ya, you're searching for somethin' and it's kinda like searching for something smaller than the atom. You *know* something's there, but it's those building blocks or the makeup or whatever that substance is that makes people good people or bad people. You know something's there, you're tryin' to search for it but I just don't think that we're there yet. I don't think we know what it is. I don't know. Everybody's different in their intellect, their ability. I'm no genius. I'm not really great with the books. I have to study real hard. I'm not super smart or anything, but I just think I was born with the right genes or something that just gave me good *common sense*. Good common sense to know right from wrong, good from bad and make good decisions in my life. And every once in a while we blow it.

I remember the first time I ever recognized discrimination in my life. I was on a bus and this great big, huge black lady gets on the bus and sits down and faces me and the bus driver stopped the bus and said, "I'm sorry, lady, you're gonna have to move to the back of the bus." And she says somethin' like, "Look I have a right to sit here. I don't have to sit

[2]*George Bernard Shaw:* Irish-born English playwright and critic (1856–1950).

back there. My feet are hurtin' me. I've been working all day. I don't want to walk back down there." Just like Rosa Parks.[3] And he says, "Look, that's the law! Either you sit in the back of the bus or this bus don't go anywhere." So she was at that tired, worn-out stage and says okay, I'm ready for a rest. So *she* was a principled dissenter as far as I'm concerned. First one I ever heard of. And she says, "Then you do what you have to do. I'm gonna sit here, I'm tired." So he got off the bus, went to the corner, and got this cop who was directin' traffic, and this cop come on and like put a handcuff on her and took her off the bus. Boy! I thought, what's goin' on here? I never realized, see, up until that time that black people had to sit in the back of the bus. I just thought, they wanted to sit there, that they liked it there. I guess I was about nine. I thought, well, I guess I'm always sittin' near white people 'cause I want to, but I never thought about goin' back there. I just never thought of it. And then, all of a sudden, boom! I started thinking' about it. All the way when I was goin' home I was thinkin', what'd she do? I didn't see her do anything. I thought maybe she had pickpocketed or robbed a purse. I didn't know. Why did they take her off the bus? I didn't know anything about it. And so I went home and I said to my mother, "What happened? This lady was arrested. I don't understand. Why couldn't she sit there?" And my mother said, "That's just the way things are. They've always been like that and that's the way they're always gonna be. Don't worry about it. Go outside and play." So I went outside and I remember sittin' on the porch for a long time and thinkin' about it, and *knowin'* that, now, I'm not getting the right answer here. Somethin's goin' on here, you know, like, even if it's always been that way and it's always goin' to be that way, well, why? Why is it that way? That's what I asked. I didn't get any answer to my question and back then that's probably the first time I started questioning like an adult would do. You know, I never thought of that again from that time on until after I got shot and I was in the VA hospital. The nurses were leavin' at four-thirty to go out and stand on the bus stop and take the bus and somebody said, "Why don't we go and take a bus and go down and have a drink with the nurses?" And everybody laughed. Ha. Ha. And there it went — boy! When that guy said that, I went back, back, seeing that person on the bus. And all of a sudden I went, "I don't believe this!" That's the first time that I had ever been discriminated against in my life!

I had been fortunate to live until that time as a white person in this 20 racist society, and I'd never experienced any kind of discrimination, none. All of a sudden I realized — you know my life was so screwed up, it was like a big jigsaw puzzle and I had found one piece to start putting

[3]*Rosa Parks:* the Black woman whose refusal to give up her seat to a white passenger initiated a bus boycott in Montgomery, Alabama, in 1955.

my life back together and I wanted to talk about it. Like, hey! There's a big puzzle out here and I know that if we can fit all the pieces together I'll understand everything that's happening to me. And that was the first significant piece of the puzzle I found out.

Listen, I'll tell you a story. This happened to me in New York. I came back from Los Angeles on TWA and I got to the terminal at Kennedy International and I was getting a transfer to Delta, okay? It had nothin' to do with the blanket, but another problem. Delta's terminal is in a separate terminal. It's about a half a mile around. And there's no curb cuts or anything. So I get there, it's midnight, and I get my bags on my lap and I'm goin' out and I figure I'll catch a cab around. So I ask a guy about cabs and he says, "Well, you're gonna have a hard time. Those cabbies have been sittin' in the line two hours and they want a big fare to go downtown." I says, "Well, I'll get one." So I went out and I told this lady who was the dispatcher. "I want a cab." She says, "Where ya goin'?" I said, "Delta Airlines." She says, "Nope! Nobody'll take ya!" So I say, "Look, then if I can't get over there, I want to go downtown, stay in a hotel overnight." She says, "Okay." Cab comes up, I get in, the guy puts my chair in the trunk and he says, "Where ya goin'?" "Delta Airlines." "Nope. I'm waiting here for a fare to go downtown." And I says, "Well, I ain't goin' downtown, I want to go to Delta Airlines." The dispatcher says, "You said you were goin' downtown." I said, "I changed my mind." He says, "Get out of the cab, I'm not goin' to take you over there. I've been sittin' here two hours." "No, I'm not going to get out." So *he* gets out and he takes my chair out of the trunk. I locked his doors. And he says, "Look, I'll call the police." And I said, "Call 'em. You call 'em and then I'll sue *you*." I says, "If you call 'em you're gonna be involved the whole damn night, you won't get another fare the whole night. Either you want to do that or take me to Delta. I don't know specifically what the law is here but I guarantee you you can't refuse to take me where I want to go. That's discrimination. Besides, if you don't take me to Delta, I'm not gonna letcha back in the cab!" And he says, "Look, man, don't make me break into my own cab!" I says, "I'm gonna tell ya, take me to Delta or I'm gonna crawl over this seat and drive this goddamned cab myself over there!" We went to Delta Airlines. That has happened to me, like, three times! I've locked the door. I'm just not gonna do that you know. And I know damn well ninety-nine percent of disabled people would *never* do anything like that because the movement is in its infancy stage. But we're getting there.

It *bugs* me that people in this country are always talkin' about civil rights, you know. When I think of rights, I think of something more — a civil right is something that is written in law and that's all bullshit anyway. We don't need any laws, we don't need any constitution, we don't need the Declaration of Independence. All we need to do is treat people with respect.

I grew up about twenty miles from this town called Alvin, Texas, and there used to be a sign out there — I was in junior high school the last time I saw it. I think since then they've had to take the thing down. It was a sign out in front of the town that said, "Nigger, don't let the sun set on your head." Not until I was twenty years old did I get out of South Texas. I'm not a racist. I might have been. I remember one time I pushed the button on the water fountain marked "white" and no water would come out of it, so I pushed the button marked "colored" and water came out, but I would not drink it. At that time we would think nothing about tellin' a racist joke — and laughing. Maybe that's a way of finding out who's a real racist. Something's happened to me. I don't think I've lost my sense of humor, I'm pretty funny, I laugh — we've been laughing here — but I just don't appreciate those kinds of jokes. The important thing was, I think, not just one incident, but I kept seeing incidents like that.

When I went into the army I was in Germany and I had never associated a whole lot with black people before, and suddenly I'm sleeping next to black people and showering with black people, drinkin' with black people and *fightin'* with black people. And I remember we were sittin' down on a cot and it was Christmastime and this one guy who was black got this big long bar of candy with these nuts all around it and he took this big bite out of it and handed it to me for me to get a bite of. Man! It was like somebody had handed me a piece of *shit* to take a bite of. Boy! Did that candy look good! But I hesitated you know, and he says, "Oh, forget it!" And I said, "Hey, no, give it here." I still think of it and that was 1967 and Jesus! It makes you realize that, you know, they got me. They got a piece of me. There we were, havin' a good time, drinkin' beer and everything's great until I did somethin' like that, and I realized, well here I am, I'm a prejudiced ass. We grow though, we grow, hopefully.

What made me not like what was happening, those jokes, the water fountain, what made me dislike that or understand that it's not right, I don't know. I think that's what you're really looking for. Why would somebody young and immature know in his soul and his heart and his mind that this is not right? Actually I did think about it a lot then. When I would see things like that happening, I would dwell on them. And I could look in the eyes of people when they were being done a number on and I could see it. I could see the hate, frustration, anger and I could see that what was happening here, this policy that would create that kind of reaction by somebody, is a policy that should be eliminated. We should have no policies that create that kind of tension in somebody, that kind of anxiety, that sense of disaster. I think I probably always felt that way. Not just for the racist-type things I saw, but as I grew up if I saw some kid being punished by his father or something, you know, when the punishment far surpassed what was just, if I saw somebody getting beat up on the playground, I was just the kind of person that would kind of go help the person.

I remember one time. It got me in really bad trouble. I was in eighth grade and I was a big kid. I was six feet tall and we had this one guy who was the only disabled person I'd ever met in my life. He had CP[4] and he couldn't talk very good and we were friends. Well, it had been rainin' on the playground and some kid threw him in this hole. Just for fun! Boy, I'll tell ya, when they threw this guy into the mud, it just made me sick and I ran over there to help him and these people were gonna throw *me* in the mud! And then we were both so muddy — it was raining like cats and dogs. And then when we were almost out of the hole, these kids kicked mud in our faces. So I told the kid, "I want to see you after school. I'll get you." And before I realized what I was sayin', I was talkin' to like one of the toughest guys in the school! And later I was sittin' in my class and my knees were almost shakin'. I'm thinkin', "I'm gonna get killed. What do I do now? If I back down now I'll be *dirt* for four years, all through high school." So I said, "Jeez, I gotta go get beat up." So I went over and met him at the drugstore. And I thought, "If I let this guy hit me, I'm gonna die, so I'm gonna get the first punch in anyway." So I walked out of this drugstore door, it was like eight steps down to the sidewalk and the glass door was framed in wood and it was closing behind this guy and he walked out and took that first step and I caught him in midair. I turned around and *smacked* this guy right in the face. I connected so good in his face that I could just feel the guy's nose crack. Blood went all over and he flew back and went right through the glass door. Just flew! And then all of a sudden I changed from being wimpo, like "I'm gonna get killed," to "Come on, man! Let's get going!" Yeah, I was *bad* you know. Next thing I knew, I was worried 'cause the guy wasn't wakin' up. And I'm goin', "Wheow! What power!" Next thing I know, they call the police and I ran. No one squealed on me. I got away with the whole thing. I mean, the guy was so bad, if it had ever been a fair fight, I would have been dead. But the guy had some kind of respect for that kind of power and I just didn't. I had no respect for myself, see, 'cause I had sucker punched the guy, right? I hadn't really used any kind of power and after that he's thinkin' I'm this bad dude, don't mess with Sabatier, man. I had this great big reputation for nothin'. I said, "Thank God, nobody else'd pick a fight with me!" So I never really had much respect, I think, for strength as far as authority over other people. Maybe those kinds of things that happen

---

[4]*CP*: cerebral palsy, a condition caused by damage to the brain before or during birth, characterized by muscular uncoordination and speech disturbances.

throughout your life kinda teach that just because somebody has authority over you, has the power to do a number on you, doesn't make them the kind of person you have to respect. I don't think, when you fight, there's anything fair about it. When you fight, it's kinda like war — you win. The *only* thing that counts is to win. You defend yourself by destroying another person, that's all there is to it. I don't care what anybody says.

I enjoyed the fighting and I enjoyed being able to defend myself. That's a nice thing — to know that you can defend yourself. That you don't take much guff. That's good and every kid needs that, at least men in our society need that. It was just demanded when we were kids. If you grow up wimpy, brother! People are going to start stepping on you so you have to be able to take care of yourself. No one ever really got hurt. That's the thing women miss most, I think, the fact that there's nothin' like winnin' a fight. If you get in a fight and you win, boy! The feeling of success and victory and power — there's somethin' about it that is a *good* feeling. And that's why when we get to be adults we get into violence. We like the violence.

It's kinda strange what happened to me. Just killing somebody, you know, is something that you never get over, and when I left Vietnam I think I was more committed to learning as much as I could and trying to understand and be empathetic about people and I gained more respect for human life than I ever had before. I was put in a situation that had little respect for human life — either on our side or theirs. We had free fire zones and in the free-fire zone, anybody walking, you kill. You know, no respect. You don't ask any questions, in the free-fire zone you just kill 'em. And I think killin' somebody close up is more of an experience than doing a number on somebody in a bush that you don't see. You just fire at the bush or something and you walk by and you don't know what happened.

I had some really close experiences where I have actually killed somebody *very* close. And I killed a woman who was unarmed and *that* was somethin' I will *never* shake. We had set up this perimeter and we were there eleven days and every day we'd run out, search and destroy, and come back. Well, it just so happened that there were about thirty Vietcong who were digging these tunnels, and we had caught them out in the open and didn't know it and when we set up our perimeter it was right on top of them. They hadn't dug the other entrance and so they were all closed in. They were like, after eleven days, tryin' to sneak out of the perimeter. They didn't have any food, they'd run out of water, and they were on their way out. And it was about four o'clock in the morning. I'd just got off guard duty and I was going to sleep and I heard this guy on this tank next to my armored personnel carrier. He started yelling, "Infantry, there's somebody in the perimeter. There's gooks in the perimeter!" And I said, "Okay, we'll go check it out." So I jumped up, I took a couple of guys from my squad and I went to the other side of this tank and he says. "There's somebody in the bomb crater. I killed two on the side of the bomb crater." We saw their bodies, they weren't moving and we could hear someone in the bomb crater. I had this tunnel light, this big flashlight that we used when we'd go through tunnels, and I shined it in the bomb crater and this guy's got these two big old bullet holes right on each side of his neck and he's breathing, erh, arh, erh, arh, like that, and blood's burbling right out of the holes in his neck and he's *buck* naked and he's got a grenade in each hand and he's layin' on his back and the tanker yells, "Go get a medic." And I says, "There's no medic going to go down there. The guy's dyin', man," I says. "Besides, he's got grenades in his hands. What fool's goin' to go down there?" So the guy calls the medic and the medic wouldn't go down there and the guy ended up, like five minutes later he died. But I wouldn't have gone down there either. And so I said, "Look, let's fan out around this bomb crater." I'm right next to the bomb crater and there's a guy like two feet to my left and two feet to his left there's another and we're gonna walk around this bomb crater and then I realize, hey! I'm the guy that has the light! So I thought, I can use my power here, you know, I'm a sergeant. I could say, "Hey, psst, take this light." But they'd say, "Take *this*." So I didn't say that. I said to myself, "Wow! What am I gonna do?" So I held this light wa-a-ay out to my left and I could feel this guy's hand pushing it back over toward me, so I went way over to my right, where nobody was and I take one step and it was so dark I couldn't see anything and I took one step and this gal jumped up in front of me on her knees and screamed out something, two or three words, and I just *instinctively* pulled the trigger on my M-16 and I just used up a whole ammo pack, twenty rounds, just destroyed her. Blood flew on me and she like flew forward and then backward and she hit me as I jumped down. I thought any second, after that, everybody's gonna open up and this guy's gonna start shootin' back or his friends will or something, but no one did. I jumped down and when I jumped down I jumped on her and I rolled off and I reached over. I was ready to fight this person, right? And of course she was dead and I grabbed her and when I grabbed her I thought, "Boy this is a little person," you know, "this is like grabbing my little niece or something." So, it was real quiet. We just lay there for a second or two and then I took the light and I said, "Let's take a look." And I put the light on her and she had her hair all up on top of her head and I cut this string that she had tied it with and boy! She had beautiful hair. It went all the way down, like past her knees.

Beautiful long black hair. And I searched her and she had this wallet, the only thing in it was a picture of her and a guy that was probably her husband and two little kids and a razor blade, an old rusty razor blade. I don't know why she had that, but that's all that was in her wallet. So I took the picture. We went around and ended up killing three or four more people and capturing about eight others and the next morning, the sun came up and the CO[5] called me over and said, "What's the statistics here?" And I told him how many dead and how many captured and he says, "Was there a woman there?" And I said, "Yeah, there was a woman." And he said, "Was she armed?" And I says, "No, we didn't find any weapons." But hell, I didn't have time to say, "Hey, do you have a weapon?" There were bullet holes in her ankles, in her arms, in her face, it was terrible. So he says, "Well, who killed her?" And I says, "I did." And this fool, he's got one of these guys that we captured and he happened to be her husband. He's in his tent and he's having this conversation with this guy with the interpreter and the interpreter tells the guy that I'm the one that killed his wife. So right away, man, the guy comes *runnin'* at me, you know, his hands are tied behind his back, and I just threw him down on the ground. And the guy just went berserk, you know, crazy. I mean, he was like a chicken with its head cut off. He wasn't comin' at anybody, he just went runnin' into everything, throwing dirt up into the air and kicking and hollerin' and screamin' and like he'd lost his mind, which he did. So there I was, you know, and that night everybody's callin' me the woman killer. Like it's a big joke. You know, the woman killer, it's a joke. That was the heaviest thing that's ever happened to me. And so I think, Jesus, I don't know whatever happened to that guy. Whether he ever got his mind together. I don't know what happened to her kids. I don't know if they're dead or alive. Unbelievable! The next day we ended up gettin' in a big firefight and burning down by accident, by all the fire and ammo and everything, all these hooches[6] and stuff and the captain told me that that was the village that this lady lived in. So in a day I had killed an unarmed lady, seen her husband go crazy, and then burned down her village — and I'm the *good* guy! I'm the good guy? And I'm thinkin', "I've gotta get out of here." God, she wasn't even armed. She was diggin' a tunnel, you know, carrying water back and forth for these people and what are they doin? They're trying to get these foreigners out of their country, you know. That was us.

You know, I called them gooks. I used this term and everything. I played that game but I never, never really thought that I was going to be in a position — that's how stupid and naïve I was — I never thought that *I* would really have to shoot somebody and that I would get shot. It was just stupid, just so stupid. I am convinced, I've talked to all those guys, you know, *none* of those people ever thought that they were actually gonna pull a trigger on somebody or that they would ever get killed. You know, what happens is that the country confused the war

[5]*CO:* commanding officer.
[6]*hooches:* G.I. slang for Vietnamese village houses.

with the warriors. We lost the war, therefore the warriors are losers. We can make jokes about them. They're psychos, they're nuts, they're baby killers, they're losers! We are discriminated against as much as if we had been the ones over there being killed!

I thought a *lot* about that when I didn't have nothin' to do except think. I was always in the field and sneakin' all the time and walkin' down trails and thinking, what am I doing? If I get killed today, will I go to hell or heaven? Am I guilty or innocent? Am I a war criminal? Am I violating people's human rights? Would I appreciate them in my country doing this? I'd walk in people's hooches and I mean, we'd go through a village at four-thirty in the morning. We don't knock on the door, we walk through and they're sleeping with their wives and babies and they're scared, you know, and you see these people, their faces. I felt like I was the Gestapo[7] in World War II, walking in somebody's house without knocking on the door. 'Course that bothers me. I don't like doin' that. I'm not that kind of a person. But what am I gonna do? Refuse to go on a search-and-destroy mission? Jesus, so all I was hopin' to do was stay alive and get home and never find myself in that position again.

And so I *really* started thinking about all this right and wrong, good and bad and human rights, and what I would die for, what I wouldn't die for. And I came to the conclusion that there's just human rights. Human rights, not civil rights. And human rights are not conditional. Any commitment to a *conditional* human right is no commitment at all. And that's exactly what we got, we disabled people. Here's a President who says he's committed to social justice and all this business and at the same time it's being conditioned on your ability to get on the bus, or on your ability to see something. Things that really shouldn't matter. And so a commitment for conditional human rights to me is no commitment at all. Exactly none. And I'll do everything in my power to make sure that people understand that if you're gonna be committed toward something you can't talk commitment and in your actions do something else. You can't say you're in favor of affirmative action[8] and then go out and discriminate.

I mean all the people of the different populations should recognize things like that. Not many people look inward. They look outward to see where the problem is. They don't look in and say, "Yeah, I've wasted twenty people off the face of the earth and for what? You know, I'm guilty, okay, from there I'll make sure this never happens again and I'll try to stop it whenever I see it." You know, whenever I see that current

[7]*Gestapo:* secret police in Nazi Germany.

[8]*affirmative action:* government policies aimed at redressing inequities caused by racism. Affirmative action programs have attempted to offer increased opportunity for education, employment, and career advancement to members of historically underrepresented groups.

of hate or that current of discrimination, or see that president or that mayor or the governor or somebody making bad decisions, whenever I see it, I got to stand up and stop it. At least I owe those people, or their souls that! I have to. I figure, if *I* don't, who will? I owe it.

Engaging the Text

1. Sabatier places great value on learning to question one's assumptions; how and why does he learn to question his?

2. Do you agree with Sabatier and Shaw that "all progress depends on the unreasonable man" (para. 16)? Why or why not?

3. Debate Sabatier's assertion that "we don't need any laws, we don't need any constitution, we don't need the Declaration of Independence. All we need to do is treat people with respect" (para. 22).

4. Do individual acts of protest like Sabatier's constitute genuine democratic action? In what sense are such actions "democratic"? Is it possible to see them as just a matter of personal gripes? Under what conditions do individual acts of defiance become expressions of larger democratic principles?

5. Why does Sabatier say that his act of protest would strike many people as an "unnatural thing to do" (para. 17)? What forces or ideas in our culture make such actions seem "unnatural"?

Exploring Connections

6. Analyze Charlie Sabatier as an example of Lewis H. Lapham's "spirit of democracy" (p. 701). How well does Sabatier illustrate Lapham's ideal?

7. Compare Sabatier's attitudes toward his disability and the challenges he faces with the attitudes expressed by Sucheng Chan in "You're Short, Besides!" (p. 99).

8. How well does Carol Gilligan's analysis of male psychology (p. 233) explain Sabatier's attraction to fighting and violence? To what extent does Sabatier's story confirm or challenge her thesis?

9. Compare the transformation that Sabatier experiences with that of C. P. Ellis (p. 336). What causes each to change? What does each learn?

Extending the Critical Context

10. Write a journal entry describing a time in your life when you began to question your own assumptions: What led you to re-evaluate your beliefs? Did you change as a result?

11. Watch Oliver Stone's *Born on the Fourth of July* (1989), the film version of paraplegic war veteran Ron Kovic's autobiography. How do Kovic's personal background, Vietnam experience, and subsequent transformation compare with Sabatier's? What do their stories tell us about democracy in America?

12. Interview someone you know who, like Sabatier, has made an individual protest against some injustice or unfairness. Then write an oral history, like Gwaltney's, using the person's own words to tell the story. Share your history in class and see what conclusions you can draw from it and those of your classmates. Do you agree with Sabatier that "we are a nation of dissenters" (para. 16)?

Women, Home, and Community: The Struggle in an Urban Environment

Cynthia Hamilton

In 1986 the Los Angeles City Council voted to build a mammoth waste incinerator in a poor inner-city neighborhood. To the council's surprise, the African American and Latino communities, led primarily by mothers and working women, fought and eventually defeated the project. Cynthia Hamilton documents their struggle against city hall in this essay, originally anthologized in Reweaving the World: The Emergence of Ecofeminism *(1990). Hamilton is a community advocate and professor of Pan-African Studies at California State University, Long Beach.*

In 1956, women in South Africa began an organized protest against the pass laws.[1] As they stood in front of the office of the prime minister, they began a new freedom song with the refrain "now you have touched the women, you have struck a rock." This refrain provides a description of the personal commitment and intensity women bring to social change. Women's actions have been characterized as "spontaneous and dramatic," women in action portrayed as "intractable and uncompromising."[2] Society has summarily dismissed these as negative attributes. When in 1986 the City Council of Los Angeles decided that a 13-acre incinerator called LANCER (for Los Angeles City Energy Recovery Project), burning 2,000 tons a day of municipal waste, should be built in a poor residential, Black, and Hispanic community, the women

[1]*pass laws:* statutes that regulated the travel of Black South Africans.
[2]See Cynthia Cockburn, "When Women Get Involved in Community Action," in Marjorie Mayo (ed.), *Women in the Community* (London: Routledge & Kegan Paul, 1977). [Author's note]

there said "No." Officials had indeed dislodged a boulder of opposition. According to Charlotte Bullock, one of the protestors, "I noticed when we first started fighting the issue how the men would laugh at the women . . . they would say, 'Don't pay no attention to them, that's only one or two women . . . they won't make a difference.' But now since we've been fighting for about a year the smiles have gone."[3]

Minority communities shoulder a disproportionately high share of the by-products of industrial development: waste, abandoned factories and warehouses, leftover chemicals and debris. These communities are also asked to house the waste and pollution no longer acceptable in White communities, such as hazardous landfills or dump sites. In 1987, the Commission for Racial Justice of the United Church of Christ published *Toxic Wastes and Race.* The commission concluded that race is a major factor related to the presence of hazardous wastes in residential communities throughout the United States. Three out of every five Black and Hispanic Americans live in communities with uncontrolled toxic sites; 75 percent of the residents in rural areas in the Southwest, mainly Hispanics, are drinking pesticide-contaminated water; more than 2 million tons of uranium tailings are dumped on Native-American reservations each year, resulting in Navajo teenagers having seventeen times the national average of organ cancers; more than 700,000 inner city children, 50 percent of them Black, are said to be suffering from lead poisoning, resulting in learning disorders. Working-class minority women are therefore motivated to organize around very pragmatic environmental issues, rather than those associated with more middle-class organizations. According to Charlotte Bullock, "I did not come to the fight against environmental problems as an intellectual but rather as a concerned mother. . . . People say, 'But you're not a scientist, how do you know it's not safe?' I have common sense. I know if dioxin and mercury are going to come out of an incinerator stack, somebody's going to be affected."

When Concerned Citizens of South Central Los Angeles came together in 1986 to oppose the solid waste incinerator planned for the community, no one thought much about environmentalism or feminism. These were just words in a community with a 78 percent unemployment rate, an average income ($8,158) less than half that of the general Los Angeles population, and a residential density more than twice that of the whole city. In the first stages of organization, what motivated and directed individual actions was the need to protect home and children; for the group this individual orientation emerged as a community-centered battle. What was left in this deteriorating district on the periphery of the central business and commercial district had to

[3]All of the quotes from Charlotte Bullock and Robin Cannon are personal communications, 1986. [Author's note]

be defended — a "garbage dump" was the final insult after years of neglect, watching downtown flourish while residents were prevented from borrowing enough to even build a new roof.

The organization was never gender restricted but it became apparent after a while that women were the majority. The particular kind of organization the group assumed, the actions engaged in, even the content of what was said, were all a product not only of the issue itself, the waste incinerator, but also a function of the particular nature of women's oppression and what happens as the process of consciousness begins.

Women often play a primary part in community action because it is about things they know best. Minority women in several urban areas have found themselves part of a new radical core as the new wave of environmental action, precipitated by the irrationalities of capital-intensive growth, has catapulted them forward. These individuals are responding not to "nature" in the abstract but to the threat to their homes and to the health of their children. Robin Cannon, another activist in the fight against the Los Angeles incinerator, says, "I have asthma, my children have asthma, by brothers and sisters have asthma, there are a lot of health problems that people living around an incinerator might be subjected to and I said, 'They can't do this to me and my family.'"

Women are more likely than men to take on these issues precisely because the home has been defined and prescribed as a woman's domain. According to British sociologist Cynthia Cockburn, "In a housing situation that is a health hazard, the woman is more likely to act than the man because she lives there all day and because she is impelled by fear for her children. Community action of this kind is a significant phase of class struggle, but it is also an element of women's liberation."[4]

This phenomenon was most apparent in the battle over the Los Angeles incinerator. Women who had had no history of organizing responded as protectors of their children. Many were single parents, others were older women who had raised families. While the experts were convinced that their smug dismissal of the validity of the health concerns these women raised would send them away, their smugness only reenforced the women's determination. According to Charlotte Bullock:

> People's jobs were threatened, ministers were threatened . . . but I said, "I'm not going to be intimidated." My child's health comes first, . . . that's more important than my job.
>
> In the 1950s the city banned small incinerators in the yard and yet they want to build a big incinerator . . . the Council is going to build

[4]Cockburn, "When Women," p. 62. [Author's note]

something in my community which might kill my child. . . . I don't need a scientist to tell me that's wrong.

None of the officials were prepared for the intensity of concern or the consistency of agitation. In fact, the consultants they hired had concluded that these women did not fit the prototype of opposition. The consultants had concluded:

> Certain types of people are likely to participate in politics, either by virtue of their issue awareness or their financial resources, or both. Members of middle or higher socioeconomic strata (a composite index of level of education, occupational prestige, and income) are more likely to organize into effective groups to express their political interests and views. All socioeconomic groupings tend to resent the nearby siting of major facilities, but the middle and upper socioeconomic strata possess better resources to effectuate their opposition. Middle and higher socioeconomic strata neighborhoods should not fall at least within the one mile and five mile radii of the proposed site.
> . . . although environmental concerns cut across all subgroups, people with a college education, young or middle aged, and liberal in philosophy are most likely to organize opposition to the siting of a major facility. Older people, with a high school education or less, and those who adhere to a free market orientation are least likely to oppose a facility.[5]

The organizers against the incinerator in South Central Los Angeles are the antithesis of the prototype: they are high school educated or less, above middle age and young, nonprofessionals and unemployed and low-income, without previous political experience. The consultants and politicians thus found it easy to believe that opposition from this group could not be serious.

The intransigence of the City Council intensified the agitation, and the women became less willing to compromise as time passed. Each passing month gave them greater strength, knowledge, and perseverance. The council and its consultants had a more formidable enemy than they had expected, and in the end they have had to compromise. The politicians have backed away from their previous embrace of incineration as a solution to the trash crisis, and they have backed away from this particular site in a poor, Black and Hispanic residential area. While the issues are far from resolved, it is important that the willingness to compromise has become the official position of the city as a result of the determination of "a few women."

The women in South Central Los Angeles were not alone in their battle. They were joined by women from across the city, White, middle- 10

---

[5]Cerrell Associates, *Political Difficulties Facing Waste to Energy Conversion Plant Siting* (Los Angeles: California Waste Management Board, 1984), pp. 42–43. [Author's note]

class, and professional women. As Robin Cannon puts it, "I didn't know we all had so many things in common . . . millions of people in the city had something in common with us — the environment." These two groups of women, together, have created something previously unknown in Los Angeles — unity of purpose across neighborhood and racial lines. According to Charlotte Bullock, "We are making a difference . . . when we come together as a whole and stick with it, we can win because we are right."

This unity has been accomplished by informality, respect, tolerance of spontaneity, and decentralization. All of the activities that we have been told destroy organizations have instead worked to sustain this movement. For example, for a year and a half the group functioned without a formal leadership structure. The unconscious acceptance of equality and democratic process resulted practically in rotating the chair's position at meetings. Newspeople were disoriented when they asked for the spokesperson and the group responded that everyone could speak for the neighborhood.

It may be the case that women, unlike men, are less conditioned to see the value of small advances.[6] These women were all guided by their vision of the possible: that it *was* possible to completely stop the construction of the incinerator, that it is possible in a city like Los Angeles to have reasonable growth, that it is possible to humanize community structures and services. As Robin Cannon says, "My neighbors said, 'You can't fight City Hall . . . and besides, you work there.' I told them I would fight anyway."

None of these women was convinced by the consultants and their traditional justifications for capital-intensive growth: that it increases property values by intensifying land use, that it draws new businesses and investment to the area, that it removes blight and deterioration — and the key argument used to persuade the working class — that growth creates jobs. Again, to quote Robin Cannon, "They're not bringing real development to our community. . . . They're going to bring this incinerator to us, and then say 'We're going to *give* you fifty jobs when you get this plant.' Meanwhile they're going to shut down another factory [in Riverside] and eliminate two hundred jobs to buy more pollution rights. . . . They may close more shops."

Ironically, the consultants' advice backfired. They had suggested that emphasizing employment and a gift to the community (of $2 million for a community development fund for park improvement) would persuade the opponents. But promises of heated swimming pools, air-conditioned basketball courts, and fifty jobs at the facility were more insulting than encouraging. Similarly, at a public hearing, an expert witness's assurance that health risks associated with dioxin exposure

[6]See Cockburn, "When Women," p. 63. [Author's note]

were less than those associated with "eating peanut butter" unleashed a flurry of derision.

The experts' insistence on referring to congenital deformities and   15
cancers as "acceptable risks" cut to the hearts of women who rose to speak of a child's asthma, or a parent's influenza, or the high rate of cancer, heart disease, and pneumonia in this poverty-stricken community. The callous disregard of human concerns brought the women closer together. They came to rely on each other as they were subjected to the sarcastic rebuffs of men who referred to their concerns as "irrational, uninformed, and disruptive." The contempt of the male experts was directed at professionals and the unemployed, at Whites and Blacks — all the women were castigated as irrational and uncompromising. As a result, new levels of consciousness were sparked in these women.

The reactions of the men backing the incinerator provided a very serious learning experience for the women, both professionals and nonprofessionals, who came to the movement without a critique of patriarchy. They developed their critique in practice. In confronting the need for equality, these women forced the men to a new level of recognition — that working-class women's concerns cannot be simply dismissed.

Individual transformations accompanied the group process. As the struggle against the incinerator proceeded to take on some elements of class struggle, individual consciousness matured and developed. Women began to recognize something of their own oppression as women. This led to new forms of action not only against institutions but to the transformation of social relations in the home as well. As Robin Cannon explains:

> My husband didn't take me seriously at first either. . . . He just saw a whole lot of women meeting and assumed we wouldn't get anything done. . . . I had to split my time . . . I'm the one who usually comes home from work, cooks, helps the kids with their homework, then I watch a little TV and go to bed to get ready for the next morning. Now I would rush home, cook, read my materials on LANCER . . . now the kids were on their own . . . I had my own homework. . . . My husband still wasn't taking me seriously. . . . After about six months everyone finally took me seriously. My husband had to learn to allocate more time for baby sitting. Now on Saturdays, if they went to the show or to the park, I couldn't attend . . . in the evening there were hearings . . . I was using my vacation time to go to hearings during the workday.

As parents, particularly single parents, time in the home was strained for these women. Children and husbands complained that meetings and public hearings had taken priority over the family and relations in the home. According to Charlotte Bullock, "My children understand, but then they don't want to understand. . . . They say, 'You're not spending time with me.' " Ironically, it was the concern for family, their love of their families, that had catapulted these women into action to begin with. But, in a pragmatic sense, the home did have to come second in order for health and safety to be preserved. These were hard learning experiences. But meetings in individual homes ultimately involved children and spouses alike — everyone worked and everyone listened. The transformation of relations continued as women spoke up at hearings and demonstrations and husbands transported children, made signs, and looked on with pride and support at public forums.

The critical perspective of women in the battle against LANCER went far beyond what the women themselves had intended. For these women, the political issues were personal and in that sense they became feminist issues. These women, in the end, were fighting for what they felt was "right" rather than what men argued might be reasonable. The coincidence of the principles of feminism and ecology that Carolyn Merchant explains in *The Death of Nature* (San Francisco: Harper & Row, 1981) found expression and developed in the consciousness of these women: the concern for Earth as a home, the recognition that all parts of a system have equal value, the acknowledgment of process, and, finally, that capitalist growth has social costs. As Robin Cannon says, "This fight has really turned me around, things are intertwined in ways I hadn't realized. . . . All these social issues as well as political and economic issues are really intertwined. Before, I was concerned only about health and then I began to get into the politics, decision making, and so many things."

In two years, what started as the outrage of a small group of mothers has transformed the political climate of a major metropolitan area. What these women have aimed for is a greater level of democracy, a greater level of involvement, not only in their organization but in the development process of the city generally. They have demanded accountability regarding land use and ownership, very subversive concerns in a capitalist society. In their organizing, the group process, collectivism, was of primary importance. It allowed the women to see their own power and potential and therefore allowed them to consolidate effective opposition. The movement underscored the role of principles. In fact, we citizens have lived so long with an unquestioning acceptance of profit and expediency that sometimes we forget that our objective is to do "what's right." Women are beginning to raise moral concerns in a very forthright manner, emphasizing that experts have left us no other choice but to follow our own moral convictions rather than accept neutrality and capitulate in the face of crisis.

The environmental crisis will escalate in this decade and women are 20
sure to play pivotal roles in the struggle to save our planet. If women are able to sustain for longer periods some of the qualities and behavioral forms they have displayed in crisis situations (such as direct participatory democracy and the critique of patriarchal bureaucracy), they may

be able to reintroduce equality and democracy into progressive action. They may also reintroduce the value of being moved by principle and morality. Pragmatism has come to dominate all forms of political behavior and the results have often been disastrous. If women resist the "normal" organizational thrust to barter, bargain, and fragment ideas and issues, they may help set new standards for action in the new environmental movement.

Engaging the Text

1. Why, according to Hamilton, do minority women often bear the burden of industrial expansion? What other factors, in her opinion, make them natural leaders in opposing such developments?

2. Why didn't the architects of the LANCER project worry about the women who were organizing against it? In what ways did the men who backed the project misjudge their opponents?

3. Explain in your own words what Hamilton means when she says that women have to resist "normal" political strategies and ways of doing business. Why does she feel women need to "set new standards?"

Exploring Connections

4. Write a conversation on democracy and democratic action with Cynthia Hamilton, Septima Clark (p. 742), Ira Katznelson and Mark Kesselman (p. 714), and Gregory Mantsios (p. 72). How might the experiences of the two African American women confirm or complicate the observations of the professional political theorists?

5. How might Susan Griffin (p. 175) explain the interest the LANCER protesters took in their environment, the way this issue unified women of different backgrounds, and the women's insistence on sticking to their principles?

6. To what extent does the action of the Concerned Citizens of South Central Los Angeles illustrate Ira Katznelson and Mark Kesselman's definition of substantive democracy (p. 714)?

7. Drawing on the experiences of Charlie Sabatier (p. 751), Septima Clark (p. 742), and the Concerned Citizens of South Central Los Angeles, write your own definition of direct democratic action. In what ways does this concept differ from what we normally think of as democracy? Is this kind of direct action a viable alternative to the wholesale restructuring of government suggested by Frank Bryan and John McClaughry (p. 726)?

Extending the Critical Context

8. Watch the documentary film *Harlan County, U.S.A.* and compare the role that women played in the coal strike it documents with the role they played in the LANCER action. What obstacles did the women have to overcome in each

case? What motivated them? What did they learn about themselves in the process? Would you consider union strikes a form of direct democratic action?

9. Research the locations of dumps, toxic disposal sites, and toxin-producing industries in your area. Does your research confirm or challenge Hamilton's statement that "minority communities shoulder a disproportionately high share of the by-products of industrial development" (para. 2)?

Let America Be America Again

Langston Hughes

Our survey of American dreams and nightmares closes with a reflection on the power that cultural myths have to inspire both hope and despair. Written nine years into the Great Depression, "Let America Be America Again" (1938) offers a stinging indictment of the hypocrisy that Langston Hughes perceived everywhere in American life. Yet Hughes transcends his rage and dares to hope for America's future; in so doing he pays homage to ideals that retain their potency even in the 1990s. (James) Langston Hughes (1902–1967) was a major figure in the Harlem Renaissance — a flowering of African American artists, musicians, and writers in New York City in the 1920s. His poems, often examining the experiences of urban African American life, use the rhythms of jazz, spirituals, and the blues. Among the most popular of his works today are The Ways of White Folks *(1934), a collection of short stories, and* Montage of a Dream Deferred *(1951), a selection of his poetry.*

Let America be America again.
Let it be the dream it used to be.
Let it be the pioneer on the plain
Seeking a home where he himself is free.

(America never was America to me.)   5

Let America be the dream the dreamers dreamed —
Let it be that great strong land of love
Where never kings connive nor tyrants scheme
That any man be crushed by one above.

(It never was America to me.)   10

O, let my land be a land where Liberty
Is crowned with no false patriotic wreath,

But opportunity is real, and life is free,
Equality is in the air we breathe.

(There's never been equality for me, 15
Nor freedom in this "homeland of the free.")

Say who are you that mumbles in the dark?
And who are you that draws your veil across the stars?

I am the poor white, fooled and pushed apart,
I am the red man driven from the land. 20
I am the refugee clutching the hope I seek —
But finding only the same old stupid plan
Of dog eat dog, of mighty crush the weak.
I am the Negro, "problem" to you all.
I am the people, humble, hungry, mean — 25
Hungry yet today despite the dream.
Beaten yet today — O, Pioneers!
I am the man who never got ahead,
The poorest worker bartered through the years.
Yet I'm the one who dreamt our basic dream 30
In that Old World while still a serf of kings,
Who dreamt a dream so strong, so brave, so true,
That even yet its mighty daring sings
In every brick and stone, in every furrow turned
That's made America the land it has become. 35
O, I'm the man who sailed those early seas
In search of what I meant to be my home —
For I'm the one who left dark Ireland's shore,
And Poland's plain, and England's grassy lea,
And torn from Black Africa's strand I came 40
To build a "homeland of the free."

The free?
Who said the free? Not me?
Surely not me? The millions on relief today?
The millions who have nothing for our pay 45
For all the dreams we've dreamed
And all the songs we've sung
And all the hopes we've held
And all the flags we've hung,
The millions who have nothing for our pay — 50
Except the dream we keep alive today.

O, let America be America again —
The land that never has been yet —
And yet must be — the land where *every* man is free.
The land that's mine — the poor man's, Indian's, Negro's, ME — 55

Who made America,
Whose sweat and blood, whose faith and pain,
Whose hand at the foundry, whose plow in the rain,
Must bring back our mighty dream again.

O, yes,   60
I say it plain,
America never was America to me,
And yet I swear this oath —
America will be!

Engaging the Text

1. Explain the two senses of the word "America" as Hughes uses it in the title and refrain of the poem.

2. According to Hughes, who must rebuild the dream and why?

3. Why does Hughes reaffirm the dream of an ideal America in the face of so much evidence to the contrary?

4. Explain the irony of lines 40–41 ("And torn from Black Africa's strand I came/To build a 'homeland of the free.' ")

5. Examine the way Hughes uses line length, repetition, stanza breaks, typography, and indentation to call attention to particular lines of the poem. Why does he emphasize these passages?

Exploring Connections

6. Review some or all of the poems in *Rereading America*:

> Aurora Levins Morales's "Class Poem" (p. 95)
> Gail Tremblay's "The Returning" (p. 162)
> Lucille Clifton's "being property once myself" (p. 174)
> Wendy Rose's "Three Thousand Dollar Death Song" (p. 331)
> Janice Mirikitani's "We, the Dangerous" (p. 334)
> Aurora Levins Morales's "Child of the Americas" (p. 396)
> Inés Hernández's "Para Teresa" (p. 554)
> Louise Erdrich's "Dear John Wayne" (p. 674)
> Sam Cornish's "Fannie Lou Hamer" (p. 749)
> Langston Hughes's "Let America Be America Again" (p. 776)

Then write an essay on poetry as a form of direct democratic action. What are the characteristics of this type of poetry? How does it differ from the poetry you have read in school before?

Extending the Critical Context

7. Working in groups, "stage" a reading of the poem, using multiple speakers. Consider carefully how to divide up the lines for the most effective presenta-

tion. After the readings, discuss the choices made by the different groups in the class.

8. Working in pairs or in groups, write prose descriptions of the two versions of America Hughes evokes. Read these aloud and discuss which description more nearly matches your own view of the United States.

Acknowledgments (continued from p. iv)

Paula Gunn Allen, "Where I Come from Is Like This" from *The Sacred Hoop* by Paula Gunn Allen. Copyright © 1986 by Paula Gunn Allen. Reprinted by permission of Beacon Press.

Gordon W. Allport, "Formation of In-Groups." From *The Nature of Prejudice* by Gordon W. Allport. Copyright © 1954 by Addison-Wesley. Reprinted by permission of Addison-Wesley Publishing Co.

Jean Anyon, "Social Class and the Hidden Curriculum of Work," edited, from *Journal of Education*, vol. 162, no. 1, Winter 1980. Reprinted by permission of the author and the *Journal of Education*.

Gloria Anzaldúa, "*La conciencia de la mestiza*/Towards a New Consciousness" from *Borderlands/La Frontera* by Gloria Anzaldúa. Copyright © 1987. Reprinted by permission of Aunt Lute Books. (415) 558-8116.

Toni Cade Bambara, "The Lesson" from *Gorilla, My Love* by Toni Cade Bambara. Copyright © 1972 by Toni Cade Bambara. Reprinted by permission of Random House, Inc.

Frank Bryan and John McClaughry, excerpts from "Recreating Democracy on a Human Scale" were first published in *The Vermont Papers: Recreating Democracy on a Human Scale*, by Frank Bryan and John McClaughry (Chelsea Green), 1989.

Bebe Moore Campbell, "Envy" from *Sweet Summer* by Bebe Moore Campbell. Copyright © 1989 by Bebe Moore Campbell. Reprinted by permission of the Putnam Publishing Group.

Janet Saltzman Chafetz, "Some Individual Costs of Gender Role Conformity" from *Masculine, Feminine, or Human? An Overview of the Sociology of Gender Roles*, pp. 47–55. Copyright © 1974. Reproduced by permission of the publisher, F. E. Peacock Publishers, Inc., Itasca, Illinois.

Sucheng Chan, "You're Short, Besides!" from *Making Waves* by Asian Women United of California. Copyright © 1989 by Asian Women United of California. Reprinted by permission of Beacon Press.

Sandra Cisneros, "Little Miracles, Kept Promises." Copyright © by Sandra Cisneros 1991. Published in *Woman Hollering Creek* published by Random House, Inc., New York. Published in *Grand Street*, vol. 9, no. 4, 1990. Reprinted by permission of Susan Bergholz Literary Services, New York.

Septima Clark and Cynthia Stokes Brown, "All Over the Deep South" from *Ready from Within*. Reprinted by permission of Cynthia Stokes Brown.

Lucille Clifton, "being property once myself." Copyright © 1987 by Lucille Clifton from *Good Woman: Poems and a Memoir 1969–1980* by Lucille Clifton, with the permission of BOA Editions, Ltd., 92 Park Avenue, Brockport, NY 14420.

Blythe McVicker Clinchy, Mary Field Belenky, Nancy Goldberger, Jill Mattuck Tarule, "Connected Education for Women," *Journal of Education*, vol. 167, no. 3, 1985. Reprinted by permission of the *Journal of Education* and the authors.

Sam Cornish, "Fannie Lou Hamer" from *Songs of Jubilee* by Sam Cornish. Copyright © 1986 by Sam Cornish. Reprinted by permission of Unicorn Press.

Hisaye Yamamoto DeSoto, "A Fire in Fontana" in *Rafu Shimpo*, December 21, 1985. Reprinted by permission of the author.

Maurine Doerken, "What's Left After Violence and Advertising?" From *Classroom Combat: Teaching and Television*. Copyright © 1983 by Educational Technology Publications. Reprinted by permission of Educational Technology Publications.

Louise Erdrich, "Dear John Wayne." Reprinted by permission of the author.

Henry Louis Gates, Jr., "TV's Black World Turns — But Stays Unreal." Copyright © 1989 by The New York Times Company. Reprinted by permission.

Carol Gilligan, "Images of Relationships" reprinted by permission of the publishers from *In a Different Voice: Psychological Theory and Women's Development* by Carol Gilligan, Cambridge, Mass.: Harvard University Press. Copyright © 1982 by Carol Gilligan.

Chellis Glendinning, "The Spell of Technology" (editor's title) excerpted from *When Technology Wounds*. Copyright © 1990 by Chellis Glendinning. Reprinted by permission of William Morrow & Company, Inc., Publishers, New York.

Richard Goldstein, "The Gay Family." Copyright © 1986 by Richard Goldstein. First appeared in *The Village Voice*, July 1, 1986. Reprinted by permission of the author.

Suzanne Gordon, "Women at Risk" from *Prisoners of Men's Dreams: Striking Out for a New Feminine Future* by Suzanne Gordon. Copyright © 1991 by Suzanne Gordon. Reprinted by permission of Little, Brown and Company.

Susan Griffin, "Split Culture" from *Healing the Wounds*, Judith Plant, ed. Reprinted by permission of Susan Griffin.

John Langston Gwaltney, "Charlie Sabatier" from *The Dissenters* by John Langston Gwaltney. Copyright © 1986 by John Langston Gwaltney. Reprinted by permission of Random House, Inc.

Cynthia Hamilton, "Women, Home and Community: The Struggle in an Urban Environment" from *Reweaving the World*, Irene Diamond and Gloria Feman Orenstein, editors. Sierra Club Books. Reprinted by permission of the editors.

Virginia R. Harris and Trinity A. Ordoña, "In Alliance, In Solidarity" from *Making Face, Making Soul/Haciendo Caras*, ed. Gloria Anzaldúa. Copyright © 1990. Reprinted by permission of Aunt Lute Books. (415) 558-8116.

Inés Hernández, "Para Teresa" from *Con Razón, Corazón: Poetry*. Copyright © 1987 by Inés Hernández. Reprinted by permission of the author.

bell hooks, "Yearning" from *The Looking Glass World of Nonfiction TV* by Elayne Rapping. Reprinted with permission from the publisher, South End Press, 116 St. Botolph Street, Boston, MA 02115.

Langston Hughes, "Let America Be America Again" from *International Workers Order*. Copyright © 1938 by Langston Hughes. Copyright renewed 1965 by Langston Hughes. Reprinted by permission of Harold Ober Associates, Incorporated.

Roger Jack, "An Indian Story" from *Dancing on the Rim of the World*, Andrea Lerner, editor. University of Arizona Press.

Ira Katznelson and Mark Kesselman, "Capitalism and Democracy" from *The*

Politics of Power, Third Edition, by Ira Katznelson and Mark Kesselman. Copyright © 1987 by Harcourt Brace Jovanovich, Inc. Reprinted by permission of the publisher.

Sam Keen, excerpt from Chapter Five of *Fire in the Belly* by Sam Keen. Copyright © 1991 by Sam Keen. Used by permission of Bantam Books, a division of Bantam Doubleday Dell Publishing Group, Inc.

Jamaica Kincaid, "Girl" from *At the Bottom of the River* by Jamaica Kincaid. Copyright © 1985 by Jamaica Kincaid. Reprinted by permission of Vintage Books, a Division of Random House, Inc.

Martin Luther King, Jr., "Racism and the White Backlash" from *Where Do We Go from Here: Chaos or Community?* by Martin Luther King, Jr. Copyright © 1967 by Martin Luther King, Jr. Reprinted by permission of HarperCollins Publishers, Inc.

Maxine Hong Kingston, "Silence" from *The Woman Warrior* by Maxine Hong Kingston. Copyright © 1975, 1976 by Maxine Hong Kingston. Reprinted by permission of Alfred A. Knopf, Inc.

John (Fire)Lame Deer and Richard Erdoes, "Talking to the Owls and Butterflies" from *Lame Deer: Seeker of Visions.* Copyright © 1972 by John (Fire)Lame Deer and Richard Erdoes. Reprinted by permission of Simon and Schuster, Inc.

Lewis H. Lapham, "Democracy in America?" Copyright © 1990 by Harper's Magazine. All rights reserved. Reprinted from the November issue by special permission.

Christopher Lasch, "The Original Meaning of the Work Ethic" from *The Culture of Narcissism, American Life in an Age of Diminishing Expectations*, by Christopher Lasch, by permission of W. W. Norton & Company, Inc. Copyright © 1979 by W. W. Norton & Company, Inc.

Patricia Nelson Limerick, "Empire of Innocence." Edited with the author's permission from *The Legacy of Conquest: The Unbroken Past of the American West.* Copyright © 1987 by Patricia Nelson Limerick. Reprinted by permission of W. W. Norton & Company, Inc.

Karen Lindsey, from *Friends as Family* by Karen Lindsey. Copyright © 1981 by Karen Lindsey. Reprinted by permission of Beacon Press.

Richard Louv, "The Children of Sex, Drugs, and Rock 'n' Roll" from *Childhood's Future* by Richard Louv. Copyright © 1990 by Richard Louv. Reprinted by permission of Houghton Mifflin Company.

Gregory Mantsios, "Class in America: Myths and Realities" from *Racism and Sexism: An Integrated Study*, Paula S. Rothenberg, editor. Reprinted by permission of the author.

Gina Marchetti, "Action-Adventure as Ideology" from *Cultural Politics in Contemporary America*, Ian Angus and Sut Jhally, editors. Reprinted by permission of the author.

Mark Crispin Miller, "The Cosby Show" from *Watching Television* by Todd Gitlin, Editor. Compilation Copyright © 1986 by Todd Gitlin. Reprinted by permission of Pantheon Books, a Division of Random House, Inc.

Janice Mirikitani, "We, the Dangerous" reprinted from *Awake in the River, Poetry and Prose*, by Janice Mirikitani, Isthmus Press, 1978, San Francisco, Calif. Copyright © 1978 by Janice Mirikitani.

Aurora Levins Morales, "Class Poem" and "Child of the Americas" from *Get*

Index of Authors and Titles